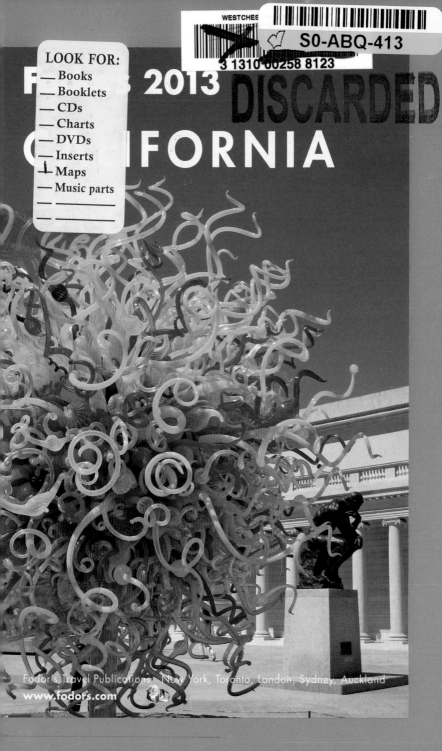

FODOR'S 2013

DISCARDED

CALIFORNIA

Fodor's Travel Publications · New York, Toronto, London, Sydney, Auckland
www.fodors.com

917.94
Fod
pb

FODOR'S CALIFORNIA 2013

Writers: Cheryl Crabtree, Denise M. Leto, Kathy A. MacDonald, Reed Parsell, Christine Vovakes, Bobbi Zane

Editors: Daniel Mangin, Michael Nalepa, Maria Teresa Hart, Jess Moss, Doug Stallings

Production Editor: Evangelos Vasilakis

Maps & Illustrations: David Lindroth and Mark Stroud, *cartographers;* Rebecca Baer, *map editor;* William Wu, *information graphics*

Design: Fabrizio La Rocca, *creative director;* Tina Malaney, Chie Ushio, Jessica Ramirez, *designers;* Melanie Marin, *associate director of photography;* Jennifer Romains, *photo research*

Cover Photo: (Beach at Natural Bridges State Park in Santa Cruz): Bill Stevenson/age fotostock

Production Manager: Angela L. McLean

COPYRIGHT

ISBN 978-0-307-92948-8

ISSN 0192-9925

SPECIAL SALES

This book is available at special discounts for bulk purchases for sales promotions or premiums. Special editions, including personalized covers, excerpts of existing books, and corporate imprints, can be created in large quantities for special needs. For more information, write to Special Markets/Premium Sales, 1745 Broadway, MD 3-1, New York, NY 10019, or e-mail specialmarkets@randomhouse.com.

AN IMPORTANT TIP & AN INVITATION

Although all prices, opening times, and other details in this book are based on information supplied to us at press time, changes occur all the time in the travel world, and Fodor's cannot accept responsibility for facts that become outdated or for inadvertent errors or omissions. So **always confirm information when it matters,** especially if you're making a detour to visit a specific place. Your experiences—positive and negative— matter to us. If we have missed or misstated something, **please write to us.** Share your opinion instantly through our online feedback center at fodors.com/contact-us.

PRINTED IN SINGAPORE

10 9 8 7 6 5 4 3 2 1

CONTENTS

CONTENTS

MAPS

CONTENTS

ABOUT THIS GUIDE

Fodor's Ratings

Everything in this guide is worth doing—we don't cover what isn't—but exceptional sights, hotels, and restaurants are recognized with additional accolades. **Fodor's Choice**★ indicates our top recommendations; ★ highlights places we deem highly recommended; and **Best Bets** call attention to notable hotels and restaurants in various categories. Care to nominate a new place? Visit Fodors.com/contact-us.

Trip Costs

We list prices wherever possible to help you budget well. Hotel and restaurant price categories from $ to $$$$ are noted alongside each recommendation. For hotels, we include the lowest cost of a standard double room in high season. For restaurants, we cite the average price of a main course at dinner or, if dinner isn't served, at lunch. For attractions, we always list adult admission fees; discounts are usually available for children, students, and senior citizens.

Hotels

Our local writers vet every hotel to recommend the best overnights in each price category, from budget to expensive. Unless otherwise specified, you can expect private bath, phone, and TV in your room. For expanded hotel reviews, facilities, and deals visit Fodors.com.

TripAdvisor ⊙⊙

Our expert hotel picks are reinforced by high ratings on TripAdvisor. Look for representative quotes in this guide, and the latest TripAdvisor ratings and feedback at Fodors.com.

Restaurants

Unless we state otherwise, restaurants are open for lunch and dinner daily. We mention dress code only when there's a specific

Ratings		Hotels &
★	Fodor's Choice	**Restaurants**
★	Highly	🔝 Hotel
	recommended	📭 Number of
🕲	Family-friendly	rooms
		❧○❧ Meal plans
Listings		✗ Restaurant
⊠	Address	🖎 Reservations
⊠	Branch address	🏛 Dress code
🖀	Telephone	🖃 No credit cards
🖷	Fax	$ Price
⊕	Website	
🖎	E-mail	**Other**
🖅	Admission fee	⇨ See also
⊙	Open/closed	☞ Take note
	times	🏌 Golf facilities
Ⓜ	Subway	
⊹	Directions or	
	Map coordinates	

requirement and reservations only when they're essential or not accepted. To make restaurant reservations, visit Fodors.com.

Credit Cards

The hotels and restaurants in this guide typically accept credit cards. If not, we'll say so.

Experience
California

WHAT'S NEW IN CALIFORNIA

Foodie's Paradise

Great dining is a staple of the California lifestyle, and a new young generation of chefs is challenging old ideas about preparing and presenting great food. Food-truck frenzy has created a movable feast up and down the state. Esteemed chefs and urban foodies follow the trucks on Twitter as they move around cities 24/7 purveying delicious, cheap, fresh meals. In L.A., chef Roy Choi started the movement when he began serving up his Korean/Mexican Pacman burgers from his Kogi BBQ truck. The Spencer on the Go truck hangs out in SoMa in San Francisco, dishing such delicacies as escargot puff lollipops. In SoCal, you can find food-laden trucks at sports and entertainment venues, near parks and attractions, and on busy roads and boulevards—and the ensuing lines of hungry patrons.

California chefs continue to shop locally for produce and farmer-sourced meat. Tender Greens (with locations in Hollywood, Pasadena, and Walnut Creek) sets the bar high by serving hand-raised produce from an Oxnard farm; grain-fed, hormone-free beef; hand-raised chickens; and line-caught tuna.

Kid-ding Around

California's theme parks work overtime to keep current and attract patrons of all ages. LEGOLAND California Resort keeps expanding with new attractions such as Pirate Reef and LEGOLAND Water Park. And LEGOLAND is opening its 250-room LEGO-theme hotel in 2013. *Captain EO*, a 3-D film starring Michael Jackson, is back at Disneyland. *Star Tours: The Adventures Continue*, also 3-D, has a new look, and World of Color in Disney California Adventure Park, presents an outdoor light and water show.

With trees as tall as they come, the Children's Redwood Forest in Humboldt Redwoods State Park is open after a major fire in 2003.

Grape Expectations

Evidence that California wine culture is alive and well comes from Temecula, which is emerging as an exciting wine destination in the Inland Empire. The number and quality of the wineries continue to grow: Thornton, Ponte, and Mount Palomar wineries offer fine dining to pair with their delicious Rhône-style wines. Hotels are springing up among the vineyards, and events such as the Balloon and Wine Festival draw thousands of visitors to the region. Winemaking is also expanding in the Central Valley and Shasta Cascade areas. In SoCal, vineyards are going up in unlikely places, such as in the hillsides of San Diego County, where Escondido-based Orfila keeps snagging awards, and on Catalina Island, where the Rusack family planted the first wine grapes ever on the historic Escondido Ranch. The Turkovich Family Winery opened in the Central Valley town of Winters just west of Sacramento. The Truckee River Winery, near Lake Tahoe, claims to be the highest and coldest winery in the nation.

Suite Dreams

Hotels are coming back to life in a big way. The luxurious new JW Marriott and Ritz-Carlton stand side by side in the burgeoning L.A. LIVE sports and entertainment complex. The W Hollywood now occupies the famed corner of Hollywood and Vine, another hot spot just steps from the Pantages Theatre. Visitors to Yountville in the Napa Valley have another lodging choice, the Bardessono, a LEED-certified hotel that sports an eco spa and an underground geothermal system. Park Hyatt Aviara has taken over and renovated the former Four Seasons in Carlsbad.

All Aboard

Riding the rails can be a satisfying experience, particularly in California where the distances between destinations sometimes run into the hundreds of miles. You can save money on gas and parking, avoid freeway traffic, and see some of the best the state has to offer.

The best trip is on the luxuriously appointed Coast Starlight, a long-distance train with sleeping cars that runs between Seattle and Los Angeles, passing some of California's most beautiful coastline as it hugs the beach. For the best surfside viewing, get a seat or a room on the left side of the train and ride south to north from San Diego to Oakland.

Amtrak has frequent Pacific Surfliner service between San Diego and Los Angeles, and San Diego and Santa Barbara. These are coach cars, but many of the trains have been upgraded and are comfortable and convenient, especially if you want to get off and on the train at several destinations—Anaheim near Disneyland, downtown Los Angeles, coastal Ventura and Santa Barbara, San Luis Obispo, and Oakland (just a BART ride to San Francisco).

It's Easy Being Green

The Golden State is glowing green all over. It's the only state in the nation to mandate green building codes for all new construction to reduce greenhouse emissions. Santa Barbara's car-free program can save you up to 50% on lodging, meals, and, of course, transportation. Palm Desert is also pushing green, not only in sustainable construction but also in encouraging use of golf carts for local transportation.

Homegrown Hospitality

Agritourism in California isn't new (remember, Knott's Berry Farm once *was* a berry farm), but it is on the rise, with farm tours and agricultural festivals sprouting up everywhere.

Wine country is a particularly fertile area—spurred by the success of vineyards, the area's lavender growers and olive-oil producers have started welcoming visitors. Sonoma Farm Trail Tours include walking the land and a farm-driven dinner with paired wines.

In the Central Valley, America's number-one producer of stone fruit, you can travel themed tourist routes (like Fresno County's Blossom Trail) and tour herb gardens, fruit orchards, organic dairies, and pumpkin patches.

State of the Arts

California's beauty-obsessed citizens aren't the only ones opting for a fresh look these days: its esteemed art museums are also having a bit of work done.

Following a trend set by the de Young Museum in San Francisco and the Getty Villa in L.A., Long Beach's Museum of Latin American Art doubled its exhibition space. Meanwhile, San Jose's Institute of Contemporary Art and the Museum of Contemporary Art in San Diego (MCASD Downtown) have both expanded into new digs. And the Palm Springs Museum of Art has morphed into a world-class showcase for contemporary work. The L.A. County Museum of Art keeps expanding its Wilshire Boulevard campus; the latest addition is the Renzo Piano–designed Resnick Pavilion, which will hold special exhibits.

WHAT'S WHERE IN SOUTHERN CALIFORNIA

The following numbers refer to chapters.

2 San Diego. San Diego's historic Gaslamp Quarter and Mexican-theme Old Town have a human scale—but it's big-ticket animal attractions like SeaWorld and the San Diego Zoo that pull in planeloads of visitors.

3 Orange County. The real OC is a diverse destination with premium resorts and shopping, first-rate restaurants, strollable waterfront communities, and kid-friendly attractions.

4 Los Angeles. Go for the glitz of the entertainment industry, but stay for the rich cultural attributes and myriad communities of people from different cultures.

5 The Central Coast. Three of the state's top stops—swanky Santa Barbara, Hearst Castle, and Big Sur—sit along the scenic 200-mile route.

6 Channel Islands National Park. Only 60 miles northwest of Los Angeles, this park accessible only by boat seems worlds away from urban sprawl and tangled freeways.

13 The Inland Empire. The San Bernardino Mountains provide seasonal escapes at Lake Arrowhead and Big Bear Lake, and the Temecula Valley will challenge your ideas of "California Wine Country."

14 Palm Springs and the Desert Resorts. Golf on some of the West's finest courses, lounge at some of its most fabulous resorts, indulge yourself at luxurious spas, check out Midcentury Modern architectural gems, and experience the simple life at primitive desert parks.

15 Joshua Tree National Park. Proximity to major urban areas—as well as world-class rock climbing and nighttime celestial displays—help make this one of the most visited national parks in the United States.

16 The Mojave Desert. In this hardscrabble country, material pleasures are in short supply, but Mother Nature's stark beauty more than compensates.

17 Death Valley National Park. America's second-largest national park isn't just vast and lonely—it's also beautiful and often the hottest place in the nation.

19 The Southern Sierra. In the Mammoth Lakes region, sawtooth mountains and deep powdery snowdrifts combine to create the state's premier conditions for skiing and snowboarding.

20 Yosemite National Park. The views immortalized by photographer Ansel Adams—of towering granite monoliths, verdant glacial valleys, and lofty waterfalls—are still camera-ready.

21 Sequoia and Kings Canyon National Parks. The sight of ancient redwoods towering above jagged mountains will take your breath away.

WHAT'S WHERE IN
NORTHERN CALIFORNIA

The following numbers refer to chapters.

7 Monterey Bay Area. Postcard-perfect Monterey, Victorian-flavored Pacific Grove, and exclusive Carmel all share this stretch of California coast. To the north, Santa Cruz boasts a boardwalk, a UC campus, ethnic clothing shops, and plenty of surfers.

8 San Francisco. To see why so many have left their hearts here, you need to the city's iconic neighborhoods—posh Pacific Heights, the Hispanic Mission, and gay-friendly Castro.

9 The Bay Area. The area that rings San Francisco is nothing like the city—but it is home to some of the nation's great universities, fabulous bay views, and Alice Waters's Chez Panisse.

10 The Wine Country. Napa and Sonoma counties retain their title as *the* California wine country, by virtue of award-winning vintages, luxe lodgings, and epicurean eats.

11 The North Coast. The star attractions here are the natural ones, from the secluded beaches and wave-battered bluffs of Point Reyes National Seashore to the towering redwood forests.

12 Redwood National Park. More than 200 miles of trails, ranging from easy to strenuous, allow visitors to see these spectacular trees in their primitive environments.

18 The Central Valley. Travelers along Highway 99 will enjoy attractions like Fresno's Forestiere Underground Gardens, the wineries of Lodi, and white-water rafting on the Stanislaus River.

22 Sacramento and the Gold Country. The 1849 gold rush that built San Francisco and Sacramento began here, and the former mining camps strung along 185 miles of Highway 49 replay their past to the hilt.

23 Lake Tahoe. With miles of crystalline water reflecting the peaks of the High Sierra, Lake Tahoe is the perfect setting for activities like hiking and golfing in summer and skiing and snowmobiling in winter.

24 The Far North. California's far northeast corner is home to snowcapped Mount Shasta, the pristine Trinity Wilderness, and abundant backwoods character that appeals to outdoorsy types.

12

Crescent City
Yreka
Klamath
Redwood National Park
Mt. Shasta
Alturas
Goose Lake
Burney
CASCADE RANGE
Arcata
Eureka
Weaverville
Shasta Lake
Ferndale
Redding
24
Lassen Volcanic National Park
Susanville
Pyramid Lake
NEVADA
Garberville
Red Bluff
Leggett
Chico
Paradise
Reno
Fort Bragg
Willits
Willows
Oroville
Grass Valley
Truckee
CARSON CITY
Mendocino
Ukiah
Sacramento Valley
Yuba City
99
23
Boonville
Clear Lake
49
Auburn
Lake Tahoe
South Lake Tahoe
Point Arena
80
Gualala
11
Healdsburg
Woodland
Placerville
Jenner
10
SACRAMENTO
Santa Rosa
Napa
Elk Grove
22
Novato
Fairfield
Sonoma
Lodi
Jackson
Bridgeport
Point Reyes National Seashore
8
Berkeley
Stockton
Sonora
Mono Lake
SAN FRANCISCO
Oakland
Modesto
SIERRA NEVADA
Mammoth Lakes
9
Fremont
Turlock
Yosemite Village
Palo Alto
San Jose
Merced
Bishop
Santa Cruz
Gilroy
Chowchilla
Big Pine
Castroville
San Luis Res.
Los Banos
Madera
PACIFIC OCEAN
Monterey
Salinas
18
Fresno
Pacific Grove
7
Soledad
5
Visalia
Carmel
Big Sur
Tulare Lake Bed
Porterville
Coalinga
Kernville
China Lake
99
San Simeon
Paso Robles
Bakersfield
Ridgecrest
San Luis Obispo
McKittrick
Santa Maria
Tejon Pass
TEHACHAPI MTS.
Lancaster
Lompoc
Santa Barbara
Ojai
Santa Barbara Channel
Ventura
Oxnard
Pasadena

0   75 mi
0   75 km

CALIFORNIA PLANNER

Driving Around

Driving may be a way of life in California, but it isn't cheap (gas prices here are usually among the highest in the nation). It's also not for the fainthearted; you've surely heard horror stories about L.A.'s freeways, but even the state's scenic highways and byways have their own hassles. For instance, on the dramatic coastal road between San Simeon and Carmel, twists, turns, and divinely distracting vistas frequently slow traffic; in rainy season, mud slides can close the road altogether. ⚠ Never cross the double line when driving these roads. If you see that cars are backing up behind you on a two-lane, no-passing stretch, do everyone (and yourself) a favor and use the first available pullout.

On California's notorious freeways, other rules apply. Nervous Nellies must resist the urge to stay in the two slow-moving ones on the far right, used primarily by trucks. To drive at least the speed limit, get yourself in a middle lane. If you're ready to bend the rules a bit, the second (lanes are numbered from 1 starting at the center) lane moves about 5 mph faster. But avoid the far-left lane (the one next to the carpool lane), where speeds range from 75 mph to 90 mph.

Flying In

Air travelers beginning or ending their vacation in San Francisco have two main airports to choose from: San Francisco International (SFO) or Oakland International (OAK) across the Bay. The former lands you closer to the city core (ground transportation will take about 20 minutes versus 35), but the latter is less heavily trafficked and less prone to pesky fog delays. BART, the Bay Area's affordable rapid-transit system, serves both airports. So your decision will probably rest on which one has the best fares and connections for your particular route.

If your final destination is Monterey or Carmel, San Jose International Airport (SJC), about 40 miles south of San Francisco, is another alternative.

Around Los Angeles, the options grow exponentially. LAX, the world's fifth-busiest airport, gets most of the attention— and not usually for good reasons. John Wayne Airport (SNA), about 25 miles south in Orange County, is a solid substitute—especially if you're planning to visit Disneyland or Orange County beaches. Depending on which part of L.A. you're heading to, you might also consider Bob Hope Airport (BUR) in Burbank (close to Hollywood and its studios) or Long Beach Airport (LGB), convenient if you're catching a cruise ship. The smaller size of these airports means easier access and shorter security lines. Another advantage is that their lower landing costs often attract budget carriers (like Southwest and JetBlue).

Convenience is the allure of San Diego's Lindbergh International Airport (SAN), located minutes from the Gaslamp Quarter, Balboa Park and Zoo, Sea World, and the cruise ship terminal.

WHEN TO GO

Because they offer activities indoors and out, the top California cities rate as all-season destinations. Ditto for Southern California's coastal playgrounds. Dying to see Death Valley or Joshua Tree National Park? They are best appreciated in spring when desert blooms offset their austerity and temperatures are still manageable. Early spring—when the gray whale migration overlaps with the end of the elephant seal breeding season and the start of the bird migration—is the optimal time to visit Point Reyes National Seashore. Yosemite is ideal in the late spring because roads closed in winter are reopened, and the park's waterfalls—swollen with melting snow—run fast. Autumn is "crush time" in all the wine destinations, from Napa/Sonoma in the north, central coast, and Temecula in the south. Snowfall makes winter peak season for skiers in Mammoth Mountain and Lake Tahoe, where runs typically open around Thanksgiving. (They sometimes remain in operation into June.)

Climate

It's difficult to generalize much about the state's weather beyond saying that precipitation comes in winter and summer is dry in most places. As a rule, inland regions are hotter in summer and colder in winter, compared with coastal areas, which are relatively cool year-round. Fog is a potential hazard any day of the year in coastal regions. As you climb into the mountains, seasonal variations are more apparent: winter brings snow (at elevations above 3,000 feet), autumn is crisp, spring can go either way, and summer is sunny and warm, with only an occasional thundershower in the southern part of the state.

Microclimates

Mountains separate the California coastline from the state's interior, and the weather can sometimes vary dramatically within a 15-minute drive. On a foggy summer day in San Francisco, you'll be grateful for a sweater—but head 50 miles north inland to Napa Valley, and you'll likely be content in short sleeves. Day and nighttime temperatures can also vary greatly. In August, Palm Springs's thermometers can soar to 110°F at noon, and drop to 75°F at night. Temperature swings elsewhere can be even more extreme. Take Sacramento: On August afternoons the mercury hits the 90s and occasionally exceeds 100°F. Yet as darkness falls, it sometimes plummets to 40°F.

Forecasts

National Weather Service ⊕ *www.wrh.noaa. gov.*

CALIFORNIA TODAY

The People

California is as much a state of mind as a state in the union—a kind of perpetual Promised Land that has represented many things to many people. In the 18th century, Spanish missionaries came seeking converts. In the 19th, miners rushed here to search for gold. And, in the years since, a long line of Dust Bowl farmers, land speculators, Haight-Ashbury hippies, migrant workers, dot-commers, real estate speculators, and would-be actors has come chasing their own dreams.

The result is a population that leans toward idealism—without necessarily being as liberal as you might think. (Remember, this is Ronald Reagan's old stomping ground.) And despite the stereotype of the blue-eyed, blond surfer, California's population is not homogeneous either. Ten million people who live here (more than 28% of Californians) are foreign born—including former Governor Schwarzenegger. Almost half hail from neighboring Mexico; another third emigrated from Asia, following the waves of Chinese workers who arrived in the 1860s to build the railroads and subsequent waves of Indochinese refugees from the Vietnam War.

The Politics

What's blue and red and green all over? California: a predominantly Democratic state with an aggressive "go green" agenda. Democratic Governor Jerry Brown, who was elected to the office for the second time in 30 years on a promise to clean up the financial mess created under his predecessor Arnold Schwarzenegger, is moving the progressive agenda ahead with policies that make California the greenest state in the nation supporting more green construction, wind farms, and solar panels.

The Economy

Leading all other states in terms of the income generated by agriculture, tourism, and industrial activity, California has the country's most diverse state economy. Moreover, with a gross state product of more than $2 trillion, California would be one of the top 10 economies *in the world* if it were an independent nation. But due to its wealth ($61,000 median household income) and productivity, California took a large hit in the recession that began in 2007. This affected all levels of government from local to statewide and resulted in reduction of services that Californians have long taken for granted.

But the Golden State's economic history is filled with boom and bust cycles—beginning with the mid-19th-century gold rush that started it all. Optimists already have their eyes on the next potential boom: high-tech and bio research, "green companies" focused on alternative energy, renewables, electric cars, and the like.

The Culture

Cultural organizations thrive in California. San Francisco—a city with only about 775,000 residents—has well-regarded ballet, opera, and theater companies, and is home to one of the continent's most noteworthy orchestras. Museums like San Francisco Museum of Modern Art (SFMOMA) and the de Young also represent the city's ongoing commitment to the arts. Art and culture thrive farther south in San Diego as well. Balboa Park alone holds 15 museums, opulent gardens, and three performance venues, in addition to the San Diego Zoo. The Old Globe Theater and La Jolla Playhouse routinely originate plays that capture coveted Tony Awards in New York.

But California's *real* forte is pop culture, and L.A. and its environs are the chief arbiters. Movie, TV, and video production have been centered here since the early 20th century. Capitol Records set up shop in L.A. in the 1940s, and this area has been instrumental in the music industry ever since. And while these industries continue to influence national trends, today they are only part of the pop culture equation. Websites are also a growing part of that creativity—Facebook, YouTube, and Google are California creatures.

The Parks and Preserves

Cloud-spearing redwood groves, snow-tipped mountains, canyon-slashed deserts, primordial lava beds, and a seemingly endless coast: California's natural diversity is staggering—and efforts to protect it started early. The first national park here was established in 1890, and the National Park Service now oversees 30 sites in California (more than in any other state). When you factor in 278 state parks—which encompass underwater preserves, historic sites, wildlife reserves, dune systems, and other sensitive habitats—the number of acres involved is almost as impressive as the topography itself.

Due to encroaching development and pollution, keeping these natural treasures in pristine condition is an ongoing challenge. For instance, Sequoia and Kings Canyon (which is plagued by pesticides and other agricultural pollutants blown in from the San Joaquin Valley) has been named America's "smoggiest park" by the National Parks Conservation Association, and the Environmental Protection Agency has designated it as an "ozone non-attainment area with levels of ozone pollution that threaten human health."

There is no question that Californians love their 278 state parks, 70 of which were scheduled to close in July 2012 due to budget cuts. Nearly every park has its grass-roots supporters, who volunteer to raise money, volunteer as rangers, and work other jobs to keep the parks open.

The Cuisine

California gave us McDonald's, Denny's, Carl's Jr., Taco Bell, and, of course, In-N-Out Burger. Fortunately for those of us with fast-clogging arteries, the state also kick-started the organic food movement. Back in the 1970s, California-based chefs put American cuisine on the culinary map by focusing on freshly prepared seasonal ingredients.

Today, this focus has spawned the "locavore" or sustainable food movement—followers try to only consume food produced within a 100-mile radius of where they live, since processing and refining food and transporting goods over long distances is bad for both the body and the environment. This isn't much of a restriction in California, where a huge variety of crops grow year-round. Some 350 cities and towns have certified farmers' markets—and their stalls are bursting with a variety of goods. California has been America's top agricultural producer for the last 50 years, growing more fruits and vegetables than any other state. Dairies and ranches also thrive here, and fishing fleets harvest fish and shellfish from the rich waters offshore.

CALIFORNIA
TOP ATTRACTIONS

San Diego

(A) San Diego is a thoroughly modern metropolis set on the sunny Pacific, filled with tourist attractions (think the Balboa Park, Zoo, SeaWorld, and LEGO-LAND) and blissful beaches. But this is also a city steeped in history—in 1769 Spaniards established a settlement here near Old Town, site of the first Spanish outpost and now a state park dedicated to illustrating San Diego's raucous early days. The city's rousing downtown dining and entertainment district, the Gaslamp Quarter, is a contemporary recreation of bawdy Stingaree of the late 1800s.

Channel Islands National Park

(B) This five-island park northwest of Los Angeles is a remote but accessible eco escape. There are no phones, no cars, and no services—but there are more than 2,000 species of plants and animals (among them blue whales and brown pelicans), plus ample opportunities for active pursuits. On land, hiking tops the itinerary. Underwater preserves surround the park, so snorkeling, scuba diving, fishing, and kayaking around lava tubes and natural arches are other memorable options.

Los Angeles

(C) Tinseltown, Lala Land, City of Angels: L.A. goes by many names and has many personas. Recognized as America's capital of pop culture, it also has highbrow appeal with arts institutions like the Getty Center, the Geffen Contemporary at MOCA, Walt Disney Concert Hall, the Norton Simon Museum, and Huntington Library. But you can go wild here, too—and not just on the Sunset Strip. Sprawling Griffith Park, Will Rogers State Historic Park, and Malibu Lagoon State Beach all offer a natural break from the concrete jungle.

Palm Springs and Beyond

(D) Celebrities used to flee to the desert for rest, relaxation, a few rays of sun, and to indulge in some high jinks beyond the watchful eyes of the media. You don't have to spend much time in Palm Springs to realize those days are *long* gone. In this improbably situated bastion of Bentleys and bling, worldly pleasures rule. Glorious golf courses, tony shops and restaurants, decadent spa resorts—they're all here. Solitude seekers can still slip away to nearby Joshua Tree National Park or Anza-Borrego Desert State Park.

Death Valley

(E) On the surface, a vacation in Death Valley sounds about as attractive as a trip to hell. Yet for well-prepared travelers, the experience is more awe-inspiring than ominous. Within the largest national park in the contiguous United States you'll find the brilliantly colored rock formations of Artists Palette, the peaks of the Panamint

Mountains, and the desolate salt flats of Badwater, 282 feet below sea level. You can't get any lower than this in the Western Hemisphere—and, in summer, you can't get much hotter.

San Francisco

(F) Population-wise, San Francisco is smaller than Indianapolis. But when it comes to sites (and soul), this city is a giant. Start working through the standard travelers' "to do" list by strolling across the Golden Gate Bridge, taking a ferry to Alcatraz, and hopping on the Powell–Hyde cable car. Just leave enough time to explore the diverse neighborhoods where San Francisco's distinctive personality—an amalgam of gold-rush history, immigrant traditions, counterculture proclivities, and millennial materialism—is on display.

Yosemite National Park

(G) Nature looms large here, both literally and figuratively. In addition to hulking Half Dome, the park is home to El

Capitan (the world's largest exposed granite monolith, rising 3,593 feet above the glacier-carved valley floor) and Yosemite Falls (North America's tallest cascade). In Yosemite's signature stand of giant sequoias—the Mariposa Grove—even the trees are Bunyanesque. Needless to say, crowds can be super-size.

Lake Tahoe

(H) Deep, clear, and intensely blue, this forest-rimmed body of water straddling the California–Nevada border is one of the continent's prettiest alpine lakes. That environmental controls can keep it that way is something of a miracle, given Tahoe's popularity. Throngs of outdoor adventurers flock to the California side to ski, hike, bike, and boat. On the Nevada side, where casinos are king, gambling often wins out over fresh-air activities—but natural wonders are never far away.

Point Reyes National Seashore

(I) Aside from the namesake seashore, this Marin County preserve encompasses ecosystems that range from woodlands and marshlands to heathlike grasslands. The range of wildlife here is equally diverse—depending on when you visit, expect to see gray whales, rare Tule elk, and almost 500 species of birds. December through March you can also see male elephant seals compete for mates.

Wine Country

(J) Although the vineyard-blanketed hills of California's original Wine Country are undeniably scenic, the wine itself (preferably accompanied by the area's famed cuisine) remains the big draw here. Budding oenophiles can educate their palettes on scores of tours and tasting sessions—provided they can elbow their way through the high-season hordes.

CALIFORNIA'S TOP EXPERIENCES

Hit the Road

Kings Canyon Highway, Redwood Highway, Tioga Pass, 17-Mile Drive, the Lake Tahoe loop: California has some splendid and challenging roads. You'll drive through a tunnel formed by towering redwood trees on the Redwood Highway. If you venture over the Sierras by way of Tioga Pass (through Yosemite in summer only), you'll see emerald green meadows, gray granite monoliths, and pristine blue lakes—and very few people.

Ride a Wave

Surfing—which has influenced everything from fashion to moviemaking to music—is a quintessential California activity. You can find great surf breaks in many places along the coast between Santa Cruz and San Diego. But one of the best places to try it is Huntington Beach. Lessons are widely available. If you're not ready to hang 10, you can hang out at "Surf City's" International Surfing Museum or stroll the Surfing Walk of Fame.

Go for the Gold

Though California's gold rush ended more than a hundred years ago, you can still feel the

49er fever on the western face of the Sierra Nevada in Columbia, a well-preserved town populated by costumed interpreters, where you can pan for gold or tour a mine. Or visit Bodie, an eerie ghost town in the eastern Sierra that remains in a state of "arrested decay."

Think Globally, Eat Locally

Over the years California cuisine has evolved from a mere trend into a respected gastronomic tradition: one that pairs local, often organic or sustainable, ingredients with techniques inspired by European, Asian, and, increasingly, Indian and Middle Eastern cookery.

Embrace Your Inner Eccentric

California has always drawn creative and, well, eccentric people. And all that quirkiness has left its mark in the form of oddball architecture that makes for some fun sightseeing. Begin by touring Hearst Castle—the beautifully bizarre estate William Randolph Hearst built above San Simeon. Scotty's Castle, a Moorish confection in Death Valley, offers a variation on the theme, as does Marta Becket's one-woman Amargosa Opera House. And Lake Tahoe's Vikingsholm (a re-created Viking castle) is equally odd.

Get Reel

In L.A. it's almost obligatory to do some Hollywood-style stargazing. Cue the action with a behind-the-scenes tour of one of the dream factories. (Warner Bros. Studios' five-hour deluxe version, which includes lunch in the commissary, is just the ticket for cinephiles.) Other must-sees include the Kodak Theatre, permanent home to the Cirque du Soleil and Academy Awards; Grauman's Chinese Theatre, where celebs press feet and hands into cement for posterity's sake; Hollywood Boulevard's star-paved Walk of Fame; and the still-iconic Hollywood sign.

People-Watch

Opportunities for world-class people-watching abound in California. Just saunter the rainbow-flagged streets of San Francisco's Castro neighborhood or the century-old boardwalk in time-warped, resiliently boho Santa Cruz. Better yet, hang around L.A.'s Venice Boardwalk, where chain-saw jugglers, surfers, fortune-tellers, and well-oiled bodybuilders take beachfront exhibitionism to a new high (or low, depending on your point of view). The result is pure eye candy.

QUINTESSENTIAL CALIFORNIA

The Beach

California's beach culture is, in a word, legendary. Of course, it only makes sense that folks living in a state with a 1,264-mile coastline (a hefty portion of which sees the sun upward of 300 days a year) would perfect the art of beach-going. True aficionados begin with a reasonably fit physique, plus a stylish wardrobe consisting of flip-flops, bikinis, wet suits, and such. Mastery of at least one beach skill—surfing, boogie boarding, kayaking, Frisbee tossing, or looking fab while catching rays—is also essential. As a visitor, though, you need only a swimsuit and some rented equipment for most sports. You can then hit the beach almost anywhere, thanks to the California belief in coastal access as a birthright. The farther south you go, the wider, sandier, and sunnier the beaches become; moving north they are rockier and foggier, with colder and rougher surf.

The Automobile

Americans may have a love affair with the automobile, but Californians have an out-and-out obsession. Even when gas prices rev up and freeway traffic slows down, their passion burns as hot as ever. You can witness this ardor any summer weekend at huge classic- and custom-car shows held statewide. Even better, you can feel it yourself by taking the wheel. Drive to the sea following Laguna Canyon Road to Laguna Beach; trace an old stagecoach route through the mountains above Santa Barbara on Highway 154; track migrating whales up the coast to Big Sur; or take 17-Mile Drive along the precipitous edge of the Monterey Peninsula. Glorious for the most part, but authentically congested in some areas in the south, Highway 1 runs almost the entire length of the state, hugging the coast most of the way.

Californians live in such a large and splashy state that they sometimes seem to forget about the rest of the country. They've developed a distinctive culture all their own, which you can delve into by doing as the locals do.

The Wine

If California were a country, it would rank as the world's fourth-largest wine producer, after Italy, France, and Spain. In those countries, where vino is barely considered an alcoholic beverage, wine drinking has evolved into a relaxing ritual best shared with friends and family. A modern, Americanized version of that mentality integrates wine into daily life in California, and there are many places to sample it. The Napa and Sonoma valleys come to mind first. However, there are other destinations for oenophiles who want a vintage vacation. You can find great wineries around Santa Barbara County, San Luis Obispo, Monterey Bay, Gold Country's Shenandoah Valley, and the Inland Empire's Temecula Valley, too. All are respected appellations, and their winery tours and tastings will show you what all the buzz is about.

The Outdoors

One of California's greatest assets—the mild year-round weather enjoyed by most of the state—inspires residents to spend as much time outside as they possibly can. They have a tremendous enthusiasm for every imaginable outdoor sport, and, up north especially, fresh-air adventures are extremely popular (which may explain why everyone there seems to own at least one pair of hiking boots). But the California-alfresco creed is more broadly interpreted, and the general rule when planning any activity is "if it can happen outside, it will!" *Plein air* vacation opportunities include dining on patios, decks, and wharves; shopping in street markets or elaborate open-air malls; hearing almost any kind of music at moonlight concerts; touring the sculpture gardens that grace major art museums; and celebrating everything from gay pride to garlic at outdoor fairs.

IF YOU LIKE

One-of-a-Kind Accommodations

Hoteliers statewide have done their utmost to create accommodations that match the glories of the region's landscape, in the process creating lodgings that boast character as well as comfort. Some are unconventional, while others are genuine old-school gems.

Hotel Del Coronado, Coronado. A turreted beauty and veritable Victorian extravaganza, this spot inspired L. Frank Baum's description of Oz. Iconic architecture aside, Hotel Del Coronado is also famous as the filming locale for *Some Like It Hot*, and has hosted most of the U.S. presidents in the last century. Today it caters more to tour groups than Tinseltown stars, but fans remain loyal.

Mission Inn, Riverside. This sprawling Spanish Revival estate has welcomed a who's who of politicos. Ronald and Nancy Reagan spent their wedding night here; Richard and Pat Nixon were married in its chapel; and eight U.S. heads of state have patronized its Presidential Lounge.

Movie Colony Hotel, Palm Springs. Hollywood's 1930s heyday comes alive at this glamorous boutique hotel designed by Albert Frey, who created mid-century minimalism in Palm Springs. The glam now attracts a lively clientele and has a cool vibe.

Fairmont San Francisco, San Francisco. It got off to a shaky start (the 1906 earthquake delayed its opening by exactly a year), but this Nob Hill hotel has hosted groundbreaking events like the drafting of the United Nations Charter and Tony Bennett's debut of "I Left My Heart in San Francisco."

Off-the-Beaten-Path Adventures

Mother Nature has truly outdone herself in California. But at the state's most popular sites, it can be hard to approach her handiwork with a sense of awe when you're encircled by souvenir hawkers and camera-wielding tourists. Step off the beaten path, though, and all you'll be able to hear will be the echo of your own voice saying "wow."

Hiking. Steam is the theme at Lassen Volcanic National Park: especially along the 3-mile Bumpass Hell Trail, which has hot springs, steam vents, and mud pots. If you're looking for a cooler hiking experience (temperature-wise), it's hard to top the rugged beauty of Point Reyes National Seashore.

Climbing. Joshua Tree National Park is California's epicenter for climbing; within the park there are hundreds of formations and thousands of routes to choose from. No experience? No problem. J-Tree outfitters offers crash courses for beginners.

Kayaking. Paddling around the lichen-covered sea caves of Channel Islands National Park or surreal tufa towers of Mono Lake, you'll feel like you're on another planet. But kayaking in San Francisco or La Jolla proves you needn't travel far to lose the mob.

Ballooning. Wanna get high? Hot-air ballooning—whether over Wine Country, Temecula, Palm Desert, Mammoth Lakes, or Shasta Valley—lets you sightsee from a totally new perspective.

Amusement Parks

You're on vacation, so why not enjoy some carefree pleasures? For concentrated doses of old-fashioned fun, indulge in creaky waterfront amusements—like Musée Mécanique on San Francisco's Fisherman's Wharf and the antique carousel at Santa Monica Pier. Or opt for a full day at an over-the-top theme park.

Disneyland, Anaheim. Walt Disney set the gold standard for theme parks, and his original "magic kingdom" (the only one built during his lifetime) remains at the top of its class due to innovative rides, animatronics, and a liberal sprinkling of pixie dust.

LEGOLAND California, Carlsbad. Dedicated to the plastic bricks that have been a playtime staple for almost 60 years, this park has more than 50 LEGO-inspired attractions (including the popular Driving School, Fun Town Fire Academy, plus get-all-wet Splash Battle and Treasure Falls) and some 15,000 LEGO models ranging from teeny working taxis to a 9-foot-tall dinosaur.

San Diego Zoo Safari Park, Escondido. Get up close and personal with lions and tigers at this huge park where animals appear to be roaming free. You can feed a giraffe, talk to the gorillas, and track herds of elk as they cross the plain. Cheetahs bound, hippos huff, and zebras zip.

Santa Cruz Beach Boardwalk, Santa Cruz. Now well over 100 years old (its centennial was in 2007), the state's oldest amusement park is a sentimental favorite. Expect vintage rides (most notably a 1911 carousel and wooden roller coaster) alongside contemporary attractions, as well as corn dogs, cotton candy, and loads of kitsch.

Spas

Ancient Romans coined the word "spa" as an acronym for *solus per aqua* (or "health by water"). There's plenty of the wet stuff in the Golden State, yet California spas—like California kitchens—are known for making the most of any indigenous ingredient. The resulting treatments are at once distinctive, decadent, and most important, relaxing.

The Golden Door, Escondido. Relax and renew at this destination spa tucked into a secluded canyon north of San Diego. Serenity and simplicity rule here, where every moment reflects its Zen-like ambience.

Glen Ivy Hot Springs Spa, Corona. Forget Club Med. In the Inland Empire, it's Club Mud that counts. The outdoor bath at this historic day spa couples red clay from Temescal Canyon with naturally heated, mineral-rich water from its own thermal springs.

Post Ranch Inn & Spa, Big Sur. Like its organic architecture, this luxe retreat's spa treatments are designed to capture the tone of Big Sur. Case in point, the Crystal and Gemstone Therapy. It combines Native American tradition (a ceremonial burning of sage) with an aromatherapy massage that employs jade collected from nearby beaches and essences of local wildflowers.

Spa Terra, Napa. While other Wine Country spas often overlook vineyards, the one at the new Meritage Resort occupies an estate cave 40 feet below them. Appropriately, the facility specializes in vinotherapy treatments incorporating—you guessed it—the fruit of the vine.

GREAT ITINERARIES

SOUTHERN CALIFORNIA DREAMING: LOS ANGELES, PALM SPRINGS, AND SAN DIEGO

Day 1: Arrival/Los Angeles

As soon as you land at LAX, make like a local and hit the freeway. Even if L.A.'s top-notch art, history, and science museums don't tempt you, the hodgepodge of art-deco, beaux-arts, and futuristic architecture begs at least a drive-by. Heading east from Santa Monica, Wilshire Boulevard cuts through a historical and cultural cross section of the city. Two stellar sights on its Miracle Mile are the encyclopedic Los Angeles County Museum of Art and the fossil-filled La Brea Tar Pits. Come evening, the open-air Farmers Market and its many eateries hum. Hotels in Beverly Hills or West Hollywood beckon, just a few minutes away.

Day 2: Hollywood and the Movie Studios

Every L.A. tourist should devote at least one day to the movies and take at least one studio tour. For fun, choose the special-effects theme park at Universal Studios Hollywood; for the nitty-gritty, choose Warner Bros. Studios. Nostalgic musts in half-seedy, half-preening Hollywood include the Walk of Fame along Hollywood Boulevard, the celebrity footprints cast in concrete outside Grauman's Chinese Theatre, and the 1922 Egyptian Theatre (Hollywood Boulevard's original movie palace). When evening arrives, the Hollywood scene boasts a bevy of trendy restaurants and nightclubs.

TIPS

❶ No matter how carefully you plan your movements to avoid busy routes at peak hours, you will inevitably encounter heavy traffic in L.A., Orange County, and San Diego.

❷ Allow yourself twice as much time as you think you'll need to negotiate LAX.

Day 3: Beverly Hills and Santa Monica

Even without that extensive art collection, the Getty Center's pavilion architecture, hilltop gardens, and frame-worthy L.A. views would make it a dazzling destination. Descend to the sea via Santa Monica Boulevard for lunch along Third Street Promenade, followed by a ride on the historic carousel on the pier. The buff and the bizarre meet on the boardwalk at Venice Beach (strap on some Rollerblades if you want to join them!). Rodeo Drive in Beverly Hills specializes in exhibitionism with a heftier price tag, but voyeurs are still welcome.

Day 4: Los Angeles to Palm Springs

Freeway traffic permitting, you can drive from the middle of L.A. to the middle of the desert in a couple of hours. Somehow in harmony with the harsh environment, midcentury "modern" homes and businesses with clean, low-slung lines define the Palm Springs style. The city seems far away, though, when you hike in hushed Tahquitz or Indian Canyon; cliffs and palm trees shelter rock art, irrigation works, and other remnants of Agua Caliente culture. If your boots aren't made for walking, you can always practice your golf game or indulge in some sublime or funky spa treatments at an area resort instead.

Day 5: The Desert
If riding a tram up an 8,516-foot mountain for a stroll or even a snowball fight above the desert sounds like fun to you, then show up at the Palm Springs Aerial Tramway before the first morning tram leaves (later, the line can get discouragingly long). Afterward stroll through the Palm Springs Art Museum where you can see a shimmering display of contemporary studio glass, an array of enormous Native American baskets, and significant works of 20th-century sculpture by Henry Moore and others.

Day 6: Palm Springs to San Diego
South through desert and mountains via the Palms to Pines Highway on your way to San Diego, you might pause in the Temecula Valley for lunch at a local winery. Otherwise go straight for the city's nautical heart by exploring the restored ships of the Maritime Museum at the waterfront downtown. Victorian buildings—and plenty of other tourists—surround you on a stroll through the Gaslamp Quarter, but the 21st century is in full swing at the quirky and colorful Horton Plaza retail and entertainment complex. Plant yourself at a downtown hotel and graze your way through the neighborhood's many restaurants and nightspots.

Day 7: San Diego Zoo and Coronado
Malayan tapirs in a faux-Asian rain forest, polar bears in an imitation Arctic—the San Diego Zoo maintains a vast and varied collection of creatures in a world-renowned facility comprised of meticulously designed habitats. Come early, wear comfy shoes, and stay as long as you can stand the sea of children. Boutique-y Coronado—anchored by the gracious Hotel Del Coronado—offers a more adult antidote. Tea, cocktails, or perhaps dinner at the Del makes a civilized end to an untamed day.

Day 8: SeaWorld and Old Town
Resistance is futile: you're going to SeaWorld. So what if it screams commercial? This humongous theme park, with its walk-through shark tanks and killer-whale shows, also screams fun. Surrender to the experience and try not to sit in anything sticky. Also touristy (but with genuine historical significance), Old Town drips with Mexican and early Californian heritage. Soak it up in the plaza at Old Town San Diego State Historic Park; then browse the stalls and shops at Bazaar del Mundo and along San Diego Avenue.

GREAT ITINERARIES

Day 9: La Jolla to Laguna Beach

Positioned above an idyllic cove, La Jolla invites lingering. So slow down long enough to enjoy its chic shop-lined streets, sheltered beaches, and cultural institutions like the low-key Birch Aquarium at Scripps and the well-curated Museum of Contemporary Art. At Mission San Luis Rey, in Oceanside, and Mission San Juan Capistrano, you can glimpse life as it was during the Spanish missionary days. Once a haven for artists, Laguna Beach still abounds with galleries. Its walkable downtown streets would abut busy Main Beach Park if the Pacific Coast Highway didn't run through the middle of town.

Day 10: Catalina Island

Having spent so much time looking at the ocean, it's high time you got out *on* it—a quick excursion to Catalina, 75 minutes from the coast, will do the trick. Get an early start, catching the boat from Newport Beach, then use the day to explore this nostalgia-inducing spot. The harbor town of Avalon has a charming, retro feel, while the island's mountains, canyons, and coves are ideal spots for outdoor adventures. Take the 4:30 boat back to the mainland and overnight in Anaheim.

Day 11: Disneyland

Disney's original park is a blast even without kids in tow. So go ahead: skirt the lines at the box office—advance-purchased ticket in hand—and storm the gates of the Magic Kingdom. You can cram the highlights into a single day if you arrive at opening time with a strategy already mapped out. Alternatively, you can spend your final full day next door at Disneyland's sister park, California Adventure, which is a fitting homage to the Golden State. In either case, cap your holiday with a nighttime toast at Downtown Disney.

Day 12: Departure/Los Angeles

Pack up your Mouseketeer gear and give yourself ample time to reach the airport. Without traffic the 35-mile drive from Anaheim to LAX *should* take about 45 minutes. But don't count on it.

SIERRA RICHES: YOSEMITE, GOLD COUNTRY, AND TAHOE

Day 1: Arrival/San Francisco

Straight from the airport, drop your bags at the lighthearted Hotel Monaco near Union Square and request a goldfish for your room. Chinatown, chock-full of dim sum shops, storefront temples, and open-air markets, promises unfamiliar tastes for lunch. Catch a Powell Street cable car to the end of the line and get off to see the bay views and the antique arcade games at Musée Mécanique, the hidden gem of otherwise mindless Fisherman's Wharf. No need to go any farther than cosmopolitan North Beach for cocktail hour, dinner, and live music.

Day 2: San Francisco

A Union Square stroll packs a wallop of people-watching, window-shopping, and architecture-viewing. In Golden Gate Park, linger amid the flora of the conservatory and the arboretum, soak up some art at the de Young Museum, and find serene refreshment at the Japanese Tea Garden. The Pacific surf pounds the cliffs below the Legion of Honor art museum, which has an exquisite view of the Golden Gate Bridge—when the fog stays away. Sunset cocktails at the circa-1909 Cliff House include a prospect over Seal Rock (actually occupied by sea lions). Eat dinner elsewhere: Pacific Heights, the

Mission, and SoMa teem with excellent restaurants.

Day 3: Into the High Sierra

First thing in the morning, pick up your rental car and head for the hills. A five-hour drive due east brings you to Yosemite National Park, where Bridalveil Fall and El Capitan, the 350-story granite monolith, greet you on your way to Yosemite Village. Ditch the car and pick up information and refreshment before hopping on the year-round shuttle to explore. Justly famous sights cram Yosemite Valley: massive Half Dome and Sentinel Dome, thundering Yosemite Falls, and wispy Ribbon Fall and Nevada Fall. Invigorating short hikes off the shuttle route lead to numerous vantage points. Celebrate your arrival in one of the world's most sublime spots with dinner in the dramatic Ahwahnee Hotel Dining Room.

Day 4: Yosemite National Park

Ardent hikers consider John Muir Trail a must-do, tackling the rigorous 12-hour round-trip to the top of Half Dome in search of life-changing vistas. The merely mortal hike downhill from Glacier Point on Four-Mile Trail or Panorama Trail, the latter an all-day trek past waterfalls. Less demanding still is a drive to Wawona for a stroll in the Mariposa Grove of Big Trees and lunch at the 19th-century Wawona Hotel. In bad weather, take shelter in the Ansel Adams Gallery and Yosemite Museum; in fair conditions, drive up to Glacier Point for a breathtaking sunset view.

Day 5: Gold Country South

Highway 49 traces the mother lode that yielded many fortunes in gold in the 1850s and 1860s. Step into a living gold-rush town at Columbia State Historic Park, where you can ride a stagecoach and pan for riches. Sutter Creek's well-preserved downtown bursts with shopping opportunities, but the vintage goods displayed at J. Monteverde General Store are not for sale. A different sort of vintage powers the present-day bonanza of Shenandoah Valley, heart of the Sierra Foothills wine country. Taste your way through Zinfandels and Syrahs at boutique wineries such as Domaine de la Terre Rouge, Renwood, and Sobon Estate. Amador City's 1879 Imperial Hotel places you firmly in the past for the night.

Day 6: Gold Country North

In Placerville, a mineshaft invites investigation at Hangtown's Gold Bug Mine, while Marshall Gold Discovery State Historic Park encompasses most of Coloma and preserves the spot where James

Marshall's 1849 find set off the California gold rush. Old Town Auburn, with its museums and courthouse, makes a good lunch stop, but if you hold out until you reach Grass Valley you can try authentic miners' pasties. A tour of Empire Mine State Historic Park takes you into a mine, and a few miles away horse-drawn carriages ply the narrow, shop-lined streets of downtown Nevada City. Backtrack to Auburn or Placerville to overnight in historic or modern lodgings.

Day 7: To the Lake

Jewel-like Lake Tahoe is a straight shot east of Placerville on Highway 50; stop for picnic provisions in commercial South Lake Tahoe. A stroll past the three magnificent estates in Pope-Baldwin Recreation area hints at the sumptuous lakefront summers once enjoyed by the elite. High above a glittering cove, Emerald Bay State Park offers one of the best lake views as well as a steep hike down to (and back up from) Vikingsholm, a replica 9th-century Scandinavian castle. Another fine, old mansion—plus a nature preserve and many hiking trails—lies in Sugar Pine Point State Park. Tahoe City offers more history and ample dining and lodging choices.

Day 8: Lake Tahoe

With advance reservations, you can tour the ultraluxe 1936 Thunderbird Lodge and its grounds. The picture-perfect beaches and bays of Lake Tahoe–Nevada State Park line the Nevada shoreline, a great place to bask in the sun or go mountain biking. For a different perspective of the lake, get out on the azure water aboard the stern-wheeler MS *Dixie II* from Zephyr Cove. In South Lake Tahoe, another view unfurls as the Heavenly Gondola travels 2½ miles up a mountain.

TIPS

❶ Try to time your trip for late spring or early fall to avoid the worst of the crowds and the road-closing snowfalls in Yosemite and around Lake Tahoe. Yosemite's falls peak in spring and early summer, while fall brings the grape harvest in the Sierra Nevada foothills.

❷ Parking in San Francisco is expensive and scarce. When you fly in, take a shuttle or taxi from the airport to the city, then use the excellent public transportation to get around.

❸ For a visit in any season, reserve your hotel or campground accommodations in Yosemite as far in advance as possible—up to a year ahead.

Keep your adrenaline pumping into the evening with some action at the massive casinos clustered in Stateline, Nevada.

Day 9: Back to the City

After a morning of driving, return your rental car in San Francisco and soak up some more urban excitement. Good options include lunch at the Ferry Building, followed by a visit to the San Francisco Museum of Modern Art, or lunch in Japantown followed by shopping in Pacific Heights. People-watching excels in the late afternoon bustle of the Castro and the Haight. Say good-bye to Northern California at one of the plush lounges or trendy bars in the downtown hotels.

Day 10: Departure/San Francisco

Check the weather before you start out for the airport: Fog sometimes causes delays at SFO. On a clear day, your flight path might give you one last fabulous glimpse of the City by the Bay.

FAQ

I'm not particularly active. Will I still enjoy visiting a national park? Absolutely, the most popular parks really do have something for everyone. Take Yosemite. When the ultrafit embark on 12-hour trail treks, mere mortals can hike Cook's Meadow—an easy 1-mile loop that's also wheelchair accessible. If even that seems too daunting, you can hop on a free shuttle or drive yourself to sites like Glacier Point or the Mariposa Grove of Giant Sequoias.

What's the single best place to take the kids? Well, that depends on your children's ages and interests, but for its sheer smorgasbord of activities, San Diego is hard to beat. Between the endless summer weather and sites such as SeaWorld, the San Diego Zoo, and LEGOLAND (about 30 minutes away), California's southernmost city draws families in droves. Once you've covered the mega-attractions, enjoy an easy-to-swallow history lesson in Old Town or the Maritime Museum. Want to explore different ecosystems? La Jolla Cove has kid-friendly tidal pools and cliff caves, while Anza-Borrego Desert State Park is a doable two-hour drive east.

If you're traveling in Northern California, San Francisco is also chockablock with kid-friendly attractions. A cable-car ride is a no-brainer—but if you have a Thomas the Tank engine fan in tow, be sure to also take a spin on the historic F-line trolleys. Other classic kid-friendly SF sights include the Exploratorium, the San Francisco Zoo, Alcatraz, the Ferry Building, and the California Academy of Sciences. Take the kids for dim sum in Chinatown; odds are they'll enjoy picking their dishes from a rolling buffet filled with foods they've likely never seen before. Or head to Musée Mécanique to see what kids played (way) before Nintendo's Wii came out.

That said, there are kid-friendly attractions all over the state—your kids are going to have to try really hard to be bored.

California sounds expensive. How can I save on sightseeing? CityPass (☎ 888/330–5008 ⊕ www.citypass.com) includes admission and some upgrades for main attractions in San Francisco, Hollywood, and Southern California (Disneyland, Universal Studios, and SeaWorld). Also, many museums set aside free-admission days. Prefer the great outdoors? An America the Beautiful annual pass (☎ 888/275–8747 ⊕ www.nps.gov) admits you to every site under the National Park Service umbrella. Better yet, depending on the property, passengers in your vehicle get in free, too.

Any tips for a first-time trip into the desert? The desert's stark, sun-blasted beauty will strip your mind of everyday clutter. But it is a brutal, punishing place for anyone ill-prepared. So whether it's your first or 15th visit, the same dos and don'ts apply. Stick to a state or national park. Pick up pamphlets at its visitor center and *follow the instructions* they set out. Keep your gas tank full. Bring lots of water and drink at least two gallons a day—even if you're not thirsty. Wear a hat and sunscreen, and don't expect to move too fast at midday when the sun is kiln-hot.

THE ULTIMATE ROAD TRIP

CALIFORNIA'S LEGENDARY HIGHWAY 1

by Cheryl Crabtree

One of the world's most scenic drives, California's State Route 1 (also known as Highway 1, the Pacific Coast Highway, the PCH) stretches along the edge of the state for nearly 660 miles, from Southern California's Dana Point to its northern terminus near Leggett, about 40 miles north of Fort Bragg. As you travel south to north, the water's edge transitions from long, sandy beaches and low-lying bluffs to towering dunes, craggy cliffs, and ancient redwood groves. The ocean changes as well; the relatively tame and surfable swells lapping the Southern California shore give way to the frigid, powerful waves crashing against weatherbeaten rocks in the north.

HIGHWAY 1 TOP 10

- Santa Monica
- Santa Barbara
- Hearst San Simeon State Historical Monument
- Big Sur
- Carmel
- 17–Mile Drive
- Monterey
- San Francisco
- Marin Headlands
- Point Reyes National Seashore

Give yourself lots of extra time to pull off the road and enjoy the scenery

STARTING YOUR JOURNEY

You may decide to drive the road's entire 660-mile route, or bite off a smaller piece. In either case, a Highway 1 road trip allows you to experience California at your own pace, stopping when and where you wish. Hike a beachside trail, dig your toes in the sand, and search for creatures in the tidepools. Buy some artichokes and strawberries from a roadside farmstand. Talk to people along the way (you'll run into everyone from soul-searching meditators, farmers, and beatniks to city-slackers and working-class folks), and take lots of pictures. Don't rush—you could easily spend a lifetime discovering secret spots along this route.

To help you plan your trip, we've broken the road into three regions (Santa Monica to Carmel, Carmel to San Francisco, and San Francisco to Fort Bragg); each region is then broken up into smaller segments—many of which are suitable for a day's drive. If you're pressed for time, you can always tackle a section of Highway 1, and then head inland to U.S. 101 or I-5 to reach your next destination more quickly.

WHAT'S IN A NAME?

Though it's often referred to as the Pacific Coast Highway (or PCH), sections of Highway 1 actually have different names. The southernmost section (Dana Point to Oxnard) is the Pacific Coast Highway. After that, the road becomes the Cabrillo Highway (Las Cruces to Lompoc), the Big Sur Coast Highway (San Luis Obispo County line to Monterey), the North Coast Scenic Byway (San Luis Obispo city limit to the Monterey County line), the Cabrillo Highway again (Santa Cruz County line to Half Moon Bay), and finally the Shoreline Highway (Marin City to Leggett). To make matters more confusing, smaller chunks of the road have additional honorary monikers.

Just follow the green triangular signs that say "California 1."

HIGHWAY 1 DRIVING

- Rent a convertible. (You will not regret it.)
- Begin the drive north from Santa Monica, where congestion and traffic delays pose less of a problem.
- Take advantage of turnouts. Let cars pass you as you take in the ocean view and snap a picture.
- Mind your manners: Don't tailgate or glare at other drivers.
- If you're prone to motion sickness, take the wheel yourself. Focusing on the landscape outside should help you feel less queasy.
- If you're afraid of heights, drive from south to north so you'll be on the mountain rather than the cliff side of the road.
- Driving PCH is glorious during winter, but check weather conditions before you go as landslides are frequent after storms.

HIGHWAY 1: SANTA MONICA TO BIG SUR

Hearst Castle

Santa Barbara

THE PLAN

Distance: approx. 335 mi

Time: 3-5 days

Good Overnight Options: Malibu, Santa Barbara, Pismo Beach, San Luis Obispo, Cambria, Carmel

For more information on the sights and attractions along this portion of Highway 1, please see Los Angeles and Central Coast chapters

SANTA MONICA TO MALIBU (approx. 26 mi)

Highway 1 begins in Dana point, but it seems more appropriate to begin a PCH adventure in **Santa Monica.** Be sure to experience the beach culture, then balance the tacky pleasures of Santa Monica's amusement pier with a stylish dinner in a neighborhood restaurant.

MALIBU TO SANTA BARBARA (approx. 70 mi)

The PCH follows the curve of Santa Monica Bay all the way to **Malibu** and **Point Mugu,** near **Oxnard.** Chances are you'll experience *déjà vu* driving this 27-mile stretch: mountains on one side, ocean on the other, opulent homes perched on hillsides; you've seen this piece of coast countless times on TV and film. Be sure to walk out on the **Malibu Pier** for a great photo opp, then check out **Surfrider Beach,** with three famous points where perfect waves ignited a worldwide surfing rage in the 1960s.

After Malibu you'll drive through miles of protected, largely unpopulated coastline. Ride a wave at **Zuma Beach**, scout for offshore whales at **Point Dume State Preserve,** or hike the trails at **Point Mugu State Park.** After skirting Point Mugu, Highway 1 merges with U.S. 101 for about 70 mi before reaching **Santa Barbara.** A mini-tour of the city includes a real Mexican lunch at **La Super-Rica,** a visit to the magnificent Spanish **Mission Santa Barbara,** and a walk down hopping **State Street to Stearns Wharf.**

SANTA BARBARA TO SAN SIMEON (approx. 147 mi)

North of Santa Barbara, Highway 1 morphs into the Cabrillo Highway, separating from and then rejoining U.S. 101. The route winds through rolling vineyards and rangeland to **San Luis Obispo,** where any legit road trip includes a photo stop at the quirky **Madonna Inn.** Be sure to also climb the humungous dunes at **Guadalupe-Nipomo Dunes Preserve.**

In downtown San Luis Obispo, the **Mission San Luis Obispo de Tolosa** stands by a tree-shaded creek edged with shops and cafés. Highway 1 continues to **Morro Bay** and up the coast. About 4 mi north of Morro Bay, you'll reach **Cayucos,** a classic old California beach town with an 1875 pier, restaurants, taverns, and shops in historic buildings. The road continues through **Cambria** to solitary **Hearst San Simeon State Historical Monument**—the art-filled pleasure palace at **San Simeon.** Just four miles north of the castle, elephant seals grunt and cavort at the

Santa Monica

Big Sur

TOP 5 PLACES TO LINGER

- Point Dume State Preserve
- Santa Barbara
- Hearst San Simeon State Historical Monument
- Big Sur/Julia Pfeiffer Burns State Park
- Carmel

Piedras Blancas Elephant Seal Rookery, just off the side of the road.

SAN SIMEON TO CARMEL (approx. 92 mi) Heading north, you'll drive through **Big Sur**, a place of ancient forests and rugged shoreline stretching 90 mi from San Simeon to **Carmel**. Much of Big Sur lies within several state parks and the 165,000-acre **Ventana Wilderness**, itself part of the **Los Padres National Forest**. This famously scenic stretch of the coastal drive, which twists up and down bluffs above the ocean, can last hours. Take your time.

At **Julia Pfeiffer Burns State Park** one easy but rewarding hike leads to an iconic waterfall off a beach-front cliff. When you reach lovely **Carmel,** stroll around the picture-perfect town's mission, galleries, and shops.

HIGHWAY 1: CARMEL TO SAN FRANCISCO

San Francisco

THE PLAN

Distance: approx. 123 mi

Time: 2-4 days

Good Overnight Options: Carmel, Monterey, Santa Cruz, Half Moon Bay, San Francisco

For more information on the sights and attractions along this portion of Highway 1, please see chapters Monterey Bay, San Francisco, and Bay Area.

CARMEL TO MONTEREY (approx. 4 mi)

Between **Carmel** and **Monterey,** Highway 1 cuts across the base of the Monterey Peninsula. Pony up the toll and take a brief detour to follow famous **17-Mile Drive,** which traverses a surf-pounded landscape of cypress trees, sea lions, gargantuan estates, and the world famous **Pebble Beach Golf Links.** Take your time here as well, and be sure to allow lots of time for pulling off to enjoy the gorgeous views.

If you have the time, spend a day checking out the sights in **Monterey,** especially the kelp forests and bat rays of the **Monterey Bay Aquarium** and the adobes and artifacts of **Monterey State Historic Park.**

MONTEREY TO SANTA CRUZ (approx. 42 mi)

From Monterey the highway rounds the gentle curve of Monterey Bay, passing through sand dunes and artichoke fields on its way to **Moss Landing** and the **Elkhorn Slough National Estuarine Marine Preserve.** Kayak near or walk through the protected wetlands here, or board a pontoon safari boat—don't forget your binoculars. The historic seaside villages of **Aptos, Capitola,** and **Soquel,** just off the highway near the bay's midpoint, are ideal stopovers for beachcombing, antiquing, and hiking through redwoods. In boho **Santa Cruz,** just 7 mi north, walk along the **wharf,** ride the historic roller coaster on the **boardwalk,** and perch on the cliffs to watch surfers peel through tubes at **Steamer Lane.**

SANTA CRUZ TO SAN FRANCISCO (approx. 77 mi)

Highway 1 hugs the ocean's edge once again as it departs Santa Cruz and runs

Davenport cliffs, Devenport

northward past a string of secluded beaches and small towns. Stop and stretch your legs in the tiny, artsy town of **Davenport,** where you can wander through several galleries and enjoy sumptuous views from the bluffs. At **Año Nuevo State Reserve,** walk down to the dunes to view gargantuan elephant

FRIGID WATERS

If you're planning to jump in the ocean in Northern California, wear a wetsuit or prepare to shiver. Even in summer, the water temperatures warm up to just barely tolerable. The fog tends to burn off earlier in the day at relatively sheltered beaches near Monterey Bay's midpoint, near Aptos, Capitola and Santa Cruz. These beaches also tend to attract softer waves than those on the bay's outer edges.

Half Moon Bay

TOP 5 PLACES TO LINGER

- 17-Mile Drive
- Monterey
- Santa Cruz
- Año Nuevo State Reserve
- Half Moon Bay

seals lounging on shore, then break for a meal or snack in **Pescadero** or **Half Moon Bay**.

From Half Moon Bay to **Daly City,** the road includes a number of shoulderless twists and turns that demand slower speeds and nerves of steel. Signs of urban development soon appear: mansions holding fast to Pacific cliffs and then, as the road veers slightly inland to merge with Skyline Boulevard, boxlike houses sprawling across **Daly City** and **South San Francisco.**

HIGHWAY 1: SAN FRANCISCO TO FORT BRAGG

Mendocino Coast Botanical Garden

THE PLAN

Distance: 177 mi

Time: 2-4 days

Good Overnight Options: San Francisco, Olema, Bodega Bay, Gualala, Mendocino, Fort Bragg

For more information on the sights and attractions along this portion of Highway 1, please see San Francisco, Bay Area, and North Coast chapters

SAN FRANCISCO

The official Highway 1 heads straight through **San Francisco** along 19th Avenue through **Golden Gate Park** and the **Presidio** toward the **Golden Gate Bridge.** For a more scenic tour, watch for signs announcing exits for 35 North/Skyline Boulevard, then Ocean Beach/The Great Highway (past Lake Merced). The Great Highway follows the coast along the western border of San Francisco; you'll cruise past entrances to the **San Francisco Zoo, Golden Gate Park,** and the **Cliff**

Golden Gate Bridge

House. Hike out to **Point Lobos** or **Land's End** for awesome vistas, then drive through **Lincoln Park** and the **Palace of the Legion of Honor** and follow El Camino del Mar/Lincoln Boulevard all the way to the Golden Gate Bridge.

The best way to see San Francisco is on foot and public transportation. A **Union Square** stroll—complete with people-watching, window-shopping, and architecture-viewing—is a good first stop. In **Chinatown,** department stores give way to storefront temples, open-air markets, and delightful dim-sum shops. After lunch in one, catch a **Powell Street cable car** to the end of the line and get off to see the bay views and the antique arcade games at **Musée Mécanique** (the gem of otherwise mindless **Fisherman's Wharf**). For dinner and live music, try cosmopolitan **North Beach.**

SAN FRANCISCO TO OLEMA

(approx. 37 mi)

Leaving the city the next day, your drive across the Golden Gate Bridge and a stop at a **Marin Headlands** overlook will yield memorable views (if fog hasn't socked in the bay). So will a hike in **Point Reyes National Seashore,** farther up Highway 1 (now

Point Reyes National Seashore

called Shoreline Highway). On this wild swath of coast you'll likely be able to claim an unspoiled beach for yourself. You should expect company, however, around the lighthouse at the tip of Point Reyes because year-round views—and seasonal elephant seal- and whale-watching—draw crowds. If you have time, poke around tiny **Olema,** which has some excellent restaurants, and is home to the historic Olema Inn & Restaurant.

OLEMA TO MENDOCINO

(approx. 131 mi)

Passing only a few minuscule towns, this next stretch of Highway 1 showcases the northern coast in all its rugged glory. The reconstructed compound of eerily foreign buildings at **Fort Ross State Historic Park** recalls the era of Russian fur trading in California. Pull into **Gualala** for an espresso, a sandwich, and a little human contact

Point Reyes National Seashore

TOP 5 PLACES TO LINGER

- San Francisco
- Marin Headlands
- Point Reyes National Seashore
- Fort Ross State Historic Park
- Mendocino

before rolling onward. After another 50 mi of tranquil state beaches and parks you'll return to civilization in **Mendocino**.

MENDOCINO TO FORT BRAGG

(approx. 9 mi)

Exploring Mendocino you may feel like you've fallen through a rabbit hole: the weather screams Northern California, but the 19th-century buildings—erected by homesick Yankee loggers—definitely say New England. Once you've browsed around the artsy shops, continue on to the **Mendocino Coast Botanical Gardens;** then travel back in time on the **Skunk Train,** which follows an old logging route from **Fort Bragg** deep into the redwood forest.

San Diego

WORD OF MOUTH

"The highlight of the day was the Backstage Pass [at the San Diego Zoo] . . . We saw a rare owl, a biturong (bear cat), an Arctic wolf, a serval, a cheetah, and we hand-fed a rhino . . . We spent from 9–5 at the zoo, arriving just as they opened and leaving just as they closed, and we still didn't get to see every animal!"

—amyb

WELCOME TO SAN DIEGO

TOP REASONS TO GO

★ **Beautiful beaches:** San Diego's shore shimmers with crystalline Pacific waters rolling up to some of the prettiest stretches of sand on the West Coast.

★ **Good eats:** Taking full advantage of the region's bountiful vegetables, fruits, herbs, and seafood, San Diego's chefs dazzle and delight diners with inventive California-colorful cuisine.

★ **History lessons:** The well-preserved and reconstructed historic sites in California's first European settlement help you imagine what the area was like when explorers first arrived.

★ **Stellar shopping:** Westfield Horton Plaza, the Gaslamp Quarter, Seaport Village, Coronado, Old Town, La Jolla . . . no matter where you go in San Diego, you'll find great places to do a little browsing.

★ **Urban oasis:** Balboa Park's 1,200 acres contain world-class museums and the zoo, but also well-groomed lawns and gardens and wild, undeveloped canyons.

1 Downtown. San Diego's Downtown area is delightfully urban and accessible, filled with walkable A-list attractions like the Gaslamp Quarter, Horton Plaza, and the waterfront.

2 Balboa Park. San Diego's cultural heart is where you'll find most of the city's museums and its world-famous zoo.

3 Coronado. Home to the Hotel Del, this island-like peninsula is a favorite celebrity haunt.

4 Harbor and Shelter Islands and Point Loma. Yachts and resorts, fast-food shacks and motels—plus gorgeous views of Coronado and the Downtown skyline.

5 Mission Bay and SeaWorld. Home to 27 miles of shoreline, this 4,600 acre aquatic park is San Diego's monument to sports and fitness.

6 Old Town. California's first permanent European settlement is now preserved as a state historic park.

7 La Jolla. This luxe, bluff-top enclave fittingly means "the jewel" in Spanish. Come here for fantastic upscale shopping and unspoiled stretches of the coast.

2

GETTING ORIENTED

Exploring San Diego may be an endless adventure, but there are limitations, especially if you don't have a car. San Diego is more a chain of separate communities than a cohesive city, and many of the major attractions are miles apart. Walking is good for getting an up-close look at how San Diegans live, but true Southern Californians use the freeways that crisscross the county. Interstate 5 runs a direct north–south route through the coastal communities from Orange County in the north to the Mexican border. Interstates 805 and 15 do much the same inland. Interstate 8 is the main east–west route. Routes 163, 52, and 94 serve as connectors.

Updated by
Bobbi Zane

San Diego is a big California city—second only to Los Angeles in population—with a small-town feel. It also covers a lot of territory, roughly 400 square miles of land and sea. To the north and south of the city are 70 miles of beaches. Inland, a succession of chaparral-covered mesas is punctuated with deep-cut canyons that step up to forested mountains, separating the coast from the arid Anza-Borrego Desert.

The San Diego area, the birthplace of California, was claimed for Spain by explorer Juan Rodríguez Cabrillo in 1542 and eventually came under Mexican rule. You'll find reminders of San Diego's Spanish and Mexican heritage throughout the region—in architecture and place-names, in distinctive Mexican cuisine, and in the historic buildings of Old Town.

In 1867 developer Alonzo Horton, who called the town's bay front "the prettiest place for a city I ever saw," began building a hotel, a plaza, and prefab homes on 960 Downtown acres. The city's fate was sealed in 1908, when President Theodore Roosevelt's Great White Fleet sailed into the bay. The U.S. Navy, impressed by the city's excellent harbor and temperate climate, decided to build a destroyer base on San Diego Bay in the 1920s. The newly developed aircraft industry soon followed (Charles Lindbergh's plane *Spirit of St. Louis* was built here). The military, which operates many bases and installations throughout the county (which, added together, form the largest military base in the world), continues to contribute to the local economy.

PLANNING

GETTING HERE AND AROUND
AIR TRAVEL
The major airport is San Diego International Airport, called Lindbergh Field locally. The airport's three-letter code is SAN. Major airlines depart and arrive at Terminal 1 and Terminal 2; commuter flights identified on your ticket with a 3000 sequence flight number depart from a

third commuter terminal. A red shuttle bus provides free transportation between terminals.

Airport San Diego International Airport ⊠ *3225 N. Harbor Dr., off I–5* ☎ *619/400–2400* ⊕ *www.san.org.*

Airport Transfers Access Shuttle ☎ *800/690–9090* ⊕ *www.accessshuttle. net.* **Cloud 9 Shuttle/SuperShuttle** ☎ *800/974–8885* ⊕ *www.cloud9shuttle. com.* **San Diego Transit** ☎ *619/233–3004, 800/568–7097 TTY and TDD* ⊕ *transit.511sd.com.*

BUS AND TROLLEY TRAVEL

San Diego County is served by a coordinated, efficient network of bus and rail routes that includes service to Oceanside in the north, the Mexican border at San Ysidro, and points east to the Anza-Borrego Desert. Under the umbrella of the Metropolitan Transit System, there are two major transit agencies: San Diego Transit and North County Transit District (NCTD). The bright-red trolleys of the San Diego Trolley light-rail system serve Downtown San Diego, Mission Valley, Old Town, South Bay, the U.S. border, and East County. The trolley system connects with San Diego Transit bus routes. All the services can be accessed by dialing 511 on your phone or at ⊕ *transit.511sd.com.*

Bus and Trolley Contacts North County Transit District ☎ *511, 619/233–3004* ⊕ *transit.511sd.com.* **San Diego Transit** ☎ *511, 800/568–7097 TTY and TDD* ⊕ *transit.511sd.com.* **Transit Store** ⊠ *102 Broadway, at 1st Ave., Downtown* ☎ *619/234–1060.*

CAR TRAVEL

When traveling in the San Diego area, it pays to consider the big picture to avoid getting lost. Water lies to the west of the city. To the east and north, mountains separate the urban areas from the desert. Interstate 5, which stretches from Canada to the Mexican border, bisects San Diego. Interstate 8 provides access from Yuma, Arizona, and points east. Drivers coming from Nevada and the mountain regions beyond can reach San Diego on Interstate 15. During rush hour there are jams on Interstate 5 and on Interstate 15 between Interstate 805 and Escondido.

TAXI TRAVEL

Taxi stands are at shopping centers and hotels; otherwise you must call and reserve a cab. The companies listed below do not serve all areas of San Diego County. If you're going someplace other than Downtown, ask if the company serves that area.

Taxi Companies Orange Cab ☎ *619/223–5555* ⊕ *www.orangecabsandiego. com.* **Silver Cabs** ☎ *619/280–5555* ⊕ *www.sandiegosilvercab.com.* **Yellow Cab** ☎ *619/444–4444* ⊕ *www.driveu.com.*

TRAIN TRAVEL

Amtrak serves Downtown San Diego's Santa Fe Depot with daily trains to and from Los Angeles, Santa Barbara, and San Luis Obispo. Connecting service to Oakland, Seattle, Chicago, Texas, Florida, and points beyond is available in Los Angeles. Amtrak trains stop in San Diego North County at Solana Beach and Oceanside.

Coaster commuter trains, which run between Oceanside and San Diego Monday through Saturday, stop at the same stations as Amtrak plus others. The Sprinter runs between Oceanside and Escondido with many stops along the way.

Information Amtrak ⊠ *Santa Fe Depot, 1050 Kettner Blvd., at Broadway* ☎ *800/872-7245* ⊕ *www.amtrak.com.* **Coaster** ☎ *619/233-3004, 511* ⊕ *transit.511sd.com.* **Metrolink** ☎ *800/371-5465* ⊕ *www.metrolinktrains.com.*

TOURS

Recommended Tours/Guides DayTripper Tours ⊠ *624 El Cajon Blvd., El Cajon* ☎ *619/299-5777, 800/679-8747* ⊕ *www.daytripper.com.* **San Diego Scenic Tours** ⊠ *2255 Garnet Ave., #3* ☎ *858/273-8687* ⊕ *www. sandiegoscenictours.com.* **Secret San Diego** ⊠ *611 K St., #B224* ☎ *619/917-6037* ⊕ *www.wheretours.com.*

Boat Tours Flagship Cruises/San Diego Harbor Excursions ⊠ *1050 N. Harbor Dr.* ☎ *619/234-4111, 800/442-7847* ⊕ *www.flagshipsd.com.* **H&M Landing** ⊠ *2803 Emerson St.* ☎ *619/222-1144* ⊕ *www.hmlanding.com.* **Hornblower Cruises & Events** ⊠ *1066. N. Harbor Dr.* ☎ *619/234-8687, 800/668-4322* ⊕ *www.hornblower.com.*

Bus and Trolley Tours Gray Line San Diego ⊠ *3888 Beech St.* ☎ *800/331-5077, 619/266-7635* ⊕ *www.grayline.com.* **Old Town Trolley Tours** ⊠ *2115 Kurtz St.* ☎ *619/298-8687* ⊕ *www.trolleytours.com/san-diego.*

Walking Tours Coronado Walking Tours ⊠ *1630 Glorietta Blvd.* ☎ *619/435-5993* ⊕ *coronadowalkingtour.com.* **Gaslamp Quarter Historical Foundation** ⊠ *410 Island Ave.* ☎ *619/233-4692* ⊕ *www.gaslampquarter.org.*

Urban Safaris ☎ *619/944-9255* ⊕ *www.walkingtoursofsandiego.com.*

VISITOR INFORMATION

City Contacts International Visitor Information Center ⊠ *SDCVB, 1140 N. Harbor Dr., at B Street Cruise Ship Terminal, Downtown* ☎ *619/236-1212* ⊕ *www.sandiego.org* ☉ *June–Sept., daily 9–5; Oct.–May, daily 9–4.***San Diego Convention & Visitors Bureau** ☎ *619/232-3101* ⊕ *www.sandiego.org.*

San Diego County Contacts Carlsbad Convention & Visitors Bureau ⊠ *400 Carlsbad Village Dr., Carlsbad* ☎ *800/227-5722* ⊕ *www.visitcarlsbad.com.* **Coronado Visitor Center** ⊠ *1100 Orange Ave., Coronado* ☎ *619/437-8788* ⊕ *www. coronadovisitorcenter.com.* **Encinitas Chamber of Commerce** ⊠ *527 Encinitas Blvd., Suite 106, Encinitas* ☎ *760/753-6041* ⊕ *www.encinitaschamber.com.* **La Jolla Village Merchants Association** ⊠ *7734 Herschel Ave., Suite G, La Jolla* ☎ *858/454-5718* ⊕ *www.lajollabythesea.com.*

EXPLORING SAN DIEGO

DOWNTOWN

Nearly written off in the 1970s, today Downtown San Diego is a testament to conservation and urban renewal. The turnaround began with the revitalization of the Gaslamp Quarter Historic District and massive redevelopment that gave rise to the Horton Plaza shopping center and the San Diego Convention Center, as well as to elegant hotels, upscale condominium complexes, and trendy restaurants and cafés. Like many modern U.S. cities, Downtown San Diego's story is as much about its rebirth as its history.

Many people think of the Gaslamp Quarter as Downtown, but Downtown comprises eight neighborhoods, among them East Village, Little Italy, and Embarcadero. Gaslamp is the liveliest, especially along 4th and 5th avenues, which are peppered with trendy nightclubs and lounges, chic restaurants, and boisterous sports pubs.

Nearby East Village encompasses 130 blocks between the railroad tracks and J Street, and from 6th Avenue east to around 10th Street. Sparking the rebirth of this former warehouse district was construction of the San Diego Padres' baseball stadium, PETCO Park. As the city's largest Downtown neighborhood, East Village is continually broadening its boundaries with its urban design of redbrick cafés, spacious galleries, rooftop bars, sleek hotels, and warehouse restaurants.

There are reasonably priced ($4–$7 per day) parking lots along Harbor Drive, Pacific Highway, and lower Broadway and Market Street. Most restaurants offer valet parking at night, but beware of fees of $15 and up.

TOP ATTRACTIONS

Embarcadero. The bustle of Embarcadero comes less these days from the activities of fishing folk than from the throngs of tourists, but this waterfront walkway remains the nautical soul of the city. There are sea vessels of every variety—cruise ships, ferries, tour boats, and Navy aircraft carriers.

On the north end of the Embarcadero at Ash Street you'll find the **Maritime Museum.** South of it, the **B Street Pier** is used by ships from major cruise lines. The terminal for the **Coronado Ferry** comes next, then the **Broadway Pier,** where tickets for harbor tours and whale-watching trips are sold. One block south of the Broadway Pier at **Tidelands Park** is Military Heritage Art, a collection of works that commemorate the service of the U.S. military.

Lining the pedestrian promenade between the Cruise Ship Terminal and Hawthorn Street are 30 "**urban trees**" sculpted by local artists. At the Navy pier is the **USS Midway Museum.**

The pleasant **Tuna Harbor Park** offers a great view of boating on the bay and across to any aircraft carriers docked at the North Island naval base.

The next bit of seafront greenery is a few blocks south at **Embarcadero Marina Park North,** an extension into the harbor from the center of the **Seaport Village** complex of retail stores, restaurants, and cafés. The park is usually full of kite fliers, in-line skaters, and picnickers. Seasonal celebrations are held here and at the similar **Embarcadero Marina Park South.** The **San Diego Convention Center,** on Harbor Drive between 1st and 6th avenues, is a waterfront landmark designed by Canadian architect Arthur Erickson.

Gaslamp Quarter Historic District. The heart of Downtown San Diego, the Gaslamp Quarter occupies 16½ blocks in a formerly run-down neighborhood holding the largest collection of commercial Victorian-building in the nation. Now a vibrant dining and entertainment district, the quarter contains restaurants, hotels, nightclubs and music venues, theaters, and the Horton Plaza shopping complex. Many of these carefully restored old buildings are downright gorgeous. This is a great place to walk and shop. PETCO Park, where the San Diego Padres play baseball, and the convention center are nearby. ■TIP➔ Metered street parking is available throughout Downtown, but a spot can be difficult to find. One alternative is the Horton Plaza parking structure, where you can get three free hours with validation.

The majority of the quarter's landmark buildings are on 4th and 5th avenues, between Island Avenue and Broadway. If you don't have much time, stroll down 5th Avenue, where highlights include the **Louis Bank of Commerce Building** (No. 835), the **Old City Hall Building** (No. 664), the **Nesmith-Greeley Building** (No. 825), and the **Yuma Building** (No. 631). The Romanesque-revival **Keating Hotel** (432 F Street) was designed by the same firm that created the famous Hotel Del Coronado. At the corner of 4th Avenue and F Street, peer into the **Hard Rock Cafe,** which occupies a restored turn-of-the-20th-century tavern. The Hard Rock has a 12-foot mahogany bar and a spectacular stained-glass domed ceiling.

The section of G Street between 6th and 9th avenues is a haven for galleries; stop in one of them to pick up a map of the Downtown arts district. Just to the north, on E and F streets from 6th to 12th avenues, the evolving **Urban Art Trail** has added pizzazz to drab city thoroughfares by transforming such things as trash cans and traffic-controller boxes into works of art.

During baseball season, the streets flood with Padres fans, and festivals, such as Mardi Gras in February, ShamROCK on St. Patrick's Day, and Monster Bash in October, bring in partygoers. To miss the Gaslamp Quarter would be to miss San Diego's most exciting neighborhood. The Gaslamp Quarter Association is a good source for information about the district. ⊠ *Gaslamp Quarter Association* ☎ *619/233–4692* ⊕ *www.gaslamp.org.*

Gaslamp Museum at the William Heath Davis House. The oldest wooden house in San Diego houses the Gaslamp Quarter Historical Foundation, the district's curator. Before developer Alonzo Horton came to town, Davis, a prominent San Franciscan, had made an unsuccessful attempt to develop the waterfront area. In 1850 he had this prefab saltbox-style house, built in Maine, shipped around Cape Horn and assembled in San Diego (it originally stood at State and Market streets). Audio-guided or brochure-guided museum tours are available with museum admission. Regularly scheduled two-hour walking tours of the historic district leave from the house on Saturday at 11 and cost $10. If you can't time your visit with the weekly tour, a self-guided tour map is available for purchase for $2. ⊠ *410 Island Ave., at 4th Ave., Gaslamp Quarter*

☎ 619/233–4692 ⊕ *www.gaslampquarter.org* 🎫 *$5* ⊙ *Tues.–Sat. 10–5, Sun. noon–4.*

OFF THE
BEATEN
PATH

Hillcrest. The large retro Hillcrest sign over the intersection of University and 5th avenues marks the epicenter of this vibrant Uptown neighborhood, the heart of San Diego's large gay community. Along 4th, 5th, and 6th avenues from Washington Street to Robinson Avenue, national chains such as American Apparel and Pinkberry coexist alongside local boutiques, bookstores, restaurants, and coffee shops. A few blocks east along University Avenue lie other interesting stores and restaurants. If you are visiting Hillcrest on Sunday between 9 and 2, be sure to explore the Hillcrest farmers' market. ⊠ *Centered around University Ave. and 5th Ave., Hillcrest.*

International Visitor Information Center. Located in front of the B Street Cruise Ship Terminal, this office is a great resource. ■ TIP→ The free planning kit available here has discounts on tours and attractions. ⊠ *1140 N. Harbor Dr. , at B St., Embarcadero* ☎ *619/236–1212* ⊕ *www. sandiego.org* ⊙ *June–Sept., daily 9–5; Oct.–May, daily 9–4.*

Ⓒ
Fodor's Choice
★

Maritime Museum. From sailing ships to submarines, this collection of restored and replica ships provides a fascinating glimpse of San Diego during its heyday as a commercial seaport. The collection's jewel, the *Star of India,* is often considered a symbol of the city. An iron windjammer built in 1863, the *Star of India* made 21 trips around the world in the late 1800s, when it traveled the East Indian trade route, shuttled immigrants from England to New Zealand, and served the Alaskan salmon trade. Now beautifully restored, the *Star of India* is the oldest active iron sailing ship in the world.

You can take to the water in the museum's other sailing ship, the *Californian.* This replica of a 19th-century revenue cutter that patrolled the shores of California is designated the state's official tall ship. Weekend sails, typically from noon to 4, cost $43. Tickets may be purchased online or at the museum on the day of sail. The voyages are popular on sunny days, when it's recommended to show up at least one hour ahead of desired departure.

Other vessels to tour in port include the popular **HMS** *Surprise.* A replica of an 18th-century British Royal Navy frigate, the *Surprise* appears in the film *Master and Commander: The Far Side of the World.* The *Berkeley,* an 1898 steam-driven ferryboat, served the Southern Pacific Railroad in San Francisco until 1958; now it's the museum's headquarters. Its ornate detailing carefully restored, the main deck has permanent exhibits on West Coast maritime history and hosts temporary exhibits. The museum also has a **Soviet B-39** "Foxtrot" class submarine and the **USS** *Dolphin* research submarine. Take a peek at the harbor from a periscope, get up close with the engine control room, and wonder at the tight living quarters onboard.

■ TIP→ At Spanish Landing Park, about 2 miles to the west, the museum is constructing a full-scale working replica of the *San Salvador,* the first European ship to land on the western coast of the future United States. To view this work-in-progress (daily 11–4:30), obtain directions at the *Berkeley.* ⊠ *1492 N. Harbor Dr., Embarcadero* ☎ *619/234–9153* ⊕ *www.*

2

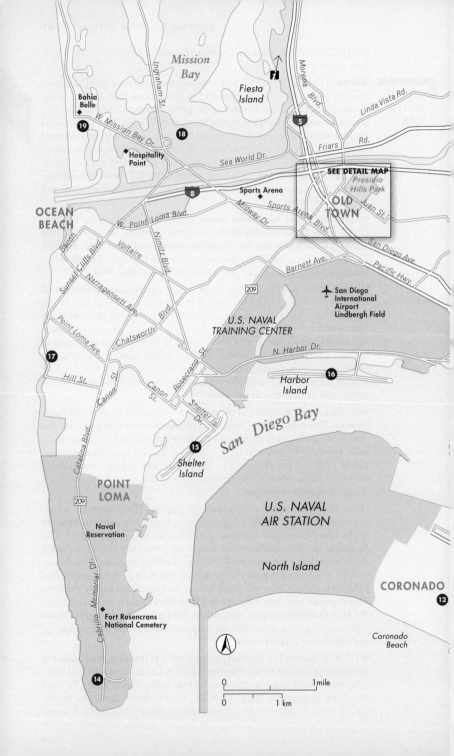

Mission Bay

Fiesta Island

Bahia Belle ◆

19

W. Mission Bay Dr.

18

Ingraham St.

Hospitality Point ◆

Morena Blvd.

5

Linda Vista Rd.

Friars Rd.

Sea World Dr.

SEE DETAIL MAP
Presidio Hills Park

OLD TOWN

Juan St.

OCEAN BEACH

8

Sports Arena ◆

Midway Dr.

Sports Arena Blvd.

San Diego Ave.

W. Point Loma Blvd.

Bacon

Sunset Cliffs Blvd.

Voltaire

Nimitz Blvd.

Narragansett Ave.

Pacific Hwy.

Barnett Ave.

209

San Diego International Airport Lindbergh Field ✈

Point Loma Ave.

Chatsworth

Blvd.

U.S. NAVAL TRAINING CENTER

17

Hill St.

Canon St.

Catalina Blvd.

Rosecrans St.

N. Harbor Dr.

Harbor Island

16

Canon St.

Shelter Is. Dr.

San Diego Bay

15

Shelter Island

POINT LOMA

209

Naval Reservation

U.S. NAVAL AIR STATION

North Island

CORONADO

12

Cabrillo Memorial Dr.

Fort Rosecrans National Cemetery

14

Coronado Beach

0   1 mile

0   1 km

Central San Diego and Mission Bay

KEY

🚤 Ferry

🛈 Tourist information

Be sure to enjoy a walk along San Diego's lovely waterfront sometime during your visit.

sdmaritime.org ✉ *$15 includes entry to all ships except Californian* ⊙ *Daily 9–8.*

Fodor's Choice
★

Museum of Contemporary Art San Diego (MCASD). At the Downtown branch of the city's contemporary art museum (the original is in La Jolla), explore the works of international and regional artists in a modern, urban space. The Jacobs Building—formerly the baggage building at the historic Santa Fe Depot—features large gallery spaces, high ceilings, and natural lighting, giving artists the flexibility to create large-scale installations. MCASD's collection includes many Pop Art, minimalist, and conceptual works from the 1950s to the present. The museum showcases both established and emerging artists in temporary exhibitions, and has permanent, site-specific commissions by Jenny Holzer and Richard Serra. ■TIP➔ Admission, good for seven days, includes the Downtown and La Jolla locations. ✉ *1100 and 1001 Kettner Blvd., Downtown* ☎ *858/454–3541* ⊕ *www.mcasd.org* ✉ *$10; free 3rd Thurs. of the month 5–7* ⊙ *Thurs.–Tues. 11–5; 3rd Thurs. until 7* ⊙ *Closed Wed.*

Fodor's Choice
★

USS Midway Museum. After 47 years of worldwide service, the retired USS *Midway* began a new tour of duty on the south side of the Navy pier in 2004. Launched in 1945, the 1,001-foot-long ship was the largest in the world for the first 10 years of its existence. Now it dominates the north Embarcadero as a floating interactive museum—an appropriate addition to the town that is home to one-third of the Pacific fleet and the birthplace of naval aviation. Free guided tours depart from the flight deck every 10 minutes. Self-guided audio tours are also available. As you clamber through passageways and up and down ladder wells,

The *Star of India*, the oldest active sailing ship in the world, still occasionally plies San Diego Bay.

you'll get a feel for how the *Midway*'s 4,500 crew members lived and worked on this "city at sea."

The entire tour is impressive, but you'll find yourself saying "wow" when you step out onto the 4-acre flight deck—not only the best place to get an idea of the ship's scale, but also one of the most interesting vantage points for bay and city skyline views. An F-14 Tomcat jet fighter is just one of many vintage aircraft on display. Many of the docents stationed throughout the ship served in the Navy, some even on the *Midway*, and they are eager to answer questions or share stories. The museum also offers multiple flight simulators for an additional fee, climb-aboard cockpits, and interactive exhibits focusing on naval aviation. There is a gift shop and a café with pleasant outdoor seating. This is a wildly popular stop, with most visits lasting several hours. ⚠ **Despite efforts to provide accessibility throughout the ship, some areas can only be reached via fairly steep steps; a video tour of these areas is available on the hangar deck.** ✉ *910 N. Harbor Dr., Embarcadero* ☎ *619/544–9600* ⊕ *www.midway.org* 💲*$18* ◷ *Mid-Aug.–June, daily 10–5; July–mid-Aug., daily 9–5; last admission 4 pm.*

☃ **Seaport Village.** You'll find some of the best views of the harbor at Seaport Village, three bustling shopping plazas designed to reflect the New England clapboard and Spanish Mission architectural styles of early California. On a prime stretch of waterfront the dining, shopping and entertainment complex connects the harbor with hotel towers and the convention center. Specialty shops offer everything from a kite store and swing emporium to a shop devoted to hot sauces. You can dine at snack bars and restaurants, many with harbor views. Seaport Village's shops are open daily 10 to 9; a few eateries open early for breakfast, and many have extended nighttime hours, especially in summer. Restaurant prices here are high and the food is only average, so your best bet is to go elsewhere for a meal.

Live music can be heard daily from noon to 4 at the main food court. Additional free concerts take place every Sunday from 1 to 4 at the East Plaza Gazebo. If you happen to visit San Diego in late November or early December, you might be lucky enough to catch Surfing Santa's Arrival and even have your picture taken with Santa on his wave. In April the Seaport Buskers Fest presents an array of costumed street performers. The **Seaport Village Carousel** (rides $2) has 54 animals, hand-carved and hand-painted by Charles Looff in 1895. ⊠ *849 W. Harbor Dr., Downtown* ☎ *619/235–4014 office and events hotline* ⊕ *www. seaportvillage.com.*

Westfield Horton Plaza. This Downtown shopping, dining, and entertainment mecca fronts Broadway and G Street from 1st to 4th avenues and covers more than six city blocks. Designed by Jon Jerde and completed in 1985, Westfield Horton Plaza is a collage of colorful tile work, banners waving in the air, and modern sculptures. The complex rises in uneven, staggered levels to five floors; great views of Downtown from the harbor to Balboa Park and beyond can be had here.

Macy's and Nordstrom department stores anchor the plaza, and more than 130 clothing, sporting-goods, jewelry, book, and gift shops flank them. Other attractions include the country's largest Sam Goody music store, a movie complex, restaurants, and a long row of take-out ethnic food shops and dining patios on the uppermost tier—and the respected San Diego Repertory Theatre below ground level. In 2008 the **Balboa Theater**, contiguous with the shopping center, reopened its doors after a $26.5 million renovation. The historic 1920s theater seats 1,400 and offers live arts and cultural performances throughout the week.

The mall has a multilevel parking garage; even so, lines to find a space can be long. ■ TIP➔ **Entering the parking structure on G Street rather than 4th Avenue generally means less traffic and more parking space.** Parking validation is complimentary whether you spend a bundle or just window-shop. Validation machines (open 7 am–9 pm) throughout the center allow for three hours' free parking; after that it's $8 per hour (or $2 per 15-minute increment). If you use this notoriously confusing fruit-and-vegetable–themed garage, be sure to remember at which produce level you've left your car. If you're staying Downtown, the Old Town Trolley Tour will drop you directly in front of Westfield Horton Plaza. ⊠ *324 Horton Plaza, Gaslamp Quarter* ☎ *619/238–1596* ⊕ *www. westfield.com/hortonplaza* ⊗ *Weekdays 10–9, Sat. 10–8, Sun. 11–7.*

BALBOA PARK AND SAN DIEGO ZOO

Balboa Park, at 1,200-acres the cultural heart of San Diego, is ranked as one of the world's best parks by the Project for Public Spaces. It's also where you can find most of the city's museums and the San Diego Zoo. Balboa Park also holds botanical gardens, performance spaces, and outdoor playrooms endeared in the hearts of residents and visitors alike.

Thanks to Kate Sessions, who suggested hiring a landscape architect in 1889, wild and cultivated gardens are an integral part of the park, featuring 350 species of trees.

The captivating architecture of Balboa's buildings, fountains, and courtyards gives the park an enchanted feel. Buildings dating from San Diego's 1915 Panama–California International Exposition are strung along the park's main east–west thoroughfare, El Prado. The parkland across the Cabrillo Bridge, at the west end of El Prado, is set aside for picnics and athletics. East of Plaza de Panama, El Prado becomes a pedestrian mall and ends at a footbridge that crosses over Park Boulevard, to rose and desert gardens.

TOP ATTRACTIONS

★ **Alcazar Garden.** The gardens surrounding the Alcazar Castle in Seville, Spain, inspired the landscaping here; you'll feel like royalty resting on the benches by the exquisitely tiled fountains. The flower beds are ever-changing horticultural exhibits featuring more than 7,000 annuals for a nearly perpetual bloom. A replica of a garden created in 1935 by San Diego architect Richard Requa, the garden is open year-round offering a changing color palette. ⊠ *1439 El Prado, Balboa Park* ⊕ *www.balboapark.org.*

Fodor's Choice **Botanical Building.** The graceful redwood-lath structure, built for the
★ 1915 Panama–California International Exposition, now houses more than 2,000 types of tropical and subtropical plants plus changing seasonal flower displays. Ceiling-high tree ferns shade fragile orchids and feathery bamboo. There are benches beside miniature waterfalls for resting in the shade. The rectangular pond outside, filled with lotuses and water lilies that bloom in spring and fall, is popular with photographers. ⊠ *1549 El Prado, Balboa Park* ☎ *619/239–0512* ⊕ *www.balboapark.org* 🖾 *Free* ☉ *Fri.–Wed. 10–4.*

Fodor's Choice **Inez Grant Parker Memorial Rose Garden and Desert Garden.** These neigh-
★ boring gardens sit just across the Park Boulevard pedestrian bridge and offer gorgeous views over Florida Canyon. The formal rose garden contains 2,500 roses representing nearly 200 varieties; peak bloom is usually in April and May. The adjacent Desert Garden provides a striking contrast, with 2.5 acres of succulents and desert plants seeming to blend into the landscape of the canyon below. ⊠ *2525 Park Blvd., Balboa Park* ⊕ *www.balboapark.org.*

☺ **San Diego Air and Space Museum.** By day, the streamlined edifice looks
★ like any other structure in the park; at night, outlined in blue neon, the round building appears—appropriately enough—to be a landed UFO. Every available inch of space in the rotunda is filled with exhibits about aviation and aerospace pioneers, including examples of enemy planes from the world wars. In all, there are 63 full-size aircraft on the floor and hanging from the rafters. You can ride in a two-seat Max Flight simulator or try out the F-35 interactive simulator. Space-related exhibits include the Apollo 9 command module. ⊠ *2001 Pan American Plaza, Balboa Park* ☎ *619/234–8291* ⊕ *www.sandiegoairandspace.org* 🖾 *Museum $17.50 (more for special exhibitions), Max Flight Simula-*

tor $8 extra, restoration tour $5 extra ⊙ Daily 10–4:30, until 5:30 Memorial Day–Labor Day.

★ **San Diego Museum of Art.** Known primarily for its Spanish baroque and Renaissance paintings, including works by El Greco, Goya, Rubens, and van Ruisdael, San Diego's most comprehensive art museum also has strong holdings of South Asian art, Indian miniatures, and contemporary California paintings. An outdoor Sculpture Court and Garden exhibits both traditional and modern pieces. The IMAGE (Interactive Multimedia Art Gallery Explorer) system allows you to call up the highlights of the museum's collection on a computer screen and custom-design a tour, call up historical information on the works and artists, and print color reproductions. The museum's goal is to "connect people to art and art to people," so its exhibits tend to have broad appeal, and if traveling shows from other cities come to town, you can expect to see them here. Free docent tours are offered throughout the day. If you become hungry, head to the **Sculpture Court Café by Giuseppe,** which serves artisan pizzas, gourmet salads and sandwiches, and grilled burgers and steak. ⊠ *1450 El Prado, Balboa Park* ☎ *619/232–7931* ⊕ *www.sdmart.org* ✑ *$12 ⊙ Tues.–Sat. 10–5, Sun. noon–5; Memorial Day–Labor Day Thurs. until 9.*

Ↄ **San Diego Natural History Museum.** There are 7.5 million fossils, dinosaur models, and even live reptiles and other specimens under this roof. Favorite exhibits include the Foucault Pendulum, suspended on a 43-foot cable and designed to demonstrate the Earth's rotation, and *Ocean Oasis,* the world's first large-format film about Baja California and the Sea of Cortés. Regional environment exhibits are highlighted, and traveling exhibits also make a stop here. Included in admission are 3-D films shown at the museum's giant-screen theater. Call ahead for information about films, lectures, and free guided nature walks. ⊠ *1788 El Prado, Balboa Park* ☎ *619/232–3821* ⊕ *www.sdnhm.org* ✑ *$15 ⊙ Sun.–Fri. 10–5, Sat. 9–5.*

Ↄ **San Diego Zoo.**

Fodor's Choice
★   ⇨ *See the highlighted listing in this chapter.*

WORTH NOTING

Ↄ **Carousel.** Suspended an arm's length away on this antique merry-go-
★ round is the brass ring that could earn you an extra free ride (it's one of the few carousels in the world that continue this bonus tradition). Hand-carved in 1910, the carousel features colorful murals, big-band music, and bobbing animals including zebras, giraffes, and dragons; real horsehair was used for the tails. ⊠ *1889 Zoo Pl., behind zoo parking lot, Balboa Park* ☎ *619/239–0512* ✑ *$2 ⊙ 11–5; Mid-June–Labor Day, daily; rest of yr, weekends and school holidays.*

House of Hospitality. A late-1990s replica of the 1915 original, this structure has won awards for the attention paid to historical detail; 2,000 paint scrapes were taken, for example, to get the art-deco colors exactly right. The structure houses the Balboa Park visitor center and its very fine gift shop. The center distributes a guide to current museum and theater offerings and the schedules and route maps for the park's free tram service. Also available are **discount passes** that offer substantial

Continued on page 66

Polar bear, San Diego Zoo

LIONS AND TIGERS AND PANDAS:
The World-Famous San Diego Zoo

From cuddly pandas and diving polar bears to 6-ton elephants and swinging great apes, San Diego's most famous attraction has it all. Nearly 4,000 animals representing 800 species roam the 100-acre zoo in expertly crafted habitats that replicate the animals' natural environments. While the pandas get top billing, there are plenty of other cool creatures to see here, from teeny-tiny mantella frogs to two-story-tall giraffes. But it's not all just fun and games. Known for its exemplary conservation programs, the zoo educates visitors on how to go green and explains its efforts to protect endangered species.

SAN DIEGO ZOO TOP ATTRACTIONS

Underwater viewing area at the Hippo Trail

❶ Children's Zoo (Discovery Outpost). Goats and sheep beg to be petted, and there is a viewer-friendly nursery where you may see baby animals bottle-feed and sleep peacefully in large cribs.

❷ Monkey Trails and Forest Tales (Lost Forest). Follow an elevated trail at treetop level and trek through the forest floor observing African mandrill monkeys, Asia's clouded leopard, the rare pygmy hippopotamus, and Visayan warty pigs.

❸ Orangutan and Siamang Exhibit (Lost Forest). Orangutans and siamangs climb and swing in this lush, tropical environment lined with 110-foot-long and 12-foot-high viewing windows.

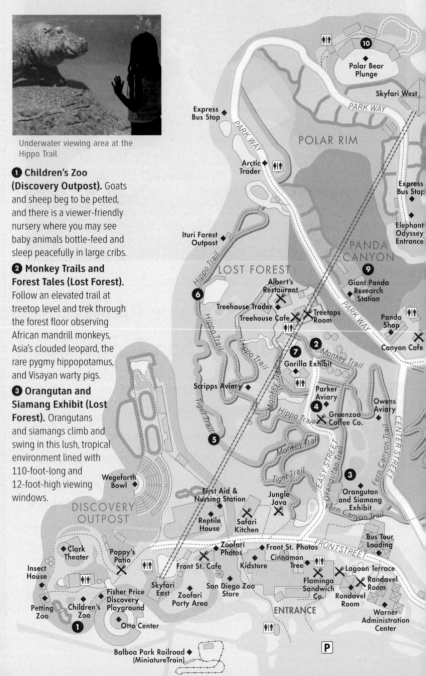

Express Bus Stop

PARK WAY

POLAR RIM

Polar Bear Plunge — ❿

Skyfari West

Express Bus Stop

Elephant Odyssey Entrance

PANDA CANYON

Arctic Trader

Ituri Forest Outpost

Hippo Trail

LOST FOREST

Albert's Restaurant

Giant Panda Research Station — ❾

Panda Shop

❻

Treehouse Trader

Treehouse Cafe

Treetops Room

PARK WAY

❼

Gorilla Exhibit

❷

Monkey Trail

Canyon Cafe

Scripps Aviary

Parker Aviary

Owens Aviary

❹

Greenzoo Coffee Co.

❺

Hippo Trail

Monkey Trail

Tiger Trail

EASY STREET

Orangutan Trail

Fern Canyon Trail

CENTER STREET

Wegeforth Bowl

First Aid & Nursing Station

Jungle Java

Orangutan and Siamang Exhibit — ❸

DISCOVERY OUTPOST

Reptile House

Safari Kitchen

Fern Canyon Trail

Bus Tour Loading

Clark Theater

Poppy's Patio

Zoofari Photos

Front St. Photos

Cinnamon Tree

FRONT STREET

Lagoon Terrace

Insect House

Front St. Cafe

Kidstore

Flamingo Sandwich Co.

Rondavel Room

Petting Zoo

Children's Zoo

Fisher Price Discovery Playground

Skyfari East

Zoofari Party Area

San Diego Zoo Store

Rondavel Room

Warner Administration Center

❶

Otto Center

ENTRANCE

Balboa Park Railroad (MiniatureTrain)

P

❹ Scripps, Parker, and Owens Aviaries (Lost Forest). Wandering paths climb through the enclosed aviaries where brightly colored tropical birds swoop between branches inches from your face.

❺ Tiger Trail (Lost Forest). The mist-shrouded trails of this simulated rainforest wind down a canyon. Tigers, Malayan tapirs, and Argus pheasants wander among the exotic trees and plants.

❻ Hippo Trail (Lost Forest). Glimpse huge but surprisingly graceful hippos frolicking in the water through an underwater viewing

window and buffalo cavorting with monkeys on dry land.

❼ Gorilla Exhibit (Lost Forest). The gorillas live in one of the zoo's bioclimatic zone exhibits modeled on their native habitat with waterfalls, climbing areas, and an open meadow. The sounds of the tropical rain forest emerge from a 144-speaker sound system that plays CDs recorded in Africa.

❽ Sun Bear Forest (Asian Passage). Playful beasts claw apart the trees and shrubs that serve as a natural playground for climbing, jumping, and general merrymaking.

❾ Giant Panda Research Station (Panda Canyon). An elevated pathway provides visitors with great access

Lories at Owen's Aviary

to the zoo's most famous residents in their side-by-side viewing areas. The adjacent discovery center features lots of information about these endangered animals and the zoo's efforts to protect them.

❿ Polar Bear Plunge (Polar Rim). Watch polar bears take a chilly dive from the underwater viewing room. There are also Siberian reindeer, white foxes, and other Arctic creatures here. Kids can learn about the Arctic and climate change through interactive exhibits.

⓫ Elephant Odyssey. Get a glimpse of the animals that roamed Southern California 12,000 years ago and meet their living counterparts. The 7.5-acre, multispecies habitat features elephants, California condors, jaguars, and more.

⓬ Koala Exhibit (Outback). The San Diego Zoo houses the largest number of koalas outside Australia. Walk through the exhibit for photo ops of these marsupials from Down-Under curled up on their perches or dining on eucalyptus branches.

SIAN SSAGE

ELEPHANT ODYSSEY ⓫

Elephant Care Center

press s Stop

Big Cat Trail

PARK WAY

Hunte Amphitheater

Big Cat Trail

Hunte Trail

Sabertooth Grill

n Bear rest

URBAN JUNGLE

Big Cat Trail

Sun Bear Trail

AFRICA ROCKS

Tusker's Trunk

Express Bus Stop

PARK WAY

Tour oading

CENTER STREET

Sydney's Grill

OUTBACK

Elephant Odyssey Exit

Express Bus Stop

RONT STREET

FRONT STREET

⓬ Sydney's Shoppe

Koala Exhibit

MUST-SEE ANIMALS

❶ GORILLA

This troop of primates engages visitors with their human-like expressions and behavior. The youngsters are sure to delight, especially when hitching a ride on mom's back. Up-close encounters might involve the gorillas using the glass partition as a backrest while peeling cabbage. By dusk the gorillas head inside to their sleeping quarters, so don't save this for your last stop.

❷ ELEPHANT

Asian and African elephants coexist at the San Diego Zoo. The larger African elephant is distinguished by its big flapping ears—shaped like the continent of Africa—which it uses to keep cool. An elephant's trunk has over 40,000 muscles in it—that's more than humans have in their whole body.

❸ GIANT PANDA

The San Diego Zoo is well-known for its giant panda research and conservation efforts, and has had five successful panda births. You'll likely see parents Bai Yun ("White Cloud") and Gao-Gao ("Big-Big") with their youngest baby Yun Zi ("Son of Cloud").

❹ KOALA

While this collection of critters is one of the cutest in the zoo, don't expect a lot of activity from the koala habitat. These guys spend most of their day curled up asleep in the branches of the eucalyptus tree—they can sleep up to 20 hours a day. Although eucalyptus leaves are poisonous to most animals, bacteria in koalas' stomachs allow them to break down the toxins.

❺ POLAR BEAR

The trio of polar bears is one of the San Diego Zoo's star attractions, and their brand-new exhibit gets you up close and personal. Visitors sometimes worry about polar bears living in the warm San Diego climate, but there is no cause for concern. The San Diego-based bears eat a lean diet, thus reducing their layer of blubber and helping them keep cool.

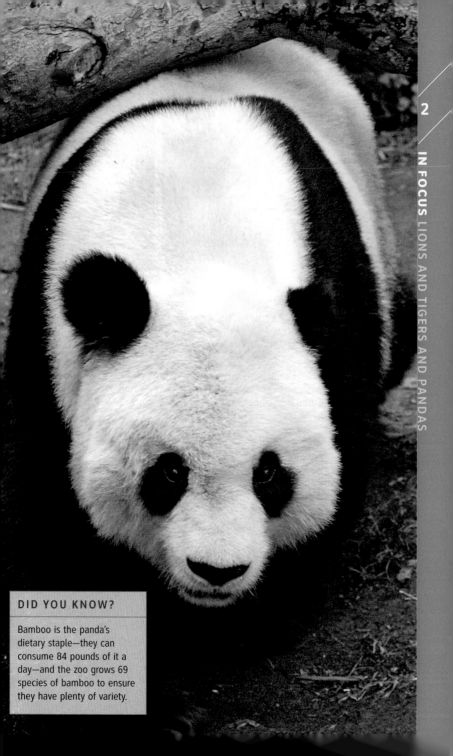

DID YOU KNOW?

Bamboo is the panda's dietary staple—they can consume 84 pounds of it a day—and the zoo grows 69 species of bamboo to ensure they have plenty of variety.

PLANNING YOUR DAY AT THE ZOO

Left: Main entrance of the San Diego Zoo. Right: Sunbear

PLANNING YOUR TIME

Plan to devote at least a half-day to exploring the zoo, but with so much to see it is easy to stay a full day or more.

If you're on a tight schedule, opt for the guided **35 minute bus tour** that lets you zip through three-quarters of the exhibits. However, lines to board the busses can be long, and you won't get as close to the animals.

Another option is to take the **Skyfari Aerial Tram** to the far end of the park, choose a route, and meander back to the entrance. The Skyfari trip gives a good overview of the zoo's layout and a spectacular view.

The **Elephant Odyssey,** while accessible from two sides of the park, is best entered from just below the Polar Rim. The extremely popular **Panda exhibit** can develop long lines, so get there early.

The zoo has three **live shows:** *Sea Lions Rock!* and *Soar-A Symphony in Flight* feature trained animal performers, and the *Dr. Zoolittle Show* is a zany science demonstration.

BEFORE YOU GO

■ To avoid ticket lines, purchase and print tickets online using the zoo's Web site.

■ To avoid excessive backtracking or a potential meltdown, plan your route along the zoo map before setting out. Try not to get too frustrated if you lose your way, as there are exciting exhibits around every turn and many paths intersect at several points.

■ The zoo offers a variety of program extras, including behind-the-scenes tours, backstage pass animal encounters, and sleepover events. Call in advance for pricing and reservations.

AT THE ZOO

■ Don't forget to explore at least some of the exhibits on foot—a favorite is the lush Tiger Trail.

■ If you visit on the weekend, find out when the Giraffe Experience is taking place. You can purchase leaf–eater biscuits to hand feed the giraffes!

■ Splurge a little at the gift shop: your purchases help support zoo programs.

■ The zoo rents strollers, wheelchairs, and lockers; it also has a first-aid office, a lost and found, and an ATM.

Fern Canyon, San Diego Zoo

GETTING HERE AND AROUND
The zoo is easy to get to, whether by bus or car.

Bus Travel: Take Bus No. 7 and exit at Park Boulevard and Zoo Place.

Car Travel: From Downtown, take Route 163 north through Balboa Park. Exit at Zoo/Museums (Richmond Street) and follow signs.

Several options help you get around the massive park: express buses loop through the zoo and the Skyfari Aerial Tram will take you from one end to the other. The zoo's topography is fairly hilly, but moving sidewalks lead up the slopes between some exhibits.

QUICK BITES
There is a wide variety of food available for purchase at the zoo from food carts to ethnic restaurants such as the Pan-Asian **Canyon Cafe**.

One of the best restaurants is **Albert's** ($), near the Gorilla exhibit, which features grilled fish, homemade pizza, and fresh pasta along with a full bar.

SERVICE INFORMATION

✉ 2920 Zoo Dr., Balboa Park

☎ 619/234–3153; 888/697–2632 Giant panda hotline

⊕ www.sandiegozoo.org

💳 $40 adult, $30 children (3–11) includes Skyfari and bus tour; 2-Visit Pass ($76 adult, $56 children age 3–11); zoo parking free

⊟ AE, D, MC, V

☉ June 24–Sept. 5, daily 9–9; Sept. 6–Oct. 2, daily 9–6; Oct. 3–Dec. 8, daily 9–5; Dec. 9–June 23, daily 9–6; Children's Zoo and Skyfari ride generally close 1 hr earlier.

SAN DIEGO ZOO SAFARI PARK

About 45 minutes north of the zoo in Escondido, the 1,800-acre San Diego Zoo Safari Park is an extensive wildlife sanctuary where animals roam free—and guests can get close in escorted caravans and on backcountry trails. This park and the zoo operate under the auspices of the San Diego Zoo's non-profit organization; joint tickets are available. ⇨ *See Chapter 15: North County and Environs for more information.*

savings if you'll be visiting many museums. Excellent free park tours depart from the center. ⊠ *1549 El Prado, Balboa Park* ☎ *619/239–0512* ⊕ *www.balboapark.org* ✉ *Passport to Balboa Park with Zoo $83, 14 museums and zoo, good for 7 days; Passport to Balboa Park $49, museums only; Stay-for-the-Day Pass $39, same-day admission to any 5 museums* ⊘ *Daily 9:30–4:30.*

House of Pacific Relations. This is not really a house but a cluster of red tile–roof stucco cottages representing some 30 foreign countries. The word "pacific" refers to the goal of maintaining peace. The cottages, decorated with crafts and pictures, are open Sunday afternoons, when you can chat with transplanted natives and try out different ethnic foods. From the first Sunday in March through the last Sunday in October, folk-song and dance performances are presented on the outdoor stage around 2 pm—check the schedule at the park visitor center. Across the road from the cottages, but not affiliated with them, is the Spanish colonial–style **United Nations Building.** Inside, the United Nations Association's International Gift Shop, open daily, has reasonably priced crafts, cards, and books. ⊠ *2191 Pan American Pl., Balboa Park* ☎ *619/234–0739* ⊕ *www.sdhpr.org* ✉ *Free, donations accepted* ⊘ *Sun. noon–4.*

Japanese Friendship Garden. A koi pond with a cascading waterfall, a 60-foot-long wisteria arbor, a tea pavilion, and a large activity center are highlights of the park's authentic Japanese garden, designed to inspire contemplation and evoke tranquillity. You can wander the various peaceful paths and meditate in the traditional stone and Zen garden. The development of an additional 9 acres is underway and will include a traditional teahouse and a cherry orchard. ⊠ *2215 Pan American Rd., Balboa Park* ☎ *619/232–2721* ⊕ *www.niwa.org* ✉ *$4* ⊘ *Summer weekdays 10–5, weekends 10–4; rest of yr Tues.–Sun. 10–4.*

Mingei International Museum. All ages can enjoy the Mingei's colorful and creative exhibits of folk art, featuring toys, pottery, textiles, costumes, jewelry, and curios from around the globe. Traveling and permanent exhibits in the high-ceilinged, light-filled museum include everything from antique American carousel horses to the latest in Japanese ceramics. The name "Mingei" comes from the Japanese words *min*, meaning "all people," and *gei*, meaning "art." Thus the museum's name describes what you'll find under its roof: "art of all people." The gift shop carries artwork from cultures around the world, from Zulu baskets to Turkish ceramics to Mexican objects, plus special items related to major exhibitions. ⊠ *House of Charm, 1439 El Prado, Balboa Park* ☎ *619/239–0003* ⊕ *www.mingei.org* ✉ *$8* ⊘ *Tues.–Sun. 10–4.*

Palm Canyon. Heading down into this lush canyon near the House of Charm provides an instant escape into another landscape. More than 450 palms are planted in two acres, with a small hiking trail emerging by the Balboa Park Club. ⊠ *South of the House of Charm, Balboa Park.*

Ⓒ **San Diego Model Railroad Museum.** When the impressive exhibits at this 27,000-square-foot museum are in operation, you can hear the sounds of chugging engines, screeching brakes, and shrill whistles. Local model railroad clubs built and maintain the four main displays, which

2

represent California railroads in "miniature," with the track laid on scale models of San Diego County terrain. A Toy Train Gallery contains an interactive Lionel exhibit that includes a camera car hooked up to a TV set showing an engineer's-eye view of the layout. ⊠ *Casa de Balboa, 1649 El Prado, Balboa Park* ☎ *619/696–0199* ⊕ *www.sdmrm. org* ✉ *$8; children under 15 free with adult* ⊙ *Tues.–Fri. 11–4, weekends 11–5.*

⊙ **San Diego Museum of Man.** If the facade of this building—the landmark California Building—looks familiar, it's because filmmaker Orson Welles used it and its dramatic tower as the principal features of the Xanadu estate in his 1941 classic, *Citizen Kane*. Inside, exhibits at this highly respected anthropological museum focus on Southwestern, Mexican, and South American cultures. Carved monuments from the Mayan city of Quirigua in Guatemala, cast from the originals in 1914, are particularly impressive. Exhibits might include examples of intricate beadwork from across the Americas, the history of Egyptian mummies, or the lifestyles of the Kumeyaay peoples, Native Americans who live in the San Diego area. Especially cool for kids is the hands-on Children's Discovery Center. ⊠ *California Bldg., 1350 El Prado, Balboa Park* ☎ *619/239–2001* ⊕ *www.museumofman.org* ✉ *$12.50* ⊙ *Daily 10–4:30.*

★ **Spanish Village Art Center.** More than 200 local artists, including glass-blowers, enamel workers, wood-carvers, sculptors, painters, jewelers, and photographers rent space in these 41 red tile–roof studio-galleries that were set up for the 1935–36 exposition in the style of an old Spanish village, and they give demonstrations of their work on a rotating basis. Spanish Village is a great source for memorable gifts. ⊠ *1770 Village Pl., Balboa Park* ☎ *619/233–9050* ⊕ *www.spanishvillageart. com* ✉ *Free* ⊙ *Daily 11–4.*

★ **Spreckels Organ Pavilion.** The 2,400-bench-seat pavilion, dedicated in 1915 by sugar magnates John D. and Adolph B. Spreckels, holds the 4,518-pipe Spreckels Organ, the largest outdoor pipe organ in the world. You can hear this impressive instrument at one of the year-round, free, 2 pm Sunday concerts, regularly performed by civic organist Carol Williams and guest artists—a highlight of a visit to Balboa Park. On Monday evenings from late June to mid-August, internationally renowned organists play evening concerts. At Christmastime the park's Christmas tree and life-size Nativity display turn the pavilion into a seasonal wonderland. ⊠ *2211 Pan American Rd., Balboa Park* ☎ *619/702–8138* ⊕ *www.sosorgan.org.*

CORONADO

Although it's actually an isthmus, easily reached from the mainland if you head north from Imperial Beach, Coronado has always seemed like an island and is often referred to as such. Located just 15 miles east of Downtown San Diego, Coronado was an uninhabited sandbar until the late 1800s; it was named after Mexico's Coronados Islands.

As if freeze-framed in the 1950s, Coronado's quaint appeal is captured in its old-fashioned storefronts, well-manicured gardens, and the charming Coronado Ferry Landing. Today's residents, many of whom live in grand Victorian homes handed down for generations, can usually be seen walking their dogs or chatting with neighbors in this safe, non-gated community. Naval Air Station North Island was established in 1911 on Coronado's north end, across from Point Loma, and was the site of Charles Lindbergh's departure on the transcontinental flight that preceded his famous solo flight across the Atlantic. Coronado's long relationship with the U.S. Navy and its desirable real estate have made it an enclave for military personnel; it's said to have more retired admirals per capita than anywhere else in the United States.

Coronado is accessible via the arching blue 2.2-mile-long San Diego–Coronado Bay Bridge, which handles some 68,000 cars each day. The view of the harbor, Downtown, and the island is breathtaking, day and night. Until the bridge was completed in 1969, visitors and residents relied on the Coronado Ferry, which today has become quite popular with bicyclists, who shuttle their bikes across the harbor and ride Coronado's wide, flat boulevards for hours.

San Diego's Metropolitan Transit System runs a shuttle bus, No. 904, around Coronado; you can pick it up where you disembark the ferry and ride it out as far as Silver Strand State Beach. Bus No. 901 runs daily between the Gaslamp Quarter and Coronado.

San Diego Harbor Excursions. Fifteen-minute ferries connect the Broadway Pier on the Embarcadero and Coronado Ferry Landing. Boats depart on the hour from the Embarcadero and on the half hour from Coronado, daily 9–9 from San Diego (9–10 Friday and Saturday), 9:30–9:30 from Coronado (9:30–10:30 Friday and Saturday). Service to Coronado also departs from the convention center every other hour. Buy tickets at the Broadway Pier, 5th Avenue Landing, or Coronado Ferry Landing. San Diego Harbor Excursions also offers water taxi service weekdays 9 am–9 pm, and Friday and Saturday 9 am–11 pm. ☎ 619/234–4111, 800/442–7847, 619/235–8294 water taxi ⊕ www.sdhe.com ⊠ Ferry $4.25 each way; water taxi $7 per person.

EXPLORING CORONADO

Coronado Museum of History and Art. The neoclassical First Bank of Commerce building, constructed in 1910, holds the headquarters and archives of the Coronado Historical Association, a museum, the Coronado Visitor Center, the Coronado Museum Store, and Tent City Restaurant. The museum's collection celebrates Coronado's history with photographs and displays of its formative events and major sights. *Promenade Through the Past: A Brief History of Coronado and its Architectural Wonders,* available at the museum store, traces a 60-minute walking tour of the area's architecturally and historically significant buildings. A guided tour of them departs from the museum lobby on Wednesday mornings at 10:30 and costs $10 (reservations required). ⊠ 1100 Orange Ave., at Park Pl., Coronado ☎ 619/435–7242 ⊕ www.coronadohistory.org ⊠ $4 suggested donation ☉ Weekdays 9–5, Sat. 10–5, Sun. 11–4.

☺ **Coronado Ferry Landing.** This collection of shops at Ferry Landing is on
★ a smaller scale than the Embarcadero's Seaport Village, but you do get

a great view of the Downtown San Diego skyline. The little bay-side shops and restaurants resemble the gingerbread domes of the Hotel Del Coronado. **Bikes and Beyond** (☎ 619/435–7180 ⊕ hollandsbicycles. com) rents bikes, surreys, and in-line skates for riding or gliding through town and Coronado's scenic bike path. ✉ 1201 1st St., at B Ave., Coronado ☎ 619/435–8895 ⊕ www.coronadoferrylandingshops.com.

Fodor's Choice **Hotel Del Coronado.** One of San Diego's best-known sites, the hotel has
★ been a National Historic Landmark since 1977. The Hotel Del, as locals call it, was the brainchild of financiers Elisha Spurr Babcock Jr. and H. L. Story, who saw the potential of Coronado's virgin beaches and its view of San Diego's emerging harbor. The hotel opened in 1888, just 11 months after construction began.

The Del's distinctive red-tile roofs and Victorian gingerbread architecture have served as a set for many movies, political meetings, and extravagant social happenings. It's speculated that the Duke of Windsor may have first met Wallis Simpson here. Eleven presidents have been guests of the Del, and the film *Some Like It Hot*—starring Marilyn Monroe, Jack Lemmon, and Tony Curtis—used the hotel as a backdrop.

Broad steps lead up to the main, balconied lobby, which is adorned with grand oak pillars and ceiling and opens out onto a central courtyard and gazebo. To the right is the cavernous **Crown Room,** whose arched ceiling of notched sugar pine was constructed without nails. A lavish Sunday brunch is served here from 9:30 to 1. During the holidays, the hotel hosts Skating by the Sea, an outdoor beachfront ice-skating rink open to the public.

Although the pool area is reserved for hotel guests, several surrounding dining patios make great places to sit back and imagine the scene during the 1920s, when the hotel rocked with good times. To the right, the Windsor Lawn provides a green oasis between the hotel and the beach. Behind the pool area, an attractive shopping arcade features a classic candy shop as well as several fine clothing and accessories stores.
■ TIP→ Even if you don't happen to be staying at the Del, gazing out over the ocean while enjoying a drink at the Sun Deck Bar and Grill makes for a great escape. If it's chilly, the fire pits and sofa seating are very inviting.

The History Gallery displays photos from the Del's early days, and books elaborating on its history and that of Kate Morgan, the hotel's resident ghost, are sold along with logo apparel and gifts in the hotel's 15-plus shops. Tours of the Del take place on Tuesday and Friday at 10:30, Saturday and Sunday at 2. Reservations are required. ✉ 1500 Orange Ave., at Glorietta Blvd., Coronado ☎ 619/435–6611, 619/437–8788 tour reservations (through Coronado Visitor Center) ⊕ www. hoteldel.com ◱ Tours $15.

Orange Avenue. Coronado's business district and its villagelike heart, this is surely one of the most charming spots in Southern California. Slow-paced and very "local" (the city fights against chain stores), it's a blast from the past, although entirely up to date in other respects. The military presence—Coronado is home to the U.S. Navy Sea, Air and Land (SEAL) forces—is reflected in shops selling military gear and places like **McP's Irish Pub,** at No. 1107. A family-friendly stop for a good,

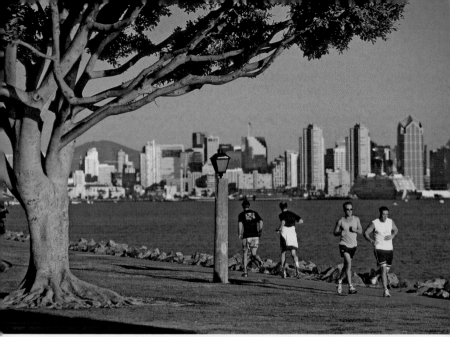

San Diego's myriad coastal trails and paths provide great views of natural and man-made wonders alike.

all-American meal, it's the unofficial SEALs headquarters. Many clothing boutiques, home-furnishings stores, and upscale restaurants cater to visitors with deep pockets, but you can buy plumbing supplies, too, or get a genuine military haircut at **Crown Barber Shop,** at No. 947. If you need a break, stop for a latte at the sidewalk café of **Bay Books** (⊠ *1029 Orange Ave.* ☎ *619/435–0070* ⊕ *www.baybookscoronado. com*), San Diego's largest independent bookstore.

HARBOR AND SHELTER ISLANDS AND POINT LOMA

The populated outcroppings that jut into the bay just west of Downtown and the airport demonstrate the potential of human collaboration with nature. Point Loma, Mother Nature's contribution to San Diego's attractions, has always protected the center city from the Pacific's tides and waves. It's shared by military installations, funky motels and fast-food shacks, stately family homes, huge estates, and private marinas packed with sailboats and yachts. Newer to the scene, Harbor and Shelter islands are landfill. Created out of sand dredged from the San Diego Bay in the second half of the past century, they've become tourist hubs—their high-rise hotels, seafood restaurants, and boat-rental centers looking as solid as those anywhere else in the city.

EXPLORING HARBOR AND SHELTER ISLANDS AND POINT LOMA

Ⓒ
Fodor'sChoice
★ **Cabrillo National Monument.** This 160-acre preserve marks the site of the first European visit to San Diego, made by 16th-century explorer Juan Rodríguez Cabrillo. Cabrillo landed at this spot on September 15, 1542. Today the site, with its rugged cliffs and shores and outstanding

overlooks, is one of the most frequently visited of all the national monuments.

The **visitor center** presents films and lectures about Cabrillo's voyage, the sea-level tide pools, and migrating gray whales. **Interpretive stations** have been installed along the walkways that edge the cliffs. The moderately steep **Bayside Trail**, 2½ miles round-trip, winds through coastal sage scrub, curving under the cliff-top lookouts and taking you ever closer to the bay-front scenery. You cannot reach the beach from this trail, and must stick to the path to protect the cliffs from erosion and yourself from thorny plants and snakes—including rattlers. You'll see prickly pear cactus and yucca, black-eyed Susans, fragrant sage, and maybe a lizard, rabbit, or hummingbird. The climb back is long but gradual, leading up to the **Old Point Loma Lighthouse.**

The western and southern cliffs of Cabrillo National Monument are prime whale-watching territory. A sheltered **viewing station** has wayside exhibits describing the great gray whales' yearly migration from Baja California to the Bering and Chukchi seas near Alaska. High-powered telescopes help you focus on the whales' waterspouts. Whales are visible on clear days from late December through early March, with the highest concentration in January and February. More-accessible sea creatures (starfish, crabs, anemones) can be seen in the **tide pools** at the foot of the monument's western cliffs. Drive north from the visitor center to Cabrillo Road, which winds down to the Coast Guard station and the shore. ⊠ *1800 Cabrillo Memorial Dr., Point Loma* ☎ *619/557–5450* ⊕ *www.nps.gov/cabr* ⊠ *$5 per car, $3 per person entering on foot or by bicycle* ☉ *Daily 9–5.*

Harbor Island. Restaurants and high-rise hotels dot the inner shore of this 1½-mile-long man-made peninsula adjacent to the airport. The bay's shore is lined with pathways, gardens, and scenic picnic spots. On the east end point, **Island Prime and C-level Lounge** (*880 Harbor Island Dr., 619/298–6802, www.cohnrestaurants.com*) offers a killer view of the Downtown skyline. On the west point, the restaurant **Tom Ham's Lighthouse** (*2150 Harbor Island Dr., 619/291–9110, www.tom-hamslighthouse.com*) has a U.S. Coast Guard–approved beacon shining from its tower and a sweeping view of San Diego's bay front. ⊠ *Harbor Island Dr., Harbor Island.*

Shelter Island. This reclaimed peninsula now supports towering palms and resorts, restaurants, and side-by-side marinas. The center of San Diego's yacht-building industry, boats in every stage of construction are visible in Shelter Island's yacht yards. A long sidewalk runs past boat brokerages to the hotels and marinas that line the inner shore, facing Point Loma. On the bay side, fishermen launch their boats and families relax at picnic tables along the grass, where there are fire rings and permanent barbecue grills. Within walking distance is the huge Friendship Bell, given to San Diegans by the people of Yokohama, Japan, in 1960 and the Tunaman's Memorial, a statue commemorating San Diego's once-flourishing fishing industry. ⊠ *Shelter Island Dr., Shelter Island.*

★ **Sunset Cliffs.** As the name suggests, the 60-foot-high bluffs on the western side of Point Loma south of Ocean Beach are a perfect place to watch the sun set over the sea. To view the tide pools along the shore, use the staircase off Sunset Cliffs Boulevard at the foot of Ladera Street.

The dramatic coastline here seems to have been carved out of ancient rock. The impact of the waves is very clear: each year more sections of the cliffs are posted with caution signs. Don't ignore these warnings—it's easy to slip in the crumbling sandstone, and the surf can be extremely rough. The small coves and beaches that dot the coastline are popular with surfers drawn to the pounding waves. The homes along the boulevard—pink stucco mansions beside shingled Cape Cod–style cottages—are fine examples of Southern California luxury. ⊠ *Sunset Cliffs Blvd., Point Loma.*

MISSION BAY AND SEAWORLD

Mission Bay Park is San Diego's monument to sports and fitness. This 4,600-acre aquatic park has 27 miles of shoreline including 19 of sandy beach. Playgrounds and picnic areas abound on the beach and low grassy hills of the park. On weekday evenings, joggers, bikers, and skaters take over. In the daytime, swimmers, water-skiers, anglers, and boaters—some in single-person kayaks, others in crowded powerboats—vie for space in the water. One Mission Bay caveat: swimmers should note signs warning about water pollution; on occasions when heavy rains or other events cause pollution, swimming is dangerous.

EXPLORING MISSION BAY AND SEAWORLD

Ⓒ **Belmont Park.** The once-abandoned amusement park between the bay ★ and Mission Beach Boardwalk is now a shopping, dining, and recreation complex. Twinkling lights outline the **Giant Dipper,** an antique wooden roller coaster on which screaming thrill-seekers ride more than 2,600 feet of track and 13 hills (riders must be at least 4 feet, 2 inches tall). Created in 1925 and listed on the National Register of Historic Places, this is one of the few old-time roller coasters left in the United States. The **Plunge,** an indoor swimming pool, also opened in 1925, and was the largest—60 feet by 125 feet—saltwater pool in the world at the time (it's had freshwater since 1951). Johnny Weismuller and Esther Williams are among the stars who were captured on celluloid swimming here. Other Belmont Park attractions include a video arcade, a submarine ride, bumper cars, a tilt-a-whirl, and an antique carousel. Belmont Park also has the most consistent wave in the county at the **Wave House,** where the FlowRider provides surfers and bodyboarders a near-perfect simulated wave on which to practice their skills. The rock wall challenges both junior climbers and their elders. ⊠ *3146 Mission Blvd., Mission Bay* ☎ *858/488–1549 for rides, 858/228–9300 for pool* ⊕ *www.belmontpark.com* ✉ *full-day unlimited ride package $27 for 48" and over, $16 for under 48"; pool $7 for one-time entry, $15 full day* ☉ *Park opens at 11 daily, ride operation varies seasonally; pool weekdays noon–4 pm and 8–10 pm, weekends noon–8 pm.*

Ⓒ **SeaWorld San Diego.** One of the world's largest marine-life amusement Fodor'sChoice parks, SeaWorld is spread over 189 tropically landscaped bay-front ★ acres—and it seems to be expanding into every available square inch of space with new exhibits, shows, and activities. **Journey to Atlantis** involves a cruise on an eight-passenger "Greek fishing boat" down a heart-stopping 60-foot plunge to explore a lost, sunken city. **Riptide Rescue** spins passengers on a rescue mission to Turtle Reef, and you can tumble through raging rapid and roaring waterfalls on **Shipwreck Rapids.**

The majority of SeaWorld's exhibits are walk-through marine environments. Kids get a particular kick out of the **Shark Encounter,** where they come face-to-face with sand, tiger, nurse, bonnethead, black-tipped, and white-tipped reef sharks by walking through a 57-foot clear acrylic tube that passes through the 280,000-gallon shark habitat. The hands-on **California Tide Pool** exhibit gives you a chance to get to know San Diego's indigenous marine life. At **Forbidden Reef** you can feed bat rays and go nose-to-nose with creepy moray eels. At **Rocky Point Preserve** you can view bottlenose dolphins, as well as Californian sea otters. At **Wild Arctic,** which starts out with a simulated helicopter ride to a research post at the North Pole, beluga whales, walruses, and polar bears can be viewed in areas decked out like the wrecked hulls of two 19th-century sailing ships. **Manatee Rescue** lets you watch the gentle-giant marine mammals cavorting in a 215,000-gallon tank. Various **freshwater and saltwater aquariums** hold underwater creatures from around the world. And for younger kids who need to release lots of energy, **Sesame Street Bay of Play at SeaWorld** is a hands-on fun zone that features three family-friendly Sesame Street–theme rides.

SeaWorld's highlights are its large-arena entertainments. You can get front-row seats if you arrive 30 minutes in advance, and the stadiums are large enough for everyone to get a seat in the off-season. **One Ocean** stars a synchronized team of killer whales who leap out of the water to the tunes of surround-sound music, illuminated by brilliantly colored lights. **Blue Horizons** combines dolphins, pilot whales, tropical birds, and aerialists in a spectacular performance.

Another favorite is *Sesame Street Presents: Lights, Camera, Imagination!* in 4-D, a new film that has Cookie Monster, Elmo, and other favorites swimming through an imaginary ocean and flying through a cinematic sky. **Clyde and Seamore's Sea Lions LIVE,** the sea lion and otter production, also is widely popular.

Not all the shows are water-oriented. **Pets Rule!** showcases the antics of more-common animals like dogs, cats, birds, and even a pig. One segment of the show actually has regular house cats climbing ladders and hanging upside down as they cross a high wire.

The **Dolphin Interaction Program** gives guests the chance to interact with SeaWorld's bottlenose dolphins in the water. The one-hour experience (20 minutes in the water), during which visitors can feed, touch, and give behavior signals, costs $190. You can also **Breakfast with Shamu** ($26) or **Dine with Shamu** ($39 per adult), which includes a buffet meal and allows you the thrill of eating while the whales swim up to you or play nearby. To see everything from on high, ride **Skytower,** a glass elevator that ascends 265 feet. The views of San Diego County are especially spectacular in early morning and late evening. The **Bayside**

Skyride, a five-minute aerial tram ride located on the west side of the park, travels across Mission Bay.

The San Diego 3-for-1 Pass ($135 for adults, $105 for children ages 3 to 9) offers seven consecutive days of unlimited admission to Sea-World, the San Diego Zoo, and the San Diego Zoo's Safari Park. This is a good idea, because if you try to get your money's worth by fitting everything in on a single day, you're likely to end up tired and cranky. Many hotels, especially those in the Mission Bay area, also offer Sea-World specials that may include rate reductions or two-days' entry for the price of one. ⊠ *500 SeaWorld Dr., near west end of I–8, Mission Bay* ☎ *800/257–4268* ⊕ *www.seaworldsandiego.com* ⊠ *$73 adults, $65 kids; parking $14 cars, $8 motorcycles, $17 RVs and campers; 1-hr behind-the-scenes walking tours $13 extra adults, $11 extra kids* ☉ *Daily 10–dusk; extended hrs in summer.*

OLD TOWN

San Diego's Spanish and Mexican roots are most evident in Old Town, the area north of Downtown at Juan Street, near the intersection of Interstates 5 and 8, which was the site of the first European settlement in Southern California. Although Old Town was largely a 19th-century phenomenon, the pueblo's true beginnings took place much earlier and on a hill overlooking it, where soldiers from New Spain established a military outpost in May 1769. Two months later Father Junípero Serra established the first of the California's missions, San Diego de Alcalá.

On San Diego Avenue, the district's main drag, art galleries and expensive gift shops are interspersed with tacky curio shops, restaurants, and open-air stands selling inexpensive Mexican pottery, jewelry, and blankets. The Old Town Esplanade on San Diego Avenue between Harney and Conde streets is the best of several mall-like affairs constructed in mock Mexican-plaza style. Shops and restaurants also line Juan and Congress streets. Bazaar del Mundo, a much-loved collection of shops holding handmade arts and crafts, is at 4133 Taylor Street.

Access to Old Town is easy thanks to the nearby Transit Center. Ten bus lines stop here, as do the San Diego Trolley and the Coaster commuter rail line. Two large parking lots linked to the park by an underground pedestrian walkway ease some of the parking congestion, and signage leading from Interstate 8 to the Transit Center is easy to follow.

EXPLORING OLD TOWN

Fiesta de Reyes. North of San Diego's Old Town Plaza lies the area's unofficial center, built to represent a colonial Mexican plaza. This collection of shops and restaurants around a central courtyard in blossom with magenta bougainvillea, scarlet hibiscus, and other flowers in season reflect what it might have looked like in the early California days, from 1821 to 1872, complete with shops stocked with items reminiscent of that era. More than a dozen shops are open, and there are also three restaurants, including **Casa de Reyes,** serving Mexican food. If you are lucky, you might catch a mariachi band or folklorico dance performance on the plaza stage—check the website for times and upcoming

Fodor'sChoice
★

special events. ✉ *Juan St. between Wallace and Mason Sts., Old Town* ☎ *619/297–3100* ⊕ *www.fiestadereyes.com* ⊙ *Shops 10–9 daily.*

Heritage Park. A number of San Diego's important Victorian buildings are the focus of this 7.8-acre park, up the Juan Street hill near Harney Street. The buildings, moved here and restored by Save Our Heritage Organization, include Southern California's first synagogue, a one-room Classical Revival structure built in 1889 for Congregation Beth Israel. The most interesting of the park's six former residences might be the Sherman-Gilbert House, which has a widow's walk and intricate carving on its decorative trim. It was built for real-estate dealer John Sherman in 1887 at the then-exorbitant cost of $20,000—indicating just how profitable the booming housing market could be. All the houses, some of which may seem surprisingly colorful, accurately represent the bright tones of the era. For visitors looking to stay overnight in a historic setting, four of the houses are being converted into "The Inns at Heritage Park." The park remains open during this process, with the synagogue and Senlis Cottage open to visitors daily from 9 to 5. The McConaughy House hosts the Old Town Gift Emporium, a gift shop specializing in Victorian porcelain dolls. ✉ *2454 Heritage Park Row, Old Town* ☎ *619/819–6009* ⊕ *www.heritageparksd.com.*

Ⓒ
Fodor's Choice
★
Old Town San Diego State Historic Park. The six square blocks on the site of San Diego's original pueblo are the heart of Old Town. Most of the 20 historic buildings preserved or re-created by the park cluster around **Old Town Plaza,** bounded by Wallace Street on the west, Calhoun Street on the north, Mason Street on the east, and San Diego Avenue on the south. The plaza is a pleasant place to rest, plan your tour of the park, and watch passersby. San Diego Avenue is closed to vehicle traffic here.

Some of Old Town's buildings were destroyed in a fire in 1872, but after the site became a state historic park in 1968, reconstruction and restoration of the remaining structures began. Five of the original adobes are still intact. The tour pamphlet available at Robinson-Rose House gives details about all the historic houses on the plaza and in its vicinity; *a few of the more interesting ones are noted below.* Several reconstructed buildings serve as restaurants or as shops purveying wares reminiscent of those that might have been available in the original Old Town; Racine & Laramie, a painstakingly reproduced version of San Diego's first (1868) cigar store, is especially interesting. Free tours depart daily from the Robinson-Rose House at 11 and 2. Due to budget cuts some historic sites here may have shortened hours. ∎TIP→ The covered wagon in Old Town Plaza makes for a great photo opportunity.

Casa de Estudillo. San Diego's first County Assessor, Jose Antonio Estudillo, built this home in 1827 in collaboration with his father, the commander of the San Diego Presidio, José Maria Estudillo. The largest and most elaborate of the original adobe homes, it was occupied by members of the Estudillo family until 1887. It was purchased and restored in 1910 by sugar magnate and developer John D. Spreckels, who advertised it in bold lettering on the side as "Ramona's Marriage Place." Spreckels's claim that the small chapel in the house was the site of the wedding in Helen Hunt Jackson's popular novel *Ramona* had

TIP SHEET: SEAWORLD SAN DIEGO

Who Will Especially Love This Park?

The park, on 180 tropically land-scaped acres, caters to adults and kids of all ages. The Sesame Street Bay of Play—for toddlers less than 42 inches tall—is a 2-acre area with familiar television characters, live performances, Sesame Street rides, and interactive educational exhibits like the California Tide Pool.

What's This Really Gonna Cost?

In addition to tickets, you'll need to pay $14 for parking. Meals are about $6–$29 per person. There are also additional fees for Bayside Skyride ($4) and Skytower ($4); you can buy a combo ticket for both for $6. Sea-World offers a broad range of public and private tours and animal interaction experiences, which start at $16 per person for a one-hour Up Close tour and run up to $190 per person for the Dolphin Interaction Program.

TOP 5 ATTRACTIONS:

Believe: This multimedia Shamu show blends killer whale behaviors with theatrical set pieces, music, and choreography. For an additional $39, you can Dine with Shamu.

Blue Horizons: Super-intelligent bottlenose dolphins and pilot whales perform alongside birds and acrobats for huge crowds in this spectacular show.

Penguin Encounter: Enjoy a close-up look at 250 penguins representing five species—including the only successful emperor penguin breeding colony outside Antarctica.

Shark Encounter: This 280,000-gallon tank is home to 12 shark species that swim above and around you as you walk through a clear acrylic tube.

Wild Arctic: Board a simulated jet helicopter, and disembark at a realistic Arctic research station with beluga whales, polar bears, walruses, and seals.

TIPS:

Cool Down: If it's hot when you visit, be sure to ride Journey to Atlantis, a cruise on an eight-passenger Greek ship that plunges 60 feet to the lost city—creating a nice, refreshing splashdown.

Up, Up and Away: Don't miss the Bayside Skyride over Mission Bay. It's an extra $4, but well worth the time and money—you'll get a great overview of the park and surrounding area.

Get Good Seats: Arrive at shows at least 30 minutes early to get front-row seats.

Save Some Cash: Look for Sea-World specials at Mission Bay area hotels; some offer reduced rates and/or two-days-for-the-price-of-one admission deals. Be sure to ask when you book.

Elmo's Flying Fish, in SeaWorld's Sesame Street Bay of Play.

Acrobatic dolphins perform in SeaWorld's Dolphin Discovery show.

no basis; that didn't stop people from coming to see it, however. *4001 Mason St.*

Cosmopolitan Hotel and Restaurant. A Peruvian, Juan Bandini, built a hacienda on this site in 1829, and the house served as Old Town's social center during Mexican rule. Albert Seeley, a stagecoach entrepreneur, purchased the home in 1869, built a second story, and turned it into the Cosmopolitan Hotel, a way station for travelers on the daylong trip south from Los Angeles. It later served as a cannery before being revived (a few times over the years) as a hotel and restaurant. *2660 Calhoun St.*

Robinson-Rose House. Facing Old Town Plaza, this was the original commercial center of Old San Diego, housing railroad offices, law offices, and the first newspaper press. Built in 1853 but in ruins at the end of the 19th century, it has been reconstructed and now serves as the park's visitor center. Inside are a model of Old Town as it looked in 1872, as well as various historic exhibits. Ghosts came with the rebuild, as the house is now considered haunted. Just behind the Robinson-Rose House is a replica of the Victorian-era Silvas-McCoy house, originally built in 1869. *4002 Wallace St.*

Seeley Stable. Next door to the Cosmopolitan Hotel, the stable became San Diego's stagecoach stop in 1867 and was the transportation hub of Old Town until 1887, when trains became the favored mode of travel. The stable houses horse-drawn vehicles, some so elaborate that you can see where the term "carriage trade" came from. Also inside are Western memorabilia, including an exhibit on the California vaquero, the original American cowboy, and a collection of Native American artifacts. *2630 Calhoun St.*

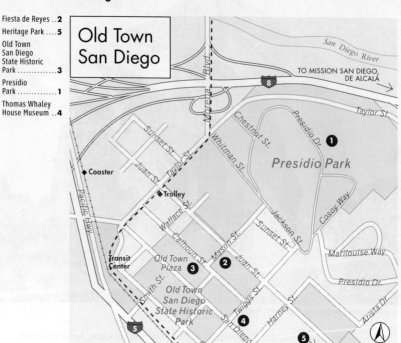

Old Town
San Diego

TO MISSION SAN DIEGO,
DE ALCALÁ

Presidio Park

◆ Coaster

◆ Trolley

Transit
Center

Old Town
Plaza

Old Town
San Diego
State Historic
Park

0   1/8 mile

0   200 meters

Also worth exploring: The San Diego Union Museum, Dental Museum, Mason Street School, Wells Fargo History Museum, First San Diego Courthouse, Casa de Machado y Silvas Commercial Restaurant Museum, and the Casa de Machado y Stewart. Ask at the visitor center for locations. ⊠ *Visitor Center (Robinson-Rose House), 4002 Wallace St., Old Town* ☎ *619/220–5422* ⊕ *www.parks.ca.gov/?page_id=663* ☑ *Free* ⊙ *Oct.–Apr., daily 10–4; May–Sept., daily 10–5; hrs may vary at individual sites.*

Presidio Park. The hillsides of the 50-acre green space overlooking Old Town from the north end of Taylor Street are popular with picnickers, and many couples have taken their wedding vows on the park's long stretches of lawn, some of the greenest in San Diego. The park offers a great ocean view from the top, more than 2 miles of hiking trails, and terrain for enthusiasts of the sport of grass-skiing, gliding over the grass and down the hills on their wheeled-model skis. It's a nice walk from Old Town to the summit if you're in good shape and wearing the right shoes—it should take about half an hour. You can also drive to the top of the park via Presidio Drive, off Taylor Street.

If you walk, look in at the **Presidio Hills Golf Course** on Mason Street. It has an unusual clubhouse that incorporates the ruins of Casa de Carrillo, the town's oldest adobe, constructed in 1820. At the end of

Mason Street, veer left on Jackson Street to reach the **presidio ruins,** where adobe walls and a bastion have been built above the foundations of the original fortress and chapel. Also on-site is the 28-foot-high **Serra Cross,** built in 1913 out of brick tiles found in the ruins. Take Presidio Drive southeast and you'll come to the site of **Fort Stockton,** built to protect Old Town and abandoned by the United States in 1848. Plaques and statues also commemorate the Mormon Battalion, which enlisted here to fight in the battle against Mexico. ✉ *Taylor and Jackson Sts., Old Town* ⊕ *www.sandiego.gov/park-and-recreation/parks.*

★ **Thomas Whaley House Museum.** Thomas Whaley was a New York entrepreneur who came to California during the gold rush. He wanted to provide his East Coast wife with all the comforts of home, so in 1857 he had Southern California's first two-story brick structure built, making it the oldest double-story brick building on the West Coast. The house, which served as the county courthouse and government seat during the 1870s, stands in strong contrast to the Spanish-style adobe residences that surround the nearby historic plaza and marks an early stage of San Diego's "Americanization." A garden out back includes many varieties of prehybrid roses from before 1867. The place is perhaps most famed, however, for the ghosts that are said to inhabit it. Starting at 5 pm, admission is by guided tour offered every half hour with the last tour departing at 9:30 pm. The nighttime tours are geared more toward the supernatural aspects of the house than the daytime self-guided tour. ✉ *2476 San Diego Ave., Old Town* ☎ *619/297–7511* ⊕ *www.whaleyhouse.org* 💲 *$6 before 5 pm, $10 after 5* ☼ *Sept.–May, Sun.–Tues. 10–5, Thurs.–Sun. 10–9:30; June–Aug., daily 10–9:30.*

LA JOLLA

La Jollans have long considered their village to be the Monte Carlo of California. Its coastline curves into natural coves backed by verdant hillsides dotted with homes worth millions. Although La Jolla is a neighborhood of the city of San Diego, it has its own postal zone and a coveted sense of class; the ultrarich from around the globe own second homes here—the seaside zone between the neighborhood's bustling Downtown and the cliffs above the Pacific has a distinctly European flavor—and old-moneyed residents maintain friendships with the visiting film stars and royalty who frequent the area's exclusive luxury hotels and private clubs. The town has a cosmopolitan air that makes it a popular vacation resort.

To reach La Jolla from Interstate 5, if you're traveling north, take the La Jolla Parkway exit, which veers into Torrey Pines Road, and turn right onto Prospect Street. If you're heading south, get off at the La Jolla Village Drive exit, which also leads into Torrey Pines Road. Prospect Street and Girard Avenue, the village's main drags, are lined with expensive shops and office buildings. Through the years the shopping and dining district has spread to Pearl and other side streets. Although there is metered parking on the streets, parking is otherwise hard to find.

TOP ATTRACTIONS

🕲 **La Jolla Cove.** This shimmering blue inlet is what first attracted everyone
Fodor'sChoice to La Jolla, from Native Americans to the glitterati; it's the secret to the
★ village's enduring cachet. You'll find the cove—as locals always refer to
it, as though it were the only one in San Diego—beyond where Girard
Avenue dead-ends into Coast Boulevard, marked by towering palms
that line a promenade where people strolling in designer clothes are as
common as Frisbee throwers.

Smaller beaches appear and disappear with the tides, which carve
small coves in cliffs covered with ice plants. Pathways lead down to
the beaches. Keep an eye on the tide to avoid getting trapped once the
waves come in. A long layer of sandstone stretching out above the
waves provides a perfect sunset-watching spot. Be careful, these rocks
can get slippery.

An underwater preserve at the north end of La Jolla Cove makes the
adjoining beach the most popular one in the area. On summer days,
when water visibility reaches down to 20 feet, the small beach is covered with blankets, towels, and umbrellas, and the lawns at the top of
the stairs leading down to the cove are staked out by groups of scuba
divers, complete with wet suits and tanks. The **Children's Pool**, at the
south end of the park, has a curving beach protected by a seawall from
strong currents and waves. Since the pool and its beach have become
home to an ever-growing colony of harbor seals, it cannot be used
by swimmers. It is however the best place on the coast to view these
engaging creatures. ■**TIP→ Take a walk through Ellen Browning Scripps
Park, past the groves of twisted junipers to the cliff's edge. Perhaps one of
the open-air shelters overlooking the sea will be unoccupied, and you can
spread your picnic out on a table and enjoy the scenery.** ✉ *From Torrey
Pines Rd., turn right on Prospect, then right on Coast Blvd. The park is
at the bottom of the hill* ⊕ *www.lajollabythesea.com/activities/beaches.*

Fodor'sChoice **Museum of Contemporary Art San Diego.** The oldest section of La Jolla's
★ branch of San Diego's contemporary art museum was originally a residence, designed by Irving Gill for philanthropist Ellen Browning Scripps
in 1916. In the mid-1990s the compound was updated and expanded
by architect Robert Venturi, who respected Gill's original geometric
structure and clean Mission-style lines while adding his own distinctive
touches. The result is a striking contemporary building that looks as
though it's always been here.

California artists figure prominently in the museum's permanent collection of post-1950s art, but the museum also includes examples of every
major art movement through the present—works by Andy Warhol,
Robert Rauschenberg, Frank Stella, Joseph Cornell, and Jenny Holzer,
to name a few. Important pieces by artists from San Diego and Tijuana
were acquired in the 1990s. The museum also hosts major visiting
shows. ✉ *700 Prospect St., La Jolla* ☎ *858/454–3541* ⊕ *www.mcasd.
org* 🖃 *$10, good for one visit here and at MCASD Downtown within
7 days; free 3rd Thurs. of the month 5–7* ⊙ *Thurs.–Tues. 11–5; 3rd
Thurs. of month open 11–7* ⊙ *Closed Wed.*

QUICK BITES

Brockton Villa Restaurant. This charming café overlooking La Jolla Cove has indoor and outdoor seating, as well as scrumptious desserts and coffee drinks; the beans are locally roasted. A popular breakfast spot, the café closes at 9 pm. ⊠ *1235 Coast Blvd., La Jolla* ☎ *858/454–7393* ⊕ *www. brocktonvilla.com.*

Fodor'sChoice **Torrey Pines State Natural Reserve.** *Pinus torreyana*, the rarest native pine
★ tree in the United States, enjoys a 1,700-acre sanctuary at the northern edge of La Jolla. About 6,000 of these unusual trees, some as tall as 60 feet, grow on the cliffs here. The park is one of only two places in the world (the other is Santa Rosa Island, off Santa Barbara) where the Torrey pine grows naturally. The reserve has several hiking trails leading to the cliffs, 300 feet above the ocean; trail maps are available at the park station. Wildflowers grow profusely in spring, and the ocean panoramas are always spectacular. When in this upper part of the park, respect the restrictions. Not permitted: picnicking, smoking, leaving the trails, dogs, alcohol, or collecting plant specimens.

You can unwrap your sandwiches, however, at **Torrey Pines State Beach,** just below the reserve. When the tide is out, it's possible to walk south all the way past the lifeguard towers to Black's Beach over rocky promontories carved by the waves (avoid the bluffs, however; they're unstable). **Los Peñasquitos Lagoon** at the north end of the reserve is one of the many natural estuaries that flow inland between Del Mar and Oceanside. It's a good place to watch shorebirds. Volunteers lead guided nature walks at 10 and 2 on most weekends. ⊠ *N. Torrey Pines Rd. exit off I–5 onto Carmel Valley Rd. going west, then turn left (south) on Coast Hwy. 101, 12600 N. Torrey Pines Rd., La Jolla* ☎ *858/755–2063* ⊕ *www.torreypine.org* ☜ *Parking $10–$15* ⊙ *Daily 9–dusk.*

WORTH NOTING

☾ **Birch Aquarium at Scripps.** The largest oceanographic exhibit in the United States, maintained by the Scripps Institution of Oceanography, sits at the end of a signposted drive leading off North Torrey Pines Road. More than 60 tanks are filled with colorful saltwater fish, and a 70,000-gallon tank simulates a La Jolla kelp forest. A special exhibit on sea horses features several examples of the species, plus mesmerizing sea dragons and a sea horse nursery. Besides the fish themselves, attractions include a gallery based on the institution's ocean-related research, and interactive educational exhibits on a variety of environmental issues. ⊠ *2300 Expedition Way, La Jolla* ☎ *858/534–3474* ⊕ *www.aquarium.ucsd.edu* ☜ *$14* ⊙ *Daily 9–5.*

☾ **La Jolla Caves.** It's a walk of 145 sometimes slippery steps down a tunnel to Sunny Jim, the largest of the caves in La Jolla Cove and the only one reachable by land. This is a one-of-a-kind local attraction, and worth the time if you have a day or two to really enjoy La Jolla. The man-made tunnel took two years to dig, beginning in 1902; later, a shop was built at its entrance. Today the Sunny Jim Cave Store, a throwback to that early day, is still the entrance to the cave. The shop sells jewelry and watercolors by local artists. ⊠ *1325 Coast Blvd. S, La Jolla* ☎ *858/459–0746* ⊕ *www.cavestore.com* ☜ *$4* ⊙ *Daily 10–5.*

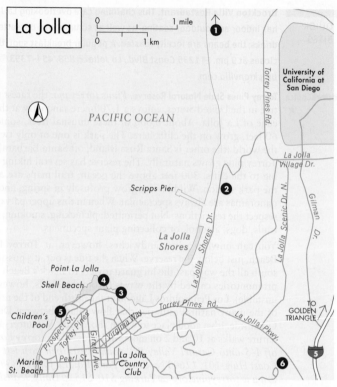

Mount Soledad. La Jolla's highest spot can be reached by taking Nautilus Street to La Jolla Scenic Drive South, and then turning left. Proceed a few blocks to the park, where parking is plentiful and the views are astounding, unless the day is hazy. The top of the mountain is an excellent vantage point from which to get a sense of San Diego's geography: looking down from here you can see the coast from the county's northern border to the south far beyond Downtown. ⊠ 6905 La Jolla Scenic Dr. S, La Jolla.

WHERE TO EAT

San Diego's unbeatable sunny and warm weather combined with gorgeous ocean views and the abundance of locally grown produce make it a satisfying place to be a chef or a diner. While most of the top restaurants offer seasonal California cuisine, San Diego also boasts excellent examples of ethnic cuisines available at all prices. Local specialties include fish tacos and spiny lobster.

While "Appropriate Dress Required" signs are sometimes displayed in the entrances to restaurants, this generally means nothing more than clean and reasonably neat clothing. Meal prices in San Diego have caught up with those of other major metropolitan areas, especially in districts like La Jolla, the Gaslamp Quarter, and Coronado, where high rents and popularity with the tourists lead to more expensive entrées. Reservations are always a good idea; we mention them only when they're essential or not accepted.

Use the coordinate (✛ A1) at the end of each listing to locate a site on the corresponding map.

RESTAURANT COSTS

Prices in the restaurant reviews are the average cost of a main course at dinner or, if dinner is not served, at lunch (excluding sales tax).

CORONADO AND SOUTH BAY

$$$ ✕ **1500 Ocean.** The fine-dining restaurant at Hotel Del Coronado right
AMERICAN on the beach offers a memorable evening that showcases the best organic and naturally raised ingredients the region has to offer. Chef Brian Sinnott presents sublimely subtle dishes such as roasted-beet salad with wild arugula, tangerine, pistachios, goat cheese, and Sauvignon Blanc; and Maine lobster lasagna with tomato confit, pickled radish, and Chardonnay. The elegant interior evokes a posh cabana, while the terrace offers ocean views. An excellent international wine list and clever desserts and artisanal cheeses complete the experience. $ *Average main: $34* ⊠ *Hotel Del Coronado, 1500 Orange Ave., Coronado* ☎ *619/522–8490* ⊕ *www.hoteldel.com/1500-ocean.aspx* ⊘ *Reservations essential* ⊘ *Closed. Sun. and Mon. No lunch* ✛ *D6.*

$$$ ✕ **Chez Loma.** A favorite with guests at nearby Hotel Del Coronado,
FRENCH this restaurant is tucked away on a side street. Chez Loma is located in a former private home with plenty of windows, attractive lighting, and an upstairs Victorian parlor where coffee and dessert are served. The more elaborate dishes among the carefully prepared French bistro menu are *boeuf bourguignon,* rack of lamb with balsamic marinade, and roasted salmon in a horseradish crust. The solid selection of desserts includes classics like chocolate soufflé and crème caramel. A specially priced early dinner menu, and two choices of fixed-price menus for $40 or $45 offer more value than the à la carte selections. $ *Average main: $31* ⊠ *1132 Loma Ave., Coronado* ☎ *619/435–0661* ⊘ *Reservations essential* ⊘ *Closed Mon. No lunch* ✛ *D6.*

DOWNTOWN

$$ ✕ **Café Chloe.** The intersection of 9th and G is now the meeting point
FRENCH for San Diego's café society, thanks to the superchic and friendly Café
Fodor's Choice Chloe. Surrounded by luxury high-rises, hotels, and boutiques, this
★ pretty, Parisian spot is frequented by the area's residents for breakfast, lunch, dinner, and weekend brunch. Start the day with whole-wheat pancakes and sour-cherry sauce; lunch on smoked trout and apple salad or a casserole of macaroni, pancetta, and Gorgonzola; or enjoy duck confit or steak frites for dinner. Enjoy wines by the glass, imported teas, and coffee with desserts like seasonal fruit tarts or chocolate pot de crème. It's a lovely place to spend the afternoon. $ *Average main:*

A surfer prepares to head out before sunset at La Jolla's Torrey Pines State Beach and Preserve.

$21 ⊠ 721 9th Ave., East Village ☎ 619/232–3242 ⊕ www.cafechloe. com ✛ E4.

$$$
MEXICAN
✕ **Candelas.** The scents and flavors of imaginative Mexican cuisine with a European flair permeate this handsome, romantic restaurant and nightspot in the shadow of San Diego's tallest residential towers. Candles glow everywhere around the small, comfortable dining room. Fine openers such as black bean soup and watercress salad with bacon and pistachios give way to main courses like Maine lobster accompanied by Angus steak and jumbo prawns. ⑤ *Average main: $28* ⊠ *416 3rd Ave., Gaslamp Quarter* ☎ 619/702–4455 ⊕ *www.candelas-sd.com* ⌕ *Reservations essential* ⊘ *No lunch* ✛ *H3.*

$$
AMERICAN
☾
Fodor's Choice
★
✕ **Jsix.** Creative and carefully prepared seafood reigns on this menu that reflects the diverse flavors found along the West Coast from Mexico to Washington. Chef Christian Graves favors fresh, light fare, using locally sourced sustainably raised seafood in dishes such as the tarragon and Dijon mussels and seared albacore with avocado puree. Nonseafood options include vegetarian butternut squash ravioli, chicken with green garlic-bacon risotto, and pork chop with rosemary garlic potatoes. The cheeses, salami, and house-made pickles are excellent. Desserts are made with equal care, and the bar boasts cocktails made with seasonal fruit. The eclectic decor includes blown-glass pendant lights, a series of culinary paintings by a local artist, and a dramatically backlighted bar. ⑤ *Average main: $23* ⊠ *616 J St., Gaslamp Quarter* ☎ 619/531–8744 ⊕ *www.jsixrestaurant.com* ⌕ *Reservations essential* ✛ *H3.*

$$$
SEAFOOD
✕ **The Oceanaire Seafood Room.** Engineered to recall an ocean liner from the 1940s, Oceanaire is a bit put-on but admirable for the long bar serving classic cocktails, oysters, and sashimi, and a carefully prepared

2

menu of up to 25 daily "fresh catches," with many specialties ranging from convincing Maryland crab cakes and oysters Rockefeller to richly stuffed California sole, a luxurious one-pound pork chop, and irresistible hash brown potatoes. The menu might also include the deliciously hot, spice-fired "angry" pink snapper. Service is a casual thing in San Diego, which makes the professional staff here all the more notable. ⑤ *Average main: $31* ✉ *400 J St., Gaslamp Quarter* ☎ *619/858–2277* ⊕ *www.theoceanaire.com* ☾ *No lunch* ⊹ *H3.*

$$$
AMERICAN

✕ **Searsucker.** The much-hyped first restaurant of *Top Chef* finalist Brian Malarkey opened in summer 2010 in the middle of the Gaslamp Quarter. Since then it has maintained its buzz, attracting patrons with its fun urban decor and experimental dishes like swordfish with drunken cherries and beef cheeks over goat cheese dumplings. The flavor combinations are mostly successful, particularly when paired with comfort-food sides like bacon grits and grilled asparagus. Chef Malarkey adds to the lively vibe when he makes his rounds to chat with diners. ⑤ *Average main: $30* ✉ *611 5th Ave., Gaslamp Quarter* ☎ *619/233–7327* ⊕ *www. searsucker.com* ⚖ *Reservations essential* ⊹ *H2.*

$
SEAFOOD

✕ **The Tin Fish.** On the rare rainy day, the staff takes it easy at this eatery less than 100 yards from the PETCO Park baseball stadium (half of its 100-odd seats are outdoors). It's a walk-up place where you can dine under umbrellas. Musicians entertain some evenings, making this a lively spot for dinners of grilled and fried fish, as well as seafood burritos and tacos. The quality here routinely surpasses that at grander establishments. Whether it's baseball season or not, the service hours vary, but Tin Fish usually stays open until 8 for much of the week and until 11 pm on Friday and Saturday. ⑤ *Average main: $10* ✉ *170 6th Ave., Gaslamp Quarter* ☎ *619/238–8100* ⊕ *www.thetinfish.net* ⚖ *Reservations not accepted* ⊹ *H3.*

LITTLE ITALY

$$
ITALIAN

✕ **Buon Appetito.** This charmer serves old world–style cooking in a casual but somewhat sophisticated environment. Choose a table on the sidewalk or in a room jammed with art and fellow diners. Baked eggplant in a mozzarella-topped tomato sauce is a dream of a dish—in San Diego, tomato sauce doesn't get better than this. Consider also sea bass in mushroom sauce, hearty cioppino, and expert osso buco paired with affordable and varied wines. The young Italian waiters' good humor makes the experience fun. ⑤ *Average main: $19* ✉ *1609 India St., Little Italy* ☎ *619/238–9880* ⊕ *www.buonappetito.signonsandiego.com* ⊹ *E5.*

$$$
ITALIAN

✕ **Po Pazzo Bar and Grille.** An eye-catching creation from leading Little Italy restaurateurs Joe and Lisa Busalacchi, Po Pazzo earns its name, which means "a little crazy," by mixing a lively bar with a restaurant serving modern Italian fare. A steak house with an accent, this stylish eatery offers attractive salads and thick cuts of prime beef, as well as a top-notch presentation of veal chops Sinatra style with mushrooms, tomatoes, and onions; and Sicilian rib-eye steak that defines richness. ⑤ *Average main: $29* ✉ *1917 India St., Little Italy* ☎ *619/238–1917* ⊕ *www.popazzo.com* ⊹ *E5.*

BEST BETS FOR SAN DIEGO DINING

With hundreds of restaurants to choose from, how will you decide where to eat? We've selected our favorite restaurants by price, cuisine, and experience in the Best Bets list below. In the first column, Fodor's Choice properties represent the "best of the best" in every price category. Bon appétit!

Fodor's Choice ★

Bread & Cie, $, p. 87
Café Chloe, $$ p. 83
Cucina Urbana, $$$, p. 87
George's at the Cove, $$$$, p. 91
Jsix, $$, p. 84
Nine-Ten, $$$, p. 92
Ortega's Bistro, $$, p. 90
Sushi on the Rock, $, p. 93

By Price

$

Bread & Cie, p. 87
El Zarape, p. 87
Sushi on the Rock, p. 93

$$

Café Chloe, p. 83
Jsix, p. 84
Ortega's Bistro, p. 90
Sushi Ota, p. 91

$$$

Cucina Urbana, p. 87
Nine-Ten, p. 92

1500 Ocean, p. 83
Searsucker, p. 85

$$$$

George's at the Cove, p. 91

Best by Cuisine

AMERICAN

George's at the Cove, $$$$, p. 91
Jsix, $$, p. 84
Nine-Ten, $$$, p. 92
Searsucker, $$$, p. 85

ASIAN

Sushi on the Rock, $, p. 93
Sushi Ota, $$, p. 91

CAFÉS

Bread & Cie, $, p. 87
Café Chloe, $$, p. 83

ITALIAN

Caffe Bella Italia, $$, p. 90
Cucina Urbana, $$$, p. 87

LATIN/MEXICAN

El Zarape, $, p. 87
Ortega's Bistro, $$, p. 90

PIZZA

Cucina Urbana, $$$, p. 87

SEAFOOD

Oceanaire Seafood Room, $$$, p. 84

Best By Experience

BRUNCH

Bread & Cie, $, p. 87
Café Chloe, $$, p. 83
Nine-Ten, $$$, p. 92

DINING WITH KIDS

Ortega's Bistro, $$, p. 90
Rimel's Rotisserie, $$, p. 92

GOOD FOR GROUPS

Oceanaire Seafood Room, $$$, p. 84

HOTEL DINING

Jsix, $$, p. 84
Nine-Ten, $$$, p. 92

OUTDOOR DINING

1500 Ocean, $$$, p. 83
Café Chloe, $$, p. 83
Osteria Romantica, $, p. 92

ROMANTIC

Chez Loma, $$$, p. 83
George's at the Cove, $$$$, p. 91
Whisknladle, $$, p. 93

SINGLES SCENE

George's at the Cove, $$$$, p. 91
Oceanaire Seafood Room, $$$, p. 84

TRENDY

Jsix, $$, p. 84
Searsucker, $$$, p. 85

WATER VIEWS

George's at the Cove, $$$$, p. 91
Marine Room, $$$$, p. 92

UPTOWN

$$ **INDIAN** ✕ **Bombay Exotic Cuisine of India.** Notable for its elegant dining room with a waterfall, Bombay employs a chef whose generous hand with raw and cooked vegetables gives each course a colorful freshness reminiscent of California cuisine, though the flavors definitely hail from India. Try the tandoori lettuce-wrap appetizer and any of the stuffed *kulchas* (a stuffed flatbread). The unusually large selection of curries may be ordered with meat, chicken, fish, or tofu. The curious should try the *dizzy noo shak,* a sweet-and-spicy banana curry. $ *Average main: $19* ✉ *Hillcrest Center, 3960 5th Ave., Hillcrest* ☎ *619/297–7777* ⊕ *www. bombayrestaurant.com* ✛ *E4.*

$ **CAFÉS** **Fodor'sChoice** ★ ✕ **Bread & Cie.** There's an East Coast air to this artsy urban bakery and café known for being one of San Diego's first and best artisanal bread bakers. Owner Charles Kaufman is a former New Yorker and filmmaker, who gave Bread & Cie a sense of theater by putting bread ovens imported from France on center stage. The mix served from daybreak to sunset includes warm focaccia covered in cheese and vegetables, crusty loaves of black olive bread, gourmet granola with Mediterranean yogurt, bear claws, and first-rate cinnamon rolls. Lunch on house-made quiche; paninis filled with pastrami, turkey, and pesto; or Brie and honey. $ *Average main: $7* ✉ *350 University Ave., Hillcrest* ☎ *619/683–9322* ⊕ *www.breadandcie.com* ✛ *E4.*

$$$ **ITALIAN** **Fodor'sChoice** ★ ✕ **Cucina Urbana.** Proprietor Tracy Borkum's casual and stylish Cal-Italian spot remains one of the most popular tables in town. Everything is reasonably priced, and diners can pop into the retail wine room, select a bottle, and drink it with dinner for a modest corkage fee. The ricotta gnudi bathed in brown butter and fried sage are the best yet; fried squash blossoms sing; and polenta boards mixed tableside are creative and satisfying. Also good are the lasagna, the short rib pappardelle, and the goat-cheese-and-toasted-almond ravioli. Sit at the cozy bar and watch the chefs turn out bubbly, thin-crust pizzas topped with wild mushroom and taleggio cheese or pancetta fried egg and potatoes, or find a spot at the main bar for a clever cocktail crafted from seasonal fruit and Italian liqueurs. $ *Average main: $26* ✉ *505 Laurel St., Banker's Hill* ☎ *619/239–2222* ⊕ *www.cucinaurbana.com* ☖ *Reservations essential* ✛ *E5.*

$ **MEXICAN** ✕ **El Zarape.** There's a humble air to this cozy Mexican taqueria, but one bite of the signature scallop tacos and you'll realize something special is happening in the kitchen. Inside the satiny corn tortilla, seared bay scallops mingle with tangy white sauce and shredded cheese. Or perhaps you'll prefer sweet pieces of lobster meat in oversize quesadillas; burritos filled with chiles rellenos; or the original beef, ham, and pineapple Aloha burrito. No matter, nearly everything is fantastic at this busy under-the-radar eatery. Mexican beverages, including the sweet-tart hibiscus-flower drink *jamaica* and the cinnamon rice drink *horchata,* and house-made flan and rice pudding round out the menu. $ *Average main: $6* ✉ *4642 Park Blvd., University Heights* ☎ *619/692–1652* ⊕ *elzarape.menutoeat.com* ✛ *E4.*

$$$ **AMERICAN** ✕ **Hash House A Go Go.** Expect to wait an hour or more for weekend breakfast at this splashy Hillcrest eatery, whose walls display photos of

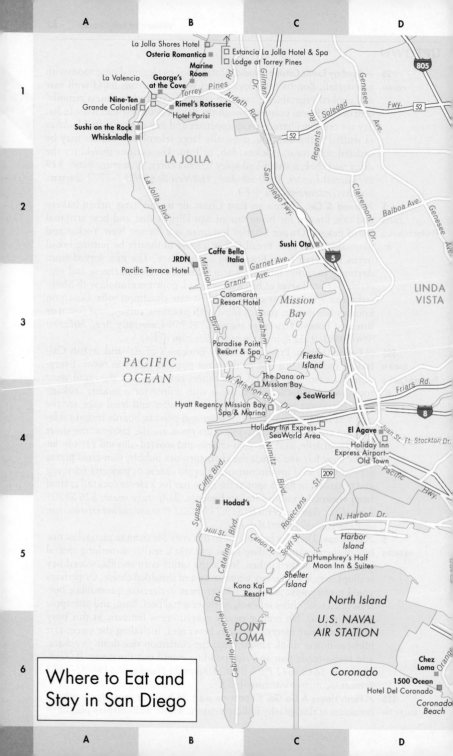

Where to Eat and Stay in San Diego

A

1
La Jolla Shores Hotel
Osteria Romantica
Estancia La Jolla Hotel & Spa
Lodge at Torrey Pines
Marine Room
La Valencia
George's at the Cove
Nine-Ten
Rimel's Rotisserie
Grande Colonial
Hotel Parisi
Sushi on the Rock
Whisknladle

LA JOLLA

2

JRDN
Pacific Terrace Hotel
Caffe Bella Italia
Sushi Ota

Catamaran Resort Hotel

Mission Bay

LINDA VISTA

3
PACIFIC OCEAN
Paradise Point Resort & Spa
Fiesta Island
The Dana on Mission Bay
SeaWorld
Hyatt Regency Mission Bay Spa & Marina

4
Holiday Inn Express–SeaWorld Area
El Agave
Holiday Inn Express Airport–Old Town
Ft. Stockton Dr.

Hodad's

5
Harbor Island
Humphrey's Half Moon Inn & Suites
Shelter Island
Kona Kai Resort
North Island
U.S. NAVAL AIR STATION

6
POINT LOMA
Coronado
Chez Loma
1500 Ocean
Hotel Del Coronado
Coronado Beach

farm machinery and other icons of Middle America, but whose menu takes a Southern-accented look at national favorites. The supersize portions are the main draw here; at breakfast, huge platters carpeted with fluffy pancakes sail out of the kitchen, while at noon customers favor the overflowing chicken potpies crowned with flaky pastry. The parade of old-fashioned good eats continues at dinner with hearty meat and seafood dishes, including sage-flavored fried chicken, bacon-studded waffles, and meat loaf stuffed with roasted red pepper, spinach, and mozzarella with a side of mashed potatoes. ⑤ *Average main: $27* ✉ *3628 5th Ave., Hillcrest* ☎ *619/298–4646* ⊕ *www.hashhouseagogo. com* ✛ *E4.*

$$ ╳ **The Linkery.** The menu at this earthy farm-to-table-style restau-
AMERICAN rant reads like a Who's Who of seasonal produce and the area's top
ⓒ organic farms. House-made sausages such as chicken-mushroom and *kaisekreiner* (spicy Vienna-style pork sausage with cheese) and smoky poblano pork lend the casual restaurant its name, but there's lots of vegetarian fare, too, including a vegan roast with eggplant and squash, and lasagna stuffed with garden vegetables. Entrées include black cod with pickled ginger and haricots verts, and a ranch-style ham-and-egg sandwich. The chefs also house-cure country ham, Italian coppa, and lardo, and they fire up the grill for Sunday cookouts. The well-chosen wine and beer list includes cask-conditioned ales and even mead. ⑤ *Average main: $23* ✉ *3794 30th St., North Park* ☎ *619/255–8778* ⊕ *www. thelinkery.com* ⌦ *Reservations essential* ✛ *F4.*

$$ ╳ **Ortega's Bistro.** Californians have long flocked to Puerto Nuevo,
MEXICAN the "lobster village" south of San Diego in Baja California. When a
ⓒ member of the family that operates several Puerto Nuevo restaurants
Fodor's Choice opened Ortega's, it became an instant sensation, since it brought no-
★ nonsense, authentic Mexican fare straight to the heart of Hillcrest. The specialty of choice is a whole lobster prepared Baja-style and served with superb beans, rice, and made-to-order tortillas, but there are other fine options, including melt-in-the-mouth carnitas (slow-cooked pork), made-at-the-table guacamole, and grilled tacos filled with *huitlacoche* corn mushrooms and Mexican herbs. The pomegranate margaritas are a must, as is the special red salsa if you like authentic spice. ⑤ *Average main: $18* ✉ *141 University Ave., Hillcrest* ☎ *619/692–4200* ⊕ *www. ortegasbistro.com* ✛ *E4.*

BEACHES

$$ ╳ **Caffe Bella Italia.** Contemporary northern Italian cooking as prepared
ITALIAN in Italy is the rule at this simple dinner-only restaurant near one of the main intersections in Pacific Beach. The menu presents Neapolitan-style squid ink ravioli stuffed with lobster, pizzas baked in a wood-fired oven, plus formal entrées like chicken breast sautéed with Marsala wine and mushrooms and slices of rare filet mignon tossed with herbs and topped with arugula and Parmesan shavings. Impressive daily specials include beet-stuffed ravioli in creamy saffron sauce. ⑤ *Average main: $21* ✉ *1525 Garnet Ave., Pacific Beach* ☎ *858/273–1224* ⊕ *www. caffebellaitalia.com* ☾ *No lunch* ✛ *B2.*

$ ✕ **Hodad's.** No, it's not a flashback. The 1960s live on at this fabulously
AMERICAN funky burger joint. Walls are covered with license plates, and the ami-
☺ able servers with tattoos. Still, this is very much a family place, and
the clientele often includes toddlers and octogenarians. Huge burgers
are the thing, loaded with onions, pickles, tomatoes, lettuce, and con-
diments, and so gloriously messy that you might wear a swimsuit so
you can stroll to the beach for a bath afterward. The minihamburger
is good, the double bacon cheeseburger is breathtaking (and artery-
clogging), as are the onion rings and seasoned potato wedges. ⑤ *Aver-*
age main: $9 ✉ *5010 Newport Ave., Ocean Beach* ☎ *619/224–4623*
⊕ *hodadies.com* ✛ *B5.*

$$$ ✕ **JRDN.** With some 300 seats, this ocean-facing restaurant, pronounced
AMERICAN Jordan, in the beach-chic boutique-style Tower23 Hotel might seem
overwhelming, but the seating is divided between a long, narrow out-
door terrace and a series of relatively intimate indoor rooms. Chef
David Warner presents modern steak-house fare including chops and
steaks with sauces of the diner's choosing, lightened with lots of sea-
sonal produce and a raw bar menu. Weekend brunch and lunch have
a similar appeal, with dishes like blue-crab eggs Benedict with citrus
hollandaise, eggplant panini sandwich, or a salad of smoked tri-tip
over spinach and fingerling potatoes. On Friday and Saturday the bar
is the place to see and be seen in Pacific Beach for under-30 types, and
it's jammed after 9 pm. The hotel only serves breakfast to guests dur-
ing the week. ⑤ *Average main: $33* ✉ *723 Felspar St., Pacific Beach*
☎ *858/270–5736* ⊕ *www.jrdn.com* ⌂ *Reservations essential* ✛ *B2.*

$$ ✕ **Sushi Ota.** Wedged into a minimall between a convenience store and
JAPANESE a looming medical building, Sushi Ota initially seems less than auspi-
cious. Still, San Diego–bound Japanese businesspeople frequently call
for reservations before boarding their trans-Pacific flights. Look closely
at the expressions on customers' faces as they stream in and out of
the doors, and you can see the eager anticipation and satisfied glows
that are products of San Diego's best sushi. Besides the usual California roll and tuna and shrimp sushi, sample the specialties that change
daily such as sea urchin or surf clam sushi, and the soft-shell crab roll
or the *omakase* tasting menu. Sushi Ota offers the cooked as well as
the raw. There's additional parking behind the mall. It's hard not to
notice that Japanese speakers get the best spots, and servers can be
abrupt. ⑤ *Average main: $17* ✉ *4529 Mission Bay Dr., Pacific Beach*
☎ *858/270–5670* ⊕ *sushiota.menutoeat.com* ⌂ *Reservations essential*
⊗ *No lunch Sat.–Mon.* ✛ *C2.*

LA JOLLA

$$$$ ✕ **George's at the Cove.** An extensive makeover brought an updated look
AMERICAN to this eternally popular restaurant overlooking La Jolla Cove. Hol-
Fodor'sChoice lywood types and other visiting celebrities can be spotted in George's
★ California Modern, the sleek main dining room with its wall of windows. Simple casual preparations of fresh seafood, beef, and lamb reign
on the menu chef Trey Foshee enlivens with seasonal produce from
local specialty growers. Give special consideration to succulent roasted
chicken with preserved lemon and Chino farms spinach, smoked Maine

lobster with curried apple puree and lobster hollandaise, and cider-glazed Niman Ranch pork chops. For more informal dining and a sweeping view of the coast, try the rooftop Ocean Terrace, which is open for lunch. ⑤ *Average main: $39* ✉ *1250 Prospect St., La Jolla* ☎ *858/454–4244* ⊕ *www.georgesatthecove.com* ⚑ *Reservations essential* ✚ *B1.*

$$$$
NEWAMERICAN

✕ **Marine Room.** Gaze at the ocean from this venerable La Jolla Shores mainstay and, if it's during an especially high tide, feel the waves race across the sand and crash against the glass. Long-running executive chef Bernard Guillas takes a bold approach to combining ingredients. Creative seasonal menus score with "trilogy" plates that combine three meats, sometimes including game, in distinct preparations. Exotic ingredients show up in a variety of dishes, among them absinthe butter–basted lobster tail, pomelo-glazed organic tofu, and rack of lamb with mission fig compote. ⑤ *Average main: $35* ✉ *2000 Spindrift Dr., La Jolla* ☎ *866/644–2351* ⊕ *www.marineroom.com* ⚑ *Reservations essential* ✚ *B1.*

$$$
AMERICAN
Fodor's Choice
★

✕ **Nine-Ten.** Many years ago, the elegant Grande Colonial Hotel in the heart of La Jolla "village" housed a drugstore owned by actor Gregory Peck's father. In the sleekly contemporary dining room that now occupies the space, acclaimed chef (2011 *Iron Chef* challenger) Jason Knibb serves satisfying seasonal fare at breakfast, lunch, and dinner. At night the perfectly executed menu may include tantalizing appetizers like Jamaican jerk pork belly or lamb sugo and main dishes such as the roasted leg of rabbit stuffed with Swiss chard, lemons, raisins, and cumin, and the beef short ribs, braised with Alesmith stout and served with Chino Farms root vegetables. Delicious desserts include cilantro basil cake and strawberry sorbet with candied kumquats. Three- and five-course pix-fixe menus are also available for the whole table. ⑤ *Average main: $34* ✉ *910 Prospect St., La Jolla* ☎ *858/964–5400* ⊕ *www.nine-ten.com* ✚ *B1.*

$
ITALIAN

✕ **Osteria Romantica.** The name means "Romantic Inn," and with a sunny location a few blocks from the beach in La Jolla Shores, the look suggests a trattoria in Positano. The kitchen's wonderfully light hand shows up in the tomato sauce that finishes the scampi and other dishes, and in the pleasing Romantica salad garnished with figs and walnuts. Savory pasta choices include lobster-filled *mezzelune* (half moons) in saffron sauce, and wonderfully rich spaghetti *alla carbonara.* The breaded veal cutlets crowned with chopped arugula and tomatoes is a worthy main course. The warm, informal service suits the neighborhood. ⑤ *Average main: $17* ✉ *2151 Ave. de la Playa, La Jolla* ☎ *858/551–1221* ⊕ *www.osteriaromantica.com* ✚ *B1.*

$$
SEAFOOD
☾

✕ **Rimel's Rotisserie.** An affordable option in pricey La Jolla, this comfy spot often serves seafood caught the same morning by fishermen who work for the owner. Other than market-priced "fresh catches" and the grass-fed filet mignon from the owner's Home Grown meat shop, many items come in under $12, such as grilled mahimahi tacos (served with a powerful green chili-garlic salsa), grain-fed chicken grilled on a mesquite-fire rotisserie, and "steaming rice bowls" that actually are plates spread with jasmine rice, wok-cooked vegetables, and grilled seafood

The quality of the food complements the spectacular views at George's at the Cove.

with a variety of vegetables. This is a good choice for families. $ *Average main: $22* ⊠ *1030 Torrey Pines Rd., La Jolla* ☎ *858/454–6045* ⊕ *www.rimelsrestaurants.com/rimels/lajolla* ✛ *B1.*

$ ✕ **Sushi on the Rock.** There's something fun about Sushi on the Rock,
JAPANESE   from the young friendly chefs to the comically named California-style
Fodor's Choice sushi specialties, like the Slippery When Wet roll featuring tempura
★   shrimp, eel, crab, and cucumber. Loads of original rolls include the Bar-
rio Roll stuffed with fried white fish and spicy tomato salsa, the Ashley
Roll that pairs seared tuna with soft-shell crab and tangy whole-grain
mustard sauce, and the Bruce Lee, with spicy crab, tuna, and avocado.
Also try the Japanese-inspired dishes, including pot stickers, Asian-style
Caesar salad, and lobster mac and cheese. This popular spot, which has
a patio with an ocean view, gets busy in the late afternoon with people
wanting to grab a seat for the daily happy hour (5–6:30 pm). $ *Average main: $16* ⊠ *1025 Prospect St., #250, La Jolla* ☎ *858/459–3208* ⊕ *www.sushiontherock.com* ⟋ *Reservations not accepted* ✛ *B1.*

$$ ✕ **Whisknladle.** This hip, popular eatery that doubles as a fashion show
SEAFOOD   of La Jolla ladies who lunch has earned national acclaim with its com-
bination of casual comfort and a menu of ever-changing local fare. In
nice weather, request a patio table when reserving. Appetizers include
dishes like warm spinach salad with grilled butternut squash and seared
scallops with caramelized endive. Larger plates feature local halibut
with Chino Farms vegetables or English pea risotto with pecorino. And
the bar is worth a visit, too, with its original menu of cocktails like the
tamarind margarita, passion-fruit vanilla mimosa, and pomegranate
mojito. $ *Average main: $23* ⊠ *1044 Wall St., La Jolla* ☎ *858/551–7575* ⊕ *www.whisknladle.com* ⟋ *Reservations essential* ✛ *B1.*

OLD TOWN

$$$

MEXICAN

✕ **El Agave.** A Mexico City native brings authentic regional Mexican fare to an otherwise touristy area. Be sure to try quesadillas filled with mushrooms; pork bathed in bright, smoky guajillo chili sauce; and chicken in a slow-simmered mole sauce. Try one of the more than 2,000 tequilas, which make El Agave the largest "tequileria" in the United States. The collection includes artisanal tequilas dating to the 1930s and some infused with jalapeño chilies. ⑤ *Average main: $30* ⊠ *2304 San Diego Ave., Old Town* ☎ *619/220–0692* ⊕ *www.elagave.com* ⊹ *D4.*

WHERE TO STAY

When you make reservations, ask about specials. Many hotels promote discounted weekend packages to fill rooms after convention and business customers leave town. Since the weather is great year-round, don't expect substantial discounts in winter. That being said, you can find affordable rooms in even the most expensive areas. If an ocean view is important, request it when booking, but be aware that it will cost significantly more. You can save on hotels and attractions by visiting the San Diego Convention & Visitors Bureau website (⊕ *www.sandiego.org*) for a free Vacation Planning Kit with a Travel Value Coupon booklet.

Use the coordinate (⊹ A1) at the end of each listing to locate a site on the corresponding map.

HOTEL COSTS

Prices in the hotel reviews are the lowest cost of a standard double room in high season. Prices do not include taxes (as high as 14%, depending on the region).

CORONADO

For expanded reviews, facilities, and current deals, visit Fodors.com.

$$$

RESORT

☺

⌨ **Coronado Island Marriott Resort.** Near San Diego Bay, this snazzy hotel has rooms with great Downtown skyline views. **Pros:** spectacular views; on-site spa; close to water taxis. **Cons:** not in Downtown Coronado; difficult to find. **TripAdvisor:** "beautiful property," "wonderful location," "a quieter side of beautiful Coronado." ⑤ *Rooms from: $329* ⊠ *2000 2nd St., Coronado* ☎ *619/435–3000, 800/543–4300* ⊕ *www.marriotthotels.com/sanci* ↙ *273 rooms, 27 suites* �ⓝⓞ *No meals* ⊹ *E6.*

$$$

HOTEL

⌨ **Glorietta Bay Inn.** The main building on this property is an Edwardian-style mansion built in 1908 for sugar baron John D. Spreckels, who once owned much of Downtown San Diego. **Pros:** great views; friendly staff; close to beach. **Cons:** mansion rooms are small; lots of traffic nearby. **TripAdvisor:** "nice hotel in a beautiful location," "very friendly staff," "super cozy beds." ⑤ *Rooms from: $179* ⊠ *1630 Glorietta Blvd., Coronado* ☎ *619/435–3101, 800/283–9383* ⊕ *www.gloriettabayinn.com* ↙ *100 rooms* ⓝⓞⓛ *Breakfast* ⊹ *E6.*

$$$

HOTEL

☺

Fodor's Choice

★

⌨ **Hotel Del Coronado.** The Victorian-styled "Hotel Del," situated along 28 oceanfront acres, is as much of a draw today as it was when it opened in 1888. **Pros:** romantic; on the beach; hotel spa. **Cons:** some rooms are small; expensive dining; public areas are very busy. **TripAdvisor:** "nice beach," "a perfect and relaxing spa vacation," "wonderful staff."

Ⓢ *Rooms from: $289* ⊠ *1500 Orange Ave., Coronado* ☎ *800/468–3533, 619/435–6611* ⊕ *www.hoteldel.com* ↩ *757 rooms, 65 suites, 43 villas, 35 cottages* |○| *No meals* ✛ *D6.*

DOWNTOWN

For expanded reviews, facilities, and current deals, visit Fodors.com.

$ 🖭 **Gaslamp Plaza Suites.** On the National Register of Historic Places, this
HOTEL 10-story structure a block from Horton Plaza was built in 1913 as one of San Diego's first "skyscrapers." **Pros:** historic building; good location; well priced. **Cons:** books up early; smallish rooms. **TripAdvisor:** "comfortable," "vintage charm," "huge spacious clean suites." Ⓢ *Rooms from: $189* ⊠ *520 E St., Gaslamp Quarter* ☎ *619/232–9500, 800/874–8770* ⊕ *www.gaslampplaza.com* ↩ *12 rooms, 52 suites* |○| *Breakfast* ✛ *H2.*

$$ 🖭 **Hard Rock Hotel.** Self-billed as a hip playground for rock stars and
HOTEL people who just want to party like them, the Hard Rock Hotel is con-
Fodor'sChoice veniently located near PETCO Park overlooking glimmering San Diego
★ Bay. **Pros:** central location; great scene; luxurious rooms. **Cons:** pricey drinks; some attitude. **TripAdvisor:** "great bar," "rock star experience," "very hip." Ⓢ *Rooms from: $204* ⊠ *207 5th Ave., Gaslamp Quarter* ☎ *619/702–3000, 866/751–7625* ⊕ *www.hardrockhotelsd.com* ↩ *244 rooms, 176 suites* |○| *No meals* ✛ *H3.*

$$ 🖭 **Hilton San Diego Bayfront.** This modern 30-story hotel overlooking
HOTEL San Diego Bay isn't a typical Hilton. **Pros:** close to the convention cen-
☺ ter; new rooms. **Cons:** awkward layout; pricey drinks; $27 for park-ing. **TripAdvisor:** "elegant and classy," "super modern and beautiful," "great location and service." Ⓢ *Rooms from: $179* ⊠ *1 Park Blvd., Downtown* ☎ *619/564–3333* ⊕ *www.hiltonsdbayfront.com* ↩ *1,160 rooms, 30 suites* |○| *No meals* ✛ *E6.*

$$ 🖭 **Hotel Palomar San Diego.** Now a member of the Kimpton Hotel group,
HOTEL the Palomar (formerly the Sè San Diego) still retains its luxurious
☺ ambience. **Pros:** new rooms; centrally located; luxury amenities. **Cons:** expensive parking; sliding glass doors in bathrooms provide limited privacy. **TripAdvisor:** "lovely hotel," "beautiful room," "amazing ser-vice." Ⓢ *Rooms from: $208* ⊠ *1047 5th Ave., Downtown* ☎ *619/515–3000* ⊕ *www.hotelpalomar-sandiego.com* ↩ *181 rooms, 37 suites, 20 condos, 3 penthouses* ✛ *H1.*

$$ 🖭 **Hotel Solamar.** For its first entry onto San Diego's hotel scene, the
HOTEL Kimpton boutique hotel chain renovated an old warehouse, hitting the
☺ right notes with striking, high style. **Pros:** great restaurant; attentive
Fodor'sChoice service; upscale rooms. **Cons:** busy valet parking; bars are crowded
★ and noisy on weekends. **TripAdvisor:** "staff was amazing," "another Kimpton gem," "treated like royalty." Ⓢ *Rooms from: $242* ⊠ *435 6th Ave., Gaslamp Quarter* ☎ *619/819–9500, 877/230–0300* ⊕ *www. hotelsolamar.com* ↩ *217 rooms, 16 suites* |○| *No meals* ✛ *H2.*

$$ 🖭 **U.S. Grant.** Stepping into the regal U.S. Grant not only puts you in
HOTEL the lap of luxury, but also back into San Diego history; the century-old

BEST BETS FOR SAN DIEGO LODGING

Fodor's offers a selective listing of quality lodging experiences. Here we've compiled our top recommendations. The very best properties—in other words, those that provide a particularly remarkable experience in their price range—are designated in the listings with a Fodor's Choice logo.

Fodor'sChoice★

Grande Colonial, $$, p. 98

Hard Rock Hotel, $$ p. 95

Hotel Del Coronado, $$$, p. 94

Hotel Solamar, $$, p. 95

Lodge at Torrey Pines, $$$, p. 98

Best by Price

$

Holiday Inn Express-SeaWorld Area, p. 97

Holiday Inn Express Airport-Old Town, p. 97

$$

The Dana on Mission Bay, p. 101

Grande Colonial, p. 98

Hard Rock Hotel, p. 95

Hotel Solamar, p. 95

La Valencia, p. 98

Paradise Point Resort & Spa, p. 101

$$$

Hotel Del Coronado, p. 94

Lodge at Torrey Pines, p. 98

Pacific Terrace Hotel, p. 101

Best by Experience

BEST BEACH

Hotel Del Coronado, $$$, p. 94

La Jolla Shores Hotel, $$$, p. 98

Paradise Point Resort & Spa, $$, p. 101

BEST POOL

Hotel Solamar, $$, p. 95

Hyatt Regency Mission Bay Spa & Marina, $$, p. 101

Kona Kai Resort, $, p. 97

BEST FOR ROMANCE

Hotel Del Coronado, $$$, p. 94

Hotel Parisi, $$, p. 98

Hotel Solamar, $$, p. 95

The Lodge at Torrey Pines, $$$, p. 98

BEST SPA

Estancia La Jolla Hotel & Spa, $$, p. 97

Hotel Palomar San Diego, $$, p. 95

The Lodge at Torrey Pines, $$$, p. 98

BEST VIEWS

Hilton San Diego Bayfront, $$, p. 95

Hyatt Regency Mission Bay Spa & Marina, $$, p. 101

La Valencia, $$, p. 98

MOST TRENDY

Hotel Palomar San Diego, $$, p. 95

building on the National Register of Historic Sites is totally au courant on the inside. **Pros:** modern rooms; great location; near shopping and restaurants. **Cons:** small elevators; the hotel's many special events can make for a hectic atmosphere. **TripAdvisor:** "elegant," "absolutely a classic," "beautiful hotel and kind staff." ⑤ *Rooms from: $161* ⊠ *326 Broadway, Gaslamp Quarter* ☎ *619/232–3121, 800/237–5029* ⊕ *www. luxurycollection.com/usgrant* ➤ *270 rooms, 47 suites* � *No meals* ⊹ *H1.*

HARBOR ISLAND, SHELTER ISLAND, AND POINT LOMA

For expanded reviews, facilities, and current deals, visit Fodors.com.

$
HOTEL
☺ ⊞ **Holiday Inn Express–SeaWorld Area.** In Point Loma near the West Mission Bay exit off Interstate 8, this is a surprisingly cute and quiet lodging option despite proximity to bustling traffic. **Pros:** near SeaWorld; kids eat free; good service. **Cons:** not a scenic area; somewhat hard to find. **TripAdvisor:** "excellent customer service," "close to everything," "very nice staff." ⑤ *Rooms from: $144* ⊠ *3950 Jupiter St., Point Loma* ☎ *619/226–8000, 800/320–0208* ⊕ *www.seaworldhi.com* ➤ *69 rooms, 2 suites* � *Multiple meal plans* ⊹ *C4.*

$$
RESORT
⊞ **Humphrey's Half Moon Inn & Suites.** This sprawling South Seas–style resort has grassy open areas with palms and tiki torches. **Pros:** water views; near marina; free admission to Backstage Live. **Cons:** vast property; not centrally located. **TripAdvisor:** "so close to the city," "just like Hawaii but not as far," "quiet getaway." ⑤ *Rooms from: $229* ⊠ *2303 Shelter Island Dr., Shelter Island* ☎ *619/224–3411, 800/542–7400* ⊕ *www.halfmooninn.com* ➤ *128 rooms, 54 suites* �PIN *No meals* ⊹ *C5.*

$
RESORT
⊞ **Kona Kai Resort.** This 11-acre property blends Hawiian and Mediterranean styles. **Pros:** quiet area; near marina; water views. **Cons:** not centrally located; small rooms. **TripAdvisor:** "great service," "beautiful location," "history and romance." ⑤ *Rooms from: $97* ⊠ *1551 Shelter Island Dr., Shelter Island* ☎ *619/221–8000, 800/566–2524* ⊕ *www. resortkonakai.com* ➤ *124 rooms, 5 suites* � *No meals* ⊹ *C5.*

OLD TOWN AND VICINITY

For expanded reviews, facilities, and current deals, visit Fodors.com.

$
HOTEL
⊞ **Holiday Inn Express Airport–Old Town.** Already an excellent value for Old Town, this cheerful property throws in such perks as a free breakfast buffet. **Pros:** good location; hot Continental breakfast. **Cons:** smallish rooms; few nightlife options. **TripAdvisor:** "outstanding experience," "great location," "great service." ⑤ *Rooms from: $105* ⊠ *3900 Old Town Ave., Old Town* ☎ *619/543–1130, 888/465–4329* ⊕ *www. hiexpress.com* ➤ *125 rooms, 2 suites* � *Breakfast* ⊹ *D4.*

LA JOLLA

For expanded reviews, facilities, and current deals, visit Fodors.com.

$$
RESORT
⊞ **Estancia La Jolla Hotel & Spa.** La Jolla's newest resort was once the site of a famous equestrian ranch, Blackhorse Farms, where Thoroughbreds

were trained. **Pros:** upscale rooms; nice spa; landscaped grounds. **Cons:** spotty service; not centrally located. **TripAdvisor:** "great place to relax," "most beautiful hotel I've ever stayed in," "the perfect vacation hotel." ⑤ *Rooms from: $179* ✉ *9700 N. Torrey Pines Rd., La Jolla* ☎ *858/550–1000, 877/437–8262* ⊕ *www.estancialajolla.com* ⇨ *200 rooms, 10 suites* ♥◎♥ *No meals* ✛ *B1.*

$$
HOTEL
Fodor'sChoice
★
🖬 **Grande Colonial.** This white wedding cake–style hotel has ocean views and is in the heart of La Jolla village. **Pros:** near shopping; near beach; superb restaurant. **Cons:** somewhat busy street. **TripAdvisor:** "small but charming," "nice little getaway," "beautiful room and view." ⑤ *Rooms from: $209* ✉ *910 Prospect St., La Jolla* ☎ *858/454–2181, 800/826–1278* ⊕ *www.thegrandecolonial.com* ⇨ *52 rooms, 41 suites* ♥◎♥ *No meals* ✛ *B1.*

$$
HOTEL
🖬 **Hotel Parisi.** A Zen-like peace welcomes you in the lobby, which has a skylighted fountain and is filled with Asian art. **Pros:** upscale amenities; wellness services; centrally located. **Cons:** one-room "suites"; staff can be aloof. **TripAdvisor:** "fabulous chic hotel," "great attention to detail," "European style." ⑤ *Rooms from: $249* ✉ *1111 Prospect St., La Jolla* ☎ *858/454–1511* ⊕ *www.hotelparisi.com* ⇨ *29 suites* ♥◎♥ *Breakfast* ✛ *B1.*

$$$
HOTEL
☯
🖬 **La Jolla Shores Hotel.** One of the few San Diego hotels actually on the beach, La Jolla Shores is located at La Jolla Beach and Tennis Club. **Pros:** on beach; great views; quiet area. **Cons:** not centrally located; some rooms are dated. **TripAdvisor:** "perfect location," "awesome accommodations," "beautiful place to stay." ⑤ *Rooms from: $303* ✉ *8110 Camino del Oro, La Jolla* ☎ *858/459–8271, 877/346–6714* ⊕ *www.ljshoreshotel.com* ⇨ *127 rooms, 1 suite* ✛ *B1.*

$$
HOTEL
🖬 **La Valencia.** This pink Spanish-Mediterranean confection drew Hollywood film stars in the 1930s and 40s with its setting and views of La Jolla Cove. **Pros:** upscale rooms; views; near beach. **Cons:** expensive; lots of traffic outside. **TripAdvisor:** "classic beach hotel," "a gem in La Jolla," "beautiful setting." ⑤ *Rooms from: $250* ✉ *1132 Prospect St., La Jolla* ☎ *858/454–0771, 800/451–0772* ⊕ *www.lavalencia.com* ⇨ *82 rooms, 16 villas, 15 suites* ✛ *B1.*

$$$
RESORT
Fodor'sChoice
★
🖬 **Lodge at Torrey Pines.** This beautiful Craftsman-style lodge sits on a bluff between La Jolla and Del Mar and commands a coastal view. **Pros:** spacious upscale rooms; good service; Torrey Pines Golf Club on property. **Cons:** not centrally located; expensive. **TripAdvisor:** "great service and sublime architecture," "extreme luxury and relaxation," "epitome of first class." ⑤ *Rooms from: $375* ✉ *11480 N. Torrey Pines Rd., La Jolla* ☎ *858/453–4420, 800/995–4507* ⊕ *www.lodgetorreypines.com* ⇨ *164 rooms, 6 suites* ✛ *B1.*

MISSION BAY AND THE BEACHES

For expanded reviews, facilities, and current deals, visit Fodors.com.

$$
RESORT
☯
🖬 **Catamaran Resort Hotel.** Exotic macaws perch in the lush lobby of this appealing hotel on Mission Bay. **Pros:** spa; free cruises. **Cons:** not centrally located; dated room decor. **TripAdvisor:** "exceeded our expectations," "relaxing," "nice place to stay." ⑤ *Rooms from: $229*

Hotel del Coronado

Hard Rock Hotel

Lodge at Torrey Pines

Hotel Solamar

Hotel Solamar

Grande Colonial

Grande Colonial

✉ *3999 Mission Blvd., Mission Beach* ☏ *858/488–1081, 800/422–8386* ⊕ *www.catamaranresort.com* ⤴ *311 rooms, 50 suites* ✦ *B3.*

$$　🏨 **The Dana on Mission Bay.** There's a modern-chic feel to the earth-tone
RESORT lobby of this beach hotel, making it feel you've arrived somewhere much
more expensive. **Pros:** water views; two pools. **Cons:** slightly confusing
layout; not centrally located. **TripAdvisor:** "nice rooms with comfort-
able beds," "location can't be beat," "a wonderful view." ⑤ *Rooms
from: $249* ✉ *1710 W. Mission Bay Dr., Mission Bay* ☏ *619/222–6440,
800/445–3339* ⊕ *www.thedana.com* ⤴ *259 rooms, 12 suites* ❘❍❘ *No
meals* ✦ *C4.*

$$　🏨 **Hyatt Regency Mission Bay Spa & Marina.** This modern and stunning
RESORT property has many desirable amenities, including balconies with excel-
♨ lent views of the garden, bay, ocean, or swimming pool courtyard (pools
have 120-foot waterslides, plus a smaller slide on the kiddie pool).
Pros: modern decor; great pet program; water views. **Cons:** slightly
hard to navigate surrounding roads; thin walls; not centrally located.
TripAdvisor: "relies on the location," "a week of bliss," "perfect for
families." ⑤ *Rooms from: $203* ✉ *1441 Quivira Rd., Mission Bay*
☏ *619/224–1234, 800/233–1234* ⊕ *www.hyatt.com* ⤴ *354 rooms, 76
suites* ❘❍❘ *No meals* ✦ *C4.*

$$$　🏨 **Pacific Terrace Hotel.** Travelers love this terrific beachfront hotel and
RESORT the ocean views from most rooms; it's a perfect place for watching sun-
sets over the Pacific. **Pros:** beach views; large rooms; friendly service.
Cons: busy area; four-night minimum stay in summer; lots of traffic.
TripAdvisor: "amazing people," "what an unbelievable gem," "beauti-
ful hotel and great service." ⑤ *Rooms from: $380* ✉ *610 Diamond St.,
Pacific Beach* ☏ *858/581–3500, 800/344–3370* ⊕ *www.pacificterrace.
com* ⤴ *61 rooms, 12 suites* ✦ *B2.*

$$　🏨 **Paradise Point Resort & Spa.** The beautiful landscape of this 44-acre
RESORT resort on Vacation Isle has been the setting for a number of movies.
♨ **Pros:** water views; pools; good service. **Cons:** not centrally located;
summer minimum stays; motel-thin walls; parking and resort fees. **Trip-
Advisor:** "very nice location," "great hotel for families with children,"
"truly paradise." ⑤ *Rooms from: $250* ✉ *1404 Vacation Rd., Mis-
sion Bay* ☏ *858/274–4630, 800/344–2626* ⊕ *www.paradisepoint.com*
⤴ *462 cottages* ✦ *C3.*

NIGHTLIFE AND THE ARTS

Downtown is the obvious neighborhood for party animals of all ages.
Its streets are lined with sleek lounges, massive nightclubs, and quirky
dive bars. The Gaslamp Quarter is party central, with the most bars
and clubs located on its 16-block stretch. The late-night commotion is
spreading to East Village, the area surrounding PETCO Park. A few
neighborhoods on the outskirts of Downtown—Golden Hill, Hillcrest,
and North and South Park, in particular—offer plenty of hip underground treasures for intrepid visitors.

The beach areas tend to cater to the casual and collegiate, though certain haunts have their share of former flower children and grizzled
bikers. Hillcrest is the heart of San Diego's gay community, and home

to loads of gay-popular bars. Coffeehouses are another important element of San Diego nightlife culture, especially for the under-21 set. Singer Jewel got her start in local coffee shops, and plenty of other acts have launched to fame from an active area music scene, including pop-punkers Blink-182 and Grammy-winning gospel group Nickel Creek. Locals rely on alt-weeklies like the *Reader* and *San Diego CityBeat*, as well as glossy monthlies like *San Diego* and *Riviera* magazines for nightlife info. You can't buy booze after 2 am, which means last call is around 1:30. Smoking is only allowed outside, and even then it can be tricky. And be sure to hail a taxi if you've tied one on—drunk driving laws in California are stringent. ■ TIP→ All of San Diego's trendiest, flashiest, busiest clubs and bars have dress codes and require identification. Call ahead for details.

NIGHTLIFE

CASUAL BARS AND PUBS

Fodor's Choice ★ **The Waterfront Bar & Grill.** It isn't really *on* the waterfront, but this joint was the gathering spot for the Italian fishermen who used to live here. Now a local landmark, San Diego's oldest bar actually had an apartment building constructed around it rather than be torn down. Still the hangout of working-class heroes, even if most of the collars are now white, it's famous for its burgers. There's live jazz and blues many evenings. ⊠ *2044 Kettner Blvd., Little Italy* ☎ *619/232–9656* ⊕ *www.waterfrontbarandgrill.com.*

COFFEEHOUSES

Fodor's Choice ★ **Extraordinary Desserts.** This café lives up to its name, which explains why there's often a line here, even though it has ample seating. Paris-trained Karen Krasne turns out award-winning cakes, tortes, and pastries of exceptional beauty. The Japanese-theme patio invites you to linger over yet another coffee drink. A second location is in Little Italy. ⊠ *2929 5th Ave., Hillcrest* ☎ *619/294–2132* ⊕ *www.extraordinarydesserts.com.*

DANCE CLUBS

★ **Stingaree.** In the posh Gaslamp Quarter, Stingaree occupies a smashing three-story space with translucent "floating" staircases and floor-to-ceiling water walls. There's a high-end restaurant and a dance club inside (the music tends to be of the Top 40 variety). Dress nicely. The air of exclusivity at this hangout is palpable, and to further prove the point, the drink prices are steep. ⊠ *454 6th Ave., at Island St., Gaslamp Quarter* ☎ *619/544–9500* ⊕ *www.stingsandiego.com.*

GAY NIGHTLIFE

Fodor's Choice ★ **Baja Betty's.** Although it draws plenty of gay customers, Baja Betty's is popular with just about everyone in the Hillcrest area. It's a low-key but elegant space with chandeliers and soft lighting, and it stocks more than 100 brands of tequila and mixes plenty of fancy cocktails. ⊠ *1421 University Ave., Hillcrest* ☎ *619/269–8510* ⊕ *www.bajabettyssd.com.*

Urban Mo's Bar and Grill. Mo's rounds up cowboys for line dancing and two-stepping on its wooden dance floor—but be forewarned, yee-hawers, it can get pretty wild on Western nights. There are also Latin,

Craft Beer Capital

San Diego claims to be the craft beer–making capital of the planet. What exactly *is* a craft beer? The term can include brews from small family-operated breweries—where you might get something different every time you go in for a sip of suds—to some fairly large, commercial operations that turn out standard (although still not mainstream) brews. Most craft brewmeisters started out as home beer makers, and the beer produced for sale reflects abundant creativity (and sometimes outright experimentation) in the use of grain, hops, and other things that go into a great glass of beer.

The brew culture continues to grow in San Diego, and enthusiasts are noticing. Escondido-based **Stone Brewing** (⊕ www.stonebrew.com) was declared the best brewery on the planet by readers of *Beer Advocate* magazine in 2009, and other San Diego breweries on the list are **AleSmith** (⊕ www.alesmith.com) and **O'Brien's Pub** (⊕ www.obrienspub.net) in Kearny Mesa. The largest and oldest of the San Diego craft brewers is **Karl Strauss Brewing** (⊕ www.karlstrauss.com), which operates a number of brewpubs in the region.

So if you're looking for a cold one, you've come to the right place.

hip-hop, and drag revue, but the real allure is in the creative drinks ("Gone Fishing"—served in a fishbowl, for example) and the breezy patio where love (or something like it) is usually in the air. ⊠ *308 University Ave., Hillcrest* ☎ *619/491–0400* ⊕ *urbanmos.com.*

HIP LOUNGES AND TRENDY SINGLES BARS

Altitude Sky Lounge. Altitude occupies the San Diego Marriott Gaslamp Quarter's 22nd-story rooftop. Location is everything—the views from here of the Downtown skyline and PETCO Park will give you a natural high. ⊠ *660 K St., Gaslamp Quarter* ☎ *619/696–0234.*

Fodor'sChoice
★ **Ivy Rooftop and Ivy Nightclub.** These two bars offer a chiller version of nightlife for Andaz San Diego hotel guests and visitors. Sink into a deep leather couch in the posh lobby Ivy Nightclub and Wine Bar or head to the spacious Ivy Rooftop, where you can sip cocktails poolside while gazing at gorgeous people or views of the city—both are abundant. ⊠ *600 F St., Gaslamp Quarter* ☎ *619/814–2055* ⊕ *ivyentertainment-sandiego.com.*

★ **JRDN.** This contemporary lounge occupies the ground floor of Pacific Beach's chicest boutique hotel, Tower23. JRDN, pronounced "Jordan," captures both the laid-back personality of the neighborhood and the increasingly sophisticated sensibility of San Diego, with sleek walls of windows and an expansive patio overlooking the boardwalk. ⊠ *723 Felspar St., Pacific Beach* ☎ *858/270–5736* ⊕ *www.t23hotel.com.*

JAZZ

Croce's. Ingrid Croce books superb acoustic-jazz musicians, among others, in this intimate dinner joint and jazz cave. Son A.J. Croce frequently performs here. ⊠ *802 5th Ave., Gaslamp Quarter* ☎ *619/233–4355* ⊕ *www.croces.com.*

Humphrey's by the Bay. Surrounded by water, Humphrey's is the summer stomping ground of musicians such as the Cowboy Junkies and Chris Isaak. From June through September this dining and drinking oasis hosts the city's best outdoor jazz, folk, and light-rock concert series. The rest of the year the music moves indoors for first-rate jazz, blues, and more. Dinner and room packages are available. ✉ *2241 Shelter Island Dr., Shelter Island* ☎ *619/224–3577* ⊕ *humphreysconcerts.com.*

LIVE MUSIC CLUBS

Belly Up Tavern. A fixture on local papers' "best of" lists, BUT has been drawing crowds since it opened in the mid-'70s. Its longevity attests to the quality of the eclectic entertainment on its stage. Within converted Quonset huts, critically acclaimed artists play everything from reggae and folk to—well, you name it. ✉ *143 S. Cedros Ave., Solana Beach* ☎ *858/481–8140* ⊕ *www.bellyup.com.*

Fodor's Choice ★ **The Casbah.** A small club near the airport, the Casbah has a national reputation for showcasing up-and-coming acts. Nirvana, Smashing Pumpkins, and the White Stripes all played here on the way to stardom. At this unofficial headquarters of the city's indie music scene, you can hear every type of band—except those that sound like Top 40. ✉ *2501 Kettner Blvd., Middletown* ☎ *619/232–4355* ⊕ *www.casbahmusic.com.*

★ **House of Blues.** The cavernous branch of the renowned chain is decorated floor to ceiling with colorful folk art. There's something going on here just about every night of the week, and Sunday's gospel brunch is one of the most praiseworthy events in town. Can we get a hallelujah? ✉ *1055 5th Ave., Downtown* ☎ *619/299–2583* ⊕ *www.houseofblues.com.*

THE ARTS

Arts Tix. You can buy advance tickets, many at half price, to theater, music, and dance events at Arts Tix. ✉ *Horton Plaza, Gaslamp Quarter* ☎ *858/381–5595* ⊕ *www.sdartstix.com.*

DANCE

★ **California Ballet Company.** The company performs high-quality contemporary and classical works from September through May. The *Nutcracker* is staged annually at the **Civic Theatre** (✉ *3rd Ave. and B St., Downtown* ☎ *619/570–1100*). Other ballets are presented at **Balboa Theatre** (✉ *868 4th Ave., Downtown* ☎ *619/570–1100 or 858/560–6741*). ⊕ *www.californiaballet.org.*

MUSIC

Fodor's Choice ★ **Copley Symphony Hall.** The great acoustics here are surpassed only by the incredible Spanish baroque interior. Not just the home of the San Diego Symphony Orchestra, the renovated 2,200-seat 1920s-era theater has also hosted major stars like Elvis Costello and Sting. ✉ *750 B St., Downtown* ☎ *619/235–0804* ⊕ *www.sandiegosymphony.org.*

La Jolla Music Society. The society presents internationally acclaimed chamber ensembles, orchestras, and soloists, and a dance series, at several venues. ✉ *Box office, 7946 Ivanhoe Ave., La Jolla* ☎ *858/459–3728* ⊕ *www.ljms.org.*

★ **San Diego Opera.** Drawing international artists, the opera's season runs from January through April. Past performances have included *Die Fledermaus, Faust, Idomeneo,* and *La Bohème,* plus concerts by such talents as Renee Fleming. ✉ *Civic Theatre, 3rd Ave. and B St., Downtown* ☎ *619/533–7000* ⊕ *www.sdopera.com.*

San Diego Symphony Orchestra. The orchestra's events include classical concerts and summer and winter pops, nearly all of them at Copley Symphony Hall. The Summer Pops series is held on the Embarcadero, on North Harbor Drive beyond the convention center. ✉ *Box office, 750 B. St., Downtown* ☎ *619/235–0800* ⊕ *www.sandiegosymphony. org.*

★ **Spreckels Organ Pavilion.** This is the home of a giant outdoor pipe organ donated to the city in 1915 by sugar magnates John and Adolph Spreckels. The beautiful Spanish baroque pavilion hosts concerts by civic organist Carol Williams and guest organists on most Sunday afternoons and on Monday evenings in summer. Local military bands, gospel groups, and barbershop quartets also perform here. All shows are free. ✉ *Balboa Park* ☎ *619/702–8138* ⊕ *sosorgan.com.*

THEATER

Fodor's Choice ★ **La Jolla Playhouse.** Under the artistic direction of Christopher Ashley, the playhouse presents exciting and innovative productions on three stages. Many Broadway shows—among them *Memphis, Tommy,* and *Jersey Boys*—have previewed here before their East Coast premieres. ✉ *University of California at San Diego, 2910 La Jolla Village Dr., La Jolla* ☎ *858/550–1010* ⊕ *www.lajollaplayhouse.org.*

★ **Lamb's Players Theatre.** The theater's regular season of five mostly uplifting productions runs from February through November. It also stages an original musical, *Festival of Christmas,* in December. The company has two performance spaces, the one used for most productions in Coronado, and the Horton Grand Theatre in the Gaslamp Quarter. ✉ *1142 Orange Ave., Coronado* ☎ *619/437–0600* ⊕ *www.lambsplayers.org.*

Fodor's Choice ★ **The Old Globe.** This complex, comprising the Sheryl and Harvey White Theatre, the Lowell Davies Festival Theatre, and the Old Globe Theatre, offers some of the finest theatrical productions in Southern California. Theater classics such as *The Full Monty* and *Dirty Rotten Scoundrels,* both of which later performed on Broadway, premiered on these famed stages. The Old Globe presents a renowned summer Shakespeare Festival with three to four plays in repertory. The theaters, done in a California version of Tudor style, sit between the sculpture garden of the San Diego Museum of Art and the California Tower. ✉ *1363 Old Globe Way, Balboa Park* ☎ *619/234–5623* ⊕ *www.oldglobe.org.*

SPORTS AND THE OUTDOORS

BASEBALL

Fodor's Choice ★ Long a favorite spectator sport in San Diego, where games are rarely rained out, baseball gained even more popularity in 2004 with the opening of PETCO Park, a stunning 42,000-seat facility in the heart of Downtown. In March 2006, the semifinals and the final game of the first-ever World Baseball Classic, scheduled to be a quadrennial event fielding teams from around the world, took place here.

San Diego Padres. The Padres slug it out for bragging rights in the National League West from April into October. Tickets are usually available on game day, but games with such rivals as the Los Angeles Dodgers and the San Francisco Giants often sell out quickly. For an inexpensive day at the ballpark, go for the park pass ($5–$12, depending on demand, available for purchase at the park only) and have a picnic on the grass, while watching the game on one of several giant-screen TVs. ⊠ *100 Park Blvd., East Village* ☎ *619/795–5000, 877/374–2784* ⊕ *sandiego.padres.mlb.com.*

BEACHES

Water temperatures are generally chilly, ranging from 55°F to 65°F from October through June, and 65°F to 73°F from July through September. For a surf and weather report, call ☎ *619/221–8824.* San Diego's beaches are well maintained and very clean during summertime, when rainfall is infrequent. Beaches along San Diego County's northern cities are typically cleaner than ones farther south. Pollution is generally worse near river mouths and storm-drain outlets, especially after heavy rainfall. The weather page of the *San Diego Union-Tribune* includes pollution reports along with listings of surfing and diving conditions (⊕ *www.utsandiego.com/surf-report*).

Lifeguards are stationed at city beaches from Sunset Cliffs up to Black's Beach in the summertime, but coverage in winter is provided by roving patrols only. Pay attention to signs listing illegal activities; undercover police often patrol the beaches. Smoking and alcoholic beverages are completely banned on city beaches. Drinking in beach parking lots, on boardwalks, and in landscaped areas is also illegal. Certain beaches also prohibit skateboarding. Fires are allowed only in fire rings or elevated barbecue grills. Although it may be tempting to take a starfish or some other sea creature as a souvenir from a tide pool, it upsets the delicate ecological balance and is illegal, too.

Finding a parking spot near the ocean can be hard in summer, but for the time being, unmetered parking is at all San Diego city beaches. Del Mar has a pay lot and metered street parking around the 15th Street beach.

Beaches are listed geographically, south to north.

CORONADO

☺ **Coronado Beach.** With the famous Hotel Del Coronado as a backdrop,
★ this stretch of sandy beach is one of San Diego County's largest and
most picturesque. It's perfect for sunbathing, people-watching, or Frisbee tossing. Exercisers include Navy SEAL teams as well as the occasional Marine Recon unit, who do training runs on the beaches in and around Coronado. Parking can be difficult on the busiest days. There are plenty of restrooms and service facilities, as well as fire rings on the north end. **Best for:** dogs, families, long walks, swimming. **Amenities:** lifeguard year-round, grills/fire pits at north end, parking (free on street), picnic tables, playground, showers, toilets. ⊠ *From the San Diego–Coronado bridge, turn left on Orange Ave. and follow signs, Coronado.*

Silver Strand State Beach. This quiet Coronado beach is ideal for families. The water is relatively calm, lifeguards and rangers are on duty year-round, and there are places to rollerblade or ride bikes. Three day-use parking lots provide room for more than 1,000 cars. Foot tunnels under Route 75 lead to a bay-side beach that has great views of the San Diego skyline. Across from the beach are the Coronado Cays, an exclusive community popular with yacht owners and celebrities, and the Loews Coronado Bay Resort. **Best For:** camping, families, long walks, swimming. **Amenities:** lifeguard year-round, camping facilities, food concessions open in summer, grills/fire pits, parking ($10), picnic tables, showers, toilets. ⊠ *From San Diego–Coronado Bridge, turn left onto Orange Ave., which becomes Rte. 75, and follow signs, Coronado* ☎ *619/435–5184.*

POINT LOMA

Sunset Cliffs. One of the more secluded beaches in the area, Sunset Cliffs is popular with surfers and locals. A few miles long, it lies beneath the jagged cliffs on the west side of the Point Loma peninsula. At the south end of the peninsula, near Cabrillo Point, tide pools teeming with small sea creatures are revealed at low tide. Farther north the waves lure surfers and the lonely coves attract sunbathers. Stairs at the foot of Pescadero and Bermuda avenues provide beach access, as do some cliff trails, which are treacherous at points. There are few facilities. A visit here is more enjoyable at low tide; check the local newspaper for tide schedules. **Best for:** couples/romance, scenic drives, scenic views, tide pools. **Amenities:** parking in lots and on street, picnic tables. ⊠ *Take I–8 west to Sunset Cliffs Blvd. and head west, Point Loma.*

MISSION BAY AND BEACHES

☺ **Mission Beach.** San Diego's most popular beach draws huge crowds on
★ hot summer days, but it's lively year-round. The 2-mile-long stretch extends from the north entrance of Mission Bay to Pacific Beach. A wide boardwalk paralleling the beach is popular with walkers, joggers, roller skaters, rollerbladers, and bicyclists. Surfers, swimmers, and volleyball players congregate at the south end. Scantily clad volleyball players practice on Cohasset Court year-round. Toward its north end, near the Belmont Park roller coaster, the beach narrows and the water becomes rougher. The crowds grow thicker and somewhat rougher as

well. For parking, you can try for a spot on the street, but your best bets are the two big lots at Belmont Park. **Best for:** accessibility, bicycling, boardwalk, families, volleyball. **Amenities:** lifeguard year-round, grills/fire pits, parking widely available at Belmont Park, picnic tables, showers, toilets. ⊠ *Exit I–5 at Grand Ave. and head west to Mission Blvd.; turn south and look for parking near roller coaster at West Mission Bay Dr., Mission Bay.*

Ocean Beach. Much of this mile-long beach is a haven for volleyball players, sunbathers, and swimmers. The area around the municipal pier at the south end is a hangout for surfers and transients. The pier itself is open to the public 24 hours a day for fishing and walking, and there's a restaurant midpier. The beach is south of the channel entrance to Mission Bay. You'll find fire rings as well as plenty of casual places to grab a snack on adjoining streets. Swimmers should beware of strong rip currents around the main lifeguard tower. There's a dog beach at the north end where Fido can run leash-free. During the summer there can be as many as 100 dogs running in the sand. For picnic areas and a paved path, check out Ocean Beach Park across from Dog Beach. **Best for:** dogs, fishing pier, sunbathing, surfing, volleyball. **Amenities:** lifeguard year-round, grills/fire pits, parking in lots and on street, picnic tables, showers, toilets. ⊠ *Take I–8 west to Sunset Cliffs Blvd. and head west; a right turn off Sunset Cliffs Blvd. takes you to the water, Point Loma.*

Pacific Beach/North Pacific Beach. The boardwalk of Mission Beach turns into a sidewalk here, but there are still bike paths and picnic tables along the beach. Pacific Beach runs from the north end of Mission Beach to Crystal Pier. North Pacific Beach extends from the pier north. The scene here is particularly lively on weekends. There are designated surfing areas, and fire rings are available. Parking can be a challenge, but there are plenty of restrooms, showers, and restaurants in the area. **Best for:** couples/romance, nightlife, singles scene, surfing, swimming. **Amenities:** lifeguard year-round, grills/fire pits, parking in lots and on street, picnic tables, showers, toilets. ⊠ *Exit I–5 at Grand Ave. and head west to Mission Blvd. Turn north and look for parking, Mission Bay.*

Tourmaline Surfing Park. Year-round, this is one of the area's most popular beaches for surfing and sailboarding. Separate areas designated for swimmers and surfers are strictly enforced. There's a 175-space parking lot at the foot of Tourmaline Street that normally fills to capacity by midday. **Best for:** boating, surfing. **Amenities:** lifeguard year-round, parking in lots and on street, picnic tables, showers, toilets. ⊠ *Take Mission Blvd. north (it turns into La Jolla Blvd.) and turn west on Tourmaline St., 600 Tourmaline St., Mission Bay.*

LA JOLLA

★ **Black's Beach.** The powerful waves at this beach, which is officially known as Torrey Pines City Park beach, attract world-class surfers, and its relative isolation appeals to nudist nature lovers (although by law nudity is prohibited) as well as gays and lesbians. Backed by cliffs whose colors change with the angle of the sun, Black's can be accessed from Torrey Pines State Beach to the north, or by a narrow path descending the cliffs from Torrey Pines Glider Port. Access to parts of the

Experts and beginners alike head to San Diego for its excellent surfing.

shore coincides with low tide. There are no lifeguards on permanent duty, although they do patrol the area between spring break and mid-October. Strong rip currents are common—only experienced swimmers should take the plunge. Storms have weakened the cliffs in the past few years; they're dangerous to climb and should be avoided. Part of the fun here is watching hang gliders and paragliders ascend from the Torrey Pines Glider Port atop the cliffs. **Best for:** solitude, sunbathing (nude), surfing. **Amenities:** lifeguard sometimes, parking available at the Torrey Pines Glider Port and La Jolla Farms. ⊠ *Take Genesee Ave. west from I–5 and follow signs to Torrey Pines Glider Port; easier access, via a paved path, available on La Jolla Farms Rd., but parking is limited to 2 hrs., La Jolla.*

La Jolla Cove. This shimmering blue inlet is what first attracted everyone to La Jolla, from Native Americans to the glitterati; it's the secret to the village's enduring cachet. You'll find "the Cove"—as locals refer to it, as though it were the only one in San Diego—beyond where Girard Avenue dead-ends into Coast Boulevard, marked by towering palms that line a promenade where people strolling in designer clothes are as common as Frisbee throwers. A palm-lined park sits on top of cliffs formed by the incessant pounding of the waves. At low tide the pools and cliff caves are a destination for explorers. Divers, snorkelers, and kayakers can check out the underwater delights of the **San Diego–La Jolla Underwater Park Ecological Reserve.** The cove is also a favorite of rough-water swimmers. **Best for:** diving, long walks, scenic views, snorkeling, tide pools. **Amenities:** lifeguard year-round (reduced hours in winter), parking on side streets, picnic tables, showers, toilets. ⊠ *Follow*

Fodor's Choice
★

Coast Blvd. north to signs, or take La Jolla Village Dr. exit from I–5, head west to Torrey Pines Rd., turn left, and drive downhill to Girard Ave.; turn right and follow signs, La Jolla.

La Jolla Shores. This is one of San Diego's most popular beaches, so get here early on summer weekends. The lures are an incredible view of La Jolla peninsula, a wide sandy beach, an adjoining grassy park, adjacent to San Diego La Jolla Underwater Park Ecological Reserve, and the gentlest waves in San Diego. Several surf and scuba schools teach here, and kayak rentals are nearby. A concrete boardwalk parallels the beach. Arrive early to get a parking spot in the lot at the foot of Calle Frescota. **Best for:** boogie boarding, families, long walks, sunbathing, surfing, swimming. **Amenities:** lifeguard year-round, grills/fire pits, parking in lots and on side streets, picnic tables, playground, showers, toilets. ⊠ *8200 Camino del Oro, From I–5 take La Jolla Village Dr. west and turn left onto La Jolla Shores Dr.; head west to Camino del Oro or Vallecitos St., turn right, La Jolla.*

Marine Street Beach. Wide and sandy, this strand often teems with sunbathers, swimmers, walkers, and joggers. The water is known as a great spot for bodysurfing, although the waves break in extremely shallow water and you'll need to watch out for riptides. **Best for:** body boarding, solitude, swimming. **Amenities:** lifeguard, street parking, picnic tables, showers and toilets near cove. ⊠ *Accessible from Marine St., off La Jolla Blvd., La Jolla.*

Windansea Beach. Named for a hotel that burned down in the late 1940s, Windansea Beach has increasingly gained notoriety due to its association with surfers. The reef break here forms an unusual A-frame wave, making it one the most popular (and crowded) surf spots in San Diego County. With its incredible views and secluded sunbathing spots set among sandstone rocks, Windansea is also one of the most romantic of West Coast beaches, especially at sunset. You can usually find nearby street parking. **Best for:** couples/romance, sunsets, surfing, solitude, tide pools. **Amenities:** lifeguard in summer, street parking. ⊠ *Take Mission Blvd. north (it turns into La Jolla Blvd.) and turn west on Nautilus St., La Jolla.*

DEL MAR

Del Mar Beach. The numbered streets of Del Mar, from 15th north to 29th, end at a wide beach popular with volleyball players, surfers, and sunbathers. Parking can be a problem in town; there's metered parking along the beach, making it challenging to stay for more than a few hours. The portion of Del Mar south of 15th Street is lined with cliffs and rarely crowded. Leashed dogs are permitted on most sections of the beach year-round; from October through May, dogs may run free at Rivermouth, Del Mar's northernmost beach. Food, hotels, and shopping are all within an easy walk of the beach. **Best for:** dogs, families, picnicking, swimming. **Amenities:** lifeguard year-round (reduced hours in winter), food concession at 17th Street, metered parking on streets, picnic tables, playground, showers, toilets. ⊠ *Take Via de la Valle exit from I–5 west to Rte. S21 (also known as Camino del Mar in Del Mar) and turn left.*

★ **Torrey Pines State Beach and Reserve.** One of San Diego's best beaches encompasses 2,000 acres of bluffs and bird-filled marshes. A network of meandering trails leads to the sandy shoreline below. Along the way enjoy the rare Torrey pine trees, found only here and on Santa Rosa Island, offshore. Guided tours of the nature preserve are offered on weekends. Torrey Pines tends to get crowded in summer, but you'll find more isolated spots heading south under the cliffs leading to Black's Beach. **Best for:** families, hiking, scenic views, sunbathing, swimming. **Amenities:** lifeguard year-round (reduced hours in winter), parking in two small lots, showers, toilets. ⊠ *Take Carmel Valley Rd. exit west from I–5, turn left on Rte. S21, 12600 N. Torrey Pines Rd.* ☎ *858/755– 2063* ⊕ *www.torreypine.org* ⊠ *Parking $10-$15.*

ENCINITAS

★ **Swami's.** The palms and the golden lotus-flower domes of the nearby Self-Realization Center temple and ashram earned this picturesque beach its name. Extreme low tides expose tide pools that harbor anemones, starfish, and other sea life. The beach is also a top surfing spot; the only access is by a long stairway leading down from the cliff-top Seaside Roadside Park, where there's free parking. On big winter swells, the bluffs are lined with gawkers watching the area's best surfers take on, and be taken down by, some of the best big waves in the county. Offshore, divers do their thing at North County's underwater park, Encinitas Marine Life Refuge. **Best for:** diving, surfing, tide pools. **Amenities:** lifeguard year-round, parking, picnic tables, toilets. ⊠ *Follow Rte. S21 north from Cardiff, or exit I–5 at Encinitas Blvd., go west to Rte. S21, and turn left.*

BICYCLING

Leisurely routes near tourist areas include Mission Bay, San Diego Harbor, and the Mission Beach boardwalk, all of which are flat and scenic. Rent a bike and get rolling!

Cheap Rentals Mission Beach. Right on the boardwalk, this place has good daily and weekly prices for bike rentals, which include beach cruisers, tandems, hybrids, and two-wheeled baby carriers. ⊠ *3689 Mission Blvd., Mission Beach* ☎ *858/488–9070, 800/941–7761* ⊕ *www. cheap-rentals.com.*

Hike Bike Kayak San Diego. This outfitter offers a wide range of guided bike tours, from easy excursions around Mission Bay and Coronado Island to slightly more rigorous trips through coastal La Jolla. Mountain-biking tours are also available, and the company also rents bikes of all types (and can van-deliver them to your hotel). ⊠ *2246 Ave. de la Playa, La Jolla* ☎ *858/551–9510, 866/425–2925* ⊕ *www. hikebikekayak.com.*

Holland's Bicycles. This great bike rental source on Coronado Island has a sister store (**Bikes and Beyond** ☎ *619/435–7180)* located at the ferry landing, so you can jump on your bike as soon as you cross the harbor from Downtown San Diego. ⊠ *977 Orange Ave., Coronado* ☎ *619/435–3153* ⊕ *www.hollandsbicycles.com.*

Route S21. On many summer days, Route S21, aka Old Highway 101, from La Jolla to Oceanside looks like a freeway for cyclists. About 24 miles long, it's easily the most popular and scenic bike route around, never straying far from the beach. Although the terrain is fairly easy, the long, steep Torrey Pines grade is famous for weeding out the weak. Another Darwinian challenge is dodging slow-moving pedestrians and cars pulling over to park in towns like Encinitas and Del Mar.

DIVING

Mission Beach. The HMCS *Yukon,* a decommissioned Canadian warship, was intentionally sunk off Mission Beach to create the main diving destination in San Diego. A mishap caused it to settle on its side, creating a surreal, M.C. Escher–esque diving environment. This is a technical dive and should be attempted only by experienced divers; even diving instructors have become disoriented inside the wreck.

Ocean Enterprises Scuba Diving. Stop in for everything you need to plan a diving adventure, including equipment, advice, and instruction. ⊠ *7710 Balboa Ave., Suite 101, Clairemont Mesa* ☎ *858/565–6054* ⊕ *www. oceanenterprises.com.*

San Diego–La Jolla Underwater Park Ecological Preserve. Diving enthusiasts the world over come to San Diego to snorkel and scuba dive off La Jolla at the underwater preserve. Because all sea life is protected here, this 533-acre preserve (all of La Jolla Cove to La Jolla Shores) is the best place to see large lobster, sea bass, and sculpin (scorpion fish), as well as numerous golden garibaldi damselfish, the state marine fish. It's common to see hundreds of beautiful (and harmless) leopard sharks schooling at the north end of the cove, near La Jolla Shores, especially in summer. ⊕ *www.lajollaparks.com/underwater-park.*

Scripps Canyon. Off the south end of Black's Beach, the rim of Scripps Canyon lies in about 60 feet of water and holds the Marine Life Refuge. The canyon plummets more than 900 feet in some sections. ⊕ *www. lajollaparks.com/underwater-park.*

Scuba San Diego. This center is well regarded for its top-notch instruction and certification programs, as well as for guided dive tours of kelp reefs in La Jolla Cove, night diving at La Jolla Canyon, and unguided charter boat trips to Mission Bay's Wreck Alley or to the Coronado Islands (in Mexico, just south of San Diego). ⊠ *San Diego Hilton Hotel, 1775 E. Mission Bay Dr., Mission Bay* ☎ *619/260–1880* ⊕ *www.scubasandiego. com.*

FOOTBALL

San Diego Chargers. The Chargers play their NFL home games at Qualcomm Stadium. Games with AFC West rivals the Oakland Raiders are particularly intense. ⊠ *9449 Friars Rd., Mission Valley* ☎ *858/874–4500 Charger Park, 877/242–7437 Season Tickets* ⊕ *www.chargers.com.*

GOLF

COURSES

Balboa Park Municipal Golf Course. Because it's in the heart of Balboa Park, this course is convenient for Downtown visitors. ✉ *2600 Golf Course Dr., Balboa Park* ☎ *619/235–1184* ⊕ *www.balboaparkgolf.com* 🏌 *18 holes. 6267 yds. Par 72. Green Fee: $40/$50* ☞ *Facilities: Driving range, putting green, pitching area, golf carts, pull carts, rental clubs, pro shop, golf academy/lessons, restaurant, bar.*

★ **Coronado Municipal Golf Course.** Views of San Diego Bay and the Coronado Bridge from the front 9 make this course popular—it's difficult to get on unless you reserve a tee time, 8 to 14 days in advance, for an additional $60. ✉ *2000 Visalia Row, Coronado* ☎ *619/435–3121* ⊕ *www.golfcoronado.com* 🏌 *18 holes. 6590 yds. Par 72. Green Fee: $30/$35. Reservations essential* ☞ *Facilities: Driving range, putting green, pitching area, golf carts, pull carts, rental clubs, pro shop, golf academy/lessons, restaurant, bar.*

★ **La Costa Resort and Spa.** One of the premier golf resorts in Southern California, La Costa is home to the PGA Tour Golf Academy, whose instructors include past and present touring pros and coaches. The resort recently remodeled its Champions Course, host to more than three dozen PGA events. After a day on the links you can wind down with a massage, steam bath, and dinner at the resort. ✉ *2100 Costa del Mar Rd., Carlsbad* ☎ *800/854-4000* ⊕ *www.lacosta.com* 🏌 *Champions: 18 holes, 6608 yds. Par 72. Green Fee: $210/$225. South: 18 holes, 6524 yds. Par 72. Green Fee: $140–$185. Reservations essential* ☞ *Facilities: Driving range, putting green, pitching area, golf carts, caddies, rental clubs, pro shop, golf academy/lessons, restaurant, bar.*

Fodor's Choice ★ **Park Hyatt Aviara Golf Club.** Designed by Arnold Palmer, this top-quality course includes views of the protected adjacent Batiquitos Lagoon and the Pacific Ocean. The carts, which are fitted with GPS systems that tell you the distance to the pin, are included in the cost. ✉ *7447 Batiquitos Dr., Carlsbad* ☎ *760/603–6900* ⊕ *www.golfaviara.com* 🏌 *18 holes. 7007 yds. Par 72. Green Fee: $215/$235* ☞ *Facilities: Driving range, putting green, pitching area, golf carts, rental clubs, pro shop, golf academy/lessons, restaurant, bar.*

★ **Rancho Bernardo Inn and Country Club.** The course management here is JC Golf, which has a golf school as well as several other respected courses throughout Southern California that are open to guests of the Rancho Bernardo Inn. The restaurant here, El Bizcocho, serves one of the best Sunday brunches in the county. ✉ *17550 Bernardo Oaks Dr., Rancho Bernardo* ☎ *858/385–8733* ⊕ *www.ranchobernardoinn.com* 🏌 *18 holes. 6631 yds. Par 72. Green Fee: $100/$135* ☞ *Facilities: Driving range, putting green, golf carts, rental clubs, pro shop, golf academy/ lessons, restaurant, bar.*

Fodor's Choice ★ **Torrey Pines Golf Course.** One of the best public golf courses in the United States, Torrey Pines was the site of the 2008 U.S. Open and has been the home of the Buick Invitational (now the Farmers Insurance Open) since 1968. The par-72 South Course receives rave reviews from the touring pros. Redesigned by Rees Jones in 2001, it's longer, more challenging, and more expensive than the North Course. Tee times may be booked from 8 to 90 days in advance at ☎ 877/581–7171 and are subject to an advance booking fee ($43). A full-day or half-day instructional package includes cart, green fee, and a golf-pro escort for the first 9 holes. ✉ *11480 N. Torrey Pines Rd., La Jolla* ☎ *858/452–3226, 800/985–4653* ⊕ *www.torreypinesgolfcourse.com* 🏌 *36 holes. South: 7,227 yds., North: 6874 yds. North and South: Par 72. Green Fee: South: $183/$229, North: $100/$125* ☞ *Facilities: Driving range, putting green, pitching area, golf carts, pull carts, caddies upon request in advance, rental clubs, pro shop, golf academy/lessons, restaurant, bar.*

SAILING AND BOATING

Harbor Sailboats. You can rent sailboats from 22 to 41 feet long here for open-ocean adventures. The company also offers skippered charter boats for whale-watching, sunset sails, and bay tours. ✉ *2040 Harbor Island Dr., Harbor Island* ☎ *619/291–9568, 800/854–6625* ⊕ *www. harborsailboats.com.*

Seaforth Boat Rentals. Call here to arrange a charter for an ocean adventure or to rent a sailboat, powerboat, or skiff from their Mission Bay, Coronado, or Downtown San Diego locations. ✉ *1641 Quivira Rd., Mission Bay* ☎ *888/834–2628 reservations* ⊕ *www.seaforthboatrental. com.*

SURFING

Cheap Rentals Mission Beach. Many local surf shops rent both surf and bodyboards. Cheap Rentals Mission Beach is right on the boardwalk, just steps from the waves. They rent wet suits, bodyboards, and skimboards in addition to soft surfboards and long and short fiberglass rides. ✉ *3689 Mission Blvd., Mission Beach* ☎ *858/488–9070, 800/941–7761* ⊕ *www.cheap-rentals.com.*

Hansen's. A short walk from Swami's beach, Hansen's is one of San Diego's oldest and most popular surf shops. It has an extensive selection of boards, wet suits, and clothing for sale, and a rental department as well. ✉ *1105 S. Coast Hwy. 101, Encinitas* ☎ *760/753–6595, 800/480–4754* ⊕ *www.hansensurf.com.*

★ **Surf Diva Surf School.** Check out clinics, surf camps, surf trips, and private lessons especially formulated for girls and women. Clinics and trips are for women only, but guys can book private lessons from the nationally recognized staff. ✉ *2160 Ave. de la Playa, La Jolla* ☎ *858/454–8273* ⊕ *www.surfdiva.com.*

SHOPPING

CORONADO

Fodor's Choice ★ **Coronado Ferry Landing.** A staggering view of San Diego's Downtown skyline across the bay and a dozen boutiques make this a delightful place to shop while waiting for a ferry. ✉ *1201 1st St., at B Ave., Coronado* ☎ *619/435–8895* ⊕ *www.coronadoferrylandingshops.com* ⊗ *Shops daily 10–7* ⌖ *Farmers' market Tues. 2:30–6; some restaurants daily late-afternoon happy hr.*

DOWNTOWN

★ **Seaport Village.** Quintessentially San Diego, this waterfront complex of more than 50 shops and restaurants has sweeping bay views, fresh breezes, and great strolling paths. You'll find sunglasses, surf gear, kites, toys, and books here. ✉ *849 W. Habor Dr., at Pacific Hwy., Downtown* ☎ *619/235–4014* ⊕ *www.spvillage.com.*

★ **Westfield Horton Plaza.** Macy's and Nordstrom anchor this multilevel complex that has 130 smaller stores, plus fast-food and upscale dining, cinemas, and a game arcade. Park in the plaza garage and use validation machines to get three free hours parking (no purchase necessary). ■TIP→ Horton Plaza sets aside parking spaces for expectant moms and families with small children; ask the attendant to direct you. ✉ *Bordered by Broadway, 1st Ave., G St., and 4th Ave., Gaslamp Quarter* ☎ *619/238–1596* ⊕ *www.westfield.com/hortonplaza.*

GASLAMP QUARTER

Long a place where fine restaurants and clubs have catered to conventioneers and partying locals, the historic heart of San Diego has recently seen an explosion of specialty shops, art galleries, and boutiques take up residence in the Victorian buildings and renovated warehouses along 4th and 5th avenues. Some stores in this area tend to close early, starting as early as 5 pm. But a trip to the Gaslamp to shop is worth it. Here, you'll find the usual mall denizens as well as hip fashion boutiques and gift shops.

UPTOWN

Located north and northeast of Downtown, the Uptown area includes Hillcrest, North Park, South Park, Mission Hills, and University Heights. The boundaries between the neighborhoods tend to blur, but you'll find that each area has unique shops. Hillcrest has a large gay community and boasts many avant-garde apparel shops alongside gift, book, and music stores. North Park, east of Hillcrest, is a retro buff's paradise with many resale shops, trendy boutiques, and stores that sell a mix of old and new. University Avenue offers a mélange of affordably priced furniture, gift, and specialty stores appealing to college students, singles, and young families. South Park's 30th, Juniper, and Fern streets have everything from the hottest new denim lines to baby gear and craft supplies. The shops and art galleries in upscale Mission Hills, west of Hillcrest, have a modern and sophisticated ambience that suits the well-heeled residents just fine.

LA JOLLA

Known as San Diego's answer to Rodeo Drive in Beverly Hills, La Jolla has chic boutiques, art galleries, and gift shops and plenty of celebrity sightings. Prospect Street and Girard Avenue are the primary shopping stretches, and North Prospect is chockablock with art galleries. The Upper Girard Design District stocks home decor accessories and luxury furnishings. Parking is tight in the village. Most shops on Prospect Street stay open until 10 pm on weeknights to accommodate evening strollers. On the east side of Interstate 15, office buildings surround the Westfield UTC mall, where you'll find department and chain stores.

SIDE TRIPS TO NORTH COUNTY

DEL MAR

23 miles north of Downtown San Diego on I–5, 9 miles north of La Jolla on Rte. S21.

Del Mar is best known for its quaint old section west of Interstate 5 marked with a glamorous racetrack, half-timber buildings, chic shops, tony restaurants, celebrity visitors, and wide beaches.

☼ **Del Mar Fairgrounds.** The Spanish Mission–style fairground is the home
★ of the **Del Mar Thoroughbred Club** (☎ 858/755–1141 ⊕ www.dmtc. com). Crooner Bing Crosby and his Hollywood buddies—Pat O'Brien, Gary Cooper, and Oliver Hardy, among others—organized the club in the 1930s, and the racing here (usually July–September, Wednesday–Monday, post time 2 pm) remains a fashionable affair. Del Mar Fairgrounds hosts more than 100 different events each year, including the San Diego County Fair, which draws more than a million visitors annually. ⊠ 2260 Jimmy Durante Blvd. ☎ 858/793–5555 ⊕ www. delmarfairgrounds.com.

WHERE TO EAT

$$$$ ✕ **Addison.** Sophisticated and stylish, Addison challenges ideas about
FRENCH what fine dining is all about. The dining room and adjacent bar feel Ital-
Fodor'sChoice ian and clubby, with intricately carved dark-wood motifs. The tables,
★ by contrast, are pure white, adorned with a single flower. Acclaimed chef William Bradley serves up explosive flavors in his four-course prix-fixe dinners, such as Prince Edward Island mussels with champagne sabayon and lemon verbena jus or foie gras de canard with Le Puy lentils, port wine, and smoked bacon mousse. Entrées might include spring lamb *persille* (parsely and garlic topping) with pistachio pâté brisée and caramelized garlic puree or wild Scottish salmon with sauce *vin jaune* (white wine from France's Jura region). Addison challenges wine lovers with 160 pages of choices. ⑤ *Average main: $158* ⊠ *5200 Grand Del*

Mar Way ☎ *858/314–1900* ⊕ *www.addisondelmar.com* ⚑ *Reservations essential* ⊗ *Closed Sun. and Mon. No lunch.*

WHERE TO STAY

For expanded reviews, facilities, and current deals, visit Fodors.com.

$$$$ 🖩 **The Grand Del Mar.** Mind-blowing indulgence in serene surroundings
ⓒ sets the Grand Del Mar apart from any other luxury hotel in the San
Fodor'sChoice Diego area. **Pros:** ultimate luxury; secluded, on-site golf course. **Cons:**
★ service can be slow; hotel is not on the beach. **TripAdvisor:** "beautiful,"
"quietly elegant," "isolated gem." ⑤ *Rooms from: $425* ⊠ *5200 Grand
Del Mar Ct.* ☎ *858/314–2000, 888/314–2030* ⊕ *www.thegranddelmar.
com* ⬎ *218 rooms, 31 suites.*

CARLSBAD

*6 miles north of Encinitas on Rte. S21, 36 miles north of Downtown
San Diego on I–5.*

Once-sleepy Carlsbad has long been popular with beachgoers and sun
seekers. On a clear day in this village you can take in sweeping ocean
views that stretch from La Jolla to Oceanside by walking the 2-mile-
long seawalk running between the Encina power plant and Pine Street.
En route, you'll find several stairways leading to the beach and quite a
few benches. Inland are LEGOLAND California and other attractions
in its vicinity.

ⓒ **Flower Fields at Carlsbad Ranch.** In spring the hillsides are abloom on
Fodor'sChoice this, the largest bulb production farm in Southern California, when
★ thousands of Giant Tecolote ranunculus produce a stunning 50-acre
display of color against the backdrop of the blue Pacific Ocean. Other
knockouts include the rose gardens—with examples of every All-American Rose Selection award-winner since 1940—and a historical display of Paul Ecke poinsettias. Family activities include a LEGO Flower
Garden and a kids' playground. ⊠ *5704 Paseo del Norte, east of I–5*
☎ *760/431–0352* ⊕ *www.theflowerfields.com* ⊡ *$11* ⊗ *Mar.–May,
daily 9–6.*

ⓒ **LEGOLAND California Resort.** The centerpiece of a development that
Fodor'sChoice includes resort hotels, a designer discount shopping mall, an aquarium,
★ and a water park, LEGOLAND offers up rides and diversions geared
toward kids ages 2 to 12. The main events:

Lost Kingdom Adventure: Armed with a laser blaster, you'll journey
through ancient Egyptian ruins in a desert roadster, scoring points as
you hit targets.

Star Wars **Miniland:** Follow the exploits of Yoda, Princess Leia, Obi-
Wan, Anakin, R2, Luke, and the denizens of the six *Star Wars* films.
Some kids loop back several times to take it all in.

Miniland U.S.A: This miniature, animated, interactive collection of U.S.
icons was constructed out of 24 million LEGO bricks!

Soak-N-Sail: Hundreds of gallons of water course through 60 interactive features including a pirate shipwreck–theme area. You'll need your
swimsuit for this one.

Dragon Coaster: Little kids love this popular indoor/outdoor steel roller coaster that goes through a castle. Don't let the name frighten you—the motif is more humorous than scary.

Volvo Driving School: Kids 6–13 can drive speed-controlled cars (not on rails) on a miniature road; driver's licenses are awarded after the course. Volvo Junior is the pint-sized version for kids 3–5.

■ TIP→ The best value is one of the Hopper Tickets that give you one admission to LEGOLAND plus Sea Life Aquarium and/or the LEGOLAND Water Park. These can be used on the same day or on different days. Go midweek to avoid the crowds. ✉ *1 Legoland Dr., Exit I–5 at Cannon Rd. and follow signs east ¼ mi* ☎ *760/918–5346* ⊕ *california.legoland.com* ⊑ *LEGOLAND $72 adults, $62 children; Hopper prices vary; parking $12* ☺ *Late May–early Sept. daily (hrs vary), early Sept.–late May closed Tues. and Wed. except holiday weeks; check website or call.*

OCEANSIDE

8 miles north of Carlsbad on Rte. S21, 37 miles north of Downtown San Diego on I–5.

ⓒ   **Old Mission San Luis Rey.** Known as the King of the Missions, this struc-
Fodor's Choice   ture was built in 1798 by Franciscan friars under the direction of Father
★   Fermin Lasuen to help educate and convert local Native Americans. Once a location for filming Disney's *Zorro* TV series, the well-preserved mission, still owned by the Franciscans, was the 18th and largest and most prosperous of California's missions. The *sala* (parlor), the kitchen, a friar's bedroom, a weaving room, and a collection of religious art and old Spanish vestments convey much about early mission life. ✉ *4050 Mission Ave.* ☎ *760/757–3651* ⊕ *www.sanluisrey.org* ⊑ *$5* ☺ *Weekdays 9–5; weekends 10–5.*

ESCONDIDO

8 miles north of Rancho Bernardo on I–15, 31 miles northeast of Downtown San Diego on I–15.

ⓒ   **San Diego Zoo Safari Park.** An extension of the San Diego Zoo, 35 miles to
Fodor's Choice   the south, the 1,800-acre preserve in the San Pasqual Valley is designed
★   to protect endangered species from around the world. Exhibit areas have been carved out of the dry, dusty canyons and mesas to represent the animals' natural habitats in various parts of Africa, the Australian rain forest, and Asian swamps and plains.

The best way to see these preserves is to take the 45-minute, 2½-mile Journey into Africa bus tour. As you pass in front of the large, naturally landscaped enclosures, you can see animals bounding across prairies and mesas as they would in the wild. More than 3,500 animals of more than 400 species roam or fly above the expansive grounds. Predators are separated from prey by deep moats, but only the elephants, tigers, lions, and cheetahs are kept in isolation. Photographers with zoom lenses can get spectacular shots of zebras, gazelles, and rhinos. In summer, when the park stays open late, the trip is especially enjoyable in the early evening, when the heat has subsided and the animals are active

A LEGOLAND model worker puts the finishing touches on the San Francisco portion of Miniland U.S.A.

and feeding. When the bus travels through the park after dark, sodium-vapor lamps illuminate the active animals.

The park is as much a botanical garden as a zoo, serving as a "rescue center" for rare and endangered plants. Unique gardens include cacti and succulents from Baja California, a bonsai collection, a fuchsia display, native plants, and protea. The park sponsors a number of garden events throughout the year, including a winter camellia show and a spring orchid show.

The **Lion Camp** gives you a close-up view of the king of beasts in a slice of African wilderness complete with sweeping plains and rolling hills. As you walk through this exhibit, you can watch the giant cats lounging around through a 40-foot-long window. The last stop is a research station where you can see them all around you through glass panels.

The ticket booths at **Nairobi Village,** the park's center, are designed to resemble the tomb of an ancient king of Uganda. Animals in the **Petting Kraal** here affectionately tolerate tugs and pats and are quite adept at posing for pictures with toddlers. At the **Congo River Village** 10,000 gallons of water pour each minute over a huge waterfall into a large lagoon. **Hidden Jungle,** an 8,800-square-foot greenhouse, is a habitat for creatures that creep, flutter, or just hang out in the tropics. Gigantic cockroaches and bird-eating spiders share the turf with colorful butterflies and hummingbirds and oh-so-slow-moving two-toed sloths. **Lorikeet Landing,** simulating the Australian rain forest, holds 75 of the loud and colorful small parrots—you can buy a cup of nectar at the aviary entrance to induce them to land on your hand. Along the trails of 32-acre **Heart of Africa** you can travel in the footsteps of an

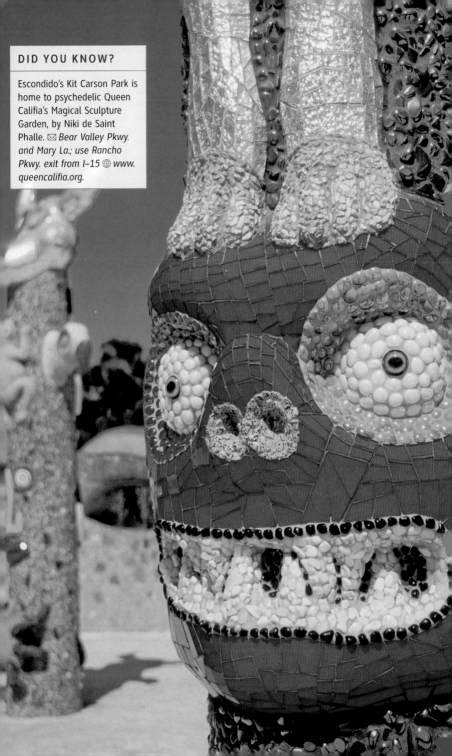

DID YOU KNOW?

Escondido's Kit Carson Park is home to psychedelic Queen Califia's Magical Sculpture Garden, by Niki de Saint Phalle. ✉ *Bear Valley Pkwy. and Mary La.; use Rancho Pkwy. exit from I–15* ⊕ *www. queencalifia.org.*

early explorer through forests and lowlands, across a floating bridge to a research station, where an expert is on hand to answer questions; finally you arrive at Panorama Point for an up-close-and-personal view of cheetahs, a chance to feed the giraffes, and a distant glimpse of the expansive savanna where rhinos, impalas, wildebeest, oryx, and beautiful migrating birds reside. At **Condor Ridge,** the Safari Park, which conducts captive breeding programs to save rare and endangered species, shows off one of its most successful efforts, the California condor. The exhibit, perched like one of the ugly black vultures it features, occupies nearly the highest point in the park, and affords a sweeping view of the surrounding San Pasqual Valley. Also on exhibit here is a herd of rare desert bighorn sheep.

All the park's animal shows are entertainingly educational. The gift shops here offer wonderful merchandise, much of it limited-edition items. Rental camcorders, strollers, and wheelchairs are available. Serious shutterbugs might consider joining one of the special Photo Caravan Safari tours ($90–$150 plus park admission). You can also stay overnight in the park in summer on a Roar and Snore Sleepover (adults $140–$220, kids 8–11 $120–$160, plus admission). ⊠ *15500 San Pasqual Valley Rd. Take I–15 north to Via Rancho Pkwy. and follow signs, 6 mi* ☎ *760/747–8702* ⊕ *www.sandiegozoo.org/wap* 🎟 *$40 includes Journey into Africa tour and Conservation Carousel; $76 two-visit pass includes a 1-day pass to San Diego Zoo and Safari Park or two 1-day passes to either; parking $10* ☉ *Daily 9-dusk, later in summer (call ahead for closing time).*

Orange County and Catalina Island

WITH DISNEYLAND AND KNOTT'S BERRY FARM

WORD OF MOUTH

"I love Catalina. I love the boat trip over; you'll often see dolphins. I love the beauty and clarity of the water; go snorkeling or [take a] glass-bottom boat. I love the untouched wild California inland; take a tour or rent a golf cart."

—logandog

WELCOME TO ORANGE COUNTY AND CATALINA ISLAND

TOP REASONS TO GO

★ **Disney magic:** Walking down Main Street, U.S.A., with Cinderella's Castle straight ahead, you really will feel like you're in one of the happiest places on Earth.

★ **Beautiful beaches:** Surf, swim, sail, or just relax on one of the state's most breathtaking stretches of coastline.

★ **Island getaways:** Just a short hydrofoil away, Catalina Island feels 1,000 miles away from California. Wander around charming Avalon, or explore the unspoiled beauty of the island's wild interior.

★ **The fine life:** Some of the state's wealthiest communities are in coastal Orange County, so spend at least part of your stay here experiencing how the other half lives.

★ **Family fun:** Spend some quality time with the kids riding roller coasters, eating ice cream, fishing off ocean piers, and bodysurfing.

1 Disneyland Resort. Southern California's top family destination has expanded from the humble park of Walt Disney's vision to a megaresort with more attractions spilling over into Disney's California Adventure. But kids still consider it the happiest place on Earth!

2 Knott's Berry Farm. Amusement park lovers should check out this Buena Park attraction, with thrill rides, the *Peanuts* gang, and lots of fried chicken and boysenberry pie.

3 Coastal Orange County. The OC's beach communities may not be quite as glamorous as seen on TV, but coastal spots like Huntington Beach, Newport Harbor, and Laguna Beach are perfect for chilling out in a beachfront hotel.

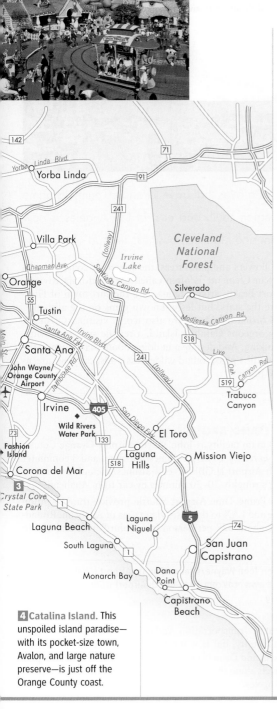

3

GETTING ORIENTED

Like Los Angeles, Orange County stretches over a large area, lacks a singular focal point, and has limited public transportation. You'll need a car and a sensible game plan to make the most of your visit. Try staying at a midpoint location such as Irvine or Costa Mesa, both equidistant from inland tourist attractions and the coast. These towns are less crowded than Anaheim and less expensive than the beach cities. Of course, if you can afford it, staying at the beach is always recommended.

4 Catalina Island. This unspoiled island paradise—with its pocket-size town, Avalon, and large nature preserve—is just off the Orange County coast.

Updated by Kathy A. McDonald

Few of the citrus groves that gave Orange County its name remain. This region south and east of Los Angeles is now ruled by tourism and high-tech business instead of farmers.

With its tropical flowers and palm trees, the stretch of coast between Seal Beach and San Clemente is often called the California Riviera. Exclusive Newport Beach, artsy Laguna, and the surf town of Huntington Beach are the stars, but lesser-known gems on the glistening coast—such as Corona del Mar—are also worth visiting. Offshore, meanwhile, lies gorgeous Catalina Island, a terrific spot for diving, snorkeling, and hiking. And despite a building boom that began in the 1990s, the area is still a place to find wilderness trails, canyons, greenbelts, and natural parks.

PLANNING

GETTING HERE AND AROUND

Orange County's main facility is John Wayne Airport Orange County (SNA), which is served by 10 major domestic airlines and 3 commuter lines. Long Beach Airport (LGB) serves 4 airlines, including its major player, JetBlue. It's roughly 20–30 minutes by car from Anaheim.

Airport Bus and Prime Time Airport Shuttle provide transportation from John Wayne and LAX to the Disneyland area of Anaheim. Round-trip fares average about $27 per person from John Wayne and $22 to $32 from LAX.

AIR TRAVEL

Airport Information John Wayne/Orange County Airport (*SNA*). ☎ *949/252–5006* ⊕ *www.ocair.com.* **Long Beach Airport** (*LGB*). ☎ *562/570–2600* ⊕ *www.lgb.org.*

BUS TRAVEL

The Orange County Transportation Authority will take you virtually anywhere in the county, but it will take time; OCTA buses go from Knott's Berry Farm and Disneyland to Huntington Beach and Newport Beach. Bus 1 travels along the coast; buses 701 and 721 provide express service to Los Angeles.

Information Orange County Transportation Authority (OCTA) ☎ *714/560–6282* ⊕ *www.octa.net.*

CAR TRAVEL

The San Diego Freeway (Interstate 405), the coastal route, and the Santa Ana Freeway (Interstate 5), the inland route, run north–south through Orange County. South of Laguna Interstate 405 merges into Interstate 5 (called the San Diego Freeway south from this point). A toll road, the 73 Highway, runs 15 miles from Newport Beach to San Juan Capistrano; it costs $3.95–$5.75 (lower rates are for weekends and off-peak hours) and is usually less jammed than the regular freeways. Do your best to avoid all Orange County freeways during rush hours (6–9 am and 3:30–6:30 pm). Highway 55 leads to Newport Beach. The Pacific Coast Highway (Highway 1) allows easy access to beach communities and is the most scenic route.

FERRY TRAVEL

There are two ferries that service Catalina Island; Catalina Express runs from Long Beach (about 90 minutes) and from Newport Beach (about 75 minutes). Reservations are advised for summers and weekends.

TRAIN TRAVEL

When planning train travel, consider where the train stations are in relation to your ultimate destination. You may need to make extra transportation arrangements once you've arrived in town. Amtrak makes daily stops in Orange County at all major towns. Metrolink is a weekday commuter train that runs to and from Los Angeles and Orange County.

Information Amtrak ☎ *800/872–7245* ⊕ *www.amtrak.com.* **Metrolink** ☎ *800/371–5465* ⊕ *www.metrolinktrains.com.*

For more information on Getting Here and Around, see Travel Smart California.

RESTAURANTS

Much like L.A., restaurants in Orange County are generally casual, and you'll rarely see men in jackets and ties. However, at top resort hotel dining rooms, many guests choose to dress up.

Of course, there's also a swath of super-casual places along the beachfronts—fish-taco takeout, taquerias, burger joints—that won't mind if you wear flip-flops. Reservations are recommended for the nicest restaurants.

Many places don't serve past 11 pm, and locals tend to eat early. Remember that according to California law, smoking is prohibited in all enclosed areas.

Prices in the restaurant reviews are the average cost of a main course at dinner or, if dinner is not served, at lunch (excluding sales tax).

HOTELS

Along the coast there are remarkable luxury resorts; if you can't afford a stay, pop in for the view at Laguna Beach's Montage or the recently refreshed Ritz-Carlton at Dana Point. For a taste of the OC glam life, have lunch near the stunning circular pool at the Resort at Pelican Hill on the Newport Coast.

As a rule, lodging prices tend to rise the closer the hotels are to the beach. If you're looking for value, consider a hotel that is inland along the Interstate 405 freeway corridor.

In most cases, you can take advantage of some of the facilities of the high-end resorts, such as restaurants and spas, even if you aren't an overnight guest.

Prices in the hotel reviews are the lowest cost of a standard double room in high season. Prices do not include taxes (as high as 14%, depending on the region).

VISITOR INFORMATION

The Anaheim-Orange County Visitor and Convention Bureau is an excellent resource for both leisure and business travelers and can provide materials on many area attractions. It's on the main floor of the Anaheim Convention Center.

The Orange County Tourism Council's website is also a useful source of information.

Information Anaheim/Orange County Visitor & Convention Bureau
⊠ *Anaheim Convention Center, 800 W. Katella Ave., Anaheim* ☎ *714/765–8888* ⊕ *www.anaheimoc.org.* **Orange County Tourism Council** ⊕ *www.visittheoc. com.*

DISNEYLAND RESORT

26 miles southeast of Los Angeles, via I–5.

The snowcapped Matterhorn, the centerpiece of the Magic Kingdom, punctuates the skyline of Anaheim. Since 1955, when Walt Disney chose this once-quiet farming community for the site of his first amusement park, Disneyland has attracted more than 600 million visitors and tens of thousands of workers, and Anaheim has been their host.

To understand the symbiotic relationship between Disneyland and Anaheim, you need only look at the $4.2 billion spent in a combined effort by the Walt Disney Company and Anaheim, the latter to revitalize the city's tourist center and run-down areas, the former to expand and renovate the Disney properties into what is known now as Disneyland Resort.

The resort is a sprawling complex that includes Disney's two amusement parks; three hotels; and Downtown Disney, a shopping, dining, and entertainment promenade. Anaheim's tourist center includes Angel Stadium of Anaheim, home of baseball's 2002 World Series Champion Los Angeles Angels of Anaheim; Arrowhead Pond, which hosts concerts and the hockey team the Anaheim Ducks; and the enormous Anaheim Convention Center.

GETTING THERE

Disney is about a 30-mile drive from either LAX or downtown. From LAX, follow Sepulveda Boulevard south to the Interstate 105 freeway and drive east 16 miles to the Interstate 605 north exit. Exit at the Santa Ana Freeway (Interstate 5) and continue south for 12 miles to the Disneyland Drive exit. Follow signs to the resort. From downtown, follow Interstate 5 south 28 miles and exit at Disneyland Drive. **Disneyland Resort Express** (☎ *714/978–8855* ⊕ *graylineanaheim.com*) offers daily nonstop bus service between LAX, John Wayne Airport, and Anaheim. Reservations are not required. The cost is $22 one-way for adults, $19 for children, for LAX, and $17 and $14 one-way for John Wayne Airport.

SAVING TIME AND MONEY

If you plan to visit for more than a day, you can save money by buying three-, four-, and five-day Park Hopper tickets that grant same-day "hopping" privileges between Disneyland and Disney's California Adventure. You get a discount on the multiple-day passes if you buy online through the Disneyland website.

A one-day Park Hopper pass costs $105 for anyone 10 or older, $99 for kids ages 3–9. Admission to either park (but not both) is $80 or $74 for kids 3–9; kids 2 and under are free.

In addition to tickets, parking is $15–$20 (unless your hotel has a shuttle or is within walking distance), and meals in the parks and at Downtown Disney range from $10 to $30 per person.

If you're staying in a hotel near the park, ask if any discount packages are available when you book.

A full-day pass for adults is $57.99; Southern California residents pay $47.99 and children three and older, up to 48 inches tall, are $28.99. Tickets can be purchased online and printed out ahead of time, for a discounted price and to avoid waiting in line.

In addition to tickets, you'll need to pay $15 for parking. Meals are about $10–$14 per person. The Laser Tag attraction is an extra $10, and the Big Swing ride is an additional $5.

DISNEYLAND

⟲ **Disneyland.** One of the biggest misconceptions people have about Disneyland is that they've "been there, done that" if they've visited either Florida's mammoth Walt Disney World or one of the Disney parks overseas. But Disneyland, opened in 1955 and the only one of the kingdoms to be overseen by Walt himself, has a genuine historic feel and occupies a unique place in the Disney legend. There's plenty here that you won't find anywhere else: for example, Storybook Land, with its miniature replicas of animated Disney scenes from classics such as *Pinocchio* and *Alice in Wonderland,* and the Indiana Jones Adventure ride.

Fodor's Choice ★

Characters appear for autographs and photos throughout the day; guidebooks at the entrances give times and places. You can also meet some of the animated icons at one of the character meals served at the three Disney hotels (open to the public). Belongings can be stored in lockers just off Main Street; purchases can also be sent back to guests' hotels. ⊠ *1313 S. Disneyland Dr., between Ball Rd. and Katella Ave., Anaheim* ☎ *714/781–4565 Guest information* ⊕ *www.disneyland.com* ⊡ *$80; kids 3–9 $74; parking $15* ⊗ *Hrs vary.*

PARK NEIGHBORHOODS

Neighborhoods for Disneyland are arranged in geographic order.

MAIN STREET, U.S.A. Walt's hometown of Marceline, Missouri, was the inspiration behind this romanticized image of small-town America, circa 1900. The sidewalks are lined with a penny arcade and shops that sell everything from tradable pins to Disney-theme clothing and photo supplies. It opens half an hour before the rest of the park, so it's a good place to explore if you're getting an early start to beat the crowds (it's also open an hour after the other attractions close, so you may want to save your shopping for the end of the day). **Main Street Cinema** offers a cool respite from the crowds and six classic Disney animated shorts, including *Steamboat Willie*. There's rarely a wait to enter. Board the **Disneyland Railroad** here to save on walking; it tours all the lands, plus offers unique views of Splash Mountain and the Grand Canyon and Primeval World dioramas.

NEW ORLEANS SQUARE A mini–French Quarter with narrow streets, hidden courtyards, and live street performances, this is home to two iconic attractions and the Cajun-inspired Blue Bayou restaurant. **Pirates of the Caribbean** now features Jack Sparrow and the cursed Captain Barbossa, in a nod to the blockbuster movies of the same name, plus enhanced special effects and battle scenes (complete with cannonball explosions). Nearby **Haunted Mansion** continues to spook guests with its stretching room and "doombuggy" rides (plus there's now an expanded storyline for the beating-heart bride). Its *Nightmare Before Christmas* holiday overlay is an annual tradition. This is a good area to get a casual bite to eat; the clam chowder in sourdough bread bowls, sold at the French Market Restaurant and Royal Street Veranda, is a popular choice.

FRONTIERLAND Between Adventureland and Fantasyland, Frontierland transports you to the wild, wild West with its rustic buildings, shooting gallery, mountain range, and foot-stompin' dance hall. The marquee attraction, **Big Thunder Mountain Railroad,** is a relatively tame roller coaster ride (no steep descents) that takes the form of a runaway mine car as it rumbles past desert canyons and an old mining town. Tour the Rivers of America on the **Mark Twain Riverboat** in the company of a grizzled old river pilot or circumnavigate the globe on the **Sailing Ship Columbia,** though its operating hours are usually limited to weekends. You can also raft over from here to Pirate's Lair on **Tom Sawyer Island,** which now features pirate-theme caves, treasure hunts, and music along with plenty of caves and hills to climb and explore. If you don't mind tight seating,

BEST TIPS FOR DISNEYLAND

Buy entry tickets in advance. Many nearby hotels sell park admission tickets; you can also buy them through the Disney website. If you book a package deal, such as those offered through AAA, tickets are included, too.

The lines at the ticket booths can take more than an hour on busy days, so you'll definitely save time by buying in advance, especially if you're committed to going on a certain day regardless of the weather.

Come midweek. Weekends, especially in summer, are a mob scene. A winter weekday is often the least crowded time to visit.

Plan your times to hit the most popular rides. If you're at the park when the gates open, make a beeline for the top rides before the crowds reach a critical mass. Another good time is the evening, when the hordes thin out somewhat, and during a parade or other show. Save the quieter attractions for midafternoon.

Look into Fastpasses. These passes allow you to reserve your place in line at some of the most crowded attractions (only one at a time). Distribution machines are posted near the entrances of each attraction. Feed in your park admission ticket, and you'll receive a pass with a printed time frame (generally up to 1–1½ hours later) during which you can return to wait in a much shorter line.

Plan your meals to avoid peak mealtime crowds. Start the day with a big breakfast so you won't be too hungry at noon, when restaurants and vendors get swarmed. Wait to have lunch until after 1.

If you want to eat at the **Blue Bayou** in New Orleans Square, it's best to make reservations in person as soon as you get to the park. Another (cheaper) option is to bring your own food. There are areas just outside the park gates with picnic tables set up for this. And it's always a good idea to bring water and a few nonmeltable snacks with you. (No bottles or coolers allowed.)

Check the daily events schedule online or at the park entrance. During parades, fireworks, and other special events, sections of the parks clog with crowds. This can work for you or against you. An event could make it difficult to get around a park—but if you plan ahead, you can take advantage of the distraction to hit popular rides.

Send the Teens Next Door: Disneyland's newer sister park, California Adventure, features more intense rides suitable for older kids (Park Hopper passes include admission to both parks).

have a snack at the Golden Horseshoe Restaurant while enjoying the always-entertaining comedy and bluegrass show of Billy Hill and the Hillybillies. Children won't want to miss **Big Thunder Ranch,** a small petting zoo of real pigs, goats, and cows beyond Big Thunder Mountain.

CRITTER COUNTRY   Down-home country is the theme in this shady corner of the park, where Winnie the Pooh and Davy Crockett make their homes. Here you can find **Splash Mountain,** a classic flume ride accompanied by music and appearances by Brer Rabbit and other characters from Song of the

South. Don't forget to check out your photo (the camera snaps close-ups of each car just before it plunges into the water) on the way out. The patio of the popular Hungry Bear Restaurant has great views of Tom Sawyer's Island and Davy Crockett's Explorer Canoes.

ADVEN-
TURELAND

Modeled after the lands of Africa, Polynesia, and Arabia, this tiny tropical paradise is worth braving the crowds that flock here for the ambience and better-than-average food. Sing along with the animatronic birds and tiki gods in the **Enchanted Tiki Room,** sail the rivers of the world with joke-cracking skippers on **Jungle Cruise,** and climb the Disneyodendron semperflorens (aka always-blooming Disney tree) to **Tarzan's Treehouse,** where you can walk through scenes, some interactive, from the 1999 animated film. Cap off the visit with a wild jeep ride at **Indiana Jones Adventure,** where the special effects and decipherable hieroglyphics distract you while you're waiting in line. The kebabs at Bengal Barbecue and pineapple whip at Tiki Juice Bar are some of the best fast-food options in the park.

FANTASYLAND

Sleeping Beauty Castle marks the entrance to Fantasyland, a visual wonderland of princesses, spinning teacups, flying elephants, and other classic storybook characters. Rides and shops (such as the princess-theme Once Upon a Time and Gepetto's Toys and Gifts) take precedence over restaurants in this area of the park, but outdoor carts sell everything from churros to turkey legs. Tots love the **King Arthur Carousel, Casey Jr. Circus Train,** and **Storybook Land Canal Boats.** This is also home to **Mr. Toad's Wild Ride, Peter Pan's Flight,** and **Pinocchio's Daring Journey,** classic, movie-theater-dark rides that immerse riders in Disney fairy tales and appeal to adults and kids alike. The Abominable Snowman pops up on the **Matterhorn Bobsleds,** a roller coaster that twists and turns you up and around a made-to-scale model of the real Swiss mountain. Anchoring the east end of Fantasyland is **it's a small world,** a smorgasbord of dancing animatronic dolls, cuckoo clock–covered walls, and variations of the song everyone knows, or soon *will* know, by heart. Beloved Disney characters like Ariel from *Under the Sea* are also part of the mix.

MICKEY'S
TOONTOWN

Geared toward small fry, this lopsided cartoonlike downtown, complete with cars and trolleys that invite exploring, is where Mickey, Donald, Goofy, and other classic Disney characters hang their hats. One of the most popular attractions is **Roger Rabbit's Car Toon Spin,** a twisting, turning cab ride through the Toontown of *Who Framed Roger Rabbit?* You can also walk through **Mickey's House** to meet and be photographed with the famous mouse, take a low-key ride on **Gadget's Go Coaster,** or bounce around the fenced-in playground in front of **Goofy's House.**

TOMOR-
ROWLAND

This popular section of the park continues to tinker with its future, adding and enhancing rides regularly. One of the newest attractions, Star Tours, is a 3-D immersive experience in the world of Star Wars. **Finding Nemo's Submarine Voyage** updates the old Submarine Voyage ride with the exploits of Nemo, Dory, Marlin, and other characters from the Pixar film. Try to visit this popular ride early in the day if you can and be prepared for a wait. The interactive **Buzz Lightyear Astro**

DID YOU KNOW?

Apparently, the plain purple teacup in Disneyland's Mad Tea Party ride spins the fastest—though no one knows why.

Blasters lets you zap your neighbors with laser beams and compete for the highest score. Hurtle through the cosmos on **Space Mountain,** refurbished in 2005, or check out mainstays like the futuristic **Astro Orbiter** rockets, **Innoventions,** a self-guided tour of the latest toys of tomorrow, and **Caption EO,** a 3-D film featuring the music and talents of the late Michael Jackson. Disneyland Monorail and Disneyland Railroad both have stations here. There's also a video arcade and dancing water fountain that makes a perfect playground for kids on hot summer days.

Besides the eight lands, the daily live-action shows and parades are always crowd-pleasers. **Fantasmic!** is a musical, fireworks, and laser show in which Mickey and friends wage a spellbinding battle against Disneyland's darker characters. ■TIP➔ Arrive early to secure a good view; if there are two shows scheduled for the day, the second one tends to be less crowded. A fireworks display sparks up Friday and Saturday evenings. Brochures with maps, available at the entrance, list show and parade times.

DISNEY CALIFORNIA ADVENTURE

Disney California Adventure. The sprawling Disney California Adventure, right next to Disneyland (their entrances face each other), pays tribute to the Golden State with six theme areas. In 2007 the park began a major five-year overhaul aimed at infusing more of Walt Disney's spirit throughout the park. Added attractions include World of Color, a nighttime water-effects show, and Toy Story Mania!, an interactive adventure ride hosted by Woody, Buzz Lightyear, and friends. Goofy's Sky School is the latest zany roller coaster. As of summer 2012, Buena Vista Street is the new art-deco-style entrance that leads to a vintage Red Car Trolley and a fine dining spot, Carthay Circle Theatre, modeled after a historic L.A. theater. Also new: Ariel's Undersea Adventure and a 12-acre section called Cars Land based on the Pixar films. ✉ *1313 S. Disneyland Dr., between Ball Rd. and Katella Ave., Anaheim* ☎ *714/781–4565 Guest information* ⊕ *www.disneyland.com* 💲 *$80; kids 3–9 $74; parking $15* ☉ *Hrs vary.*

PARK NEIGHBORHOODS

GOLDEN STATE Celebrate California's history and natural beauty with nature trails, a winery, and a tortilla factory (with free samples). The area of Condor Flats has **Soarin' Over California,** a spectacular simulated hang-glider ride over California terrain, and the **Redwood Creek Challenge Trail,** a challenging trek across net ladders and suspension bridges. **Grizzly River Run** simulates the river rapids of the Sierra Nevadas; be prepared to get soaked. The Wine Country Trattoria at the Golden Vine Winery is a great place for a relaxing outdoor lunch.

HOLLYWOOD PICTURES BACKLOT With a main street modeled after Hollywood Boulevard, a fake blue-sky backdrop, and real soundstages, this area celebrates California's most famous industry. **Disney Animation** gives you an insider's look at the work of animators and how they create characters. **Turtle Talk with Crush** lets kids have an unrehearsed talk with computer-animated Crush, a sea turtle from *Finding Nemo.* The Hyperion Theater hosts **Aladdin—A Musical Spectacular,** a 45-minute live performance with terrific visual effects. ■TIP➔ **Plan on getting in line about half an hour in advance: the show is well worth the wait.** On the latest film-inspired ride, **Monsters, Inc. Mike & Sulley to the Rescue,** you climb into taxis and travel the streets of Monstropolis on a mission of safely returning Boo to her bedroom. A major draw for older kids is the looming **Twilight Zone Tower of Terror,** which drops riders 13 floors.

A BUG'S LAND Inspired by the 1998 film *A Bug's Life,* this section skews its attractions to an insect's point of view. Kids can spin around in giant takeout Chinese food boxes on **Flik's Flyers,** and hit the bug-shape bumper cars on **Tuck and Roll's Drive Em Buggies.** The short show *It's Tough to Be a Bug!* gives you a 3-D look at insect life.

PARADISE PIER This section re-creates the glory days of California's seaside piers. If you're looking for thrills, the **California Screamin'** roller coaster takes its riders from 0 to 55 mph in about four seconds and proceeds through scream tunnels, steeply angled drops, and a 360-degree loop. **Goofy's Sky School** is a rollicking roller coast ride that goes up three stories and covers more than 1,200 feet of track. **Mickey's Fun Wheel,** a giant Ferris wheel, provides a good view of the grounds at a more leisurely pace. There's also carnival games, a fish-theme carousel, and Ariel's Grotto, where future princesses can dine with the mermaid and her friends (reservations a must).

CAR LANDS New in 2012, Cars Land offers Radiator Springs Racers, Luigi's Flying Tires, and Mater's Junkyard Jamboree. A new entrance leads to Buena Vista Street that recreates the Southern California of the 1920s that Walt Disney first encountered.

OTHER ATTRACTIONS

Downtown Disney. Downtown Disney is a 20-acre promenade of dining, shopping, and entertainment that connects the Disneyland Resort hotels and theme parks. Restaurant-nightclubs here include the **House of Blues,** which spices up its Delta-inspired ribs and seafood with various live music acts on an intimate two-story stage. At **Ralph Brennan's Jazz Kitchen** you can dig into New Orleans–style food and music. Sports fans gravitate to **ESPN Zone,** a sports bar–restaurant–entertainment center with American grill food, interactive video games, and 175 video screens telecasting worldwide sports events. There's also an **AMC** multiplex movie theater with stadium-style seating that plays the latest blockbusters and, naturally, a couple of kids' flicks. Promenade shops sell everything from Disney goods to antique jewelry; don't miss **Vault 28,** a hip boutique that sells one-of-kind vintage and couture clothes and accessories from Disney, Betsey Johnson, and other designers. ⊠ *Disneyland Dr., between Ball Rd. and Katella Ave., Anaheim* ☎ *714/300–7800* ⊕ *www.disneyland.com* 🎫 *Free* ☉ *Daily 7 am–2 am; hrs at shops and restaurants vary.*

WHERE TO EAT

$$$ ✕ **Anaheim White House.** Several small dining rooms are set with crisp linens and candles in this flower-filled 1909 mansion. The northern Italian menu includes steak, rack of lamb, and fresh seafood. Try the signature Ravioli Arragosta, lobster-filled pasta on a bed of ginger and citrus. A three-course prix-fixe low-calorie lunch, served weekdays, costs $23.

ITALIAN

Where to Eat and Stay in Anaheim

KEY
① *Hotels*
❶ *Restaurants*

$ *Average main: $26* ⊠ *887 S. Anaheim Blvd., Anaheim* ☎ *714/772–1381* ⊕ *www.anaheimwhitehouse.com* ⊘ *No lunch weekends.*

$$$
MEDITERRANEAN

✕ **Catal Restaurant & Uva Bar.** Famed chef Joachim Splichal of L.A.'s Patina empire takes a more relaxed approach at this bi-level Mediterranean spot—with tapas breaking into the finger-food territory. People-watch at the outdoor Uva (Spanish for "grape") bar on the ground level, where there are specialty cocktails and more than 40 wines by the glass. Upstairs, Catal's menu has tapas, a variety of paellas, and charcuterie. $ *Average main: $30* ⊠ *1580 S. Disneyland Dr., Suite 103, Anaheim* ☎ *714/774–4442* ⊕ *www.patinagroup.com.*

$$
ITALIAN

✕ **Luigi's D'Italia.** Despite the simple surroundings—red vinyl booths and plastic checkered tablecloths—Luigi's serves outstanding old-school Italian cuisine: spaghetti marinara, veal Parmesan, homemade pizza, and other classics. Kids will feel right at home here; there's even a children's menu. It's an easy five-minute drive from Disneyland, but less crowded and expensive than many restaurants adjacent to the park. $ *Average main: $17* ⊠ *801 S. State College Blvd., Anaheim* ☎ *714/490–0990* ⊕ *www.luigisditalia.net.*

$$$$
AMERICAN

✕ **Mr. Stox.** Intimate booths and linen tablecloths create a sophisticated, old-school setting at this family-owned restaurant. Prime rib, Maryland crab cakes, and fresh fish specials are excellent; the pasta, bread, and pastries are made in-house; and the wine list is wide-ranging. $ *Average* *main: $35* ✉ *1105 E. Katella Ave., Anaheim* ☎ *714/634–2994* ⊕ *www. mrstox.com* ⊙ *No lunch weekends.*

$$$$ ✕ **Napa Rose.** In sync with its host hotel, Disney's Grand Californian,
AMERICAN   this restaurant is done in a lovely Arts and Crafts style. The contempo-
★   rary cuisine here is matched with an extensive wine list (1,000 labels on
hand). For a look into the open kitchen, sit at the counter and watch the
chefs as they whip up signature dishes such as pan-roasted diver scallops
in a sauce of lemon, lobster, and vanilla and duck à l'orange topped with
a blood-orange-and- almond jus. The four-course, $90 prix-fixe menu
changes weekly; with wine pairings it's $135. ⑤ *Average main: $36*
✉ *Disney's Grand Californian Hotel, 1600 S. Disneyland Dr., Anaheim*
☎ *714/300–7170, 714/381–3463 Disney dining* ⊕ *disneyland.disney.
go.com/grand-californian-hotel/napa-rose/* ⚓ *Reservations essential.*

WHERE TO STAY
For expanded reviews, facilities, and current deals, visit Fodors.com.

$ ⊞ **The Anabella.** This Spanish Mission–style hotel on the convention cen-
HOTEL   ter campus is a good value. **Pros:** attentive service; landscaped grounds;
walk to Disney California Adventure. **Cons:** some say the room walls
are thin. **TripAdvisor:** "comfortable," "fantastic staff," "very convenient." ⑤ *Rooms from: $112* ✉ *1030 W. Katella Ave., Anaheim*
☎ *714/905–1050, 800/863–4888* ⊕ *www.anabellahotel.com* ⇲ *234
rooms, 124 suites* ⊙ *No meals.*

$$ ⊞ **Anaheim Fairfield Inn by Marriott.** Attentive service and proximity to
HOTEL   Disneyland (a 10-minute walk away) make this high-rise hotel a big
draw for families. **Pros:** all new decor in 2011; close to many restau-
rants; dicounted Park Hopper passes are available. **Cons:** small pool
abuts the parking lot; lack of green space. **TripAdvisor:** "great value
for families," "comfortable," "great location." ⑤ *Rooms from: $139*
✉ *1460 S. Harbor Blvd., Anaheim* ☎ *714/772–6777, 888/236–2427*
⊕ *www.marriott.com* ⇲ *467 rooms* ⊙ *No meals.*

$$ ⊞ **Candy Cane Inn.** One of the Disneyland area's first hotels (deeds were
HOTEL   executed Christmas Eve, hence the name), the Candy Cane is one of Ana-
★   heim's most relaxing properties. **Pros:** proximity to Disneyland; friendly
service; well-lighted, landscaped property. **Cons:** rooms and lobby are
on the small side; all rooms face parking lot. **TripAdvisor:** "excellent
location," "outstanding inn," "never fails to deliver." ⑤ *Rooms from:
$139* ✉ *1747 S. Harbor Blvd., Anaheim* ☎ *714/774–5284, 800/345–
7057* ⊕ *www.candycaneinn.net* ⇲ *171 rooms* ⊙ *Breakfast.*

$$$$ ⊞ **Disney's Grand Californian Hotel & Spa.** The most opulent of Disney's
RESORT   Anaheim hotels, this Craftsman-style luxury property has guest rooms
Fodor's Choice   with views of the California Adventure park and Downtown Disney.
★   **Pros:** large, gorgeous lobby; direct access to California Adventure.
Cons: the self-parking lot is across the street from the hotel; standard
rooms are on the small side. **TripAdvisor:** "exceptional all around,"
"so many perks," "great service." ⑤ *Rooms from: $316* ✉ *1600 S. Dis-
neyland Dr., Anaheim* ☎ *714/635–2300, 714/956–6425 reservations*
⊕ *www.disneyland.com* ⇲ *901 rooms, 44 suites, 50 villas* ⊙ *No meals.*

$$ ⊞ **Doubletree Guest Suites Anaheim Resort-Convention Center.** This upscale
HOTEL   hotel near the convention center caters to business travelers and fami-
★   lies alike. **Pros:** huge suites; elegant lobby; within walking distance of

a variety of restaurants. **Cons:** some say the hotel seems far-removed from Disneyland; pool area is small. **TripAdvisor:** "great location," "fabulous room," "home away from home." $ *Rooms from: $129* ✉ *2085 S. Harbor Blvd., Anaheim* ☎ *714/750–3000, 800/215–7316* ⤳ *50 rooms, 202 suites* ❄ *Breakfast.*

$$$
HOTEL

🖵 **Hilton Anaheim.** Next to the Anaheim Convention Center, this busy Hilton is one of the largest hotels in Southern California with a restaurant and food court, cocktail lounges, a full-service gym, and its own Starbucks. **Pros:** friendly efficient service; great seasonal kids' programs. **Cons:** huge size can be daunting; $16 fee to use health club. **TripAdvisor:** "very busy," "good service," "convenient for conventioneers." $ *Rooms from: $179* ✉ *777 Convention Way, Anaheim* ☎ *714/750–4321, 800/445–8667* ⊕ *www.anaheim.hilton.com* ⤳ *1,572 rooms, 93 suites* ❄ *No meals.*

$$
HOTEL

🖵 **Park Vue Inn.** This bougainvillea-trimmed two-story Spanish-style inn is one of the closest hotels you can find to Disneyland's main gate. **Pros:** easy walk to Disneyland and many restaurants; good value. **Cons:** all rooms face the parking lot; some complain about early-morning street noise. **TripAdvisor:** "fantastic location," "can't get closer to the Disneyland gate," "great place for our family vacation." $ *Rooms from: $146* ✉ *1570 S. Harbor Blvd., Anaheim* ☎ *714/772–3691, 800/334–7021* ⊕ *www.parkvueinn.com* ⤳ *76 rooms, 8 suites* ❄ *No meals.*

$$
HOTEL
★

🖵 **Sheraton Anaheim Hotel.** If you're hoping to escape from the commercial atmosphere of the hotels near Disneyland, consider this sprawling replica of a Tudor castle. **Pros:** large, attractive lobby; game room; spacious rooms with comfortable beds. **Cons:** confusing layout; hotel sits close to a busy freeway and is not within walking distance of Disneyland. **TripAdvisor:** "comfortable and clean," "outstanding start to finish," "all-around great experience." $ *Rooms from: $149* ✉ *900 S. Disneyland Dr., Anaheim* ☎ *714/778–1700, 866/716-8130* ⊕ *www.starwoodhotels.com* ⤳ *460 rooms, 29 suites* ❄ *No meals.*

SPORTS

Anaheim Ducks. The National Hockey League's Anaheim Ducks, winners of the 2007 Stanley Cup, play at Honda Center (formerly Arrowhead Pond). ☎ *714/704–2400* ⊕ *ducks.nhl.com.*

Los Angeles Angels of Anaheim. Pro baseball's Los Angeles Angels of Anaheim play at Angel Stadium of Anaheim. An "Outfield Extravaganza" celebrates great plays on the field, with fireworks and a geyser exploding over a model evoking the California coast. ☎ *714/940–2211* ⊕ *www.angelsbaseball.com.*

KNOTT'S BERRY FARM

25 miles south of Los Angeles, via I–5, in Buena Park.

☾
★

Knott's Berry Farm. The land where the boysenberry was invented (by crossing red raspberry, blackberry, and loganberry bushes) is now occupied by Knott's Berry Farm. In 1934 Cordelia Knott began serving chicken dinners on her wedding china to supplement her family's income. Or so the story goes. The dinners and her boysenberry pies proved more profitable than husband Walter's berry farm, so the two moved first into the restaurant business and then into the entertainment business. The park is now a 160-acre complex with 100-plus rides, dozens of restaurants and shops, and even a brick-by-brick replica of Philadelphia's Independence Hall. Although it has some good attractions for small children, the park is best known for its roster of awesome thrill rides. And, yes, you can still get that boysenberry pie (and jam, juice—you name it). ■ **TIP➔ If you think you'll only need a few hours at Knott's Berry Farm, you can save money by coming after 4 pm, when admission fees drop to $29. This deal is offered any day the park is open after 6.** ✉ *8039 Beach Blvd.* ✛ *Between La Palma Ave. and Crescent St., 2 blocks south of Hwy. 91* ☎ *714/220–5200* ⊕ *www.knotts. com* ✉ *$57.99; kids 3 years or older and under 48 inches tall $28.99.*

PARK NEIGHBORHOODS

THE
BOARDWALK

Not-for-the-squeamish thrill rides and skill-based games dominate the scene at the **boardwalk.** Go head over heels on the **Boomerang** roller coaster, then do it again—backward. The **Perilous Plunge,** once billed as the world's tallest, steepest, and—thanks to its big splash—wettest thrill ride, sends riders down an almost-vertical chute. The boardwalk is also home to a string of test-your-skill games that are fun to watch whether you're playing or not, and Johnny Rockets, the park's newest restaurant.

CAMP SNOOPY

It can get gridlocked on weekends, but small fry love this miniature High Sierra wonderland where the *Peanuts* gang hangs out. They can push and pump their own mini-mining cars on **Huff and Puff,** zip around a pint-size racetrack on **Charlie Brown Speedway,** and hop aboard **Woodstock's Airmail,** a kids' version of the park's Supreme Scream ride. Most of the rides here are geared toward kids only, leaving parents to cheer them on from the sidelines. **Sierra Sidewinder,** a roller coaster near the entrance of Camp Snoopy, is aimed at older children with spinning saucer-type vehicles that go a maximum speed of 37 mph.

FIESTA
VILLAGE

Over in **Fiesta Village** are three more musts for adrenaline junkies: **Montezooma's Revenge,** a roller coaster that goes from 0 to 55 mph in less than five seconds, and **Jaguar!,** which simulates the motions of a cat stalking its prey, twisting, spiraling, and speeding up and slowing down as it takes you on its stomach-dropping course. Windseeker, opened in 2011, whisks passengers on an unforgettable gondola ride 301 feet above the park. There's also **Hat Dance,** a version of the spinning teacups but with sombreros, and a 100-year-old Dentzel Carousel, complete with an antique organ and menagerie of hand-carved animals.

GHOST TOWN

Clusters of authentic old buildings relocated from their original mining-town sites mark this section of the park. You can stroll down the street, stop and chat with a blacksmith, pan for gold (for a fee), crack open a geode, check out the chalkboard of a circa-1875 schoolhouse, and ride an original Butterfield stagecoach. Looming over it all is **GhostRider,** Orange County's first wooden roller coaster. Traveling up to 56 mph and reaching 118 feet at its highest point, the park's biggest attraction is riddled with sudden dips and curves, subjecting riders to forces up to three times that of gravity. On the Western-theme **Silver Bullet,** riders are sent to a height of 146 feet and then back down 109 feet.

Riders spiral, corkscrew, fly into a cobra roll, and experience over-banked curves. The **Calico Mine** ride descends into a replica of a working gold mine. The **Timber Mountain Log Ride** is a worthwhile flume ride, especially if you're with kids who don't make the height requirements for the flumes at Disneyland. Also found here is the park's newest thrill ride, the **Pony Express,** a roller coaster that lets riders saddle up on packs of "horses" tethered to platforms that take off on a series of hairpin turns and travel up to 38 mph. Don't miss the **Western Trails Museum,** a dusty old gem full of Old West memorabilia, plus menus from the original chicken restaurant, and Mrs. Knott's antique button collection. **Calico Railroad** departs regularly from Ghost Town station for a round-trip tour of the park (bandit holdups notwithstanding).

This section is also home to **Big Foot Rapids,** a splash-fest of white-water river rafting over towering cliffs, cascading waterfalls, and wild rapids. Don't miss the visually stunning show at **Mystery Lodge,** which tells the story of Native Americans in the Pacific Northwest with lights, music, and beautiful images.

INDIAN LANDS   Celebrate Native American traditions through interactive exhibits like tepees and daily dance and storytelling performances.

Knott's Soak City Water Park is directly across from the main park on 13 acres next to Independence Hall. It has a dozen major water rides; the latest is **Pacific Spin,** an oversize waterslide that drops riders 75 feet into a catch pool. There's also a children's pool, 750,000-gallon wave pool, and funhouse. Soak City is open daily after Memorial Day; weekends only after Labor Day.

WHERE TO EAT AND STAY

$$ ✕ **Mrs. Knott's Chicken Dinner Restaurant.** Cordelia Knott's fried chicken
AMERICAN and boysenberry pies drew crowds so big that Knott's Berry Farm was built to keep the hungry customers occupied while they waited. The restaurant's current incarnation (outside the park's entrance) still serves crispy fried chicken, along with fluffy biscuits, corn, mashed potatoes, and Mrs. Knott's signature chilled cherry-rhubarb compote. The wait, unfortunately, can be an hour or more on weekends; another option is to order a bucket of the same tasty chicken from the adjacent takeout counter and have a picnic at the duck pond next to Independence Hall across the street. Jump start a visit to the park with a hearty breakfast here. ⑤ *Average main: $16* ⊠ *Knott's Berry Farm Marketplace Area, 8039 Beach Blvd.* ☎ *714/220–5055.*

$$$$ ✕ **Pirate's Dinner Adventure.** During this interactive pirate-theme dinner
AMERICAN show, 150 actors/singers/acrobats (some quite talented) perform on a galleon while you eat a three-course meal. Food—barbecue pork, roast chicken, salad, veggies, rice, and unlimited soda and coffee— is mediocre and seating is tight, but kids love making a lot of noise to cheer on their favorite pirate, and the action scenes are breathtaking. ■ TIP→ **Purchase tickets online for a discount.** ⑤ *Tickets: $58 per adult; $39 per child* ⊠ *7600 Beach Blvd., Buena Park* ☎ *866/439–2469* ⊕ *www.piratesdinneradventure.com.*

$$ 🏨 **Knott's Berry Farm Resort Hotel.** Knott's Berry Farm runs this conve-
RESORT nient high-rise hotel on park grounds. **Pros:** easy access to Knott's Berry

Farm; plenty of kids' activities; basketball court. **Cons:** lobby and hall-ways can be noisy and chaotic. **TripAdvisor:** "the kids loved it," "clean and convenient," "superb." ⑤ *Rooms from: $129* ✉ *7675 Crescent Ave.* ☎ *714/995–1111, 866/752–2444* ⊕ *www.knottshotel.com* ⟿ *320 rooms* ⦿ *No meals.*

THE COAST

Running along the Orange County coastline is scenic Pacific Coast Highway (Highway 1, known locally as the PCH). Older beachfront settlements, with their modest bungalow-style homes, are joined by posh new gated communities. The pricey land between Newport Beach and Laguna Beach is where Laker Kobe Bryant, novelist Dean Koontz, and a slew of Internet and finance moguls live.

Though the coastline is rapidly being filled in, there are still a few stretches of beautiful, protected open land. And at many places along the way you can catch an idealized glimpse of the Southern California lifestyle: surfers hitting the beach, boards under their arms.

LONG BEACH AND SAN PEDRO

About 25 miles southeast of Los Angeles, I–110 south.

EXPLORING

🅒 **Aquarium of the Pacific.** Sea lions, nurse sharks, and octopuses, oh my!—this aquarium focuses primarily on ocean life from the Pacific Ocean, with a detour into Australian birds. The main exhibits include lively sea lions, large tanks of various sharks and sting rays, and ethereal sea dragons, which the aquarium has successfully bred in captivity. Welcoming visitors to the aquarium's Great Hall is the multimedia attraction, *Penguins,* a panoramic film that captures the world of this endangered species. (Ask for show times at the information desk.) Be sure to say hello to newest resident Ollie, a sea otter rescued off the Santa Cruz coast as a baby in 2010. For a nonaquatic experience, head over to Lorikeet Forest, a walk-in aviary full of the friendliest parrots from down under. Buy a cup of nectar and smile as you become a human bird perch. If you're a true tropical animal lover, book an up-close-and-personal Animal Encounters Tour ($90) to learn about and assist in care and feeding of the animals; or find out how the aquarium functions with the extensive Behind the Scenes Tour ($38.95). Certi-fied divers can book a supervised dive in the aquarium's Tropical Reef Habitat ($299). ✉ *100 Aquarium Way, Long Beach* ☎ *562/590–3100* ⊕ *www.aquariumofpacific.org* ⊡ *$24.95* ⊙ *Daily 9–6.*

🅒 **Cabrillo Marine Aquarium.** Dedicated to the marine life that flourishes off the Southern California coast, this Frank Gehry–designed center gives an intimate and instructive look at local sea creatures. Head to the Exploration Center and S. Mark Taper Foundation Courtyard for kid-friendly interactive exhibits and activity stations. Especially fun is the "Crawl In" aquarium, where you can be surrounded by fish without getting wet. ■TIP➜ From March through July the aquarium organizes a legendary grunion program, when you can see the small, silvery fish as they

A mural at Huntington Beach

come ashore at night to spawn on the beach. After visiting the museum, you can stop for a picnic or beach stroll along Cabrillo Beach. ✉ *3720 Stephen M. White Dr., San Pedro* ☎ *310/548–7562* ⊕ *www.cabrilloaq. org* ✉ *$5 suggested donation, parking $1 per hr* ⊗ *Tues.–Fri. noon–5, weekends 10–5.*

🕲 **Queen Mary.** The reason to see this impressive example of 20th-century cruise ship opulence is because it's the last of its kind. And there's a saying among staff members that the more you get to know the *Queen Mary,* the more you realize she has an endearing personality to match her wealth of history.

The beautifully preserved ocean liner was launched in 1934 and made 1,001 transatlantic crossings before finally berthing in Long Beach in 1967. It has gone through many periods of renovations since, but in 1993, the RMS Foundation took over ownership and restored its original art-deco style. Delaware North Companies took over management in 2009 with plans to continue restoration and renovation of the ship.

On board, you can take one of 12 tours, such as the informative Behind the Scenes walk or the downright spooky Haunted Encounters tour. (Spirits have been spotted in the pool and engine room.) You could stay for dinner at one of the ship's restaurants, listen to live jazz in the original first-class lounge, or even spend the night in one of the wood-paneled cabins. The ship's neighbor, a geodesic dome originally built to house Howard Hughes's *Spruce Goose* aircraft, now serves as a terminal for Carnival Cruise Lines, making the *Queen Mary* the perfect pit stop before or after a cruise. And anchored next to the *Queen* is the *Scorpion,* a Russian submarine you can tour for a look at Cold War history. ✉ *1126 Queens Hwy., Long Beach* ☎ *877/342–0738* ⊕ *www. queenmary.com* ⌖ *Tours $24.95–$32.95, includes a self-guided audio tour* ⊙ *Call for times and frequency of guided tours.*

HUNTINGTON BEACH

40 miles southeast of Los Angeles, I–5 south to I–605 south to I–405 south to Beach Blvd.

Once a sleepy residential town with little more than a string of rugged surf shops, Huntington Beach has transformed itself into a resort destination. The town's appeal is its broad white-sand beaches with often-towering waves, complemented by a lively pier, shops, and restaurants on Main Street and a growing collection of resort hotels.

A draw for sports fans and partiers of all stripes is the U.S. Open professional surf competition, which brings a festive atmosphere to town annually in late July. There's even a Surfing Walk of Fame, with plaques set in the sidewalk around the intersection of PCH and Main Street.

ESSENTIALS

Huntington Beach Marketing and Visitors Bureau ✉ *301 Main St., Suite 208* ☎ *714/969–3492, 800/729–6232* ⊕ *www.surfcityusa.com.*

EXPLORING

★ **Bolsa Chica Ecological Reserve.** Wildlife lovers and bird-watchers flock to Bolsa Chica Ecological Reserve, which has a 1,180-acre salt marsh where 321 out of Orange County's 420 bird species—including great blue herons, snowy and great egrets, and brown pelicans—have been spotted in the past decade. Throughout the reserve are trails for bird-watching, including a comfortable 1½-mile loop. Free guided tours depart from the walking bridge on the second Saturday of each month at 10 am. ✉ *Off PCH, 1 mile south of Warner Ave., opposite Bolsa Chica State Beach at traffic light* ☎ *714/846–1114* ⊕ *www.bolsachica. org* ⌖ *Free* ⊙ *Daily dawn–dusk.*

Huntington Pier. This pier stretches 1,800 feet out to sea, well past the powerful waves that made Huntington Beach reach for the title of "Surf City U.S.A." A farmers' market is held on Friday; an informal arts fair sets up most weekends.

NEED A BREAK?

Ruby's. At the end of the Huntington Pier sits this restaurant, part of a California chain of 1940s-style burger joints ☎ *714/969–7829* ⊕ *www.rubys. com*

International Surfing Museum. Just up Main Street from the pier, the International Surfing Museum pays tribute to the sport's greats with the Surfing Hall of Fame, which has an impressive collection of surfboards and related memorabilia. They've even got the Bolex camera used to shoot the 1966 surfing documentary *The Endless Summer.* ✉ *411 Olive St.* ☎ *714/960–3483* ⊕ *www.surfingmuseum.org* ⌖ *Free, donations accepted* ⊙ *Weekdays noon–5, Tuesdays until 9, weekends 11–6.*

The Orange County Coast

5 mi

5 km

Riding the waves at Newport Beach

WHERE TO EAT

$$$
SEAFOOD

✕ **Duke's.** Oceanfront vistas and fresh-caught seafood reign supreme at this homage to surfing legend Duke Kahanamoku, which is a prime people-watching spot right at the beginning of the pier. Choose from several fish-of-the-day selections—many Hawaiian—prepared in one of five ways. Or try the crispy coconut shrimp or tuna tacos with Maui onions. Duke's mai tai is not to be missed. ⑤ *Average main: $24* ✉ *317 PCH* ☎ *714/374–6446* ⊕ *www.dukeshuntington.com.*

$$
AMERICAN

✕ **Lou's Red Oak BBQ.** You won't find any frills at Lou's Red Oak BBQ—just barbecue pork, grilled linguica, rotisserie chicken, and a lot of beef. Try the tri-tip (either as an entrée or on a toasted bun smothered with traditional Santa Maria–style salsa) or a Hawaiian teriyaki plate to get into the surfing spirit. ⑤ *Average main: $15* ✉ *21501 Brookhurst St.* ☎ *714/965–5200* ⊕ *www.lousbbq.com.*

SPORTS AND THE OUTDOORS

BEACHES

Bolsa Chica State Beach. At the northern section of the city, Bolsa Chica State Beach has barbecue pits and RV campsites and is usually less crowded than its southern neighbors. **Amenities:** food and drink; lifeguards; parking; showers; toilets. **Best for:** sunset; surfing; swimming; walking. ✉ *Off PCH, between Seapoint St. and Warner Ave.* ☎ *714/846–3460* ⊕ *www.parks.ca.gov/?page_id=642* ✑ *$15 parking.*

Huntington City Beach. Stretching for 3 miles north and south of the pier from Bolsa Chica State Beach to Huntington State Beach on the south, Huntington City Beach is most crowded around the pier; amateur and professional surfers brave the waves daily on its north side. **Amenities:**

food and drink; lifeguards; parking; showers; toilets. **Best for:** sunset; surfing; swimming; walking. ⊠ *PCH, from Beach Blvd. to Seapoint St.* ☎ *714/536–5281* ⊕ *www.ci.huntington-beach.ca.us* ◨ *Parking $15 ($17 weekends/holidays).*

Huntington State Beach. As you continue south, Huntington State Beach parallels Pacific Coast Highway. On the state and city beaches there are changing rooms, concessions, lifeguards, Wi-Fi, and ample parking; the state beach also has fire pits for bonfires. A 6 mile bike path connects Huntington State Beach to the city beach and Bolsa Chica to the north. **Amenities:** food and drink; lifeguards; parking; showers; toilets. **Best for:** sunset; surfing; swimming; walking. ⊠ *PCH, from Beach Blvd. south to Santa Ana River* ☎ *714/536–1454* ⊕ *www.parks.ca.gov* ◨ *$15 parking.*

SURFING

Corky Carroll's Surf School. This surf school organizes lessons, weeklong workshops, and surfing trips. ☎ *714/969–3959* ⊕ *www.surfschool.net.*

Dwight's. You can rent surf- or boogie boards at Dwight's, one block south of the pier. ⊠ *201 PCH* ☎ *714/536–8083.*

NEWPORT BEACH

6 miles south of Huntington Beach, PCH.

Newport Beach has evolved from a simple seaside village to an icon of chic coastal living. Its ritzy reputation comes from megayachts bobbing in the harbor, boutiques that rival those in Beverly Hills, and spectacular homes overlooking the ocean.

Newport is said to have the highest per-capita number of Mercedes-Benzes in the world; inland Newport Beach's concentration of high-rise office buildings, shopping centers, and luxury hotels drive the economy. But on the city's Balboa Peninsula, you can still catch a glimpse of a more innocent, down-to-earth beach town scattered with taco spots, tackle shops, and sailor bars.

ESSENTIALS

Visitor and Tour Information Visit Newport Beach Inc. ⊠ *1600 Newport Center Dr., Suite 120* ☎ *949/719–6100, 800/942–6278* ⊕ *www. visitnewportbeach.com.*

EXPLORING

Balboa Island. This sliver of terra firma in Newport Harbor boasts quaint streets tightly packed with impossibly charming multimillion-dollar cottages. The island's main drag, Marine Avenue, is lined with equally picturesque cafés and shops.

Basilic. This intimate French-Swiss bistro adds a touch of elegance to the island with its white linen and flower-topped tables. Head here for charcuterie, steak au poivre, and a fine Bordeaux. ⊠ *217 Marine Ave.* ☎ *949/673–0570* ⊕ *www.basilicrestaurant.com*

Olive Oil & Beyond. At Olive Oil & Beyond, you can sample and purchase premium oils from around the globe. There's also a lineup of unique balsamic vinegars—some flavored with fig or tangerine—and other gourmet goodies. ⊠ *210 Marine Ave.* ☎ *949/566–9380* ⊕ *www. oliveoilandbeyond.com*

Sugar & Spice. Stop by ice cream parlor Sugar & Spice for a Balboa Bar—a slab of vanilla ice cream dipped first in chocolate and then in a topping of your choice such as hard candy or Oreo crumbs. Other parlors serve the concoction, but Sugar & Spice claims to have invented it back in 1945. ⊠ *310 Marine Ave., Balboa Island* ☎ *949/673–8907*

Balboa Pavilion. Located on the bay side of the peninsula, the Balboa Pavilion was built in 1905 as a bath- and boathouse. Today it is home to a restaurant and shops; it also serves as a departure point for harbor- and whale-watching cruises. Look for it on Main Street, off Balboa Boulevard. Adjacent to the pavilion is the three-car ferry that connects the peninsula to Balboa Island. In the blocks around the pavilion you can find restaurants, beachside shops, and the small **Fun Zone**—a local kiddie hangout with a Ferris wheel and a nautical museum. On the other side of the narrow peninsula is **Balboa Pier.** On its end is the original branch of Ruby's, a 1940s-esque burger-and-shake joint.

Balboa Peninsula. Newport's best beaches are on Balboa Peninsula, where many jetties pave the way to ideal swimming areas. The most intense bodysurfing place in Orange County and arguably on the West Coast, known as the **Wedge,** is at the south end of the peninsula. Created by accident in the 1930s when the Federal Works Progress Administration built a jetty to protect Newport Harbor, the break is pure euphoria for highly skilled bodysurfers. ■**TIP→** Since the waves generally break very close to shore and rip currents are strong, lifeguards strongly discourage visitors from attempting it—but it sure is fun to watch an experienced local ride it.

Fashion Island. Shake the sand out of your shoes to head inland to the ritzy Fashion Island outdoor mall, a cluster of arcades and courtyards complete with koi pond, fountains, and a Venetian-style carousel—plus some awesome ocean views. It has the luxe department store Neiman Marcus and expensive spots like L'Occitane, Kate Spade, Ligne Roset, and Michael Stars. Chains, restaurants, and the requisite movie theater fill out the rest. ⊠ *410 Newport Center Dr., between Jamboree and MacArthur Blvds., off PCH* ☎ *949/721–2000* ⊕ *www. shopfashionisland.com.*

★ **Newport Harbor.** Newport Harbor, which shelters nearly 10,000 small boats, may seduce even those who don't own a yacht. Spend an afternoon exploring the charming avenues and surrounding alleys. Within Newport Harbor are eight small islands, including Balboa and Lido. The houses framing the shore may seem modest, but this is some of the most expensive real estate in the world. Several grassy areas on primarily residential Lido Isle have views of Newport Harbor.

Newport Harbor Nautical Museum. The Newport Harbor Nautical Museum, in the Balboa Fun Zone (a small, historic amusement park), has exhibits on the history of the harbor as well as of the Pacific as a whole. There's a fleet of ship models, some dating to 1798; one is made entirely of gold and silver. Another fun display is a touch tank holding local sea creatures. A new exhibit features simulated and submersion experiences through live feeds from underwater archaeological sites and a replicated yacht race. ✉ *600 E. Bay Ave.* ☎ *949/675–8915* ⊕ *www. nhnm.org* ☜ *$4* ⊗ *Call for hours.*

★ **Orange County Museum of Art.** The Orange County Museum of Art gathers a collection of modernist paintings and sculpture by California artists and cutting-edge, international contemporary works. Works by such key California artists as Richard Diebenkorn, Ed Ruscha, Robert Irwin, and Chris Burden are included in the collection. The museum also displays some of its digital art, Internet-based art, and sound works in the Orange Lounge, a satellite gallery at South Coast Plaza; free of charge, it's open the same hours as the mall. ✉ *850 San Clemente Dr.* ☎ *949/759–1122* ⊕ *www.ocma.net* ☜ *$12* ⊗ *Wed. and Fri.–Sun. 11–5, Thurs. 11–8.*

WHERE TO EAT

$$$

AMERICAN

✕ **3-Thirty-3.** If there's a nightlife "scene" to be had in Newport Beach, this is it. This swank and stylish eatery attracts a convivial crowd—both young and old—for midday, sunset, and late-night dining; a long list of small, shareable plates heightens the camaraderie. Pair a cocktail with Chinese-spiced lollipop lamb chops or chicken satay while you check out the scene, or settle in for a dinner of Kobe flatiron steak or potato-crusted halibut. ⑤ *Average main: $25* ✉ *333 Bayside Dr.* ☎ *949/673–8464* ⊕ *www.3thirty3nb.com.*

$$$$

SEAFOOD

✕ **The Cannery.** This 1920s cannery building still teems with fish, but now they go into dishes on the eclectic Pacific Rim menu rather than being packed into crates. Settle in at the sushi bar, dining room, or patio before choosing between sashimi, bouillabaisse, or pan-seared Chilean sea bass topped with a lively citrus beurre blanc. The menu includes a selection of steaks, ribs, and seafood. Fodor's readers recommend the crème brûlée for dessert. ⑤ *Average main: $35* ✉ *3010 Lafayette Rd.* ☎ *949/566–0060* ⊕ *www.cannerynewport.com.*

WHERE TO STAY

For expanded reviews, facilities, and current deals, visit Fodors.com.

$$$

RESORT

⊞ **Balboa Bay Club and Resort.** Sharing the same frontage as the private Balboa Bay Club where Humphrey Bogart, Lauren Bacall, and the Reagans hung out, this hotel has one of the best bay views around. **Pros:** exquisite bayfront views; comfortable beds; romantic. **Cons:** service is helpful but can be slow; not much within walking distance. **Trip-Advisor:** "your boat has come in," "full service," "lovely." ⑤ *Rooms from: $249* ✉ *1221 W. Coast Hwy.* ☎ *949/645–5000, 888/445–7153* ⊕ *www.balboabayclub.com* ⇆ *150 rooms, 10 suites* ⦿ *No meals.*

$$$$

HOTEL

⊞ **The Island Hotel.** A suitably stylish hotel in a very chic neighborhood (it's across the street from the Fashion Island shopping center), this 20-story tower caters to luxury seekers by offering weekend golf packages in conjunction with the nearby Pelican Hill golf course. **Pros:** proximity to Fashion Island; 24-hour exercise facilities; first-class spa. **Cons:** steep valet parking prices; some rooms have views of mall; pricey. **Trip-Advisor:** "pleasant stay," "loved the location," "great views." ⑤ *Rooms from: $440* ✉ *690 Newport Center Dr.* ☎ *949/759–0808, 866/554–4620* ⊕ *www.theislandhotel.com* ⇆ *295 rooms, 83 suites* ⦿ *No meals.*

SPORTS AND THE OUTDOORS
BOAT RENTALS
Balboa Boat Rentals. You can tour Lido and Balboa isles by renting kayaks ($15 an hour), sailboats ($45 an hour), small motorboats ($75 an hour), and electric boats ($75–$90 an hour) at Balboa Boat Rentals. You must have a driver's license, and some knowledge of boating is helpful; rented boats must stay in the bay. ⊠ *510 E. Edgewater Ave.* ☎ *949/673–7200* ⊕ *www.boats4rent.com.*

BOAT TOURS
Catalina Flyer. The Catalina Flyer, at the Balboa Pavilion, operates a 90-minute daily round-trip passage to Catalina Island for $69. Reservations are required. ⊠ *400 Main St.* ☎ *800/830–7744 Reservations* ⊕ *www.catalinainfo.com.*

Hornblower Cruises & Events. This operator books three-hour weekend dinner cruises with dancing for $82; the two-hour Sunday brunch cruise is $61. ⊠ *2431 West Coast Hwy.* ☎ *949/650–2412, 888/467–6256* ⊕ *www.hornblower.com.*

GOLF
Newport Beach Golf Course. An 18-hole executive course, Newport Beach Golf Course is also lighted for night play. Rates start at $20 (Monday through Thursday and twilight). Reservations are accepted up to one week in advance, but walk-ins are accommodated when possible. ⊠ *3100 Irvine Ave.* ☎ *949/852–8681* ⊕ *www.npbgolf.com.*

SPORTFISHING
Davey's Locker. In addition to a complete tackle shop, Davey's Locker operates sportfishing trips starting at $46.50 (half day), as well as private charters and whale-watching trips for $36. ⊠ *Balboa Pavilion, 400 Main St.* ☎ *949/673–1434* ⊕ *www.daveyslocker.com.*

CORONA DEL MAR

2 miles south of Newport Beach, via PCH.

A small jewel on the Pacific Coast, Corona del Mar (known by locals as "CDM") has exceptional beaches that some say resemble their majestic Northern California counterparts. South of CDM is an area referred to as the Newport Coast or Crystal Cove—whatever you call it, it's another dazzling spot on the California Riviera.

ESSENTIALS
Visitor and Tour Information Visit Newport Beach Inc. ⊠ *1600 Newport Center Dr., Suite 120, Newport Beach* ☎ *949/719–6100, 800/942–6278* ⊕ *www. visitnewportbeach.com.*

EXPLORING
Corona del Mar State Beach. This beach is actually made up of two beaches, Little Corona and Big Corona, separated by a cliff. Facilities include fire pits and volleyball courts. ■ **TIP→ Two colorful reefs (and the fact that it's off-limits to boats) make Corona del Mar great for snorkelers and for beachcombers who prefer privacy.** Parking in the lot is a steep $15, $25 on holidays, but you can often find a spot on the street on weekdays. **Amenities:** food and drink; lifeguards; parking; showers;

A whimbrel hunts for mussels at Crystal Cove State Park.

toilets. **Best for:** snorkeling; sunset; swimming. ✉ *Iris St. and Ocean Blvd.* ☎ *949/644–3151* ⊕ *www.parks.ca.gov.*

Crystal Cove Promenade. Further adding to Orange County's overwhelming supply of high-end shopping and dining is Crystal Cove Promenade, which might be described as the toniest strip mall in America. The storefronts of this Mediterranean–inspired center are lined up across the street from Crystal Cove State Park, with the shimmering Pacific waters in plain view. There is plenty of sidewalk and courtyard seating at this center that is both a regional destination and dog-friendly neighborhood hangout for the lucky locals. ✉ *7772–8112 E. Coast Hwy.* ⊕ *crystalcove.com/beach-living/shopping.*

Fodor's Choice
★

Crystal Cove State Park. Midway between Corona del Mar and Laguna, stretching along both sides of Pacific Coast Highway, Crystal Cove State Park is a favorite of local beachgoers and wilderness trekkers. It encompasses a 3.2-mile stretch of unspoiled beach and has some of the best tide-pooling in Southern California. Here you can see starfish, crabs, and other sea life on the rocks. The park's 2,400 acres of back-country are ideal for hiking, horseback riding, and mountain biking, but stay on the trails to preserve the beauty. Hike-in, backcountry camping is allowed in one of the three campgrounds. Bring water, food, and other supplies; there's a pit toilet but no shower. Open fires and pets are forbidden. **Crystal Cove Historic District** holds a collection of 46 handmade historic cottages (22 of which are available for overnight rental), decorated and furnished to reflect the 1935–55 beach culture that flourished here. On the sand above the high tide line and on a bluff above the beach, the cottages offer a funky look at beach life 50 years

Looking for shells on Laguna Beach, one of the nicest stretches of sand in Southern California

ago. Reservations are essential for cottage overnight stays. ☎ 949/494–3539, 800/444–7275 Reserve America ⊕ www.crystalcovestatepark.com ✉ $15 parking ☉ Daily 6–dusk.

NEED A BREAK? **Bluefin.** Stop in here for the area's most renowned sushi bar. ✉ *7952 E. Coast Hwy.* ☎ *949/715–7373* ⊕ *www.bluefinbyabe.com*

LAGUNA BEACH

Fodor's Choice ★ *10 miles south of Newport Beach on PCH, 60 miles south of Los Angeles, I–5 south to Hwy. 133, which turns into Laguna Canyon Rd.*

Even the approach tells you that Laguna Beach is exceptional. Driving in along Laguna Canyon Road from the Interstate 405 freeway gives you the chance to cruise through a gorgeous coastal canyon, large stretches of which remain undeveloped. You'll arrive at a glistening wedge of ocean, at the intersection with PCH.

Laguna's welcome mat is legendary. For decades in the mid-20th century a local booster, Eiler Larsen, greeted everyone downtown. (There's now a statue of him on the main drag.) On the corner of Forest and Park avenues you can see a 1930s gate proclaiming, "This gate hangs well and hinders none, refresh and rest, then travel on." A gay community has long been established here; until relatively recently, this was quite the exception in conservative Orange County. The Hare Krishnas have a temple where they host a Sunday vegetarian feast, environmentalists rally, artists continue to gravitate here—there seems to be room for everyone.

There's a definite creative slant to this tight-knit community. The California plein air art movement coalesced here in the early 1900s; by 1932 an annual arts festival was established. Art galleries now dot the village streets, and there's usually someone daubing up in Heisler Park, overlooking the beach. The town's main street, Pacific Coast Highway, is referred to as either South Coast or North Coast Highway, depending on the address. From this waterfront, the streets slope up steeply to the residential areas. All along the highway and side streets, you'll find dozens of fine art and crafts galleries, clothing boutiques, jewelry shops, and cafés.

ESSENTIALS

Visitor and Tour Information Laguna Beach Visitors Center ⊠ *381 Forest Ave.* ☎ *949/497-9229, 800/877-1115* ⊕ *www.lagunabeachinfo.com.*

EXPLORING

Laguna Art Museum. The Laguna Art Museum displays American art, with an emphasis on California artists from all periods. Special exhibits change quarterly. ■**TIP→ The museum, along with galleries throughout the city, stays open until 9 for Art Walk on the first Thursday of each month** (⊕ *www.firstthursdaysartwalk.com*). A free shuttle service runs from the museum to galleries and studios (except in July and August). ⊠ *307 Cliff Dr.* ☎ *949/494-8971* ⊕ *www.lagunaartmuseum.org* ⊡ *$7* ☉ *Fri.– Tues. 11–5, Thurs. 11–9; closed Wed.*

Main Beach Park. Laguna's central beach gives you a perfect slice of local life. A stocky 1920s lifeguard tower marks Main Beach Park, at the end of Broadway at South Coast Highway. A wooden boardwalk separates the sand from a strip of lawn. Walk along this, or hang out on one of its benches, to watch people bodysurfing, playing sand volleyball, or scrambling around one of two half-basketball courts. The beach also has children's play equipment, picnic areas, restrooms, and showers. Across the street is a historic Spanish Renaissance movie theater.

WHERE TO EAT

$$
VEGETARIAN

✕ **Café Zinc & Market.** Families flock to this small Laguna Beach institution for well-priced breakfast and lunch. Try the signature quiches or poached egg dishes in the morning, or swing by later in the day for healthy salads, quesadillas, lasagna, or one of their pizzettes. The café also has great artisanal cheese and gourmet goodies to go, and your four-legged friends are welcome in the outdoor patio area. Dinner is served Wednesday through Sunday in summer. ⑤ *Average main: $12* ⊠ *350 Ocean Ave.* ☎ *949/494-6302* ⊕ *www.zinccafe.com.*

$$$$
AMERICAN
★

✕ **Studio.** In a nod to Laguna's art history, Studio has food that entices the eye as well as the palate. You can't beat the location, on a 50-foot bluff overlooking the Pacific Ocean—every table has an ocean view. And because the restaurant occupies its own Craftsman-style bungalow, it doesn't feel like a hotel dining room. Under the deft direction of Chef Craig Strong, the menu changes seasonally to reflect the finest seafood and the freshest local ingredients on hand. You might begin with Kumamoto oysters or hamachi sashimi with edible flowers before moving on to lamb rib eye or sous-vide wild Alaskan salmon. The wine list here is bursting, with nearly 2,500 labels. $ *Average main: $58* ⊠ *Montage Laguna Beach, 30801 S. Coast Hwy.* ☎ *949/715–6420* ⊕ *www. studiolagunabeach.com* ⚓ *Reservations essential* ⊘ *Closed Mon. No lunch.*

WHERE TO STAY

For expanded reviews, facilities, and current deals, visit Fodors.com.

$$$
HOTEL
★

⛭ **La Casa del Camino.** This historic Spanish-style hotel opened in 1929 and was once a favorite of Hollywood stars. **Pros:** breathtaking views from rooftop lounge; personable service; close to beach. **Cons:** some rooms front traffic-filled highway; frequent on-site events can make hotel busy and noisy. **TripAdvisor:** "quirky and quaint," "lovely old-world charm," "a great beach getaway." $ *Rooms from: $189* ⊠ *1289 S. Coast Hwy.* ☎ *949/497–2446, 888/367–5232* ⊕ *www. lacasadelcamino.com* ⟿ *26 rooms, 10 suites* ❙○❙ *No meals.*

$$$$
RESORT
Fodor'sChoice
★

⛭ **Montage Laguna Beach.** Laguna's connection to the Californian plein air artists is mined for inspiration at this head-turning, lavish hotel. **Pros:** top-notch service; idyllic coastal location; special programs for all interests, from art to marine biology. **Cons:** pricey; food inconsistent given the prices. **TripAdvisor:** "pamper yourself," "truly first class," "beautiful property with exceptional service." $ *Rooms from: $395* ⊠ *30801 S. Coast Hwy.* ☎ *949/715–6000, 888/715–6700* ⊕ *www. montagelagunabeach.com* ⟿ *190 rooms, 60 suites* ❙○❙ *No meals.*

$$$$
RESORT
★

⛭ **Surf & Sand Resort.** One mile south of downtown, this Laguna Beach property has been made over and is now even more fantastic than longtime locals remember. **Pros:** easy beach access; intimate property; central location slightly removed from Main Street crowds. **Cons:** $30 valet parking; surf is quite loud. **TripAdvisor:** "just beautiful," "a relaxing getaway," "wonderful ocean views." $ *Rooms from: $395* ⊠ *1555 S. Coast Hwy.* ☎ *949/497–4477, 888/869–7569* ⊕ *www. surfandsandresort.com* ⟿ *155 rooms, 13 suites* ❙○❙ *No meals.*

NIGHTLIFE AND THE ARTS

Laguna Playhouse. Dating to the 1920s, the Laguna Playhouse mounts a variety of productions, from classics to youth-oriented plays. ⊠ *606 Laguna Canyon Rd.* ☎ *949/497–2787* ⊕ *www.lagunaplayhouse.com.*

SPORTS AND THE OUTDOORS

BEACHES

There is a handful of lovely beaches around town besides the Main Beach.

1,000 Steps Beach. Off South Coast Highway at 9th Street, 1,000 Steps Beach is a hard-to-find locals' spot with great waves. There aren't really 1,000 steps down (but when you hike back up, it'll certainly feel like it). **Amenities:** parking. **Best for:** sunset; surfing; swimming. ⊠ *South Coast Hwy. at 9th St.*

Wood's Cove. Wood's Cove, off South Coast Highway at Diamond Street, is especially quiet during the week. Big rock formations hide lurking crabs. Climbing the steps to leave, you can see a Tudor-style mansion that was once the home of Bette Davis. Parking—on the street—is limited. This is a prime scuba diving spot. **Amenities:** none. **Best for:** snorkeling; sunset. ⊠ *Diamond St. and Ocean Way.*

HIKING

Laguna Coast Wilderness Park. The Laguna Coast Wilderness Park is spread over 19 acres of fragile coastal territory, including the canyon. The trails are great for hiking and mountain biking and are open daily, weather permitting. Docent-led hikes are given regularly; call for information. ☎ *949/923–2235* ⊕ *www.lagunacanyon.org* ⚏ *$3 Parking.*

WATER SPORTS

Hobie Sports. Because its entire beach area is a marine preserve, Laguna Beach is ideal for snorkelers. Scuba divers should head to the Marine Life Refuge area, which runs from Seal Rock to Diver's Cove. Rent bodyboards at Hobie Sports. ⊠ *294 Forest Ave.* ☎ *949/497–3304* ⊕ *www.hobiesurfshop.com.*

DANA POINT

10 miles south of Laguna Beach, via PCH.

Dana Point's claim to fame is its small-boat marina tucked into a dramatic natural harbor and surrounded by high bluffs.

ESSENTIALS

Visitor and Tour Information Dana Point Chamber of Commerce. The Dana Point Chamber of Commerce offers a useful visitor's guide. ☎ 949/496–1555 ⊕ www.danapointchamber.com.

EXPLORING

Dana Point Harbor. Dana Point Harbor was first described more than 100 years ago by its namesake, Richard Henry Dana, in his book *Two Years Before the Mast.* At the marina are docks for private boats and yachts, marine-oriented shops, restaurants, and boat and bike rentals. ☎ *949/923–2255* ⊕ *www.danapointharbor.com.*

Dana Point Festival of Whales. In early March the Dana Point Festival of Whales celebrates the passing gray whale migration with concerts, 40-foot-long balloon whales on parade, films, sports competitions, and a weekend street fair. ☎ *949/496–1045, 888/440–4309* ⊕ *www. festivalofwhales.org*

Doheny State Beach. At the south end of Dana Point, Doheny State Beach is one of Southern California's top surfing destinations, but there's a lot more to do within this 61-acre area. Divers and anglers hang out at the beach's western end, and during low tide, the tide pools beckon both young and old. You'll also find five indoor tanks and an interpretive center devoted to the wildlife of the Doheny Marine Refuge. There are food stands and shops, picnic facilities, volleyball courts, and a pier for fishing. The beachfront campground here is one of the most popular in the state with 120 no-hookup sites that rent for $35 (inland) or $60 (beachfront) per night; reservations, made through Reserve America, are essential. ■TIP➔ Be aware that the waters here periodically do not meet health standards established by California (warning signs are posted if that's the case). **Amenities:** food and drink; lifeguards; parking; showers; toilets. **Best for:** partiers; sunset; surfing; swimming; walking. ☎ 949/496–6172, 714/433–6400 *water quality information,* 800/444–7275 *Reserve America* ⊕ *www.dohenystatebeach.org* ⊨ *$15 parking.*

WHERE TO EAT

$$
ITALIAN

✕ **Luciana's Ristorante.** This intimate family-owned eatery serves simply prepared, tasty Italian food. Try one of the homemade soups or gnocchi classico—Grandma's homemade potato dumplings with marinara sauce. If you don't have a reservation, be prepared to wait at the bar with a glass of one of the many reasonably priced Italian wines, chatting with the predominantly local clientele. $ *Average main: $18* ☒ *24312 Del Prado Ave.* ☎ *949/661–6500* ⊕ *www.lucianas.com* ☾ *No lunch.*

$$
AMERICAN

✕ **Wind & Sea.** An unblocked marina view makes this a particularly great place for lunch or a sunset dinner. The Sunday breakfast buffet is good value at $15 per person. Among the entrées, the macadamia-crusted mahimahi and the grilled teriyaki shrimp stand out. On warm days, patio tables beckon you outside, and looking out on the Pacific might put you in the mood for a retro cocktail like a mai tai. $ *Average main: $22* ☒ *34699 Golden Lantern St.* ☎ *949/496–6500* ⊕ *www.windandsearestaurants.com.*

WHERE TO STAY

For expanded reviews, facilities, and current deals, visit Fodors.com.

$$
B&B/INN
★

⌂ **Blue Lantern Inn.** Combining New England–style architecture with a Southern California setting, this white-clapboard B&B rests on a bluff overlooking the harbor and ocean. **Pros:** gas fireplaces; amazing harbor views from Room 304; afternoon wine and cheese; breakfast buffet. **Cons:** nearby restaurant can be noisy; understaffed compared to larger resorts. **TripAdvisor:** "lovely setting for a getaway," "what wonderful amenities," "great rooms." $ *Rooms from: $230* ☒ *34343 St. of the Blue Lantern* ☎ *949/661–1304, 800/950–1236* ⊕ *www.bluelanterninn. com* ⌁ *29 rooms* ⦿ *Breakfast.*

$$$$
RESORT
Fodor's Choice
★

⌂ **Ritz-Carlton, Laguna Niguel.** Take Ritz-Carlton's top-tier level of service coupled with an unparalleled view of the Pacific and you're in the lap of complete luxury at this oceanside resort. **Pros:** beautiful grounds and views; luxurious bedding; seamless service. **Cons:** some rooms are small for the price; culinary program has room to grow. **TripAdvisor:** "luxury as standard," "Ritz Carlton at its finest," "excellent staff." $ *Rooms from: $425* ☒ *1 Ritz-Carlton Dr.* ☎ *949/240–2000, 800/241–3333* ⊕ *www.ritzcarlton.com* ⌁ *367 rooms, 29 suites* ⦿ *No meals.*

SPORTS AND THE OUTDOORS

Rental stands for surfboards, windsurfers, small powerboats, and sailboats can be found near most of the piers.

Capt. Dave's Dolphin & Whale Safari. You have a good chance of getting a water's-eye view of resident dolphins and migrating whales if you take one of these tours on a 35-foot catamaran. Dave, a marine naturalist–filmmaker, and his wife run the safaris year-round. The endangered blue whale is sometimes seen in summer. Reservations are required for

3

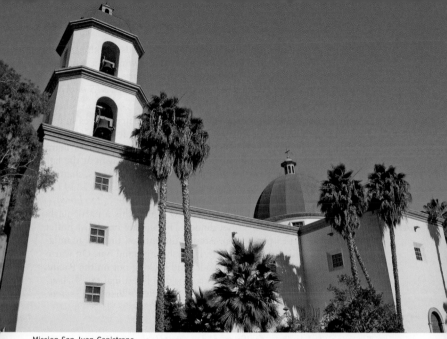
Mission San Juan Capistrano

the safaris, which last 2½ hours and cost $55. ⊠ *24440 Dana Point Harbor Dr.* ☏ *949/488–2828* ⊕ *www.dolphinsafari.com.*

Dana Wharf Sportfishing & Whale Watching. Charters and whale-watching excursions are offered by Dana Wharf Sportfishing & Whale Watching from early November to late April. Tickets cost $29; reservations are required. ⊠ *34675 Golden Lantern St.* ☏ *949/496–5794* ⊕ *www. danawharf.com.*

SAN JUAN CAPISTRANO

5 miles north of Dana Point, Hwy. 74, 60 miles north of San Diego, I–5.

San Juan Capistrano is best known for its historic mission, where the swallows traditionally return each year, migrating from their winter haven in Argentina, but these days they are more likely to choose other local sites for nesting. St. Joseph's Day, March 19, launches a week of fowl festivities. After summering in the arches of the old stone church, the swallows head south on St. John's Day, October 23. Charming antiques stores, which range from pricey to cheap, line Camino Capistrano.

If you arrive by train, which is far more romantic and restful than battling freeway traffic, you'll be dropped off across from the mission at the San Juan Capistrano depot. With its appealing brick café and preserved Santa Fe cars, the depot retains much of the magic of early American railroads. If driving, park near Ortega and Camino Capistrano, the city's main streets.

ESSENTIALS

Visitor and Tour Information San Juan Capistrano Chamber of Commerce and Visitors Center ⊠ *31421 La Matanza St.* ☎ *949/493–4700* ⊕ *www. sanjuanchamber.com.*

EXPLORING

Fodor's Choice ★ **Mission San Juan Capistrano.** Mission San Juan Capistrano, founded in 1776 by Father Junípero Serra, was one of two Roman Catholic outposts between Los Angeles and San Diego. The Great Stone Church, begun in 1797, is the largest structure created by the Spanish in California. Many of the mission's adobe buildings have been preserved to illustrate mission life, with exhibits of an olive millstone, tallow ovens, tanning vats, metalworking furnaces, and the padres' living quarters. The gardens, with their fountains, are a lovely spot in which to wander. The bougainvillea-covered Serra Chapel is believed to be the oldest church still standing in California and is the only building remaining in which Fr. Serra actually led Mass. Mass takes place weekdays at 7 am in the chapel. ⊠ *Camino Capistrano and Ortega Hwy.* ☎ *949/234–1300* ⊕ *www.missionsjc.com* ☞ *$9* ⊙ *Daily 8:30–5.*

WHERE TO EAT

$$

AMERICAN

✗**The Ramos House Cafe.** It may be worth hopping the Amtrak for San Juan Capistrano just for the chance to have breakfast or lunch at one of Orange County's most beloved restaurants. Here's your chance to visit one of Los Rios Historic District's simple, board-and-batten homes dating back to 1881. This café sits practically on the railroad tracks across from the depot—nab a table on the patio and dig into a hearty breakfast, such as the mountainous wild-mushroom scramble. The $35 weekend brunch includes champagne, memorable mac-and-cheese with smoked veggies, and huckleberry coffee cake. Every item on the menu illustrates chef-owner John Q. Humphreys' creative hand. ⑤ *Average main: $15* ⊠ *31752 Los Rios St.* ☎ *949/443–1342* ⊕ *www.ramoshouse. com* ⊙ *Closed Mon. No dinner.*

CATALINA ISLAND

Fodor's Choice ★ Just 22 miles out from the L.A. coastline, across from Newport Beach and Long Beach, Catalina has virtually unspoiled mountains, canyons, coves, and beaches; best of all, it gives you a glimpse of what undeveloped Southern California once looked like.

Water sports are a big draw, as divers and snorkelers come for the exceptionally clear water surrounding the island. The main town, Avalon, is a charming, old-fashioned beach community, where yachts bob in the crescent bay. Wander beyond the main drag and find brightly painted little bungalows fronting the sidewalks, with the occasional golf cart purring down the street.

Perhaps it's no surprise that Catalina has long been a destination for filmmakers and movie stars. In its earlier past, however, the island also sheltered Russian fur trappers (seeking sea-otter skins), pirates, gold miners, and bootleggers (carrier pigeons were used to communicate with the mainland).

In 1919, William Wrigley Jr., the chewing-gum magnate, purchased a controlling interest in the company developing Catalina Island, whose most famous landmark, the Casino, was built in 1929 under his orders. Because he owned the Chicago Cubs baseball team, Wrigley made Catalina the team's spring training site, an arrangement that lasted until 1951.

In 1975, the Santa Catalina Island Conservancy, a nonprofit foundation, acquired about 86% of the island to help preserve the area's natural flora and fauna, including the bald eagle and the Catalina Island fox. These days the conservancy is restoring the rugged interior country with plantings of native grasses and trees. Along the coast you might spot oddities like electric perch, saltwater goldfish, and flying fish.

GETTING HERE AND AROUND

FERRY TRAVEL Two companies offer ferry service to Catalina Island. The boats have both indoor and outdoor seating and snack bars. Excessive baggage is not allowed, and there are extra fees for bicycles and surfboards. The waters around Santa Catalina can get rough, so if you're prone to seasickness, come prepared.

Catalina Express makes an hour-long run from Long Beach or San Pedro to Avalon and a 90-minute run from Dana Point to Avalon with some stops at Two Harbors. Round-trip fares begin at $70.50, with discounts for seniors and kids. On busy days, a $15 upgrade to the Commodore Lounge, when available, is worth it. Service from Newport Beach to Avalon is available through the Catalina Flyer. Boats leave from Balboa Pavilion at 9 am (in season), take 75 minutes to reach the island, and cost $69 round-trip. Return boats leave Catalina at 4:30 pm. Reservations are advised in summer and on weekends for all trips. ■TIP➔ Keep an eye out for dolphins, which sometimes swim alongside the ferries.

GOLF CARTS Golf carts constitute the island's main form of transportation for sightseeing in the area, but they can't be used on the streets in town. You can rent them along Avalon's Crescent Avenue and Pebbly Beach Road for about $40 per hour with a $40 deposit, payable via cash or traveler's checks only.

HELICOPTER TRAVEL Island Express helicopters depart hourly from San Pedro and Long Beach (8 am–dusk). The trip takes about 15 minutes and costs $110 one-way, $211 round-trip (plus tax). Reservations a week in advance are recommended (☎ 800/228-2566).

TIMING

Although Catalina can be seen in a day, several inviting hotels make it worth extending your stay for one or more nights. A short itinerary might include breakfast along the boardwalk, a tour of the interior, a snorkeling excursion at Casino Point, and a romantic waterfront dinner in Avalon.

After late October, rooms are much easier to find on shorter notice, rates drop dramatically, and many hotels offer packages that include transportation from the mainland and/or sightseeing tours. If you'd rather stay at a charming freestanding cottage or home, contact a local real estate office such as Catalina Island Vacation Rentals.

TO
DANA
POINT

TO
NEWPORT BEACH

TO
SAN PEDRO
AND LONG BEACH

1 hr 30mn

1 hr 15mn

1 hr 15mn

1 hr 15mn

San Pedro Channel

Casino Point
Underwater Park

Underwater Bay

Underwater Marine Park

Avalon

Toyon Bay

Wrigley Memorial
and Botanical Garden

East Mtn.

East Peak

Church
Rock

Long Point

Whites Landing

Echo Lake

PALISADES

SILVER CANYON

Catalina Canyon

Bullrush

Salta
Verde Point

MIDDLE CANYON

SALTA VERDE

Black Jack Mtn.

Mt. Orizaba

Middle Canyon Trail

Cactus Peak

China Point

Catalina
Airport

Escondido Rd.

Empire Landing Rd.

Little Harbor Rd.

Little Harbor

Ben Weston Beach
Ben Weston Point

Overlook

Isthmus
Cove

Two Harbors

West End Rd.

Lobster
Bay

Catalina Head

Catalina Harbor

Silver Peak Trail

Silver
Peak

Iron Bound Bay

Emerald Bay

Star Bay

Starlight
Beach

West
End

PACIFIC OCEAN

4 mi

4 km

0

0

Catalina Island

TOURS

Santa Catalina Island Company runs the following Discovery Tours: a summer-only coastal cruise to Seal Rocks; the *Flying Fish* boat trip (summer evenings only); a comprehensive inland motor tour (which includes an Arabian horse performance); a tour of Skyline Drive; a Casino tour; a scenic tour of Avalon; a glass-bottom-boat tour; an undersea tour on a semisubmersible vessel; a eco-theme zip line tour of the interior; and a tour of the Botanical Garden. Reservations are highly recommended for the inland tours. Tours cost $18 to $120. There are ticket booths on the Green Pleasure Pier, at the Casino, in the plaza, and at the boat landing. Catalina Adventure Tours, which has booths at the boat landing and on the pier, arranges similar excursions at comparable prices.

The Santa Catalina Island Conservancy organizes custom ecotours and hikes of the interior. Naturalist guides drive open jeeps through some gorgeously untrammeled parts of the island. Tours start at $109 per person for a three-hour trip (two-person minimum); you can also book half- and full-day tours. The tours run year-round.

ESSENTIALS

Ferry Contacts Catalina Express ☏ *800/481–3470* ⊕ *www.catalinaexpress. com.* **Catalina Flyer** ☏ *949/673–5245, 800/830–7744* ⊕ *www.catalinainfo.com.*

Golf Cart Rentals Island Rentals ✉ *125 Pebbly Beach Rd., Avalon* ☏ *310/510–1456* ⊕ *www.catalinagolfcartrentals.com.*

Visitor and Tour Information Catalina Adventure Tours ☏ *877/510–2888* ⊕ *www.catalinaadventuretours.com.* **Catalina Island Chamber of Commerce & Visitors' Bureau** ✉ *#1 Green Pleasure Pier, Avalon* ☏ *310/510–1520* ⊕ *www. catalinachamber.com.* **Santa Catalina Island Company** ☏ *310/510–2800, 800/626–1496* ⊕ *www.visitcatalinaisland.com.* **Catalina Island Conservancy** ✉ *125 Claressa Ave., Avalon* ☏ *310/510–2595* ⊕ *www.catalinaconservancy.org.*

AVALON

A 1- to 2-hr ferry ride from Long Beach, Newport Beach, or San Pedro; a 15-min helicopter ride from Long Beach or San Pedro.

Avalon, Catalina's only real town, extends from the shore of its natural harbor to the surrounding hillsides. Its resident population is about 3,500 but it swells with tourists on summer weekends. Most of the city's activity, however, is centered on the pedestrian mall on Crescent Avenue, and most sights are easily reached on foot. Private cars are restricted and rental cars aren't allowed, but taxis, trams, and shuttles can take you anywhere you need to go. Bicycles and golf carts can be rented from shops along Crescent Avenue.

EXPLORING

★ **Casino.** On the northwest point of Avalon Bay (looking to your right from Green Pleasure Pier) is the majestic landmark Casino. This circular white structure is one of the finest examples of art- deco architecture anywhere. Its Spanish-inspired floors and murals gleam with brilliant blue and green Catalina tiles. In this case, *casino,* the Italian word for "gathering place," has nothing to do with gambling. Rather, Casino life revolves around the magnificent ballroom.

Santa Catalina Island Company leads tours of the Casino, lasting about 55 minutes, for $18.75. You can also visit the **Catalina Island Museum,** in the lower level of the Casino, which investigates 7,000 years of island history; or stop at the **Casino Art Gallery** to see works by local artists. First-run movies are screened nightly at the **Avalon Theatre,** noteworthy for its classic 1929 theater pipe organ. ⊠ *1 Casino Way* ☎ *310/510–2414 museum, 310/510–0179 Avalon Theatre* ⊕ *www.catalinamuseum. com* 🖾 *Museum $5* ☯ *Call for hrs.*

Casino Point Underwater Park. In front of the Casino are the crystal-clear waters of the Casino Point Underwater Park, a marine preserve protected from watercraft where bright orange Garibaldi, moray eels, bat rays, spiny lobsters, halibut, and other sea animals cruise around kelp forests and along the sandy bottom. It's a terrific site for scuba diving, with some shallow areas suitable for snorkeling. Scuba and snorkeling equipment can be rented on and near the pier. The shallow waters of **Lover's Cove,** east of the boat landing, are also good for snorkeling.

Crescent Avenue. A walk along Crescent Avenue is a nice way to begin a tour of the town. Vivid art-deco tiles adorn the avenue's fountains and planters—fired on the island by the now-defunct Catalina Tile Company, the tiles are a coveted commodity.

Green Pleasure Pier. Head to the Green Pleasure Pier, at the center of Crescent Avenue, for a good vantage point of Avalon. At the top of the hill you'll spot a big white building, the Inn at Mt. Ada, now a top-of-the-line B&B but originally built by William Wrigley Jr. for his wife. On the pier you can find the Catalina Island Chamber of Commerce, snack stands, the Harbor Patrol, and scads of squawking seagulls.

Wrigley Memorial and Botanic Garden. Two miles south of the bay via Avalon Canyon Road is Wrigley Memorial and Botanic Garden. Here you can find plants native to Southern California, including several that grow only on Catalina Island: Catalina ironwood, wild tomato, and rare Catalina mahogany. The Wrigley family commissioned the garden as well as the monument, which has a grand staircase and a Spanish mausoleum inlaid with colorful Catalina tile. (The mausoleum was never used by the Wrigleys, who are buried in Los Angeles.) Taxi service from Avalon is available, or you can take a tour bus from the downtown Tour Plaza or ferry landing. ⊠ *Avalon Canyon Rd.* ☎ *310/510–2897* ⊕ *www.catalinaconservancy.org* 🖾 *$7* ☯ *Daily 8–5.*

WHERE TO EAT

$
AMERICAN

× **Eric's on the Pier.** This little snack bar has been an Avalon family–run institution since the 1920s. A favorite of Fodor's readers, it's a good place to people-watch while munching a breakfast burrito, hot dog, or signature buffalo burger. Most of the action (and seating) is outside, but you can also sit down at a table inside and dine on a bowl of homemade clam chowder in a baked bread bowl or an order of fish-and-chips. ⑤ *Average main: $7* ⊠ *Green Pier No. 2* ☎ *310/510–0894* ☯ *Closed Thurs. No dinner Nov.–May.*

WHERE TO STAY

For expanded reviews, facilities, and current deals, visit Fodors.com.

$ **Hotel Villa Portofino.** Steps from the beach and the Pleasure Pier, this
HOTEL hotel has a European flair and creates an intimate feel with brick courtyards and walkways. **Pros:** romantic; close to beach; incredible sun deck.
Cons: though quiet in general, ground floor rooms can be noisy; some
rooms are on small side; no elevator. **TripAdvisor:** "convenient and comfortable," "amazing for a low-key romantic getaway," "great service."
⑤ *Rooms from: $175* ✉ *111 Crescent Ave.* ☎ *310/510–0555, 800/346–
2326* ⊕ *www.hotelvillaportofino.com* ⤢ *35 rooms* ⦿*Breakfast.*

$$ **Hotel Vista del Mar.** On the middle of Main Street, this beautiful prop-
HOTEL erty is just steps from the beach, where complimentary towels, chairs,
★ and umbrellas await guests. **Pros:** comfortable king beds; central; mod-
ern decor. **Cons:** no restaurant or spa facilities; only two rooms have
ocean views or balconies; no elevator. **TripAdvisor:** "amazing gem,"
"very convenient," "relaxing." ⑤ *Rooms from: $225* ✉ *417 Crescent
Ave.* ☎ *310/510–1452, 800/601–3836* ⊕ *www.hotel-vistadelmar.com*
⤢ *11 rooms, 3 suites* ⦿*Breakfast.*

$$$$ **Inn on Mt. Ada.** If you stay in the mansion where Wrigley Jr. once
B&B/INN lived, you'll enjoy all the comforts of a millionaire's home—at a million-
Fodor's Choice aire's prices. **Pros:** timeless charm; shuttle from heliport and dock; first-
★ class service. **Cons:** smallish rooms and bathrooms; pricey. **TripAdvisor:**
"amazing lunch," "sleep like a king and queen," "such luxury and
comfort." ⑤ *Rooms from: $430* ✉ *398 Wrigley Rd.* ☎ *310/510–2030,
800/608–7669* ⊕ *www.innonmtada.com* ⤢ *6 rooms* ⦿*Some meals.*

SPORTS AND THE OUTDOORS

BICYCLING

To bike beyond the paved roads of Avalon, you must buy an annual
permit from the Catalina Conservancy. Individual passes start at $35;
family passes cost $125. You may not ride on hiking paths.

Bike rentals are widely available in Avalon starting at $5 per hour and
$12 per day.

Brown's Bikes. Look for rentals on Crescent Avenue and Pebbly Beach
Road such as Brown's Bikes. ✉ *107 Pebbly Beach Rd., next to Island
Rentals* ☎ *310/510–0986* ⊕ *www.catalinabiking.com.*

DIVING AND SNORKELING

The Casino Point Underwater Park, with its handful of wrecks, is best
suited for diving. Lover's Cove is better for snorkeling (no scuba diving
allowed, but you'll share the area with glass-bottom boats). Both are
protected marine preserves.

Catalina Divers Supply. Head to Catalina Divers Supply to rent equip-
ment, take guided scuba and snorkel tours, and attend certification
classes. It also has an outpost at Casino Point. ✉ *7 Green Pleasure Pier*
☎ *800/353–0330* ⊕ *www.catalinadiverssupply.com.*

HIKING

Santa Catalina Island Conservancy. Permits from the Santa Catalina
Island Conservancy are required for hiking into Catalina Island's inte-
rior. ■**TIP**➔ If you plan to backpack overnight, you'll need a camping

reservation. The interior is dry and desertlike; bring plenty of water and sunblock. The permits are free and can be picked up at the main house of the conservancy or at the airport. You don't need a permit for shorter hikes, such as the one from Avalon to the Botanical Garden. The conservancy has maps of the island's east-end hikes, such as Hermit's Gulch Trail. It's possible to hike between Avalon and Two Harbors, starting at the Hogsback Gate, above Avalon, though the 28-mile journey has an elevation gain of 3,000 feet and is not for the weak. ■TIP→ For a pleasant 4-mile hike out of Avalon, take Avalon Canyon Road to Wrigley Gardens and follow the trail to Lone Pine. At the top, you'll have an amazing view of the Palisades cliffs and, beyond them, the sea. ⊠ *125 Claressa Ave.* ☎ *310/510–1445* ⊕ *www.catalinaconservancy.org.*

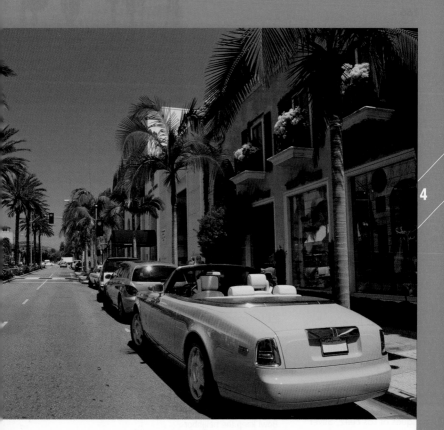

Los Angeles

WORD OF MOUTH

"Downtown L.A. has a magnificence that I'd never appreciated from a distance. . . . For an amateur architectural buff, there's a lot to be taken in here.

—MRand

WELCOME TO LOS ANGELES

TOP REASONS TO GO

★ **Hollywood magic:** A massive chunk of the world's entertainment is developed, written, filmed, edited, distributed, and sold here; you'll hear people discussing "the Industry" wherever you go.

★ **The beach:** Getting some sand on the floor of your car is practically a requirement here, and the beach is an integral part of the SoCal lifestyle.

★ **Chic shopping:** From Beverly Hills's Rodeo Drive and Downtown's Fashion District to the funky boutiques of Los Feliz, Silver Lake, and Echo Park, L.A. is a shopper's paradise.

★ **Trendy restaurants:** Celebrity is big business here, so it's no accident that the concept of the celebrity chef is a key part of the city's dining scene.

★ **People-watching:** Celeb-spotting in Beverly Hills, trying to get past the velvet rope at hip clubs, hanging out on the Venice Boardwalk . . . there's always something (or someone) interesting to see.

1 Downtown Los Angeles. Downtown L.A. shows off spectacular modern architecture with the swooping Walt Disney Concert Hall and the stark Cathedral of Our Lady of the Angels. The Music Center and the Museum of Contemporary Art anchor a world-class arts scene, while Olvera Street, Chinatown, and Little Tokyo reflect the city's history and diversity.

2 Hollywood and the Studios. Glitzy and tarnished, good and bad—Hollywood is just like the entertainment business itself. The Walk of Fame, Grauman's Chinese Theatre, Paramount Pictures studio, and the Hollywood Bowl keep the neighborhood's romantic past alive. Universal Studios Hollywood, Warner Bros., and NBC Television Studios are in the Valley.

3 The Westside and Beverly Hills. Go for the glamour, the restaurants, and the scene. Rodeo Drive is particularly good for a look at wretched or ravishing excess. But don't forget the Westside's cultural attractions—especially the dazzling Getty Center. West Hollywood's an area for urban indulgences—shopping, restaurants, nightspots— rather than sightseeing. Its main arteries are the Sunset Strip (Sunset Boulevard), and Melrose Avenue, lined with shops ranging from punk to postmodern.

4 Santa Monica, Venice, and Malibu. These desirable beach communities move from ultrarich, ultracasual Malibu to bohemian/ transitioning Venice, with liberal, Mediterranean-style Santa Monica in between.

5 Pasadena Area. Its own separate city, Pasadena is a quiet area with outstanding Arts and Crafts homes, good dining, and a pair of exceptional museums.

Sepulveda Dam Recreation Area

Ventura Fwy.

101

VAN NUY

SANTA MONICA MTS.

Mulholland Dr.

SHERMAN OAKS

405

Topanga State Park

Getty Center

BEVERLY HILLS

BRENTWOOD

WESTWOO

←TO MALIBU

Sunset Blvd.

PACIFIC PALISADES

Santa Monic

San Diego Fwy.

2

10

1

SANTA MONICA

1

Venice Boardwalk

VENICE

MARINA DEL REY

PACIFIC OCEAN

GETTING ORIENTED

Looking at a map of sprawling Los Angeles, first-time visitors are sometimes overwhelmed. Where to begin? What to see first? And what about all those freeways? Here's some advice: relax. Begin by setting your priorities—movie and television buffs should first head to Hollywood, Universal Studios, and a taping of a television show. Beach lovers and nature types might start out in Santa Monica, Venice, or Malibu, or spend an afternoon in Griffith Park, one of the largest city parks in the country. Culture vultures should make a beeline for the twin Gettys (the center in Brentwood and the villa near Malibu), the Los Angeles County Museum of Art (LACMA), or the Norton Simon Museum. And urban explorers might begin with Downtown Los Angeles.

Updated by Kathy A. McDonald Los Angeles is as much a fantasy as it is a physical city. A mecca for face-lifts, film noir, shopping starlets, beach bodies, and mind-numbing traffic, it sprawls across 467 square miles; add in the surrounding five-county metropolitan area, and you've got an area of close to 34,000 square miles.

Contrary to popular myth, however, that doesn't mean you have to spend all your time in a car. In fact, getting out of your car is the only way to really get to know the various entertainment-industry-centered, financial, beachfront, wealthy, and fringe neighborhoods and mini-cities that make up the vast L.A. area. But remember, no single locale—whether it be Malibu, Downtown, Beverly Hills, or Burbank—fully embodies Los Angeles. It's in the mix that you'll discover the city's character.

PLANNING

WHEN TO GO

Almost any time of the year is the right time to go to Los Angeles; the climate is mild and pleasant year-round. Winter brings crisp, sunny, unusually smogless days from about November to May (expect brief rains from December to April). Los Angeles summers, which are virtually rainless, can lead to air-quality alerts. Prices skyrocket and reservations are a must when tourism peaks from July through early October.

GETTING HERE AND AROUND

AIR TRAVEL

It's generally easier to navigate the secondary airports than to get through sprawling LAX, the city's major gateway. Bob Hope Airport in Burbank is closest to Downtown L.A., and domestic flights to it can be cheaper than flights to LAX—it's definitely worth checking out. From Long Beach Airport it's equally convenient to go north to central Los Angeles or south to Orange County. Flights to Orange County's John Wayne Airport are often more expensive than those to the other secondary airports. Parking at the smaller airports is cheaper than at LAX.

Airports Bob Hope Airport (*BUR*). ☎ *818/840–8840* ⊕ *www.bobhopeairport. com*. **John Wayne/Orange County Airport** (*SNA*). ☎ *949/252–5006* ⊕ *www. ocair.com*. **Long Beach Airport** (*LGB*). ☎ *562/570–2600* ⊕ *www.lgb.org*. **Los Angeles International Airport** (*LAX*). ☎ *310/646–5252* ⊕ *www.lawa.org or www.airport-la.com*. **Ontario International Airport** (*ONT*). ☎ *909/937–2700* ⊕ *www.lawa.org*.

Shuttles Prime Time ☎ *800/733–8267* ⊕ *www.primetimeshuttle.com*. **SuperShuttle** ☎ *323/775–6600, 310/782–6600, 800/258–3826* ⊕ *www. supershuttle.com*. **Xpress by ExecuCar** ☎ *800/427–7483* ⊕ *www. execucarexpress.com*.

BUS TRAVEL

Inadequate public-transportation systems have been an L.A. problem for decades. That said, many local trips can be made, with time and patience, by bus. In certain cases, it may be your best option; for example, visiting the Getty Center, going to Universal Studios and/or the adjacent CityWalk, or venturing into Downtown. The Metropolitan Transit Authority DASH (Downtown Area Short Hop) minibuses cover nine different circular routes in Hollywood, Mid-Wilshire, and the Downtown area. The buses stop every two blocks or so. The Santa Monica Municipal Bus Line, also known as the Big Blue Bus, is a pleasant and inexpensive way to move around the Westside, where the MTA lines leave off. There's also an express bus to and from Downtown L.A., and a shuttle bus, the Tide Shuttle, which runs between Main Street and the Third Street Promenade and stops at hotels along the way. Culver CityBus Lines run seven routes through Culver City.

Bus Information Commute Smart ☎ ⊕ *www.commutesmart.info*. **Culver CityBus Lines** ☎ *310/253–6500* ⊕ *www.culvercity.org*. **DASH** ☎ *310/808–2273*, ⊕ *www.ladottransit.com/dash*. **Los Angeles County Metropolitan Transit Authority (LACMTA)** ☎ *323/466–3876* ⊕ *www.metro.net*. **Santa Monica Municipal Bus Line** ☎ *310/451–5444* ⊕ *www.bigbluebus.com*.

CAR TRAVEL

Most freeways are known by a name and a number; for example, the San Diego Freeway is Interstate 405, the Hollywood Freeway is U.S. 101, the Ventura Freeway is a different stretch of U.S. 101, the Santa Monica Freeway is Interstate 10, and the Harbor Freeway is Interstate 110. It helps, too, to know which direction you're traveling; say, west toward Santa Monica or east toward Downtown Los Angeles. Distance in miles doesn't mean much, depending on the time of day you're traveling: the short 10-mile drive between the San Fernando Valley and Downtown Los Angeles might take an hour to travel during rush hour but only 20 minutes at other times.

Be aware that a number of major streets have similar-sounding names (Beverly Drive and Beverly Boulevard, or numbered streets north to south Downtown and east to west in Hollywood, West Hollywood, and Beverly Hills) or exactly the same name (San Vicente Boulevard in West L.A., Brentwood, Santa Monica, and West Hollywood). Also, some smaller streets seem to exist intermittently for miles, so unless you have good directions, you should use major streets rather than try for an alternative that is actually blocked by a dead end or detours, like the side streets off Sunset Boulevard. Try to get clear directions and stick to them.

If you get discombobulated while on the freeway, remember the rule of thumb: even-numbered freeways run east and west, odd-numbered freeways run north and south.

Information California Highway Patrol ☎ *800/427–7623 for road conditions.* **City of Los Angeles** ⊕ *www.sigalert.com.*

Emergency Services Metro Freeway Service Patrol ☎ *213/922–2957 general information, 323/982–4900 for breakdowns.*

METRO RAIL TRAVEL

Metro Rail covers a limited area of L.A.'s vast expanse, but what there is, is helpful and frequent. The underground Red Line runs from Union Station Downtown through Mid-Wilshire, Hollywood, and Universal City on its way to North Hollywood, stopping at the most popular tourist destinations along the way. The light commuter rail Green Line stretches from Redondo Beach to Norwalk, while the partially underground Blue Line goes from Downtown to the South Bay (Long Beach/San Pedro). The Green and Blue lines are not often used by visitors, though the Green is gaining popularity as an alternative, albeit time-consuming, way to reach LAX. The monorail-like Gold Line begins at Union Station and heads northeast to Pasadena and Sierra Madre. The Orange Line, a 14-mile bus corridor, connects the North Hollywood subway station with the western San Fernando Valley. The new Expo line to Culver City begins operation in late 2012.

The website is the best way to get info on Metro Rail.

Metro Rail Information Los Angeles County Metropolitan Transit Authority (LACMTA) ☎ *323/466–3876* ⊕ *www.metro.net.*

TAXI AND LIMOUSINE TRAVEL

Don't even try to hail a cab on the street in Los Angeles. Instead, phone one of the many taxi companies. The metered rate is $2.85 per mile. Taxi rides from LAX have an additional $4 surcharge. Be aware that distances between sights in L.A. are vast, so cab fares add up quickly. On the other end of the price spectrum, limousines come equipped with everything from a full bar and telephone to a hot tub. If you open any L.A.–area yellow pages, the number of limo companies will astound you. Most charge by the hour, with a three-hour minimum.

Limo Companies ABC Limousine & Sedan Service ☎ *818/980–6000, 888/753–7500.* **American Executive** ☎ *800/927–2020.* **Black & White Transportation Services** ☎ *800/924–1624.* **Chauffeur's Unlimited** ☎ *888/546–6019.* **Dav El Chauffeured Transportation Network** ☎ *800/922–0343* ⊕ *www. davel.com.* **First Class Limousine Service by Norman Lewis** ☎ *800/400–9771* ⊕ *www.first-classlimo.com.* **ITS** ☎ *800/487–4255* ⊕ *www.itslimo.com.*

Taxi Companies Beverly Hills Cab Co. ☎ *800/398–5221.* **Checker Cab** ☎ *800/300–5007.* **Independent Cab Co.** ☎ *800/521–8294* ⊕ *www.taxi4u. com.* **United Independent Taxi** ☎ *800/822–8294.* **Yellow Cab/LA Taxi Co-Op** ☎ *800/200–1085, 800/200–0011.*

TRAIN TRAVEL

Union Station in Downtown Los Angeles is one of the great American railroad stations. The interior is well kept and includes comfortable seating, a restaurant, and snack bars. As the city's rail hub, it's the place to catch an Amtrak train. Among Amtrak's Southern California routes are 12 daily trips to San Diego and four to Santa Barbara. Amtrak's luxury *Coast Starlight* travels along the spectacular coastline from Seattle to Los Angeles in just a day and a half (though it's often a little late). The *Sunset Limited* goes to Los Angeles from Florida (via New Orleans and Texas), and the *Southwest Chief* from Chicago. You can make reservations in advance by phone or at the station. As with airlines, you usually get a better deal the farther in advance you book. You must show your ticket and a photo ID before boarding. Smoking is not allowed on Amtrak trains.

Information Amtrak ☎ 800/872-7245 ⊕ www.amtrak.com. **Union Station** ⊠ 800 N. Alameda St. ☎ 213/683-6979.

VISITOR INFORMATION

Contacts Beverly Hills Conference and Visitors Bureau ☎ 310/248-1000, 800/345-2210 ⊕ www.lovebeverlyhills.com, www.beverlyhillschamber. com. **California Office of Tourism** ☎ 916/444-4429, 800/862-2543 ⊕ www.visitcalifornia.com. **Hollywood Chamber of Commerce Info Center** ☎ 323/469-8311 ⊕ www.hollywoodchamber.net. **L.A. Inc./The Convention and Visitors Bureau** ☎ 213/624-7300, 800/228-2452 ⊕ www. discoverlosangeles.com. **Pasadena Convention and Visitors Bureau** ☎ 626/795-9311 ⊕ www.pasadenacal.com. **Redondo Beach Chamber of Commerce and Visitors Bureau** ☎ 310/376-6911, 800/282-0333 ⊕ www.redondochamber.org. **Santa Monica Convention & Visitors Bureau** ☎ 310/393-7593, 800/544-5319 ⊕ www.santamonica.com. **West Hollywood Marketing and Visitors Bureau** ☎ 310/289-2525, 800/368-6020 ⊕ www. visitwesthollywood.com.

EXPLORING LOS ANGELES

Star-struck . . . excessive . . . smoggy . . . superficial. There's a modicum of truth to each of the adjectives regularly applied to L.A. But Angelenos—and most objective visitors—dismiss their prevalence as signs of envy from people who hail from places less blessed with fun and sun. Pop culture, for instance, *does* permeate life in LaLaLand: A massive economy employing millions of Southern Californians is built around it.

However, this city also boasts highbrow appeal, having amassed an impressive array of world-class museums and arts venues. Moreover, it has burgeoning neighborhoods that bear little resemblance to those featured on *The Real Housewives of Beverly Hills* or *Entourage*. America's second-largest city has more depth than paparazzi shutters can ever capture.

DOWNTOWN LOS ANGELES

Once the lively heart of Los Angeles, Downtown has been a glitz-free businessman's domain of high-rises for the past few decades. But if there's one thing Angelenos love, it's a makeover, and now city planners have put the wheels in motion for a dramatic revitalization. Glance in every direction and you'll find construction crews building luxury lofts and retail space in hopes of attracting new high-class residents.

TOP ATTRACTIONS

Fodor'sChoice **Cathedral of Our Lady of the Angels.** A half block away from the giant
★ rose-shaped steel grandeur of Frank Gehry's curvaceous Disney Concert Hall sits Cathedral of Our Lady of the Angels. Not only is it a spiritual draw but an architectural attraction. The exterior is all strict soaring angles and the building is as heavy, solid, and hunkering as the Gehry building is feminine and ethereal.

Controversy surrounded Spanish architect José Rafael Moneo's unconventional, costly, austere design for the seat of the Archdiocese of Los Angeles. But judging from the swarms of visitors and the standing-room-only holiday masses, the church has carved out a niche for itself in Downtown's daily life.

Opened in 2002, the ocher-concrete cathedral looms up by the Hollywood Freeway. The plaza in front is relatively austere, glaringly bright on sunny days; a children's play garden with bronze animals helps relieve the stark space.

Imposing bronze entry doors, designed by local artist Robert Graham, are decorated with multicultural icons and New World images of the Virgin Mary. The canyonlike interior of the church is spare, polished, and airy. By day, sunlight illuminates the sanctuary through translucent curtain walls of thin Spanish alabaster, a departure from the usual stained glass.

Artist John Nava used residents from his hometown of Ojai, California, as models for some of the 135 figures in the tapestries that line the nave walls. Make sure to go underground to wander the bright, mazelike white-marble corridors of the mausoleum.

Free guided tours start at the entrance fountain at 1 on weekdays. Check for free concerts inside of the Cathedral on Wednesday at 12:45 pm. There's plenty of underground visitor parking; the vehicle entrance is on Hill Street. ■TIP→ The café in the plaza has become one of Downtown's favorite lunch spots. You can pick up a fresh, reasonably priced meal to eat at one of the outdoor tables. ⊠ *555 W. Temple St., Downtown* ☏ *213/680–5200* ⊕ *www.olacathedral.org* ⊠ *Free, parking $4 every 15 mins, $18 maximum* ☉ *Weekdays 6–6, Sat. 9–6, Sun. 7–6.*

★ **The Geffen Contemporary at MOCA.** Frank Gehry transformed what was a 40,000-square-foot former police warehouse in Little Tokyo into this top-notch museum, originally built as a temporary exhibit hall while the **Museum of Contemporary Art (MOCA)** was under construction at California Plaza. Thanks to its popular reception, it remains one of two satellite museums of MOCA (the other is outside the Pacific Design Center in West Hollywood) and houses a sampling of its permanent

Downtown Los Angeles

TO DODGER STADIUM

Hollywood Fwy

Sunset Blvd

Pasadena Fwy

Bernard St.

110

College St.

CHINATOWN

Court St.

Cotton St.

Alpine St.

Ord St.

Cesar E. Chavez Ave.

N. Broadway

N. High St.

Spring St.

N. Main St.

Glendale Blvd

2nd St.

3rd St.

4th St.

Beaudry Ave.

Boylston St.

Temple St.

Arcadia St.

Olvera St.

4

5

6

M
3
Union Station

Aliso St.

101

Commercial St.

Harbor Fwy

Figueroa St.

1st St.

7

8

M

2nd St.

Flower St.

Hope St.

Grand Ave.

Olive St.

Bunker Hill Steps

◆ Watercourt

Grand Central Market ◆

9

Central Library

Pershing Square

M

Hill St.

5th St.

4th St.

LITTLE TOKYO

2

1

Banning St.

Alameda St.

Rose St.

1st St.

2nd St.

Tracion Ave.

3rd St.

10 - 12

Wilshire Blvd

6th St.

7th St.

8th St.

9th St.

Broadway

Spring St.

Main St.

Los Angeles St.

Maple Ave.

Wall St.

3rd St.

Central Ave.

San Pedro St.

Crocker St.

Towne Ave.

Stanford Ave.

Gladys Ave.

TO WATTS TOWERS

5th St.

TO EXPOSITION PARK

FASHION DISTRICT

Olympic Blvd

11th St.

Flower Market

Agatha St.

| 0 | 1/2 mi |
| 0 | 800 meters |

KEY

M Metro stops

collection. In addition, it puts on one or two special exhibits yearly. Call before you visit because the museum sometimes closes for installations. ✉ *152 N. Central Ave., Downtown* ☎ *213/626–6222* ⊕ *www. moca-la.org* 🖾 *$10, free with MOCA admission on same day and on Thurs. evenings.* ⊙ *Mon. and Fri. 11–5, Thurs. 11–8, weekends 11–6.*

Fodor'sChoice
★
The Museum of Contemporary Art (MOCA). The MOCA's permanent collection of American and European art from 1940 to the present divides itself among three spaces: this linear red-sandstone building at California Plaza, the **Geffen Contemporary,** in nearby Little Tokyo, and the satellite gallery at West Hollywood's **Pacific Design Center.** Likewise, its exhibitions are split between the established and the cutting edge.

Heavy hitters such as Mark Rothko, Franz Kline, Susan Rothenberg, Diane Arbus, and Robert Frank are part of the permanent collection that's rotated into the museum exhibits at different times, while additional theme shows are featured annually. It's a good idea to check the schedule in advance, as some galleries occasionally close for exhibit installations. ✉ *250 S. Grand Ave., Downtown* ☎ *213/626–6222* ⊕ *www.moca.org* 🖾 *Grand Ave. and Geffen Contemporary $10, free Thurs. 5–8; Pacific Design Center free* ⊙ *Mon. and Fri. 11–5, Thurs. 11–8, weekends 11–6; Pacific Design Center, Tues.–Fri. 11–5, weekends 11–6.*

★ **The Music Center.** Serving as L.A.'s major performing arts venue since its opening in 1964, this was where the Academy Awards was held until it moved to the Dolby Theatre.

The Music Center is reminiscent of New York's Lincoln Center because the buildings that house the Los Angeles Philharmonic, the Los Angeles Opera, the Center Theater Group, and the Los Angeles Master Chorale all surround a large courtyard. Glorya Kaufman presents Dance at the Music Center is another program that features the best of dance, from global to traditional ballet. At intermission, patrons spill into the plaza to drink wine, enjoy the lighted "dancing" fountain or occasional art exhibits, adding magic to an evening already filled with artistic excellence.

The largest of the center's four theaters is the **Dorothy Chandler Pavilion,** named after the philanthropic wife of former *Los Angeles Times* publisher Norman Chandler. The **Ahmanson,** at the north end, is a flexible venue for major musicals and plays. In between these two sits the round **Mark Taper Forum,** an intimate 700-seat theater.

Activity isn't limited to merely ticketed events; free tours of the entire Music Center campus are available by volunteer docents who provide a wealth of architectural and behind-the-scenes information while escorting you through elaborate, art-punctuated VIP areas. ✉ *135 N. Grand Ave., at 1st St., Downtown* ☎ *213/972–7211, 213/972–4399 for tour information* ⊕ *www.musiccenter.org.*

Walt Disney Concert Hall. L.A.'s crown jewel, designed by Frank Gehry, opened in 2003 and instantly became a stunning icon of the city. The gorgeous stainless-steel-clad exterior soars upward, seeming to defy the laws of engineering.

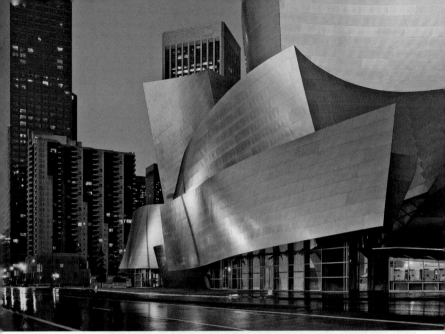

Frank Gehry's Walt Disney Concert Hall is the crown jewel of the Music Center, if not all of Downtown Los Angeles.

Inside, the Hall has a billowing ceiling of Douglas fir, and an enormous pine-clad organ centerpiece said to have been inspired by a box of McDonald's french fries. The carpet, named "Lily," is a wild collage of petals inspired by Lillian Disney's love of flowers, as is the "Rose for Lily" fountain—made entirely of bits of Delftware, Mrs. Disney's favorite collectible—in the tranquil outdoor public garden.

Docent-led and self-guided audio tours of the Hall are available free to the public for parties of 14 and less, but note that entry to the performance space is subject to rehearsal schedules. Your chances are better in summer when the Philharmonic moves to the Hollywood Bowl.

Additional children's performances, lectures, and experimental works are held in surrounding smaller theater spaces: the indoor BP Hall, two outdoor mini-amphitheaters, and CalArts's intimate 266-seat REDCAT Theatre. ⊠ *111 S. Grand Ave.* ☎ *323/850–2000* ⊕ *www.laphil.com*

Olvera Street Visitors Center. For information, stop by the Olvera Street Visitors Center, in the Sepulveda House, a Victorian building built in 1887 as a hotel and boardinghouse. The center is open weekdays and weekends 9–4. Free hour-long walking tours leave here at 10, 11, and noon Tuesday through Saturday. Tours ⊕ *www.lasangelitas.org.* ⊠ *622 N. Main St., Downtown* ☎ *213/628–1274* ⊕ *www.olvera-street.com.*

★ **Union Station.** Once the key entry point into Los Angeles prior to LAX, Union Station is worth a visit even if you don't plan to go anywhere but merely want to wallow in the ambience of one of the country's last great rail stations.

VISITING THE STUDIOS

If you've never been to L.A.—or if you have, and are coming back with your kids—it's hard to resist the allure of being where the magic happens among the cameras, props, and backlots of Tinseltown's studios.

(above) Go to Universal Studios for a big-bang theme park experience of moviemaking. (lower right) Warner Bros. Studios. (upper right) Paramount Pictures.

Nearly 70% of all L.A.'s entertainment productions happen in the Valley. And to really get behind the scenes, studio tours are the best way for mere mortals to get close to where celebs and the Industry's crème-de-la-crème work.

Most tours last several hours, and allow you to see where hit television shows are filmed, spot actors on the lot, and visit movie soundstages—some directors even permit visitors on the set while shooting.

Specific sights change daily, so if there's something in particular you're dying to see, it's best to call ahead and ask.

IT'S ALL ABOUT LOCATION

Many L.A. first-timers make the incorrect assumption that because Hollywood is where all the action takes place, it's also where the stars work.

The only studio that's still located in Hollywood is Paramount; Warner Bros., Universal Studios Hollywood, and NBC Television Studios are north of Hollywood, in Universal City and Burbank.

PARAMOUNT PICTURES

BEST FOR

Paramount offers an intimate—maximum of eight people at a time—two-hour tour of its 65-acre lot. It's probably the most authentic studio tour you can take, giving you a real sense of the film industry's history. Paramount is the only studio left in Hollywood—all the others are in Burbank, Universal City, or Culver City.

TOURING BASICS

Guests are driven around the lot in a tricked-out golf cart and primarily visit sets and soundstages that are not in use. Other stops include the New York backlot and the studio's iconic Bronson Gate.

WHAT'S BEEN FILMED HERE

Chinatown, The Godfather, The Untouchables, Breakfast at Tiffany's, Austin Powers, Cloverfield, Star Trek, and the final *Indiana Jones* are just a few of the notable films shot here. Ongoing TV productions include Dr. Phil and Community.

TIPS FOR TOURING

Guests can grab a quick coffee before embarking on the tour at the lot's coffee shop. The four-hour VIP tour package ($128) on Friday includes a catered lunch at the studio commissary.

GETTING HERE

From Melrose Avenue, enter on Windsor Boulevard at the main gate. Parking is just north of the gate on the left, and there's additional parking at the lot on the southwest corner of Windsor and Melrose. Parking is $7.

VISITOR INFORMATION

Kids must be 12 or older to tour the studio. ⊠ *5555 Melrose Ave., Hollywood* ☎ *323/956–1777* ⊕ *www. paramountstudiotour.com* 🎟 *Tours weekdays by reservation only, $48, $128 (VIP tour).*

WARNER BROS. STUDIOS

BEST FOR

If you're looking for an authentic behind-the-scenes look at how films and TV shows are made, head to this major studio center, one of the world's busiest. There aren't many bells and whistles here, but you'll get a much better idea of production work than you will at Universal Studios.

TOURING BASICS

On the VIP Tour, which lasts 2 hours and 25 minutes, you'll see the studio from inside an electric cart with 11 others. The specifics of what you'll actually see changes daily, but after viewing a short film on WB movies and shows, you'll be taken by tram to visit sets like the often-recycled Anytown U.S.A.,

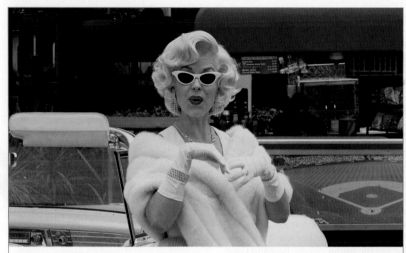

The Universal Studios Tour pays tribute to Hollywood stars of the past and present.

as well as soundstages and back-lot locations for popular films and shows. The studio's museum has a floor dedicated to *Casablanca* and 85 years of WB history; another belongs exclusively to *Harry Potter*. The tour ends here, and you can explore it at your leisure.

The Deluxe Tour is a five-hour affair that takes you onto working production sets and includes lunch at the commissary (great stargazing ops). Note: photography is not permitted!

WHAT'S BEEN FILMED HERE

Without A Trace, The Mentalist, Friends, the original *Ocean's Eleven, Casablanca*, and *Rebel Without a Cause*.

TIPS FOR TOURING

Showing up about 20 minutes before the scheduled time of your tour is recommended. VIP Tours leave continuously throughout the day; the Deluxe Tour leaves daily at 10:20 am.

GETTING HERE

The studio's website (⊕ *vipstudiotour. warnerbros.com*) provides good directions from all parts of the city, including Downtown (take 101 north).

VISITOR INFORMATION

✉ *3400 W. Riverside Dr., Burbank* ☎ *877/492–8687*   ⊕ *vipstudiotour. warnerbros.com* ✉ *VIP Tour is $49 per person; the Deluxe Tour is $250 per person* ⊙ *Weekdays 8:30–4:30. Children under 8 are not admitted. Advance booking is recommended. Parking is $7 at Gate 6.*

UNIVERSAL STUDIOS HOLLYWOOD

BEST FOR

This studio is more a theme park with lots of roller coasters and thrill rides than a backstage pass, though its studio tour does provide a good firsthand look at familiar TV shows and major movie sets.

TOURING BASICS

The tour lasts about an hour and you'll sit on a tram with nearly 100 other people. You'll pass back-lots, dressing rooms, and production offices.

There's also a VIP Tour where you can explore a historic, working movie studio's back-lot and score a closer view of sets, costumes, and props. It's a full-day outing that includes a two-hour studio tour, lunch, valet parking, and front-of-the-line privileges for the theme park's thrill rides.

WHAT'S BEEN FILMED HERE
See the airplane wreckage from *War of the Worlds*, the *Desperate Housewives'* Wisteria Lane, *Psycho*'s infamous Bates Motel, and the animatronic great white shark from *Jaws*.

TIPS FOR TOURING
You may be tempted to get the $139 pass that takes you to the front of the line. Try to resist this splurge. Once inside, you'll find that the lines, if any, move quickly. Pass on the premium and spend it on a decent lunch outside the park.

GETTING HERE
The park is located in Universal City. From Hollywood, take the 101 Hollywood Freeway north to Universal Studios Boulevard.

VISITOR INFORMATION
✉ *100 Universal City Plaza, Universal City* ☎ *800/864–8377* ⊕ *www. universalstudioshollywood.com* 🎫 *Ticket prices for the studio tour are included in park admission ($77); $249 VIP tour; parking is $15; preferred parking is available for $20* ☯ *Contact park for seasonal hrs.*

visit an old broadcast booth, listen to bands rehearsing, view setups for jokes, check out rehearsals, see sets under construction, and visit the prop warehouse and the studios where shows are taped.

WHAT'S FILMED HERE
The Tonight Show with Jay Leno, Days of Our Lives, The Ellen DeGeneres Show, and *Access Hollywood.*

TIPS FOR TOURING
If you decide to take a last-minute studio tour, definitely call ahead; low ticket prices and advance purchase means tickets tend to sell out quickly the day of.

GETTING HERE
The studio is located in Burbank. The best way to get here from Downtown or the Hollywood area is to take the Hollywood Freeway 101 North to Barham Boulevard, which forks off onto West Olive Avenue. Make a right on West Alameda Avenue and then a right on Bob Hope Drive. The studio is on the right.

VISITOR INFORMATION
✉ *3000 W. Alameda Ave., Burbank* ☎ *818/840–3537* ⊕ *www.nbc*.com 🎫 *Tours $8.50. There's no minimum age requirement for children; those under 4 are free.*

NBC TELEVISION STUDIOS

BEST FOR
In contrast to other studio tours, you get to walk on the set rather than being confined to a tram. It's the only TV studio that offers a behind-the-scenes look at production.

TOURING BASICS
The guided 70-minute tour—a rare opportunity to see the inside of a TV studio—emphasizes the history of the station from its roots in radio. You'll

Jurassic Park—the Ride at Universal Studios

Evoking an era when travel and style went hand in hand, Union Station will transport you to another destination, and another time. Built in 1939 and designed by City Hall architects John and Donald Parkinson, it combines Spanish colonial revival and art-deco styles that have retained their classic warmth and quality.

The waiting hall's commanding scale and enormous chandeliers have provided the setting for countless films, TV shows, and music videos. The indoor restaurant, **Traxx,** offers a glamorous vintage setting for lunch and dinner. ⊠ *800 N. Alameda St., Downtown.*

WORTH NOTING

★ **Bradbury Building.** Stunning wrought-iron railing, blond-wood and brick interior, ornate moldings, pink marble staircases, Victorian-style skylighted atrium that rises almost 50 feet, and a birdcage elevator: it's easy to see why the Bradbury leaves visitors awestruck.

Designed in 1893 by a novice architect who drew his inspiration from a science-fiction story and a conversation with his dead brother via a Ouija board, the office building was originally the site of turn-of-the-20th-century sweatshops, but now houses a variety of business that try to keep normal working conditions despite the barrage of daily tourist visits and filmmakers. *Blade Runner, Chinatown,* and *Wolf* were filmed here.

For that reason, visits (and photo-taking) are limited to the lobby and the first-floor landing. The building is open daily 9–5 for a peek, as long as you don't wander beyond visitor-approved areas. ⊠ *304 S. Broadway, southeast corner Broadway and 3rd St., Downtown* ☎ *213/626–1893.*

California African American Museum. Works by 20th-century African-American artists and contemporary art of the African diasporas are the backbone of this museum's permanent collection. Its exhibits document the African-American experience from Emancipation and Reconstruction through the 20th century, especially as expressed by artists in California and elsewhere in the West. ⊠ *600 Exposition Park, Exposition Park* ☎ *213/744–7432* ⊕ *www.caamuseum.org* ⊠ *Free, parking $10* ☉ *Tues.–Sat. 10–5, Sun. 11–5.*

Ⓒ **California Science Center.** You're bound to see excited kids running up to the dozens of interactive exhibits here that illustrate the relevance of science to everyday life, from bacteria to airplanes. Clustered in different "Worlds," this center provides opportunities to examine such topics as structures and communications, where you can be an architect and design your own building and learn how to make it earthquake-proof, to "Life" itself where Tess, the 50-foot animatronic star of the exhibit "Body Works," dramatically demonstrates how the body's organs work together. Air and Space Exhibits show what it takes to go to outer space with Gemini 11, a real capsule flown into space by Pete Conrad and Dick Gordon in September 1966. An IMAX theater shows large-format releases.

The museum is also home to NASA's Space Shuttle Endeavor, which at this writing was expected to be delivered in late 2012. Funds are currently being raised to build a new Air and Space Center, which will be the shuttle's permanent home, but in the meantime visitors can view the spacecraft in the temporary Endeavor Display Pavilion until construction is complete. ✉ *700 State Dr., Exposition Park* ☎ *213/744–7400, 323/724–3623* ⊕ *www.californiasciencecenter.org* ✉ *Free, except for IMAX, prices vary; parking $10* ⊙ *Daily 10–5.*

Japanese American National Museum. What was it like to grow up on a sugar plantation in Hawaii? How difficult was life for Japanese-Americans interned in concentration camps during World War II? These questions are addressed by changing exhibits at this museum in Little Tokyo. Insightful volunteer docents are on hand to share their own stories and experiences. The museum occupies an 85,000-square-foot adjacent pavilion as well as its original site in a renovated 1925 Buddhist temple. ✉ *369 E. 1st St., at Central Ave., next to Geffen Contemporary, Downtown* ☎ *213/625–0414* ⊕ *www.janm.org* ✉ *$9, free Thurs. 5–8 and 3rd Thurs. of month* ⊙ *Tues., Wed., and Fri.–Sun. 11–5; Thursday noon–8.*

☾ **Natural History Museum of Los Angeles County.** The completed renovation of the museum's 1913 beaux arts building sets the stage for new visitor experiences leading up to the centennial in 2013.

In summer 2011 the new Dinosaur Hall opened, featuring more than 300 fossils, 20 full-body specimens, manual and digital interactivity, and large-format video, as well as a T. rex series that includes adult, juvenile, and baby specimens. At this writing, an exhibit focusing on the natural and cultural history of Southern California dating from prehistoric times to modern-day Hollywood was expected to open in late 2012.

The museum has the same quaint feel of many natural history museums, with enclosed dioramas of animals in their natural habitats. But it mixes it up with interactive displays such as a seasonal Butterfly Pavilion in a separate small building in front of the museum; the Discovery Center, where kids can touch real animal pelts; the Insect Zoo; and their Dino Lab, where you can watch actual paleontologists work on dinosaur fossils.

In addition, there are also exhibits typifying various cultural groups, including pre-Columbian artifacts and a display of crafts from the South Pacific as well as marine-life exhibits. ✉ *900 Exposition Blvd., Exposition Park* ☎ *213/763–3466* ⊕ *www.nhm.org* ✉ *$12, free 1st Tues. of month except July and Aug.* ⊙ *Daily 9:30–5.*

HOLLYWOOD AND THE STUDIOS

The Tinseltown mythology of Los Angeles was born in Hollywood. Daytime attractions can be found on foot around the home of the Academy Awards at the Dolby Theatre, part of the Hollywood & Highland entertainment complex. The adjacent Grauman's Chinese Theatre delivers silver screen magic with its cinematic facade and ornate interiors from a bygone era. Walk the renowned Hollywood Walk of Stars to find your favorite celebrities' hand- and footprints. In summer, visit the crown jewel of Hollywood, the Hollywood Bowl, which features shows by the Los Angeles Philharmonic.

The San Fernando Valley gets a bad rap. There are even some Angelenos who swear, with a sneer, that they will never set foot in "the Valley." But despite all the snickering, it's where the majority of studios that have made Los Angeles famous are located.

TOP ATTRACTIONS

★ **Grauman's Chinese Theatre.** A place that inspires the phrase "only in Hollywood," these stylized Chinese pagodas and temples have become a shrine to stardom. Although you have to buy a movie ticket to appreciate the interior trappings, the courtyard is open to the public. The main theater itself is worth visiting, if only to see a film in the same seats as hundreds of celebrities who have attended big premieres here.

And then, of course, outside in front are the oh-so-famous cement hand- and footprints. This tradition is said to have begun at the theater's opening in 1927, with the premiere of Cecil B. DeMille's *King of Kings,* when actress Norma Talmadge just happened to step into wet cement. Now more than 160 celebrities have contributed imprints for posterity, including some oddball specimens, such as ones of Whoopi Goldberg's dreadlocks. ⊠ *6925 Hollywood Blvd., Hollywood* ☎ *323/464–8111* ⊕ *www.chinesetheatres.com.*

★ **Griffith Observatory.** High on a hillside overlooking the city, the Griffith Observatory is one of the most celebrated icons of Los Angeles. And now its interior is as impressive as its exterior after a massive expansion and cosmic makeover. Highlights of the building include the Foucoult's pendulum hanging in the main lobby, the planet exhibitions on the lower level, and the playful wall display of galaxy-themed jewelry along the twisty indoor ramp.

In true L.A. style, the Leonard Nimoy Event Horizon Theater presents guest speakers and shows on current space-related topics and discoveries. The planetarium now features a new dome, laser digital projection system, theatrical lighting, and a stellar sound system. Shows are $7.

Grab a meal at the Café at the End of the Universe, which serves up dishes created by celebrity chef Wolfgang Puck of Spago. For a fantastic view, come is at sunset to watch the sky turn fiery shades of red with the city's skyline silhouetted. ⊠ *2800 E. Observatory Rd., Griffith Park* ☎ *213/473–0800* ⊕ *www.griffithobservatory.org* ◷ *Wed.–Fri. noon–10, weekends 10–10.*

Fodor's Choice **Hollywood Museum.** Lovers of Hollywood's glamorous past will be sing-
★ ing "Hooray for Hollywood" when they stop by this gem of cinema history. It's inside the Max Factor Building, purchased in 1928. Factor's famous makeup was made on the top floors and on the ground floor was a salon. After its renovation, this art-deco landmark now holds more than 10,000 bits of film memorabilia.

The extensive exhibits inside include those dedicated to Marilyn Monroe and Bob Hope and to costumes and set props from such films as *Moulin Rouge, The Silence of the Lambs,* and *Planet of the Apes.* There's an impressive gallery of photos showing movie stars frolicking at such venues as the Brown Derby, Ciro's, the Trocadero, and the Mocambo.

Hollywood

4

Hollywood Fwy. 101

Franklin Ave.
Orchid Ave.
Hillcrest Rd.
Franklin Pl.
Las Palmas Ave.
Cherokee Ave.
Whitley Ave.
Grace Ave.
Hudson Ave.
Yucca St.
Ivar Ave.
Vista del Mar Ave.
Cahuenga Blvd.
Vine St.
Argyle Ave.
Gower St.
Cartos Ave.
Carltos Way
Selma Ave.
Schrader Blvd.
Cassil Pl.
Sunset Blvd.
Highland Ave.
Hawthorn Ave.
Orange Dr.
Sycamore Ave.
McCadden Pl.
Wilcox Ave.
Cosmo St.
Morningside Ct.

Hollywood Blvd.

◆ Hollywood Roosevelt Hotel
◆ Hollywood High School
◆ Snow White Cafe
◆ Hollywood Wax Museum
◆ Ripley's Believe It Or Not
◆ Guiness World of Records
◆ Egyptian Theatre
◆ Pig 'n Whistle
◆ Musso & Frank Grill
◆ Avalon Theatre
◆ Capitol Records Tower
◆ Pantages Theatre
Ⓜ Hollywood & Vine
◆ The Music Box @ Fonda Theatre
◆ Arclight/ Cinema Dome
▶ Gower Gulch

Ⓜ Hollywood/ Highland

➀ ➁ ➂ ➃ ➄ ➅ ➆ ➇ ➈

0   1/4 km
0   1/4 mi

Hallway walls are covered with the stunning autograph collection of ultimate fan Joe Ackerman; aspiring filmmakers will want to check out an exhibit of early film equipment. The museum's showpiece, however, is the Max Factor exhibit, where separate dressing rooms are dedicated to Factor's "color harmony": creating distinct looks for "brownettes" (Factor's term), redheads, and of course, bombshell blondes. You can practically smell the peroxide of Marilyn Monroe getting her trademark platinum look here, and see makeup cases owned by Lucille Ball, Lana Turner, Ginger Rogers, Bette Davis, Rita Hayworth, and others who made the makeup as popular as the starlets who wore it. ✉ *1660 N. Highland Ave., Hollywood* ☎ *323/464–7776* ⊕ *www. thehollywoodmuseum.com* 🎫 *$15* ⊙ *Wed.–Sun. 10–5.*

★ **Hollywood Walk of Fame.** Along Hollywood Boulevard runs a trail of affirmations for entertainment-industry overachievers. On this mile-long stretch of sidewalk, inspired by the concrete handprints in front of Grauman's Chinese Theatre, names are embossed in brass, each at the center of a pink star embedded in dark-gray terrazzo. They're not all screen deities; many stars commemorate people who worked in a technical field. The first eight stars were unveiled in 1960 at the northwest corner of Highland Avenue and Hollywood Boulevard: Olive Borden, Ronald Colman, Louise Fazenda, Preston Foster, Burt Lancaster, Edward Sedgwick, Ernest Torrence, and Joanne Woodward (some of these names have stood the test of time better than others). Since then, more than 2,000 others have been immortalized, though that honor doesn't come cheap—upon selection by a special committee, the personality in question (or more likely his or her movie studio or record company) pays about $30,000 for the privilege. To aid you in spotting celebrities you're looking for, stars are identified by one of five icons: a motion-picture camera, a radio microphone, a television set, a record, or a theatrical mask. Contact the **Hollywood Chamber of Commerce** (✉ *7018 Hollywood Blvd.* ☎ *323/469–8311* ⊕ *www.walkof-fame.com*) for celebrity-star locations and information on future star installations.

WORTH NOTING

★ **Dolby Theatre.** Taking a half-hour tour of the theater that hosts the Academy Awards isn't cheap, but it's a worthwhile expense for movie buffs who just can't get enough insider information.

Tour guides share plenty of behind-the-scenes tidbits about Oscar ceremonies as they take you through the theater. You'll get to step into the VIP lounge, where celebrities mingle on the big night, and get a bird's-eye view from the balcony seating.

The interior design was inspired by European opera houses, but underneath all the trimmings, the space has one of the finest technical systems in the world.

If you aren't one of the lucky few with a ticket to the Oscars, get a glimpse of the inside by attending a performance of *Cirque du Soleil's* long-running *Iris,* a musical and acrobatic tour of cinematic history. ✉ *6801 Hollywood Blvd., Hollywood* ☎ *323/308–6300* ⊕ *www. dolbytheatre.com* 🎫 *Free; tours $15* ⊙ *Daily 10:30–4.*

★ **Hollywood & Highland.** Bringing some glitz, foot traffic, and commerce back to Hollywood, the hotel-retail-entertainment complex here has become a huge tourist magnet. The design pays tribute to the city's film legacy with a grand staircase leading up to a pair of white stucco 33-foot-high elephants, a nod to the 1916 movie *Intolerance.* (Something tells us that the reference is lost on most visitors.) ■TIP→ **Pause at the entrance arch, Babylon Court, which frames the "Hollywood" sign in the hills above for a picture-perfect view.**

There are plenty of clothing stores and eateries, and you may find yourself ducking into these for a respite from the crowds and street artists. In summer and during Christmas vacation—when the complex is at its busiest—special music programs and free entertainment keep strollers entertained.

A Metro Red Line station provides easy access to and from other parts of the city, and there's plenty of underground parking accessible from Highland Avenue. ✉ *Hollywood Blvd. and Highland Ave., Hollywood* ☎ *323/467–6412 visitor center* ⊕ *www.hollywoodandhighland.com* 🎫 *Parking $2 with validation* ☉ *Mon.–Sat. 10–10, Sun. 10–7.*

Hollywood Bowl. Classic Hollywood doesn't get better than this. Summer-evening concerts have been a tradition since 1922 at this amphitheater cradled in the Hollywood Hills. The Bowl is the summer home of the Los Angeles Philharmonic, but the musical fare also includes pop and jazz. A new much larger shell arrived in 2004, improving the acoustics and allowing the occasional dance and theater performance on stage with the orchestra.

Evoking the 1929 shell structure, the revised shell ripples out in a series of concentric rings. The 17,000-plus seating capacity ranges from boxes (where alfresco preconcert meals are catered) to concrete bleachers in the rear. Most of the box seats are reserved for season ticket holders, but the ideally located Super Seats, with comfortable armrests and great sight lines, are a great alternative. Dollar tickets are available for some weeknight classical and jazz performances. Come early to picnic on the grounds. ✉ *2301 N. Highland Ave., Hollywood* ☎ *323/850–2000* ⊕ *www.hollywoodbowl.com* 🎫 *Museum free* ☉ *Grounds daily dawn–dusk, call or check online for performance schedule.*

  Hollywood Bowl Museum. Before the concert, or during the day, visit the Hollywood Bowl Museum for a time-capsule version of the Bowl's history. The microphone used during Frank Sinatra's 1943 performance is just one of the pieces of rare memorabilia on display.

Throughout the gallery, drawers open to reveal vintage programs or letters written by fans tracing their fondest memories of going to the Bowl. Headphones let you listen to recordings of such great Bowl performers as Amelita Galli-Curci, Ella Fitzgerald, and Paul McCartney, and videos give you a tantalizing look at performances by everyone from the Beatles to Esa-Pekka Salonen. Be sure to pick up a map and take the "Bowl Walk" to explore the parklike grounds of this beautiful setting. During the summer, the store stays open until showtime. ☎ *323/850–2058* ☉ *Tues.–Fri. 10–5, Sat. by appointment*

★ **Hollywood Sign.** With letters 50 feet tall, Hollywood's trademark sign can be spotted from miles away. The sign, which originally read "Hollywoodland," was erected on Mt. Lee in the Hollywood Hills in 1923 to promote a real-estate development. In 1949 the "land" portion of the sign was taken down. By 1973, the sign had earned landmark status, but since the letters were made of wood, its longevity came into question. A makeover project was launched and the letters were auctioned off (rocker Alice Cooper bought the "o," singing cowboy Gene Autry sponsored an "l") to make way for a new sign made of sheet metal. Inevitably, the sign has drawn pranksters who have altered it over the years, albeit temporarily, to spell out "Yollyweed" (in the 1970s, to commemorate lenient marijuana laws), "go navy" (before a Rose Bowl game), and "Perotwood" (during the 1992 presidential election). A fence and surveillance equipment have since been installed to deter intruders. Use caution if driving up to the sign on residential streets since many cars speed around the blind corners. ⊕ *www.hollywoodsign.org.*

BEVERLY HILLS AND THE WESTSIDE

If you only have a day to see L.A., see Beverly Hills. Love it or hate it, it delivers on a dramatic, cinematic scale of wealth and excess. West Hollywood is not a place to see things (like museums or movie studios)

A mural depicting Hollywood's legends (John Wayne, Elvis Presley, and Marilyn Monroe are pictured here) adorns a wall of West Hollywood's Stella Adler Academy on Highland Avenue.

as much as it is a place to do things—like go to a nightclub, eat at a world-famous restaurant, or attend an art gallery opening.

The three-block stretch of Wilshire Boulevard known as Museum Row, east of Fairfax Avenue, racks up five intriguing museums and a prehistoric tar pit to boot. Only a few blocks away are the historic Farmers Market and The Grove shopping mall, a great place to people-watch over breakfast. Wilshire Boulevard itself is something of a cultural monument—it begins its grand 16-mile sweep to the sea in Downtown Los Angeles.

For some privileged Los Angelenos, the city begins west of La Cienega Boulevard, where keeping up with the Joneses becomes an epic pursuit. Chic, attractive neighborhoods with coveted postal codes—Bel Air, Brentwood, Westwood, West Los Angeles, and Pacific Palisades—are home to power couples pushing power kids in power strollers. Still, the Westside is rich in culture—and not just entertainment-industry culture. It's home to UCLA, the monumental Getty Center, and the engrossing Museum of Tolerance.

TOP ATTRACTIONS

Fodor'sChoice
★ **Farmers Market and The Grove.** The saying "Meet me at 3rd and Fairfax" became a standard line for generations of Angelenos who ate, shopped, and spotted the stars who drifted over from the studios for a breath of unpretentious air. Starting back in 1934 when two entrepreneurs convinced oil magnate E.B. Gilmore to open a vacant field for a bare-bones market, this spot became a humble shop for farmers selling produce out of their trucks. From this seat-of-the-pants situation grew a European-

style open-air market and local institution at the corner of 3rd Street and Fairfax Avenue.

Now the market includes 110 stalls and more than 30 restaurants, plus the landmark 1941 Clock Tower. The Grove celebrated its 10th anniversary in 2012, and the outdoor mall, with its pseudo-European facade, cobblestones, marble mosaics, and pavilions has never been more popular or packed, especially on weekends and holidays.

Los Angeles history gets a nod with the electric steel-wheeled Red Car trolley, which shuttles two blocks through the Farmers Market and The Grove. If you hate crowds, try visiting The Grove before noon for the most comfortable shopping experience. By afternoon, it bustles with shoppers and teens hitting the movie theaters and chain stores such as Banana Republic, Crate & Barrel, Barnes & Noble, and J. Crew. Fashionistas find a haven at the Barney's Co-Op store. The parking structure on the east side for The Grove handles the cars by monitoring the number of spaces available as you go up each level, combined with the first hour free and a second hour free if you get your ticket validated, which helps to make parking less of a pain. Surface parking for the Farmers Market is two hours free with validation. ■TIP➔ **The Grove really dazzles around Christmas, with an enormous Christmas tree and a nightly faux snowfall until New Year's Day.** ⊠ *Farmers Market, 6333 W. 3rd St.; The Grove, 189 The Grove Dr., Fairfax District* ☎ *323/965–9594 Farmers Market, 323/900–8080 The Grove* ⊕ *www.farmersmarketla.com; www.thegrovela.com* ◷ *Farmers Market weekdays 9–9, Sat. 9–8, Sun. 10–7; The Grove Mon.–Thurs. 10–9, Fri. and Sat. 10–10, Sun. 10–8.*

ⓒ **The Getty Center.** With its curving walls and isolated hilltop perch, the
Fodor'sChoice Getty Center resembles a pristine fortified city of its own. You may have
★ been lured up by the beautiful views of L.A. (on a clear day stretching all the way to the Pacific Ocean), but the architecture, uncommon gardens, and fascinating art collections will be more than enough to capture and hold your attention. When the sun is out, the complex's rough-cut travertine marble skin seems to soak up the light.

J. Paul Getty, the billionaire oil magnate and art collector, began collecting Greek and Roman antiquities and French decorative arts in the 1930s. He opened the J. Paul Getty Museum at his Malibu estate in 1954, and in the 1970s, he built a re-creation of an ancient Roman village to house his initial collection. When Getty died in 1976, the museum received an endowment of $700 million that grew to a reported $4.5 billion. The Malibu villa, reopened in 2006, is devoted to the antiquities. The Getty Center, designed by Richard Meier, opened in 1998 and pulled together the rest of the collections, along with the museum's affiliated research, conservation, and philanthropic institutes.

Getting to the center involves a bit of anticipatory lead-up. At the base of the hill, a pavilion disguises the underground parking structure. From there you either walk or take a smooth, computer-driven tram up the steep slope, checking out the Bel Air estates across the humming 405 freeway. The five pavilions that house the museum surround a central courtyard and are bridged by walkways. From the courtyard, plazas,

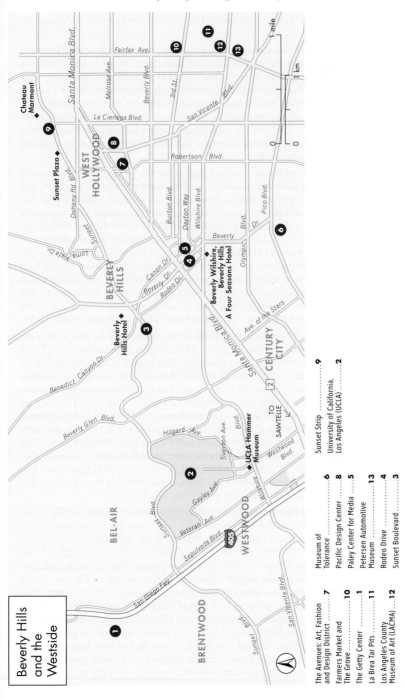

Beverly Hills and the Westside

The Avenues: Art, Fashion
and Design District **7**
Farmers Market and
The Grove **10**
The Getty Center **1**
La Brea Tar Pits **11**
Los Angeles County
Museum of Art (LACMA) ...**12**

Museum of
Tolerance **6**
Pacific Design Center **8**
Paley Center for Media ...**5**
Petersen Automotive
Museum **13**
Rodeo Drive **4**
Sunset Boulevard **3**

Sunset Strip **9**
University of California,
Los Angeles (UCLA) **2**

and walkways, you can survey the city from the San Gabriel Mountains to the ocean.

In a ravine separating the museum and the Getty Research Institute, conceptual artist Robert Irwin created the playful Central Garden in stark contrast to Meier's mathematical architectural geometry. The garden's design is what Hollywood feuds are made of: Meier couldn't control Irwin's vision, and the two men sniped at each other during construction, with Irwin stirring the pot with every loose twist his garden path took. The result is a refreshing garden walk whose focal point is an azalea maze (some insist the Mickey Mouse shape is on purpose) in a reflecting pool.

Inside the pavilions are the galleries for the permanent collections of European paintings, drawings, sculpture, illuminated manuscripts, and decorative arts, as well as American and European photographs. The Getty's collection of French furniture and decorative arts, especially from the early years of Louis XIV (1643–1715) to the end of the reign of Louis XVI (1774–92), is renowned for its quality and condition; you can see a pair of completely reconstructed salons. In the paintings galleries, a computerized system of louvered skylights allows natural light to filter in, creating a closer approximation of the conditions in which the artists painted. Notable among the paintings are Rembrandt's *The Abduction of Europa,* Van Gogh's *Irises,* Monet's *Wheatstack, Snow Effects,* and *Morning,* and James Ensor's *Christ's Entry into Brussels.*

If you want to start with a quick overview, pick up the brochure in the entrance hall that guides you to 15 highlights of the collection. There's also an instructive audio tour ($5) with commentaries by art historians. Art information rooms with multimedia computer stations contain more details about the collections. The Getty also presents lectures, films, concerts, and special programs for kids and families. The complex includes an upscale restaurant and downstairs cafeteria with panoramic window views, and two outdoor coffee bar cafés. ■ TIP➔ **On-site parking is subject to availability and can fill up by late afternoon on holidays and summer weekends, so try to come early in the day.** You may also take public transportation (MTA Bus 761). ⊠ *1200 Getty Center Dr., Brentwood* ☎ *310/440–7300* ⊕ *www.getty.edu* ▨ *Free, parking $15* ☉ *Tues.–Fri. 10–5:30, Sat. 10–9, Sun. 10–5:30.*

Ⓒ ★ **La Brea Tar Pits.** Do your children have prehistoric animals on the brain? Show them where Ice Age fossils come from by taking them to the stickiest park in town. About 40,000 years ago, deposits of oil rose to the earth's surface, collected in shallow pools, and coagulated into asphalt. In the early 20th century, geologists discovered that all that goo contained the largest collection of Pleistocene, or Ice Age, fossils ever found at one location: more than 600 species of birds, mammals, plants, reptiles, and insects. Roughly 100 tons of fossil bones have been removed in excavations over the last 100 years, making this one of the world's most famous fossil sites. You can see most of the pits through chain-link fences. (They can be a little smelly, but your kids are sure to love it.) Pit 91 and Project 23 are ongoing excavation projects; tours are available, and you can volunteer to help with the excavations in summer. There are several pits scattered around Hancock Park and the surrounding neighborhood; construction in the area has often had to accommodate them, and in nearby streets and along sidewalks, little bits of tar occasionally ooze up, unstoppable. The nearby **Page Museum at the La Brea Tar Pits** displays fossils from the tar pits and has a "Fishbowl Lab," which is a glass-walled laboratory that allows visitors a rare look behind-the-scenes of the museum where paleontologists and volunteers work on specimens. ✉ *5801 Wilshire Blvd., Hancock Park, Miracle Mile* ☎ *323/934–7243* ⊕ *www.tarpits.org* 🖻 *$7, Children under 5 free, free on 1st Tues. of each month* ☉ *Daily 9:30–5.*

Fodor's Choice ★ **Los Angeles County Museum of Art (LACMA).** Without a doubt, LACMA is the focal point of the museum district that runs along Wilshire Boulevard. Chris Burden's *Urban Light* sculpture, composed of more than two hundred restored cast iron antique street lamps, elegantly illuminate building's front.

Inside, visitors will find one of the country's most comprehensive collections of more than 100,000 objects dating from ancient times to the present. Since opening in 1965, the museum has grown into a complex of several different buildings interconnected via walkways, stretching across a 20-acre campus.

Works from the museum's rotating permanent collection include Latin American artists such as Diego Rivera and Frida Kahlo, prominent Southern California artists, collections of Islamic and European art, paintings by Henri Matisse and Rene Magritte, as well as works by Paul Klee and Wassily Kandinsky. There's also has a solid collection of art representing the ancient civilizations of Egypt, the Near East, Greece, and Rome, plus a vast costume and textiles collection dating back to the 16th century.

As part of an ambitious 10-year face-lift plan that is becoming a work of art on its own, entitled "Transformation: The LACMA Campaign," the museum is adding buildings, exhibition galleries, and redesigning public spaces and gardens.

In early 2008, the impressive Broad Contemporary Art Museum (BCAM) opened. With three vast floors, BCAM's integrates contemporary art into LACMA's collection, exploring the interplay of current times with that of the past. Then in 2010, the Lynda and Stewart Resnick Exhibition Pavilion was added, a stunning, light-filled space designed by Renzo Piano.

LACMA other buildings include the Ahmanson Building, which contains African, Middle Eastern, South and Southeast Asian collections, as well as the Gore Rifkind Gallery for German Expressionism; the Art of the Americas building; the Pavilion for Japanese Art, featuring scrolls, screens, drawings, paintings, textiles, and decorative arts from Japan; the Bing Center, a research library, resource center, and film theater; and the Boone's Children's Gallery, located inside the Korean art galleries in the Hammer Building, where kids can take advantage of activities such as story time and learning how to brush paint. The museum organizes special exhibitions and hosts major traveling shows.

■TIP→ Temporary exhibits sometimes require tickets purchased in advance, so check the calendar ahead of time. ✉ *5905 Wilshire Blvd., Miracle Mile* ☎ *323/857–6000* ⊕ *www.lacma.org* ☞ *$15, free for children under 17* ☉ *Mon., Tues., and Thurs. noon–8, Fri. noon–9, weekends 11–8.*

☺ **Museum of Tolerance.** Using interactive technology, this important museum (part of the Simon Wiesenthal Center) challenges visitors to confront bigotry and racism. One of the most affecting sections covers the Holocaust, with film footage of deportation scenes and simulated sets of concentration camps. Each visitor is issued a "passport" bearing the name of a child whose life was dramatically changed by the German Nazi rule and by World War II; as you go through the exhibit, you learn the fate of that child. Anne Frank artifacts are part of the museum's permanent collection as is Wiesenthal's Vienna office, set exactly as the famous "Nazi hunter" had it while performing his research that brought more than 1,000 war criminals to justice. Interactive exhibits include the "Millennium Machine," which engages visitors in finding solutions to human rights abuses around the world; Globalhate.com, which examines hate on the Internet by exposing problematic sites via touch-screen computer terminals; and the "Point of View Diner," a re-creation of a 1950s diner, red booths and all, that "serves" a menu of controversial topics on video jukeboxes. Renovations brought a new youth action floor and revamped 300-seat theater space. To ensure a visit to this popular museum, make reservations in advance (especially for Friday, Sunday, and holidays) and plan to spend at least three hours there. Testimony from Holocaust survivors is offered at specified times. Museum entry stops at least two hours before the actual closing time. Although every exhibit may not be appropriate for children, school tours regularly visit the museum. ✉ *9786 W. Pico Blvd., just south of Beverly Hills* ☎ *310/553–8403* ⊕ *www.museumoftolerance. com* ☞ *$15.50* ☉ *Weekdays 10–5, closed Sat., Sun. 11–5, early close at 3 pm Fri. Nov.–Mar.*

☺ **Petersen Automotive Museum.** You don't have to be a gearhead to appreciate this building full of antique and unusual cars. The Petersen is likely to be one of the coolest museums in town with its take on some of the most unusual creations on wheels and rotating exhibits of the icons who drove them. Lifelike dioramas and street scenes spread through the ground floor help to establish a local context for the history of the automobile. The second floor may include displays of Hollywood-celebrity and movie cars, "muscle" cars (like a 1969 Dodge Daytona 440 Magnum), alternative-powered cars, motorcycles, and a showcase of the Ferrari. You can also learn about the origins of our modern-day car-insurance system, as well as the history of L.A.'s formidable freeway network. A children's interactive Discovery Center illustrates the mechanics of the automobile and fun child-inspired creations; there is also a gift shop. ✉ *6060 Wilshire Blvd., Miracle Mile* ☎ *323/930–2277* ⊕ *www.petersen.org* ☞ *$10* ☉ *Tues.–Sun. 10–6.*

★ **Sunset Boulevard.** One of the most fabled avenues in the world, Sunset Boulevard began humbly enough in the 18th century as a route from El Pueblo de Los Angeles (today's Downtown L.A.) to the ranches in the west and then to the Pacific Ocean. Now as it winds its way across the L.A. basin to the ocean, it cuts through gritty urban neighborhoods and what used to be the working center of Hollywood's movie industry. In West Hollywood, it becomes the sexy and seductive Sunset Strip, then slips quietly into the tony environs of Beverly Hills and Bel Air, twisting and winding past gated estates. Continuing on past UCLA in Westwood, through Brentwood and Pacific Palisades, Sunset finally descends to the beach, the edge of the continent, and the setting sun.

WORTH NOTING

The Avenues: Art, Fashion and Design District. Established in 1996, the area defined by Melrose Avenue and Robertson and Beverly boulevards is The Avenues: Art, Fashion & Design District. More than 300 businesses including art galleries, antiques shops, contemporary furniture and interior design stores, high-end boutiques, and about 40 restaurants are clustered here. Note that some showrooms are reserved for design professionals and require trade credentials, and not open to the public. ✉ *Melrose Ave. and Robertson and Beverly Blvds.* ☎ *310/289–2534* ⊕ *www.avenueswh.com.*

Pacific Design Center. World-renowned architect Cesar Pelli's original vision for the Pacific Design Center was three buildings that together housed designer showrooms, office buildings, parking and more—a virtual multi-building shrine to design. These architecturally intriguing buildings were built years apart: the building sheathed in blue glass (known as the Blue Whale) opened in 1975; the green building opened in 1988. In 2013 the final "Red" building is scheduled to open, completing Pelli's grand vision of all of these many years later. All together the 1.2 million-square-foot vast complex covers over 14 acres, housing more than 120 design showrooms as well as 2,100 interior product lines; it's the largest interior design complex in the western United States. You'll also find restaurants such as Red Seven by Wolfgang Puck, the Silverscreen movie theater, an outpost of the Museum of Contemporary Art, as well as myriad special events. Focused on the professional trade, some showrooms are open only to professionals such as credentialed decorators, but many other showrooms are open to the public. The PDC also has a Designer Service to help non-professionals shop and get access to certain designers and showrooms. ✉ *8687 Melrose Ave., West Hollywood* ☎ *310/657–0800* ⊕ *www.pacificdesigncenter. com* ☾ *Weekdays 9–5.*

MOCA at Pacific Design Center. The Downtown Museum of Contemporary Art has a small satellite MOCA Gallery here that shows works from current artists and designers and hosts exhibit-related talks. ✉ *8687 Melrose Ave., West Hollywood* ☎ *310/657–0800* ⊕ *www.moca. org.*

Paley Center for Media. Formerly the Museum of Television and Radio, this institution changed its name in 2007 with a look toward a future that encompasses all media in the ever-evolving world of entertainment and information. Reruns are taken to a curated level in this sleek stone-and-glass building, designed by Getty architect Richard Meier. A sister to the New York location, the Paley Center carries a duplicate of its collection: more than 100,000 programs spanning eight decades. Search for your favorite commercials and television shows on easy-to-use computers. A radio program listening room provides cozy seats supplied with headphones playing snippets of a variety of programming from a toast to Dean Martin to an interview with John Lennon. Frequent seminars with movers n' shakers from the film, television, and radio world are big draws, as well as screenings of documentaries and short films. Free parking is available in the lot off Santa Monica Boulevard. ⊠ *465 N. Beverly Dr., Beverly Hills* ☏ *310/786–1000* ⊕ *www.paleycenter.org* ☉ *Wed.–Sun. noon–5.*

Rodeo Drive. The ultimate shopping indulgence—Rodeo Drive is one of Southern California's bona fide tourist attractions. The art of window-shopping is prime among the retail elite: Tiffany & Co., Gucci, Jimmy Choo, Valentino, Harry Winston, Prada—you get the picture. Several nearby restaurants have patios where you can sip a drink while watching career shoppers in their size 2 threads saunter by with shopping bags stuffed with superfluous delights. At the southern end of Rodeo Drive (at Wilshire Boulevard), **Via Rodeo,** a curvy cobblestone street designed to resemble a European shopping area, makes the perfect backdrop to strike a pose for that glamour shot. The holidays bring a special magic to Rodeo and the surrounding streets with twinkling lights, swinging music, and colorful banners. ⊠ *Beverly Hills.*

University of California, Los Angeles (UCLA). With spectacular buildings such as a Romanesque library, the parklike UCLA campus makes for a fine stroll through one of California's most prestigious universities. In the heart of the north campus, the **Franklin Murphy Sculpture Garden** contains more than 70 works of artists such as Henry Moore and Gaston Lachaise. The **Mildred E. Mathias Botanic Garden,** which contains some 5,000 species of plants from all over the world in a 7-acre outdoor garden, is in the southeast section of the campus and is accessible from Tiverton Avenue. West of the main-campus bookstore, the **J.D. Morgan Center and Athletic Hall of Fame** displays the sports memorabilia and trophies of the university's athletic departments and championship teams.

Campus maps and information are available at drive-by kiosks at major entrances daily, and free 90-minute walking tours of the campus are given most weekdays at 10:15 and 2:15 and Saturday at 10:15. Call 310/825–8764 for reservations, which are required three to four weeks in advance. The campus has cafés, plus bookstores selling UCLA Bruins paraphernalia. The main-entrance gate is on Westwood Boulevard. Campus parking costs $11. ⊠ *Bordered by Le Conte, Hilgard, and Gayley Aves. and Sunset Blvd., Westwood* ⊕ *www.ucla.edu.*

Fowler Museum at UCLA. Many visitors head straight to the Fowler Museum at UCLA, which presents exhibits on the world's diverse cultures and visual arts, especially those of Africa, Asia, the Pacific, and Native and Latin America. The museum is open Wednesday through Sunday noon–5, Thursday until 8 pm. ☏ *310/825–4361* ⊕ *www.fowler. ucla.edu* ▨ *Free, parking $11, use lot 4 off Sunset Blvd.*

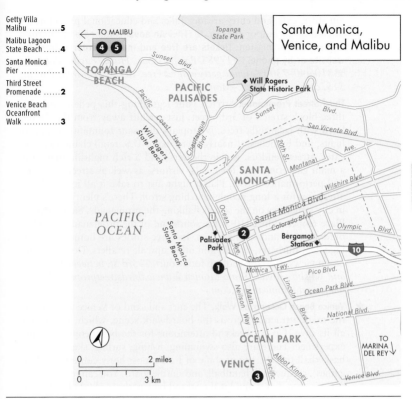

SANTA MONICA, VENICE, AND MALIBU

Hugging the Santa Monica Bay in an arch, the desirable communities of Malibu, Santa Monica, and Venice move from the ultrarich, ultracasual Malibu to the bohemian, borderline seedy Venice. What they have in common, however, is cleaner air, mild temperatures, horrific traffic, and an emphasis on the beach-focused lifestyle that many people consider the hallmark of Southern California.

TOP ATTRACTIONS

Fodor's Choice **Getty Villa Malibu.** Feeding off the cultures of ancient Rome, Greece, ★ and Etruria, the remodeled Getty Villa opened in 2006 with much fanfare—and some controversy concerning the acquisition and rightful ownership of some of the Italian artifacts on display. The antiquities are astounding, but on a first visit even they take a backseat to their environment. This megamansion sits on some of the most valuable coastal property in the world. Modeled after an Italian country home, the Villa dei Papiri in Herculaneum, the Getty Villa includes beautifully manicured gardens, reflecting pools, and statuary. The largest and most lovely garden, the Outer Peristyle, gives you glorious views over a rectangular reflecting pool and geometric hedges to the Pacific. The new structures blend thoughtfully into the rolling terrain and significantly improve the public spaces, such as the new outdoor amphitheater, gift store, café, and entry arcade. Talks and educational programs are offered at an indoor theater. ■TIP→ An advance timed entry ticket is required for admission. Tickets are free and may be ordered from the website or by phone. ⊠ *17985 Pacific Coast Hwy., Pacific Palisades* ☎ *310/440–7300* ⊕ *www.getty.edu* ⊠ *Free, tickets required. Parking $15, cash only* ☉ *Wed.–Mon. 10–5.*

Third Street Promenade. Stretch your legs along this pedestrians-only three-block stretch of 3rd Street, just a whiff away from the Pacific, lined with jacaranda trees, ivy-topiary dinosaur fountains, strings of lights, and branches of nearly every major U.S. retail chain. Outdoor cafés, street vendors, movie theaters, and a rich nightlife make this a main gathering spot for locals, visitors, as well as street musicians and performance artists. Plan a night just to take it all in or take an afternoon for a long people-watching stroll. There's plenty of parking in city structures on the streets flanking the promenade. **Santa Monica Place** reopened in 2010 at the south end of the promenade as a sleek outdoor mall and foodie haven. Its three stories are home to Bloomingdale's, Burberry, Coach, and other upscale retailers. Don't miss the ocean views from the rooftop food court. ⊠ *3rd St. between Colorado and Wilshire Blvds., Santa Monica* ⊕ *www.thirdstreetpromenade.com, www.santamonicaplace.com.*

★   **Venice Beach Oceanfront Walk.** The surf and sand of Venice are fine, but the main attraction here is the boardwalk scene, which is a cosmos all its own. Go on weekend afternoons for the best people-watching experience. There are also swimming, fishing, surfing, skateboarding, basketball (it's the site of some of L.A.'s most hotly contested pickup games), racquetball, handball, and shuffleboard. You can rent a bike or some in-line skates and hit the Strand bike path. ⊠ *1800 Ocean Front Walk, west of Pacific Ave., Venice* ☎ *310/392–4687* ⊕ *www.westland.net/venice.*

WORTH NOTING

Malibu Lagoon State Beach. Bird-watchers, take note: in this 5-acre marshy area you can spot egrets, blue herons, avocets, and gulls. (You need to stay on the boardwalks so as not to disturb their habitats.) The path leads out to a rocky stretch of Surfrider Beach and makes for a pleasant stroll. You're also likely to spot a variety of marine life. Look for the signs to help identify these sometimes exotic-looking creatures. The lagoon is particularly enjoyable in the early morning and at sunset. The parking lot has limited hours, but street-side parking is usually available at off-peak times. **Amenities:** parking. **Best for:** sunset; walking. ⊠ *23200 Pacific Coast Hwy., Malibu* ☎ *310/457–8143* ⊕ *www.parks.ca.gov* ⊠ *$12 parking.*

☾   **Santa Monica Pier.** Souvenir shops, a psychic adviser, carnival games, arcades, eateries, an outdoor trapeze school, and **Pacific Park** are all part the festive atmosphere of this truncated pier at the foot of Colorado Boulevard below Palisades Park. The pier's indoor trademark 46-horse Looff Carousel, built in 1922, has appeared in several films, including *The Sting*. Free concerts are held on the pier in summer. ⊠ *Colorado Ave. and the ocean, Santa Monica* ☎ *310/458–8900*

Pasadena Area

⊕ *www.santamonicapier.org* ⊙ *Hrs vary by season; check website before visiting.*

PASADENA AREA

Although seemingly absorbed into the general Los Angeles sprawl, Pasadena is a separate and distinct city. Noted for its Tournament of Roses, seen around the world each New Year's Day, the city brims with noteworthy spots, from its gorgeous Craftsman homes to its exceptional museums, particularly the Norton Simon and the Huntington Library, Art Collections, and Botanical Gardens. Where else can you see a Chaucer manuscript and rare cacti in one place?

TOP ATTRACTIONS

Fodor's Choice **Huntington Library, Art Collections, and Botanical Gardens.** If you have
★ time for only one stop in the Pasadena area, it should be the Huntington, built in the early 1900s as the home of railroad tycoon Henry E. Huntington. You can truly forget you're in a city here wandering the ground's 150 acres, just over the Pasadena line in San Marino.

Henry and his wife, Arabella (who was his aunt by marriage), voraciously collected rare books and manuscripts, botanical specimens, and 18th-century British art. The institution they established became one of the most extraordinary cultural complexes in the world. ■TIP→ Ongoing gallery renovations occasionally require some works from the permanent collection to be shifted to other buildings for display.

Among the highlights are John Constable's intimate *View on the Stour near Dedham* and the monumental *Sarah Siddons as the Tragic Muse,* by Joshua Reynolds. In the Virginia Steele Scott Gallery of American Art, which reopened in May 2009 after extensive renovations, you can see paintings by Mary Cassatt, Frederic Remington, and more.

The library contains more than 700,000 books and 4 million manuscripts, including such treasures as a Gutenberg Bible, the Ellesmere manuscript of Chaucer's *Canterbury Tales,* George Washington's genealogy in his own handwriting, scores of works by William Blake, and a world-class collection of early editions of Shakespeare. You'll find some of these items in the Library Hall with more than 200 important works on display. In 2006 the library acquired more than 60,000 rare books and reference volumes from the Cambridge, Massachusetts–based Bundy Library, making the Huntington the source of one of the biggest history of science collections in the world.

Although the art collections are increasingly impressive here, don't resist being lured outside into the stunning Botanical Gardens. From the main buildings, lawns and towering trees stretch out toward specialty areas. The 10-acre Desert Garden, for instance, has one of the world's largest groups of mature cacti and other succulents, arranged by continent. Visit this garden on a cool morning or in the late afternoon, or a hot midday walk may be a little too authentic.

In the remodeled Japanese Garden, an arched bridge curves over a pond; the area also has stone ornaments, a ceremonial Japanese tea house, a bonsai court, and a Zen rock garden. There are collections of azaleas and 1,500 varieties of camellias. The 3-acre rose garden is displayed chronologically, so the development leading to modern varieties of roses can be observed; on the grounds is the charming Rose Garden Tea Room, where traditional afternoon tea is served. (Reservations required for English tea.) There are also herb, palm, and jungle gardens, plus the Shakespeare Garden, which blooms with plants mentioned in Shakespeare's works.

The Rose Hills Foundation Conservatory for Botanical Science, a massive greenhouse–style center with dozens of kid-friendly, hands-on exhibits illustrate plant diversity in various environments. (These rooms are quite warm and humid, especially the central rotunda, which displays rain-forest plants.)

The Bing Children's Garden is a tiny tot's wonderland filled with opportunities for children to explore the ancient elements of water, fire, air, and earth. A classical Chinese Garden "Liu Fang Yuan" (or Garden of Flowing Fragrance) opened in spring 2008, the largest of its kind outside China. The quaint Chinese Garden Tea House overlooks the small lagoon and serves dim sum. A 1¼-hour guided tour of the botanical gardens is led by docents at posted times, and a free brochure with map and highlights is available in the entrance pavilion. ⊠ *1151 Oxford Rd., San Marino* ☎ *626/405–2100* ⊕ *www.huntington.org* ☎ *$15 weekdays,*

$20 weekends, free 1st Thurs. of month (reservations required) ☉ Mon. and Wed.–Fri. noon–4:30, weekends 10:30–4:30; call for summer hrs.

Fodor'sChoice   **Norton Simon Museum.** Long familiar to television viewers of the New
★   Year's Day Rose Parade, this low-profile brown building is more than just a background for the passing floats. It's one of the finest small museums anywhere, with an excellent collection that spans more than 2,000 years of Western and Asian art. It all began in the 1950s when Norton Simon (Hunt-Wesson Foods, McCalls Corporation, and Canada Dry) started collecting the works of Degas, Renoir, Gauguin, and Cézanne. His collection grew to include old masters, impressionists, and modern works from Europe and Indian and Southeast Asian art. After he retired, Simon reorganized the failing Pasadena Art Institute and continued to assemble one of the world's finest collections.

Today the Norton Simon Museum is richest in works by Rembrandt, Goya, Picasso, and, most of all, Degas: this is one of the only two U.S. institutions to hold the complete set of the artist's model bronzes (the other is New York's Metropolitan Museum of Art). Renaissance, baroque, and rococo masterpieces include Raphael's profoundly spiritual *Madonna with Child with Book* (1503), Rembrandt's *Portrait of a Bearded Man in a Wide-Brimmed Hat* (1633), and a magical Tiepolo ceiling, *The Triumph of Virtue and Nobility Over Ignorance* (1740–50). The museum's collections of Impressionist (Van Gogh, Matisse, Cézanne, Monet, Renoir) and Cubist (Braque, Gris) works are extensive. Several Rodin sculptures are placed throughout the museum. Head down to the bottom floor to see rotating exhibits and phenomenal Southeast Asian and Indian sculptures and artifacts, where graceful pieces like a Ban Chiang blackware vessel date to well before 1000 BC. Don't miss a living artwork outdoors: the garden, conceived by noted southern California landscape designer Nancy Goslee Power. The tranquil pond was inspired by Monet's gardens at Giverny. ⊠ *411 W. Colorado Blvd., Pasadena* ☎ *626/449–6840* ⊕ *www.nortonsimon.org* ⊠ *$10, free 1st Fri. of month 6–9 pm* ☉ *Wed., Thurs., and Sat.–Mon. noon–6, Fri. noon–9.*

WORTH NOTING

★   **Gamble House.** Built by Charles and Henry Greene in 1908, this is a spectacular example of American Arts and Crafts bungalow architecture. The term *bungalow* can be misleading, since the Gamble House is a huge three-story home. To wealthy Easterners such as the Gambles (as in Procter & Gamble), this type of vacation home seemed informal compared with their mansions back home. What makes admirers swoon is the incredible amount of handcraftsmanship, including a teak staircase and cabinetry, Greene and Greene–designed furniture, and an Emil Lange glass door. The dark exterior has broad eaves, with sleeping porches on the second floor. An hour-long, docent-led tour of the Gamble's interior will draw your eye to the exquisite details. If you want to see more Greene and Greene homes, buy a self-guided tour map of the neighborhood in the bookstore. ⊠ *4 Westmoreland Pl., Pasadena* ☎ *626/793–3334* ⊕ *www.gamblehouse.org* ⊠ *$10* ☉ *Thurs.–*

Sun. noon–3; tickets go on sale Thurs.–Sat. at 10, Sun. at 11:30. 1-hr tour every 15–30 mins.

★ **Old Town Pasadena.** Once the victim of decay, the area was revitalized in the 1990s as a blend of restored 19th-century brick buildings with a contemporary overlay. A phalanx of chain stores has muscled in, but there are still some homegrown shops and plenty of tempting cafés and restaurants. In the evening and on weekends, streets are packed with people, and Old Town crackles with energy. The 12-block historic district is anchored along Colorado Boulevard between Pasadena Avenue and Arroyo Parkway.

Rose Bowl. With an enormous rose, the city of Pasadena's logo, adorned on its exterior, it's hard to miss this 100,000-seat stadium, host of many Super Bowls and home to the UCLA Bruins. Set in Brookside Park at the wide bottom of an arroyo, the facility is closed except during games and special events such as the monthly Rose Bowl Flea Market, which is considered the granddaddy of West Coast flea markets. If you want the best selection of items, show up early. People start arriving here at the crack of dawn, but note you will also pay a higher entry fee for having first dibs on the selection. The best bargaining takes place at the end of the day when vendors would rather settle for a few less dollars then have to lug their goods home. ⊠ *1001 Rose Bowl Dr., at Rosemont Ave., Pasadena* ☎ *626/577–3100* ⊕ *www.rosebowlstadium. com for flea market, www.rgcshows.com for shows* ⊠ *$8 from 9 am on, $10 for 8–9 am entrance, $15 for 7–8 am entrance* ☉ *Flea market 2nd Sun. of month 9–3.*

WHERE TO EAT

Dining out in Los Angeles tends to be a casual affair, and even at some of the most expensive restaurants you're likely to see customers in jeans (although this is not necessarily considered in good taste). Despite its veneer of decadence, L.A. is not a particularly late-night city for eating. (The reenergized Hollywood dining scene is emerging as a notable exception.) The peak dinner times are from 7 to 9, and most restaurants won't take reservations after 10 pm. Generally speaking, restaurants are closed either Sunday or Monday; a few are shuttered both days. Most places—even the upscale spots—are open for lunch on weekdays, when Hollywood megadeals are conceived.

Use the coordinate (✛ 1:A1) at the end of each listing to locate a site on the corresponding map.

RESTAURANT COSTS
Prices in the restaurant reviews are the average cost of a main course at dinner or, if dinner is not served, at lunch (excluding sales tax).

The map contains the following labels:

Little Flower Candy Co.
Langham Huntington Pasadena
TO PASADENA
101
Cesar Chavez Ave.
Ord St.
N. Broadway
New High St.
Spring St.
Philippe the Original
Alameda St.
2nd St.
Boylston St.
Miramar St.
3rd St.
4th St.
Maryland St.
5th St.
6th St.
Bixel St.
Boylston St.
Beaudry Ave.
Harbor Fwy.
110
Figueroa St.
Flower St.
Hope St.
Grand Ave.
Olive St.
Temple St.
Hollywood Fwy.
Aliso St.
1st St.
Arcadia St.
N. Main St.
Patina
Wilshire Blvd.
The Standard, Downtown L.A.
Hilton Checkers Los Angeles
Millennium Biltmore Hotel
Water Grill
4th St.
5th St.
Hill St.
Broadway
Spring St.
Main St.
2nd St.
1st St.
Central Ave.
Alameda St.
Pershing Square
3rd St.
TO CONVENTION CENTER
Hope St.
7th St.
Bottega Louie
8th St.
6th St.
Wood Spoon
Los Angeles St.
Maple Ave.
Figueroa Hotel
9th St.

0   1/4 mile
0   400 meters

DOWNTOWN WITH LOS FELIZ

DOWNTOWN

$$
ITALIAN
Fodor's Choice
★

✕ **Bottega Louie.** This former Brooks Brother's suit store was reincarnated into a lively Italian restaurant and gourmet market in 2008 and quickly crowned Downtown's new culinary darling. Vast open space, stark white walls and long windows that stretch from floor to ceiling give it a grand and majestic appeal. An army of stylish servers weave in-and-out of the crowds carrying bowls of pasta, trays of bubbly Prosecco, and thin-crust pizzas. Pick and choose from a bevy of salads, pastas, pizzas, and entrées that range from shrimp scampi to a hearty New York strip steak. Or simply order from its small-plates menu with favorites: asparagus with fried egg, burrata and roasted vine tomatoes, tomato bruschetta, and fried calamari. Don't let the crowd of people waiting for a table deter you.Order a cocktail from the bar, peruse the gourmet *patisserie*, and nibble on a brightly colored macaroon. $ *Average main: $18 ⊠ 700 S. Grand Ave., Downtown ☎ 213/802–1470 ⊕ www. bottegalouie.com ⌕ Reservations not accepted ✦ 1:A3.*

$$$$
FRENCH

✕ **Patina.** Formed by chef Joachim Splichal, the Patina Group's flagship restaurant has Downtown's most striking address: inside the Frank Gehry–designed Walt Disney Concert Hall. The contemporary space, surrounded by a rippled "curtain" of rich walnut, is an elegant, dramatic stage for the acclaimed restaurant's contemporary French cuisine. Seasonally changing specialties include copious amounts of foie gras,

BEST BETS FOR LOS ANGELES DINING

With thousands of restaurants to choose from, how will you decide where to eat? Fodor's writers and editors have selected their favorite restaurants by price and cuisine in the Best Bets lists below. You can also search by neighborhood—just peruse the following pages to find specific details about a restaurant in the full reviews later in the chapter.

Fodor's Choice★

Angelini Osteria, $$$, p. 212

A.O.C. $$$, p. 212

The Apple Pan, $, p. 214

Bouchon Bistro, $$$, p. 208

Bottega Louie, $$, p. 202

Cube Café and Marketplace, $$, p. 207

Little Dom's, $$, p. 204

Mélisse, $$$$, p. 215

Philippe the Original, $, p. 204

Pizzeria Mozza, $$, p. 207

Providence, $$$$, p. 208

Urasawa, $$$$, p. 209

Yuca's Hut, $, p. 205

By Price

$

The Apple Pan, p. 214

Artisan Cheese Gallery, p. 208

Father's Office, p. 215

Little Flower Candy Company, p. 216

Philippe the Original, p. 204

Pink's Hot Dogs, p. 207

Porto's Bakery, p. 205

Wood Spoon, p. 204

Yuca's Hut, p. 205

Zankou Chicken, p. 208

$$

Bombay Café, p. 215

Bottega Louie, p. 202

Cube Café and Marketplace, p. 207

Gjelina, p. 216

La Serenata Gourmet, p. 215

Little Dom's, p. 204

Pizzeria Mozza, p. 207

$$$

Angelini Osteria, p. 212

Animal, p. 205

A.O.C., p. 212

Bouchon Bistro, p. 208

Campanile, p. 213

Oliverio, p. 209

Osteria Mozza, p. 207

$$$$

Gordon Ramsay at The London, p. 213

Mélisse, $$$$, p. 215

Providence, p. 208

Urasawa, p. 209

Water Grill, p. 204

By Cuisine

AMERICAN

The Apple Pan, $, p. 214

Gjelina, $$, p. 216

Philippe the Original, $, p. 204

Pink's Hot Dogs, $, p. 207

CHINESE

Mandarette, $, p. 214

FRENCH

Mélisse, $$$$, p. 215

INDIAN

Bombay Café, $$, p. 215

ITALIAN

Angelini Osteria, $$$, p. 212

Cube Café and Marketplace, $$, p. 207

Osteria Mozza, $$$, p. 207

Pizzeria Mozza, $$, p. 207

Valentino, $$$$, p. 216

JAPANESE

Urasawa, $$$$, p. 209

MEDITERRANEAN

A.O.C., $$$, p. 212

Campanile, $$$, p. 213

MEXICAN

La Serenata Gourmet, $$, p. 215

Yuca's Hut, $, p. 205

SEAFOOD

Providence, $$$$, p. 208

Water Grill, $$$$, p. 204

4

butter-poached lobster, and medallions of venison served with lady apples. Finish with a hard-to-match cheese tray (orchestrated by a genuine *maître fromager*) and the elegant fromage blanc soufflé served with house-made bourbon ice cream. $ *Average main: $46* ⊠ *Walt Disney Concert Hall, 141 S. Grand Ave., Downtown* ☎ *213/972–3331* ⊕ *www. patinagroup.com* ⌕ *Reservations essential* ⊙ *Closed Mon.* ✛ *1:B2*

$ ✕ **Philippe the Original.** L.A.'s oldest restaurant (1908), Philippe claims
AMERICAN the French dip sandwich originated here. You can get one made with
☺ beef, pork, ham, lamb, or turkey on a freshly baked roll; the house hot
Fodor'sChoice mustard is as famous as the sandwiches. Its reputation is earned by
★ maintaining traditions, from sawdust on the floor to long communal
tables where customers debate the Dodgers or local politics. The home cooking—orders are taken at the counter where some of the motherly servers have managed their long lines for decades—includes huge breakfasts, chili, pickled eggs, and a generous pie selection. The best bargain: a cup of java for 49¢. $ *Average main: $7* ⊠ *1001 N. Alameda St., Downtown* ☎ *213/628–3781* ⊕ *www.philippes.com* ⌕ *Reservations not accepted* ▭ *No credit cards* ✛ *1:D1.*

$$$$ ✕ **Water Grill.** There's a bustling, enticing rhythm here as platters of glis-
SEAFOOD tening shellfish get whisked from the oyster bar to the newly renovated and brightened dining room with blond-wood accents. The menu is seasonally driven; all the seafood greats are represented. Start with steamed mussels, the Fijian albacore tuna Niçoise salad or a New England–style lobster roll. For entrées, consider the line caught Baja mahi-mahi sautéed with pomegranate glaze, the Atlantic cod fish-and-chips, and the bigeye tuna rubbed with maitake mushrooms and sizzling oil. Excellent desserts and a fine wine list round out this top-notch (albeit pricey) Downtown dining experience. $ *Average main: $36* ⊠ *544 S. Grand Ave., Downtown* ☎ *213/891–0900* ⊕ *www.watergrill.com* ⌕ *Reservations essential* ⊙ *No lunch weekends* ✛ *1:B3.*

$ ✕ **Wood Spoon.** There's no sign for this cozy bistro in Downtown's fash-
BRAZILIAN ion district, just a big wood spoon that locals have come to know as
☺ the beacon for great Brazilian food. Loved by students from the fashion institute, Brazilian expats, and concertgoers heading to the Orpheum Theatre for a show, this place is an affordable gem in a high-priced dining area. Order from the small plate's selection, such as *coxinha* (a Brazilian street snack made with chicken), calabreza sausage with potatoes, and salt cod *croquette*. The house favorite is a Brazilian chicken potpie or pork burger served with yam fries. $ *Average main: $15* ⊠ *107 W. 9th St., Downtown* ☎ *213/629–1765* ⊕ *www.woodspoonla. com* ⊙ *Closed Sun. and Mon.* ✛ *1:B3*

LOS FELIZ

$$ ✕ **Little Dom's.** With a $15 Monday night supper, a vintage bar with
ITALIAN a barkeep who mixes up seasonally inspired retro cocktails, and an
Fodor'sChoice attached Italian deli where one can pick up a pork cheek sub, it's not
★ surprising why Little Dom's is a neighborhood favorite. Cozy and inviting with big leather booths one can sink into for the night, the menu blends classic Italian fare with a modern sensibility, with dishes like the baked ricotta and wild boar soppressatta, rigatoni with homemade sausage, whitefish picatta, and a New York strip steak with fennel

béarnaise. This is a terrific spot for weekend brunch; order a bottle of the well-priced house wine and take a seat in the sidewalk patio. $ *Average main: $24* ✉ *2128 Hillhurst Ave., Los Feliz* ☎ *323/661–0055* ⊕ *www.littledoms.com* ⌦ *Reservations essential* ✛ *2:F1*.

$ ✕ **Yuca's Hut.** Blink and you can miss this place, whose reputation far
MEXICAN exceeds its size (it may be the tiniest place to have ever won a James
ℭ   Beard award). It's known for *carne asada*, carnitas, and *cochinita pibil*
Fodor's Choice (Yucatán-style roasted pork) tacos, burritos, and banana leaf-wrapped
★   tamales (Sat. only). This is a fast-food restaurant in the finest tradition—independent, family-owned, and sticking to what it does best. The liquor store next door sells lots of Coronas to Yuca's customers soaking up the sun on the makeshift parking-lot patio. There's no chance of satisfying a late-night craving, though; it closes at 6 pm. $ *Average main: $10* ✉ *2056 N. Hillhurst Ave., Los Feliz* ☎ *323/662–1214* ⊕ *www.yucasla.com* ⌦ *Reservations not accepted* ▭ *No credit cards* ☾ *Closed Sun.* ✛ *2:F1*

HOLLYWOOD AND THE STUDIOS

BURBANK

$ ✕ **Porto's Bakery.** Waiting in line at Porto's is as much as part of the
CUBAN experience as is indulging in a roasted pork sandwich and chocolate-
ℭ   dipped croissant. Locals love this neighborhood bakery and café that has been an L.A. staple for more than 50 years. This is its second location, just minutes away from the studios; it's a great spot to take a stroll and peruse the consignment shops run by former movie stylists. The crowded café bustles with an ambitious lunch crowd, but counter service is quick and efficient. Go for one of its tasty Cuban sandwiches like the media noche or the *pan con lechon* (roasted pork) sandwich, or try the filling *ropa vieja* (shredded beef) plate. Skipping dessert here would just be wrong. Your sweet tooth will thank you later. $ *Average main: $10* ✉ *3614 W. Magnolia Blvd., Burbank* ☎ *818/846–9100* ⊕ *www.portosbakery.com* ✛ *2:E1*.

HOLLYWOOD

$$$ ✕ **Animal.** When foodies in Los Angeles need a culinary thrill, they come
AMERICAN to this minimalist restaurant in the Fairfax District, which is light on the flash but heavy on serious food. The James Beard award–winning restaurant is owned by Jon Shook and Vinny Dotolo, two young chefs who shot to fame with a stint on *Iron Chef* and later with their own Food Network show, *Two Dudes Catering*. With a closing time of 1 am, the small restaurant is an L.A. anomaly. That assessment is also true for the restaurant's diverse clientele, which ranges from neighborhood dwellers to young Hollywood celebrities to food snobs in search of their new favorite dish. The changing daily menu consists of small plates and entrées that make it easy to explore many items, like barbecue pork belly sandwiches, *poutine* with oxtail gravy, foie gras *loco moco* (a hamburger topped with foie gras, quail egg, and Spam), and grilled quail served with plum *char-siu*. For dessert, the house specialty is a multi-layered bacon-chocolate crunch bar. $ *Average main: $25* ✉ *435 N.*

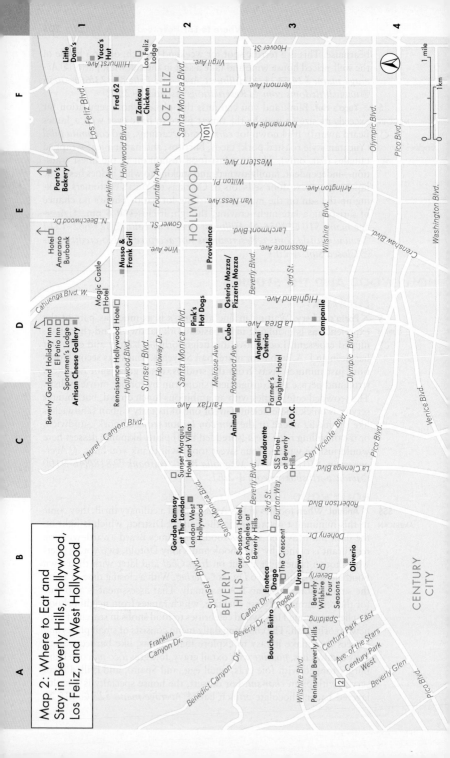

Map 2: Where to Eat and
Stay in Beverly Hills, Hollywood,
Los Feliz, and West Hollywood

Fairfax Ave., Hollywood ☎ *323/782–9225* ⊕ *www.animalrestaurant. com* ⌖ *Reservations essential* ☉ *No lunch* ✛ *2:C2.*

$$
ITALIAN
Fodor's Choice
★

✕ **Cube Café & Marketplace.** Cheese, charcuterie, and pasta lovers take heed: this dark and cozy Italian restaurant will ruin you for all the others. With more than 30 varieties of cheese, an enviable salami selection, pasta made in-house, and a passionate and earnest staff, this former pasta company turned upscale café and gourmet market is one of L.A.'s more affordable culinary gems. Take a seat at the cheese bar, order the cheesemonger's choice, and pair it with a glass of Italian wine. For dinner, order the antipasti of braised octopus, and then move onto the seasonally driven pasta dishes, like the English pea tortellini. $ *Average main: $22* ✉ *615 N. La Brea Blvd., Hollywood* ☎ *323/939–1148* ⊕ *www.eatatcube.com* ☉ *Closed Sun. and Mon.* ✛ *2:D2*

$$$
AMERICAN

✕ **Musso & Frank Grill.** Liver and onions, lamb chops, shrimp Louie salad, dry gin martinis, gruff waiters—you'll find all the old favorites here in Hollywood's oldest restaurant. A film-industry hangout since it opened in 1919, Musso & Frank still attracts the working studio set to its maroon faux-leather booths, along with tourists and locals nostalgic for Hollywood's golden era. Great breakfasts are served all day, but the kitchen's famous "flannel cakes" (pancakes) are served only until 3 pm. $ *Average main: $30* ✉ *6667 Hollywood Blvd., Hollywood* ☎ *323/467–7788* ⊕ *www.mussoandfrank.com* ☉ *Closed Sun. and Mon.* ✛ *2:E1*

$$$
ITALIAN

✕ **Osteria Mozza.** Born from the immensely popular collaboration between celebrated bread maker Nancy Silverton (founder of L.A.'s La Brea Bakery and Campanile), restaurateur Joe Bastianich, and Iron Chef Mario Batali, Osteria Mozza features candlelit, linen-clad tables surrounding a central marble-topped mozzarella bar, ideal for solo diners. From that bar come several presentations of velvety *burrata* cheese and perfectly dressed salads, while the kitchen turns out an oversize *raviolo* oozing ricotta and egg in brown butter sauce, blissful sweetbreads piccata and grilled whole *orata* (Mediterranean sea bream), capped off with Italian cheeses and delicious rosemary–olive oil cakes. If you can't score a reservation here, treat yourself to the partners' pizzeria next door. $ *Average main: $34* ✉ *6602 Melrose Ave., Hollywood* ☎ *323/297–0100* ⊕ *www.mozza-la.com* ⌖ *Reservations essential* ☉ *No lunch* ✛ *2:D2.*

$
AMERICAN
☺

✕ **Pink's Hot Dogs.** Orson Welles ate 18 of these hot dogs in one sitting, and you, too, will be tempted to order more than one. The chili dogs are the main draw, but the menu has expanded to include a Martha Stewart Dog (a 10-inch frank topped with mustard, relish, onions, tomatoes, sauerkraut, bacon, and sour cream). Since 1939, Angelenos and tourists alike have been lining up to plunk down some modest change for one of the greatest guilty pleasures in L.A. Pink's is open until 3 am on weekends. $ *Average main: $4* ✉ *709 N. La Brea Ave., Hollywood* ☎ *323/931–4223* ⊕ *www.pinkshollywood.com* ⌖ *Reservations not accepted* ▭ *No credit cards* ✛ *2:D2.*

$$
ITALIAN
Fodor's Choice
★

✕ **Pizzeria Mozza.** The other, more casual half of Batali, Bastianich, and Silverton's partnership (the first being Osteria Mozza), this casual venue gives newfound eminence to the humble "pizza joint." With traditional

Mediterranean items like white anchovies, lardo, squash blossoms, and Gorgonzola, Mozza's pies—thin-crusted delights with golden, blistered edges—are much more Campania than California, and virtually every one is a winner. Antipasti include simple salads, roasted bone marrow, and platters of *salumi*. All sing with vibrant flavors thanks to superb market-fresh ingredients, and daily specials may include favorites like lasagna. Like the menu, the Italian-only wine list is both interesting and affordable. Walk-ins are welcomed for dining at the bar. $ *Average main: $20* ⊠ *641 N. Highland Ave., Hollywood* ☎ *323/297–0101* ⊕ *www.pizzeriamozza.com* ⌕ *Reservations essential* ✛ *2:D2.*

$$$$
SEAFOOD
Fodor'sChoice
★

✕ **Providence.** Chef-owner Michael Cimarusti has elevated Providence to the ranks of America's finest seafood restaurants. The elegant dining room, outfitted with subtle nautical accents, is smoothly overseen by co-owner–general manager Donato Poto. Obsessed with quality and freshness, the meticulous chef maintains a network of specialty purveyors, some of whom tip him off to their catch before it even hits the dock. This exquisite seafood then gets the Cimarusti treatment of French technique, traditional American themes, and Asian accents, often presented in elaborate tasting menus. Pastry chef David Rodriguez's exquisite desserts are not to be missed; consider the six-course dessert tasting menu. $ *Average main: $43* ⊠ *5955 Melrose Ave., Hollywood* ☎ *323/460–4170* ⊕ *www.providencela.com* ⌕ *Reservations essential* ◎ *No lunch Mon.–Thurs. and weekends* ✛ *2:D2.*

$
MIDDLE EASTERN
☺

✕ **Zankou Chicken.** Forget the Colonel. Zankou's aromatic, Armenian-style rotisserie chicken with perfectly crisp, golden skin is one of L.A.'s truly great budget meals. It's served with pita bread, veggies, hummus, and unforgettable garlic sauce. If this doesn't do it for you, try the kebabs, falafel, or sensational *shawarma* (spit-roasted lamb or chicken) plates. $ *Average main: $9* ⊠ *5065 W. Sunset Blvd., Hollywood* ☎ *323/665–7845* ⌕ *Reservations not accepted* ✛ *2:F2.*

STUDIO CITY

$
DELI
☺

✕ **Artisan Cheese Gallery.** Taste your way through triple creams, blues, goats milk, and stinky cheeses from all over the globe at this charming locale that offers cheese and charcuterie plates, sandwiches, oversize salads, and hot panini sandwiches. Taste-testing is encouraged, so don't be shy to ask. Grab a table in small outdoor patio and enjoy the neighborhood scenery; it's a great way to experience the Valley. $ *Average main: $10* ⊠ *12023 Ventura Blvd., Studio City* ☎ *818/505–0207* ⊕ *www.artisancheesegallery.com* ⌕ *Reservations not accepted* ✛ *2:D1.*

BEVERLY HILLS AND THE WESTSIDE

BEVERLY HILLS

$$$
FRENCH
Fodor'sChoice
★

✕ **Bouchon Bistro.** Famed chef Thomas Keller finally made it back to Los Angeles and has set up his French bistro in swanky Beverly Hills. Grand and majestic, but still casual and friendly, there is nothing about an afternoon or night at Bouchon that doesn't make you feel pampered. With little details that separate it from the pack, there's filtered Norwegian water served at every table, a twig-shaped baguette made fresh in the kitchen, and an expansive wine list celebrating California and French wines. It's a foodie scene that welcomes L.A.'s high-profile chefs, celebrities, and locals. Start with its classic onion soup that arrives with a bubbling lid of cheese or the salmon rillettes, which are big enough to share. For dinner, there's a traditional steak and frites, roasted chicken, steamed Maine mussels, and a delicious grilled *croque madame*. Bouchon Bistro is also known for its beautiful French pastries. For a sweet bite, order an espresso and the profiteroles or the Bouchons (bite-size brownies served with homemade vanilla ice cream). Special dining menus can come with a tour of the multi-million dollar kitchen. ⑤ *Average main: $27* ✉ *235 N. Canon Dr., Beverly Hills* ☏ *310/271–9910* ⊕ *www.bouchonbistro.com* ⚐ *Reservations essential* ✛ *2:B3.*

$$ **✕ Enoteca Drago.** High-flying Sicilian chef Celestino Drago scores with
ITALIAN this sleek but unpretentious version of an *enoteca* (a wine bar serving small snacks). It's an ideal spot for skipping through an Italian wine list—more than 50 wines are available by the glass—and enjoying a menu made up of small plates such as stuffed olives, an assortment of cheeses and *salumi*, ricotta-stuffed zucchini flowers, or *crudo* (Italy's answer to ceviche) from the raw bar. Although the miniature mushroom-filled ravioli bathed in foie gras–truffle sauce is a bit luxurious for an enoteca, it's one of the city's best pasta dishes. Larger portions and pizzas are also available here, but the essence of an enoteca is preserved. ⑤ *Average main: $17* ✉ *410 N. Cañon Dr., Beverly Hills* ☏ *310/786–8236* ⊕ *www.celestinodrago.com* ⚐ *Reservations essential* ⊗ *Closed Sun.* ✛ *2:B3*

$$$ **✕ Oliverio.** This restaurant in the Avalon Hotel, an eco-friendly property
ITALIAN in a renovated 1950s apartment complex, feels straight out of the *Valley of the Dolls* movie. Mid-century design gives vintage appeal that blends in with the restaurant's modern Italian cuisine and Californian sensibility. Fresh food concepts are created by chef Mirko Paderno who favors seasonal ingredients. Enjoy a starter of fritto misto or a cauliflower soufflé, for dinner try the classic chicken diavolo, beef short ribs, or a risotto Milanese. Private poolside cabanas are a favorite for celebratory occasions. ⑤ *Average main: $25* ✉ *9400 W. Olympic Ave., Beverly Hills* ☏ *310/277–5221* ⊕ *www.avalonbeverlyhills.com* ✛ *2:B4.*

$$$$ **✕ Urasawa.** Shortly after celebrated sushi chef Masa Takayama packed
JAPANESE his knives for the Big Apple, his soft-spoken protégé Hiroyuki Urasawa
Fodor's Choice settled into the master's former digs. The understated sushi bar has few
★ precious seats, resulting in incredibly personalized service. At a minimum of $375 per person for a strictly *omakase* (chef's choice) meal, Urasawa remains the priciest restaurant in town, but the endless parade of masterfully crafted, exquisitely presented dishes renders few regrets. The maple sushi bar, sanded daily to a satin-like finish, is where most of the action happens. You might be served velvety bluefin toro paired with beluga caviar, slivers of foie gras to self-cook *shabu shabu* style, or egg custard layered with *uni* (sea urchin), glittering with gold leaf. This is also the place to come during *fugu* season, when the legendary, potentially deadly blowfish is artfully served to adventurous diners. ⑤ *Average main: $375* ✉ *2 Rodeo, 218 N. Rodeo Dr., Beverly Hills* ☏ *310/247–8939* ⚐ *Reservations essential* ⊗ *Closed Sun. and Mon. No lunch.* ✛ *2:B3*

SOUTH-OF-THE-BORDER FLAVOR

From Cal-Mex burritos to Mexico City–style tacos, Southern California is a top stateside destination for experiencing Mexico's myriad culinary styles.

Many Americans are surprised to learn that the Mexican menu goes far beyond Tex-Mex (or Cal-Mex) favorites like burritos, chimichangas, enchiladas, fajitas, and nachos—many of which were created or popularized stateside. Indeed, Mexico has rich, regional food styles, like the complex *mole* sauces of Puebla and Oaxaca and the fresh *ceviches* of Veracruz, as well as the trademark snack of Mexico City: tacos.

In Southern California, tacos are an obsession, with numerous blogs and websites dedicated to the quest for the perfect taco. They're everywhere—in ramshackle taco stands, roving taco trucks, and strip-mall taquerias. Whether you're looking for a cheap snack or a lunch on-the-go, SoCal's taco selection can't be beat. But be forewarned: there may not be an English menu. Here we've noted unfamiliar taco terms, along with other potentially new-to-you items from the Mexican menu.

THIRST QUENCHERS

Spanish for "fresh water," *agua fresca* is a nonalcoholic Mexican drink made from fruit, rice, or seeds that are blended with sugar and water. Fruit flavors like lemon, lime, and watermelon are common. Other varieties include *agua de Jamaica*, flavored with red hibiscus petals; *agua de horchata*, a cinnamon-scented rice milk; and *agua de tamarindo*, a bittersweet variety flavored with tamarind. If you're looking for something with a little more kick, try a *Michelada*, a beer that has been enhanced with a mixture of lime juice, chili sauce, and other savory ingredients. It's typically served in a salt-rimmed glass with ice.

DECODING THE MENU

Ceviche—Citrus-marinated seafood appetizer from the Gulf shores of Veracruz. Often eaten with tortilla chips.

Chile relleno—Roasted poblano pepper that is stuffed with ingredients like ground meat or cheese, then dipped in egg batter, fried, and served in tomato sauce.

Clayuda—A Oaxacan dish similar to pizza. Large corn tortillas are baked until hard, then topped with ingredients like refried beans, cheese, and salsa.

Fish taco—A specialty in Southern California, the fish taco is a soft corn tortilla stuffed with grilled or fried white fish (mahi-mahi, tilapia, or wahoo), pico de gallo, crema and shredded cabbage.

Gordita—"Little fat one" in Spanish, this dish is like a taco, but the cornmeal shell is thicker, similar to pita bread.

Mole—A complex, sweet sauce with Aztec roots made from more than 20 ingredients, including chilies, cinnamon, cumin, anise, black pepper, sesame seeds, and Mexican chocolate. There are many types of mole using various chilies and ingredient combinations, but the most common is *mole poblano* from the Puebla region.

Quesadilla—A snack made from a fresh tortilla that is folded over and stuffed with simple fillings like cheese, then toasted on a griddle. Elevated versions

of the quesadilla may be stuffed with sautéed *flor de calabaza* (squash blossoms) or *huitlacoche* (corn mushrooms).

Salsa—A class of cooked or raw sauces made from chilies, tomatoes, and other ingredients. Popular salsas include *pico de gallo*, a fresh sauce made from chopped tomatoes, onions, chilies, cilantro, and lime; *salsa verde*, made with tomatillos instead of tomatoes; and *salsa roja*, a cooked sauce made with chilies, tomatoes, onion, garlic, and cilantro.

Sopes—A small, fried corn cake topped with ingredients like refried beans, shredded chicken, and salsa.

Taco—In Southern California, as in Mexico, tacos are made from soft, palm-sized corn tortillas folded over and filled with meat, chopped onion, cilantro, and salsa. Common taco fillings include *al pastor* (spiced pork), *barbacoa* (braised beef), *carnitas* (roasted pork), *cecina* (chili-coated pork), *carne asada* (roasted, chopped beef), *chorizo* (spicy sausage), *lengua* (beef tongue), *sesos* (cow brain), and *tasajo* (spiced, grilled beef).

Tamales—Sweet or savory corn cakes that are steamed, and may be filled with cheese, roasted chilies, shredded meat, or other fillings.

Torta—A Mexican sandwich served on a crusty sandwich roll. Fillings often include meat, refried beans, and cheese.

A feeling of refined elegance comes through in the food (and decor) at Patina, in Downtown Los Angeles.

WEST HOLLYWOOD

$$$
ITALIAN
Fodor'sChoice
★

✗ Angelini Osteria. You might not guess it from the modest, rather congested dining room, but this is one of L.A.'s most celebrated Italian restaurants. The key is chef-owner Gino Angelini's thoughtful use of superb ingredients, evident in dishes such as a salad of baby greens, Gorgonzola, and pear; and pumpkin tortelli with butter, sage, and asparagus. An awesome lasagna verde, inspired by Angelini's grandmother, is not to be missed. Whole branzino, crusted in sea salt, and boldly flavored rustic specials (e.g., tender veal kidneys, rich oxtail stew) consistently impress. An intelligent selection of mostly Italian wines complements the menu. ⑤ *Average main: $32* ⊠ *7313 Beverly Blvd., West Hollywood* ☎ *323/297–0070* ⊕ *www.angeliniosteria.com* ⚞ *Reservations essential* ☉ *Closed Mon. No lunch weekends* ✛ *2:D3.*

$$$
MEDITERRANEAN
Fodor'sChoice
★

✗ A.O.C. Since it opened in 2002, this restaurant and wine bar has revolutionized dining in L.A., pioneering the small-plate format that has now swept the city. The space is dominated by a long, candle-laden bar serving more than 50 wines by the glass. There's also a charcuterie bar, an L.A. rarity. The tapas-like menu is perfectly calibrated for the wine list; you could pick duck confit, lamb roulade with mint pistou, an indulgent slice of ricotta tartine, or just plunge into one of the city's best cheese selections. Named for the acronym for Appellation d'Origine Contrôlée, the regulatory system that ensures the quality of local wines and cheeses in France, A.O.C. upholds the standard of excellence. ⑤ *Average main: $35* ⊠ *8022 W. 3rd St., West Hollywood* ☎ *323/653–6359* ⊕ *www.aocwinebar.com* ⚞ *Reservations essential* ☉ *No lunch weekdays.* ✛ *2:C3*

CLOSE UP

Local Chains Worth Stopping For

It's said that the drive-in burger joint was invented in L.A., probably to meet the demands of an ever-mobile car culture. Burger aficionados line up at all hours outside **In-N-Out Burger** (⊕ www.in-n-out.com, multiple locations), still a family-owned operation whose terrific made-to-order burgers are revered by Angelenos. Visitors may recognize the chain as the infamous spot where Paris Hilton got nabbed for drunk driving, but locals are more concerned with getting their burger fix off the "secret" menu, with variations like "Animal Style" (mustard-grilled patty with grilled onions and extra spread), a "4 x 4" (four burger patties and four cheese slices, for big eaters) or the bun-less "Protein Style" that comes wrapped in Bibb lettuce. The company's website lists explanations for other popular secret menu items.

Tommy's sells a delightfully sloppy chili burger; the original location (⊠ 2575 Beverly Blvd.,

☎ 213/389–9060) is a no-frills 24/7 culinary landmark. For rotisserie chicken that will make you forget the Colonel forever, head to **Zankou Chicken** (⊠ 5065 Sunset Blvd., Hollywood ☎ 323/665–7845), noted for its golden crispy-skinned birds, potent garlic sauce, and Armenian specialties. Homesick New Yorkers will appreciate **Jerry's Famous Deli** (⊠ 10925 Weyburn Ave., Westwood ☎ 310/208–3354 ⊕ www.jerrysfamousdeli.com), where the massive menu includes all the classic deli favorites. With a lively bar scene, good barbecued ribs, and contemporary takes on old favorites, the more upscale **Houston's** (⊠ 202 Wilshire Blvd., Santa Monica ☎ 310/576–7558 ⊕ www.hillstone. com) is a popular local hangout. And **Señor Fish** (⊠ 422 E. 1st St., Downtown ☎ 213/625–0566 ⊕ www.senor-fish.com) is known for its healthy Mexican seafood specialties, such as scallop burritos and ceviche tostadas.

4

$$$

MEDITERRANEAN

✕ **Campanile.** Chef-owner Mark Peel has mastered the mix of robust Mediterranean flavors with homey Americana. The 1926 building (which once housed the offices of Charlie Chaplin) exudes a lovely Renaissance charm, and Campanile is one of L.A.'s most acclaimed and beloved restaurants. Appetizers may include duck meatballs or a pretty Bibb lettuce and herb salad, while wild striped sea bass with cherry tomatoes and grilled pork chop with wild mushrooms are likely to appear as entrées. Thursday night, grilled cheese sandwiches are a huge draw, as the beloved five-and-dime classic is morphed into exotic creations. For an ultimate L.A. experience, come for weekend brunch on the enclosed patio. $ *Average main: $35* ⊠ *624 S. La Brea Ave., West Hollywood* ☎ *323/938–1447* ⊕ *www.campanilerestaurant.com* ⌂ *Reservations essential* ✦ *2:D3.*

$$$$

FRENCH

✕ **Gordon Ramsay at the London.** The foul-mouthed celebrity chef from Fox's *Hell's Kitchen* demonstrates why he nevertheless ranks among the world's finest chefs at this fine-dining restaurant in a West Hollywood boutique hotel. Two pastel-color dining rooms with city views flank a formidable white marble bar, creating a space that feels trendy yet surprisingly unpretentious. A menu of small plates accommodates both light suppers and indulgent feasts alike. Highlights include Ramsay's

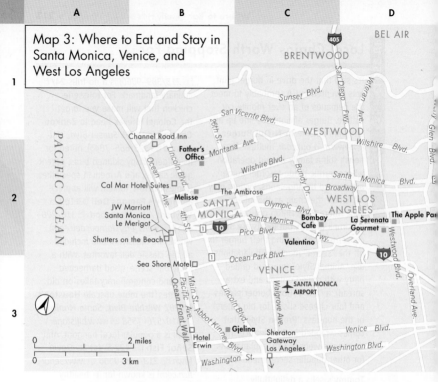

Map 3: Where to Eat and Stay in Santa Monica, Venice, and West Los Angeles

signature beef Wellington for two, filet mignon and braised short ribs, and a Maine lobster with coconut froth and mushroom ravioli. To maximize the experience, consider one of the flexible tasting menus ($120 on average), artfully crafted by Ramsay's local culinary team and orchestrated by a polished, gracious serving staff. ⑤ *Average main: $38 ⊠ The London, 1020 N. San Vicente Blvd., West Hollywood* ☎ *310/358–7788* ⊕ *www.thelondonwesthollywood.com/gordon-ramsay* ⚐ *Reservations essential* ✛ *2:B2.*

$ ✕ **Mandarette.** Clad in warm wood and copper finishes, this inviting
CHINESE café began as a casual spin-off of the Mandarin in Beverly Hills, but the
ⓒ casual concept has outlasted its high-end originator. Start with chicken salad with red ginger, scallion pancakes, or shrimp dumplings before indulging in *kung pao* scallops or crispy sesame beef. ⑤ *Average main: $17 ⊠ 8386 Beverly Blvd., West Hollywood* ☎ *323/655–6115* ⊕ *www. mandarettecafe.com* ✛ *2:C3.*

WEST LOS ANGELES

$ ✕ **The Apple Pan.** A burger-insider haunt since 1947, this unassuming
AMERICAN joint with a horseshoe-shaped counter—no tables here—turns out one
Fodor's Choice heck of a good burger topped with Tillamook cheddar, plus an excel-
★ lent hickory burger with barbecue sauce. You can also find great fries and, of course, an apple pie indulgent enough to christen the restaurant (although many regulars argue that the banana cream deserves

the honor). Be prepared to wait, but the veteran countermen turn the stools at a quick pace. In the meantime, grab a cup of Sanka and enjoy a little L.A. vintage. $ *Average main: $10* ⊠ *10801 W. Pico Blvd., West L.A.* ☎ *310/475–3585* ⚐ *Reservations not accepted* ⊟ *No credit cards* ⏱ *Closed Mon.* ✛ *3:D2*

$$ ✕ **Bombay Café.** Some of the menu items at Bombay Café are strictly
INDIAN   authentic, others have been lightened up a bit to suit Southern California sensibilities, and a few are truly innovative (e.g., ginger margarita, California tandoori salad with lemon-cilantro dressing). Regulars (and there are many) swear by the chili-laden lamb *frankies* (burritolike snacks sold by vendors on the beaches of Bombay), *sev puri* (wafers topped with onions, potatoes, and chutneys), and Sindhi chicken, a complex poached-then-sautéed recipe with an exotically seasoned crust. $ *Average main: $20* ⊠ *12021 W. Pico Blvd., West L.A.* ☎ *310/473–3388* ⊕ *www.bombaycafe-la.com* ✛ *3:C2.*

$$ ✕ **La Serenata Gourmet.** With uncomfortable chairs and crowds from the
MEXICAN   nearby Westside Pavilion boosting decibel levels, this branch of the East L.A. original isn't ideal for leisurely conversation. But the restaurant scores big points for its boldly flavored Mexican cuisine. Pork dishes and moles are delicious, but seafood is the real star—there are chubby *gorditas* (cornmeal pockets stuffed with shrimp), juicy shrimp enchiladas in tomatillo sauce, and flavorful grilled fish with cilantro or garlic sauce. If your experience with Mexican food has been on the Tex-Mex end of the spectrum, come here to broaden your taste buds' horizons. $ *Average main: $18* ⊠ *10924 W. Pico Blvd., West L.A.* ☎ *310/441–9667* ⊕ *www.laserenataonline.com* ✛ *3:D2.*

SANTA MONICA AND VENICE

SANTA MONICA

$ ✕ **Father's Office.** With a facade distinguished only by a vintage neon
AMERICAN   sign, Father's Office is a congested, gentrified pub famous for handcrafted beers and what has been called L.A.'s best burger. Topped with Gruyère and Maytag blue cheeses, arugula, caramelized onions, and applewood-smoked bacon compote, the "Office Burger" is a guilty pleasure worth waiting in line for (which is usually required). Other options include steak frites and Spanish tapas, with side orders of addictive sweet potato fries served in a miniature shopping cart with aïoli—don't even think of asking for ketchup, because FO enforces a strict no-substitutions policy. So popular is the Office Burger that chef-owner Sang Yoon opened a second location in Culver City. Note: Because Father's Office is a bar, it's strictly 21 and over. $ *Average main: $15* ⊠ *1018 Montana Ave., Santa Monica* ☎ *310/393–2337* ⊕ *www.fathersoffice. com* ⚐ *Reservations not accepted* ⏱ *No lunch weekdays* ✛ *3:B2.*

$$$$ ✕ **Mélisse.** In a city where informality reigns, this is one of L.A.'s more
FRENCH   dressy, but not stuffy, restaurants. The dining room is contemporary
Fodor's Choice   yet elegant, with well-spaced tables topped with flowers and fine china.
★   Chef-owner Josiah Citrin enhances his modern French cooking with seasonal California produce. Consider seared sweet white corn ravioli

in brown butter–truffle froth, lobster Bolognese, and elegant table-side presentations of Dover sole and stuffed rotisserie chicken. The cheese cart is packed with domestic and European selections. The tasting menus offered here including a creative vegetarian option. ⑤ *Average main: $115* ✉ *1104 Wilshire Blvd., Santa Monica* ☎ *310/395–0881* ⊕ *www.melisse.com* ⌖ *Reservations essential* ⊘ *Closed Sun. and Mon. No lunch* ✢ *3:B2.*

$$$$
ITALIAN

✕ **Valentino.** Renowned as one of the country's top Italian restaurants, Valentino has a truly awe-inspiring wine list. With nearly 2,800 labels consuming 130 pages, backed by a cellar overflowing with more than 80,000 bottles, this restaurant is nothing short of heaven for serious oenophiles. In the 1970s, suave owner Piero Selvaggio introduced L.A. to his exquisite modern Italian cuisine, and he continues to impress guests with dishes like a timballo of wild mushrooms with rich Parmigiano-Reggiano–saffron *fonduta*, a fresh risotto with farmers' market vegetables, a memorable osso buco, and sautéed branzino with lemon emulsion. A welcome addition to this exalted venue is its more casual wine bar for wine tasting and nibbles like *crudo* and carpaccio. ⑤ *Average main: $40* ✉ *3115 Pico Blvd., Santa Monica* ☎ *310/829–4313* ⊕ *www.valentinosantamonica.com* ⌖ *Reservations essential* ⊘ *Closed Sun. No lunch Sat. and Mon.–Thurs.* ✢ *2:C2*

VENICE

$$
AMERICAN

✕ **Gjelina.** This handsome restaurant comes alive with personality the minute you walk through its oversize rustic wooden door. There are long communal tables, hanging light fixtures that soften the room and make it glow, and an outdoor patio. The menu is smart and seasonal with small plates, cheese and charcuterie, pastas, and pizza. Begin with a mushroom, goat cheese, and truffle oil pizza, heirloom spinach salad, mussels with chorizo, or grilled squid with lentils and salsa verde. For the main course, there's the duck leg confit or the Niman Ranch hanger steak with watercress salsa verde. Typically crowded and noisy, the outdoor patio is the spot. However, service is not on par with the setting. Open until midnight daily. ⑤ *Average main: $22* ✉ *1429 Abbot Kinney Blvd., Venice* ☎ *310/450–1429* ⊕ *www.gjelina.com* ⌖ *Reservations essential* ⊘ ✢ *2:B3.*

PASADENA

$
CAFÉ
☾

✕ **Little Flower Candy Company.** Just off-the-beaten-path of Old Town Pasadena sits this quaint café that has charmed the hearts and taste buds of locals with its seasonally driven menu of sandwiches, salads, fresh soups, and incredible baked goods. The café is owned by Christine Moore, who made a name for herself in the candy world as a creator of addicting sea salt caramels and oversize sugar marshmallow. She opened shop a few years ago to sell her sweets, but also ended up creating a neighborhood hub for northeast Los Angeles. The café is nestled up against the sloping hills for a small-town feel (even though Downtown L.A. is a few miles away). It's a terrific place to grab a coffee, a fresh berry pastry, or a light lunch before heading out for an afternoon of shopping. ⑤ *Average main: $10* ✉ *1424 W. Colorado Blvd.,*

Pasadena ☎ *626/304–4800* ⊕ *www.littleflowercandyco.com* ⊘ *Closed Sun.* ✛ *1:B1*

WHERE TO STAY

When looking for a hotel, don't write off the pricier establishments immediately. Price categories are determined by "rack rates"—the list price of a hotel room, which is usually discounted. Specials abound, particularly Downtown on the weekends. Many hotels have packages that include breakfast, theater tickets, spa services, or exotic rental cars. Pricing is very competitive, so always check out the hotel website in advance for current special offers. When making reservations, particularly last-minute ones, check the hotel's website for exclusive Internet specials or call the property directly.

For expanded reviews, facilities, and current deals, visit Fodors.com.

Use the coordinate (✛ 1:B2) at the end of each listing to locate a site on the corresponding map.

HOTEL COSTS

Prices in the hotel reviews are the lowest cost of a standard double room in high season. Prices do not include taxes (as high as 14%, depending on the region).

DOWNTOWN WITH LOS FELIZ

DOWNTOWN

$
HOTEL
Figueroa Hotel. On the outside, it feels like Spanish Colonial; on the inside, this 12-story hotel, built in 1926, is a mix of Mexican, Mediterranean, and Moroccan styles, with earth tones, hand-glazed walls, and wrought-iron beds. **Pros:** a short walk to Nokia Theatre, L.A. Live, Convention Center; well-priced; great poolside bar. **Cons:** somewhat funky room decor; small bathrooms; gentrifying neighborhood. **TripAdvisor:** "very funky in a good way," "fun and exotic," "impeccable service." $ *Rooms from: $148* ⊠ *939 S. Figueroa St., Downtown* ☎ *213/627–8971, 800/421–9092* ⊕ *www.figueroahotel.com* ⊅ *285 rooms, 6 suites* ⊠ *No meals* ✛ *1:A3.*

$$
HOTEL
Fodor's Choice
★
Hilton Checkers Los Angeles. Opened as the Mayflower Hotel in 1927, Checkers retains much of its original character; its various-size rooms all have charming period details, although they also have contemporary luxuries like pillow-top mattresses, coffeemakers, 24-hour room service, and plasma TVs. **Pros:** historic charm; business-friendly; rooftop pool and spa. **Cons:** no on-street parking; some rooms compact; urban setting. **TripAdvisor:** "retro glam," "elegant," "superb staff." $ *Rooms from: $189* ⊠ *535 S. Grand Ave., Downtown* ☎ *213/624–0000, 800/445–8667* ⊕ *www.hiltoncheckers.com* ⊅ *188 rooms, 5 suites* ⊠ *No meals* ✛ *1:B2.*

$$$
HOTEL
Millennium Biltmore Hotel. One of Downtown L.A.'s true treasures, the gilded 1923 Beaux Arts masterpiece exudes ambience and history. **Pros:** historic character; famed filming location; club-level rooms have many hospitable extras. **Cons:** pricey valet parking; standard rooms

BEST BETS FOR
LOS ANGELES LODGING

Fodor's offers a selective listing of lodging experiences at every price range. Here, we've compiled our top recommendations by price and experience. The very best properties are designated in the listings with the Fodor's Choice logo.

Fodor's Choice ★

Channel Road Inn, $$, p. 224

The Crescent Beverly Hills, $$, p. 221

Farmer's Daughter Hotel, $$, p. 220

Hilton Checkers Los Angeles, $$, p. 217

Hotel Erwin, $$, p. 224

The Langham Huntington, Pasadena, $$, p. 225

Peninsula Beverly Hills, $$$$, p. 221

Renaissance Hollywood Hotel, $$, p. 220

Shutters on the Beach, $$$$, p. 224

Sunset Marquis Hotel & Villas, $$$, p. 223

By Price

$

The Beverly Garland Holiday Inn, p. 220

El Patio Inn, p. 221

Figueroa Hotel, p. 217

Los Feliz Lodge, p. 219

Sea Shore Motel, p. 224

$$

The Ambrose, p. 223

Cal Mar Hotel Suites, p. 224

Channel Road Inn, p. 224

The Crescent Beverly Hills, p. 221

Farmer's Daughter Hotel, p. 220

Hilton Checkers Los Angeles, p. 217

Hotel Erwin, p. 224

The Langham Huntington, Pasadena, p. 225

The London West Hollywood, p. 223

Magic Castle Hotel, p. 220

Renaissance Hollywood Hotel, p. 220

Sheraton Gateway Los Angeles, p. 223

Sportsmen's Lodge, p. 221

The Standard, Downtown L.A., p. 219

$$$

Hotel Amarano Burbank, p. 220

JW Marriott Santa Monica Le Merigot, p. 224

Millennium Biltmore Hotel, p. 217

Sunset Marquis Hotel & Villas, p. 223

$$$$

Beverly Wilshire, a Four Seasons Hotel, p. 221

Four Seasons Hotel, Los Angeles at Beverly Hills, p. 221

Peninsula Beverly Hills, p. 221

Shutters on the Beach, p. 224

SLS Hotel at Beverly Hills, p. 223

By Experience

BEST DESIGN

Figueroa Hotel, $, p. 217

The Standard, Downtown L.A., $$, p. 219

BEST SPAS

Four Seasons Hotel, Los Angeles at Beverly Hills, $$$$, p. 221

Renaissance Hollywood Hotel, $$, p. 220

Shutters on the Beach, $$$$, p. 224

GREEN FOCUS

The Ambrose, $$, p. 223

Los Feliz Lodge, $, p. 219

MOST KID-FRIENDLY

Magic Castle Hotel, $$, p. 220

Renaissance Hollywood Hotel, $$, p. 220

Shutters on the Beach, $$$$, p. 224

The Rooftop Bar at The Standard, Downtown L.A., is a super casual place to enjoy a nightcap.

are truly compact. **TripAdvisor:** "a nice surprise," "gorgeous," "old-fashioned luxury." ⑤ *Rooms from: $359* ✉ *506 S. Grand Ave., Downtown* ☎ *213/624–1011, 866/866–8086* ⊕ *www.thebiltmore.com* ☞ *635 rooms, 48 suites* ❑ *No meals* ✢ *1:B3.*

$$ ⊡ **The Standard, Downtown L.A.** Built in 1955 as Standard Oil's company's

HOTEL headquarters, the building was completely revamped under the sharp eye of owner André Balazs. **Pros:** on-site Rudy's barbershop for grooming; 24/7 coffee shop for dining; rooftop pool and lounge for fun. **Cons:** disruptive party scene weekends and holidays; street noise; pricey valet parking. **TripAdvisor:** "back to the future," "quirky doesn't even begin to describe," "fun place to stay." ⑤ *Rooms from: $245* ✉ *550 S. Flower St., Downtown* ☎ *213/892–8080* ⊕ *www.standardhotels.com* ☞ *171 rooms, 36 suites* ❑ *No meals* ✢ *1:A2.*

LOS FELIZ

$ ⊡ **Los Feliz Lodge.** Checking into this bungalow-style lodge is like crash-

RENTAL ing at an eco-minded and artsy friend's place: you let yourself into an apartment with fully stocked kitchen, washer and dryer, and a communal patio. **Pros:** homey feel; walking distance to restaurants. **Cons:** no on-site restaurant or pool. **TripAdvisor:** "charming apartment," "nice owners," "lovely." ⑤ *Rooms from: $150* ✉ *1507 N. Hoover St., Los Feliz* ☎ *323/660–4150* ⊕ *www.losfelizlodge.com* ☞ *4 rooms* ❑ *No meals* ✢ *2:F2.*

HOLLYWOOD AND THE STUDIOS

BURBANK

$$$
HOTEL

🏨 **Hotel Amarano Burbank.** Close to Burbank's TV and movie studios, the smartly designed Amarano feels like a Beverly Hills boutique hotel. **Pros:** boutique style in a Valley location; pleasant breakfast room. **Cons:** Pass Avenue street noise. **TripAdvisor:** "still in love," "friendly staff," "great bartender." Ⓢ *Rooms from: $365* ✉ *322 N. Pass Ave., Burbank* ☎ *818/842–8887, 888/956–1900* ⊕ *www.hotelamarano.com* ⤳ *108 rooms, 24 suites* ⦿| *No meals* ✢ *2:E1.*

HOLLYWOOD

$$
HOTEL
Fodor's Choice
★

🏨 **Farmer's Daughter Hotel.** Tongue-in-cheek country style is the name of the game at this motel: rooms are upholstered in blue gingham with denim bedspreads, and farm tools serve as art. **Pros:** great central city location; across from the cheap eats of the Farmers Market and The Grove's shopping and entertainment mix. **Cons:** pricey restaurant; roadside motel-size rooms; shaded pool; less than stellar service. **TripAdvisor:** "awesome stay," "amazingly cute," "fantastic part of LA." Ⓢ *Rooms from: $229* ✉ *115 S. Fairfax Ave., Farmers Market* ☎ *323/937–3930, 800/334–1658* ⊕ *www.farmersdaughterhotel.com* ⤳ *63 rooms, 2 suites* ⦿| *No meals* ✢ *2:C3.*

$$
HOTEL
☺

🏨 **Magic Castle Hotel.** Close to the action (and traffic) of Hollywood, this former apartment building faces busy Franklin Avenue and is a quick walk to the nearby Red Line stop at Hollywood & Highland. **Pros:** remarkably friendly and able staff; free Wi-Fi; good value. **Cons:** traffic-y locale; no elevator; small bathrooms. **TripAdvisor:** "service second to none," "don't stay anywhere else," "amazing." Ⓢ *Rooms from: $224* ✉ *7025 Franklin Ave., Hollywood* ☎ *323/851–0800, 800/741–4915* ⊕ *www.magiccastlehotel.com* ⤳ *7 rooms, 36 suites* ⦿| *Breakfast* ✢ *2:D1.*

$$
HOTEL
☺
Fodor's Choice
★

🏨 **Renaissance Hollywood Hotel.** Part of the massive Hollywood & Highland shopping and entertainment complex, this 20-story Renaissance is at the center of Hollywood's action. **Pros:** large rooms with new contemporary-styled furniture; Red Line Metro–station adjacent. **Cons:** corporate feeling; very touristy. **TripAdvisor:** "perfect location with great service," "beautiful," "in the center of it all." Ⓢ *Rooms from: $299* ✉ *1755 N. Highland Ave., Hollywood* ☎ *323/856–1200, 800/769–4774* ⊕ *www.renaissancehollywood.com* ⤳ *604 rooms, 33 suites* ⦿| *No meals* ✢ *2:D1.*

NORTH HOLLYWOOD

$
HOTEL
☺

🏨 **The Beverly Garland Holiday Inn.** The Hollywood connection starts in the lobby where framed photos of hotel namesake actress Beverly Garland decorate the lobby. **Pros:** large pool and play area; unpretentious and friendly feel; on-site Wi-Fi café. **Cons:** small bathrooms; touristy; $15 self-parking lot charge. **TripAdvisor:** "very good," "great food," "clean and convenient." Ⓢ *Rooms from: $159* ✉ *4222 Vineland Ave., North Hollywood* ☎ *818/980–8000, 800/238–3759* ⊕ *www.beverlygarland.com* ⤳ *238 rooms, 17 suites* ⦿| *No meals* ✢ *2:D1.*

STUDIO CITY

$ **El Patio Inn.** Behind a classic hacienda-style adobe and neon-lighted
HOTEL   facade, El Patio Inn is a throwback to 1960s-era roadside motels. **Pros:**
close to Universal Studios and a Metro line stop; Ventura Boulevard
has an endless supply of restaurants; low rates. **Cons:** no pool; service
matches the low rates; zero amenities. **TripAdvisor:** "charming," "it's
alright," "quiet room." $ *Rooms from: $94 ✉ 11466 Ventura Blvd.,
Studio City ☎ 818/508–5828 ⊕ www.elpatioinn.com ➫ 16 rooms
|◯| Breakfast ✛ 2:D1.*

$$ **Sportsmen's Lodge.** The sprawling five-story hotel is under new owner-
HOTEL   ship and management, and the lobby, bar, and popular coffee shop now
☪   have a contemporary look. **Pros:** close to Ventura Boulevard's plenti-
ful restaurants; free shuttle and discounted tickets to Universal Hol-
lywood; garden-view rooms are quietest. **Cons:** $11 daily self-parking
fee. **TripAdvisor:** "charming," "great comfortable hotel," "a relic of the
golden era." $ *Rooms from: $249 ✉ 12825 Ventura Blvd., Studio City
☎ 818/769–4700, 800/821–8511 ⊕ www.slhotel.com ➫ 177 rooms, 13
suites |◯| No meals ✛ 2:D1.*

BEVERLY HILLS AND THE WESTSIDE

BEVERLY HILLS

$$$$ **Beverly Wilshire, a Four Seasons Hotel.** Built in 1928, the Italian Renais-
HOTEL   sance–style Wilshire wing of this fabled hotel is replete with elegant
details: crystal chandeliers, oak paneling, walnut doors, crown mold-
ings, and marble. **Pros:** chic location; top-notch service; refined vibe.
Cons: small lobby; valet parking backs up at peak times; expensive din-
ing choices. **TripAdvisor:** "1950's luxury," "beautiful," "great service."
$ *Rooms from: $475 ✉ 9500 Wilshire Blvd., Beverly Hills ☎ 310/275–
5200, 800/427–4354 ⊕ www.fourseasons.com/beverlywilshire ➫ 258
rooms, 137 suites |◯| No meals ✛ 2:B3.*

$$ **The Crescent Beverly Hills.** Built in 1926 as a dorm for silent film actors,
HOTEL   the Crescent is now a sleek boutique hotel within the Beverly Hills shop-
Fodor's Choice   ping triangle. **Pros:** the on-site restaurant CBH's tasty cuisine and convi-
★   ial happy hour; the lobby is fashionista central. **Cons:** dorm-size rooms;
gym an additional fee and only accessed outside hotel via Sports ClubLA;
no elevator. **TripAdvisor:** "a great boutique find," "comfy," "stylish."
$ *Rooms from: $224 ✉ 403 N. Crescent Dr., Beverly Hills ☎ 310/247–
0505 ⊕ www.crescentbh.com ➫ 35 rooms |◯| No meals ✛ 2:B3.*

$$$$ **Four Seasons Hotel, Los Angeles at Beverly Hills.** High hedges and patio
HOTEL   gardens make this hotel a secluded retreat that even the hum of traffic can't permeate. **Pros:** expert concierge; deferential service; celebrity
magnet. **Cons:** Hollywood scene in bar and restaurant means rarefied
prices. **TripAdvisor:** "welcoming staff," "great property and service,"
"luxury refuge." $ *Rooms from: $455 ✉ 300 S. Doheny Dr., Beverly Hills ☎ 310/273–2222, 800/332–3442 ⊕ www.fourseasons.com/
losangeles ➫ 185 rooms, 100 suites |◯| No meals ✛ 2:B3.*

$$$$ **Peninsula Beverly Hills.** This French Rivera–style palace is a favorite
HOTEL   of Hollywood bold-face names, but all kinds of visitors consistently
Fodor's Choice   describe their stay as near perfect—though expensive. **Pros:** central,
★   walkable Beverly Hills location; stunning flowers; one of the best

Farmer's Daughter Hotel

Renaissance Hollywood Hotel

The Crescent Beverly Hills

Peninsula Beverly Hills

Channel Road Inn

concierges in the city. **Cons:** serious bucks required to stay here. **Trip-Advisor:** "high class," "consistent high standards," "extraordinary service from start to finish." ⑤ *Rooms from: $555* ✉ *9882 S. Santa Monica Blvd., Beverly Hills* ☎ *310/551–2888, 800/462–7899* ⊕ *www.beverlyhills.peninsula.com* ⇆ *142 rooms, 36 suites, 16 villas* ⏐⊙⏐ *No meals* ✛ *2:A3.*

$$$$ ⚉ **SLS Hotel at Beverly Hills.** Imagine dropping into Alice in Wonderland's
HOTEL rabbit hole: this is the colorful, textured, and tchotke-filled lobby of the SLS from design maestro Philippe Starck. **Pros:** a vibrant newcomer with lofty ambitions; excellent design and cuisine. **Cons:** standard rooms are compact but you pay for the scene; pricey hotel dining. **TripAdvisor:** "customer service at its best," "perfect Beverly Hills experience," "felt like a star." ⑤ *Rooms from: $599* ✉ *465 S. La Cienega Blvd., Beverly Hills* ☎ *310/247–0400* ⊕ *www.slshotels.com* ⇆ *236 rooms, 61 suites* ⏐⊙⏐ *No meals* ✛ *2:C3.*

WEST HOLLYWOOD

$$ ⚉ **The London West Hollywood.** Just off the Sunset Strip, cosmopolitan and
HOTEL chic in design, the London WeHo is a remake of 1984-built Bel Age. **Pros:** perfectly designed interiors; hillside and city views in generous-size suites all with balconies and steps from the Strip. **Cons:** too refined for kids to be comfortable; lower floors have mundane views. **TripAdvisor:** "made to feel like a movie star," "LA class," "simply stunning." ⑤ *Rooms from: $249* ✉ *1020 N. San Vicente Blvd., West Hollywood* ☎ *310/854–1111, 866/282–4560* ⊕ *www.thelondonwesthollywood.com* ⇆ *200 suites* ⏐⊙⏐ *No meals* ✛ *2:C2.*

$$$ ⚉ **Sunset Marquis Hotel & Villas.** If you're in town to cut your new hit sin-
HOTEL gle, you'll appreciate the two on-site recording studios here. **Pros:** supe-
Fodor'sChoice rior service; discreet setting just off the Strip; clublike atmosphere; free
★ passes to Equinox nearby. **Cons:** standard suites are somewhat small. **TripAdvisor:** "absolutely wonderful," "in the heart of West Holly-wood," "this hotel has the style." ⑤ *Rooms from: $315* ✉ *1200 N. Alta Loma Rd., West Hollywood* ☎ *310/657–1333, 800/858–9758* ⊕ *www.sunsetmarquis.com* ⇆ *102 suites, 52 villas* ⏐⊙⏐ *No meals* ✛ *2:C2.*

SANTA MONICA, VENICE, AND LAX

LOS ANGELES INTERNATIONAL AIRPORT

$$ ⚉ **Sheraton Gateway Los Angeles.** LAX's coolest-looking hotel is so swank
HOTEL that guests have been known to ask to buy the black-and-white pho-tos hanging behind the front desk. **Pros:** weekend rates significantly lower; free LAX shuttle. **Cons:** convenient to airport but not much else. **TripAdvisor:** "busy but comfortable," "wonderful staff," "easy stay." ⑤ *Rooms from: $219* ✉ *6101 W. Century Blvd., LAX* ☎ *310/642–1111, 800/325–3535* ⊕ *www.sheratonlosangeles.com* ⇆ *714 rooms, 88 suites* ✛ *3:C3.*

SANTA MONICA

$$ ⚉ **The Ambrose.** An air of tranquillity pervades the four-story Ambrose,
HOTEL which blends right into its mostly residential Santa Monica neighbor-hood. **Pros:** L.A.'s most eco-conscious hotel with nontoxic housekeep-ing products and recycling bins in each room. **Cons:** quiet, residential

area of Santa Monica; no restaurant on-site. **TripAdvisor:** "quiet and quaint," "modern mission style," "pleasant hotel with a great breakfast." ⑤ *Rooms from: $225* ✉ *1255 20th St., Santa Monica* ☎ *310/315–1555, 877/262–7673* ⊕ *www.ambrosehotel.com* ↩ *77 rooms* ❙�‖❙ *Breakfast* ✛ *3:B2.*

$$
HOTEL
☾
▦ **Cal Mar Suites.** On a residential street one block from the Third Street Promenade and within a short walk to the beach, this low-profile, two-story, all-suites hotel is a comparative bargain. **Pros:** lower off-season rates; full kitchens; low-key vibe. **Cons:** street noise; no air-conditioning but ocean breeze is present. **TripAdvisor:** "location and staff make this hotel great," "roomy and clean," "good area." ⑤ *Rooms from: $224* ✉ *220 California Ave., Santa Monica* ☎ *310/395–5555, 800/776–6007* ⊕ *www.calmarhotel.com* ↩ *36 suites* ❙❙❖❙ *No meals* ✛ *3:B2.*

$$
B&B/INN
Fodor's Choice
★
▦ **Channel Road Inn.** A quaint surprise in Southern California, the Channel Road Inn is every bit the country retreat B&B lovers adore, with four-poster beds with fluffy duvets and a cozy living room with fireplace. **Pros:** quiet residential neighborhood close to beach; free Wi-Fi and evening wine and hors d'oeuvres. **Cons:** no pool. **TripAdvisor:** "great friendly staff," "comfy and cozy," "beautiful." ⑤ *Rooms from: $235* ✉ *219 W. Channel Rd., Santa Monica* ☎ *310/459–1920* ⊕ *www.channelroadinn.com* ↩ *15 rooms* ❙❙❖❙ *Breakfast* ✛ *3:B2.*

$$$
HOTEL
▦ **JW Marriott Santa Monica Le Merigot.** Steps from Santa Monica's expansive beach, Le Merigot caters largely to a corporate clientele. **Pros:** steps from the beach and pier; welcoming to international travelers; walk to Third Street Promenade. **Cons:** small shaded pool; $35 valet parking. **TripAdvisor:** "nice location," "gorgeous hotel with a fantastic staff," "swanky." ⑤ *Rooms from: $349* ✉ *1740 Ocean Ave., Santa Monica* ☎ *310/395–9700, 877/637–4468* ⊕ *www.lemerigothotel.com* ↩ *173 rooms, 2 suites* ❙❙❖❙ *No meals* ✛ *3:B2.*

$
HOTEL
▦ **Sea Shore Motel.** On Santa Monica's busy Main Street, the Sea Shore is a throwback to Route 66 and to 60s-style, family-run roadside motels. **Pros:** close to beach and great restaurants; free Wi-Fi and parking. **Cons:** street noise; motel-style decor and beds. **TripAdvisor:** "sunny side of LA," "big and spacious," "great location." ⑤ *Rooms from: $160* ✉ *2637 Main St., Santa Monica* ☎ *310/392–2787* ⊕ *www.seashoremotel.com* ↩ *19 rooms, 5 suites* ❙❙❖❙ *No meals* ✛ *3:B3.*

$$$$
HOTEL
☾
Fodor's Choice
★
▦ **Shutters on the Beach.** Set right on the sand, this gray-shingle inn has become synonymous with in-town escapism. **Pros:** romantic; discreet; residential vibe. **Cons:** service not as good as it should be. **TripAdvisor:** "beautiful property," "very pristine," "very comfortable." ⑤ *Rooms from: $575* ✉ *1 Pico Blvd., Santa Monica* ☎ *310/458–0030, 800/334–9000* ⊕ *www.shuttersonthebeach.com* ↩ *186 rooms, 12 suites* ✛ *3:B2.*

VENICE

$$
HOTEL
Fodor's Choice
★
▦ **Hotel Erwin.** Formerly a Best Western, this now bona fide boutique hotel just off the Venice Beach boardwalk had a major face-lift in 2009. **Pros:** great location, great food; close to Santa Monica without hefty prices. **Cons:** some rooms face a noisy alley; no pool. **TripAdvisor:** "intimate place with a killer view," "a very pleasant stay," "the best staff ever." ⑤ *Rooms from: $229* ✉ *1697 Pacific Ave., Venice*

☎ *310/452–1111, 800/786–7789* ⊕ *www.hotelerwin.com* ↩ *119 rooms* ⦿| *No meals* ⊹ *3:B3.*

PASADENA

$$ 🏯 **The Langham Huntington, Pasadena.** An azalea-filled Japanese garden
HOTEL and the unusual Picture Bridge, with murals celebrating California's
ᠻ history, are just two of this grande dame's picturesque attributes. **Pros:**
Fodor'sChoice great for romantic escape; excellent restaurant; top-notch spa. **Cons:**
★ set in a suburban neighborhood far from local shopping and dining.
TripAdvisor: "comfy," "quiet and elegance," "perfect romantic get-
away." **⑤** *Rooms from: $269* ⊠ *1401 S. Oak Knoll Ave., Pasadena*
☎ *626/568–3900* ⊕ *www.pasadena.langhamhotels.com* ↩ *342 rooms,*
38 suites ⦿| *No meals* ⊹ *1:B1.*

NIGHTLIFE AND THE ARTS

Hollywood and West Hollywood, where hip and happening nightspots
liberally dot Sunset and Hollywood boulevards, are the epicenter of
L.A. nightlife. The city is one of the best places in the world for see-
ing soon-to-be-famous rockers as well as top jazz, blues, and classical
performers. Movie theaters are naturally well represented here, but
the worlds of dance, theater, and opera have flourished in the past few
years as well.

For a thorough listing of local events, ⊕ *www.la.com* and *Los Angeles
Magazine* are both good sources. The Calendar section of the *Los Ange-
les Times* (⊕ *www.latimes.com*) also lists a wide survey of Los Angeles
arts events, especially on Thursday and Sunday, as does the more irrev-
erent publication, *LA Weekly* (free; published every Thursday). Call
ahead to confirm that what you want to see is ongoing.

THE ARTS

CONCERT HALLS

Fodor'sChoice **Dolby Theatre.** This jewel in the crown of the Hollywood & Highland
★ Center, this theater (formerly the Kodak Theatre) was created as the per-
manent host of the Academy Awards, and the lavish 3,500-seat center is
now also home to the Cirque du Soleil's *Iris* (except for a months-long
hiatus in preparation for and just after the awards). Via jaw-dropping
acrobatics, inventive costumes, and music, *Iris* tells the story of cinema
with humor and panache. Seeing a show in this setting is worthwhile
just to witness the gorgeous, crimson-and-gold interior, with its box
seating and glittering chandeliers. ⊠ *6801 Hollywood Blvd., Holly-
wood* ☎ *323/308–6300* ⊕ *www.dolbytheatre.com.*

Fodor'sChoice **Dorothy Chandler Pavilion.** One of the Music Center's most cherished and
★ impressive music halls, the 3,200-seat landmark remains an elegant
space to see performances with its plush red seats and giant gold curtain.
It presents an array of music programs and L.A. Opera's classics from
September through June. Music director Plácido Domingo encourages
fresh work (in 2006, for instance, he ushered in *Grendel,* a new opera

staged by the hypercreative director Julie Taymor) as much as old favorites (the 2010 season marked the world renown production of Wagner's *Der Ring des Nibelungen* or *Ring Cycle* that ran in conjunction with *Ring Festival L.A.*—a celebration of the arts and L.A. style). There's also a steady flow of touring ballet and modern ballet companies. ✉ *135 N. Grand Ave., Downtown* ☎ *213/972–7211* ⊕ *www.musiccenter.org.*

Gibson Amphitheater. Adjacent to Universal Studios, this 6,189-seat space hosts more than 100 performances a year, including star-studded benefit concerts and all-star shindigs for local radio station KROQ 106.7. ✉ *100 Universal City Plaza, Universal City* ☎ *818/622–4440.*

Greek Theatre. In the beautiful tree-enclosed setting of Griffith Park, this open-air auditorium in Los Feliz is in the company of stunning Hollywood Hills homes and the nearby Griffith Observatory shining atop the hill. The Greek has hosted some of the biggest names in entertainment across all genres. Go for the laid-back California experience and the unique opportunity to experience your favorite performers in the warm western air with a view of the sparkling lights of the city flats splayed at your feet. After the concert go for a later-night snack or cocktail in the hipster neighborhood hotspots nearby. Open from May through November. 2013 marks their 82nd year. ✉ *2700 N. Vermont Ave., Los Feliz* ☎ *323/665–5857* ⊕ *www.greektheatrela.com.*

Fodor's Choice ★ **Hollywood Bowl.** Ever since it opened in 1920, in a park surrounded by mountains, trees, and gardens, the Hollywood Bowl has been one of the world's largest and most atmospheric outdoor amphitheaters. Its season runs from May through September; the L.A. Philharmonic spends its summers here. There are performances daily except Monday (and some Sundays); the program ranges from jazz to pop to classical. Concertgoers usually arrive early and bring picnic suppers (picnic tables are available). Additionally, a moderately priced outdoor grill and a more upscale restaurant are among the dining options operated by the Patina Group. ■TIP➜ Be sure to bring a sweater—it gets chilly here in the evening. You might also bring or rent a cushion to apply to the wood seats. Avoid the hassle of parking by taking one of the Park-and-Ride buses, which leave from various locations around town; call the Bowl for information. ✉ *2301 Highland Ave., Hollywood* ☎ *323/850–2000* ⊕ *www. hollywoodbowl.com.*

Shrine Auditorium. Former home of the Oscars, the 6,300-seat Arabic-inspired space was built in 1926 as Al Malaikah Temple. Touring companies from all over the world perform here, as do assorted gospel choirs, choral groups, and other musical acts. High-profile awards shows, including SAG and NAACP Image Awards, are still televised on-site. ✉ *665 W. Jefferson Blvd., Downtown* ☎ *213/748–5116* ⊕ *shrineauditorium.com.*

Fodor's Choice ★ **Walt Disney Concert Hall.** Built in 2003 as a grand addition to L.A.'s Music Center, the 2,265-seat architectural wonder is now the home of the Los Angeles Master Chorale as well as the Los Angeles Philharmonic, under the direction of passionate, new Music Director Gustavo Dudamel, an international celebrity conductor in his own right. The theater, a sculptural monument of gleaming, curved steel designed by master architect Frank Gehry, is part of a complex that includes a public park, gardens, and shops as well as two outdoor amphitheaters for children's and preconcert events. ■TIP➔ In the main hall, the audience completely surrounds the stage, so it's worth checking the seating chart when buying tickets to gauge your view of the performers. ⊠ *111 S. Grand Ave., Downtown* ☎ *323/850–2000* ⊕ *www.laphil. org.*

FILM

The American Cinemathèque Independent Film Series. Screen classics are shown here, plus recent independent films, sometimes with question-and-answer sessions with the filmmakers. The main venue is the Lloyd E. Rigler Theater, within the 1922 Egyptian Theater, which combines an exterior of pharaoh sculptures and columns with a modern, high-tech design inside. ⊠ *6712 Hollywood Blvd., Hollywood* ☎ *323/466–3456* ⊕ *www.americancinematheque.com.*

Aero Theater. The Cinemathèque also screens movies at the 1940 Aero Theater. ⊠ *1328 Montana Ave., Santa Monica* ☎ *323/466–3456* ⊕ *www.americancinematheque.com*

★ **Cinefamily at The Silent Movie Theatre.** A treasure of pretalkies, nonsilent films (the artier the better), and sneak previews of upcoming independent films are screened here. Live musical accompaniment and shorts precede some films. Each show is made to seem like an event in itself, and it's just about the only theater of its kind. The schedule—which also offers occasional DJ and live music performances—varies, but you can be sure to catch silent screenings every week. ⊠ *611 N. Fairfax Ave., Fairfax District* ☎ *323/655–2510* ⊕ *www.cinefamily.org.*

★ **UCLA and the Hammer Museum.** The museum, part of the university, presents several fine film series including those curated by the UCLA Film & Television archive.

Billy Wilder Theater. The programs of the Billy Wilder Theater might cover the works of major directors, documentaries, children's films, horror movies—just about anything. ⊠ *10899 Wilshire Blvd., Westwood* ☎ *310/206–8013* ⊕ *www.cinema.ucla.edu*

School of Film & Television. The School of Film & Television uses the James Bridges Theater (⊠ *Melnitz Hall, Sunset Blvd. and Hilgard Ave., Westwood* ☎ *310/206–8365* ⊕ *www.cinema.ucla.edu/james-bridges-theater*) and has its own program of newer, avant-garde films. Enter the campus at the northeastern most entrance. Street parking is available on Loring Avenue (a block east of the campus) after 6 pm, or park for a fee in Lot 3 (go one entrance south to Wyton Drive to pay at the kiosk before 7, after 7 at the lot itself). ⊕ *www.cinema.ucla.edu*

The musical comedy *Minsky's* had its world premiere at the Ahmanson Theater.

THEATER

Geffen Playhouse. Jason Robards and Nick Nolte got their starts here. This acoustically superior, 522-seat theater offers five new plays each season from September to July—both contemporary and classics are mixed in with musicals and comedies, and many of the productions are on their way to or from Broadway. ✉ *10886 Le Conte Ave., Westwood* ☎ *310/208–5454* ⊕ *www.geffenplayhouse.com.*

John Anson Ford Amphitheater. In addition to theater performances, there is also a wide variety of other events happening at this 1,250-seat outdoor venue in the Hollywood Hills, including lectures, children's programs, summer jazz, dance, cabaret, and occasionally Latin and rock concerts. Winter shows are typically staged at the smaller indoor theater, **Inside the Ford.** ✉ *2580 Cahuenga Blvd. E, Hollywood* ☎ *323/461–3673* ⊕ *www.fordamphitheater.org.*

LA Stage Alliance. LA Stage Alliance also gives information on what's playing in Los Angeles, albeit with capsules that are either noncommittal or overly enthusiastic. Its LAStageTIX service allows you to buy tickets online the day of the performance at roughly half price. ⊕ *www. lastagealliance.com.*

★ **The Music Center.** Three theaters are part of this big Downtown complex. ✉ *135 N. Grand Ave., Downtown* ☎ *213/972–7211* ⊕ *www. musiccenter.org.*

    Ahmanson Theatre. The 2,140-seat Ahmanson Theatre presents both classics and new plays. ☎ *213/628–2772* ⊕ *www.centertheatregroup. org*

Dorothy Chandler Pavilion. The 3,200-seat Dorothy Chandler Pavilions shows a smattering of plays between the more prevalent musical performances. ⊕ *www.musiccenter.org*

Mark Taper Forum. The 760-seat Mark Taper Forum presents new works that often go on to Broadway, such as Bruce Norris' *Clybourne Park.* ☎ *213/628–2772* ⊕ *www.centertheatregroup.org*

★ **Pantages Theatre.** The home of the Academy Awards telecast from 1949 to 1959, this is a massive (2,600-seat) and splendid example of high-style Hollywood art deco, presenting large-scale Broadway musicals such as *The Lion King* and *Wicked.* ⊠ *6233 Hollywood Blvd., Hollywood* ☎ *323/468–1770* ⊕ *www.broadwayla.org.*

Ricardo Montalbán Theatre. There's an intimate feeling here despite its 1,038-seat capacity. Plays, concerts, seminars, and workshops with an emphasis on Latin culture are all presented. ⊠ *1615 N. Vine St., Hollywood* ☎ *323/871–2420* ⊕ *www.themontalban.com.*

NIGHTLIFE

Although the ultimate in velvet-roped vampiness and glamour used to be the Sunset Strip, in the past couple of years the glitz has definitely shifted to Hollywood Boulevard and its surrounding streets. The lines are as long as the skirts are short outside the Hollywood club du jour (which changes so fast, it's often hard to keep track). But the Strip still has plenty going for it, with comedy clubs, hard-rock spots, and restaurants. West Hollywood's Santa Monica Boulevard bustles with gay and lesbian bars and clubs. For less conspicuous—and congested—alternatives, check out the events in Downtown L.A.'s performance spaces and galleries. Silver Lake and Echo Park are best for boho bars and live music clubs.

Note that parking, especially after 7 pm, is at a premium in Hollywood. In fact, it's restricted on virtually every side street along the "hot zone" of West Hollywood (Sunset Boulevard from Fairfax to Doheny). Posted signs indicate the restrictions, but these are naturally harder to notice at night. Paying $6 to $20 for valet or lot parking is often the easiest way to go.

BARS
HOLLYWOOD

★ **Beauty Bar.** This salon-themed bar offers manicures on Friday and Saturday nights along with perfect martinis, but the hotties who flock to this retro spot (the little sister of the Beauty Bars in NYC and San Fran) don't really need the cosmetic care—this is where the edgy beautiful people hang. ⊠ *1638 N. Cahuenga Blvd., Hollywood* ☎ *323/464–7676* ⊕ *www.thebeautybar.com.*

★ **Three Clubs.** This casually hip club is in a strip mall, beneath a sign that simply reads "Cocktails." The DJs segue through the many faces and phases of rock-and-roll and dance music. With dark-wood paneling, lamp-lighted tables, and even some sofas, you could be in a giant basement rec room from decades past—no fancy dress required, but fashionable looks suggested. ⊠ *1123 Vine St., Hollywood* ☎ *323/462–6441* ⊕ *www.threeclubs.com.*

★ **Yamashiro.** A lovely L.A. tradition is to meet at here for cocktails at sunset. In the elegant restaurant, waitresses glide by in kimonos, and entrées can zoom up to $42; on the terrace, a spectacular hilltop view spreads out before you. ■ **TIP→ Mandatory valet parking is $8.** ⊠ *1999 N. Syca-more Ave., Hollywood* ☎ *323/466–5125* ⊕ *www.yamashirorestaurant.com.*

WEST HOLLYWOOD

★ **Bar Marmont.** As at so many other nightspots in this neck of the woods, the popularity and clientele of this hotel bar bulged—and changed—after word got out it was a favorite of celebrities. Lately, it's gotten a second wind thanks to a strong DJ selection and luscious cocktails. The bar is next to the inimitable hotel Chateau Marmont, which bold-face names continue to haunt. ⊠ *8171 Sunset Blvd., West Hollywood* ☎ *323/650–0575* ⊕ *www.chateaumarmont.com.*

★ **Rainbow Bar & Grill.** In the heart of the Strip and next door to the legendary Roxy, the Rainbow is a landmark in its own right as *the* drinking spot of the 80s hair-metal scene—and it still attracts a music-industry crowd. ⊠ *9015 Sunset Blvd., West Hollywood* ☎ *310/278–4232* ⊕ *www.rainbowbarandgrill.com.*

★ **The Standard.** A classic Hollywood makeover—formerly a nursing home, this spot in the happening part of Sunset Strip got converted into a smart, brash-looking hotel, the Standard, for the young, hip, and connected. (Check out the live model in the lobby's terrarium.) This hotel (especially the bar) is popular with those in the biz. ⊠ *8300 Sunset Blvd., West Hollywood* ☎ *323/650–9090* ⊕ *www.standardhotels.com.*

ECHO PARK AND SILVER LAKE

★ **Cha Cha Lounge.** Seattle's coolest rock bar aims to repeat its success with this colorful, red-lighted space. Think part tiki hut, part tacky Tijuana party palace. The tabletops pay homage to the lounge's former performers; they've got portraits of Latin drag queens. ⊠ *2375 Glendale Blvd., Silver Lake* ☎ *323/660–7595* ⊕ *www.chachalounge.com.*

★ **The Echo.** This Echo Park mainstay sprang from the people behind the Silver Lake rock joint Spaceland. Most evenings this dark and divey space's tiny dance floor and well-worn booths attract artsy local bands and their followers, but things rev up when DJs spin reggae, rock, and funk. ⊠ *1154 Glendale Blvd.* ☎ *213/413–8200* ⊕ *www.attheecho.com.*

★ **Tiki-Ti.** This tiny Hawaiian-theme room is one of the most charming drinking huts in the city. You can spend hours just looking at the Polynesian artifacts strewn all about the place, but be careful—time flies in this tropical bar, and the colorful drinks can be so potent that you may have to stay marooned for a while. ⊠ *4427 Sunset Blvd., Silver Lake* ☎ *323/669–9381* ⊕ *www.tiki-ti.com.*

DOWNTOWN

Fodor's Choice
★ **Downtown L.A. Standard.** This futuristic hotel has a groovy lounge with pink sofas and DJs, as well as an all-white restaurant that looks like something out of *2001: A Space Odyssey*. But it's the rooftop bar and

biergarten, with an amazing view of the city's illuminated skyscrapers, a heated swimming pool, and private, podlike water-bed tents, that's worth waiting in line to get into. And wait you probably will, especially on weekends and in summer. Friday and Saturday $20 cover charge after 7 pm. ⊠ *550 S. Flower St., Downtown* ☎ *213/892–8080* ⊕ *www.standardhotels.com.*

COMEDY

Comedy Store. A nightly premiere comedy showcase, this venue has been going strong for more than two decades, with three stages (with covers ranging from free to $20) to supply the yuks. Famous comedians occasionally make unannounced appearances. ⊠ *8433 Sunset Blvd., West Hollywood* ☎ *323/650–6268* ⊕ *www.thecomedystore.com.*

★ **Groundlings Theatre.** For close to forty years, this renowned theater company has been a breeding ground for *Saturday Night Live* performers; alumni include Will Ferrell, Lisa Kudrow, and *Bridesmaids'* Melissa McCarthy. The primarily sketch and improv comedy shows run Wednesday through Sunday, costing $13–$19. ⊠ *7307 Melrose Ave., Hollywood* ☎ *323/934–4747* ⊕ *www.groundlings.com.*

Improv. Richard Pryor got his start at this renowned establishment, which showcases stand-up comedy. Reservations are recommended. Cover is $11–$21, and there's a two-item minimum. ⊠ *8162 Melrose Ave., West Hollywood* ☎ *323/651–2583* ⊕ *www.improv.com.*

Laugh Factory. Look for top stand-ups—and frequent celeb residents—like Bob Saget, or unannounced drop-ins, like Chris Rock. The club has shows Sunday through Thursday nights at 8 pm and 10 pm, plus an additional show on Friday and Saturday at midnight; the cover is $20–$45 plus a two-drink minimum. ⊠ *8001 Sunset Blvd., West Hollywood* ☎ *323/656–1336* ⊕ *www.laughfactory.com.*

Upright Citizens Brigade. New York's UCB marched in with a mix of sketch comedy and wild improvisations skewering pop culture. Members of the L.A. Brigade include VH1 commentator Paul Scheer and *Mad TV*'s Andrew Daly. ⊠ *5919 Franklin Ave., Hollywood* ☎ *323/908–8702* ⊕ *www.ucbtheatre.com.*

DANCE CLUBS

Though the establishments listed below are predominantly dance clubs as opposed to live music venues, there's often some overlap. A given club can vary wildly in genre from night to night, or even on the same night. ■**TIP→** Gay and promoter-driven theme nights tend to "float" from venue to venue. Call ahead to make sure you don't end up looking for retro '60s music at an industrial bondage celebration (or vice versa). Covers vary according to the night and the DJs.

★ **Boardner's.** This bar has a multidecade history (in the 20s it was a speakeasy), but with the adjoining ballroom, which was added a couple of years ago, it's now a state-of-the-art dance club. DJs may be spinning electronica, funk, or something else depending on the night—at the popular Saturday Goth event "Bar Sinister," patrons must wear black or risk not getting in. The cover here ranges from $3–$20. ⊠ *1652 N. Cherokee Ave., Hollywood* ☎ *323/462–9621* ⊕ *www.boardners.com.*

Perfect Like Me performs at the Knitting Factory in Hollywood.

GAY AND LESBIAN CLUBS

Some of the most popular gay and lesbian "clubs" are weekly theme nights at various venues, so read the preceding list of clubs, *LA Weekly* listings, and gay publications such as *Odyssey* in addition to the following recommendations.

★ **Here.** Nowhere is more gregarious than here (no pun intended), where there are hot DJs and an even hotter clientele. Some weekly highlights include "Truck Stop" on Friday, "Hooker Casino" on Saturday, and "Stripper Circus" on Wednesday. ✉ *696 N. Robertson Blvd., West Hollywood* ☎ *310/360–8455* ⊕ *www.herelounge.com.*

The Palms. A long-running gay-gal fave, this club continues to thrive thanks to great DJs spinning dance tunes as well as karaoke and comedy shows. There are also an outdoor patio, pool tables, and an occasional live performance. ✉ *8572 Santa Monica Blvd., West Hollywood* ☎ *310/652–1595* ⊕ *www.thepalmsbar.com.*

Rage. This spot is a longtime favorite of the "gym boy" set, with DJs following a different musical theme every night of the week (alternative rock, house, dance remixes, etc.). The cover ranges from free to $12. ✉ *8911 Santa Monica Blvd., West Hollywood* ☎ *310/652–7055.*

ROCK AND OTHER LIVE MUSIC

In addition to the venues listed here, many smaller bars book live music, if less frequently or with less publicity.

Avalon. The landmark, formerly known as the Palace, is now the Avalon. The multilevel art-deco building opposite Capitol Records has a fabulous sound system, four bars, and a balcony. Big-name rock and pop concerts hit the stage during the week, but on weekends the place becomes a dance club, with the most popular night the DJ-dominated Avaland on Saturday. Upstairs, but with a separate entrance, you can find celeb hub **Bardot,** a glamorous tribute to Old Hollywood where stars and their entourages are frequent visitors. ✉ *1735 N. Vine St., Hollywood* ☏ *323/462–8900* ⊕ *www.avalonhollywood.com.*

Key Club. This flashy, multitier rock club offers four bars presenting current artists of all genres (some on national tours, others local aspirants). After the concerts, there's often dancing with DJs spinning techno and house. ✉ *9039 Sunset Blvd., West Hollywood* ☏ *310/274–5800* ⊕ *www.keyclub.com.*

Largo. Musician-producer Jon Brion (Fiona Apple, Aimee Mann, and others) shows off his ability to play virtually any instrument and any song in the rock lexicon—and beyond—as host of a popular evening of music some Fridays at Largo. Other nights, low-key rock and singer-songwriter fare is offered at this cozy venue. And when comedy comes in, about one night a week, it's usually one of the best comedy nights in town, with folks like Sarah Silverman. Cash only. ✉ *366 N. La Cienega Blvd., Hollywood* ☏ *310/855–0350* ⊕ *www.largo-la.com.*

McCabe's Guitar Shop. This famous guitar shop is rootsy-retro-central, where all things earnest and (preferably) acoustic are welcome—chiefly folk, blues, bluegrass, and rock. It *is* a guitar shop (so no liquor license), with a room full of folding chairs for concert-style presentations. Shows on weekends only. Make reservations well in advance. ✉ *3101 Pico Blvd., Santa Monica* ☏ *310/828–4497 for concert information* ⊕ *www. mccabes.com.*

The Roxy. A Sunset Strip fixture for decades, this live music club hosts local and touring rock, alternative, blues, and rockabilly bands. Not the comfiest club around, but it's the site of many memorable shows. ✉ *9009 Sunset Blvd., West Hollywood* ☏ *310/278–9457* ⊕ *www. theroxyonsunset.com.*

★ **The Satellite.** The hottest bands of tomorrow, surprises from yesteryear, and unclassifiable bands of today perform at this low-key Silver Lake venue (formerly known as Spaceland), which has two bars, a jukebox, and a pool table. Monday is always free, with monthlong gigs by the indie fave du jour. There is a nice selection of beers. ✉ *1717 Silver Lake Blvd., Silver Lake* ☏ *323/661–4380* ⊕ *www.thesatellitela.com.*

Silver Lake Lounge. Neighborhoody and relaxed, this lounge draws a mixed collegiate and boho crowd. The club is very unmainstream "cool," the booking policy an adventurous mix of local and touring alt-rockers. Bands play three to five nights a week; covers vary but are low. ✉ *2906 Sunset Blvd., Silver Lake* ☏ *323/663–9636.*

The Troubadour. One of the best and most comfortable clubs in town, this live music Mecca has weathered the test of time since its 60s debut as a folk club. After surviving the 80s heavy-metal scene, this all-ages, wood-panel venue has caught a second (third? fourth?) wind by booking hot alternative rock acts. There's valet parking, but if you don't mind walking up Doheny a block or three, there's usually ample street parking (check the signs carefully). ✉ *9081 Santa Monica Blvd., West Hollywood* ⊕ *www.troubadour.com.*

Viper Room. Actor Johnny Depp sold his share of the infamous rock venue in 2004, but the place continues to rock with a motley live music lineup, if a less stellar crowd. ⊠ *8852 W. Sunset Blvd., West Hollywood* ☎ *310/358–1881* ⊕ *www.viperroom.com.*

Whisky-A-Go-Go. The Whisky, as locals call it, is the most famous rock-and-roll club on the Strip, where back in the 60s, Johnny Rivers cut hit singles and the Doors, Love, and the Byrds cut their musical eyeteeth. It's still going strong, with up-and-coming alternative, hard rock, and punk bands, though mostly of the unknown variety. ⊠ *8901 Sunset Blvd., West Hollywood* ☎ *310/652–4202* ⊕ *www.whiskyagogo.com.*

SPORTS AND THE OUTDOORS

BEACHES

Los Angeles County beaches (and state beaches operated by the county) have lifeguards on duty year-round, with expanded forces during the summer. Public parking is usually available, though fees can range anywhere from $8 to $20; in some areas, it's possible to find free street and highway parking. Both restrooms and beach access have been brought up to the standards of the Americans with Disabilities Act. Generally, the northernmost beaches are best for surfing, hiking, and fishing, and the wider and sandier southern beaches are better for tanning and relaxing. ■ TIP➔ Almost all are great for swimming in warmer months, but beware: pollution in Santa Monica Bay sometimes approaches dangerous levels, particularly after storms.

The following beaches are listed in north–south order:

Ⓒ **Leo Carrillo State Park.** On the very edge of Ventura County, this narrow beach is better for exploring than for sunning or swimming (watch that strong undertow!). On your own or with a ranger, venture down at low tide to examine the tide pools among the rocks. Sequit Point, a promontory dividing the northwest and southeast halves of the beach, creates secret coves, sea tunnels, and boulders on which you can perch and fish. Generally, anglers stick to the northwest end of the beach; experienced surfers brave the rocks to the southeast. Campgrounds are set back from the beach; campsites must be reserved well in advance. **Amenities:** lifeguards (seasonally); parking; showers; toilets. **Best for:** sunset; surfing; swimming; walking. ⊠ *35000 PCH, Malibu* ☎ *818/880–0363, 800/444–7275 for camping reservations* ⊕ *www.parks.ca.gov* ⊠ *$12 parking* ☞ *Parking, lifeguard (year-round, except only as needed in winter), restroom, showers, fire pits.*

Malibu Surfrider Beach. Steady 3- to 5-foot waves make this beach, just west of Malibu Pier, a surfing paradise. Water runoff from Malibu Canyon forms a natural lagoon that's a sanctuary for 250 species of birds. Unfortunately, the lagoon is often polluted and algae filled. If you're leery of going into the water, you can bird-watch, play volleyball, or take a walk on one of the nature trails, which are perfect for romantic sunset strolls. **Amenities:** parking; showers; toilets. **Best for:** sunset; surfing; swimming; windsurfing. ⊠ *23050 PCH, Malibu* ☎ *310/457–8143* ⊕ *www.parks.ca.gov* ⊠ *$12 parking.*

★ **Redondo Beach.** The Redondo Beach Pier marks the starting point of this wide, sandy, busy beach along a heavily developed shoreline community. Restaurants and shops flourish along the pier, excursion boats and privately owned crafts depart from launching ramps, and a reef formed by a sunken ship creates prime fishing and snorkeling conditions. If you're adventurous, you might try to kayak out to the buoys and hobnob with pelicans and sea lions. A series of free rock and jazz concerts takes place at the pier every summer. **Amenities:** food and drink; lifeguards; parking; showers; toilets; water sports. **Best for:** snorkeling; sunset; swimming; walking. ⊠ *Torrance Blvd. at Catalina Ave., Redondo Beach* ☎ *310/372–2166.*

Fodor's Choice **Robert H. Meyer Memorial State Beach.** Part of Malibu's most beautiful
★ coastal area, this beach is made up of three minibeaches: El Pescador, La Piedra, and El Matador—all with the same spectacular view. Scramble down the steps to the rocky coves via steep, steep stairways; all food and water needs to be toted in as there are no services. Portable toilets at the trailhead are the only restrooms. "El Mat" has a series of caves, Piedra some nifty rock formations, and Pescador a secluded feel; but they're all picturesque and fairly private. **Amenities:** parking; toilets; lifeguards (summer weekends). **Best for:** solitude; sunset; surfing; walking. ■TIP→ One warning: watch the incoming tide and don't get trapped between those otherwise scenic boulders. ⊠ *32350, 32700, and 32900 PCH, Malibu* ☎ *818/880–0363* ⊕ *www.parks.ca.gov.*

★ **Santa Monica State Beach.** It's the first beach you'll hit after the Santa Monica Freeway (Interstate 10) runs into the PCH, and it's one of L.A.'s best known. Wide and sandy, Santa Monica is *the* place for sunning and socializing: be prepared for a mob scene on summer weekends, when parking becomes an expensive ordeal. Swimming is fine (with the usual post-storm pollution caveat); for surfing, go elsewhere. For a memorable view, climb up the stairway over the PCH to Palisades Park, at the top of the bluffs. Free summer-evening concerts are held Thursday nights on the pier. **Amenities:** food and drink; lifeguards; parking; showers; toilets; water sports. **Best for:** sunset; surfing; swimming; walking. ⊠ *1642 Promenade, PCH at California Incline, Santa Monica* ☎ *310/458–8573* ⊕ *www.smgov.net/Portals/Beach* 🅿 *$10 parking* ⌖ *Parking, lifeguard (year-round), restrooms, showers.*

Will Rogers State Beach. This clean, sandy, 3-mile beach, with a dozen volleyball nets, gymnastics equipment, and playground equipment for kids, is an all-around favorite. The surf is gentle, perfect for swimmers and beginning surfers. However, it's best to avoid the place after a storm, when untreated water flows from storm drains into the sea. **Amenities:** food and drink; lifeguards; parking; showers; toilets. **Best for:** sunset; swimming; walking. ⊠ *17700 PCH, 2 miles north of Santa Monica Pier, Pacific Palisades* ☎ *310/305–9503* ⊕ *www.parks.ca.gov* 🅿 *$12 parking.*

Zuma Beach Park. This 2-mile stretch of white sand, usually littered with tanning teenagers, has it all: from fishing and kite surfing to swings for the kids to volleyball courts. Beachgoers looking for quiet or privacy should head elsewhere. Stay alert in the water: the surf is rough and inconsistent. **Amenities:** food and drink; lifeguards; parking; showers;

Surf City

Nothing captures the laid-back cool of California quite like surfing. Those wanting to sample the surf here should keep a few things in mind before getting wet. First, surfers can be notoriously territorial. Beginners should avoid Palos Verdes and Third Point, at the north end of Malibu Lagoon State Beach, where veterans rule the waves. Once in the water, be as polite and mellow as possible. Give other surfers plenty of space—do *not* cut them off—and avoid swimmers. Beware of rocks and undertows. Surfing calls for caution: that huge piece of flying fiberglass beneath you could kill someone. If you're not a strong swimmer, think twice before jumping in; fighting the surf to where the waves break is a strenuous proposition. The best and safest way to learn is by taking a lesson. A wet suit is a must most of the year.

When you hit the surfing hot spots, surf shops with rentals will be in long supply. Competition keeps prices comparable; most rent long and short boards and miniboards (kid-size surfboards) from $20 per day and wet suits from $10 per day (some give discounts for additional days).

Learners should never surf in a busy area; look for somewhere less crowded where you'll catch more waves anyway. Good beaches for beginners are Santa Monica State Beach, Malibu Lagoon State Beach, and Huntington City Beach north of the pier, but you should always check conditions, which change throughout the day, before heading into the water.

toilets. **Best for:** partiers; sunset; swimming; walking. ⊠ *30000 PCH, Malibu* ☎ *310/305–9503* ⊕ *beaches.lacounty.gov* 🚗 *$10 parking.*

SPORTS

BASEBALL

Dodgers. You can watch the Dodgers take on their National League rivals while munching on pizza, tacos, or a foot-long "Dodger dog" at one of the game's most comfortable ball parks, Dodger Stadium. ⊠ *Dodger Stadium, 1000 Elysian Park Ave., exit off I-110, Pasadena Fwy.* ☎ *866/363–4377 ticket information* ⊕ *www.dodgers.com.*

Los Angeles Angels of Anaheim. The Los Angeles Angels of Anaheim won the World Series in 2002, the first time since the team formed in 1961. ⊠ *Angel Stadium of Anaheim, 2000 Gene Autry Way, Anaheim* ☎ *714/663–9000* ⊕ *www.angelsbaseball.com.*

Several colleges in the area also have baseball teams worth watching, especially USC, which has been a perennial source of major-league talent.

BASKETBALL

L.A.'s pro basketball teams play at the Staples Center.

Clippers. L.A.'s "other" team, the much-maligned but newly revitalized Clippers, sells tickets that are sometimes cheaper and easier to get than those for Lakers games. ☎ *888/895–8662* ⊕ *www.nba.com/clippers.*

Los Angeles Lakers. It's not easy to get tickets, but if you can don't miss the chance to see this championship-winning team. ☎ *310/426–6000* ⊕ *www.nba.com/lakers.*

Los Angeles Sparks. After the 2010 retirement of WNBA superstar Lisa Leslie, the Los Angeles Sparks have put the spotlight on forward Candace Parker. ☎ *310/426–6031* ⊕ *www.wnba.com/sparks.*

GOLF

Griffith Park. Griffith Park has two splendid 18-hole courses along with a challenging 9-hole course. **Harding Municipal Golf Course** and **Wilson Municipal Golf Course** (☒ *4900 Griffith Park Dr., Los Feliz* ☎ *323/663–2555*) are about 1½ miles inside the park entrance, at Riverside Drive and Los Feliz Boulevard. Bridle paths surround the outer fairways, and the San Gabriel Mountains make a scenic background. ⊕ *www.golf.lacity.org.*

Los Verdes Golf Course. If you want a scenic course, the county-run, par-71 Los Verdes Golf Course has fierce scenery. You get a cliff-top view of the ocean—time it right and you can watch the sun set behind Catalina Island. ☒ *7000 W. Los Verdes Dr., Rancho Palos Verdes* ☎ *310/377–7370* ⊕ *www.americangolf.com/los-verdes-golf-course.*

Rancho Park Golf Course. The City Parks and Recreation Department lists seven public 18-hole courses in Los Angeles, and L.A. County runs some good ones, too. Rancho Park Golf Course is one of the most heavily played links in the country. It's a beautifully designed course, but the towering pines present an obstacle for those who slice or hook. There's a two-level driving range, a 9-hole pitch n' putt, a snack bar, and a pro shop where you can rent clubs. ☒ *10460 W. Pico Blvd., West L.A.* ☎ *310/838–7373* ⊕ *www.golf.lacity.org.*

Roosevelt Municipal Golf Course. The 9-hole Roosevelt Municipal Golf Course can be reached through the park's Vermont Avenue entrance. ☒ *2650 N. Vermont Ave., Los Feliz* ☎ *323/665–2011* ⊕ *www.golf. lacity.org.*

SHOPPING

AROUND BEVERLY HILLS

★ **Beverly Center.** This is one of the more traditional malls you can find in L.A., with eight levels of stores, including Macy's, Bloomingdale's, and the newer addition: luxury retailer Henri Bendel. Fashion is the biggest draw and there's a little something for everyone, from D&G to H&M, and many shops in the midrange, including Banana Republic, Club Monaco, and Coach. Look for accessories at Aldo and inexpensive accessories and fun fashion at Forever 21; there's even a destination for the race-car obsessed at the Ferrari Store.

Inside there a casual dining choices at the top floor food court, and several popular chain restaurants are outside on the ground floor. Next door is Loehmann's, which offers a huge selection of discounted

The Santa Monica Pier is packed with fun diversions and hosts free concerts in summer.

designer wear. ⊠ *8500 Beverly Blvd., bounded by Beverly, La Cienega, and San Vicente Blvds. and 3rd St., between Beverly Hills and West Hollywood* ☎ *310/854–0071* ⊕ *www.beverlycenter.com.*

Rodeo Drive. New York City has Fifth Avenue, but L.A. has famed Rodeo Drive. The triangle, between Santa Monica and Wilshire boulevards and Beverly Drive, is one of the city's biggest tourist attractions and is lined with shops featuring the biggest names in fashion.

You can see well-coifed, well-heeled ladies toting multiple packages to their Mercedes and paparazzi staking out street corners. Although the dress code in L.A. is considerably laid-back, with residents wearing flip-flops year-round, you might find them to be jewel-encrusted on Rodeo.

Steep price tags on designer labels make it a "just looking" experience for many residents and tourists alike, but salespeople are used to the ogling and window shopping. In recent years, more mid-range shops have opened up on the strip and surrounding blocks. Keep in mind that some stores are by appointment only. ⊕ *www.rodeodrive-bh.com.*

DOWNTOWN

The Jewelry District. This area resembles a slice of Manhattan, with the crowded sidewalks, diverse aromas, and haggling bargain hunters. Expect to save 50% to 70% off retail for everything from wedding bands to sparkling belt buckles. The more upscale stores are along Hill Street between 6th and 7th streets. There's a parking structure next door on Broadway. ⊠ *Between Olive St. and Broadway from 5th to 8th St., Downtown* ⊕ *www.lajd.net.*

Fodor's Choice **Olvera Street.** Historic buildings line this redbrick walkway overhung
★ with grapevines. At dozens of clapboard stalls you can browse south-
of-the-border goods—leather sandals, bright woven blankets, devo-
tional candles, and the like—as well as cheap toys and tchotchkes.
With the musicians and cafés providing background noise, the area is
constantly lively. ⊠ *Between Cesar Chavez Ave. and Arcadia St., Downtown* ⊕ *www.olvera-street.com.*

HOLLYWOOD

Local shops may be a mixed bag, but at least you can read the stars
below your feet as you browse along Hollywood Boulevard. Lingerie
and movie memorabilia stores predominate here, but there are numerous
options in the retail-hotel-dining-entertainment complex Hollywood &
Highland. Hollywood impersonators (Michael Jackson, Marilyn Monroe, and, er, Chewbacca) join break-dancers and other street entertainers in keeping tourists entertained on Hollywood Boulevard's sidewalks
near the Dolby Theatre, home to the Oscars and Cirque du Soleil's *Iris.*
Along La Brea Avenue, you'll find plenty of trendy, quirky, and hip
merchandise, from records to furniture and clothing.

Hollywood & Highland. Dozens of stores, eateries, a bowling alley, and
the Dolby Theatre fill this outdoor complex, which mimics cinematic
glamour. Find designer shops (Coach, Louis Vuitton) and chain stores
(Victoria's Secret, Fossil, Sephora, and the Hard Rock Cafe).

From the upper levels, there's a camera-perfect view of the famous
"Hollywood" sign. On the second level, next to the Dolby Theatre, is a
Visitor Information Center (☎ 323/467–6412) with a multilingual staff,
maps, attraction brochures, and information about services.

The streets nearby provide the setting for the Sunday Hollywood Farmer's Market, where you're likely to spot a celebrity or two picking
up fresh produce or stopping to eat breakfast from the food vendors.
⊠ *Hollywood Blvd. and Highland Ave., Hollywood* ☎ *323/817–0220.*

LOS FELIZ, SILVER LAKE, AND ECHO PARK

There's a hipster rock-and-roll vibe to this area, which has grown in
recent years to add just the slightest shine to its edge. Come for home-
grown, funky galleries, vintage shops, and local designers' boutiques.
Shopping areas are concentrated along Vermont Avenue and Hollywood Boulevard in Los Feliz; Sunset Boulevard in both Silver Lake
(known as Sunset Junction) and Echo Park; and Echo Park Avenue
in Echo Park. ■TIP➜ Keep in mind that things are spread out enough to
necessitate a couple of short car trips, and many shops in these neighborhoods don't open until noon but stay open later, so grab dinner or drinks at
one of the area's über-cool spots after shopping.

WEST HOLLYWOOD AND MELROSE AVENUE

West Hollywood is prime shopping real estate. And as they say with real estate, it's all about location, location, location. Depending on the street address, West Hollywood has everything from upscale art, design, and antiques stores to ladies-who-lunch clothing boutiques to megamusic stores and specialty book vendors. Melrose Avenue, for instance, is part bohemian-punk shopping district (from North Highland to Sweetzer) and part upscale art and design mecca (upper Melrose Avenue and Melrose Place). Discerning locals and celebs haunt the posh boutiques around Sunset Plaza (Sunset Boulevard at Sunset Plaza Drive), on Robertson Boulevard (between Beverly Boulevard and 3rd Street), and along upper Melrose Avenue.

The huge, blue Pacific Design Center, on Melrose at San Vicente Boulevard, is the focal point for this neighborhood's art- and interior design–related stores, including many on nearby Beverly Boulevard. The Beverly–La Brea neighborhood also claims a number of trendy clothing stores. Perched between Beverly Hills and West Hollywood, 3rd Street (between La Cienega and Fairfax) is a magnet for small, friendly designer boutiques. Finally, the Fairfax District, along Fairfax below Melrose, encompasses the flamboyant, historic Farmers Market, at Fairfax Avenue and 3rd Street; the adjacent shopping extravaganza, The Grove; and some excellent galleries around Museum Row at Fairfax Avenue and Wilshire Boulevard.

SANTA MONICA AND VENICE

The breezy beachside communities of Santa Monica and Venice are ideal for leisurely shopping. Scads of tourists (and some locals) gravitate to Santa Monica Place and the Third Street Promenade, a popular pedestrians-only strolling–shopping area that is within walking range of the beach and historic Santa Monica Pier. A number of modern furnishings stores are nearby on 4th and 5th streets. Main Street between Pico Boulevard and Rose Avenue offers upscale chain stores, cafés, and some original shops, while Montana Avenue is a great source for distinctive clothing boutiques and child-friendly shopping, especially between 7th and 17th streets. ■TIP➡ Parking in Santa Monica is next to impossible on Wednesday, when some streets are blocked off for the farmers' market, but there are several parking structures with free parking for an hour or two. In Venice, Abbot Kinney Boulevard is abuzz with mid-century furniture stores, art galleries and boutiques, and cafés.

★ **Third Street Promenade.** Whimsical dinosaur-shaped, ivy-covered fountains, and buskers of every stripe set the scene along this pedestrians-only shopping stretch. Stores are mainly the chain variety (Restoration Hardware, Urban Outfitters, Apple), but there are also Quiksilver and Rip Curl outposts for cool surf attire. Movie theaters, bookstores, pubs, and restaurants ensure that virtually every need is covered. ⊠ *3rd St., between Broadway and Wilshire Blvd.*

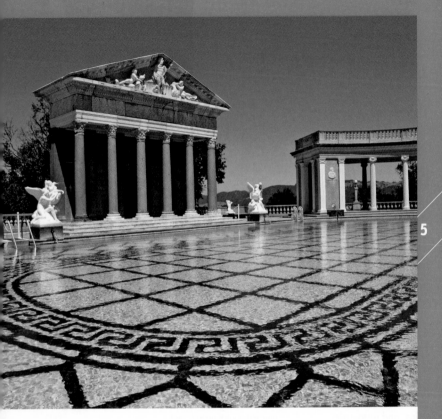

The Central Coast

FROM VENTURA TO BIG SUR

WORD OF MOUTH

"I was blown away by the immense outdoor pool at the Hearst Castle. It is huge, and yet incredibly serene in its surroundings. The Castle is situated on top of the hills in the San Simeon area and allows for massive views of nearly 360 degrees around."

— photo by L Vantreight, Fodors.com member

WELCOME TO THE CENTRAL COAST

TOP REASONS TO GO

★ **Incredible nature:** Much of the Central Coast looks as wild and wonderful as it did centuries ago. The area is home to Channel Islands National Park, two national marine sanctuaries, state parks and beaches, and the vast and rugged Los Padres National Forest.

★ **Edible bounty:** Land and sea provide enough fresh regional foods to satisfy even the savviest of foodies—grapes, strawberries, seafood, olive oil . . . the list goes on and on. Get your fill at countless farmers' markets, wineries, and restaurants.

★ **Outdoor activities:** Kick back and revel in the casual California lifestyle. Surf, golf, kayak, hike, play tennis—or just hang out and enjoy the gorgeous scenery.

★ **Small-town charm, big-city culture:** Small, friendly, uncrowded towns offer an amazing array of cultural amenities. With all the art and history museums, theater, music, and festivals, you might start thinking you're in L.A. or San Francisco.

1 Ventura County. Ventura is an up-and-coming city with a thriving arts community, miles of beaches, and a vibrant harbor—the gateway to Channel Islands National Park. Eleven miles inland, tiny, artsy Ojai plays host to folks who want to golf, meditate, and commune with tony peers in an idyllic mountain setting.

2 Santa Barbara. Down-home surfers rub elbows with Hollywood celebrities in sunny, well-scrubbed Santa Barbara, 95 miles north of Los Angeles. Its Spanish-Mexican heritage is reflected in the architectural style of its mission, courthouse, and many homes and public buildings.

3 **Santa Barbara County.**
Wineries, ranches, and
small villages dominate the
quintessentially Californian
landscape here.

4 **San Luis Obispo
County.** Friendly college
town San Luis Obispo serves
as the hub of a burgeoning
wine region that stretches
nearly 100 miles from Pismo
Beach north to Paso Robles;
the 230-plus wineries here
have earned reputations
for high-quality vintages
that rival those of northern
California.

5 **The Big Sur Coastline.** Rugged cliffs meet
the Pacific for more than
60 miles—one of the most
scenic and dramatic drives
in the world.

6 **Channel Islands
National Park.** Home to
145 species of plants and
animals found nowhere
else on Earth, this relatively
undiscovered gem of a park
encompasses five islands
and a mile of surrounding
ocean. ⇨ *See Chapter 6 for
more information.*

GETTING ORIENTED

The Central Coast region
begins about 60 miles
north of Los Angeles, near
the seaside city of Ventura.
From there the coastline
stretches north about 200
miles, winding through the
cities of Santa Barbara
and San Luis Obispo, then
north through the small
towns of Morro Bay and
Cambria to Carmel. The
drive through this region,
especially the section
of Highway 1 from San
Simeon to Big Sur, is one of
the most scenic in the state.

5

```
0              20 miles
|----|----|----|
0              30 kilometers
```

C O A S T

R A N G E S

SAN RAFAEL MOUNTAINS

ipomo 166

Santa Maria

Orcutt
101

246 **3** Los Olivos
Buellton   Santa Ynez
    Solvang 154
1
101 SANTA YNEZ MOUNTAINS
        Goleta   Montecito Mira   Ojai
                               Monte
2 Santa Barbara Carpinteria **1** Oak   Santa
                                      View Paula
TO **6**   126
CHANNEL ISLANDS   Ventura
        ↓   Oxnard   101
Santa Barbara Channel

Updated
by Cheryl
Crabtree

Balmy weather, glorious beaches, crystal-clear air, and serene landscapes have lured people to the Central Coast since prehistoric times. It's an ideal place to relax, slow down, and appreciate the good things in life.

Along the Pacific coast, the scenic variety is stunning—everything from dramatic cliffs and grass-tufted bluffs to wildlife estuaries and miles of dunes. Offshore, a pristine national park and a vast marine sanctuary protect the wild, wonderful underwater resources of this incredible corner of the planet. But not all of the Central Coast's top attractions are natural: Ventura, Santa Barbara, and San Luis Obispo are filled with sparkling examples of Spanish-Mediterranean architecture, bustling shopping districts, and first-rate restaurants showcasing regional foods and wines.

PLANNING

WHEN TO GO
The Central Coast climate is mild year-round. If you like to swim in warmer (if still nippy) ocean waters, July and August are the best months to visit. Be aware that this is also high season. Fog often rolls in along the coastal areas in early summer; you'll need a jacket, especially after sunset, close to the shore. It usually rains from December through March. From April to early June and in early fall the weather is almost as fine as in high season, and the pace is less hectic.

GETTING HERE AND AROUND
AIR TRAVEL
Alaska Air, American, Frontier, United, and US Airways fly to Santa Barbara Municipal Airport (SBA), 9 miles from downtown. United Express and US Airways provide service to San Luis Obispo County Regional Airport (SBP), 3 miles from downtown San Luis Obispo.

Santa Barbara Airbus shuttles travelers between Santa Barbara and Los Angeles for $48 one-way and $90 round-trip. The Santa Barbara Metropolitan Transit District Bus 11 ($1.75) runs every 30 minutes from the airport to the downtown transit center. A taxi between the airport and the hotel districts costs between $20 and $38.

Airport Contacts San Luis Obispo County Regional Airport ✉ 903-5 *Airport Dr., San Luis Obispo* ☎ *805/781-5205* ⊕ *www.sloairport.com.* **Santa Barbara Airport** ✉ *500 Fowler Rd., Santa Barbara* ☎ *805/683-4011* ⊕ *www.flysba. com.* **Santa Barbara Airbus** ☎ *805/964-7759, 800/423-1618* ⊕ *www.sbairbus. com.* **Santa Barbara Metropolitan Transit District** ☎ *805/963-3366* ⊕ *www. sbmtd.gov.*

BUS TRAVEL

Greyhound provides service from Los Angeles and San Francisco to San Luis Obispo, Ventura, and Santa Barbara. Local transit companies serve these three cities and several smaller towns. Buses can be useful for visiting some urban sights, particularly in Santa Barbara; they're less so for rural ones.

Bus Contacts Greyhound ☎ *800/231-2222* ⊕ *www.greyhound.com.*

CAR TRAVEL

Driving is the easiest way to experience the Central Coast. U.S. 101 and Highway 1, which run north–south, are the main routes to and through the Central Coast from Los Angeles and San Francisco. Highly scenic Highway 1 hugs the coast, and U.S. 101 runs inland. Between Ventura County and northern Santa Barbara County, the two highways are the same road. Highway 1 again separates from U.S. 101 north of Gaviota, then rejoins the highway at Pismo Beach. Along any stretch where these two highways are separate, U.S. 101 is the quicker route.

The most dramatic section of the Central Coast is the 70 miles between San Simeon and Big Sur. The road is narrow and twisting, with a single lane in each direction. In fog or rain the drive can be downright nerveracking; in wet seasons mud slides can close portions of the road.

Other routes into the Central Coast include Highway 46 and Highway 33, which head, respectively, west and south from Interstate 5 near Bakersfield.

Contacts Caltrans ☎ *800/427-7623, 888/836-0866 Hwy. 1 Visitor Hotline (Cambria north to Carmel)* ⊕ *www.dot.ca.gov.*

TRAIN TRAVEL

The Amtrak *Coast Starlight,* which runs between Los Angeles and Seattle via Oakland, stops in Paso Robles, San Luis Obispo, Santa Barbara, and Oxnard. Amtrak runs several *Pacific Surfliner* trains daily between San Luis Obispo, Santa Barbara, Los Angeles, and San Diego. Metrolink Regional Rail Service trains connect Ventura and Oxnard with Los Angeles and points between.

Train Contacts Amtrak ☎ *800/872-7245, 805/963-1015 in Santa Barbara, 805/541-0505 in San Luis Obispo* ⊕ *www.amtrakcalifornia.com.* **Metrolink** ☎ *800/371-5465* ⊕ *www.metrolinktrains.com.*

RESTAURANTS

The cuisine in Ventura and Santa Barbara is every bit as eclectic as it is in California's bigger cities; fresh seafood is a standout. A foodie renaissance has overtaken the entire region from Ventura to Paso Robles, spawning dozens of new restaurants touting locavore cuisine made with fresh organic produce and meats. Dining attire on the Central Coast is generally casual, though slightly dressy casual wear is the custom at pricier restaurants. *Prices in the reviews are the average cost of a main course at dinner or, if dinner is not served, at lunch.*

HOTELS

Lodging options abound in the Central Coast, but expect to pay top dollar for rooms along the shore, especially in summer. Moderately priced hotels and motels do exist—most just a short drive inland from their higher-price counterparts. Make your reservations as early as possible and take advantage of midweek specials to get the best rates. It's common for lodgings to require two-day minimum stays on holidays and some weekends, especially in summer, and to double rates during festivals and other events. Hot Spots provides room reservations and tourist information. *Prices in the reviews are the lowest cost of a standard double room in high season. For expanded reviews, facilities, and current deals, visit Fodors.com.*

Hot Spots ☎ *800/793–7666* ⊕ *www.hotspotsusa.com.*

TOUR OPTIONS

Cloud Climbers Jeep and Wine Tours offers four types of daily tours: wine-tasting, mountain, sunset, and a discovery tour for families. These trips to the Santa Barbara/Santa Ynez mountains and Wine Country are conducted in open-air, six-passenger jeeps. Fares range from $89 to $129 per adult. The company also offers a four-hour All Around Ojai Tour ($109) and arranges biking, horseback riding, and trap-shooting tours and Paso Robles wine tours by appointment.

Wine Edventures operates guided wine tours ($110 per person) in the Santa Ynez Valley in vans, minicoaches, and other vehicles. The Grapeline Wine Country Shuttle leads daily wine and vineyard picnic tours ($88 to $138) with flexible itineraries in San Luis Obispo County and the Santa Barbara County Wine Country.

Spencer's Limousine & Tours offers customized tours of Santa Barbara and the Wine Country via sedan, limousine, or van. A five-hour basic tour with at least four participants costs about $90 per person. Sustainable Vine Wine Tours' biodiesel-powered vans can take you on a day of eco-friendly wine touring ($125) in the Santa Ynez Valley. Trips include tastings at green-minded wineries, and a gourmet organic picnic lunch.

Many of the tour companies described above will pick you up at your hotel or central locations; ask about this when booking.

Tour Contacts Cloud Climbers Jeep and Wine Tours ☎ *805/646–3200* ⊕ *www.ccjeeps.com.* **The Grapeline Wine Country Shuttle** ☎ *888/894–6379* ⊕ *www.gogrape.com.* **Spencer's Limousine & Tours** ☎ *805/884–9700* ⊕ *www. spencerslimo.com.* **Sustainable Vine Wine Tours** ☎ *805/698–3911* ⊕ *www. sustainablevine.com.***Wine Edventures** ✉ *Santa Barbara* ☎ *805/965–9463* ⊕ *www.welovewines.com.*

VISITOR INFORMATION

Contacts Central Coast Tourism Council ⊕ *www.centralcoast-tourism.com.*

VENTURA COUNTY

Ventura County was first settled by the Chumash Indians. Spanish missionaries were the first Europeans to arrive, followed by Americans and other Europeans, who established bustling towns, transportation networks, and highly productive farms. Since the 1920s, though, agriculture has been steadily replaced as the area's main industry—first by the oil business and more recently by tourism.

VENTURA

60 miles north of Los Angeles on U.S. 101.

Like Los Angeles, the city of Ventura enjoys gorgeous weather and sun-kissed beaches—but without the smog and congestion. The miles of beautiful beaches attract athletes—bodysurfers and boogie boarders, runners and bikers—and those who'd rather doze beneath an umbrella all day. Ventura Harbor is home to myriad fishing boats, restaurants, and water-activity centers where you can rent boats and take harbor cruises. Foodies can get their fix all over Ventura—dozens of upscale cafés and wine and tapas bars have opened in recent years. Arts and antiques buffs have long trekked downtown to browse the galleries and shops there.

GETTING HERE AND AROUND

Amtrak and Metrolink trains serve the area from Los Angeles area. Greyhound buses stop in Ventura; Gold Coast Transit serves the city and the rest of Ventura County.

U.S. 101 is the north–south main route into town, but for a scenic drive, take Highway 1 north from Santa Monica. The highway merges with U.S. 101 just south of Ventura. ■TIP→ Traveling north to Ventura from Los Angeles on weekdays, it's best to depart before 6 am, between 10 and 2, or after 7, or you'll get caught in the extended rush-hour traffic. Coming south from Santa Barbara, depart before 1 or after 6. On weekends, traffic is generally fine except southbound on U.S. 101 between Santa Barbara and Ventura.

ESSENTIALS

Bus Contacts Gold Coast Transit ☎ *805/643–3158* ⊕ *www.goldcoasttransit. org.*

Visitor Information Ventura Visitors and Convention Bureau ✉ *Downtown Visitor Center, 101 S. California St.* ☎ *805/648–2075, 800/483–6214* ⊕ *www. ventura-usa.com.*

EXPLORING

Lake Casitas Recreation Area. Lunker largemouth bass, rainbow trout, crappie, redears, and channel catfish live in the waters at Lake Casitas Recreation Area, an impoundment of the Ventura River. The lake is one of the country's best bass-fishing areas, and anglers come from all over the United States to test their luck. The park, nestled below the Santa Ynez Mountains' Laguna Ridge, is also a beautiful spot for pitching a tent or having a picnic. The Casitas Water Adventure, which has two water playgrounds and a lazy river for tubing and floating, is a great place to take kids in summer ($12 for an all-day pass; $6 from 5 to 7 pm). The park is 13 miles northwest of Ventura. ⊠ *11311 Santa Ana Rd., off Hwy. 33* ☎ *805/649–2233, 805/649–1122 campground reservations* ⊕ *www.casitaswater.org* ☒ *$10–$15 per vehicle, $13 per boat* ☉ *Daily.*

Mission San Buenaventura. The ninth of the 21 California missions, Mission San Buenaventura was established in 1782 but burned to the ground in the 1790s. It was rebuilt and rededicated in 1809. A self-guided tour takes you through a small museum, a quiet courtyard, and a chapel with 250-year-old paintings. ⊠ *211 E. Main St., at Figueroa St.* ☎ *805/643–4318* ⊕ *www.sanbuenaventuramission.org* ☒ *$2* ☉ *Weekdays 10–5, Sat. 9–5, Sun. 10–4.*

Ventura Oceanfront. Four miles of gorgeous coastline stretch from the county fairgrounds at the northern border of the city of San Buenaventura, through San Buenaventura State Beach, down to Ventura Harbor in the south. The main attraction here is the San Buenaventura City Pier, a landmark built in 1872 and restored in 1993. Surfers rip the waves just north of the pier, and sunbathers relax on white-sand beaches on either side. The mile-long promenade and the Omer Rains Bike Trail north of the pier attract scores of joggers, surrey cyclers, and bikers throughout the year. ⊠ *California St. at ocean's edge.*

WHERE TO EAT

$$$
FRENCH
✕ **71 Palm Restaurant.** This elegant restaurant occupies a 1910 house, and it still has touches that make it feel like a home: lace curtains, wood floors, a dining patio for good weather, and a fireplace that's often crackling in winter. A standout appetizer is the homemade country pâté with cornichons; for dinner, try the grilled salmon on a potato pancake, the New Zealand rack of lamb Provençal, or the bouillabaise. ⑤ *Average main: $24* ⊠ *71 N. Palm St., at Poli St.* ☎ *805/653–7222* ⊕ *www.71palm.com* ☉ *Closed Sun.*

$$
SEAFOOD
✕ **Brophy Bros.** The Ventura outpost of this wildly popular Santa Barbara restaurant provides the same fresh seafood-oriented meals in a spacious second-story setting overlooking the harbor. Feast on everything from fish-and-chips and crab cakes to chowder and delectable fish—often straight from the boats moored below. ⑤ *Average main: $18* ⊠ *1559 Spinnaker Dr., in Ventura Harbor Village* ☎ *805/639–0865* ⊕ *www.brophybros.com* ☒ *Reservations not accepted.*

$
AMERICAN
✕ **Busy Bee Cafe.** A local favorite for decades, this classic 1950s diner has a jukebox on every table and serves hearty burgers and comfort food (think meat loaf and mashed potatoes, pot roast, and Cobb salad). For breakfast, tuck into a huge omelet; for a snack or dessert, order a shake or hot fudge sundae from the soda fountain. ⑤ *Average main: $10* ⊠ *478 E. Main St., near S. California St.* ☎ *805/643–4864* ⊕ *www.busybeecafe.biz.*

$
AMERICAN
✕ **Christy's.** You can get breakfast all day—don't miss the breakfast burrito—at this cozy, nautical-theme locals' hangout in the harbor, across the water from the Channel Islands. It also serves burgers, sandwiches, and soup. ⑤ *Average main: $12* ⊠ *1559 Spinnaker Dr., in Ventura Harbor Village* ☎ *805/642–3116.*

The map shows "Ventura and Santa Barbara Counties."

$$ ✗**Peirano's.** In 2012 new owners transformed the historic Peirano's
ECLECTIC building into a colorful, contemporary space filled with art from around
the globe. In keeping with this global perspective, chef Robert Grenner's
seasonal menus incorporate the flavors of California, the Mediterranean
region, and the Middle East. Starters might include braised heirloom
eggplant with sun-dried mint, cardamom, and a rich Middle Eastern
yogurt, or a traditional Caesar salad. Mains might include cioppino or
lamb kebabs marinated in a rosemary-avocado-honey sauce and served
with pearl-barley risotto. $ *Average main: $22* ⊠ *204 E. Main St.,
at Figueroa Street Mall* ☎ *805/648–4853* ⊕ *www.peiranos.com* ☽ *No
lunch.*

WHERE TO STAY
For expanded reviews, facilities, and current deals, visit Fodors.com.

$$ ⛉**Crowne Plaza Ventura Beach.** An enviable location is the main draw of
HOTEL this 12-story hotel: it's on the beach, next to a historic pier, and within
walking distance of downtown restaurants and nightlife. **Pros:** on the
beach, near downtown and attractions; steps from waterfront; near
Amtrak. **Cons:** early-morning train noise; waterfront area crowded in
summer; most rooms on the small side. **TripAdvisor:** "a beach treat,"
"clean rooms," "so friendly." $ *Rooms from: $169* ⊠ *450 E. Harbor
Blvd.* ☎ *800/842–0800* ⊕ *cpventura.com* ⇱ *254 rooms, 4 suites.*

$$ 🏨 **Four Points by Sheraton Ventura Harbor Resort.** An on-site restaurant,
RESORT   spacious rooms, and a slew of amenities make this 17-acre property
(which includes sister hotel Holiday Inn Express) a popular and practical choice for Channel Islands visitors. **Pros:** close to island transportation; mostly quiet; short drive to historic downtown Ventura. **Cons:** not in the heart of downtown; noisy seagulls sometimes congregate nearby. **TripAdvisor:** "staff is the friendliest," "really nice amenities," "super comfy beds." ⑤ *Rooms from: $145* ✉ *1050 Schooner Dr.* ☎ *805/658–1212* ⊕ *www.fourpoints.com/ventura* ⇋ *102 rooms, 4 suites.*

$$ 🏨 **Holiday Inn Express Ventura Harbor.** A favorite among Channel Islands
HOTEL   visitors, this quiet, comfortable, lodge-inspired property sits right at the Ventura Harbor entrance. **Pros:** quiet at night; easy access to harbor restaurants and activities; five-minute drive to downtown sights. **Cons:** busy area on weekends; complaints of erratic service. **TripAdvisor:** "best view and customer service in town," "perfect," "lots of room." ⑤ *Rooms from: $130* ✉ *1080 Navigator Dr.* ☎ *805/856–9533, 800/315–2621* ⊕ *www.holidayinnexpress.com/venturaca* ⇋ *69 rooms* ❍| *Breakfast.*

$$$ 🏨 **Ventura Beach Marriott.** Spacious, contemporary rooms, a peace-
HOTEL   ful location just steps from San Buenaventura State Beach, and easy access to historic downtown Ventura's arts and culture district make the Marriott a popular choice. **Pros:** walk to beach and biking/jogging trails; a block from historic pier; great value for location. **Cons:** close to highway; near busy intersection. **TripAdvisor:** "very comfortable and quiet," "exceptional service," "great place to stay and play." ⑤ *Rooms from: $189* ✉ *2055 E. Harbor Blvd.* ☎ *805/643–6000, 888/236–2427* ⊕ *www.marriottventurabeach.com* ⇋ *272 rooms, 12 suites.*

SPORTS AND THE OUTDOORS

The most popular outdoor activities in Ventura are beach-going and whale-watching. California gray whales migrate offshore through the Santa Barbara Channel from late December through March; giant blue and humpback whales feed here from mid-June through September. The channel teems with marine life year-round, so tours, which depart from Ventura Harbor, include more than just whale sightings. To learn about the spectacular hiking trails on the five islands that comprise Channel Islands National Park, check out its visitor center, also at the harbor.

Island Packers. A cruise through the Santa Barbara Channel with Island Packers will give you the chance to spot dolphins and seals—and sometimes even whales—throughout the year. ✉ *Ventura Harbor, 1691 Spinnaker Dr.* ☎ *805/642–1393* ⊕ *www.islandpackers.com.*

OJAI

15 miles north of Ventura, U.S. 101 to Hwy. 33.

The Ojai Valley, which director Frank Capra used as a backdrop for his 1936 film *Lost Horizon*, sizzles in the summer when temperatures routinely reach 90°F. The acres of orange and avocado groves here evoke postcard images of long-ago agricultural Southern California. Many artists and celebrities have sought refuge in lush Ojai from life in the fast lane.

GETTING HERE AND AROUND

From northern Ventura, Highway 33 veers east from U.S. 101 and climbs inland to Ojai. From Santa Barbara, exit U.S. 101 at Highway 150 in Carpinteria, then travel east 20 miles on a twisting, two-lane road that is not recommended at night or during poor weather. You can also access Ojai by heading west from Interstate 5 on Highway 126. Exit at Santa Paula and follow Highway 150 north for 16 miles to Ojai. Gold Coast Transit provides service to Ojai from Ventura.

Ojai can be easily explored on foot; you can also hop on the Ojai Trolley ($1), which follows two routes around Ojai and neighboring Miramonte between 7:15 and 5:15 on weekdays, and one route between 9 and 5 on weekends. If you tell the driver you're a visitor, you'll get an informal guided tour.

ESSENTIALS

Bus Contact Gold Coast Transit ☎ 805/643–3158 ⊕ *www.goldcoasttransit.org.* **Ojai Trolley** ☎ 805/646–5581 ⊕ *ojaitrolley.com.*

Visitor Information Ojai Visitors Bureau ✉ 206 N. Signal St. ☎ 888/652–4669 ⊕ *www.ojaivisitors.com* ☉ Weekdays 9–4.

EXPLORING

Ojai Art Center. California's oldest nonprofit, multipurpose art center exhibits artwork from various disciplines and presents theater, dance, and other performances. ✉ 113 S. Montgomery St. ☎ 805/646–0117 ⊕ www.ojaiartcenter.org.

Ojai Avenue. The work of local artists is displayed in the Spanish-style shopping arcade along Ojai Avenue (Highway 150). Organic and specialty growers sell their produce on Sunday between 9 and 1 at the farmers' market behind the arcade.

Ojai Valley Museum. Housed in a former chapel, the Ojai Valley Museum has exhibits on the valley's history and many Native American artifacts. ✉ 130 W. Ojai Ave. ☎ 805/640–1390 ⊕ www.ojaivalleymuseum.org ⊡ $4.

Ojai Valley Trail. The 18-mile Ojai Valley Trail is open to pedestrians, bikers, joggers, equestrians, and nonmotorized vehicles. You can access it anywhere along its route. ✉ Parallel to Hwy. 33 from Soule Park in Ojai to ocean in Ventura ☎ 888/652–4669 ⊕ www.ojaivisitors.com.

WHERE TO EAT

$$
MEDITERRANEAN
✕ **Azu.** Delectable tapas, a full bar, slick furnishings, and piped jazz music lure diners to this popular, artsy Mediterranean bistro. You can also order soups, salads, and bistro fare such as tagine roasted chicken and paella. Save room for the homemade gelato. ⑤ Average main: $16 ✉ 457 E. Ojai Ave. ☎ 805/640–7987 ⊕ www.azuojai.com ☉ No lunch Sun. and Mon., early Sept.–early May.

$
ITALIAN
✕ **Boccali's.** Edging a ranch, citrus groves, and a seasonal garden that provides much of the produce for menu items, the modest but cheery Boccali's attracts droves of loyal fans. In the warmer months, you can dine alfresco in the oak-shaded patio and lawn area and sometimes listen to live music. The family-run operation, best known for hand-rolled pizzas and homestyle pastas (don't miss the eggplant lasagna),

also serves a highly popular seasonal strawberry shortcake. $ *Average main: $15* ✉ *3277 Ojai Ave., about 2 miles east of downtown* ☎ *805/646–6116* ⊕ *www.boccalis.com* ▤ *No credit cards* ⊘ *No lunch Mon. and Tues.*

$$$

AMERICAN

★

✕ **The Ranch House.** This elegant yet laid-back eatery has been around for decades. Main dishes such as the broiled-and-roasted rack of lamb with pineapple guava chutney, and the grilled diver scallops with curried sweet-corn sauce are not to be missed. The verdant patio is a wonderful place to have Sunday brunch. $ *Average main: $27* ✉ *500 S. Lomita Ave.* ☎ *805/646–2360* ⊕ *www.theranchhouse.com* ⊘ *Closed Mon. No lunch.*

$$$

EUROPEAN

✕ **Suzanne's Cuisine.** Peppered filet mignon, linguine with steamed clams, and pan-roasted salmon with a roasted mango sauce are among the offerings at this European-style restaurant. Game, seafood, and vegetarian dishes dominate the dinner menu, and salads and soups star at lunchtime. All the breads and desserts are made on the premises. $ *Average main: $24* ✉ *502 W. Ojai Ave.* ☎ *805/640–1961* ⊕ *www.suzannescuisine.com* ⊘ *Closed Tues.*

WHERE TO STAY

For expanded reviews, facilities, and current deals, visit Fodors.com.

$$

B&B/INN

▥ **The Blue Iguana Inn & Suites.** Artists run this Southwestern-style hotel, and their work (which is for sale) decorates the rooms. **Pros:** colorful art everywhere; secluded property. **Cons:** 2 miles from the heart of Ojai; sits on the main highway to Ventura; small. **TripAdvisor:** "lovely getaway spot," "a perfect port in a storm," "has it all." $ *Rooms from: $129* ✉ *11794 N. Ventura Ave., Hwy. 33* ☎ *805/646–5277* ⊕ *www.blueiguanainn.com* ⬳ *4 rooms, 8 suites, 8 cottages* ☉ *Breakfast.*

$$

RESORT

▥ **Oaks at Ojai.** Rejuvenation is the name of the game at this comfortable spa resort. **Pros:** great place to get fit; peaceful retreat; healthful meals. **Cons:** rooms are basic; sits on the main highway through town. **TripAdvisor:** "excellent all around fitness resort experience," "amazing spa with terrific results," "great place to get your life back." $ *Rooms from: $199* ✉ *122 E. Ojai Ave.* ☎ *805/646–5573, 800/753–6257* ⊕ *www.oaksspa.com* ⬳ *44 rooms, 2 suites* ☉ *All meals* ⌖ *2-night minimum stay.*

$$$$

RESORT

★

▥ **Ojai Valley Inn & Spa.** This outdoorsy, golf-oriented resort and spa is set on beautifully landscaped grounds, with hillside views in nearly all directions. **Pros:** gorgeous grounds; exceptional outdoor activities; romantic yet kid-friendly. **Cons:** expensive; areas near restaurants can be noisy. **TripAdvisor:** "relax in the sun," "idyllic setting," "gorgeous property." $ *Rooms from: $400* ✉ *905 Country Club Rd.* ☎ *805/646–1111, 888/697–8780* ⊕ *www.ojairesort.com* ⬳ *231 rooms, 77 suites.*

$$$

B&B/INN

▥ **Su Nido Inn.** Just a short walk from downtown Ojai sights and restaurants, this posh Mission revival–style inn is nested in a quiet neighborhood a few blocks from Libbey Park. **Pros:** walking distance from downtown; homey feel. **Cons:** no pool; can get hot during summer. **TripAdvisor:** "more than we could have asked for," "serene," "lovingly appointed." $ *Rooms from: $179* ✉ *301 N. Montgomery St.* ☎ *805/646–7080, 866/646–7080* ⊕ *www.sunidoinn.com* ⬳ *3 rooms, 9 suites.*

SANTA BARBARA

27 miles northwest of Ventura and 29 miles west of Ojai on U.S. 101.

Santa Barbara has long been an oasis for Los Angelenos seeking respite from big-city life. The attractions begin at the ocean and end in the foothills of the Santa Ynez Mountains. A few miles up the coast east and west—but still very much a part of Santa Barbara—are the exclusive residential districts of Montecito and Hope Ranch. Santa Barbara is on a jog in the coastline, so the ocean is actually to the south, instead of the west; for this reason, directions can be confusing. "Up" the coast toward San Francisco is west, "down" toward Los Angeles is east, and the mountains are north.

GETTING HERE AND AROUND

U.S. 101 is the main route into Santa Barbara. If you're staying in town, a car is handy but not essential; the beaches and downtown are easily explored by bicycle or on foot. Visit the Santa Barbara Car Free website for bike route and walking-tour maps and car-free vacation packages with substantial lodging, dining, activity, and transportation discounts.

Santa Barbara Metropolitan Transit District's Line 22 bus serves major tourist sights. Several bus lines connect with the very convenient electric shuttles that cruise the downtown and waterfront every 8 to 15 minutes (25¢ each way).

Santa Barbara Trolley Co. operates a motorized San Francisco–style cable car that loops past major hotels, shopping areas, and attractions from 10 to 4. Get off whenever you like, and pick up another trolley (they come every hour) when you're ready to move on. The fare is $19 for the day.

TOURS

Land and Sea Tours. Land and Sea Tours takes visitors on narrated, 90-minute land-and-sea adventures in an amphibious 49-passenger vehicle, nicknamed the Land Shark. Tours begin with a drive through the city and continue with a plunge into the harbor for a cruise along the coast. ⊠ *State St. at Stearns Wharf* ☎ *805/683–7600* ⊕ *www.out2seesb. com* 🎫 *$25* ⊗ *Tours May–Oct., daily noon, 2, and 4; Nov.–Apr., daily noon and 2.*

ESSENTIALS

Transportation Contacts Santa Barbara Car Free ⊕ *www.santa-barbaracarfree.org.* **Santa Barbara Metropolitan Transit District** ☎ *805/963–3366* ⊕ *www.sbmtd.gov.* **Santa Barbara Trolley Co.** ☎ *805/965–0353* ⊕ *www.sbtrolley.com.*

Visitor Information Santa Barbara Chamber of Commerce Visitor Information Center ⊠ *1 Garden St., at Cabrillo Blvd.* ☎ *805/965–3021, 805/568–1811* ⊕ *www.sbchamber.org.* **Santa Barbara Conference and Visitors Bureau** ⊠ *1601 Anacapa St.* ☎ *805/966–9222* ⊕ *www.santabarbaraca.com.*

Continued on page 260

ON A MISSION

Their soul may belong to Spain, their heart to the New World, but the historic missions of California, with their lovely churches, beckon the traveler on a soulful journey back to the very founding of the American West.

by Cheryl Crabtree and Robert I.C. Fisher

California history changed forever in the 18th century when Spanish explorers founded a series of missions along the Pacific coast. Believing they were following God's will, they wanted to spread the gospel and convert as many natives as possible. The process produced a collision between the Hispanic and California Indian cultures, resulting in one of the most striking legacies of Old California: the Spanish mission churches. Rising like mirages in the middle of desert plains and rolling hills, these saintly sites transport you back to the days of the Spanish colonial period.

GOD AND MAN IN CALIFORNIA

The Alta California territory came under pressure in the 1760s when Spain feared foreign advances into the territory explorer Juan Rodríguez Cabrillo had claimed for the Spanish crown back in 1542. But how could Spain create a visible and viable presence halfway around the world? They decided to build on the model that had already worked well in Spain's Mexico colony. The plan involved establishing a series of missions, to be operated by the Catholic Church and protected by four of Spain's *presidios* (military outposts). The native Indians—after quick conversion to Christianity—would provide the labor force necessary to build mission towns.

FATHER OF THE MISSIONS

Father Junípero Serra is an icon of the Spanish colonial period. At the behest of the Spanish government, the diminutive padre—then well into his fifties, and despite a chronic leg infection— started out on foot from Baja California to search for suitable mission sites, with a goal of reaching Monterey. In 1769 he helped establish Alta California's first mission in San Diego and continued his travels until his death, in 1784, by which time he had founded eight more missions.

The system ended about a decade after the Mexican government took control of Alta California in the early 1820s and began to secularize the missions. The church lost horses and cattle, as well as vast tracts of land, which the Mexican government in turn granted to private individuals. They also lost laborers, as the Indians were for the most part free to find work and a life beyond the missions. In 1848, the Americans assumed control of the territory, and California became part of the United States. Today, these missions stand as extraordinary monuments to their colorful past.

Mission Santa Barbara Museum

MISSION ACCOMPLISHED

California's Mission Trail is the best way to follow in the fathers' footsteps. Here, below, are its 21 settlements, north to south.

Amazingly, all 21 Spanish missions in California are still standing—some in their pristine historic state, others with modifications made over the centuries. Many are found on or near the "King's Road"—El Camino Real—which linked these mission outposts. At the height of the mission system the trail was approximately 600 miles long, eventually extending from San Diego to Sonoma. Today the road is commemorated on portions of routes 101 and 82 in the form of roadside bell markers erected by CalTrans every one to two miles between San Diego and San Francisco.

San Francisco Solano, Sonoma (1823; this was the final California mission constructed.)

San Rafael, San Rafael (1817)

San Francisco de Asís (aka Mission Dolores), San Francisco (1776). Situated in the heart of San Francisco,

Mission Santa Clara de Asís

these mission grounds and nearby Arroyo de los Dolores (Creek of Sorrows) are home to the oldest intact building in the city.

Santa Clara de Asís, Santa Clara (1777). On the campus of Santa Clara University, this beautifully restored mission contains original paintings, statues, a bell, and hundreds of artifacts, as well as a spectacular rose garden.

San José, Fremont (1797)

Santa Cruz, Santa Cruz (1791)

San Juan Bautista, San Juan Bautista (1797). Immortalized in Hitchcock's *Vertigo*, this remarkably preserved pueblo contains the largest church of all the California missions, as well as 18th- and 19th-century buildings and a sprawling plaza.

San Carlos Borromeo del Río Carmelo, Carmel (1770). Carmel Mission was head-

quarters for the California mission system under Father Serra and the Father Presidents who succeeded him; the on-site museum includes Serra's tiny sleeping quarters (where he died in 1784).

Nuestra Señora de la Soledad, Soledad (1791)

San Antonio de Padua, Jolon (1771)

San Miguel Arcángel, San Miguel (1797). San Miguel boasts the only intact original interior wall painting in any of the missions, painted in 1821 by Native American converts under the direction of Spanish artist Esteban Muras.

Painting from 1818, San Juan Bautista.

Mission Santa Inés

Mission San Fernando Rey de España

now a living-history museum with a church and nearly forty craft and residence rooms.

Santa Inés, Solvang (1804). Home to one of the most significant pieces of religious art created by a California mission Indian.

Santa Bárbara, Santa Barbara (1786). The "Queen of the Missions" has twin bell towers, gorgeous gardens with heirloom plant varietals, a massive collection of rare artworks and artifacts, and lovely stonework.

San Buenaventura, Ventura (1782). This was the last mission founded by Father Serra; it is still an active parish in the Archdiocese of Los Angeles.

San Luis Obispo de Tolosa, San Luis Obispo (1772). Bear meat from grizzlies captured here saved the Spaniards from starving, which helped convince Father Serra to establish a mission.

La Purísima Concepción, Lompoc (1787). La Purísima is the nation's most completely restored mission complex. It is

San Fernando Rey de España, Mission Hills (1797)

San Gabriel Arcángel, San Gabriel (1771)

San Luis Rey de Francia, Oceanside (1798)

San Juan Capistrano, San Juan Capistrano (1776). This mission is famed for its Saint Joseph's Day (March 19) celebration of the return of swallows in the springtime. The mission's adobe walls enclose acres of lush gardens and historic buildings.

San Diego de Alcalá, San Diego (1769). This was the first California missions constructed, although the original was destroyed in 1775 and rebuilt over a number of years.

Coalinga

Paso Robles

San Miguel Arcángel

101

San Luis Obispo

McKittrick

San Luis Obispo de Tolosa

Santa Maria

La Purísima Conepción

Tejon Pass

Lompoc

Santa Bárbara

Santa Inés

Santa Barbara

101

Oxnard

Ventura

San Fernando Rey de España

Pasadena

San Buenaventura

LOS ANGELES

San Gabriel Arcángel

Huntington Beach

San Luis Rey de Francia

San Juan Capistrano

Oceanside

Julian

101

KEY

| 0 | 50 mi |

| 0 | 50 km |

✠ Mission

San Diego de Alcalá

SAN DIEGO

MEXICO

5

IN FOCUS ON A MISSION

SPANISH MISSION STYLE

(left) Mission San Luis Rey de Francia; (right) Mission San Antonio de Padua

The Spanish mission churches derive much of their strength and enduring power from their extraordinary admixture of styles. They are spectacular examples of the combination of races and cultures that bloomed along Father Serra's road through Alta California.

SPIRIT OF THE PLACE

In building the missions, the Franciscan padres had to rely on available resources. Spanish churches back in Europe boasted marble floors and gilded statues. But here, whitewashed adobe walls gleamed in the sun and floors were often merely packed earth.

However simple the structures, the art within the mission confines continued to glorify the Church. The padres imported much finery to decorate the churches and perform the mass—silver, silk and lovely paintings to teach the life of Christ to the Indians and soldiers and settlers. Serra himself com-

missioned fine artists in Mexico to produce custom works using the best materials and according to exact specifications. Sculptures of angels, Mary, Joseph, Jesus and the Franciscan heroes and saints—and of course the Stations of the Cross—adorned all the missions.

AN ENDURING LEGACY

Mission architecture reflects a gorgeous blend of European and New World influences. While naves followed the simple forms of Franciscan Gothic, cloisters (with beautiful arcades) adopted aspects of the Romanesque style, and ornamental touches of the Spanish Renaissance—including red-tiled roofs and wrought-iron grilles—added even more elegance. In the 20th century, the Mission Revival Style had a huge impact on architecture and design in California, as seen in examples ranging from San Diego's Union Station to Stanford University's main quadrangle.

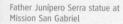

Father Junípero Serra statue at Mission San Gabriel

FOR WHOM THE BELLS TOLLED

Perhaps the most famous architectural motif of the Spanish Mission churches was the belltower. These took the form of either a campanile—a single tower called a campanario—or, more spectacularly, of an open-work espedaña, a perforated adobe wall housing a series of bells (notable examples of this form are at San Miguel Arcángel and San Diego de Alcalá). Bells were essential to maintaining the routines of daily life at the missions.

MISSION LIFE

Morning bells summoned residents to chapel for services; noontime bells introduced the main meal, while the evening bells sounded the alert to gather around 5 pm for mass and dinner. Many of the natives were happy with their new faith, and even enjoyed putting in numerous hours a week working as farmers, soapmakers, weavers, and masons.

Others, however, were less willing to abandon their traditional culture, but were coerced to abide by the new Spanish laws and mission rules. Natives were sometimes mistreated by the friars, who used a system of punishments to enforce submission to the new culture.

NATIVE TRAGEDY

In the end, mission life proved extremely destructive to the Native Californian population. European diseases and contaminated water caused the death of nearly a third, with some tribes—notably the Chumash—being virtually decimated.

Despite these losses, small numbers did survive. After the Mexican government secularized the missions in 1833, a majority of the native population was reduced to poverty. Some stayed at the missions, while others went to live in the pueblos, ranchos, and countryside.

Many Native Californian people today still work and live near the missions that are monuments to their artistry skills.

FOR MORE INFORMATION

California Missions Foundation

✉ 26555 Carmel Rancho Blvd., Ste. 7
Carmel, CA 93923

☎ 831/622-7500

🌐 www.california missionsfoundation.org

Top, Mission San Gabriel Arcángel
Bottom, Mission San Miguel Arcángel

EXPLORING

Santa Barbara's waterfront is beautiful, with palm-studded promenades and plenty of sand. In the few miles between the beaches and the hills are downtown, the old mission, and the botanic gardens.

EXPLORING
TOP ATTRACTIONS

★ **El Presidio State Historic Park.** Founded in 1782, El Presidio was one of four military strongholds established by the Spanish along the coast of California. The park encompasses much of the original site in the heart of downtown. El Cuartel, the adobe guardhouse, is the oldest building in Santa Barbara and the second oldest in California. ⊠ *123 E. Canon Perdido St., at Anacapa St.* ☎ *805/965-0093* ⊕ *www.sbthp.org* ✉ *$5* ☺ *Daily 10:30–4:30.*

Fodor's Choice **Mission Santa Barbara.** Widely referred to as the "Queen of Missions,"
★ this is one of the most beautiful and frequently photographed buildings in coastal California. Dating to 1786, the architecture evolved from adobe-brick buildings with thatch roofs to more permanent edifices as the mission's population burgeoned. An earthquake in 1812 destroyed the third church built on the site. Its replacement, the present structure, is still a functioning Catholic church. Mission Santa Barbara has a splendid Spanish/Mexican colonial art collection, as well as Chumash sculptures and the only Native American–made altar and tabernacle left in the California missions. Docents lead 90-minute tours ($8 adult) Thursday and Friday at 11 and Saturday at 10:30. ⊠ *2201 Laguna St., at E. Los Olivos St.* ☎ *805/682-4149, 805/682-4713* ⊕ *www. santabarbaramission.org* ✉ *$5* ☺ *Daily 9–4:30.*

Santa Barbara Botanic Garden. Scenic trails meander through the garden's 78 acres of native plants. The Mission Dam, built in 1806, stands just beyond the redwood grove and above the restored aqueduct that once carried water to Mission Santa Barbara. More than a thousand plant species thrive in various themed sections, including mountains, deserts, meadows, redwoods, and Channel Islands. ⊠ *1212 Mission Canyon Rd., north of Foothill Rd. (Hwy. 192)* ☎ *805/682-4726* ⊕ *www.sbbg. org* ✉ *$8* ☺ *Mar.–Oct., daily 9–6; Nov.–Feb., daily 9–5. Guided tours weekends at 11 and 2.*

★ **Santa Barbara County Courthouse.** Hand-painted tiles and a spiral staircase infuse the courthouse with the grandeur of a Moorish palace. This magnificent building was completed in 1929, part of a rebuilding process after a 1925 earthquake destroyed many downtown structures. At the time, Santa Barbara was also in the midst of a cultural awakening, and the trend was toward an architectural style appropriate to the area's climate and history. The result is the harmonious Mediterranean–Spanish look of much of the downtown area, especially the municipal buildings. An elevator rises to an arched observation area in the courthouse tower that provides a panoramic view of the city. The murals in the ceremonial chambers on the courthouse's second floor were painted by an artist who did backdrops for some of Cecil B. DeMille's films. ⊠ *1100 Anacapa St., at E. Anapamu St.* ☎ *805/962-6464* ⊕ *www.santabarbaracourthouse.org* ☺ *Weekdays 8–4:45, weekends*

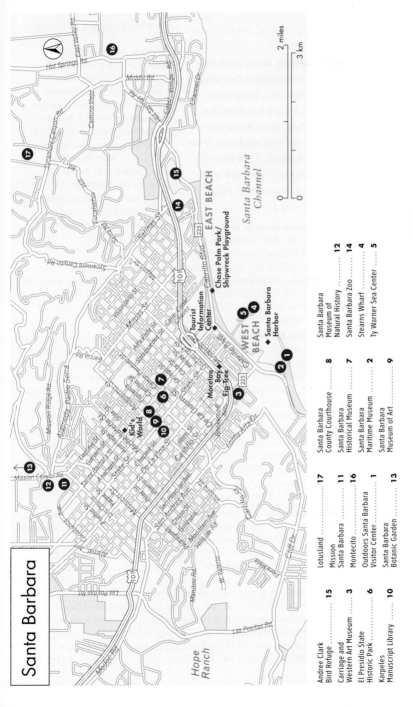

Santa Barbara

2 miles
3 km

Santa Barbara Channel

EAST BEACH

Chase Palm Park/
Shipwreck Playground

Tourist
Information
Center

WEST
BEACH

Santa Barbara
Harbor

Moreton
Bay
Fig Tree

Kid's
World

Hot Springs Rd.

Hope
Ranch

10–4:30. Free guided tours Mon., Tues., Wed., and Fri. at 10:30, daily at 2.

QUICK BITES

Cielito Taqueria. Take a break from State Street shopping at the casual taqueria attached to fancy Cielito Restaurant. Enjoy a few tacos or a Oaxacan-style tamale in the court-yard patio, and then head back to the shops. ⊠ *La Arcada, 1114 State St., at E. Figueroa St.* ☎ *805/225–4488* ⊕ *cielitorestaurant.com* ⊗ *Mon. 11–8, Tues.–Sat. 11–6.*

Santa Barbara Museum of Art. The highlights of this museum's permanent collection include ancient sculpture, Asian art, impressionist paintings, contemporary art, photography, and American works in several media. ⊠ *1130 State St., at E. Anapamu St.* ☎ *805/963–4364* ⊕ *www.sbma.net* ✉ *$9; pay what you wish on Sun.* ⊗ *Tues.–Sun. 11–5. Free guided tours Tues.–Sun. at noon and 1.*

SANTA BARBARA STYLE

Why does downtown Santa Barbara look so scrubbed and uniform? After a 1925 earth-quake, which demolished many buildings, the city seized a golden opportunity to create a Spanish-Mediterranean look. It established an architectural board of review, which, along with city commissions, created strict architectural codes for the downtown district: red tile roofs, earth-tone facades, arches, wrought-iron embellishments, and height restrictions (about four stories).

☺ **Santa Barbara Museum of Natural History.** The gigantic skeleton of a blue whale greets you at the entrance of this complex. The major draws include the planetarium, space lab, and a gem and mineral display. A room of dioramas illustrates Chumash Indian history and culture. Startlingly alive-looking stuffed specimens, complete with nests and eggs, roost in the bird diversity room. Many exhibits have interactive components. Outdoors you can stroll on nature trails that wind through the serene oak-studded grounds. Ask about the Nature Pass, which includes discounted unlimited two-day admission to both the Museum of Natural History and the Ty Warner Sea Center on Stearns Wharf. ⊠ *2559 Puesta del Sol Rd., off E. Los Olivos St.* ☎ *805/682–4711* ⊕ *www.sbnature.org* ✉ *$10 Oct.–Apr., $11 May–Sept.; free 3rd Sun. of month Sept.–May* ⊗ *Daily 10–5.*

☺ **Santa Barbara Zoo.** The grounds of this smallish zoo are so gorgeous people book their weddings here long in advance. The palm-studded lawns on a hilltop overlooking the beach are perfect spots for family picnics. The natural settings of the zoo shelter elephants, gorillas, exotic birds like the California condor, and big cats such as the rare snow leopard, a thick-furred, high-altitude dweller from Asia. For small children, there's a scenic railroad and barnyard petting zoo. Duncan, an amazingly lifelike dinosaur, stars in the live stage show *How to Train Your Dinosaur* (free with zoo admission, daily in summer, on weekends the rest of year). Duncan, designed by one of Hollywood's top creature shops, demonstrates the special techniques trainers use to care for animals. ⊠ *500 Niños Dr., off El Cabrillo Blvd.* ☎ *805/962–5339 main* *line, 805/962–6310 information ⊕ www.santabarbarazoo.org ☎Zoo $14, parking $6 ⊗ Daily 10–5.*

Stearns Wharf. Built in 1872, Stearns Wharf is Santa Barbara's most visited landmark. Expansive views of the mountains, cityscape, and harbor unfold from every vantage point on the three-block-long pier. Although it's a nice walk from the Cabrillo Boulevard parking areas, you can also park on the pier and then wander through the shops or stop for a meal at one of the wharf's restaurants. ⊠ *Cabrillo Blvd. and State St. ⊕ www.stearnswharf.org.*

🐾 **Ty Warner Sea Center.** A branch of the Santa Barbara Museum of Natural History, the center specializes in Santa Barbara Channel marine life and conservation. Though small compared to aquariums in Monterey and Long Beach, this is a fascinating, hands-on marine science laboratory that lets you participate in experiments, projects, and exhibits, including touch tanks. Two-story glass walls here open to stunning ocean, mountain, and city views. You can purchase a Nature Pass, which includes discounted two-day admission to the natural history museum and the Sea Center. Ty Warner, the Beanie Baby mogul and a local resident, is a major donor. ⊠ *211 Stearns Wharf* ☎ *805/962–2526 ⊕ www.sbnature. org* ☎ *$8 ⊗ Daily 10–5.*

WORTH NOTING

Andree Clark Bird Refuge. This peaceful lagoon and its gardens sit north of East Beach. Bike trails and footpaths, punctuated by signs identifying native and migratory birds, skirt the lagoon. ⊠ *1400 E. Cabrillo Blvd., near the zoo* ☎ *Free.*

🐾 **Carriage and Western Art Museum.** The country's largest collection of old horse-drawn vehicles—painstakingly restored—is exhibited here, everything from polished hearses to police buggies to old stagecoaches and circus vehicles. In August the Old Spanish Days Fiesta borrows many of the vehicles for a jaunt around town. This is one of the city's hidden gems. ⊠ *Pershing Park, 129 Castillo St.* ☎ *805/962–2353 ⊕ www. carriagemuseum.org* ☎ *Free ⊗ Weekdays 9–3, 3rd Sun. of month 1–4 for docent tours.*

Karpeles Manuscript Library. Ancient political tracts and old Disney cartoons are among the holdings at this facility, which also houses one of the world's largest privately owned collections of rare manuscripts. Fifty display cases contain a sampling of the archive's million-plus documents. ⊠ *21 W. Anapamu St., near Chapala St.* ☎ *805/962–5322 ⊕ www.karpeles.com* ☎ *Free ⊗ Wed.–Sun. noon–4.*

Montecito. Since the late 1800s the tree-studded hills and valleys of this town have attracted the rich and famous (Hollywood icons, business tycoons, dot-commers who divested before the crash, and old-money families who installed themselves here years ago). Shady roads wind through the community, which consists mostly of gated estates. Swank boutiques line Coast Village Road, where well-heeled residents such as Oprah Winfrey sometimes browse for truffle oil, picture frames, and designer jeans. Residents also hang out in the Upper Village, a chic shopping area with restaurants and cafés at the intersection of San

Santa Barbara's downtown is attractive, but be sure also to visit its beautiful—and uncrowded—beaches.

Ysidro and East Valley roads. Montecito is about 3 miles east of Santa Barbara off U.S. 101.

Lotusland. The 37-acre Montecito estate called Lotusland once belonged to Polish opera singer Ganna Walska. Many of the exotic trees and other subtropical flora were planted in 1882 by horticulturist R. Kinton Stevens. On the two-hour guided tour (the only option for visiting unless you're a member), you'll see an outdoor theater, a topiary garden, a huge collection of rare cycads (an unusual plant genus that has been around since the time of the dinosaurs), and a lotus pond. Tours are conducted February 15 through November 15, Wednesday through Saturday at 10 and 1:30. Reservations are required. Child-friendly family tours are available for groups with children under the age of 10; contact Lotusland for scheduling. ⊠ *695 Ashley Rd.* 🕾 *805/969–9990* ⊕ *www.lotusland.org* 🖃 *$35*

Outdoors Santa Barbara Visitor Center. The small office provides maps and information about Channel Islands National Park, Channel Islands National Marine Sanctuary, and the Santa Barbara Maritime Museum, which occupies the same harbor building. ⊠ *113 Harbor Way, off Shoreline Dr.* 🕾 *805/884–1475* ⊕ *outdoorsb.noaa.gov* 🖃 *Free* 🕑 *Daily 11–5.*

Santa Barbara Historical Museum. The historical society's museum exhibits decorative and fine arts, furniture, costumes, and documents from the town's past. Adjacent to it is the Gledhill Library, a collection of books, photographs, maps, and manuscripts. ⊠ *136 E. De La Guerra St., at Santa Barbara St.* 🕾 *805/966–1601* ⊕ *www.santabarbaramuseum.com* 🖃 *Museum by donation; library $2–$5 per hr for research* 🕑 *Museum*

Tues.–Sat. 10–5, Sun. noon–5, guided tours Sat. at 2; library Tues.–Fri. 10–4, 1st Sat. of month 10–1.

🕑 **Santa Barbara Maritime Museum.** California's seafaring history is the focus here. High-tech, hands-on exhibits, such as a sportfishing activity that lets participants catch a "big one" and a local surfing history retrospective make this a fun stop for families. ✉ *113 Harbor Way, off Shoreline Dr.* ☎ *805/962–8404* ⊕ *www.sbmm.org* 💲 *$7* ☼ *June–Aug., Thurs.– Tues. 10–6; Sept.–May, Thurs.–Tues. 10–5.*

Urban Wine Trail. More than a dozen winery tasting rooms form the Urban Wine Trail; most are within walking distance of the waterfront and the lower State Street shopping and restaurant district. **Santa Barbara Winery,** at 202 Anacapa Street, and **Au Bon Climat,** at 813 Anacapa Street, are good places to start your oenological trek. ☎ ⊕ *urbanwinetrailsb.com.*

BEACHES

Santa Barbara's beaches don't have the big surf of the shoreline farther south, but they also don't have the crowds. You can usually find a solitary spot to swim or sunbathe. In June and July, fog often hugs the coast until about noon.

Arroyo Burro County Beach. The usually gentle surf at Arroyo Burro County Beach makes it ideal for families with young children. It's a local favorite, since you can walk for miles in both directions when tides are low. Leashed dogs are allowed on the main stretch of beach and westward; they are allowed to romp off-leash east of the slough at the beach entrance. The parking lots fill early on weekends and throughout the summer, but the park is relatively quiet at other times. Walk along the beach just a few hundreds yards away from the main steps at the entrance to escape crowds on warm-weather days. Surfers, swimmers, standup paddlers, and boogie boarders regularly ply the waves, and photographers come often to catch the vivid sunsets. **Amenities:** food and drink; lifeguard in summer; parking, showers, toilets. **Best For:** sunset; surfing; swimming; walking. ✉ *Cliff Dr. and Las Positas Rd.*

🕑 **East Beach.** The wide swath of sand at the east end of Cabrillo Boulevard is a great spot for people-watching. East Beach has sand volleyball courts, summertime lifeguard and sports competitions, and arts-and-crafts shows on Sunday and holidays. You can use showers, a weight room, and lockers (bring your own towel) and rent umbrellas and boogie boards at the Cabrillo Bathhouse. Next door, there's an elaborate jungle-gym play area for kids. Hotels line the boulevard across from the beach. **Amenities:** food and drink; lifeguards in summer; parking (fee); showers; toilets; water sports. **Best For:** walking; swimming; surfing. ✉ *1118 Cabrillo Blvd., at Ninos Dr.* ☎ *805/897–2680.*

WHERE TO EAT

$$ ✕ **Arigato Sushi.** You might have to wait for a table at this trendy, two-
JAPANESE story restaurant and sushi bar—locals line up early for the wildly creative combination rolls and other delectables. Fans of authentic

Japanese food sometimes disagree about the quality of the seafood, but all dishes are fresh and artfully presented. The menu includes traditional dishes as well as innovative creations such as sushi pizza on seaweed and Hawaiian sashimi salad. ⑤ *Average main: $20* ✉ *1225 State St., near W. Victoria St.* ☎ *805/965–6074* ⊕ *www.arigatosantabarbara.com* ⟡ *Reservations not accepted* ⊘ *No lunch.*

$$
SEAFOOD

✕ **Brophy Bros.** The outdoor tables at this casual harborside restaurant have perfect views of the marina and mountains. Staffers serve enormous, exceptionally fresh fish dishes—don't miss the seafood salad and chowder—and provide

guests with a pager if there's a long wait for a table. Stroll along the waterfront until the beep lets you know your table's ready. Hugely popular, Brophy Bros. can be crowded and loud, especially on weekend evenings. ⑤ *Average main: $20* ✉ *119 Harbor Way, off Shoreline Dr.* ☎ *805/966–4418* ⊕ *www.brophybros.com.*

$
INDIAN

✕ **Flavor of India.** Feast on authentic northern Indian dishes like tandoori chicken, lamb biryani, and a host of curries at this local favorite in a residential neighborhood. Best bets include the combination dinners served in a traditional Indian tray and the all-you-can-eat lunch buffet ($9). ⑤ *Average main: $11* ✉ *3026 State St., at De La Vina St.* ☎ *805/682–6561* ⊕ *www.flavorofindiasb.com* ⊘ *Closed Sun.*

$$$$
SEAFOOD

✕ **The Hungry Cat.** The hip Santa Barbara sibling of a famed Hollywood eatery, run by chefs David Lentz and his wife Suzanne Goin, dishes up savory seafood in a small but lively nook in the downtown arts district. Feast on sea urchin, addictive peel-and-eat shrimp, and creative cocktails made from farmers' market fruits and veggies. A busy nightspot on weekends, the Cat also awakens for a popular brunch on Sunday. Night or day, come early or be prepared for a wait. ⑤ *Average main: $30* ✉ *1134 Chapala St., near W. Figueroa St.* ☎ *805/884–4701* ⊕ *www.thehungrycat.com* ⊘ *Closed Mon. Sept.–April.*

$
MEXICAN
★

✕ **La Super-Rica.** Praised by Julia Child, this food stand on the east side of town serves some of the spiciest and most authentic Mexican dishes between Los Angeles and San Francisco. Fans fill up on the soft tacos served with yummy spicy or mild sauces and legendary beans. Three specials are offered daily. Portions are on the small side; order several dishes and share. ⑤ *Average main: $9* ✉ *622 N. Milpas St., at Alphonse St.* ☎ *805/963–4940* ⊟ *No credit cards* ⊘ *Closed Wed.*

$$$
ITALIAN

✕ **Olio e Limone.** Sophisticated Italian cuisine (with an emphasis on Sicily) is served at this restaurant near the Arlington Center. The juicy veal chop is popular, but surprises abound here; be sure to try unusual dishes such as ribbon pasta with quail and sausage in a mushroom ragout, or the duck ravioli. Tables are placed close together, so this may not be the best spot for intimate conversations. For casual artisanal Italian fare, head next door to the Olio pizzeria/enoteca/bar. $ *Average main: $29* ⊠ *17 W. Victoria St., at State St.* ☎ *805/899–2699* ⊕ *www.olioelimone.com* ☉ *No lunch Sun.*

$$$
SOUTHERN
✕ **Palace Grill.** Mardi Gras energy, team-style service, lively music, and great food have made the Palace a Santa Barbara icon. Acclaimed for its Cajun and creole dishes such as blackened redfish and jambalaya with dirty rice, the Palace also serves Caribbean fare, including a delicious coconut-shrimp dish. If you're spice-phobic, you can choose pasta, soft-shell crab, or filet mignon. Be prepared to wait for a table on Friday and Saturday night (when reservations are taken for a 5:30 seating only), though the live entertainment and free appetizers, sent out front when the line is long, will whet your appetite for the feast to come. $ *Average main: $28* ⊠ *8 E. Cota St., at State St.* ☎ *805/963–5000* ⊕ *www.palacegrill.com.*

$$$
ECLECTIC
✕ **Roy.** Owner-chef Leroy Gandy serves a fixed-price dinner (selections $20, $25, and $30)—a real bargain—that includes a small salad, fresh soup, homemade organic bread, and a rotating selection of contemporary American main courses. If you're lucky, the entrée choices might include grilled local fish with a mandarin beurre blanc, or bacon-wrapped filet mignon. You can also choose from an à la carte menu of inexpensive appetizers and entrées, plus local wines. Roy is a favorite spot for late-night dining—it's open until midnight and has a full bar. $ *Average main: $25* ⊠ *7 W. Carrillo St., near State St.* ☎ *805/966–5636* ⊕ *www.restaurantroy.com* ☉ *No lunch.*

$$$$
AMERICAN
★
✕ **The Stonehouse.** The elegant Stonehouse is inside a century-old granite former farmhouse at the San Ysidro Ranch resort. Executive chef Matt Johnson creates outstanding regional cuisine centered around herbs and veggies from the on-site garden and top-quality local ingredients. The menu changes constantly but typically includes favorites such as crab cake with persimmon relish appetizer and local spiny lobster with mascarpone risotto. Dine on the radiant-heated ocean-view deck with stone fireplace, next to a fountain under a canopy of loquat trees, or in the romantic, candlelit dining room overlooking a creek. The Plow & Angel pub, downstairs, offers more casual bistro fare. $ *Average main: $47* ⊠ *900 San Ysidro La., off San Ysidro Rd., Montecito* ☎ *805/565–1700* ⊕ *www.sanysidroranch.com* ⚭ *Reservations essential* ☉ *No lunch Sun.–Wed.*

$$$
AMERICAN
✕ **Wine Cask.** A reinvention of a same-named local favorite that closed a few years back, the Wine Cask serves bistro-style meals—many of them made with ingredients from a nearby farmers' market—in a comfortable and classy dining room. The dishes are paired with wines from Santa Barbara's most extensive wine list, not a surprise given co-owner Doug Margerum's main occupation as a winemaker and wine merchant (his wine shop/tasting room is just steps away). The more casual bar-café,

Intermezzo, across the courtyard, serves pizzas, salads, small plates, wines, and cocktails and is open late. $ *Average main: $29 ⊠ El Paseo, 813 Anacapa St., at E. De La Guerra St.* ☎ *805/966–9463* ⊕ *www. winecask.com* ⌕ *Reservations essential.*

$ ✕ **Zen Yai Thai Cuisine.** As the shingle above the tiny storefront amid
THAI lower State Street's club scene states, the food here is "reminiscent of things Thai." That might drive away diners seeking absolute authenticity, but every day a trendy flock of fans packs the room for delectable dishes made from fresh local ingredients. Reserve a table or be prepared for a wait. $ *Average main: $14 ⊠ 425 State St., at W. Haley St.* ☎ *805/957–1102* ☾ *No lunch Mon. and weekends.*

WHERE TO STAY

For expanded reviews, facilities, and current deals, visit Fodors.com.

$$$$ ▦ **Canary Hotel.** The only full-service hotel in the heart of downtown, the
HOTEL Canary blends a casual, beach-getaway feel with tony urban sophistication. **Pros:** easy stroll to museums, shopping, dining; friendly, attentive service; adjacent fitness center. **Cons:** across from main bus transit center; some rooms feel cramped. **TripAdvisor:** "lovely hotel," "wonderful experience," "helpful staff." $ *Rooms from: $300 ⊠ 31 W. Carrillo St.* ☎ *805/884–0300, 877/468–3515* ⊕ *www.canarysantabarbara.com* ⇆ *77 rooms, 20 suites.*

$$$$ ▦ **Four Seasons Resort The Biltmore Santa Barbara.** Surrounded by lush,
RESORT perfectly manicured gardens and across from the beach, Santa Barbara's
★ grande dame has long been a favorite for quiet, California-style luxury. **Pros:** first-class resort; historic Santa Barbara character; personal service; steps from the beach. **Cons:** back rooms are close to train tracks; expensive. **TripAdvisor:** "gorgeous location," "beautiful hotel with very friendly staff," "well worth it." $ *Rooms from: $595 ⊠ 1260 Channel Dr.* ☎ *805/969–2261, 800/332–3442* ⊕ *www.fourseasons.com/ santabarbara* ⇆ *181 rooms, 26 suites.*

$$ ▦ **Franciscan Inn.** Part of this Spanish-Mediterranean motel, a block
HOTEL from the harbor and West Beach, dates back to the 1920s. **Pros:** walking distance from waterfront and harbor; family-friendly; great value. **Cons:** busy lobby; pool can be crowded. **TripAdvisor:** "great staff," "charming," "home away from home." $ *Rooms from: $160 ⊠ 109 Bath St.* ☎ *805/963–8845, 800/663–5288* ⊕ *www.franciscaninn.com* ⇆ *48 rooms, 5 suites* ⍥ *Breakfast.*

$$$ ▦ **Hyatt Santa Barbara.** A complex of four separate buildings on three
HOTEL landscaped acres, Hyatt Santa Barbara provides a wide range of value-laden lodging options in a prime location—right across from East Beach and the Cabrillo Pavilion Bathhouse. **Pros:** steps from the beach; many room types and rates; walk to the zoo and waterfront shuttle. **Cons:** motelish vibe; busy area in summer. **TripAdvisor:** "friendly people make the difference," "excellent customer service and staff," "lovely property." $ *Rooms from: $229 ⊠ 1111 E. Cabrillo Blvd.* ☎ *805/882-1234, 800/643–1994* ⊕ *www.santabarbara.hyatt.com* ⇆ *171 rooms, 3 suites.*

$ ▦ **Motel 6 Santa Barbara Beach.** A half block from East Beach amid fan-
HOTEL cier hotels sits this basic but comfortable motel, which was the first

Motel 6 in existence. **Pros:** less than a minute's walk from the zoo and beach; friendly staff; clean and comfortable. **Cons:** no frills; motel-style rooms; no breakfast. **TripAdvisor:** "great staff," "one of the best Motel 6s," "beautiful room." ⑤ *Rooms from: $109* ⊠ *443 Corona Del Mar Dr.* ☎ *805/564–1392, 800/466–8356* ⊕ *www.motel6.com* ⇌ *51 rooms.*

$$ ☷ **Presidio Motel.** Young globetrotting couple Chris Sewell and Kenny

HOTEL Osehan transformed the Presidio, a formerly funky motel, into a simple yet stylish oasis. **Pros:** great downtown location; friendly staff; hip, artsy vibe. **Cons:** smallish rooms; basic baths; thin walls. **TripAdvisor:** "quirky hidden gem," "California charmer," "really unique place." ⑤ *Rooms from: $159* ⊠ *1620 State St.* ☎ *805/963–1355* ⊕ *www. thepresidiomotel.com* ⇌ *16 rooms.*

$$$$ ☷ **San Ysidro Ranch.** At this romantic hideaway on an historic prop-

RESORT erty in the Montecito foothills—where John and Jackie Kennedy spent

★ their honeymoon and Oprah sends her out-of-town visitors—guest cottages are scattered among groves of orange trees and flower beds. **Pros:** ultimate privacy; surrounded by nature; celebrity hangout; pet-friendly. **Cons:** very expensive; too remote for some. **TripAdvisor:** "it doesn't get any better," "outstanding cuisine," "romance and beauty." ⑤ *Rooms from: $650* ⊠ *900 San Ysidro La., Montecito* ☎ *805/565– 1700, 800/368–6788* ⊕ *www.sanysidroranch.com* ⇌ *23 rooms, 4 suites, 14 cottages* ☞ *2-day minimum stay on weekends, 3 days on holiday weekends.*

$$$$ ☷ **Simpson House Inn.** If you're a fan of traditional B&Bs, this property,

B&B/INN with its beautifully appointed Victorian main house and acre of lush

★ gardens, is for you. **Pros:** impeccable landscaping; walking distance from everything downtown; ranked among the nation's top B&Bs. **Cons:** some rooms in the main building are small; two-night minimum stay on weekends. **TripAdvisor:** "so beautiful," "charming," "almost perfection." ⑤ *Rooms from: $250* ⊠ *121 E. Arrellaga St.* ☎ *805/963– 7067, 800/676–1280* ⊕ *www.simpsonhouseinn.com* ⇌ *11 rooms, 4 cottages* ⑩ *Breakfast.*

$$$$ ☷ **Spanish Garden Inn.** A half block from the Presidio in the heart of

B&B/INN downtown, this elegant Spanish-Mediterranean retreat celebrates Santa Barbara style, from the tile floors, wrought-iron balconies, and exotic plants, to the original art by local plein-air artists. **Pros:** walking distance from downtown; classic Spanish-Mediterranean style; caring staff. **Cons:** far from the beach; not much here for kids. **TripAdvisor:** "lovely small hotel," "perfect oasis of style and quality," "laid back." ⑤ *Rooms from: $389* ⊠ *915 Garden St.* ☎ *805/564–4700, 866/564– 4700* ⊕ *www.spanishgardeninn.com* ⇌ *23 rooms* ⑩ *Breakfast.*

NIGHTLIFE AND THE ARTS

Most major hotels present entertainment nightly during the summer and on weekends all year. The town's bar, club, and live-music scene centers on lower State Street, between the 300 and 800 blocks. The thriving arts district, with theaters, restaurants, and cafés, starts around the 900 block of State Street and continues north to the Arlington Center for the Performing Arts, in the 1300 block. The proximity to the University of California at Santa Barbara assures an endless stream of visiting artists and performers. To see what's scheduled around town, pick up a copy of the free weekly *Santa Barbara Independent* newspaper or visit its website ⊕ *www.independent.com.*

NIGHTLIFE

Blue Agave. Leather couches, a crackling fire in chilly weather, a cigar balcony, and pool tables draw a fancy crowd to Blue Agave for good food and designer martinis. ⊠ *20 E. Cota St., near State St.* ☎ *805/899–4694.*

Dargan's. All types of people hang out at Dargan's, a lively pub with four pool tables, great draft beers and Irish whiskeys, and a full menu of traditional Irish dishes. ⊠ *18 E. Ortega St., at Anacapa St.* ☎ *805/568–0702.*

James Joyce. A good place to have a few beers and while away an evening, the James Joyce sometimes hosts folk and rock performers. ⊠ *513 State St., at W. Haley St.* ☎ *805/962–2688.*

Joe's Cafe. Steins of beer accompany hearty bar food at Joe's. It's a fun, if occasionally rowdy, collegiate scene. ⊠ *536 State St., at E. Cota St.* ☎ *805/966–4638.*

Lucky's. A slick sports bar attached to an upscale steak house owned by the maker of Lucky Brand Dungarees, this place attracts hip, fashionably dressed patrons hoping to see and be seen. ⊠ *1279 Coast Village Rd., near Olive Mill Rd., Montecito* ☎ *805/565–7540.*

Milk & Honey. Artfully prepared tapas, coconut-mango mojitos, and exotic cocktails lure trendy crowds to swank M&H, despite high prices and a reputation for inattentive service. ⊠ *30 W. Anapamu St., at State St.* ☎ *805/275–4232.*

SOhO. A hip restaurant, bar, and music club, SOhO books bands, from jazz to blues to rock, every night of the week. ⊠ *1221 State St., at W. Victoria St.* ☎ *805/962–7776.*

THE ARTS

Arlington Center for the Performing Arts. This Moorish-style auditorium hosts major events during the two-week Santa Barbara International Film Festival every winter and presents touring performers and films throughout the year. ⊠ *1317 State St., at Arlington Ave.* ☎ *805/963–4408.*

Center Stage Theatre. This venue hosts plays, music, dance, and readings. ⊠ *Paseo Nuevo Center, Chapala and De la Guerra Sts., 2nd floor* ☎ *805/963–0408.*

Ensemble Theatre Company. The company stages plays by authors ranging from Tennessee Williams and Henrik Ibsen to rising contemporary dramatists. ⊠ *914 Santa Barbara St., at El Canon Perdido St.* ☎ *805/965–5400.*

Granada. A restored and modernized landmark that dates to 1924, the Granada hosts Broadway touring shows and dance, music, and other cultural events. ⊠ *1214 State St., at E. Anapamu St.* ☎ *805/899–2222 box office.*

Lobero Theatre. A state landmark, the Lobero hosts community theater groups and touring professionals. ⊠ *33 E. Canon Perdido St., at Anacapa St.* ☎ *805/963–0761.*

Music Academy of the West. The academy showcases orchestral, chamber, and operatic works every summer. ⊠ *1070 Fairway Rd., off Channel Dr.* ☎ *805/969–4726, 805/969–8787 box office.*

SPORTS AND THE OUTDOORS

BICYCLING **Cabrillo Bike Lane.** The level, two-lane, 3-mile Cabrillo Bike Lane passes the Santa Barbara Zoo, the Andree Clark Bird Refuge, beaches, and the harbor. There are restaurants along the way, and you can stop for a picnic along the palm-lined path looking out on the Pacific.

Wheel Fun Rentals. Wheel Fun Rentals has bikes, quadricycles, and skates; a second outlet around the block rents small electric cars and scooters. ⊠ *23 E. Cabrillo Blvd.* ☎ *805/966–2282.*

BOATS AND CHARTERS **Condor Express.** From SEA Landing, the *Condor Express*, a 75-foot high-speed catamaran, whisks up to 149 passengers toward the Channel Islands on dinner cruises, whale-watching excursions, and pelagic-bird trips. ☎ *805/882–0088, 888/779–4253.*

Santa Barbara Sailing Center. The center offers sailing instruction, rents and charters sailboats, and organizes dinner and sunset champagne cruises, island excursions, and whale-watching trips. ⊠ *Santa Barbara Harbor launching ramp* ☎ *805/962–2826, 800/350–9090.*

☙ **Santa Barbara Water Taxi.** Children beg to ride *L'il Toot*, a cherry yellow water taxi that cruises from the harbor to Stearns Wharf and back again. ⊠ *Santa Barbara Harbor and Stearns Wharf* ☎ *805/896–6900, 888/316–9363* ⊕ *sbwatertaxi.com* ✉ *$4 one-way* ☺ *Departures every ½ hr from noon to 6 in summer, noon to sunset in winter.*

Truth Aquatics. Departing from SEA Landing in the Santa Barbara Harbor, Truth Aquatics ferries passengers on excursions to the National Marine Sanctuary and Channel Islands National Park and takes scuba divers on single-day and multiday trips. ☎ *805/962–1127.*

GOLF **Sandpiper Golf Club.** This 18-hole, par-72 course sits on the ocean bluffs and combines stunning views with a challenging game. Greens fees are $139–$159; a cart (optional) is $16. ⊠ *7925 Hollister Ave., 14 miles north of downtown off U.S. 101* ☎ *805/968–1541.*

Santa Barbara Golf Club. The club has an 18-hole, par-70 course. The greens fees are $48–$58; a cart (optional) costs $15 per rider. ⊠ *3500 McCaw Ave., at Las Positas Rd.* ☎ *805/687–7087.*

> **BIRTHPLACE OF THE ENVIRONMENTAL MOVEMENT**
>
> In 1969, 200,000 gallons of crude oil spilled into the Santa Barbara Channel, causing an immediate outcry from residents, particularly in the UCSB community. The day after the spill, Get Oil Out (GOO) was established; the group helped lead the successful fight for legislation to limit and regulate offshore drilling in California. The Santa Barbara spill also spawned Earth Day, which is still celebrated in communities across the nation today.

5

TENNIS Many hotels in Santa Barbara have courts.

City of Santa Barbara Parks and Recreation Department. The City of Santa Barbara Parks and Recreation Department operates public courts with lighted play until 9 pm weekdays. You can purchase day permits ($8) at the courts, or call the department. ☎ 805/564–5473.

Municipal Tennis Center. The 12 hard courts at the Municipal Tennis Center include an enclosed stadium court and three lighted courts open daily. ✉ 1414 Park Pl., near Salinas St. and U.S. 101.

Pershing Park. Pershing Park has eight lighted courts available for public play after 5 pm weekdays and all day on weekends and Santa Barbara City College holidays. ✉ 100 Castillo St., near Cabrillo Blvd.

SHOPPING

SHOPPING AREAS **Brinkerhoff Avenue.** Antiques and gift shops are clustered in restored Victorian buildings on Brinkerhoff Avenue. ✉ 2 blocks west of State St. at W. Cota St.

El Paseo. Shops, art galleries, and studios share the courtyard and gardens of El Paseo, a historic arcade. ✉ Canon Perdido St., between State and Anacapa Sts.

State Street. State Street, roughly between Cabrillo Boulevard and Sola Street, is the commercial hub of Santa Barbara and a shopper's paradise. Chic malls, quirky storefronts, antiques emporia, elegant boutiques, and funky thrift shops abound here. You can do your shopping on foot or by a battery-powered trolley (25¢) that runs between the waterfront and the 1300 block. Nordstrom and Macy's anchor **Paseo Nuevo**, an open-air mall in the 700 block of State that also contains arts institutions such as Center Stage Theater.

Summerland. Serious antiques hunters head southeast of Santa Barbara to Summerland, which is full of shops and markets. Several good ones are along Lillie Avenue and Ortega Hill Road.

CLOTHING **Channel Islands Surfboards.** Come here for the latest in California beachwear, sandals, and accessories. ✉ 36 Anacapa St., at E. Mason St. ☎ 805/966–7213.

Diani. This upscale, European-style women's boutique dresses clients in designer clothing from around the world. A sibling shoe shop is nearby. ✉ 1324 State St., at Arlington Ave. ☎ 805/966-3114, 805/966-7175 shoe shop ⊕ www.dianiboutique.com.

Santa Barbara Outfitters. Kayakers, climbers, cyclists, runners, hikers, and other active folks shop here for stylish, functional clothing, shoes, and accessories. ✉ 1200 State St., at E. Anapamu St. ☎ 805/564–1007.

Surf 'N Wear's Beach House. This shop carries surf clothing, gear, and collectibles; it's also the home of Santa Barbara Surf Shop and the exclusive local dealer of Surfboards by Yater. ✉ 10 State St., at Cabrillo Blvd. ☎ 805/963–1281.

Territory Ahead. The flagship of the outdoorsy catalog company sells fashionably rugged clothing for men and women. ✉ 515 State St., near W. Haley St. ☎ 805/962–5558.

WORD OF MOUTH

"California's Central Coast is a popular place for surfers and windsurfers. If you're not up to surfing yourself, spend some time relaxing on the beach and watching the action." —photo by Doreen Miller, Fodors.com member

Wendy Foster. This store sells casual-chic clothing for women. ✉ *833 State St., at W. Canon Perdido St.* ☎ *805/966–2276.*

┌─
│ EN
│ ROUTE
└─ If you choose to drive north via U.S. 101 without detouring to the Solvang/Santa Ynez area, you will drive right past some good beaches. In succession from east to west, **El Capitan, Gaviota, and Refugio state beaches** all have campsites, picnic tables, and fire rings.

SANTA BARBARA COUNTY

Residents refer to the glorious 30-mile stretch of coastline from Carpinteria to Gaviota as the South Coast. The Santa Ynez Mountains divide the county geographically; U.S. 101 passes through a mountain tunnel leading inland. Northern Santa Barbara County used to be known for its sprawling ranches and strawberry and broccoli fields. Today its 100-plus wineries and 22,000 acres of vineyards dominate the landscape from the Santa Ynez Valley in the south to Santa Maria in the north. The hit film *Sideways* was filmed almost entirely in the North County Wine Country; when the movie won Golden Globe and Oscar awards in 2005, it sparked national and international interest in visits to the region.

GETTING HERE AND AROUND

Two-lane Highway 154 over San Marcos Pass is the shortest and most scenic route from Santa Barbara into the Santa Ynez Valley. You can also drive along U.S. 101 north 43 miles to Buellton, then 7 miles east through Solvang to Santa Ynez. Santa Ynez Valley Transit shuttle buses serve Santa Ynez, Los Olivos, Ballard, Solvang, and Buellton. COLT Wine Country Express buses connect Lompoc, Buellton, and Solvang weekdays except holidays.

ESSENTIALS

Bus Contacts COLT Wine Country Express ✉ *Lompoc* ☎ *805/736–7666* ⊕ *www.cityoflompoc.com/transit.* **Santa Ynez Valley Transit** ☎ *805/688–5452* ⊕ *www.syvt.com.*

Visitor Information Santa Barbara County Vintners' Association ☎ *805/688–0881* ⊕ *www.sbcountywines.com.* **The Santa Barbara Conference & Visitors Bureau** ☎ *805/966–9222* ⊕ *www.santabarbaraca.com.*

SANTA YNEZ

31 miles north of Goleta via Hwy. 154.

Founded in 1882, the tiny town of Santa Ynez still has many of its original frontier buildings. You can walk through the three-block downtown area in a few minutes, shop for antiques, and hang around the old-time saloon. At some of the eponymous valley's best restaurants, you just might bump into one of the celebrities who own nearby ranches.

GETTING HERE AND AROUND

Take Highway 154 over San Marcos Pass or U.S. 101 north 43 miles to Buellton, then 7 miles east.

ESSENTIALS

Visitor Information Santa Ynez Valley Visitors Association ☎ *805/686–0053, 800/742–2843* ⊕ *www.visitthesantaynezvalley.com.*

EXPLORING

Chumash Casino Resort. Just south of Santa Ynez on the Chumash Indian Reservation lies this Las Vegas–style casino with 2,000 slot machines, three restaurants, a spa, and an upscale hotel. ⊠ *3400 E. Hwy. 246* ☎ *800/248–6274.*

WHERE TO EAT AND STAY

For expanded reviews, facilities, and current deals, visit Fodors.com.

$$
ITALIAN
★

✕ **Trattoria Grappolo.** Authentic Italian fare, an open kitchen, and festive, family-style seating make this trattoria equally popular with celebrities from Hollywood and ranchers from the Santa Ynez Valley. Thin-crust pizza, homemade ravioli, risottos, and seafood linguine are among the menu favorites. The noise level tends to rise in the evening, so this isn't the best spot for a romantic getaway. $ *Average main: $22* ⊠ *3687-C Saguno St.* ☎ *805/688–6899* ⊕ *www.trattoriagrappolo.com* ⊗ *No lunch Mon.*

$$$
B&B/INN

🏨 **Santa Ynez Inn.** This posh two-story Victorian inn in downtown Santa Ynez was built from scratch in 2002, and the owners have furnished all the rooms with authentic historical pieces. **Pros:** near restaurants; unusual antiques; spacious rooms. **Cons:** high price for location; not a historic building. **TripAdvisor:** "gateway to great hospitality," "comfortable elegance," "every modern luxury." $ *Rooms from: $245* ⊠ *3627 Saguno St.* ☎ *805/688–5588, 800/643–5774* ⊕ *www. santaynezinn.com* ⤢ *20 rooms, 3 suites* ⦿ *Breakfast.*

LOS OLIVOS

4 miles north of Santa Ynez on Hwy. 154.

This pretty village in the Santa Ynez Valley was once on Spanish-built El Camino Real (Royal Highway) and later a stop on major stagecoach and rail routes. It's so sleepy today, though, that the movie *Return to Mayberry* was filmed here. Tasting rooms, art galleries, antiques stores, and country markets line Grand Avenue and intersecting streets for several blocks.

GETTING HERE AND AROUND

From U.S. 101 north or south, exit at Highway 154 and drive east about 8 miles. From Santa Barbara, travel 30 miles northwest on Highway 154.

EXPLORING

Carhartt Vineyard Tasting Room. At this intimate space, you're likely to meet owners and winemakers Mike and Brooke Carhartt, who pour samples of their small-lot, handcrafted vintages most days. ⊠ *2990-A Grand Ave.* ☎ *805/693–5100* ⊕ *www.carharttvineyard.com.*

Daniel Gehrs Tasting Room. Heather Cottage, built in the early 1900s as a doctor's office, houses the Gehrs tasting room, where you can sample various varietals produced in limited small-lot quantities. ⊠ *2939 Grand Ave.* ☎ *805/693–9686* ⊕ *www.danielgehrswines.com.*

Firestone Vineyard. This winery has been around since 1972. It has daily tours, grassy picnic areas, and hiking trails in the hills overlooking the valley. The views are fantastic. ⊠ *5000 Zaca Station Rd., off U.S. 101* ☎ *805/688–3940* ⊕ *www.firestonewine.com.*

WHERE TO EAT AND STAY

For expanded reviews, facilities, and current deals, visit Fodors.com.

$$ ✕ **Los Olivos Cafe.** Part wine store and part local social hub, this café
AMERICAN that appeared in the film *Sideways* focuses on wine-friendly fish, pasta, and meat dishes, plus salads, pizzas, and burgers. Don't miss the homemade muffuletta and olive tapenade spreads. Other house favorites include an artisanal cheese plate, baked Brie with honey-roasted hazelnuts, and braised pot roast with whipped potatoes. Ⓢ *Average main: $20* ⊠ *2879 Grand Ave.* ☎ *805/688–7265, 888/946–3748* ⊕ *www. losolivoscafe.com.*

$$$ ✕ **Sides Hardware & Shoes: A Brothers Restaurant.** For more than a decade,
AMERICAN chef-owners and brothers Matt and Jeff Nichols operated one of the
★ valley's best restaurants at historic Mattei's Tavern. In spring 2012, they renovated and moved to another historic building, Sides Hardware & Shoes. Comfort food, which they prepare with panache, is the focus of their seasonal menu. Popular breakfast dishes include cooked-to-order beignets and eggs Benedict with house-made bacon steak. The Kobe-style burgers make a great lunch, and the dinner favorites include fried chicken and lamb sirloin with herbed gnocchi. Ⓢ *Average main: $24* ⊠ *2375 Alamo Pintado Ave.* ☎ *805/688–4820* ⊕ *www. brothersrestaurant.com.*

$$$ 🛏 **The Ballard Inn & Restaurant.** Set among orchards and vineyards in the
B&B/INN tiny town of Ballard, 2 miles south of Los Olivos, this inn makes an elegant wine-country escape. **Pros:** exceptional food; attentive staff; secluded. **Cons:** some baths could use updating; several miles from Los Olivos and Santa Ynez. **TripAdvisor:** "beautiful rooms," "fabulous escape," "extremely comfortable." Ⓢ *Rooms from: $225* ⊠ *2436 Baseline Ave., Ballard* ☎ *805/688–7770, 800/638–2466* ⊕ *www.ballardinn. com* ⇆ *15 rooms* ⦿◡ *Breakfast.*

$$$$ 🛏 **Fess Parker's Wine Country Inn and Spa.** This luxury inn includes an
B&B/INN elegant, tree-shaded French country–style main building and an equally attractive annex across the street with a pool and day spa. **Pros:** convenient wine-touring base; walking distance from restaurants and galleries; well-appointed rooms. **Cons:** pricey; staff attention is inconsistent. **TripAdvisor:** "beautifully updated hotel with spacious rooms," "homey and relaxing," "simply fabulous." Ⓢ *Rooms from: $395* ⊠ *2860 Grand Ave.* ☎ *805/688–7788, 800/446–2455* ⊕ *www.fessparker.com* ⇆ *15 rooms, 4 suites* ⦿◡ *Breakfast.*

SOLVANG

☼ *5 miles south of Los Olivos on Alamo Pintado Rd.; 3 miles east of U.S. 101 on Hwy. 246.*

You'll know you've reached the town of Solvang when the architecture suddenly changes to half-timber buildings and windmills. The town was settled in 1911 by a group of Danish educators—the flatlands and rolling green hills reminded them of home—and even today, more than two-thirds of the residents are of Danish descent. Although Solvang has attracted tourists for decades, in recent years it has become more sophisticated, with galleries, upscale restaurants, and wine-tasting rooms. Most shops are locally owned; the city has an ordinance prohibiting chain stores. To get your bearings, park your car in one of the free public lots and stroll around town. You can pick up maps and walking-tour information at the visitor center on Copenhagen Drive. Before you depart, be sure to sample the breads and pastries from the town's excellent bakeries.

5

GETTING HERE AND AROUND

Highway 246 West (Mission Drive) traverses Solvang, connecting with U.S. 101 to the west and Highway 154 to the east. Alamo Pintado Road connects Solvang with Ballard and Los Olivos to the north. Santa Ynez Valley Transit shuttle buses run between Solvang and nearby towns.

ESSENTIALS

Visitor Information Solvang Conference & Visitors Bureau ⊠ *1639 Copenhagen Dr., at 2nd St.* ☎ *805/688–6144* ⊕ *www.solvangusa.com.*

EXPLORING

Alma Rosa Winery. Richard and Thekla Sanford helped put Santa Barbara County on the international wine map with a 1989 Pinot Noir. In 2005 they started a new winery, Alma Rosa, crafting wines from grapes grown on their 100-plus-acre certified organic vineyards in the Santa Rita Hills. You can taste the current releases—the Pinot Noirs and Chardonnays are exceptional—at one of the most environmentally sensitive tasting rooms and picnic areas in the valley. ⊠ *7250 Santa Rosa Rd., off U.S. 101, Buellton* ☎ *805/688–9090* ⊕ *www.almarosawinery.com.*

Mission Santa Inés. The mission holds an impressive collection of paintings, statuary, vestments, and Chumash and Spanish artifacts in a serene bluff-top setting. Take a self-guided tour through the museum, sanctuary, and tranquil gardens. ⊠ *1760 Mission Dr., at Alisal Rd.* ☎ *805/688–4815* ⊕ *www.missionsantaines.org* ☚ *$5* ☼ *Daily 9–4:30.*

Rideau Vineyard. Housed in an 1884 adobe, Rideau's tasting room provides simultaneous blasts from the area's ranching past and from its hand-harvested, Rhône-varietal wine-making present. ⊠ *1562 Alamo Pintado Rd., 2 miles north of Hwy. 246* ☎ *805/688–0717* ⊕ *www.rideauvineyard.com.*

WHERE TO EAT

$$

SCANDINAVIAN

✕ **Bit O' Denmark.** Perhaps the most authentic Danish eatery in Solvang, this restaurant occupies an old-beam building that was a church until 1929. Two specialties of the house are the *Frikadeller* (meatballs with pickled red cabbage, potatoes, and thick brown gravy) and the *Medisterpølse* (Danish beef and pork sausage with cabbage). ⑤ *Average main: $18* ⊠ *473 Alisal Rd., at Park Way* ☎ *805/688–5426* ⊕ *www. bitodenmark.com.*

$$$ ✕ **The Hitching Post II.** You'll find everything from grilled artichokes to
AMERICAN ostrich at this casual eatery just outside Solvang, but most people come
for the wonderful smoky Santa Maria–style barbecue. Be sure to try
a glass of owner-chef-winemaker Frank Ostini's signature Highliner
Pinot Noir, a star in the film *Sideways.* ⑤ *Average main: $28* ⊠ *406 E. Hwy. 246, off U.S. 101* ☎ *805/688–0676* ⊕ *www.hitchingpost2.com* ☉ *No lunch.*

$$$ ✕ **Root 246.** The chefs at this chic restaurant tap local purveyors and
AMERICAN shop for organic ingredients at farmers' markets before deciding on the
★ day's menu. Depending on the season, you might feast on local squid
with sweet baby prawns, rib-eye steak grilled over an oak fire and served
with root vegetable gratin, or rhubarb and polenta upside-down cake.
The well-informed wait staff can recommend regional wines from the
restaurant's 1,800-bottle selection. Root 246's gorgeous design incorporates wood, stone, tempered glass, and leather elements in several
distinct areas, including a slick 47-seat dining room, a more casual bar
with sofas and chairs, and a hip lounge. ⑤ *Average main: $26* ⊠ *Hotel Corque, 420 Alisal Rd., at Molle Way* ☎ *805/686–8681* ⊕ *www.root-246.com* ☉ *Closed Mon. No lunch.*

WHERE TO STAY

For expanded reviews, facilities, and current deals, visit Fodors.com.

$$$$ 🏨 **Alisal Guest Ranch and Resort.** Since 1946 this 10,000-acre ranch
RESORT has been popular with celebrities and plain folk alike. **Pros:** Old West
★ atmosphere; tons of activities; ultraprivate. **Cons:** isolated; cut off from
the high-tech world; some units are aging. **TripAdvisor:** "the pacing
is seductive," "come to have fun," "wonderful horseback riding."
⑤ *Rooms from: $515* ⊠ *1054 Alisal Rd.* ☎ *805/688–6411, 800/425–4725* ⊕ *www.alisal.com* ⇱ *36 rooms, 37 suites* ❒⑪ *Some meals.*

$$$ 🏨 **Hotel Corque.** Sleek, stunning Hotel Corque—the Santa Ynez Valley's
HOTEL largest hotel—provides a full slate of upscale amenities on the edge of
★ town. **Pros:** front desk staff are trained concierges; short walk to shops,
tasting rooms and restaurants; smoke-free property. **Cons:** no kitchenettes or laundry facilities; pricey. **TripAdvisor:** "outstanding service
and accommodations," "kind and comfy," "beautifully remodeled."
⑤ *Rooms from: $239* ⊠ *400 Alisal Rd.* ☎ *805/688–8000, 800/624–5572* ⊕ *www.hotelcorque.com* ⇱ *122 rooms, 10 suites.*

$ 🏨 **King Frederik Inn.** If you want to stay right in Solvang and not spend a
HOTEL fortune, this is a good bet. **Pros:** great value; near main square; spacious
rooms; good for families. **Cons:** on main highway; miniature lobby;
next to major parking lot. ⑤ *Rooms from: $109* ⊠ *1617 Copenhagen Dr.* ☎ *805/688–5515, 800/549–9955* ⊕ *www.kingfrederikinn.com* ⇱ *45 rooms, 1 suite* ❒⑪ *Breakfast.*

$$ 🏨 **Petersen Village Inn.** The canopy beds here are plush, the bathrooms
B&B/INN small but sparkling, and the rates include a European buffet breakfast. **Pros:** in the heart of Solvang; easy parking; comfy beds. **Cons:**

on highway; some find atmosphere too traditional. **TripAdvisor:** "old-world charm," "delightfully retro," "superb meal and excellent service." ⓢ *Rooms from: $120* ✉ *1576 Mission Dr.* ☎ *805/688–3121, 800/321–8985* ⊕ *www.peterseninn.com* ➾ *39 rooms, 1 suite* ⓧ *Breakfast.*

$ ⌂ **Solvang Gardens Lodge.** The lush gardens with fountains and water-
B&B/INN   falls and the cheery English-country-theme rooms make for a peaceful retreat just a few blocks—but worlds away—from Solvang's main tourist area. **Pros:** homey; family-friendly; colorful gardens. **Cons:** some rooms are tiny; some need upgrades. **TripAdvisor:** "great location," "quiet," "kitschy and quaint." ⓢ *Rooms from: $119* ✉ *293 Alisal Rd.* ☎ *805/688–4404, 888/688–4404* ⊕ *www.solvanggardens.com* ➾ *16 rooms, 8 suites* ⓧ *Breakfast.*

LOMPOC

20 miles west of Solvang on Hwy. 246.

Known as the flower-seed capital of the world, Lompoc is blanketed with vast fields of brightly colored flowers that bloom from May through August.

GETTING HERE AND AROUND

Driving is the easiest way to get to Lompoc. From Santa Barbara, follow U.S. 101 north to Highway 1 exit off Gaviota Pass, or Highway 246 west at Buellton.

EXPLORING

La Purisima Mission State Historic Park. The most fully restored mission in the state, Mission La Purisima Concepción, founded in 1787, stands in a stark and still remote location that powerfully evokes the lives and isolation of California's Spanish settlers. Docents lead tours every afternoon, and displays illustrate the secular and religious activities that were part of mission life. From March through October the mission holds special events, including crafts demonstrations by costumed docents. ✉ *2295 Purisima Rd., off Hwy. 246* ☎ *805/733–3713* ⊕ *www.lapurisimamission.org* ⌧ *$6 per vehicle* ☉ *Daily 9–5; tour daily at 1.*

Lompoc Valley Flower Festival. Around the last weekend of June, Lompoc celebrates its floral heritage with a parade, a carnival, and a crafts show. ☎ *805/735–8511* ⊕ *www.flowerfestival.org.*

EN ROUTE   **Guadalupe-Nipomo Dunes Preserve.** This spectacular preserve straddles the coast for 18 miles between Santa Barbara and San Luis Obispo counties. The largest and most ecologically diverse dune system in the state, this habitat shelters more than 200 species of birds as well as sea otters, black bears, bobcats, coyotes, and deer. The 1,500-foot Mussel Rock is the highest beach dune in the western states. About two dozen movies have been filmed here, including Cecil B. DeMille's 1923 silent feature *The Ten Commandments*. At the **Dunes Center** (check ahead for hours), in downtown Guadalupe, you can get nature information and view an exhibit about DeMille's movie set. The main Santa Barbara County entrance to the preserve is at the far west end of Highway 166 (Main Street) in Guadalupe. ✉ *Hwy. 166/Main St., 5 miles west of Hwy. 1 and 15 miles west from Santa Maria, off U.S. 101, Guadalupe*

☎ *805/343–2455* ⊕ *www.dunescenter.org* ✉ *Free, donation suggested; dogs not permitted on this section of dunes.*

SAN LUIS OBISPO COUNTY

San Luis Obispo County's pristine landscapes and abundant wildlife areas, especially those around Morro Bay and Montaña de Oro State Park, have long attracted nature lovers. In the south, Pismo Beach and other coastal towns have great sand and surf; inland, a booming wine region stretches from the Edna and Arroyo Grande valleys in the south to Paso Robles in the north. With historical attractions, a photogenic downtown, and busy shops and restaurants, the college town of San Luis Obispo is at the heart of the county.

GETTING HERE AND AROUND

San Luis Obispo Regional Transit Authority operates buses in San Luis Obispo and serves Paso Robles as well as Pismo Beach and other coastal towns.

ESSENTIALS

Transportation Contacts San Luis Obispo Regional Transit Authority ☎ *805/541–2228* ⊕ *www.slorta.org.*

Visitor Information San Luis Obispo County Visitors and Conference Bureau ✉ *811 El Capitan Way, Suite 200, San Luis Obispo* ☎ *805/541–8000* ⊕ *www.sanluisobispocounty.com.*

PISMO BEACH

U.S. 101/Hwy. 1, about 40 miles north of Lompoc.

About 20 miles of sandy shoreline—nicknamed the Bakersfield Riviera for the throngs of vacationers who come here from the Central Valley—begins at the town of Pismo Beach. The southern end of town runs along sand dunes, some of which are open to cars and off-road vehicles. Sheltered by the dunes, a grove of eucalyptus trees attracts thousands of migrating monarch butterflies from November through February. A long, broad beach fronts the center of town, where a municipal pier extends into the sea at the foot of shop-lined Pomeroy Street. To the north, hotels and homes perch atop chalky oceanfront cliffs.

Fewer than 10,000 people live in this quintessential surfer haven, but Pismo Beach has a slew of hotels and restaurants with great views of the Pacific Ocean. Still, rooms can sometimes be hard to come by. Each Father's Day weekend the Pismo Beach Classic, one of the West Coast's largest classic-car and street-rod shows, overruns the town. A Dixieland jazz festival in February also draws crowds.

GETTING HERE AND AROUND

Pismo Beach straddles both sides of U.S. 101. If you're traveling from Santa Barbara and have time for a scenic drive, exit U.S. 101 in Santa Maria and take Highway 166 west for 8 miles to Guadalupe and follow Highway 1 north 16 miles to Pismo Beach. South County Area Transit (SCAT; ⊕ *www.slorta.org*) buses run throughout the city and connects

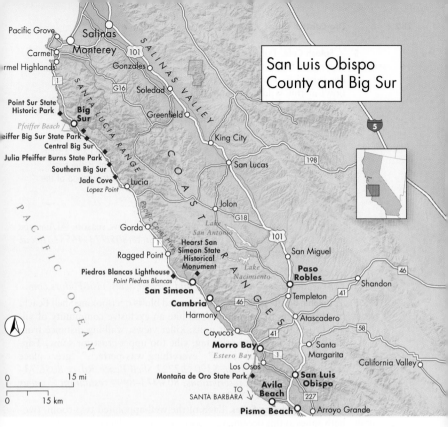

with nearby towns and the city of San Luis Obispo. On summer weekends, the free Avila Trolley extends service to Pismo Beach.

WHERE TO EAT

$$$
SEAFOOD
✕ **Cracked Crab.** This traditional New England–style crab shack imports fresh seafood daily from Australia, Alaska, and the East Coast. Fish is line-caught, much of the produce is organic, and everything is made from scratch. For a real treat, don a bib and chow through a bucket of steamed shellfish with Cajun sausage, potatoes, and corn on the cob, all dumped right onto your table. $ *Average main: $23 ✉ 751 Price St., near Main St.* ☎ *805/773–2722* ⊕ *www.crackedcrab.com* ⌫ *Reservations not accepted.*

$$
ITALIAN
✕ **Giuseppe's Cucina Italiana.** The classic flavors of southern Italy are highlighted at this lively downtown spot. Most recipes originate from Bari, a seaport on the Adriatic; the menu includes breads and pizzas baked in the wood-burning oven, hearty dishes such as osso buco and lamb, and homemade pastas. The wait for a table can be long at peak dinner hours, but sometimes an accordion player gets the crowd singing. $ *Average main: $22 ✉ 891 Price St., at Pismo Ave.* ☎ *805/773–2870* ⊕ *www.giuseppesrestaurant.com* ⌫ *Reservations not accepted* ⊘ *No lunch weekends.*

$ ✕ **Splash Café.** Folks stand in line
SEAFOOD   down the block for clam chowder served in a sourdough bread
bowl at this wildly popular seafood stand. You can also order
beach food such as fresh steamed
clams, burgers, and fried calamari
at the counter (no table service).
Many items on the menu cost
$8 or less. The grimy, cramped,
but cheery hole-in-a-wall is open
daily for lunch and dinner (plus
a rock-bottom basic breakfast),

> **VOLCANOES?**
>
> Those funny looking, sawed-
> off peaks along the drive from
> Pismo Beach to Morro Bay are the
> Seven Sisters—a series of ancient
> volcanic plugs. Morro Rock, the
> northernmost sibling and a state
> historic monument, is the most
> famous and photographed of the
> clan.

but closes early on weekday evenings during low season. ⑤ *Average
main: $8* ⌧ *197 Pomeroy St., at Cypress St.* ☎ *805/773–4653* ⊕ *www.
splashcafe.com.*

WHERE TO STAY
For expanded reviews, facilities, and current deals, visit Fodors.com.

$$$$ ⬚ **Dolphin Bay.** Perched on grass-covered bluffs overlooking Shell Beach,
RESORT   this luxury resort looks and feels like an exclusive community of villas. **Pros:** lavish apartment units; killer views; walking distance from
the beach. **Cons:** hefty price tag; vibe too upper-crust for some. **Trip-
Advisor:** "wonderful room," "everything was perfect," "great place
to relax." ⑤ *Rooms from: $390* ⌧ *2727 Shell Beach Rd.* ☎ *805/773–
4300, 800/516–0112 reservations, 805/773–8900 restaurant* ⊕ *www.
thedolphinbay.com* ⇨ *62 suites.*

$$$ ⬚ **Pismo Lighthouse Suites.** Each of the well-appointed two-room, two-
HOTEL   bath suites at this oceanfront resort has a private balcony or patio. **Pros:**
lots of space for families and groups; nice pool area. **Cons:** not easy
to walk to main attractions; some units are next to busy road. **Trip-
Advisor:** "home away from home," "could have stayed much longer,"
"nice property." ⑤ *Rooms from: $239* ⌧ *2411 Price St.* ☎ *805/773–
2411, 800/245–2411* ⊕ *www.pismolighthousesuites.com* ⇨ *70 suites*
⦿❘ *Breakfast.*

$$$ ⬚ **Sea Venture Resort.** The bright, homey rooms at this hotel all have
HOTEL   fireplaces and featherbeds; most have balconies with private hot tubs,
and some have beautiful ocean views. **Pros:** on the beach; excellent
food; romantic rooms. **Cons:** touristy area; some rooms and facilities
are beginning to age; dark hallways. **TripAdvisor:** "romantic getaway,"
"can't ask for more," "nice location." ⑤ *Rooms from: $179* ⌧ *100
Ocean View Ave.* ☎ *805/773–4994, 800/662-5545* ⊕ *www.seaventure.
com* ⇨ *50 rooms.*

$ ⬚ **Shell Beach Inn.** Just 2½ blocks from the beach, this basic but cozy
HOTEL   motor court is a great bargain for the area. **Pros:** walking distance from
the beach; clean rooms; friendly and dependable service. **Cons:** sits on
a busy road; small rooms; tiny pool. **TripAdvisor:** "loved the owners
and the rooms," "a hidden gem in a wonderful setting," "great service." ⑤ *Rooms from: $100* ⌧ *653 Shell Beach Rd.* ☎ *805/773–4373,
800/549–4727* ⊕ *www.shellbeachinn.com* ⇨ *10 rooms.*

AVILA BEACH

⏱ *4 miles north of Pismo Beach on U.S. 101/Hwy. 1.*

Because the village of Avila Beach and the sandy, cove-front shoreline for which it's named face south into the Pacific Ocean, they get more sun and less fog than any other stretch of coast in the area. It can be bright and warm here while the surrounding hillside communities shiver under the marine layer. With its fortuitous climate and protected waters, Avila's public beach draws plenty of sunbathers and families; weekends are very busy. Downtown Avila Beach has a lively seaside promenade and some shops and hotels, but for real local color, head to the far end of the cove and watch the commercial fishers offload their catch on the old Port San Luis wharf. A few seafood shacks and fish markets do business on the pier while sea lions congregate below. On Friday from mid-April through mid-September, a fish and farmers' market livens up the beach area with music, fresh local produce and seafood, and children's activities.

GETTING HERE AND AROUND

Exit U.S. 101 at Avila Beach Drive and head 3 miles west to reach the beach. The free Avila Trolley operates weekends year-round, plus Friday afternoon/evenings from April to September. The minibuses connect Avila Beach and Port San Luis to Shell Beach, with multiple stops along the way. Service extends to Pismo Beach in summer.

WHERE TO STAY

For expanded reviews, facilities, and current deals, visit Fodors.com.

$$$$ 🏨 **Avila La Fonda.** Modeled after a village in early California's Mexican
HOTEL   period, Avila La Fonda surrounds guests with rich jewel tones, fountains, and upscale comfort. **Pros:** one-of-a-kind theme and artwork; flexible room combinations; a block from the beach. **Cons:** pricey; most rooms don't have an ocean view. **TripAdvisor:** "a special getaway," "a hidden gem," "great staff." ⑤ *Rooms from: $300* ✉ *101 San Miguel St.* ☎ *805/595–1700* ⊕ *www.avilalafondahotel.com* ⇆ *28 rooms, 1 suite.*

$$ 🏨 **Sycamore Mineral Springs Resort.** This wellness resort's hot mineral
RESORT   springs bubble up into private outdoor tubs on an oak-and-sycamore-forest hillside. **Pros:** great place to rejuvenate; nice hiking; incredible spa services. **Cons:** rooms vary in quality; 2½ miles from the beach. **TripAdvisor:** "great place for a relaxing time," "quaint," "a little piece of heaven." ⑤ *Rooms from: $169* ✉ *1215 Avila Beach Dr., San Luis Obispo* ☎ *805/595–7302, 800/234–5831* ⊕ *www.sycamoresprings.com* ⇆ *26 rooms, 50 suites.*

SAN LUIS OBISPO

8 miles north of Avila Beach on U.S. 101/Hwy. 1.

About halfway between San Francisco and Los Angeles, San Luis Obispo—nicknamed SLO—spreads out below gentle hills and rocky extinct volcanoes. Its main appeal lies in its architecturally diverse and commercially lively downtown, especially several blocks of Higuera Street. The pedestrian-friendly district bustles with shoppers, restaurant goers, and students from California Polytechnic State University, known

as Cal Poly. On Thursday from 6 pm to 9 pm a farmers' market fills Higuera Street with local produce, entertainment, and food stalls. SLO is less a vacation destination than a pleasant stopover along Highway 1; it's a nice place to stay while touring the Wine Country south of town.

GETTING HERE AND AROUND

U.S. 101/Highway 1 traverses the city for several miles. From the north, Highway 1 jogs inland from the coast and merges with the interstate when it reaches the city of San Luis Obispo. SLO City Transit buses operate daily; Regional Transit Authority (SLORTA) buses connect with towns throughout the north county. The Downtown Trolley lumbers through the city's hub on Thursday, Friday, and Saturday.

ESSENTIALS

Visitor Information San Luis Obispo Chamber of Commerce ✉ *1039 Chorro St.* ☎ *805/781-2777* ⊕ *www.visitslo.com.* **San Luis Obispo City Visitor Information** ☎ ⊕ *www.sanluisobispovacations.com.* **San Luis Obispo Vintners Association** ☎ *805/541-5868* ⊕ *www.slowine.com.*

EXPLORING

TOP ATTRACTIONS

Edna Valley/Arroyo Grande Valley wine country. San Luis Obispo is the commercial center of a wine region whose appellations stretch west toward the coast and east toward the inland mountains. Many of the nearly 30 wineries here line Highway 227 and connecting roads. The region is known for Chardonnay and Pinot Noir, although many wineries experiment with other varietals and blends. Wine-touring maps are available around town. Many wineries charge a small tasting fee; most tasting rooms close at 5.

Ↄ **History Center of San Luis Obispo County.** Across the street from the old Spanish mission, the center presents exhibits that survey topics such as Native American life in the county, the California ranchos, and the impact of railroads. A separate children's room has theme activities for kids. On the center's website are links to free downloadable video-podcast walking tours of historic San Luis Obispo. ✉ *696 Monterey St., at Broad St.* ☎ *805/543–0638* ⊕ *historycenterslo.org* ⬛ *Free* ☽ *Daily 10–4.*

★ **Mission San Luis Obispo de Tolosa.** Special events often take place on sun-dappled Mission Plaza in front of Mission San Luis Obispo de Tolosa, established in 1772. Its small museum exhibits artifacts of the Chumash Indians and early Spanish settlers, and docents sometimes lead tours of the church and grounds. ✉ *751 Palm St., at Chorro St.* ☎ *805/543–6850* ⊕ *www.missionsanluisobispo.org* ⬛ *$3 suggested donation* ☽ *Apr.–late-Oct., daily 9–5; late Oct.–Mar., daily 9–4.*

San Luis Obispo Museum of Art. San Luis Obispo Museum of Art displays a mix of traditional work and cutting-edge arts and crafts by Central Coast, national, and international artists. The permanent collection focuses on the artistic legacy of the Central Coast. ✉ *Mission Plaza, 1010 Broad St., at Monterey St.* ☎ *805/543–8562* ⊕ *www.sloma.org* ☽ *Daily 11–5* ☽ *Closed Tues. early Sept.–late June.*

WORTH NOTING

Baileyana Winery. A refurbished 1909 schoolhouse serves as tasting room for Baileyana, which produces chardonnays, pinot noirs, and syrahs. Four sister wineries share the tasting facility. ⊠ *5828 Orcutt Rd., at Righetti Rd.* ☎ *805/269–8200* ⊕ *www.baileyana.com.*

> **DEEP ROOTS**
>
> Way back in the 1700s, the Spanish padres who accompanied Father Junípero Serra planted grapevines from Mexico along California's Central Coast, and began using European wine-making techniques to turn the grapes into delectable vintages.

Claiborne & Churchill. An eco-friendly winery built from straw bales, Claiborne & Churchill makes small lots of exceptional Alsatian-style wines such as dry Riesling and gewürztraminer, plus pinot noir and chardonnay. ⊠ *2649 Carpenter Canyon Rd., at Price Canyon Rd.* ☎ *805/544–4066* ⊕ *www.claibornechurchill.com.*

Edna Valley Vineyard. For sweeping views of the Edna Valley while you sample estate-grown chardonnay, go to the modern tasting bar at Edna Valley Vineyard. ⊠ *2585 Biddle Ranch Rd., off Edna Rd.* ☎ *805/544–5855* ⊕ *www.ednavalleyvineyard.com.*

Old Edna. While touring Edna Valley wine country, be sure to stop at Old Edna, a peaceful, 2-acre site that once was the town of Edna. Browse local art, peek at the vintage 1908 farmhouse (now a B&B), taste wines, pick up sandwiches at the gourmet deli, and stroll along Old Edna Lane. ⊠ *1655 Old Price Canyon Rd., at Hwy. 227* ☎ *805/544–8062, 805/543–0900 deli* ⊕ *www.oldedna.com.*

☺ **San Luis Obispo Children's Museum.** Indoor and outdoor activities at this delightful museum present a kid-friendly version of the city of San Luis Obispo. An "imagination-powered" elevator transports visitors to a series of underground caverns, and simulated lava and steam sputters from an active volcano. Kids can pick rubber fruit at a farmers' market, race in a fire engine to fight a fire, and learn about solar energy from a 15-foot sunflower. The facility is geared to kids under eight; older children may lose interest quickly. ⊠ *1010 Nipomo St., at Monterey St.* ☎ *805/545–5874* ⊕ *www.slocm.org* 💲 *$8* ☉ *Apr.–Sept., Tues.–Fri. 10–4, Sat. 10–5, Sun. and some Mon. holidays 11–5; Oct.–Mar., Tues. and Wed. 10–3, Thurs.–Sat. 10–5, Sun. and some Mon. holidays 1–5.*

WHERE TO EAT

$$ ✕ **Big Sky Café.** A quintessentially Californian, family-friendly (and
ECLECTIC sometimes noisy) café, Big Sky turns local and organically grown ingre-
★ dients into global dishes, starting with breakfast. Brazilian churasco chicken breast, Thai catfish, New Mexican *pozole* (hominy stew): just pick your continent. Vegetarians have lots to choose from. 💲 *Average main: $17* ⊠ *1121 Broad St., at Higuera St.* ☎ *805/545–5401* ⊕ *www.bigskycafe.com* ⚊ *Reservations not accepted.*

$$ ✕ **Buona Tavola.** Homemade pasta with river shrimp in a creamy tomato
ITALIAN sauce and porcini-mushroom risotto are among the northern Italian dishes served at this casual spot. Daily fresh fish and salad specials and an impressive wine list attract a steady stream of regulars. In good weather you can dine on the flower-filled patio. The Paso Robles branch

is equally enjoyable. $ *Average main: $20* ✉ *1037 Monterey St., near Osos St.* ☎ *805/545–8000* ⊕ *www.btslo.com* �Ⓝ *No lunch weekends.*

$ ✕ **Mo's Smokehouse BBQ.** Barbecue joints abound on the Central Coast,

SOUTHERN but this one excels. Various Southern-style sauces season tender hickory-smoked ribs and shredded-meat sandwiches; sides such as baked beans, coleslaw, homemade potato chips, and garlic bread extend the pleasure. $ *Average main: $9* ✉ *1005 Monterey St., at Osos St.* ☎ *805/544–6193* ⊕ *www.smokinmosbbq.com.*

$$ ✕ **Novo Restaurant & Lounge.** In the colorful dining room or on the large

ECLECTIC creek-side deck, this animated downtown eatery will take you on a culinary world tour: The salads, small plates, and entrées come from nearly every continent. The wine and beer list also covers the globe and includes local favorites. Many of the decadent desserts are baked at the restaurant's sister property in Cambria, the French Corner Bakery. $ *Average main: $18* ✉ *726 Higuera St., at Broad St.* ☎ *805/543–3986* ⊕ *www.novorestaurant.com.*

WHERE TO STAY

For expanded reviews, facilities, and current deals, visit Fodors.com.

$$$ ▦ **Apple Farm.** Decorated to the hilt with floral bedspreads and watercol-

HOTEL ors by local artists, this Victorian country-style hotel is one of the most popular places to stay in San Luis Obispo. **Pros:** flowers everywhere; convenient to Cal Poly and U.S. 101; creek-side setting. **Cons:** hordes of tourists during the day; too floral for some people's tastes. **TripAdvisor:** "a wonderful picture of Americana," "lots of little extras," "charming and restful." $ *Rooms from: $209* ✉ *2015 Monterey St.* ☎ *800/255–2040, 805/544-2040* ⊕ *www.applefarm.com* ⇆ *104 rooms.*

$$$ ▦ **Garden Street Inn.** From this fully restored 1887 Italianate Queen

B&B/INN Anne, the only lodging in downtown SLO, you can walk to many restaurants and attractions. **Pros:** classic B&B; walking distance from everywhere downtown; nice wine-and-cheese reception. **Cons:** city noise filters through some rooms; not great for families. **TripAdvisor:** "nice location," "close to everything," "incredible charm." $ *Rooms from: $189* ✉ *1212 Garden St.* ☎ *805/545–9802, 800/488–2045* ⊕ *www. gardenstreetinn.com* ⇆ *9 rooms, 4 suites* ⑩ *Breakfast.*

$$$ ▦ **Madonna Inn.** From its rococo bathrooms to its pink-on-pink frou-

HOTEL frou steak house, the Madonna Inn is fabulous or tacky, depending on your taste. **Pros:** fun, one-of-a-kind experience. **Cons:** rooms vary widely; must appreciate kitsch. **TripAdvisor:** "very fun," "great place for a unique experience," "for something different." $ *Rooms from: $179* ✉ *100 Madonna Rd.* ☎ *805/543–3000, 800/543–9666* ⊕ *www. madonnainn.com* ⇆ *106 rooms, 4 suites.*

$ ▦ **Peach Tree Inn.** Extra touches such as rose gardens, a porch with

HOTEL rockers, and flower-filled vases turn this modest, family-run motel into a relaxing creek-side haven. **Pros:** bargain rates; cozy rooms; decent breakfast. **Cons:** near a busy intersection and freeway; basic amenities. **TripAdvisor:** "nice personal touch," "very clean rooms," "wonderful staff." $ *Rooms from: $89* ✉ *2001 Monterey St.* ☎ *805/543–3170, 800/227–6396* ⊕ *www.peachtreeinn.com* ⇆ *37 rooms* ⑩ *Breakfast.*

$$ ▦ **Petit Soleil.** A cobblestone courtyard, country-French custom furnish-

B&B/INN ings, and Gallic music piped through the halls evoke a Provençal mood at this cheery inn on upper Monterey Street's motel row. **Pros:** French details throughout; scrumptious breakfasts; cozy rooms. **Cons:** sits on a busy avenue; cramped parking. **TripAdvisor:** "quaint and comfortable," "peaceful and relaxing," "what an unexpected delight." ⑤ *Rooms from: $159* ✉ *1473 Monterey St.* ☎ *805/549–0321, 800/676–1588* ⊕ *www.psslo.com* ⤺ *15 rooms, 1 suite* ⦿ *Breakfast.*

NIGHTLIFE AND THE ARTS
NIGHTLIFE
The club scene in this college town is centered on Higuera Street off Monterey Street.

Frog and Peach. This is a decent spot to nurse an English beer and listen to live music. ✉ *728 Higuera St., at Broad St.* ☎ *805/595–3764.*

Koberl at Blue. A trendy crowd hangs out at the slick bar at Koberl at Blue, an upscale restaurant with late-night dining, exotic martinis, and a huge list of local and imported beer and wine. ✉ *998 Monterey St., at Osos St.* ☎ *805/783–1135.*

Linnaea's Cafe. A mellow java joint, Linnaea's sometimes hosts poetry readings, as well as blues, jazz, and folk music performances. ✉ *1110 Garden St., at Higuera St.* ☎ *805/541–5888.*

MoTav. Chicago-style MoTav draws crowds with good pub food and live entertainment in a turn-of-the-20th-century setting (complete with antique U.S. flags and a wall-mounted moose head). ✉ *725 Higuera St., at Broad St.* ☎ *805/541–8733.*

THE ARTS
Festival Mozaic. Held each year in mid-July, the festival celebrates five centuries of classical music. ☎ *805/781–3008* ⊕ *www.festivalmozaic. com.*

Performing Arts Center, San Luis Obispo. The center hosts live theater, dance, and music performances by artists from around the world. ✉ *Cal Poly, 1 Grand Ave., off U.S. 101* ☎ *805/756–7222, 805/756–2787 box office, 888/233–2787 toll-free* ⊕ *www.pacslo.org.*

SPORTS AND THE OUTDOORS
Parks and Recreation Department. Hilly greenbelts with extensive hiking trails surround San Luis Obispo. For information about trailheads, call the parks department or download a trail map on its website. ☎ *805/781–7300* ⊕ *www.slocity.org/parksandrecreation.*

EN ROUTE

Montaña de Oro State Park. Instead of continuing north on U.S. 101/Highway 1 from San Luis Obispo to Morro Bay, consider detouring west along Los Osos Valley Raod past farms and ranches to Montaña de Oro State Park, where miles of nature trails traverse rocky shoreline, wild beaches, and hills that overlook dramatic scenery. Check out the tide pools, watch the waves roll into the bluffs, and picnic in the eucalyptus groves. From Montaña de Oro you can reach Morro Bay by following the coastline along South Bay Boulevard 8 miles through the quaint residential villages of Los Osos and Baywood Park. ✉ *West about 13 miles on Madonna Rd., to Los Osos Valley Rd., to Pecho Valley Rd.; to continue on to Morro Bay, backtrack east to Los Osos*

Valley Rd., then head north on S. Bay Blvd., and west on State Park Rd. ☎ *805/528–0513, 805/772–7434* ⊕ *www.parks.ca.gov.*

MORRO BAY

14 miles north of San Luis Obispo on Hwy. 1.

Commercial fishermen slog around Morro Bay in galoshes, and beat-up fishing boats bob in the bay's protected waters. Nature-oriented activities take center stage here: kayaking, hiking, biking, fishing, and wildlife watching around the bay and national marine estuary and along the state beach.

GETTING HERE AND AROUND

From U.S. 101 south or north, exit at Highway 1 in San Luis Obispo and head west. Scenic Highway 1 passes through the eastern edge of town. From Atascadero, two-lane Highway 41 West treks over the mountains to Morro Bay. San Luis Obispo RTA Route 12 buses travel year-round between Morro Bay, San Luis Obispo, Cayucos, Cambria, San Simeon, and Hearst Castle. The Morro Bay Shuttle picks up riders throughout the town from Friday through Monday in summer ($1.25).

ESSENTIALS

Visitor Information Morro Bay Visitors Center ⊠ *845 Embarcadero Rd., near Harbor St.* ☎ *805/772–4467, 800/231–0592* ⊕ *www.morrobay.org* ⊙ *Daily 9–5.*

EXPLORING

Embarcadero. The center of the action on land is the Embarcadero, where vacationers pour in and out of souvenir shops and seafood restaurants and stroll or bike along the scenic half-mile Harborwalk to Morro Rock. From here, you can get out on the bay in a kayak or tour boat. ⊠ *On waterfront from Beach St. to Tidelands Park.*

♻ ★ **Morro Bay State Park Museum of Natural History.** The entertaining and educational interactive exhibits at this spiffy museum south of downtown Morro Bay explain the natural environment and how to preserve it—in the bay and estuary and on the rest of the planet. ⊠ *State Park Rd.* ☎ *805/772–2694* ⊕ *www.ccnha.org/morrobay* ☜ *$3* ⊙ *Daily 10–5.*

Morro Rock. At the mouth of Morro Bay, which is both a state and national estuary, stands 576-foot-high Morro Rock, one of nine such small volcanic peaks, or morros, in the area. A short walk leads to a breakwater, with the harbor on one side and the crashing waves of the Pacific on the other. You may not climb the rock, where endangered falcons and other birds nest. Sea lions and otters often play in the water at the foot of the peak. ⊠ *Northern end of Embarcadero.*

WHERE TO EAT

$$
SEAFOOD
✗ **Dorn's Original Breakers Cafe.** This seafood restaurant overlooking the harbor has satisfied Morro Bay appetites since 1948. In addition to straight-ahead fish dishes such as petrale sole or calamari steaks sautéed in butter and wine, Dorn's serves breakfast. ⑤ *Average main: $18* ⊠ *801 Market Ave., at Morro Bay Blvd.* ☎ *805/772–4415* ⊕ *www. dornscafe.com.*

$ ╳ **Taco Temple.** The devout stand in line at this family-run diner that
SOUTHWESTERN serves some of the freshest food around. Seafood anchors a menu of
★ dishes—salmon burritos, superb fish tacos with mango salsa—hailing
from somewhere between California and Mexico. Desserts get rave
reviews, too. Make an effort to find this gem. It's in a supermarket
parking lot on the frontage road parallel to Highway 1, just north of
the Highway 41 junction. ⑤ *Average main: $14* ⊠ *2680 Main St., at
Elena St.* ☎ *805/772–4965* ⚲ *Reservations not accepted* ▭ *No credit
cards* ⦸ *Closed Tues.*

$$$ ╳ **Windows on the Water.** Diners at this second-floor restaurant view the
SEAFOOD sunset through giant picture windows. Meanwhile, fresh fish and other
dishes based on local ingredients emerge from the wood-fired oven in
the open kitchen, and oysters on the half shell beckon from the raw
bar. The extensive, California-centric wine list includes about 20 selec-
tions poured by the glass. ⑤ *Average main: $28* ⊠ *699 Embarcadero,
at Pacific St.* ☎ *805/772–0677* ⊕ *www.windowsmb.com* ⦸ *No lunch.*

WHERE TO STAY

For expanded reviews, facilities, and current deals, visit Fodors.com.

$$$ ▦ **Anderson Inn.** The innkeepers' friendly, personalized service and an
B&B/INN oceanfront setting keep loyal patrons returning to this Embarcadero
★ inn, built from scratch in 2008. **Pros:** walk to restaurants and sights;
well-appointed rooms; attentive service. **Cons:** waterfront area gets
crowded on weekends and in summer; not low-budget. **TripAdvisor:**
"exceptional in every way," "first class," "a lovely retreat with warm
hospitality." ⑤ *Rooms from: $239* ⊠ *897 Embarcadero* ☎ *805/772–
3434* ⊕ *www.andersoninnmorrobay.com* ⤺ *8 rooms.*

$$$ ▦ **Cass House.** In tiny Cayucos, an oceanfront enclave about 4 miles
B&B/INN north of Morro Bay, the 1867 home of shipping pioneer Captain
★ James Cass is now a luxurious B&B surrounded by rose and other
gardens. **Pros:** historic property; some ocean views; excellent meals.
Cons: not near Morro Bay nightlife or tourist attractions; not designed
for families. **TripAdvisor:** "great rooms," "peaceful oasis of comfort,"
"amazing food." ⑤ *Rooms from: $200* ⊠ *222 N. Ocean Ave., Cayucos*
☎ *805/995–3669* ⊕ *casshouseinn.com* ⤺ *5 rooms* ⦿⦿ *Breakfast.*

$$ ▦ **Embarcadero Inn.** The rooms at this waterfront hotel are cheery and
HOTEL welcoming, and many have fireplaces. **Pros:** right across from the water-
front. **Cons:** tiny lobby; no pool. **TripAdvisor:** "huge first-rate rooms,"
"great view and great people," "all around awesome." ⑤ *Rooms from:
$145* ⊠ *456 Embarcadero* ☎ *805/772–2700, 800/292–7625* ⊕ *www.
embarcaderoinn.com* ⤺ *29 rooms, 4 suites* ⦿⦿ *Breakfast.*

SPORTS AND THE OUTDOORS

Kayak Horizons. This outfit rents kayaks and gives lessons and guided
tours. ⊠ *551 Embarcadero, near Marina St.* ☎ *805/772–6444* ⊕ *www.
kayakhorizons.com.*

Lost Isle Adventures. Captain Alan Rackov cruises his Tiki-Boat into the
bay and out to Morro Rock every hour starting at 11 am daily (less
often in winter). ⊠ *Giovanni's Fish Market, 1001 Front St., on the
Embarcadero* ☎ *805/440–8170* ⊕ *lostisleadventures.com.*

Sub-Sea Tours. Sub-Sea operates glass-bottom boat and catamaran cruises, and has kayak and canoe rentals and summer whale-watching cruises. ✉ *699 Embarcadero, at Pacific St.* ☎ *805/772–9463* ⊕ *subseatours.com.*

Virg's Landing. Virg's conducts deep-sea fishing and whale-watching trips. ✉ *1215 Embarcadero* ☎ *805/772–1222* ⊕ *www.virgs.com.*

PASO ROBLES

30 miles north of San Luis Obispo on U.S. 101; 25 miles northwest of Morro Bay via Hwy. 41 and U.S. 101.

In the 1860s tourists began flocking to this dusty ranching outpost to "take the cure" in a luxurious bathhouse fed by underground mineral hot springs. An Old West town, complete with opera house, emerged, and grand Victorian homes went up, followed in the 20th century by Craftsman bungalows. A 2003 earthquake demolished or weakened several beloved downtown buildings, but historically faithful reconstruction has helped the district retain its character.

More than 200 wineries and more than 26,000 vineyard acres pepper the wooded hills of Paso Robles west of U.S. 101 and blanket the flatter, more open land on the east side. The region's brutally hot summer days and cool nights yield stellar grapes that make noteworthy wines, particularly robust reds such as Cabernet Sauvignon, Merlot, Zinfandel, and Rhône varietals such as Syrah. Exquisite whites also come out of Paso, including Chardonnay and Rhône varietals such as Viognier. Small-town friendliness prevails at most wineries, especially smaller ones, which tend to treat visitors like neighbors. Pick up a regional wine-touring map at lodgings, wineries, and attractions around town. Most tasting rooms close at 5 pm; many charge a small fee.

But more attracts people to the Paso Robles area than fine wine and fancy tasting rooms. Golfers play the four local courses and spandex-clad bicyclists race along the winding back roads. Down-home and upmarket restaurants, bars, antiques stores, and little shops fill the streets around oak-shaded City Park, where special events of all kinds—custom car shows, an olive festival, Friday-night summer concerts—take place on many weekends. Despite its increasing sophistication, Paso (as the locals call it) more or less remains cowboy country. Each year in late July and early August, the city throws the two-week California Mid-State Fair, complete with livestock auctions, carnival rides, and corn dogs.

GETTING HERE AND AROUND

U.S. 101 runs through the city of Paso Robles. Highway 46 West links Paso Robles to Highway 1 and Cambria on the coast. Highway 46 East connects Paso Robles with Interstate 5 and the San Joaquin Valley. Public transit is not convenient for wine touring and sightseeing.

ESSENTIALS

Visitor Information Paso Robles Wine Country Alliance ☎ *805/239–8463, 800/549–9463* ⊕ *www.pasowine.com.*

EXPLORING

TOP ATTRACTIONS

Eberle Winery. Even if you don't drink wine, stop at Eberle Winery for a fascinating tour of the huge wine caves beneath the east-side Paso Robles vineyard. Gary Eberle, one of Paso wine's founding fathers, is obsessed with Cabernet Sauvignon. ⊠ *3810 E. Hwy. 46, 3½ miles east of U.S. 101* ☎ *805/238–9607* ⊕ *www.eberlewinery.com.*

Firestone Walker Brewing Company. As they say around Paso Robles, it takes a lot of beer to make good wine, and to meet that need the locals turn to Firestone, where you can sample medal-winning craft beers such as Double Barrel Ale. ⊠ *1400 Ramada Dr., east side of U.S. 101; exit at Hwy. 46 W/Cambria exit, but head east* ☎ *805/238–2556* ⊕ *www. firestonebeer.com.*

Justin Vineyards & Winery. At the western end of Paso Robles wine country, swank Justin makes Bordeaux-style blends. This readers' favorite offers winery, vineyard, and barrel-tasting tours ($15 to $400). In the tasting room there's a deli bar; a high-end restaurant and B&B are also part of the complex. ⊠ *11680 Chimney Rock Rd., 15 miles west of U.S. 101's Hwy 46 E exit; take 24th St. west and follow road (name changes along the way) to Chimney Rock Rd.* ☎ *805/238–6932, 800/726–0049* ⊕ *www.justinwine.com.*

Paso Robles Wine Festival. Most local wineries pour at this mid-May outdoor festival that has live bands and diverse food vendors. Winery open houses and winemaker dinners round out the weekend. ⊠ *City Park, Spring St., between 10th and 12th Sts.* ☎ *805/239–8463, 800/549–9463* ⊕ *www.pasowine.com* 🖃 *$55 basic admission, designated driver or child $15.*

★ **Pasolivo.** While touring the idyllic west side of Paso Robles, take a break from wine by stopping at Pasolivo. Find out how the artisans here make their Tuscan-style olive oils on a high-tech Italian press, and taste the acclaimed results. ⊠ *8530 Vineyard Dr., west off U.S. 101 (Exit 224) or Hwy. 46 W (Exit 228)* ☎ *805/227–0186* ⊕ *www.pasolivo.com.*

River Oaks Hot Springs & Spa. The lakeside spa, on 240 hilly acres near the intersection of U.S. 101 and Highway 46E, is a great place to relax after wine tasting or festival-going. Soak in a private indoor or outdoor hot tub fed by natural mineral springs, or indulge in a massage or facial. ⊠ *800 Clubhouse Dr., off River Oaks Dr.* ☎ *805/238–4600* ⊕ *www.riveroakshotsprings.com* 🖃 *Hot tubs $13 to $24 per person per hr* ⊙ *Tues.–Sun. 9–9.*

Tablas Creek Vineyard. Tucked in the far-west hills of Paso Robles, Tablas Creek Vineyard makes some of the area's finest wine by blending organically grown, hand-harvested Rhône varietals such as Syrah, Grenache, Roussanne, and Viognier. Tours include a chance to graft your own grapevine; call to reserve space. ⊠ *9339 Adelaida Rd., west of Vineyard Dr.* ☎ *805/237–1231* ⊕ *www.tablascreek.com.*

WORTH NOTING

Harris Stage Lines. Former pro rodeo riders and horse trainers Tom and Debby Harris offer stagecoach rides (learn to hitch the team of horses beforehand), riding-and-driving lessons, and various Old

West-themed events at their ranch on the north side of town. ⊠ *5995 North River Rd., east of U.S. 101, Exit 230* ☎ *805/237–1860* ⊕ *www. harrisstagelines.com.*

Paso Robles Pioneer Museum. The museum's one-room schoolhouse and its displays of ranching paraphernalia, horse-drawn vehicles, hot-springs artifacts, and photos evoke Paso's rural heritage. ⊠ *2010 Riverside Ave., at 21st St.* ☎ *805/239–4556* ⊕ *www. pasoroblespioneermuseum.org* 🖘 *Free* ☉ *Thurs.–Sun. 1–4.*

Paso Wine Centre. Four dozen local wines are available for tasting via enomatic dispensers at this spacious, contemporary space downtown that's furnished with comfy sofas and handhewn oak tables. More than 200 wines are available for purchase. ⊠ *1240 Park St., at 13th St.* ☎ *805/239–9156* ⊕ *www.pasowinecentre.com.*

LAID-BACK WINE COUNTRY

Hundreds of vineyards and wineries dot the hillsides from Paso Robles to San Luis Obispo, through the scenic Edna Valley and south to northern Santa Barbara County. The wineries offer much of the variety of northern California's Napa and Sonoma valleys—without the glitz and crowds. Since the early 1980s the region has developed an international reputation for high-quality wines, most notably Pinot Noir, Chardonnay, and Zinfandel. Wineries here tend to be small, but most have tasting rooms (some have tours), and you'll often meet the winemakers themselves.

WHERE TO EAT

$$$ ✕ **Artisan.** Innovative renditions of traditional American comfort foods,
AMERICAN a well-chosen list of regional wines, a stylish full bar, and a sophisticated urban vibe lure winemakers, locals, and tourists to this small, family-run American bistro in an art-deco building near the town square. Chris Kobayashi (Chef Koby, a James Beard award nominee) uses local, organic, wild-caught ingredients to whip up regional favorites, which might include red abalone with fried green tomatoes and pancetta, scallops with laughing bird prawns, mussels, clams, Spanish chorizo, and saffron, or flatiron steak with shallots, fries, and cabernet butter. Ask for a booth facing the open kitchen, and save room for the restaurant's home-style desserts: brownies, peach crumbles, crème brûlée, and the like. ⑤ *Average main: $28* ⊠ *1401 Park St., at 14th St.* ☎ *805/237–8084* ⊕ *www.artisanpasorobles.com.*

$$$ ✕ **Bistro Laurent.** Owner-chef Laurent Grangien has created a handsome,
FRENCH welcoming French bistro in an 1890s brick building across from City
★ Park. He focuses on traditional dishes such as osso buco, cassoulet, rack of lamb, goat-cheese tart, and onion soup, but always offers a few updated dishes as daily specials. Wines, sourced from the adjacent wine shop, come from around the world. ⑤ *Average main: $28* ⊠ *1202 Pine St., at 12th St.* ☎ *805/226–8191* ⊕ *www.bistrolaurent.com* ☉ *Closed Sun. and Mon.*

$$$ ✕ **McPhee's Grill.** In an 1860s building in the tiny cow town of Templeton
AMERICAN (just south of Paso Robles), this casual chophouse serves sophisticated, contemporary versions of traditional Western fare—such as oak-grilled filet mignon and cedar-planked salmon. House-label wines, made

especially for McPhee's, are quite good. $ *Average main: $25* ✉ *416 S. Main St., at 5th St., Templeton* ☎ *805/434-3204* ⊕ *mcpheesgrill.com.*

$ ✕**Panolivo Family Bistro.** Scrumptious French bistro fare is the draw at
FRENCH this cheery downtown café, just a block north of the town square. For breakfast, try a fresh pastry or quiche, or build your own omelet. Lunch and dinner choices include traditional French dishes like snails baked in garlic-butter sauce or cassoulet as well as sandwiches, salads, and fresh pastas—including the house-made beef cannelloni. $ *Average main: $15* ✉ *1344 Park St., at 14th St.* ☎ *805/239-3366* ⊕ *www. panolivo.com.*

$$ ✕**Thomas Hill Organics.** In a casual bistro off a tiny alley, Joe and Debbie
AMERICAN Thomas serve delectable locavore cuisine made from regional ingredients; much of the produce comes from their nearby ten-acre organic farm. The menu changes weekly, depending on what's in-season and available, and includes a good selection of Central Coast wines (there's also a wine bar here). Ask for a table in the outdoor courtyard when the weather's fine. $ *Average main: $16* ✉ *1305 Park St., at 13th St., Templeton* ☎ *805/226-5888* ⊕ *thomashillorganics.com* ⊘ *Closed Tues.*

$$$ ✕**Villa Creek.** With a firm nod to the rancho and mission cuisine of
SOUTHWESTERN California's early Spanish settlers, chef Tom Fundero conjures distinctly modern magic with local and sustainable ingredients. The seasonal menu has included butternut-squash enchiladas and braised lamb shank with saffron risotto and classic beef bourguignonne with parsnip and cauliflower purée, but you might also find duck breast with sweet-potato latkes. Central Coast wines dominate the list, with a smattering of Spanish and French selections. All brick and bare wood, the dining room can get loud when winemakers start passing their bottles from table to table, but it's always festive. For lighter appetites or wallets, the bar serves smaller plates—not to mention a killer margarita. $ *Average main: $26* ✉ *1144 Pine St., at 12th St.* ☎ *805/238-3000* ⊕ *www. villacreek.com* ⊘ *No lunch.*

WHERE TO STAY

For expanded reviews, facilities, and current deals, visit Fodors.com.

$ ▦ **Adelaide Inn.** Family-owned and -managed, this clean, friendly oasis
HOTEL with meticulous landscaping offers spacious rooms and everything you
Fodor's Choice need: coffeemaker, iron, hair dryer, and peace and quiet. **Pros:** great
★ bargain; attractive pool area; ideal for families. **Cons:** not a romantic retreat; near a busy intersection and freeway. **TripAdvisor:** "pride in ownership," "awesome hotel and location," "comfortable bed." $ *Rooms from: $99* ✉ *1215 Ysabel Ave.* ☎ *805/238-2770, 800/549-7276* ⊕ *www.adelaideinn.com* ⊅ *109 rooms* ▯⊚▯ *Breakfast.*

$$$$ ▦ **Hotel Cheval.** Equestrian themes surface throughout this intimate,
HOTEL sophisticated, European-style inn just a half-block from the main square and a short walk to some of Paso's best restaurants. **Pros:** walking distance to downtown restaurants; European-style facilities; personal service. **Cons:** views aren't great; no pool or hot tub. **TripAdvisor:** "a bit of Europe," "in a class by itself," "cozy and comfy." $ *Rooms from: $315* ✉ *1021 Pine St.* ☎ *805/226-9995, 866/522-6999* ⊕ *www. hotelcheval.com* ⊅ *16 rooms* ▯⊚▯ *Breakfast.*

$$$ 🏨 **La Bellasera Hotel & Suites.** The swankest full-service hotel for miles
HOTEL around, the La Bellasera, completed in 2008, caters to those looking
for luxurious high-tech amenities and close proximity to major Cen-
tral Coast roadways. **Pros:** new property; tons of amenities. **Cons:** far
from town square; located at major intersection. **TripAdvisor:** "excel-
lent amenities," "a lovely place to stay," "hidden gem." ⑤ *Rooms from:
$229* ✉ *206 Alexa Court* ☎ *805/238–2834, 866/782–9669* ⊕ *www.
labellasera.com* ⌁ *35 rooms, 25 suites.*

$$ 🏨 **Paso Robles Inn.** On the site of a luxurious old spa hotel by the same
HOTEL name, the inn is built around a lush, shady garden with a pool. **Pros:** pri-
vate spring-fed hot tubs; historic property; across from park and town
square. **Cons:** fronts a busy street; rooms vary in size and quality. **Trip-
Advisor:** "hospitable taste of classic California," "perfect location,"
"just right." ⑤ *Rooms from: $150* ✉ *1103 Spring St.* ☎ *805/238–2660,
800/676–1713* ⊕ *www.pasoroblesinn.com* ⌁ *92 rooms, 6 suites.*

$$$$ 🏨 **Summerwood Inn.** Verdant gardens and vineyards envelop Summer-
B&B/INN wood Winery's elegant, friendly B&B in tranquility; four-poster and
sleigh beds, lace and floral fabrics, thick robes, and nightly turn-down
service bring comfort to the individually designed rooms. **Pros:** convenient wine touring base; super-friendly staff; delicious breakfast. **Cons:**
across from winery on a main highway; can be noisy during the day.
⑤ *Rooms from: $269* ✉ *2130 Arbor Rd., 1 mile west of U.S. 101,
at Hwy. 46W* ☎ *805/227–1111* ⊕ *www.summerwoodwine.com* ⌁ *9
rooms* ⑩ *Breakfast.*

CAMBRIA

*28 miles west of Paso Robles on Hwy. 46; 20 miles north of Morro
Bay on Hwy. 1.*

Cambria, set on piney hills above the sea, was settled by Welsh miners
in the 1890s. In the 1970s, the gorgeous, isolated setting attracted artists
and other independent types; the town now caters to tourists, but it still
bears the unmistakable imprint of its bohemian past. Both of Cambria's
downtowns, the original East Village and the newer West Village, are
packed with art and crafts galleries, antiques shops, cafés, restaurants,
and B&Bs. Late-Victorian homes stand along side streets, and the hills
are filled with redwood-and-glass residences. If you're driving north
up Highway 1 from Morro Bay, make a quick stop 7 miles south of
Cambria at the cute former dairy town of Harmony, population 18, to
visit its glassworks, pottery, and other enterprises.

GETTING HERE AND AROUND
Highway 1 leads to Cambria from the north and south. From U.S. 101
at Paso Robles, Highway 246 West curves through the mountains to
Cambria and the coast. San Luis Obispo RTA Route 12 buses ferry
passengers between San Luis Obispo and Hearst Castle, stopping in
Cambria along the way.

ESSENTIALS
Visitor Information Cambria Chamber of Commerce ☎ *805/927–3624*
⊕ *www.cambriachamber.org.*

EXPLORING

Leffingwell's Landing. A state picnic ground, the landing a good place for examining tidal pools and watching otters as they frolic in the surf. ⊠ *North end of Moonstone Beach Dr.* ☎ *805/927–2070.*

Moonstone Beach Drive. Lined with low-key motels, the drive runs along a bluff above the ocean. The 2-mile boardwalk that winds along the beach makes for a fine walk and a great photo op. You're apt to glimpse sea lions and even sea otters, and during winter and spring the occasional gray whale. Year-round birds aplenty fly about, and tiny creatures scurry amid the tide pools. ⊠ *Off Hwy. 1.*

Nit Wit Ridge. Arthur Beal (aka Captain Nit Wit, Der Tinkerpaw) spent 51 years building Nit Wit Ridge, a home with terraced rock gardens. For building materials, he used all kinds of collected junk: beer cans, rocks, abalone shells, car parts, TV antennas—you name it. The site, above Cambria's West Village, is a State Historic Landmark. You can drive by and peek in—from the 700 block of Main Street, head southeast on Cornwall Street and east on Hillcrest Drive. Better yet, call ahead for a guided tour of the house and grounds. ⊠ *881 Hillcrest Dr.* ☎ *805/927–2690* ⊡ *$10 suggested donation* ☉ *Daily by appointment.*

WHERE TO EAT

$$$
AMERICAN
✕ **Black Cat Bistro.** Jazz wafts through the several small rooms of this intimate East Village bistro where stylish cushions line the banquettes. Start with an order of the fried olives stuffed with Gorgonzola, accompanied by a glass from the eclectic list of local and imported wines. The daily-changing menu is centered on sustainable ingredients and might include roasted rack of elk rubbed in cocoa or breast of pheasant stuffed with caramelized apples. ⑤ *Average main: $24* ⊠ *1602 Main St.* ☎ *805/927–1600* ⊕ *www.blackcatbistro.com* ⚞ *Reservations essential* ☉ *Closed Tues. and Wed. No lunch.*

$
CAFÉ
✕ **French Corner Bakery.** Place your order at the counter and then sit outside to watch the passing East Village scene (if the fog has rolled in, take a seat in the tiny deli). The rich aroma of coffee and fresh breakfast pastries makes mouths water in the morning; for lunch, try a quiche with flaky crust or a sandwich on house-baked bread. ⑤ *Average main: $7* ⊠ *2214 Main St.* ☎ *805/927–8227* ⚞ *Reservations not accepted* ☉ *No dinner.*

$$
ECLECTIC
✕ **Robin's.** A truly multiethnic and vegetarian-friendly dining experience awaits you at this East Village cottage filled with country antiques. At dinner, choose from lobster enchiladas, pork osso buco, Thai green chicken curry, and more. Lunchtime's extensive salad and sandwich menu embraces burgers and tofu alike. Unless it's raining, ask for a table on the secluded (and heated) garden patio. ⑤ *Average main: $20* ⊠ *4095 Burton Dr., at Center St.* ☎ *805/927–5007* ⊕ *www. robinsrestaurant.com.*

$$$
SEAFOOD
✕ **The Sea Chest.** The best seafood place in town—readers give it a big thumbs-up—this Moonstone Beach restaurant fills soon after it opens at 5:30. Those in the know grab seats at the oyster bar and take in spectacular sunsets while watching the chefs broil fresh halibut and steam garlicky clams. If you can't get here early, play some cribbage

or checkers while you wait for a table. $ *Average main: $25* ✉ *6216 Moonstone Beach Dr., near Weymouth St./Hwy. 1* ☎ *805/927–4514* ⊕ *www.seachestrestaurant.com* ♣ *Reservations not accepted* ▭ *No credit cards* ⊘ *Closed Tues. mid-Sept.–May. No lunch*.

WHERE TO STAY

For expanded reviews, facilities, and current deals, visit Fodors.com.

$ **Bluebird Inn.** This sweet motel in Cambria's East Village sits amid
HOTEL beautiful gardens along Santa Rosa Creek; rooms include simply furnished doubles and nicer creek-side suites with patios, fireplaces, and refrigerators. **Pros:** excellent value; well-kept gardens; friendly staff. **Cons:** few frills; basic rooms; on Cambria's main drag; not on beach. **TripAdvisor:** "homey and sweet," "blast from the past," "lovely ambience." $ *Rooms from: $78* ✉ *1880 Main St.* ☎ *805/927–4634, 800/552–5434* ⊕ *bluebirdmotel.com* ⤳ *37 rooms*.

$$ **Cambria Pines Lodge.** With lots of recreational facilities and a range
RESORT of accommodations—from basic state park–style cabins to motel-style standard rooms to large fireplace suites—this 25-acre retreat up the hill from the East Village is a good choice for families. **Pros:** short walk from downtown; verdant gardens; spacious grounds. **Cons:** service and housekeeping not always top-quality; some units need updating. **TripAdvisor:** "like living in a garden," "rustic but clean," "large room with great meal." $ *Rooms from: $169* ✉ *2905 Burton Dr.* ☎ *805/927–4200, 800/966–6490* ⊕ *www.cambriapineslodge.com* ⤳ *72 rooms, 18 cabins, 62 suites* ⦿ *Breakfast*.

$$ **J. Patrick House.** Monterey pines and flower gardens surround this
B&B/INN Irish-theme inn, which sits on a hilltop above Cambria's East Village. **Pros:** fantastic breakfasts; friendly innkeepers; quiet neighborhood. **Cons:** few rooms; fills up quickly. **TripAdvisor:** "getaway from the world," "tastefully done," "great price and wonderful service." $ *Rooms from: $165* ✉ *2990 Burton Dr.* ☎ *805/927–3812, 800/341–5258* ⊕ *www.jpatrickhouse.com* ⤳ *8 rooms* ⦿ *Breakfast*.

$$ **Moonstone Landing.** Friendly staff, lots of amenities, and reasonable
HOTEL rates make this up-to-date motel a top pick with readers who like to
★ stay right on Moonstone Beach. **Pros:** sleek furnishings; across from the beach; cheery lounge. **Cons:** narrow property; some rooms overlook a parking lot. **TripAdvisor:** "charm in a beautiful location," "spacious room," "relaxing coastal getaway." $ *Rooms from: $125* ✉ *6240 Moonstone Beach Dr.* ☎ *805/927–0012, 800/830–4540* ⊕ *www. moonstonelanding.com* ⤳ *29 rooms* ⦿ *Breakfast*.

SAN SIMEON

Hwy. 1, 9 miles north of Cambria and 65 miles south of Big Sur.

Whalers founded San Simeon in the 1850s but had virtually abandoned the town by the time Senator George Hearst reestablished it 20 years later. Hearst bought up most of the surrounding ranch land, built a 1,000-foot wharf, and turned San Simeon into a bustling port. His son, William Randolph Hearst, further developed the area during the construction of Hearst Castle. Today the town, 4 miles south of the entrance to Hearst San Simeon State Historical Monument, is basically a strip of gift shops and mediocre motels along Highway 1.

GETTING HERE AND AROUND

Highway 1 is the only way to reach San Simeon. From northern California, follow Highway 1 from Big Sur south to San Simeon. From U.S. 101 north or south, exit at Highway 1 in San Luis Obispo and follow it northwest 42 miles to San Simeon. Alternative rural routes to reach Highway 1 from the 101 include Highway 41 West (Atascadero to Morro Bay) and Highway 46 West (Paso Robles to Cambria).

EXPLORING

★ **Hearst Castle.** Hearst Castle, officially known as "Hearst San Simeon State Historical Monument," sits in solitary splendor atop La Cuesta Encantada (the Enchanted Hill). Its buildings and gardens spread over 127 acres that were the heart of newspaper magnate William Randolph Hearst's 250,000-acre ranch. Hearst devoted nearly 30 years and about $10 million to building this elaborate estate. He commissioned renowned architect Julia Morgan—who also designed buildings at the University of California at Berkeley—but he was very much involved with the final product, a hodgepodge of Italian, Spanish, Moorish, and French styles. The 115-room main building and three huge "cottages" are connected by terraces and staircases and surrounded by pools, gardens, and statuary. In its heyday the castle was a playground for Hearst and his guests, many of them Hollywood celebrities. Construction began in 1919 and was never officially completed. Work was halted in 1947 when Hearst had to leave San Simeon because of failing health. The Hearst family presented the property to the State of California in 1958.

Access to the castle is through the large visitor center at the foot of the hill, which contains a collection of Hearst memorabilia and a giant-screen theater that shows a 40-minute film giving a sanitized version of Hearst's life and of the castle's construction. Buses from the visitor center zigzag up the hillside to the neoclassical extravaganza, where guides conduct three different daytime tours of various parts of the estate: grand rooms, upstairs suites, and cottages and kitchen. Daytime tours take about two hours and include the movie. In spring and fall, docents in period costume portray Hearst's guests and staff for the slightly longer evening tour, which begins at sunset. All tours include a ½-mile walk and between 150 and 400 stairs. Reservations for the tours are highly recommended. ⊠ *San Simeon State Park, 750 Hearst Castle Rd.* ☎ *800/444–4445* ⊕ *www.hearstcastle.com* ✉ *Daytime tours $25, evening tours $36* ☉ *Tours daily 9–3:20, later in summer; additional tours take place most Fri. and Sat. evenings Mar.–May and Sept.–Dec.*

Old San Simeon. Turn west from Highway 1 across from the Hearst Castle entrance to see Old San Simeon, an 1850s whaling village that morphed into an outpost for Hearst employees. There's a one-room schoolhouse and Spanish-style buildings; don't miss Sebastian's General Store in an 1852 building. Now a state historic landmark, Sebastian's houses a store, a wine tasting room, and a café that serves excellent sandwiches and salads. ⊠ *West of Hwy. 1, across from Hearst Castle entrance.*

Piedras Blancas Elephant Seal Rookery. A large colony of elephant seals (at last count 15,000 members) gathers every year at Piedras Blancas Elephant Seal Rookery, on the beaches near Piedras Blancas Lighthouse. The huge males with their pendulous, trunklike noses typically start appearing on shore in late November, and the females begin to arrive in December to give birth—most babies are born in the last two weeks of January. The newborn pups spend about four weeks nursing before their mothers head out to sea, leaving them on their own; the "weaners" leave the rookery when they are about 3½ months old. The seals return in the spring and summer months to molt or rest, but not en masse as in winter. You can watch them from a boardwalk along the bluffs just a few feet above the beach; do not attempt to approach them, as they are wild animals. Docents are often on hand to give background information and statistics. The nonprofit Friends of the Elephant Seal runs a small visitor center and gift shop at its office, at 250 San Simeon Avenue in San Simeon. ⊠ *Off Hwy. 1, 4½ miles north of Hearst Castle, just south of Piedras Blancas Lighthouse* ☎ 805/924–1628 ⊕ *www. elephantseal.org.*

Piedras Blancas Light Station. If you think traversing craggy, twisting Highway 1 is tough, imagine trying to navigate a boat up the rocky coastline (piedras blancas means "white rocks" in Spanish) near San Simeon before lighthouses were built. Captains must have cheered wildly when the beam began to shine here in 1875. Try to time a visit to include a morning tour (reservations not required). ■ TIP➔ **Do not meet at the gate to the lighthouse—you'll miss the tour. Meet your guide instead at the former Piedras Blancas Motel, a mile and a half north of the light station.** ☎ 805/927–7361 ⊕ *piedrasblancas.org* ⊠ $10 ☉ *Tours at 9:45, mid-June–Aug. Mon–Sat.; Sept.–mid-June Tues., Thurs., and Sat.; no tours on national holidays* ↷ *No pets allowed.*

WHERE TO STAY

For expanded reviews, facilities, and current deals, visit Fodors.com.

$$
HOTEL
Best Western Cavalier Oceanfront Resort. Reasonable rates, an ocean-front location, evening bonfires, and well-equipped rooms—some with wood-burning fireplaces and private patios—make this motel one of the best choices in San Simeon. **Pros:** on the bluffs; fantastic views; close to Hearst Castle; bluff bonfires. **Cons:** room amenities and sizes vary; pools are small and sometimes crowded. **TripAdvisor:** "nice grounds," "the most relaxing ever," "breathtaking ocean views." ⑤ *Rooms from: $159* ⊠ *9415 Hearst Dr.* ☎ 805/927–4688, 800/826–8168 ⊕ *www. cavalierresort.com* ↷ *90 rooms.*

$$
HOTEL
The Morgan San Simeon. On the ocean side of Highway 1, near San Simeon restaurants and shops, the Morgan offers motel-style rooming options while paying tribute to Hearst Castle architect Julia Morgan. **Pros:** fascinating artwork; easy access to Hearst Castle and Highway 1; some ocean views. **Cons:** not right on beach; no fitness room or laundry facilities. **TripAdvisor:** "loved it," "big clean rooms," "wonderful stay."

⑤ *Rooms from: $149* ✉ *9135 Hearst Dr.* ☎ *805/927–3878, 800/451–9900* ⊕ *www.hotel-morgan.com* ⤵ *54 rooms, 1 suite* �ⓄⅠ *Breakfast.*

BIG SUR COASTLINE

Long a retreat of artists and writers, Big Sur is a place of ancient forests and rugged shoreline, stretching 90 miles from San Simeon to Carmel. Residents have protected it from overdevelopment, and much of the region lies within several state parks and the more than 165,000-acre Ventana Wilderness, itself part of the Los Padres National Forest.

ESSENTIALS

Visitor Information Big Sur Chamber of Commerce ☎ *831/667–2100* ⊕ *www.bigsurcalifornia.org.*

SOUTHERN BIG SUR

Hwy. 1 from San Simeon to Julia Pfeiffer Burns State Park.

This especially rugged stretch of oceanfront is a rocky world of mountains, cliffs, and beaches.

GETTING HERE AND AROUND

Highway 1 is the only major access route from north or south. From the south, access Highway 1 from U.S. 101 in San Luis Obispo. From the north, take rural routes Highway 46 West (Paso Robles to Cambria) or Highway 41 West (Atascadero to Morro Bay). Nacimiento-Fergusson Road snakes through mountains and forest from U.S. 101 at Jolon about 25 miles to Highway 1 at Kirk Creek, about 4 miles south of Lucia; this curving, at times precipitous road is a motorcyclist favorite, not recommended for the faint of heart or during inclement weather.

EXPLORING

Fodor'sChoice **Highway 1.** One of California's most spectacular drives, Highway 1
★ snakes up the coast north of San Simeon. Numerous pullouts along the way offer tremendous views and photo ops. On some of the beaches, huge elephant seals lounge nonchalantly, seemingly oblivious to the attention of rubberneckers—but keep your distance.

   CalTrans. In rainy seasons, portions of Highway 1 north and south of Big Sur are sometimes shut down by mud slides. Contact CalTrans for road conditions. ☎ *888/836–0866* ⊕ *www.dot.ca.gov.*

Jade Cove. In Los Padres National Forest just north of the town of Gorda is Jade Cove, a well-known jade-hunting spot. Rock hunting is allowed on the beach, but you may not remove anything from the walls of the cliffs. ✉ *Hwy. 1, 34 miles north of San Simeon.*

Julia Pfeiffer Burns State Park. Julia Pfeiffer Burns State Park provides some fine hiking, from an easy ½-mile stroll with marvelous coastal views to a strenuous 6-mile trek through the redwoods. The big attraction here, an 80-foot waterfall that drops into the ocean, gets crowded in summer; still, it's an astounding place to sit and contemplate nature. Migrating whales, harbor seals, and sea lions can sometimes be spotted not far from shore. ⊠ *Hwy. 1, 53 miles north of San Simeon, 15 miles north of Lucia* ☎ *831/667–2315* ⊕ *www.parks.ca.gov* ⌑ *$10* ☉ *Daily sunrise–sunset.*

WHERE TO STAY

For expanded reviews, facilities, and current deals, visit Fodors.com.

$$
HOTEL

⌑ **Ragged Point Inn.** At this cliff-top resort—the only inn and restaurant for miles around—glass walls in most rooms open to awesome, unobstructed ocean views. **Pros:** on the cliffs; great food; idyllic views. **Cons:** busy road stop during the day; often booked for weekend weddings. **TripAdvisor:** "very cool," "all about the location and the views," "beautiful place to get away." ⑤ *Rooms from: $169* ⊠ *19019 Hwy. 1, 20 miles north of San Simeon, Ragged Point* ☎ *805/927–4502, 805/927–5708 restaurant* ⊕ *raggedpointinn.com* ↬ *30 rooms.*

$$$
RESORT

⌑ **Treebones Resort.** Perched on a hilltop, surrounded by national forest and stunning, unobstructed ocean views, this yurt resort opened in 2004. **Pros:** 360-degree views; spacious pool area; comfortable beds. **Cons:** steep paths; no private bathrooms; more than a mile to the nearest store; not good for families with young children. **TripAdvisor:** "perfect way to commune with nature," "great accommodations," "given me vitality." ⑤ *Rooms from: $189* ⊠ *71895 Hwy. 1, Willow Creek Rd., 32 miles north of San Simeon, 1 mile north of Gorda* ☎ *805/927–2390, 877/424–4787* ⊕ *www.treebonesresort.com* ↬ *16 yurts, 5 campsites, 1 human nest w/campsite* ❍❘ *Breakfast.*

CENTRAL BIG SUR

Hwy. 1, from Partington Cove to Bixby Bridge.

The countercultural spirit of Big Sur—which instead of a conventional town is a loose string of coast-hugging properties along Highway 1—is alive and well today. Its few residents include the very wealthy, the enthusiastically outdoorsy, and the thoroughly evolved: since the 1960s the Esalen Institute, a center for alternative education and East–West philosophical study, has attracted seekers of higher consciousness and devotees of the property's hot springs. Today, posh and rustic resorts hidden among the redwoods cater to visitors drawn from near and far by the extraordinary scenery and serene isolation.

GETTING HERE AND AROUND

From the north, follow Highway 1 south from Carmel. From the south, continue the drive north from Julia Pfeiffer Burns State Park *(above)* on Highway 1. Monterey-Salinas Transit operates the Line 22 Big Sur bus from Monterey and Carmel to Central Big Sur (the last top is Nepenthe), daily from late May to early September and weekends only the rest of the year.

Bus Contact Monterey-Salinas Transit ☎ *888/678–2871* ⊕ *www.mst.org.*

EXPLORING

Bixby Creek Bridge. The graceful arc of Bixby Creek Bridge is a photographer's dream. Built in 1932, it spans a deep canyon, more than 100 feet wide at the bottom. From the parking area on the north side you can admire the view or walk across the 550-foot span. ⊠ *Hwy. 1, 6 miles north of Point Sur State Historic Park, 13 miles south of Carmel.*

Pfeiffer Big Sur State Park. Among the many hiking trails at Pfeiffer Big Sur State Park, a short route through a redwood-filled valley leads to a waterfall. You can double back or continue on the more difficult trail along the valley wall for views over miles of treetops to the sea. Stop in at the Big Sur Station visitor center, off Highway 1, less than ½ mile south of the park entrance, for information about the entire area; it's open Wednesday to Sunday from 9 to 4. ⊠ *47225 Hwy. 1* 📷 *831/667-2315* ⊕ *www.parks.ca.gov* ⌇ *$10 per vehicle* ⊙ *Daily dawn–dusk.*

★   **Point Sur State Historic Park.** An 1889 lighthouse still stands watch from atop a large volcanic rock at this state park. Four lighthouse keepers lived here with their families until 1974, when the light station became automated. Their homes and working spaces are open to the public only on 2½- to 3-hour ranger-led tours. Considerable walking, including up two stairways, is involved. Strollers are not allowed. ⊠ *Hwy. 1, 7 miles north of Pfeiffer Big Sur State Park* 📷 *831/625–4419* ⊕ *www.pointsur. org* ⌇ *$10* ⊙ *Tours generally Nov.–Mar., weekends at 10, Wed. at 1; Apr.–Oct., Sat. and Wed. at 10 and 2, Sun. at 10; call to confirm.*

BEACHES

Pfeiffer Beach. Through a hole in one of the gigantic boulders at secluded Pfeiffer Beach, you can watch the waves break first on the sea side and then on the beach side. Keep a sharp eye out for the unsigned, ungated road to the beach: it branches west of Highway 1 between the post office and Pfeiffer Big Sur State Park. The 2-mile, one-lane road descends sharply. **Amenities:** parking (fee); toilets. **Best For:** solitude; sunset. ⊠ *Off Hwy. 1, 1 mile south of Pfeiffer Big Sur State Park* ⌇ *$5 per vehicle per day* ⊙ *Daily 9–8.*

WHERE TO EAT

$$$ ✕ **Deetjen's Big Sur Inn.** The candlelighted, creaky-floor restaurant in the
AMERICAN   main house at the historic inn of the same name is a Big Sur institution. It serves spicy seafood paella, steak, and rack of lamb for dinner and wonderfully flavorful eggs Benedict for breakfast. The chef procures much of the fish, meats, and produce from purveyors who practice sustainable farming and fishing practices. ⑤ *Average main: $30* ⊠ *Hwy. 1, 3½ mile south of Pfeiffer Big Sur State Park* 📷 *831/667–2377* ⊕ *www. deetjens.com* ⊙ *No lunch.*

$$$ ✕ **Nepenthe.** It may be that no other restaurant between San Francisco
AMERICAN   and Los Angeles has a better coastal view than Nepenthe. The food and drink are overpriced but good; there are burgers, sandwiches, and salads for lunch, and fresh fish and hormone-free steaks for dinner. For the real show, settle on the terraced deck in the late afternoon, order a glass from the extensive wine list, and watch the sun slip into the Pacific Ocean. The less expensive, outdoor Café Kevah serves brunch and lunch. ⑤ *Average main: $26* ⊠ *Hwy. 1, 2½ miles south of Big Sur Station* 📷 *831/667–2345* ⊕ *www.nepenthebigsur.com.*

$$$$ ✕ **The Restaurant at Ventana.** The redwood, copper, and cedar elements at
AMERICAN   the Ventana Inn's restaurant pay tribute to the historic natural setting,

while gleaming new fixtures and dining accoutrements place the facility firmly in the 21st century. Chef Truman Jones's seasonal menu showcases meat, fish, and produce—such as rabbit loin, California white sea bass, artichokes, and abalone—grown or caught in California. (Much of the produce comes from the restaurant's organic vegetable garden.) A full slate of regional and international wines complements his dishes. The restaurant is also open for lunch. If the day is sunny, ask for a table on the outdoor terrace and take in the ocean views. $ *Average main: $36* ⊠ *Hwy. 1, 1½ miles south of Pfeiffer Big Sur State Park* ☎ *831/667–2242* ⊕ *www.ventanainn.com* ⌔ *Reservations essential.*

$$$$
AMERICAN
✕ **Sierra Mar.** Ocean-view dining doesn't get much better than this. Perched at cliff's edge 1,200 feet above the Pacific at the ultra-chic Post Ranch Inn, Sierra Mar serves cutting-edge American food made from mostly organic, seasonal ingredients. The four-course prix-fixe option is stellar. The restaurant's wine list is one of the most extensive in the nation. $ *Average main: $90* ⊠ *Hwy. 1, 1½ miles south of Pfeiffer Big Sur State Park* ☎ *831/667–2800* ⌔ *Reservations essential.*

WHERE TO STAY
For expanded reviews, facilities, and current deals, visit Fodors.com.

$$$
HOTEL
🏨 **Big Sur Lodge.** Modern motel-style cottages with Mission-style furnishings and vaulted ceilings sit in a meadow, surrounded by trees and flowering shrubbery. **Pros:** near trailheads; good camping alternative. **Cons:** basic rooms; walk to main lodge. **TripAdvisor:** "Spartan but comfortable," "spectacular setting," "good restaurant." $ *Rooms from: $199* ⊠ *Pfeiffer Big Sur State Park, 47225 Hwy. 1* ☎ *831/667–3100, 800/424–4787* ⊕ *www.bigsurlodge.com* ⌔ *61 rooms.*

$
B&B/INN
🏨 **Deetjen's Big Sur Inn.** This historic 1930s Norwegian-style property is endearingly rustic and charming, especially if you're willing to go with a camplike flow. **Pros:** surrounded by Big Sur history; tons of character; wooded grounds. **Cons:** rustic; thin walls; some rooms don't have private baths. **TripAdvisor:** "bucolic charm," "rustic bliss," "so romantic." $ *Rooms from: $105* ⊠ *Hwy. 1, 3½ miles south of Pfeiffer Big Sur State Park* ☎ *831/667–2377* ⊕ *www.deetjens.com* ⌔ *20 rooms, 15 with bath.*

$$$$
HOTEL
🏨 **Glen Oaks Big Sur.** At this rustic-modern cluster of adobe-and-redwood buildings in the heart of Big Sur, you can choose between motel-style rooms and cottages in the woods. **Pros:** in the heart of town; walking distance of restaurants. **Cons:** near busy road and parking lot; no TVs. **TripAdvisor:** "contemporary and cozy gem," "relaxing and welcoming," "best little cabin in the woods." $ *Rooms from: $275* ⊠ *Hwy. 1, 1 mile north of Pfeiffer Big Sur State Park* ☎ *831/667–2105* ⊕ *www.glenoaksbigsur.com* ⌔ *16 rooms, 2 cottages, 7 cabins.*

$$$$
RESORT
Fodor's Choice
★
🏨 **Post Ranch Inn.** This luxurious retreat, designed exclusively for adult getaways, has remarkably environmentally conscious architecture. **Pros:** world-class resort; spectacular views; gorgeous property with hiking trails. **Cons:** expensive; austere design; not a good choice if you're scared of heights. **TripAdvisor:** "a special retreat," "this is the best," "bliss." $ *Rooms from: $700* ⊠ *Hwy. 1, 1½ miles south of Pfeiffer Big*

5

Sur State Park ☎ 831/667–2200, 888/524–4787 ⊕ *www.postranchinn. com* ☞ *39 units* ⊚| *Breakfast.*

$$$$ 🖵 **Ventana Inn & Spa.** Hundreds of celebrities, from Oprah Winfrey to
HOTEL   Sir Anthony Hopkins, have escaped to Ventana, a romantic resort on
Fodor's Choice   243 tranquil acres 1,200 feet above the Pacific. **Pros:** nature trails every-
★   where; great food; secluded. **Cons:** simple breakfast; some rooms have
no ocean view. **TripAdvisor:** "really neat place," "absolutely lovely,"
"beautiful." ⑤ *Rooms from: $600* ⊠ *Hwy. 1, almost 1 mile south of
Pfeiffer Big Sur State Park* ☎ 831/667–2331, 800/628–6500 ⊕ *www.
ventanainn.com* ☞ *25 rooms, 31 suites* ⊚| *Breakfast.*

Channel Islands
National Park

WORD OF MOUTH

"Channel Island park is unique and very undeveloped very nice if you are into ecotravel. There will probably be lots of whale-watching in that area in December . . . might be nice!"

—Lisa_Foley

WELCOME TO CHANNEL ISLANDS NATIONAL PARK

TOP REASONS TO GO

★ **Rare flora and fauna:** The Channel Islands are home to 145 species of terrestrial plants and animals found nowhere else on Earth.

★ **Time travel:** With no cars, phones, or services, these undeveloped islands provide a glimpse of what California was like hundreds of years ago, away from hectic modern life.

★ **Underwater adventures:** The incredibly healthy channel waters rank among the top 10 diving destinations on the planet—but you can also visit the kelp forest virtually via an underwater video program.

★ **Marvelous marine mammals:** More than 30 species of seals, sea lions, whales, and other marine mammals ply the park's waters at various times of year.

★ **Sea-cave kayaking:** Paddle around otherwise inaccessible portions of the park's 175 miles of gorgeous coastline—including one of the world's largest sea caves.

1 **Anacapa.** Tiny Anacapa is a 5-mile stretch of three islets, with towering cliffs, caves, natural bridges, and rich kelp forests.

2 **San Miguel.** Isolated, windswept San Miguel, the park's westernmost island, has an ancient caliche forest and hundreds of archaeological sites chronicling the Chumash Indians' 11,000-year history on the island. More than 100,000 pinnipeds (seals and sea lions) hang out on the island's beaches during certain times of year.

3 **Santa Barbara.** Nearly 6 miles of scenic trails crisscross this tiny island, known for its excellent wildlife viewing and native plants. It's a favorite destination for diving, snorkeling, and kayaking.

Goleta

Montecito

Santa Barbara

Goleta Point

Carpinteria

SANTA YNEZ MOUNTAINS

154

150

33

101

126

Ventura

Visitor Center

El Rio

101

6

Oxnard

Point Mugu

1

Channel

Painted Cave

Scorpion Ranch

San Pedro Point

Summit Peak 936 ft

Prisoners Harbor

4

Light Station & Museum

Anacapa Island

Mount Diablo 2,450 ft

Main Ranch

Central Valley

Smugglers Cove

Santa Cruz Island

Morse Point

Anacapa Passage

0   10 mi

0   10 km

Santa Barbara island is approximately 52 miles southeast of Santa Cruz Island

Santa Barbara Island Light

3

Santa Barbara Island

GETTING ORIENTED

Channel Islands National Park includes five of the eight Channel Islands and the one nautical mile of ocean that surrounds them. Six nautical miles of surrounding channel waters are designated a National Marine Sanctuary and are teeming with life, including dolphins, whales, seals, sea lions, and seabirds. The islands range in size from 1-square-mile Santa Barbara to 96-square-mile Santa Cruz. Together they form a magnificent nature preserve with 145 endemic or unique species of plants and animals.

4 Santa Cruz. The park's largest island offers some of the best hikes and kayaking opportunities, one of the world's largest and deepest sea caves, and more species of flora and fauna than any other park island.

5 Santa Rosa. Campers love to stay on Santa Rosa, with its myriad hiking opportunities, stunning white-sand beaches, and rare grove of Torrey pines. It's also the only island accessible by plane.

Updated
by Cheryl
Crabtree

On crystal-clear days the craggy peaks of the Channel Islands are easy to see from the mainland, jutting from the Pacific in such sharp detail it seems you could reach out and touch them. The islands really aren't that far away—a high-speed boat will whisk you to the closest ones in less than an hour—yet very few people ever visit them. Those fearless, adventurous types who do will experience one of the most splendid land-and-sea wilderness areas on the planet.

CHANNEL ISLANDS PLANNER

WHEN TO GO

Channel Islands National Park records about 620,000 visitors each year, but many never venture beyond the visitor center. The busiest times are holidays and summer weekends; if you're going then, make your transportation and accommodations arrangements in advance.

The warm, dry summer and fall months are the best time to go camping. Humpback and blue whales arrive to feed from late June through early fall. The rains usually come from December through March—but this is also the best time to spot gray whales and to get discounts at area hotels. In the late spring, thousands of migratory birds descend on the islands to hatch their young, and wildflowers carpet the slopes. The water temperature is nearly always cool, so bring a wet suit if you plan to spend much time in the ocean, even in the summer. Fog, high winds, and rough seas can happen any time of the year.

GETTING HERE AND AROUND

AIR TRAVEL

Channel Islands Aviation flies solely to Santa Rosa Island. You can catch a flight to Santa Rosa Island from the Camarillo Airport, near Oxnard, and the Santa Barbara Airport.

Channel Islands Aviation. Channel Islands Aviation provides day excursions, surf fishing, and camper transportation year-round, flying from Camarillo Airport, about 10 miles east of Oxnard, to an airstrip on Santa Rosa (25-minute flight). The operator will also pick up groups of six or more at Santa Barbara Airport. ⊠ *305 Durley Ave., Camarillo* ☎ *805/987–1301* ⊕ *www.flycia.com* ✉ *$160 per person, $300 per person if camping.*

BOAT TRAVEL
The visitor center for Channel Islands National Park is on California's mainland, in the town of Ventura, off U.S. 101. From the harbors at Ventura, Santa Barbara, and Oxnard you can board a boat to one of the islands. If you have your own boat, you can land at any of the islands, but each island has certain closed and restricted areas, so boaters should visit the park website for instructions. Boaters landing at San Miguel must contact the park ranger beforehand.

Island Packers. Sailing on high-speed catamarans from Ventura or a mono-hull vessel from Oxnard, Island Packers goes to Santa Cruz Island daily most of the year, weather permitting. The boats also go to Anacapa several days a week, and to the outer islands two weekends a month, from May through October. They also cruise along Anacapa's north shore on three-hour wildlife tours (non-landing) several times a week. ⊠ *3600 S. Harbor Blvd., Oxnard* ☎ *805/642–1393* ⊕ *www. islandpackers.com* ⊠ *1691 Spinnaker Dr., Ventura* ☎ *805/642–1393* ⊕ *www.islandpackers.com* ✉ *$33–$140.*

CAR TRAVEL
To reach the Ventura harbor, exit U.S. 101 in Ventura at Seaward Boulevard or Victoria Avenue and follow the signs to Ventura Harbor/Spinnaker Drive. To access Channel Islands Harbor in Oxnard, exit U.S. 101 at Victoria Avenue and head south approximately 7 miles to Channel Islands Boulevard. To access dive and whale-watching boats in Santa Barbara, exit U.S. 101 at Castillo Street and head south to Cabrillo Boulevard, then turn right for the harbor entrance. Private vehicles are not permitted on the islands. Pets are also not allowed in the park.

PARK ESSENTIALS
PARK FEES AND PERMITS
There is no fee to enter Channel Islands National Park, but unless you have your own boat, you will pay $33 or more per person for a ride with a boat operator. The cost of taking a boat to the park varies depending on which operator you choose. Also, there is a $15-per-day fee for staying in one of the islands' campgrounds.

If you take your own boat, landing permits are not required to visit Channel Islands National Park. If you anchor in a nearby cove, at least one person should remain aboard the boat at all times. Boaters who want to land on the Nature Conservancy preserve on Santa Cruz Island should visit ⊕ *www.nature.org/cruzpermit* for permit information; allow 10 to 15 business days to process and return your permit application. To hike on San Miguel, call ☎ *805/658–5711* to be matched up with a ranger, who must accompany you there. Anglers must have a state fishing license; for details, call the California Department of

Fish and Game at ☎ *916/653–7664* or visit ⊕ *www.dfg.ca.gov.* Thirteen Marine Protected Areas (MPAs) with special resource protection regulations surround the islands, so read the guidelines carefully before you depart.

PARK HOURS

The islands are open every day of the year. Channel Islands National Park Visitor Center in Ventura is closed on Thanksgiving and Christmas. Channel Islands National Park is located in the Pacific time zone.

VISITOR INFORMATION

PARK CONTACT INFORMATION

Channel Islands National Park Visitor Center ⊠ *1901 Spinnaker Dr., Ventura* ☎ *805/658–5730* ⊕ *www.nps.gov/chis.*

VISITOR CENTERS

Channel Islands National Park Robert J. Lagomarsino Visitor Center. The park's main visitor center has a museum, a bookstore, a three-story observation tower with telescopes, and exhibits about the islands. There's also a marine life exhibit where you can see sea stars clinging to rocks, anemones waving their colorful, spiny tentacles, and a brilliant orange Garibaldi darting around. The center also has full-size reproductions of a male northern elephant seal and the pygmy mammoth skeleton unearthed on Santa Rosa Island in 1994. Rangers lead various free public programs describing park resources on weekends and holidays at 11 and 3; they can also give you a detailed map and trip-planning packet if you're interested in visiting the actual islands. In summer you can watch live ranger broadcasts of underwater dives and hikes on Anacapa Island, shown at the center Wednesday through Saturday (hike at 11, dive at 2). ⊠ *1901 Spinnaker Dr., Ventura* ☎ *805/658–5730* ⊕ *www. nps.gov/chis* ⊗ *Daily 8:30–5.*

EXPLORING

THE ISLANDS

Anacapa Island. Although most people think of it as an island, Anacapa Island is actually comprised of three narrow islets. The tips of these volcanic formations nearly touch but are inaccessible from one another except by boat. All three islets have towering cliffs, isolated sea caves, and natural bridges; Arch Rock, on East Anacapa, is one of the best-known symbols of Channel Islands National Park. Wildlife viewing is the reason most people come to East Anacapa—particularly in summer when seagull chicks are newly hatched and sea lions and seals lounge on the beaches. Trips to Middle Anacapa Island require a ranger escort.

The compact **museum** on East Anacapa tells the history of the island and houses, among other things, the original lead-crystal Fresnel lens from the island's 1932 lighthouse.

Depending on the season and the number of desirable species lurking about there, a limited number of boats travel to **Frenchy's Cove** at West Anacapa, where there are pristine tide pools where you might see anemones, limpets, barnacles, mussel beds, and colorful marine algae. The rest of West Anacapa is closed to protect nesting brown pelicans.

San Miguel Island. The westernmost of the Channel Islands, San Miguel Island is frequently battered by storms sweeping across the North Pacific. The 15-square-mile island's wild, windswept landscape is lush with vegetation. Point Bennett, at the western tip, offers one of the world's most spectacular wildlife displays when more than 100,000 pinnipeds hit its beach. Explorer Juan Rodríguez Cabrillo was the first European to visit this island; he claimed it for Spain in 1542. Legend holds that Cabrillo died on one of the Channel Islands—no one knows where he's buried, but there's a memorial to him on a bluff above Cuyler Harbor.

> **PLANTS AND WILDLIFE ON THE CHANNEL ISLANDS**
>
> The Channel Islands National Park is home to species found nowhere else on Earth: mammals such as the island fox and the island deer mouse and birds like the island scrub jay live forever on the endangered species list. Thousands of western gulls hatch each summer on Anacapa, then fly off to the mainland where they spend about four years learning all their bad habits. Then they return to the island to roost and have chicks of their own.

Santa Barbara Island. At about 1 square mile, Santa Barbara Island is the smallest of the Channel Islands and nearly 35 miles south of the others. Triangular in shape, Santa Barbara's steep cliffs—which offer a perfect nesting spot for the Xantus's murrelet, a rare seabird—are topped by twin peaks. In spring, you can enjoy a brilliant display of yellow coreopsis. Learn about the wildlife on and around the islands at the island's small museum.

★ **Santa Cruz Island.** Five miles west of Anacapa, 96-square-mile Santa Cruz Island is the largest of the Channel Islands. The National Park Service manages the easternmost 24% of the island; the rest is owned by the Nature Conservancy, which requires a permit to land. When your boat drops you off on the 70 miles of craggy coastline, you see two rugged mountain ranges with peaks soaring to 2,500 feet and deep canyons traversed by streams. This landscape is the habitat of a remarkable variety of flora and fauna—more than 600 types of plants, 140 kinds of land birds, 11 mammal species, five varieties of reptiles, and three amphibian species live here. Bird-watchers may want to look for the endemic island scrub jay, which is found nowhere else in the world.

The largest and deepest sea cave in the world, **Painted Cave,** lies along the northwest coast of Santa Cruz. Named for the colorful lichen and algae that cover its walls, Painted Cave is nearly ¼ mile long and 100 feet wide. In spring a waterfall cascades over the entrance. Kayakers may encounter seals or sea lions cruising alongside their boats inside the cave. The Channel Islands hold some of the richest archaeological resources in North America; all artifacts are protected within the park. Remnants of a dozen Chumash villages can be seen on the island. The largest of these villages, at the eastern end of the island, occupied the area now called **Scorpion Ranch.** The Chumash mined extensive chert deposits on the island for tools to produce shell-bead money, which they traded with people on the mainland. You can learn about Chumash history and view artifacts, tools, and exhibits on native plant and wildlife at the interpretive visitor center near the landing dock. Visitors can also explore remnants of the early-1900s ranching era in the restored historic adobe and outbuildings.

Santa Rosa Island. Set between Santa Cruz and San Miguel, Santa Rosa Island is the second largest of the Channel Islands and has a relatively low profile, broken by a central mountain range rising to 1,589 feet. The coastal areas range from broad sandy beaches to sheer cliffs. The island is home to about 500 species of plants, including the rare Torrey pine. Three unusual mammals—the endemic island fox, spotted skunk, and deer mouse—are among those that make their home here. They hardly compare to the mammoths that once roamed the island; a nearly complete skeleton of a 6-foot-tall pygmy mammoth was unearthed here in 1994.

SPORTS AND THE OUTDOORS

DIVING

Some of the best snorkeling and diving in the world can be found in the cool waters surrounding the Channel Islands. The best time to scuba dive is in the summer and fall, when the water is often clear up to a 100-foot depth.

KAYAKING

The most remote parts of the Channel Islands are accessible only by a sea kayak. Some of the best kayaking in the park can be found on Anacapa, Santa Barbara, and the eastern tip of Santa Cruz. It's too far to kayak from the mainland out to the islands, but outfitters have tours that take you to the islands. Tours are offered year-round, but high seas may cause trip cancellations between December and March. ⚠ Channel waters can be unpredictable and challenging. Don't venture out alone unless you are an experienced kayaker; guided trips are highly recommended.

WHALE-WATCHING

About a third of the world's cetacean species (27 to be exact) can be seen in the Santa Barbara Channel. In July and August, humpback and blue whales feed off the north shore of Santa Rosa. From late December through March, up to 10,000 gray whales pass through the Santa Barbara Channel on their way from Alaska to Mexico and back again, and on a whale-watching trip during this time frame, you should see one or more of them. Other types of whales, but fewer in number, swim the channel June through August.

7

The Monterey Bay Area

FROM CARMEL TO SANTA CRUZ

WORD OF MOUTH

"To be able to see, up close, the wonders of the ocean, is an amazing experience at the wonderful Monterey Bay Aquarium."
—photo by mellifluous, Fodors.com member

WELCOME TO THE MONTEREY BAY AREA

TOP REASONS TO GO

★ **Marine life:** Monterey Bay is the location of the world's third-largest marine sanctuary, home to whales, otters, and other underwater creatures.

★ **Getaway central:** For more than a century, urbanites have come to the Monterey Bay area to unwind, relax, and have fun. It's a great place to browse unique shops and galleries, ride a giant roller coaster, or play a round of golf on a world-class course.

★ **Nature preserves:** More than the sea is protected here—the region boasts nearly 30 state parks, beaches, and preserves, fantastic places for walking, jogging, hiking, and biking.

★ **Wine and dine:** The area's rich agricultural bounty translates to abundant fresh produce, great wines, and fabulous dining. It's no wonder more than 300 culinary events take place here every year.

★ **Small-town vibes:** Even the cities here are friendly, walkable places where you'll feel like a local.

1 Carmel and Pacific Grove. Exclusive Carmel-by-the-Sea and Carmel Valley Village burst with historic charm, fine dining, and unusual boutiques that cater to celebrity residents and well-heeled visitors. Nearby 17-Mile Drive—quite possibly the prettiest stretch of road you'll ever travel—runs between Carmel-by-the-Sea and Victorian-studded Pacific Grove, home to thousands of migrating monarch butterflies between October and February.

2 Monterey. A former Spanish military outpost, Monterey's well-preserved historic district is a hands-on history lesson. Cannery Row, the former center of Monterey's once-thriving sardine industry, has been reborn as a tourist attraction with shops, restaurants, hotels, and the Monterey Bay Aquarium.

3 Around Monterey Bay. Much of California's lettuce, berries, artichokes, and Brussels sprouts come from Salinas and Watsonville. Salinas is also home of the National Steinbeck Center, and Moss Landing and Watsonville encompass pristine wildlife wetlands. Aptos, Capitola, and Soquel are former lumber towns that became popular seaside resorts more than a century ago. Today they're filled with antiques shops, restaurants, and wine-tasting rooms; you'll also find some of the bay's best beaches along the shore here.

4 Santa Cruz. Santa Cruz shows its colors along an old-time beach boardwalk and municipal wharf. A University of California campus imbues the town with arts and culture and a liberal mind-set.

The Forest of Nisene Marks State Park

152

quel
Aptos
Capitola
Rio
del Mar
Soquel Cove
Freedom

1

Watsonville
129
Pajaro

Las Lomas

M O N T E R E Y   B A Y

3

1

Moss Landing
Prunedale

156

Castroville
101

Salinas R.

1

183

S A L I N A S

Marina
Salinas
G17

V A L L E Y

Spreckels

Point
Pinos

sh Bay
Pacific
Grove
Seaside
Sand City

17 Mile Dr.

1

Monterey 2
Del Rey Oaks
68

*press
nt*
68
Pebble
Beach

68

S I E R R A   D E   S A L I N A S

Carmel
G16
Carmel Valley Rd.
G20

*Carmel
Bay
oint
os*

1

Carmel River

Carmel
Highlands

G16
Carmel
Valley

GETTING ORIENTED

North of Big Sur the coast-line softens into lower bluffs, windswept dunes, pristine estuaries, and long, sandy beaches, bordering one of the world's most amazing marine environ-ments—the Monterey Bay. On the Monterey Peninsula, at the southern end of the bay, are Carmel-by-the-Sea, Pacific Grove, and Monterey; Santa Cruz sits at the northern tip of the crescent. In between, Highway 1 cruises along the coastline, passing wind-swept beaches piled high with sand dunes. Along the route are wetlands, artichoke and strawberry fields, and workaday towns such as Castroville and Watsonville.

7

Updated by Cheryl Crabtree

Natural beauty is at the heart of this region's enormous appeal—you sense it everywhere, whether you're exploring one of Monterey Bay's attractive coast-side towns, relaxing at a luxurious resort, or touring the coast on the lookout for marine life.

It's been this way for a long time: an abiding current of plenty runs through the region's history. Military buffs see it in centuries' worth of battles for control of the rich territory. John Steinbeck saw it in the success of a community built on the elbow grease of farm laborers in the Salinas Valley and fishermen along Cannery Row. Biologists see it in the ocean's potential as a more sustainable source of food.

Downtown Carmel-by-the-Sea and Monterey are walks through history. The bay itself is protected by the Monterey Bay National Marine Sanctuary, the nation's largest undersea canyon—bigger and deeper than the Grand Canyon. And of course, the backdrop of natural beauty is still everywhere to be seen.

MONTEREY BAY PLANNER

WHEN TO GO

Summer is peak season; mild weather brings in big crowds. In this coastal region, a cool breeze generally blows and fog often rolls in from offshore; you will frequently need a sweater or windbreaker. Off-season, from November through April, fewer people visit and the mood is mellower. Rainfall is heaviest in January and February, but autumn through spring days are crystal clear more often than in summer.

GETTING HERE AND AROUND

AIR TRAVEL

Monterey Peninsula Airport, 3 miles east of downtown Monterey off Highway 68, is served by Alaska, Allegiant, American Eagle, United/United Express, and US Airways. Taxi service to downtown runs about $15 to $17; to Carmel the fare is $23 to $32. To and from San Jose International Airport and San Francisco International Airport, Monterey Airbus starts at $35 and the Early Bird Airport Shuttle runs $75 to $190.

Airport Contacts Monterey Regional Airport ✉ *200 Fred Kane Dr., at Olmsted Rd., off Hwy. 68, Monterey* ☎ *831/648–7000* ⊕ *www.montereyairport.com.*

Ground Transportation Central Coast Cab Company ☎ *831/626–3333.* **Early Bird Airport Shuttle** ☎ *831/462–3933* ⊕ *www.earlybirdairportshuttle.com.* **Monterey Airbus** ☎ *831/373-7777* ⊕ *www.montereyairbus.com.* **Yellow Cab** ☎ *831/646–1234.*

BUS TRAVEL

Greyhound serves Santa Cruz and Salinas from San Francisco and San Jose. The trips take about 3 and 4½ hours, respectively. Monterey-Salinas Transit (MST) provides frequent service in Monterey County (fares $1 to $3; day pass $8), and Santa Cruz METRO ($2; day pass $10) buses operate throughout Santa Cruz County. You can switch between the two lines in Watsonville, in southern Santa Cruz County.

Bus Contacts Greyhound ☎ *800/231–2222* ⊕ *www.greyhound.com.* **Monterey-Salinas Transit** ☎ *888/678–2871* ⊕ *www.mst.org.*

CAR TRAVEL

Highway 1 runs south–north along the coast, linking the towns of Carmel-by-the-Sea, Monterey, and Santa Cruz; some sections have only two lanes. The freeway, U.S. 101, lies to the east, roughly parallel to Highway 1. The two roads are connected by Highway 68 from Pacific Grove to Salinas; Highway 156 from Castroville to Prunedale; Highway 152 from Watsonville to Gilroy; and Highway 17 from Santa Cruz to San Jose. ⚠ **Traffic near Santa Cruz can crawl to a standstill during commuter hours. In the morning, avoid traveling between 7 and 9; in the afternoon avoid traveling between 4 and 7.**

The drive south from San Francisco to Monterey can be made comfortably in three hours or less. The most scenic way is to follow Highway 1 down the coast past flower, pumpkin, and artichoke fields and small seaside communities. Unless you drive on sunny weekends when locals are heading for the beach, the two-lane coast highway may take no longer than the freeway. A sometimes-faster route is Interstate 280 south from San Francisco to Highway 17, north of San Jose.

From Los Angeles the drive to Monterey can be made in five to six hours by heading north on U.S. 101 to Salinas and then west on Highway 68. You can also follow Highway 1 all or part of the way north from Southern California.

TRAIN TRAVEL

Amtrak's *Coast Starlight* runs between Los Angeles, Oakland, and Seattle. From the train station in Salinas, you can connect with buses serving Carmel, Monterey, and Santa Cruz.

Train Contacts Amtrak ☎ *800/872-7245* ⊕ *www.amtrakcalifornia.com.*

TOUR OPTIONS

California Parlor Car Tours operates motor-coach tours from San Francisco that include one or two days in Monterey and Carmel. Ag Venture Tours runs wine-tasting, sightseeing, and agricultural tours to several towns.

Tour Contacts Ag Venture Tours ☎ *831/761–8463* ⊕ *www.agventuretours. com.* **California Parlor Car Tours** ☎ *415/474–7500, 800/227–4250* ⊕ *www. calpartours.com.*

RESTAURANTS

The Monterey Bay area is a culinary paradise. The surrounding waters are full of fish, wild game roams the foothills, and the inland valleys are some of the most fertile in the country—local chefs draw on this bounty for their fresh, truly Californian cuisine. Except at beachside stands and inexpensive eateries, where anything goes, casual but neat dress is the norm. *Prices in the restaurant reviews are the average cost of a main course at dinner or, if dinner is not served, at lunch (excluding sales tax).*

HOTELS

Accommodations in the Monterey area range from no-frills motels to luxurious hotels. Pacific Grove, amply endowed with ornate Victorian houses, is the region's B&B capital; Carmel also has charming inns. Lavish resorts cluster in exclusive Pebble Beach and pastoral Carmel Valley.

High season runs from April through October. Rates in winter, especially at the larger hotels, may drop by 50% or more, and B&Bs often offer midweek specials. Whatever the month, some properties require a two-night stay on weekends. *Prices in the hotel reviews are the lowest cost of a standard double room in high season. For expanded reviews, facilities, and current deals, visit Fodors.com.* △ Many of the fancier accommodations aren't suitable for children; if you're traveling with kids, ask before you book.

Lodging Contact Bed and Breakfast Inns of Santa Cruz County. This association of innkeepers can help you find a bed-and-breakfast. ⊕ *www. santacruzbnb.com.*

VISITOR INFORMATION

Contacts Monterey County Convention & Visitors Bureau ☎ *877/666–8373* ⊕ *www.seemonterey.com.* **Monterey County Vintners and Growers Association** ☎ *831/375–9400* ⊕ *www.montereywines.org.* **Santa Cruz County Conference and Visitors Council** ✉ *303 Water St., Santa Cruz* ☎ *831/425–1234, 800/833–3494* ⊕ *www.santacruz.org.* **Santa Cruz Mountain Winegrowers Association** ✉ *7605-A Old Dominion Ct., Aptos* ☎ *831/685–8463* ⊕ *www. scmwa.com.*

CARMEL AND PACIFIC GROVE

As Highway 1 swings inland about 30 miles north of Big Sur, historic Carmel-by-the-Sea anchors the southern entry to the Monterey Peninsula—a gorgeous promontory at the southern tip of Monterey Bay. Just north of Carmel along the coast, the legendary 17-Mile Drive wends its way through private Pebble Beach and the town of Pacific Grove.

Highway 1 skirts the peninsula to the east with more direct access to Pebble Beach and Pacific Grove.

CARMEL-BY-THE-SEA

26 miles north of Big Sur on Hwy. 1.

Although the community has grown quickly through the years and its population quadruples with tourists on weekends and in summer, Carmel-by-the-Sea, commonly referred to as Carmel, retains its identity as a quaint village. Self-consciously charming, the town is populated by many celebrities, major and minor, and has its share of quirky ordinances. For instance, women wearing high heels do not have the right to pursue legal action if they trip and fall on the cobblestone streets, and drivers who hit a tree and leave the scene are charged with hit-and-run.

Buildings have no street numbers (street names are written on discreet white posts) and consequently no mail delivery (if you want to see the locals, go to the post office). Artists started this community, and their legacy is evident in the numerous galleries.

GETTING HERE AND AROUND

From north or south follow Highway 1 to Carmel. Head west at Ocean Avenue to reach the main village hub. In summer the MST Carmel-by-the-Sea Trolley loops around town to the beach and mission every 30 minutes or so.

TOURS

For insight into Carmel's history and culture, join a guided two-hour Carmel Walks tour through hidden courtyards, gardens, and pathways. Tours ($25) depart from the Pine Inn courtyard on Lincoln Street. Call to reserve a spot.

ESSENTIALS

Tour Contacts Carmel Walks ⊠ *Lincoln St. at 6th Ave.* ☎ *831/642–2700* ⊕ *www.carmelwalks.com* ☉ *Tues.–Fri. at 10, Sat. at 10 and 2.*

Visitor Information Carmel Chamber of Commerce ⊠ *Visitor Center, San Carlos, between 5th and 6th* ☎ *831/624–2522, 800/550–4333* ⊕ *www. carmelcalifornia.org* ☉ *Daily 10–5.*

EXPLORING

TOP ATTRACTIONS

★ **Carmel Mission.** Long before it became a shopping and browsing destination, Carmel was an important religious center during the establishment of Spanish California. That heritage is preserved in the Mission San Carlos Borroméo del Rio Carmelo, more commonly known as the Carmel Mission. Founded in 1771, it served as headquarters for the mission system in California under Father Junípero Serra. Adjoining the stone church is a tranquil garden planted with California poppies. Museum rooms at the mission include an early kitchen, Serra's spartan sleeping quarters, and the first college library in California. ⊠ *3080 Rio Rd., at Lasuen Dr.* ☎ *831/624–3600* ⊕ *www.carmelmission.org* ⊠ *$6.50* ☉ *Mon.–Sat. 9:30–4:30, Sun. 10:30–4:30.*

Map: Monterey Bay Area

★ **Point Lobos State Reserve.** A 350-acre headland harboring a wealth of marine life, this reserve lies a few miles south of Carmel. The best way to explore here is to walk along one of the many trails. The Cypress Grove Trail leads through a forest of Monterey cypress (one of only two natural groves remaining), which clings to the rocks above an emerald-green cove. Sea Lion Point Trail is a good place to view sea lions. From those and other trails you may also spot otters, harbor seals, and (in winter and spring) migrating whales. An additional 750 acres of the reserve is an undersea marine park open to qualified scuba divers. ■ TIP➔ **Arrive early (or in late afternoon) to avoid crowds; the parking lots fill up.** No pets are allowed. ⊠ *Hwy. 1* ☎ *831/624–4909, 831/624–8413 for scuba-diving reservations* ⊕ *www.pointlobos.org* ⊠ *$10 per vehicle* ⊙ *Daily 8 am–½ hr after sunset in winter, closes 6:30 pm rest of year.*

WORTH NOTING

Carmel Plaza. Carmel Plaza, in the east end of the village proper, holds more than 50 shops and restaurants. ⊠ *Ocean Ave. and Mission St.* ☎ *831/624–1385* ⊕ *www.carmelplaza.com.*

Carmel Wine Walk By-the-Sea. Park the car and sample local wines at tasting rooms and shops in downtown Carmel, all within a few blocks of each other. Purchase a Wine Walk Passport, good for seven tastings within a year; participating venues will stamp it each time you visit. ⊠ *Carmel Chamber of Commerce Visitor Center, San Carlos St., between 5th and 6th Aves.* ☎ *831/624–2522, 800/550–4333* ⊕ *www.carmelcalifornia.org* ✉ *$50.*

Ocean Avenue. Downtown Carmel's chief lure is shopping, especially along its main street, Ocean Avenue, between Junipero Avenue and Camino Real; the architecture here is a mishmash of ersatz Tudor, Mediterranean, and other styles.

Tor House. Scattered throughout the pines in Carmel-by-the-Sea are houses and cottages originally built for the writers, artists, and photographers who discovered the area decades ago. Among the most impressive dwellings is Tor House, a stone cottage built in 1919 by poet Robinson Jeffers on a craggy knoll overlooking the sea. Portraits, books, and unusual art objects fill the low-ceiling rooms. The highlight of the small estate is Hawk Tower, a detached edifice set with stones from the Carmel coastline—as well as one from the Great Wall of China. The docents who lead tours (six people maximum) are well informed about the poet's work and life. Reservations for tours, via email at ✎ *thf@torhouse.org*, are recommended. ⊠ *26304 Ocean View Ave.* ☎ *831/624–1813, 831/624–1840 direct docent office line, available Fri. and Sat. only* ⊕ *www.torhouse.org* ✉ *$10* ☉ *Tours on hr Fri. and Sat. 10–3* ☞ *No children under 12.*

BEACHES

Carmel Beach. Carmel-by-the-Sea's greatest attraction is its rugged coastline, with pine and cypress forests and countless inlets. Carmel Beach, an easy walk from downtown shops, has sparkling white sands and magnificent sunsets. ■**TIP**➔ **Dogs are allowed to romp off-leash here. Amenities:** parking (no fee); toilets. **Best For:** sunset; surfing; walking. ⊠ *End of Ocean Ave.*

Carmel River State Beach. This sugar-white beach, stretching 106 acres along Carmel Bay, is adjacent to a bird sanctuary, where you might spot pelicans, kingfishers, hawks, and sandpipers. **Amenities:** none. **Best For:** sunrise; sunset; walking. ⊠ *Off Scenic Rd. south of Carmel Beach* ☎ *831/624–4909, 831/649–2836* ⊕ *www.parks.ca.gov* ✉ *Free* ☉ *Daily 8 am–½ hr after sunset in winter; closes 6:30 pm rest of year.*

WHERE TO EAT

$$$

FRENCH

★

✕ **André's Bouchée.** The food here presents an innovative bistro-style take on local ingredients. A Monterey Bay sea scallop reduction adorns pan-seared veal tenderloin; grilled rib-eye steaks are topped with a shallot–cabernet sauvignon sauce. With its copper wine bar, the dining room feels more urban than most of Carmel; perhaps that's why this is the "cool" place in town to dine. The stellar wine list sources the selection at the in-house wineshop. ⑤ *Average main: $28* ⊠ *Mission St.,* *between Ocean and 7th Aves.* ☎ *831/626–7880* ⊕ *www.andresbouchee. com* ⌂ *Reservations essential* ⊘ *No lunch Mon. and Tues.*

$$$
EUROPEAN

✕ **Anton and Michel.** Carefully prepared European cuisine is the draw at this airy restaurant. The rack of lamb is carved at the table, the grilled Halloumi cheese and tomatoes are meticulously stacked and served with basil and kalamata olive tapenade, and the desserts are set aflame before your eyes. ⑤ *Average main: $30* ✉ *Mission St. and 7th Ave.* ☎ *831/624–2406* ⊕ *www.antonandmichel.com* ⌂ *Reservations essential.*

$$$
MEDITERRANEAN
★

✕ **Casanova.** This cozy restaurant inspires European-style celebration and romance—accordions hang from the walls, and tiny party lights dance along the low ceilings. The food consists of delectable seasonal dishes from southern France and northern Italy. Private dining and a special menu are offered at Van Gogh's Table, a special table imported from France's Auberge Ravoux, the artist's final residence. ⑤ *Average main: $30* ✉ *5th Ave., between San Carlos and Mission Sts.* ☎ *831/625–0501* ⊕ *www.casanovarestaurant.com* ⌂ *Reservations essential.*

$
AMERICAN

✕ **The Cottage Restaurant.** This family-friendly spot serves sandwiches, pizzas, and homemade soups at lunch and simple entrées at dinner, but the best meal is breakfast (good thing it's served all day). The menu offers six variations on eggs Benedict, and all kinds of sweet and savory crepes. ⑤ *Average main: $14* ✉ *Lincoln St., between Ocean and 7th Aves.* ☎ *831/625–6260* ⊕ *www.cottagerestaurant.com* ⊘ *No dinner Sun.–Wed.*

$$$
SEAFOOD

✕ **Flying Fish Grill.** Simple in appearance yet bold with its flavors, this Japanese–California seafood restaurant is one of Carmel's most inventive eateries. Among the best entrées is the almond-crusted sea bass served with Chinese cabbage and rock shrimp stir-fry. The warm, wood-lined dining room is broken up into very private booths. ⑤ *Average main: $24* ✉ *Mission St., between Ocean and 7th Aves.* ☎ *831/625–1962* ⊕ *flyingfishgrill.com* ⊘ *No lunch.*

$$$
AMERICAN

✕ **Grasing's Coastal Cuisine.** Chef Kurt Grasing draws from fresh Carmel Coast and Central Valley ingredients to whip up contemporary adaptations of European-provincial and American cooking. Longtime menu favorites include artichoke lasagna in a roasted tomato sauce, duck with fresh cherries and green peppercorns in a port wine sauce, a savory paella, and grilled steaks and chops. ⑤ *Average main: $30* ✉ *6th Ave. and Mission St.* ☎ *831/624–6562* ⊕ *www.grasings.com* ⌂ *Reservations essential.*

$
AMERICAN

✕ **Jack London's.** This publike local hangout is the only Carmel restaurant to serve food late at night, often until 11 pm or midnight. The menu includes everything from nachos to steaks. ⑤ *Average main: $15* ✉ *Su Vecino Court on Dolores St., between 5th and 6th Aves.* ☎ *831/624–2336* ⊕ *jacklondons.com.*

$
AMERICAN

✕ **Katy's Place.** Locals flock to Katy's cozy, country-style eatery to fill up on hearty eggs Benedict dishes. (There are 16 types to choose from, each made with three fresh eggs.) The huge breakfast menu also includes omelets, pancakes, and eight types of Belgian waffles. Salads, sandwiches, and burgers are available for lunch—try the grilled calamari burger with melted Monterey Jack cheese. ⑤ *Average main: $15*

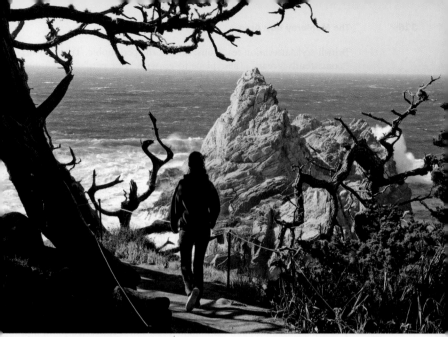

Point Lobos Reserve State Park is home to one of the only two natural stands of Monterey Cypress in the world.

✉ *Mission St., between 5th and 6th Aves.* ☎ *831/624–0199* ⊕ *www. katysplacecarmel.com* ⊟ *No credit cards* ⊘ *No dinner.*

$$$
FRENCH
✕ **L'Escargot.** Chef-owner Kericos Loutas personally sees to each plate of food served at this romantic, unpretentious French restaurant. Order the pan-roasted duck breast or the bone-in steak in truffle butter; or, if you can't decide, choose the three-course prix-fixe dinner. $ *Average main: $30* ✉ *Mission St., between 4th and 5th Aves.* ☎ *831/620–1942* ⊕ *www.escargot-carmel.com* ⚔ *Reservations essential* ⊘ *No lunch.*

$
AMERICAN
✕ **Tuck Box.** This bright little restaurant is in a cottage right out of a fairy tale, complete with stone fireplace. Handmade scones, good for break-fast or afternoon tea, are the specialty. $ *Average main: $12* ✉ *Dolores St., between Ocean and 7th Aves.* ☎ *831/624–6365* ⊕ *www.tuckbox. com* ⚔ *Reservations not accepted* ⊟ *No credit cards* ⊘ *No dinner.*

$$$
ITALIAN
✕ **Vesuvio.** Chef and restaurateur Rich Pèpe's heats up the night with his latest venture, a lively trattoria downstairs and a swinging rooftop terrace, Starlight Lounge 65°. Pèpe's elegant take on traditional Italian cuisine yields dishes such as wild-boar Bolognese pappardelle, lobster ravioli, and velvety limoncello mousse cake. Pizzas and small plates are served in the restaurant and two bars. Upstairs, relax in comfy chairs by fire pits and enjoy bird's-eye views of the village and, most nights in summer, take in live music. $ *Average main: $24* ✉ *6th and Junipero Aves.* ☎ *831/626–7373 ext. 2* ⊕ *pepemag.com* ⊘ *No lunch.*

WHERE TO STAY

For expanded reviews, facilities, and current deals, visit Fodors.com.

$$$$
B&B/INN
▥ **Cypress Inn.** The decorating style here is luxurious but refreshingly simple. **Pros:** luxury without snobbery; popular lounge; traditional

British-style afternoon tea. **Cons:** not for the pet-phobic. **TripAdvisor:** "consistently great," "best place to go with your pet," "nice atmosphere." ⑤ *Rooms from: $235 ⊠ Lincoln St. and 7th Ave., Box Y* ☎ *831/624–3871, 800/443–7443* ⊕ *www.cypress-inn.com* ⌐⤴ *39 rooms, 5 suites* ¶⊙¶ *Breakfast.*

$$$$ 🛏 **Highlands Inn, A Hyatt Hotel.** High on a hill overlooking the Pacific,
HOTEL   this place has superb views; accommodations include king rooms with
★   fireplaces, suites with personal Jacuzzis, and full town houses with all
        the perks. **Pros:** killer views; romantic getaway; great food. **Cons:** thin
        walls; must drive to Carmel. **TripAdvisor:** "spectacular views," "very
        good room," "exceptional service." ⑤ *Rooms from: $439 ⊠ 120 Highlands Dr.* ☎ *831/620–1234, 800/233–1234* ⊕ *highlandsinn.hyatt.com*
        ⌐⤴ *46 rooms, 2 suites.*

$$$$ 🛏 **L'Auberge Carmel.** Stepping through the doors of this elegant inn is like
B&B/INN being transported to a little European village. **Pros:** in town but off the
Fodor'sChoice main drag; four blocks from the beach; full-service luxury. **Cons:** tour-
★   isty area; not a good choice for families. **TripAdvisor:** "fantastic service
        and even better food," "perfect location with every luxury," "very cap-
        tivating." ⑤ *Rooms from: $385 ⊠ Monte Verde at 7th Ave.* ☎ *831/624–
        8578* ⊕ *www.laubergecarmel.com* ⌐⤴ *20 rooms* ¶⊙¶ *Breakfast.*

$$ 🛏 **Mission Ranch.** Movie star Clint Eastwood owns this sprawling prop-
HOTEL   erty whose accommodations include rooms in a converted barn, and
        several cottages, some with fireplaces. **Pros:** farm setting; pastoral views;
        great for tennis buffs. **Cons:** busy parking lot; must drive to the heart of
        town. **TripAdvisor:** "lovely and quaint," "spectacular setting," "relax-
        ing with a gorgeous view." ⑤ *Rooms from: $140 ⊠ 26270 Dolores St.*
        ☎ *831/624–6436, 800/538–8221, 831/625–9040 restaurant* ⊕ *www.
        missionranchcarmel.com* ⌐⤴ *31 rooms* ¶⊙¶ *Breakfast.*

$$$ 🛏 **Sea View Inn.** In a residential area a few hundred feet from the beach,
B&B/INN this restored 1905 home has a double parlor with two fireplaces, Orien-
        tal rugs, canopy beds, and a spacious front porch. **Pros:** quiet; private;
        close to the beach. **Cons:** small building; uphill trek to the heart of town.
        TripAdvisor: "great location," "excellent staff," "fantastic service."
        ⑤ *Rooms from: $180 ⊠ Camino Real, between 11th and 12th Aves.*
        ☎ *831/624–8778* ⊕ *www.seaviewinncarmel.com* ⌐⤴ *8 rooms, 6 with
        private bath* ¶⊙¶ *Breakfast.*

$$$$ 🛏 **Tickle Pink Inn.** Atop a towering cliff, this inn has views of the Big
B&B/INN Sur coastline, which you can contemplate from your private balcony.
        Pros: close to great hiking; intimate; dramatic views. **Cons:** close to
        a big hotel; lots of traffic during the day. **TripAdvisor:** "divine prop-
        erty," "breathtaking views," "a gem within the cliffs." ⑤ *Rooms from:
        $289 ⊠ 155 Highland Dr.* ☎ *831/624–1244, 800/635–4774* ⊕ *www.
        ticklepink.com* ⌐⤴ *23 rooms, 10 suites, 1 cottage* ¶⊙¶ *Breakfast.*

$$$ 🛏 **Tradewinds Carmel.** Its sleek decor inspired by the South Seas, this
B&B/INN converted motel encircles a courtyard with waterfalls, a meditation
★   garden, and a fire pit. **Pros:** serene; within walking distance of res-
        taurants; friendly service. **Cons:** no pool; long walk to the beach.
        TripAdvisor: "tranquil and plush," "cozy in Carmel," "romantic."
        ⑤ *Rooms from: $250 ⊠ Mission St., at 3rd Ave.* ☎ *831/624–2776*
        ⊕ *www.tradewindscarmel.com* ⌐⤴ *26 rooms, 2 suites* ¶⊙¶ *Breakfast.*

SHOPPING

ART GALLERIES **Carmel Art Association.** The association exhibits the original paintings and sculptures of local artists. ⊠ *Dolores St., between 5th and 6th Aves.* ☎ *831/624–6176* ⊕ *www.carmelart.org.*

Galerie Plein Aire. The gallery showcases the oil paintings of a group of local artists. ⊠ *Dolores St., between 5th and 6th Aves.* ☎ *831/625–5686* ⊕ *www.galeriepleinaire.com.*

Weston Gallery. Run by the family of the late Edward Weston, this hands down the best photography gallery around, with contemporary color photography complemented by classic black-and-whites. ⊠ *6th Ave., between Dolores and Lincoln Sts.* ☎ *831/624–4453* ⊕ *www. westongallery.com.*

SPECIALTY **Bittner.** The shop carries a fine selection of collectible and vintage pens
SHOPS from around the world. ⊠ *Ocean Ave., between Mission and San Carlos Sts.* ☎ *831/626–8828* ⊕ *www.bittner.com.*

Intima. Find European lingerie that ranges from lacy to racy here. ⊠ *Mission St., between Ocean and 7th Aves.* ☎ *831/625–0599* ⊕ *www. intimacarmel.com.*

Jan de Luz. This shops monograms and embroiders fine linens (including bathrobes) while you wait. ⊠ *Dolores St., between Ocean and 7th Aves.* ☎ *831/622–7621* ⊕ *www.jandeluz.com.*

Madrigal. Sportswear, sweaters, and accessories for women are the specialties here. ⊠ *Carmel Plaza and Mission St.* ☎ *831/624–3477.*

CARMEL VALLEY

10 miles east of Carmel, Hwy. 1 to Carmel Valley Rd.

Carmel Valley Road, which heads inland from Highway 1 south of Carmel, is the main thoroughfare through this valley, a secluded enclave of horse ranchers and other well-heeled residents who prefer the area's sunny climate to coastal fog and wind. Once thick with dairy farms, the valley has evolved into an esteemed wine appellation. Carmel Valley Village has crafts shops, art galleries, and the tasting rooms of numerous local wineries.

GETTING HERE AND AROUND

From U.S. 101 north or south, exit at Highway 68 and head west toward the coast. Scenic, two-lane Laureles Grade winds west over the mountains to Carmel Valley Road north of the village.

TOURS

The Carmel Valley Grapevine Express, aka MST's Line 24 bus, travels between downtown Monterey and Carmel Valley Village, with stops near wineries, restaurants, and shopping centers. At $8 for a ride-all-day pass, it's an incredible bargain.

Bus Contact Carmel Valley Grapevine Express ☎ *888/678–2871* ⊕ *www. mst.org.*

EXPLORING

Bernardus Tasting Room. At this tasting room you can sample many of Bernardus Winery's offerings, including older vintages and reserve wines. ⊠ *5 W. Carmel Valley Rd., at El Caminito Rd.* ☎ *831/298–8021, 800/223–2533* ⊕ *www.bernardus.com* ☉ *Daily 11–5.*

Château Julien. The expansive winery, recognized internationally for its Chardonnays and Merlots, offers tours by appointment only, but the tasting room is open daily. ⊠ *8940 Carmel Valley Rd., at Schetter Rd., Carmel* ☎ *831/624–2600* ⊕ *www.chateaujulien.com* ☉ *Weekdays 8–5, weekends 11–5; tours weekdays at 10:30 and 2:30, weekends at 12:30 and 2:30, by appointment.*

Earthbound Farm. Pick up fresh veggies, ready-to-eat meals, gourmet groceries, flowers, and gifts at Earthbound Farm, the world's largest grower of organic produce. You can also take a romp in the kid's garden, cut your own herbs, and stroll through the chamomile aromatherapy labyrinth. Special events, on Saturdays from April through December, include bug walks and garlic-braiding workshops. ⊠ *7250 Carmel Valley Rd., Carmel* ☎ *831/625–6219* ⊕ *www.ebfarm.com* ☎ *Free* ☉ *Mon.–Sat. 8–6:30, Sun. 9–6.*

Garland Ranch Regional Park. Hiking trails stretch across much of this park's 4,500 acres of meadows, forested hillsides, and creeks. ⊠ *Carmel Valley Rd., 9 miles east of Carmel-by-the-Sea* ☎ *831/659–4488* ⊕ *www.mprpd.org.*

WHERE TO EAT

$$
ITALIAN
✕ **Café Rustica.** Italian-inspired country cooking is the focus at this lively roadhouse. Specialties include roasted meats, pastas, and thin-crust pizzas from the wood-fired oven. It can get noisy inside; for a quieter meal, request a table outside. ⑤ *Average main: $18* ⊠ *10 Delfino Pl., at Pilot Rd., off Carmel Valley Rd.* ☎ *831/659–4444* ⊕ *www.caferusticacarmel. com* ⌕ *Reservations essential* ☉ *Closed Mon.*

$
ECLECTIC
✕ **LokaL.** Slang for "local" in Czech, LokaL infuses Carmel Valley Village with youth and vitality. After stints in Spain and Prague, where he ran a popular bar, local boy and chef Brendan Jones fashioned his hip new restaurant to encourage social interaction. Order Czech-style beer on tap at the 29-foot, recycled-redwood bar and dine on inventive tapas, among them orange-cardamom paella, sardine bocadillo with mojito aioli, and crispy-pig-cheek salad (exotic!), that riff off Jones' Spanish and Czech influences. ⑤ *Average main: $15* ⊠ *13750 Center St., off Village Dr.* ☎ *831/659–5886* ☉ *Closed Sun. No breakfast or lunch on weekends. No dinner Mon.–Wed.*

$
AMERICAN
✕ **Wagon Wheel Coffee Shop.** This local hangout decorated with wagon wheels, cowboy hats, and lassos serves up terrific hearty breakfasts, including oatmeal and banana pancakes, eggs Benedict, and biscuits and gravy. The lunch menu includes a dozen different burgers and other sandwiches. ⑤ *Average main: $11* ⊠ *Valley Hill Center, 7156 Carmel Valley Rd., next to Quail Lodge, Carmel* ☎ *831/624–8878* ⊟ *No credit cards* ☉ *No dinner.*

$$$
AMERICAN
✕ **Will's Fargo.** Around since the 1920s, this restaurant calls itself a "dressed-up saloon." Steer horns and gilt-frame paintings adorn the

walls of the Victorian-style dining room; you can also eat on the patios. The menu is mainly seafood and steaks, including a 20-ounce porterhouse. ⑤ *Average main: $28* ✉ *16 E. Carmel Valley Rd.* ☎ *831/659–2774* ⊕ *www.bernardus.com* ⊙ *Closed Wed. No lunch Oct.–Mar.*

WHERE TO STAY

For expanded reviews, facilities, and current deals, visit Fodors.com.

$$$$
RESORT
Fodor'sChoice
★

Bernardus Lodge. The spacious guest rooms at this luxury spa resort have vaulted ceilings, featherbeds, fireplaces, patios, and bathtubs for two. **Pros:** exceptional personal service; outstanding food and wine. **Cons:** some guests can seem snooty; pricey. **TripAdvisor:** "lovely retreat," "fantastic service," "unbelievable luxury." ⑤ *Rooms from: $435* ✉ *415 W. Carmel Valley Rd.* ☎ *831/658–3400, 888/648–9463* ⊕ *www.bernardus.com* ⤳ *56 rooms, 1 suite.*

$$$$
RESORT

Carmel Valley Ranch. Hotel scion John Pritzker bought this 500-acre all-suites resort in 2009 and committed more than $30 million to transform the property into an upscale experiential getaway. **Pros:** stunning natural setting; tons of activities; state-of-the-art amenities. **Cons:** must drive several miles to shops and nightlife; pricey. **TripAdvisor:** "quiet getaway," "lovely resort in a spectacular setting," "great place to relax." ⑤ *Rooms from: $275* ✉ *1 Old Ranch Rd., Carmel* ☎☎ *831/626–2510* ☎ *855/687–7262* ⊕ *www.carmelvalleyranch.com* ⤳ *139 suites.*

$$$$
RESORT
Fodor'sChoice
★

Stonepine Estate Resort. Set on 330 pastoral acres, this former estate of the Crocker banking family has been converted to a luxurious inn. **Pros:** supremely exclusive. **Cons:** difficult to get a reservation; far from the coast. **TripAdvisor:** "beautiful and over the top," "a special treat," "what a fulfillment of a fantasy." ⑤ *Rooms from: $300* ✉ *150 E. Carmel Valley Rd.* ☎ *831/659–2245* ⊕ *www.stonepineestate.com* ⤳ *10 rooms, 2 suites, 3 cottages.*

SPAS

Refuge. Relax and recharge in a co-ed, European-style relaxation center on 2 serene acres—without breaking the bank. Heat up in the eucalyptus steam room or cedar sauna, plunge in cold pools, and relax indoors in zero-gravity chairs or outdoors in Adirondack chairs around fire pits. Repeat the cycle a few times, then lounge around the thermal waterfall pools. Talk is limited to whispers, and bathing suits are required. Optional 50-minute massages ($60) are available. ✉ *27300 Rancho San Carlos Rd., south off Carmel Valley Rd., Carmel* ☎ *831/620–7360* ✆ *$39* ⊙ *Daily 10–10.*

SPORTS AND THE OUTDOORS

GOLF
Quail Lodge Golf Club. The Quail Lodge Golf Club incorporates several lakes into its course. Depending on the season and day of the week, greens fees range from $75 to $150, including cart rental. ✉ *8000 Valley Greens Dr., Carmel* ☎ *831/624–2888, 831/620–8808 golf shop.*

Rancho Cañada Golf Club. Rancho Cañada Golf Club is a public course with 36 holes, some of them overlooking the Carmel River. Fees range from $40 to $70, plus $19 per rider for cart rental, depending on course and tee time. ✉ *4860 Carmel Valley Rd., 1 mile east of Hwy. 1, Carmel* ☎ *831/624–0111.*

17-MILE DRIVE

Fodor's Choice *Off North San Antonio Rd. in Carmel-by-the-Sea or off Sunset Dr. in*
★ *Pacific Grove.*

Primordial nature resides in quiet harmony with palatial estates along 17-Mile Drive, which winds through an 8,400-acre microcosm of the Monterey coastal landscape. Dotting the drive are rare Monterey cypress, trees so gnarled and twisted that Robert Louis Stevenson described them as "ghosts fleeing before the wind." The $9.75-per-car fee collected at the gates is well worth the price.

GETTING HERE AND AROUND

If you drive south from Monterey on Highway 1, exit at 17-Mile-Drive/Sunset Drive in Pacific Grove to find the northern entrance gate. Coming from Carmel, exit at Ocean Avenue and follow the road almost to the beach; turn right on North San Antonio Road to the Carmel Gate. You can also enter through the Highway 1 Gate at Scenic Drive/Sunridge Road. Monterey-Salinas Transit buses provide regular service in and around Pebble Beach.

EXPLORING

Bird Rock. Bird Rock, the largest of several islands at the southern end of the Monterey Peninsula Country Club's golf course, teems with harbor seals, sea lions, cormorants, and pelicans.

Crocker Marble Palace. Many of the stately homes along 17-Mile Drive reflect the classic Monterey or Spanish Mission style typical of the region. A standout is the Crocker Marble Palace, about a mile south of the Lone Cypress (⇨ *below)*. It's a private waterfront estate inspired by a Byzantine castle, easily identifiable by its dozens of marble arches.

Lone Cypress. The most-photographed tree along 17-Mile Drive is the weather-sculpted Lone Cypress, which grows out of a precipitous outcropping above the waves about 1½ miles up the road from Pebble Beach Golf Links. You can stop for a view of the Lone Cypress at a parking area, but you can't walk out to the tree.

Seal Rock. Sea creatures and birds—as well as some very friendly ground squirrels—make use of Seal Rock, the largest of a group of islands about 2 miles north of Lone Cypress.

WHERE TO STAY

For expanded reviews, facilities, and current deals, visit Fodors.com.

$$$$
RESORT
★
Casa Palmero. This exclusive spa resort evokes a stately Mediterranean villa. **Pros:** ultimate in pampering; more private than sister resorts; right on the golf course. **Cons:** pricey; may be *too* posh for some. **TripAdvisor:** "lovely hideaway," "pampered luxury," "amazing service in a beautiful place." ⑤ *Rooms from: $875* ✉ *1518 Cypress Dr.* ☎ *831/622–6650, 800/654–9300* ⊕ *www.pebblebeach.com* ⇗ *21 rooms, 3 suites.*

$$$$
RESORT
Inn at Spanish Bay. This resort sprawls across a breathtaking stretch of shoreline, and has lush, 600-square-foot rooms. **Pros:** attentive service; tons of amenities; spectacular views. **Cons:** huge hotel; 4 miles from other Pebble Beach Resort facilities. **TripAdvisor:** "great place to stay for Pebble Beach golf," "beautiful," "simply spectacular." ⑤ *Rooms*

from: $615 ✉ *2700 17-Mile Dr.* ☎ *831/647–7500, 800/654–9300*
⊕ *www.pebblebeach.com* ⬆ *252 rooms, 17 suites.*

$$$$ ▦ **Lodge at Pebble Beach.** All rooms have fireplaces and many have won-
RESORT derful ocean views at this circa-1919 resort. **Pros:** world-class golf; bor-
★ ders the ocean and fairways; fabulous facilities. **Cons:** some rooms are
on the small side; very pricey. **TripAdvisor:** "everything we anticipated
and more," "stunning," "can't put a price on this." ⑤ *Rooms from:*
$715 ✉ *1700 17-Mile Dr.* ☎ *831/624–3811, 800/654–9300* ⊕ *www.*
pebblebeach.com ⬆ *142 rooms, 19 suites.*

SPORTS AND THE OUTDOORS

GOLF **Links at Spanish Bay.** This course, which hugs a choice stretch of shoreline, is designed in the rugged manner of a traditional Scottish course,
with sand dunes and coastal marshes interspersed among the greens.
The greens fee is $260, plus $35 per person for cart rental (cart is
included for resort guests); nonguests can reserve tee times up to two
months in advance. ✉ *17-Mile Dr., north end* ☎ *800/654–9300.*

Pebble Beach Golf Links. Pebble Beach Golf Links attracts golfers from
around the world, despite a greens fee of $495, plus $35 per person for
an optional cart (complimentary cart for guests of the Pebble Beach and
Spanish Bay resorts). The ocean plays a major role in the 18th hole of
the famed links. Each February the course is the main site of the AT&T
Pebble Beach Pro-Am, where show-business celebrities and golf pros
team up for one of the nation's most glamorous tournaments. Tee times
are available to guests who book a minimum two-night stay. Nonguests
can reserve a tee time only one day in advance on a space-available basis
(up to a year for groups); resort guests can reserve up to 18 months in
advance. ✉ *17-Mile Dr., near Lodge at Pebble Beach* ☎ *800/654–9300.*

Peter Hay. A 9-hole, par-3 course, Peter Hay charges $30 per person, no
reservations necessary. ✉ *17-Mile Dr.* ☎ *831/622–8723.*

Poppy Hills. Poppy Hills, a splendid 18-hole course designed in 1986 by
Robert Trent Jones Jr., has a greens fee of $200; an optional cart costs
$18 per person. Individuals may reserve up to one month in advance,
groups up to a year. ✉ *3200 Lopez Rd., at 17-Mile Dr.* ☎ *831/625–2035*
⊕ *www.poppyhillsgolf.com.*

Spyglass Hill. Spyglass Hill is among the most challenging Pebble Beach
courses. With the first five holes bordering on the Pacific and the other
13 reaching deep into the Del Monte Forest, the views offer some conso-
lation. The greens fee is $360, and an optional cart costs $35 (the cart is
complimentary for resort guests). Reservations are essential and may be
made up to one month in advance (18 months for guests). ✉ *Stevenson*
Dr. and Spyglass Hill Rd. ☎ *800/654–9300.*

PACIFIC GROVE

3 miles north of Carmel-by-the-Sea on Hwy. 68.

This picturesque town, which began as a summer retreat for church
groups more than a century ago, recalls its prim and proper Victorian
heritage in its host of tiny board-and-batten cottages and stately mansions. However, long before the church groups flocked here the area

DID YOU KNOW?

The Lone Cypress has stood on this rock for more than 250 years. The tree is the official symbol of Pebble Beach.

received thousands of annual pilgrims—in the form of bright orange-and-black monarch butterflies. They still come, migrating south from Canada and the Pacific Northwest to take residence in pine and euca-lyptus groves from October through March. In Butterfly Town USA, as Pacific Grove is known, the sight of a mass of butterflies hanging from the branches like a long, fluttering veil is unforgettable.

A prime way to enjoy Pacific Grove is to walk or bicycle the 3 miles of city-owned shoreline along Ocean View Boulevard, a cliff-top area landscaped with native plants and dotted with benches meant for sitting and gazing at the sea. You can spot many types of birds here, includ-ing the web-footed cormorants that crowd the massive rocks rising out of the surf. Two Victorians of note along Ocean View are the Queen Anne–style Green Gables, at No. 301—erected in 1888, it's now a B&B—and the 1909 Pryor House, at No. 429, a massive, shingled, private residence with a leaded- and beveled-glass doorway.

GETTING HERE AND AROUND

Reach Pacific Grove via Highway 68 off Highway 1, just south of Monterey. From Cannery Row in Monterey, head north until the road merges with Ocean Boulevard and follow it along the coast. MST buses travel within Pacific Grove and surrounding towns.

EXPLORING

Lovers Point Park. The coastal views are gorgeous from this waterfront park whose sheltered beach has a children's pool and a picnic area. The main lawn has a volleyball court and a snack bar. ⊠ *Ocean View Blvd. northwest of Forest Ave.* ☎ *831/648–5730.*

Monarch Grove Sanctuary. The Monarch Grove Sanctuary is a fairly reli-★ able spot for viewing the butterflies between October and February. ⊠ *1073 Lighthouse Ave., at Ridge Rd.* ⊕ *www.pgmuseum.org.*

Pacific Grove Museum of Natural History. Contact the museum for the lat-est information about the butterfly population. Year-round, you can view the well-crafted butterfly tree exhibit here. ⊠ *165 Forest Ave., at Central Ave.* ☎ *831/648–5716* ⊕ *www.pgmuseum.org* ⊠ *$3 suggested donation; $5 per family* ⊗ *Tues.–Sun. 10–5.*

Point Pinos Lighthouse. At the 1855-vintage Point Pinos Lighthouse, the ★ oldest continuously operating lighthouse on the West Coast, you can learn about the lighting and foghorn operations and wander through a small museum containing U.S. Coast Guard memorabilia. ⊠ *Asilomar Ave., between Lighthouse Ave. and Del Monte Blvd.* ☎ *831/648–3176* ⊕ *www.pgmuseum.org* ⊠ *$2 suggested donation* ⊗ *Thurs.–Mon. 1–4.*

BEACHES

★ **Asilomar State Beach.** Asilomar State Beach, a beautiful coastal area, stretches between Point Pinos and the Del Monte Forest. The 100 acres of dunes, tidal pools, and pocket-size beaches form one of the region's richest areas for marine life—including surfers, who migrate here most winter mornings. **Amenities:** none. **Best For:** sunrise; sunset; surfing; walking. ⊠ *Sunset Dr. and Asilomar Ave.* ☎ *831/646–6440* ⊕ *www. parks.ca.gov.*

WHERE TO EAT

$$$
MEDITERRANEAN

✕ Fandango. The menu here is mostly Mediterranean and southern French, with such dishes as calves' liver and onions and paella served in a skillet. The decor follows suit: stone walls and country furniture give the restaurant the earthy feel of a European farmhouse. This is where locals come when they want to have a big dinner with friends, drink wine, have fun, and generally feel at home. $ *Average main: $25* ✉ *223 17th St., south of Lighthouse Ave.* ☎ *831/372–3456* ⊕ *www. fandangorestaurant.com.*

$$
SEAFOOD

✕ Fishwife. Fresh fish with a Latin accent makes this a favorite of locals for lunch or a casual dinner. Standards are the sea garden salads topped with your choice of fish and the fried seafood plates with fresh veggies. Diners with large appetites appreciate the fisherman's bowls—fresh fish served with rice, black beans, spicy cabbage, salsa, vegetables, and crispy tortilla strips. $ *Average main: $22* ✉ *1996½ Sunset Dr., at Asilomar Blvd.* ☎ *831/375–7107* ⊕ *www.fishwife.com.*

$$$
ITALIAN

✕ Joe Rombi's La Mia Cucina. Pastas, fish, steaks, and chops are the specialties at this modern trattoria, which is the best in town for Italian food. The look is spare and clean, with colorful antique wine posters decorating the white walls. Next door, Joe Rombi's La Piccola Casa Pizzeria & Coffee House serves breakfast (baked goods), lunch, and early dinner Wednesday through Sunday. $ *Average main: $23* ✉ *208 17th St., at Lighthouse Ave.* ☎ *831/373–2416* ⊕ *www.joerombi.com* ☾ *Closed Mon. and Tues. No lunch.*

$$$
MODERN
AMERICAN
★

✕ Passionfish. South American artwork and artifacts decorate Passionfish, and Latin and Asian flavors infuse the dishes. Chef Ted Walter shops at local farmers' markets several times a week to find the best produce, fish, and meat available, then pairs it with creative sauces. The menu might include crispy squid with spicy orange-cilantro vinaigrette. $ *Average main: $23* ✉ *701 Lighthouse Ave., at Congress Ave.* ☎ *831/655–3311* ⊕ *www.passionfish.net* ☾ *No lunch.*

$
MEXICAN

✕ Peppers Mexicali Cafe. This cheerful white-walled storefront serves traditional dishes from Mexico and Latin America, with an emphasis on fresh seafood. Excellent red and green salsas are made throughout the day, and there's a large selection of beers, along with fresh lime margaritas. $ *Average main: $15* ✉ *170 Forest Ave., between Lighthouse and Central Aves.* ☎ *831/373–6892* ⊕ *www.peppersmexicalicafe.com* ☾ *Closed Tues. No lunch Sun.*

$$
AMERICAN

✕ Red House Café. When it's nice out, sun pours through the big windows of this cozy restaurant and across tables on the porch; when fog rolls in, the fireplace is lighted. The American menu changes with the seasons, but typically includes grilled lamb fillets atop mashed potatoes for dinner and Dungeness crab cakes over salad for lunch. Breakfast on weekends is a local favorite. $ *Average main: $20* ✉ *662 Lighthouse Ave., at 19th St.* ☎ *831/643–1060* ⊕ *www.redhousecafe.com* ☾ *Closed Mon.*

$$
AMERICAN

✕ Taste Café and Bistro. Grilled marinated rabbit, roasted half chicken, filet mignon, and other meats are the focus at Taste, which serves hearty European-inspired food in a casual, open-kitchen setting. $ *Average main: $20* ✉ *1199 Forest Ave.* ☎ *831/655–0324* ⊕ *www.tastecafebistro. com* ☾ *Closed Sun. and Mon.*

WHERE TO STAY
For expanded reviews, facilities, and current deals, visit Fodors.com.

$$$
B&B/INN
★
⛧ **Green Gables Inn.** Stained-glass windows and ornate interior details compete with spectacular ocean views at this Queen Anne–style mansion, built by a businessman for his mistress in 1888. **Pros:** exceptional views; impeccable attention to historic detail. **Cons:** some rooms are small; thin walls. **TripAdvisor:** "beautiful ocean views," "wonderful B&B," "great service." ⑤ *Rooms from: $215* ✉ *301 Ocean View Blvd.* ☎ *831/375–2095, 800/722–1774* ⊕ *www.greengablesinnpg.com* ⊋ *10 rooms, 3 with bath; 1 suite* ⦿⦿ *Breakfast.*

$$$
B&B/INN
⛧ **The Inn at 213 Seventeen Mile Drive.** Set in a residential area just past town, this carefully restored 1920s Craftsman-style home and cottage are surrounded by gardens and redwood, cypress, and eucalyptus trees. **Pros:** killer gourmet breakfast; historic charm; verdant gardens. **Cons:** far from restaurants and shops; few extra amenities. **TripAdvisor:** "great getaway," "great hospitality," "elegant yet cozy Craftsman charm." ⑤ *Rooms from: $195* ✉ *213 17-Mile Dr., at Lighthouse Dr.* ☎ *831/642–9514, 800/526–5666* ⊕ *www.innat17.com* ⊋ *14 rooms* ⦿⦿ *Breakfast.*

$$
HOTEL
⛧ **Lighthouse Lodge and Suites.** Near the tip of the peninsula, this complex straddles Lighthouse Avenue—the lodge is on one side, the all-suites Lighthouse Resort facility on the other. **Pros:** near lighthouse and 17-Mile Drive; friendly reception; many room options. **Cons:** next to a cemetery; lodge rooms are basic. **TripAdvisor:** "beautiful rooms," "perfect," "a regular guest for 10 years." ⑤ *Rooms from: $139* ✉ *1150 and 1249 Lighthouse Ave.* ☎ *831/655–2111, 800/858–1249* ⊕ *www.lhls.com* ⊋ *64 rooms, 31 suites* ⦿⦿ *Breakfast.*

$$$
B&B/INN
⛧ **Martine Inn.** The glassed-in parlor and many guest rooms at this 1899 Mediterranean-style villa have stunning ocean views; thoughtful details such as robes, rocking chairs, and nightly turndown create an ambience of luxuriant comfort. **Pros:** romantic; fancy breakfast; ocean views. **Cons:** not child-friendly; sits on a busy thoroughfare. **TripAdvisor:** "beautiful spot," "pure heaven," "friendly hospitable attention to detail." ⑤ *Rooms from: $199* ✉ *255 Ocean View Blvd.* ☎ *831/373–3388, 800/852–5588* ⊕ *www.martineinn.com* ⊋ *25 rooms* ⦿⦿ *Breakfast.*

MONTEREY

2 miles southeast of Pacific Grove via Lighthouse Ave.; 2 miles north of Carmel-by-the-Sea via Hwy. 1.

Early in the 20th century Carmel Martin, the first mayor of the city of Monterey, saw a bright future for his town: "Monterey Bay is the one place where people can live without being disturbed by manufacturing and big factories. I am certain that the day is coming when this will be the most desirable place in the whole state of California." His Honor was not far off the mark.

GETTING HERE AND AROUND

From San Jose or San Francisco, take U.S. 101 south to Highway 156 West at Prunedale. Head west about 8 miles to Highway 1 and follow it about 15 miles south. From San Luis Obispo, take U.S. 101 north to Salinas and drive west on Highway 68 about 20 miles.

Many MST bus lines connect at the Monterey Transit Center, at Pearl Street and Munras Avenue. In summer (daily from 10 until at least 7), the free MST Monterey Trolley travels from downtown Monterey along Cannery Row to the Aquarium and back.

ESSENTIALS

Visitor Information Monterey County Convention & Visitors Bureau
☎ 877/666–8373 ⊕ www.seemonterey.com.

EXPLORING

TOP ATTRACTIONS

Cannery Row. When John Steinbeck published the novel *Cannery Row* in 1945, he immortalized a place of rough-edged working people. The waterfront street, edging a mile of gorgeous coastline, once was crowded with sardine canneries processing, at their peak, nearly 200,000 tons of the smelly silver fish a year. During the mid-1940s, however, the sardines disappeared from the bay, causing the canneries to close. Through the years the old tin-roof canneries have been converted into restaurants, art galleries, and malls with shops selling T-shirts, fudge, and plastic sea otters. Recent tourist development along the row has been more tasteful, however, and includes several stylish inns and hotels, wine tasting rooms, and upscale specialty shops. ⊠ *Cannery Row, between Reeside and David Aves.* ⊕ *www.canneryrow.com.*

Colton Hall. A convention of delegates met here in 1849 to draft the first state constitution. The stone building, which has served as a school, a courthouse, and the county seat, is a city-run museum furnished as it was during the constitutional convention. The extensive grounds outside the hall surround the Old Monterey Jail. ⊠ *570 Pacific St., between Madison and Jefferson Sts.* ☎ *831/646–5640* ⊕ *www.monterey.org/museums* ⌑ *Free* ☉ *Daily 10–4.*

Cooper-Molera Adobe. The restored 2-acre complex includes a house dating from the 1820s, a bookstore, and a large garden enclosed by a high adobe wall. The mostly Victorian-era antiques and memorabilia that fill the house provide a glimpse into the life of a prosperous sea merchant's family. If the house is closed, you can still stop by the visitor center and pick up walking-tour maps and stroll the grounds. ⊠ *Monterey State Historic Park, Polk and Munras Sts.* ☎ *831/649–7111* ⊕ *www.parks.ca.gov/mshp* ⌑ *$5* ☉ *Store open 10–4; tours on weekends, call for hrs.*

Custom House. Built by the Mexican government in 1827 and now California's oldest standing public building, the Custom House was the first stop for sea traders whose goods were subject to duties. In 1846, Commodore John Sloat raised the American flag over this adobe structure and claimed California for the United States. The house is presently closed (state budget cuts), but you can visit the cactus gardens

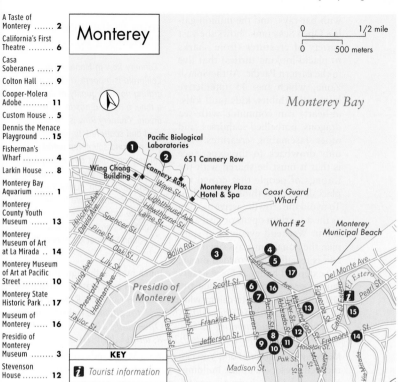

Monterey

Monterey Bay

Pacific Biological Laboratories
651 Cannery Row
Wing Chong Building
Cannery Row
Wave St.
Lighthouse Ave.
Hawthorne St.
Laine St.
Monterey Plaza Hotel & Spa
Coast Guard Wharf
Wharf #2
Monterey Municipal Beach
Spencer St.
Pine St.
Oak St.
Bolio Rd.
Lily Ave.
Irving Ave.
Prescott Ave.
Hoffman Ave.
Taylor Ave.
Cedar St.
Presidio of Monterey
Scott St.
Franklin St.
Jefferson St.
Van Buren St.
Pacific St.
Calle Principal
Tyler St.
Alvarado St.
Washington St.
Figueroa St.
Del Monte Ave.
Camino El Estero
Pearl St.
Abrego St.
Webster St.
Houston St.
Fremont St.
Polk St.
Madison St.
Murras St.
Via Mirada

KEY

🛈 *Tourist information*

and stroll the plaza. ✉ *Monterey State Historic Park, 1 Custom House Plaza, across from Fisherman's Wharf* ☎ *831/649–7118* ⊕ *www.parks. ca.gov/mshp* 🎟 *Free.*

🅒 **Fisherman's Wharf.** The mournful barking of sea lions provides a steady sound track all along Monterey's waterfront, but the best way to actually view the whiskered marine mammals is to walk along one of the two piers across from Custom House Plaza. Lined with souvenir shops, the wharf is undeniably touristy, but it's lively and entertaining. At Wharf No. 2, a working municipal pier, you can see the day's catch being unloaded from fishing boats on one side, and fishermen casting their lines into the water on the other. The pier has a couple of low-key restaurants, from whose seats lucky customers may spot otters and harbor seals. ✉ *At end of Calle Principal* ⊕ *www.montereywharf.com.*

🅒 **Monterey Bay Aquarium.** The minute you hand over your ticket at this
Fodor's Choice extraordinary aquarium you're surrounded by sea creatures; right at
★ the entrance, you can see dozens of them swimming in a three-story-tall, sunlit kelp forest tank. The beauty of the exhibits here is that they are all designed to give a sense of what it's like to be in the water with the animals—sardines swim around your head in a circular tank, and jellyfish drift in and out of view in dramatically lighted spaces that suggest the ocean depths. A petting pool gives you a hands-on experience

with bat rays, and the million-gallon Open Seas tank shows the vast variety of creatures (from sharks to placid-looking turtles) that live in the eastern Pacific. At the Splash Zone, which has 45 interactive bilingual exhibits, kids (and kids-at-heart) can commune with sea dragons, potbellied seahorses, and other fascinating creatures. The only drawback to the experience is that it must be shared with the throngs of people that crowd the place daily; most think it's worth it. To avoid the crowds, arrive as soon as the aquarium opens or visit after 2 pm. Weekend evenings in summer, the aquarium stays open later and is usually less crowded during

> ### JOHN STEINBECK'S CANNERY ROW
>
> "Cannery Row in Monterey in California is a poem, a stink, a grating noise, a quality of light, a tone, a habit, a nostalgia, a dream. Cannery Row is the gathered and scattered, tin and iron and rust and splintered wood, chipped pavement and weedy lots and junk heaps, sardine canneries of corrugated iron, honky tonks, restaurants and whore houses, and little crowded groceries, and laboratories and flophouses."
>
> —John Steinbeck, *Cannery Row*

the extended hours. ■TIP➜ Reserve a lunch table at the aquarium's restaurant, perched on ocean's edge. Otters and other sea creatures often frolic just outside the floor-to-ceiling windows. ✉ *886 Cannery Row, at David Ave.* ☎ *800/555–3656 info, 800/756–3737 for advance tickets* ⊕ *www. montereybayaquarium.org* 🖃 *$33* ☉ *Open daily 10–6; summer/holidays 9:30–6; summer weekends 9:30–8; winter daily 10–5.*

Monterey State Historic Park. You can glimpse Monterey's early history in the well-preserved adobe buildings scattered along several city blocks. Far from being a hermetic period museum, the park facilities are an integral part of the day-to-day business life of the town—within some of the buildings are a store, a theater, and government offices. At some of the historic houses, the gardens (open daily 10 to 5 in summer, 10 to 4 the rest of the year) are worthy sights themselves. ■TIP➜ At this writing, many buildings are closed and tours on hiatus due to state park budget cuts. Visit the park's website for up-to-date information. ✉ *20 Custom House Plaza* ☎ *831/649–7118* ⊕ *www.parks.ca.gov/mshp* 🖃 *Free* ☉ *Call for hrs.*

Museum of Monterey. The former Monterey Maritime Museum still displays maritime artifacts but has expanded its focus to include art, photography, and costumes from Monterey's earliest days to the present. The jewel in the museum's crown remains the enormous Fresnel lens from the Point Sur Light Station. ✉ *Stanton Center, 5 Custom House Plaza* ☎ *831/372–2608* ⊕ *museumofmonterey.org* 🖃 *$10. Free 1st Tues. of month* ☉ *Tues.–Sat. 10–5, Sun. noon–5.*

WORTH NOTING

A Taste of Monterey. Without driving the back roads, you can taste the wines of more than 90 area vintners while taking in fantastic bay views. Purchase a few bottles and pick up a map and guide to the county's wineries and vineyards. ✉ *700 Cannery Row, Suite KK* ☎ *831/646–5446, 888/646–5446* ⊕ *www.tastemonterey.com* 🖃 *Wine tastings $10–$20* ☉ *Daily 11–6.*

Trained "seals" that perform in circuses are actually California sea lions, intelligent, social animals that live (and sleep) close together in groups.

California's First Theatre. This adobe began its life in 1846 as a saloon and lodging house for sailors. Four years later stage curtains were fashioned from army blankets, and some U.S. officers staged plays to the light of whale oil lamps. As of this writing, the building is not open but you can stroll in the garden. ⊠ *Monterey State Historic Park, Scott and Pacific Sts.* ☏ *831/649–7118* ⊕ *www.parks.ca.gov/mshp* ✈ *Free* ⊙ *Call for hrs.*

Casa Soberanes. A classic low-ceiling adobe structure built in 1842, this was once a Custom House guard's residence. The building is closed, but you can visit the peaceful rear garden and its rose-covered arbor. ⊠ *Monterey State Historic Park, 336 Pacific St., at Del Monte Ave.* ☏ *831/649–7118* ⊕ *www.parks.ca.gov/mshp* ✈ *Free.*

☺ **Dennis the Menace Playground.** This play area was designed by the late cartoonist Hank Ketcham. The equipment is on a grand scale and made for Dennis-like daredevils: there's a roller slide, a clanking suspension bridge, and a real Southern Pacific steam locomotive. You can rent a rowboat or a paddleboat for cruising around U-shaped Lake El Estero, populated with an assortment of ducks, mud hens, and geese. ⊠ *El Estero Park, Pearl St. and Camino El Estero* ☏ *831/646–3866* ⊙ *Daily 10–dusk in summer* ⊙ *Closed Tues., Sept.–May.*

Larkin House. A veranda encircles the second floor of this 1835 adobe, whose design bears witness to the Mexican and New England influences on the Monterey style. Many of the antiques inside were brought from New Hampshire by the building's namesake, Thomas O. Larkin, an early California statesman. The building is closed weekdays, but you can peek in the windows and stroll the gardens. ⊠ *Monterey State Historic Park, 464 Calle Principal, between Jefferson and Pacific Sts.*

☎ 831/649–7118 ⊕ www.parks.
ca.gov/mshp 🎫 $5 ⊙ Weekends;
call for hrs.

☾ **Monterey County Youth Museum (MY Museum).** Monterey Bay comes to life from a child's perspective in this fun-filled, interactive indoor exploration center. The seven exhibit galleries showcase the science and nature of the Big Sur coast, theater arts, Pebble Beach golf, and beaches. There's also a live-performance theater, a creation station, a hospital emergency room, and an agriculture corner where kids follow artichokes, strawberries, and other fruits and veggies on their evolution from sprout to harvest to farmers' markets. ⊠ 425 Washington St., between E. Franklin St. and Bonifacio Pl. ☎ 831/649–6444 ⊕ www. mymuseum.org 🎫 $7 ⊙ Tues.–Sat. 10–5, Sun. noon–5.

> **MONTEREY: FORMER CAPITAL OF CALIFORNIA**
>
> In 1602 Spanish explorer Sebastián Vizcaíno stepped ashore on a remote California peninsula. He named it after the viceroy of New Spain—Count de Monte Rey. Soon the Spanish built a military outpost, and the site was the capital of California until the state came under American rule.

Monterey Museum of Art at La Mirada. Asian and European antiques fill this 19th-century adobe house. A newer 10,000-square-foot gallery space, designed by Charles Moore, houses Asian and California regional art. Outdoors are magnificent rose and rhododendron gardens. ⊠ 720 Via Mirada, at Fremont St. ☎ 831/372–3689 ⊕ www.montereyart. org 🎫 $10, also good for admission to museum's Pacific Street facility ⊙ Wed.–Sat. 11–5, Sun. 1–4.

Monterey Museum of Art at Pacific Street. Photographs by Ansel Adams and Edward Weston, as well as works by other artists who have spent time on the peninsula, are on display here, along with international folk art, from Kentucky hearth brooms to Tibetan prayer wheels. ⊠ 559 Pacific St., across from Colton Hall ☎ 831/372–5477 ⊕ www.montereyart. org 🎫 $10, also good for admission to museum's La Mirada facility ⊙ Wed.–Sat. 11–5, Sun. 1–4.

Presidio of Monterey Museum. This spot has been significant for centuries. Its first incarnation was as a Native American village for the Rumsien tribe. The Spanish explorer Sebastián Vizcaíno landed here in 1602, and Father Junípero Serra arrived in 1770. Notable battles fought here include the 1818 skirmish in which the corsair Hipólito Bruchard conquered the Spanish garrison that stood on this site and claimed part of California for Argentina. The indoor museum tells the stories; plaques mark the outdoor sites. ⊠ Presidio of Monterey, Corporal Ewing Rd., off Lighthouse Ave. ☎ 831/646–3456 ⊕ www.monterey.org/museums 🎫 Free ⊙ Mon. 10–1, Thurs.–Sat. 10–4, Sun. 1–4.

Stevenson House. This house was named in honor of author Robert Louis Stevenson, who boarded here briefly in a tiny upstairs room. Items from his family's estate furnish Stevenson's room; period-decorated chambers elsewhere in the house include a gallery of memorabilia and a children's nursery stocked with Victorian toys and games. ⊠ Monterey State His-

CLOSE UP

The Underwater Kingdom

Although Monterey's coastal landscapes are stunning, their beauty is more than equaled by the wonders that lie offshore. The huge Monterey Bay National Marine Sanctuary—which stretches 276 miles, from north of San Francisco almost all the way down to Santa Barbara—teems with abundant life, and has topography as diverse as that aboveground.

The preserve's 5,322 square miles include vast submarine canyons, which reach down 10,663 feet at their deepest point. They also encompass dense forests of giant kelp—a kind of seaweed that can grow more than a hundred feet from its roots on the ocean floor. These kelp forests are especially robust off Monterey.

The sanctuary was established in 1992 to protect the habitat of the many species that thrive in the bay. Some animals can be seen quite easily from land. In summer and winter you might glimpse the offshore spray of gray whales as they migrate between their summer feeding grounds in Alaska and their breeding grounds in Baja. Clouds of marine birds—including white-faced ibis, three types of albatross, and more than 15 types of gull—skim the waves, or roost in the rock islands along 17-Mile Drive. Sea otters dart and gambol in the calmer waters of the bay; and of course, you can watch the sea lions—and hear their round-the-clock barking—on the wharves in Santa Cruz and Monterey.

The sanctuary supports many other creatures, however, that remain unseen by most on-land visitors. Some of these are enormous, such as the giant blue whales that arrive to feed on plankton in summer; others, like the more than 22 species of red algae in these waters, are microscopic. So whether you choose to visit the Monterey Bay Aquarium, take a whale-watch trip, or look out to sea with your binoculars, remember you're seeing just a small part of a vibrant underwater kingdom.

toric Park, 530 Houston St., near Pearl St. ☎ 831/649–7118 ⊕ www. parks.ca.gov/mshp ⌨ Free ☉ Sat. 1–4 and last Sun. of month 1–4.

WHERE TO EAT

$
AMERICAN
✕ **Café Lumiere.** Attached to the lobby of Monterey's art-house cinema, this café shows work by local artists. Eat a light breakfast, lunch, or dinner; order beer on tap; drink coffee; or choose a pot of tea from the extensive selection. The menu includes baked goods, cakes, sandwiches, granola, and other breakfast items. Most patrons bring their laptops for the free Wi-Fi, and most tables are shared. Close to downtown bars, it's open until 10 pm. ⓢ *Average main: $8* ⌧ *365 Calle Principal* ☎ *831/920–2451.*

$$
SEAFOOD
✕ **Monterey's Fish House.** Casual yet stylish and always packed, this seafood restaurant is removed from the hubbub of the wharf. If the dining room is full, you can wait at the bar and savor deliciously plump oysters on the half shell. The bartenders and waitstaff will gladly advise you on the perfect wine to go with your poached, blackened, or oak-grilled

seafood. $ *Average main: $21* ✉ *2114 Del Monte Ave., at Dela Vina St.* ☎ *831/373–4647* ⚔ *Reservations essential* ⊘ *No lunch weekends.*

$$$
AMERICAN
Fodor's Choice
★

╳ **Montrio Bistro.** This quirky, converted firehouse, with its rawhide walls and iron indoor trellises, has a wonderfully sophisticated menu. Chef Tony Baker uses organic produce and meats and sustainably sourced seafood to create imaginative dishes that reflect local agriculture, such as baby artichoke risotto fritters, and pesto-rubbed prime sirloin with marinated prawns, spinach, and a red wine–veal reduction sauce. The wine list also draws primarily on California—Monterey-area wineries are well represented—and signature cocktails are infused with local fruits, herbs, and veggies. $ *Average main: $24* ✉ *414 Calle Principal, at W. Franklin St.* ☎ *831/648–8880* ⊕ *www.montrio.com* ⚔ *Reservations essential* ⊘ *No lunch.*

$
AMERICAN

╳ **Old Monterey Café.** Breakfast here gets constant local raves. The café's fame rests on familiar favorites: a dozen kinds of omelets, and pancakes from blueberry to cinnamon-raisin-pecan. For lunch are good soups, salads, and sandwiches. This is a fine place to relax with an afternoon cappuccino. $ *Average main: $12* ✉ *489 Alvarado St., at Munras Ave.* ☎ *831/646–1021* ⊕ *www.cafemonterey.com/about.html* ⚔ *Reservations not accepted* ⊘ *No dinner.*

$$
AMERICAN

╳ **Tarpy's Roadhouse.** Fun, dressed-up American favorites—a little something for everyone—are served in this renovated early-1900s stone farmhouse several miles east of town. The kitchen cranks out everything from Cajun-spiced prawns to meat loaf with marsala-mushroom gravy to grilled ribs and steaks. Eat indoors by a fireplace or outdoors in the courtyard. $ *Average main: $22* ✉ *2999 Monterey–Salinas Hwy., Hwy. 68* ☎ *831/647–1444* ⊕ *www.tarpys.com.*

WHERE TO STAY

For expanded reviews, facilities, and current deals, visit Fodors.com.

$$
RESORT

▦ **Best Western Beach Resort Monterey.** With a great waterfront location about 2 miles north of Monterey—with views of the bay and the city skyline—and a surprising array of amenities, this hotel is one of the area's best values. **Pros:** on the beach; great value; family-friendly. **Cons:** several miles from major attractions; big-box mall neighborhood. **Trip-Advisor:** "can't get any closer to the beach," "great location," "amazing view." $ *Rooms from: $159* ✉ *2600 Sand Dunes Dr.* ☎ *831/394–3321, 800/242–8627* ⊕ *www.montereybeachresort.com* ⤶ *196 rooms.*

$$$
RESORT
☾

▦ **InterContinental The Clement Monterey.** Spectacular bay views, assiduous service, a slew of upscale amenities, and a superb waterfront location next to the aquarium propelled this full-service luxury hotel to immediate stardom. **Pros:** a block from the aquarium; fantastic views from some rooms; great for families. **Cons:** a tad formal; not budget-friendly. **TripAdvisor:** "amazing views," "excellent service," "comfortable." $ *Rooms from: $225* ✉ *750 Cannery Row* ☎ *831/375–4500, 866/781–2406 toll free* ⊕ *www.ictheclementmonterey.com* ⤶ *192 rooms, 16 suites.*

$$
HOTEL
★

▦ **Monterey Bay Lodge.** Location (on the edge of Monterey's El Estero Park) and superior amenities give this cheerful facility an edge over other motels in town. **Pros:** within walking distance of beach and playground; quiet at night; good family choice. **Cons:** near busy boulevard. **TripAdvisor:** "can't be beat," "good value," "great location." $ *Rooms from: $129 ⊠ 55 Camino Aguajito ☎ 831/372–8057, 800/558–1900 ⊕ www.montereybaylodge.com ↩ 43 rooms, 3 suites.*

$$$$ **Monterey Plaza Hotel and Spa.**
HOTEL This hotel commands a waterfront location on Cannery Row, where you can see frolicking sea otters from the wide outdoor patio and many room balconies. **Pros:** on the ocean; lots of amenities; attentive service. **Cons:** touristy area; heavy traffic. **TripAdvisor:** "excellent service," "great experience," "out of this world." $ *Rooms from: $279 ⊠ 400 Cannery Row ☎ 831/646–1700, 800/334–3999 ⊕ www.montereyplazahotel.com ↩ 280 rooms, 10 suites.*

$$$$ **Old Monterey Inn.** This three-story manor house was the home of
B&B/INN Monterey's first mayor, and today it remains a private enclave within
Fodor's Choice walking distance of downtown. **Pros:** gorgeous gardens; refined luxury;
★ serene. **Cons:** must drive to attractions and sights; fills quickly. **TripAdvisor:** "luxurious retreat," "welcoming and relaxing," "literally the best of the best." $ *Rooms from: $269 ⊠ 500 Martin St. ☎ 831/375–8284, 800/350–2344 ⊕ www.oldmontereyinn.com ↩ 6 rooms, 3 suites, 1 cottage ⊙ Breakfast.*

$ **Quality Inn Monterey.** This attractive motel has a friendly, country-inn
HOTEL feeling. **Pros:** indoor pool; bargain rates; cheerful innkeepers. **Cons:** street is busy during the day; some rooms are dark. **TripAdvisor:** "exceptional quality," "genuinely awesome staff," "quaint accommodation gem." $ *Rooms from: $105 ⊠ 1058 Munras Ave. ☎ 831/372–3381 ⊕ www.qualityinnmonterey.com ↩ 55 rooms ⊙ Breakfast.*

$$$ **Spindrift Inn.** This boutique hotel on Cannery Row has beach access
HOTEL and a rooftop garden that overlooks the water. **Pros:** close to aquarium; steps from the beach; friendly staff. **Cons:** throngs of visitors outside; can be noisy; not good for families. **TripAdvisor:** "very romantic," "a heavenly place on the ocean," "nice and cozy." $ *Rooms from: $200 ⊠ 652 Cannery Row ☎ 831/646–8900, 800/841–1879 ⊕ www.spindriftinn.com ↩ 45 rooms ⊙ Breakfast.*

THE ARTS

Bruce Ariss Wharf Theater. American musicals past and present are the focus here, with dramas and comedies also in the mix. ⊠ 1 Fisherman's Wharf ☎ 831/649–2332.

★ **Dixieland Monterey.** Traditional jazz bands play waterfront venues during this festival, held on the first full weekend of March. ☎ 831/675–0298, 888/349–6879 ⊕ www.dixieland-monterey.com.

THE FIRST ARTICHOKE QUEEN

Castroville, a tiny town off Highway 1 between Monterey and Watsonville, produces about 95% of U.S. artichokes. Back in 1948, the town chose its first queen to preside during its Artichoke Festival—a beautiful young woman named Norma Jean Mortenson, who later changed her name to Marilyn Monroe.

7

Monterey Bay Blues Festival. Blues fans flock to the Monterey Fairgrounds for this festival, held the last weekend in June. ☎ *831/394–2652* ⊕ *www. montereyblues.com.*

Monterey Jazz Festival. The world's oldest jazz festival attracts top-name performers to the Monterey Fairgrounds on the third full weekend of September. ☎ *888/248–6499 ticket office, 831/373–3366* ⊕ *www. montereyjazzfestival.org.*

SPORTS AND THE OUTDOORS

Throughout most of the year, the Monterey Bay area is a haven for those who love tennis, golf, surfing, fishing, biking, hiking, scuba diving, and kayaking. In the rainy winter months, when the waves grow larger, adventurous surfers flock to the water.

Monterey Bay National Marine Sanctuary. The sanctuary, home to mammals, seabirds, fishes, invertebrates, and plants, encompasses a 276-mile shoreline and 5,322 square miles of ocean. Ringed by beaches and campgrounds, it's a place for kayaking, whale-watching, scuba diving, and other water sports. ☎ *831/647–4201* ⊕ *montereybay.noaa.gov.*

BICYCLING

Adventures by the Sea, Inc. You can rent surreys and tandem and standard bicycles from Adventures by the Sea, which also offers bike tours. ⊠ *299 Cannery Row* ☎ *831/372–1807, 831/648–7236* ⊕ *adventuresbythesea. com* ⊠ *210 Alvarado Mall* ⊠ *Stillwater Cove, 17-Mile Drive, Pebble Beach* ⊠ *Beach at Lovers Point, Pacific Grove.*

Bay Bikes. For bicycle and surrey rentals and tours, visit Bay Bikes. ⊠ *585 Cannery Row* ☎ *831/655–2453* ⊕ *www.baybikes.com.*

FISHING

Randy's Fishing and Whale Watching Trips. A family-run business, Randy's has been in business since 1949. ⊠ *66 Fisherman's Wharf* ☎ *831/372–7440, 800/251–7440* ⊕ *www.randysfishingtrips.com.*

SCUBA DIVING

Monterey Bay waters never warm to the temperatures of their Southern California counterparts (the warmest they get is the low 60s), but that's one reason why the marine life here is among the world's most diverse.

Aquarius Dive Shop. Staffers at Aquarius give diving lessons and tours, and rent equipment. The diving-conditions information line is updated daily. ⊠ *2040 Del Monte Ave.* ☎ *831/375–1933, 831/657–1020 diving conditions* ⊕ *www.aquariusdivers.com.*

WALKING

Monterey Bay Coastal Trail. From Custom House Plaza, you can walk along the coast in either direction on this 29-mile-long trail for spectacular views of the sea. The trail runs from north of Monterey to Pacific Grove, with sections continuing around Pebble Beach. ☎ *831/372–3196* ⊕ *www.mtycounty.com/pgs-parks/bike-path.html.*

WHALE-WATCHING

Thousands of gray whales pass close by the Monterey Coast on their annual migration between the Bering Sea and Baja California. The gigantic creatures are sometimes visible through binoculars from shore, but a whale-watching cruise is the best way to get a close look at these magnificent mammals. The migration south takes place from December through March; January is prime viewing time. The whales migrate north from March through June. In addition, some 2,000 blue whales and 600 humpbacks pass the coast and are easily spotted in late summer and early fall.

★ **Monterey Bay Whale Watch.** The marine biologists here lead three- to five-hour whale-watching tours. ⊠ *84 Fisherman's Wharf* ☎ *831/375–4658* ⊕ *www.montereybaywhalewatch.com.*

Princess Monterey Whale Watching. Tours are offered daily on a 150-passenger high-speed cruiser and a large 75-foot boat. ⊠ *96 Fisherman's Wharf #1* ☎ *831/372–2203, 800/979–3370* ⊕ *www.montereywhalewatching.com.*

AROUND MONTEREY BAY

As Highway 1 follows the curve of the bay between Monterey and Santa Cruz, it passes through a rich agricultural zone. Opening right onto the bay, where the Salinas and Pajaro rivers drain into the Pacific, a broad valley brings together fertile soil, an ideal climate, and a good water supply to create optimum growing conditions for crops such as strawberries, artichokes, brussels sprouts, and broccoli. Several beautiful beaches line this part of the coast. Salinas and Moss Landing are in Monterey County; the other cities and towns covered here are in Santa Cruz County.

GETTING HERE AND AROUND

All the towns in this area are on or just off Highway 1. MST buses serve Monterey County destinations, connecting in Watsonville with Santa Cruz METRO buses, which operate throughout Santa Cruz County.

SALINAS

17 miles east of Monterey on Hwy. 68.

Salinas, a hard-working city surrounded by vineyards and fruit and vegetable fields, honors the memory and literary legacy of John Steinbeck, its most famous native, with the National Steinbeck Center. The facility spurred the revival of Old Town Salinas, where renovated turn-of-the-20th-century stone buildings house shops and restaurants.

ESSENTIALS

Transportation Information Salinas Amtrak Station ⊠ *30 Railroad Ave., Salinas* ☎ *800/872–7245.*

Visitor Information Salinas Valley Chamber of Commerce ⊠ *119 E. Alisal St., Salinas* ☎ *831/751–7725* ⊕ *www.salinaschamber.com.*

EXPLORING

National Steinbeck Center. The center's exhibits document the life of Pulitzer- and Nobel-prize winner John Steinbeck and the history of the nearby communities that inspired novels such as *East of Eden.* Highlights include reproductions of the green pickup-camper from *Travels with Charley* and of the bunkroom from *Of Mice and Men.* **Steinbeck House,** the author's Victorian birthplace, at 132 Central Avenue, is two blocks from the center in a so-so neighborhood. Now a decent lunch spot, it displays memorabilia. ⊠ *1 Main St., at Central Ave.* ☎ *831/775–4721* ⊕ *www.steinbeck.org* ⊠ *$11* ⊙ *Daily 10–5.*

MOSS LANDING

17 miles north of Monterey on Hwy. 1; 12 miles north of Salinas on Highway 183.

Moss Landing is not much more than a couple of blocks of cafés and restaurants, art galleries, and studios plus a busy fishing port, but therein lies its charm. It's a fine place to overnight or stop for a meal and get a dose of nature.

GETTING HERE AND AROUND

From Highway 1 north or south, exit at Moss Landing Road on the ocean side. MST buses serve Moss Landing via Watsonville.

ESSENTIALS

Visitor Information Moss Landing Chamber of Commerce ☎ *831/633–4501* ⊕ *www.mosslandingchamber.com.*

EXPLORING

★ **Elkhorn Slough National Estuarine Research Reserve.** In the Elkhorn Slough National Estuarine Research Reserve, 1,400 acres of tidal flats and salt marshes form a complex environment that supports some 300 species of birds. A walk along the meandering waterways and wetlands can reveal hawks, white-tailed kites, owls, herons, and egrets. Sea otters, sharks, rays, and many other animals also live or visit here. On weekends, guided walks from the visitor center to the heron rookery begin at 10 and 1. ⊠ *1700 Elkhorn Rd.* ☎ *831/728–2822* ⊕ *www.elkhornslough.org* ⊠ *$4* ⊙ *Wed.–Sun. 9–5.*

WHERE TO EAT AND STAY

For expanded reviews, facilities, and current deals, visit Fodors.com.

$ ✕ **Phil's Fish Market & Eatery.** Exquisitely fresh, simply prepared seafood
SEAFOOD   (try the cioppino) is on the menu at this warehouselike restaurant on the harbor; all kinds of glistening fish are for sale at the market in the front. ■ TIP→ Phil's Snack Shack, a tiny sandwich-and-smoothie joint, serves quicker meals at the north end of town. ⑤ *Average main: $15* ⊠ *7600 Sandholdt Rd.* ☎ *831/633–2152* ⊕ *www.philsfishmarket.com.*

$$ ⌕ **Captain's Inn.** Commune with nature and pamper yourself with upscale
B&B/INN   creature comforts at this green-certified getaway in the heart of town. **Pros:** walk to restaurants and shops; tranquil natural setting; homey atmosphere **Cons:** rooms in historic building don't have water views; far from urban amenities; not appropriate for young children. **TripAdvisor:** "beautiful views," "excellent hospitality," "a quiet getaway."

⑤ *Rooms from: $165* ✉ *8122 Moss Landing Rd.* ☎ *831/633–5550*
⊕ *www.captainsinn.com* ⌁ *10 rooms* ⦿ *Breakfast.*

SPORTS AND THE OUTDOORS

Elkhorn Slough Safari. This outfit's naturalists lead two-hour tours of Elkhorn Sough aboard a 27-foot pontoon boat. Reservations are required. ✉ *Moss Landing Harbor* ☎ *831/633–5555* ⊕ *www.elkhornslough.com* ✉ *$35.*

WATSONVILLE

7 miles north of Moss Landing on Hwy. 1.

If ever a city was built on berries, Watsonville is it. Produce has long driven the economy here, and this is where the Santa Cruz County Fair takes place each September.

GETTING HERE AND AROUND

From Santa Cruz or Monterey, follow Highway 1 to Watsonville. From U.S. 101, take Highway 152 West from Gilroy (a curving but scenic road over the mountains) or Highway 129 West from just north of San Juan Bautista. MST and Santa Cruz METRO buses connect at the Watsonville Transit Center, at Rodriguez Street and West Lake Avenue.

EXPLORING

☾ **Agricultural History Project.** One feature of the Santa Cruz County Fairgrounds is the Agricultural History Project, which preserves the history of farming in the Pajaro Valley. In the Codiga Center and Museum you can examine antique tractors and milking machines, peruse an exhibit on the era when Watsonville was the "frozen food capital of the West," and watch experts restore farm implements and vehicles. ✉ *2601 E. Lake Ave., Hwy. 152, at Carlton Rd.* ☎ *831/724–5898* ⊕ *www. aghistoryproject.org* ✉ *$2 suggested donation* ☉ *Thurs.–Sun. noon–4.*

☾ **Watsonville Fly-in & Air Show.** Every Labor Day weekend, aerial performers execute elaborate aerobatics at the Watsonville Fly-in & Air Show. More than 300 classic, experimental, and military aircraft are on display; concerts and other events fill three days. ✉ *Watsonville Municipal Airport, 100 Aviation Way* ☎ *831/763–5600* ⊕ *www.watsonvilleflyin. org* ✉ *$15.*

APTOS

7 miles north of Watsonville on Hwy. 1.

Backed by a redwood forest and facing the sea, downtown Aptos—known as Aptos Village—is a place of wooden walkways and false-fronted shops. Antiques dealers cluster along Trout Gulch Road, off Soquel Drive east of Highway 1.

GETTING HERE AND AROUND

Use Highway 1 to reach Aptos from Santa Cruz or Monterey. Exit at State Park Drive to reach the main shopping hub and Aptos Village. You can also exit at Freedom Boulevard or Rio del Mar. Soquel Drive is the main artery through town.

SAN JUAN BAUTISTA

About as close to early-19th-century California as you can get, San Juan Bautista (15 miles east of Watsonville on Highway 156) has been protected from development since 1933, when much of it became a state park. Small antiques shops and restaurants occupy the Old West and art-deco buildings that line 3rd Street.

The wide green plaza of San Juan Bautista State Historic Park is ringed by 18th- and 19th-century buildings, many of them open to the public.

The cemetery of the long, low, colonnaded mission church contains the unmarked graves of more than 4,300 Native American converts. Nearby is an adobe home furnished with Spanish-colonial antiques, a hotel frozen in the 1860s, a blacksmith shop, a stable, a pioneer cabin, and a jailhouse.

The first Saturday of each month, costumed volunteers engage in quilting bees, tortilla making, and other frontier activities. ⊕ *www.san-juan-bautista.ca.us.*

ESSENTIALS

Visitor Information Aptos Chamber of Commerce ⊠ *7605-A Old Dominion Ct.* ☎ *831/688–1467* ⊕ *www.aptoschamber.com.*

BEACHES

Seacliff State Beach. Sandstone bluffs tower above popular Seacliff State Beach. You can fish off the pier, which leads out to a sunken World War I tanker ship built of concrete. **Amenities:** food and drink; lifeguards; parking (fee); showers; toilets. **Best For:** sunset; swimming; walking. ⊠ *201 State Park Dr., off Hwy. 1* ☎ *831/685–6442* ⊕ *www.parks.ca.gov* 🖃 *$10 per vehicle.*

WHERE TO EAT AND STAY

For expanded reviews, facilities, and current deals, visit Fodors.com.

$$$
MEDITERRANEAN
★

✕ **Bittersweet Bistro.** A large old tavern with cathedral ceilings houses this popular bistro, where chef-owner Thomas Vinolus draws culinary inspiration from the Mediterranean. The menu changes seasonally, but regular highlights include pan-seared Monterey Bay petrale sole, seafood puttanesca (pasta with a spicy sauce of garlic, tomatoes, anchovies, and olives), and fire-roasted pork tenderloin. The decadent chocolate desserts are not to be missed. Breakfast and lunch are available in the casual Bittersweet Café. Pets are welcome on the outdoor patio. $ *Average main: $25* ⊠ *787 Rio Del Mar Blvd., off Hwy. 1* ☎ *831/662–9799* ⊕ *www.bittersweetbistro.com.*

$$$
HOTEL
☺

🛏 **Best Western Seacliff Inn.** Families and business travelers like this 6-acre property near Seacliff State Beach that's more resort than hotel. **Pros:** walking distance to the beach; family-friendly; hot breakfast buffet. **Cons:** close to freeway; occasional nighttime bar noise. **TripAdvisor:** "affordable accommodation," "fun," "choose your room wisely." $ *Rooms from: $180* ⊠ *7500 Old Dominion Ct.* ☎ *831/688–7300, 800/367–2003* ⊕ *www.seacliffinn.com* 🖛 *139 rooms, 10 suites* ⭐ *Breakfast.*

$$$
B&B/INN

🛏 **Flora Vista.** Multicolor fields of flowers, strawberries, and veggies unfold in every direction at this luxury neo-Georgian inn set on 2 serene acres just south of Aptos. **Pros:** super-private; near Sand Dollar Beach; flowers everywhere. **Cons:** no restaurants or nightlife within walking distance; not a good place for kids. **TripAdvisor:** "warm innkeepers," "excellent food," "beautiful setting." $ *Rooms from: $195* ⊠ *1258 San Andreas Rd., La Selva Beach* ☎ *831/724–8663, 877/753–5672* ⊕ *www. floravistainn.com* ↪ *5 rooms* ⚲ *Breakfast.*

$$$$
RESORT
☃

❂ **Seascape Beach Resort.** On a bluff overlooking Monterey Bay, Seascape is a full-fledged resort that makes it easy to unwind. **Pros:** time-share-style apartments; access to miles of beachfront; superb views. **Cons:** far from city life; most bathrooms are small. **TripAdvisor:** "everything you desire," "cool setting," "lovely room and staff." $ *Rooms from: $300* ⊠ *1 Seascape Resort Dr.* ☎ *831/688–6800, 800/929–7727* ⊕ *www. seascaperesort.com* ↪ *285 suites.*

CAPITOLA AND SOQUEL

4 miles northwest of Aptos on Hwy. 1.

On the National Register of Historic places as California's first seaside resort town, the village of Capitola has been in a holiday mood since the late 1800s. Casual eateries, surf shops, and ice-cream parlors pack its walkable downtown. Inland, across Highway 1, antiques shops line Soquel Drive in the town of Soquel. Wineries dot the Santa Cruz Mountains beyond.

GETTING HERE AND AROUND

From Santa Cruz or Monterey, follow Highway 1 to the Capitola/Soquel (Bay Avenue) exit about 7 miles south of Santa Cruz and head west to reach Capitola and east to access Soquel Village. On summer weekends, park for free in the lot behind the Crossroads Center, a block west of the freeway, and hop aboard the free Capitola Shuttle to the village.

ESSENTIALS

Visitor Information Capitola-Soquel Chamber of Commerce ⊠ *716-G Capitola Ave.* ☎ *831/475–6522, 800/474–6522* ⊕ *www.capitolachamber.com.*

BEACHES

New Brighton State Beach. New Brighton State Beach, once the site of a Chinese fishing village, is now a popular surfing and camping spot. Its Pacific Migrations Visitor Center traces the history of the Chinese and other peoples who settled around Monterey Bay, as well as the migratory patterns of the area's wildlife, such as monarch butterflies and gray whales. ■**TIP**➡ New Brighton Beach connects with Seacliff Beach, and at low tide you can walk or run along this scenic stretch of sand for nearly 16 miles south (you might have to wade through a few creeks). The 1½-mile stroll from New Brighton to Seacliff's cement ship is a local favorite. **Amenities:** parking (fee); showers; toilets. **Best For:** sunset; swimming; walking. ⊠ *1500 State Park Dr., off Hwy. 1* ☎ *831/464–6330* ⊕ *www. parks.ca.gov* ⌾ *$10 per vehicle.*

WHERE TO EAT

$ **✕ Carpo's.** Locals love this casual
SEAFOOD counter. Seafood predominates,
but Carpo's also serves burgers, salads, and steaks. Favorites include the baskets of fresh
battered snapper, calamari and
prawns, seafood kebabs, and
homemade olallieberry pie. Nearly
everything costs less than $10. Go
early to beat the crowds. $ *Aver-
age main: $9* ⊠ *2400 Porter St., at
Hwy. 1* ☎ *831/476–6260* ⊕ *www.
carposrestaurant.com.*

$ **✕ Gayle's Bakery & Rosticceria.**
CAFÉ Whether you're in the mood for an
orange-olallieberry muffin, a wild
rice and chicken salad, or tri-tip on
garlic toast, this bakery-cum-deli's
varied menu is likely to satisfy.
Munch your chocolate macaroon on the shady patio or dig into the daily
blue-plate dinner amid the whirl inside. $ *Average main: $10* ⊠ *504
Bay Ave., at Capitola Ave.* ☎ *831/462–1200* ⊕ *www.gaylesbakery.com.*

$$ **✕ Michael's on Main.** Creative variations on classic comfort food draw
AMERICAN lively crowds to this upscale-but-casual creek-side eatery. Chef Michael
Clark's menu changes seasonally, but you can always count on finding
such home-style dishes as pork osso bucco in red-wine tomato-citrus
sauce, as well as unusual entrées like pistachio-crusted salmon with
mint vinaigrette. For a quiet conversation spot, ask for a table on the
romantic patio overlooking the creek. The busy bar area hosts live
music from Wednesday through Saturday. $ *Average main: $22* ⊠ *2591
Main St., at Porter St.* ☎ *831/479–9777* ⊕ *www.michaelsonmain.net*
☾ *Closed Mon.*

$$$ **✕ Shadowbrook.** To get to this romantic spot overlooking Soquel Creek,
EUROPEAN you can take a cable car or walk the stairs down a steep, fern-lined bank
beside a running waterfall. Dining room options include the rooftop
Redwood Room, the wood-paneled Wine Cellar, and the airy, glass-
enclosed Garden Room. Prime rib and grilled seafood are the stars
of the simple menu. A cheaper menu of light entrées is available in
the lounge. $ *Average main: $28* ⊠ *1750 Wharf Rd., at Lincoln Ave.*
☎ *831/475–1511, 800/975–1511* ⊕ *www.shadowbrook-capitola.com*
☾ *No lunch.*

WHERE TO STAY

For expanded reviews, facilities, and current deals, visit Fodors.com.

$$$$ **⌂ Inn at Depot Hill.** This inventively designed B&B in a former rail
B&B/INN depot sees itself as a link to the era of luxury train travel. **Pros:** short
walk to beach and village; historic charm; excellent service. **Cons:** fills
quickly; hot tub conversation on the patio may irk second-floor guests.
TripAdvisor: "always lovely," "perfect romantic getaway," "oasis of

rest." 🏵 *Rooms from: $279* ✉ *250 Monterey Ave.* ☎ *831/462–3376, 800/572–2632* ⊕ *www.innatdepothill.com* ➵ *12 rooms* 🍽 *Breakfast.*

SANTA CRUZ

5 miles west of Capitola on Hwy. 1; 48 miles north of Monterey on Hwy. 1.

The big city on this stretch of the California coast, Santa Cruz (pop. 57,500) is less manicured than Carmel or Monterey. Long known for its surfing and its amusement-filled beach boardwalk, the town is a mix of grand Victorian-era homes and rinky-dink motels. The opening of the University of California campus in the 1960s swung the town sharply to the left politically, and the counterculture more or less lives on here. At the same time, the revitalized downtown and an insane real-estate market reflect the city's proximity to Silicon Valley and to a growing wine country in the surrounding mountains.

GETTING HERE AND AROUND

From the San Francisco Bay Area, take Highway 17 south over the mountains to Santa Cruz, where it merges with Highway 1. Use Highway 1 to get around the area. The Santa Cruz Transit Center is at 920 Pacific Avenue, at Front Street, a short walk from the Wharf and Boardwalk, with connections to public transit throughout the Monterey Bay and San Francisco Bay areas. You can purchase Santa Cruz METRO bus day passes here.

ESSENTIALS

Transportation Information Santa Cruz METRO ☎ *831/425–8600* ⊕ *www. scmtd.com.*

Visitor Information Santa Cruz County Conference and Visitors Council ✉ *303 Water St.* ☎ *831/425–1234, 800/833–3494* ⊕ *www.santacruz.org.*

EXPLORING

TOP ATTRACTIONS

Pacific Avenue. When you've had your fill of the city's beaches and waters, take a stroll in downtown Santa Cruz, especially on Pacific Avenue between Laurel and Water streets. Vintage boutiques and mountain sports stores, sushi bars and Mexican restaurants, day spas, and nightclubs keep the main drag and the surrounding streets hopping mid-morning until late evening.

Santa Cruz Beach Boardwalk. Santa Cruz has been a seaside resort since the mid-19th century. Along one end of the broad, south-facing beach, the Boardwalk has entertained holidaymakers for more than a century. Its Looff carousel and classic wooden Giant Dipper roller coaster, both dating from the early 1900s, are surrounded by high-tech thrill rides and easygoing kiddie rides with ocean views. Video and arcade games, a mini-golf course, and a laser-tag arena pack one gigantic building, which is open daily even if the rides aren't running. You have to pay to play, but you can wander the entire boardwalk for free while sampling delicacies such as corn dogs and garlic fries. ✉ *Along Beach St.*

☎ *831/426–7433 info line* ⊕ *www.beachboardwalk.com* 🖃 *$30 day pass for unlimited rides, or pay per ride* ☉ *Apr.–early Sept., daily; early Sept.–late May, weekends, weather permitting; call for hrs.*

🔄 **Santa Cruz Municipal Wharf.** Jutting half a mile into the ocean near one end of the Boardwalk, the Municipal Wharf is lined with seafood restaurants, a wine bar, souvenir shops, and outfitters offering bay cruises, fishing trips, and boat rentals. A salty sound track drifts up from under the wharf, where barking sea lions lounge in heaps on crossbeams. ⊠ *Beach St. at Pacific Ave.* ☎ *831/420–6025* ⊕ *www.santacruzwharf. com.*

★ **Santa Cruz Surfing Museum.** This museum inside the Mark Abbott Memorial Lighthouse chronicles local surfing history. Photographs show old-time surfers, and a display of boards includes rarities such as a heavy redwood plank predating the fiberglass era and the remains of a modern board chomped by a great white shark. On-site surfer-docents talk about the good old days. ⊠ *Lighthouse Point Park, 701 W. Cliff Dr., near Pelton Ave.* ☎ *831/420–6289* ⊕ *www.santacruzsurfingmuseum. org* 🖃 *$2 suggested donation* ☉ *Sept.–June, Thurs.–Mon. noon–4; July and Aug., Wed.–Mon. 10–5.*

West Cliff Drive. The road that winds along an oceanfront bluff from the municipal wharf to Natural Bridges State Beach makes for a spectacular drive, but it's even more fun to walk, blade, or bike the paved path that parallels the road. Surfers bob and swoosh in Monterey Bay at several points near the foot of the bluff, especially at a break known as Steamer Lane. Named for a surfer who died here in 1965, the nearby Mark Abbott Memorial Lighthouse stands at Point Santa Cruz, the cliff's major promontory. From here you can watch pinnipeds hang out, sunbathe, and frolic on Seal Rock.

WORTH NOTING

Mystery Spot. Hokey tourist trap or genuine scientific enigma? Since 1940, curious throngs baffled by the Mystery Spot have made it one of the most visited attractions in Santa Cruz. The laws of gravity and physics don't appear to apply in this tiny patch of redwood forest, where balls roll uphill and people stand on a slant. Advance online tickets ($6) are recommended for weekend and holiday visits. ⊠ *465 Mystery Spot Rd., off Branciforte Dr. (north off Hwy. 1)* ☎ *831/423–8897* ⊕ *www.mysteryspot.com* 🖃 *$5 on site, $6 in advance, parking $5* ☉ *Late May–early Sept., daily 10–7; early Sept.–late May, weekdays 10–4, weekends 10–5.*

Santa Cruz Mission State Historic Park. On the northern fringes of downtown is the site of California's 12th Spanish mission, built in the 1790s and destroyed by an earthquake in 1857. A museum in a restored 1791 adobe and a half-scale replica of the mission church are part of the complex. ⊠ *144 School St., at Adobe St.* ☎ *831/425–5849* ⊕ *www.parks. ca.gov* 🖃 *Free* ☉ *Thurs.–Sat. 10–4.*

OFF THE BEATEN PATH

Santa Cruz Mountains wineries. Highway 9 heads northeast from Santa Cruz into hills densely timbered with massive coastal redwoods. The road winds through the lush San Lorenzo Valley, past hamlets consisting of a few cafés, antiques shops, and old-style tourist cabins. Residents of the hunting-and-fishing persuasion coexist with hardcore flower-power survivors and wannabes here, and a new generation has joined the pioneers who opened wineries decades ago. Mountain grapes produce some superb Chardonnays, Pinot Noirs, and Cabernet Sauvignons, among other wines. To sample some, you can start a **winery tour** in downtown Santa Cruz at Storrs Winery, at 303 Potrero Street—a

> **HAWAIIAN ROYALTY SURFS THE BAY**
>
> In 1885 relatives of Hawaiian Queen Kapiolani reputedly visited Santa Cruz and surfed near the mouth of the San Lorenzo River. Nearly 20 years later, legendary Hawaiian surfer Duke Kahanamoku also surfed the Santa Cruz swells.

block off River Street, which, heading north from here becomes Highway 9. Drive north to Felton to visit the Organic Wine Works, just west of Highway 9 on Felton Empire Road downtown. Continue north on Highway 9 and east on Bear Creek Road to the classy Byington and David Bruce wineries, both in Los Gatos. ■ TIP→ The Santa Cruz Mountains Winegrowers Association (⊕ www.scmwa.com) distributes a wine-touring map at member wineries and many lodgings and attractions around Santa Cruz.

Seymour Marine Discovery Center. Part of Long Marine Laboratory at UCSC's Institute of Marine Sciences, the center looks more like a research facility than a slick aquarium. Interactive exhibits demonstrate how scientists study the ocean, and the aquarium displays creatures of interest to marine biologists. The 87-foot blue whale skeleton is one of the world's largest. Tours (sign up when you arrive) take place at 11, 1, 2, and 3. ⊠ *100 Shaffer Rd., off Delaware Ave., west of Natural Bridges State Beach* ☎ *831/459–3800* ⊕ *seymourcenter.ucsc.edu* ⊠ *$6* ⊙ *Tues.–Sat. 10–5, Sun. noon–5.*

University of California at Santa Cruz. The 2,000-acre UC Santa Cruz campus nestles in the forested hills above town. Its sylvan setting, sweeping ocean vistas, and redwood architecture make the university worth a visit. Wander about on your own (maps available at the office of admissions) or on a guided tour (reservations required). Either way, the free campus shuttles can help you get around. ⊠ *Main entrance at Bay and High Sts.* ☎ *831/459–0111* ⊕ *www.ucsc.edu/visit.*

UCSC Arboretum. Half a mile beyond the main campus entrance, the arboretum contains a stellar collection of gardens arranged by geography. A walking path leads through areas dedicated to the plants of California, Australia, New Zealand, and South Africa. ⊠ *1156 High St.* ☎ *831/427–2998* ⊕ *arboretum.ucsc.edu* ⊠ *$5* ⊙ *Daily 9–5, guided tours by appointment*

Wilder Ranch State Park. In the park's Cultural Preserve you can visit the homes, barns, workshops, and bunkhouse of a 19th-century dairy farm. Nature has reclaimed most of the ranch land, and native plants and wildlife have returned to the 7,000 acres of forest, grassland, canyons, estuaries, and beaches. Hike, bike, or ride horseback on miles of ocean-view trails. ⊠ *Hwy. 1, 1 mile north of Santa Cruz* ☎ *831/426–0505*

7

Interpretive Center, 831/423–9703 trail information ⊕ *www.parks. ca.gov* 🅿 *Parking $10* ⊙ *Daily 8 am–sunset.*

BEACHES

♻ **Natural Bridges State Beach.** At the end of West Cliff Drive lies Natural Bridges State Beach, a stretch of soft sand edged with tide pools and sea-sculpted rock bridges. ■ TIP➜ From October to early March a colony of monarch butterflies roosts in a eucalyptus grove. **Amenities:** lifeguards; parking (fee); toilets. **Best For:** sunrise; sunset; surfing; swimming. ⊠ *2531 W. Cliff Dr.* ☎ *831/423–4609* ⊕ *www.parks.ca.gov* 🅿 *Beach free, parking $10* ⊙ *Daily 8 am–sunset. Visitor center Oct.–Feb., daily 10–4; Mar.–Sept., weekends 10–4.*

WHERE TO EAT

$$ ✕ **Crow's Nest.** This classic California beachside eatery sits right on the
SEAFOOD water in Santa Cruz Harbor. Vintage surfboards and local surf pho-
★ tography line the walls in the main dining room; nearly every table overlooks the sand and surf. Seafood and steaks, served with local veggies, dominate the menu; favorite appetizers include the chilled shrimp-stuffed artichoke and crispy tempura prawns, served with rice pilaf. No need to pile high on your first trip to the endless salad bar—you can return as often as you like. For sweeping ocean views and more casual fare (think fish tacos and burgers), head upstairs to the Breakwater Bar & Grill. Live entertainment several days a week makes for a dynamic atmosphere year-round. ⑤ *Average main: $18* ⊠ *2218 E. Cliff Dr., west of 7th Ave.* ☎ *831/476–4560* ⊕ *www.crowsnest-santacruz.com.*

$$ ✕ **Gabriella Café.** The work of local artists hangs on the walls of this
ITALIAN petite, romantic café in a tile-roof cottage. Featuring organic pro-duce from area farms, the seasonal Italian menu has included wild-mushroom risotto, roast rabbit tenderloin wrapped in prosciutto, and roasted beet salad with arugula, goat cheese and pistachios. ⑤ *Average main: $22* ⊠ *910 Cedar St., at Church St.* ☎ *831/457–1677* ⊕ *www. gabriellacafe.com.*

$$$ ✕ **La Posta.** Authentic Italian fare made with fresh local produce lures
ITALIAN diners into cozy, modern-rustic La Posta. Nearly everything is house-made, from the pizzas and breads baked in the brick oven to the pasta and the vanilla-bean gelato. The seasonal menu includes flavorful dishes such as fried artichokes, ravioli filled with crab, chicken with brussels sprouts, or sautéed fish from local waters. Come Sunday for the family-style, fixed-price dinner—four courses for just $30. ⑤ *Average main: $26* ⊠ *538 Seabright Ave., at Logan St.* ☎ *831/457–2782* ⊕ *www. lapostarestaurant.com* ⊙ *Closed Mon. No lunch.*

$$$ ✕ **Oswald.** Sophisticated yet unpretentious European-inspired Califor-
EUROPEAN nia cooking is the order of the day at this intimate and stylish bistro.
★ The menu changes seasonally, but might include such items as perfectly prepared sherry-steamed mussels or sautéed duck breast. Sit at the slick marble bar and order a creative concoction like whiskey mixed with aperol and organic strawberry and lemon juices or tequila with celery juice and lime. ⑤ *Average main: $25* ⊠ *121 Soquel Ave., at Front St.*

☎ *831/423–7427* ⊕ *www.oswaldrestaurant.com* ☺ *Closed Mon. Lunch Fridays only.*

$ ✕**Seabright Brewery.** Great burgers, big salads, and stellar microbrews

AMERICAN make this a favorite hangout in the youthful Seabright neighborhood east of downtown. Sit outside on the patio or inside at a comfortable, spacious booth; both are popular with families. ⑤ *Average main: $12* ⊠ *519 Seabright Ave., at Murray St.* ☎ *831/426–2739* ⊕ *www.seabrightbrewery.com.*

$$ ✕**Soif.** Wine reigns at this sleek bistro and wineshop that takes its name

MEDITERRANEAN from the French word for thirst. The lengthy list includes selections from near and far, many of which you can order by the taste or glass. Infused with the tastes of the Mediterranean, small plates and mains are served at the copper-top bar, the big communal table, and private tables. A jazz combo or solo pianist plays some evenings. ⑤ *Average main: $22* ⊠ *105 Walnut Ave., at Pacific Ave.* ☎ *831/423–2020* ⊕ *www.soifwine.com* ☺ *No lunch.*

$ ✕**Zachary's.** This noisy café filled with students and families defines

AMERICAN the funky essence of Santa Cruz. It also dishes up great breakfasts: stay simple with sourdough pancakes, or go for Mike's Mess—eggs scrambled with bacon, mushrooms, and home fries, then topped with sour cream, melted cheese, and fresh tomatoes. ■**TIP**➜ **If you arrive after 9 am, expect a long wait for a table; lunch is a shade calmer (closing time is 2:30 pm).** ⑤ *Average main: $10* ⊠ *819 Pacific Ave.* ☎ *831/427–0646* ⌧ *Reservations not accepted* ☺ *Closed Mon. No dinner.*

WHERE TO STAY

For expanded reviews, facilities, and current deals, visit Fodors.com.

$$$ ⌂**Babbling Brook Inn.** Though it's smack in the middle of Santa Cruz, this

B&B/INN B&B has lush gardens, a running stream, and tall trees that make you feel like you're in a secluded wood. **Pros:** close to UCSC; within walking distance of downtown shops; woodsy feel. **Cons:** near a high school; some rooms close to a busy street. **TripAdvisor:** "beautiful gardens," "serene and friendly," "pristine and cozy rooms." ⑤ *Rooms from: $219* ⊠ *1025 Laurel St.* ☎ *831/427–2437, 800/866–1131* ⊕ *www.babblingbrookinn.com* ⮑ *13 rooms* ⍟**|**⍟ *Breakfast.*

$$$$ ⌂**Chaminade Resort & Spa.** A full-on renovation of the entire property,

RESORT completed in 2009, sharpened this hilltop resort's look, enhanced its amenities, and qualified it for regional green certification. **Pros:** far from city life; spectacular property; ideal spot for romance and rejuvenation. **Cons:** must drive to attractions and sights; near major hospital. **TripAdvisor:** "the hidden jewel," "comfortable and convenient," "beautiful." ⑤ *Rooms from: $299* ⊠ *1 Chaminade La.* ☎ *800/283–6569 reservations, 831/475–5600* ⊕ *www.chaminade.com* ⮑ *112 rooms, 44 suites.*

$ ⌂**Harbor Inn.** Family-run, friendly, and funky, this basic but sparkling-

B&B/INN clean lodge offers exceptional value just a few blocks from Santa Cruz Harbor and Twin Lakes Beach. **Pros:** affordable; free Wi-Fi; park your car and walk to the beach. **Cons:** not fancy; not near downtown. **TripAdvisor:** "nice place with character," "clean and comfortable," "staff is wonderful." $ *Rooms from: $89* ✉ *645 7th Ave.* ☎ *831/479–9731* ⊕ *www.harborinn.info* ⬅ *17 rooms, 2 suites.*

$$$
B&B/INN

🏨 **Pacific Blue Inn.** Green themes reign in this three-story, eco-friendly B&B, built from scratch in 2009 on a sliver of prime property downtown. **Pros:** free bicycles; five-minute walk to boardwalk and wharf; right in downtown. **Cons:** tiny property; not suitable for children. **TripAdvisor:** "stylish," "wonderfully appointed," "Santa Cruz secret." $ *Rooms from: $189* ✉ *636 Pacific Ave.* ☎ *831/600–8880* ⊕ *www. pacificblueinn.com* ⬅ *9 rooms* ⑩ *Breakfast.*

$$$$
B&B/INN
★

🏨 **Santa Cruz Dream Inn.** Just a short stroll from the boardwalk and wharf, this full-service luxury hotel is the only lodging in Santa Cruz directly on the beach. **Pros:** directly on the beach; easy parking; walk to boardwalk and downtown. **Cons:** expensive; area gets congested on busy weekends. **TripAdvisor:** "can't get any closer to the sand," "courtesy and service still exist," "comfortable luxury." $ *Rooms from: $309* ✉ *175 W. Cliff Dr.* ☎ *831/426–4330, 866/774–7735 reservations* ⊕ *www.dreaminnsantacruz.com* ⬅ *149 rooms, 16 suites.*

$$$
B&B/INN
★

🏨 **West Cliff Inn.** Perched on the bluffs across from Cowell Beach, this posh nautical-theme inn commands sweeping views of the boardwalk and Monterey Bay. **Pros:** killer views; walking distance of the beach; close to downtown. **Cons:** boardwalk noise; street traffic. **TripAdvisor:** "outstanding accommodations," "diamond in Santa Cruz," "beautifully restored." $ *Rooms from: $200* ✉ *174 West Cliff Dr.* ☎ *800/979–0910 toll free, 831/457–2200* ⊕ *www.westcliffinn.com* ⬅ *7 rooms, 2 suites, 1 cottage* ⑩ *Breakfast.*

NIGHTLIFE AND THE ARTS

NIGHTLIFE

★ **Catalyst.** Dance with the crowds at this huge, grimy club that regularly features big names, from Neil Young to the Red Hot Chili Peppers. ✉ *1011 Pacific Ave.* ☎ *831/423–1338* ⊕ *www.catalystclub.com.*

Kuumbwa Jazz Center. The renowned center draws top performers such as Herbie Hancock, Pat Metheny, and Charlie Hunter; the café serves meals an hour before most shows. ✉ *320–2 Cedar St.* ☎ *831/427–2227* ⊕ *kuumbwajazz.org.*

Moe's Alley. Blues, salsa, reggae, funk: Moe's has it all (and more), six nights a week. ✉ *1535 Commercial Way* ☎ *831/479–1854* ⊕ *www. moesalley.com.*

THE ARTS

Cabrillo Festival of Contemporary Music. Each August, the Cabrillo Festival of Contemporary Music brings some of the world's finest artists to the Santa Cruz Civic Auditorium to play groundbreaking symphonic music, including major world premieres. ☎ *831/426–6966, 831/420–5260 box office* ⊕ *www.cabrillomusic.org.*

Santa Cruz Baroque Festival. Using period and reproduction instruments, the festival presents classical music at various venues. As the name suggests, the focus is on 17th- and 18th-century composers such as Bach and Handel. ☎ *831/457–9693* ⊕ *www.scbaroque.org.*

Shakespeare Santa Cruz. This six-week festival in July and August occasionally includes a modern dramatic performance. Most performances are outdoors under the redwoods. A holiday program takes place in December. ⊠ *SSC/UCSC Theater Arts Center, 1156 High St.* ☎ *831/459–2121 administration, 831/459–2159 tickets* ⊕ *www. shakespearesantacruz.org.*

SPORTS AND THE OUTDOORS

BICYCLING

Another Bike Shop. Mountain bikers should head here for tips on the best area trails and to browse cutting-edge gear made and tested locally. ⊠ *2361 Mission St., at King St.* ☎ *831/427–2232* ⊕ *www. anotherbikeshop.com.*

BOATS AND CHARTERS

Chardonnay Sailing Charters. The 70-foot *Chardonnay II* departs year-round from Santa Cruz yacht harbor on whale-watching, sunset, and other cruises around Monterey Bay. Most regularly scheduled excursions cost $50; food and drink are served on many of them. Reservations are essential. ☎ *831/423–1213* ⊕ *www.chardonnay.com.*

Stagnaro Sport Fishing. Stagnaro operates salmon, albacore, and rock-cod fishing expeditions; the fees ($50 to $75) include bait. The company also runs whale-watching, dolphin, and sea-life cruises ($45) year-round. ⊠ *June–Aug., Santa Cruz Municipal Wharf; Sept.–May, Santa Cruz West Harbor* ☎ *831/427–2334* ⊕ *www.stagnaros.com.*

GOLF

Pasatiempo Golf Club. Designed by famed golf architect Dr. Alister MacKenzie in 1929, this semiprivate course, set amid undulating hills just above the city, is among the nation's top championship courses. Golfers rave about the spectacular views and challenging terrain. The greens fee is $220; an electric cart is $30 per player. ⊠ *20 Clubhouse Rd.* ☎ *831/459–9155* ⊕ *www.pasatiempo.com.*

KAYAKING

Kayak Connection. In March, April, and May, participants on this outfit's tours mingle with gray whales and their calves on their northward journey to Alaska. Throughout the year, the company rents kayaks and paddle boards and conducts tours of Natural Bridges State Beach, Capitola, and Elkhorn Slough. Most regularly scheduled tours cost between $20 and $55. ⊠ *Santa Cruz Harbor, 413 Lake Ave. #3* ☎ *831/479–1121* ⊕ *www.kayakconnection.com.*

Venture Quest Kayaking. Explore hidden coves and kelp forests on guided nature tours that depart from Santa Cruz Wharf or Harbor, depending on the season. A two-hour kayak nature tour and introductory lesson costs $58. A three-hour kayak rental is $30 and includes wet suit and gear. Venture Quest also arranges tours at other Monterey Bay destinations, including Capitola and Elkhorn Slough. ⊠ *#2 Santa Cruz Wharf* ☎ *831/427–2267 kayak hotline, 831/425–8445 rental office* ⊕ *www. kayaksantacruz.com.*

CLOSE UP

O'Neill: A Santa Cruz Icon

O'Neill wet suits and beachwear weren't exactly born in Santa Cruz, but as far as most of the world is concerned, the O'Neill brand is synonymous with Santa Cruz and surfing legend.

The O'Neill wet-suit story began in 1952, when Jack O'Neill and his brother Robert opened their first Surf Shop in a garage across from San Francisco's Ocean Beach. While shaping balsa surfboards and selling accessories, the O'Neills experimented with solutions to a common surfer problem: frigid waters. Tired of being forced back to shore, blue-lipped and shivering, after just 20 or 30 minutes riding the waves, they played with various materials and eventually designed a neoprene vest.

In 1959 Jack moved his Surf Shop 90 miles south to Cowell Beach in Santa Cruz. It quickly became a popular surf hangout, and O'Neill's new wet suits began to sell like hotcakes. In the early 1960s the company opened a warehouse for manufacturing on a larger scale. Santa Cruz soon became a major surf city, attracting waveriders to prime breaks at Steamer Lane, Pleasure Point, and The Hook. In 1965 O'Neill pioneered the first wet-suit boots, and in 1971 Jack's son invented the surf leash. By 1980, O'Neill stood at the top of the world wet-suit market.

O'Neill operates two flagship stores, one downtown and one close to Jack O'Neill's home on Pleasure Point, along with a smaller outlet on the Santa Cruz Wharf. Sporting stores all over town also carry the line (it's everywhere). ⊕ www.oneill.com

SURFING

Pleasure Point. Surfers gather for the spectacular waves and sunsets here. ⊠ *E. Cliff and Pleasure Point Drs.*

Steamer Lane. This area near the lighthouse on West Cliff Drive has a decent break. Steamer Lane hosts several competitions in summer.

EQUIPMENT AND LESSONS **Club-Ed Surf School and Camps.** Find out what all the fun is about at Club-Ed. Your first private or group lesson ($85 and up) includes all equipment. ⊠ *Cowell Beach, at Santa Cruz Dream Inn* ☎ *831/464–0177* ⊕ *www.club-ed.com.*

Cowell's Beach Surf Shop. This shop sells gear, clothing, and swimwear; rents surfboards, standup paddle boards, and wet suits; and offers lessons. ⊠ *30 Front St.* ☎ *831/427–2355* ⊕ *www.cowellssurfshop.com.*

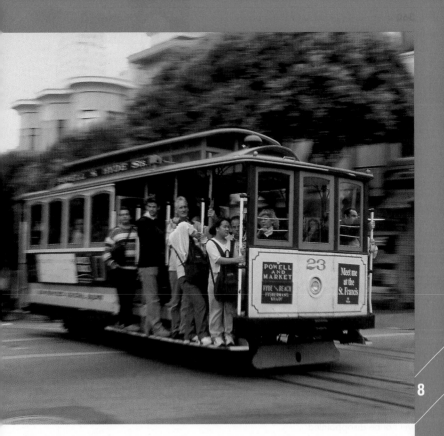

San Francisco

WORD OF MOUTH

"The part I was really looking forward to was walking down [Telegraph Hill] and looking for parrots. I'd seen the movie *The Wild Parrots of Telegraph Hill,* and the neighborhood was one of the things that meant 'San Francisco' to me. The neighborhood itself was beautiful, and we did indeed see parrots."

—sunny16

WELCOME TO
SAN FRANCISCO

TOP REASONS
TO GO

★ **The bay:** It's hard not to gasp as you catch sight of sunlight dancing on the water when you crest a hill, or watch the Golden Gate Bridge vanish and reemerge in the summer fog.

★ **The food:** San Franciscans are serious about what they eat, and with good reason. Home to some of the nation's best chefs, top restaurants, and finest local produce, it's hard not to eat well here.

★ **The shopping:** Shopaholics visiting the city will not be disappointed: San Francisco is packed with browsing destinations, everything from quirky boutiques to massive malls.

★ **The good life:** A laid-back atmosphere, beautiful surroundings, and oodles of cultural, culinary, and aesthetic pleasures . . . if you spend too much time here, you might not leave!

★ **The great outdoors:** From Golden Gate Park to sidewalk cafés in North Beach, San Franciscans relish their outdoor spaces.

1 Union Square and Chinatown. Union Square has hotels, public transportation, and shopping; walking through Chinatown is like visiting another country.

2 SoMa and Civic Center. SoMa is anchored by SFMOMA and Yerba Buena Gardens; the city's performing arts venues are in Civic Center.

3 Nob Hill and Russian Hill. Nob Hill is old money San Francisco; Russian Hill's steep streets have excellent eateries and shopping.

4 North Beach. This small Italian neighborhood is a great place to enjoy an espresso.

5 On the Waterfront. Head here to visit the exquisitely restored Ferry Building, Fisherman's Wharf, Pier 39, and Ghirardelli Square.

6 The Marina and the Presidio. The Marina has trendy boutiques, restaurants, and cafés; the wooded Presidio offers great views of the Golden Gate Bridge.

5 WATERFRONT
Fisherman's Wharf ◆ Pier 39
Marina Green
4 NORTH BEACH
Ghirardelli Square ◆ Bay St.
6 MARINA
Palace of Fine Arts
Lombard St.
RUSSIAN HILL
Coit Tower
TELEGRAPH HILL
Broadway
NOB HILL
(tunnel)
3 CHINATOWN
Ferry Building
PACIFIC HEIGHTS
Washington St.
Sacramento St. California St.
FINANCIAL DISTRICT
Pine St.
Bush St.
Post St.
Geary St.
1 **UNION SQUARE**
San Francisco Bay
JAPANTOWN
Turk St.
Geary Blvd.
Golden Gate Ave.
Fulton St.
CIVIC CENTER
Hayes St.
2 **SOMA**
Harrison St.
HAIGHT
Haight St.
Duboce
Buena Vista Park
CASTRO
8
Castro Theater
9 17th St.
MISSION
20th St.
Central Basin
Twin Peaks
24th St.
25th St.
Cesar Chavez St.
Islais Cr. Channel

---

7 **Golden Gate Park and the Western Shoreline.** San Francisco's 1,000-acre backyard has sports fields, windmills, museums, and gardens; the windswept Western Shoreline stretches for miles.

8 **The Haight, the Castro, and Noe Valley.** After you've seen the blockbuster sights, come to these neighborhoods to see where the city's heart beats.

9 **The Mission.** This Latino neighborhood has destination restaurants, bargain ethnic eateries, and a hip bar scene.

10 **Pacific Heights and Japantown.** Pacific Heights has some of the city's most opulent real estate; Japantown is packed with authentic Japanese shops and restaurants.

GETTING ORIENTED

San Francisco is a compact city; just 46½ square miles. Essentially a tightly packed cluster of extremely diverse neighborhoods, the city dearly rewards walking. The areas that most visitors cover are easy (and safe) to reach on foot, but many have steep— make that *steep*—hills.

8

Updated by
Denise M.
Leto, Michele
Bigley, Marcia
Gagliardi,
Fiona G.
Parrott, Jerry
James Stone

"You could live in San Francisco a month and ask no greater entertainment than walking through it," wrote Inez Hayes Irwin, author of *The Californiacs*, an effusive 1921 homage to the Golden State and the City by the Bay. Follow in her footsteps, and you'll find that her claim still rings true today: simply wandering around this beautiful metropolis on foot is the best way to experience all of its diverse wonders.

Snuggling on a 46½-square-mile strip of land between San Francisco Bay and the Pacific Ocean, San Francisco is a relatively small city of about 750,000 residents. San Franciscans cherish their city for the same reasons visitors do: the proximity to the bay and its pleasures, rows of Victorian homes clinging precariously to the hillsides, the sun setting behind the Golden Gate Bridge. But the city's attraction goes much deeper, from the diversity of its neighborhoods to the progressive free spirit here. Take all these things together, and you'll begin to understand why many San Franciscans can't imagine calling anyplace else home—despite the dizzying cost of living.

San Francisco's charms are great and small. You won't want to miss Golden Gate Park, the Palace of Fine Arts, the Golden Gate Bridge, or a cable car ride over Nob Hill. But a walk down the Filbert Street Steps or through Macondray Lane or an hour gazing at murals in the Mission or the thundering Pacific from the cliffs of Lincoln Park can be equally inspiring.

PLANNING

WHEN TO GO
You can visit San Francisco comfortably any time of year. Possibly the best time to visit San Francisco is September and October, when the city's summerlike weather brings outdoor concerts and festivals. The climate here always feels Mediterranean and moderate—with a foggy, sometimes chilly bite. The temperature rarely drops below 40°F, and anything warmer than 80°F is considered a heat wave. Be prepared for

rain in winter, especially December and January. Winds off the ocean can add to the chill factor. That old joke about summer in SF feeling like winter is true at heart, but once you move inland, it gets warmer. (And some locals swear the thermostat has inched up in recent years.)

GETTING HERE AND AROUND

AIR TRAVEL

The major gateway to San Francisco is San Francisco International Airport (SFO), 15 miles south of the city. It's off U.S. 101 near Millbrae and San Bruno. Oakland International Airport (OAK) is across the bay, not much farther away from downtown San Francisco (via Interstate 80 east and Interstate 880 south), but rush-hour traffic on the Bay Bridge may lengthen travel times considerably. San Jose International Airport (SJC) is about 40 miles south of San Francisco; travel time depends largely on traffic flow, but plan on an hour and a half with moderate traffic.

Airports San Francisco International Airport (*SFO*) ☎ *800/435–9736, 650/821–8211* ⊕ *www.flysfo.com.* **Oakland International Airport** (*OAK*) ☎ *510/563–3300* ⊕ *www.flyoakland.com.* **San Jose International Airport** (*SJC*) ☎ *408/392–3600* ⊕ *www.flysanjose.com.*

Airport Transfers American Airporter ☎ *415/202–0733* ⊕ *www. americanairporter.com.* **BayPorter Express** ☎ *415/467–1800* ⊕ *www. bayporter.com.* **Caltrain** ☎ *800/660–4287* ⊕ *www.caltrain.com.* **East Bay Express Airporter** ☎ *877/526–0304* ⊕ *www.eastbaytransportation.com.* **Lorrie's Airport Service** ☎ *415/334–9000* ⊕ *www.gosfovan.com.* **Marin Airporter** ☎ *415/461–4222* ⊕ *www.marinairporter.com.* **Marin Door to Door** ☎ *415/457–2717* ⊕ *www.marindoortodoor.com.* **SamTrans** ☎ *800/660–4287* ⊕ *www.samtrans.com.* **South & East Bay Airport Shuttle** ☎ *800/548–4664* ⊕ *www.southandeastbayairportshuttle.com.* **SuperShuttle** ☎ *800/258–3826* ⊕ *www.supershuttle.com.* **VIP Airport Shuttle** ☎ *408/986–6000, 800/235–8847* ⊕ *www.viptransportgroup.com.*

8

BART TRAVEL

Bay Area Rapid Transit (BART) trains, which run until midnight, travel under the bay via tunnel to connect San Francisco with Oakland, Berkeley, Pittsburgh/Bay Point, Richmond, Fremont, Dublin/Pleasanton, and other small cities and towns in between. Within San Francisco, stations are limited to downtown, the Mission, and a couple of outlying neighborhoods.

Trains travel frequently from early morning until evening on weekdays. After 8 pm weekdays and on weekends there's often a 20-minute wait between trains on the same line. Trains also travel south from San Francisco as far as Millbrae. BART trains connect downtown San Francisco to San Francisco International Airport; a ride is $8.10.

Intracity San Francisco fares are $1.75; intercity fares are $2.90 to $5.95. BART bases its ticket prices on miles traveled, and does not offer price breaks by zone. The easy-to-read maps posted in BART stations list fares based on destination, radiating out from your starting point of the current station.

Contact BART. ☎ *415/989–2278 San Francisco/Daly City, 510/465–2278 East Bay* ⊕ *www.bart.gov.*

BOAT AND FERRY TRAVEL

Several ferry lines run out of San Francisco. Blue & Gold Fleet operates a number of routes, including service to Sausalito ($10.50 one-way) and Tiburon ($10.50 one-way). Tickets are sold at Pier 41 (between Fisherman's Wharf and Pier 39), where the boats depart. Alcatraz Cruises, owned by Hornblower Yachts, operates the ferries to Alcatraz Island ($28 including audio tour and National Park Service ranger-led programs) from Pier 33, about a half mile east of Fisherman's Wharf. Boats leave 10 times a day (14 times a day in summer), and the journey itself is 30 minutes. Allow roughly 2½ hours for a round-trip jaunt. Golden Gate Ferry runs daily to and from Sausalito ($9.25 one way) and Larkspur ($8.75 one-way), leaving from Pier 1, behind the San Francisco Ferry Building. The Alameda/Oakland Ferry operates daily between Alameda's Main Street Ferry Building, Oakland's Jack London Square, and San Francisco's Pier 41 and the Ferry Building ($6.25 one-way); some ferries go only to Pier 41 or the Ferry Building, so ask when you board. Purchase tickets onboard.

Ferry Lines Alameda/Oakland Ferry ☎ *510/522–3300* ⊕ *www.eastbayferry. com.* **Alcatraz Cruises** ☎ *415/981–7625* ⊕ *www.alcatrazcruises.com.* **Blue & Gold Fleet** ☎ *415/705–8200* ⊕ *www.blueandgoldfleet.com.* **Golden Gate Ferry** ☎ *415/455–2000* ⊕ *www.goldengateferry.org.* **San Francisco Ferry Building** ✉ *1 Ferry Bldg., at foot of Market St. on Embarcadero* ☎ *415/983–8030.*

CABLE CAR TRAVEL

The fare (for one direction) is $6. You can buy tickets on board (exact change isn't necessary) or at the kiosks at the cable car turnarounds at Hyde and Beach streets and at Powell and Market streets.

The heavily traveled Powell–Mason and Powell–Hyde lines begin at Powell and Market streets near Union Square and terminate at Fisherman's Wharf; lines for these routes can be long, especially in summer. The California Street line runs east and west from Market and California streets to Van Ness Avenue; there is often no wait to board this route.

CAR TRAVEL

Driving in San Francisco can be a challenge because of the one-way streets, snarly traffic, and steep hills. The first two elements can be frustrating enough, but those hills are tough for unfamiliar drivers. ■TIP→ Remember to curb your wheels when parking on hills—turn wheels away from the curb when facing uphill, toward the curb when facing downhill. You can get a ticket if you don't do this.

MUNI TRAVEL

The San Francisco Municipal Railway, or Muni, operates light-rail vehicles, the historic F-line streetcars along Fisherman's Wharf and Market Street, trolley buses, and the world-famous cable cars. Light rail travels along Market Street to the Mission District and Noe Valley (J line), the Ingleside District (K line), and the Sunset District (L, M, and N lines); during peak hours (weekdays 6 am–9 am and 3 pm–7 pm) the J line continues around the Embarcadero to the Caltrain station at 4th and King streets. The T line light rail runs from the Castro, down Market Street, around the Embarcadero, and south past Hunters Point and

Candlestick Park to Sunnydale Avenue and Bayshore Boulevard. Muni provides 24-hour service on select lines to all areas of the city.

On buses and streetcars the fare is $2. Exact change is required, and dollar bills are accepted in the fare boxes. For all Muni vehicles other than cable cars, 90-minute transfers are issued free upon request at the time the fare is paid. These are valid for two additional transfers in any direction. Cable cars cost $6 and include no transfers (*see Cable Car Travel, above*).

One-day ($14), three-day ($21), and seven-day ($27) Passports valid on the entire Muni system can be purchased at several outlets, including the cable car ticket booth at Powell and Market streets and the visitor information center downstairs in Hallidie Plaza. A one-day passport can be purchased from cable-car drivers. A monthly ticket, called a Fast Pass, is available for $72, and can be used on all Muni lines (including cable cars) and on BART within city limits. The San Francisco CityPass ($69), a discount ticket booklet to several major city attractions, also covers all Muni travel for seven consecutive days.

The San Francisco Municipal Transit and Street Map ($3) is a useful guide to the extensive transportation system. You can buy the map at most bookstores and at the San Francisco Visitor Information Center, on the lower level of Hallidie Plaza at Powell and Market streets.

Outside the city, AC Transit serves the East Bay, and Golden Gate Transit serves Marin and Sonoma counties.

Bus Lines AC Transit ☎ *510/839–2882* ⊕ *www.actransit.org.***Golden Gate Transit** ☎ *511, 415/455–2000* ⊕ *www.goldengate.org.***San Francisco Municipal Railway System** (*Muni*) ☎ *311, 415/701–3000* ⊕ *www.sfmta.com.*

8

TAXI TRAVEL

Taxi service is notoriously bad in San Francisco, and hailing a cab can be frustratingly difficult in some parts of the city, especially on weekends. Popular nightspots such as the Mission, SoMa, North Beach, the Haight, and the Castro have a lot of cabs but a lot of people looking for taxis, too. Midweek, and during the day, you shouldn't have much of a problem—unless it's raining. In a pinch, hotel taxi stands are an option, as is calling for a pick-up. But be forewarned: taxi companies frequently don't answer the phone in peak periods. The absolute worst time to find a taxi is Friday afternoon and evening; plan well ahead, and if you're going to the airport, make a reservation or book a shuttle instead. Most taxi companies take advance reservations for airport and out-of-town runs but not in-town transfers.

Taxis in San Francisco charge $3.50 for the first 1/5 mile (one of the highest base rates in the United States and rising), 55¢ for each additional 1/5 mile, and 55¢ per minute in stalled traffic. There is no charge for additional passengers; there is no surcharge for luggage. For trips outside city limits, multiply the metered rate by 1.5.

Taxi Companies DeSoto Cab ☎ *415/970–1300.* **Luxor Cab** ☎ *415/282–4141.* **Veteran's Taxicab** ☎ *415/648–1313.* **Yellow Cab** ☎ *415/626–2345.*

Complaints San Francisco Police Department Taxi Complaints ☎ *415/553–1447.*

TRAIN TRAVEL

Amtrak trains travel to the Bay Area from some cities in California and the United States. The *Coast Starlight* travels north from Los Angeles to Seattle, passing the Bay Area along the way, but contrary to its name, the train runs inland through the Central Valley for much of its route through Northern California; the most scenic stretch is in Southern California, between San Luis Obispo and Los Angeles. Amtrak also has several routes between San Jose, Oakland, and Sacramento. The *California Zephyr* travels from Chicago to the Bay Area, and has spectacular alpine vistas as it crosses the Sierra Nevada mountains. San Francisco doesn't have an Amtrak train station but does have an Amtrak bus station, at the Ferry Building, which provides service to trains in Emeryville, just over the Bay Bridge. Shuttle buses also connect the Emeryville train station with downtown Oakland, the Caltrain station, and other points in downtown San Francisco.

Caltrain connects San Francisco to Palo Alto, San Jose, Santa Clara, and many smaller cities en route. In San Francisco, trains leave from the main depot, at 4th and Townsend streets, and a rail-side stop at 22nd and Pennsylvania streets. One-way fares are $2.75 to $12.75, depending on the number of zones through which your travel tickets are valid for four hours after purchase time. A ticket is $6.75 from San Francisco to Palo Alto, at least $8.75 to San Jose. You can also buy a day pass ($5.50–$25.50) for unlimited travel in a 24-hour period. It's worth waiting for an express train for trips that last 1 to 1¾ hours. On weekdays, trains depart three or four times per hour during the morning and evening, twice per hour during daytime non-commute hours, and as little as once per hour in the evening. Weekend trains run once per hour. The system shuts down at midnight. There are no onboard ticket sales. You must buy tickets before boarding the train or risk paying a $250 fine for fare evasion.

Train Contacts **Amtrak** ☎ *800/872–7245* ⊕ *www.amtrak.com.* **Caltrain** ☎ *800/660–4287* ⊕ *www.caltrain.com.* **San Francisco Caltrain station** ✉ *700 4th St., at King St.* ☎ *800/660–4287.*

VISITOR INFORMATION

The San Francisco Convention and Visitors Bureau can mail you brochures, maps, and festivals and events listings. Once you're in town, you can stop by their info center near Union Square. Information about the Wine Country, redwood groves, and northwestern California is available at the California Welcome Center on Pier 39.

Contacts **San Francisco Visitor Information Center** ✉ *Hallidie Plaza, lower level, 900 Market St., at Powell St., Union Sq.* ☎ *415/391–2000 TDD* ⊕ *www. onlyinsanfrancisco.com.*

EXPLORING SAN FRANCISCO

UNION SQUARE AND CHINATOWN

The Union Square area bristles with big-city bravado, while just a stone's throw away is a place that feels like a city unto itself, Chinatown. The two areas share a strong commercial streak, although manifested very differently. In Union Square the crowds zigzag among international brands, trailing glossy shopping bags. A few blocks north in Chinatown, people dash between small neighborhood stores, their arms draped with plastic totes filled with groceries or souvenirs.

EXPLORING IN UNION SQUARE

Maiden Lane. Known as Morton Street in the raffish Barbary Coast era, this former red-light district reported at least one murder a week during the late 19th century. Things cooled down after the 1906 fire destroyed the brothels, and these days Maiden Lane is a chic, boutique-lined pedestrian mall stretching two blocks, between Stockton and Kearny streets. Wrought-iron gates close the street to traffic most days between 11 and 5, when the lane becomes a patchwork of umbrella-shaded tables.

At **140 Maiden Lane** you can see the only Frank Lloyd Wright building in San Francisco. Walking through the brick archway and recessed entry feels a bit like entering a glowing cave. The interior's graceful, curving ramp and skylights are said to have been his model for the Guggenheim Museum in New York. Xanadu Gallery, which showcases Baltic, Latin American, and African folk art, now occupies the space. ⊠ *Between Stockton and Kearny Sts., Union Sq.*

San Francisco Visitor Information Center. A multilingual staff operates this facility below the cable-car terminus. Staffers answer questions and provide maps and pamphlets. You can also pick up discount coupons—the savings can be significant, especially for families—and hotel brochures here. If you're planning to hit the big-ticket stops like the California Academy of Sciences, the Exploratorium, and SFMOMA, and ride the cable cars, consider picking up a CityPass here (or at any of the attractions it covers). ■TIP➔ The CityPass ($69, $39 ages 5–12), good for nine days including seven days of transit, will save you about 50%. Also buy your Muni Passport here. ⊠ *Hallidie Plaza, lower level, Powell and Market Sts., Union Sq.* ☎ *415/391–2000, 415/283–0177* ⊕ *www. sanfrancisco.travel* ⊙ *Weekdays 9–5, Sat. 9–3; also Sun. 9–3 May–Oct.*

Union Square. Ground zero for big-name shopping in the city and within walking distance of most hotels, Union Square is home base for many visitors. The St. Francis and Macy's line two sides of the square, with Saks, Neiman-Marcus, and Tiffany & Co. bordering the other sides, and shopping titan Bloomie's lies just a few blocks down the cable-car tracks. Considered the heart of San Francisco's downtown since 1850, the landscaped, 2½-acre square is about the only place you can sit for free in this part of town. Back in 2002, the public responded to Union Square's redesign with a resounding shrug. With its pretty landscaping, easier street access, and the addition of a café (welcome,

8

Union Square and Chinatown

Jackson Square Historic District

CHINATOWN

Chinese Culture Center

NOB HILL

Old St. Mary's Cathedral

St. Mary's Sq.

San Francisco Museum of Craft & Design

Hallidie Building

UNION SQUARE

Lotta's Fountain

Pacific Telephone Bldg.

MONTGOMERY ST.

POWELL ST.

Yerba Buena Gardens

Moscone Convention Center

Old U.S. Mint

KEY

🅱 *Bart Stop*

.... *Cable Car*

0   350 M

0   1,000 ft.

but nothing special), it certainly was an improvement over the previous concrete wasteland. Four globular lamp sculptures by the artist R.M. Fischer preside over the space; there's also a café, an open-air stage, a visitor information booth, and a front-row seat to the cable-car tracks. And there's a familiar kaleidoscope of characters: office workers sunning and brown-bagging, street musicians, shoppers taking a rest, kids chasing pigeons, and a fair number of homeless people.

The square takes its name from the violent pro-Union demonstrations staged here before the Civil War. At

> **CABLE CAR TERMINUS**
>
> Two of the three cable car lines begin and end their runs at Powell and Market streets, a couple of blocks south of Union Square. These two lines are the most scenic, and both pass near Fisherman's Wharf, so they're usually clogged with first-time sightseers. The wait to board a cable car at this intersection is longer than at any other stop in the system. If you'd rather avoid the mob, board the less-touristy California line at the bottom of Market Street, at Drumm Street.

center stage, Robert Ingersoll Aitken's *Victory Monument* commemorates Commodore George Dewey's victory over the Spanish fleet at Manila in 1898. The 97-foot Corinthian column, topped by a bronze figure symbolizing naval conquest, was dedicated by Theodore Roosevelt in 1903 and withstood the 1906 earthquake. After the earthquake and fire of 1906, the square was dubbed Little St. Francis because of the temporary shelter erected for residents of the St. Francis Hotel. Actor John Barrymore (grandfather of actress Drew Barrymore and a notorious carouser) was among the guests pressed into volunteering to stack bricks in the square. His uncle, thespian John Drew, remarked, "It took an act of God to get John out of bed and the United States Army to get him to work."

On the eastern edge of Union Square, **TIX Bay Area** (☎ *415/433–7827 info only ⊕ www.theatrebayarea.org*) provides half-price day-of-performance tickets to all types of performing-arts events, as well as regular full-price box-office services.

Union Square covers a convenient four-level garage, allegedly the first underground garage in the world. ⊠ *Bordered by Powell, Stockton, Post, and Geary Sts., Union Sq.*

Westin St. Francis Hotel. The second-oldest hotel in the city, established in 1904, was conceived by railroad baron and financier Charles Crocker and his associates as a hostelry for their millionaire friends. Swift service and sumptuous surroundings have always been hallmarks of the property. After the hotel was ravaged by the 1906 fire, a larger, more luxurious Italian Renaissance–style residence was opened in 1907 to attract loyal clients from among the world's rich and powerful. The hotel's checkered past includes the ill-fated 1921 bash in the suite of the silent-film comedian Fatty Arbuckle, at which a woman became ill and later died. Arbuckle endured three sensational trials for rape and murder before being acquitted, by which time his career was kaput. In 1975 Sara Jane Moore, standing among a crowd outside the hotel, attempted to shoot then-president Gerald Ford. As might be imagined, no plaques in the lobby commemorate these events. ■TIP➔ One of the best views in the city is from the glass elevators here—and best of all, a ride is free. Zip up to the 32nd floor for a bird's-eye view; the lights of the nighttime cityscape are particularly lovely. Don't be shy if you're not a guest: some visitors make this a stop every time they're in town. Every November the hotel's pastry chef adds a new touch to his spectacular, rotating 12-foot gingerbread castle, on display in the grand lobby—a fun holiday treat for families. ✉ *335 Powell St., at Geary St., Union Sq.* ☎ *415/397–7000* ⊕ *www. westinstfrancis.com.*

> **LOOK UP!**
>
> When wandering around Chinatown, don't forget to look up! Above the chintziest souvenir shop might loom an ornate balcony or a curly pagoda roof. The best examples are on the 900 block of Grant Avenue (at Washington Street) and at Waverly Place.

EXPLORING IN CHINATOWN

Chinatown Gate. This is the official entrance to Chinatown. Stone lions flank the base of the pagoda-topped gate; the lions, dragons, and fish up top symbolize wealth, prosperity, and other good things. The four Chinese characters immediately beneath the pagoda represent the philosophy of Sun Yat-sen (1866–1925), the leader who unified China in the early 20th century. Sun Yat-sen, who lived in exile in San Francisco for a few years, promoted the notion of friendship and peace among all nations based on equality, justice, and goodwill. The vertical characters under the left pagoda read "peace" and "trust," the ones under the right pagoda "respect" and "love." The whole shebang telegraphs the internationally understood message of "photo op." ✉ *Grant Ave. at Bush St., Chinatown.*

Chinese Historical Society of America Museum and Learning Center. This airy, light-filled gallery has displays about the Chinese-American experience from 19th-century agriculture to 21st-century food and fashion trends, including a moving collection of racist games and toys. A separate room hosts rotating exhibits by contemporary Chinese-American artists. ✉ *965 Clay St., Chinatown* ☎ *415/391–1188* ⊕ *www.chsa.org* 💲 *$5, free 1st Thurs. of month* ⊙ *Tues.–Fri. noon–5, Sat. 11–4.*

☪ **Golden Gate Fortune Cookie Factory.** Follow your nose down Ross Alley to this tiny but fragrant cookie factory. Workers sit at circular motorized griddles and wait for dollops of batter to drop onto a tiny metal plate, which rotates into an oven. A few moments later out comes a cookie that's pliable and ready for folding. It's easy to peek in for a moment, and hard to leave without a few free samples. A bagful of cookies—with mildly racy "adult" fortunes or more benign ones—costs $4.50. You can also purchase the cookies "fortuneless" in their waferlike unfolded state, which makes snacking that much more efficient. Being allowed to photograph the cookie makers at work will set you back 50¢. ✉ *56 Ross Alley, west of and parallel to Grant Ave., between Washington and Jackson Sts., Chinatown* ☎ *415/781–3956* 💲 *Free* ⊙ *Daily 9–8.*

Continued on page 377

CHINATOWN

Chinatown's streets flood the senses. Incense and cigarette smoke mingle with the scents of briny fish and sweet vanilla. Rooflines flare outward, pagoda-style. Loud Cantonese bargaining and honking car horns rise above the sharp clack of mah-jongg tiles and the eternally humming cables beneath the street.

Most Chinatown visitors march down Grant Avenue, buy a few trinkets, and call it a day. Do yourself a favor and dig deeper. This is one of the largest Chinese communities outside Asia, and there is far more to it than buying a back-scratcher near Chinatown Gate. To get a real feel for the neighborhood, wander off the main drag. Step into a temple or an herb shop and wander down a flag-draped alley. And don't be shy: residents welcome guests warmly, though rarely in English.

Whatever you do, don't leave without eating something. Noodle houses, bakeries, tea houses, and dim sum shops seem to occupy every other storefront. There's a feast for your eyes as well: in the market windows on Stockton and Grant, you'll see hanging whole roast ducks, fish, and shellfish swimming in tanks, and strips of shiny, pink-glazed Chinese-style barbecued pork. (For the scoop on dim sum, *see* the Union Square and Chinatown spotlight in the Where to Eat chapter.)

CHINATOWN'S HISTORY

Sam Brannan's 1848 cry of "Gold!" didn't take long to reach across the world to China. Struggling with famine, drought, and political upheaval at home, thousands of Chinese jumped at the chance to try their luck in California. Most came from the Pearl River Delta region, in the Guangdong province, and spoke Cantonese dialects. From the start, Chinese businesses circled around Portsmouth Square, which was conveniently central. Bachelor rooming houses sprang up, since the vast majority of new arrivals were men. By 1853, the area was called Chinatown.

The Street of Gamblers (Ross Alley), 1898 (top). The first Chinese telephone operator in Chinatown (bottom).

COLD WELCOME

The Chinese faced discrimination from the get-go. Harrassment became outright hostility as first the gold rush, then the work on the Transcontinental Railroad petered out. Special taxes were imposed to shoulder aside competing "coolie labor." Laws forbidding the Chinese from moving outside Chinatown kept the residents packed in like sardines, with nowhere to go but up and down—thus the many basement establishments in the neighborhood. State and federal laws passed in the 1870s deterred Chinese women from immigrating, deeming them prostitutes. In the late 1870s, looting and arson attacks on Chinatown businesses soared.

The coup de grace, though, was the Chinese Exclusion Act, passed by the U.S.

Chinatown's Grant Avenue.

Women and children flooded into the neighborhood after the Great Quake.

Congress in 1882, which slammed the doors to America for "Asiatics." This was the country's first significant restriction on immigration. The law also prevented the existing Chinese residents, including American-born children, from becoming naturalized citizens. With a society of mostly men (forbidden, of course, from marrying white women), San Francisco hoped that Chinatown would simply die out.

OUT OF THE ASHES

When the devastating 1906 earthquake and fire hit, city fathers thought they'd seize the opportunity to kick the Chinese out of Chinatown and get their hands on that desirable piece of downtown real estate. Then Chinatown businessman Look Tin Eli had a brainstorm of Disneyesque proportions.

He proposed that Chinatown be rebuilt, but in a tourist-friendly, stylized, "Oriental" way. Anglo-American architects would design new buildings with pagoda roofs and dragon-covered columns. Chinatown would attract more tourists—the curious had been visiting on the sly

for decades—and add more tax money to the city's coffers. Ka-ching: the sales pitch worked.

PAPER SONS

For the Chinese, the 1906 earthquake turned the virtual "no entry" sign into a flashing neon "welcome!" All the city's immigration records went up in smoke, and the Chinese quickly began to apply for passports as U.S. citizens, claiming their old ones were lost in the fire. Not only did thousands of Chinese become legal overnight, but so did their sons in China, or "sons," if they weren't really related. Whole families in Chinatown had passports in names that weren't their own; these "paper sons" were not only a windfall but also an uncomfortable neighborhood conspiracy. The city caught on eventually and set up an immigration center on Angel Island in 1910. Immigrants spent weeks or months being inspected and interrogated while their papers were checked. Roughly 250,000 people made it through. With this influx, including women and children, Chinatown finally became a more complete community.

A GREAT WALK THROUGH CHINATOWN

■ Start at the Chinatown Gate and walk ahead on Grant Avenue, entering the souvenir gauntlet. (You'll also pass Old St. Mary's Cathedral.)

■ Make a right on Clay Street and walk to Portsmouth Square. Sometimes it feels like the whole neighborhood's here, playing chess and exercising.

■ Head up Washington Street to the elaborately pagodaed Old Chinese Telephone Exchange building, now the Bank of Canton. Across Grant, look left for Waverly Place. Here Republic of China flags flap over some of the neighborhood's most striking buildings, including Tin How Temple.

■ At the Sacramento Street end of Waverly Place stands the oddly beautiful brick First Chinese Baptist Church of 1908. Just across the way, the Clarion Music Center is chock-full of unusual instruments, as well as exquisite lion-dance sets.

■ Head back to Washington Street and check out the herb shops, like the Superior Trading Company (No. 839) and the Great China Herb Co. (No. 857).

■ Follow the scent of vanilla from Washington Street down Ross Alley (entrance across

from Superior Trading Company) to the Golden Gate Fortune Cookie Factory. Then head across the alley to Sam Bo Trading Co., where religious items are stacked chockablock in the narrow space. Tell the friendly owners your troubles and they'll prepare a package of joss papers, joss sticks, and candles, and tell you how and when to offer them up.

■ Turn left on Jackson Street; ahead is the real Chinatown's main artery, Stockton Street. This is where most residents do their grocery shopping; if it's Saturday, get ready for throngs (and their elbows). Look toward the back of stores for Buddhist altars with offerings of oranges and grapefruit. From here you can loop one block east back to Grant.

ALL THE TEA IN CHINATOWN

Preparing a perfect brew at Red Blossom Tea.

San Francisco's close ties to Asia have always made it more tea-conscious than other American burgs, but these days the city is in the throes of a tea renaissance, with new tasting rooms popping up in every neighborhood. Below are our favorite spots for every tea under the sun.

Blest Tea. Chinatown's smallest tea shop is a calm, modern space with a thoughtful selection of teas by the pound. The Taiwane owners sell teas from many Asian countries, but their offerings emphasize Taiwan. Regulars rave about the service. ⊠ *752 Grant Ave.* ☎ *415/951–8516.*

Red Blossom Tea. A light and modern shop—the staff really know their stuff. It's a favorite among younger tea enthusiasts, who swear by its excellent bang-for-the-buck value. While Red Blossom doesn't do formal tastings or sell tea by the cup, they'll gladly brew up perfect samples of the teas you're interested in. ⊠ *831 Grant Ave.* ☎ *415/395–0868.*

Vital Tea Leaf. Tastings here work like those for wine—one of the gregarious, knowledgeable servers chooses the teas and describes them as you sample. It's a great spot for tea newbies to get their feet wet without a hard sell, but local connoisseurs grumble about the high prices and the self-promotion. ⊠ *1044 Grant Ave.* ☎ *415/981–2388.*

Imperial Tea Court. If you want to visit the most respected of traditional tea purveyors, you'll need to venture outside of Chinatown. Imperial Tea Court's serene Powell Street oasis closed unexpectedly in 2007, but you'll find the same great selection and expertise at their fancy new digs in the Ferry Building. ☎ *415/544–9830.*

WAITING FOR CUSTARD

As you're strolling down Grant Avenue, past the plastic Buddhas and yin/yang balls, be sure to stop at the Golden Gate Bakery (No. 1029) for some delicious eggy *dan tat* (custard tarts). These flaky-crusted treats are heaven for just a buck. There's often a line, but it's worth the wait.

DON'T-MISS SHOPS

Locals snap up flowers from an outdoor vendor.

If you're in the market for a pair of chirping metal crickets (oh you'll hear them, trust us), you can duck into any of the obvious souvenir-stuffed storefronts. But if you're looking for something special, head for these tempting sources.

■ TIP→ Fierce neighborhood competition keeps prices within reason, but for popular wares like jade, it pays to shop around before making a serious investment. Many stores accept cash only.

Chinatown Kite Shop. Family-run shop selling bright, fun-shaped kites—dragons, butterflies, sharks—since the 1960s. ⊠ *717 Grant Ave.* ☎ *415/ 989–5182.*

Dragon House. A veritable museum: the store sells authentic, centuries-old antiques like ivory carvings. ⊠ *455 Grant Ave.* ☎ *415/421–3693.*

Old Shanghai. One of the largest selections of hand-painted robes, formal dresses, and jackets in Chinatown, plus chic Asian-inspired pieces. ⊠ *645 Grant Ave.* ☎ *415/986–1222.*

CHINATOWN WITH KIDS

It can be tough for the little ones to keep their hands to themselves, especially when all sorts of curios spill out onto the sidewalk at just the right height. To burn off some steam (in them) and relieve some stress (in you), take them to the small but spruce playground in St. Mary's Square, across California from Old St. Mary's. If that setting's too tranquil, head to the more boisterous Willie Wong Playground, on Sacramento Street at Waverly Place.

Kong Chow Temple. This ornate temple sets a somber, spiritual tone right away with a sign warning visitors not to touch *anything*. The god to whom the members of this temple pray represents honesty and trust. Chinese stores and restaurants often display his image because he's thought to bring good luck in business. Chinese immigrants established the temple in 1851; its congregation moved to this building in 1977. Take the elevator up to the fourth floor, where incense fills the air. You can show respect by placing a dollar or two in the donation box and by leaving your camera in its case. Amid the statuary, flowers, and richly colored altars (red wards off evil spirits and signifies virility, green symbolizes longevity, and gold connotes majesty), a couple of plaques announce that "Mrs. Harry S. Truman came to this temple in June 1948 for a prediction on the outcome of the election . . . this fortune came true." The temple's balcony has a good view of Chinatown. ⊠ *855 Stockton St., Chinatown* 🖻 *Free* ⊙ *Mon.–Sat. 9–4.*

Old Chinese Telephone Exchange. After the 1906 earthquake, many Chinatown buildings were rebuilt in Western style with pagoda roof and fancy balconies slapped on. This building—today the Bank of Canton—is the exception, an example of top-to-bottom Chinese architecture. The intricate three-tier pagoda was built in 1909. The exchange's operators were renowned for their prodigious memories, about which the San Francisco Chamber of Commerce boasted in 1914: "These girls respond all day with hardly a mistake to calls that are given (in English or one of five Chinese dialects) by the name of the subscriber instead of by his number—a mental feat that would be practically impossible to most high-schooled American misses." ⊠ *Bank of Canton, 743 Washington St., Chinatown.*

Portsmouth Square. Chinatown's living room buzzes with activity. The square, with its pagoda-shape structures, is a favorite spot for morning tai chi; by noon dozens of men huddle around Chinese chess tables, engaged in not-always-legal competition. Kids scamper about the square's two grungy playgrounds (warning: the bathrooms are sketchy). Back in the late 19th century this land was near the waterfront. The square is named for the U.S.S. *Portsmouth*, the ship helmed by Captain John Montgomery, who in 1846 raised the American flag here and claimed the then-Mexican land for the United States. A couple of years later, Sam Brannan kicked off the gold rush at the square when he waved his loot and proclaimed, "Gold from the American River!" Robert Louis Stevenson, the author of *Treasure Island*, often dropped by, chatting up the sailors who hung out here. Some of the information he gleaned about life at sea found its way into his fiction. A bronze galleon sculpture, a tribute to Stevenson, anchors the square's northwest corner. ⊠ *Bordered by Walter Lum Pl. and Kearny, Washington, and Clay Sts., Chinatown.*

Tin How Temple. Duck into the inconspicuous doorway, climb three flights of stairs—on the second floor is a mah-jongg parlor whose patrons hope the spirits above will favor them—and be assaulted by the aroma of incense in this tiny, altar-filled room. Day Ju, one of the first three Chinese to arrive in San Francisco, dedicated this temple to the Queen of the Heavens and the Goddess of the Seven Seas in 1852. In the temple's entryway, elderly ladies can often be seen preparing "money" to be burned as offerings to various Buddhist gods or as funds for ancestors to use in the afterlife. Hundreds of red-and-gold lanterns cover the ceiling; the larger the lamp, the larger its donor's contribution to the temple. Gifts of oranges, dim sum, and money left by the faithful, who kneel mumbling prayers, rest on altars to various gods. Tin How presides over the middle back of the temple, flanked by one red and one green lesser god. Take a good look around, since taking photographs is not allowed. ⊠ 125 Waverly Pl., Chinatown ☎ Free, donations accepted ⊙ Daily 9–4.

SOMA AND CIVIC CENTER

To a newcomer, SoMa (short for "south of Market") and Civic Center may look like cheek-by-jowl neighbors—they're divided by Market Street. To locals, though, these areas are firmly separate entities, especially since Market Street itself is considered such a strong demarcation line. SoMa is less a neighborhood than it is a sprawling area of wide, traffic-heavy boulevards lined with office high-rises and pricey live-work lofts. Across Market Street from the western edge of SoMa is Civic Center, with San Francisco's eye-catching, gold-domed City Hall. Tickets to a show at one of the neighborhood's grand performance halls are the main reason to venture here.

EXPLORING SOMA

California Historical Society. If you're not a history buff, the CHS might seem like an obvious skip—who wants to look at fading old photographs and musty artifacts? If the answer is an indignant "I do!" or if you're just curious, these airy galleries are well worth a stop. A rotating selection draws from the society's vast repository of Californiana—hundreds of thousands of photographs, publications, paintings, and gold-rush paraphernalia. ■TIP➔ From out front, take a look across the street: this is the best view of the Museum of the African Diaspora's three-story photo mosaic. ⊠ 678 Mission St., SoMa ☎ 415/357–1848 ⊕ www.californiahistoricalsociety.org ☜ $3 ⊙ Wed.–Sat. noon–5; galleries close between exhibitions.

Cartoon Art Museum. Krazy Kat, Zippy the Pinhead, Batman, and other colorful cartoon icons greet you at the Cartoon Art Museum, established with an endowment from cartoonist-icon Charles M. Schulz. The museum's strength is its changing exhibits, which explore such topics as America from the perspective of international political cartoons, and the output of women and African-American cartoonists. Serious fans of cartoons—especially those on the quirky underground side—will likely enjoy the exhibits; those with a casual interest may be disappointed. The museum store carries loads of cool titles to add to your collection. ⊠ 655 Mission St., SoMa ☎ 415/227–8666 ⊕ www.cartoonart.org ☜ $7, pay what you wish 1st Tues. of month ⊙ Tues.–Sun. 11–5.

Contemporary Jewish Museum. Daniel Liebeskind designed the postmodern CJM, whose impossible-to-ignore diagonal blue cube juts out of a painstakingly restored power substation. A physical manifestation of the Hebrew phrase l'chaim (to life), the cube may have obscure

SoMa and Civic Center

Transbay Terminal

Palace Hotel ◆

San Francisco Craft and
Folk Art Museum ◆

Old U.S.
Mint

San Francisco
Public Library ◆

KEY

🚇 Bart Stop

Asian Art Museum **10**

California Historical
Society **7**

Cartoon Art Museum **6**

City Hall **11**

Contemporary Jewish
Museum **1**

Museum of
African Diaspora **4**

Rincon Center **8**

San Francisco
Museum of Modern Art **5**

United Nations Plaza **9**

Yerba Buena Center
for the Arts **3**

Yerba Buena Gardens **2**

Veterans Building ◆

War Memorial
Opera House ◆

Louise M. Davies
Symphony Hall ◆

philosophical origins, but Liebeskind created a unique, light-filled space that merits a stroll through the lobby even if current exhibits don't entice you into the galleries. Be sure to check out the seam where old building meets new. ■TIP➔ At the end of 2012 look for *The Snowy Day and the Art of Ezra Jack Keats,* the first major U.S. exhibit to showcase this award-winning author and illustrator. ⊠ *736 Mission St., between 3rd and 4th Sts., SoMa* ☏ *415/655–7800* ⊕ *www.thecjm.org* ⊠ *$12, $5 Thurs. after 5 pm, free 1st Tues. of the month* ☉ *Thurs. 1–8, Fri.–Tues. 11–5.*

Museum of the African Diaspora (MoAD). Dedicated to the influence that people of African descent have had all over the world, MoAD provokes discussion from the get-go with the question, "When did you discover you are African?" painted on the wall at the entrance. With no permanent collection, the museum is light on displays and heavy on interactive exhibits. For instance, you can sit in a darkened theater and listen to the moving life stories of slaves; hear snippets of music that helped create genres from gospel to hip-hop; and see videos about the Civil Rights movement or the Haitian Revolution. Some grumble that sweeping generalities replace specific information, but almost everyone can appreciate the museum's most striking exhibit in the front window. The three-story mosaic, made from thousands of photographs, forms the image of a little girl's face. Walk up the stairs inside the museum and view the photographs up close—Malcolm X is there, Muhammad Ali, too, along with everyday folks—but the best view is from across the street. ⊠ *685 Mission St., SoMa* ☏ *415/358–7200* ⊕ *www.moadsf. org* ⊠ *$10* ☉ *Wed.–Sat. 11–6, Sun. noon–5.*

Rincon Center. The only reason to visit what is basically a modern office building is the striking Works Project Administration mural by Anton Refregier in the lobby of the streamlined moderne–style former post office on the building's Mission Street side. The 27 panels depict California life from the days when Native Americans were the state's sole inhabitants through World War I. Completion of this significant work was interrupted by World War II (which explains the swastika in the final panel) and political infighting. The latter led to some alteration in Refregier's "radical" historical interpretations; they exuded too much populist sentiment for some of the politicians who opposed the artist. A permanent exhibit below the murals contains photographs and artifacts of life in the Rincon area in the 1800s. A sheer five-story column of water resembling a mini-rainstorm is the centerpiece of the indoor arcade around the corner from the mural. ⊠ *Bordered by Steuart, Spear, Mission, and Howard Sts., SoMa.*

Fodor'sChoice **San Francisco Museum of Modern Art (SFMOMA).** With its brick facade and
★ a striped central tower lopped at a lipstick-like angle, architect Mario Botta's SFMOMA building fairly screams "modern-art museum." The stripes continue inside, from the black marble and gray granite of the floors to the wooden slats on the ceiling. ■TIP➔ Taking in all four exhibit floors can be overwhelming, but keep in mind that the heavy hitters are on floors 2 and 3. Floor 2 gets the big-name traveling exhibits and collection highlights such as Matisse's Woman with the Hat, Diego Rivera's The Flower Carrier, and Georgia O'Keeffe's Black Place 1. Photography

Light streams in through the skylight atop the bold striped cylinder of the San Francisco Museum of Modern Art (SFMOMA).

buffs should hustle up to floor 3, with its works by Ansel Adams and Alfred Stieglitz. Large-scale contemporary exhibits unfold on floors 4 and 5. If it's on display, don't miss sculptor Jeff Koons' memorably creepy, life-size gilded porcelain Michael Jackson and Bubbles, on the fifth floor at the end of the Turret Bridge, a vertiginous catwalk dangling under the central tower. (Look down if you dare.) The window at the bridge's other (west) end offers a great view of the Yerba Buena Gardens below. Back on the fifth floor's east side is the garage-top sculpture garden.

SFMOMA highlights in late 2012 and into 2013 include Jasper Johns: Seeing with the Mind's Eye and the documentary photography exhibit South Africa in Apartheid and After.

Caffè Museo, accessible from the street, provides a refuge with reasonably priced drinks and light meals. The museum's large store sells fun gadgets, artsy doodads of all kinds, very modern furniture, and has a superb collection of kids' books. ■ TIP➔ No ticket is required to visit the lobby, so if it's the architecture you're interested in, you can peek for free.

Note: the SFMOMA will be closed for a massive expansion project starting June 2013 and ending in 2016. The portions of the collection will temporarily move to neighboring museums like the Exploratorium and the Museum of the African Diaspora. See their website for details. ✉ 151 3rd St., SoMa ☎ 415/357–4000 ⊕ www.sfmoma.org ✉ $18, free 1st Tues. of month, ½ price Thurs. 6–9 ⊙ Labor Day–Memorial Day, Fri.–Tues. 11–5:45, Thurs. 11–8:45; Memorial Day–Labor Day, Fri.–Tues. 10–5:45, Thurs. 10–8:45.

Yerba Buena Center for the Arts. You never know what's going to be on display at this facility in Yerba Buena Gardens, but whether it's an exhibit of Mexican street art (graffiti to laypeople), innovative modern dance, or baffling video installations, it's likely to be memorable. The productions here tend to draw a young, energetic crowd, and lean hard toward the cutting edge. ✉ *701 Mission St., SoMa* ☎ *415/978–2787* ⊕ *www.ybca.org* ✉ *Galleries $7, free 1st Tues. of month* ⊙ *Thurs.–Sat. noon–8, Sun. noon–6, 1st Tues. of the month noon–8.*

☾ ★ **Yerba Buena Gardens.** There's not much south of Market that encourages lingering outdoors, or indeed walking at all, with this notable exception. These two blocks

HAYES VALLEY

Hayes Valley, right next door to the Civic Center, is an offbeat neighborhood with terrific eateries, cool watering holes, and great browsing in its funky clothing and home-decor boutiques. Swing down main drag Hayes Street, between Franklin and Laguna, and you can hit the highlights, including two very popular restaurants, Absinthe and Suppenküche. Comfy Place Pigalle (at Hayes and Octavia streets) is also a favorite for its living-room atmosphere, wines, and microbrews. Locals love this quarter, but without any big-name draws it remains off the radar for most visitors.

encompass the Center for the Arts, Metreon, Moscone Convention Center, and the convention center's rooftop Children's Creativity Museum, but the gardens themselves are the everyday draw. Office workers escape to the green swath of the East Garden. The memorial to Martin Luther King Jr. is the focal point here. Powerful streams of water surge over large, jagged stone columns, mirroring the enduring force of King's words that are carved on the stone walls and on glass blocks behind the waterfall. Moscone North is behind the memorial, and an overhead walkway leads to Moscone South and its rooftop attractions. ■**TIP→** The gardens are liveliest during the week and especially during the Yerba Buena Gardens Festival (May through October, ⊕ *www.ybgf.org*), when free performances run from Latin music to Balinese dance.

Atop the Moscone Convention Center perch a few lures for kids. The historic Looff carousel ($3 for two rides) twirls daily 11 to 6. South of the carousel is the Children's Creativity Museum (☎ *415/820–3320* ⊕ *creativity.org*), a high-tech, interactive arts-and-technology center ($10) geared to children ages eight and over. Kids can make Claymation videos, work in a computer lab, check out new games and apps, and perform and record music videos. The museum is open 10–4 Wednesday through Sunday. Also part of the rooftop complex are gardens, an ice-skating rink, and a bowling alley. ✉ *Bordered by 3rd, 4th, Mission, and Folsom Sts., SoMa* ⊕ *www.yerbabuenagardens.com* ✉ *Free* ⊙ *Daily sunrise–10 pm.*

EXPLORING CIVIC CENTER

★ **Asian Art Museum.** Expecting a building full of Buddhas and jade? Well, yeah, you can find plenty of that here. Happily, though, you don't have to be a connoisseur of Asian art to appreciate a visit to this splendidly renovated museum, whose monumental exterior conceals a light, open, and welcoming space. The fraction of the museum's items on display (about 2,500 pieces from a 15,000-plus-piece collection) is laid out thematically and by region, making it easy to follow developments.

Begin on the third floor, where highlights of Buddhist art in Southeast Asia and early China include a large, jewel-encrusted, exquisitely painted 19th-century Burmese Buddha and clothed rod puppets from Java. On the second floor you can find later Chinese works, as well as pieces from Korea and Japan. Look for a cobalt tiger jauntily smoking a pipe on a whimsical Korean jar and delicate Japanese tea implements. The ground floor displays rotating exhibits, including contemporary and traveling shows. ■TIP➜ If you'd like to attend one of the occasional tea ceremonies and tastings at the Japanese Teahouse, call ahead, since preregistration is required. ✉ *200 Larkin St., between McAllister and Fulton Sts., Civic Center* 🕿 *415/581–3500* ⊕ *www.asianart.org* 🎟 *$12, free 1st Sun. of month; $10 some Thurs. 5–9; tea ceremony $27, includes museum* ☉ *Tues.–Sun. 10–5; Jan.–Oct., Thurs. until 9.*

City Hall. This imposing 1915 structure with its massive gold-leaf dome—higher than the U.S. Capitol's—is about as close to a palace as you're going to get in San Francisco. (Alas, the metal detectors take something away from the grandeur.) The classic granite-and-marble behemoth was modeled after St. Peter's Cathedral in Rome. Architect Arthur Brown Jr., who also designed Coit Tower and the War Memorial Opera House, designed an interior with grand columns and a sweeping central staircase. San Franciscans were thrilled, and probably a bit surprised, when his firm built City Hall in just a few years. The 1899 structure it replaced had taken 27 years to erect, as corrupt builders and politicians lined their pockets with funds earmarked for it. That building collapsed in about 27 seconds during the 1906 earthquake, revealing trash and newspapers mixed into the construction materials.

City Hall was spruced up and seismically retrofitted in the late 1990s, but the sense of history remains palpable. Some noteworthy events that have taken place here include the marriage of Marilyn Monroe and Joe DiMaggio (1954); the hosing—down the central staircase—of civil-rights and freedom-of-speech protesters (1960); the murders of Mayor George Moscone and openly gay supervisor Harvey Milk (1978); the torching of the lobby by angry members of the gay community in response to the light sentence given to the former supervisor who killed both men (1979); and the registrations of scores of gay couples in celebration of the passage of San Francisco's Domestic Partners Act (1991). February 2004 has come to be known as the Winter of Love: thousands of gay and lesbian couples responded to Mayor Gavin Newsom's decision to issue marriage licenses to same-sex partners, turning City Hall into the site of raucous celebration and joyful nuptials for a month before the state Supreme Court ordered the practice stopped. That celebratory scene replayed during 2008, when scores of couples were wed between the court's June ruling that everyone enjoys the civil right to marry and the November passage of California's ballot proposition banning same-sex marriage. (Stay tuned as the issue moves through the courts and perhaps back to the voters.) Free tours are offered weekdays at 10, noon, and 2.

The South Light Court houses a modest, rotating display from the collection of the **Museum of the City of San Francisco** (⊕ *www.sfmuseum. org*), including historical items, maps, and photographs. That enormous, 700-pound iron head once crowned the *Goddess of Progress* statue, which topped the old City Hall building when it crumbled during the 1906 earthquake.

Across Polk Street is **Civic Center Plaza,** with lawns, walkways, seasonal flower beds, a playground, and an underground parking garage. This sprawling space is generally clean but somewhat grim. A large part of the city's homeless population hangs out here, despite frequently being shunted away, so the plaza can feel dodgy. ⊠ *Bordered by Van Ness Ave. and Polk, Grove, and McAllister Sts., Civic Center* ☎ *415/554–6023* ⊕ *www.sfgov.org/site/cityhall* ☒ *Free* ☽ *Weekdays 8–8.*

United Nations Plaza. Locals know this plaza for two things: its Wednesday and Sunday farmers' market—cheap and earthy to the Ferry Building's pricey and beautiful—and its homeless population, which seems to return no matter how many times the city tries to shunt them aside. Brick pillars listing various nations and the dates of their admittance into the United Nations line the plaza, and its floor is inscribed with the goals and philosophy of the United Nations charter, which was signed at the War Memorial Opera House in 1945. ⊠ *Fulton St. between Hyde and Market Sts., Civic Center.*

NOB HILL AND RUSSIAN HILL

In place of the quirky charm and cultural diversity that mark other San Francisco neighborhoods, Nob Hill exudes history and good breeding. Topped with some of the city's most elegant hotels, Gothic Grace Cathedral, and private blue-blood clubs, it's the pinnacle of privilege. One hill over, across Pacific Avenue, is another old-family bastion, Russian Hill. It may not be quite as wealthy as Nob Hill, but it's no slouch—and it's known for its jaw-dropping views.

Nob Hill was officially dubbed during the 1870s when "the Big Four"—Charles Crocker, Leland Stanford, Mark Hopkins, and Collis Huntington, who were involved in the construction of the transcontinental railroad—built their hilltop estates. The lingo is thick from this era: those on the hilltop were referred to as "nabobs" (originally meaning a provincial governor from India) and "swells," and the hill itself was called Snob Hill, a term that survives to this day. By 1882 so many estates had sprung up on Nob Hill that Robert Louis Stevenson called it "the hill of palaces." But the 1906 earthquake and fire destroyed all the palatial mansions except for portions of the Flood brownstone. History buffs may choose to linger here, but for most visitors, a casual glimpse from a cable car will be enough.

Essentially a tony residential neighborhood of spiffy pieds-à-terre, Victorian flats, Edwardian cottages, and boxlike condos, Russian Hill also has some of the city's loveliest stairway walks, hidden garden ways, and steepest streets—brave drivers can really have some fun here—not to mention those bay views. Several stories explain the origin of Russian Hill's name. One legend has it that Russian farmers raised vegetables here for Farallon Islands seal hunters; another attributes the name to a Russian sailor of prodigious drinking habits who drowned when he fell into a well on the hill. A plaque at the top of the Vallejo Steps gives credence to the version that says sailors of the Russian-American company were buried here in the 1840s. Be sure to visit the sign for yourself—its location offers perhaps the finest vantage point on the hill.

EXPLORING NOB HILL

Cable Car Museum. The Cable Car Museum is one of the city's best free offerings and an absolute must for kids. (You can even ride a cable car there, since all three lines stop between Russian Hill and Nob Hill.) The museum, which is inside the city's last cable-car barn, takes the top off the system to let you see how it all works. Eternally humming and squealing, the massive powerhouse cable wheels steal the show. You can also climb aboard a vintage car and take the grip, let the kids ring a cable-car bell (briefly), and check out vintage gear dating from 1873.

The gift shop sells cable-car paraphernalia, including an authentic grip-man's bell for $600 (it'll sound like Powell Street in your house every day). For significantly less, you can pick up a key chain made from a piece of worn-out cable. ⊠ *1201 Mason St., at Washington St., Nob Hill* ☎ *415/474–1887* ⊕ *www.cablecarmuseum.com* ☎ *Free* ☉ *Oct.–Mar., daily 10–5; Apr.–Sept., daily 10–6.*

Grace Cathedral. Not many churches can boast an altarpiece by Keith Haring and not one but two labyrinths. The seat of the Episcopal Church in San Francisco, this soaring Gothic-style structure, erected on the site of Charles Crocker's mansion, took 53 years to build, wrapping up in 1964. The gilded bronze doors at the east entrance were taken from casts of Lorenzo Ghiberti's incredible Gates of Paradise, which are on the Baptistery in Florence, Italy. A black-and-bronze stone sculpture of St. Francis by Beniamino Bufano greets you as you enter.

The 35-foot-wide limestone labyrinth is a replica of the 13th-century stone maze on the floor of Chartres Cathedral. All are encouraged to walk the ¼-mile-long labyrinth, a ritual based on the tradition of meditative walking. There's also a terrazzo outdoor labyrinth on the church's north side. The AIDS Interfaith Chapel, to the right as you enter Grace, contains a metal triptych by the late artist Keith Haring and panels from the AIDS Memorial Quilt. ■ TIP→ Especially dramatic times to view the cathedral are during Thursday-night evensong (5:15) and during special holiday programs. ✉ *1100 California St., at Taylor St., Nob Hill* ☎ *415/749–6300* ⊕ *www.gracecathedral.org* ⊙ *Weekdays 7–6, Sat. 8–6, Sun. 8–7.*

Pacific Union Club. The former home of silver baron James Flood cost a whopping $1.5 million in 1886, when even a stylish Victorian like the Haas-Lilienthal House cost less than $20,000. All that cash did buy some structural stability. The Flood residence (to be precise, its shell) was the only Nob Hill mansion to survive the 1906 earthquake and fire. The Pacific Union Club, a bastion of the wealthy and powerful, purchased the house in 1907 and commissioned Willis Polk to redesign it; the architect added the semicircular wings and third floor. (The ornate fence design dates from the mansion's construction.) West of the house, Huntington Park is the site of the Huntington mansion, destroyed in 1906. Mrs. Huntington donated the land to the city for use as a park; the Crockers purchased the Fountain of the Tortoises, based on the original in Rome. ■ TIP→ The benches around the fountain offer a welcome break after climbing Nob Hill. It's hard to get the skinny on the club itself; its 700 or so members allegedly follow the directive "no women, no Democrats, no reporters." Those who join usually spend years on the waiting list and undergo a stringent vetting process, the rigors of which might embarrass the NSA. Needless to say, the club is closed to the public. ✉ *1000 California St., Nob Hill.*

EXPLORING RUSSIAN HILL

Feusier House. Octagonal houses were once thought to make the best use of space and enhance the physical and mental well-being of their occupants. A brief mid-19th-century craze inspired the construction of several in San Francisco. Only the Feusier House, built in 1857, and the Octagon House in Pacific Heights remain standing. A private residence, the Feusier House is easy to overlook unless you look closely—it's dwarfed by the large-scale apartments around it. Across from the Feusier House is the **1907 Firehouse** (✉ *1088 Green St.*). Louise M. Davies, the local art patron for whom Symphony Hall is named, bought it from the city in 1957. The firehouse is closed to the public, but it's worth taking in the exterior. ✉ *1067 Green St., Russian Hill.*

Continued on page 391

CABLE CARS

The moment it dawns on you that you severely underestimated the steepness of the San Francisco hills will likely be the same moment you look down and realize those tracks aren't just for show—or just for tourists.

Sure, locals rarely use the cable cars for commuting these days. (That's partially due to the $6 fare—hear that, Muni?) So you'll likely be packed in with plenty of fellow sightseers. You may even be approaching cable-car fatigue after seeing its image on so many souvenirs. But if you fear the magic is gone, simply climb on board, and those jaded thoughts will dissolve. Grab the pole and gawk at the view as the car clanks down an insanely steep grade toward the bay. Listen to the humming cable, the clang of the bell, and the occasional quip from the gripman. It's an experience you shouldn't pass up, whether on your first trip or your fiftieth.

HOW CABLE CARS WORK

The mechanics are pretty simple: cable cars grab a moving subterranean cable with a "grip" to go. To stop, they release the grip and apply one or more types of brakes. Four cables, totaling 9 miles, power the city's three lines. If the gripman doesn't adjust the grip just right when going up a steep hill, the cable will start to slip and the car will have to back down the hill and try again. This is an extremely rare occurrence—imagine the ribbing the gripman gets back at the cable car barn!

Gripman: Stands in front and operates the grip, brakes, and bell. Favorite joke, especially at the peak of a steep hill: "This is my first day on the job folks…"

Conductor: Moves around the car, deals with tickets, alerts the grip about what's coming up, and operates the rear wheel brakes.

❶ Cable: Steel wrapped around flexible sisal core; 2 inches thick; runs at a constant 9½ mph.

❷ Bells: Used for crew communication; alerts other drivers and pedestrians.

❸ Grip: Vice-like lever extends through the center slot in the track to grab or release the cable.

❹ Grip Lever: Left-hand lever; operates grip.

❺ Car: Entire car weighs 8 tons.

❻ Wheel Brake: Steel brake pads on each wheel.

❼ Wheel Brake Lever: Foot pedal; operates wheel brakes.

❽ Rear Wheel Brake Lever: Applied for extra traction on hills.

❾ Track Brake: 2-foot long sections of Monterey pine push down against the track to help stop the car.

❿ Track Brake Lever: Middle lever; operates track brakes.

⓫ Emergency Brake: 18-inch steel wedge, jams into street slot to bring car to an immediate stop.

⓬ Emergency Brake Lever: Right-hand lever, red; operates emergency brake.

ROUTES

Powell–Hyde line: Most scenic, with classic Bay views. Begins at Powell and Market streets, then crosses Nob Hill and Russian Hill before a white-knuckle descent down Hyde Street, ending near the Hyde Street Pier.

Powell–Mason line: Also begins at Powell and Market streets, but winds through North Beach to Bay and Taylor streets, a few blocks from Fisherman's Wharf.

California line: Runs from the foot of Market Street, at Drumm Street, up Nob Hill and back. Great views (and aromas and sounds) of Chinatown on the way up. Sit in back to catch glimpses of the Bay. ■TIP→ Take the California line if it's just the cable-car experience you're after—the lines are shorter, and the grips and conductors say it's friendlier and has a slower pace.

Cars run at least every 15 minutes, from around 6 AM to about 1 AM.

RULES OF THE RIDE

Tickets. A whopping $6 each way. There are ticket booths at all three turnarounds, or you can pay the conductor after you board (they can make change). Try not to grumble about the price—they're embarrassed enough as it is.

■TIP→ If you're planning to use public transit a few times, or if you'd like to ride back and forth on the cable car without worrying about the price, consider a one-day Muni passport ($14). You can get passports online, at the Powell Street turnaround, the TIX booth on Union Square, or the Fisherman's Wharf cable-car ticket booth at Beach and Hyde streets.

All Aboard. You can board on either side of the cable car. It's legal to stand on the running boards and hang on to the pole, but keep your ears open for the gripman's warnings. ■TIP→ Grab a seat on the outside bench for the best views.

Most people wait (and wait) in line at one of the cable car turnarounds, but you can also hop on along the route. Board wherever you see a white sign showing a figure climbing aboard a brown cable car; wave to the approaching driver, and wait until the car stops.

Riding on the running boards can be part of the thrill.

CABLE CAR HISTORY

HALLIDIE FREES THE HORSES

In the 1850s and '60s, San Francisco's streetcars were drawn by horses. Legend has it that the horrible sight of a car dragging a team of horses downhill to their deaths roused Andrew Smith Hallidie to action. The English immigrant had invented the "Hallidie Ropeway," essentially a cable car for mined ore, and he was convinced that his invention could also move people. In 1873, Hallidie and his intrepid crew prepared to test the first cable car high on Russian Hill. The anxious engineer peered down into the foggy darkness, failed to see the bottom of the hill, and promptly turned the controls over to Hallidie. Needless to say, the thing worked . . . but rides were free for the first two days because people were afraid to get on.

SEE IT FOR YOURSELF

The **Cable Car Museum** is one of the city's best free offerings and an absolute must for kids. (You can even ride a cable car there, since all three lines stop between Russian Hill and Nob Hill.) The museum, which is inside the city's last cable-car barn, takes the top off the system to let you see how it all works.

Eternally humming and squealing, the massive powerhouse cable wheels steal the show. You can also climb aboard a vintage car and take the grip, let the kids ring a cable-car bell (briefly, please!), and check out vintage gear dating from 1873.

✉ *1201 Mason St., at Washington St., Nob Hill* ☎ *415/474–1887* ⊕ *www. cablecarmuseum.com* 🎟 *Free* ⊙ *Oct.– Mar., daily 10–5; Apr.–Sept., daily 10–6*

■ **TIP→** The gift shop sells cable car paraphernalia, including an authentic gripman's bell for $600 (it'll sound like Powell Street in your house every day). For significantly less, you can pick up a key chain made from a piece of worn-out cable.

CHAMPION OF THE CABLE CAR BELL

Each June the city's best and brightest come together to crown a bell-ringing champion at Union Square. The crowd cheers gripmen and conductors as they stomp, shake, and riff with the rope. But it's not a popularity contest; the ringers are judged by former bell-ringing champions who take each ping and gong very seriously.

★ **Ina Coolbrith Park.** If you make it all the way up here, you may have the place all to yourself, or at least feel like you do. The park's terraces are carved from a hill so steep that it's difficult to see if anyone else is there or not. Locals love this park because it feels like a secret no one else knows about—one of the city's magic hidden gardens, with a meditative setting and spectacular views of the bay peeking out from among the trees. A poet, Oakland librarian, and niece of Mormon prophet Joseph Smith, Ina Coolbrith (1842–1928) introduced Jack London and Isadora Duncan to the world of books. For years she entertained literary greats in her Macondray Lane home near the park. In 1915 she was named poet laureate of California. ⊠ *Vallejo St. between Mason and Taylor Sts., Russian Hill.*

★ **Lombard Street.** The block-long "Crookedest Street in the World" makes eight switchbacks down the east face of Russian Hill between Hyde and Leavenworth streets. Residents bemoan the traffic jam outside their front doors, but the throngs continue. Join the line of cars waiting to drive down the steep hill, or avoid the whole mess and walk down the steps on either side of Lombard. You take in super views of North Beach and Coit Tower whether you walk or drive—though if you're the one behind the wheel, you'd better keep your eye on the road lest you become yet another of the many folks who ram the garden barriers. ■**TIP➜** Can't stand the traffic? Thrill seekers of a different stripe may want to head two blocks south of Lombard to Filbert Street. At a gradient of 31.5%, the hair-raising descent between Hyde and Leavenworth streets is the city's steepest. Go slowly! ⊠ *Lombard St. between Hyde and Leavenworth Sts., Russian Hill.*

Fodor's Choice
★ **Macondray Lane.** San Francisco has no shortage of impressive, grand homes, but it's the tiny fairy-tale lanes that make most folks want to move here, and Macondray Lane is the quintessential hidden garden. Enter under a lovely wooden trellis and proceed down a quiet, cobbled pedestrian lane lined with Edwardian cottages and flowering plants and trees. Watch your step—the cobblestones are quite uneven in spots. A flight of steep wooden stairs at the end of the lane leads to Taylor Street—on the way down you can't miss the bay views. If you've read any of Armistead Maupin's *Tales of the City* books, you may find the lane vaguely familiar. It's the thinly disguised setting for part of the series' action. ⊠ *Between Jones and Taylor Sts., and Union and Green Sts., Russian Hill.*

★ **San Francisco Art Institute.** A Moorish-tile fountain in a tree-shaded courtyard draws the eye as soon as you enter the institute. The number-one reason for a visit is Mexican master Diego Rivera's *Making of a Fresco Showing the Building of a City* (1931), in the student gallery to your immediate left inside the entrance. Rivera himself is in the fresco—his broad behind is to the viewer—and he's surrounded by his assistants. They in turn are surrounded by a construction scene, laborers, and city notables such as sculptor Robert Stackpole and architect Timothy Pfleuger. *The Making of a Fresco* is one of three San Francisco murals painted by Rivera. The number-two reason to come here is the café, or more precisely the eye-popping, panoramic view from the café, which serves surprisingly decent food for a song.

The older portions of the Art Institute, including the lovely Mission-style bell tower, were erected in 1926. To this day, otherwise pragmatic people claim that ghostly footsteps can be heard in the tower at night. Ansel Adams created the school's fine-arts photography department in 1946, and school directors established the country's first fine-arts film program. Notable faculty and alumni have included painter Richard Diebenkorn and photographers Dorothea Lange, Edward Weston, and Annie Leibovitz.

The **Walter & McBean Galleries** (☎ 415/749–4563 ⊙ Tues.–Sat. 11–6) exhibit the often provocative works of established artists. ⊠ 800 Chestnut St., North Beach ☎ 415/771–7020 ⊕ www.sfai.edu ᐃ Galleries free ⊙ Student gallery daily 8:30–8:30.

NORTH BEACH

San Francisco novelist Herbert Gold calls North Beach "the longest-running, most glorious American bohemian operetta outside Greenwich Village." Indeed, to anyone who's spent some time in its eccentric old bars and cafés, North Beach evokes everything from the Barbary Coast days to the no-less-rowdy Beatnik era. Italian bakeries appear frozen in time, homages to Jack Kerouac and Allen Ginsberg pop up everywhere, and the modern equivalent of the Barbary Coast's "houses of ill repute," strip joints, do business on Broadway. With its outdoor café tables, throngs of tourists, and holiday vibe, this is probably the part of town Europeans are thinking of when they say San Francisco is the most European city in America.

EXPLORING NORTH BEACH

★ **City Lights Bookstore.** Take a look at the exterior of the store: the replica of a revolutionary mural destroyed in Chiapas, Mexico, by military forces; the poetry in the windows; and the sign that says "Turn your sell [sic] phone off. Be here now." This place isn't just doling out best sellers. Designated a city landmark, the hangout of Beat-era writers—Allen Ginsberg and store founder Lawrence Ferlinghetti among them—remains a vital part of San Francisco's literary scene. Browse the three levels of sometimes haphazardly arranged poetry, philosophy, politics, fiction, history, and local zines, to the tune of creaking wood floors. ■ TIP→ Be sure to check the calendar of literary events.

Back in the day, the basement was a kind of literary living room, where writers like Ginsberg and Jack Kerouac would read and even receive mail. Ferlinghetti cemented City Lights's place in history by publishing Ginsberg's *Howl and Other Poems* in 1956. The small volume was ignored in the mainstream . . . until Ferlinghetti and the bookstore manager were arrested for corruption of youth and obscenity. In the landmark First Amendment trial that followed, the judge exonerated both men, declaring that a work that has "redeeming social significance" can't be obscene. *Howl* went on to become a classic.

Kerouac Alley, branching off Columbus Avenue next to City Lights, was rehabbed in 2007. Embedded in the pavement are quotes from

Ferlinghetti, Maya Angelou, Confucius, John Steinbeck, and the street's namesake. ⊠ *261 Columbus Ave.* ☎ *415/362–8193* ⊕ *www.citylights. com* ☉ *Daily 10 am–midnight.*

★ **Coit Tower.** Whether or not you agree that it resembles a fire-hose nozzle, this 210-foot tower is among San Francisco's most distinctive skyline sights. Although the monument wasn't intended as a tribute to firemen, it's often considered as such because of the donor's special attachment to the local fire company. As the story goes, a young gold rush–era girl, Lillie Hitchcock Coit (known as Miss Lil), was a fervent admirer of her local fire company—so much so that she once deserted a wedding party and chased down the street after her favorite engine, Knickerbocker No. 5, while clad in her bridesmaid finery. She became the Knickerbocker Company's mascot and always signed her name "Lillie Coit 5." When Lillie died in 1929 she left the city $125,000 to "expend in an appropriate manner . . . to the beauty of San Francisco."

You can ride the elevator to the top of the tower—the only thing you have to pay for here—to enjoy the view of the Bay Bridge and the Golden Gate Bridge; due north is Alcatraz Island. ■TIP➜ The views from the base of the tower are also expansive—and free. Parking at Coit Tower is limited; in fact, you may have to wait (and wait) for a space. Save yourself some frustration and take the 39 bus, which goes all the way up to the tower's base, or, if you're in good shape, hike up. ⇨ *For more details on the lovely stairway walk, see the Telegraph Hill listing.*

Inside the tower, 19 Depression-era murals depict California's economic and political life. The federal government commissioned the paintings from 25 local artists, and ended up funding a controversy. The radical Mexican painter Diego Rivera inspired the murals' socialist-realist style, with its biting cultural commentary, particularly about the exploitation of workers. At the time the murals were painted, clashes between management and labor along the waterfront and elsewhere in San Francisco were widespread. ⊠ *Telegraph Hill Blvd. at Greenwich St. or Lombard St., North Beach* ☎ *415/362–0808* ☐ *Free; elevator to top $7* ☉ *Mar.– Sept., daily 10–5:30; Oct.–Feb., daily 9–4:30.*

FodorsChoice
★ **Telegraph Hill.** Residents here have some of the city's best views, as well as the most difficult ascents to their aeries. The hill rises from the east end of Lombard Street to a height of 284 feet and is capped by Coit Tower *(see above)*. Imagine lugging your groceries up that! If you brave the slope, though, you can be rewarded with a "secret treasure" SF moment. Filbert Street starts up the hill, then becomes the Filbert Steps when the going gets too steep. You can cut between the Filbert Steps and another flight, the Greenwich Steps, on up to the hilltop. As you climb, you can pass some of the city's oldest houses and be surrounded by beautiful, flowering private gardens. In some places the trees grow over the stairs so it feels like you're walking through a green tunnel; elsewhere, you'll have wide-open views of the bay. And the telegraphic name? It comes from the hill's status as the first Morse code signal station back in 1853. ⊠ *Bordered by Lombard, Filbert, Kearny, and Sansome Sts., North Beach.*

8

North Beach and On the Waterfront

East
Harbor

Mexican
Museum

Fort
Mason

Aquatic Park

Pier 45

14

San Francisco Bay

12

Pier 47

13

The Cannery at
Del Monte Square

11

Pier 41

Jefferson St.

**NORTH
BEACH**

North Point St.

10

Pier 35

Pier 33

Pier 31

Pier 29

Pier 27

*Russian
Hill Park*

North Point St.

Francisco St.

Bay St.

Beach St.

North Point St.

Bay St.

Taylor St.

Mason St.

Powell St.

Stockton St.

Pfeiffer St.

Kearny St.

Chestnut St.

Pier 23

**Levi Strauss
Headquarters**

Pier 19

Pier 17

Pier 15

Pier 9

Pier 7

Pier 5

Pier 3

Pier 1

Bay St.

Francisco St.

Chestnut St.

Lombard St.

Greenwich St.

Filbert St.

Union St.

Green St.

Vallejo St.

Broadway

*Washington
Square*

7

8

9

Columbus Ave.

Grant Ave.

Varennes St.

Sergent St.

Jasper St.

Kearny St.

Union St.

Green St.

Lombard St.

Chestnut St.

Montgomery St.

Sansome St.

Battery St.

Front St.

Davis St.

The Embarcadero

5

Van Ness Ave.

Polk St.

Larkin St.

Hyde St.

Leavenworth St.

Jones St.

Taylor St.

Mason St.

Stockton St.

**RUSSIAN
HILL**

Broadway

Pacific Ave.

Jackson St.

Washington St.

Pleasant St.

Tunnel

**Cable Car
Museum**

*Huntington
Park*

NOB HILL

6

Pacific Ave.

Jackson St.

Clay St.

Washington St.

Sacramento St.

California St.

Drumm St.

4

3

Taylor St.

Mason St.

Powell St.

Pine St.

Tunnel

Bush St.

Sutter St.

Post St.

*Union
Square*

St. Mary's
Sq.

**Wells Fargo Bank
History Museum**

DOWNTOWN

*Justin
Herman
Plaza*

MONTGOMERY ST.

🚇

Market St.

EMBARCADERO

Mission St.

**Hyatt
Regency
Hotel**

1

2

**Audiffred
Building**

4th St.

Jessie St.

Annie St.

Mission St.

New Montgomery St.

Ecker
Al.

Elim
Al.

Fremont St.

Beale St.

Main St.

Spear St.

Steuart St.

**CITY
FRONT**

**Yerba Buena
Gardens**

Minna St.

Natoma St.

Howard St.

Hawthorne St.

Tehama St.

Clementina St.

Folsom St.

1st St.

2nd St.

Essex St.

Harrison St.

80

San Francisco - Oakland Bay Bridge

Taber Pl.

Bryant St.

Pier 26

KEY	
🚇	*Bart Stop*
....	*Cable Car*

0   350 meters

0   1,000 ft

The Birds

While on Telegraph Hill, you might be startled by a chorus of piercing squawks and a rushing sound of wings. No, you're not about to have a Hitchcock bird-attack moment. These small, vivid green parrots with cherry-red heads number in the hundreds; they're descendants of former pets that escaped or were released by their owners. (The birds dislike cages and they bite if bothered...must've been some disillusioned owners along the way.)

The parrots like to roost high in the aging cypress trees on the hill, chattering and fluttering, sometimes taking wing en masse. They're not popular with most residents, but they did find a champion in local bohemian Mark Bittner, a former street musician. Bittner began chronicling their habits, publishing a book and battling the homeowners who wanted to cut down the cypresses. A documentary, *The Wild Parrots of Telegraph Hill*, made the issue a cause célèbre. In 2007 City Hall, which recognizes a golden goose when it sees one, stepped in and brokered a solution to keep the celebrity birds in town. The city will cover the homeowners' insurance worries and plant new trees for the next generation of wild parrots.

—Denise M. Leto

Washington Square. Once the daytime social heart of Little Italy, this grassy patch has changed character numerous times over the years. The Beats hung out in the 1950s, hippies camped out in the 1960s and early 70s, and nowadays you're just as likely to see kids of Southeast Asian descent tossing a Frisbee as Italian men or women chatting about their children and the old country. In the morning elderly Asians perform the motions of tai chi, but by mid-morning groups of conservatively dressed Italian men in their seventies and eighties begin to arrive. Any time of day, the park may attract a number of homeless people, who stretch out to rest on the benches and grass, and young locals sunbathing or running their dogs. Lillie Hitchcock Coit, in yet another show of affection for San Francisco's firefighters, donated the statue of two firemen with a child they rescued. ■TIP→ The North Beach Festival, the city's oldest street fair, celebrates the area's Italian culture here each June. ⊠ *Bordered by Columbus Ave. and Stockton, Filbert, and Union Sts., North Beach.*

ON THE WATERFRONT

San Francisco's waterfront neighborhoods have fabulous views and utterly different personalities. Kitschy, overpriced Fisherman's Wharf struggles to maintain the last shreds of its existence as a working wharf, while Pier 39 is a full-fledged consumer circus. The Ferry Building draws well-heeled locals with its culinary pleasures, firmly reconnecting the Embarcadero to downtown. Between the Ferry Building and Pier 39 a former maritime no-man's-land is filling in with Alcatraz Landing, fashionable waterfront restaurants, restored pedestrian-friendly piers, and in 2013, the new Exploratorium.

Today's shoreline was once Yerba Buena Cove, filled in during the latter half of the 19th century, when San Francisco was a brawling, extravagant gold-rush town. Jackson Square, now a genteel and upscale corner of the inland Financial District, was the heart of the Barbary Coast, bordering some of the roughest wharves in the world. Below Montgomery Street (in today's Financial District), between California Street and Broadway, lies a remnant of these wild days: more than 100 ships abandoned by frantic crews and passengers caught up in gold fever lie under the foundations of buildings here.

EXPLORING THE WATERFRONT

Alcatraz. Thousands of visitors come every day to walk in the footsteps of Alcatraz's notorious criminals. The stories of life and death on "the Rock" may sometimes be exaggerated, but it's almost impossible to resist the chance to wander the cellblock that tamed the country's toughest gangsters and saw daring escape attempts of tremendous desperation. Fewer than 2,000 inmates ever did time on the Rock, and though they weren't the worst criminals, they were definitely the worst prisoners, include Al "Scarface" Capone, Robert "The Birdman" Stroud, and George "Machine Gun" Kelly.

Some tips for escaping to Alcatraz: 1) Buy your ticket in advance. Visit the website for Alcatraz Cruises (*www.alcatrazcruises.com*) to scout out available departure times for the ferry. Prepay by credit card and keep a receipt record; the ticket price covers the boat ride and the audio tour. Pick up your ticket at the "will call" window at Pier 33 up to an hour before sailing. 2) Dress smart. Bring a jacket to ward off the chill from the boat ride and wear comfortable shoes. 3) Go for the evening tour. You'll get even more out of your Alcatraz experience at night. The evening tour has programs not offered during the day, the bridge-to-bridge view of the city twinkles at night, and your "prison experience" will be amplified as darkness falls. 4) Be mindful of scheduled and limited-capacity talks. Some programs are only given once a day (the schedule is posted in the cell house). Certain talks have limited-capacity seating, so keep an eye out for a cell-house staffer handing out passes shortly before the start time.

The boat ride to the island is brief (15 minutes), but affords beautiful views of the city, Marin County, and the East Bay. The audio tour, highly recommended, includes observations by guards and prisoners about life in one of America's most notorious penal colonies. Plan your schedule to allow at least three hours for the visit and boat rides combined. ⊠ *Pier 33, Embarcadero* ☎ *415/981–7625* ⊕ *www.nps.gov/alca* ⊠ *$28, including audio tour; $35 evening tour, including audio* ☉ *Ferry departs every 30–45 mins Sept.–late May, daily 9:30–2:15, 4:20 for evening tour Thurs.–Mon. only; late May–Aug., daily 9:30–4:15, 6:30 and 7:30 for evening tour.*

☾ **Exploratorium.** Walking into this fascinating "museum of science, art, and
★ human perception" is like visiting a mad scientist's laboratory. Most of the exhibits are supersize, and you can play with everything. After moving into its new, larger digs on the Embarcadero in April 2013, the Exploratorium will have even more space for its signature experiential

Thousands of visitors take ferries to Alcatraz each day to walk in the footsteps of the notorious criminals who were held on "The Rock."

exhibits, including a new Tinkering Studio and a brand-new glass Bay Observatory building, where exhibits inside will help visitors better understand what they see outside. Look for surprises outside the building, too. Quintessential Exploratorium exhibits remain: Get an Alice in Wonderland feeling in the distortion room, where you seem to shrink and grow as you walk across the slanted, checkered floor. In the shadow room, a powerful flash freezes an image of your shadow on the wall; jumping is a favorite pose. "Pushover" demonstrates cow-tipping, but for people: stand on one foot and try to keep your balance while a friend swings a striped panel in front of you (trust us, you're going to fall).

More than 650 other exhibits focus on sea and insect life, computers, electricity, patterns and light, language, the weather, and much more. "Explainers"—usually high-school students on their days off—demonstrate cool scientific tools and procedures, like DNA sample-collection and cow-eye dissection. One surefire hit is the pitch-black, touchy-feely Tactile Dome, newly built in the Embarcadero space. In this geodesic dome strewn with textured objects, you crawl through a course of ladders, slides, and tunnels, relying solely on your sense of touch. Not surprisingly, lovey-dovey couples sometimes linger in the "grope dome," but be forewarned: the staff will turn on the lights if they have to. ■ TIP➔ Reservations are required for the Tactile Dome, and will get you 75 minutes of access. You have to be at least seven years old to go through the dome, and the space is not for the claustrophobic. The Exploratorium plans to remain open in its Marina home through January 2013. Call ahead to confirm which location is open when you visit and the hours it's open. ⌧ Piers 15–17, Embarcadero ☎ 415/561–0360 general *information, 415/561–0362 Tactile Dome reservations ⊕ www. exploratorium.edu ☞ $15, free 1st Wed. of month; Tactile Dome $5 extra ⊙ Tues.–Sun. 10–5.*

Fodor's Choice
★

Ferry Building. The jewel of the Embarcadero, erected in 1896, is topped by a 230-foot clock tower modeled after the campanile of the cathedral in Seville, Spain. On the morning of April 18, 1906, the tower's four clock faces, powered by the swinging of a 14-foot pendulum, stopped at 5:17—the moment the great earthquake struck—and stayed still for 12 months.

Today San Franciscans flock to the street-level marketplace, stocking up on supplies from local favorites such as Acme Bread, Scharffen Berger Chocolate, Cowgirl Creamery, and Blue Bottle Coffee. Lucky diners claim a coveted table at Slanted Door, the city's beloved high-end Vietnamese restaurant. The seafood bars at Hog Island Oyster Company and Ferry Plaza Seafood have fantastic city panoramas—or you can take your purchases around to the building's bay side, where benches face views of the Bay Bridge. On Saturday mornings the plazas outside the building buzz with an upscale farmers' market where you can buy exotic sandwiches and other munchables. Extending from the piers on the north side of the building south to the Bay Bridge, the waterfront promenade is a favorite among joggers and picnickers, with a front-row view of the sailboats slipping by. The Ferry Building also serves actual ferries: from behind the building they sail to Sausalito, Larkspur, Tiburon, and the East Bay. ⊠ *Embarcadero at foot of Market St., Embarcadero* ☎ *415/983–8030* ⊕ *www.ferrybuildingmarketplace. com.*

▌QUICK
BITES

Buena Vista Café. Smack-dab at the end of the Hyde Street cable-car line, the Buena Vista packs 'em in for its famous Irish coffee—which, according to owners, was the first served stateside (in 1952). The place oozes nostalgia, drawing devoted locals as well as out-of-towners relaxing after a day of sightseeing. It's narrow and can get crowded, but this spot is a welcome respite from the overpriced generic tourist joints nearby. ⊠ *2765 Hyde St., at Beach St., Fisherman's Wharf* ☎ *415/474–5044* ⊕ *www.thebuenavista. com.*

↻ **Fisherman's Wharf.** It may be one of the city's best-known attractions, but the Wharf is a no-go zone for most locals, who shy away from the difficult parking, overpriced food, and cheesy shops at third-rate shopping centers like the Cannery at Del Monte Square. If you can't resist a visit here, come early to avoid the crowds and get a sense of the Wharf's functional role—it's not just an amusement park replica.

Most of the entertainment at the Wharf is schlocky and overpriced, with one notable exception: the splendid **Musée Mécanique** (☎ *415/346–2000* ☺ *Weekdays 10–7, weekends 10–8*), a time-warped arcade with antique mechanical contrivances, including peep shows and nickelodeons. Some favorites are the giant and rather creepy "Laffing Sal," an arm-wrestling machine, the world's only steam-powered motorcycle, and mechanical fortune-telling figures that speak from their curtained boxes. Note the depictions of race that betray the prejudices of the time: stoned Chinese figures in the "Opium-Den" and clown-faced African-Americans eating watermelon in the "Mechanical Farm." Admission is free, but you'll need quarters to bring the machines to life.

Just outside, the USS *Pampanito* (Pier 45, ☎ *415/775–1943* ⊕ *www. maritime.org/pamphome.htm* ☺ *Oct.–Memorial Day, Sun.–Thurs. 9–6, Fri. and Sat. 9–8; Memorial Day–Sept., Thurs.–Tues. 9–8, Wed. 9–6*) provides an intriguing if mildly claustrophobic glimpse into life on a submarine during World War II. The sub sank six Japanese warships and damaged four others. Admission is $10; the family pass is a great deal at $20 for two adults and up to four kids.

Among the two floors of exhibits at **Ripley's Believe It or Not! Museum** (⊠ *175 Jefferson St.,* ☎ *415/771–6188* ⊕ *www.ripleysf.com* ☞ *$19.99* ☺ *Late June–Labor Day, Sun.–Thurs. 9 am–11 pm, Fri. and Sat. 9 am–midnight; Labor Day–early June, Sun.–Thurs. 10–10, Fri. and Sat. 10 am–midnight*) is a tribute to San Francisco—an 8-foot-long scale model of a cable car, made entirely of matchsticks.

Notables from local boy Robin Williams to King Tut await at the **Wax Museum** (⊠ *145 Jefferson St.* ☎ *415/202–0400, 800/439–4305* ⊕ *www.waxmuseum.com*), open daily 10–9. Admission is $14. ⊠ *Jefferson St. between Leavenworth St. and Pier 39, Fisherman's Wharf.*

Ghirardelli Square. Most of the redbrick buildings in this early-20th-century complex were once part of the Ghirardelli factory. Now tourists come here to pick up the famous chocolate, though you can purchase it all over town and save yourself a trip to what is essentially a mall. But this is the only place to watch the cool chocolate manufactory in action. (If you're a chocoholic, this definitely beats the Cannery.) There are no fewer than three Ghirardelli stores here, as well as gift shops and a couple of restaurants—including Ana Mandara—that even locals love. Fairmont recently opened an upscale urban time-share directly on the square. Placards throughout the square describe the factory's history. ⊠ *900 N. Point St., Fisherman's Wharf* ☎ *415/775–5500* ⊕ *www. ghirardellisq.com.*

Hyde Street Pier. Cotton candy and souvenirs are all well and good, but if you want to get to the heart of the Wharf—boats—there's no better place to do it than at this pier, one of the Wharf area's best bargains. Depending on the time of day, you might see boatbuilders at work or children pretending to man an early-1900s ship.

Don't pass up the centerpiece collection of historic vessels, part of the **San Francisco Maritime National Historic Park,** almost all of which can be boarded. The *Balclutha,* an 1886 full-rigged three-masted sailing vessel that's more than 250 feet long, sailed around Cape Horn 17 times; kids especially love the *Eureka,* a side-wheel passenger and car ferry, for her onboard collection of vintage cars; the *Hercules* is a steam-powered tugboat. The *C.A. Thayer,* a three-masted schooner, recently underwent a painstaking restoration.

Across the street from the pier and almost a museum in itself is the San Francisco Maritime National Historic Park's **Visitor Center** (⊠ *499 Jefferson St.* 🕾 *415/447–5000* ☽ *June–Aug., daily 9:30–5:30; Sept.–May, daily 9:30–5*), happily free of mind-numbing, text-heavy displays. Instead, fun large-scale exhibits, such as a huge First Order Fresnel lighthouse lens and a shipwrecked boat, make this an engaging and relatively quick stop. ⊠ *Hyde and Jefferson Sts., Fisherman's Wharf* 🕾 *415/561–7100* ⊕ *www.nps.gov/safr* ⊐ *Ships $5* ☽ *June–Aug., daily 9:30–5:30; Sept.–May, daily 9:30–5.*

Jackson Square. This was the heart of the Barbary Coast of the Gay 90s (the 1890s, that is). Although most of the red-light district was destroyed in the fire that followed the 1906 earthquake, old redbrick buildings and narrow alleys recall the romance and rowdiness of San Francisco's early days. The days of brothels and bar fights are long gone—now Jackson Square is a genteel, quiet corner of the Financial District. It's of interest to the historically inclined and antiques-shop browsers, but otherwise safely skipped.

Some of the city's first business buildings, survivors of the 1906 quake, still stand between Montgomery and Sansome streets. After a few decades of neglect, these old-timers were adopted by preservation-minded interior designers and wholesale furniture dealers for use as showrooms. In 1972 the city officially designated the area—bordered by Columbus Avenue on the west, Broadway and Pacific Avenue on the north, Washington Street on the south, and Sansome Street on the east—San Francisco's first historic district. When property values soared, many of the fabric and furniture outlets fled to Potrero Hill. Advertising agencies, attorneys, and antiques dealers now occupy the Jackson Square–area structures.

It takes a bit of conjuring to evoke the wild Barbary Coast days when checking out the now-gentrified gold rush–era buildings in the 700 block of **Montgomery Street.** But this was an especially colorful block. Author Mark Twain was a reporter for the spunky *Golden Era* newspaper, which occupied No. 732 (now part of the building at No. 744). From 1959 to 1996 the late ambulance-chaser extraordinaire, lawyer Melvin Belli, had his headquarters at Nos. 722 and 728–730. There was never a dull moment in Belli's world; he represented clients from Mae West to Gloria Sykes (who in 1964 claimed that a cable-car accident turned her into a nymphomaniac) to Jim and Tammy Faye Bakker. Whenever he won a case, he fired a cannon and raised the Jolly Roger. Belli was also known for receiving a letter from the never-caught Zodiac killer. It seems fitting that the building sat for years, deteriorating and moldering, while the late attorney's sons fought wife number five (joined with Belli in holy matrimony just three months before his death). She eventually won, but today the dilapidated building is for sale.

Restored 19th-century brick buildings line Hotaling Place, which connects Washington and Jackson streets. The lane is named for the head of the **A.P. Hotaling Company whiskey distillery** (✉ *451 Jackson St., at Hotaling Pl.*), which was the largest liquor repository on the West Coast in its day. (Hotaling whiskey is still made in the city, by the way; look for their single malts for a sip of truly local flavor.) ✉ *Jackson Sq. district, bordered by Broadway and Washington, Kearny, and Sansome Sts., Financial District.*

☙ **Pier 39.** The city's most popular waterfront attraction draws millions of visitors each year who come to browse through its shops and concessions hawking every conceivable form of souvenir. The pier can be quite crowded, and the numerous street performers may leave you feeling more harassed than entertained. Arriving early in the morning ensures you a front-row view of the sea lions, but if you're here to shop—and make no mistake about it, Pier 39 wants your money—be aware that most stores don't open until 9:30 or 10 (later in winter).

Pick up a buckwheat hull–filled otter neck wrap or a plush sea lion to snuggle at the **Marine Mammal Center Store** (☎ *415/289–7373*), whose proceeds benefit Sausalito's respected wild-animal hospital, the Marine Mammal Center.

Brilliant colors enliven the double-decker **San Francisco Carousel** ($3 per ride), decorated with images of such city landmarks as the Golden Gate Bridge and Lombard Street.

Follow the sound of barking to the northwest side of the pier to view the sea lions that flop about the floating docks.

At **Aquarium of the Bay** (☎ *415/623–5300 or 888/732–3483* ⊕ *www.aquariumofthebay.org* 💰 *$16.95* ⏱ *June–Sept., daily 9–8; Mar.–May and Oct., Mon.–Thurs. 10–7, Fri.–Sun. 10–8; Nov.–Feb., daily 10–7*) moving walkways transport you through a space surrounded on three sides by water filled with indigenous San Francisco Bay marine life, from fish and plankton to sharks. Many find the aquarium overpriced; if you can, take advantage of the family rate ($46 for two adults and two kids under 12).

The **California Welcome Center** (☎ *415/981–1280* ⊕ *www.visitcwc.com* ⏱ *Daily 10–6*), on Pier 39's second level, can help you reserve tours and plan your time in the city.

Parking (free with validation from a Pier 39 restaurant) is at the Pier 39 Garage, off Powell Street at the Embarcadero. ✉ *Beach St. at Embarcadero, Fisherman's Wharf* ⊕ *www.pier39.com.*

☙ **San Francisco Railway Museum.** A labor of love brought to you by the same vintage-transit enthusiasts responsible for the F-line's revival, this one-room museum and store celebrates the city's storied streetcars and cable cars with photographs, models, and artifacts. The permanent exhibit includes the replicated end of a streetcar with a working cab—complete with controls and a bell—for kids to explore; the cool, antique Wiley birdcage traffic signal; and models and display cases to view. Right on the F-line track, just across from the Ferry Building, this is a great quick stop. ⊠ *77 Steuart St., Embarcadero* ☎ *415/974–1948* ⊕ *www.streetcar. org* ☑ *Free* ⊙ *Tues.–Sun. 10–6.*

Transamerica Pyramid. It's neither owned by Transamerica nor is it a pyramid, but this 853-foot-tall obelisk *is* the most photographed of the city's high-rises. Excoriated in the design stages as "the world's largest architectural folly," the icon was quickly hailed as a masterpiece when it opened in 1972. Today it's probably the city's most recognized structure after the Golden Gate Bridge. A fragrant redwood grove along the east side of the building, replete with benches and a cheerful fountain, is a placid patch in which to unwind. ⊠ *600 Montgomery St., Financial District* ⊕ *www.transamerica.com.*

THE MARINA AND THE PRESIDIO

Yachts bob at their moorings, satisfied-looking folks jog along the Marina Green, and multimillion-dollar homes overlook the bay in this picturesque, if somewhat sterile, neighborhood. Does it all seem a bit too perfect? Well, it got this way after the hard knock of Loma Prieta—the current pretty face was put on after hundreds of homes collapsed in the 1989 earthquake. Just west of this waterfront area is a more natural beauty: the Presidio. Once a military base, this beautiful, sprawling park is mostly green space, with hills, woods, and the marshlands of Crissy Field.

EXPLORING THE MARINA

Fort Mason Center. Originally a depot for the shipment of supplies to the Pacific during World War II, the fort was converted into a cultural center in 1977. Here you can find the vegetarian restaurant Greens and shops, galleries, and performance spaces, most of which are closed Monday. You have to be seriously into Italian-American culture to appreciate the text- and photograph-heavy exhibits at the **Museo Italo-Americano** (⊠ *Bldg. C* ☎ *415/673–2200* ⊕ *museoitaloamericano.org* ⊙ *Tues.–Sun. noon–4*), but depending on the exhibit, it might be worth a glance if you're already at Fort Mason. Plus, it's free. The temporary exhibits downstairs at the free **SFMOMA Artists Gallery** (⊠ *Bldg. A* ☎ *415/441–4777*) can be great, but head upstairs and check out the paintings, sculptures, prints, and photographs for sale and for rent. It's a fun scene, with folks flipping through the works like posters. You won't find a Picasso or a Rembrandt here, but you can find works of high quality by emerging Northern California artists—and where else can you get a $50,000 work of art to hang on your wall for $400 (a month)? It's open Tuesday through Saturday 11:30–5:30. While waiting for its permanent home downtown, the **Mexican Museum** (⊠ *Bldg. D* ☎ *415/202–9700*) hosts temporary exhibits in this small space. It's open Wednesday through Sunday noon to 4 and admission is free. ⊠ *Buchanan St. and Marina Blvd., Marina* ☎ *415/345–7500 event information* ⊕ *www.fortmason.org.*

Fodor's Choice   **Palace of Fine Arts.** At first glance this stunning, rosy rococo palace seems
★   to be from another world, and indeed, it's the sole survivor of the many tinted-plaster structures (a temporary classical city of sorts) built for

the 1915 Panama-Pacific International Exposition, the world's fair that celebrated San Francisco's recovery from the 1906 earthquake and fire. The expo buildings originally extended about a mile along the shore. Bernard Maybeck designed this faux–Roman classic beauty, which was reconstructed in concrete and reopened in 1967. A victim of the elements, the Palace required a piece-by-piece renovation that was completed in 2008.

The pseudo-Latin language adorning the Palace's exterior urns continues to stump scholars. The massive columns (each topped with four "weeping maidens"), great rotunda, and swan-filled lagoon have been used in countless fashion layouts, films, and wedding photo shoots. After admiring the lagoon, look across the street to the house at 3460 Baker Street. If the maidens out front look familiar, they should—they're original casts of the lovely "garland ladies" you can see in the Palace's colonnade. ⊠ *3301 Lyon St., at Beach St., Marina* ☎ *415/561–0364 Palace history tours* ⊕ *www.palaceoffinearts.org* ⊠ *Free* ☼ *Daily 24 hrs.*

EXPLORING THE PRESIDIO

♻ **Fort Point.** Dwarfed today by the Golden Gate Bridge, this brick fortress constructed between 1853 and 1861 was designed to protect San Francisco from a Civil War sea attack that never materialized. It was also used as a coastal-defense fortification post during World War II, when soldiers stood watch here. This National Historic Site is now a sprawling museum filled with military memorabilia, surrounding a lonely, windswept courtyard. The building has a gloomy air and is suitably atmospheric. (It's usually chilly and windy, too, so bring a jacket.) On days when Fort Point is staffed, guided group tours and cannon drills take place. The top floor affords a unique angle on the bay. ■ TIP→ Take care when walking along the front side of the building, as it's slippery, and the waves have a dizzying effect. Note that the fort is open only Friday through Sunday. The fort's popular guided candlelight tours, available only in winter, sell out in advance, so be sure to book ahead. Southeast of this structure is the **Fort Point Mine Depot,** an army facility that functioned as the headquarters for underwater mining operations throughout World War II. Today it's the Warming Hut, a National Park Service café and bookstore. ⊠ *Marine Dr. off Lincoln Blvd., Presidio* ☎ *415/556–1693* ⊕ *www.nps.gov/fopo* ⊠ *Free* ☼ *Fri.–Sun. 10–5.*

Fodor'sChoice **Golden Gate Bridge.** The suspension bridge that connects San Francisco with Marin County has long wowed sightseers with its simple
★ but powerful art-deco design. Completed in 1937 after four years of construction, the 1.7-mile span and its 750-foot towers were built to withstand winds of more than 100 mph. It's also not a bad place to be in an earthquake: designed to sway up to 27.7 feet, the Golden Gate Bridge, unlike the Bay Bridge, was undamaged by the 1989 Loma Prieta quake. (If you're on the bridge when it's windy, stand still and you can feel it swaying a bit.) Though it's frequently gusty and misty—always bring a jacket, no matter what the weather's like—the bridge provides unparalleled views of the Bay Area. Muni buses 28 and 76 make stops at the Golden Gate Bridge toll plaza, on the San Francisco side. However, drive to fully appreciate the bridge from multiple vantage points in and around the Presidio; you'll be able to park at designated areas.

8

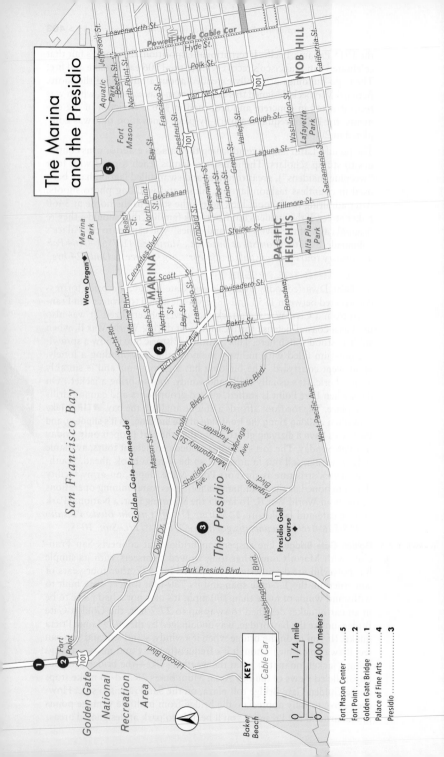

The Marina
and the Presidio

San Francisco Bay

Golden Gate
National
Recreation
Area

Golden Gate Promenade

The Presidio

Presidio Golf Course

MARINA

Fort Mason

NOB HILL

PACIFIC HEIGHTS

Powell-Hyde Cable Car

Wave Organ

Marina Park

Baker Beach

Lincoln Blvd.

Mason St.

Doyle Dr.

Park Presidio Blvd.

Washington Blvd.

Lincoln Blvd.

Presidio Blvd.

West Pacific Ave.

Arguello Blvd.

Funston Ave.

Moraga Ave.

Sheridan Ave.

Montgomery St.

Richardson Ave.

Yacht Rd.

Marina Blvd.

Cervantes Blvd.

Beach St.

North Point St.

Bay St.

Francisco St.

Scott St.

Divisadero St.

Broadway

Steiner St.

Fillmore St.

Baker St.

Lyon St.

Beach St.

North Point St.

Bay St.

Francisco St.

Buchanan

North Point

Beach St.

Tombard St.

Greenwich St.

Filbert St.

Union St.

Green St.

Vallejo St.

Laguna St.

Gough St.

Franklin St.

Van Ness Ave.

Polk St.

Hyde St.

Leavenworth St.

Jefferson St.

Beach St.

North Point St.

Aquatic Park

Chestnut St.

Washington St.

Sacramento St.

California St.

Lafayette Park

Alta Plaza Park

101

101

101

1

KEY
...... Cable Car

0   1/4 mile

0   400 meters

Fort Mason Center	5
Fort Point	2
Golden Gate Bridge	1
Palace of Fine Arts	4
Presidio	3

From the bridge's eastern-side walkway—the only side pedestrians are allowed on—you can take in the San Francisco skyline and the bay islands; look west for the wild hills of the Marin Headlands, the curving coast south to Land's End, and the Pacific Ocean. On sunny days sailboats dot the water, and brave windsurfers test the often-treacherous tides beneath the bridge. A vista point on the Marin side gives you a spectacular city panorama.

But there's a well-known, darker side to the bridge's story, too. The bridge is perhaps the world's most popular suicide platform, with an average of about 20 jumpers per year. (The first leaped just three months after the bridge's completion, and the official count was stopped in 1995 as the 1,000th jump approached.) Signs along the bridge read "There is hope. Make the call," referring the disconsolate to the special telephones on the bridge. Bridge officers, who patrol the walkway and watch by security camera to spot potential jumpers, successfully talk down two-thirds to three-quarters of them each year. Documentary filmmaker Eric Steel's controversial 2006 movie *The Bridge* once again put pressure on the Golden Gate Bridge Highway and Transportation District to install a suicide barrier. The unobtrusive net supported by most locals is finally in the design phase, though funding hasn't been secured. ✉ *Lincoln Blvd. near Doyle Dr. and Fort Point, Presidio* ☎ *415/921–5858* ⊕ *www.goldengatebridge.org* ☾ *Pedestrians Mar.–Oct., daily 5 am–9 pm; Nov.–Feb., daily 5 am–6 pm; hrs change with daylight saving time. Bicyclists daily 24 hrs.*

★ **Presidio.** When San Franciscans want to spend a day in the woods, they head here. The Presidio has 1,400 acres of hills and majestic woods, two small beaches, and stunning views of the bay, the Golden Gate Bridge, and Marin County. Famed environmental artist Andy Goldsworthy's sculpture greets visitors at the Arguello Gate entrance. The 100-plus-foot *Spire*, made of 37 cypress logs reclaimed from the Presidio, looks like a rough, natural version of a church spire. ■ TIP➔ The best lookout points lie along Washington Boulevard, which meanders through the park.

Part of the **Golden Gate National Recreation Area,** the Presidio was a military post for more than 200 years. Don Juan Bautista de Anza and a band of Spanish settlers first claimed the area in 1776. It became a Mexican garrison in 1822, when Mexico gained its independence from Spain; U.S. troops forcibly occupied the Presidio in 1846. The U.S. Sixth Army was stationed here until October 1994.

Today the area is being transformed into a self-sustaining national park with a combination of public, commercial, and residential projects. In 2005 Bay Area filmmaker George Lucas opened the **Letterman Digital Arts Center,** his 23-acre digital studio "campus," along the eastern edge of the land. Seventeen of those acres are exquisitely landscaped and open to the public. If you have kids in tow or are a *Star Wars* fan yourself, sidle over to the **Yoda Fountain** (Letterman Dr. and Dewitt Rd.), between two of the ILM buildings.

The battle over the fate of the rest of the Presidio is ongoing. Many older buildings have been reconstructed; the issue now is how to fill them. The original plan described a nexus for arts, education, and environmental

Armed with only helmets, safety harnesses, and painting equipment, a full-time crew of 38 painters keeps the Golden Gate Bridge clad in International Orange.

groups. Since the Presidio's overseeing trust was tasked with making the park financially self-sufficient by 2013, which means generating enough revenue to keep afloat without the federal government's monthly $20 million checks, many fear that money will trump culture. The Asian-theme SenSpa and a new Walt Disney museum have opened, and a lodge at the Main Post is in the planning stages. With old military housing now repurposed as apartments and homes with rents up to $10,000 a month, there's some concern that the Presidio will become an incoherent mix of pricey real estate. Still, the $6 million that Lucas shells out annually for rent does plant a lot of saplings.

The Presidio also has two beaches, a golf course, a visitor center, and picnic sites; the views from the many overlooks are sublime.

Especially popular is **Crissy Field,** a stretch of restored marshland along the sand of the bay. Kids on bikes, folks walking dogs, and joggers share the paved path along the shore, often winding up at the Warming Hut, a combination café and fun gift store at the end of the path, for a hot chocolate in the shadow of the Golden Gate Bridge. Midway along the Golden Gate Promenade that winds along the shore is the Gulf of the Farallones National Marine Sanctuary Visitor Center, where kids can get a close-up view of small sea creatures and learn about the rich ecosystem offshore. Temporarily relocated to East Beach, just across from the Palace of Fine Arts, Crissy Field Center offers great children's programs and has cool science displays; grab lunch at the Beach Hut Café next door. West of the Golden Gate Bridge is sandy **Baker Beach,** beloved for its spectacular views and laid-back vibe (read: you'll see naked people here). This is one of those places that inspires local pride.

✉ *Between Marina and Lincoln Park, Presidio* ⊕ *www.nps.gov/prsf and www.presidio.gov.*

GOLDEN GATE PARK AND THE WESTERN SHORELINE

More than 1,000 acres, stretching from the Haight all the way to the windy Pacific coast, Golden Gate Park is a vast patchwork of woods, trails, lakes, lush gardens, sports facilities, museums—even a herd of buffalo. There's more natural beauty beyond the park's borders, along San Francisco's wild Western Shoreline.

EXPLORING GOLDEN GATE PARK

California Academy of Sciences. With its native plant–covered living roof, retractable ceiling, three-story rain forest, gigantic planetarium, living coral reef, and frolicking penguins, the Cal Academy is one of the city's most spectacular treasures. Dramatically designed by Renzo Piano, it's an eco-friendly, energy-efficient adventure in biodiversity and green architecture. The roof's large mounds and hills mirror the local topography, and Piano's audacious design completes the dramatic transformation of the park's Music Concourse. Moving away from a restrictive role as a backward-looking museum that catalogued natural history, the new academy is all about sustainability and the future, but you'll still find those beloved dioramas in African Hall.

By the time you arrive, hopefully you've decided which shows and programs to attend, looked at the academy's floor plan, and designed a plan to cover it all in the time you have. And if not, here's the quick version: Head left from the entrance to the wooden walkway over otherworldly rays in the Philippine Coral Reef, then continue to the Swamp to see the famous albino alligator. Swing through African Hall and gander at the penguins, take the elevator up to the living roof, then return to the main floor and get in line to explore the Rainforests of the World, ducking free-flying butterflies and watching for other live surprises. You'll end up below ground in the Amazonian Flooded Rainforest, where you can explore the academy's other aquarium exhibits. Phew. ✉ *55 Music Concourse Dr.* ☎ *415/379–8000* ⊕ *www.calacademy.org* 🖃 *$29.95, free one Sun. per quarter* ⊗ *Mon.–Sat. 9:30–5, Sun. 11–5.*

Conservatory of Flowers. Whatever you do, be sure to at least drive by the Conservatory of Flowers—it's just too darn pretty to miss. The gorgeous, white-framed 1878 glass structure is topped with a 14-ton glass dome. Stepping inside the giant greenhouse is like taking a quick trip to the rain forest, with its earthy smell and humid warmth. The undeniable highlight is the Aquatic Plants section, where lily pads float and carnivorous plants dine on bugs to the sounds of rushing water. On the east side of the conservatory (to the right as you face the building), cypress, pine, and redwood trees surround the Dahlia Garden, which blooms in summer and fall. To the west is the Rhododendron Dell, which contains 850 varieties, more than any other garden in the country. It's a favorite local Mother's Day picnic spot. ✉ *John F. Kennedy Dr. at Conservatory Dr., Golden Gate Park* ☎ *415/666–7001* ⊕ *www.conservatoryofflowers.org* 🖃 *$7, free 1st Tues. of month* ⊗ *Tues.–Sun. 10–4:30.*

8

Golden Gate Park and the Western Shoreline

The Presidio

TO THE GOLDEN GATE BRIDGE

RICHMOND

SEACLIFF

China Beach

Land's End

Point Lobos

Seal Rocks

Pacific Ocean

Ocean Beach

Sutro Heights Park

Great Highway

Geary Blvd.

Arguello Blvd.

8th Ave.

Park Presidio Blvd.

19th Ave.

25th Ave.

34th Ave.

40th Ave.

43rd Ave.

Balboa St.

Cabrillo St.

Clement St.

Lake St.

Pine St.

Anza St.

Fulton St.

Hayes St.

Fell St.

Stanyan St.

Judah St.

Irving St.

Lincoln Way

Funston Ave.

28th Ave.

41st Ave.

Sunset Blvd.

J.F. Kennedy Dr.

M.L. King Jr. Dr.

M.L. King Jr. Dr.

Cross Over Dr.

El Camino Del Mar

Legion of Honor Dr.

Seal Rock Dr.

Point Lobos Ave.

Golden Gate Park

McLaren Lodge (Park HQ)

National AIDS Memorial Grove

Kezar Stadium

Koret Children's Playground

Shakespeare Garden

Strawberry Hill

Stowe Lake

Boat House

Portals of the Past

Marx Meadow

Lindley Meadow

Speedway Meadow

Golden Gate Park Stadium (Polo Field)

Spreckels Lake

Buffalo Paddock

North Lake

Middle Lake

South Lake

Floating Island

Metson Lake

Mallard Lake

Dutch Windmill

Beach Chalet and Park Chalet

Murphy Windmill

Archery Field

Bercut Equitation Field

Golf Course

Ft. Miley, Veterans Administration Medical Center

Sutro Heights Park

1

2

3

4

5

6

7

8

9

10

11

1 mile

km

0

de Young Museum. It seems that everyone in town has a strong opinion about the de Young Museum: Some adore its striking copper facade, while others just hope that the green patina of age will mellow the effect. Most maligned is the 144-foot tower, but the view from its ninth-story observation room, ringed by floor-to-ceiling windows and free to the public, is worth a trip here by itself. The building almost overshadows the de Young's respected collection of American, African, and Oceanic art. The museum also plays host to major international exhibits, such as 2010's showing of postimpressionist works on loan from the Musée d'Orsay and 2011's exhibit of 100 works from Paris's Musée National Picasso. ⊠ *50 Hagiwara Tea Garden Dr., Golden Gate Park* 🕾 *415/750–3600* ⊕ *deyoung.famsf.org* 🖃 *$10, free 1st Tues. of month* ☉ *Tues.–Sun. 9:30–5:15; mid-Jan.–Nov., Fri. until 8:45.*

San Francisco Japanese Tea Garden. As you amble through the manicured landscape, past Japanese sculptures and perfect miniature pagodas, over ponds of carp that have been here since before the 1906 quake, you may be transported to a more peaceful plane. Or maybe the shrieks of kids clambering over the almost vertical "humpback" bridges will keep you firmly in the here and now. Either way, this garden is one of those tourist spots that's truly worth a stop (a half hour will do). And at 5 acres, it's large enough that you'll always be able to find a bit of serenity, even when the tour buses drop by. The garden is especially lovely in April, when the cherry blossoms are in bloom. ⊠ *Hagiwara Tea Garden Dr., off John F. Kennedy Dr., Golden Gate Park* 🕾 *415/752–4227* ⊕ *www.japaneseteagardensf.com* 🖃 *$7, free Mon., Wed., and Fri. if you enter by 10 am* ☉ *Mar.–Oct., daily 9–6; Nov.–Feb., daily 9–4:45.*

San Francisco Botanical Garden at Strybing Arboretum. One of the best picnic spots in a very picnic-friendly park, the 55-acre arboretum specializes in plants from areas with climates similar to that of the Bay Area. Walk the Eastern Australian garden to see tough, pokey shrubs and plants with cartoon-like names, such as the hilly-pilly tree. Kids gravitate toward the large shallow fountain and the pond with ducks, turtles, and egrets. Alas, the city began charging admission to the gardens in 2010, so it's a slightly less alluring picnic spot compared to the free stretches in front of the Conservatory of Flowers and on the Music Concourse between the de Young and the Cal Academy. ⊠ *Enter the park at 9th Ave. at Lincoln Way, Golden Gate Park* 🕾 *415/661–1316* ⊕ *www.sfbotanicalgarden.org* 🖃 *$7, free 2nd Tues. of month* ☉ *Apr.–Oct., daily 9–6; Nov.–Mar., daily 10–5.*

EXPLORING THE WESTERN SHORELINE

Cliff House. A meal at the Cliff House isn't about the food—the spectacular ocean view is what brings folks here. The vistas, which include offshore Seal Rock (the barking marine mammals who reside there are actually sea lions), can be 30 miles or more on a clear day—or less than a mile on foggy days. ■ TIP→ Come for drinks just before sunset; then head back into town for dinner.

Three buildings have occupied this site since 1863. The current building dates from 1909; a 2004 renovation has left a strikingly attractive res-

8

taurant and a squat concrete viewing platform out back. The complex, owned by the National Park Service, includes a gift shop.

Sitting on the observation deck is the **Giant Camera,** a camera obscura with its lens pointing skyward housed in a cute yellow-painted wooden shack. Built in the 1940s and threatened many times with demolition, it's now on the National Register of Historic Places. Step into the dark, tiny room inside (for a $3 fee); a fascinating 360-degree image of the surrounding area—which rotates as the "lens" on the roof rotates—is projected on a large, circular table. ■TIP→ In winter and spring you may also glimpse migrating gray whales from the observation deck.

To the north of the Cliff House are the ruins of the once-grand glass-roof **Sutro Baths,** which you can explore on your own (they look a bit like water-storage receptacles). Adolf Sutro, eccentric onetime San Francisco mayor and Cliff House owner, built the bath complex, including a train out to the site, in 1896, so that everyday folks could enjoy the benefits of swimming. Six enormous baths (some freshwater and some seawater), more than 500 dressing rooms, and several restaurants covered 3 acres north of the Cliff House and accommodated 25,000 bathers. Likened to Roman baths in a European glass palace, the baths were for decades the favorite destination of San Franciscans in search of entertainment. The complex fell into disuse after World War II, was closed in 1952, and burned down (under officially questionable circumstances, wink wink) during demolition in 1966. ✉ *1090 Point Lobos Ave., Outer Richmond* ☏ *415/386–3330* ⊕ *www.cliffhouse.com* ✆ *Free* ⊙ *Weekdays 9 am–9:30 pm, weekends 9 am–10 pm.*

Fodor's Choice ★ **Legion of Honor.** The old adage of real estate—location, location, location—is at full force here. You can't beat the site of this museum of European art atop cliffs overlooking the ocean, the Golden Gate Bridge, and the Marin Headlands. A pyramidal glass skylight in the entrance court illuminates the lower-level galleries, which exhibit prints and drawings, English and European porcelain, and ancient Assyrian, Greek, Roman, and Egyptian art. The 20-plus galleries on the upper level display the permanent collection of European art (paintings, sculpture, decorative arts, and tapestries) from the 14th century to the present day.

The noteworthy Auguste Rodin collection includes two galleries devoted to the master and a third with works by Rodin and other 19th-century sculptors. An original cast of Rodin's *The Thinker* welcomes you as you walk through the courtyard. As fine as the museum is, the setting and view outshine the collection and make a trip here worthwhile.

The **Legion Café,** on the lower level, serves tasty light meals (soup, sandwiches, grilled chicken) inside and on a garden terrace. (Unfortunately, there's no view.) Just north of the museum's parking lot is George Segal's *The Holocaust,* a stark white installation that evokes life in concentration camps during World War II. It's haunting at night, when backlighted by lights in the Legion's parking lot. ■TIP→ Admission to the Legion also counts as same-day admission to the de Young Museum. ✉ *34th Ave. at Clement St., Outer Richmond* ☏ *415/750–3600* ⊕ *legionofhonor.famsf.org* ✆ *$10, $2 off with Muni transfer, free 1st Tues. of month* ⊙ *Tues.–Sun. 9:30–5:15.*

★ **Lincoln Park.** Although many of the city's green spaces are gentle and welcoming, Lincoln Park is a wild 275-acre park with windswept cliffs and panoramic views. The newly renovated Coastal Trail, the park's most dramatic one, leads out to **Lands End**; pick it up west of the Legion of Honor (at the end of El Camino del Mar) or from the parking lot at Point Lobos and El Camino del Mar. Time your hike to hit Mile Rock at low tide, and you might catch a glimpse of two wrecked ships peeking up from their watery graves. ⚠ Do be careful if you hike here; landslides are frequent, and many people have fallen into the sea by standing too close to the edge of a crumbling bluff top.

On the tamer side, large Monterey cypresses line the fairways at Lincoln Park's 18-hole golf course, near the Legion of Honor. At one time this land was the Golden Gate Cemetery, where the dead were segregated by nationality; most were indigent and interred without ceremony in the potter's field. In 1900 the Board of Supervisors voted to ban burials within city limits, and all but two city cemeteries (at Mission Dolores and the Presidio) were moved to Colma, a small town just south of San Francisco. When digging has to be done in the park, bones occasionally surface again. ✉ *Entrance at 34th Ave. at Clement St, Outer Richmond.*

Ocean Beach. Stretching 3 miles along the western side of the city from the Richmond to the Sunset, this sandy swath of the Pacific coast is good for jogging or walking the dog—but not for swimming. The water is so cold that surfers wear wet suits year-round, and riptides are strong. As for sunbathing, it's rarely warm enough here; think meditative walking instead of sun worshipping.

Paths on both sides of the Great Highway lead from Lincoln Way to Sloat Boulevard (near the zoo); the beachside path winds through landscaped sand dunes, and the paved path across the highway is good for biking and in-line skating. (Though you have to rent bikes elsewhere.) The **Beach Chalet** restaurant and brewpub is across the Great Highway from Ocean Beach, about five blocks south of the Cliff House. ✉ *Along Great Hwy. from Cliff House to Sloat Blvd. and beyond.*

☕ **San Francisco Zoo.** Ever since one of its tigers escaped its enclosure and killed a visitor on Christmas Day 2007, the city's zoo has concentrated on polishing its image, raising funds to update its habitats, and restoring its reputation with animal welfare organizations. Occupying prime oceanfront property, the zoo is touting its metamorphosis into the "New Zoo," a wildlife-focused recreation center that inspires visitors to become conservationists. Integrated exhibits group different species of animals from the same geographic areas together in enclosures that don't look like cages. More than 250 species reside here, including endangered species such as the snow leopard, Sumatran tiger, grizzly bear, and as of 2011, a new Siberian tiger.

The zoo's superstar exhibit is **Grizzly Gulch,** where orphaned sisters Kachina and Kiona enchant visitors with their frolicking and swimming. When the bears are in the water, the only thing between you and them is (thankfully thick) glass. Grizzly feedings are 11:30 am daily.

The **Lemur Forest** has five varieties of the bug-eyed, long-tailed primates from Madagascar. You can help hoist food into the lemurs' feeding towers and watch the fuzzy creatures climb up to chow down. African Kikuyu grass carpets the circular outer area of **Gorilla Preserve,** one of the largest and most natural gorilla habitats of any zoo in the world. Trees and shrubs create communal play areas.

Ten species of rare monkeys—including black howler monkeys, black-and-white ruffed lemurs, and macaques—live and play at the two-tier **Primate Discovery Center,** which contains 23 interactive learning exhibits on the ground level.

Magellanic penguins waddle about the rather sad concrete **Penguin Island,** splashing and frolicking in its 200-foot pool. Feeding times are 10:15 and 3:30. Koalas peer out from among the trees in **Koala Crossing,** and kangaroos and wallabies headline the **Australian Walkabout** exhibit. The 7-acre **Puente al Sur** (Bridge to the South) re-creates habitats in South America, replete with giant anteaters and capybaras.

An **African Savanna** exhibit mixes giraffes, zebras, kudus, ostriches, and many other species, all living together in a 3-acre section with a central viewing spot accessed by a covered passageway.

The 6-acre **Children's Zoo** has about 300 mammals, birds, and reptiles, plus an insect zoo, a meerkat and prairie-dog exhibit, a nature trail, a nature theater, a restored 1921 Dentzel carousel, and a mini–steam train. A ride on the train costs $4, and you can hop astride one of the carousel's 52 hand-carved menagerie animals for $2. ⊠ *Sloat Blvd. and 47th Ave.(Muni L–Taraval streetcar from downtown), Sunset* ☎ *415/753–7080* ⊕ *www.sfzoo.org* ✉ *$15, $1 off with Muni transfer* ☉ *Mid-Mar.–Oct., daily 10–5; Nov.–mid-Mar., daily 10–4.*

Sutro Heights Park. Crows and other large birds battle the heady breezes at this cliff-top park on what were once the grounds of the home of Adolph Sutro, an eccentric mining engineer and former San Francisco mayor. An extremely wealthy man, Sutro may have owned about 10% of San Francisco at one point, but he couldn't buy good taste: a few remnants of his gaudy, faux-classical statue collection still stand (including the lions at what was the main gate). Monterey cypresses and Canary Island palms dot the park, and photos on placards depict what things looked like before the house burned down in 1896, from the greenhouse to the ornate carpet-bed designs.

All that remains of the main house is its foundation. Climb up for a sweeping view of the Pacific Ocean and the Cliff House below (which Sutro owned), and try to imagine what the perspective might have been like from one of the upper floors. San Francisco City Guides (☎ 415/557–4266) runs a free Saturday tour of the park that starts at 2 (meet at the lion statue at 48th and Point Lobos avenues). ⊠ *Point Lobos and 48th Aves., Outer Richmond.*

THE HAIGHT, THE CASTRO, AND NOE VALLEY

Once you've seen the blockbuster sights and you're getting curious about the neighborhoods where the city's soul resides, come out to these three areas. They wear their personalities large and proud, and all are perfect for just strolling around. You can move from the Haight's residue of 1960s counterculture to the Castro's connection to 1970s and '80s gay life to 1990s gentrification in Noe Valley. Although history thrust the Haight and the Castro onto the international stage, both are anything but stagnant—they're still dynamic areas well worth exploring. Noe Valley may lack the headlines, but a mellow morning walk here will make you feel like a local.

EXPLORING THE HAIGHT

Haight-Ashbury Intersection. On October 6, 1967, hippies took over the intersection of Haight and Ashbury streets to proclaim the "Death of Hip." If they thought hip was dead then, they'd find absolute confirmation of it today, what with the only tie-dye in sight on the famed corner being Ben & Jerry's storefront.

Everyone knows the Summer of Love had something to do with free love and LSD, but the drugs and other excesses of that period have tended to obscure the residents' serious attempts to create an America that was more spiritually oriented, more environmentally aware, and less caught up in commercialism. The Diggers, a radical group of actors and populist agitators, for example, operated a free shop a few blocks off Haight Street. Everything really was free at the free shop; people brought in things they didn't need and took things they did. (The group also coined immortal phrases like "Do your own thing.")

Among the folks who hung out in or near the Haight during the late 1960s were writers Richard Brautigan, Allen Ginsberg, Ken Kesey, and Gary Snyder; anarchist Abbie Hoffman; rock performers Marty Balin, Jerry Garcia, Janis Joplin, and Grace Slick; LSD champion Timothy Leary; and filmmaker Kenneth Anger. If you're keen to feel something resembling the hippie spirit these days, there's always Hippie Hill, just inside the Haight Street entrance of Golden Gate Park. Think drum circles, guitar players, and whiffs of pot smoke. ⊠ *Haight.*

EXPLORING THE CASTRO

★ **Castro Theatre.** Here's a classic way to join in the Castro community: grab some popcorn and catch a flick at this gorgeous, 1,500-seat art-deco theater; opened in 1922, it's the grandest of San Francisco's few remaining movie palaces. The neon marquee, which stands at the top of the Castro strip, is the neighborhood's great landmark. The Castro was the fitting host of 2008's red-carpet preview of Gus Van Sant's film *Milk,* starring Sean Penn as openly gay San Francisco supervisor Harvey Milk. The theater's elaborate Spanish baroque interior is fairly well preserved. Before many shows the theater's pipe organ rises from the orchestra pit and an organist plays pop and movie tunes, usually ending with the Jeanette McDonald standard "San Francisco" (go ahead, sing along). The crowd can be enthusiastic and vocal, talking back to the screen as loudly as it talks to them. Classics such as *Who's Afraid of Virginia Woolf?* take on a whole new life, with the assembled beating the actors to the punch and fashioning even snappier comebacks for Elizabeth Taylor. Head here to catch classics, a Fellini film retrospective, or the latest take on same-sex love. ⊠ *429 Castro St., Castro* ☎ *415/621–6120* ⊕ *www.castrotheatre.com.*

8

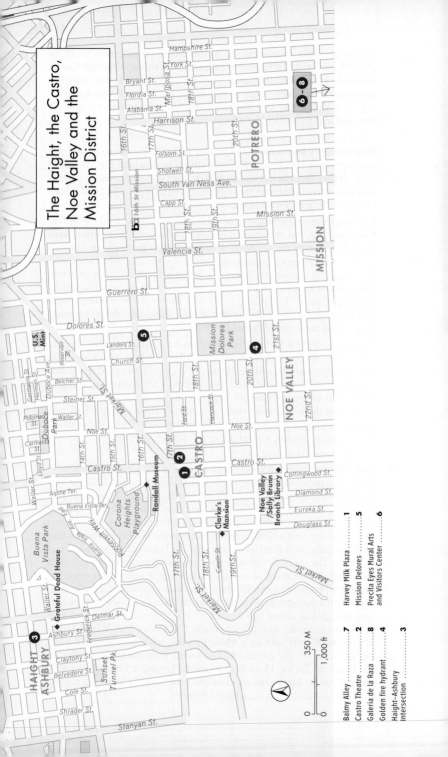

The Haight, the Castro, Noe Valley and the Mission District

POTRERO

MISSION

NOE VALLEY

CASTRO

HAIGHT ASHBURY

Hampshire St.
York St.
Bryant St.
Flordia St.
Alabama St.
Harrison St.
Folsom St.
Shotwell St.
South Van Ness Ave.
Capp St.
Mission St.
Valencia St.
Guerrero St.
Dolores St.
Landers St.
Church St.
Belcher St.
Steiner St.
Noe St.
Castro St.
Alpine Ter.
Buena Vista Ter.
Market St.
Mariposa St.
16th St.
17th St.
18th St.
19th St.
20th St.
21st St.
22nd St.
Ford St.
Hancock St.
Noe St.
Collingwood St.
Diamond St.
Eureka St.
Douglass St.

16th St. Mission
U.S. Mint
Reservoir St.
Germania St.
Herman St.
DuBoce Ave.
DuBoce Park
Potomac St.
Carmelita St.
Walter St.
Lloyd St.
Waller St.
Buena Vista Park
Buena Vista Ave. East
Buena Vista Ave. West
Roosevelt Way
Corona Heights Playground
Randall Museum
Clarke's Mansion
Noe Valley / Sally Brunn Branch Library
Mission Dolores Park

Grateful Dead House
Waller St.
Ashbury St.
Frederick St.
Delmar St.
Clayton St.
Belvedere St.
Cole St.
Shrader St.
Stanyan St.
Sunset Tunnel Pk.
Market St.
Greenfield St.

1 ... (Randall Museum area)
2 ...
5 ...
4 ...
6 ...

0   350 M
0   1,000 ft

A colorful mosaic mural in the Castro

Harvey Milk Plaza. An 18-foot-long rainbow flag, the symbol of gay pride, flies above this plaza named for the man who electrified the city in 1977 by being elected to its Board of Supervisors as an openly gay candidate. In the early 1970s Milk had opened a camera store on the block of Castro Street between 18th and 19th streets. The store became the center for his campaign to open San Francisco's social and political life to gays and lesbians.

The liberal Milk hadn't served a full year of his term before he and Mayor George Moscone, also a liberal, were shot in November 1978 at City Hall. The murderer was a conservative ex-supervisor named Dan White, who had recently resigned his post and then became enraged when Moscone wouldn't reinstate him. Milk and White had often been at odds on the board, and White thought Milk had been part of a cabal to keep him from returning to his post. Milk's assassination shocked the gay community, which became infuriated when the infamous "Twinkie defense"—that junk food had led to diminished mental capacity—resulted in a manslaughter verdict for White. During the so-called White Night Riot of May 21, 1979, gays and their allies stormed City Hall, torching its lobby and several police cars.

Milk, who had feared assassination, left behind a tape recording in which he urged the community to continue the work he had begun. His legacy is the high visibility of gay people throughout city government; a bust of him was unveiled at City Hall on his birthday in 2008, and the 2008 film *Milk* gives insight into his life. A plaque at the base of the flag-pole lists the names of past and present openly gay and lesbian state and local officials. ⊠ *Southwest corner of Castro and Market Sts., Castro.*

EXPLORING NOE VALLEY

Golden fire hydrant. When all the other fire hydrants went dry during the fire that followed the 1906 earthquake, this one kept pumping. Noe Valley and the Mission District were thus spared the devastation wrought elsewhere in the city, which explains the large number of pre-quake homes here. Every year on April 18 (the anniversary of the quake) folks gather here to share stories about the earthquake, and the famous hydrant gets a fresh coat of gold paint. ⊠ *Church and 20th Sts., southeast corner, across from Dolores Park, Noe Valley.*

CASTRO AND NOE WALK

The Castro and Noe Valley are both neighborhoods that beg to be walked—or ambled through, really, without time pressure or an absolute destination. Hit the Castro first, beginning at **Harvey Milk Plaza** under the gigantic rainbow flag. If you're going on to Noe Valley, first head east down **Market Street** for the cafés, bistros, and shops, then go back to **Castro Street** and head south, past the glorious art-deco **Castro Theatre**, checking out boutiques and cafés along the way (Cliff's Variety, at 479 Castro St., is a must). To tour Noe Valley, go east down **18th Street** to Church (at Dolores Park), and then either strap on your hiking boots and head south over the hill or hop the J–Church to **24th Street**, the center of this rambling neighborhood.

MISSION DISTRICT

The Mission has a number of distinct personalities: it's the Latino neighborhood, where working-class folks raise their families and where gangs occasionally clash; it's the hipster hood, where tattooed and pierced twenty- and thirtysomethings hold court in the coolest cafés and bars in town; it's a culinary epicenter, with the strongest concentration of destination restaurants and affordable ethnic cuisine in the city; and it's the artists' quarter, where murals adorn literally blocks of walls. It's also the city's equivalent of the Sunshine State—this neighborhood's always the last to succumb to fog.

EXPLORING THE MISSION DISTRICT

Balmy Alley. Mission District artists have transformed the walls of their neighborhood with paintings, and Balmy Alley is one of the best-executed examples. Murals fill the one-block alley, with newer ones continually filling in the blank spaces. Local children working with adults started the project in 1971. Since then dozens of artists have steadily added to it, with the aim of promoting peace in Central America, as well as community spirit and AIDS awareness. ■ TIP➜ Be alert here: the 25th Street end of the alley adjoins a somewhat dangerous area. ⊠ *24th St. between and parallel to Harrison and Treat Sts., alley runs south to 25th St., Mission.*

Galería de la Raza. San Francisco's premier showcase for contemporary Latino art, the gallery exhibits the works of mostly local artists. Events include readings and spoken word by local poets and writers, screenings of Latin American and Spanish films, and theater works by local minority theater troupes. Just across the street, amazing art festoons the 24th Street/York Street Minipark, a tiny urban playground. A mosaic-covered

Quetzalcoatl serpent plunges into the ground and rises, creating hills for little ones to clamber over, and mural-covered walls surround the space. ⊠ *2857 24th St., at Bryant St., Mission* 🕾 *415/826–8009* ⊕ *www. galeriadelaraza.org* ⊙ *Gallery Tues. 1–7, Wed.–Sat. noon–6.*

★ **Mission Dolores.** Two churches stand side by side at this mission, including the small adobe **Mission San Francisco de Asís,** the oldest standing structure in San Francisco. Completed in 1791, it's the sixth of the 21 California missions founded by Father Junípero Serra in the 18th and early 19th centuries. Its ceiling depicts original Ohlone Indian basket designs, executed in vegetable dyes. The tiny chapel includes frescoes and a hand-painted wooden altar. There's a hidden treasure here, too. In 2004 an archaeologist and an artist crawling along the ceiling's rafters opened a trap door behind the altar and rediscovered the mission's original mural, painted with natural dyes by Native Americans in 1791. The centuries have taken their toll, so the team photographed the 20-by-22-foot mural and began digitally restoring the photographic version. Among the images is a dagger-pierced Sacred Heart of Jesus. There's a small museum covering the mission's founding and history, and the pretty little mission cemetery (made famous by a scene in Alfred Hitchcock's *Vertigo*) maintains the graves of mid-19th-century European immigrants. (The remains of an estimated 5,000 Native Americans lie in unmarked graves.) Services are held in both the Mission San Francisco de Asís and next door in the handsome multi-dome basilica. ⊠ *Dolores and 16th Sts., Mission* 🕾 *415/621–8203* ⊕ *www.missiondolores. org* ⊠ *$5 donation, audio tour $7* ⊙ *Nov.–Apr., daily 9–4; May–Oct., daily 9–4:30.*

Precita Eyes Mural Arts and Visitors Center. Founded by muralists, this nonprofit arts organization designs and creates murals. The artists themselves lead informative guided walks of murals in the area. Most tours start with a 45-minute slide presentation. The bike and walking trips, which take between one and three hours, pass several dozen murals. May is Mural Awareness Month, with visits to murals-in-progress and presentations by artists. You can pick up a map of 24th Street's murals at the center and buy art supplies, T-shirts, postcards, and other mural-related items. Bike tours are available by appointment; Saturday's 11 am walking tour meets at Cafe Venice, at 24th and Mission streets. (All other tours meet at the center.) ⊠ *2981 24th St., Mission* 🕾 *415/285–2287* ⊕ *www.precitaeyes.org* ⊠ *Center free, tours $12–$15* ⊙ *Center weekdays 10–5, Sat. 10–4, Sun. noon–4; walks weekends at 11 and 1:30 or by appointment.*

PACIFIC HEIGHTS AND JAPANTOWN

Pacific Heights and Japantown are something of an odd couple: privileged, old-school San Francisco and the workaday commercial center of Japanese-American life in the city, stacked virtually on top of each other. The sprawling, extravagant mansions of Pacific Heights gradually give way to the more modest Victorians and unassuming housing tracts of Japantown. The most interesting spots in Japantown huddle in the Japan Center, the neighborhood's two-block centerpiece, and along

Post Street. You can find plenty of authentic Japanese treats in the shops and restaurants, if you have a special interest in these.

■TIP→ Japantown is a relatively safe area, but the Western Addition, south of Geary Boulevard, can be dangerous even during the daytime. Avoid going too far west of Fillmore Street on either side of Geary.

EXPLORING PACIFIC HEIGHTS

Alta Plaza Park. Golden Gate Park's longtime superintendent, John McLaren, designed Alta Plaza in 1910, modeling its terracing on that of the Grand Casino in Monte Carlo, Monaco. From the top you can see Marin to the north, downtown to the east, Twin Peaks to the south, and Golden Gate Park to the west. Kids love the many play structures at the large, enclosed playground at the top; everywhere else is dog territory. ⊠ *Bordered by Clay, Steiner, Jackson, and Scott Sts., Pacific Heights.*

Franklin Street buildings. What at first looks like a stone facade on the **Golden Gate Church** (1901 Franklin St.) is actually redwood painted white. A Georgian-style residence built in the early 1900s for a coffee merchant sits at 1735 Franklin. On the northeast corner of Franklin and California streets is a **Christian Science church**; built in the Tuscan revival style, it's noteworthy for its terra-cotta detailing. The **Coleman House** (1701 Franklin St.) is an impressive twin-turret Queen Anne mansion that was built for a gold-rush mining and lumber baron. Don't miss the large, brilliant-purple stained-glass window on the house's north side. ⊠ *Franklin St. between Washington and California Sts., Pacific Heights.*

Haas-Lilienthal House. A small display of photographs on the bottom floor of this elaborate, gray 1886 Queen Anne house makes clear that despite its lofty stature and striking, round third-story tower, the house was modest compared with some of the giants that fell victim to the 1906 earthquake and fire. The Foundation for San Francisco's Architectural Heritage operates the home, whose carefully kept rooms provide an intriguing glimpse into late-19th-century life through period furniture, authentic details (antique dishes in the kitchen built-in), and photos of the family who occupied the house until 1972. Volunteers conduct one-hour house tours three days a week and informative two-hour walking tours ($8) of the Civic Center, Broadway, and Union Street areas on Saturday afternoon, and of the eastern portion of Pacific Heights on Sunday afternoon (call or check website for schedule). ⊠ *2007 Franklin St., between Washington and Jackson Sts., Pacific Heights* ☏ *415/441–3004* ⊕ *www.sfheritage.org* ⌦ *Entry $8* ☉ *1-hr tour Wed. and Sat. noon–3, Sun. 11–4; 2-hr tour Sun. at 12:30.*

Noteworthy Victorians. Two **Italianate Victorians** (1818 and 1834 California St.) stand out on the 1800 block of California. A block west is the Victorian-era **Atherton House** (1990 California St.), whose mildly daffy design incorporates Queen Anne, Stick-Eastlake, and other architectural elements. Many claim the house—now apartments—is haunted by the ghosts of its 19th-century residents, who regularly whisper, glow, and generally cause a mild fuss. The oft-photographed **Laguna Street Victorians,** on the west side of the 1800 block of Laguna Street, cost between $2,000 and $2,600 when they were built in the 1870s. No

DID YOU KNOW?

These soft-colored Victorian homes in Pacific Heights are closer to the original hues sported back in the 1900s. It wasn't until the 1960s that the bold, electric colors now seen around SF gained popularity. Before that, the most typical house paint color was a standard gray.

Pacific Heights
and Japantown

bright colors here though—most of the paint jobs are in soft beiges or pastels. ✉ *California St. between Franklin and Octavia Sts., and Laguna St. between Pine and Bush Sts., Pacific Heights.*

Octagon House. This eight-sided home sits across the street from its original site on Gough Street; it's one of two remaining octagonal houses in the city (the other is on Russian Hill), and the only one open to the public. White quoins accent each of the eight corners of the pretty blue-gray exterior, and a colonial-style garden completes the picture. Inside, it's full of antique American furniture, decorative arts (paintings, silver, rugs), and documents from the 18th and 19th centuries. A deck of Revolutionary-era hand-painted playing cards takes an antimonarchist position: in place of kings, queens, and jacks, the American upstarts substituted American statesmen, Roman goddesses, and Indian chiefs. ✉ *2645 Gough St., Pacific Heights* ☎ *415/441–7512* 🖼 *Free, donations encouraged* ☉ *Feb.–Dec., 2nd Sun. and 2nd and 4th Thurs. of month noon–3; group tours weekdays by appointment.*

Spreckels Mansion. Shrouded behind tall juniper hedges at the corner of lovely winding, brick Octavia Street, overlooking Lafayette Park, the estate was built for sugar heir Adolph Spreckels and his wife Alma. Mrs. Spreckels was so pleased with her house that she commissioned George Applegarth to design another building in a similar vein: the

Legion of Honor. One of the city's great iconoclasts, Alma Spreckels was the model for the bronze figure atop the Victory Monument in Union Square. Today this house belongs to prolific romance novelist Danielle Steel. ⊠ *2080 Washington St., at Octavia St., Pacific Heights.*

Whittier Mansion. With a Spanish-tile roof and scrolled bay windows on all four sides, this is one of the most elegant 19th-century houses in the state. Unlike other grand mansions lost in the 1906 quake, the Whittier Mansion was built so solidly that only a chimney toppled over during the disaster. ⊠ *2090 Jackson St., Pacific Heights.*

EXPLORING JAPANTOWN

★ **Japan Center.** Cool and curious trinkets, noodle houses and sushi joints, a destination bookstore, and a peek at Japanese culture high and low await at this 5-acre complex designed in 1968 by noted American architect Minoru Yamasaki. The Japan Center includes the shop- and restaurant-filled Kintetsu and Kinokuniya buildings; the excellent Kabuki Springs & Spa; the Hotel Kabuki; and the Sundance Kabuki, Robert Redford's fancy, reserved-seating cinema/restaurant complex. Unfortunately, the development hasn't aged well, and its Peace Plaza, where seasonal festivals are held, is an unwelcoming sea of cement.

The Kinokuniya Bookstores, in the Kinokuniya Building, have an extensive selection of Japanese-language books, *manga* (graphic novels), books on design, and English-language translations and books on Japanese topics. Just outside, follow the Japanese teenagers to Pika Pika, where you and your friends can step into a photo booth and then use special effects and stickers to decorate your creation. On the bridge connecting the center's two buildings, check out Shige Antiques for *yukata* (lightweight cotton kimonos) for kids and lovely silk kimonos, and Asakichi and its tiny incense shop for tinkling wind chimes and display-worthy teakettles. Continue into the Kintetsu Building for a selection of Japanese restaurants.

Between the Miyako Mall and Kintetsu Building are the five-tier, 100-foot-tall **Peace Pagoda** and the Peace Plaza. The pagoda, which draws on the 1,200-year-old tradition of miniature round pagodas dedicated to eternal peace, was designed in the late 1960s by Yoshiro Taniguchi to convey the "friendship and goodwill" of the Japanese people to the people of the United States. The plaza itself is a shadeless, unwelcoming stretch of cement with little seating. Continue into the Miyako Mall to Ichiban Kan, a Japanese dollar store where you can pick up fun Japanese kitchenware, tote bags decorated with hedgehogs, and erasers shaped like food. ⊠ *Bordered by Geary Blvd. and Fillmore, Post, and Laguna Sts., Japantown.*

Japan Center Mall. The buildings lining this open-air mall are of the shoji school of architecture. The shops are geared more toward locals—travel agencies, electronics shops—but there are some fun Japanese-goods stores. Arrive early in the day and you may score some fabulous mochi (a soft, sweet Japanese rice treat) at Benkyodo (⊠ *1747 Buchanan St.* ☎ *415/922–1244*). It's easy to spend hours among the fabulous origami and craft papers at Paper Tree (⊠ *1743 Buchanan St.* ☎ *415/921–7100*). You can have a seat on local artist Ruth Asawa's twin origami-style fountains, which sit in the middle of the mall; they're squat circular structures made of fieldstone, with three levels for sitting and a brick floor. ⊠ *Buchanan St. between Post and Sutter Sts., Japantown.*

★ **Kabuki Springs & Spa.** This serene spa is one Japantown destination that draws locals from all over town, from hipster to grandma, Japanese-American or not. Balinese urns decorate the communal bath area of this house of tranquillity.

The massage menu has also expanded well beyond traditional shiatsu technique. The experience is no less relaxing, however, and the treatment regimen includes facials, salt scrubs, and mud and seaweed wraps. You can take your massage in a private room with a bath or in a curtained-off area.

The communal baths ($22 weekdays, $25 weekends) contain hot and cold tubs, a large Japanese-style bath, a sauna, a steam room, and showers. Bang the gong for quiet if your fellow bathers are speaking too loudly. The clothing-optional baths are open for men only on Monday, Thursday, and Saturday; women bathe on Wednesday, Friday, and Sunday. Bathing suits are required on Tuesday, when the baths are coed.

Men and women can reserve private rooms daily. An 80-minute massage-and-private-bath package costs $120; a package that includes a 50-minute massage and the use of the communal baths costs $100. ⊠ *1750 Geary Blvd., Japantown* ☎ *415/922–6000* ⊕ *www.kabukisprings.com* ☉ *Daily 10–10.*

WHERE TO EAT

San Francisco is a vital culinary crossroads, with nearly every ethnic cuisine represented. Although locals have long headed to the Mission District for Latin food, Chinatown for Asian food, and North Beach for Italian food, they also know that every part of the city offers dining experiences beyond the neighborhood tradition.

Some renowned restaurants are booked weeks or even months in advance. But you can get lucky at the last minute if you're flexible—and friendly. Most restaurants keep a few tables open for walk-ins and VIPs. Show up for dinner early (5:30 pm) or late (after 9 pm) and politely inquire about any last-minute vacancies or cancellations. *Prices in the restaurant reviews are the average cost of a main course at dinner or, if dinner is not served, at lunch (excluding sales tax).*

Use the coordinate (✛ A1) at the end of each listing to locate a site on the corresponding map.

UNION SQUARE

$$$ ✕ **Canteen.** Blink, and you'll miss this place. Chef-owner Dennis Leary
AMERICAN   has transformed this narrow coffee shop into a popular spot where locals and visiting gourmands rub elbows. The intimate dining room has just 20 seats (7 at a counter and a quartet of booths). But that's all Leary, with a modest open kitchen and a single assistant, can handle. The inspired dinner menu, which changes often, offers only four first

courses, four mains, and three or four desserts. A typical meal might start with chestnut soup and rabbit confit, followed by a gratin of chanterelles and tomatoes, or pork tenderloin with braised cranberry beans and fig-olive jus, and then a stellar vanilla soufflé. On Tuesday and Saturday nights a three-course prix-fixe menu is in force (no choices within each course) for $43–$50. Because this is a one-man band, there are set times to dine: 6 pm and 8 pm on Tuesday and 6 pm, 7:30 pm, and 9:15 pm Wednesday through Sunday. Brunch (only on Sunday 8 am until 2 pm) is a popular option; don't miss the eggs Benedict. ⑤ *Average main: $26* ⊠ *817 Sutter St., Union Sq.* ☎ *415/928–8870* ⊕ *www.sfcanteen. com* ⌲ *Reservations essential* ⊗ *Closed Mon* ✛ *D4.*

CHINATOWN

$$ ✕ **R&G Lounge.** The name conjures up an image of a dark, smoky bar with a piano player, but this Cantonese restaurant is actually as bright as a new penny. On the lower level (entrance on Kearny Street) is a no-tablecloth dining room that's packed at lunch and dinner. The classy upstairs space (entrance on Commercial Street) is a favorite stop for Chinese businessmen on expense accounts and special-occasion banquets. The street-level room on Kearny is a comfortable spot to wait for an open table. A menu with photographs helps you pick from the many wonderful, sometimes pricey, always authentic dishes, such as the famous salt-and-pepper Dungeness crab, roast squab, and shrimp-stuffed tofu (and much of the seafood is fresh from the tank). ⑤ *Average main: $20* ⊠ *631 Kearny St., Chinatown* ☎ *415/982–7877* ⊕ *www. rnglounge.com* ✛ *F3.*

CHINESE
☺

SOMA

$$$$ ✕ **Benu.** Chef-owner Corey Lee launched his contemporary American restaurant, one of the most high-profile restaurants to open in the city, much to the delight of food-obsessed locals and travelers alike. His pedigree spans 15 years in fine dining (including a position as chef de cuisine at The French Laundry), but Benu is decidedly more relaxed—no jacket required. The dining room is very minimalist, with bare wood tables and high-backed banquettes along the walls. While some guests come early in the week to dine on the à la carte menu, the 17-course tasting menu (mandatory on Friday and Saturday nights) is the way to go if your pocketbook can handle it. Each dish is a marvel, from the meticulous presentation (Lee has had pieces specifically designed for the restaurant and each course) to the sophisticated flavors and textures. Fans of Asian cuisine will be particularly thrilled to see his elegant handling of ingredients like *xiao long bao* dumplings and sea cucumber. He utilizes many modern techniques, but never in an alienating way. You may find dishes like Hokkaido sea cucumber stuffed with shrimp, pork belly, eggplant, fermented pepper or eel, feuille de brick, crème fraiche, and lime. An extremely professional staff is behind the quick pacing and on-point wine pairings. Couples expecting an ultra-romantic environment may be a bit disappointed by the stark atmosphere, but culinary adventurers will be thrilled. ⑤ *Prix-fixe: $160* ⊠ *22 Hawthorne St.,*

MODERN
AMERICAN
Fodor'sChoice
★

8

SoMa ☎ *415/685–4860* ⊕ *www.benusf.com* ⊜ *Reservations essential* ⊙ *Closed Sun. and Mon.* ✛ *G5*

HAYES VALLEY

$$$$ ✕ **Jardinière.** A special anniversary? An important business dinner? A
MODERN fat tax refund? These are the reasons you book a table at Jardinière.
AMERICAN The restaurant takes its name from chef-owner Traci Des Jardins, and
the sophisticated interior, with its eye-catching oval atrium and curving
staircase, fills nightly with locals and out-of-towners alike. An equally
sophisticated French-Californian dining room menu, served upstairs in
the atrium, changes daily, but regularly includes such high-priced adorn-
ments as caviar, foie gras, and truffles. (The tasting menu is available for
$120.) Downstairs, the lounge menu, with smaller plates and smaller
prices ($8 to $18), is ideal for when you want to eat light while visiting
with friends or tame your hunger before or after the nearby opera or
symphony. Cheese lovers will appreciate the wide variety of choices—
both Old World and New—housed in the glassed-in cheese-aging chamber in the rear of the restaurant. The choice wine selection is worthy
of celebration in and of itself. Ⓢ *Average main: $38* ✉ *300 Grove St.,
Hayes Valley* ☎ *415/861–5555* ⊕ *www.jardiniere.com* ⊜ *Reservations
essential* ⊙ *No lunch* ✛ *C5.*

$$$ ✕ **Zuni Café.** After one bite of chef Judy Rodgers's succulent brick-oven-
MEDITERRANEAN roasted whole chicken with Tuscan bread salad, you'll understand why
Fodor's Choice she's a national star (and why it's the most well-known chicken dish in
★ town). Food is served here on two floors; the rabbit warren of rooms
on the second level includes a balcony overlooking the main dining
room. Mingle among a disparate mix that reflects the makeup of the
city—casual and dressy, young and old, hip and staid—at the long
copper bar where trays of briny-fresh oysters on the half shell are dis-
pensed along with cocktails and wine. The southern French–Italian
menu changes daily, though the signature chicken, prepared for two, is
a fixture (and, alas, its cost reflects its popularity). Rotating dishes are
simple but made with excellent ingredients, like house-cured ancho-
vies with Parmigiano-Reggiano, deep-fried squid and lemons, ricotta
gnocchi with seasonal vegetables, and brick-oven squab with polenta.
Desserts include crumbly crusted tarts and a cream-laced coffee granita.
The lunchtime (and late-night) burger on rosemary focaccia with a side
of shoestring potatoes is a favorite with locals. Ⓢ *Average main: $28*
✉ *1658 Market St., Hayes Valley* ☎ *415/552–2522* ⊕ *www.zunicafe.
com* ⊙ *Closed Mon.* ✛ *C6*

FINANCIAL DISTRICT

$$ ✕ **Bocadillos.** The name means "sandwiches," but that's only half the
SPANISH story here. You'll find 13 bocadillos at lunchtime: plump rolls filled
with everything from serrano ham to Catalan sausage with arugula to
a memorable lamb burger (pick two for $10). But at night chef-owner
Gerald Hirigoyen, who also owns the high-profile Piperade, focuses
on tapas, offering some two dozen choices, including a savory octopus
carpaccio, an equally superb pig's trotters with chopped egg salad, and

BEST BETS FOR
SAN FRANCISCO DINING

With thousands of restaurants to choose from, how will you decide where to eat? Fodor's writers and editors have selected their favorite restaurants by price, cuisine, and experience in the Best Bets lists below. In the first column, Fodor's Choice designations represent the "best of the best" in every price category. You can also search by neighborhood for excellent eats—just peruse the following pages.

Fodor's Choice ★

Acquerello, $$$$, p. 431
Aziza, $$$, p. 440
Benu, $$$$, p. 423
Boulevard, $$$$, p. 434
Coi, $$$$, p. 433
Delfina, $$$, p. 438
Dosa on Fillmore, $$, p. 439
Dosa on Valencia, $$, p. 438
Gary Danko, $$$$, p. 434
L'Osteria del Forno, $, p. 433
Nopalito, $$, p. 437
Quince, $$$$, p. 430
Swan Oyster Depot, $$, p. 433
Zuni Café, $$$, p. 424

By Price

$

Good Noodle, p. 440

L'Osteria del Forno, p. 433
SanJalisco, p. 438

$$

Dosa on Fillmore, p. 439
Dosa on Valencia, p. 438
Nopalito, p. 437
Swan Oyster Depot, p. 433

$$$

A16, p. 436
Aziza, p. 440
Canteen, p. 422
Delfina, p. 438
Zuni Café, p. 424

$$$$

Acquerello, p. 431
Benu, p. 423
Boulevard, p. 434
Coi, p. 433
Gary Danko, p. 434
Quince, p. 430

By Cuisine

AMERICAN

Boulevard, $$$$, p. 434
Canteen, $$$, p. 422
Gary Danko, $$$$, p. 434
Nopa, $$$, p. 437

CHINESE

R&G Lounge, $$, p. 423
Yank Sing, $$, p. 430

INDIAN

Dosa on Fillmore, $$, p. 439
Dosa on Valencia, $$, p. 438
Indian Oven, $$, p. 436

ITALIAN

A16, $$$, p. 436
Delfina, $$$, p. 438
L'Osteria del Forno, $, p. 433

Quince, $$$$, p. 430

MEDITERRANEAN

Zuni Café, $$$, p. 424

MEXICAN

Nopalito, $$, p. 437
SanJalisco, $, p. 438

SEAFOOD

Hog Island Oyster Company, $$, p. 434
Plouf, $$, p. 430
Swan Oyster Depot, $$, p. 433

VIETNAMESE

Good Noodle, $, p. 440
Slanted Door, $$$, p. 435

By Experience

BAY VIEWS

Slanted Door, $$$, p. 435

BRUNCH

Rose's Café, $$, p. 436

CHILD-FRIENDLY

Mifune, $, p. 440
Yank Sing, $$, p. 430

SPECIAL OCCASION

Boulevard, $$$$, p. 434
Gary Danko, $$$$, p. 434

8

NORCAL'S LOCAVORE FOOD MOVEMENT

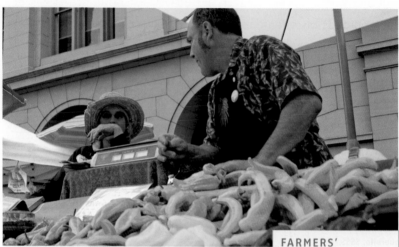

Organic, *local*, and *sustainable* are buzzwords in Northern California, home to hundreds of small family farmers, sustainable ranchers, and artisan producers leading the country's back-to-the-earth food movement.

When Alice Waters opened Chez Panisse in Berkeley in 1971, she sparked a culinary revolution that continues today. Initially called California cuisine, the cooking style showcased local, seasonal ingredients in fresh preparations. It also marked a new willingness by American chefs to experiment with international influences. As the movement spread, it became known as New American cooking. This "eat local, think global" ethos has led to a resurgence of artisanal producers across the country.

The *locavore* (focused on sustainable, local foods) movement's epicenter is still Northern California. At the Ferry Plaza Farmers Market in San Francisco alone, farmers bring over 1,200 varieties of fruits and vegetables to market every year. Chefs proudly call out their purveyors on menus and websites, elevating humble vegetable growers to starring culinary roles.

FARMERS' MARKETS

One of the best ways to taste Northern California's bounty is by stopping by the Ferry Plaza Farmers Market, held outside of the Ferry Building on the Embarcadero, at Market Street on Tuesday and Saturday mornings. The market offers produce, meats, fish, and flowers from small regional farmers and ranchers, many of whom are certified organic.

It is also a great place to pick up items for a picnic. Prepared foods like tamales and pasta are available, as are specialties like jams, breads, and cheeses from local artisan producers.

Check ⊕ *www.cuesa.org* for hours.

FRUIT

Northern California's diverse climate makes it an ideal place to grow all types of fruit, from berries to stone fruit. Farmers' markets and restaurants abound with a staggering selection of produce: Blossom Bluff Orchards, south of San Francisco, offers more than 150 varieties of stone fruits, like apricots, nectarines, and peaches. North of the city, the Apple Farm grows 80 varieties of apples, pears, persimmons, quince, and French plums. The Bay Area is also one of the best places in the country to find rare fruit varieties like aprium, cherimoya, cactus pear, jujube, and loquat; California's famous Meyer lemons—sweeter and less acidic than common lemons—are celebrated in restaurant desserts.

VEGETABLES

Some chefs give top billing to their produce purveyors, like a recently observed menu touting a salad of Star Route Farm field greens with Picholine olives, sweet herbs, and goat cheese. Along with these tantalizing items, be on the lookout for locally grown artichokes, Asian vegetables, multihued beets and carrots, and heirloom varieties of tomatoes, squash, and beans.

MEAT

Family-owned ranches and farms are prominent in the region, with many raising organic or "humane certified" beef, pork, lamb, and poultry. Upscale Bay Area restaurants are fervent about recognizing their high-quality protein producers. From recent menus at two well-known San Francisco restaurants: Wolfe Ranch quail and foie gras crostini with Murcott mandarins, smoked bacon and bok choy, and vanilla gastrique; and Prather Ranch lamb with fava greens, cranberry beans, crispy artichokes, and salsa verde.

FISH

Diners and shoppers will find myriad seafood from local waters, from farm-raised scallops to line-caught California salmon. On menus, look for Hog Island Oysters, a local producer that raises more than 3 million oysters a year in Tomales Bay. Sardines netted in Monterey Bay are popular in preparations like mesquite-grilled sardines with fava beans, French radish and fennel salad, and preserved Meyer lemon.

CHEESE

Restaurant cheese plates, often served before—or in lieu of—dessert, are a great way to experience the region's excellent local cheeses. Look for selections from Cypress Grove Chevre, popular for its artisan goat cheeses, and Cowgirl Creamery, a renowned local producer of fresh and aged cow's milk cheeses. Additionally, some shops and bakeries offer fresh local butter and cheeses.

8

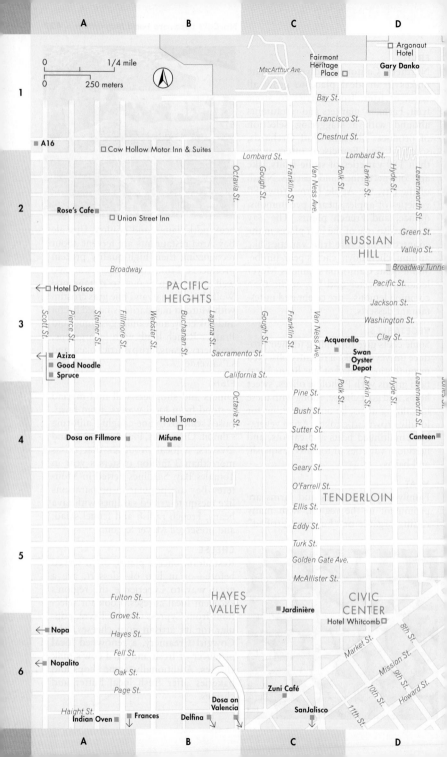

Map labels

Grid columns: A B C D
Grid rows: 1, 2, 3, 4, 5, 6

Scale bar: 0 — 1/4 mile · 0 — 250 meters

MacArthur Ave.

Argonaut Hotel

Fairmont Heritage Place

Gary Danko

Bay St.

Francisco St.

Chestnut St.

A16

Cow Hollow Motor Inn & Suites

Lombard St.

Lombard St.

Octavia St.

Gough St.

Franklin St.

Van Ness Ave.

Polk St.

Larkin St.

Hyde St.

Leavenworth St.

Rose's Cafe

Union Street Inn

RUSSIAN HILL

Green St.

Vallejo St.

Broadway

Broadway Tunnel

PACIFIC HEIGHTS

Hotel Drisco

Pacific St.

Jackson St.

Washington St.

Clay St.

Scott St.

Pierce St.

Steiner St.

Fillmore St.

Webster St.

Buchanan St.

Laguna St.

Gough St.

Franklin St.

Van Ness Ave.

Acquerello

Swan Oyster Depot

Aziza

Good Noodle

Spruce

Sacramento St.

California St.

Pine St.

Polk St.

Larkin St.

Hyde St.

Leavenworth St.

Jones St.

Octavia St.

Bush St.

Hotel Tomo

Sutter St.

Dosa on Fillmore

Mifune

Post St.

Canteen

Geary St.

O'Farrell St.

TENDERLOIN

Ellis St.

Eddy St.

Turk St.

Golden Gate Ave.

McAllister St.

Fulton St.

HAYES VALLEY

CIVIC CENTER

Grove St.

Jardinière

Hotel Whitcomb

Nopa

Hayes St.

8th St.

Market St.

Mission St.

Fell St.

Nopalito

9th St.

Oak St.

10th St.

Howard St.

Page St.

Zuni Café

11th St.

Haight St.

Dosa on Valencia

Indian Oven

Frances

Delfina

SanJalisco

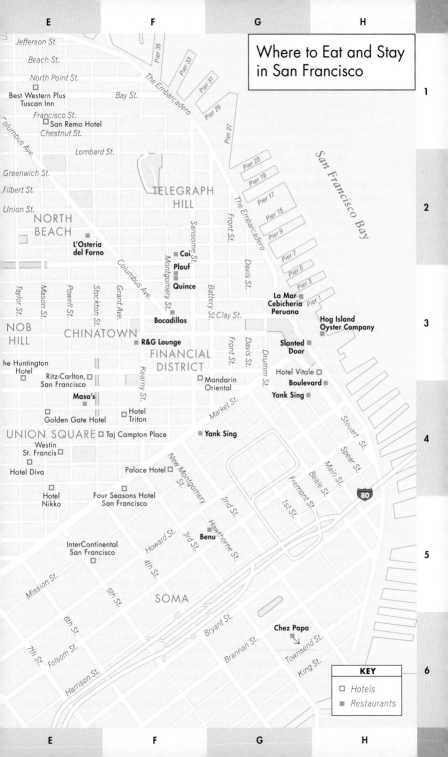

E | F | G | H

Jefferson St.

Beach St.

North Point St.

Best Western Plus
Tuscan Inn

Bay St.

Francisco St.

San Remo Hotel

Chestnut St.

Columbus Ave.

Lombard St.

Greenwich St.

Filbert St.

Union St.

NORTH
BEACH

L'Osteria
del Forno

Pier 35
Pier 33
Pier 31
Pier 29
Pier 27

The Embarcadero

Pier 23
Pier 19
Pier 17
Pier 15
Pier 9
Pier 7
Pier 5
Pier 3
Pier 1

The Embarcadero

San Francisco Bay

TELEGRAPH
HILL

Sansome St.
Front St.
Davis St.

Coi

Plouf

Quince

Montgomery St.

Columbus Ave.

Grant Ave.

Battery St.

Clay St.

La Mar
Cebicheria
Peruana

Hog Island
Oyster Company

Bocadillos

NOB
HILL

CHINATOWN

Taylor St.
Mason St.
Powell St.
Stockton St.

R&G Lounge

FINANCIAL
DISTRICT

Front St.
Davis St.
Drumm St.

Slanted
Door

Hotel Vitale

Boulevard

Yank Sing

he Huntington
Hotel

Ritz-Carlton,
San Francisco

Kearny St.

Mandarin
Oriental

Masa's

Golden Gate Hotel

Hotel
Triton

Market St.

Steuart St.

Spear St.

UNION SQUARE

Taj Campton Place

Yank Sing

Westin
St. Francis

Hotel Diva

New Montgomery St.

Palace Hotel

2nd St.

Fremont St.

Beale St.

Main St.

1st St.

Spear St.

80

Hotel
Nikko

Four Seasons Hotel
San Francisco

InterContinental
San Francisco

Howard St.

3rd St.

Benu

Hawthorne St.

Mission St.

5th St.

6th St.

7th St.

Folsom St.

SOMA

4th St.

Bryant St.

Brannan St.

Chez Papa

Townsend St.

King St.

Harrison St.

KEY	
□	Hotels
■	Restaurants

patatas bravas (potatoes) with *romesco* sauce (a thick combination of red pepper, tomato, almonds, and garlic). His wine list is well matched to the dishes. A youngish crowd typically piles into the dining space, decorated with redbrick walls, wire chairs, and small square light fixtures. Be prepared to wait for a seat. The large communal table is a good perch for singles. If you're in the neighborhood at breakfast time, there is plenty here to keep you happy, including a scrambled-eggs-and-cheese bocadillo or house-made chorizo and eggs. ⑤ *Average main: $22* ⊠ *710 Montgomery St., Financial District* ☎ *415/982–2622* ⊕ *www.bocasf. com* ⌲ *Reservations not accepted* ⊘ *Closed Sun. No lunch Sat.* ✥ *F3*

$$
SEAFOOD
✕ **Plouf.** A gold mine for mussel lovers, this French-friendly spot offers seven preparations to choose from, plus a variety of clam dishes, all at a modest price. Among the best are *marinière* (white wine, garlic, and parsley) and one combining coconut milk, lime juice, and chili. Add a side of the skinny fries and that's all most appetites need. The rest of the menu includes meaty dishes like lamb shank and New York strip to satisfy any unrepentant carnivores, but many of the presentations seem to be stuck in the last decade (same story with the lackluster desserts, complete with squeeze-bottle squiggles adorning the plates). The tables are clustered together in the lively dining room, so you might overhear neighboring conversations. Solo diners will find a bar where they can dine. On temperate days and nights, try for one of the tables outdoors. ⑤ *Average main: $22* ⊠ *40 Belden Pl., Financial District* ☎ *415/986– 6491* ⊕ *www.ploufsf.com* ⊘ *Closed Sun. No lunch Sat.* ✥ *F3*

$$$$
ITALIAN
Fodor's Choice
★
✕ **Quince.** Previously housed in a small space in Pacific Heights, this smart, wildly praised restaurant has moved and expanded to a much bigger more elegant space in Jackson Square. Chef-owner Michael Tusk, who has cooked at the legendary Chez Panisse and Oliveto, oversees the kitchen, where he uses only the finest local ingredients to turn out his Italian-inspired cuisine. The four-course menu ($95) or chef's tasting menu ($140) changes regularly, featuring a delicious selection of their famed pastas and seasonal dishes, such as tortelloni with robiola and cardoons, quail with cabbage and sausage, suckling pig and sweetbreads, and bosc pear with Medjool date genoise. Don't pass up the cheese course ($16 supplement)—it's one of the city's finer selections. The 800-bottle-strong wine list is top-notch, but can get pricey (a $35 corkage fee means you won't save much by bringing your own bottle), and the seamless service is both refined and welcoming. The lounge is an optimal place to swing by for an excellent cocktail. (You can also slink next door to Quince's new casual offshoot, Cotogna, for an affordable and rustic meal, at either lunch or dinner.) ⑤ *Prix-fixe: $95* ⊠ *470 Pacific Ave., Financial District* ☎ *415/775–8500* ⊕ *www. quincerestaurant.com* ⌲ *Reservations essential* ⊘ *No lunch* ✥ *F3.*

$$
CHINESE
☾
✕ **Yank Sing.** The granddaddy of SF dim sum teahouses, Yank Sing opened in a plain-Jane storefront in Chinatown in 1959, but left its Cantonese neighbors behind for the high-rises of downtown by the 1970s. This brightly decorated location on quiet Stevenson Street (there's also a big, brassy branch in the Rincon Center) serves some of San Francisco's best dim sum to office workers on weekdays and to big, boisterous families on weekends. The kitchen cooks up some 100 varieties of dim sum

on a rotating basis, offering 60 different types daily. These include both the classic (steamed pork buns, shrimp dumplings, egg custard tartlets) and the creative (scallion-skewered prawns tied with bacon, lobster and *tobiko* roe dumplings, basil seafood dumplings). The Shanghai soup dumplings are a classic—and some of the best in the city. The carts will keep whirring up to your table, and the tab can rise quickly, so diners should pace themselves. A take-out counter makes a meal on the run a satisfying and penny-wise compromise when office duties—or touring—won't wait. ⑤ *Average main: $16 ⊠ 49 Stevenson St., Financial District* ☎ *415/541–4949* ⊕ *www.yanksing.com* ⊗ *No dinner* ✛ *G4.*

NOB HILL

$$$$ ✕**Masa's.** Although the toque has been passed to several chefs since
FRENCH the tragic death of founding chef Masataka Kobayashi in 1984, this 25-year-old restaurant, with its chocolate-brown walls, white fabric ceiling, and vermilion-silk-shaded lanterns, remains a noted destination for fine dining in San Francisco. Chef Gregory Short, who worked alongside Thomas Keller at the famed French Laundry for seven years, has been at the helm since 2004. His tasting menus of four or seven courses, including a vegetarian option, all showcase the bounty of the seasons, from winter root vegetables to summer peaches. The California-French cuisine also features Japanse flair (an homage to Masa), and all the dishes are laced with luxe ingredients, from foie gras to Maine lobster to prime beef. In fall, when northern Italy's exquisite white truffles are in season, Short typically puts together a tasting menu that tucks them into every course, which will hopefully include a silky truffle custard whose perfume you can smell before it arrives at the table. The mignardise cart of candies, cookies, and chocolates is a famous component to the dining experience here. Wine drinkers are in excellent hands, with an award-winning list by sommelier Alan Murray that includes many small-production wines from around the globe. The elegant room has a formal atmosphere that is thankfully far from stuffy or suffocating, although a jacket is preferred for gentlemen. ⑤ *Prix-fixe: $98 ⊠ Hotel Vintage Court, 648 Bush St., Nob Hill* ☎ *415/989–7154* ⊕ *www.masasrestaurant.com* ⌂ *Reservations essential. Jacket required* ⊗ *Closed Sun. and Mon. No lunch* ✛ *E4.*

VAN NESS/POLK

$$$$ ✕**Acquerello.** For years, devotees of chef-owner Suzette Gresham-
ITALIAN Tognetti's high-end but soulful Italian cooking have been swooning
Fodor's Choice over her incomparable Parmesan *budino* (pudding), ridged pasta with
★ foie gras and truffles, and veal loin rolled and stuffed with seasonal vegetables. Dishes are complex, refined, and also feature some cutting-edge touches and techniques. Dinners are prix-fixe, with three ($70), four ($82), or five ($96) courses and at least six choices within each course. Tognetti also tempts with a chef's eight-course tasting menu ($195, with wine pairings). The cheese course is definitely worth indulging in since each one has been lovingly selected. Co-owner Giancarlo Paterlini (and his son) oversee the service and the deep list of Italian wines, both of

Eating with Kids

Kids can be fussy eaters, but parents can be, too, so picking places that will satisfy both is important. Fortunately, there are plenty of excellent possibilities all over town.

Sears Fine Food. If you're downtown for breakfast, stop at the touristy but venerable Sears Fine Food, home of "the world-famous Swedish pancakes." Eighteen of the silver-dollar-size beauties cost less than a movie ticket. ⊠ 439 Powell St., near Post St. ☎ 415/986–0700.

City View Restaurant. Nearby in Chinatown, City View Restaurant serves a varied selection of dim sum, with tasty pork buns for kids and more-exotic fare for adults. ⊠ 662 Commercial St., near Kearny St. ☎ 415/398–2838.

Pluto's. Try Pluto's after a visit to Golden Gate Park. Small kids love the chicken nuggets and mac and cheese, whereas bigger kids will likely opt for one of the two-fisted sandwiches or make-your-own salads. Everyone will want a double fudge brownie for dessert. ⊠ 627 Irving St., between 7th and 8th Sts. ☎ 415/753–8867.

Barney's Gourmet Burgers. With locations all over the Bay Area, including this one not far from Fort Mason, this chain caters to older kids and their parents with mile-high burgers and giant salads. But Barney's doesn't forget "kids under 8," who have their own menu featuring a burger, an all-beef frank, chicken strips with ranch dressing, and more. ⊠ 3344 Steiner St., near Union St. ☎ 415/563–0307 ⊕ www.barneyshamburgers.com.

The Ferry Building on the Embarcadero has plenty of kid-friendly options, from **Mijita Cocina Mexicana,** which has its own kids' menu,

to **Gott's Roadside Tray Gourmet,** for burgers, shakes, and more. (And the outdoor access can help keep the little ones entertained.)

La Corneta. The Mission has dozens of no-frills taco-and-burrito parlors; especially worthy is bustling La Corneta, which has a baby burrito and well-made quesadillas. ⊠ 2731 Mission St., between 23rd and 24th Sts. ☎ 415/643–7001.

St. Francis Fountain. Banana splits and hot-fudge sundaes are what St. Francis Fountain is known for, along with its vintage decor (and popularity with hipsters for weekend brunch). Opened in 1918, it recalls the early 1950s, and the menu, with its burgers, BLTs, grilled-cheese sandwiches, and chili with corn bread, is timeless. ⊠ 2801 24th St., at York St. ☎ 415/826–4200.

Rosamunde Sausage Grill. In Lower Haight, the small Rosamunde Sausage Grill serves just that—a slew of different sausages, from Polish to duck to Weisswurst (Bavarian veal). You get your choice of two toppings, like grilled onions, sauerkraut, and chili, and since there are only six stools, plan on takeout. Hint: head to nearby Duboce Park, with its cute playground. ⊠ 545 Haight St., between Steiner and Fillmore Sts. ☎ 415/437–6851.

Park Chalet. Finally, both kids and adults love to be by the ocean, and the Park Chalet, hidden behind the two-story Beach Chalet, offers pizza, mac and cheese, sticky ribs, and a big banana split. ⊠ 1000 Great Hwy., at Fulton St. ☎ 415/386–8439.

which are superb. The room, with its vaulted ceiling and terra-cotta and pale-ocher palette, suits the refined food. This is a true San Francisco dining gem that is worth every penny. $ *Prix-fixe: $70* ⊠ *1722 Sacramento St., Van Ness/Polk* ☎ *415/567–5432* ⊕ *www.acquerello. com* ⊗ *Closed Sun. and Mon. No lunch* ✚ *C3*.

$$ ✕ **Swan Oyster Depot.** Half fish market and half diner, this small, slim,
SEAFOOD family-run seafood operation, open since 1912, has no tables, just a
Fodor's Choice narrow marble counter with about a dozen and a half stools. Most
★ people come in to buy perfectly fresh salmon, halibut, crabs, and other seafood to take home. Everyone else hops onto one of the rickety stools to enjoy a bowl of clam chowder—the only hot food served—a dozen oysters, half a cracked crab, a slice of crusty sourdough, a big shrimp salad, or a smaller shrimp cocktail. And it's all served up with a side of big personality from the jovial folks behind the counter who make you feel like a regular. Come early or late to avoid a long wait. And since this place is notoriously cash only (and seafood is not exactly cheap!), be sure to come with a full wallet. $ *Average main: $18* ⊠ *1517 Polk St., Van Ness/Polk* ☎ *415/673–1101* ⊜ *Reservations not accepted* ⊟ *No credit cards* ⊗ *Closed Sun. No dinner* ✚ *D3*.

NORTH BEACH

$$$$ ✕ **Coi.** Daniel Patterson, who has made a name for himself internation-
MODERN ally both as a chef and as a pundit on contemporary restaurant trends,
AMERICAN has created a destination restaurant, an enchanting spot on the gritty
Fodor's Choice end of Broadway. There are two dining rooms: the front room, a bit
★ more casual with rustic wood tables and banquettes with pillows, and the 30-seat formal dining room, with soft lighting, luxe linens, and gold-taupe banquettes along the two walls. On offer is an 11-course tasting menu ($165), full of the bounty of Bay Area produce and ingredients. The highly seasonal and obsessively sourced food (some of it is even for-aged by chef Patterson) matches the space in sophistication, with such inspired dishes as Dungeness crab raviolo with sheep sorrel and butter crab broth; aged duck breast with stuffed cabbage, roasted beets, horse-radish, and dill; and Monterey Bay abalone with heirloom chicories and shellfish sauce. The kitchen is always tinkering and innovating, so the menu feels like a new and often exciting culinary experience. $ *Prix-fixe: $165* ⊠ *373 Broadway, North Beach* ☎ *415/393–9000* ⊕ *www. coirestaurant.com* ⊗ *Closed Sun., Mon. and Tues. No lunch* ✚ *F2*.

$ ✕ **L'Osteria del Forno.** Pass through the door of this modest storefront
ITALIAN and you'll feel as if you've stumbled into a homey trattoria in Italy,
♨ with the staff chattering in Italian and seductive aromas drifting from
Fodor's Choice the open kitchen through the sunny yellow dining room. Each day the
★ kitchen produces small plates of simply cooked vegetables (grilled pep-pers, roasted potatoes with yams and carrots), a few baked pastas, a daily special or two, lamb skewers, a roast of the day, creamy polenta, and thin-crust pizzas—including a memorable "white" pie topped with porcini mushrooms and mozzarella. (All the hot dishes come out of an oven—no stove here, so don't come expecting a large selection of pastas.) Wine drinkers will find a good match for any dish they order on the all-Italian list, which showcases gems from limited-production

8

vineyards. At lunch try one of North Beach's best focaccia sandwiches. The space is petite, so don't come with a large group, and there can often be a wait for a table. ⑤ *Average main: $15* ⊠ *519 Columbus Ave., North Beach* ☏ *415/982–1124* ⊕ *www.losteriadelforno.com* ▬ *No credit cards* ⊘ *Closed Tues.* ✛ *E2*

FISHERMAN'S WHARF

$$$$ ✕ **Gary Danko.** Be prepared to wait your turn for a table behind chef
MODERN Gary Danko's legion of loyal fans, who typically keep the reservation
AMERICAN book chock-full here (plan on reserving two months in advance). The
Fodor'sChoice cost of a meal ($69–$102) is pegged to the number of courses, from
★ three to five. The decadent menu spans a classic yet Californian style
that changes seasonally; it may include risotto with lobster and rock
shrimp, lemon pepper duck breast with duck hash, and herb-crusted
lamb loin. A diet-destroying chocolate soufflé with two sauces is usually among the desserts. So, too, is a "no-cholesterol" Grand Marnier
soufflé with raspberry sorbet, perfect for diners with a conscience or
a heart problem. But then there's the amazing cheese cart. The wine
list is the size of a small-town phone book, and the banquette-lined
rooms, with beautiful wood floors and stunning (but restrained) floral
arrangements, are as memorable as the food and impeccable service.
⑤ *Prix-fixe: $69* ⊠ *800 N. Point St., Fisherman's Wharf* ☏ *415/749–
2060* ⊕ *www.garydanko.com* ⌦ *Reservations essential. Jacket required*
⊘ *No lunch* ✛ *D1.*

EMBARCADERO

$$$$ ✕ **Boulevard.** Two of San Francisco's top restaurant celebrities—chef
AMERICAN Nancy Oakes and designer Pat Kuleto—are responsible for this high-
Fodor'sChoice profile, high-priced eatery in the magnificent 1889 Audiffred Building,
★ a Parisian look-alike and one of the few downtown structures to survive the 1906 earthquake. Kuleto's Belle-Époque interior and Oakes's
sophisticated-American-food-with-a-French-accent attract well-dressed
locals and flush out-of-towners. The menu changes seasonally, but count
on standout appetizers and generous portions of dishes like Maine
lobster ravioli, grilled king salmon with wild rice and vegetables that
include chanterelle mushrooms, and a wood-grilled pork prime rib chop
with Kabocha squash gnocchi (all the entrées come with delicious side
dishes). Save room (and calories) for one of the dynamite desserts, such
as dark chocolate brioche custard. There's counter seating for folks too
hungry to wait for a table, and an American Kobe beef burger at lunchtime that lets you eat with the swells without raiding your piggy bank.
The well-chosen wine list and excellent service are also hallmarks here.
⑤ *Average main: $36* ⊠ *1 Mission St., Embarcadero* ☏ *415/543–6084*
⊕ *www.boulevardrestaurant.com* ⌦ *Reservations essential* ⊘ *No lunch
weekends* ✛ *H4.*

$$ ✕ **Hog Island Oyster Company.** Hog Island, a thriving oyster farm in
SEAFOOD Tomales Bay, north of San Francisco, serves up its harvest at this attrac-
tive raw bar and retail shop in the busy Ferry Building. The U-shape
counter and a handful of tables seat no more than three dozen diners,

who come here for impeccably fresh oysters (from Hog Island and elsewhere) or clams (from Hog Island) on the half shell. Other mollusk-centered options include a first-rate oyster stew, baked oysters, clam chowder, and "steamer" clams with Israeli couscous. The bar also turns out what is arguably one of the city's best grilled-cheese sandwiches (with three artisanal cheeses on artisanal bread) this side of Wisconsin. You need to eat early, however, as the bar closes at 8 on weekdays and 6 on weekends. Happy hour, 5 to 7 on Monday and Thursday, is an oyster lover's dream and jam-packed: chef's choice of oysters for a buck apiece and a pint of beer for $4. ⑤ *Average main: $20* ⊠ *Ferry Bldg., Embarcadero at Market St., Embarcadero* ☎ *415/391–7117* ⊕ *www. hogislandoysters.com* ✛ *H3.*

$$$ ✕ **La Mar Cebicheria Peruana.** Set right on the water's edge, this casually
PERUVIAN chic restaurant is divided into three areas: a lounge with a long ceviche bar where diners watch chefs put together their plates; the savvy Pisco Bar facing the Embarcadero, where bartenders make a dozen different cocktails based on Peru's famed Pisco brandy; and a bright blue and whitewashed dining room overlooking an outdoor patio and the bay. Your waiter will start you out with a pile of potato and plantain chips with three dipping sauces, but then you're on your own, choosing from a long list of ceviches, can't-miss *causas* (whipped potatoes topped with a choice of fish, shellfish, or vegetable salads), and everything from crisp, lightly deep-fried fish and shellfish to soups and stews and rice dishes, many spiked with Peruvian chilies. The original La Mar is in Lima, Peru. San Francisco is the first stop in its campaign to open a string of cebicherias across the United States and Latin America. The view of the water is especially enjoyable during lunch or a warm evening. ⑤ *Average main: $25* ⊠ *Pier 1½ between Washington and Jackson Sts., Embarcadero* ☎ *415/397–8880* ⊕ *www.lamarcebicheria. com* ✛ *G3.*

$$$ ✕ **Slanted Door.** If you're looking for homey Vietnamese food served in
VIETNAMESE a down-to-earth dining room at a decent price, *don't* stop here. Celebrated chef-owner Charles Phan has mastered the upmarket, Western-accented Vietnamese menu. To showcase his cuisine, he built a big space with sleek wooden tables and chairs, white marble floors, a cocktail lounge, a bar, and an enviable bay view. Among his popular cult dishes are green papaya salad, daikon rice cakes, cellophane crab noodles, chicken clay pot, and shaking beef (tender beef cubes with garlic and onion)—and they don't come cheap, although the dishes are made with quality ingredients. Alas, the crush of fame means that no one speaking in a normal voice can be heard. To avoid the midday and evening crowds (and to save some bucks), stop in for the afternoon-tea menu (spring rolls, grilled pork over rice noodles), dine at the bar, or visit Out the Door, Phan's take-out counter around the corner from the restaurant. A second Out the Door, complete with table service, is a popular location in the Lower Pacific Heights (and the quality of the food seems to be better). ⑤ *Average main: $29* ⊠ *Ferry Bldg., Embarcadero at Market St., Embarcadero* ☎ *415/861–8032* ⊕ *www.slanteddoor.com* ✍ *Reservations essential* ✛ *G3.*

8

MARINA

$$$ **✕A16.** Marina residents—and, judging from the crowds, everybody
ITALIAN   else—gravitate to this lively trattoria, named for the autostrada that
winds through Italy's sunny south. The kitchen serves the food of
Naples and surrounding Campania, with a twist of seasonal Califor-
nia ingredients. Cult classics on the menu include creamy burrata with
olive oil and crostini and crisp-crust pizzas, including a classic Nea-
politan Margherita (mozzarella, tomato, and basil). Among the regu-
larly changing pastas are rustic favorites like *maccaronara* with *ragu
napoletana* and house-made ricotta salata, and dishes like petrale sole
with Monterey squid, sunchokes, and grilled lemon with *salmoriglio* (a
southern Italian sauce with garlic and herbs). An expertly chosen wine
list of primarily southern Italian with some California wines suits the
fare perfectly, along with a newly expanded beer list. The long dining
room includes an animated bar scene near the door; ask for a table in
the quieter alcove at the far end. Reservations are easier to snag mid-
week. ⑤ *Average main: $24* ⊠ *2355 Chestnut St., Marina* ☎ *415/771–
2216* ⊕ *www.a16sf.com* ⊘ *No lunch Sat.–Tues.* ✛ *A1*

COW HOLLOW

$$ **✕Rose's Café.** Sleepy-headed locals turn up at Rose's for the break-
ITALIAN   fast pizza of smoked ham, eggs, and fontina; house-baked pastries and
🕑   breads; poached eggs with Yukon Gold potato and mushroom hash;
or soft polenta with mascarpone and jam. Midday is time for a roasted
chicken and fontina sandwich; pizza with wild nettles; or linguine with
clams. Evening hours find customers eating their way through more
pizza and pasta if they are on a budget, and skirt steak and roasted
chicken if they aren't. The ingredients are top-notch, the service is
friendly, and the seating is in comfortable booths, at tables, and at a
counter. At the outside tables, overhead heaters keep you toasty when
the temperature dips. Expect long lines for Sunday brunch. ⑤ *Average
main: $22* ⊠ *2298 Union St., Cow Hollow* ☎ *415/775–2200* ⊕ *www.
rosescafesf.com* ✛ *A2.*

THE HAIGHT

$$ **✕Indian Oven.** This white-tablecloth northern Indian restaurant draws
INDIAN   diners from all over the city who come for the tandoori specialties—
chicken, lamb, breads. Classics like *saag paneer* (spinach with Indian
cheese), *aloo gobhi* (potato, cauliflower, and spices), and *bengan bartha*
(roasted eggplant with onions and spices) are also excellent. The chef
wants to keep his clientele around for the long haul, too, and puts a
little "heart healthy" icon next to some of the menu items. On Friday
and Saturday nights famished patrons overflow onto the sidewalk as
they wait for open tables. If you try to linger over a mango *lassi* or an
order of the excellent *kheer* (rice pudding) on one of these nights, you'll
probably be hurried along by a waiter. For better service, come on a
slower weeknight or for lunch. ⑤ *Average main: $16* ⊠ *233 Fillmore
St., Lower Haight* ☎ *415/626–1628* ⊕ *www.indianovensf.com* ✛ *A6.*

$$$ ✕ **Nopa.** In the mid-2000s North of the Panhandle became the city's
AMERICAN newest talked-about neighborhood in part because of the big, bustling
Nopa, which was cleverly named after it. This casual space, with its
high ceilings, concrete floor, long bar, and sea of tables, suits the high-
energy crowd of young professionals mixed with stylish neighborhood
residents that fill it every night (and since the kitchen doesn't close until
1 am, plenty of restaurant industry types come in and pack the bar
late into the night). Diners come primarily for the rustic fare, like an
always winning flat bread topped with fennel sausage and caramelized
onions; the vegetable tagine with lemon yogurt; smoky, crisp-skinned
rotisserie chicken; a juicy grass-fed hamburger with thick-cut fries; one
of the city's best pork chops; and for dessert, the donutlike sopapillas.
But they also love the lively spirit of the place. Unfortunately, that buzz
sometimes means that raised voices are the only way to communicate
with fellow diners. A big communal table and the friendly bar ease the
way for anyone dining out on his or her own. Wine lovers are happily
satisfied here with the excellent list, and weekend brunch is one of the
city's best (and most popular—arrive a few minutes before they open
at 11 am to score a table). ⑤ *Average main: $24* ✉ *560 Divisadero St.,
Haight* ☎ *415/864–8643* ⊕ *www.nopasf.com* ☽ *No lunch* ✛ *A6.*

$$ ✕ **Nopalito.** This is one of the more unusual (and delicious) Mexican
MEXICAN restaurants in the city—the two chefs here were originally cooks in
☺ the kitchen at Nopa around the corner, and their staff/family meals
Fodor's Choice were so delicious that the Nopa owners were inspired to create this
★ restaurant around their cooking. The menu features authentic recipes
prepared skillfully with excellent ingredients, from a bright ceviche and
seasonal salads to the succulent pork carnitas and a fulfilling posole. All
the tortillas are made from an organic house-ground masa (also used
in the delicious tortilla chips layering the *chilaquiles* during weekend
brunch). It's a casual space with a variety of tables, communal seating,
and a counter, quite popular with families and equally pleasing for
adult groups perusing its well-selected tequila list. Expect a steady wait
in the evening—you'll have to leave your name on a list, but you can
call before heading over to get your name on the waitlist in advance.
There's also a take-out window if you're feeling impatient. ⑤ *Average main: $15* ✉ *306 Broderick St., Haight* ☎ *415/437–0303* ⊕ *www.
nopalitosf.com* ✛ *A6.*

THE CASTRO

$$$ ✕ **Frances.** One of the hottest tickets in town, Frances is located, ironi-
FRENCH cally, on a sleepy residential street in the Castro. Chef-owner Melissa
Perello's menu of California and French cuisine is well executed, bal-
anced, and notably affordable for the high quality. Bacon beignets,
tender gnocchi, and a savory bavette steak are becoming favorites on
the seasonally driven menu, while new entries like baked clams with
bacon cream and a duck confit and kale salad are angling to become
standbys as well. An apple galette for dessert hits all the right notes.
The small space is simply designed and casual, with a limited number
of close tables (hence the difficulty in landing a reservation). Service
here is both very professional and warm, and there's a small bar area

8

for desperate diners who want to try their luck for a walk-in spot at the counter. $ *Average main: $27* ✉ *3870 17th St., Castro* ☎ *415/621–3870* ⊕ *www.frances-sf.com* ☜ *Reservations essential* ⊘ *Closed Mon. No lunch* ✛ *A6.*

THE MISSION

$$$
ITALIAN
Fodor'sChoice
★

✕ **Delfina.** "Irresistible." That's how countless die-hard fans describe Craig and Anne Stoll's Delfina. Such wild enthusiasm has made patience the critical virtue for anyone wanting a reservation here (although walk-ins can find some success at a counter and in the bar area). The urban interior is comfortable, with hardwood floors, aluminum-top tables, a tile bar, and a casual, friendly atmosphere. The menu changes daily, and among the usual offerings are grilled squid with warm white-bean salad and excellent tripe (they're also known for their spaghetti). If Piemontese fresh white truffles have made their way to San Francisco, you are likely to find hand-cut tagliarini dressed with butter, cream, and the pricey aromatic fungus on the menu alongside dishes built on more-prosaic ingredients. The panna cotta is the best in its class. The storefront next door is home to pint-size Pizzeria Delfina. And for folks who can't get to the Mission, the Stolls have opened a second pizzeria on California Street in lively Lower Pacific Heights. $ *Average main: $25* ✉ *3621 18th St., Mission* ☎ *415/552–4055* ⊕ *www.delfinasf.com* ☜ *Reservations essential* ⊘ *No lunch* ✛ *B6.*

$$
INDIAN
Fodor'sChoice
★

✕ **Dosa on Valencia.** Like Indian food but crave more than chicken tikka masala and naan? Dosa is your answer. This temple of South Indian cuisine, done in cheerful tones of tangerine and turmeric, serves not only the large, thin savory pancake for which it is named, but also curries, *uttapam* (open-face pancakes), and various starters, breads, rice dishes, and chutneys. You can select from about 10 different dosa fillings, ranging from traditional potatoes, onions, and cashews to spinach and fennel stems. Each comes with tomato and fresh coconut chutneys and *sambar* (lentil curry) for dipping. Tamil lamb curry with fennel and tomatoes and poppy seed prawns are popular, as are starters like Chennai chicken (chicken marinated in yogurt and spices and lightly fried), and the new Indian street-food additions, like *vada pav* (a vegetarian slider). The wine and beer lists are top drawer, and both include some Indian labels; the cocktail list is also very food friendly. Weekend brunch offers a nice change from the usual brunch suspects (the flavorful *pani puri* are a must). Queues for this Mission District spot convinced the owners to open a second, splashier branch on the corner of Fillmore and Post in Japantown. $ *Average main: $15* ✉ *995 Valencia St., at 21st St., Mission* ☎ *415/642–3672* ⊕ *www.dosasf.com* ⊘ *No lunch* ✛ *B6.*

$
MEXICAN
☺

✕ **San Jalisco.** This old-time, sun-filled, colorful, family-run restaurant is a neighborhood gem (and it's not just because it serves breakfast all day). At brunch, try the hearty *chilaquiles,* made from day-old tortillas cut into strips and cooked with cheese, eggs, chilies, and sauce. Or order eggs scrambled with cactus or with *chicharrones* (crisp pork skins) and served with freshly made tortillas. Soup offerings change daily, with Tuesday's *albondigas* (meatballs) comfort food at its best. On weekends, adventurous eaters may opt for *birria,* a spicy goat stew, or *menudo,* a tongue-searing soup made from tripe, calf's foot, and hominy. The latter is a time-honored hangover cure—but don't come expecting margaritas here (although you will find beer and sangria). Bring plenty of change for the jukebox loaded with Latin hits. $ *Average main: $11* ⊠ *901 S. Van Ness Ave., Mission* ☎ *415/648–8383* ⊕ *www.sanjalisco.com* ✛ *C6.*

POTRERO HILL

$$$
FRENCH

✕ **Chez Papa Bistrot.** France arrived on Potrero Hill with this restaurant, which delivers food, waiters, and charm that would be right at home in Provence. The modest corner restaurant, with a Mediterranean blue awning, big windows overlooking the street, and a small heated patio, caters to a lively crowd that can make conversation difficult. Small plates include bistro classics like mussels in pastis, beef tartare, and a leek and tomato tart. Big plates range from duck confit, to grilled flat-iron steak and frites, to homey lamb daube. The lavender crème brûlée or chocolate fondant provides a sweet ending. The $34.95 prix-fixe (Sunday through Thursday) is also a good deal for the penny-wise. To accommodate the overflow of Hill residents who have packed this place since day one, the owners opened the tiny (and more casual) Chez Maman (crepes, burgers, salads) a few doors down the block. $ *Average main: $23* ⊠ *1401 18th St., Potrero Hill* ☎ *415/824–8205* ⊕ *www. chezpapasf.com* ☾ *No lunch Sun.* ✛ *G6*

PACIFIC HEIGHTS

$$$$
MODERN
AMERICAN

✕ **Spruce.** One of the hottest reservations in town from the day it opened, Spruce caters to the city's social set, with the older crowd sliding into oversized faux ostrich chairs in the early hours and the younger set taking their places after 8 (there's also quite the lunch club during the week). The large space, a former 1930s auto barn, shelters a high-style dining room and a more casual bar and library lounge. Charcuterie, bavette steak with bordelaise sauce and duck-fat potatoes, and sweetbreads reflect the French slant of the modern American menu. The wine list is a star here (especially a delight for Riesling fans). If you can't wrangle a table, stop in at the take-out café next door, which carries not only sandwiches, salads, and pastries (like the exquisite palmiers) but also anything from the dining room menu to go. And if you are watching your pocketbook, you can graze off the bar menu (which includes their excellent burger and *boudin blanc*) and watch the swells come and go over a well-crafted cocktail. $ *Average main: $34* ⊠ *3640 Sacramento St., Pacific Heights* ☎ *415/931–5100* ⊕ *www.sprucesf.com* ⌂ *Reservations essential* ☾ *No lunch weekends* ✛ *A3.*

JAPANTOWN

$$
INDIAN
Fodor'sChoice
★

✕ **Dosa on Fillmore.** As soon as the large door swings open to this happening two-level space, diners are greeted with a sexy atmosphere with bright colors, vivid artwork, upbeat music, a lively bar scene, and the smell of spices in the air. This is the second location of the popular Dosa on Valencia, but it's definitely the glamorous younger sister, with a full

8

bar, an expanded menu, and much more room. The menu entices with savory fish dishes, fall-off-the-bone pepper chicken, and papery dosas stuffed with a variety of fillings. The restaurant handles group dining often, and has a special menu you can customize. Return for lunch and indulge in the Indian street-food selections, and the famed *pani puri* (little crisp puffs you fill with mint and tamarind water and pop all at once into your mouth). ⑤ *Average main: $17* ✉ *1700 Fillmore St., Japantown* ☎ *415/441–3672* ⊕ *www.dosasf.com* ⊗ *No lunch Mon. and Tues.* ✛ *A4*

$ ✕ **Mifune.** Thin brown soba and thick white udon are the stars at this
JAPANESE   long-popular North American outpost of an Osaka-based noodle
ⓒ   empire. A line regularly snakes out the door, but the house-made noodles, served both hot and cold and with a score of toppings, are worth the wait (and the line moves quickly). Seating is at wooden tables, where diners of every age can be heard slurping down big bowls of such traditional Japanese combinations as *nabeyaki udon,* wheat noodles topped with tempura, chicken, and fish cake; and *tenzaru,* cold noodles and hot tempura with gingery dipping sauce served on lacquered trays. The noodle-phobic can choose from a few rice dishes and sushi. ⑤ *Average main: $9* ✉ *Japan Center, Kintetsu Bldg., 1737 Post St., Japantown* ☎ *415/922–0337* ⊕ *www.mifune.com* ✛ *B4.*

RICHMOND

$$$ ✕ **Aziza.** Chef-owner Mourad Lahlou's California-Moroccan food
MOROCCAN   boasts a healthy dose of modernity that keeps locals coming back for
Fodor's Choice   his unique flavors and thoughtfully sourced ingredients. Diners enjoy
★   inspired and gorgeously plated first courses that are always changing with the seasons, like big fin squid with artichoke, citrus, piquillo, and olive, or sweetbreads with winter squash, cornichon, and marash pepper. The main courses are equally elegant, ranging from squab with smoked farro to lamb shank with apricot, turnips, and barley. The basteeya is one delicious holdover from the restaurant's earlier rustic days, although it's now made with duck confit. Desserts here are as sophisticated as the savory dishes. The attractive three-room dining area, done in blue, saffron, and white, is a warm, inviting sea of tiles, arches, and candlelight. The wine list is very food-friendly, with some organic and biodynamic options, while cocktail enthusiasts can pick from more than two dozen inspired drinks that use ingredients like tarragon, Kaffir lime, and cumin. ⑤ *Average main: $27* ✉ *5800 Geary Blvd., Richmond* ☎ *415/752–2222* ⊕ *www.aziza-sf.com* ⊗ *Closed Tues. No lunch* ✛ *A3.*

$ ✕ **Good Noodle.** The menu at this no-frills Formica-and-linoleum spot is
VIETNAMESE   big and remarkably cheap. You can order everything from Vietnamese
ⓒ   salads to rice dishes and noodle plates. But the soups are what take up the most space on the menu, from the two dozen varieties of *pho,* rice noodles in beef broth, to a dozen types of *hu tieu,* seafood and pork noodle soups. All of them are served in three sizes—small, medium, and large—usually separated by just 75¢, and no bowl is skimpy. Regulars, many of whom hail from Southeast Asia, favor the shrimp, fish ball, and pork slices soup with clear noodles and the special combo pho with rare

steak, well-done brisket, tendon, and tripe. ⑤ *Average main: $8* ✉ *239 Clement St., Inner Richmond* ☎ *415/379–9008* ⊕ *A3.*

WHERE TO STAY

San Francisco is one of the country's best hotel towns, offering a rich selection of properties that satisfy most tastes and budgets. Whether you're seeking a cozy inn, a kitschy motel, a chic boutique, or a grande dame hotel, this city has got the perfect room for you.

Prices in the hotel reviews are the lowest cost of a standard double room in high season. Prices do not include taxes (as high as 14%, depending on the region).

Use the coordinate (⊕ A1) at the end of each listing to locate a site on the corresponding map.

UNION SQUARE/DOWNTOWN

For expanded reviews, facilities, and current deals, visit Fodors.com.

$
B&B/INN
☺
Fodor's Choice
★

Golden Gate Hotel. Families looking for accommodations in the Union Square area will delight in this homey, family-run B&B. **Pros:** friendly staff; spotless rooms; comfortable bedding; good location if you're a walker. **Cons:** only some of the rooms have private baths. **TripAdvisor:** "very nice," "great location," "wonderful bed and breakfast." ⑤ *Rooms from: $105* ✉ *775 Bush St., Union Sq.* ☎ *415/392–3702, 800/835–1118* ⊕ *www.goldengatehotel.com* ⬎ *25 rooms, 14 with bath* ⦿ *Breakfast* ⊕ *E4.*

$$
HOTEL
☺
Fodor's Choice
★

Hotel Diva. Entering this hotel requires stepping over footprints, handprints, and autographs embedded into the sidewalk by visiting stars; with two major theaters, the Curran and the American Conservatory Theater, just across the street, this hotel has long been a magnet for actors, musicians, writers, and artists. **Pros:** clean; safe; in the heart of the theater district; accommodating service. **Cons:** no frills; tiny bathrooms. **TripAdvisor:** "excellent location," "friendly staff," "what's not to love." ⑤ *Rooms from: $199* ✉ *440 Geary St., Union Sq.* ☎ *415/885–0200, 800/553–1900* ⊕ *www.hoteldiva.com* ⬎ *115 rooms, 3 suites* ⦿ *No meals* ⊕ *E4.*

$$$$
HOTEL
☺
Fodor's Choice
★

Hotel Nikko, San Francisco. The vast surfaces of gray-flecked white marble and gurgling fountains in the neoclassical lobby of this business-traveler hotel have the sterility of an airport; however the crisply designed rooms in muted tones, with flat-screen TVs, modern (and newly renovated) bathrooms with sinks that sit on top of granite bases, plus separate showers and tubs, please jet-setters. **Pros:** friendly multilingual staff; large indoor pool; very clean. **Cons:** rooms and antiseptic lobby lack color; some may find the atmosphere cold; expensive parking. **TripAdvisor:** "great room," "comfy beds," "very convenient." ⑤ *Rooms from: $265* ✉ *222 Mason St., Union Sq.* ☎ *415/394–1111, 800/248–3308* ⊕ *www.hotelnikkosf.com* ⬎ *510 rooms, 22 suites* ⦿ *No meals* ⊕ *E4.*

$$
HOTEL
Fodor's Choice
★

Hotel Triton. The spirit of fun has taken up full-time residence in this Kimpton property, which has a youngish, superfriendly staff; pink-and-blue-neon elevators; and a colorful psychedelic lobby mural depicting the San Francisco art and music scene—think flower power mixed with

8

Andy Warhol. **Pros:** attentive service; refreshingly funky atmosphere; hip arty environs; good location. **Cons:** rooms and baths are on the small side. **TripAdvisor:** "a triumph over calamity," "quirky," "customer service at its finest."[$] *Rooms from: $179 ⊠ 342 Grant Ave., Union Sq.* ☏ *415/394–0500, 800-800-1299* ⊕ *www.hoteltriton.com* ⤳ *133 rooms, 7 suites* ⦿| *No meals* ✛ *F4.*

$$$$
HOTEL
Fodor's Choice
★
⚏ **Taj Campton Place San Francisco.** Beauty and highly attentive service remain the hallmarks of this exquisite jewel-like, top-tier hotel. **Pros:** attentive service; first-class restaurant; abundant natural light; the most lavish robes in town. **Cons:** pricey (but worth it). **TripAdvisor:** "lovely boutique property," "over and above customer service," "luxury on Union Square."[$] *Rooms from: $615 ⊠ 340 Stockton St., Union Sq.* ☏ *415/781–5555, 866/332–1670* ⊕ *www.camptonplace.com* ⤳ *101 rooms, 9 suites* ⦿| *No meals* ✛ *E4.*

$$$$
HOTEL
⚏ **Westin St. Francis.** The site of sensational, headline-making scandals, this hotel's past is shrouded as much in infamy as in stardust: This is where Sara Jane Moore tried to assassinate President Gerald Ford and where singer Al Jolson died playing poker—not to mention the tempest that erupted after a booze fest hosted by silent-film comedian Fatty Arbuckle in Suite 1219–21 ended with the death of an aspiring actress. **Pros:** fantastic beds; prime location; spacious rooms, some with great views. **Cons:** some guests comment on the long wait at check-in; rooms in original building can be small; glass elevators are not for the faint of heart. **TripAdvisor:** "perfect location," "we loved it," "gracious service."[$] *Rooms from: $299 ⊠ 335 Powell St., Union Sq.* ☏ *415/397–7000, 800/917–7458* ⊕ *www.westinstfrancis.com* ⤳ *1,157 rooms, 38 suites* ⦿| *No meals* ✛ *E4.*

SOMA

$$$$
HOTEL
☾
Fodor's Choice
★
⚏ **Four Seasons Hotel San Francisco.** Occupying floors 5 through 17 of a skyscraper, this exclusive, award-winning hotel is sandwiched between multimillion-dollar condos, elite shops, and a premier sports-and-fitness complex. **Pros:** near museums, galleries, restaurants, shopping and clubs; terrific fitness facilities; luxurious rooms and amenities. **Cons:** pricey; staff can be uppity. **TripAdvisor:** "luxury," "exceptional experience," "cradle of comfort."[$] *Rooms from: $415 ⊠ 757 Market St., SoMa* ☏ *415/633–3000, 800/332–3442, 800/819–5053* ⊕ *www.fourseasons.com/sanfrancisco* ⤳ *231 rooms, 46 suites* ⦿| *No meals* ✛ *F4.*

$$$$
HOTEL
⚏ **InterContinental San Francisco.** The arctic-blue glass exterior and subdued, Zen-like lobby of this sparkling hotel may be as bland as an airport concourse, but they're merely a prelude to the spectacularly light, expansive, thoughtfully laid-out guest rooms, which have all the ultramodern conveniences. **Pros:** a stone's throw from the Moscone Center; well-equipped gym; near hip clubs and edgy eateries. **Cons:** conservative decor is a bit short on character; borders a rough neighborhood; a few blocks off from many major points of interest for tourists. **TripAdvisor:** "excellent service," "amazing views and perfect location," "lovely."[$] *Rooms from: $289 ⊠ 888 Howard St., SoMa* ☏ *415/616–*

6500, 866/781–2364 ⊕ www.intercontinentalsanfrancisco.com ⟋ 536 rooms, 14 suites ⎮◎⎮ No meals ✛ E5.

$$$$ ⛫ **Palace Hotel, San Francisco.** "Majestic" is the word that best sums up
HOTEL this landmark hotel, which was the world's largest and most luxurious when it opened in 1875. **Pros:** gracious service; close to Union Square; near BART. **Cons:** design from another era; smallish rooms with even smaller baths; many nearby establishments closed on weekends; west-facing rooms can be warm and stuffy. **TripAdvisor:** "ideal location and beautiful surroundings," "historic beauty," "old-world elegance." ⑤ Rooms from: $599 ⊠ 2 New Montgomery St., SoMa ☏ 415/512–1111, 888/627–7196 ⊕ www.sfpalace.com ⟋ 518 rooms, 34 suites ⎮◎⎮ No meals ✛ F4.

CIVIC CENTER/VAN NESS

$ ⛫ **Hotel Whitcomb.** Built in 1910, this historic hotel was the temporary
HOTEL seat of city government from 1912 to 1915 before becoming a hotel in 1916. **Pros:** good location; rich architectural and historic legacy; opulent lobby; airport shuttle; free Wi-Fi. **Cons:** difficult to find street parking; area can be dodgy at night; rooms are not as flashy as the lobby. **TripAdvisor:** "New York in San Francisco," "outstanding service," "old-time elegance." ⑤ Rooms from: $129 ⊠ 1231 Market St., Civic Center ☏ 415/626–8000, 800/227–4747 ⊕ www.hotelwhitcomb. com ⟋ 447 rooms, 13 suites ⎮◎⎮ No meals ✛ D6.

FINANCIAL DISTRICT

$$$$ ⛫ **Mandarin Oriental, San Francisco.** Two towers connected by glass-
HOTEL enclosed sky bridges compose the top 11 floors of one of San Francisco's tallest buildings, offering spectacular panoramas from every room; the windows open so you can hear that trademark San Francisco sound: the "ding ding" of the cable cars some 40 floors below (and some rooms even include binoculars). **Pros:** spectacular "bridge-to-bridge" views; attentive service; in the running for the most comfy beds in the city. **Cons:** located in a business area that's quiet on weekends; extremely pricey. **TripAdvisor:** "spectacular view," "amazing and magical," "quiet, pretty rooms." ⑤ Rooms from: $445 ⊠ 222 Sansome St., Financial District ☏ 415/276–9600, 800/622–0404 ⊕ www.mandarinoriental.com/ sanfrancisco ⟋ 151 rooms, 7 suites ⎮◎⎮ No meals ✛ F3.

NOB HILL

$$$$ ⛫ **The Huntington Hotel.** The venerable ivy-covered hotel, a family-owned
HOTEL property for three generations, has provided gracious personal service
Fodor's Choice to everyone from Bogart and Bacall to Picasso and Pavarotti. **Pros:**
★ personal service; an aura of old San Francisco; guests have access to the primo spa with city views; cable car passes by right out front. **Cons:** up a steep hill from downtown. **TripAdvisor:** "classic San Francisco hotel," "large rooms," "the bar and spa are the highlights." ⑤ Rooms from: $410 ⊠ 1075 California St., Nob Hill ☏ 415/474–5400, 800/227–4683 ⊕ www.huntingtonhotel.com ⟋ 96 rooms, 40 suites ⎮◎⎮ No meals ✛ E4.

Fairmont Heritage Place, Ghirardelli Square

The Huntington Hotel

Argonaut Hotel

Hotel Vitale

Ritz-Carlton, San Francisco.

Hotel Drisco

Hotel Tomo

Union Street Inn

BEST BETS FOR SAN FRANCISCO LODGING

Fodor's offers a selective listing of quality lodging experiences at every price range, from the city's best budget motel to its most sophisticated luxury hotel. Here we've compiled our top recommendations by price and experience. The very best properties—in other words, those that provide a particularly remarkable experience in their price range—are designated in the listings with the Fodor's Choice logo.

Fodor's Choice ★

Argonaut Hotel, $$$$, p. 447

Cow Hollow Motor Inn and Suites, $, p. 448

Fairmont Heritage Place, Ghirardelli Square, $$$$, p. 448

Four Seasons Hotel San Francisco, $$$$, p. 442

Golden Gate Hotel, $, p. 441

Hotel Diva, $$, p. 441

Hotel Drisco, $$$$, p. 449

Hotel Nikko, San Francisco, $$$$, p. 441

Hotel Tomo, $, p. 448

Hotel Triton, $$, p. 441

Hotel Vitale, $$$$, p. 448

Huntington Hotel, $$$$, p. 443

Ritz-Carlton, San Francisco, $$$$, p. 447

San Remo Hotel, $, p. 447

Taj Campton Place San Francisco, $$$$, p. 442

Union Street Inn, $$$, p. 449

By Price

$

Cow Hollow Motor Inn and Suites, p. 448

Golden Gate Hotel, P. 441

Hotel Tomo, p. 448

San Remo Hotel, p. 447

$$

Hotel Triton, p. 441

Hotel Diva, p. 441

$$$

Union Street Inn, p. 449

$$$$

Argonaut Hotel, p. 447

Fairmont Heritage Place, Ghirardelli Square, p. 448

Four Seasons Hotel San Francisco, p. 442

Hotel Drisco, p. 449

Hotel Nikko, San Francisco, p. 441

Hotel Vitale, p. 448

Huntington Hotel, p. 443

Ritz-Carlton, San Francisco, p. 447

Taj Campton Place San Francisco, p. 442

By Experience

BUSINESS TRAVELERS

Four Seasons Hotel San Francisco, $$$$, p. 442

Hotel Nikko, San Francisco, $$$$, p. 441

GREAT CONCIERGE

Ritz-Carlton, San Francisco, $$$$, p. 447

HISTORICAL FLAVOR

Hotel Whitcomb, $, p. 443

Palace Hotel, San Francisco, $$$$, p. 443

Westin St. Francis, $$$$, p. 442

MOST KID-FRIENDLY

Argonaut Hotel, $$$$, p. 447

Four Seasons Hotel San Francisco, $$$$, p. 442

Hotel Tomo, $, p. 448

MOST ROMANTIC

Hotel Drisco, $$$$, p. 449

Huntington Hotel, $$$$, p. 443

Palace Hotel, San Francisco, $$$$, p. 443

Union Street Inn, $$$, p. 449

TOP B&BS

Hotel Drisco, $$$$, p. 449

TOP SPAS

Huntington Hotel, $$$$, p. 443

Mandarin Oriental San Francisco, $$$$, p. 443

$$$$
HOTEL
Fodor'sChoice
★
Ritz-Carlton, San Francisco. A preferred destination for travel-industry honchos, movie stars, and visitors alike, this hotel—a stunning tribute to beauty and attentive, professional service—is completing a $12.5-million renovation to offer a modern luxurious experience with Ritz style. **Pros:** terrific service; all-day food service on Club Level; beautiful surroundings; fantastic new restaurant and lobby lounge; renovated fitness center. **Cons:** expensive; hilly location; no pool. **TripAdvisor:** "as good as it gets," "excellent service," "definitely lovely."⑤ *Rooms from: $399* ⊠ *600 Stockton St., at California St., Nob Hill* ☎ *415/296–7465* ⊕ *www.ritzcarlton.com* ⌁ *276 rooms, 60 suites* ⑩ *No meals* ✛ *E4.*

NORTH BEACH

$
HOTEL
Fodor'sChoice
★
San Remo Hotel. A few blocks from Fisherman's Wharf, this three-story 1906 Italianate Victorian—once home to longshoremen and Beat poets—has a narrow stairway from the street leading to the front desk and labyrinthine hallways; rooms are small but charming, with lace curtains, forest-green-painted wood floors, and brass beds and other antique furnishings. **Pros:** inexpensive; historic; cozy. **Cons:** some rooms are dark; no private bath; spartan amenities. **TripAdvisor:** "an authentic taste of old San Francisco," "clean and beautiful," "excellent hotel in a quiet area."⑤ *Rooms from: $65* ⊠ *2237 Mason St., North Beach* ☎ *415/776–8688, 800/352–7366* ⊕ *www.sanremohotel.com* ⌁ *64 rooms with shared baths, 1 suite* ⑩ *No meals* ✛ *E1.*

FISHERMAN'S WHARF

$$$$
HOTEL
☺
Fodor'sChoice
★
Argonaut Hotel. When the four-story Haslett Warehouse was a fruit-and-vegetable canning complex in 1907, boats docked right up against the building; today it's a hotel with a nautical decor—think anchors, ropes, compasses, and a row of cruise-ship deck chairs in the lobby—that makes perfect sense given the fact that the Argonaut is part of the San Francisco Maritime National Historical Park (whose visitors center occupies the ground floor). **Pros:** bay views; near Hyde Street cable car; sofa beds; toys for the kids. **Cons:** nautical theme isn't for everyone; cramped public areas; service can be hit or miss; location is a bit of a trek from other parts of town. **TripAdvisor:** "can't get a better location," "a brilliant experience," "very pleased."⑤ *Rooms from: $319* ⊠ *495 Jefferson St., at Hyde St., Fisherman's Wharf* ☎ *415/563–0800, 866/415–0704* ⊕ *www.argonauthotel.com* ⌁ *239 rooms, 13 suites* ⑩ *No meals* ✛ *D1.*

$$$
HOTEL
Best Western Plus Tuscan Inn. Described by some Fodors.com users as a "hidden treasure," this hotel's redbrick facade barely hints at the Tuscan country villa that lies within. **Pros:** wine and beer hour; down-home feeling; great location near Fisherman's Wharf. **Cons:** congested touristy area; small rooms. **TripAdvisor:** "great location," "excellent service," "nice comfortable hotel."⑤ *Rooms from: $249* ⊠ *425 N. Point St., at Mason St., Fisherman's Wharf* ☎ *415/561–1100, 800/648–4626* ⊕ *www.tuscaninn.com* ⌁ *212 rooms, 12 suites* ⑩ *No meals* ✛ *E1.*

8

$$$$ 🖼 **Fairmont Heritage Place, Ghirardelli Square.** Housed in the former Ghi-
RENTAL rardelli chocolate factory, these one-to-three-bedroom serviced apart-
🕃 ments might possibly be the most luxurious accommodations in San
Fodor'sChoice Francisco. **Pros:** luxury at its finest; gigantic apartments with heaps of
★ amenities; bay views from most apartments; free hotel car to deliver you
within a 2-mile radius. **Cons:** a bit of a trek from downtown; expensive.
TripAdvisor: "the only way to travel," "comfort and style," "great
rooms."⑤ *Rooms from: $599* ⊠ *950 North Point St., Fisherman's
Wharf* ☎ *415/268–9900* ⊕ *www.fairmont.com/ghirardelli* ⦿ *Breakfast* ⊹ *D1.*

EMBARCADERO

$$$$ 🖼 **Hotel Vitale.** "Luxury, naturally," the theme of this eight-story ter-
HOTEL raced bay-front hotel, is apparent in every thoughtful detail: little vases
🕃 of aromatic herbs mounted outside each room; the penthouse day spa
Fodor'sChoice with soaking tubs set in a rooftop bamboo forest; and the aromatherapy
★ garden off the patio of restaurant Americano, whose outdoor terrace is
packed with hip jet-setters. **Pros:** family-friendly studios; great views;
fanciful spa; luxurious amenities throughout. **Cons:** cramped rooms
can be noisy; some guests report inconsistent service from staff and find
the hotel pricey. **TripAdvisor:** "great staff and pleasant views," "truly
dog friendly," "a comfortable relaxing stay."⑤ *Rooms from: $399* ⊠ *8
Mission St., Embarcadero* ☎ *415/278–3700, 888/890–8688* ⊕ *www.
hotelvitale.com* ➶ *190 rooms, 9 suites* ⦿ *No meals* ⊹ *H3.*

JAPANTOWN

$ 🖼 **Hotel Tomo.** Japanese Pop, or J-Pop as it is known across the pond,
HOTEL comes alive in this Japantown boutique hotel, located just a couple of
🕃 blocks from the chic Fillmore district, Yoshi's, and the famous Fillmore
Fodor'sChoice concert venue. **Pros:** J-Pop style; anime playing on the lobby TV and
★ manga in your room; great price in a fun neighborhood. **Cons:** tight
quarters; a trek from downtown. **TripAdvisor:** "charming refuge from
the typical SFO hotel," "nice rooms," "fun and modern."⑤ *Rooms
from: $149* ⊠ *1800 Sutter St., Japantown* ☎ *415/921–4000* ⊕ *www.
hoteltomo.com* ➶ *125 rooms, 1 suite* ⦿ *No meals* ⊹ *B4.*

PACIFIC HEIGHTS/COW HOLLOW

$ 🖼 **Cow Hollow Motor Inn and Suites.** Newly refreshed suites at this large,
RENTAL family-owned modern motel are more spacious than average, featur-
Fodor'sChoice ing one or two bedrooms, hardwood floors, sitting and dining areas,
★ Oriental rugs, marble wood-burning fireplaces, big living rooms, and
fully equipped kitchens. **Pros:** suites are the size of apartments; good
for families; covered parking in building. **Cons:** congested neighbor-
hood has a frat-boy feel; standard rooms are on a loud street. **Trip-
Advisor:** "comfortable and conveniently located," "great base for San
Francisco," "clean with great service."⑤ *Rooms from: $140* ⊠ *2190
Lombard St., Marina* ☎ *415/921–5800* ⊕ *www.cowhollowmotorinn.
com* ➶ *117 rooms, 12 suites* ⦿ *No meals* ⊹ *A1.*

$$$$
B&B/INN
Fodor'sChoice
★

▒ **Hotel Drisco.** Pretend you're a resident of one of the wealthiest and most beautiful residential neighborhoods in San Francisco at this under-stated, elegant 1903 Edwardian hotel. **Pros:** great service; comfortable rooms; quiet residential retreat. **Cons:** small rooms; far from down-town. **TripAdvisor:** "traditional charm and warmth," "everyone was friendly and helpful," "live like a tycoon." $ *Rooms from: $335* ✉ *2901 Pacific Ave., Pacific Heights* ☎ *415/346–2880, 800/634–7277* ⊕ *www. hoteldrisco.com* ⇗ *29 rooms, 19 suites* ⦿*Breakfast* ✛ *A3.*

$$$
B&B/INN
Fodor'sChoice
★

▒ **Union Street Inn.** Precious family antiques and unique artwork helped British innkeepers Jane Bertorelli and David Coyle (former chef for the Duke and Duchess of Bedford) transform this green-and-cream 1902 Edwardian into a delightful B&B. **Pros:** personal service; Jane's excellent full breakfast; romantic setting. **Cons:** parking in the neigh-borhood is tricky; no air-conditioning; no elevator. **TripAdvisor:** "a wonderful retreat," "a relaxing garden," "Victorian beauty." $ *Rooms from: $219* ✉ *2229 Union St., Cow Hollow* ☎ *415/346–0424* ⊕ *www. unionstreetinn.com* ⇗ *6 rooms* ⦿*Breakfast* ✛ *A2.*

NIGHTLIFE

This small city packs the punch of a much larger metropolis after dark. Downtown cool, trendy, relaxed, quirky, and downright outrageous could all be used to describe San Francisco's diverse and vibrant col-lection of bars, clubs, and performance venues.

THE 4-1-1

Entertainment information is printed in the pink Sunday "Datebook" section (⊕ *www.sfgate.com/datebook*) and the more calendar-based Thursday "96 Hours" section (⊕ *www.sfgate.com/96hours*) in the *San Francisco Chronicle*. Also consult any of the free alternative weeklies, notably the *SF Weekly* (⊕ *www.sfweekly.com*), which blurbs nightclubs and music, and the *San Francisco Bay Guardian* (⊕ *www.sfbg.com*), which lists neighborhood, avant-garde, and budget events. SF Station (⊕ *www.sfstation.com*; online only) has an up-to-date calendar of enter-tainment goings-on.

8

BARS AND LOUNGES

Bourbon & Branch. The address and phone are unlisted, the black outer door unmarked, and when you make your reservation (required), you get a password for entry. In short, Bourbon & Branch reeks of Prohibi-tion-era speakeasy cool. It's not exclusive, though: everyone is granted a password. The place has sex appeal, with tin ceilings, bordello-red silk wallpaper, intimate booths, and low lighting; loud conversations and cell phones are not allowed. The menu of expertly mixed cocktails and quality bourbon and whiskey is substantial, but the servers aren't always authorities. ■**TIP→** **This place is small, so couples or groups of four or fewer are ideal.** Your reservation dictates your exit time, which is strictly enforced. ✉ *501 Jones St., at O'Farrell St., Tenderloin* ⊕ *www. bourbonandbranch.com.*

★ **Cliff House.** Classier than the nearby Beach Chalet, with a more impressive view of Ocean Beach, the Cliff House is our pick if you must choose just one oceanfront restaurant/bar. Sure, it's the site of many high-school prom dates, and you could argue that the food and drinks are overpriced, and some say the sleek facade looks like a mausoleum—but the views are terrific. The best window seats are reserved for diners, but there's a small upstairs lounge where you can watch gulls sail high above the vast blue Pacific. Come before sunset. ⊠ *1090 Point Lobos, at Great Hwy., Lincoln Park* ☎ *415/386–3330* ⊕ *www.cliffhouse.com.*

★ **Hôtel Biron.** Sharing an alleylike block with the backs of Market Street restaurants, this tiny, cavelike (in a good way) spot displays rotating artwork of the Mission School aesthetic on its brick walls. The clientele is well-behaved twenty- to thirtysomethings who enjoy the cramped quarters, good range of wines and prices, off-the-beaten path location, soft lighting, and hip music. ⊠ *45 Rose St., off Market St. near Gough St., Hayes Valley* ☎ *415/703–0403* ⊕ *www.hotelbiron.com.*

Redwood Room. Opened in 1933 and updated by designer Philippe Starck in 2001, the Redwood Room at the Clift Hotel is a San Francisco icon. The entire room, floor to ceiling, is paneled with the wood from a single redwood tree, giving the place a rich, monochromatic look. The gorgeous original art-deco sconces and chandeliers still hang, but bizarre video installations on plasma screens also adorn the walls. It's packed on weekend evenings after 10, when young scenesters swarm the hotel; for maximum glamour, visit on a weeknight. ⊠ *Clift Hotel, 495 Geary St., at Taylor St., Union Sq.* ☎ *415/929–2372 for table reservations, 415/775–4700 for hotel* ⊕ *www.clifthotel.com.*

Smuggler's Cove. With the decor of a pirate ship and a slew of rum-based cocktails, you half expect Captain Jack Sparrow to sidle up next to you at this offbeat, Disney-esque hangout. But don't let the kitschy ambience fool you. The folks at Smuggler's Cove take rum so seriously that they even make their own, which you can sample along with more than 200 other offerings, some of them vintage and very hard to find. A punch card is provided so you can try all 70 cocktails and remember where you left off without getting shipwrecked. The small space has won numerous awards and fills up quickly, so arrive early. ⊠ *650 Gough St., at McAllister St., Hayes Valley* ☎ *415/869–1900* ⊕ *www.smugglerscovesf.com.*

Tonga Room. Since 1947 the Tonga Room has given San Francisco a taste of high Polynesian kitsch. Fake palm trees, grass huts, a lagoon (three-piece combos play pop standards on a floating barge), and faux monsoons—courtesy of sprinkler-system rain and simulated thunder and lightning—grow more surreal as you quaff fruity cocktails. ⊠ *Fairmont San Francisco, 950 Mason St., at California St., Nob Hill* ☎ *415/772–5278* ⊕ *www.tongaroom.com.*

★ **Vesuvio Café.** If you're only hitting one bar in North Beach, it should be this one. The low-ceiling second floor of this raucous boho hangout, little altered since its 1960s heyday (when Jack Kerouac frequented the place), is a fine vantage point for watching the colorful Broadway and Columbus Avenue intersection. Another part of Vesuvio's appeal is its diverse clientele (twenties to sixties), from neighborhood regulars and young couples to Bacchanalian posses of friends. ⊠ *255 Columbus Ave., at Broadway, North Beach* ☎ *415/362–3370* ⊕ *www.vesuvio.com.*

GAY AND LESBIAN NIGHTLIFE

Bay Area Reporter. The *Bay Area Reporter*, a weekly newspaper, lists gay and lesbian events in its calendar and has a special nightlife site (⊕ *www. bartabsf.com).* ☎ *415/861–5019* ⊕ *www.ebar.com.*

San Francisco Bay Times. The biweekly *San Francisco Bay Times* is aimed at gay and lesbian readers. ☎ *415/626–0260* ⊕ *www.sfbaytimes.com.*

Lexington Club. According to its slogan, "every night is ladies' night" at this all-girl club geared to urban alterna-dykes in their twenties and thirties (think piercings and tattoos, not lipstick). ■ **TIP➜** The women's room has awesome graffiti. ⊠ *3464 19th St., at Valencia, Mission* ☎ *415/863–2052* ⊕ *www.lexingtonclub.com.*

★ **Martuni's.** A mixed crowd enjoys cocktails in the semirefined environment of this elegant bar at the intersection of the Castro, the Mission, and Hayes Valley; variations on the martini are a specialty. ■ **TIP➜** The Godiva Chocolate Martini is a crowd favorite. In the intimate back room a pianist plays nightly, and patrons take turns boisterously singing show tunes. It's a favorite post-theater spot—especially after the symphony or opera, which are within walking distance. ⊠ *4 Valencia St., at Market St., Mission* ☎ *415/241–0205.*

★ **The Mint Karaoke Lounge.** A mixed gay-straight crowd that's drop-dead serious about its karaoke—to the point where you'd think an *American Idol* casting agent was in attendance—comes here seven nights a week. Regulars sing everything from Simon and Garfunkel songs to disco classics in front of an attentive audience. Do *not* walk onstage unprepared! Check out the songbook online to perfect your debut before you attempt to take the mike. ⊠ *1942 Market St., between Duboce Ave. and Laguna St., Hayes Valley* ☎ *415/626–4726* ⊕ *www.themint.net.*

★ **The Stud.** Open since 1966, the Stud is the bar for glam trannies, bears, tight-teed pretty boys, ladies and their ladies, and a handful of straight onlookers who dance to the live DJ and watch world-class drag performers on the small stage. The entertainment is often campy, pee-your-pants funny, and downright fantastic. At Frolic, the Stud's most outrageous party, club-goers dance the night away dressed as bunnies, kittens, and even stranger creatures. Each night's music is different— from funk, soul, and hip-hop to 80s tunes and disco favorites. ⊠ *1284 Harrison St., at 9th St., SoMa* ☎ *415/863–6623* ⊕ *www.studsf.com.*

JAZZ CLUBS

★ **Yoshi's.** The legendary Oakland club that has pulled in some of the world's best jazz musicians—Pat Martino, Branford Marsalis, Betty Carter, and Dizzy Gillespie, to name just a few—opened a San Francisco location in 2007. The new club has terrific acoustics, a 9-foot Steinway grand piano (broken in by Chick Corea), and seating for 411; it's been hailed as "simply the best jazz club in the city." Yoshi's serves Japanese food in an adjoining restaurant set in a soaring two-story space, decorated with blond wood and hanging paper lanterns (you can also order food at café tables in the club). And yes, the coupling of sushi and jazz *is* as elegant as it sounds. Sightlines are good from just about any vantage point, including the back balcony. Yoshi's is in the Fillmore District, which was known as the "Harlem of the West" in its 1940s and '50s heyday. The club is on a tough block in an even tougher neighborhood, so take advantage of the valet parking. ⊠ *1330 Fillmore St., at Eddy St., Japantown* ☎ *415/655–5600* ⊕ *www.yoshis.com.*

ROCK, POP, HIP-HOP, FOLK, AND BLUES CLUBS

★ **Bimbo's 365 Club.** The plush main room and adjacent lounge of this club, here since 1951, retain a retro vibe perfect for the "Cocktail Nation" programming that keeps the crowds entertained. For a taste of the old-school San Francisco nightclub scene, you can't beat this place. Indie low-fi and pop bands like Stephen Malkmus and the Jicks and Camera Obscura fill the bill. ⊠ *1025 Columbus Ave., at Chestnut St., North Beach* ☎ *415/474–0365* ⊕ *www.bimbos365club.com.*

Fodor'sChoice **BooM BooM RooM.** John Lee Hooker's old haunt has been an old-school
★ blues haven for years, attracting top-notch acts from all around the country. Luck out with legendary masters like James "Super Chikan" Johnson, or discover new blues and funk artists. ⊠ *1601 Fillmore St., at Geary Blvd., Japantown* ☎ *415/673–8000* ⊕ *www.boomboomblues. com.*

★ **Bottom of the Hill.** This is a great live-music dive—in the best sense of the word—and truly the epicenter for independent rock in the Bay Area. The club has hosted some great acts over the years, including the Strokes and the Throwing Muses. Rap and hip-hop acts occasionally make it to the stage. ⊠ *1233 17th St., at Texas St., Potrero Hill* ☎ *415/621–4455* ⊕ *www.bottomofthehill.com.*

★ **The Fillmore.** This is *the* club that all the big names, from Coldplay to Clapton, want to play. San Francisco's most famous rock-music hall serves up a varied menu of national and local acts: rock, reggae, grunge, jazz, folk, acid house, and more. Most tickets cost $20–$30, and some shows are open to all ages. ■TIP➜ Avoid steep service charges by purchasing tickets at the Fillmore box office on Sunday (10–4). At the end of each show, apples are set near the door and free for the taking, and staffers hand out collectible posters that at the very least will sell well on eBay. ⊠ *1805 Geary Blvd., at Fillmore St., Western Addition* ☎ *415/346–6000* ⊕ *www.thefillmore.com.*

Fodor'sChoice **Great American Music Hall.** You can find top-drawer entertainment at
★ this eclectic nightclub. Acts range from the best in blues, folk, and jazz to up-and-coming college-radio and American-roots artists to of-the-moment indie rock stars (OK Go, Mates of State) and the establishment (Cowboy Junkies). The colorful marble-pillared emporium (built in 1907 as a bordello) also accommodates dancing at some shows. Pub grub is available most nights. ⊠ *859 O'Farrell St., between Polk and Larkin Sts., Tenderloin* ☎ *415/885–0750* ⊕ *www.slimspresents.com.*

THE ARTS

San Francisco's symphony, opera, and ballet all perform in the Civic Center area, also home to the 928-seat Herbst Theatre, which hosts many fine soloists and ensembles.

TICKETS

City Box Office. This charge-by-phone service, sells tickets for many performances and lectures. You can buy tickets in person at its downtown location weekdays 9:30–5:30. ⌧ *180 Redwood St., Suite 100, off Van Ness Ave. between Golden Gate Ave. and McAllister St., Civic Center* ☎ *415/392–4400* ⊕ *www.cityboxoffice.com.*

San Francisco Performances. SFP brings an eclectic array of top-flight global music and dance talents to various venues—mostly the Yerba Buena Center for the Arts, Davies Symphony Hall, and Herbst Theatre. Artists have included the Los Angeles Guitar Quartet, Edgar Meyer, the Paul Taylor Dance Company, and Midori. Tickets can be purchased in person, online, or by phone. ⌧ *500 Sutter St., Suite 710* ☎ *415/392–2545* ⊕ *www.performances.org.*

Tickets.com. You can charge tickets for everything from jazz concerts to Giants games by phone or online through **Tickets.com.** ☎ *800/955–5566* ⊕ *www.tickets.com.*

TIX Bay Area. Half-price, same-day tickets for many local and touring stage shows go on sale (cash only) at 11 am Tuesday through Saturday at the Union Square booth of **TIX Bay Area.** TIX is also a full-service ticket agency for theater and music events around the Bay Area, open Tuesday through Friday 11–6, Saturday 10–6, and Sunday 10–3. ⌧ *Powell St. between Geary and Post Sts., Union Sq.* ☎ *415/433–7827* ⊕ *www.tixbayarea.com.*

THE 4-1-1

The best guide to the arts is the Sunday "Datebook" section (⊕ *www.sfgate.com/datebook*), printed on pink paper, in the *San Francisco Chronicle.* The four-day entertainment supplement "96 Hours" (⊕ *www.sfgate.com/96hours*) is in the Thursday *Chronicle.* Also be sure to check out the city's free alternative weeklies, including *SF Weekly* (⊕ *www.sfweekly.com*) and the more avant-garde *San Francisco Bay Guardian* (⊕ *www.sfbg.com*).

Online, SF Station (⊕ *www.sfstation.com*) has a frequently updated arts and nightlife calendar. San Francisco Arts Monthly (⊕ *www.sfarts.org*), which is published at the end of the month, has arts features and events, plus a helpful "Visiting San Francisco?" section. For offbeat, emerging artist performances, consult CounterPULSE (⊕ *www.counterpulse.org*).

DANCE

Fodor's Choice ★ **San Francisco Ballet.** For ballet-lovers, this company is reason alone to visit the Bay Area. Under artistic director Helgi Tomasson, the San Francisco Ballet's works—both classical and contemporary—have won critical raves. The primary season runs from February through May. The repertoire includes full-length ballets such as *Don Quixote* and

Built as a bordello in 1907, the Great American Music Hall now pulls in top-tier performers.

Sleeping Beauty; the December presentation of *The Nutcracker* is truly spectacular. The company also performs bold new dances from star choreographers such as William Forsythe and Mark Morris, alongside modern classics by George Balanchine and Jerome Robbins. Tickets and information are available at the **War Memorial Opera House.** ⊠ *War Memorial Opera House, 301 Van Ness Ave., at Grove St., Civic Center* ☎ *415/865–2000* ⊕ *www.sfballet.org* ⊙ *Weekdays 10–4.*

MUSIC

Fodor's Choice ★   **San Francisco Symphony.** One of America's top orchestras, the San Francisco Symphony performs from September through May, with additional summer performances of light classical music and show tunes; visiting artists perform here the rest of the year. The orchestra and its charismatic music director, Michael Tilson Thomas, who is known for his daring programming of 20th-century American works (most notably his Grammy Award–winning Mahler cycle), often perform with soloists of the caliber of Andre Watts, Gil Shaham, and Renée Fleming. The adventuresome side of the organization is amply illustrated by this symphony's collaboration with the heavy-metal group Metallica. David Byrne has performed here, as well. Tickets run from $15 to $100. ⊠ *Davies Symphony Hall, 201 Van Ness Ave., at Grove St., Civic Center* ☎ *415/864–6000* ⊕ *www.sfsymphony.org.*

Summer in the City. Many members of the San Francisco Symphony perform in the Summer in the City concert series, held in the 2,400-seat Davies Symphony Hall. The schedule includes light classics and Broadway, country, and movie music. ☎ 415/864–6000 ⊕ *www.sfsymphony.org*

MUSIC FESTIVALS

Stern Grove Festival. The nation's oldest continual free summer music festival hosts Sunday-afternoon performances of symphony, opera, jazz, pop music, and dance. The amphitheater is in a beautiful eucalyptus grove below street level, perfect for picnicking before the show. (Dress for cool weather.) ⊠ *Sloat Blvd. at 19th Ave., Sunset* ☎ 415/252–6252 ⊕ *www.sterngrove.org*.

OPERA

Fodor's Choice ★ **San Francisco Opera.** Founded in 1923, this world-renowned company has resided at the Civic Center's War Memorial Opera House since the building's completion in 1932. Over its split season—September through January and June through July—the opera presents about 70 performances of 10 to 12 operas. Translations are projected above the stage during almost all non-English operas. Long considered a major international company and the most important operatic organization in the United States outside New York, the opera frequently embarks on productions with European opera companies and unconventional projects, some with a popular cultural edge designed to attract younger audiences. Ticket prices can range from $25 to $195. The full-time box office (Monday 10–5, Tuesday through Friday 10–6) is at 199 Grove Street, at Van Ness Avenue. ⊠ *War Memorial Opera House, 301 Van Ness Ave., at Grove St., Civic Center* ☎ 415/864–3330 tickets ⊕ *www.sfopera.com*.

THEATER

★ **American Conservatory Theater.** Not long after its founding in the mid-1960s, the city's major nonprofit theater company became one of the nation's leading regional theaters. During its season, which runs from early fall to late spring, ACT presents approximately eight plays, from classics to contemporary works, often in rotating repertory. In December ACT stages a much-loved version of Charles Dickens's *A Christmas Carol.* ⊠ *415 Geary St., Union Sq.* ☎ 415/749-2228 ⊕ *www.act-sf.org*.

ACT ticket office. The **ACT ticket office** is next door to the American Conservatory Theater. ⊠ *405 Geary St., Union Sq.* ☎ 415/749–2228

Fodor's Choice ★ **Teatro ZinZanni.** Contortionists, chanteuses, jugglers, illusionists, and circus performers entertain the audiences who dine on a surprisingly good five-course dinner in a fabulous antique Belgian traveling-dance-hall tent (slated for a permanent relocation to Broadway and the Embarcadero in late 2012). Be ready to laugh, and arrive early for a front-and-center table. Reservations are essential; tickets are $125 to $150; call or check the website for prices. And dress fancy. ⊠ *Broadway and the Embarcadero, Northern Waterfront* ☎ 415/438–2668 ⊕ *www.zinzanni.org*.

8

SPORTS AND THE OUTDOORS

BASEBALL

San Francisco Giants. The National League's New York Giants became the San Francisco Giants when they moved to California in 1958, the same year that the Brooklyn Dodgers moved to Los Angeles. Today the classic design of the Giants' AT&T Park and the team's 2010 World Series title have created a new legion of fans. Buy your tickets in advance—nearly every game sells out. ⊠ *AT&T Park, 24 Willie Mays Plaza, between 2nd and 3rd Sts., SoMa* ☎ *415/972–2000, 800/734–4268* ⊕ *sanfrancisco.giants.mlb.com.*

Fodor's Choice ★

Tickets.com. Tickets.com sells game tickets over the phone and charges a per-ticket fee of $5–$24, plus a per-call processing fee of up to $3.50. ☎ *877/473–4849* ⊕ *www.tickets.com.*

Giants Dugout. The team sells tickets at the ballpark and numerous Dugout locations, among them Embarcadero Center and Union Square. A surcharge is added except at the ballpark. ⊠ *AT&T Park, 24 Willie Mays Plaza, at 3rd St., SoMa* ☎ *415/972–2000, 800/734–4268* ⊕ *sanfrancisco.giants.mlb.com/sf/ballpark/dugout_stores.jsp* ⊠ *4 Embarcadero Center, Embarcadero* ☎ *415/951–8888.*

BICYCLING

San Francisco Bicycle Coalition. The San Francisco Bicycle Coalition has extensive information about the policies and politics of riding and lists local events for cyclists on its website. You can download (but not print) a PDF version of the *San Francisco Bike Map and Walking Guide.* ☎ *415/431–2453* ⊕ *www.sfbike.org.*

WHERE TO RENT

Bike and Roll. You can rent bikes at this operator's locations for $8 per hour or $32 per day; discounted weekly rates are available, and complimentary maps are provided. ⊠ *899 Columbus Ave., at Lombard St., North Beach* ☎ *415/229–2000* ⊕ *www.bicyclerental.com* ⊠ *353 Jefferson St., between Jones and Leavenworth Sts., Fisherman's Wharf* ⊠ *2800 Leavenworth St., at Beach St., Fisherman's Wharf.*

Blazing Saddles. This outfitter rents bikes for $8 to $9 an hour, depending on the type of bike, or $32 to $88 a day, and shares tips on sights to see along the paths. ⊠ *2715 Hyde St., at Beach St., Fisherman's Wharf* ☎ *415/202–8888* ⊕ *www.blazingsaddles.com* ⊠ *433 Mason St., at Post St., Union Sq.* ⊠ *Pier 41, Fisherman's Wharf* ⊠ *465 Jefferson St., at Hyde St., Fisherman's Wharf* ⊠ *2555 Powell St., at the Embarcadero, Fisherman's Wharf* ⊠ *1095 Columbus, at Francisco St., North Beach* ⊠ *721 Beach St., at Hyde St., North Beach.*

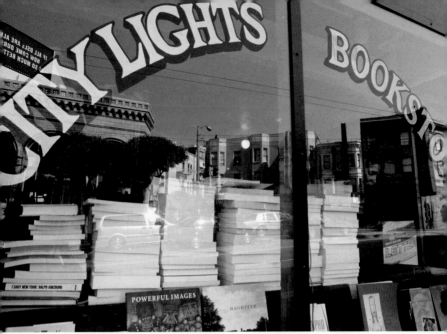

The beat movement of the 1950s was born in San Francisco's most famous bookstore, City Lights.

SHOPPING

UNION SQUARE

Fodor'sChoice
★ **Diptyque.** The original Diptyque boutique in Paris has long attracted a following of celebrities. You can find the full line of scented candles and fragrances in this chic shop that would be at home on the Boulevard St-Germain. Trademark black-and-white labels adorn the popular L'eau toilet water, scented with geranium and sandalwood. Candles come in both traditional and esoteric scents, including lavender, basil, leather, and fig tree. Also available is a collection of French Mariage Frères teas. ☒ *171 Maiden La., between Grant Ave. and Stockton St., Union Sq.* ☎ *415/402–0600.*

★ **Gump's.** It's a San Francisco institution, dating to the 19th century, and it's a strikingly luxurious one. The airy store exudes a museum-like vibe, with its large decorative vases, sumptuous housewares, and a gobsmacking Tahitian pearl display. Locals line up to register for weddings here. But it's also a great place to pick up gifts, such as the Golden Gate Bridge note cards or the silver-plated butter spreaders in a signature Gump's box. ☒ *135 Post St., between Grant Ave. and Kearny St., Union Sq.* ☎ *415/982–1616.*

Fodor'sChoice
★ **Hang Art.** A spirit of fun imbues this inviting second-floor space that showcases emerging artists. Prices range from a few hundred dollars to several thousand, making it an ideal place for novice art collectors to get their feet wet. A rental program lets you take a piece home before

buying it. ✉ *567 Sutter St., between Mason and Powell Sts., Union Sq.* ☎ *415/434–4264.*

Fodor'sChoice
★ **Lang Antiques and Estate Jewelry.** Dozens of diamond bracelets in the window attract shoppers to one of the city's best vintage jewelry shops, where rings, brooches, and other glittering items represent various eras and styles, from Victorian and Edwardian to art nouveau and Arts and Crafts. The shop has been selling fine jewelry, including engagement rings and a small number of vintage watches, since 1969. ✉ *323 Sutter St., at Grant Ave., Union Sq.* ☎ *415/982–2213.*

Fodor'sChoice
★ **Margaret O'Leary.** If you can only buy one piece of clothing in San Francisco, make it a hand-loomed, locally made cashmere sweater by this Irish-born local legend. The perfect antidote to the city's wind and fog, the sweaters are so beloved by San Franciscans that some people literally never wear anything else. Pick up an airplane wrap for your trip home and a media cozy to keep your iPod toasty, too. Another store is located in Pacific Heights on Fillmore Street. ✉ *1 Claude La., at Sutter St., Union Sq.* ☎ *415/391–1010.*

★ **Nordstrom.** Somehow Nordstrom manages to be all things to all people, and this location, with spiral escalators circling a four-story atrium, is no exception. Whether you're an elegant lady of a certain age shopping for a new mink coat or a teen on the hunt for a Roxy hoodie, the salespeople are known for being happy to help. Nordstrom carries the best selections in town of new designers like Tory Burch, but its own brands have loyal followings, too. The café upstairs is a superb choice for a ladies-who-lunch shopping break. ✉ *San Francisco Shopping Centre, 865 Market St., at 5th St., Union Sq.* ☎ *415/243–8500.*

CHINATOWN

Chinatown Kite Shop. Kites at this family-owned business range from basic diamond shapes to box- and animal-shape configurations. Colorful dragon kites make great Chinatown souvenirs. ✉ *717 Grant Ave., between Clay and Sacramento Sts., Chinatown* ☎ *415/989–5182.*

SOMA

★ **K&L Wine Merchants.** More than any other wine store, this one has an ardent cult following around town. The friendly staffers promise not to sell what they don't taste themselves, and weekly events (Thursday from 5 pm and 6:30 pm and Saturday from noon to 3 pm) open the tastings to customers. The best-seller list for varietals and regions for both the under- and over-$30 categories appeals to the wine lover in everyone. ✉ *638 4th St., between Brannan and Townsend Sts., SoMa* ☎ *415/896–1734.*

HAYES VALLEY

★ **Miette Confiserie.** There is truly nothing sweeter than a cellophane bag tied with blue-and-white twine and filled with malt balls or chocolate sardines from this European-style apothecary. The lovely pastel-color cake stands make even window-shopping a treat. ⊠ *449 Octavia Blvd., between Hayes and Fell Sts., Hayes Valley* ☎ *415/626–6221.*

NORTH BEACH

Fodor's Choice ★ **City Lights Bookstore.** The city's most famous bookstore is where the Beat movement of the 1950s was born. Neal Cassady and Jack Kerouac hung out in the basement, and now regulars and tourists while hours away in this well-worn space. The upstairs room highlights impressive poetry and Beat literature collections. Poet Lawrence Ferlinghetti, the owner, remains active in the workings of this three-story shop. City Lights Publishers, which issued the poet Allen Ginsberg's *Howl* in 1956, publishes a dozen new titles each year. ⊠ *261 Columbus Ave., at Broadway, North Beach* ☎ *415/362–8193.*

Fodor's Choice ★ **Molinari Delicatessen.** Billing itself as the oldest delicatessen west of the Rockies, the store has been making its own salami, sausages, and cold cuts since 1896. Other homemade specialties include meat and cheese ravioli, tomato sauces, and fresh pastas. ■TIP➜ **Do like the locals: grab a made-to-order sandwich for lunch and eat it at one of the sidewalk tables.** ⊠ *373 Columbus Ave., at Vallejo St., North Beach* ☎ *415/421–2337.*

EMBARCADERO

Fodor's Choice ★ **Ferry Plaza Farmers' Market.** The most upscale and expensive of the city's farmers' markets, in front of the restored Ferry Building, places baked goods and fancy pots of jam alongside organic basil and heirloom tomatoes. The Saturday market is the grandest, with about 100 vendors packed along three sides of the building. The Tuesday and Thursday markets are smaller. At the Sunday garden market, vegetable and ornamental plants crop up next to a small selection of food items. (The Thursday and Sunday markets don't operate in winter, generally December or January through March.) ■TIP➜ **On Saturday, don't miss the coffee at Blue Bottle—and yes, the line is worth it.** ⊠ *Ferry Plaza, The Embarcadero at Market St., Embarcadero* ☎ *415/291–3276* ☉ *Tues. and Sun. 10–2, Thurs. 4–8, Sat. 8–2.*

THE HAIGHT

Fodor's Choice ★ **Amoeba Music.** With more than 2.5 million new and used CDs, DVDs, and records, this warehouselike store (and the original Berkeley location) carries titles you can't find on Amazon at bargain prices. No niche is ignored—from electronica and hip-hop to jazz and classical—and the stock changes daily. Weekly in-store performances attract large crowds. ⊠ *1855 Haight St., between Stanyan and Shrader Sts., Haight* ☎ *415/831–1200.*

THE MISSION

Fodor's Choice ★ **Paxton Gate.** Elevating gardening to an art, this serene shop offers beautiful earthenware pots, amaryllis and narcissus bulbs, decorative garden items, and coffee-table books such as *An Inordinate Fondness for*

Beetles. The collection of taxidermy and preserved bugs provides more unusual gift ideas. ✉ 824 *Valencia St., between 19th and 20th Sts., Mission* ☎ *415/824–1872.*

PACIFIC HEIGHTS

★ **BeneFit.** You can find the locally based BeneFit line of cosmetics and skin-care products at Macy's and Sephora, but it's much more fun to come to one of the eponymous boutiques. No-pressure salespeople dab you with whimsical makeup such as Ooh La Lift concealer and Tinted Love, a stain for lips and cheeks. ✉ 2117 *Fillmore St., between California and Sacramento Sts., Pacific Heights* ☎ *415/567–0242.*

JAPANTOWN

★ **Kinokuniya Bookstore.** The selection of English-language books about Japanese culture—everything from medieval history to origami instructions—is one of the finest in the country. Kinokuniya is the city's biggest seller of Japanese-language books. Dozens of glossy Asian fashion magazines attract the young and trendy, and books and DVDs related to the Japanese anime director Hayao Miyazaki are the latest trend. ✉ *Kinokuniya Bldg., 1581 Webster St., at Geary Blvd., Japantown* ☎ *415/567–7625.*

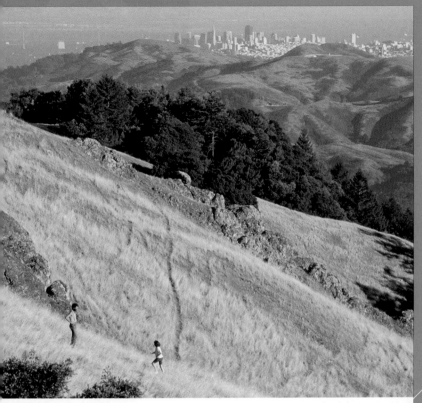

The Bay Area

WITH MARIN COUNTY, BERKELEY, OAKLAND, AND THE COASTAL PENINSULA

WORD OF MOUTH

"We . . . caught the ferry over to Sausalito. A stroll along the sheltered waterfront and a close-quarters view of Alcatraz on the way back rounded out a perfect stay in the City by the Bay."

—kiwi_rob

WELCOME TO THE BAY AREA

TOP REASONS TO GO

★ **Walk among giants:** Walking into Muir Woods, a mere 12 miles north of the Golden Gate Bridge, is like entering a cathedral built by God.

★ **Sip some coffee:** Lytton Square in downtown Mill Valley is a tranquil place to soak up some sun, caffeine, and a real local "hanging out" kind of vibe.

★ **Bite into the "Gourmet Ghetto":** Eat your way through this area of Berkeley, starting with a slice of pizza from the Cheese Board.

★ **Sit on a dock by the bay:** Admire the beauty of the Bay Area from the rocky, picturesque shores of Sausalito.

★ **Find solitude at Point Reyes National Seashore:** Head here to hike beautifully rugged—and deserted—beaches.

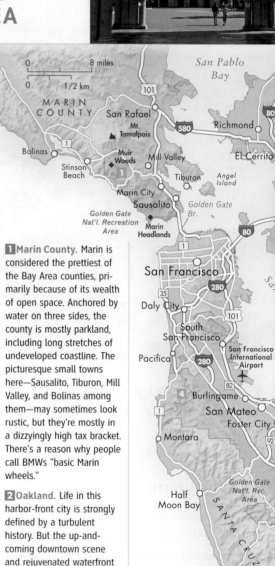

1 Marin County. Marin is considered the prettiest of the Bay Area counties, primarily because of its wealth of open space. Anchored by water on three sides, the county is mostly parkland, including long stretches of undeveloped coastline. The picturesque small towns here—Sausalito, Tiburon, Mill Valley, and Bolinas among them—may sometimes look rustic, but they're mostly in a dizzyingly high tax bracket. There's a reason why people call BMWs "basic Marin wheels."

2 Oakland. Life in this harbor-front city is strongly defined by a turbulent history. But the up-and-coming downtown scene and rejuvenated waterfront are signals of good things ahead.

3 **Berkeley.** This college town has long been known for its liberal ethos, stimulating university community (and perhaps even more stimulating coffee shops), and activist streak. But these days the booming restaurant and arts scenes are luring even those who wouldn't be caught dead in Birkenstocks.

4 **The Coastal Peninsula.** The coastal towns between Santa Cruz and San Francisco have long been agricultural outposts, supplying food for the missions and towns. Today, artichokes and grapes still grow in the fields, but the big attraction here is the beaches.

GETTING ORIENTED

Cross the Golden Gate Bridge and head north to reach Marin County's rolling hills and green expanses, where residents enjoy an haute-suburban lifestyle. Farther afield, the wild landscapes of the Marin Headlands, Muir Woods, Mt. Tamalpais, Stinson Beach, and Point Reyes National Seashore await. East of the city, across the San Francisco Bay, are Berkeley and Oakland, which most Bay Area residents refer to as the East Bay. These two towns have distinct personalities, but life here feels more relaxed than in the city—though every bit as vibrant.

9

Updated by
Fiona G.
Parrott

It's rare for a metropolis to compete with its suburbs for visitors, but the view from any of San Francisco's hilltops shows that the Bay Area's temptations extend far beyond the city limits. To the north is Marin County, the beauty queen, with small but chic villages like Tiburon and Mill Valley, plus dramatic coastal scenery. East of town are two energetic urban centers, Berkeley and Oakland. Formerly radical Berkeley is getting more glam, while Oakland is shaking off its image as San Francisco's ugly stepsister and developing its own brand of hipness.

Up in Marin, the birthplace of mountain biking, trail-veined Mt. Tamalpais and the woods below draw hikers and cyclists. Beaches lure families and thrill seekers, while little towns offer respite to harried urbanites. In the mid-1960s and '70s alternative lifestyle seekers established Marin's reputation as ground zero for gurus, granola, and redwood hot tubs. Despite the influx of stock-market millionaires and chic boutiques, the counterculture identity still sticks. Immediately after crossing the Golden Gate Bridge on U.S. 101 northbound, you'll pass through a tunnel whose archway is painted with a rainbow that welcomes you to magical Marin, "Land of Oz."

Meanwhile, the town often referred to as the People's Republic of Berkeley retains its liberal image, though it's drastically tamer than it was in the late 1960s. It's now as famous for chef and food activist Alice Waters (and her pricey restaurant Chez Panisse) as it is for its role as the birthplace of the Free Speech movement. Oakland is polishing some of its rough edges, too, with a successful port and a revitalized downtown, an alternative arts scene, and hipster cafés and boutiques.

PLANNING

WHEN TO GO

Berkeley is a university town, and the rhythm of the school year might affect your visit. It's easier to navigate the streets and find parking near the university between semesters, but there's also less buzz around town. Surprisingly, summer is chock-full of students attending the many summer sessions on campus. Moving-in weeks, before the fall semester starts, bring a massive influx of students *and* parents and other family members—definitely not the best time to take a campus tour.

BART trains can be packed during the morning and evening rush hours, but things are less congested at other times. BART can get you from downtown San Francisco to a coffee shop in Rockridge in about 25 minutes. (It's closer to 30 minutes for farther points in Berkeley.)

It'll take about the same amount of time by car to reach Tiburon if traffic is clear on the Golden Gate Bridge (also depending, of course, on what part of the city you're departing from).

GETTING HERE AND AROUND
BART TRAVEL

Using public transportation to reach Berkeley or Oakland is ideal. The under- and above-ground BART (Bay Area Rapid Transit) trains make stops in both towns. Trips to either take 30 to 45 minutes one way from the center of San Francisco.

Contacts BART ☎ 510/465–2278 ⊕ www.bart.gov.

BOAT AND FERRY TRAVEL

For sheer romance, nothing beats the ferry; there's service from San Francisco to Sausalito and Tiburon in Marin County, and to Alameda and Oakland in the East Bay.

The Golden Gate Ferry crosses the bay to Sausalito from San Francisco's Ferry Building (⊠ *Market St. and the Embarcadero*). Blue & Gold Fleet ferries depart daily for Sausalito and Tiburon from Pier 41 at Fisherman's Wharf; weekday commuter ferries leave from the Ferry Building for Tiburon. The trip to Sausalito takes 30 minutes; to Tiburon, it takes 20 minutes.

The Angel Island–Tiburon Ferry sails to the island daily April through September and weekends the rest of the year.

The Alameda/Oakland Ferry runs several times daily between San Francisco's Ferry Building or Pier 39, Alameda, and the Clay Street dock near Oakland's Jack London Square; one-way tickets are $6.25. The trip lasts 30 to 45 minutes, depending on your departure point, and leads to Oakland's waterfront shopping and restaurant district. Purchase tickets on board.

Boat and Ferry Lines Alameda/Oakland Ferry ☎ 510/522–3300 ⊕ www.eastbayferry.com. **Angel Island–Tiburon Ferry** ☎ 415/435–2131 ⊕ www.angelislandferry.com. **Blue & Gold Fleet** ☎ 415/705–8200 ⊕ www.blueandgoldfleet.com. **Golden Gate Ferry** ☎ 415/923–2000 ⊕ www.goldengateferry.org.

BUS TRAVEL

Golden Gate Transit buses travel to Sausalito, Tiburon, and Mill Valley from 1st and Mission streets and from other points in San Francisco. For Mt. Tamalpais State Park and West Marin (e.g., Stinson Beach, Bolinas, and Point Reyes Station), take Bus 10, 70, or 80 to Marin City; in Marin City transfer to the West Marin Stagecoach (schedules vary). San Francisco MuniBus 76 runs hourly from 4th and Townsend streets to the Marin Headlands Visitor Center on Sunday and major holidays only. The trip takes roughly 45 minutes.

Though much less convenient than BART, AC Transit buses run between San Francisco's Transbay Temporary Terminal (on the block bordered by Main, Folsom, Beale and Howard streets) and the East Bay. AC Transit's F and FS lines stop near the university and 4th Street shopping in Berkeley. Lines C and P travel to Piedmont in Oakland. The O bus stops at the edge of Chinatown near downtown Oakland.

Bus Lines AC Transit ☎ 511 ⊕ www.actransit.org. **Golden Gate Transit** ☎ 415/455–2000 ⊕ www.goldengate.org. **San Francisco Muni** ☎ 415/701–2311 ⊕ www.sfmuni.com. **West Marin Stagecoach** ☎ 415/526–3239 ⊕ www.marintransit.org/stage.html.

CAR TRAVEL

Head north on U.S.101 and cross the Golden Gate Bridge to reach all points in Marin by car, which is essential to visit the outer reaches unless you want to spend all day on the bus. From San Francisco, the towns of Sausalito and Tiburon and the Marin Headlands and Point Reyes National Seashore are accessed off U.S. 101. The coastal route, Highway 1, also known as Shoreline Highway, can be accessed off U.S. 101 as well. Follow this road to Mill Valley, Muir Woods, Mt. Tamalpais State Park, Stinson Beach, and Bolinas. From Bolinas, you can continue north on Highway 1 to Point Reyes. Depending on traffic, it takes from 20 to 45 minutes to get to Sausalito, Tiburon, and the Marin Headlands; driving directly to Point Reyes from San Francisco takes about 90 minutes in moderate traffic if you drive north on U.S. 101 and west on Sir Francis Drake Boulevard. Trips to Muir Woods take from 35 minutes to an hour from San Francisco. Add another 30 minutes for the drive to Stinson Beach (the curving roads make the going slower), 10 more if you continue on to Bolinas. The drive from Bolinas to Point Reyes takes an additional half hour.

To reach the East Bay from San Francisco, take Interstate 80 East across the Bay Bridge. For most of Berkeley, take the University Avenue exit through downtown Berkeley to the campus or take the Ashby Avenue exit and turn left on Telegraph Avenue; there's a parking garage on Channing Way near the campus. For Oakland, take Interstate 580 off the Bay Bridge to the Grand Avenue exit for Lake Merritt. To reach downtown and the waterfront, take Interstate 980 from Interstate 580 and exit at 12th Street. Both trips take about 30 minutes unless it's rush hour or a weekend afternoon, when you should count on an hour.

SIGHTSEEING GUIDES

Blue & Gold Fleet has a 3½-hour narrated tour of the San Francisco Bay, for $46, with frequent daily departures from Pier 39 in San Francisco. Super Sightseeing offers a 4-hour bus tour of Muir Woods. The tour, which stops in Sausalito en route, leaves at 9 am and 2 pm daily from North Point and Taylor Street at Fisherman's Wharf and costs $52 ($50 senior citizens, $27 ages 5–11); 24-hour advance reservations are recommended. Great Pacific Tour Co. runs 4-hour morning and afternoon tours of Muir Woods and Sausalito for $55 ($53 senior citizens, $43 ages 5–11), with hotel pickup, in 14-passenger vans with excellent interpretation.

By Bus and Van Blue & Gold Fleet ☎ *415/705–8200* ⊕ *www.blueandgoldfleet. com.* **Great Pacific Tour Co.** ☎ *415/626–4499* ⊕ *www.greatpacifictour.com.* **Super Sightseeing** ☎ *415/353–5310* ⊕ *www.supersightseeing.com.*

RESTAURANTS

The Bay Area is home to some of the most popular and innovative restaurants in the country, including Chez Panisse Café & Restaurant, in Berkeley, and the Buckeye, in Mill Valley—for which reservations must be made well in advance. Expect an emphasis on locally grown produce, hormone-free meats, and California wine. Keep in mind that many Marin cafés don't serve dinner, and when dinner it is offered, service ends on the early side. (No 10 pm reservations in this neck of the woods.)

Prices in the restaurant reviews are the average cost of a main course at dinner or, if dinner is not served, at lunch (excluding sales tax).

HOTELS

Hotels in Berkeley or Oakland tend to be standard issue, but many Marin hotels package themselves as cozy retreats. Summer is often booked well in advance, despite weather that is sometimes downright chilly. Check for special packages during this season.

Prices in the hotel reviews are the lowest cost of a standard double room in high season. Prices do not include taxes (as high as 14%, depending on the region).

Hotel reviews have been condensed for this book. For expanded reviews, facilities, and current deals, visit Fodors.com.

VISITOR INFORMATION

Contact Marin Convention & Visitors Bureau ✉ *1 Mitchell Blvd., Suite B, San Rafael* ☎ *415/925–2060* ⊕ *www.visitmarin.org.*

MARIN COUNTY

Marin is quite simply a knockout—some go so far as to call it spectacular and wild. This isn't an extravagant claim, since more than 40% of the county (180,000 acres), including the majority of the coastline, is parkland. The territory ranges from chaparral, grassland, and coastal scrub to broadleaf and evergreen forest, redwood, salt marsh, and rocky shoreline.

Regardless of its natural beauty, what gave the county its reputation was Cyra McFadden's 1977 book *The Serial,* a literary soap opera that depicted the county as a bastion of hot-tubbing and "open" marriages. Indeed old-time bohemian, but also increasingly jet-set, Marinites still spend a lot of time outdoors, and surfing, cycling, and hiking are common after-work and weekend activities. Adrenaline junkies mountain bike down Mt. Tamalpais, and those who want solitude take a walk on one of Point Reyes's many empty beaches. The hot tub remains a popular destination, but things have changed since the boho days. Artists and musicians who arrived in the 1960s have set the tone for mellow country towns, but Marin is now undeniably chic, with BMWs supplanting VW buses as the cars of choice.

Most cosmopolitan is Sausalito, the town just over the Golden Gate Bridge from San Francisco. Across the inlet from Sausalito, Tiburon and Belvedere are lined with grand homes that regularly appear on fund-raising circuits, and to the north, landlocked Mill Valley is a hub of wining and dining and tony boutiques. The next town, Corte Madera, hosts regular readings by top-notch authors and Larkspur, San Anselmo, and Fairfax beyond have walkable downtown areas, each a bit folksier than the next but all with good restaurants and shops and a distinct sense of place.

In general, the farther you get from the Golden Gate Bridge the more country things become, and West Marin is about as far as you can get from the big city, both physically and ideologically. Separated from the inland county by the slopes and ridges of giant Mt. Tamalpais, this territory beckons to mavericks, artists, ocean lovers, and other free spirits. Stinson Beach has tempered its isolationist attitude to accommodate out-of-towners, as have Inverness and Point Reyes Station. Bolinas, on the other hand, would prefer you not know its location.

SAUSALITO

2 miles north of Golden Gate Bridge.

Bougainvillea-covered hillsides and an expansive yacht harbor give Sausalito the feel of an Adriatic resort. The town sits on the northwestern edge of San Francisco Bay, where it's sheltered from the ocean by the Marin Headlands; the mostly mild weather here is perfect for strolling and outdoor dining. Nevertheless, morning fog and afternoon winds can roll over the hills without warning, funneling through the central part of Sausalito once known as Hurricane Gulch.

South on Bridgeway (toward San Francisco), which snakes between the bay and the hills, a waterside esplanade is lined with restaurants on piers that lure diners with good seafood and even better views. Stairs along the west side of Bridgeway climb the hill to wooded neighborhoods filled with both rustic and opulent homes. As you amble along Bridgeway past shops and galleries, you'll notice the absence of basic services. If you need an aspirin or some groceries (or if you want to see the locals), you'll have to head to Caledonia Street, which runs parallel to Bridgeway, north of the ferry terminus and inland a couple of blocks. The streets closest to the ferry landing flaunt their fair share of

The crowded piers and rolling hillside of the Sausalito waterfront

shops selling T-shirts and kitschy souvenirs. Venture into some of the side streets or narrow alleyways to catch a bit more of the town's taste for eccentric jewelry and handmade crafts.

■TIP➜ The ferry is the best way to get to Sausalito from San Francisco; you get more romance (and less traffic) and disembark in the heart of downtown.

Sausalito had a raffish reputation before it went upscale. Discovered in 1775 by Spanish explorers and named Sausalito (Little Willow) for the trees growing around its springs, the town served as a port for whaling ships during the 19th century. By the mid-1800s wealthy San Franciscans were making Sausalito their getaway across the bay. They built lavish Victorian summer homes in the hills, many of which still stand. In 1875 the railroad from the north connected with ferryboats to San Francisco, bringing the merchant and working classes with it. This influx of hardworking, fun-loving folk polarized the town into "wharf rats" and "hill snobs," and the waterfront area grew thick with saloons, gambling dens, and bordellos. Bootleggers flourished during Prohibition, and shipyard workers swelled the town's population in the 1940s.

Sausalito developed its bohemian flair in the 1950s and '60s, when creative types, led by a charismatic Greek portraitist named Varda, established an artists' colony and a houseboat community here. Today more than 450 houseboats are docked in Sausalito, which has since also become a major yachting center. Some of the houseboats are ragged, others deluxe, but all are quirky (one, a miniature replica of a Persian castle, even has an elevator inside). For a close-up view of the community, head north on Bridgeway—Sausalito's main thoroughfare—from downtown, turn right on Gate Six Road, and park where it dead-ends

Marin County

at the public shore. Keep a respectful distance; these are homes, after all, and the residents become a bit prickly from too much ogling.

ESSENTIALS

Visitor Information Sausalito Chamber of Commerce ✉ *780 Bridgeway* ☎ *415/332–0505, 415/331–7262* ⊕ *www.sausalito.org.*

GETTING HERE AND AROUND

From San Francisco by car or bike, follow U.S. 101 north across the Golden Gate Bridge and take the first exit, Alexander Avenue, just past Vista Point; continue down the winding hill to the water to where the road becomes Bridgeway. Buses 10 and 22 will drop you off in downtown Sausalito, and the ferries dock downtown as well. The center of town is flat, with plenty of sidewalks and bay views. It's a pleasure and a must to explore on foot.

EXPLORING

Bay Area Discovery Museum. Sitting at the base of the Golden Gate Bridge, this indoor-outdoor museum offers entertaining and enlightening hands-on exhibits for children under eight. Kids can fish from a boat at the indoor wharf, imagine themselves as marine biologists in the Wave Workshop, and play outdoors at Lookout Cove (made up of scaled-down sea caves, tidal pools, and even a re-created shipwreck). At Tot Zone, toddlers and preschoolers dress up in animal costumes and crawl through miniature tunnels. From San Francisco, take U.S. 101's Alexander Avenue exit and follow signs to East Fort Baker. ✉ *557 McReynolds Rd., at East Rd. off Alexander Ave.* ☎ *415/339–3900* ⊕ *www.baykidsmuseum.org* ✍ *$11; children under 6 months free* ☺ *Tues.–Fri. 9–4, weekends 10–5.*

Bay Model. An anonymous-looking World War II shipyard building holds a great treasure: the sprawling (more than 1½ acres) Bay Model of the entire San Francisco Bay and the San Joaquin–Sacramento River delta, complete with flowing water. The U.S. Army Corps of Engineers uses the model to reproduce the rise and fall of tides, the flow of currents, and the other physical forces at work on the bay. Science becomes tangible as interactive displays draw children in and adults also learn more about some real California flow. ✉ *2100 Bridgeway, at Marinship Way* ☎ *415/332–3870 recorded information, 415/332–3871 operator assistance* ⊕ *www.spn.usace.army.mil/bmvc* ✍ *Free* ☺ *Memorial Day– Labor Day, Tues.–Fri. 9–4, weekends 10–5; Labor Day–Memorial Day, Tues.–Sat. 9–4.*

Drinking Fountain. On the waterfront between the Hotel Sausalito and the Sausalito Yacht Club is an unusual historic landmark—a drinking fountain. It's inscribed with "Have a drink on Sally" in remembrance of Sally Stanford, the former San Francisco madam who later became the town's mayor in the 1970s. Sassy Sally, as they called her, would have appreciated the fountain's eccentric custom attachment: a knee-level basin that reads "Have a drink on Leland," in memory of her beloved dog.

QUICK BITES

Hamburgers. Judging by the crowds gathered outside Hamburgers, you'd think someone was juggling flaming torches out front. They're really gaping at the juicy hand-formed beef patties sizzling on a rotating grill. Brave the line (it moves fast), get your food to go, and head for the esplanade to enjoy the sweeping views. Hours are 11 am–5 pm. ✉ *737 Bridgeway, at Humboldt Ave.* ☎ *415/332–9471.*

Plaza Viña del Mar. The landmark Plaza Viña del Mar, named for Sausalito's sister city in Chile, marks the center of town. Flanked by two 14-foot-tall elephant statues (created in 1915 for the Panama-Pacific International Exposition), the fountain is a great setting for snapshots and people-watching. ✉ *Bridgeway and Park St.*

Sausalito Visitors Center and Historical Exhibit. Get your bearings and find out what's happening in town at the Sausalito Visitors Center and Historical Exhibit, operated by the town's historical society. The center is closed Monday. ✉ *780 Bridgeway, at Bay St.* ☎ *415/332–0505.*

WHERE TO EAT

$$
ITALIAN

✕ **Bar Bocce.** Few Bay Area eateries can boast of having a beach adjoining the outdoor dining area. And when you play a game of bocce here, it's framed by Richardson Bay. Modern Californian cuisine is served, including pizzas, salads, and signature dishes such as the meatball sliders and the fire-roasted game hen. Reservations aren't taken, so be prepared to wait for a table—time you can spend sipping local beer

9

and wine by the outdoor fire pit. $ *Average main: $17* ✉ *1250 Bridge-way, between Pine and Turney Sts.* ☎ *415/331–0555* ⊕ *barbocce.com* ⌒ *Reservations not accepted.*

$$
SEAFOOD
Fodor'sChoice
★
☾

✕ **Fish.** When locals want fresh seafood, they head to this gleaming dockside fish house a mile north of downtown. Order at the counter and then grab a seat by the floor-to-ceiling windows or at a picnic table on the pier, overlooking the yachts and fishing boats. Most of the sustainably caught fish is hauled in from the owner's boats, docked right outside. Try the ceviche, crab Louis, cioppino, barbecue oysters, or anything fresh that's being grilled over the oak-wood fire. Outside, kids can doodle with sidewalk chalk on the pier. $ *Average main: $22* ✉ *350 Harbor Dr., off Bridgeway* ☎ *415/331–3474* ⊕ *www.331fish.com* ⌒ *Reservations not accepted* ▬ *No credit cards.*

$$$
BISTRO
★

✕ **Le Garage.** Brittany-born Olivier Souvestre serves traditional French bistro fare in a relaxed, sidewalk café–style bayside setting. The menu is small, but the dishes are substantial in flavor and presentation. Standouts include frisée salad with poached egg, bacon, croutons, and pancetta vinaigrette; steak frites with a shallot confit and crispy fries; and a chef's selection of cheese or charcuterie with soup and mixed greens. The restaurant only seats 35 inside and 15 outside, so to avoid a long wait for lunch, arrive before 11:30 or after 1:30. $ *Average main: $23* ✉ *85 Liberty Ship Way, off Marinship Way* ☎ *415/332–5625* ⊕ *www.legaragebistrosausalito.com* ⌒ *Reservations essential* ☾ *No dinner Sun.*

$
SCANDINAVIAN

✕ **Lighthouse Cafe.** A cozy spot with a long coffee bar and dose of Scandinavian flair, this local establishment has been a favorite brunch destination for nearly two decades. The hearty Norwegian salmon omelet with spinach and cream cheese or fruit pancakes, as well as the grilled burgers, sandwiches, and Danish specials like meatballs with potato salad always hit the spot, especially on chilly days. Expect a wait on weekends and at lunch hour. $ *Average main: $12* ✉ *1311 Bridgeway, near Turney St.* ☎ *415/331–3034* ⊕ *www.lighthouse-restaurants.com* ⌒ *Reservations not accepted* ☾ *No dinner.*

$$$
MODERN
AMERICAN

✕ **Plate Shop.** Sausalito's newest shrine to farm-to-table organic, sustainable, and seriously local cuisine sits tucked neatly away from traffic. The seasonal menu is ever-changing, but the bar favorites include the grilled Monterey squid and the smoked trout; for dinner entrées, if they're offered, consider the fried chicken with fingerling potatoes or the rabbit braised in mustard sauce. The bar scene's fun here, too. $ *Average main: $23* ✉ *39 Caledonia St., between Pine and Johnson Sts.* ☎ *415/887–9047.*

$$
ITALIAN
★

✕ **Poggio.** One of the few restaurants in Sausalito to attract both food-savvy locals and tourists, Poggio serves modern Tuscan cuisine in a handsome, open-wall space that spills onto the street. Expect dishes such as grilled lamb chops with roasted eggplant, braised artichokes with polenta, feather-light gnocchi, and pizzas from the open kitchen's wood-fired oven. $ *Average main: $21* ✉ *777 Bridgeway, at Bay St.* ☎ *415/332–7771* ⌒ *Reservations essential.*

$$
SUSHI
★

✕ **Sushi Ran.** Sushi aficionados swear that this is the Bay Area's best option for raw fish, but don't overlook the excellent Pacific Rim fusions, a melding of Japanese ingredients and French cooking techniques, served up in unusual presentations. Because Sushi Ran is so highly ranked among area foodies, book two to seven days in advance for dinner. Otherwise, expect a long wait, which you can soften by sipping one of the 45 by-the-glass sakes from the outstanding wine-and-sake bar. ■TIP→ **If you arrive without a reservation and can't get a table, you can sometimes dine in the noisy bar.** ⑤ *Average main: $18* ✉ *107 Caledonia St., at Pine St.* ☎ *415/332–3620* ⚑ *Reservations essential* ⊘ *No lunch weekends.*

$ ✕**Wellingtons Wine Bar.** British memorabilia decorates the walls of this
WINE BAR establishment that celebrates English and Californian liquid culture. The space is bright, warm, and welcoming with hardwood floors, leather sofas, and actual Wellington boots mounted beside the big glass windows. When the weather is nice, you can sit on the boat dock and drink your pint of lager or sip a glass of wine while scooping up hummus with garlic pita chips. The menu is as big as a book—no one leaves this place hungry (or thirsty). ⑤ *Average main: $10* ✉ *1306 Bridgeway, at Turney St.* ☎ *415/331–9463* ⊕ *www.wellingtonswinebar.com* ⚑ *Reservations not accepted.*

WHERE TO STAY
For expanded reviews, facilities, and current deals, visit Fodors.com.

$$$$ 🏨**Cavallo Point.** Set in Golden Gate National Park, this luxury hotel
HOTEL and resort's location is truly one of a kind, featuring turn-of-the-20th-century buildings converted into well-appointed yet eco-friendly rooms. **Pros:** stunning views and numerous activities: a cooking school, yoga classes, and nature walks; spa with a tea bar; art gallery. **Cons:** landscaping feels incomplete; isolated from urban amenities. **TripAdvisor:** "hidden gem in the Bay area," "fantastic stay," "wonderful place to bring a toddler." ⑤ *Rooms from: $310* ✉ *601 Murray Circle, Fort Baker* ☎ *415/339–4700* ⊕ *www.cavallopoint.com* ⇄ *68 historic and 74 contemporary guest rooms.*

$$ 🏨**Hotel Sausalito.** Handmade furniture and tasteful original art and
B&B/INN reproductions give this well-run inn the feel of a small European hotel. **Pros:** great staff; excellent central location; feels like home away from home. **Cons:** no room service; some rooms feel cramped. **TripAdvisor:** "best of Sausalito," "great location," "delightful." ⑤ *Rooms from: $170* ✉ *16 El Portal* ☎ *415/332–0700, 888/442–0700* ⊕ *www.hotelsausalito.com* ⇄ *14 rooms, 2 suites.*

$$$$ 🏨**The Inn Above Tide.** This is the only hotel in the Bay Area with bal-
B&B/INN conies literally hanging over the water, and each of its rooms has a perfect-10 view that takes in wild Angel Island as well as the city lights across the bay. **Pros:** great complimentary breakfast; minutes from restaurants/attractions; free in-room binoculars let you indulge in the incredible views. **Cons:** costly parking; some rooms are on the small side. **TripAdvisor:** "what a view," "sweet and stunning," "comfortable luxury." ⑤ *Rooms from: $340* ✉ *30 El Portal* ☎ *415/332–9535, 800/893–8433* ⊕ *www.innabovetide.com* ⇄ *29 rooms, 3 suites.*

9

SPORTS AND THE OUTDOORS

Sea Trek Ocean Kayaking Center. The center offers guided half-day sea-kayaking trips underneath the Golden Gate Bridge and full- and half-day trips to Angel Island, both for beginners. Starlight and full-moon paddles are particularly popular. Trips for experienced kayakers, classes, and rentals are also available. Prices start at $20 per hour for rentals; $65 for a three-hour guided trip. ✉ *Schoonmaker Point Marina, off Libertyship Way* ☎ *415/488–1000* ⊕ *www.seatrekkayak.com.*

SF Bay Adventures. This outfit's expert skippers conduct sunset and full-moon sails around the bay, as well as fascinating eco and great-white-shark tours. If you're interested, they can arrange for you to spend the night in a lighthouse or even barbecue on Angel Island. ✉ *60 Liberty Ship Way, Suite 4* ☎ *415/331–0444* ⊕ *www.sfbayadventures.com.*

THE ARTS

Sausalito Art Festival. The annual festival, held over Labor Day weekend, attracts more than 50,000 people to the northern waterfront area; Blue & Gold Fleet ferries from San Francisco dock at the pier adjacent to the festival. Tickets are $25. ☎ *415/332–3555, 415/331–3757* ⊕ *www.sausalitoartfestival.org.*

SHOPPING

♻ **Sausalito Ferry Co.** Eccentric and fun, this shop is a great place to buy trendy T-shirts, wallets, and clocks—not to mention solar-powered bobbleheads, outrageous cocktail napkins, even one-of-a-kind key chains. ✉ *688 Bridgeway, near Princess St.* ☎ *415/332–9590* ⊕ *www.sausalitoferry.com.*

Something/Anything Gallery. Where Bridgeway ends and curves toward the dock, this gallery with a friendly staff carries jewelry and gifts, from unique watches to humorous pendants. It's a good spot to pick up your Sausalito memento. ✉ *20 Princess St., at Broadway* ☎ *415/339–8831.*

TIBURON

2 miles north of Sausalito, 7 miles north of Golden Gate Bridge.

On a peninsula that was called Punta de Tiburon (Shark Point) by the Spanish explorers, this beautiful Marin County community retains the feel of a village—it's more low-key than Sausalito—despite the encroachment of commercial establishments from the downtown area. The harbor faces Angel Island across Raccoon Strait, and San Francisco is directly south across the bay—which makes the views from the decks of harbor restaurants a major attraction. Since its incarnation, in 1884, when ferries from San Francisco connected the point with a railroad to San Rafael, the town has centered on the waterfront. ■ TIP→ The ferry is the most relaxing (and fastest) way to get here, particularly in summer, allowing you to skip traffic and parking problems. If visiting midweek, keep in mind that many shops close either Tuesday or Wednesday, or both.

ESSENTIALS

Visitor InformationTiburon Peninsula Chamber of Commerce ✉ *96-B Main St.* ☎ *415/435–5633* ⊕ *www.tiburonchamber.org.*

GETTING HERE AND AROUND

By car, head north from San Francisco on U.S. 101 and get off at CA 131/Tiburon Boulevard/East Blithedale Avenue (Exit 447). Turn right onto Tiburon Boulevard and drive just over 4 miles to downtown. Golden Gate Transit buses 8 and 19 serve downtown Tiburon from San Francisco, as does the Blue & Gold Fleet Ferry service. Tiburon's Main Street is made for wandering, as are the footpaths that frame the water's edge.

EXPLORING

Ark Row. Past the pink-brick bank building, Main Street is known as Ark Row, and has a tree-shaded walk lined with antiques and specialty stores. Some of the buildings are actually old houseboats. They floated in Belvedere Cove before being beached and transformed into stores. If you're curious about architectural history, the Tiburon Heritage & Arts Commission prints a self-guided walking-tour map, available at local businesses. ⊠ *Ark Row, parallel to Main St.* ⊕ *www.landmarks-society.org.*

Old St. Hilary's Landmark and Wildflower Preserve. The stark-white Old St. Hilary's Landmark and Wildflower Preserve, an 1886 Carpenter Gothic church barged over from Strawberry Point in 1957, overlooks the town and the bay from its hillside perch. ■**TIP→ The church is surrounded by a wildflower preserve that's spectacular in May and June, when the rare black jewel flower blooms.** Expect a steep walk uphill to reach the preserve. The hiking trails behind the landmark wind up to a peak that has 360-degree views of the entire Bay Area (great photo op). ⊠ *201 Esperanza St., off Mar West St.* ☎ *415/435–1853* ⊕ *www.landmarks-society.org* ⊠ *$3 suggested donation* ⊙ *Apr.–Oct., Wed. and Sun. 1–4 and by appointment.*

WHERE TO EAT

$$$
AMERICAN

✕**The Caprice.** For more than 50 years this Tiburon landmark, perched on a cliff overlooking the bay, has been the place to come to mark special occasions. The views are spectacular, and soft-yellow walls and starched white tablecloths help to make the space bright and light. Elegant comfort food is the premise, with choices like seared day boat scallops or pan-roasted filet mignon. Polishing off the warm chocolate cake with almond ice cream while gazing out at the sunset and porpoises bobbing in the waves below is a near perfect end to the evening. ⑤ *Average main: $27* ⊠ *2000 Paradise Dr.* ☎ *415/435–3400* ⊕ *www. thecaprice.com* ⊙ *Closed Mon. No lunch.*

$$
MODERN
MEXICAN

✕**Guaymas.** The festive Guaymas restaurant at the ferry terminal claims a knockout view of the bay, handsome whitewashed adobe walls, tile floors, and a heated terrace bar—and it serves a top-notch margarita. A large open kitchen churns out fairly authentic Mexican dishes such as ceviche, *carnitas uruapan* (slow-roasted pork with salsa and black beans), mesquite-grilled fish, tamales, and a long list of others. ■**TIP→ Sunday lunch is very popular, so make a reservation.** ⑤ *Average main: $19* ⊠ *5 Main St.* ☎ *415/435–6300.*

$
AMERICAN

✕**New Morning Cafe.** Omelets and scrambles are served all day long at this homey café. If you're past morning treats, choose from the many soups, salads, and sandwiches. New Morning is open 6:30 am–2:30 pm

9

weekdays and 6:30 am–4 pm weekends. ⑤ *Average main: $11* ✉ *1696 Tiburon Blvd.* ☎ *415/435–4315* ✆ *No dinner.*

$$ ✕ **Sam's Anchor Cafe.** Open since 1921, this casual dockside restaurant
AMERICAN   with mahogany wainscoting is the town's most famous eatery. Today
★   most people flock here for the deck, where out-of-towners and old
salts sit shoulder to shoulder for bay views, beer, seafood, and Ramos
fizzes. The lunch menu has the usual suspects—burgers, sandwiches,
salads, fried fish with tartar sauce—and you'll sit on plastic chairs at
tables covered with blue-and-white-checked oilcloths. At night you
can find standard seafood dishes with vegetarian and meat options.
Expect a wait for outside tables on sunny summer days or weekends
(there are no reservations for deck seating or weekend lunch). Mind
the seagulls; they know no restraint. ⑤ *Average main: $22* ✉ *27 Main
St.* ☎ *415/435–4527.*

$$ ✕ **Waypoint Pizza.** A nautical decor theme and a tasty "between the
PIZZA   sheets" pizza-style sandwich are signatures of this creative pizzeria that
also serves slices and whole gourmet pies. Booths are brightened with
blue-checked tablecloths, and a playful air is added by indoor deck
chairs, a picnic table complete with umbrella, and lighthouse salt-and-
pepper shakers. ⑤ *Average main: $15* ✉ *15 Main St.* ☎ *415/435–3440.*

WHERE TO STAY

For expanded reviews, facilities, and current deals, visit Fodors.com.

$$ ⛫ **The Lodge at Tiburon.** A block from Main Street and framed by stone
HOTEL   pillars and sloped rooftops, the Lodge at Tiburon has the feel of a winter
ski chalet, though the outdoor pool and its cabanas provide a summery
counterpoint. **Pros:** spacious work desks in each room; plush bath-
robes; L'Occitane bath products; room service from the Tiburon Grill.
Cons: breakfast for a fee; some rooms have a few too many mirrors; no
bay views. **TripAdvisor:** "clean modern rooms," "beautiful common
areas," "perfect spot for a quiet romantic evening." ⑤ *Rooms from:
$170* ✉ *1651 Tiburon Blvd., at Beach St.* ☎ *415/435–3133* ⊕ *lodgeat-
tiburon.com* ⤶ *102 rooms.*

$$$ ⛫ **Waters Edge Hotel.** Checking into this elegant hotel feels like tucking
B&B/INN   away into an inviting retreat by the water—the views are stunning and
★   the lighting is perfect. **Pros:** complimentary wine and cheese for guests
every evening; restaurants/sights are minutes away; free bike rentals
for guests. **Cons:** except for breakfast delivery, no room service; fitness
center is off-site; not a great place to bring small children. **TripAdvisor:**
"just about perfect," "a beautiful haven," "comfortable and relaxing."
⑤ *Rooms from: $209* ✉ *25 Main St., off Tiburon Blvd.* ☎ *415/789-
5999, 877/789–5999* ⊕ *www.marinhotels.com* ⤶ *23 rooms.*

SHOPPING

☺ **The Candy Store on Main Street.** This store is every child's (and many
adults') dream come true, with rows of fresh homemade fudge, barrels of rainbow-colored jelly beans, and neat boxes of truffles with
pin-striped ribbons. A train in the window drives figure eights through
chocolate mountains and around M&M houses. ✉ *7 Main St., at Tiburon Blvd.* ☎ *415/435–0434.*

Nasimiyu. The beaded jewelry sold here—necklaces, earrings, and bracelets—is big, vibrant, and very colorful. The shop's namesake owner, Nasimiyu Wekesa, who greets all customers with her warm smile, draws inspiration from her African heritage, making her crafts not just something to wear but also to be proud of. ⊠ *80D Main St.* ☎ *415/435–3429.*

Ruth Livingston Studio. The namesake owner of this design showcase and walk-in shop will greet you and explain the concepts behind her neomodern pieces. Find everything from striking vases to one-of-a-kind furniture. ⊠ *74 Main St.* ☎ *415/435–5264.*

Schoenberg Guitars. Small, narrow, and chockablock with handmade guitars, this shop is a treat even for those who don't play music. Dozens, if not hundreds, of guitars varying in size, shape, and color hang from the walls and stand against the polished wood floor. There is an organized beauty to the layout of this place and a comforting sense of musical harmony. ⊠ *106 Main St.* ☎ *415/789–0846.*

MILL VALLEY

2 miles north of Sausalito, 4 miles north of Golden Gate Bridge.

Chic and woodsy Mill Valley has a dual personality. Here, as elsewhere in the county, the foundation is a superb natural setting. Virtually surrounded by parkland, the town lies at the base of Mt. Tamalpais and contains dense redwood groves traversed by countless creeks. But this is no lumber camp. Smart restaurants and chichi boutiques line the streets, and more rock stars than one might suspect live here.

The rustic village flavor is not a modern conceit but a holdover from the town's early days as a logging camp. In 1896 the Mill Valley and Mt. Tamalpais Scenic Railroad—called "the crookedest railroad in the world" because of its curvy tracks—began transporting visitors from Mill Valley to the top of Mt. Tam and down to Muir Woods, and the town soon became a vacation retreat for city slickers. The trains stopped running in the 1940s, but you can see the old railway depot: the 1924 building has been transformed into the popular Depot Bookstore & Cafe, at 87 Throckmorton Avenue.

The small downtown area has the constant bustle of a leisure community; even at noon on a Tuesday, people are out shopping for fancy cookware and lacy pajamas.

ESSENTIALS

Visitor Information Mill Valley Chamber of Commerce ⊠ *85 Throckmorton Ave.* ☎ *415/388–9700* ⊕ *www.millvalley.org.*

GETTING HERE AND AROUND

By car, from San Francisco head north on U.S. 101 and get off at CA 131/Tiburon Boulevard/East Blithedale Avenue (Exit 447). Turn left onto East Blithedale and continue west to Throckmorton Avenue; turn left to reach Lytton Square, then park. Golden Gate Transit bus 4 leaves for Mill Valley from 8th and Folsom streets in San Francisco every 30 minutes during commute hours. Once here, explore the town on foot; it's great for strolling.

9

EXPLORING

🌀 **Lytton Square.** Mill Valley locals congregate on weekends to socialize in the many coffeehouses near the town's central square, but it bustles most any time of day. Shops, restaurants, and cultural venues line the nearby streets. ✉ *Miller and Throckmorton Aves.*

OFF THE BEATEN PATH

Marin County Civic Center. This wonder of arches, circles, and skylights was Frank Lloyd Wright's last major architectural undertaking. You can wander about on your own or take a docent-led tour of the complex. Tours ($5) leave from the gift shop, on the second floor, on Wednesday mornings at 10:30. If you can't make it on a Wednesday, pick up the self-guided tour map for 50¢ at the gift shop. Don't miss the photographs on the first floor, which show Marin County homes designed by Wright. There's also an excellent California library here for bibliophiles and oral-history buffs. ✉ *3501 Civic Center Dr., off N. San Pedro Rd., San Rafael* 🕾 *415/499–7009* 🖃 *Free* ◷ *Weekdays 8–5.*

🌀 **Old Mill Park.** To see one of the numerous outdoor oases that make Mill Valley so appealing, follow Throckmorton Avenue ¼ mile west from Lytton Square to Old Mill Park, a shady patch of redwoods that shelters a playground and reconstructed sawmill. From the park, Cascade Way winds its way past creek-side homes to the trailheads of several forest paths. ✉ *Throckmorton Ave. and Cascade Dr.*

WHERE TO EAT

$$$
AMERICAN

✕ **The Balboa Café.** With intimate lighting, rich wood accents, and fresh-pressed white linens, this café offers an upscale dining experience. The bar is so busy that you'll be lucky if your elbow gets anywhere near it. Although the cocktails aren't as stiff as their price tags, the food is creative, local, and beautifully presented. Try the Black Angus rib eye, wild-mushroom risotto, or seared sea scallops—and be sure to save room for the blueberry brioche bread pudding. The extensive wine list includes a few wines from Marin County. 🖫 *Average main: $26* ✉ *38 Miller Ave., at Sunnyside Ave.* 🕾 *415/381–7321* ⌕ *Reservations essential.*

$$$
AMERICAN

✕ **Buckeye Roadhouse.** This is Mill Valley's secret den of decadence, where house-smoked meats and fish, grilled steaks, and old-fashioned dishes such as brisket bring the locals coming back for more. The restaurant also serves beautiful organic, locally grown salads and desserts so heavenly—like the rich but light crème brûlée—you'll just about melt into the floor. The look of the 1937 roadhouse is decidedly hunting-lodge chic, with trophy heads and a river-rock fireplace dominating one wall. Marin County's Jaguar-driving bon vivants pack the place every night. The busy but cozy bar with elegant mahogany paneling and soft lighting is a good place to quench your thirst for a Marin martini or Californian Merlot. 🖫 *Average main: $23* ✉ *15 Shoreline Hwy., off U.S. 101* 🕾 *415/331–2600* ⌕ *Reservations essential.*

$$
MODERN
AMERICAN

✕ **Bungalow 44.** Banana plants and tropical lighting set the mood at this glowing space that serves Californian comfort and glistening cocktails (the restaurant is as popular for its bar as it is for its food). The dance of flames is everywhere—in the crackling dining-room fireplace, and the kitchen's wood oven. House specialties include goat-cheese ravioli in a tomato vodka sauce, fried chicken with local-honey coleslaw, and braised short ribs with horseradish cream. In nice weather, you can eat outdoors. $ *Average main: $21* ⊠ *44 E. Blithedale Ave., at Sunnyside Ave.* ☎ *415/381–2500* ⊕ *www.bungalow44.com.*

$

FRENCH

✕**Champagne.** This adorable little bakery/café on Mill Valley's main shopping street is a nice place to pop into for breakfast, a light lunch, dinner, or afternoon pick-me-up. Filled with light, authentic French decor and only a dozen tables, Champagne serves amazing crepes with roasted chicken, creamed spinach, and Swiss cheese, as well as an assortment of savory flat breads—try the pesto-and-tomato version. It's a popular place for breakfast, too. The perennial favorite: brioche French toast with bacon. The afternoon crowd chats over cappuccinos, raspberry-almond croissants, and meringue cookies. $ *Average main: $11* ⊠ *41 Throckmorton Ave., at Miller Ave.* ☎ *415/380–0410.*

$$

AMERICAN

🄲

✕**The Dipsea Cafe.** There is no better place for breakfast than the Dipsea, which is named after the gorgeous trail that stretches from Mill Valley to Stinson Beach. Locals crowd its cozy interior most mornings, but weekends are especially popular. Choose from huge plates of French toast, eggs Benedict, and huevos rancheros; the homemade fries and jam that accompany the breakfast entrées are to die for. The café also serves hearty lunches and dinners, like the Chinese salad with seared salmon and the enormous BLTs. After 4 pm you can order from the Greek-influenced menu. This is a great spot to fuel up on your way to or from Muir Woods and Stinson Beach. $ *Average main: $14* ⊠ *200 Shoreline Hwy., west of Tennessee Valley Rd.* ☎ *415/381–0298* ◔ *No dinner Mon. and Tues.*

$$$

CONTEMPORARY

Fodor'sChoice

★

✕**El Paseo House of Chops.** Chef Tyler Florence and rocker Sammy Hagar teamed up to restore El Paseo, which was established in 1947 and remains *the* place for a romantic and culinary night out. You'll feel as if you're on one of Spain's tiny cobbled lanes as you enter the secluded brick walkway that wraps around a candlelit dining room. If you reserve well in advance you can sit in the bougainvillea-framed courtyard, but the dining room casts its own atmospheric charms, with soft leather chairs, white tablecloths, and dark wooden walls. And then there's Tyler Florence's famous seasonal Californian cuisine. The spinach-and-artichoke dip is rich and full of fresh flavors, as is the bacon-wrapped pork tenderloin with spiced-apple pulp and glazed turnips. Don't overlook the decadent desserts. $ *Average main: $30* ⊠ *17 Throckmorton Ave., at E. Blithedale Ave.* ☎ *415/388–0741* ⊱ *Reservations essential* ◔ *No lunch.*

$

MEXICAN

🄲

✕**Joe's Taco Lounge.** A funky, bright lounge (and it really does feel like someone's lounge), this is a fun place to go for a casual, cheap, and delicious Mexican meal. There are all sorts of colorful relics on the walls, and chili-pepper lights adorn the windows. The signature dishes are fish tacos and snapper burritos—which are generous in both size and flavor. The organic burger with spicy fries and the fire-grilled corn on the cob are also yummy. Choose from a wide selection of Mexican beers, or go for a refreshing wine-based margarita. Between 5 and 7 pm, this place is popular with families. $ *Average main: $11* ⊠ *382 Miller Ave., and Montford Ave.* ☎ *415/383–8164.*

$$ ✕ **La Ginestra.** In business since 1964, La Ginestra is a Mill Valley institu-
ITALIAN   tion renowned for its no-pretense, family-style Italian meals—the great-
est hits include thin-crusted pizzas, homemade pastas, breaded veal, and
chicken with artichokes—and impressive wine list. An adorable little
bar sits off to the side of the dining room, just right for a martini or two
and a plate of antipasto. $ *Average main: $19* ⊠ *127 Throckmorton
Ave., at Miller Ave.* ☎ *415/388–0224* ⊘ *Closed Mon. No lunch.*

$ ✕ **Pearl's Phat Burgers.** Families, couples, and teenagers flock to Pearl's
BURGER   for juicy, grass-fed organic burgers stacked high with tomatoes, lettuce,
bacon, and cheese; sweet-potato fries that are not too crispy and not
too soft; and thick, creamy milk shakes. The food here is among the
freshest, biggest, and fastest in town. No wonder there's always a line
out the door. $ *Average main: $9* ⊠ *8 E. Blithedale Ave., at Sunnyside
Ave.* ☎ *415/381–6010* ⊕ *www.pearlsdeluxe.com.*

$$ ✕ **Piazza D'Angelo.** In the heart of downtown, busy D'Angelo's is known
ITALIAN   for its osso buco and veal saltimbocca, as well as pastas and delicious
crème brûlée. The food is authentic and fresh, but another draw is the
scene, especially in the lounge area, which hosts a lively cocktail hour
packed with beautiful people and serves food until 10 or 11 pm—late
for Mill Valley. The sprawling space encompasses a bright front room,
romantic booths, and a warm patio. $ *Average main: $21* ⊠ *22 Miller
Ave., near Sunnyside Ave.* ☎ *415/388–2000* ⊕ *www.piazzadangelo.
com.*

WHERE TO STAY

For expanded reviews, facilities, and current deals, visit Fodors.com.

$$ ⌗ **Acqua Hotel.** Astride Richardson Bay, this boutique hotel has modern,
HOTEL   elegant rooms decorated in deep purples and classic golds. **Pros:** eve-
ning cookie hour; complimentary bikes; hearty breakfast. **Cons:** next
to freeway; traffic audible in rooms facing east. **TripAdvisor:** "beauti-
ful view and walking path," "nice amenities," "well located and clean
design." $ *Rooms from: $189* ⊠ *555 Redwood Hwy., off U.S. 101*
☎ *415/388–9353* ⊕ *www.marinhotels.com* ⇱ *49 rooms* ⦿| *Breakfast.*

$ ⌗ **Larkspur Hotel.** In the shadow of Mt. Tamalpais and practically sur-
HOTEL   rounded by water, the Larkspur Hotel is central to Marin's attractions.
Pros: central location; complimentary breakfast; popular restaurant
(Frantoio) next door. **Cons:** hallway is disorienting; lobby is cold;
new-carpet smell lingers in the air. **TripAdvisor:** "pleasant staff,"
"nice rooms," "an oasis of quiet." $ *Rooms from: $149* ⊠ *160 Shore-
line Hwy, at U.S. 101* ☎ *415/332–5700* ⊕ *www.larkspurhotels.com/
larkspur-hotels/mill-valley* ⇱ *100 rooms* ⦿| *Breakfast.*

$$$ ⌗ **Mill Valley Inn.** The only hotel in downtown Mill Valley has smart-
B&B/INN   looking rooms done up in Tuscan colors of ocher and olive, with hand-
crafted beds, armoires, and lamps by local artisans. **Pros:** minutes from
local shops and restaurants; great complimentary Continental breakfast. **Cons:** dark in winter because of surrounding trees; some rooms
are not accessible via elevator; no in-room coffeemakers. **TripAdvisor:**
"awesome gem in Mill Valley," "personal service with care," "nice hotel
in a gorgeous area." $ *Rooms from: $239* ⊠ *165 Throckmorton Ave.,
near Miller Ave.* ☎ *415/389–6608, 800/595–2100* ⊕ *www.marinhotels.
com* ⇱ *25 rooms, 1 suite, 2 cottages* ⦿| *Breakfast.*

$$$$
B&B/INN
Fodor'sChoice
★

⊞ **Mountain Home Inn.** Abutting 40,000 acres of state and national parks, the inn sits on the skirt of Mt. Tamalpais, where you can follow hiking trails all the way to Stinson Beach. **Pros:** amazing deck and views; peaceful, remote setting. **Cons:** nearest town is a 20-minute drive away; restaurant can get crowded on sunny weekend days. **TripAdvisor:** "brilliant location and restaurant," "stunning view and tranquil setting," "outstanding service." ⑤ *Rooms from: $279* ⊠ *810 Panoramic Hwy., at Edgewood Ave.* ☎ *415/381–9000* ⊕ *www.mtnhomeinn.com* ⇆ *10 rooms* ⫩⦶ *Breakfast.*

NIGHTLIFE AND THE ARTS

142 Throckmorton Theatre. This ultra-quirky venue presents plays, musical acts, and comedy shows, along with visual and related arts. Top events include the DjangoFest Mill Valley, celebrating the gypsy-jazz artist Django Reinhardt; a film series hosted by comedian Mort Sahl; and the annual Writers with Attitude festival of short-play readings. Stunning murals cover the theater's ceiling, and the foyer has on old-fashioned popcorn maker. ⊠ *142 Throckmorton Ave., at Madrona St.* ☎ *415/383–9600* ⊕ *www.142throckmortontheatre.com.*

Beerworks. A fine place to rest your feet after shopping or hiking, Beerworks serves more than 100 local, national, and international beers, from ale to port to lager. For food, you'll find cheese plates, olives, homemade pretzels, and sandwiches. ⊠ *173 Throckmorton Ave., at Madrona St.* ☎ *415/336–3596* ⊕ *millvalleybeerworks.com.*

★ **Sweetwater Saloon.** With the help of part-owner Bob Weir of the Grateful Dead, this renowned club reopened in an old Masonic Hall. The location may be new, but the Sweetwater's reputation as the best music club and bar in Marin remains. In its former life it hosted the likes of John Lee Hooker and Jerry Garcia. Today, famous as well as up-and-coming bands play nightly, and local stars such as Bonnie Raitt and Huey Lewis have been known to stop in for a pickup session. ⊠ *19 Corte Madera Ave., between Throckmorton and Lovell Aves.* ☎ *415/388–3850.*

SHOPPING

The area around Throckmorton Avenue downtown brims with stylish and quirky stores, indies as well as chains.

Book Passage. This sprawling independent bookstore north of Mill Valley in Corte Madera is beloved for its many author events, with readings by notables like Alice Walker, Val McDermid, Michael Connelly, and Peter Mayle. Coffee and snacks are available at the in-store café. ⊠ *The Marketplace, 51 Tamal Vista Blvd., between Madera Blvd. and Wornum Dr., Corte Madera* ☎ *415/927–0960, 800/999–7909.*

Jaylina's. Budget fashionistas flock to this chic consignment store, where Prada dresses, Seven jeans, even Chanel bags sell for reasonable prices. The items are carefully selected and easy to find; no need to rummage through crowded racks. ⊠ *19 E. Blithedale Ave., at Throckmorton Ave.* ☎ *415/388–4682.*

Summer House. All sorts of surprises pile up here. For the home: furniture, lavish pillows, and decorative objects. For the body: scented potions and soaps. To decorate both: stunning jewelry, tableware, and tempting shirts. ✉ *21 Throckmorton Ave., at W. Blithedale Ave.* ☎ *415/383–6695.*

Tyler Florence Shop. Stock up here on everything you need for cooking—the celebrity chef's shop has the works, from chicken-shape hard-boiled-egg holders to copper frying pans. If you want to escape into one of Florence's many cookbooks, there's a library in back with leather sofas. ✉ *59 Throckmorton Ave., at Corte Madera Ave.* ☎ *415/380–9200.*

THE MARIN HEADLANDS

Due west of the Golden Gate Bridge's northern end.

★ The term "Golden Gate" may now be synonymous with the world-famous bridge, but it originally referred to the grassy, poppy-strewn hills flanking the passageway into San Francisco Bay. To the north of the gate lie the Marin Headlands, part of the Golden Gate National Recreation Area (GGNRA) and the most dramatic scenery in these parts. Windswept hills plunge down to the ocean, and creek-fed thickets shelter swaying wildflowers.

The headlands stretch from the Golden Gate Bridge to Muir Beach. Photographers perch on the southern headlands for shots of the city, with the bridge in the foreground and the skyline on the horizon. Equally remarkable are the views north along the coast and out to sea, where the Farallon Islands are visible on clear days. ■ TIP→ Almost any of the roads, all very windy, offer great coast views, especially as you drive at higher elevations.

The headlands' strategic position at the mouth of San Francisco Bay made them a logical site for World War II military installations. Today you can explore the crumbling concrete batteries where naval guns protected the approaches from the sea. The headlands' main attractions are centered on Forts Barry and Cronkhite, which lie just across Rodeo Lagoon from each other. Fronting the lagoon is Rodeo Beach, a dark stretch of sand that attracts sand-castle builders and dog owners.

⚠ Note: The beaches at the Marin Headlands are not safe for swimming. The giant cliffs are steep and unstable, so hiking down them can be dangerous. Stay on trails.

GETTING HERE AND AROUND
Driving from San Francisco, head north on U.S. 101. Just after you cross the Golden Gate Bridge, take the Alexander Avenue exit. From there take the first left (signs read "San Francisco/U.S. 101 South"), go through the tunnel under the freeway, and turn right up the hill where the sign reads: "Forts Barry and Cronkhite." The MuniBus 76 runs hourly from 4th and Townsend streets to the Marin Headlands Visitor Center on Sunday and major holidays only. Once here, you can explore this beautiful countryside on foot.

EXPLORING
Green Gulch Zen Center. Giant eucalyptus trees frame the long winding road that leads to this tranquil retreat. There are mediation programs on Sunday, workshops, and events, as well as an extensive organic garden. Visitors are welcome to roam freely through the acres of gardens

Shutterbugs rejoice in catching a scenic Muir Beach sunset.

that reach down toward Muir Beach. If you follow the main dirt road it will take you to a walking path that brings you to the beach. It's a peaceful walk surrounded by trees, birds, and the ocean breeze. ⊠ *1601 Shoreline Hwy., at Green Gulch Rd., Muir Beach* ☏ *415/383–3134* ⊕ *www.sfzc.org* 🌐 *Free* ⊙ *Tues.–Sat. 9–noon and 2–4, Sun. 9–10 am.*

Headlands Center for the Arts. The center's main building, formerly the barracks, exhibits contemporary art in a rustic natural setting; the downstairs "archive room" contains objects found and created by residents, such as natural rocks, interesting glass bottles filled with collected items, and unusual masks. Stop by the industrial gallery space, two flights up, to see what the resident visual artists are up to—most of the work is quite contemporary. ⊠ *Fort Barry, Field and Bunker Rds., Bldg. 944* ☏ *415/331–2787* ⊕ *www.headlands.org* ⊙ *Weekdays 10–5, Sun. noon–5.*

⟳ **Marin Headlands Visitor Center.** Open daily 9:30–4:30, the center sells a guide to historic sites and wildlife and has exhibits on the area's history and ecology. Pick up the park newspaper for a schedule of guided walks. Kids will enjoy the "please touch" educational sites and small play area inside. ⊠ *Fort Barry, Field and Bunker Rds., Bldg. 948* ☏ *415/331–1540* ⊕ *www.nps.gov/goga/marin-headlands.htm.*

★ **Muir Beach.** Small but scenic, this beach—a rocky patch of shoreline off
⟳ Highway 1 in the northern headlands—is a good place to stretch your legs and gaze out at the Pacific. Locals often walk their dogs here; families and cuddling couples come for picnicking and sunbathing. At one end of the sand is a cluster of waterfront homes, and at the other are the bluffs of Golden Gate National Recreation Area. The beach itself

has an interesting history. Janis Joplin's ashes were scattered here among the sands, and this is where author Ken Kesey hosted the second of his famed Acid Tests. ⊠ *190 Pacific Way, off Shoreline Highway, Muir Beach* ⊕ *www.parksconservancy.org/visit/park-sites/muir-beach.html.*

★ **Point Bonita Lighthouse.** At the end of Conzelman Road, in the southern
☾ headlands, is the Point Bonita Lighthouse, a restored beauty that still guides ships to safety with its original 1855 refractory lens. Half the fun of a visit is the steep ½-mile walk from the parking area down to the lighthouse, which takes you through a rock tunnel and across a suspension bridge. Signposts along the way detail the bravado of surfmen, as the early lifeguards were called, and the tenacity of the "wickies," the first keepers of the light. ⊠ *End of Conzelman Rd.* 🎫 *Free* ☾ *Sat.–Mon. 12:30–3:30.*

WHERE TO STAY

For expanded reviews, facilities, and current deals, visit Fodors.com.

$$$ 🛏 **Pelican Inn.** From its slate roof to its whitewashed plaster walls, this
B&B/INN inn looks so Tudor that it's hard to believe it was built in the 1970s.
★ **Pros:** five-minute walk to beach; great bar and restaurant; peaceful setting. **Cons:** 20-minute drive to nearby attractions; no Wi-Fi or wheelchair access to bedrooms. **TripAdvisor:** "quaint inn with lots of charm," "very British," "fantastic getaway." 💲 *Rooms from: $210* ⊠ *10 Pacific Way, off Hwy. 1, Muir Beach* ☎ *415/383–6000* ⊕ *www.pelicaninn.com* ⤴ *7 rooms* 🍽 *Breakfast.*

MUIR WOODS NATIONAL MONUMENT

12 miles northwest of the Golden Gate Bridge.

GETTING HERE AND AROUND

To get here from San Francisco by car, take U.S. 101 north across the Golden Gate Bridge to the Mill Valley/Stinson Beach exit, then follow signs to Highway 1 north. On weekends and holidays, Memorial Day through Labor Day, Golden Gate Transit operates a shuttle ($3 round-trip) from Mill Valley every half hour. Park in Marin City at the Gateway Shopping Center (look for lighted signs directing you from U.S. 101) or at the Manzanita Park-and-Ride, at the Highway 1 exit off U.S. 101 (look for the lot under the elevated freeway), or take connecting bus service from San Francisco with Golden Gate Transit. Once here, you can wander by foot through this pristine patch of nature.

EXPLORING

☾ **Muir Woods National Monument.** One hundred fifty million years ago,
Fodor's Choice ancestors of redwood and sequoia trees grew throughout the United
★ States. Today the *Sequoia sempervirens* can be found only in a narrow, cool coastal belt from Monterey to Oregon. The 550 acres of Muir Woods National Monument contain some of the most majestic redwoods in the world—some nearly 250 feet tall and 1,000 years old. The stand was saved from destruction in 1905, when it was purchased by a couple who donated it to the federal government. Three years later it was named after naturalist John Muir, whose environmental campaigns helped to establish the national park system. His response: "Saving

DID YOU KNOW?

The gorgeous old-growth redwood trees in Muir Woods are often enveloped in fog, a useful dampness for the trees, especially to counteract the dry summers.

these woods from the ax and saw is in many ways the most notable service to God and man I have heard of since my forest wandering began."

Muir Woods, part of the Golden Gate National Recreation Area, is a pedestrian's park. The trails vary in difficulty and length. Beginning from the park headquarters, a 2-mile, wheelchair-accessible **loop trail** crosses streams and passes ferns and azaleas, as well as magnificent redwood groves. Among the most famous are **Bohemian Grove** and the circular formation called **Cathedral Grove.** On summer weekends, visitors oohing and aahing in a dozen languages line the trail. If you prefer a little serenity, consider the challenging **Dipsea Trail,** which climbs west from the forest floor to soothing views of the ocean and the Golden Gate Bridge. For a complete list of trails, check with rangers, who can also help you pick the best one for your ability level.

■ TIP➜ **The weather in Muir Woods is usually cool and often wet, so wear warm clothes and shoes appropriate for damp trails.** Picnicking and camping aren't allowed, and pets aren't permitted. Parking can be difficult here—the lots are small and the crowds are large—so try to come early in the morning or late in the afternoon. The fine **Muir Woods Visitor Center** has books and exhibits about redwood trees and the woods' history. ⊠ *1 Muir Woods Trail, off Panoramic Hwy., Mill Valley* ☎ *415/388–2595 park information, 415/925–4501 shuttle information* ⊕ *www.nps.gov/muwo* ☏ *$7* ⊙ *Daily 8 am–sunset.*

MT. TAMALPAIS STATE PARK

16 miles northwest of Golden Gate Bridge.

GETTING HERE AND AROUND

By car, take the Highway 1–Stinson Beach exit off U.S. 101 and follow the road west and then north. From San Francisco the trip can take from 30 minutes up to an hour, depending on traffic. By bus, take the 10, 70 or 80 to Marin City; in Marin City transfer to the West Marin Stagecoach (☎ *415/226–0855* ⊕ *www.marintransit.org/stage.html*). Once here, the only way to explore is on foot or by bike.

EXPLORING

Mt. Tamalpais State Park. Although the summit of Mt. Tamalpais is only 2,571 feet high, the mountain rises practically from sea level, dominating the topography of Marin County. Adjacent to Muir Woods National Monument, Mt. Tamalpais State Park affords views of the entire Bay Area and the Pacific Ocean to the west. The mountain was sacred to Native Americans, who saw in its profile—as you can see today—the silhouette of a sleeping Indian maiden. Locals fondly refer to it as the "Sleeping Lady." For years the 6,300-acre park has been a favorite destination for hikers. There are more than 200 miles of trails, some rugged but many developed for easy walking through meadows, grasslands, and forests and along creeks. Mt. Tam, as it's called by locals, is also the birthplace (in the 1970s) of mountain biking, and today many spandex-clad bikers whiz down the park's winding roads.

The park's major thoroughfare, the Panoramic Highway, snakes its way up from U.S. 101 to the **Pantoll Ranger Station** (⊠ *Pantoll Rd.*). The office is staffed sporadically, depending on funding. From the ranger station, the Panoramic Highway drops down to the town of Stinson Beach. Pantoll Road branches off the highway at the station, connecting up with Ridgecrest Boulevard. Along these roads are numerous parking areas, picnic spots, scenic overlooks, and trailheads. Parking is free along the roadside, but there's a fee at the ranger station and at some of the other parking lots.

The **Mountain Theater** (⊠ *Richardson Blvd. off Panoramic Hwy.*), also known as the Cushing Memorial Amphitheatre, is a natural amphitheater with terraced stone seats (for nearly 4,000 people) constructed in its current form by the Civilian Conservation Corps in the 1930s.

The **Rock Spring Trail** starts at the Mountain Theater and gently climbs about 1¾ mile to the **West Point Inn,** once a stop on the Mt. Tam railroad route. Relax at a picnic table and stock up on water before forging ahead, via Old Railroad Grade Fire Road and the Miller Trail, to Mt. Tam's Middle Peak, about 2 miles uphill.

Starting from the Pan Toll Ranger Station, the precipitous **Steep Ravine Trail** brings you past stands of coastal redwoods and, in the springtime, numerous small waterfalls. Take the connecting **Dipsea Trail** to reach the town of Stinson Beach and its swath of golden sand. If you're too weary to make the 3½-mile trek back up, Golden Gate Transit Bus 63 (Saturday, Sunday, and holidays from mid-March through early December) takes you from Stinson Beach back to the ranger station. ⊠ *Pantoll Ranger Station, 3801 Panoramic Hwy., at Pantoll Rd.* ☎ *415/388–2070* ⊕ *www.parks.ca.gov.*

NIGHTLIFE AND THE ARTS

☙ **Mountain Play.** Every May and June, locals tote overstuffed picnic baskets to the Mountain Theater to see the Mountain Play, popular musicals such as *The Music Man* and *My Fair Lady.* Depending on the play, this can be a great family activity. Summer 2013 marks the 100th anniversary of this Bay Area tradition. ⊠ *Richardson Blvd. off Panoramic Hwy.* ☎ *415/383–1100* ⊕ *www.mountainplay.org* ▱ *$40.*

STINSON BEACH

20 miles northwest of Golden Gate Bridge.

GETTING HERE AND AROUND

If you're driving, take the Highway 1–Stinson Beach exit off U.S. 101 and follow the road west and then north. The journey from San Francisco can take from 35 minutes to more than an hour, depending on traffic. By bus, take the 10, 70, or 80 to Marin City; in Marin City transfer to the West Marin Stagecoach. The intimate town is perfect for casual walking.

EXPLORING

☙ **Stinson Beach.** Stinson Beach is the most expansive stretch of sand in Marin County. It's as close (when the fog hasn't rolled in) as you can get to the stereotypical feel of a Southern California beach. ⚠ Swimming here is recommended only from early May through September, when lifeguards are on duty, because the undertow can be strong and shark sightings, although infrequent, aren't unusual. There are several clothing-optional areas (such as Red Rock Beach). On any hot summer weekend, every road to Stinson Beach is jam-packed, so factor this into your plans. The town itself is down to earth—like tonier Mill Valley, but more relaxed. ⊠ *1 Calle Del Sierra, off Shoreline Hwy. 1.*

WHERE TO EAT AND STAY

For expanded reviews, facilities, and current deals, visit Fodors.com.

$$ ✕ **Parkside Cafe.** The Parkside is popular for its beachfront snack bar
AMERICAN (cash only), but inside is Stinson's best restaurant, with classic Cal-cuisine offerings such as the day-boat-scallop and ceviche appetizers, and mains like the lamb with goat-cheese-stuffed red peppers. Breakfast is served until 2 pm. Creeping vines on the sunny patio shelter diners from the wind; for a cozier atmosphere eat by the fire in the dining room. ⑤ *Average main: $20* ⊠ *43 Arenal Ave., off Shoreline Hwy. 1* ☎ *415/868–1272.*

$ ✕ **Sand Dollar.** The town's oldest restaurant still attracts all the old salts
AMERICAN from Muir Beach to Bolinas, but these days they sip whiskey over an up-to-date bar or beneath market umbrellas on the spiffy deck. The food is good—try the panfried sand dabs (small flatfish) and pear salad with blue cheese—but the big draw is the lively atmosphere. Musicians play on weekends in summer, and on sunny afternoons the deck gets so packed that people sit on the fence rails sipping beer. ⑤ *Average main: $13* ⊠ *3458 Shoreline Hwy.* ☎ *415/868–0434* ⊘ *No lunch Tues. Nov.–Mar.*

$$ 🔲 **The Sandpiper.** Recharge, rest, and enjoy the local scenery at this
B&B/INN ultra-popular lodging that books up months, even years, in advance. **Pros:** bright rooms; lush gardens; minutes from the beach. **Cons:** not exactly on the beach; walls are thin. **TripAdvisor:** "hospitable," "ideal spot for quiet beach vacation," "peaceful getaway." ⑤ *Rooms from: $180* ⊠ *1 Marine Way, at Arenal Ave.* ☎ *415/868–1632* ⊕ *www.sandpiperstinsonbeach.com* ⤳ *10 rooms.*

BOLINAS

7 miles north of Stinson Beach.

The tiny town of Bolinas wears its 1960s idealism on its sleeve, attract-ing potters, poets, and peace lovers to its quiet streets. With a funky gallery, a general store selling organic produce, a café, and an offbeat saloon, the main thoroughfare, Wharf Road, looks like a hippie-fied version of Main Street, USA.

GETTING HERE AND AROUND

Bolinas isn't difficult to find: heading north from Stinson Beach follow Highway 1 west and then north. Make a left at the first road just past the Bolinas Lagoon (⊠ *Olema–Bolinas Rd.*), and then turn left at the stop sign. The road dead-ends smack-dab in the middle of town. By bus, take the 10, 70, or 80 to Marin City; in Marin City transfer to the West Marin Stagecoach. Walking is the only way to see this small town.

WHERE TO EAT

$$
AMERICAN

✕ **Coast Cafe.** Decked out in a nautical theme with surfboards and buoys, the dining room at the Coast serves dependably good American fare, including specials such as shepherd's pie, pot roast, local fresh fish, grass-fed steaks, and gorgeous salads. The café is open for breakfast on weekends. $ *Average main: $16* ⊠ *46 Wharf Rd., off Olema–Bolinas Rd.* ☎ *415/868–2298* ⊕ *www.bolinascafe.com.*

POINT REYES NATIONAL SEASHORE

Bear Valley Visitor Center is 12 miles northwest of Bolinas.

GETTING HERE AND AROUND

From San Francisco, take U.S. 101 north, head west at Sir Francis Drake Boulevard (Exit 450B), and follow the road just under 20 miles to Bear Valley Road. From Stinson Beach or Bolinas, drive north on Highway 1 and turn left on Bear Valley Road. If you're going by bus, take the 10, 70, or 80 to Marin City; in Marin City transfer to the West Marin Stagecoach. Once at the visitor center, the best way to get around is on foot.

EXPLORING

Fodor's Choice
★

Point Reyes National Seashore. One of the Bay Area's most spectacular treasures and the only national seashore on the West Coast, the 66,500-acre Point Reyes National Seashore encompasses hiking trails, secluded beaches, and rugged grasslands as well as Point Reyes itself, a triangular peninsula that juts into the Pacific. The town of **Point Reyes Station** is a quaint, one-main-drag affair, with a charming bakery, some good gift shops with locally made and imported goods, and a few places to eat. It's nothing fancy, but that's part of its relaxed charm.

When explorer Sir Francis Drake sailed along the California coast in 1579, he missed the Golden Gate and San Francisco Bay, but he did land at what he described as a convenient harbor, now thought to be Drake's Bay, which flanks the point on the east. Today Point Reyes's hills and dramatic cliffs attract other kinds of explorers: hikers, whale-watchers, and solitude seekers.

The infamous San Andreas Fault runs along the eastern edge of the park and up the center of Tomales Bay; take the short **Earthquake Trail** from the visitor center to see the impact near the epicenter of the 1906 earthquake that devastated San Francisco. A ½-mile path from the visitor center leads to **Kule Loklo,** a brilliantly reconstructed Miwok village that sheds light on the daily lives of the region's first inhabitants. From here, trails also lead to the park's free campgrounds (camping permits are required).

■ TIP→ In late winter and spring, take the short walk at Chimney Rock, just before the lighthouse, to the Elephant Seal Overlook. Even from the cliff, the male seals look enormous as they spar for resident females.

You can experience the diversity of Point Reyes's ecosystems on the scenic **Coast Trail,** which starts at the Palomarin Trailhead, just outside Bolinas. From here it's a 3-mile trek through eucalyptus groves and pine forests and along seaside cliffs to beautiful and tiny Bass Lake. To reach the Palomarin Trailhead, take Olema–Bolinas Road toward Bolinas, follow signs to the Point Reyes Bird Observatory, and then continue until the road dead-ends.

The 4.7-mile-long (one-way) **Tomales Point Trail** follows the spine of the park's northernmost finger of land through a Tule Elk Preserve, providing spectacular ocean views from the high bluffs. Expect to see elk, but keep your distance from the animals. To reach the fairly easy hiking trail, look for the Pierce Point Road turnoff on the right, just north of the town of Inverness; park at the end of the road by the old ranch buildings. ⊕ *www.nps.gov/pore.*

Bear Valley Visitor Center. The center's informative exhibits explain the park's wildlife and history. Rangers here dispense information about beaches, whale-watching, hiking trails, and camping. ⊠ *Bear Valley Visitor Center Access Rd., west of Hwy. 1* ☎ 415/464–5100 ⊕ *www. nps.gov/pore/planyourvisit* ☉ *Weekdays 9–5, weekends 8–5.*

Duxbury Reef. Mile-long Duxbury Reef is the largest shale intertidal reef in North America. Look for starfish, barnacles, sea anemones, purple urchins, limpets, sea mussels, and the occasional abalone. But check a tide table (⊕ *www.wrh.noaa.gov/mtr/marine.php*) or the local papers if you plan to explore the reef—it's accessible only at low tide. To get here, take Mesa Road and turn left onto Overlook Drive and then right on Elm Avenue.

Point Reyes Bird Observatory. Birders adore the observatory, which lies in the southernmost part of Point Reyes National Seashore and is accessed through Bolinas. (Those not interested in birds might find it ho-hum.) The compact visitor center has excellent interpretive exhibits, including a comparative display of real birds' talons, and the surrounding woods, well worth a visit, harbor more than 200 bird species. As you hike the quiet trails through forest and along ocean cliffs, you're likely to see biologists banding birds to aid in the study of their life cycles. ⊠ *Mesa Rd., Bolinas* ☎ 415/868–0655 ⊕ *www.prbo.org* ≊ *Free* ☉ *Daily 9–5.*

★
☾ **Point Reyes Lighthouse.** In operation since December 1, 1870, this lighthouse is one of the premier attractions of the Point Reyes National Seashore. It occupies the tip of Point Reyes, 22 miles from the Bear Valley Visitor Center, a scenic 45-minute drive over hills scattered with longtime cattle ranches. The lighthouse originally cast a rotating beam lighted by four wicks that burned lard oil. Keeping the wicks lighted and the lens soot-free in Point Reyes's perpetually foggy climate was a constant struggle that reputedly drove the early attendants to alcoholism and insanity. On busy whale-watching weekends (late December through mid-April), parking at the forged-iron-plate lighthouse may be restricted by park staff; on these days buses shuttle visitors from the Drakes Beach lot to the top of the stairs leading down to the lighthouse (bus $5, admission free). Once there, consider whether you have it in you to walk down—and up—the 308 steps to the lighthouse. The view from the bottom is worth the effort, but the whales are visible from the cliffs above the lighthouse. ⊠ *Western end of Sir Francis Drake Blvd.* ☎ 415/669–1534 ☉ *Thurs.–Mon. 10–4:30; weather lens room 2:30–4, except during very windy weather.*

WHERE TO EAT

$ ✕**Pine Cone Diner.** A block off the main drag, this oh-so-cute diner
AMERICAN serves great traditional breakfasts as well as Mexican specialties such
ⓒ as huevos rancheros. At lunch expect hearty homemade soups, fresh
salads, and thick sandwiches, all made with local, organic ingredients. ■TIP→ Kids love the outdoor picnic tables. Ⓢ *Average main: $11*
✉ *60 4th St., at B St., Point Reyes Station* ☎ *415/663–1536* ⊕ *www.
pineconediner.com* ⊗ *No dinner.*

$$ ✕**Station House Cafe.** In good weather, hikers fresh from the park fill
AMERICAN the Station House's garden to enjoy alfresco dining, and on weekends
there's not a spare seat on the banquettes in the dining room. The focus
is on local, seasonal, and sustainable food: oyster shooters, Niman
Ranch braised lamb, Californian white sea bass, and sweet bread pud-
ding are the standbys. The place is also open for breakfast, and there's
a full bar. Ⓢ *Average main: $22* ✉ *11180 Hwy. 1, Point Reyes Station*
☎ *415/663–1515* ⊕ *www.stationhousecafe.com* ⊗ *Closed Wed.*

$$$ ✕**Tomales Bay Foods.** A renovated hay barn off the main drag houses this
AMERICAN collection of food shops, a favorite stopover among Bay Area foodies.
★ Watch workers making Cowgirl Creamery cheese; then buy some at a
counter that sells exquisite artisanal cheeses from around the world.
Tomales Bay Foods showcases local organic fruits and vegetables and
premium packaged foods, and the kitchen turns the best ingredients
into creative sandwiches, salads, and soups. You can eat at a small café
table or on the lawn. The shops are open until 6 pm. Ⓢ *Average main:
$23* ✉ *80 4th St., at B. St., Point Reyes Station* ☎ *415/663–9335 cheese
shop, 415/663–8478 deli* ⊗ *Closed Mon. and Tues.*

WHERE TO STAY

For expanded reviews, facilities, and current deals, visit Fodors.com.

$$$$ 🏨**Manka's Inverness Lodge.** Chef-owner Margaret Grade takes rustic
B&B/INN fantasy to extravagant heights in her 1917 hunting lodge and cabins,
Fodor's Choice where mica-shaded lamps cast an amber glow, and bearskin rugs warm
★ wide-planked floors. **Pros:** extremely romantic, remote and quiet. **Cons:**
no on-site restaurant; sounds from neighboring room are easily heard.
TripAdvisor: "pristine oasis in Inverness," "rustic luxury," "relaxed
setting." Ⓢ *Rooms from: $450* ✉ *30 Callendar Way, at Argyle Way,
Inverness* ☎ *415/669–1034* ⊕ *www.mankas.com* ⇆ *8 rooms, 1 boathouse, 4 cabins.*

$$$$ 🏨**Olema Druids Hall.** Set on a quiet hill beneath towering eucalyptus
B&B/INN trees, the inn, built in 1885 as a meeting hall for the Ancient Order
of Druids, now holds gorgeously appointed rooms, each of which
seems like a designer showcase. **Pros:** heated hardwood floors; wood-
burning fireplaces. **Cons:** not much to do at night; some traffic noise.
TripAdvisor: "comfortable luxury," "old-world heaven," "casual and
comfortable." Ⓢ *Rooms from: $325* ✉ *9870 Shoreline Hwy., Box 96,
Olema* ☎ *415/663–8727, 866/554–4255* ⊕ *www.olemadruidshall.com*
⇆ *3 rooms, 1 suite, 1 cottage* ❙◉❙ *Breakfast.*

$$$ 🏨**Olema Inn & Restaurant.** Built in 1876, this inn retains all of its 19th-
B&B/INN century architectural charm but has been decorated in a sophisticated,
uncluttered style. **Pros:** great restaurant; magnificent scenery. **Cons:** no
elevator means carrying your luggage up the stairs; the carpets need to

9

DID YOU KNOW?

The majestic Point Reyes
National Seashore offers
many attractions for nature
lovers: hiking, bird-watching,
camping, or whale-watching
depending on the season.
But flower picking isn't an
approved activity; the wild
flowers here are protected.

be replaced. **TripAdvisor:** "clean and quiet," "amazing hospitality," "largely very nice." $ *Rooms from: $222* ✉ *10000 Sir Francis Drake Blvd., Olema* ☎ *415/663–9559* ⊕ *www.theolemainn.com* �'t *6 rooms* ⊙ *Closed Tues. No lunch weekdays.*

$$
B&B/INN

⌐ **Ten Inverness Way.** This is the kind of down-to-earth place where you sit around after breakfast and share tips for hiking Point Reyes or linger around the living room with its stone fireplace and library. **Pros:** great base for exploring nearby wilderness; peaceful garden and friendly staff. **Cons:** overly folksy decor; some rooms are on the small side; poor cell-phone reception. **TripAdvisor:** "romantic," "great host," "lovely setting." $ *Rooms from: $182* ✉ *10 Inverness Way, Inverness* ☎ *415/669–1648* ⊕ *www.teninvernessway.com* ➮ *4 rooms, 1 suite.*

SPORTS AND THE OUTDOORS

Blue Waters Kayaking. This outfit rents kayaks and offers tours and lessons. ✉ *12938 Sir Francis Drake Blvd., Inverness* ☎ *415/669–2600* ⊕ *www.bwkayak.com.*

Five Brooks Stable. Tour guides here lead horse rides lasting from one to six hours; trails from the stable wind through Point Reyes National Seashore and along the beaches. ✉ *8001 Hwy. 1, north of town, Olema* ☎ *415/663–1570* ⊕ *www.fivebrooks.com* ➯ *$40–$240.*

THE EAST BAY

When San Franciscans refer to it, the East Bay often means nothing more than what you can see across the bay from the city—mainly Oakland and Berkeley, both of which are in Alameda County. In fact, the East Bay stretches north and east of Alameda to Contra Costa County, which itself has emerged as a powerful business nexus.

OAKLAND

Directly east of Bay Bridge.

Often overshadowed by San Francisco's beauty and Berkeley's storied counterculture, Oakland's allure lies in its amazing diversity. Here you can find a Nigerian clothing store, a beautifully renovated Victorian home, a Buddhist meditation center, and a lively salsa club, all within the same block. Oakland's multifaceted nature reflects its colorful and often tumultuous history. Once a cluster of Mediterranean-style homes and gardens that served as a bedroom community for San Francisco, the city became a hub of shipbuilding and industry almost overnight when the United States entered World War II. New jobs in the city's shipyards and factories attracted thousands of workers, including some of the first female welders, and the city's neighborhoods were imbued with a proud but gritty spirit. In the 1960s and '70s this intense community pride gave rise to such militant groups as the Black Panther Party and the Symbionese Liberation Army, but they were little match for the economic hardships and racial tensions that plagued Oakland. In many neighborhoods the reality was widespread poverty and gang violence—subjects that dominated the songs of such Oakland-bred rappers as the late Tupac Shakur. The highly publicized protests of the Occupy Oakland movement in 2011 and 2012 illustrated just how much Oakland remains a mosaic of its past.

The affluent reside in the city's hillside homes, which provide a warmer, more spacious, and more affordable alternative to San Francisco, and a constant flow of newcomers—many from Central America and Asia—ensures continued diversity, vitality, and growing pains. Many neighborhoods to the west and south of the city center remain run-down and unsafe, but a renovated downtown area—sparking a vibrant arts scene—and the thriving though sterile Jack London Square have injected new energy into the city.

Everyday life here revolves around the neighborhood, with a main business strip attracting both shoppers and strollers. In some areas, such as high-end Piedmont and Rockridge, you'd swear you were in Berkeley or San Francisco's Noe Valley or Cow Hollow. These are perfect places for browsing, eating, or just relaxing between sightseeing trips to Oakland's architectural gems, rejuvenated waterfront, and numerous green spaces. Between Rockridge and Piedmont and to the west, you can find the Temescal District, along Telegraph Avenue just south of 51st Street, where interesting eateries and shops are beginning to congregate.

ESSENTIALS

Visitor InformationOakland Convention and Visitors Bureau ⊠ *463 11th St.* ☎ *510/839–9000* ⊕ *www.oaklandcvb.com.*

GETTING HERE AND AROUND

Driving from San Francisco, take Interstate 80 East across the Bay Bridge, then take Interstate 580 to the Grand Avenue exit for Lake Merritt. To reach downtown and the waterfront, take Interstate 980 from Interstate 580 and exit at 12th Street.

By BART, use the Lake Merritt Station for the Oakland Museum and southern Lake Merritt; the Oakland City Center–12th Street Station for downtown, Chinatown, and Old Oakland; and the 19th Street Station for the Paramount Theatre and the north side of Lake Merritt.

By bus, take the AC Transit's C and P lines to get to Piedmont in Oakland. The O bus stops at the edge of Chinatown near downtown Oakland. Once you arrive, be aware of how quickly neighborhoods can change. Walking is safe and advised downtown as well as in the Piedmont and Rockridge areas, but avoid walking west and south of downtown.

EXPLORING

Chinatown. Across Broadway from Old Oakland but worlds apart, Chinatown is a densely packed, bustling neighborhood. Unlike its San Francisco counterpart, Oakland's Chinatown makes no concessions to tourists; you won't find baskets of trinkets lining the sidewalk and souvenir displays in the shop windows. But supermarkets such as **Yuen Hop Noodle Company and Asian Food Products** (⊠ *824 Webster St.*), open since 1931, overflow with goodies. And the line for sweets, breads, and towering cakes snakes out the door of **Napoleon Super Bakery** (⊠ *810 Franklin St.*).

Fox Theater. The Fox Theater, an art-deco movie palace built in 1928, sat decaying and mostly unused for decades until the last of several redevelopment schemes culminated in a stunning renovation. The Mediterranean Moorish–style Fox and its attached buildings contain the main theater, these days used for music concerts; a charter arts school; and a restaurant space. The theater's restoration helped revive what's known as the Uptown neighborhood. ⊠ *1807 Telegraph Ave., at 18th St., Uptown* ⊕ *www.thefoxoakland.com.*

Jack London Square. Shops, restaurants, small museums, and historic sites line Jack London Square, which is named after one of California's best-known authors; London wrote *The Call of the Wild* and *The Sea Wolf,* among many other books. When he lived in Oakland, he spent many a day boozing and brawling in the waterfront area, most notably at the tiny, wonderful **Heinold's First and Last Chance Saloon** (⊠ *48 Webster St., at Embarcadero West* ☏ *510/839–6761*). The saloon has been serving since 1883, although it's a little worse for wear since the 1906 earthquake. Next door is the Klondike cabin in which London spent a summer in the late 1890s. The cabin was moved from Alaska and reassembled here in 1970.

■TIP➜ The square is an obvious spot for tourists to visit and it's worth a peek if you take a ferry that docks here; to really get a feel for Oakland,

A fun place to wet your whistle, Heinold's First and Last Chance Saloon

though, you're better off browsing downtown, or at least in Rockridge. ✉ *Embarcadero West at Broadway* ☎ *866/295–9853* ⊕ *www. jacklondonsquare.com.*

Lake Merritt. Joggers and power-walkers charge along the 3-mile path that encircles this 155-acre natural saltwater lake in downtown Oakland. Crew teams often glide across the water, and boatmen guide snuggling couples in authentic Venetian gondolas. **Lakeside Park,** which surrounds the north side of Lake Merritt, has several outdoor attractions, including a cute children's park and a waterfowl refuge. Herons, egrets, geese, and ducks nest here in spring and summer, and migrating birds pass through from September through February. Year-round, you can watch birds being fed daily at 3:30 pm. Look for the sign that says "Sailboat House, Gondola Servizio." Gondola fares start at $40 per couple for 30 minutes. ✉ *Lakeside Park, Bellevue and Grand Aves.*

★ **Oakland Museum of California.** One of Oakland's top attractions, the
☺ museum showcases the state's art, history, and natural wonders in absorbing, detailed exhibits. You can travel through myriad ecosystems in the Natural Sciences Gallery, from the sand dunes of the Pacific to the coyotes and brush of the Nevada border. Kids love the lifelike wild-animal exhibits, especially the snarling wolverine, big-eyed harbor seal, and trove of hidden creatures. The rambling Cowell Hall of California History includes everything from Spanish-era armor to a small but impressive collection of vintage vehicles, including a gorgeous, candy-apple-red "Mystery" car from the 1960s and a gleaming red, gold, and silver fire engine that battled the flames in San Francisco in 1906. The Gallery of California Art holds an eclectic collection of modern works

Oakland

and early landscapes. Of particular interest are paintings by Richard Diebenkorn, Joan Brown, Elmer Bischoff, and David Park, all members of the Bay Area Figurative School, which flourished here after World War II. Fans of Dorothea Lange won't want to miss the gallery's comprehensive collection of her work. The museum also has a sculpture garden with a view of the Oakland and Berkeley hills in the distance. ✉ *1000 Oak St., at 10th St.* ☎ *510/238–2200* ⊕ *www.museumca.org* 💵 *$12, free 1st Sun. of month* ⊙ *Wed.–Sun. 11–5.*

Old Oakland. In the shadow of the convention center and towering downtown hotels, Old Oakland was once a booming business district. Today the restored Victorian storefronts lining four historic blocks house restaurants, cafés, shops, galleries, and a lively three-block farmers' market, which takes place Friday morning. Architectural consistency distinguishes the area from surrounding streets and lends it a distinct neighborhood feel. The Italian grocer **Ratto's International Market** (✉ *827 Washington St.* ☎ *510/832–6503*) has been in business for more than a century. Stop in for a deli sandwich there, or head over to the genial **Pacific Coast Brewing Company** (✉ *906 Washington St.* ☎ *510/836–2739*) for a microbrew on the patio.

★ **Paramount Theatre.** Some truly stunning examples of late art-deco architecture can be found in the Uptown (but still downtown) neighborhood around the 19th Street BART station. Some of these buildings have fallen into disrepair, but the Paramount Theatre, perhaps the most glorious art-deco specimen in the city, if not the entire Bay Area, still operates as a venue for concerts and performances of all kinds, from the Oakland East Bay Symphony to Tom Waits and Elvis Costello. You can take a two-hour tour of the building, which starts near the box office on 21st Street at 10 am on the first and third Saturday of each month. ⊠ *2025 Broadway, at 20th St., Uptown* ☏ *510/465–6400* ⊕ *www.paramounttheatre.com* ⊠ *Tour $5.*

Rockridge. The upscale neighborhood of Rockridge is one of Oakland's most desirable places to live. Explore the tree-lined streets that radiate out from **College Avenue** just north and south of the Rockridge BART station for a look at California bungalow architecture at its finest. By day College Avenue between Broadway and Alcatraz Avenue is crowded with shoppers buying fresh flowers, used books, and clothing; by night the same folks are back for dinner and locally brewed ales in the numerous restaurants and pubs. With its pricey specialty-food shops, **Market Hall,** an airy European-style marketplace at Shafter Avenue, is a hub of culinary activity.

WHERE TO EAT

$$
MEDITERRANEAN

✕ **À Côté.** This place for Mediterranean food is all about small plates, cozy tables, family-style eating—and truly excellent food. The butternut-squash ravioli, Alsatian goose sausage, and pear-and-walnut flat bread are all lovely choices. And you won't find a better plate of pommes frites anywhere. The restaurant offers more than 40 wines by the glass. Desserts here are tempting: try the warm crème-fraîche pound cake with apple confit, vanilla ice cream, and huckleberry sauce or a tangy pomegranate sorbet. The heavy wooden tables, cool tiles, and natural light make this a coveted destination for students, families, couples, and after-work crowds. ⓢ *Average main: $18* ⊠ *5478 College Ave., at Taft Ave., Rockridge* ☏ *510/655–6469* ⌖ *Reservations not accepted* ⊗ *No lunch.*

$
AMERICAN

✕ **Brown Sugar Kitchen.** Chef and owner Tanya Holland uses local, organic, and seasonal products to craft meals influenced by her African-American heritage and her culinary education in France. Holland blends sweet and savory flavors like no one else, and pairs her dishes with well-chosen wines. The dining room is fresh and bright, with a long, sleek counter, red-leather stools, and spacious booths and tables. This is *the* place to come for chicken and waffles. ⓢ *Average main: $13* ⊠ *2534 Mandela Pkwy., at 26th St., West Oakland* ☏ *510/839–7685* ⊕ *www.brownsugarkitchen.com* ⊗ *Closed Mon. No dinner.*

$$$
AMERICAN

✕ **Camino.** The first solo venture of chef-owner Russell Moore (a Chez Panisse alum of 21 years) and co-owner Allison Hopelain focuses on simple, seasonal, and straightforward dishes cooked in the enormous, crackling *camino* (Italian for "fireplace"). Everything is made with top-notch ingredients, including local sardines; grilled lamb and sausage with shell beans; and grilled white sea bass with green beans and new potatoes. The menu changes nightly and includes vegetarian options such as eggplant gratin. The restaurant is decorated in a Craftsman-meets-refectory style, with brick walls and two long redwood communal tables. Seasonally inspired cocktails from the small bar are not to be missed; the gin-based drink with house-made cherry and hibiscus bitters is notably delicious. Ⓢ *Average main: $24* ✉ *3917 Grand Ave., at Boulevard Way, Lake Merritt* ☎ *510/547–5035* ⊙ *Closed Tues. No lunch (weekend brunch 10–2).*

$$ **MEXICAN** ✕ **Doña Tomás.** A neighborhood favorite, this spot in Oakland's up-and-coming Temescal District serves seasonal Mexican fare to a hip but low-key crowd. Mexican textiles and art adorn walls in two long rooms; there's also a vine-covered patio. Banish all images of taquería grub and tuck into starters such as quesadillas filled with butternut squash and goat cheese and entrées such as *albondigas en sopa de zanahoria* (pork-and-beef meatballs in carrot puree). A fine selection of tequilas rounds out the offerings. Ⓢ *Average main: $18* ✉ *5004 Telegraph Ave., near 51st St.* ☎ *510/450–0522* ⊙ *Closed Sun. and Mon. No lunch.*

$ **CAFÉ** ✕ **L'Amyx Tea Bar.** Light through the large windows bathes the blond-wood tables, comfy chairs, and long bar, all filled with absorbed students, chatting friends, and tired shoppers in need of a boost. A small area in the back sells first-rate tea accoutrements, but sink into a couch or private nook to bask in much more than the usual cuppa. Try a tea smoothie or an herbal remedy such as Tealaxation. Ⓢ *Average main: $4* ✉ *4179 Piedmont Ave., at Linda Ave., Piedmont* ☎ *510/594–8322.*

$ **VIETNAMESE** ✕ **Le Cheval Restaurant.** This is a good place to sample *pho,* Hanoi-style beef noodle soup fragrant with star anise. Other entrées include lemon chicken, cubed beef steak, clay-pot snapper, and shark in coconut milk. It's hard to spend more than $20 for an entire meal unless you order the special crab (about $30). The complementary mini-bowls of soup that are placed on the table as soon as you sit down are a great balm to hungry diners although service is lightning-quick anyway. Ⓢ *Average main: $12* ✉ *1019 Clay St., at 11th St., Downtown* ☎ *510/763–8495* ⊙ *No lunch Sun.*

$$ **BELGIAN** ✕ **Luka's Taproom & Lounge.** Luka's is a real taste of downtown Oakland: hip and urban, with an unpretentious vibe. Diners nibble on *frites* any Belgian would embrace and entrées like *choucroute garni* (sauerkraut with duck confit, ham hock, and pork shoulder). The brews draw 'em in, too—you'd be hard-pressed to find a larger selection of Belgian beer this side of the pond—and the DJs in the adjacent lounge keep the scene going late. Ⓢ *Average main: $22* ✉ *2221 Broadway, at West Grand Ave., Lake Merritt* ☎ *510/451–4677* ⊙ *No lunch Sat.*

$$$ **MEDITERRANEAN** ✕ **Oliveto Cafe & Restaurant.** Respected chef Jonah Rhodehamel is at the helm of this locally renowned eatery that anchors Market Hall in the Rockridge neighborhood. The first-class dining room upstairs serves straightforward Italian cuisine; the menu changes daily, but might include house-made duck prosciutto, pan-seared swordfish, or spit-roasted leg of lamb. Downstairs, in the less pricey café ($–$$), everything from a morning espresso to pizza to a full-blown Italian meal (at half the upstairs price) can be enjoyed at one of the small tables or at the bar. Ⓢ *Average main: $26* ✉ *5655 College Ave., at Keith Ave., Rockridge* ☎ *510/547–5356* ⊙ *No lunch weekends in restaurant.*

WHERE TO STAY
For expanded reviews, facilities, and current deals, visit Fodors.com.

$$
HOTEL

⊞ **Waterfront Hotel.** One of Oakland's more appealing neighborhoods is home to this thoroughly modern waterfront hotel. **Pros:** great location; dog-friendly. **Cons:** passing trains can be noisy; parking is pricey. **TripAdvisor:** "stylish remodel," "great customer service," "warm friendly charm." ⑤ *Rooms from: $159* ⊠ *10 Washington St., Jack London Square* ☎ *510/836–3800, 800/729–3638* ⊕ *www.waterfrontplaza.com* ⤴ *143 rooms.*

NIGHTLIFE AND THE ARTS

Artists have found cheap rent and loft spaces in Oakland, giving rise to an underground cultural scene—visual arts, indie music, spoken word, film—that is definitely buzzing, especially in Uptown (which is pretty much downtown). Trendy bars and clubs have also emerged—everything from artisan breweries to all-out retro dives. The nightlife scene here is less crowded and more intimate than what you'll find in San Francisco. Music is just about everywhere, though the most popular venues are downtown.

Fodor's Choice
★

Café van Kleef. Dutch artist Peter van Kleef's candle-strewn, funky café-bar crackles with creative energy. Van Kleef has a lot to do with the convivial atmosphere; the garrulous owner loves sharing tales about his quirky, floor-to-ceiling collection of mementos, including what he claims are Cassius Clay's boxing gloves and Dorothy's ruby slippers. The café also has a consistently solid calendar of live music, heavy on the jazz side. The drinks are quite possibly the stiffest in town. ⊠ *1621 Telegraph Ave., between 16th and 17th Sts., Lake Merritt* ☎ *510/763-7711* ⊕ *www.cafevankleef.com.*

Fox Theater. Willie Nelson, Counting Crows, Rebelution, and Rodrigo Y Gabriela and their band C.U.B.A. have all been booked at this recently renovated art-deco stunner that has good sight lines, a state-of-the-art sound system and acoustics, and bars and other amenities aplenty. ⊠ *1807 Telegraph Ave., at 18th St., Uptown* ☎ *510/548–3010* ⊕ *www.thefoxoakland.com.*

The Layover Music Bar and Lounge. Bright, bold, and very hip, this hangout filled with recycled furniture is constantly evolving because everything is for sale, from the artwork to the pillows, rugs, and lamps. The busy bar serves up organic cocktails, and depending on the night, the entertainment might include comedy or live or DJ music. ⊠ *1517 Franklin St., near 15th St., Uptown* ☎ *510/763-7711* ⊕ *www.oaklandlayover.com.*

Mua. Cuisine, cocktails, and culture—Mua puts it all together in a bright and airy former garage: The chefs serve up beautifully crafted meals like softshell crab and duck confit; the bartenders shake up elegant cocktails; and the rich cultural offerings include poetry readings, art shows, DJ music, and more. ⊠ *2442a Webster St., between 16th and 17th Sts., Uptown* ☎ *510/238–1100* ⊕ *www.muaoakland.com.*

Paramount Theatre. The art-deco movie palace is home to the Oakland East Bay Symphony and also presents ballet, comedy (Cedric, Sinbad, Bill Cosby), well-known rock and other musical acts, and the occasional classic film. ⊠ *2025 Broadway, at 20th St., Uptown* ☎ *510/465–6400* ⊕ *www.paramounttheatre.com.*

The Trappist. Grand pillars, brick walls, soft lighting, and the buzz of conversation set a warm and mellow tone inside this Victorian space that's been renovated to resemble a traditional Belgian pub. The setting is definitely a draw, but the real stars are the artisan beers: more than a hundred Belgian, Dutch, and North American ones. The light fare includes panini made with organic ingredients. ⊠ *460 8th St., at Broadway, Old Oakland* ☎ *510/238–8900* ⊕ *www.thetrappist.com.*

Fodor'sChoice **Yoshi's.** Oma Sosa and Charlie Hunter are among the musicians who
★ play at Yoshi's, one of the area's best jazz venues. Monday through Saturday shows start at 8 pm and 10 pm; Sunday shows usually start at 2 pm and 8 pm. The cover runs from $16 to $30. ⊠ *510 Embarcadero St., between Washington and Clay Sts., Jack London Square* ☎ *510/238–9200* ⊕ *www.yoshis.com.*

SPORTS AND THE OUTDOORS

BASEBALL

Oakland A's. Billy Beane of *Moneyball* fame is the general manager of the American League baseball team. Same-day tickets can usually be purchased at the **O.co Coliseum** box office (Gate D). To get to the game, take a BART train to the Coliseum/Oakland Airport Station. ⊠ *O.co Coliseum, 7000 Coliseum Way, off I–880, north of Hegenberger Rd.* ☎ *510/638–4900* ⊕ *oakland.athletics.mlb.com.*

BASKETBALL

Golden State Warriors. The National Basketball Association's Golden State Warriors play at the **Oracle Arena** from November through April. You can take a BART train to the game. Get off at the Coliseum/Oakland Airport Station. Warriors tickets are available through **Ticketmaster** (☎ *800/653-8000* ⊕ *www.ticketmaster.com*). ⊠ *Oracle Arena, 7000 Coliseum Way, off I–880, north of Hegenberger Rd.* ☎ *510/986–2200, 888/479–4667* ⊕ *www.nba.com/warriors.*

FOOTBALL

Oakland Raiders. The National Football League's brawling Oakland Raiders play at **O.co Coliseum.** Purchase Raiders tickets through **Tickets.com** (☎ *800/653-8000* ⊕ *www.tickets.com*); except for high-profile games, they're easy to come by. ⊠ *O.co Coliseum, 7000 Coliseum Way, off I–880, north of Hegenberger Rd.* ☎ *510/864–5000* ⊕ *www.raiders. com.*

SHOPPING

College Avenue is great for upscale strolling, shopping, and people-watching. The more casual streets around Lake Merritt and Grand Lake have smaller, less fancy boutiques.

Diesel. Wandering bibliophiles collect armfuls of the latest fiction and nonfiction here. The loftlike space, with its high ceilings and spare design, encourages airy contemplation, and on chilly days (a rarity) there's a fire going in the hearth. Keep an eye out for the excellent reading series. ⊠ *5433 College Ave., at Kales Ave., Rockridge* ☎ *510/653–9965.*

Maison d'Etre. Close to the Rockridge BART station, this store epitomizes the Rockridge neighborhood's funky-chic shopping scene. Look for impulse buys like whimsical watches, imported fruit-tea blends, and a basket of funky slippers near the back. ✉ *5640 College Ave., at Keith Ave., Rockridge* ☎ *510/658–2801.*

BERKELEY

2 miles northeast of Bay Bridge.

The birthplace of the Free Speech Movement, the radical hub of the 1960s, the home of arguably the nation's top public university, and the city whose government condemned the bombing of Afghanistan—Berkeley is all of those things. The city of 100,000 facing San Francisco across the bay is also culturally diverse, a breeding ground for social trends, a bastion of the counterculture, and an important center for Bay Area writers, artists, and musicians. Berkeley residents, students, and faculty spend hours nursing various coffee concoctions while they read, discuss, and debate at any of the dozens of cafés that surround the campus. Oakland may have Berkeley beat when it comes to cutting-edge arts, and the city may have forfeited some of its renegade 1960s spirit, as some residents say, but unless a guy in a hot-pink satin body suit, skullcap, and cape rides a unicycle around *your* town, you'll likely find that Berkeley remains plenty offbeat.

It's the quintessential university town, and many who graduated years ago still bask in daily intellectual conversation, great weather, and good food. Residents will walk out of their way to go to the perfect bread shop or consult with their favorite wine merchant. And every September, residents gently lampoon themselves during the annual "How Berkeley Can You Be?" parade and festival where they celebrate their tie-dyed past and consider its new incarnations.

ESSENTIALS

Visitor Information Berkeley Convention and Visitors Bureau ✉ *2030 Addison St., #102* ☎ *510/549–7040* ⊕ *www.visitberkeley.com.*

GETTING HERE AND AROUND

BART is the easiest way to get to Berkeley from San Francisco. Alight at the Berkeley (not North Berkeley) Station, and walk a block up Center Street to get to the western edge of campus. AC Transit buses F and FS lines stop near the university and 4th Street shopping. By car, take Interstate 80 east across the Bay Bridge then take the University Avenue exit through downtown Berkeley to the campus or take the Ashby Avenue exit and turn left on Telegraph Avenue to the traditional campus entrance. Once you arrive, explore on foot. Berkeley is very pedestrian friendly.

EXPLORING

4th Street. An industrial area on 4th Street north of University Avenue has been converted into a pleasant shopping stretch, with popular eateries and shops selling handcrafted and eco-conscious goods. About six blocks long, this compact area (the action has spilled onto neighboring streets) is busiest on bright weekend afternoons. Stained Glass Garden, Hear Music, and the Crate and Barrel Outlet are among shoppers' favorites, along with a mini-slew of upscale boutiques and wonderful paper stores. ✉ *4th St., between University Ave. and Delaware Sts.*

Cheese Board Pizzeria. With a jazz combo playing in the storefront and a long line snaking down the block, Cheese Board taps into the pulse of the Gourmet Ghetto. The cooperatively owned takeout spot draws devoted customers with the smell of just-baked garlic, fresh vegetables, and perfect sauces. For just a nibble, bakery–cheese shop next door sells cookies, muffins, scones, bialys—you name it, they bake it. ✉ *1504–1512 Shattuck Ave., at Vine St.* ☎ *510/549-3055* ⊙ *Tues.–Fri. 11:30–2 and 4:30–7, Sat. 11:30–3.*

QUICK BITES

Elmwood. Shops and cafés pack two pleasant blocks of College Avenue in the Elmwood neighborhood south of the U.C. campus. You'll know you're here when you see the logo for the beloved art-house cinema and performance space, the **Elmwood theater,** near College and Ashby avenues, though you're just as apt to see a line snaking outside nearby **Ici Ice Cream,** at 2948 College. All the treats here are made on the premises. While you're waiting, check out the architectural details of the nearby pre–World War II storefronts. Century-old shingled houses line the tree-shaded streets nearby. ✉ *College Ave. between Russell and Webster Sts., Elmwood.*

9

Gourmet Ghetto. The success of Chez Panisse restaurant attracted other food-related enterprises to its stretch of Shattuck Avenue, and the area surrounding the intersection of Shattuck and Vine Street became known as the Gourmet Ghetto. If you love food at all, it's worth a couple of hours to poke around the food shops and grab a quick bite or a full meal at one of the neighborhood's eateries. Of special note are the small food stands of **Epicurious Garden,** at 1509–1513 Shattuck, which sell everything from sushi to gelato. Outside, you can find a terraced garden—the best place to sit—that winds up four levels and ends at the **Imperial Tea Court.** Around the corner on Vine Street is **Walnut Square,** whose shops include **Love at First Bite,** a cupcakery that sells scrumptious confections. Across Vine Street from Walnut Square, the **Vintage Berkeley** wineshop occupies the historic former pump house at No. 2113; the offerings here are shrewdly selected and reasonably priced. Coffee lovers of the Peet's persuasion may want to pay brief respects at No. 2124, at Walnut Street, where the famed roaster got its start and still maintains a presence. In the block north of Vine Street on Shattuck is popular **Saul's** deli and restaurant, and **Cheese Board Pizzeria** is across Shattuck from Epicurious Garden. We could go on, but you get the idea. ⊠ *Shattuck Ave. between Cedar and Rose Sts., North Berkeley* ⊕ *www.gourmetghetto.org.*

Telegraph Avenue. Berkeley's student-oriented thoroughfare, Telegraph Avenue is the best place to get a dose of the city's famed counterculture. On any given day you might encounter a troop of chanting Hare Krishnas or a drumming band of Rastafarians. First and foremost, however, Telegraph is a place for socializing and shopping, the only uniquely Berkeley shopping experience in town and a definite don't-miss. ■TIP→ **Take care at night, as things get edgier on Telegraph. The nearby People's Park, mostly harmless by day, is best avoided after sunset.** Cafés, bookstores, poster shops, and street vendors line the avenue. T-shirt vendors and tarot-card readers come and go on a whim, but a few establishments—**Rasputin Music** (No. 2401), **Amoeba Music** (No. 2455), and **Moe's Books** (No. 2476)—are neighborhood landmarks. Allen Ginsberg wrote his acclaimed poem "Howl" at **Caffe Mediterraneum** (No. 2475), a relic of 1960s-era café culture that also lays claim to inventing the café latte.

★ **Tilden Regional Park.** The **Regional Parks Botanic Garden** is the star of
☼ this beautiful 2,000-acre park to the east of the Cal campus. Botanically speaking, a stroll through the garden, which focuses on native plants of California, provides a whirlwind tour of the entire state. You can pick up information about Tilden's other attractions, including its picnic spots, Lake Anza swimming site, golf course, and hiking trails (the paved **Nimitz Way** is a popular hike with wonderful views) at the garden's visitors center. Children love Tilden Park's miniature steam trains; Little Farm, where kids can feed the animals; and the vintage carousel with wooden animals. ⊠ *Regional Parks Botanic Garden, Wildcat Canyon Rd. and South Park Dr., Tilden Park* ☎ *510/544–2747* ⊕ *www.ebparks.org/parks/tilden* ⊡ *Free to park and botanic garden* ☉ *Daily 8 am–10 pm.*

University of California. The founding campus of California's university system, chartered in 1868, sits on a rising plain of oak trees split by Strawberry Creek. Frederick Law Olmsted, who designed New York City's Central Park, proposed the first campus plan. University architects over the years have included Bernard Maybeck as well as Julia Morgan, who designed Hearst Castle at San Simeon. The central campus occupies 178 acres, bounded by Bancroft Way to the south, Hearst Avenue to the north, Oxford Street to the west, and Gayley Road to the east. With more than 30,000 students and a full-time faculty of 1,400, the university, known simply as "Cal," is one of the leading intellectual centers in the United States and a major site for scientific research.

The **Berkeley Visitor Information Center** (⊠ *University Hall, Room 101, 2200 University Ave., at Oxford St.* ☎ *510/642–5215* ☉ *Weekdays 8:30–4:30*) is the starting point for the free, student-guided tours of the campus, which last 1½ hours and start at 10 on weekdays. (Weekend tours depart from Sather Tower.)

Student-guided campus tours leave from **Sather Tower** (⊠ *South of University Dr.* 🎫 *$2* ☉ *Weekdays 10–4, Sat. 10–5, Sun. 10–1:30 and 3–5*), the campus landmark popularly known as the Campanile, at 10 on Saturday and 1 on Sunday. The 307-foot structure, modeled on St. Mark's Tower in Venice and completed in 1914, can be seen for miles. The carillon is played daily at 7:50 am, noon, and 6 pm and for an extended 45-minute concert Sunday at 2. Take the elevator up 175 feet; then walk another 38 steps to the observation deck for a view of the campus and a close-up look at the iron bells, each of which weighs up to 10,500 pounds.

Sproul Plaza (⊠ *Telegraph Ave. and Bancroft Way*), just inside the U.C. Berkeley campus border on Bancroft Way, was the site of several free-speech and civil-rights protests in the 1960s. Today a lively panorama of political and social activists, musicians, and students show off Berkeley's flair for the bizarre. Preachers orate atop milk crates, amateur entertainers bang on makeshift drum sets, and protesters distribute leaflets about everything from marijuana to the Middle East. No matter what the combination, on weekdays when school is in swing, it always feels like a carnival. ■TIP➔ **Walk through at noon for the liveliest show of student spirit.**

The collection at the **University of California, Berkeley Art Museum & Pacific Film Archive** (⊠ *2626 Bancroft Way, between College Ave. and Bowditch St.* ☎ *510/642–0808, 510/642–1124 film-program information* ⊕ *www.bampfa.berkeley.edu* 🎫 *$10, free 1st Thurs. of month* ☉ *Wed.–Sun. 11–5, Fri. 11–9*) spans five centuries. Look for Jonathan Borofsky's enormous orange-red *Hammering Man* sculpture, which can be seen from the outside through the museum's floor-to-ceiling windows. Among the other noteworthy holdings here are a series of vibrant paintings by abstract expressionist Hans Hofmann. The downstairs galleries, which house rotating exhibits, are always free. The museum's raw foods café is famous, and you can also find some cooked options, too. The Pacific Film Archive, on the ground floor, has a library and hosts programs about historic and contemporary films, but its main theater sits across the street at 2575 Bancroft Way, near Bowditch Street.

Thanks to Berkeley's temperate climate, about 13,500 species of plants from all over the world flourish in the 34-acre **University of California Botanical Garden** (⊠ *200 Centennial Dr.* ☎ *510/643–2755* ⊕ *botanicalgarden.berkeley.edu* ⊒ *$9, free 1st Thurs. of month* ⊙ *Daily 9–5. Closed 1st Tues. of month*). Free garden tours are given Thursday, Saturday, and Sunday at 1:30. Benches and shady picnic tables make this a relaxing place to take in breathtaking views.

A TASTING TOUR

For an unforgettable foodie experience, take Lisa Rogovin's **Culinary Walking Tour** (☎ *510/540-6444* ⊕ *www.gourmetghetto.org*). You'll taste your way through the Gourmet Ghetto, learn some culinary history, and meet the chefs behind the food. Tours run Thursday 11 am–2:15 pm and cost $75 per person.

At this dazzling hands-on **Lawrence Hall of Science** (⊠ *Centennial Dr. near Grizzly Peak Blvd.* ☎ *510/642–5132* ⊕ *www.lawrencehallofscience.org* ⊒ *$12* ⊙ *Daily 10–5*), kids can look at insects under microscopes, solve crimes using chemical forensics, and explore the physics of baseball. On weekends there are special lectures, demonstrations, and planetarium shows. Popular (and free) stargazing sessions take place on the first and third Saturday of each month, weather permitting.

⊕ *www.berkeley.edu.*

WHERE TO EAT

Dining in Berkeley is a low-key affair; even in the finest restaurants, most folks dress casually. Late diners be forewarned: Berkeley is an "early to bed" kind of town.

$
SOUTHERN

✕ **Angeline's Louisana Kitchen.** There's always a line winding out the door for the delicious food at Angeline's. The brick walls, maps of Louisana, ceiling fans, and true New Orleans music create a festive atmosphere that is both welcoming and exciting. Specialties include Voo Doo shrimp with blue lake beans, crawfish étouffée, and buttermilk fried chicken. A lot of love goes into the food here and the Creole pecan pie is so good, you'll be coming back for more. ⓢ *Average main: $14* ⊠ *2261 Shattuck Ave* ☎ *510/548-6900.*

$
AMERICAN

✕ **Bette's Oceanview Diner.** Buttermilk pancakes are just one of the specialties at this 1930s-inspired diner complete with checkered floors and burgundy booths. Huevos rancheros and lox and eggs are other breakfast options; kosher franks, generous slices of pizza, and a slew of sandwiches are available for lunch. The wait for a seat can be quite long; thankfully, 4th Street was made for strolling. ■TIP→ **If you're starving, head to Bette's to Go, next door, for takeout.** ⓢ *Average main: $10* ⊠ *1807 4th St., near Delaware St., 4th Street* ☎ *510/644–3230* ⊘ *Reservations not accepted* ⊙ *No dinner.*

$$
MEDITERRANEAN

✕ **Café Rouge.** You can recover from 4th Street shopping in this spacious two-story bistro complete with zinc bar, skylights, and festive lanterns. The short, seasonal menu ranges from the sophisticated, such as rack of lamb and juniper-berry-cured pork chops, to the homey, like spit-roasted chicken or pork loin, or cheddar-topped burgers. If you visit by day, be certain to peek at the meat market in the back. ⑤ *Average main: $21* ⊠ *1782 4th St., at Delaware St., 4th Street* ☎ *510/525–1440* ⊙ *No dinner Mon.*

$ ✗ **César.** In true Spanish style, dinners are served late at César, whose
SPANISH kitchen closes at 11:30 pm on Friday and Saturday and at 11 pm the rest of the week. Couples spill out from its street-level windows on warm nights, or rub shoulders at the polished bar or center communal table. Founded by a trio of former Chez Panisse chefs, César is like a first cousin to Chez Panisse, each restaurant recommending the other if there's a long wait ahead. For tapas and perfectly grilled *bocadillos* (small sandwiches), there's no better choice. The bar also makes a mean martini and has an impressive wine list. ■TIP➜ **Come early to get seated quickly and also to hear your tablemates; the room gets loud when the bar is in full swing.** ⑤ *Average main: $10* ⊠ *1515 Shattuck Ave., at Vine St., North Berkeley* ☎ *510/883–0222* ⚑ *Reservations not accepted.*

$$$$ ✗ **Chez Panisse Café & Restaurant.** At Chez Panisse even humble pizza is
AMERICAN reincarnated, with innovative toppings of the freshest local ingredients.
Fodor's Choice The downstairs portion of Alice Waters's legendary eatery is noted
★ for its formality and personal service. The daily-changing multicourse dinners are prix-fixe ($$$$), with the cost slightly lower on weekdays. Upstairs, in the informal café, the crowd is livelier, the prices are lower ($$–$$$), and the ever-changing menu is à la carte. The food is simpler, too: penne with new potatoes, arugula, and sheep's-milk cheese; fresh figs with Parmigiano-Reggiano cheese and arugula; and grilled tuna with Savoy cabbage, for example. Legions of loyal fans insist that Chez Panisse lives up to its reputation and delivers a dining experience well worth the price. Visiting foodies won't want to miss a meal here; be sure to make reservations a few weeks ahead of time. ⑤ *Prix-fixe: $95* ⊠ *1517 Shattuck Ave., at Vine St., North Berkeley* ☎ *510/548–5525 restaurant, 510/548–5049 café* ⊕ *www.chezpanisse.com* ⚑ *Reservations essential* ⊙ *Closed Sun. No lunch in the restaurant.*

$ ✗ **Freehouse.** High ceilings, a warm fireplace, worn leather sofas, and a
MODERN BRITISH snooker table lend this restaurant the feel of a British country pub. The bar is bright, busy, and well stocked with whiskies and local beers on tap. The food, from sustainable sources, includes items like pot pies, cider-brined pork chops, and Loch Duart salmon burgers. There's a spacious patio outside. ⑤ *Average main: $14* ⊠ *2700 Brancroft Way, at College Ave.* ☎ *510/647–2300* ⊕ *berkeleyfreehouse.com* ⚑ *Reservations not accepted.*

$$ ✗ **Gather.** Here organic, sustainable and all things Berkeley reside har-
MODERN moniously beneath one tasty roof. This vibrant, well-lighted eatery
AMERICAN boasts an inviting patio, comfy leather chairs, and a variety of shiny wood furnishings. Everything feels contemporary and local, especially the food. The stinging nettles pizza is refreshing and the grilled chicken with beluga lentils is oh so juicy. This is a haven for vegetarian, vegan, and gluten-free eaters, but there's plenty for meat eaters to choose from, too. And the desserts don't get much better than the chocolate budino with braised cherries and Sonoma salt. Yum, yum. ⑤ *Average main: $20* ⊠ *2200 Oxford St.* ☎ *510/809-0400.*

9

The pioneer restaurant Chez Panisse focuses on seasonal local ingredients.

$$ ✕ **Lalime's.** Inside a charming, flower-covered house, this restaurant
MEDITERRANEAN serves dishes that reflect the entire Mediterranean region. The menu,
★ constantly changing and unfailingly great, depends on the availability
of fresh seasonal ingredients. Choices might include grilled ahi tuna
or creamy Italian risotto. Light colors used in the dining room, which
has two levels, help to create a cheerful mood. A star in its own right,
Lalime's is a good second choice if Chez Panisse is booked. $ *Average
main: $22* ⊠ *1329 Gilman St., at Tevlin St., North Berkeley* ☎ *510/527–
9838* ⌨ *Reservations essential* ☾ *No lunch.*

$ ✕ **Picante.** A barnlike space full of cheerful Mexican tiles and folk-art
MEXICAN masks, Picante is a find for anyone seeking good Mexican food for a
song. The *masa* (flour) is freshly ground for the tortillas and tamales,
the salsas are complex, and the flavor combinations are inventive. Try
tamales filled with butternut squash and chilies or a simple taco of
roasted poblanos and sautéed onions; we challenge you to finish a plate
of supernachos. $ *Average main: $11* ⊠ *1328 6th St., North Berkeley*
☎ *510/525–3121* ⌨ *Reservations not accepted.*

$ ✕ **Rick & Ann's.** Haute comfort food is the focus here. The brunches are
AMERICAN legendary for quality and value, and customers line up outside the door
before the restaurant opens on the weekend. If you come during prime
brunch hours, expect a long wait, but the soft-style eggs are worth it.
Pancakes, waffles, and French toast are more flavorful than usual, with
variations such as potato-cheese and orange-rice pancakes. Lunch and
dinner offer burgers, favorites such as Mom's macaroni and cheese,
and chicken potpie, but always with a festive twist. Reservations are
accepted 48 hours in advance for dinner and for lunch parties of six
or more, but, alas, you can't reserve a table for brunch. $ *Average*

main: $14 ⊠ 2922 Domingo Ave., Claremont ☎ 510/649–8538 ⊗ No dinner Mon.

$ ✕ **Saul's.** Well known for its homemade sodas and enormous sand-
AMERICAN   wiches, the Saul's of today also uses sustainably sourced seafood, grass-fed beef, and organic eggs. The restaurant is a Berkeley institution, and has a loyal clientele that swears by the pastrami sandwiches, stuffed cabbage rolls, and tuna melts. For breakfast, the challah French toast is so thick it's almost too big to bite and the deli omelets are served pancake style. The high ceilings and red-leather booths add to the friendly atmosphere. Don't overlook the glass deli case where you can order food to go. ⑤ *Average main: $13 ⊠ 1475 Shattuck Ave., near Vine St., North Berkeley ☎ 510/848–3354 ⊕ www.saulsdeli.com ⌲ Reservations not accepted ⊗ Closed Thanksgiving and Yom Kippur.*

WHERE TO STAY

For inexpensive lodging, investigate University Avenue, west of campus. The area is noisy, congested, and somewhat dilapidated, but does include a few decent motels and chain properties. All Berkeley lodgings, except for the swanky Claremont, are strictly midrange.

For expanded reviews, facilities, and current deals, visit Fodors.com.

$ 🏨 **The Bancroft Hotel.** Lovingly remodeled in 2012, this new green hotel
HOTEL   is fresh, stylish and completely eco-friendly. **Pros:** heating under the floorboards; great rooftop deck; closest hotel in Berkeley to campus. **Cons:** some of the rooms are on the small side; bathrooms could be freshened up. **TripAdvisor:** "great staff," "beautiful but noisy," "great breakfast." ⑤ *Rooms from: $120 ⊠ 2680 Bancroft Way ☎ 510/549-1000 ⌲ 22 rooms ⎮⎮ Breakfast.*

$$$ 🏨 **Claremont Resort and Spa.** Straddling the Oakland–Berkeley border, the
HOTEL   hotel beckons like a gleaming white castle in the hills, luring traveling
Fodor's Choice   executives that come for the business amenities, including T-1 Internet
★   connections, guest email addresses, and oversize desks. **Pros:** amazing spa; supervised child care; some rooms have great views of the bay. **Cons:** parking is pricey; additional facilities charge for use of spa, tennis courts, pool, gym etc.; no Wi-Fi in rooms; breakfast is an additional fee. **TripAdvisor:** "excellent gym and good food," "Claremont bliss," "great facilities." ⑤ *Rooms from: $249 ⊠ 41 Tunnel Rd., at Ashby and Domingo Aves., Claremont ☎ 510/843–3000, 800/551–7266 ⊕ www.claremontresort.com ⌲ 249 rooms, 30 suites.*

$$ 🏨 **Hotel Shattuck Plaza.** In 2009 this elegant boutique hotel in the heart
HOTEL   of Berkeley underwent a major multimillion-dollar renovation, which
★   successfully combined turn-of-the-20th-century glamour (the hotel was built in 1910) with all the contemporary amenities. **Pros:** central location; modern facilities; good views; great restaurant. **Cons:** pricey parking; limited fitness center. **TripAdvisor:** "very comfortable," "nice staff," "charming original Berkeley hotel." ⑤ *Rooms from: $185 ⊠ 2086 Allston Way, at Shattuck Ave. ☎ 510/845-7300 ⊕ www.hotelshattuckplaza.com ⌲ 199 rooms, 17 suites.*

9

NIGHTLIFE AND THE ARTS

Berkeley Repertory Theatre. One of the region's highly respected resident professional companies and a Tony Award winner for Outstanding Regional Theatre (in 1997), the theater performs classic and contemporary plays from autumn to spring. Well-known pieces such as *Mother Courage* and *Oliver Twist* mix with edgier fare. The theater's complex is near BART's Downtown Berkeley Station. ⊠ *2025 Addison St.* ☎ *510/647–2949* ⊕ *www.berkeleyrep.org.*

Berkeley Symphony Orchestra. The works of 20th-century composers are a focus of this prominent orchestra, but traditional pieces are also performed. BSO plays a handful of concerts each year, in Zellerbach Hall and other locations. ⊠ *1942 University Ave., Suite 207* ☎ *510/841–2800* ⊕ *www.berkeleysymphony.org.*

★ **Cal Performances.** The series, running from September through May at Zellerbach Hall and various other U.C. Berkeley venues, offers the Bay Area's most varied bill of internationally acclaimed artists in all disciplines, from classical soloists to the latest jazz, world-music, theater, and dance ensembles. Look for frequent campus colloquiums or preshow talks featuring Berkeley's professors. ⊠ *Zellerbach Hall, Telegraph Ave. and Bancroft Way* ☎ *510/642–9988* ⊕ *calperformances.org.*

Fodor'sChoice
★ **Freight & Salvage Coffeehouse.** Some of the most talented practitioners of folk, blues, Cajun, and bluegrass perform in this alcohol-free space, one of the finest folk houses in the country. Most tickets are less than $20. ⊠ *2020 Addison St., between Shattuck and Milvia Sts.* ☎ *510/644–2020* ⊕ *www.thefreight.org.*

SHOPPING

Fodor'sChoice
★ **Amoeba Music.** Heaven for audiophiles, this legendary Berkeley favorite is *the* place to head for new and used CDs, records, cassettes, and DVDs. The dazzling stock includes thousands of titles for all music tastes. The store even has its own record label. There are now branches in San Francisco and Hollywood, but this is the original. ⊠ *2455 Telegraph Ave., at Haste St.* ☎ *510/549–1125.*

Body Time. Founded in Berkeley in 1970, this local chain emphasizes the premium-quality ingredients it uses in its natural perfumes and skin-care and aromatherapy products. Sustainably harvested essential oils that you can combine and dilute to create your own personal fragrances are the specialty. Its distinct Citrus, Lavender-Mint, and China Rain scents are all popular. ⊠ *1942 Shattuck Ave., at Berkeley Way* ☎ *510/841–5818.*

Kermit Lynch Wine Merchant. Lynch's newsletters describing his finds are legendary, as is his friendship with Alice Waters of Chez Panisse. Credited with taking American appreciation of French wine to another level, this shop is a great place to peruse as you educate your palate. The friendly salespeople can direct you to the latest French bargains. ⊠ *1605 San Pablo Ave., at Dwight Way* ☎ *510/524–1524.*

★ **Moe's Books.** The spirit of Moe—the cantankerous, cigar-smoking late proprietor—lives on in this four-story house of books. Students and professors come here for used books, including large sections of literary and cultural criticism, art books, and literature in foreign languages. ✉ *2476 Telegraph Ave., near Haste St.* ☎ *510/849–2087.*

THE COASTAL PENINSULA

Bookended by San Francisco and Silicon Valley are some surprisingly low-key and unspoiled natural treasures. The vistas here are the Pacific and rolling hills, making it easy to forget the hustle and bustle that's just out of sight.

MOSS BEACH

20 miles south of San Francisco on Hwy. 1.

Moss Beach was a busy outpost during Prohibition, when regular shipments of liquid contraband from Canada were unloaded at the secluded beach and hauled off to San Francisco. The town stayed under the radar out of necessity, with only one local hotel and bar (now the Distillery) where Bay Area politicians and gangsters could go for a drink while waiting for their shipments. Today, although it has grown into a cheerful surfing town with charming inns and restaurants, it is still all but invisible from the highway—a good hideaway for those allergic to crowds.

GETTING HERE AND AROUND

To get to Moss Beach from San Francisco, take Highway 1, also known as the Coast Highway, south along the San Mateo coast.

Fitzgerald Marine Reserve. Arguably, the biggest Moss Beach attraction is this 3-mile stretch of bluffs and tide pools. Since the reserve was protected in 1969, scientists have discovered 25 new aquatic species here; depending on the tide, you'll most likely find shells, anemones, or starfish. ✉ *California and North Lake Sts.* ☎ *650/728–3584*

9

Mavericks. Just off the coast at Moss Beach is one of the biggest surfing breaks in the world. Waves here have reportedly reached 60 feet in height, and surfers get towed out to them by Jet Skis. The break is a mile offshore, so seeing it from the coast can be tough and requires a challenging hike.

WHERE TO EAT

$$
SEAFOOD
✕ **Sam's Chowder House.** An East Coast–style seafood joint in the Bay Area? This waterfront restaurant isn't textbook Cape Cod, but that's OK—dine here, and you'll get the best of both coasts: true New England–style clam chowder and lump crab cakes and ahi tuna poke with sesame oil and scallions or local halibut with mango salsa. Indoor seats are in one of several long dining rooms; outdoor seats are warmed by gas fire pits and heaters on chilly days; and every seat in the house looks out to the water. The attached market sells fresh fish and picnic food. Ⓢ *Average main: $22* ✉ *4210 N. Hwy. 1* ☎ *650/712–0245* ⊕ *www. samschowderhouse.com.*

HALF MOON BAY

7 miles south of Moss Beach on Hwy. 1.

It may be the largest and most visited of the coastal communities, but Half Moon Bay is still by all measures a small town. Looking from the highway you'd hardly even know it was there. Turn onto Main Street, though, and you'll find five blocks of galleries, shops, and cafés, many of which occupy renovated 19th-century buildings. While traditionally this was an agricultural center for local growers of artichokes and other coastal crops, in recent years it has also come to be a haven for Bay Area retirees.

GETTING HERE AND AROUND

To get to Half Moon Bay from San Francisco, take Highway 1, also known as the Coast Highway, south along the length of the San Mateo coast.

Half Moon Bay Art and Pumpkin Festival The town comes to life on the third weekend in October, when 250,000 people gather for this festival. Highlights include a parade, pie-eating contests, street performers, and a "weigh-off" of giant pumpkins, some as big as 1,200 pounds.

Half Moon Bay State Beach. This 4-mile stretch of is perfect for long walks, kite flying, and picnic lunches, though the 50°F water and dangerous currents make swimming inadvisable. There are three access points, one in Half Moon Bay and two south of town off the highway. To find them, look for road signs that have a picture of footsteps. ⊠ *Hwy. 1, west of Main St.* ☎ *650/726–8819.*

WHERE TO EAT

$$$ ✕ **Pasta Moon.** As one of the best restaurants on the coast between San
ITALIAN   Francisco and Monterey, Pasta Moon boasts a friendly, laid-back staff
★   and fun, jovial crowd. Local produce flavors the seasonal menu, which includes such highlights as wood-fired pizzas and braised lamb shank. Beware: the dining room can get slightly noisy on weekend nights, when live music plays in the bar and lounge. $ *Average main: $24* ⊠ *315 Main St.* ☎ *650/726–5125* ⊕ *www.pastamoon.com.*

WHERE TO STAY

$$$$ 🛏 **The Ritz-Carlton.** With its enormous and elegantly decorated rooms,
★   secluded oceanfront property, and a staff that waits on guests hand and foot, this golf and spa resort defines opulence. **Pros:** four-star service; total luxury; ocean views. **Cons:** formal; not within walking distance of anything. $ *Rooms from: $475* ⊠ *1 Miramontes Point Rd.* ☎ *650/712–7000 or 800/241–3333* ⊕ *www.ritzcarlton.com* 🛏 *239 rooms, 22 suites.*

PESCADERO

17 miles south of Half Moon Bay on Hwy. 1.

As you walk down Stage Road, Pescadero's main street, it's hard to believe you're only 30 minutes from Silicon Valley. If you could block out the throngs of weekend cyclists, the downtown area could almost serve as the backdrop for a western movie.

GETTING HERE AND AROUND

Pescadero is 2 miles inland from Highway 1 on Pescadero Creek Road.

Harley Farms. There's cuteness overload at this farm, a restored 1910 farm with 200 alpine goats on 12 acres of pasture. It's a fully operational dairy, renowned for its delicious cheeses: chevre, fromage blanc, ricotta, and feta. A two-hour tour follows the milk trail as it moves from goat to dairy, then from curd to cheese. During the week you can walk around the yard and read detailed signage describing the buildings and operations. Purchase a ticket for the tour and you may get to hold a newborn kid. The Harley Farms Shop sells cheese (samples available), lotions, soaps, and gift items. Monthly dinners in the old hay loft showcase local, in-season produce. ✉ *205 North St.* ☎ *650/879–0480* ⊕ *www.harleyfarms.com* 🎟 *Tours $20* ⊙ *Shop daily 11 to 5; tours weekends at 11 and 1.*

Pescadero State Beach. If a quarantine is not in effect (watch for signs), from November through April you can look for mussels amid tidal pools and rocky outcroppings at this beach, then roast them at the barbecue pits. Any time of year is good for exploring the beach, the north side of which has several secluded spots along sandstone cliffs. Across U.S. 101, the **Pescadero Marsh Natural Preserve** has hiking trails that cover 600 acres of marshland. Early spring and fall are the best times to come, when there are lots of migrating birds and other wildlife to see. ✉ *14½ miles south of Half Moon Bay on Hwy. 1* ☎ *650/879–2170* 🎟 *Free, parking $8* ⊙ *Daily 8 am–sunset.*

AÑO NUEVO STATE RESERVE

13 miles south of Pescadero on Hwy. 1.

GETTING HERE AND AROUND

You need your own vehicle to get here. The reserve is on Highway 1, 13 miles south of Pescadero and 21 miles north of Santa Cruz.

⊙ ★ **Año Nuevo State Reserve.** At the height of mating season, upward of 4,000 elephant seals congregate at Año Nuevo, one of the world's only approachable mainland rookeries. The seals are both vocal and spectacularly big (especially the males, which can weigh up to 2½ tons), and some are in residence year-round. An easy, 1½-hour round-trip walk takes you to the dunes, from which you can look down onto the animals lounging on the shoreline. Note that during mating season (mid-December through March), visitors may do the hike only as part of a 2½-hour guided tour, for which reservations must be made well in advance. The area's visitor center has a fascinating film about the seals and some natural-history exhibits (including a sea otter's pelt that you can touch). Dogs are not allowed, even in cars in the parking lot. ✉ *Hwy. 1, 13 miles south of Pescadero* ☎ *650/879–2025, 800/444–4445 for tour reservations* 🎟 *Tour $7, parking $10* ⊙ *Guided tours leave every 15 mins, mid-Dec.–Mar., daily 8:45–3.*

9

BIG BASIN REDWOODS STATE PARK

17 miles north of Santa Cruz on Hwy. 1.

GETTING HERE AND AROUND

You need your own vehicle to get here. Coming from the coast, access the park at Waddell Creek (off Highway 1, 17 miles north of Santa Cruz), where a confluence of waterways pours out of the redwoods and into the ocean.

Big Basin Redwoods State Park. California's oldest state park is the best place to see old-growth redwoods without going north of San Francisco (and it's far less crowded than Muir Woods and other famous spots). The parkland ranges from sea level up to 2,000 feet in elevation, which means the landscape changes often, from dark redwood groves to oak pastures that are deep green in winter and bleached nearly white in summer. The mountain setting also makes for countless waterfalls, most visible during the winter rains. The visitor center is inland, at park headquarters in Boulder Creek. Staffing at the park's coastal entrance is spotty, but there are always park information and camping check-in available at a self-service kiosk.

Ꮿ A short walk on the Marsh Trail leads to the **Rancho Del Oso Nature Center** (🕾 831/427–2288 ☉ *Weekends noon–4*), which has natural-history exhibits and is the starting point for several self-guided nature walks.

Mountain bikers, horseback riders, and hikers can take the nearly level Canyon Road (a dirt fire road) back up the creek and into the woods. Hikers looking for solitude might consider a more strenuous, uphill climb on Clark Connection to Westridge Trail, which rewards hard work with spectacular views of the ocean. Those who don't want to go anywhere can just stay on the windswept beach, where the main attraction is watching kite surfers get huge air on the windy shoreline waves. ⊠ *21600 Big Basin Way, Boulder Creek* 🕾 *831/338–8860* 🖭 *$10 parking fee.*

The Wine Country

WORD OF MOUTH

"The entire Napa Valley is much smaller than the Sonoma County Wine Country area. The farther north you go, the more expensive it is for hotels . . . Calistoga is at the north end, the city of Napa is at the south end. From there it's about a 30-minute drive through the Alexander Valley to Healdsburg."

—elnap29

WELCOME TO WINE COUNTRY

TOP REASONS TO GO

★ **Biking:** Cycling is one of the best ways to see the Wine Country—the Russian River and Dry Creek valleys, in Sonoma County, are particularly beautiful.

★ **Browsing the farmers' markets:** Many towns in Napa and Sonoma have seasonal farmers' markets, each rounding up an amazing variety of local produce.

★ **Wandering di Rosa:** Though this art and nature preserve is just off the busy Carneros Highway, it's a relatively unknown treasure. The galleries and gardens are filled with hundreds of pieces of art.

★ **Canoeing on the Russian River:** Trade in your car keys for a paddle and glide down the Russian River in Sonoma County. May through October is the best time to be on the water.

★ **Touring Wineries:** Let's face it: this is the reason you're here, and the range of excellent sips to sample would make any oenophile (or novice drinker, for that matter) giddy.

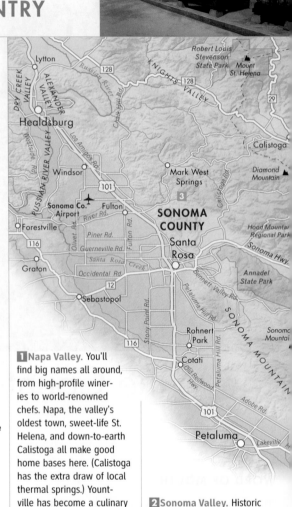

1 Napa Valley. You'll find big names all around, from high-profile wineries to world-renowned chefs. Napa, the valley's oldest town, sweet-life St. Helena, and down-to-earth Calistoga all make good home bases here. (Calistoga has the extra draw of local thermal springs.) Yountville has become a culinary boomtown, while the tiny communities of Oakville and Rutherford are home to major wineries such as Robert Mondavi and Grgich Hills. Rutherford in particular is the source for outstanding Cabernet Sauvignon.

2 Sonoma Valley. Historic attractions and an unpretentious attitude prevail here. The town of Sonoma, with its picture-perfect central plaza, is rich with 19th-century buildings. Glen Ellen, meanwhile, has a special connection with author Jack London.

GETTING ORIENTED

The Napa and Sonoma valleys run roughly parallel, northwest to southeast, and are separated by the Mayacamas Mountains. Northwest of the Sonoma Valley are several more important viticultural areas in Sonoma County, including the Dry Creek, Alexander, and Russian River valleys. The Carneros region, which spans southern Sonoma and Napa counties, is just north of San Pablo Bay. Coombsville, recently recognized as a discrete wine region, sits in the southeastern corner of Napa Valley and is the closest of all local wine regions to San Francisco.

10

3 Elsewhere in Sonoma.
The winding, rural roads here feel a world away from Napa's main drag. The lovely Russian River, Dry Creek, and Alexander valleys are all excellent places to seek out Pinot Noir, Zinfandel, and Sauvignon Blanc. The small town of Healdsburg gets lots of attention, thanks to its terrific restaurants, bed-and-breakfasts, and chic boutiques.

Updated by
Matt Villano

Life is lived well in the California Wine Country. Eating and drinking are cultivated as high arts. If you've been day-dreaming about driving through vineyards, stopping for a wine tasting or a picnic, well, that fantasy is just everyday life here.

It's little wonder that so many visitors to San Francisco take a day or two—or five or six—to unwind in the Napa and Sonoma valleys. They join the locals in the tasting rooms, from serious wine collectors making their annual pilgrimages to wine newbies who don't know the difference between a Merlot and Mourvèdre but are eager to learn.

The state's wine industry is booming, and the Napa and Sonoma valleys have long led the field. For instance, in 1975 Napa Valley had no more than 20 wineries; today there are nearly 400. A recent up-and-comer is the Carneros region, which overlaps Napa and Sonoma counties at the head of the San Francisco Bay. Another exciting area: Coombsville, in southeastern Napa, which recently received an official AVA (American Viticultural Area) designation recognizing its unique characteristics.

Great dining and wine go hand in hand, and the local viticulture has naturally encouraged a robust passion for food. Several outstanding chefs have taken root here, sealing the area's reputation as one of the best restaurant destinations in the country. The lust for fine food doesn't stop at the doors of the bistros, either. Whether you visit an artisanal olive-oil producer, nibble locally made cheese, or browse the fresh vegetables in the farmers' markets, you'll soon see why Napa and Sonoma are a food-lover's paradise.

Napa and Sonoma counties are also rich in history. In the town of Sonoma, for example, you can explore buildings from California's Spanish and Mexican past. Some wineries, such as Napa Valley's Beringer, have cellars or tasting rooms dating to the late 1800s. The town of Calistoga is a flurry of Steamboat Gothic architecture, gussied up with the fretwork favored by late-19th-century spa goers. Modern architecture is the exception rather than the rule, but one standout example is the postmodern extravaganza of Clos Pegase winery in Calistoga.

Binding all these temptations together is the sheer scenic beauty of the place. Much of Napa Valley's landscape unspools in orderly, densely planted rows of vines. Sonoma's vistas are broken by rolling hills or stands of ancient oak and madrone trees. Even the climate cooperates, as the warm summer days and refreshingly cool evenings that make the area one of the world's best grape-growing regions make perfect weather for traveling, too. If you're inspired to dig further into the Wine Country, grab a copy of *Fodor's InFocus Napa & Sonoma* or the in-depth *Compass American Guide: California Wine Country*.

PLANNING

WHEN TO GO

"Crush," the term used to indicate the season when grapes are picked and crushed, usually takes place in September or October, depending on the weather. From September until November the entire Wine Country celebrates its bounty with street fairs and festivals. The Sonoma County Harvest Fair, with its famous grape stomp, is held the first weekend in October. Golf tournaments, wine auctions, and art and food fairs occur throughout fall.

In season (April through November), Napa Valley draws crowds of tourists, and traffic along Highway 29 from St. Helena to Calistoga is often backed up on weekends. The Sonoma Valley, Santa Rosa, and Healdsburg are less crowded (though even that is changing). In season and over holiday weekends it's best to book lodging, restaurant, and winery reservations at least a month in advance. Many wineries give tours at specified times and require appointments.

To avoid crowds, visit the Wine Country during the week and get an early start (most wineries open around 10). Because many wineries close as early as 4 or 4:30—and few are open past 5—you'll need to get a reasonably early start if you want to fit in more than one or two, especially if you're going to enjoy the leisurely lunch customary in the Wine Country. Summer is usually hot and dry, and autumn can be even hotter, so dress appropriately if you go during these times.

GETTING HERE AND AROUND

AIR TRAVEL

If you'd like to bypass San Francisco or Oakland, you can fly directly to the small Charles M. Schulz Sonoma County Airport (STS) in Santa Rosa on Horizon Air, which has direct flights from Los Angeles, Portland, Las Vegas, and Seattle. Rental cars are available from Avis, Budget, Enterprise, and Hertz at the airport.

BUS TRAVEL

Bus travel is an inconvenient way to explore the Wine Country. Service is infrequent and buses from San Francisco can only get you to Santa Rosa or the town of Vallejo, south of Napa—neither of which is close to the vineyards. Sonoma County Transit offers daily bus service to points all over the county. VINE (Valley Intracity Neighborhood Express) provides bus service within the city of Napa and between other Napa Valley towns.

10

Bus Lines Greyhound ☎ *800/231–2222* ⊕ *www.greyhound.com.* **Sonoma County Transit** ☎ *707/576–7433, 800/345–7433* ⊕ *www.sctransit.com.* **VINE** ☎ *707/251–2800, 800/696–6443* ⊕ *www.nctpa.net/routes-schedules/vine.html.*

CAR TRAVEL

Driving your own car is by far the best way to explore the Wine Country. Well-maintained roads zip through the centers of the Napa and Sonoma valleys, while scenic routes thread through the backcountry. Distances between towns are fairly short, and you can often drive from one end of the Napa or Sonoma valley to the other in less than an hour—if there's no significant traffic. This may be a relatively rural area, but the usual rush hours still apply, and high-season weekend traffic can be excruciatingly slow, especially on Highway 29.

Five major roads cut through the Napa and Sonoma valleys. U.S. 101 and Highways 12 and 121 travel through Sonoma County. Highway 29 heads north from Napa. The 25-mile Silverado Trail, which runs parallel to Highway 29 north from Napa to Calistoga, is Napa Valley's more scenic, less-crowded alternative to Highway 29.

■ TIP→ If you're wine tasting, either select a designated driver or be careful of your wine intake. (When you're taking just a sip or two of any given wine, it can be hard to keep track of how much you're drinking.) Also, keep in mind that you'll likely be sharing the road with cyclists and joggers; keep a close eye on the shoulder.

When calculating the time it will take you to drive between the Napa and Sonoma valleys, remember that the Mayacamas Mountains are between the two. If it's not too far out of your way, you might want to travel between the two valleys along Highway 12/121 to the south, or along Highway 128 to the north, to avoid the slow, winding drive on the Oakville Grade, which connects Oakville, in Napa, and Glen Ellen, in Sonoma.

From San Francisco to Napa: Cross the Golden Gate Bridge, then go north on U.S. 101. Next go east on Highway 37 toward Vallejo, then north on Highway 121, also called the Carneros Highway. Turn left (north) when Highway 121 runs into Highway 29. This should take about 1½ hours when traffic is light.

From San Francisco to Sonoma: Cross the Golden Gate Bridge, then go north on U.S. 101, east on Highway 37 toward Vallejo, and north on Highway 121, aka the Carneros Highway. When you reach Highway 12, take it north. If you're going to any of the Sonoma County destinations north of the valley, take U.S. 101 all the way north through Santa Rosa to Healdsburg. This should take about an hour, not counting substantial traffic.

From Berkeley and other East Bay towns: Take Interstate 80 north to Highway 37 west, then on to Highway 29 north. To head up the Napa Valley, continue on Highway 29; to reach Sonoma County, turn off Highway 29 onto Highway 121 heading north. Getting from Berkeley to Napa will take at least 45 minutes, from Berkeley to Sonoma at least an hour.

RESTAURANTS

Star chefs from around the world have come into the Wine Country's orbit, drawn by the area's phenomenal produce, artisanal foods, and wines. These days, many visitors come to Napa and Sonoma as much for the restaurants' tasting menus as for the wineries' tasting rooms.

Although excellent meals can be found virtually everywhere in the region, the small town of Yountville has become a culinary crossroads under the influence of chef Thomas Keller. If a table at Keller's famed French Laundry is out of reach, keep in mind that he's also behind a number of more modest restaurants in town. In St. Helena the elegant Restaurant at Meadowood has achieved almost as much critical acclaim as the French Laundry, yet is considerably easier to get into. And the buzzed-about restaurants in Sonoma County, including Cyrus and Farmhouse Inn, offer plenty of mouthwatering options.

Inexpensive eateries include high-end delis that serve superb picnic fare, and brunch is a cost-effective strategy at pricey restaurants, as is sitting at the bar and ordering a few appetizers instead of sitting down to a full-blown meal.

With few exceptions (*which are noted in individual restaurant listings*), dress is informal. Where reservations are indicated as essential, you may need to make them a week or more ahead. In summer and early fall you may need to book several weeks ahead.

Prices in the restaurant reviews are the average cost of a main course at dinner or, if dinner is not served, at lunch (excluding sales tax).

HOTELS

Napa and Sonoma know the tourism ropes well; their inns and hotels range from low-key to utterly luxurious, and generally maintain high standards. Most of the bed-and-breakfasts are in historic Victorian and Spanish buildings, and the breakfast part of the equation often involves fresh local produce. The newer hotels tend to have a more modern, streamlined aesthetic and elaborate, spa-like bathrooms. Many hotels and B&Bs have excellent restaurants on their grounds, and those that don't are still just a short drive away from gastronomic bliss.

10

However, all of this comes with a hefty price tag. As the cost of vineyards and grapes has risen, so have lodging rates. Santa Rosa, the largest population center in the area, has the widest selection of moderately priced rooms. Try there if you've failed to reserve in advance or have a limited budget. In general, all accommodations in the area often have lower rates on weeknights, and prices are about 20% lower in winter.

On weekends, two- or even three-night minimum stays are commonly required, especially at smaller inns and B&Bs. If you'd prefer to stay a single night, though, innkeepers are usually more flexible in winter. Many B&Bs book up long in advance of the summer and fall seasons. Many B&Bs and small inns also discourage the presence of children though fall short of actually prohibiting them. If you're traveling with children, be sure to ask about them when booking to make sure they will receive a warm welcome.

Prices in the hotel reviews are the lowest cost of a standard double room in high season. Prices do not include taxes (as high as 14%, depending on the region).

Hotel reviews have been condensed for this book. Please go to Fodors. com for expanded reviews of each property.

BED-AND-BREAKFAST ASSOCIATIONS

Contacts Bed & Breakfast Association of Sonoma Valley ☎ 800/969–4667 ⊕ www.sonomabb.com. **The Wine Country Inns of Sonoma County** ☎ 800/946–3268 ⊕ www.winecountryinns.com.

TOURS

Full-day guided tours of the Wine Country generally include lunch, and cost about $60–$100 per person. Reservations are usually required.

Beau Wine Tours. Based in downtown Sonoma, this outfitter organizes personalized tours of Napa and Sonoma in limos, vans, and shuttle buses. ⊠ *21707 8th St. E, Sonoma* ☎ *707/938–8001, 800/387–2328* ⊕ *www.beauwinetours.com.*

Gray Line. The national outfitter offers a tour that covers the southern Napa and Sonoma valleys in a single day, with stops for shopping and sightseeing at Sonoma Plaza and lunch in Yountville. ⊠ *Pier 43½, Embarcadero, San Francisco* ☎ *415/434–8687, 888/428–6937* ⊕ *www.grayline.com.*

Great Pacific Tour Co. This friendly outfitter operates full-day tours of Napa and Sonoma, including a restaurant lunch and a tour at Domaine Chandon. Tours are offered in passenger vans that seat 14. ⊠ *518 Octavia St., Hayes Valley, San Francisco* ☎ *415/626–4499* ⊕ *www.greatpacifictour.com.*

Wine Country Bikes. This family-owned Healdsburg outfitter rents bikes by the day and organizes one-day and multi-day trips throughout Sonoma County. ⊠ *61 Front St., Healdsburg* ☎ *707/473–0610, 866/922–4537* ⊕ *www.winecountrybikes.com.*

VISITOR INFORMATION

Napa Valley Welcome Center. Visitors love the Napa Valley Wecome Center, a downtown storefront offering everything from baked goods to information about winery tours and recreation. ⊠ *600 Main St., Napa* ☎ *707/251–5895* ⊕ *www.legendarynapavalley.com.*

THE NAPA VALLEY

When it comes to wine production in the United States, Napa Valley rules the roost, with nearly 400 wineries and many of the biggest brands in the business. Vastly diverse soils and microclimates give Napa winemakers the chance to make a tremendous variety of wines. But what's the area like beyond the glossy advertising and boldface names?

The small towns strung along Highway 29 are where wine-industry workers live, and they're also where most of the area lodging is. Napa—the valley's largest town—lures with its growing cultural attractions and accommodations that are (relatively) reasonably priced. A few miles

Continued on page 532

Napa Valley

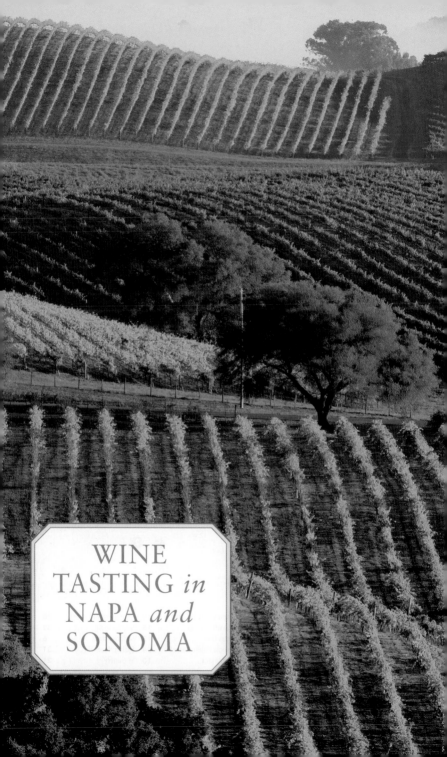

WINE
TASTING *in*
NAPA *and*
SONOMA

The tantalizing pop of a cork. Roads unspooling through hypnotically even rows of vines. Sun glinting through a glass of sparkling wine or ruby colored cabernet. If these are your daydreams, you won't be disappointed when you get to Napa and Sonoma. The vineyard-blanketed hills, shady town squares, and ivy-draped wineries—not to mention the luxurious restaurants, hotels, and spas— really *are* that captivating.

(opposite page) Carneros vineyards in autumn, Napa Valley. (top) Pinot Gris grapes (bottom) Bottles from Far Niente winery.

VISITING WINERIES

Napa and Sonoma are outstanding destinations for both wine newcomers and serious wine buffs. Tasting rooms range from modest to swanky, offering everything from a casual conversation over a few sips of wine to in-depth tours of winemaking facilities and vineyards. And there's a tremendous variety of wines to taste. The one constant is a deep, shared pleasure in the experience of wine tasting.

Wineries in Napa and Sonoma range from faux châteaux with vast gift shops to rustic converted barns where you might have to step over the vintner's dog in the doorway. Many are regularly open to the public, usually daily from around 10 am to 5 pm. Others require advance reservations to visit, and still others are closed to the public entirely. When in doubt, call ahead.

There are many, many more wineries in Napa and Sonoma than we could possibly include here. Free maps pinpointing most of them are widely available, though; ask the staff at the tasting rooms you visit or look for the ubiquitous free tourist magazines.

Pick a designated driver before setting out for the day. Although wineries rarely advertise it, many will provide a free nonalcoholic drink for the designated driver; it never hurts to ask.

Fees. In the past few years, tasting fees have skyrocketed. Most Napa wineries charge $10 to $20 to taste four or so wines, though $30, $40 or even $50 fees aren't unheard of. Sonoma wineries are often a bit cheaper, in the $5 to $15 range, and you'll still find the occasional freebie.

Some winery tours are free, in which case you're usually required to pay a separate fee if you want to taste the wine. If you've paid a fee for the tour—often $15 to $30—your wine tasting is usually included in that price.

MAKING THE MOST OF YOUR TIME

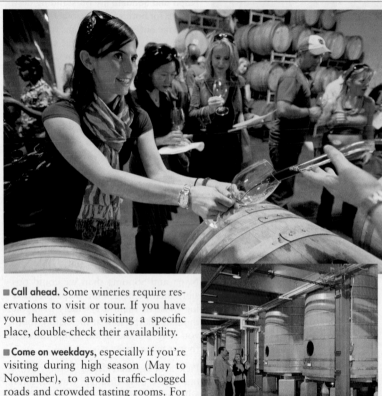

(top) Sipping and swirling in the De Loach tasting room. (bottom) Learning about barrel aging at Robert Mondavi Winery.

■ **Call ahead.** Some wineries require reservations to visit or tour. If you have your heart set on visiting a specific place, double-check their availability.

■ **Come on weekdays**, especially if you're visiting during high season (May to November), to avoid traffic-clogged roads and crowded tasting rooms. For more info on the best times of year to visit, see this chapter's Planner.

■ **Get an early start.** Tasting rooms are often deserted before 11 am or so, when most visitors are still lingering over a second cup of coffee. If you come early, you'll have the staff's undivided attention. You'll usually encounter the largest crowds between 3 and 5 pm.

■ **Consider skipping Napa.** If you've got less than two days to spend in the Wine Country, dip into the Carneros area or the Sonoma Valley rather than Napa Valley or northern Sonoma County. Though you might find fewer big-name wineries and critically acclaimed

restaurants, these regions are only about an hour and half away from the city . . . if you don't hit traffic.

■ **Divide your attention.** If you're lucky enough to have three nights or more here, split your overnights between Napa and Sonoma to easily see the best that both counties have to offer.

Domaine Carneros.

AT THE BAR

In most tasting rooms, you'll be handed a list of the wines available that day. The wines will be listed in a suggested tasting order, starting with the lightest-bodied whites, progressing to the most intense reds, and ending with dessert wines. If you can't decide which wines to choose, tell the server what types of wines you usually like and ask for a recommendation.

The server will pour you an ounce or so of each wine you select. As you taste it, feel free to take notes or ask questions. Don't be shy—the staff are there to educate you about their wine. If you don't like a wine, or you've simply tasted enough, feel free to pour the rest into one of the dump buckets on the bar.

TOURS

Tours tend to be the most exciting (and the most crowded) in September and October, when the harvest and crush-

ing are underway. Tours typically last from 30 minutes to an hour and give you a brief overview of the winemaking process. At some of the older wineries, the tour guide might focus on the history of the property.

■TIP➜ If you plan to take any tours, wear comfortable shoes, since you might be walking on wet floors or dirt or gravel pathways or stepping over hoses or other equipment.

MONEY-SAVING TIPS

■ Many hotels and B&Bs distribute coupons for free or discounted tastings to their guests—don't forget to ask.

■ If you and your travel partner don't mind sharing a glass, servers are happy to let you split a tasting.

■ Some wineries will refund all or part of the tasting fee if you buy a bottle, making it so much easier to rationalize buying that $80 bottle of cabernet.

■ Almost all wineries will also waive the fee if you join their wine club program. However, this typically commits you to buying a certain number of bottles of their wine for a period of time, so be sure you really like their wines before signing up.

Preston Vineyards bottles only estate-grown grapes.

TOP 2-DAY ITINERARIES

First-Timer's Napa Tour

Start: Oxbow Public market, Napa. Get underway by browsing the shops selling wines, spices, locally grown produce, and other fine foods, for a taste of what the Wine Country has to offer.

Inglenook, Rutherford. The tour here is a particularly fun way to learn about the history

of Napa winemaking—and you can see the old, atmospheric, ivy-covered château.

Frog's Leap, Rutherford. Friendly, unpretentious, and knowledgeable staff makes this place great for wine newbies. (Make sure you get that advance reservation lined up.)

Dinner and Overnight: St. Helena. Spluge at Meadowood Resort and you won't need to leave the property for an

Map

Domaine Carneros

121
12

Old Sonoma Rd.

di Rosa Preserve

Oxbow Public Market

Napa 29

NAPA COUNTY

Robert Mondavi

Far Niente

🏠✕

Yountville Oakville

KEY
━━━ First-Timer's Napa Tour
━━━ Wine Buff's Tour

Silverado Trail

Stag's Leap Wine Cellars

Wine Buff's Tour

Start: Stag's Leap Wine Cellars, Yountville. Famed for its cabernet sauvignon and Bordeaux blends.

Beaulieu Vineyard, Rutherford. Pony up the extra fee to visit the reserve tasting room to try their flagship cabernet sauvignon.

Mumm Napa, Rutherford. Come for the bubbly—which is available in a variety of tastings—stay for the photography exhibits.

Dinner and Overnight: Yountville. Have dinner at one of the Thomas Keller restaurants. Splurge at Bardessono; save at

Maison Fleurie.

Next Day: Robert Mondavi, Oakville. Spring for the reserve room tasting so you can sip the top-of-the-line wines, especially the stellar cabernet. Head across Highway 29 to the Oakville Grocery to pick up a picnic lunch.

extravagant dinner at their restaurant. Save at El Bonita Motel with dinner at Gott's.

Next Day: Poke around St. Helena's shops, then drive to Yountville for lunch.

di Rosa, Napa. Call ahead to book a one- or two-hour tour of the acres of gardens and galleries, which

are chock-full of thousands of works of art.

Domaine Carneros, Napa. Toast your trip with a glass of outstanding bubbly.

Inglenook

Rutherford

Beaulieu Vineyard

Frog's Leap

Mumm Napa

NAPA VALLEY

St. Helena

128 29

Far Niente, Oakville. You have to reserve in advance and the fee for the tasting and tour is steep, but the

payoff is an especially intimate winery experience. You'll taste excellent cabernet and chardonnay, then end your trip on a sweet note with a dessert wine.

Sonoma Backroads

Healdsburg

Gary Farrell & Rochioli

Hartford Family Winery

Forestville

Iron Horse Vineyards

Westside Rd.

Los Amigos Rd.

Russian R.

Eastside Rd.

SONOMA COUNTY

101

116

Bodega Hwy.

12

Santa Rosa

12

Bennett Valley Rd.

Matanzas Creek Winery

101

TO SONOMA

0 ——— 3 miles
0 ——— 3 km

Start: Iron Horse Vineyards, Russian River Valley.
Soak up a view of vine-covered hills and Mount St. Helena while sipping a sparkling wine or pinot noir at this beautifully rustic spot.

Hartford Family Winery, Russian River Valley.
A terrific source for pinot noir and chardonnay, the stars of this valley.

Dinner and Overnight: Forestville. Go all out with a stay at the Farmhouse Inn, whose award-winning restaurant is one of the best in all of Sonoma.

Next Day: Westside Road, Russian River Valley.
This scenic route, which follows the river, is crowded with worthwhile wineries like Gary Farrell and Rochioli—but it's not crowded with visitors. Pinot fans will find a lot to love. Picnic at Rochioli and enjoy the lovely view.

Matanzas Creek Winery, near Santa Rosa.
End on an especially relaxed note with a walk through their lavender fields (best in June).

IN FOCUS WINE TASTING IN NAPA AND SONOMA

10

WINE TASTING 101

TAKE A GOOD LOOK.
Hold your glass by the stem, raise it to the light, and take a close look at the wine. Check for clarity and color. (This is easiest to do if you can hold the glass in front of a white background.) Any tinge of brown usually means that the wine is over the hill or has gone bad.

Swirl

BREATHE DEEP.
1. Sniff the wine once or twice to see if you can identify any smells.

2. Swirl the wine gently in the glass. Aerating the wine this way releases more of its aromas. (It's called "volatilizing the esters," if you're trying to impress someone.)

3. Take another long sniff. You might notice that experienced wine tasters spend more time sniffing the wine than drinking it. This is because this step is where the magic happens. The number of scents you might detect is almost endless, from berries, apricots, honey, and wildflowers to leather, cedar, or even tar. Does the wine smell good to you? Do you detect any "off" flavors, like wet dog or sulfur?

Sniff

AT LAST! TAKE A SIP.
1. Swirl the wine around your mouth so that it makes contact with all your taste buds and releases more of its aromas. Think about the way the wine feels in your mouth. Is it watery or rich? Is it crisp or silky? Does it have a bold flavor, or is it subtle? The weight and intensity of a wine are called its body.

2. Hold the wine in your mouth for a few seconds and see if you can identify any developing flavors. More complex wines will reveal many different flavors as you drink them.

Sip

SPIT OR SWALLOW.
The pros typically spit, since they want to preserve their palate (and sobriety!) for the wines to come, but you'll find that swallowers far outnumber the spitters in the winery tasting rooms. Whether you spit or swallow, notice the flavor that remains after the wine is gone (the finish).

DODGE THE CROWDS

To avoid bumping elbows in the tasting rooms, look for wineries off the main drags of Highway 29 in Napa and Highway 12 in Sonoma. The back roads of the Russian River, Dry Creek, and Alexander valleys, all in Sonoma, are excellent places to explore. In Napa, try the northern end. Also look for wineries that are open by appointment only; they tend to schedule visitors carefully to avoid a big crush at any one time.

HOW WINE IS MADE

1. CRUSHING
Harvested grapes go into a stemmer-crusher, which separates stems from fruit and crushes the grapes to release "free-run" juice.

2. PRESSING
Remaining juice is gently extracted from grapes. Usually done by pressing grapes against the walls of a tank with an inflatable bladder.

3. FERMENTING
Extracted juice (and also grape skins and pulp, when making red wine) goes into stainless-steel tanks or oak barrels to ferment. During fermentation, sugars convert to alcohol.

4. AGING
Wine is stored in stainless-steel or oak casks or barrels to develop flavors.

5. RACKING
Wine is transferred to clean barrels; sediment is removed. Wine may be filtered and fined (clarified) to improve its clarity, color, and sometimes flavor.

6. BOTTLING
Wine is bottled either at the winery or at a special facility, then stored again for bottle-aging.

WHAT'S AN APPELLATION?

A specific region with a particular set of grape-growing conditions, such as soil type, climate, and elevation, is called an appellation. What makes things a little confusing is that appellations, which are defined by the Alcohol and Tobacco Tax and Trade Bureau, often overlap. California is an appellation, for example, but so is the Napa Valley. Napa and Sonoma counties are each county appellations, but they, too, are divided into even smaller regions, usually called subappellations or AVAs (American Viticultural Areas). You'll hear a lot about these AVAs from the staff in the tasting rooms; they might explain, for example, why the Russian River Valley AVA is such an excellent place to grow pinot noir grapes.

By law, if the label on a bottle of wine lists the name of an appellation, then at least 85% of the grapes in that wine must come from that appellation.

Wine and contemporary art find a home at di Rosa.

farther north, compact Yountville is a culinary boomtown, densely packed with top-notch restaurants and hotels, including a few luxury properties. Continuing north, St. Helena teems with elegant boutiques and restaurants; mellow Calistoga, known for spas and hot springs, feels a bit like an Old West frontier town, and has a more casual attitude.

ESSENTIALS

Contacts Napa Valley Destination Council ☎ 707/226–5813, 707/251-5895 ⊕ www.legendarynapavalley.com.

NAPA

46 miles from San Francisco via I–80 east and north, Hwy. 37 west, and Hwy. 29 north.

The town of Napa is the valley's largest, and visitors who get a glimpse of the strip malls and big-box stores from Highway 29 often speed right past on the way to smaller and more seductive Yountville or St. Helena. But Napa is changing. After many years as a blue-collar town that more or less turned its back on the Wine Country scene, Napa has spent the last few years attempting to increase its appeal to visitors. A walkway that follows the river through town, completed in 2008, makes the city more pedestrian-friendly, and in the last two years a surprising number of high-profile new restaurants have popped up. Of course there's also the Oxbow Public Market, a klatch of high-end food purveyors. At night, catch a show at either the circa-1880 Napa Valley Opera House, or the recently renovated Uptown Theatre.

Many visitors choose to stay in Napa after experiencing hotel sticker shock; prices in Napa are marginally more reasonable than elsewhere. If you set up your home base here, you'll undoubtedly want to spend some time getting out of town and into the beautiful countryside, but don't neglect taking a stroll to see what the valley's least pretentious town has to offer, or checking out the ever-changing culinary landscape.

GETTING HERE AND AROUND

To get to downtown Napa from Highway 29, take the 1st Street exit and follow the signs for Central Napa less than a mile through town until you reach the corner of 2nd Street and Main Street. Most of the town's sights and many of its restaurants are clustered in an easily walkable area near this intersection.

EXPLORING

Artesa Vineyards & Winery. With its modern, minimalist look in the tasting room, which is dug into a Carneros hilltop, and contemporary sculptures and fountains on the property, Artesa Vineyards & Winery is a far cry from the many faux French châteaus and rustic Italianstyle villas in the region. Although the Spanish owners once made only sparkling wines, now they also produce still wines, mostly Chardonnay and Pinot Noir, but also Cabernet Sauvignon and a smattering of other limited-release wines such as Syrah and Albariño. Call ahead to reserve a spot on one of the specialty tours, such as a wine-and-cheese pairing, a wine-and-chocolate pairing, or the walk through the vineyard ($45). ⊠ *1345 Henry Rd., north off Old Sonoma Rd. and Dealy La.* ☎ *707/224–1668* ⊕ *www.artesawinery.com* 🍷 *Tasting $10–$15, tour $20* ☉ *Daily 10–5; tour daily at 11 and 2.*

Clos du Val. Although this austere winery doesn't seduce you with dramatic architecture or lush grounds, it doesn't have to: the wines, crafted by winemaker John Clews, have a wide following, especially among those who are patient enough to cellar the wines for a number of years. Though Clews and his team make great Pinot Noir and Chardonnay (grown in the nearby Carneros region), the real claim to fame is the intense reserve Cabernet, made with fruit from the Stags Leap District. The few picnic tables (in a peaceful olive grove) fill up early on summer weekends, and anyone is welcome to try a hand at the boccie-style French game of pétanque. ⊠ *5330 Silverado Trail* ☎ *707/261–5251, 800/993–9463* ⊕ *www.closduval.com* 🍷 *Tasting $15–$25* ☉ *Daily 10–5; tour by appointment.*

Fodor's Choice ★ **di Rosa.** While you're driving along the Carneros Highway on your way to Napa from San Francisco, it would be easy to zip by one of the region's best-kept secrets: di Rosa. Metal sculptures of sheep grazing in the grass mark the entrance to this sprawling, art-stuffed property. Thousands of 20th-century artworks by hundreds of Northern California artists crop up everywhere—in galleries, in the former di Rosa residence, on every lawn, in every courtyard, and even on the lake. Some of the works were commissioned especially for the preserve, such as Paul Kos's meditative *Chartres Bleu,* a video installation in a chapellike setting that replicates a stained-glass window of the cathedral in Chartres, France. If you stop by without a reservation, you'll only gain

10

access to the Gatehouse Gallery, where there's a small collection of riotously colorful figurative and abstract sculpture and painting, as well as rotating modern-art exhibits throughout the year. ■ **TIP→ To see the rest of the property and artwork, you'll have to sign up for one of the various tours of the grounds (from 1 to 2½ hours).** Tour reservations are recommended, but walk-ins are sometimes accommodated. ⊠ *5200 Sonoma Hwy./Carneros Hwy.* ☎ *707/226–5991* ⊕ *www.dirosaart.org* 🖅 *Suggested donation $5, tour $10–$15* ☉ *Wed.–Sat. 9–3; tours 10–3.*

★ **Domaine Carneros.** The majestic château here looks for all the world like it belongs in France, and in fact it does: it's modeled after the Château de la Marquetterie, an 18th-century mansion owned by the Taittinger family near Epernay, France. Carved into the hillside beneath the winery, Domaine Carneros's cellars produce delicate sparkling wines reminiscent of those made by Taittinger, using only grapes grown locally in the Carneros wine district. The winery sells full glasses, flights, and bottles of their wines, which also include still wines like Pinot Noir, Merlot, and Chardonnay, and serves them with cheese plates, charcuterie plates, caviar, or smoked salmon. Seating is in the Louis XV–inspired salon or on the terrace overlooking the vineyards. Though this makes a visit here a tad more expensive than some stops on a winery tour, it's also one of the most opulent ways to enjoy the Carneros District, especially on fair days, when the views over the vineyards are spectacular. ⊠ *1240 Duhig Rd., at Carneros Hwy.* ☎ *707/257–0101, 800/716–2788* ⊕ *www. domainecarneros.com* 🖅 *Tasting $6.50–$85, tour $25* ☉ *Daily 10–6; tour daily at 11, 1, and 3.*

Fodor'sChoice
★ **Hess Collection Winery.** Nine miles northwest of the city of Napa, up a winding road ascending Mt. Veeder, this winery is a delightful discovery. The simple limestone structure, rustic from the outside but modern and airy within, contains Swiss owner Donald Hess's personal art collection, including mostly large-scale works by such contemporary European and American artists as Robert Motherwell, Andy Goldsworthy, and Frank Stella. Cabernet Sauvignon is the real strength here, though Hess also produces some fine Chardonnays. A number of wine-and-food pairings also are available. Self-guided tours of the art collection and guided tours of the winery's production facilities are both free. On weekdays, ask to borrow an iPod for the free audio tour, which includes commentary by Donald Hess and some of the artists featured in the collection. ⊠ *4411 Redwood Rd., west of Hwy. 29* ☎ *707/255–1144* ⊕ *www. hesscollection.com* 🖅 *Tasting $10–$50* ☉ *Daily 10–5:30; guided tours daily, usually hourly 10:30–3:30.*

★ **Oxbow Public Market.** Though not terribly large, this collection of about 25 small shops, wine bars, and artisanal food producers is a fun place to begin your introduction to the wealth of food and wine available in the Napa Valley. Swoon over the decadent charcuterie at the Fatted Calf, slurp down some oysters on the half shell at Hog Island Oyster Company, chow down on tacos with homemade tortillas at C Casa, or get a whiff of the hard-to-find seasonings at the Whole Spice Company before sitting down to a glass of wine at the Oxbow Wine Merchant & Wine Bar. A branch of the retro fast-food joint Gott's Roadside tempts those who prefer hamburgers (or egg-and-cheese breakfast sandwiches)

Climbing ivy and lily pads decorate the Hess Collection's rustic exterior.

to duck-liver mousse. ✉ *610 and 644 1st St., at McKinstry St.* ☎ *No phone* ⊕ *www.oxbowpublicmarket.com* ✉ *Free* ☼ *Generally weekdays 9–9, weekends 10–9; hrs of some merchants vary.*

Sodaro Estate Winery. Upscale-yet-modest Sodaro is a great introduction to Coombsville, Napa's newest AVA. Tours start on the crush pad, with a view of rolling vineyards, then head inside the wine cave, to a marble banquet table, for a seated tasting of the winery's signature wines: a Cabernet Sauvignon and a Bordeaux-style blend. You might also taste a special limited release, perhaps a Malbec or a Cabernet Franc. All wines are paired with local cheese and breadsticks. The tour concludes with a walk through the wine cave itself. It's no surprise the vibe here is so luxurious: owners Don and Deedee Sodaro also own the Hanford Hotels chain. ✉ *24 Blue Oak La., off 3rd Ave.* ☎ *707/251–8216* ⊕ *www.sodarowines.com* ✉ *Tour and tasting $30* ☼ *Open by appointment only.*

WHERE TO EAT

$$$

FRENCH

✕ **Angèle.** An 1890s boathouse with a vaulted wood-beam ceiling sets the scene for romance at this cozy French bistro. Though the style is casual—tables are close together, and the warm, crusty bread is plunked right down on the paper-top tables—the food is always well executed. Look for classic French dishes like duck breast accompanied with confit, guinea hen wrapped in house-cured pancetta, or a starter of *ris de veau* (veal sweetbreads). Save room for the homemade desserts. In fair weather, ask for one of the charming outdoor tables. ⑤ *Average main: $30* ✉ *540 Main St., at 5th St.* ☎ *707/252–8115* ⊕ *www. angelerestaurant.com.*

10

Where to Eat and Stay in Napa Valley

Lake Berryessa Recreation Area

Lake Hennessy City Recreation Area

KEY

- **1** *Restaurants*
- ① *Hotels*

$$$ ✕ **Bistro Don Giovanni.** Co-owner and host Giovanni Scala might be
ITALIAN around to warmly welcome you to this lively bistro, where you can peek
★ past the copper pots hanging in the open kitchen to see the 750-degree
☾ wood-burning oven. The Cal-Italian food is simultaneously inventive
and comforting: an excellent fritto misto usually comprised of onions,
fennel, calamari, and plump rock shrimp; pizza with Brussels sprouts
and garlic; and whole roasted fish. Children are unusually welcome
here, catered to with crayons and paper-topped tables and a menu
with items like pizza topped with cheese, french fries, and "no green
stuff." Fodors.com Forum users suggest angling for a table on the
covered patio for a "more intimate and quiet" experience. ⑤ *Average
main: $27* ✉ *4110 Howard La. /Hwy. 29* ☎ *707/224–3300* ⊕ *www.
bistrodongiovanni.com.*

$$$ ✕ **Bounty Hunter.** A triple threat, Bounty Hunter is a wine store, a wine
SOUTHERN bar, and a restaurant in one. You can stop by for just wine—about 40
★ choices available by the glass in both 2- and 5-ounce pours, and 400 by
the bottle—but it's best to come with an appetite. A miniscule kitchen
means the menu is also small, but every dish is a standout, including
the pulled-pork and beef brisket sandwiches served with three types of
barbecue sauce, the signature beer-can chicken, and meltingly tender
St. Louis–style ribs. The space is whimsically rustic, with stuffed game
trophies mounted on the wall and leather saddles standing in for seats
at a couple of tables. ■ TIP→ The restaurant remains open until midnight
on Friday and Saturday, making it a popular spot for a late-night bite. ⑤ *Average main: $24* ✉ *975 1st St., at Main St.* ☎ *707/226–3976* ⊕ *www.
bountyhunterwinebar.com* ⚐ *Reservations not accepted.*

$$$$ ✕ **Morimoto Napa.** Masuharu Morimoto, known to many as the star of
JAPANESE Iron Chef but also well regarded for his eponymous restaurants around
the world, is the big name behind this hot restaurant in downtown
Napa. Organic materials like twisting grapevines above the bar and
rough-hewn wooden tables seem simultaneously earthy and modern,
which seems a fitting setting for the gorgeously plated Japanese fare,
from super-fresh sashimi served with grated fresh wasabi to more-elab-
orate concoctions like sea-urchin carbonara, made with udon noodles.
For the full experience, consider the omakase menu ($120). If no tables
are available, you can still order many dishes in the lounge, where a
young and lively crowd drinks specialty cocktails along with appetizers
like a tempura calamari salad and pork gyoza. ⑤ *Average main: $44*
✉ *610 Main St., at 5th St.* ☎ *707/252–1600* ⊕ *www.morimotonapa.
com.*

$$ ✕ **Norman Rose Tavern.** If downtown Napa has its own version of the bar
AMERICAN in *Cheers*, the Norman Rose Tavern is it. Casual and family-friendly,
"The Rose," as locals call it, serves up classic American fare such as
hamburgers, sandwiches, and fish-and-chips, and proudly pours local
wines and regional beers until 9 or 10 pm. Happy Hour, held week-
nights from 3 to 6 pm, is particularly rollicking, with $4 draft beers,
$6 glasses of wine, $6 hot wings (by the pound), and $2.50 sliders. On
warm days, arrive early for a spot on the open-air patio. ⑤ *Average
main: $17* ✉ *1401 1st St., at Franklin St.* ☎ *707/258–1516.*

10

WHERE TO STAY

For expanded reviews, facilities, and current deals, visit Fodors.com.

$
HOTEL
🏨 **Avia Napa.** Hands down, this boutique hotel, now part of the Hyatt family, is the hippest place to stay in Napa; the rooms, most of them suites, are modern but welcomingly so. **Pros:** proximity to restaurants, theaters, and tasting rooms downtown; modern fitness center. **Cons:** on-site restaurant and bar lack identity; parking can be a challenge on popular weekends. **TripAdvisor:** "beautiful and comfortable," "modern," "great breakfast." 💲 *Rooms from: $189* ✉ *1450 1st St.* ☎ *707/224–3900* ⊕ *avianapa.hyatt.com/hyatt/hotels* ⬦ *50 rooms, 91 suites.*

$$$$
RESORT
Fodor's Choice
★
🏨 **Carneros Inn.** Freestanding board-and-batten cottages with rocking chairs on each porch are simultaneously rustic and chic at this luxurious property. **Pros:** cottages have lots of privacy; beautiful views from the hilltop pool and hot tub; heaters on each private patio encourage lounging outside in the evening. **Cons:** a long drive from destinations up-valley; smallish rooms with limited seating options. **TripAdvisor:** "everything you need," "great vistas," "beautiful location and relaxing accommodation." 💲 *Rooms from: $550* ✉ *4048 Sonoma Hwy.(Hwy. 121)* ☎ *707/299–4900, 888/400–9000* ⊕ *www.thecarnerosinn.com* ⬦ *76 cottages, 10 suites.*

$$$
B&B/INN
🏨 **Milliken Creek Inn.** Wine and cheese at sunset set a romantic mood in the intimate lobby, with its terrace overlooking the Napa River and a lush lawn. **Pros:** soft-as-clouds beds; serene hotel-guests-only spa; breakfast delivered to your room (or wherever you'd like to eat on the grounds); gratuities are not accepted (except at the spa). **Cons:** expensive; road noise can be heard from the admittedly beautiful outdoor areas. **TripAdvisor:** "very friendly attentive staff," "romantic getaway," "consistent elegance." 💲 *Rooms from: $350* ✉ *1815 Silverado Trail* ☎ *707/255–1197, 800/835–6112* ⊕ *www.millikencreekinn.com* ⬦ *12 rooms.*

$$
B&B/INN
🏨 **Napa River Inn.** Almost everything's close here: this waterfront inn is part of a complex of restaurants, shops, a gallery, and a spa, all within easy walking distance of downtown Napa. **Pros:** a pedestrian walkway connects the hotel to downtown Napa; unusual pet-friendly policy; wide range of room sizes and prices. **Cons:** river views could be more scenic; some rooms get noise from nearby restaurants. **TripAdvisor:** "first class," "great location," "clean and comfortable." 💲 *Rooms from: $300* ✉ *500 Main St.* ☎ *707/251–8500, 877/251–8500* ⊕ *www. napariverinn.com* ⬦ *65 rooms, 1 suite.*

$
HOTEL
🏨 **Westin Verasa.** Across the street from the Wine Train depot and just behind the Oxbow Public Market, this spacious hotel-condo complex, opened in 2008, is sophisticated and soothing, with pristine white bedding and furniture in warm earth tones. **Pros:** pool is heated year-round; most rooms have well-equipped kitchenettes; spacious double-headed showers. **Cons:** $20 "amenities fee" charged in addition to room rate. **TripAdvisor:** "wonderful property," "needs a few extra touches," "great food on-site." 💲 *Rooms from: $239* ✉ *1314 McKinstry St.* ☎ *707/257–1800, 800/937–8461* ⊕ *www.westinnapa.com* ⬦ *130 rooms, 50 suites.*

NIGHTLIFE AND THE ARTS

Napa Valley Opera House. The interior of the 1879 Italianate Victorian Napa Valley Opera House isn't quite as majestic as the facade, but the intimate 500-seat venue is still an excellent place to see all sorts of performances, from Pat Metheny and Mandy Patinkin to the Napa Valley Film Festival and, yes, even the occasional opera. ⊠ *1030 Main St., at 1st St.* ☎ *707/226–7372* ⊕ *www.nvoh.org.*

Uptown Theatre. This Napa icon opened as a movie house in 1937. After years in disrepair, it was renovated and in 2010 reopened as a live-music venue that has attracted the likes of Lucinda Williams and Devo. ⊠ *1350 3rd St., at Franklin St.* ☎ *707/259–0123* ⊕ *www.uptowntheatrenapa.com.*

MAKING TRACKS IN NAPA

Napa Valley Wine Train. Turn the driving over to someone else—a train conductor. The Napa Valley Wine Train runs a scenic route between Napa and St. Helena with several restored 1915–17 Pullman railroad cars. The ride often includes a meal, such as brunch or dinner. While it's no bargain (starting at around $99 for lunch, $109 for dinner) and can feel a bit hokey, the train gives you a chance to enjoy the vineyard views without any driving worries. ⊠ *1275 McKinstry St., off 1st St.* ☎ *707/253–2111, 800/427–4124* ⊕ *www.winetrain.com.*

SPORTS AND THE OUTDOORS

Thanks to the scenic country roads that wind through the region, bicycling is a practically perfect way to get around the Wine Country. And whether you're interested in an easy spin to a few wineries or a strenuous haul up a mountainside, there's a way to make it happen. Another fine way to take in the scenery is by kayak. ■TIP➔ There are almost no designated bike lanes in the Wine Country, though, so be sure to pay attention to traffic.

Napa Valley Adventure Tours. Operating out of the Oxbow Public Market in downtown Napa, this outfitter offers a variety of half- and full-day outdoor trips, including kayaking along the Napa River in the southern part of the valley. ⊠ *610 1st St., at McKinstry St.* ☎ *707/259–1833, 877/548–6877.*

Napa Valley Bike Tours. Napa Valley Bike Tours will deliver the bikes, which go for $39 to $78 a day, to many hotels in the Napa Valley if you're renting at least two bikes for a full day. In addition to hourly rentals, guided and self-guided winery tours are available. ⊠ *6795 Washington St., at Madison St., Yountville* ☎ *707/944–2953* ⊕ *www.napavalleybiketours.com.*

YOUNTVILLE

13 miles north of the town of Napa on Hwy. 29.

These days Yountville is something like Disneyland for food lovers. It all started with Thomas Keller's French Laundry, simply one of the best restaurants in the United States. Now Keller is also behind two more-casual restaurants a few blocks from his mother ship—and that's only the tip of the iceberg. You could stay here for a week and not exhaust all the options in this tiny town with a big culinary reputation.

Yountville is full of small inns and high-end hotels that cater to those who prefer to walk (not drive) after an extravagant meal. It's also well located for excursions to many big-name Napa wineries, especially those in the Stags Leap District, from which big, bold Cabernet Sauvignons helped put the Napa Valley on the wine-making map.

GETTING HERE AND AROUND

To get to Yountville from Highway 29 traveling north, take the Yountville exit and then take the first left, onto Washington Street. Almost all of Yountville's business and restaurants are clustered along Washington Street in the first half mile. Yountville Cross Road connects tiny downtown Yountville to the Silverado Trail, along which many of the area's best wineries are located.

EXPLORING

Domaine Chandon. On a knoll west of downtown dotted with whimsical sculptures and shaded with ancient oak trees, this French-owned winery claims one of Yountville's prime pieces of real estate. Basic tours of the sleek, modern facilities are available for $12 (not including a tasting), but other tours ($32 each), which focus on various topics (food-and-wine pairing or Pinot production, for example), end with a seated tasting. The top-quality sparklers are made using the laborious *méthode champenoise*. For the complete experience, order hors d'oeuvres to accompany the wines in the tasting room; although Chandon is best known for its bubblies, still wines like the Chardonnay, Pinot Noir, and Pinot Meunier are also worth a try. Only wine club members are welcome to bring young children. ✉ *1 California Dr., west of Hwy. 29* ☎ *707/944–2280, 888/242–6366* ⊕ *www.chandon.com* ✉ *Tasting $8–$22 by the glass, $18–$25 by the flight* ☉ *Daily 10–5; tours daily at 11:30, 3:30.*

Napa Valley Museum. Although it's not worth a long detour, this small museum, next to Domaine Chandon on the grounds of the town's Veterans Home, is a great respite from a day of wine tasting. Downstairs, the permanent exhibit, The Land and People of Napa Valley, focuses on the geology and history of the area, from the Native Americans who once lived here through the pioneer period to the modern winemakers who made it famous. The rotating fine-arts shows upstairs feature the work of Napa Valley artists. The museum also hosts regular Family Fun Days, which include arts-and-crafts projects for young kids. ✉ *55 Presidents Circle, at California Dr.* ☎ *707/944–0500* ⊕ *www.napavalleymuseum. org* ✉ *$10* ☉ *Wed.–Mon. 10–5.*

Robert Sinskey Vineyards. Although the winemaker here produces well-regarded Cabernet blends and a variety of aromatic white wines from all-organic, certified biodynamic vineyards, Sinskey is best known for its intense, brambly Pinot Noirs, grown in the cooler Carneros District, where the grape thrives. The influence of Rob's wife, Maria Helm Sinskey—a chef and cookbook author and the winery's culinary director—is evident during the tastings, which come with a few bites of food paired with each wine (her books and other culinary items are also available in the gift shop, next to the open kitchen). But for the best sense of how Sinskey wines pair with food, reserve a spot on the ($75) culinary tour, which takes you through the winery's gardens and ends with a seated pairing of foods and wine. ⊠ *6320 Silverado Trail, at Yountville Cross Rd., Napa* ☎ *707/944–9090* ⊕ *www.robertsinskey.com* ⊠ *Tasting $25; tour $75* ☉ *Daily 10–4:30; tours daily at 11 (by appointment).*

Stag's Leap Wine Cellars. The 1973 Cabernet Sauvignon produced by Stag's Leap Wine Cellars put the winery—and the Napa Valley—on the map by placing first in the famous Paris tasting of 1976. Today, a visit to the winery is a no-frills affair. Visitors in the tasting room are clearly serious about tasting wine, and aren't interested in distractions like a gift shop. It costs $30 to taste the top-of-the-line wines, including the limited-production estate-grown Cabernets, a few of which sell for well over $100. If you're interested in more-modestly priced wines, try the $15 tasting, which usually includes a Sauvignon Blanc, Chardonnay, Merlot, and Cabernet. (Note: Don't conflate this winery with Stag's Leap; that's a different operation entirely.) ⊠ *5766 Silverado Trail, at Wappo Hill Rd., Napa* ☎ *707/944–2020, 866/422–7523* ⊕ *www. cask23.com* ⊠ *Tasting $15–$30, tour $40* ☉ *Daily 10–4:30; tours by appointment.*

V Marketplace. In between bouts of eating and drinking, you might stop by V Marketplace. The vine-covered brick complex, which once housed a winery, a livery stable, and a brandy distillery, contains a smattering of clothing boutiques, art galleries, and gift stores. NapaStyle, a large store, deli, and wine bar, sells cookbooks, luxury food items, and kitchenware, as well as an assortment of prepared foods perfect for picnics. The complex's signature restaurant, Bottega, features the food of celebrity chef Michael Chiarello (⇨ *see Bottega*). ⊠ *6525 Washington St., near Mulberry St.* ☎ *707/944–2451* ⊕ *www.vmarketplace.com.*

WHERE TO EAT

$$$$
MODERN
AMERICAN
Fodor's Choice
★

✕ **Ad Hoc.** When superstar chef Thomas Keller opened this relatively casual spot in 2006, he meant to run it for only six months until he opened a burger joint in the same space, but locals were so charmed by the homey food that they clamored for the stopgap to stay. Now a single, seasonal, fixed-price menu ($52) is served nightly, with a small menu of decadent brunch items served on Sunday. The selection might include a juicy pork loin and buttery polenta, served family style, or a delicate *panna cotta* with a citrus glaze. The dining room is warmly low-key, with zinc-top tables, wine served in tumblers, and rock and jazz on the stereo. If you just can't wait to know what's going be served before you visit, you can call a day in advance for the menu or sign up for daily email blasts. ⑤ *Prix-fixe: $52* ⊠ *6476 Washington St., at Oak Circle* ☎ *707/944–2487* ⊕ *www.adhocrestaurant.com* ☉ *No lunch Mon.–Sat. No dinner Tues. and Wed.*

$$$$
ITALIAN

✕ **Bottega.** The food at this lively trattoria is simultaneously soulful and inventive, transforming local ingredients into regional Italian dishes with a twist. The antipasti in particular shine: you can order olives grown on chef Michael Chiarello's own property in St. Helena, house-made charcuterie, or an incredibly fresh fish crudo. Potato gnocchi might be served with duck and a chestnut ragu, and hearty main courses

10

like braised short ribs could come on a bed of spinach prepared with preserved lemons. The vibe is more festival than formal, with exposed brick walls, an open kitchen, and paper-topped tables, but service is spot on, and the reasonably priced wine list offers lots of interesting choices from both Italy and California. $ *Average main: $35* ⊠ *6525 Washington St., near Mulberry St.* ☎ *707/945–1050* ⊕ *www.botteganapavalley. com* ⊗ *No lunch Mon.*

$$$
FRENCH

✕ **Bouchon.** The team that brought French Laundry to its current pinnacle is also behind this place, where everything—the lively and crowded zinc bar, the elbow-to-elbow seating, the traditional French onion soup—could have come straight from a Parisian bistro. Roast chicken with mustard greens and fingerling potatoes and steamed mussels served with crispy, addictive *frites* (french fries) are among the hearty dishes served in the high-ceilinged room. ■ TIP➔ Late-night meals from a limited menu are served until midnight—a rarity in the Wine Country, where it's often difficult to find a place to eat after 10. $ *Average main: $25* ⊠ *6534 Washington St., near Humboldt St.* ☎ *707/944–8037* ⊕ *www. bouchonbistro.com.*

$$$$
AMERICAN

✕ **Étoile.** Housed at Domaine Chandon, this quietly elegant stunner seems built for romance, with delicate orchids on each table and views of the wooded winery grounds from the large windows. The restaurant's young chef Perry Hoffman turns out sophisticated California cuisine. Starters such as lobster carpaccio with pickled carrots play with a variety of textures, and luxe ingredients like shavings of black truffle dress up pappardelle with maitake mushrooms. Four- and six-course tasting menus can be ordered with or without wine pairings. The wine list naturally features plenty of Domaine Chandon sparklers, but it's strong in wines from throughout other regions of California as well. $ *Average main: $34* ⊠ *1 California Dr., at Hwy. 29* ☎ *888/242–6366* ⊕ *www. chandon.com/etoile-restaurant* ⊗ *Closed Tues. and Wed.*

$$$$
AMERICAN
Fodor'sChoice
★

✕ **French Laundry.** An old stone building laced with ivy houses the most acclaimed restaurant in Napa Valley—and, indeed, one of the most highly regarded in the country. The restaurant's two nine-course prix-fixe menus (both $270), one of which is vegetarian, vary, but "oysters and pearls," a silky dish of pearl tapioca with oysters and white sturgeon caviar, is a signature starter. Some courses rely on luxe ingredients like foie gras, while others take humble foods like fava beans and elevate them to art. Many courses also offer the option of "supplements," such as sea urchin or black truffles. Reservations at French Laundry are hard-won, and not accepted more than two months in advance. ■ TIP➔ Call two months ahead to the day at 10 am, on the dot. Didn't get a reservation? Call on the day you'd like to dine here to be considered if there's a cancellation. $ *Prix-fixe: $270* ⊠ *6640 Washington St., at Creek St.* ☎ *707/944–2380* ⊕ *www.frenchlaundry.com* ⌂ *Reservations essential* 🏛 *Jacket required* ⊗ *No lunch Mon.–Thurs.*

$$$
AMERICAN

✕ **Mustards Grill.** There's not an ounce of pretension at Cindy Pawlcyn's longtime Napa favorite, despite the fact that it's filled every day and night with fans of her hearty cuisine. The menu mixes updated renditions of traditional American dishes (what the restaurant likes to call "deluxe truck-stop classics"), such as barbecued baby back pork ribs and a lemon-lime tart piled high with browned meringue, with a handful of more innovative choices such as sweet corn tamales with tomatillo-avocado salsa and wild mushrooms. A black-and-white marble tile floor and upbeat artwork set a scene that one Fodors.com reader describes as "pure fun, if not fancy." ⑤ *Average main: $25* ✉ *7399 St. Helena Hwy. (Hwy. 29), 1 mile north of town* ☎ *707/944–2424* ⊕ *www. mustardsgrill.com.*

WHERE TO STAY
For expanded reviews, facilities, and current deals, visit Fodors.com.

$$$$ **Bardessono.** Although Bardessono bills itself as the "greenest luxury hotel in America," there's nothing spartan about its large, sparce rooms. **Pros:** large rooftop lap pool; exciting restaurant on-site; polished service. **Cons:** expensive; the view from many rooms is uninspiring. **TripAdvisor:** "long weekend in paradise," "an exquisite favorite," "heavenly beds." ⑤ *Rooms from: $500* ✉ *6526 Yount St.* ☎ *707/204–6000* ⊕ *www.bardessono.com* ⟿ *50 rooms, 12 suites.*

RESORT

$$$ **Hotel Luca.** This 20-room Yountville inn that opened in 2009 embodies a rustic Tuscan style, with dark-wood furniture and soothing decor in brown and sage. **Pros:** extremely comfortable beds; attentive service; breakfast, included in rates, is served in the restaurant or delivered to your room. **Cons:** rooms are soundproofed, but outdoor areas get some traffic noise. **TripAdvisor:** "most comfortable bed in the world," "impeccable service," "laid-back luxury." ⑤ *Rooms from: $350* ✉ *6757 Washington St.* ☎ *707/944–8080* ⊕ *www.hotellucanapa.com* ⟿ *20 rooms* ❚❘❙ *Breakfast.*

B&B/INN

$ **Maison Fleurie.** If you'd like to be within easy walking distance of most of Yountville's best restaurants, and possibly score a great bargain, look into this casual, comfortable inn. **Pros:** smallest rooms are some of the most affordable in town; free bike rental; refrigerator stocked with free bottled water and soda. **Cons:** breakfast room can be crowded at peak times; bedding could be nicer. **TripAdvisor:** "very cozy and romantic," "very relaxing," "charming." ⑤ *Rooms from: $175* ✉ *6529 Yount St.* ☎ *707/944–2056, 800/788–0369* ⊕ *www.maisonfleurienapa.com* ⟿ *13 rooms* ❚❘❙ *Breakfast.*

B&B/INN
★

$ **Napa Valley Railway Inn.** Budget-minded travelers and those with kids appreciate these very basic accommodations—inside actual railcars—just steps away from most of Yountville's best restaurants. **Pros:** central Yountville location; guests have access to adjacent gym. **Cons:** minimal service, since the office is often unstaffed; rooms on the parking-lot side get some noise. **TripAdvisor:** "a gem in Yountville," "great carriages," "great location." ⑤ *Rooms from: $175* ✉ *6523 Washington St.* ☎ *707/944–2000* ⊕ *www.napavalleyrailwayinn.com* ⟿ *9 rooms.*

HOTEL

$$$ **Villagio Inn & Spa.** The luxury here is quiet and refined: streamlined furnishings, subdued color schemes, and high ceilings create a sense of spaciousness in the guest rooms, each of which has a fireplace and, beyond louvered doors, a balcony or a patio. **Pros:** amazing buffet breakfast; no extra charge for hotel guests to use the spa facilities; steps away from Yountville's best restaurants. **Cons:** can be bustling with large groups; you can hear highway noise from many of the rooms' balconies or patios. **TripAdvisor:** "perfect place for wine and food lovers,"

RESORT
★

10

"extra perks," "heaven in Yountville." $ *Rooms from: $375* ✉ *6481 Washington St.* ☎ *707/944–8877, 800/351–1133* ⊕ *www.villagio.com* ↝ *86 rooms, 26 suites* ⦿ *Breakfast.*

$$$ ⊞ **Vintage Inn.** Rooms in this lavish inn are housed in two-story villas
RESORT scattered around a lush, landscaped 3½-acre property. **Pros:** spacious bathrooms with spa tubs; lavish breakfast buffet; luscious bedding. **Cons:** highway noise is audible in some exterior rooms; pool area is smaller than the one at its sister property, the Villagio Inn & Spa. **TripAdvisor:** "lovely grounds," "well located hotel with comfortable amenities," "quiet place to stay." $ *Rooms from: $350* ✉ *6541 Washington St.* ☎ *707/944–1112* ⊕ *www.vintageinn.com* ↝ *68 rooms, 12 suites* ⦿ *Breakfast.*

OAKVILLE

2 miles west of Yountville on Hwy. 29.

There are three reasons to visit the town of Oakville: its gourmet grocery store; its scenic mountain road; and its magnificent, highly exclusive wineries.

GETTING HERE AND AROUND

Those driving along Highway 29 will know they've reached Oakville when they see the Oakville Grocery on the east side of the road. Here the Oakville Cross Road provides access to the Silverado Trail, which runs parallel to Highway 29. Oakville wineries are scattered along Highway 29, Oakville Cross Road, and the Silverado Trail in roughly equal measure.

You can reach Oakville from the town of Glen Ellen in Sonoma County by heading east on Trinity Road from Highway 12. The twisting route, along the mountain range that divides Napa and Sonoma, eventually becomes the Oakville Grade. The views of both valleys on this drive are breathtaking, though the continual curves make it unsuitable for those who suffer from motion sickness.

EXPLORING

Fodor'sChoice **Far Niente.** Though the fee for the combined tour and tasting is at the
★ high end, Far Niente is especially worth visiting if you're tired of elbowing your way through crowded tasting rooms and are looking for a more personal experience. Here you're welcomed by name and treated to a glimpse of one of the most beautiful Napa properties. Small groups are shepherded through the historic 1885 stone winery, including some of the 40,000 square feet of caves, for a lesson on the labor-intensive method for making Far Niente's two wines, a Cabernet blend and a Chardonnay. (The latter is made without undergoing malolactic fermentation, so it doesn't have that buttery taste that's characteristic of many California Chards.) The next stop is the Carriage House, where you can see the founder's gleaming collection of classic cars. The tour zips by the property's floating solar panel installation upon request, and ends back in the tasting room with a seated tasting of wines and cheeses. ✉ *1350 Acacia Dr., off Oakville Grade Rd.* ☎ *707/944–2861, 800/363–6523* ⊕ *www.farniente.com* ✉ *$50* ☉ *Tasting and tour by appointment.*

Far Niente's wine cellars have a touch of ballroom elegance.

Oakville Grocery. Built in 1881 as a general store, this popular spot carries unusual and high-end groceries and prepared foods. Unbearable crowds pack the narrow aisles on weekends, but it's still a fine place to sit on a bench out front and sip an espresso between winery visits. ✉ *7856 St. Helena Hwy. (Hwy. 29)* ☎ *707/944–8802.*

Opus One. The combined venture of the late California winemaker Robert Mondavi and the late French Baron Philippe de Rothschild, Opus One produces only one wine: a big, inky Bordeaux blend that was the first of Napa's ultra-premium wines, fetching unheard-of prices before it was overtaken by cult wines like Screaming Eagle. The winery's futuristic limestone-clad structure, built into the hillside, seems to be pushing itself out of the earth. Although the tours, which focus on why it costs so much to produce this exceptional wine, can come off as "stuffy" (in the words of one Fodors.com reader), the facilities are undoubtedly impressive, with gilded mirrors, exotic orchids, and a large semicircular cellar modeled on the Château Mouton Rothschild winery in France. You can also taste the current vintage without the tour ($35), as long as you've called ahead for a reservation. ■TIP➜ Take your glass up to the rooftop terrace if you want to appreciate the views out over the vineyards. ✉ *7900 St. Helena Hwy. (Hwy. 29)* ☎ *707/944–9442, 800/292–6787* ⊕ *www.opusonewinery.com* 🎫 *Tours $50-$70; tastings $35* ⊗ *Daily 10–4; tasting and tour by appointment.*

PlumpJack. If Opus One is the Rolls-Royce of the Oakville District—expensive, refined, and a little snooty—then PlumpJack is the Mini Cooper: fun, casual, and sporty. With its metal chandelier and wall hangings, the tasting room looks like it could be the stage set for a modern Shakespeare production. (The name "PlumpJack" is a nod to Shakespeare's Falstaff.) The reserve Chardonnay has a good balance of baked fruit and fresh citrus flavors, while a Merlot is blended with a bit of Cabernet Sauvignon, giving the wine enough tannins to ensure it can be aged for another five years or more. Visitors also can taste wines from the sister winery, Cade Estate. If the tasting room is crowded, take a breather under the shady arbor on the back patio, where you can enjoy a close-up view of the vines. ⊠ *620 Oakville Cross Rd., off Hwy 29* ☎ *707/945–1220* ⊕ *www.plumpjack.com* 🖂 *Tastings $15* ⊘ *Daily 10–4.*

Robert Mondavi. The arch at the center of the sprawling Mission-style building here perfectly frames the lawn and the vineyard behind, inviting a stroll under the lovely arcades. You can head straight for one of the two tasting rooms, but if you've never taken a winery tour before, the comprehensive Signature Tour and Tasting ($25), which concludes with a seated tasting, is a good way to learn about enology, as well as the late Robert Mondavi's role in California wine making. Those new to tasting and mystified by all that swirling and sniffing should consider the 45-minute Wine Tasting Basics experience ($20). Serious wine lovers should consider springing for the one-hour $55 Exclusive Cellar tasting, where a well-informed server pours and explains limited-production, reserve, and older-vintage wines. Concerts, mostly jazz and R&B, take place in summer on the lawn; call ahead for tickets. ⊠ *7801 St. Helena Hwy.(Hwy. 29)* ☎ *888/766–6328* ⊕ *www.robertmondaviwinery.com* 🖂 *Tours and tastings $20–$55* ⊘ *Daily 10–5; tour times vary.*

RUTHERFORD

2 miles northwest of Oakville on Hwy. 29.

From a fast-moving car, Rutherford is a quick blur of vineyards and a rustic barn or two, but don't speed by this tiny hamlet. With its singular microclimate and soil, this is an important viticultural center, with more big-name wineries than you can shake a corkscrew at. Cabernet Sauvignon is king here. The well-drained, loamy soil is ideal for those vines, and since this part of the valley gets plenty of sun, the grapes develop exceptionally intense flavors. The late, great winemaker André Tchelistcheff claimed that "it takes Rutherford dust to grow great Cabernet."

GETTING HERE AND AROUND

Wineries around Rutherford are dotted along Highway 29 and the parallel Silverado Trail just north and south of Rutherford Road/Conn Creek Road, which connect these two major thoroughfares.

EXPLORING

Beaulieu Vineyard. The Cabernet Sauvignon produced at the ivy-covered Beaulieu Vineyard is a benchmark of the Napa Valley. The legendary André Tchelistcheff, who helped define the California style of wine making, worked his magic here from 1938 until his death in 1973. This helps explain why Beaulieu's flagship, the Georges de Latour Private Reserve Cabernet Sauvignon, still garners high marks from major wine publications. The wines being poured in the main tasting room, which might include anything from a zesty Gewürztraminer to a lush Petite

Syrah, are notably good. Still, it's worth the $50 fee to taste that special Cabernet in the less-crowded reserve tasting room. ⊠ *1960 St. Helena Hwy.(Hwy. 29)* ☎ *707/967–5200, 800/373–5896* ⊕ *www.bvwines.com* ⊡ *Tasting $15–$50, tour $20* ⊙ *Daily 10–5.*

Cakebread Cellars. Jack and Dolores Cakebread snapped up the property at Cakebread Cellars in 1973, after Jack fell in love with the area while visiting on a photography assignment. Since then, they've been making luscious Chardonnays, as well as Merlot, a great Sauvignon Blanc, and a beautifully complex Cabernet Sauvignon. You must make an appointment for a tasting, for which there are several different options. The most basic usually involves a stroll through the winery's barrel room and crush pad and past Dolores's kitchen garden before ending in a taste of current releases. Other options focus on red, reserve, or library wines, and might take place in the winery's modern wing, where an elevator is crafted out of a stainless-steel fermentation tank and the ceiling is lined with thousands of corks. ⊠ *8300 St. Helena Hwy.(Hwy 29)* ☎ *707/963–5222, 800/588–0298* ⊕ *www.cakebread.com* ⊡ *Tastings $15–$45, tour $25* ⊙ *Daily 10–4; tasting and tour by appointment.*

☾ **Frog's Leap.** The owner, John Williams, maintains a goofy sense of humor **Fodor'sChoice** about wine that translates into an entertaining yet informative experi-
★ ence, making Frog's Leap the perfect place for wine novices to begin their education. You'll also find some fine Zinfandel, Cabernet Sauvignon, Merlot, Chardonnay, Sauvignon Blanc, Rosé, and also the German dessert wine Trockenbeerenauslese. The winery includes a red barn built in 1884, 5 acres of organic gardens, an eco-friendly visitor center, and, naturally, a frog pond topped with lily pads. The fun tour ($20) is highly recommended, but you can also just do a seated tasting that takes place on a porch overlooking the garden. ⊠ *8815 Conn Creek Rd.* ☎ *707/963–4704, 800/959–4704* ⊕ *www.frogsleap.com* ⊡ *Tasting $20, tour $20* ⊙ *Daily 10–4; tour by appointment.*

☾ **Honig Vineyard and Winery.** Sustainable farming is the big story at this small, family-run winery in the heart of Rutherford. Michael Honig, the grandson of founder Louis Honig, helped write the code of Sustainable Practices for the Wine Institute, and was a key player in developing the first certification programs for wineries across California. Some of the modern applications of this mind-set: solar panels that generate a majority of the winery's power and an on-site bee colony that helps with pollination. Four wines, including a stellar Cabernet Sauvignon and a renowned Sauvignon Blanc, reflect this commitment to excellence. Because the Honigs have three young children, the winery is incredibly family-friendly, with a special area for toddlers to play. ⊠ *850 Rutherford Rd.* ☎ *800/929–2217* ⊕ *www.honigwine.com* ⊡ *Tasting $10* ⊙ *Daily 10–4:30; tastings by appointment only.*

Inglenook. It's the house *The Godfather* built. Literally. Filmmaker Francis Ford Coppola began his wine-making career in 1975, when he bought part of the historic, renowned Inglenook estate. He eventually reunited the original Inglenook land and purchased the ivy-covered 19th-century château to boot. In 2006 he renamed the property Rubicon Estate, intending to focus on his premium wines, including the

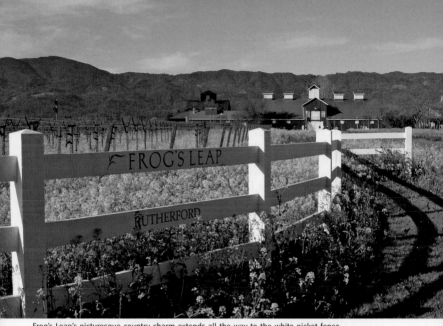

Frog's Leap's picturesque country charm extends all the way to the white picket fence.

namesake Cabernet Sauvignon–based blend. (The less expensive wines are showcased at the Francis Ford Coppola Winery in Sonoma County's Geyserville.) Then, in 2011, he renamed the place Inglenook. Various tours cover topics that include the estate's history, the Rutherford climate and geology, and the sensory evaluation of wine. Two distinctly different tastings are held in an opulent, high-ceilinged tasting room. The Bistro, an on-site bistro, has seating in a picturesque courtyard. ⊠ *1991 St. Helena Hwy. (Hwy. 29)* ☎ *707/968–1100, 800/782–4266* ⊕ *www.inglenook.com* ✉ *Tastings $25–$50, tours free–$95* ☉ *Daily 10–5; call for tour times.*

Mumm Napa. Although this is one of California's best-known sparkling-wine producers, enjoying the bubbly from the light-filled tasting room—available in either single flutes or by the flight—isn't the only reason to visit Mumm. There's also an excellent photography gallery with 30 Ansel Adams prints and rotating exhibits that feature local photographers. You can even take that glass of wonderfully crisp Brut Rosé with you as you wander. For a leisurely tasting of a flight of library wines while seated on their outdoor terrace ($30), reserve in advance. ⊠ *8445 Silverado Trail* ☎ *707/967–7700* ⊕ *www.mummnapa.com* ✉ *Tasting $7–$65, tour free–$20* ☉ *Daily 10–4:45; tour daily at 10 (free; tasting not included), 11, 1, and 3 ($20, tasting included).*

★ **Round Pond.** This winery makes Cabernet Sauvignon, Sauvignon Blanc and a host of other wines, but it's not all grapevines here—you can switch your focus to olives at will. The small farm grows five varieties of Italian olives and three types of Spanish olives. Within an hour of being handpicked, the olives are crushed in the mill on the property to produce pungent, peppery oils that are later blended and sold. Call at least a day or two in advance to arrange a tour of the mill, followed by an informative tasting, during which you can sample several types of oil, both alone and with Round Pond's own red-wine vinegars and other tasty foods. ■TIP➔ If you visit between mid-November and the end of December, you might be lucky enough to see the mill in action. ✉ *875 Rutherford Rd.* ☎ *707/302–2575, 888/302–2575* ⊕ *www.roundpond. com* 🍽 *Tour $30* ⊙ *Tour by appointment.*

Rutherford Hill Winery. A Merlot lover's paradise in a Cabernet Sauvignon world. When the winery's founders were deciding what grapes to plant, they discovered that the climate and soil conditions of their vineyards resembled those of Pomerol, a region of Bordeaux where Merlot is king. The wine caves here are some of the most extensive of any California winery—nearly a mile of tunnels and passageways. You can get a glimpse of the tunnels and the 5,000 barrels inside on the tours, then cap your visit with a picnic in their oak or olive groves. With views over the valley from a perch high on a hill, the picnic grounds are more charming than many others in Napa, which tend to be rather close to one of the busy thoroughfares. ✉ *200 Rutherford Hill Rd., east of Silverado Trail* ☎ *707/963–1871* ⊕ *www.rutherfordhill.com* 🍽 *Tasting $15–$30, tour $25–$40* ⊙ *Daily 10–5; tours daily at 11:30, 1:30, and 3:30.*

St. Supéry. Major renovations in 2012 transformed the tasting experience at this Rutherford hotspot from exclusive to ultra-exclusive. The winery now offers several small venues and patios for private tastings of library Cabernet Sauvignon wines. At other, more traditional, sampling sessions, the pours might include Sauvignon Blanc, Merlot, Chardonnay, and even Cabernet Franc or Petit Verdot wines. The tours here provide behind-the-scenes perspectives; the tour that ends with a tasting in the 1882 Queen Anne Victorian is worth the $50 admission. Outside, a small demonstration vineyard allows you to contemplate the variations among grape types and even taste the grapes when they're in season. ✉ *8440 St. Helena Hwy. (Hwy. 29)* ☎ *707/963–4507, 800/942–0809* ⊕ *www.stsupery.com* 🍽 *Tastings $15–$25, tours $25–$50* ⊙ *Daily 10–5.*

WHERE TO STAY

For expanded reviews, facilities, and current deals, visit Fodors.com.

$$$$
RESORT
★

Auberge du Soleil. Taking a cue from the olive-tree-studded landscape, this hotel with a renowned restaurant and spa cultivates a luxurious Mediterranean look—earth-tone tile floors, heavy wood furniture, and terra-cotta colors—and backs it up with lavish amenities such as flat-screen TVs (in both the rooms and bathrooms), private terraces, jetted soaking tubs, and extra-large showers. **Pros:** stunning views over the valley; spectacular pool and spa areas; the most expensive suites are fit for a superstar. **Cons:** stratospheric prices; the two least expensive rooms (in the main house) get some noise from the bar and restaurant. **TripAdvisor:** "exceeded our expectations," "beautiful property," "absolutely amazing." ⑤ *Rooms from: $650* ✉ *180 Rutherford Hill Rd., off Silverado Trail north of Hwy. 128* ☎ *707/963–1211, 800/348–5406* ⊕ *www.aubergedusoleil.com* ⤵ *31 rooms, 21 suites* ⑽ *Breakfast.*

10

ST. HELENA

2 miles northwest of Oakville on Hwy. 29.

Downtown St. Helena is a symbol of how well life can be lived in the Wine Country. Sycamore trees arch over Main Street (Highway 29), a funnel of outstanding restaurants and tempting boutiques. At the north end of town looms the hulking stone building of the Culinary Institute of America. Weathered stone and brick buildings from the late 1800s give off that gratifying whiff of history.

By the time pioneering winemaker Charles Krug planted grapes in St. Helena around 1860, vineyards already existed in the area. Today the town is hemmed in by wineries, and you could easily spend days visiting vintners within a few miles.

GETTING HERE AND AROUND

Downtown St. Helena stretches along Highway 29, which is called Main Street here. Many of the shops and restaurants are clustered on two pedestrian-friendly blocks of Main Street, between Pope Street and Adams Street. Wineries in the area are found both north and south of downtown along both Highway 29 and the Silverado Trail, but some of the less touristed and more scenic spots are on the slopes of Spring Mountain, which rises southwest of town.

EXPLORING

Beringer Vineyards. Arguably the Napa Valley's most beautiful winery, the 1876 Beringer Vineyards is also the oldest continuously operating property. In 1884 Frederick and Jacob Beringer built the Rhine House Mansion to serve as Frederick's family home. Today it serves as the reserve tasting room, where you can sample wines surrounded by Belgian art-nouveau hand-carved oak and walnut furniture and stained-glass windows. The assortment includes a limited-release Chardonnay, a few big Cabernets, and a luscious white dessert wine named Nightingale. Another, less expensive tasting takes place in the original stone winery. ■ TIP→ If you're looking for an undiscovered gem, pass this one by, but first-time visitors to the valley will learn a lot about the region's winemaking history on the introductory tour. Longer tours, which might pass through a demonstration vineyard or end with a seated tasting in the Rhine House, are also offered. ⊠ *2000 Main St.(Hwy. 29)* ☎ *707/963–4812* ⊕ *www.beringer.com* ⊜ *Tastings $15–$40, tour $20–$30* ☾ *May 29–Oct. 22, daily 10–6; Oct. 23–May 28, daily 10–5; call for tour times.*

Charles Krug Winery. The first winery founded in the Napa Valley, Charles Krug Winery, opened in 1861 when Count Haraszthy lent Krug a small cider press. Today the family of Peter Mondavi (Robert's brother) runs it. Though the tasting room is modest, the knowledgeable and friendly servers ensure a relaxed visit. The winery is best known for its lush red Bordeaux blends, but its Zinfandel is also good—or go for something unusual with the New Zealand–style Sauvignon Blanc. Its zingy flavor of citrus and tropical fruit is rare in wines from this area. The picnic area behind the tasting room has a view of the redwood cellar (not open to the public), where the wines are aged. ⊠ *2800 N. Main*

St. (Hwy. 29) ☎ *707/967–2200* ⊕ *www.charleskrug.com* ⌚ *Tastings $15–$25* ⊙ *Daily 10:30–5.*

Culinary Institute of America. The West Coast headquarters of the Culinary Institute of America, the country's leading school for chefs, are in the **Greystone Winery,** an imposing building that was the largest stone winery in the world when it was built in 1889. On the ground floor you can check out the quirky corkscrew display and shop at a well-stocked culinary store that tempts aspiring chefs with gleaming gadgets and an impressive selection of cookbooks. Attached to the store, at the Flavor Bar, you can experience a guided tasting ($10 to $15) of certain types of ingredients (for example, chocolate or olive oil) to gain a greater understanding of them. Upstairs, if no special events are taking place, you can browse the Vintners Hall of Fame, where plaques fastened to 2,200-gallon redwood wine barrels commemorate winemakers past and present. One-hour cooking demonstrations ($20; reservations required) take place on Saturday and Sunday. ⊠ *2555 Main St. (Hwy. 29)* ☎ *707/967–1100* ⊕ *www.ciachef.edu/california* ⌚ *Free* ⊙ *Restaurant Sun.–Thurs. 11:30–9, Fri. and Sat. 11:30–10; store and museum daily 10:30–6.*

Fodor'sChoice ★ **Joseph Phelps Vineyards.** Although an appointment is required to taste here, it's worth the trouble. In fair weather the casual, self-paced wine tastings are held on the terrace of a huge, modern barnlike building with stunning views down the slopes over oak trees and orderly vines. Though the Sauvignon Blanc and Viognier are good, the blockbuster wines are reds. The 2002 vintage of the flagship wine, a Bordeaux-style blend called Insignia, was selected as *Wine Spectator*'s wine of the year, immediately pushing up prices and demand. Luckily, you'll get a taste of the current vintage of Insignia (which goes for around $200 a bottle). Ninety-minute tasting seminars, available by appointment, are $40. The popular blending seminar, during which you get to try your hand at mixing the various varietals that go into their Insignia blend, is $60. ⊠ *200 Taplin Rd., off Silverado Trail* ☎ *707/963–2745, 800/707–5789* ⊕ *www.jpvwines.com* ⌚ *Tastings $25–$60* ⊙ *Weekdays 9–5, weekends 10–4; tastings by appointment only.*

★ **Spring Mountain Vineyard.** Hidden off a winding road behind a security gate, Spring Mountain Vineyard has the feeling of a private estate in the countryside, even though it's only a few miles from downtown St. Helena. Though Sauvignon Blanc, Pinot Noir, and Syrah are produced, the calling card here is Cabernet—big, chewy wines that demand some time in the bottle but promise great things. A tasting of current releases ($25) gives you a good sense of the wines' charms, but consider opting for the estate ($40) or reserve tasting ($50), either of which includes a meander through the beautiful property, from the cellars to the beautifully preserved 1885 mansion. ⊠ *2805 Spring Mountain Rd., off Madrona Ave.* ☎ *707/967–4188, 877/769–4637* ⊕ *www.springmountainvineyard.com* ⌚ *Tastings $25–$50* ⊙ *Daily 10–4; tastings by appointment only.*

10

WHERE TO EAT

$$$$
MODERN
AMERICAN

✕ **Farmstead.** Housed in a former nursery barn, Farmstead revolves around an open kitchen where chef Stephen Barber cooks with as many local and organic ingredients as possible. Many of them—including grass-fed beef, vegetables, extra-virgin olive oil, and honey—come from the property of parent company Long Meadow Ranch. Others are sourced from within a 30-mile radius. On Tuesday, two-course meals ($35) include comfort food such as chicken-fried steak, ribs, or fried chicken and dessert. In warm weather, you can dine on an open-air patio beneath apple trees. Instead of charging a corkage fee, Farmstead collects $2 per bottle to donate to a local non-profit organization. ⑤ *Average main: $35* ⊠ *738 Main St., at Charter Oak Ave.* ☎ *707/963–4555, 877/627–2645* ⊕ *www.longmeadowranch.com/Farmstead-Restaurant.*

$$
AMERICAN
★

✕ **Gott's Roadside.** A slick 1950s-style outdoor hamburger stand (formerly known as Taylor's Refresher) goes upscale at this hugely popular spot, where locals are willing to brave long lines to order breakfast sandwiches, juicy burgers, root-beer floats, and garlic fries. You'll also find plenty of choices not available a half century ago, such as the ahi tuna burger and the chicken club with pesto mayo. Try to arrive early or late for lunch, or all the shaded picnic tables on the lawn might be filled. ⑤ *Average main: $15* ⊠ *933 Main St. (Hwy. 29)* ☎ *707/963–3486* ⊕ *www.gotts.com.*

$$
AMERICAN

✕ **Market.** Comfort reigns at this understated-yet-modern eatery. Executive chef and owner Eduardo Martinez spruces up American classics such as crab Louis, made with local Dungeness crab, and fried chicken served with jalapeño corn bread. Sunday brunch is popular, with locals frequently lining up outside the door. For the most relaxed experience, stroll in at lunchtime midweek and linger over local wine from the extensive list. ⑤ *Average main: $18* ⊠ *1347 Main St., Hunt and Adams Sts.* ☎ *707/963–3799* ⊕ *marketsthelena.com.*

$$$$
AMERICAN
Fodor's Choice
★

✕ **The Restaurant at Meadowood.** Chef Christopher Kostow has garnered rave reviews for transforming seasonal local products (some grown right on the property) into elaborate, elegant fare. The "composition of carrots," constructed of the tiniest carrots imaginable accompanied by delicate shavings of chocolate, foie gras, and candied tangerine (it sounds odd, but it works) is just one example of Kostow's inventiveness and playfulness. Other dishes, such as slow-cooked black cod with chorizo and lamb, demonstrate an earthier approach. The chef's menu ($225, $430 with wine pairings), composed of (roughly) seven courses, is the best way to appreciate the experience, but the gracious and well-trained servers provide some of the best service in the valley even if you're ordering a less extravagant four- or five-course menu (prices here start at $125, $230 with wine). The warm lighting and well-spaced tables in the dining room, which was renovated in early 2012, makes it a top choice for a romantic tête-à-tête. ⑤ *Prix-fixe: $125* ⊠ *900 Meadowood La.* ☎ *707/967–1205, 800/458–8080* ⊕ *www.meadowood.com* ☾ *Closed Sun. No lunch.*

$$$$
MEDITERRANEAN
★

✕ **Terra.** St. Helena may have newer, flashier, and more dramatic restaurants, but for old-school romance and service, many diners return year after year to this quiet favorite in an 1884 fieldstone building. Since

1988, chef Hiro Sone has been giving unexpected twists to Italian and southern French cuisine in dishes such as the mussel soup with caramelized onions and garlic croutons, heavily perfumed with the scent of saffron. A few, like the signature sake-marinated black cod in a *shiso* broth, draw on Sone's Japanese background. Homey yet elegant desserts, courtesy of Sone's wife, Lissa Doumani, might include a chocolate caramel tart topped with fleur de sel. Next door, Bar Terra serves inventive cocktails and local wines. $ *Average main: $35* ⊠ *1345 Railroad Ave., off Hunt Ave.* ☎ *707/963–8931* ⊕ *www.terrarestaurant.com* ☉ *Closed Tues. No lunch.*

$$$
MEDITERRANEAN
✕ **Wine Spectator Greystone Restaurant.** The Culinary Institute of America runs this place in the **Greystone Winery,** which also once served as the Christian Brothers Winery. Century-old stone walls encase a spacious restaurant that bustles at both lunch and dinner, with several cooking stations in full view. On busy nights you may find the hard-at-work chefs more entertaining than your dining companions. The tables on the terrace, shaded by red umbrellas, are away from the action, but on fair days they're even more appealing, providing a panoramic view down the hillside. The menu has a Mediterranean spirit and emphasizes locally grown produce. Typical main courses include prosciutto-wrapped cod and house-made pasta with trumpet mushrooms and a sherry cream sauce. $ *Average main: $25* ⊠ *2555 Main St. (Hwy. 29)* ☎ *707/967–1010* ⊕ *www.ciachef.edu/restaurants/wsgr/.*

WHERE TO STAY
For expanded reviews, facilities, and current deals, visit Fodors.com.

$
HOTEL
🏨 **El Bonita Motel.** Only in St. Helena would a basic room in a roadside motel cost around $200 a night in high season, but for budget-minded travelers the tidy rooms here are pleasant enough, and the landscaped grounds and picnic tables elevate this property over similar places. **Pros:** cheerful rooms; hot tub; microwaves and mini-refrigerators. **Cons:** road noise is a problem in some rooms. **TripAdvisor:** "wonderful budget bargain," "comfortable place to stay," "great location." $ *Rooms from: $149* ⊠ *195 Main St. (Hwy. 29)* ☎ *707/963–3216, 800/541–3284* ⊕ *www.elbonita.com* ⇲ *38 rooms, 4 suites* ○| *Breakfast.*

$$$$
RESORT
Fodor's Choice
★
🏨 **Meadowood Resort.** A rambling lodge and several gray clapboard bungalows are scattered across this sprawling property, giving it an exclusive New England feel, and every unit runs seamlessly—starting with the gatehouse staff, who alert the front desk to arrivals. **Pros:** site of one of Napa's best restaurants; lovely hiking trails on the property; the most gracious service in all of Napa. **Cons:** very expensive; far from shops in downtown St. Helena. **TripAdvisor:** "wonderful property in a great location," "very quiet and romantic," "over-the-top service." $ *Rooms from: $525* ⊠ *900 Meadowood La.* ☎ *707/963–3646, 800/458–8080* ⊕ *www.meadowood.com* ⇲ *85 rooms, suites and cottages.*

$
B&B/INN
🏨 **Wine Country Inn & Gardens.** A pastoral landscape of vine-covered hills surrounds this retreat, which was styled after the traditional New England inns its owners liked to visit in the 1970s—rooms are decorated with homey furniture like four-poster beds, and most have a wood-burning or gas fireplace, a large jetted tub, and a patio or balcony overlooking the vineyards. **Pros:** free shuttle to some restaurants

(reserve early); lovely grounds; swimming pool is heated year-round. **Cons:** some rooms let in noise from neighbors; some areas could use updating. **TripAdvisor:** "helpful staff," "quiet cozy country inn," "rustic feel." $ *Rooms from: $250* ✉ *1152 Lodi La., east of Hwy. 29* ☎ *707/963–7077, 888/465–4608* ⊕ *www.winecountryinn.com* ⇌ *24 rooms, 5 cottages* ⊙| *Breakfast.*

SHOPPING

Baksheesh. A member of the Fair Trade Federation, this funky store sells imported art, crafts, textiles, and other items from countries in Africa, Asia, and South America. ✉ *1327 Main St., at Hunt Ave.* ☎ *707/968–9182.*

Spice Islands Marketplace. This fun store inside the Culinary Institute of America at Greystone is the place to shop for cookbooks, kitchenware, and everything else related to cooking and preparing food. ✉ *Culinary Institute of America, 2555 Main St. (Hwy. 29)* ☎ *888/424–2433, 707/967–2309.*

Woodhouse Chocolate. Elaborate confections handmade on the premises are displayed like miniature works of art at this lovely shop that resembles an 18th-century Parisian salon. ✉ *1367 Main St. (Hwy. 29)* ☎ *707/963–8413, 800/966–3468.*

CALISTOGA

3 miles northwest of St. Helena on Hwy. 29.

With false-fronted, Old West–style shops, 19th-century hotels, and unpretentious cafés lining Lincoln Avenue, the town's main drag, Calistoga has a slightly rough-and-tumble feel that's unique in the Napa Valley. It comes across as more down-to-earth than some of the polished towns to the south. And it's easier to find a bargain here, making it a handy home base for exploring the surrounding vineyards and back roads.

Ironically, Calistoga was developed as a swell, tourist-oriented getaway. In 1859 maverick entrepreneur Sam Brannan snapped up 2,000 acres of prime property and laid out a resort, intending to use the area's natural hot springs as the main attraction. Brannan's gamble didn't pay off as he'd hoped, but the hotels and bathhouses won a local following. Many of them are still going, and you can come for an old-school experience of a mud bath or a dip in a warm spring-fed pool.

GETTING HERE AND AROUND

To get to downtown Calistoga from anywhere farther south in the valley, take Highway 29 north and then turn right on Lincoln Avenue. Most of the town's sights are found along a five-block stretch of Lincoln Avenue, or just off one of the side streets that intersect it. After about a mile, Lincoln Avenue (which changes names to Lake County Highway) intersects with the Silverado Trail.

EXPLORING

★ **Castello di Amorosa.** Possibly the most astounding sight in Napa Valley is your first glimpse of the Castello di Amorosa, which looks like a medieval castle, complete with drawbridge and moat, chapel, stables, and secret passageways. Some of the 107 rooms contain replicas of 13th-century frescoes, and the dungeon has an actual iron maiden from Nuremberg, Germany. You must pay for the tour ($33 or $43, depending on the wine you taste) to see the most of the extensive eight-level property, though basic tastings ($18 or $28) include access to a small portion of the astounding complex. All experiences include a sample of several Italian-style wines, including a "super Tuscan," a blend of Sangiovese and Merlot with Cabernet Sauvignon that has more heft than your average Italian red. ⊠ *4045 N. Saint Helena Hwy. (Hwy. 29)* ☎ *707/967–6272* ⊕ *www.castellodiamorosa.com* ☛ *Tasting $18–$28, tour $33–$44* ⊙ *Mar.–Oct., daily 9:30–6; Nov.–Feb., daily 9:30–5; tour by appointment.*

Chateau Montelena. This modest winery in northern Calistoga helped establish the Napa Valley's reputation for quality wine making when its 1973 Chardonnay took first place at a blind tasting in Paris, shocking the international wine critics in attendance. The 2008 movie *Bottle Shock* immortalized the event, and the winery milks its cinematic fame with a special tour ($25) that includes a tasting of Chardonnays and a souvenir. More traditional tastings ($20) occur in the circa-1882 château. These five-wine tastings include two stellar Cabernet Sauvignons and a limited-release Riesling. ⊠ *1429 Tubbs La., off Hwy. 29* ☎ *707/942–5105* ⊕ *www.montelena.com* ☛ *Tastings $20–$20, tours $25–$30* ⊙ *Daily 9:30–4; tours vary.*

Clos Pegase. Designed by postmodern architect Michael Graves, the Clos Pegase winery is a one-of-a-kind "temple to wine and art" packed with unusual art objects from the collection of owner and publishing entrepreneur Jan Shrem. After tasting the wines, which include a bright Sauvignon Blanc, fruity Chardonnays, and mellow Pinot Noirs, Merlots, and Cabernets (they're made in a soft, approachable style and meant to be drunk somewhat young), be sure to check out the surrealist paintings near the main tasting room, which include a Jean Dubuffet painting you may have seen on a Clos Pegase label. Better yet, bring a picnic and have lunch in the courtyard, where a curvaceous Henry Moore sculpture is one of about two dozen works of art. ⊠ *1060 Dunaweal La., off Hwy. 29* ☎ *707/942–4981* ⊕ *www.clospegase.com* ☛ *Tasting $10–$35, tour $20* ⊙ *Daily 10:30–5; tour daily at 11:30 and 2.*

Robert Louis Stevenson State Park. Encompassing the summit of Mt. St. Helena, this mostly undeveloped park is home to the area where Stevenson and his bride, Fanny Osbourne, spent their honeymoon in an abandoned bunkhouse of the Silverado Mine. This stay in 1880 inspired the writer's travel memoir *The Silverado Squatters,* and Spyglass Hill in *Treasure Island* is thought to be a portrait of Mt. St. Helena. A marble memorial marks the site of the bunkhouse. ■ TIP➜ **The hike to the summit is 10 miles round-trip; bring water and dress appropriately. The trail is steep and lacks shade in spots, but the summit is often cool and breezy.** ⊠ *Hwy. 29, 7 miles north of Calistoga* ☎ *707/942–4575* ⊕ *www.parks.ca.gov/?page_id=472* ☛ *Free* ⊙ *Daily sunrise–sunset.*

Fodor's Choice ★ Schramsberg. Founded in the 1860s, Schramsberg, one of Napa's oldest wineries, produces bubblies made using the traditional *méthode*

Floor-to-ceiling stacked bottles are no exaggeration in Schramsberg's cellars.

champenoise (which means, among other things, that the wine undergoes a second fermentation in the bottle before being "riddled," or turned every few days over a period of weeks, to nudge the sediment into the neck of the bottle). To taste, you must tour first, but what a tour: in addition to glimpsing the winery's historic architecture, you get to tour the underground cellars dug in the late 19th century by Chinese laborers. Down in the caves, a mind-boggling 2 million bottles are stacked in gravity-defying configurations. The tour fee ($45) includes generous pours of several very different sparkling wines, as well as tiny snacks to enhance the experience. ⊠ *1400 Schramsberg Rd., off Hwy. 29* ☎ *707/942–4558, 800/877–3623* ⊕ *www.schramsberg.com* ✉ *Tasting and tour $45* ☉ *Tasting and tour by appointment.*

Storybook Mountain Vineyards. Tucked into a rock face in the Mayacamas range, Storybook Mountain Vineyards occupies a picture-perfect site, with vines rising steeply from the winery in dramatic tiers. Zinfandel is king here, and there's even a Zin Gris, an unusual dry rosé of Zinfandel grapes. (In Burgundy, *Vin Gris*—pale rosé—is made from Pinot Noir grapes.) Tastings are preceded by a low-key tour, during which you take a short walk up the hillside and then visit the atmospheric tunnels, parts of which have the same rough-hewn look as they did when Chinese laborers painstakingly dug them around 1888. ⊠ *3835 Hwy. 128, 4 miles northwest of town* ☎ *707/942–5310* ⊕ *www.storybookwines.com* ✉ *Free* ☉ *Mon.–Sat.; tour and tasting by appointment.*

WHERE TO EAT

$$
ITALIAN

✕ **Barolo.** With red-leather seats, artsy light fixtures, and a marble bar indoors and café seating out, this Italian-inflected wine bar inside the Mount View Hotel is a stylish, modern spot for a glass of wine, with many from small producers you probably haven't heard of. Small plates that could have come straight from Tuscany—fried calamari, risotto croquettes, a selection of *salumi*—are great for sharing. A handful of well-executed large plates, like the pappardelle with shrimp and braised short ribs, round out the menu. ⑤ *Average main: $20* ⊠ *1457 Lincoln Ave.* ☎ *707/942–9900* ⊕ *www.barolocalistoga.com* ☽ *No lunch.*

$$$
AMERICAN

✕ **Calistoga Inn Restaurant and Brewery.** On pleasant days this riverside restaurant and its sprawling, tree-shaded patio come into their own. At lunchtime, casual plates like a grilled-turkey-and-Brie sandwich or a vegetarian black-bean chili are light enough to leave some energy for an afternoon of wine tasting. And at night, when there's often live jazz played on the patio during the warm months, you'll find heartier dishes such as braised lamb shank or Sonoma duck breast with a fennel-and-Parmesan stuffing. Service can be a bit lackadaisical, so order one of the house-made brews and enjoy the atmosphere while you're waiting. ⑤ *Average main: $25* ⊠ *1250 Lincoln Ave., at Cedar St.* ☎ *707/942–4101* ⊕ *www.calistogainn.com/restaurant.html.*

$$$$
MODERN
AMERICAN

✕ **JoLe.** Local produce plays a starring role at this modern American restaurant inside the Mount View Hotel, not surprising as chef Matt Spector is one of the area's biggest proponents of farm-to-table dining. Depending on when you visit, you might enjoy Mendocino-caught squid with crab stuffing; Forni, Brown & Welsh mixed greens with fresh Asian pears; and chicken-fried quail with fig jam. The menu is available à la carte, and there are four-, five- and six-course prix-fixe options. No visit is complete without a slice of coconut cream pie. Pastry chef Sonjia Spector also makes scrumptious cupcakes for patrons to buy and take home. ⑤ *Average main: $45* ⊠ *1457 Lincoln Ave., near Fair Way* ☎ *707/942–9538* ⊕ *jolerestaurant.com* ☽ *No Lunch.*

WHERE TO STAY

For expanded reviews, facilities, and current deals, visit Fodors.com.

$
B&B/INN

▦ **Brannan Cottage Inn.** Housed inside the only one of Sam Brannan's 1860 resort cottages still standing on its original site, this inn, a pristine Victorian house with lacy white fretwork, large windows, and a shady porch, is on the National Register of Historic Places. **Pros:** innkeepers go the extra mile; most rooms have fireplaces; a five-minute walk from most of Calistoga's restaurants. **Cons:** owners' dog may be a problem for those with allergies; beds may be too firm for some. **TripAdvisor:** "friendly and helpful operators," "authentic and unique," "lovely peaceful getaway." ⑤ *Rooms from: $180* ⊠ *109 Wapoo Ave.* ☎ *707/942–4200* ⊕ *www.brannancottageinn.com* ⬩ *6 rooms* ⏚ *Breakfast.*

$$$$
RESORT
★

▦ **Calistoga Ranch.** Spacious free-standing cedar-shingle bungalows throughout this posh, wooded property have outdoor living areas, and even the restaurant, spa, and reception space have outdoor seating areas and fireplaces. **Pros:** almost half the cottages have private hot tubs on the deck; lovely hiking trails on the property; guests have reciprocal

10

All it needs is a fair maiden: Castello di Amorosa's re-created castle.

privileges at Auberge du Soleil. **Cons:** innovative indoor-outdoor organization works better in fair weather than in rain or cold; staff, though friendly, sometimes seems inexperienced compared to similarly priced places. **TripAdvisor:** "escape to serenity," "romantic," "unbelievable property." $ *Rooms from: $750* ⊠ *580 Lommel Rd.* ☎ *707/254–2800, 800/942–4220* ⊕ *www.calistogaranch.com* ⇆ *48 rooms.*

$$ **Cottage Grove Inn.** A long driveway lined with 16 freestanding cottages, each shaded by elm trees and with rocking chairs on the porch, looks a bit like Main Street, U.S.A., but inside the skylighted buildings are all the perks needed for a romantic weekend away. **Pros:** bicycles available for loan; freestanding cottages offer privacy; huge bathtubs. **Cons:** no pool; decor may seem a bit frumpy for some. **TripAdvisor:** "terrific property," "cozy romantic wine retreat," "charming and beautiful." $ *Rooms from: $300* ⊠ *1711 Lincoln Ave.* ☎ *707/942–8400, 800/799–2284* ⊕ *www.cottagegrove.com* ⇆ *16 cottages* ⦿ *Breakfast.*

B&B/INN

$ **Indian Springs.** Since 1861, this old-time spa has welcomed clients to its mud baths, mineral pool, and steam room, all of them supplied with mineral water from its four geysers. **Pros:** lovely grounds with outdoor seating areas; stylish for the price; enormous mineral pool. **Cons:** lodge rooms are small; service could be more polished. **TripAdvisor:** "indulgent and revitalizing," "heaven on Earth," "perfect place to stay." $ *Rooms from: $240* ⊠ *1712 Lincoln Ave.* ☎ *707/942–4913* ⊕ *www. indianspringscalistoga.com* ⇆ *24 rooms, 17 suites.*

RESORT
★

$ **Meadowlark Country House.** Twenty hillside acres just north of downtown Calistoga surround this decidedly laid-back but sophisticated inn, and each of the rooms in the main house and guest wing has its own charms: one has a deep whirlpool tub looking onto a green hillside, and

B&B/INN
Fodor's Choice
★

Best Wine Country Spas

Spas in Napa and Sonoma have two special angles. First, there are the local mud baths and mineral-water sources, concentrated particularly around Calistoga. Admittedly, it can seem really strange to lower yourself into a vat of thick, muddy paste, but once you've had a few minutes to get used to the intense heat and peaty smell, you may never want to leave your cocoon. Second, there are all those grapes: their seeds, skins, and vines are credited with all sorts of antioxidant and other healthful properties by those who use them in scrubs, lotions, and other spa products.

Below are some of the best spas of the bunch.

Dr. Wilkinson's. The oldest spa in Calistoga, this kitschy spot is well loved for its reasonable prices and its unpretentious vibe. Their mud baths are a mix of volcanic ash and peat moss. ✉ *1507 Lincoln Ave., at Fair Way, Calistoga* ☎ *707/942–4102* ⊕ *www.drwilkinson.com.*

Fairmont Sonoma Mission Inn & Spa. The largest spa of its type in the Wine Country, the vast complex covers every amenity you could want in a spa, including several pools and Jacuzzis fed by local thermal mineral springs. ✉ *100 Boyes Blvd./Hwy. 12,*

Boyes Hot Springs ☎ *707/938–9000* ⊕ *www.fairmont.com/sonoma.*

Kenwood Inn & Spa. Hands down, this is the prettiest spa setting in the Wine Country. The "wine wrap" body treatment is finished off with a slathering of lotion made from various grape-seed oils and red-wine extract. ✉ *10400 Sonoma Hwy./Hwy. 12, Kenwood* ☎ *707/833–1293, 800/353–6966* ⊕ *www.kenwoodinn.com.*

Spa Solage. This eco-conscious spa has reinvented the traditional Calistoga mud and mineral water therapies. Case in point: the hour-long "Mudslide," a three-part treatment that includes a mud body mask (in a heated lounge), a soak in a geothermal bath, and a power nap in a comfy sound/vibration chair. Traditional spa services are available as well. ✉ *755 Silverado Trail, at Rosedale Rd., Calistoga* ☎ *866/942–7442.*

Spa Villagio. This 13,000-square-foot spa with fieldstone walls and a Mediterranean theme has all the latest gadgets, including men's and women's outdoor hot tubs and showers with an extravagant number of showerheads. Huge spa suites—complete with flat-panel TV screens and wet bars—are perfect for couples and groups. ✉ *6481 Washington St., Yountville* ☎ *707/948–5050, 800/351–1133.*

10

others have a deck with a view of the mountains. **Pros:** sauna next to the pool and hot tub; welcoming vibe attracts diverse guests; some of the most gracious innkeepers in Napa. **Cons:** clothing-optional pool policy isn't for everyone. **TripAdvisor:** "amazing owners," "great stay with fantastic breakfast," "we've become regulars." ⑤ *Rooms from: $250* ✉ *601 Petrified Forest Rd.* ☎ *707/942–5651, 800/942–5651* ⊕ *www. meadowlarkinn.com* ⇴ *5 rooms, 5 suites* ⧉| *Breakfast.*

$
B&B/INN
⬚ **Mount View Hotel & Spa.** A National Historic Landmark built in 1917 in the Mission revival style, the Mount View nevertheless feels up-to-date, with freshly painted rooms (some are a dramatic red and

black), feather duvets, and high-tech touches like iPod alarm clocks. **Pros:** convenient location; excellent spa treatments. **Cons:** ground-floor rooms dark; mediocre Continental breakfast; some bathrooms could use updating. **TripAdvisor:** "luxury and history," "super relaxing amenities and spa," "great service and location." ⓈⒾ *Rooms from: $249 ✉ 1457 Lincoln Ave. ☎ 707/942–6877, 800/816–6877 ⊕ www. mountviewhotel.com ⤳ 18 rooms, 13 suites and cottages* ⦿| *Breakfast.*

$$$$
RESORT
⊞ **Solage.** The cottages at this resort, which spreads over 22 acres, don't look particularly luxurious from the outside, but inside the aesthetic is Napa Valley barn meets San Francisco loft, with high ceilings, polished concrete floors, recycled walnut furniture, and all-natural fabrics in soothing muted colors. **Pros:** great service; complimentary bike cruisers available; separate pools for kids and adults. **Cons:** ascetic vibe; some rooms don't have tubs. **TripAdvisor:** "modern touches in a traditional setting," "unparalleled concierge and service," "all around perfection." Ⓢ *Rooms from: $425 ✉ 755 Silverado Trail ☎ 866/942–7442, 707/226–0800 ⊕ www.solagecalistoga.com ⤳ 83 rooms, 6 suites.*

SPORTS AND THE OUTDOORS

Calistoga Bikeshop. This bike-shop-turned-outfitter currently offers a self-guided Calistoga Cool Wine Tour package ($80), which includes free tastings at small wineries. Best of all, the shop will pick up any wine you purchase along the way if you've bought more than will fit in the handy bottle carrier on your bike. ✉ *1318 Lincoln Ave.* ☎ *707/942–9687.*

SHOPPING

Mudd Hens. Stock up on bath amenities and soaking salts at this eclectic shop on downtown Calistoga's main drag. The store also sells candles and handmade soaps, including some made from carrot seeds. ✉ *1348C Lincoln Ave., at Washington St.* ☎ *707/942–0210, 800/793–9220.*

Wine Garage. Bargain hunters love this garage-turned-wine-shop, where all the bottles go for $25 or less. It's a great way to discover the work of smaller wineries producing undervalued wines. ✉ *1020 Foothill Blvd., at Hwy. 29* ☎ *707/942–5332, 888/690–9463.*

THE SONOMA VALLEY

Although the Sonoma Valley may not have the cachet of the neighboring Napa Valley, wineries here entice with an unpretentious attitude and smaller crowds. The Napa-style glitzy tasting rooms with enormous gift shops and $25 tasting fees are the exception here. Sonoma's landscape seduces, too, its roads gently climbing and descending on their way to wineries hidden from the road by trees.

The scenic valley, bounded by the Mayacamas Mountains on the east and Sonoma Mountain on the west, extends north from San Pablo Bay nearly 20 miles to the eastern outskirts of Santa Rosa. The varied terrain, soils, and climate (cooler in the south because of the bay influence and hotter toward the north) allow grape growers to raise cool-weather varietals such as Chardonnay and Pinot Noir as well as Merlot, Cabernet Sauvignon, and other heat-seeking vines. The valley is home to dozens of wineries, many of them on or near Highway 12, which runs the length of the valley.

ESSENTIALS

Contacts Sonoma County Tourism Bureau ⊠ *3637 Westwind Blvd., Santa Rosa* ☎ *707/522–5800, 800/576–6662* ⊕ *www.sonomacounty.com.* **Sonoma Valley Visitors Bureau** ⊠ *453 1st St., E, Sonoma* ☎ *866/996–1090* ⊕ *www. sonomavalley.com.*

SONOMA

14 miles west of Napa on Hwy. 12; 45 miles from San Francisco, north on U.S. 101, east on Hwy. 37, and north on Hwy. 121/12.

Founded in the early 1800s, Sonoma is the oldest town in the Wine Country. The central Sonoma Plaza dates from the Mission era; surrounding it are 19th-century adobes, atmospheric hotels, and the swooping marquee of the 1930s Sebastiani Theatre. On summer days the plaza is a hive of activity, with children blowing off steam in the playground while their folks stock up on picnic supplies and browse the boutiques surrounding the square.

On your way into town from the south, you pass through the Carneros wine district, which straddles the southern sections of Sonoma and Napa counties.

GETTING HERE AND AROUND

To get to the town of Sonoma from San Francisco, cross the Golden Gate Bridge, then go north on U.S. 101, east on Highway 37 toward Vallejo, and north on Highway 121, aka the Carneros Highway. When you reach Highway 12, turn left and take it north. It turns into Broadway, which dead-ends at Sonoma's Central Plaza. If you park here, a pleasant stroll around the plaza will take you by many of the town's restaurants and shops. Interesting wineries can be found a mile or so east of the plaza; signs on East Spain Street or East Napa Street will direct you to most of them.

EXPLORING

Fodor'sChoice
★
Bartholomew Park Winery. Although this certified organic winery was founded only in 1994, grapes were grown in some of its vineyards as early as the 1830s. The emphasis here is on handcrafted, single-varietal wines—Cabernet, Merlot, Zinfandel, Syrah, and Sauvignon Blanc. The wines themselves, available only at the winery, make a stop worth it, but another reason to visit is its small museum, with vivid exhibits about the history of the winery and the Sonoma region. Another plus is the beautiful, slightly off-the-beaten-path location in a 375-acre private park about 2 miles from downtown Sonoma (head east on East Napa Street and follow the signs). Pack a lunch to enjoy on the woodsy grounds, one of the prettier picnic spots in Sonoma. ⊠ *1000 Vineyard La., off Castle Rd.* ☎ *707/935–9511* ⊕ *www.bartpark.com* ⌖ *Tasting $10, tour $20* ☉ *Daily 11–4:30; tour Fri. and Sat. at 11:30 by reservation.*

Buena Vista Winery. It was here in 1857, at California's oldest premium winery, that Count Agoston Haraszthy de Mokcsa laid the basis for modern California wine making, bucking the conventional wisdom that

Sonoma Valley

vines should be planted on well-watered ground by instead planting on well-drained hillsides. Chinese laborers dug tunnels 100 feet into the hillside, and the limestone they extracted was used to build the main house, which is now surrounded by redwood and eucalyptus trees and a picnic area. The best wines here are the Chardonnay, Pinot Noir, Syrah, and Merlot grown in the Ramal Vineyard in the Carneros District. ⊠ *18000 Old Winery Rd., off Napa Rd.* ☎ *800/926–1266* ⊕ *buenavistawinery.com* ⊠ *Tasting $10* ⊙ *Daily 10–5.*

Gundlach Bundschu. Wine Country visitors may mispronounce this winery's name (it's gund-lak bund-shoe), but still they flock here to sample ultrapremium wines served by some of the friendliest pourers in Sonoma County. Most of the winery's land has been in the Bundlach family since the 1850s. The Cabernet Sauvignon, Cabernet Franc, Tempranillo, and Chardonnay wines are worth trying, and all are included in the standard $10 tasting. For a more comprehensive experience that also includes a tasting, consider the cave tour ($20) or the vineyard excursion ($40; only available between May and October). ⊠ *2000 Denmark St., at Bundschu Rd, off 8th St. E* ☎ *707/938–5277* ⊕ *www.gunbun. com* ⊠ *Tasting $10, tours $20–$40* ⊙ *Daily 11–4:30.*

Robledo Family Winery. Reynaldo Robledo Sr., a former migrant worker from Michoacán, Mexico, founded this winery that remains a family affair. You're likely to encounter one of the charming Robledo sons in the tasting room, where he'll proudly tell you the story of the immigrant family while pouring tastes of Sauvignon Blanc, Pinot Noir, Merlot, Cabernet Sauvignon, and other wines, including a Chardonnay that comes from the vineyard right outside the door. All seven Robledo sons and two Robledo daughters, as well as matriarch Maria, are involved in the winery operations. ⊠ *21901 Bonness Rd., off Hwy. 116* ☎ *707/939–6903, 888/939–6903* ⊕ *www.robledofamilywinery. com* ⊠ *Tasting $5–$20* ⊙ *Mon.–Sat. 10–5, Sun. 11–4, by appointment.*

Sonoma Mission. The centerpiece of Sonoma State Historic Park, this circa-1823 structure sits just north of Sonoma Plaza. Formally known as the Mission San Francisco Solano, this is the the northernmost of the 21 missions established by Franciscan friars in California. Budget cuts have led to reduced hours, but the facility, worth a peek if you're a history buff, is open daily except Monday between at least 11 and 3. On weekends, docents lead tours every hour on the hour. The modest museum contains exhibits about the California mission network. ⊠ *114 E. Spain St., at 1st St. E* ☎ *707/938–9560* ⊕ *www.parks.ca.gov/?page_ id=479* ⊠ *$3* ⊙ *Tues.–Sun. at least 11–3.*

Two Amigos Wines. This tiny winery, just off Sonoma Plaza, has a cultish connection to stardom: Co-owner Squire Fridell was television's Ronald McDonald from 1984 to 1991, and was the spokesman for Toyota for 33 years. Vestiges of Fridell's former life abound in the tasting room—you can't miss the big red shoes on the wall. To some extent, the clown has never left; Fridell and co-owner Bob Briner don Groucho Marx glasses on all wine labels (the glasses also are for sale). The wines here, especially the Bordeaux-style Cuvée Classico, are pretty good, too. ⊠ *Sonoma Court Shops, 25 E. Napa St., at 1st St. E* ☎ *707/799–7146*

⊕ *twoamigoswines.com* ⌫ *Tasting $10* ⊙ *Thurs.–Mon. 11–6, Tues. and Wed. 1–5.*

WHERE TO EAT

$$$
AMERICAN
★

✕ **Cafe La Haye.** In a postage-stamp-size open kitchen, skillful chefs turn out main courses that star on a small but worthwhile seasonal menu emphasizing local ingredients. Chicken, beef, pasta, and fish get deluxe treatment without fuss or fanfare. The daily roasted chicken and the risotto specials are always good. Butterscotch pudding is a homey signature dessert. The dining room is compact, but the friendly owner, who is often there to greet diners, gives it a particularly welcoming vibe. $ *Average main: $25* ⌧ *140 E. Napa St., at 1st. St. E* ☎ *707/935–5994* ⊕ *www.cafelahaye.com* ⊙ *Closed Sun. and Mon. No lunch.*

$$
ITALIAN

✕ **Della Santina's.** This longtime favorite, with a charming heated brick patio out back, serves the most authentic Italian food in town. (The Della Santina family, which has been running the restaurant since 1990, hails from Lucca, Italy.) Daily fish and veal specials join classic northern Italian pastas such as linguine with pesto and lasagna Bolognese. Of special note are the roasted meat dishes and, when available, petrale sole and sand dabs. $ *Average main: $18* ⌧ *133 E. Napa St.* ☎ *707/935–0576* ⊕ *www.dellasantinas.com.*

$$$
FRENCH

✕ **The Girl & the Fig.** Chef Sondra Bernstein has turned the historic barroom of the Sonoma Hotel into a hot spot for inventive French cooking. You can always find something with the signature figs in it here, whether it's a fig-and-arugula salad or an aperitif of sparkling wine with a fig liqueur. Also look for duck confit with French lentils, a burger with matchstick fries, or braised pork shank with soft polenta. The wine list is notable for its emphasis on Rhône varietals, and a counter in the bar area sells artisanal cheese platters for eating here as well as cheese by the pound to go. Sunday brunch brings rib-sticking dishes such as steak and eggs and a Basque frittata with potatoes, onions, and tomatoes. On weekend nights, the kitchen serves until 11. $ *Average main: $28* ⌧ *Sonoma Hotel, Sonoma Plaza, 110 W. Spain St., at 1st St. W* ☎ *707/938–3634* ⊕ *www.thegirlandthefig.com.*

$$
AMERICAN
★

✕ **Harvest Moon Cafe.** It's easy to feel like one of the family at this little restaurant with an odd, zigzagging layout. Diners seated at one of the two tiny bars chat with the servers like old friends, but the husband-and-wife team in the kitchen is serious about the food, much of which relies on local produce. The daily menu sticks to homey dishes like half a grilled chicken served with polenta and tapenade, rib-eye steak with a red-wine sauce, and a marinated-beet-and-frisée salad. Everything is so perfectly executed and the vibe so genuinely warm that a visit here is deeply satisfying. In fair weather a spacious back patio, with seats arranged around a fountain, more than doubles the number of seats. $ *Average main: $22* ⌧ *487 1st St. W, at W. Napa St.* ☎ *707/933–8160* ⊕ *www.harvestmooncafesonoma.com* ⊙ *Closed Tues. No lunch Mon.–Sat.*

$$
PORTUGUESE

✕ **LaSalette.** Chef-owner Manuel Azevedo, born in the Azores and raised in Sonoma, serves dishes inspired by his native Portugal in this warmly decorated spot, where the best seats are on the patio, along a pedestrian alleyway off Sonoma Plaza. Boldly flavored dishes such as pork

10

tenderloin *recheado,* stuffed with olives and almonds and topped with a port sauce, or one of the daily seafood specials might be followed by a dish of rice pudding with Madeira-braised figs or a port from the varied list. $ *Average main: $22* ⊠ *452 E. 1st St., between E. Spain and E. Napa Sts.* ☎ *707/938–1927* ⊕ *www.lasalette-restaurant.com.*

$$$$
AMERICAN
Fodor's Choice
★

✕ **Santé.** This elegant dining room has gained a reputation as a destination restaurant through its focus on seasonal and locally sourced ingredients. The room is understated, with drapes in rich earth tones and softly lighted chandeliers, but the food is anything but. Dishes such as the roasted Sonoma duck breast with braised Swiss chard and duck confit are complex without being fussy, while others, like the butter-poached Maine lobster with flageolet beans and lardons, are pure decadence. The restaurant offers a seasonal tasting menu ($125). Brunch is served in summer. $ *Average main: $55* ⊠ *Fairmont Sonoma Mission Inn & Spa, 100 Boyes Blvd., off Hwy. 12), 2 miles north of Sonoma, Boyes Hot Springs* ☎ *707/938–9000* ⊕ *www.fairmont.com/sonoma/GuestServices/Restaurants/SanteRestaurant.htm* ⊘ *No lunch.*

$$
AMERICAN

✕ **Sunflower Caffé.** This casual café has one of Sonoma's prettiest patios. Equipped with both heating lamps and plenty of shade, it's comfortable in all but the most inclement weather. On dreary days, cheerful artworks brighten up the interior, where locals hunker over their computers and take advantage of the free Wi-Fi. The menu, composed mostly of salads and sandwiches (as well as omelets and waffles for breakfast), is simple but satisfying, and it relies largely on local ingredients. $ *Average main: $15* ⊠ *421 W. 1st St., at W. Spain St.* ☎ *707/996–6645* ⊕ *www.sonomasunflower.com* ⊘ *No dinner.*

WHERE TO STAY
For expanded reviews, facilities, and current deals, visit Fodors.com.

$
B&B/INN

▦ **El Dorado Hotel.** Rooms in this remodeled 1843 building strike a spare, modern pose, with rectilinear four-poster beds and pristine white bedding, but the Mexican-tile floors hint at Sonoma's mission-era past. **Pros:** stylish for the price; hip restaurant downstairs; central location. **Cons:** rooms are small; lighting could be better; noisy. **TripAdvisor:** "awesome food," "rustic chic," "cute place with lots of charm." $ *Rooms from: $175* ⊠ *405 1stt St. W, at W. Spain St.* ☎ *707/996–3220* ⊕ *eldoradosonoma.com/el_dorado_hotel.html* ⇨ *27 rooms.*

$$$
RESORT

▦ **Fairmont Sonoma Mission Inn & Spa.** The real draw at this Mission-style resort is the extensive, swanky spa, easily the biggest in Sonoma, with a vast array of massages and treatments, some using locally sourced grape and lavender products. **Pros:** enormous spa; excellent, well-reviewed restaurant on-site; free shuttle to downtown. **Cons:** standard rooms on the smaller side; not as intimate as some similarly priced places. **TripAdvisor:** "very relaxing," "top notch," "serenity with some fun thrown in." $ *Rooms from: $329* ⊠ *100 Boyes Blvd., off Hwy. 12, 2 miles north of Sonoma, Boyes Hot Springs* ☎ *707/938–9000* ⊕ *www.fairmont.com/sonoma* ⇨ *166 rooms, 60 suites.*

$
B&B/INN
☾

▦ **Sonoma Creek Inn.** The small but cheerful rooms at this roadside inn with a sunny yellow exterior are individually decorated with painted wooden armoires, cozy quilts, and brightly colored contemporary artwork, elevating this bargain option well above your average motel.

Pros: clean, well-lighted bathrooms; a lot of charm for the low price. **Cons:** office not staffed 24 hours a day; slightly out-of-the-way location (about a 10-minute drive from Sonoma Plaza). **TripAdvisor:** "1930's charm with today's comfort," "clean and great value," "sweet and comfy." ⑤ *Rooms from: $129* ⊠ *239 Boyes Blvd., off Hwy. 12* ☎ *707/939–9463, 888/712–1289* ⊕ *www.sonomacreekinn.com* ⇖ *16 rooms.*

NIGHTLIFE AND THE ARTS

Sebastiani Theatre. This theatre, built on Sonoma Plaza in 1934 by Italian immigrant and entrepreneur Samuele Sebastiani, schedules first-run films, as well as occasional musical and theatrical performances. ⊠ *476 1st St. E, near W. Spain St.* ☎ *707/996–2020.*

Swiss Hotel. The bar here serves up Glariffee, a cold and potent cousin to Irish coffee, as well as rollicking good times (especially during football season). ⊠ *18 W. Spain St., at 1st St. W* ☎ *707/938–2884.*

SHOPPING

Sonoma Plaza is the town's main shopping magnet, with tempting boutiques and specialty food purveyors facing the square or just a block or two away.

Sign of the Bear. This modest and locally owned shop sells the latest and greatest in kitchenware and cookware, as well as a few Wine Country–themed items, such as lazy Susans made from wine barrels. ⊠ *435 1st St. W* ☎ *707/996–3722.*

Sonoma Cheese Factory. The town's popular cheese shop offers samples of many local cheeses, though the Sonoma Jack cheese and tangy Sonoma Teleme are no longer made on the premises. The store has everything you need for a picnic, from sandwiches to wine to homemade fudge. ⊠ *2 E. Spain St.* ☎ *707/996–1931, 800/535–2855.*

Vella Cheese Company. A block east of Sonoma Plaza, this old-world Italian cheese shop has been making superb cheeses, such as raw-milk cheddars and several varieties of jack, since 1931. ⊠ *315 2nd St. E* ☎ *707/938–3232, 800/848–0505.*

10

GLEN ELLEN

7 miles north of Sonoma on Hwy. 12.

Unlike its flashier Napa Valley counterparts, craggy Glen Ellen eschews well-groomed sidewalks lined with upscale boutiques and restaurants, preferring instead its crooked streets, some with no sidewalks at all, shaded with stands of old oak trees. Jack London, who represents Glen Ellen's rugged spirit, lived in the area for many years; the town commemorates him with place-names and nostalgic establishments. Hidden among sometimes ramshackle buildings abutting Sonoma and Calabasas creeks are low-key shops and galleries worth poking through, and several fine dining establishments.

Where to Eat and Stay in Sonoma Valley

GETTING HERE AND AROUND

To get to Glen Ellen from Sonoma Plaza, drive west on East Spain Street. After about a mile, turn right onto Highway 12. Drive about 7 miles, then take the Arnold Drive exit and turn left. Many of Glen Ellen's restaurants and inns are along a half-mile stretch of Arnold Drive.

EXPLORING

Arrowood Vineyards & Winery. Although it's neither as famous or as old as some of its neighbors, Arrowood produces well-regarded wines, especially the Chardonnays, Syrahs, and age-worthy Cabernets. A wraparound porch with wicker chairs invites you to linger outside the tasting room, built to resemble a New England farmhouse. In fact, if you're more interesting in lounging than a full-on tasting ($10–$15), you can buy a glass of wine to enjoy outside. Tours ($20), offered daily at 10:30 and 2 by appointment, conclude with a seated tasting. ■ TIP➔ If you're doing a reserve tasting on a weekend and are interested in discovering what Arrowood wines taste like after several years in the bottle, ask if any library wines are available for tasting. ⊠ *14347 Sonoma Hwy. (Hwy. 12)* ☎ *707/935–2600, 800/938–5170* ⊕ *www.arrowoodwinery. com* ⊠ *Tasting $10–$15, tour $20* ☉ *Daily 10–4:30; tours daily 10:30 and 2.*

★ **Benziger Family Winery.** One of the best-known local wineries sits on a sprawling estate in a bowl with 360-degree sun exposure. Benziger is noted for its Merlot, Pinot Noir, Cabernet Sauvignon, Chardonnay, and Sauvignon Blanc. The tram tours here are especially interesting (they're first come, first served). On a ride through the vineyards, guides explain the regional microclimates and geography and provide a glimpse of the extensive cave system. Tours depart several times a day, weather permitting. Reservations are needed for smaller tours that conclude with a seated tasting ($40). ■ TIP➔ Arrive before lunch for the best shot at joining a tour (they do fill up), and bring a picnic. The grounds here are lovely. ⊠ *1883 London Ranch Rd., off Arnold Dr.* ☎ *707/935–3000, 888/490–2739* ⊕ *www.benziger.com* ⊠ *Tastings $10–$20, tours $20– $40* ☉ *Daily 10–5; tours daily at 11:15, 12:45, and 2:15.*

Jack London State Historic Park. In the hills above Glen Ellen—known as the Valley of the Moon—lies Jack London State Historic Park, where you could easily spend the afternoon hiking along the edge of vineyards and through stands of oak trees. Several of the author's manuscripts and a handful of personal effects are on view at the House of Happy Walls museum, once the home of London's widow. A short hike away from Happy Walls are the ruins of Wolf House. Designed by London, it mysteriously burned down just before he was to move in. Also open to the public are a few restored farm outbuildings, and on weekends you can visit the Cottage, a restored wood-framed building where he wrote many of his later works. London is buried on the property. Budget

Horseback riding tours loop around Jack London State Historic Park.

cuts may result in reduced hours of operation; be sure to check before you visit. ✉ *2400 London Ranch Rd.* ☎ *707/938–5216* 🅿 *Parking $8, admission to buildings free* 🕓 *Park and museum Fri.–Mon. 10–5, cottage weekends 10–4.*

WHERE TO EAT

$$
FRENCH
Fodor'sChoice
★

✕ **The Fig Cafe.** Pale sage walls, a high, sloping ceiling, and casual but very warm service set a sunny mood in this little bistro that's run by the same team behind Sonoma's The Girl & the Fig. The restaurant's eponymous fruit shows up in all sorts of places, from salads to the wintertime apple-and-fig bread pudding. The small menu focuses on California and French comfort food, like steamed mussels served with terrific crispy fries, and a roast quail served with faro and olives. ■ **TIP➔** The unusual no-corkage-fee policy makes it a great place to drink the wine you just discovered down the road. ⑤ *Average main: $20* ✉ *13690 Arnold Dr., at O'Donnell La.* ☎ *707/938–2130* ⊕ *www.thefigcafe.com* 🕓 *No lunch weekdays.*

$$$
ECLECTIC

✕ **Glen Ellen Inn Oyster Grill & Martini Bar.** Tucked inside a creekside 1940s cottage, this cozy restaurant exudes romance, especially if you sit in the shady garden or on the patio strung with tiny lights. After taking the edge off your hunger with some oysters on the half shell and an ice-cold martini, order from a menu that plucks elements from California, French, and occasionally Asian cuisines. You might find ginger tempura calamari with mango salsa or grilled rib-eye steak with Gorgonzola mashed potatoes. Desserts tend toward the indulgent; witness the warm pecan bread pudding with a chocolate center that sits in a puddle of

Hitching a ride on the Benziger Family Winery tram tour

brandy sauce. $ *Average main: $25* ✉ *13670 Arnold Dr., at O'Donnell La.* ☎ *707/996–6409* ⊕ *www.glenelleninn.com* ☺ *No lunch Wed.*

WHERE TO STAY

For expanded reviews, facilities, and current deals, visit Fodors.com.

$

B&B/INN

★

▦ **Beltane Ranch.** On a slope of the Mayacamas range a few miles from Glen Ellen, this 1892 ranch house, shaded by magnificent oak trees, contains charmingly old-fashioned rooms, each individually decorated with antiques and thick old-fashioned bedcovers. **Pros:** casual, friendly atmosphere; reasonably priced; beautiful grounds with ancient oak trees. **Cons:** downstairs rooms get some noise from upstairs rooms; cooled with ceiling fans instead of air-conditioning. **TripAdvisor:** "the beauty is in the details," "beautiful and relaxing," "straight out of Gone with the Wind." $ *Rooms from: $175* ✉ *11775 Sonoma Hwy. (Hwy. 12)* ☎ *707/996–6501* ⊕ *www.beltaneranch.com* ⇆ *3 rooms, 2 suites, 1 cottage* ☟ *Breakfast.*

$$$$

RENTAL

▦ **The Chauvet.** Originally built in 1906 as a hotel, this yellow-brick property in downtown Glen Ellen is listed on the National Registry of Historic Places and was renovated in 2007 as six upscale condominium rentals. **Pros:** spacious accommodations offer room to spread out; local artwork adorns exposed-brick walls; short (uphill) walk to Jack London State Historic Park. **Cons:** no services on-site; long drive to downtown Sonoma. **TripAdvisor:** "lovely weekend," "true luxury condominiums," "unforgettable." $ *Rooms from: $600* ✉ *13756 Arnold Dr.* ☎ *415/823–4570, 855/242–8838* ⊕ *www.chauvetcondominium. com* ⇆ *6 units.*

$$
B&B/INN
Fodor's Choice
★

🛏 **Gaige House.** Gorgeous Asian objets d'art and leather club chairs cozied up to the fireplace in the lobby are just a few of the graceful touches in this luxurious but understated B&B. **Pros:** beautiful lounge areas; cottages are very private; excellent service. **Cons:** sound carries in the main house; the least expensive rooms are on the small side. **Trip-Advisor:** "amazing boutique hotel," "laid-back Sonoma at its best," "outstanding stay in serenity." ⑤ *Rooms from: $275* ✉ *13540 Arnold Dr.* ☎ *707/935–0237, 800/935–0237* ⊕ *www.gaige.com* ⬐ *10 rooms, 13 suites* ⏐⏐*Breakfast.*

KENWOOD

3 miles north of Glen Ellen on Hwy. 12.

Blink and you might miss tiny Kenwood, which consists of little more than a few restaurants and shops and a historic train depot. But hidden in this pretty landscape of meadows and woods at the north end of Sonoma Valley are several good wineries, most just off the Sonoma Highway.

GETTING HERE AND AROUND

To get to Kenwood from Glen Ellen, drive 3 miles north on Highway 12.

EXPLORING

Deerfield Ranch Winery. Visitors to this fun Kenwood winery arrive already in the middle of the action; from the parking lot, you walk across the crush pad, past a row of barrels, and straight into the wine cave. About halfway back, owners Robert and P.J. Rex have fashioned a makeshift living room, complete with comfy couches, tables, candles and tasting bars. Robert, who is also the winemaker, likes Super Tuscan-style and Bordeaux-style blends and makes them with gusto (the 2002 DRX is a blend to be reckoned with). Standard tastings ($15) include five wines; for an additional $5, you can taste all seven in the portfolio. ✉ *10200 Sonoma Hwy. (Hwy. 12)* ☎ *707/833–5215* ⊕ *www.deerfieldranch.com* 🍷 *Tastings $15–$20* ⊗ *Daily 10:30–4:30.*

Kunde Estate Winery & Vineyards. On your way into Kunde Estate Winery & Vineyards you pass a terrace flanked with fountains, virtually coaxing you to stay for a picnic with views over the vineyard. Kunde is perhaps best known for its toasty Chardonnays, although tastings might include Sauvignon Blanc, Cabernet Sauvignon, and Zinfandel as well. For insight into the winery's approach to sustainable winemaking, take a few minutes to wander around the demonstration vineyard outside the tasting room. The (free) basic tour of the grounds includes the extensive caves, some of which stretch 175 feet below a Syrah vineyard. Reserve in advance if you want to take advantage of the Mountain Top Tasting, a tour that ends with a sampling of reserve wines at the highest point on the property ($30). ✉ *9825 Sonoma Hwy. (Hwy. 12)* ☎ *707/833–5501* ⊕ *www.kunde.com* 🍷 *Tastings $10–$40, tours free–$30* ⊗ *Daily 10:30–5; tours daily at various times.*

★ **St. Francis Winery.** Named for St. Francis of Assisi, founder of the Franciscan order, which established missions and vineyards throughout California, St. Francis Winery has one of the most scenic locations in

10

Sonoma, nestled at the foot of Mt. Hood. The visitor center beautifully replicates the California Mission style, with its red-tile roof and dramatic bell tower. The charm of the surroundings is matched by the wines, most of them red, including rich, earthy Zinfandels from both the Russian River and Sonoma valleys. In addition to the usual wine tastings, food and wine pairings are available ($20 to $35). ☒ *100 Pythian Rd., off Hwy. 12* ☎ *888/675–9463, 707/833–6146* ⊕ *www. stfranciswine.com* ☒ *Tastings $10–35, tour $30* ☉ *Daily 10–5; tours by appointment (call for times).*

WHERE TO EAT AND STAY

For expanded reviews, facilities, and current deals, visit Fodors.com.

$$ ✕ **Café Citti.** Classical music in the background and a friendly staff (as
ITALIAN   well as a roaring fire when the weather's cold) keep this no-frills roadside café from feeling too spartan. Order dishes such as roast chicken and slabs of tiramisu from the counter and they're delivered to your table, a few of which are on an outdoor patio. The array of prepared salads and sandwiches means the café does a brisk business in takeout for picnic packers, but you can also choose pasta made to order. ⑤ *Average main: $15* ☒ *9049 Sonoma Hwy. (Hwy. 12)* ☎ *707/833–2690* ⊕ *www.cafecitti.com.*

$$$$ 🏨 **Kenwood Inn and Spa.** Buildings resembling graceful old haciendas and
B&B/INN   the mature fruit trees that shade the courtyards make it seem like this
★   inn has been here for more than a century (it was actually built in 1990). **Pros:** large rooms; lavish furnishings; extremely romantic. **Cons:** Wi-Fi can be spotty in some areas; expensive. **TripAdvisor:** "Italian getaway in Sonoma," "perfect place," "pure 5-star relaxation." ⑤ *Rooms from: $499* ☒ *10400 Sonoma Hwy. (Hwy. 12)* ☎ *707/833–1293, 800/353–6966* ⊕ *www.kenwoodinn.com* ⋑ *25 rooms, 4 suites* ⦿*l Breakfast.*

ELSEWHERE IN SONOMA COUNTY

At nearly 1,598 square miles, there's more to Sonoma County than the day-tripper favorites of Sonoma, Glen Ellen, and Kenwood. To the north is Healdsburg, a small town with killer shopping. The national media have latched onto it for its swank hotels and remarkable restaurants, and many Fodors.com readers recommend it as an ideal home base for wine tasting in northern Sonoma County.

Within easy striking distance of Healdsburg are the scenic vineyards of the Alexander, Dry Creek, and Russian River valleys. These lookers produce some of the country's best Pinot Noir, Cabernet Sauvignon, Zinfandel, and Sauvignon Blanc. Though these regions are hardly unknown names, their quiet, narrow roads feel a world away from Highway 29 in Napa. The western stretches of Sonoma County are sparsely populated in comparison to the above destinations and have fewer wineries. River Road heading west from U.S. 101—the exit is about 4 miles north of Santa Rosa—intersects Westside Road, which passes through Pinot Noir paradise on its way to Healdsburg.

SANTA ROSA

8 miles northwest of Kenwood on Hwy. 12.

Santa Rosa, the Wine Country's largest city, isn't likely to charm you with its office buildings, department stores, and frequent snarls of traffic along U.S. 101. It is, however, home to a couple of interesting cultural offerings. Its moderately priced chain lodgings can be handy, especially since Santa Rosa is roughly equidistant from Sonoma, Healdsburg, and the Russian River valley, three of the most popular wine-tasting destinations.

GETTING HERE AND AROUND

To get to Santa Rosa from San Francisco, drive north over the Golden Gate Bridge and continue north on U.S. 101 to the downtown Santa Rosa exit. To get to Santa Rosa from Sonoma Valley, take Highway 12 north. Santa Rosa's hotels, restaurants, and wineries are spread over a wide area; factor in extra time when driving around Santa Rosa, especially during morning and evening commute hours.

EXPLORING

Charles M. Schulz Museum. Fans of Snoopy and Charlie Brown will love the Charles M. Schulz Museum, dedicated to the cartoonist who lived in Santa Rosa for the last 30 years of his life, until his death in 2000. Permanent installations such as a re-creation of the artist's studio share the space with temporary exhibits, which often focus on a particular theme in Schulz's work. Children and adults can take a stab at creating cartoons in the Education Room or wander through the labyrinth in the form of Snoopy's head. ⊠ *2301 Hardies La., at W. Steele La.* ☎ *707/579–4452* ⊕ *www.schulzmuseum.org* ⊠ *$10* ☉ *Labor Day– Memorial Day, Wed.–Fri. and Mon. 11–5, weekends 10–5; Memorial Day–Labor Day, weekdays 11–5, weekends 10–5.*

★ **De Loach Vineyards.** Just far enough off the beaten track to feel like a real find, this winery produces old-vine Zinfandels, Chardonnays, and a handful of other varietals, but it is best for known for its Pinot Noir, some of which is made using open-top wood fermentation vats that are uncommon in Sonoma but have been used in France for centuries. (Some think they intensify a wine's flavor.) Tours focus on the estate vineyards, where you can learn about the labor-intensive biodynamic and organic farming methods used, and take you through the culinary garden. Call a day or two in advance if you want to taste wines paired with regional cheeses ($25) or purchase a picnic basket ($30) to enjoy in their attractive picnic area. ⊠ *1791 Olivet Rd.* ☎ *707/526–9111, 800/441–9298* ⊕ *www.deloachvineyards.com* ⊠ *Tasting $10–$25, tour $15* ☉ *Daily 10–5; tours daily at 11 (or by appointment).*

Luther Burbank Home and Gardens. The Luther Burbank Home and Gardens commemorates the great botanist who lived and worked on these grounds and single-handedly developed the modern techniques of hybridization. The 1.6-acre garden and a greenhouse show the results of some of Burbank's experiments to develop spineless cactus, fruit trees, and flowers such as the Shasta daisy. Instructions for accessing the free self-guided garden tour using visitors' own cell phones is posted near the

10

carriage house. In the music room of his house, a modified Greek revival structure that was Burbank's home from 1884 to 1906, a dictionary lies open to a page on which the verb "burbank" is defined as "to modify and improve plant life." To see the house, you'll need to join one of the docent-led tours, which leave from the gift shop every half hour or so. ⊠ *204 Santa Rosa Ave., at Sonoma Ave.* ☎ *707/524–5445* ⊕ *www. lutherburbank.org* ⊠ *Gardens free, tour $7* ☉ *Gardens daily 8–dusk; museum and gift shop Apr.–Oct., Tues.–Sun. 10–4.*

Fodor'sChoice **Matanzas Creek Winery.** The visitor center at this beautiful winery sets
★ itself apart with an understated Japanese aesthetic, extending to a tranquil fountain and a koi pond. Best of all, huge windows overlook a vast field of lavender plants. ■TIP➔ The ideal time to visit is in May and June, when the lavender blooms and perfumes the air. The winery specializes in Sauvignon Blanc, Merlot, and Chardonnay, although it also produces a popular dry rosé as well as some Syrah, Pinot Noir, and Cabernet. Guided tours range from an hour-long intro to the Bennett Valley, the tiny AVA where the winery is located ($10), to a more expensive one ($35) that concludes with a taste of limited-production and library wines paired with artisanal cheeses. If you'd like to go it on your own, ask for a printed vineyard-tour guide. ⊠ *6097 Bennett Valley Rd.* ☎ *707/528–6464, 800/590–6464* ⊕ *www.matanzascreek.com* ⊠ *Tasting $5, tours $10–$35* ☉ *Daily 10–4:30; tour by appointment.*

🝔 **Safari West.** An unexpected bit of wilderness in the Wine Country, this African wildlife preserve covers 400 acres on the outskirts of Santa Rosa. Set aside an entire morning or afternoon for a visit, which begins with a stroll around enclosures housing lemurs, cheetahs, giraffes, and many varieties of rare birds, like the brightly colored scarlet ibis. Next, guests climb onto open-air vehicles that spend about two hours driving around the expansive property, where more than 80 species, such as African cape buffalo, gazelles, wildebeests, and zebras make their home on the hillsides. All the while you're accompanied by a staff member who informs you about the animals, their behavior, and the threats they face in the wild. Note that the admission price for children ages 3 to 12 is $30–$32. If you'd like to extend your stay, lodging in well-equipped tent cabins ($–$$) is available. ⊠ *3115 Porter Creek Rd.* ☎ *707/579–2551, 800/616–2695* ⊕ *www.safariwest.com* ⊠ *$68–$78.*

WHERE TO EAT

$$$ ✕ **Zazu.** A low wooden ceiling, rustic copper tables, and rock music on
ITALIAN the stereo create a casual vibe at this roadhouse. It's a few miles west
Fodor'sChoice of downtown Santa Rosa, but the hearty, soulful cooking of owners
★ Duskie Estes and John Stewart lures passionate fans from all over the Wine Country. About 30% of the produce comes from their own garden, and the meats are house-cured, so the antipasto plate or a pizza with house-made pepperoni are both excellent choices. The small seasonal menu—a mix of Italian-influenced dishes and updated American classics—tends toward rich flavors, with choices like rabbit braised in red wine and served with a mushroom risotto. On Mondays in summer, try the three-course family-style "farm supper" for $39 per person. Sunday brunch, featuring cornmeal waffles (among other great choices), is worthwhile, too. ⑤ *Average main: $30* ⊠ *3535 Guerneville Rd., at*

Willowside Rd. ☎ 707/523–4814 ⊕ www.zazurestaurant.com ⊘ Closed Tues. No lunch.

WHERE TO STAY

For expanded reviews, facilities, and current deals, visit Fodors.com.

$ **⊞ Flamingo Conference Resort & Spa.** If Don Draper from the hit show

RESORT *Mad Men* popped into Santa Rosa, he'd probably park himself in this kitschy, 1950s-style resort just beyond downtown; the rooms have been updated since the property opened in 1957, but they've still got high ceilings and that old-school flair. **TripAdvisor:** "great customer service," "well-appointed room," "neat retro atmosphere." ⑤ *Rooms from: $119 ⊠ 2777 4th St. ☎ 707/545–8530, 800/848–8300 ⊕ www. flamingoresort.com ⥱ 170 rooms.*

RUSSIAN RIVER VALLEY

10 miles northwest of Santa Rosa.

The Russian River flows from Mendocino to the Pacific Ocean, but in terms of wine making, the Russian River valley is centered on a triangle with points at Healdsburg, Guerneville, and Sebastopol. Tall redwoods shade many of the two-lane roads that access this scenic area, where, thanks to the cooling marine influence, Pinot Noir and Chardonnay are the king and queen of grapes.

ESSENTIALS

Contacts Russian River Wine Road ⊠ *498 Moore La., Healdsburg* ☎ *707/433– 4335, 800/723–6336* ⊕ *www.wineroad.com.*

GETTING HERE AND AROUND

Many people visit the Russian River valley while based in nearby Healdsburg. To get to the wineries along Westside Road from Healdsburg's central plaza, head south on Center Street and turn right at Mill Street, which turns into Westside Road after it crosses U.S. 101. From Westside Road turn left on Wohler Road and left again on Eastside Road to loop back to U.S. 101 just south of Healdsburg. Wineries are somewhat more widely spaced in this rural area than in other parts of the Wine Country, and you should plan on spending some leisurely time driving along the winding roads. This is also a particularly scenic area for biking and jogging.

EXPLORING

Gary Farrell Winery. Pass through an impressive metal gate and wind your way up a steep hill to reach Gary Farrell, a spot with knockout views over the rolling hills and vineyards below. Although the winery has changed hands a few times since Farrell sold it in 2004, it's managed to continue producing well-regarded bottles under Susan Reed, who worked alongside him. Though its earthy, full-bodied Zinfandels and Carneros and Russian River Chardonnays are winners, the winery has built its reputation on its Pinot Noirs. ⊠ *10701 Westside Rd., Healdsburg* ☎ *707/473–2900* ⊕ *www.garyfarrellwines.com ⥱ Tasting $10–$15, tour $25 ⊘ Daily 10:30–4:30; tour by appointment.*

10

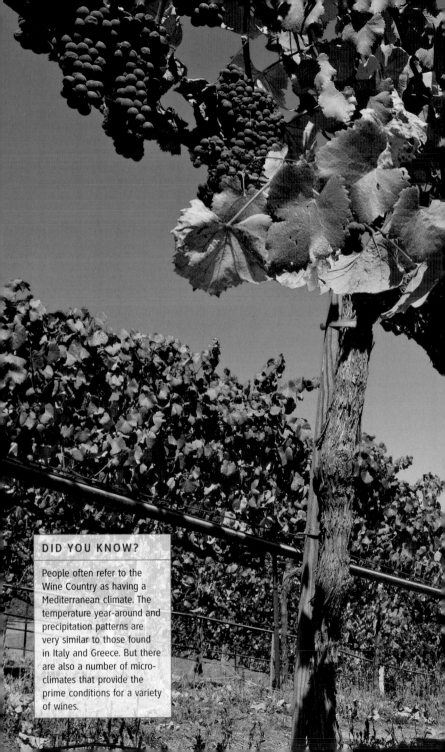

DID YOU KNOW?

People often refer to the
Wine Country as having a
Mediterranean climate. The
temperature year-around and
precipitation patterns are
very similar to those found
in Italy and Greece. But there
are also a number of microclimates that provide the
prime conditions for a variety
of wines.

Annual barrel tasting along Russian River's wine road

Hartford Family Winery. Pinot Noir fans flock to this opulent winery that sits off a meandering country road. The winemakers here turn grapes from the cooler areas of the Russian River valley, Sonoma coast, and other regions into crisp Chardonnays, old-vine Zinfandels, and Pinots, many of which are single-vineyard wines. Tours of the barrel room ($10, not including tasting) and a seated tasting of library wines ($25) are offered (call ahead). ⊠ *8075 Martinelli Rd., off Hwy. 116 or River Rd., Forestville* ☎ *707/887–1756, 800/588–0234* ⊕ *www.hartfordwines.com* ☜ *Tastings $15–$25, tour $10* ⊘ *Daily 10–4:30; tours by appointment.*

Fodor'sChoice
★ **Iron Horse Vineyards.** A one-lane country road leads to Iron Horse Vineyards, known for its sparkling wines, from the bright and austere to the rich and toasty, as well as estate Chardonnays and Pinot Noirs. Three hundred acres of rolling, vine-covered hills, barnlike buildings, and a rustic outdoor tasting area with a view of Mt. St. Helena set this winery apart from stuffier spots. Tours (by appointment) take place weekdays at 10 am. Winemaker David Munksgard leads the Friday tour. ⊠ *9786 Ross Station Rd., off Hwy. 116, Sebastopol* ☎ *707/887–1507* ⊕ *www.ironhorsevineyards.com* ☜ *Tasting $10, tour $20* ⊘ *Daily 10–4:30; tour weekdays at 10 by appointment.*

J Vineyards and Winery. The dry sparkling wines made here, all from Pinot Noir and Chardonnay grapes planted in Russian River vineyards, have wonderfully complex fruit and floral aromas and good acidity. Best known for its sparklers, J also makes fine still wines, often from Pinot and Chardonnay grapes, as well as brandy-fortified dessert wine and a pear eau-de-vie. You can sample just the wines at the tasting bar, or indulge yourself in the Bubble Room (reservations required), where top-end still and sparkling wines are paired with food. Free, 30-minute tours take place twice daily. ⊠ *11447 Old Redwood Hwy., at Eastside Rd., Healdsburg* ☎ *707/431–3646* ⊕ *www.jwine.com* ✉ *Tasting $20–$65, tours free* ☉ *Daily 11–5; Bubble Room hrs vary; tours daily 11 and 2:30.*

Rochioli Vineyards and Winery. Claiming one of the prettiest picnic sites in the area, with tables overlooking vineyards, this winery also has an airy little tasting room hung with modern artwork. Production is small—about 12,000 cases annually—and fans on the winery's mailing list snap up most of the bottles, but the wines are still worth a stop. Because of the cool growing conditions in the Russian River valley, the flavors of the Chardonnay and Sauvignon Blanc are intense and complex. It's the Pinot, though, that is largely responsible for the winery's stellar reputation; it helped cement the Russian River's status as a Pinot powerhouse. ■ TIP➔ **Though Rochioli typically pours only a couple of wines for visitors, it's one of the few wineries of its stature that still doesn't charge for a tasting.** ⊠ *6192 Westside Rd., Healdsburg* ☎ *707/433–2305* ⊕ *www. rochioliwinery.com* ✉ *Tasting free* ☉ *Thurs.–Mon. 11–4, Tues. and Wed. by appointment; closed mid-Dec.–early Jan.*

WHERE TO EAT

$$$$

FRENCH

Fodor's Choice

★

✕ **The Farmhouse Inn.** From the personable sommelier who assists you with wine choices to the servers who describe the provenance of the black truffles shaved over your intricate pasta dish, the staff matches the quality of this restaurant's outstanding French-inspired cuisine. The signature dish, "rabbit, rabbit, rabbit," a rich trio of confit of leg, rabbit loin wrapped in applewood-smoked bacon, and roasted rack of rabbit with a whole-grain mustard sauce, is typical of the preparations that are both rustic and refined, and the starters often include a seared Sonoma foie gras served with an apple cider sauce. The restaurant offers three-course, prix-fixe dinners every Monday for $49 per person. ■ TIP➔ **The inn is a favorite of wine-industry foodies, so reserve well in advance; if you haven't done so, you might still be able to dine in the small lounge area.** ⑤ *Prix-fixe: $52* ⊠ *7871 River Rd., at Wohler Rd., Forestville* ☎ *707/887–3300, 800/464–6642* ⊕ *www.farmhouseinn.com* ⌂ *Reservations essential* ☉ *Closed Tues. and Wed. No lunch.*

WHERE TO STAY

For expanded reviews, facilities, and current deals, visit Fodors.com.

$$$

B&B/INN

Fodor's Choice

★

▦ **The Farmhouse Inn.** Inside a pale yellow 1873 farmhouse and its adjacent cottages, this hotel maintains individually decorated guest rooms with comfortable touches such as down comforters and whirlpool tubs. **Pros:** one of Sonoma's best restaurants is on-site; free snacks, games, movies, and luxury bath products available; full-service spa uses many products made from local ingredients. **Cons:** rooms closest to the street get a bit of road noise. **TripAdvisor:** "in a different world," "the perfect wine country experience," "wonderful place with fantastic service." ⑤ *Rooms from: $350* ⊠ *7871 River Rd., Forestville* ☎ *707/887–3300, 800/464–6642* ⊕ *www.farmhouseinn.com* ⥩ *12 rooms, 6 suites* ⦿ *Breakfast.*

10

$ ⌨ **Sebastopol Inn.** Simple but cheerful rooms, freshly painted a sunny
HOTEL   yellow and equipped with blue-and-white striped curtains, have a spare
☾   California country style at this reasonably priced inn. **Pros:** friendly
staff; just steps from a café, wine bar, and spa. **Cons:** 30-minute drive
from most Russian River wineries; some will find the beds too firm.
TripAdvisor: "clean and convenient," "well tended," "big room."
⑤ *Rooms from: $135* ✉ *6751 Sebastopol Ave., Sebastopol* ☎ *707/829–*
2500 ⊕ *www.sebastopolinn.com* ⇆ *29 rooms, 2 suites.*

SPORTS AND THE OUTDOORS

Burke's Canoe Trips. This friendly Forestville-based outfitter rents canoes
($60 per day) for a leisurely paddle 10 miles downstream to Guerneville.
A shuttle bus will return you to your car at the end of the journey. From
late May through mid-October is the best time for canoeing. ✉ *River*
and Mirabel Rds., 1 mile north of Forestville ☎ *707/887–1222* ⊕ *www.*
burkescanoetrips.com.

HEALDSBURG

17 miles north of Santa Rosa on U.S. 101.

Just when it seems that the buzz about Healdsburg couldn't get any
more intense, there's another article published in a glossy food or wine
magazine about the restaurant Cyrus or the spanking new h2hotel. The
good news: You don't have to be a tycoon to stay here and enjoy
the town. For every ritzy restaurant there's a great bakery or relatively
modest B&B. A tin-roofed bandstand on Healdsburg's plaza hosts free
summer concerts, where you might hear anything from bluegrass to
Sousa marches. Add to that the fragrant magnolia trees shading the
square and the bright flower beds, and the whole thing is as pretty as
a Norman Rockwell painting.

The setting is no less idyllic in the nearby countryside, where stores
straddling the relatively untrafficked roads sell just-plucked fruits and
vine-ripened tomatoes. Winery buildings here are barely visible, since
they're tucked behind groves of eucalyptus or hidden high on fog-
shrouded hills.

GETTING HERE AND AROUND

To get to Healdsburg from San Francisco, cross the Golden Gate Bridge
and continue north on U.S. 101. About 65 miles from San Francisco,
take the Central Healdsburg exit and follow Healdsburg Avenue a few
blocks to the town's central plaza. Many of the town's hotels and restaurants ring the scenic town square and the few blocks radiating out
from here.

WHERE TO EAT

$$$$ ✕ **Barndiva.** This hip joint abandons the homey vibe of so many Wine
AMERICAN   Country spots for a younger, more urban feel. Electronic music plays
quietly in the background while hipster servers ferry inventive seasonal
cocktails. The food is as stylish as the well-dressed couples cozying up
next to one another on the banquette seats. Make a light meal out of
starters like goat-cheese croquettes or "The Artisan," a bountiful plate
of cheeses and charcuterie, or settle in for the evening with dishes such

as pork tenderloin with potato puree or lobster risotto. During warm weather the open-air patio is the place to be. $ *Average main: $32* ✉ *231 Center St., at Matheson St.* ☎ *707/431–0100* ⊕ *www.barndiva. com* ☾ *Closed Mon. and Tues.*

$$ ✕ **Bovolo.** Husband-and-wife team John Stewart and Duskie Estes—they
ITALIAN of Zazu fame—opened this restaurant on the Healdsburg Plaza to serve what they call "slow food . . . fast." The stars of the show: house-cured meats that are featured in pizzas, pastas, and sandwiches. For instance, the Salumist's Salad mixes a variety of cured meats with greens, white beans, and a tangy vinaigrette; and a thin-crust pizza might come topped with house-made Italian pork sausage and roasted peppers. House-made gelato served with a dark chocolate sauce or *zeppole* (Italian donuts) provide a perfect ending to a meal. On summer weekends, the restaurant serves breakfast at 9 am. Closing hours vary according to season, so call ahead if planning an evening visit. $ *Average main: $18* ✉ *106 Matheson St., at Healdsburg Ave.* ☎ *707/431–2962* ⊕ *www. bovolorestaurant.com* ⚇ *Reservations not accepted* ☾ *Often no dinner Tues. and Wed.; no dinner Sun.–Thurs. fall–spring.*

$$ ✕ **Costeaux.** This French-style bakery in downtown Healdsburg has won
FRENCH numerous awards for its bread, and the croissants and Epi breads are the best in all of Sonoma County. Also worth sampling: savory breakfast and lunch dishes, such as the homemade quiche or the omelet with sun-dried tomatoes, bacon, and Brie. Arrive early on weekends to grab a seat on the open-air patio. $ *Average main: $15* ✉ *417 Healdsburg Ave., at North St.* ☎ *707/433–1913* ⊕ *www.costeaux.com* ☾ *No dinner.*

$$$$ ✕ **Cyrus.** Hailed as the best thing to hit the Wine Country since French
AMERICAN Laundry, Cyrus has collected lots of awards and many raves from
Fodor'sChoice guests. From the moment you're seated to the minute your dessert plates
★ are whisked away, you'll be carefully tended by gracious servers and an expert sommelier. The formal dining room, with its vaulted Venetian-plaster ceiling, is a suitably plush setting for chef Douglas Keane's creative, subtle cuisine. Each night, diners have their choice of four set menus: five- and eight-course extravaganzas ($108 and $135, respectively), for both omnivores and vegetarians. Wine pairings are available for both (also $108 and $135). Set aside three hours to work your way from savory starters such as a terrine of foie gras with curried apple compote, through fragrant dishes such as a truffled wine risotto with Parmesan broth. Desserts are otherworldly, and every guest receives a box of tiny sweets to take home. If you've failed to make reservations, you can order à la carte at the bar, which has one of the best collection of cocktails and spirits in all of the Wine Country. $ *Prix-fixe: $108* ✉ *29 North St., near Healdsburg Ave.* ☎ *707/433–3311* ⊕ *www. cyrusrestaurant.com* ⚇ *Reservations essential* ☾ *Closed Tues. and Wed. in winter. No lunch.*

10

$$$ ✕ **Scopa.** At this tiny eatery chef Ari Rosen cooks up rustic Italian spe-
ITALIAN cialties such as house-made ravioli stuffed with ricotta cheese, braised chicken with greens and polenta, and *polpette Calabrese* (spicy meatballs served with smoked mozzarella in a tomato sauce). Simple thin-crust pizzas are worth ordering, too. Locals love the restaurant for its lack of pretension: wine is served in juice glasses, and the friendly

hostess visits guests frequently to make sure all are satisfied. You'll be packed in elbow-to-elbow with your fellow diners, but for a convivial evening over a bottle of Nebbiolo, there's no better choice. $ *Average main: $25* ✉ *109A Plaza St., near Healdsburg Ave.* ☎ *707/433–5282* ⊕ *www.scopahealdsburg.com* ☽ *No lunch.*

$$$

MEDITERRANEAN

✕ **Spoonbar.** Cantina doors that open wide onto Healdsburg Avenue make this trendy eatery especially appealing in summer, when the warm breeze wafts into the stylish space. Inside, concrete walls, mid-century modern chairs, and a long communal table fashioned from rough-hewn acacia wood create an urbane setting for the modern Mediterranean fare. "Small bites" like the marinated quail eggs, spicy lamb meatballs, and house-cured olives are standouts, while several of the entrée-sized dishes demonstrate a Moroccan flair (the Moorish-style chicken with grilled lemon and couscous is especially popular). The perpetually packed bar, where celebrity bartender Scott Beattie and his staff mix inventive seasonal cocktails, is the real draw for many locals. $ *Average main: $29* ✉ *h2hotel, 219 Healdsburg Ave., at Vine St.* ☎ *707/433–7222* ⊕ *www.h2hotel.com/spoonbar* ☽ *No lunch Mon.–Thurs. in winter.*

$$$

AMERICAN

✕ **Zin Restaurant and Wine Bar.** Concrete walls and floors and large canvases on the walls lend the restaurant a casual, industrial, and slightly artsy feel. The American cuisine—such as the grilled pork chop with homemade applesauce or the wine-braised lamb shank—is hearty and highly seasoned. Portions are large, so consider sharing if you hope to save room for desserts such as the brownie sundae with house-made ice cream. As you might have guessed from the name, Zinfandel is the drink of choice here: the varietal makes up roughly half of the 100 or so bottles on the wine list. From Sunday through Thursday, blue-plate specials featuring homey fare (like pot roast and chicken and dumplings) make this place a bargain. $ *Average main: $25* ✉ *344 Center St., at North St.* ☎ *707/473–0946* ⊕ *zinrestaurant.com* ☽ *No lunch weekends.*

WHERE TO STAY

For expanded reviews, facilities, and current deals, visit Fodors.com.

$

B&B/INN

Camellia Inn. In a well-preserved Italianate Victorian constructed in 1869, this colorful B&B is on a quiet residential street a block from the town's main square. **Pros:** reasonable rates; a rare family-friendly inn; within easy walking distance of restaurants. **Cons:** a few rooms have a shower but no bath; all rooms lack TVs. **TripAdvisor:** "a truly wonderful inn," "make yourself at home," "helpful staff." $ *Rooms from: $230* ✉ *211 North St.* ☎ *707/433–8182, 800/727–8182* ⊕ *www.camelliainn.com* ⇔ *8 rooms, 1 suite* ⍟ *Breakfast.*

$

B&B/INN

h2hotel. Eco-friendly touches abound at this LEED-certified newcomer, from the undulating plant-covered "green roof" to wooden decks made from salvaged lumber. **Pros:** stylish modern design; Healdsburg's most popular bar; king beds can be converted to two twins. **Cons:** least expensive rooms lack bathtubs; no fitness facilities on-site. **TripAdvisor:** "unique property," "great small touches," "modern hotel." $ *Rooms from: $200* ✉ *219 Healdsburg Ave.* ☎ *707/922–5251* ⊕ *www.h2hotel.com* ⇔ *34 rooms, 2 suites* ⍟ *Breakfast.*

$$$ ⬚ **The Honor Mansion.** An 1883
B&B/INN Italianate Victorian houses this
★ photogenic hotel, and rooms in the
main house preserve a sense of the
building's heritage, while the larger
suites are comparatively under-
stated. **Pros:** spacious grounds
with boccie and tennis courts, a
putting green, and half-court for
basketball; homemade sweets
available at all hours; spa pavilions
by pool available for massages in
fair weather. **Cons:** almost a mile
from Healdsburg's plaza; walls can
seem thin. **TripAdvisor:** "beautiful
and relaxing," "simply the best,"
"Honor Mansion defines ser-
vice." ⑤ *Rooms from: $315* ⊠ *891
Grove St.* ☎ *707/433–4277, 800/554–4667* ⊕ *www.honormansion.
com* ⇆ *5 rooms, 7 suites, 1 cottage* ⊙ *Closed 2 wks around Christmas*
†◎† *Breakfast.*

$$$ ⬚ **Hotel Healdsburg.** Across the street from Healdsburg's tidy town plaza,
RESORT this spare, sophisticated hotel caters to travelers with an urban sensi-
bility. **Pros:** several rooms overlook the town plaza; comfortable lobby
with a small attached bar; extremely comfortable beds. **Cons:** exterior
rooms get some street noise; rooms could use better lighting. **Trip-
Advisor:** "casual luxury at its best," "really comfortable," "refreshing
hotel with world-class staff." ⑤ *Rooms from: $375* ⊠ *25 Matheson St.*
☎ *707/431–2800, 800/889–7188* ⊕ *www.hotelhealdsburg.com* ⇆ *46
rooms, 10 suites* †◎† *Breakfast.*

$$$$ ⬚ **Hôtel Les Mars.** This Relais & Châteaux property takes the prize for
HOTEL opulence with guest rooms spacious and elegant enough for French
nobility, with 18th- and 19th-century antiques and reproductions,
canopied beds, and gas-burning fireplaces. **Pros:** large rooms; just off
Healdsburg's plaza; Bulgari bath products. **Cons:** very expensive. **Trip-
Advisor:** "absolutely first class," "luxurious weekend getaway destination," "finest hotel in the Sonoma wine country." ⑤ *Rooms from:
$600* ⊠ *27 North St.* ☎ *707/433–4211* ⊕ *www.hotellesmars.com* ⇆ *16
rooms* †◎† *Breakfast.*

$$ ⬚ **Madrona Manor.** The flagship 1881 Victorian mansion here is sur-
B&B/INN rounded by 8 acres of wooded and landscaped grounds, and rooms
in the three-story mansion, the carriage house, and the three separate
cottages are splendidly ornate, with mirrors in gilt frames and paintings
covering every wall. **Pros:** old-fashioned and romantic; pretty veranda
perfect for a cocktail. **Cons:** pool heated May through October only;
some might find decor too fussy. **TripAdvisor:** "romantic and relax-
ation," "beautiful grounds," "European style hotel with great service."
⑤ *Rooms from: $300* ⊠ *1001 Westside Rd.* ☎ *707/433–4231, 800/258–
4003* ⊕ *www.madronamanor.com* ⇆ *18 rooms, 5 suites* †◎† *Breakfast.*

10

SHOPPING

M Clothing. A high-end women's-clothing boutique, M carries dresses, skirts, sweaters, and accessories from Diane von Furstenberg, Nanette Lapore, and other top designers. The shop sometimes hosts fashion shows at local hotels. ✉ *333 Healdsburg Ave., at Plaza St.* ☎ *707/431–8738* ⊕ *www.martymclothing.com.*

Moustache Baked Goods. This shop specializes in sweets incorporating local, organic ingredients: cupcakes (try the one with locally sourced bacon), whoopie pies, macaroons, and Oreos. Wash everything down with Blue Bottle Coffee. ✉ *381 Healdsburg Ave., at North St.* ☎ *707/395–4111.*

DRY CREEK AND ALEXANDER VALLEYS

On the west side of U.S. 101, Dry Creek Valley remains one of the least-developed appellations in Sonoma. Zinfandel grapes flourish on the benchlands, whereas the gravelly, well-drained soil of the valley floor is better known for Chardonnay and, in the north, Sauvignon Blanc. The wineries in this region tend to be smaller, which makes them a good bet on summer weekends, when larger spots and those along the main thoroughfares fill up with tourists.

The Alexander Valley, which lies northeast of Healdsburg, is similarly rustic. The largely family-owned wineries often produce Zinfandel and Chardonnay, while the winding Highway 128 through Knights Valley is a popular destination for cyclists and joggers alike.

GETTING HERE AND AROUND

The Dry Creek Valley sits west of downtown Healdsburg, across U.S. 101. If you drive north on Healdsburg Avenue and turn left on Dry Creek Road you'll slip under the freeway and soon see signs pointing the way to wineries on that road and West Dry Creek Road, which runs roughly parallel about a mile to the west, accessible by the cross streets Lambert Bridge Road and Yoakim Bridge Road.

The Alexander Valley is just northeast of Healdsburg. To get here from the plaza, drive north on Healdsburg Avenue and veer right on Alexander Valley Road. Although there are a few wineries on Alexander Valley Road itself, most of them on are on Highway 128, which intersects after 3.3. miles.

EXPLORING

Dry Creek Vineyard. Fumé Blanc is king at Dry Creek, where the refreshing white wine is made in the style of those made in Sancerre, France. The winery also makes well-regarded Zinfandels, a zesty dry Chenin Blanc, a Pinot Noir, and a handful of Cabernet Sauvignon blends. Since many wines are priced at less than $30 a bottle (some less than $20), it's a popular stop for wine lovers looking to stock their cellars for a reasonable price. You can picnic on the lawn here next to a flowering magnolia tree. Conveniently, a general store and deli is close by. ✉ *3770 Lambert Bridge Rd., off Dry Creek Rd., Dry Creek* ☎ *707/433–1000, 800/864–9463* ⊕ *www.drycreekvineyard.com* 🍷 *Tasting $5* ☉ *Daily 10:30–4:30.*

Best Wine Country Festivals

■ **March: Wine Road Barrel Tasting weekends.** For two weekends in March, more than 100 wineries in the Russian River, Dry Creek, and Alexander valleys open their cellars to visitors who want to taste the wine as it ages in barrels, getting previews of what's to come. (☎ 707/433–4335 or 800/723–6336 ⊕ www.wineroad.com)

■ **Early April: Napa Valley Arts in April.** Dozens of wineries have amassed stunning art collections, and many promote the valley's artistic bounty with seminars, parties, and tasting specials. (☎ 707/260–0107 ⊕ www.legendarynapavalley.com/artsinapril)

■ **Late May: Sonoma Jazz + festival.** Headlining jazz, rock, and world music performers play in a large tent in downtown Sonoma, and smaller music, food, and wine events take place around town. (☎ 866/468–8355 ⊕ www.sonomajazz.org)

■ **Early June: Auction Napa Valley.** One of Napa's glitziest gatherings culminates in a dramatic auction followed by an opulent dinner and party. (☎ 707/963–3388 ⊕ www.napavintners.com)

■ **Early October: Sonoma County Harvest Fair.** This festival celebrates agriculture in Sonoma County, with wine tastings, cooking demos, livestock shows, crafts, carnival rides, and local entertainers filling the Sonoma County Fairgrounds in Santa Rosa. (⊕ www.harvestfair.org)

■ **Mid-November: Napa Valley Film Festival.** Film premieres, pre-movie wine tastings, and food- and wine-related events take place in downtown Napa and St. Helena. (⊕ www.napavalleyfilmfest.org)

Francis Ford Coppola Winery. The famous film director showcases his less-expensive wines at this majestic French-style château that he transformed into an impressive fantasyland. (Coppola's Napa winery, Inglenook, focuses on the high-end vintages.) In addition to tasting wines or ordering cocktails at the full bar, you can select from tours that include a vineyard walk and the opportunity to watch the bottling facility in action. Scattered throughout the facility are mementos of Coppola's film career, among them his Oscars and Don Corleone's desk in *The Godfather.* Kids (and some adults), though, will be most excited by the large pool. Guests rent small cabanas to shower and change into their swimsuits before spending the afternoon lounging under the striped umbrellas, perhaps even ordering food from the poolside café. The winery's restaurant, Rustic, serves a more elaborate menu from a spacious dining room and a terrace overlooking the vineyards. Prices, pool hours, and tour times change seasonally, so check before coming. ✉ *300 Via Archimedes, at Fulton Rd., Geyserville* ☎ *707/857–1400* ⊕ *www.franciscoppolawinery.com* 🍷 *Tasting free–$7; tour $20–$55; pool pass $15* ☉ *Tasting room daily 11–6, restaurant daily 11–9; pool hrs vary seasonally.*

Jordan Vineyard and Winery. A visit to this sprawling property north of Healdsburg revolves around an impressive estate built in the early 1970s to replicate a French château. Seated tastings of Cabernet Sauvignon and Chardonnay are held in the château itself, in a secluded room that once served as a private cellar. Basic tastings ($20) last 45 minutes and include food and cheese prepared by executive chef Todd Knoll. Tours ($30), which last 75 minutes and include a tasting, wind from the château past a garden and through vineyards shaded by century-old oak trees. The wines alone are worth a visit here, but don't leave without sampling the olive oil grown and milled on the estate. ✉ *1474 Alexander Valley Rd., on Greco Rd., Alexander Valley* ☎ *800/654–1213, 707/431–5250* ⊕ *www.jordanwinery.com* 🖼 *Tastings and tour $20–$30* ⊙ *Weekdays 8–4:30, weekends 9–3:30; tours and tastings daily by appointment* ⊙ *Closed Sun. Nov.–Apr.*

Papapietro Perry. Pinot Noir and Zinfandel are the only wines on the tasting list at this small winery in the heart of the Dry Creek Valley, but wine lovers hail them as some of the region's best. Most of the grapes come from the Russian River valley, though Zin made from locally sourced fruit is available as well. Standard tastings at the copper-topped bar include five pours, and it always pays to ask what else is open in the back (the 777 Clone Pinot is particularly delicious). For a break in the action, peruse the winery shop for witty T-shirts, or call for Ruby, the winery dog, who always is eager for a gentle pet. ✉ *4791 Dry Creek Rd., at Wine Creek Rd., Dry Creek* ☎ *707/433–0422, 877/467–4668* ⊕ *www.papapietro-perry.com* 🖼 *Tasting $10* ⊙ *Daily 11–4:30.*

Fodor'sChoice ★ **Preston Vineyards.** The long driveway at Preston, flanked by vineyards and punctuated by the occasional olive tree, winds down to some farmhouses encircling a shady yard. In summer a small selection of organic produce grown in the winery's gardens is sold from an impromptu stand on the front porch, and house-made bread and olive oil are available year-round. The down-home style is particularly in evidence on Sunday, the only day of the week that tasting-room staffers sell a 3-liter bottle of Guadagni Red, a primarily Zinfandel blend filled from the barrel right in front of you. Owners Lou and Susan Preston are committed to organic growing techniques, and use only estate-grown grapes in their wines, like Sauvignon Blanc, and Rhône varietals such as Syrah and Viognier. ✉ *Tasting Room, 9206 W. Dry Creek Rd., at Hartsock Rd. No. 1, Dry Creek* ☎ *707/433–3372* ⊕ *www.prestonvineyards.com* 🖼 *Tasting $10* ⊙ *Daily 11–4:30.*

Quivira. An unassuming winery in a modern wooden barn topped by solar panels, Quivira produces some of the most interesting wines in Dry Creek Valley. It's known for its dangerously drinkable reds, including a petite Syrah, and a few hearty Zinfandel blends. The excellent tour provides information about the winery's biodynamic and organic farming practices and offers a glimpse of the beautiful garden and the pigs, chickens, and beehives kept on the property. Visitors also can take a free self-guided tour through the garden. ✉ *4900 W. Dry Creek Rd., near Wine Creek Rd., Healdsburg* ☎ *707/431–8333, 800/292–8339* ⊕ *www.quivirawine.com* 🖼 *Tasting $10, tours $20–$30* ⊙ *Daily 11–5; tours by appointment.*

The North Coast

FROM THE SONOMA COAST TO REDWOOD NATIONAL PARK

WORD OF MOUTH

"You may be surprised by how (1) Small and (2) Beautiful Trinidad is! I was there for the first time a couple of months ago and it's now one of my favorite places for scenery on the whole North coast."

—roundthebend

WELCOME TO THE NORTH COAST

TOP REASONS TO GO

★ **Scenic coastal drives:** There's hardly a road here that *isn't* scenic.

★ **Wild beaches:** This stretch of California is one of nature's masterpieces. Revel in the unbridled, rugged coastline, without a building in sight.

★ **Dinnertime:** When you're done hiking the beach, refuel with delectable food; you'll find everything from burritos to bouillabaisse.

★ **Romance:** Here you can end almost every day with a perfect sunset.

★ **Wildlife:** Sea lions and otters and deer, oh my!

1 **The Sonoma Coast.** Heading up through northwestern Marin into Sonoma County, Highway 1 traverses gently rolling pastureland. North of Bodega Bay dramatic shoreline scenery takes over. The road snakes up, down, and around sheer cliffs and steep inclines—some without guardrails—where cows seem to cling precariously. Stunning vistas (or cottony fog) and hairpin turns make this one of the most exhilarating drives north of San Francisco.

2 **The Mendocino Coast.** The timber industry gave birth to most of the small towns strung along this stretch of the California coastline. Although tourism now drives the economy, the region has retained much of its old-fashioned charm. The beauty of the coastal landscape, of course, has not changed.

3 Redwood Country. There's a different state of mind in Humboldt County. Here, instead of spas, there are old-time hotels. Instead of wineries, there are breweries. The landscape is primarily thick redwood forest, which gets snow in winter and sizzles in summer while the coast sits covered in fog. Until as late as 1924, there was no road that went north of Willits; the coastal towns were reachable only by sea. That legacy is apparent in the communities here today: Eureka and Arcata, both former ports, are sizeable, but otherwise towns are tiny and nestled in the woods, and people have an independent spirit that recalls the original homesteaders. Coming from the south, Garberville is a good place to stop for picnic provisions and stretch your legs.

4 Redwood National Park. For a pristine encounter with giant redwoods, make the trek to this seldom-visited park where even casual visitors have easy access to the trees. *(See Chapter 12, Redwood National Park.)*

GETTING ORIENTED

It's all but impossible to explore the northern California coast without a car. Indeed, you wouldn't want to—driving here is half the fun. The main road is Highway 1, two lanes that twist and turn (sometimes 180 degrees) up cliffs and down through valleys. Towns appear every so often, but this is mostly a land of green pasture, dense forest, and natural, undeveloped coastline. ■TIP→ Pace yourself: Most drivers stop frequently to appreciate the views (and you can't drive faster than 20–40 mph on many portions of the highway), so don't plan to drive too far in one day.

Smith River
199
Point St. George
Crescent City
101
Klamath
Redwood National Park
4
Orick
Patrick's Point
Trinidad
McKinleyville
96
Willow Creek
Arcata Bay
3
Arcata
Eureka
Humboldt Bay
Fortuna
Ferndale
Cape Mendocino
Hydesville
36
Hayfork
Rio Dell
Point Gorda
Humboldt Redwoods State Park
KING MTN RANGE
Garberville
Richardson Grove State Park
Leggett
Laytonville
101
Fort Bragg
1
Mendocino
Little River
Willits
20
Albion
128
Elk
2
Ukiah
20
Point Arena
Point Arena
ANDERSON VALLEY
Lucerne
Gualala
Kelseyville
Clearlake
Lower Lake
Stewarts Point
1
Pacific Coast Hwy
Cloverdale
Healdsburg
Calistoga
Jenner
101
Saint Helena
Occidental
Sebastopol
Santa Rosa
29
Bodega Bay
Petaluma
Napa
Inverness
Novato
Sonoma
Point Reyes National Seashore
1
Vallejo
Concord
Bolinas
Richmond
80
Marin Headlands
Berkeley
San Francisco
Oakland
Daly City

SISKIYOU MOUNTAINS
KLAMATH MOUNTAINS
COAST RANGES
PACIFIC OCEAN

0   30 mi
0   30 km

Updated
by Christine
Vovakes

The spectacular coastline between Marin County and the Oregon border defies expectations. The landscape is defined by the Pacific Ocean, but instead of boardwalks and bikinis there are ragged cliffs and pounding waves—and the sunbathers are mostly sea lions.

Instead of strip malls and freeways, there are small towns that retire around sundown and a single-lane road that follows the fickle shoreline. And that's exactly why many Californians, especially those from the Bay Area, come here to escape the Sturm und Drang of daily life.

This stretch of Highway 1 is made up of numerous little worlds, each different from the next. From Point Reyes toward Bodega Bay, the land spreads out into green, rolling pastures and sandy beaches. The road climbs higher and higher as it heads north through Sonoma County, where cows graze on precipitous cliffs and the ocean views are breathtaking. In Mendocino the coastline follows the ins and outs of lush valleys where rivers pour down from the forests and into the ocean. At Humboldt County the highway heads inland to the redwoods, then returns to the shoreline at the tidal flats surrounding the ports of Eureka and Arcata. Heading north to the Oregon border, the coast is increasingly wild and lined with redwood trees.

Although the towns along the way vary from deluxe spa retreat to hippie hideaway, all are reliably sleepy. Most communities have fewer than 1,000 inhabitants, with main streets shuttered by 9 pm. Exceptions are Mendocino and Eureka, but even they are loved best by those who would rather cozy up in bed than paint the town.

NORTH COAST PLANNER

WHEN TO GO

The North Coast is a year-round destination, though when you go determines what you will see. The migration of the Pacific gray whales is a wintertime phenomenon, which lasts roughly from mid-December to early April. Wildflowers follow the winter rain, as early as January in southern areas through June and July farther north. Summer is the high season for tourists, but spring, fall, and even winter are arguably better times to visit when the pace is slower, towns are quieter, and lodging is cheaper.

The coastal climate is quite similar to San Francisco's, although winter nights are colder than in the city. In July and August thick fog can drop temperatures to the high 50s. If you do get caught in the summer fog, fear not! You need only drive inland to find temperatures that are often 20 degrees higher.

GETTING HERE AND AROUND

AIR TRAVEL

The only North Coast airport with commercial air service, Arcata/Eureka Airport (ACV) receives flights on United Express. The airport is in McKinleyville, which is 16 miles from Eureka.

A taxi to Eureka costs about $50 and takes roughly 25 minutes. Door-to-door airport shuttles cost $20 to Arcata and Trinidad, $24 to Eureka, and $50 to Ferndale. All prices are for the first person, and go up only $5 total for each additional person.

Airport Contact Arcata/Eureka Airport ⊠ *3561 Boeing Ave., McKinleyville* ☎ *707/839–5401.*

Shuttle Contact Door to Door Airport Shuttle ☎ *888/338–5497, 707/839–4186* ⊕ *www.doortodoorairporter.com.*

BUS TRAVEL

Greyhound buses travel along U.S. 101 from San Francisco to Eureka and Arcata. Bus drivers will stop in other towns along the route if you specify your destination when you board. You can also take Greyhound to Seattle, but you must first travel from Eureka to Oakland, with another transfer in Sacramento before continuing north on I-5. Humboldt Transit Authority connects Eureka, Arcata, and Trinidad.

Bus Contacts Greyhound ☎ *800/231–2222* ⊕ *www.greyhound.com.* **Humboldt Transit Authority** ☎ *707/443–0826* ⊕ *www.hta.org.*

CAR TRAVEL

Although there are excellent services along U.S. 101, long, lonesome stretches separate towns (with their resident gas stations and mechanics) along Highway 1, and services are even fewer and farther between on the smaller roads. ■ TIP→ If you're running low on fuel and see a gas station, stop for a refill. Driving directly to Mendocino from San Francisco is quicker if, instead of driving up the coast on Highway 1, you take U.S. 101 north to Highway 128 west (from Cloverdale) to Highway 1 north. The quickest way to the far North Coast from the Bay Area is a straight shot up U.S. 101, which runs inland all way until Eureka. Weather sometimes forces closure of parts of Highway 1, but it's rare. For information on the condition of roads in Northern California, call the Caltrans Highway Information Network's voice-activated system.

Road Conditions Caltrans Highway Information Network ☎ *800/427–7623* ⊕ *www.dot.ca.gov.*

HEALTH AND SAFETY

In an emergency, dial 911. In state and national parks, park rangers serve as police officers and will help you in any emergency. Bigger towns along the coast have hospitals, but for major medical emergencies you will need to go to San Francisco. Note that cell phones don't work along large swaths of the North Coast.

RESTAURANTS

A few restaurants with national reputations, plus several more of regional note, entice palates on the North Coast. Even the workaday local spots take advantage of the abundant fresh seafood and locally grown vegetables and herbs. Attire is usually informal, though at the pricier establishments dressy casual (somewhere between flip-flops and high heels) is the norm. As in many rural areas, plan to dine early: the majority of kitchens close at 8 or 8:30 and virtually no one serves past 9:30. Also note that many restaurants in the northern part of this region close for a winter break in January. *Prices in the reviews are the average cost of a main course at dinner or, if dinner is not served, at lunch.*

HOTELS

Restored Victorians, rustic lodges, country inns, and vintage motels are among the accommodations available here. Hardly any have air-conditioning (the ocean breezes make it unnecessary), and many have no phones or TVs in the rooms. Although several towns have only one or two places to spend the night, some of these lodgings are destinations in themselves. Budget accommodations are rare, but in winter you're likely to find reduced rates and nearly empty inns and B&Bs. In summer and on the weekends, though, make bed-and-breakfast reservations as far ahead as possible—rooms at the best inns often sell out months in advance. *Prices in the reviews are the lowest cost of a standard double room in high season. For expanded reviews, facilities, and current deals, visit Fodors.com.*

VISITOR INFORMATION

Contacts Humboldt County Convention and Visitors Bureau ✉ *1034 2nd St., Eureka* ☎ *707/443–5097, 800/346–3482* ⊕ *www.redwoods.info.* **Mendocino Coast Chamber of Commerce** ✉ *217 S. Main St., Fort Bragg* ☎ *707/961–6300* ⊕ *www.mendocinocoast.com.* **Redwood Coast Chamber: Sonoma to Mendocino** ✉ *39150 S. Hwy. 1, Gualala* ☎ *707/884–1080, 800/778–5252* ⊕ *www.redwoodcoastchamber.com.* **Sonoma County Tourism Bureau** ✉ *3637 Westwind Blvd., Santa Rosa* ☎ *707/522–5800, 800/576–6662* ⊕ *www.sonomacounty.com.* **Visit Mendocino County** ✉ *120 S. Franklin St., Ft. Bragg* ☎ *707/462–7417, 866/466–3636* ⊕ *www.visitmendocino.com.*

THE SONOMA COAST

BODEGA BAY

21 miles north of Marshall on Hwy. 1.

From the busy harbor here, commercial boats pursue fish and Dungeness crab. There's nothing quaint about this working town without a center—it's just a string of businesses along several miles of Highway 1. But some tourists still come to see where Alfred Hitchcock shot *The Birds* in 1962. The Tides Wharf complex, an important location used for the movie, has been expanded and remodeled several times and is no longer recognizable. But a few miles inland, in Bodega, you can find Potter Schoolhouse, which is now a private residence.

GETTING HERE AND AROUND

Reach Bodega Bay from Highway 101 north or south to Santa Rosa, then Highway 12 west (Bodega Highway west of Sebastopol) 23 miles to the coast. From San Francisco you can also take Valley Ford Road (Highway 1) northwest about 27 miles from Petaluma. Mendocino Transit Authority (⊕ *www.4mta.org*) Route 95 buses connect Bodega Bay with coastal towns and Santa Rosa.

WHERE TO EAT AND STAY

For expanded reviews, facilities, and current deals, visit Fodors.com.

$$
SEAFOOD

✕ **Sandpiper Restaurant.** A local favorite for breakfast, this friendly café on the marina does a good job for a fair price. Peruse the board for the day's fresh catch or order a menu regular such as crab stew or steak and prawns; clam chowder is the house specialty. $ *Average main: $21* ✉ *1400 N. Hwy. 1* ☎ *707/875–2278* ⊕ *www.sandpiperrestaurant.com.*

$$$$
HOTEL

🏨 **Bodega Bay Lodge.** Looking out to the ocean across a wetland, a group of shingle-and-river-rock buildings houses Bodega Bay's finest accommodations. **Pros:** pampering; ocean views. **Cons:** on the highway. **TripAdvisor:** "peaceful," "pretty place," "a perfect romantic getaway." $ *Rooms from: $295* ✉ *103 Coast Hwy. 1* ☎ *707/875–3525, 888/875–2250* ⊕ *www.bodegabaylodge.com* 🔑 *78 rooms, 5 suites* ⊙ *No meals.*

SPORTS AND THE OUTDOORS

Bodega Bay Sportfishing. This outfitter charters ocean-fishing boats and rents equipment; they also offer whale-watching trips mid-winter through spring. ✉ *1410 B Bay Flat Rd.* ☎ *707/875–3344* ⊕ *www.bodegabaysportfishing.com.*

Horse N Around Trail Rides. Saddle up at this ranch for guided horseback trail rides, some along the beach. Reservations are required. ✉ *2660 N. Hwy. 1* ☎ *707/875–8849* ⊕ *www.horsenaroundtrailrides.com.*

Links at Bodega Harbour. At the incredibly scenic oceanfront Links at Bodega Harbour you can play an 18-hole Robert Trent Jones–designed course. ✉ *21301 Heron Dr.* ☎ *707/875–3538, 800/503–8158* ⊕ *www.bodegaharbourgolf.com.*

OCCIDENTAL

14 miles northeast of Bodega Bay on Bohemian Hwy.

A village surrounded by redwood forests, orchards, and vineyards, Occidental is a former logging hub with a bohemian vibe. The 19th-century downtown offers a top-notch B&B, good food, and a handful of art galleries and boutiques. The neighboring town of Freestone offers much of the same, but on a smaller scale.

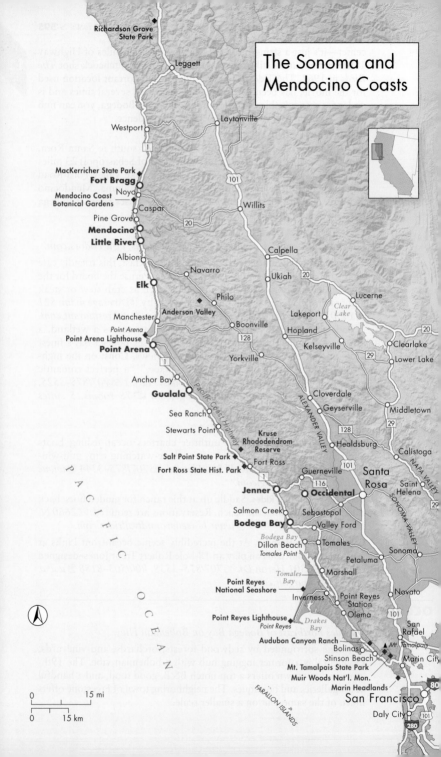

The Sonoma and Mendocino Coasts

Richardson Grove State Park

Leggett

Westport

Laytonville

MacKerricher State Park
Fort Bragg
Noyo
Mendocino Coast
Botanical Gardens
Caspar

Willits

Pine Grove
Mendocino
Little River

Albion

Navarro

Calpella

Ukiah

Elk

Philo

Lucerne

Anderson Valley

Clear Lake

Manchester

Boonville

Lakeport

Point Arena
Point Arena Lighthouse
Point Arena

Hopland

Kelseyville

Clearlake

Lower Lake

Yorkville

Anchor Bay

Gualala

Cloverdale

Geyserville

Middletown

Sea Ranch

Stewarts Point

Kruse
Rhododendrom
Reserve

Healdsburg

Calistoga

Salt Point State Park
Fort Ross State Hist. Park

Fort Ross

Guerneville

Santa Rosa

Saint Helena

Jenner

Occidental

Salmon Creek

Sebastopol

Bodega Bay

Bodega Bay
Dillon Beach
Tomales Point

Valley Ford

Tomales

Sonoma

Petaluma

Tomales Bay

Marshall

Novato

**Point Reyes
National Seashore**

Inverness

Point Reyes
Station
Olema

Point Reyes Lighthouse
Point Reyes

Drakes Bay

San Rafael

Audubon Canyon Ranch

Bolinas

San Francisco

Stinson Beach
Mt. Tamalpais State Park
Muir Woods Nat'l. Mon.
Marin Headlands

Mt. Tamalpais

Marin City

Daly City

PACIFIC OCEAN

Pacific Coast Highway

ALEXANDER VALLEY

SONOMA VALLEY

NAPA VALLEY

FARALLON ISLANDS

0   15 mi
0   15 km

GETTING HERE AND AROUND

To reach Occidental, take Highway 12 (Bodega Highway) east 5 miles from Highway 1. Take a left onto Bohemian Highway, where you'll find Freestone; another 3½ miles and you'll be in Occidental. From Highway 101 north or south take Highway 12 west from Santa Rosa about 13 miles, then head north on Bohemian Highway about 3½ miles to the village.

EXPLORING

Occidental Center for the Arts. From September through May, the Redwood Arts Council presents nine concerts featuring world-class musicians performing with passion in an intimate space. ⊠ *3850 Doris Murphy Ct.* ☎ *707/874–1124* ⊕ *www.redwoodarts.org.*

Osmosis–The Enzyme Bath Spa. A traditional Japanese detoxifying treatment awaits you at this spa, which claims to be the only such facility in America. Your bath is a deep redwood tub of damp cedar shavings and rice bran, naturally heated to 140°F by the action of enzymes. Serene attendants bury you up to the neck and during the 20-minute treatment bring you sips of water and place cool cloths on your forehead. After a shower, lie down and listen to brain-balancing music through headphones or have a massage, perhaps in one of the creek-side pagodas. A treatment and access to the gardens costs $85 per person (less for parties of two or more people); reservations are recommended. ⊠ *209 Bohemian Hwy., Freestone* ☎ *707/823–8231* ⊕ *www.osmosis. com* ☉ *Daily 9–8.*

WHERE TO EAT AND STAY

For expanded reviews, facilities, and current deals, visit Fodors.com.

$ CAFÉ | ✕ **Wild Flour Bread.** Customers at this bakery in a renovated barn line up early for delectable breads both savory and sweet, plus scones and biscotti, all baked in a wood-fired brick oven. ⑤ *Average main: $5* ⊠ *140 Bohemian Hwy., Freestone* ☎ *707/874–2938* ⊕ *www.wildflourbread. com* ⊟ *No credit cards* ☉ *Closed Tues.–Thurs.*

$$$ B&B/INN   ★ | ▦ **The Inn at Occidental.** Quilts, folk art, and original paintings and photographs fill this colorful and friendly inn. **Pros:** colorful; luxurious; friendly. **Cons:** not for those with minimalist tastes; not for kids. **TripAdvisor:** "delightful quiet hidden secret," "first-class service and character," "cute and cozy." ⑤ *Rooms from: $229* ⊠ *3657 Church St.* *707/874–1047, 800/522–6324* ⊕ *www.innatoccidental.com* ⇆ *13 rooms, 3 suites, 1 cottage* ⦿ *Breakfast.*

JENNER

10 miles north of Bodega Bay on Hwy. 1.

The broad, lazy Russian River empties into the Pacific Ocean at Jenner, a wide spot in the road where houses dot a mountainside high above the sea. Facing south, the village looks across the river's mouth to Goat Rock State Beach, home to a colony of sea lions for most of the year; pupping season is March through June. The beach, accessed for free off Highway 1 a couple of miles south of town, is open daily from 8 am to sunset. Bring binoculars and walk north from the parking lot to view the sea lions.

GETTING HERE AND AROUND

From Highway 101 in Santa Rosa head west on Highway 12 (Bodega Highway west of Sebastopol) 23 miles to the coast, then travel 10 miles north on Highway 1 to Jenner. From Santa Rosa you can also use Highway 116 west through Guerneville (about 31 miles to Jenner). Mendocino Transit Authority (⊕ *www.4mta.org*) Route 95 buses stop in Jenner and connect with Bodega Bay, Santa Rosa, and other coastal towns.

WHERE TO EAT

$$$$ ✕ **River's End.** A magnificent ocean view makes lunch or an evening here
MODERN   memorable. Come for cocktails and Hog Island oysters on the half
AMERICAN   shell and hope for a splashy sunset. If you stay for dinner, choose from elaborate entrées such as chimichurri lamb or applewood smoked filet mignon with Gorgonzola walnut butter. The execution may not always justify the prices and the dining room is plain-Jane, but just look at that view. Open hours sometimes vary, so call to confirm; reservations are essential on weekends. River's End also rents out a few ocean-view rooms and cabins ($$–$$$). ⑤ *Average main: $31* ✉ *11048 Hwy. 1* ☎ *707/865-2484* ⊕ *www.ilovesunsets.com* ⌕ *Reservations essential* ⊙ *Closed Tues. and Wed. and fall–spring.*

FORT ROSS STATE HISTORIC PARK

12 miles north of Jenner on Hwy. 1.

GETTING HERE AND AROUND

From Santa Rosa, head west on Highway 116 about 31 miles to Jenner, then north 12 miles on Highway 1 to the park entrance. Mendocino Transit Authority (⊕ *www.4mta.org*) Route 95 provides service between Fort Ross and other coastal towns and cities.

EXPLORING

♺   **Fort Ross State Historic Park.** Established in 1812, Fort Ross became Russia's major outpost in California, meant to produce crops and other supplies for northerly fur-trading operations. The Russians brought Aleut sea-otter hunters down from Alaska. By 1841 the area was depleted of seals and otters, and the Russians sold their post to John Sutter, later of gold-rush fame. After a local Anglo rebellion against the Mexicans, the land fell under U.S. domain, becoming part of California in 1850. The state park service has reconstructed Fort Ross, including its Russian Orthodox chapel, a redwood stockade, the officers' barracks, and a blockhouse. The excellent museum here documents the history of the fort and this part of the North Coast. ✉ *19005 Hwy. 1* ☎ *707/847-3286* ▣ *$8 per vehicle* ⊙ *Weekends 10–4:30* ☞ *No dogs allowed past parking lot and picnic area.*

Surfers check out the waves near Bodega Bay on the Sonoma Coast.

SALT POINT STATE PARK

6 miles north of Fort Ross on Hwy. 1.

GETTING HERE AND AROUND

Exit U.S. 101 in Santa Rosa and travel west on Highway 116 about 31 miles to Jenner, then north 18 miles on Highway 1 to reach the park. Mendocino Transit Authority (⊕ *www.4mta.org*) Route 95 buses stop at Salt Point and connect with other North Coast towns.

EXPLORING

Salt Point State Park. For 5 mi, Highway 1 winds through this park, 6,000 acres of forest, meadows, and rocky shoreline. Heading north, the first park entrance (on the right) leads to forest hiking trails and several campgrounds. The next entrance—the park's main road—winds through meadows and along the wave-splashed coastline (a great place to stop so the kids can let off steam). This is also the route to the visitor center and Gerstle Cove, a favorite spot for abalone divers and sunbathing seals. Next along the highway is Stump Beach Cove, with picnic tables, toilets, and a ¼-mile walk to the sandy beach. The park's final entrance is at Fisk Mill Cove, where centuries of wind and rain erosion have carved unusual honeycomb patterns in the sandstone called "tafonis." A five-minute walk uphill from the parking lot leads to a dramatic view of Sentinel Rock, an excellent spot for sunsets. ⊠ *25050 Hwy. 1* ☎ *707/847–3221* 🖾 *$8 per vehicle* ☉ *Daily sunrise–sunset.*

Kruse Rhododendron State Reserve. Just up the highway, narrow, unpaved Kruse Ranch Road leads to the Kruse Rhododendron State Reserve, where each May thousands of rhododendrons bloom within a quiet forest of redwoods and tan oaks. ☎ 707/847–3221 ☜ *Free* ⊙ *Daily sunrise–sunset*

BEACHES

Sonoma Coast State Beach. The gorgeous sandy coves of Sonoma Coast State Beach stretch for 17 miles along the Highway 1 shoreline from Bodega Head to 4 miles north of Jenner, encompassing numerous beaches. Rock Point, Duncan's Landing, and Wright's Beach, clustered at about the halfway mark, have picnic areas, as do several others. A long road leads from the highway to Goat Rock, near the mouth of the Russian River at Jenner, with parking areas at different stops for views of the ocean and the long beach where harbor seals lounge. Shell Beach, 2.5 miles south of Goat Rock, is known for beachcombing, tidepooling, and fishing. Duncan's Landing, about 2 miles south of Shell Beach, is the most dangerous spot on the coast because of unpredictable surf; rogue waves have come up to the parking lot and have also swept people off rocks. If you're lucky you'll catch sight of migrating whales from any of the beaches, but Bodega Head is an especially popular perch for patient gazers. During summer months a few lifeguards are on duty at different spots, but strong rip currents and heavy surf are a treacherous combination that keep would-be swimmers on shore at all the beaches. Wright's Beach and Bodega Dunes have developed campsites. Pick up information about the beaches at state park headquarters at Highway 1 and Salmon Creek, about 2 miles north of Bodega Bay. **Amenities:** parking; toilets. **Best For:** solitude; sunset; walking. ☎ 707/865–2391 ☜ *$8 per vehicle.*

THE MENDOCINO COAST

GUALALA

16 miles north of Salt Point State Park on Hwy. 1.

This former lumber port on the Gualala River has become a headquarters for exploring the coast. The busiest town between Bodega Bay and Mendocino, it has all the basic services plus a number of galleries and gift shops.

GETTING HERE AND AROUND

From San Francisco exit Highway 101 at Cloverdale and follow Highway 128 northwest 28 miles to Boonville. From Ukiah, take Highway 253 west about 17 miles to Boonville/Highway 128. From Boonville, turn west on Mountain View Road and travel 24 miles to Highway 1, then head south 18½ miles to Gualala. South Mendocino Coast Bus routes 75 and 95 (⊕ *www.4mta.org*) connect Gualala with coastal and inland towns.

EXPLORING

Gualala Point Regional Park. This park has a long, sandy beach, picnic areas ($6 day-use fee), and is an excellent whale-watching spot December through April. Along the river, shaded by redwoods, are two dozen campsites. ✉ *Hwy. 1, 1 mile south of Gualala* ☎ *707/785–2377* ☉ *Daily 8 am–sunset.*

WHERE TO EAT AND STAY

For expanded reviews, facilities, and current deals, visit Fodors.com.

$$$$ ✕ **St. Orres.** Resembling a traditional Russian dacha with two onion-
AMERICAN dome towers, this intriguing lodge stands on 42 acres of redwood forest and meadow. In one of the towers is a spectacular atrium dining
room. Here, locally farmed and foraged ingredients appear in dishes
such as garlic flan with black chanterelles and rack of venison medallions with wild huckleberries. The prix-fixe menu ($45) includes soup
and salad but no appetizer or dessert (available à la carte). $ *Average
main: $45* ✉ *36601 Hwy. 1, 3 miles north of Gualala* ☎ *707/884–3303*
⊕ *www.saintorres.com* ⟳ *Reservations essential* ☉ *Closed Tues. and
Wed. Dec.–May. No lunch weekdays.*

$$ ⚏ **Mar Vista Cottages.** The thoughtfully appointed, sparkling clean refur-
HOTEL bished 1930s cottages at Mar Vista are intentionally slim on mod-
ern gadgetry (no TV, phone, radio, or even a clock) and big on retro
charm. **Pros:** charming, peaceful retreat. **Cons:** no other businesses in
walking distance. **TripAdvisor:** "pampering for the pros," "charming
and relaxing country cottages," "retro relaxation." $ *Rooms from:
$160* ✉ *35101 S. Hwy 1, 5 miles north of Gualala* ☎ *707/884–3522,
877/855–3522* ⊕ *www.marvistamendocino.com* ⬎ *8 1-bedroom cot-
tages, 4 2-bedroom cottages* ⦿ *No meals.*

$$ ⚏ **Seacliff on the Bluff.** This motel hugs a bluff overlooking where the
HOTEL Gualala River joins the sea. **Pros:** budget choice; great views. **Cons:** less-
than-scenic setting. **TripAdvisor:** "perfect relaxation," "great view," "a
lovely surprise." $ *Rooms from: $140* ✉ *39140 S. Hwy. 1* ☎ *707/884–
1213, 800/400–5053* ⊕ *www.seacliffmotel.com* ⬎ *16 rooms* ⦿ *No
meals.*

POINT ARENA

★ *14 miles north of Gualala on Hwy. 1.*

Occupied by an eclectic mix of long-time locals and long-haired surfers, this former timber town is part New Age, part rowdy—and always
laid back. The one road going west out of downtown will lead you to
the harbor, where fishing boats unload urchins and salmon and there's
almost always someone riding the waves.

GETTING HERE AND AROUND

From the south, exit Highway 101 at Cloverdale and follow Highway 128 northwest 28 miles to Boonville. From Ukiah, take Highway
253 west about 17 miles to Boonville/Highway 128. From Boonville,
Mountain View Road dead-ends after 25 miles at Highway 1; travel
south 4 miles to reach Point Arena. South Mendocino Coast Bus Routes
75 and 95 (⊕ *www.4mta.org*) stop in Point Arena and travel to most
towns in the region.

EXPLORING

Point Arena Lighthouse. For an outstanding view of the ocean and, in winter, migrating whales, take the marked road off Highway 1 north of town to the 115-foot Point Arena Lighthouse. The lighthouse is open for tours daily from 10 until 3:30, and until 4:30 from Memorial Day until Labor Day weekends; admission is $7.50. It's possible to stay out here, in one of four rental units ($$), all of which have full kitchens. (On weekends there's a two-night minimum.) ⊠ *45500 Lighthouse Rd., off Hwy. 1* ☎ *707/882–2777, 877/725–4448* ⊕ *www.pointarenalighthouse.com.*

BEACHES

Manchester State Park. As you head north on Highway 1 from Point Arena toward Elk, you'll pass several beaches. Most notable is the one at Manchester State Park, 3 miles north of Point Arena, which has 5 miles of sandy, usually empty shoreline and lots of trails through the dunes. There's excellent seasonal steelhead fishing in the park's two streams, and you'll see beautiful coastal wildflowers beginning in early spring. Tundra swans overwinter here, and migrating whales are often spotted close to shore. Swimming and water sports are too dangerous because of strong undertows; hiking, bird-watching, and beach strolling are the popular activities. The northernmost segment of the San Andreas Fault cuts through the park and slips into the sea. Dogs are not allowed on the beach. **Amenities:** parking. **Best For:** solitude; sunset; walking. ⊠ *44500 Kinney La., off Hwy. 1, about 1½ miles north of Manchester, Manchester* ☎ *707/937–5804* ⊕ *www.parks.ca.gov.*

WHERE TO EAT AND STAY

For expanded reviews, facilities, and current deals, visit Fodors.com.

$ ✕ **Arena Market.** The simple café at this all-organic grocery store offers
CAFÉ hot soups, good sandwiches, and an ample salad bar. Picnickers can stock up on cheese, bread, and other good stuff in the market, which specializes in food from local farms. ⑤ *Average main: $7* ⊠ *185 Main St.* ☎ *707/882–3663.*

$ ✕ **Franny's Cup and Saucer.** Aided by her mother, Barbara, a former pastry
CAFÉ chef at Chez Panisse, Franny turns out baked goods that are sophisti-
★ cated and inventive. Take the coffee crunch cake: vanilla chiffon cake layered with coffee whipped cream, topped with chocolate ganache and puffs of coffee caramel "seafoam." More familiar options include berry tarts and a strawberry-apricot crisp, plus a mouthwatering assortment of cookies, candy, jams, and jellies. Open Wednesday through Saturday, this delightful bakery in the blue building on Main Street is definitely worth a visit. ⑤ *Average main: $5* ⊠ *213 Main St.* ☎ *707/882–2500* ⊕ *www.frannyscupandsaucer.com* ⊟ *No credit cards* ⊘ *Closed Sun.– Tues. No dinner.*

$$$$ ▦ **Inn at Victorian Gardens.** Set amid 92 acres of meadows and trees, this
B&B/INN exquisite Victorian house dates to 1904, but owner-architect Pauline
★ Zamboni has updated and expanded it seamlessly over the past 18 years—skylights open up bathrooms with original hardwood floors, and peaked alcoves frame windows that look out onto lush gardens, open meadows, and the sea. **Pros:** total relaxation; total quiet; total elegance.

Cons: 6 miles from the nearest town. $\boxed{\$}$ *Rooms from: $255* ✉ *14409 S. Hwy. 1, Manchester* ☎ *707/882–3606* ⊕ *www.innatvictoriangardens. com* ⌔ *4 rooms* ⏐○⏐ *Breakfast.*

ELK

33 miles north of Gualala on Hwy. 1.

This quiet town is arranged on the cliff above Greenwood Cove, and just about every spot has a view of the rocky coastline and stunning Pacific sunsets. Beyond walking the beach there's little here for visitors, aside from a handful of restaurants and inns—and that's exactly why people come. Families don't tend to stay here, perhaps because it's such a romantic place.

GETTING HERE AND AROUND

From Ukiah, take Highway 253 west about 17 miles to Boonville/ Highway 128, then follow Highway 128 northwest 29 miles until it ends at Highway 1; you'll find Elk about 6 miles south. From San Francisco, travel north on Highway 101 and exit at Cloverdale/Highway 128 West. Follow the road northwest about 56 miles to Highway 1, then head south 6 miles to Elk. South Mendocino Coast Bus Route 75 (⊕ *www.4mta.org*) stops in town.

WHERE TO EAT AND STAY

For expanded reviews, facilities, and current deals, visit Fodors.com.

$
AMERICAN

✕ **Queenie's Roadhouse Cafe.** The chrome-and-patent-leather diner-style chairs here are usually occupied by locals, as it's a good bet for big breakfasts (served all day) and casual lunches (the cheeseburgers are highly recommended). The wide windows give you a view of the Pacific to go with your coffee. Or, if the day is sunny, grab one of the two picnic tables out front. $\boxed{\$}$ *Average main: $11* ✉ *6061 S. Hwy. 1* ☎ *707/877– 3285* ⊘ *Closed Jan. and Tues. and Wed. No dinner.*

$$
B&B/INN

⊡ **Elk Cove Inn & Spa.** Perched on a bluff above pounding surf and a driftwood-strewn beach, this property has stunning views from most rooms. **Pros:** steps to the beach; gorgeous views; great breakfast. **Cons:** rooms in main house are smallish and within earshot of common TV. **TripAdvisor:** "exceeded all expectations," "beautiful," "simply perfect getaway." $\boxed{\$}$ *Rooms from: $135* ✉ *6300 S. Hwy. 1* ☎ *707/877–3321, 800/275–2967* ⊕ *www.elkcoveinn.com* ⌔ *7 rooms, 4 suites, 4 cottages* ⏐○⏐ *Breakfast.*

$$$$
B&B/INN

⊡ **Harbor House.** Constructed in 1916, this redwood Craftsman-style house is as elegant as its location is rugged. **Pros:** luxurious; romantic. **Cons:** not a place for kids. **TripAdvisor:** "a beautiful place," "divine food and location," "attentive and gracious staff." $\boxed{\$}$ *Rooms from: $315* ✉ *5600 S. Hwy. 1* ☎ *707/877–3203, 800/720–7474* ⊕ *www. theharborhouseinn.com* ⌔ *6 rooms, 4 cottages* ⏐○⏐ *Some meals.*

ANDERSON VALLEY

6 miles north of Elk on Hwy. 101, then 22 miles southeast on Hwy. 128.

At the town of Albion, Highway 128 leads southeast into the Anderson Valley, whose hot summer weather might lure those weary of persistent coastal fog. Most of the first 13 miles wind through redwood forest along the Navarro River, then the road opens up to reveal farms and vineyards. While the community here is anchored in ranching, in the past few decades a progressive, gourmet-minded counterculture has taken root and that is what defines most visitors' experience. In the towns of Philo and Boonville you'll find B&Bs with classic Victorian style as well as small eateries.

Anderson Valley is best known to outsiders for its wineries. Tasting rooms here are more low-key than in Napa; most are in farmhouses and are more likely to play reggae than classical music. That said, Anderson Valley wineries produce world-class wines, particularly Pinot Noirs and Gewürztraminers, whose grapes thrive in the cool, coastal climate. All the wineries are along Highway 128, mostly in Philo with a few east of Boonville. The following are our favorites and are listed here from west to east.

GETTING HERE AND AROUND

Highway 128 West travels through the Anderson Valley; access it from Highway 101 from Cloverdale, or from Ukiah take Highway 253 west about 17 miles. The South Mendocino Coast Bus Route 75 offers limited service in the Anderson Valley between the coast and Ukiah.

EXPLORING

Greenwood Ridge Vineyards. White Riesling is the specialty here. Awards line the walls of the tasting room (built from a single redwood), and you can picnic at tables on an island in the middle of a pond. ⊠ *5501 Hwy. 128, Philo* ☎ *707/895–2002* ⊕ *www.greenwoodridge.com* ☼ *Tasting room daily 10–5.*

Husch Vineyards. Anderson Valley's oldest winery has a cozy tasting room next to sheep pastures and picnic tables under a grapevine-covered arbor. ⊠ *4400 Hwy. 128, Philo* ☎ *800/554–8724* ⊕ *www. huschvineyards.com* ☼ *Tasting room daily 10–5.*

Navarro River Redwoods State Park. Known by locals as the "11-mile-long redwood tunnel to the sea," this park just off Highway 128 is great for walks in the second-growth redwood forest and for summer swimming in the gentle Navarro River. There's also fishing, canoeing, and kayaking in the late winter and spring, when the river is higher. The two campgrounds (one on the river "beach") are quiet and clean. ⊠ *Hwy. 128, Navarro* ☎ *707/937–5804.*

★ **Navarro Vineyards.** A visit to this family-run winery is a classic Anderson Valley experience. Make time if you can for a vineyard tour (conducted daily by appointment at 10:30 and 3); guides draw from years of hands-on experience to explain every aspect of production, from sustainable farming techniques to the choices made in aging and blending. They're best known for their Alsatian varietals, but Navarro offers a wide range of other wines as well, with up to 15 at a time open for tasting. The

You'll find excellent vintages and great places to taste wine in the Anderson Valley—but it's much more laid back than Napa.

tasting room sells cheese and charcuterie for picnickers. ⊠ *5601 Hwy. 128, Philo* ☎ *707/895–3686* ⊕ *www.navarrowine.com* ⊗ *Apr.–Oct. daily 9–6; Nov.–Mar. daily 9–5.*

Roederer Estate. To experience the more polished side of Anderson Valley wine production, stop in at Roederer to sample one of their delicious sparkling wines and take in the beautiful view from the patio. ⊠ *4501 Hwy. 128, Philo* ☎ *707/895–2288* ⊕ *www.roedererestate.com* ⊗ *Tasting room daily 11–5.*

WHERE TO EAT AND STAY

For expanded reviews, facilities, and current deals, visit Fodors.com.

$
CAFÉ
✕ **The Boonville General Store.** The café menu here is nothing surprising, but the exacting attention paid to ingredients elevates each dish above the ordinary. Sandwiches are served on fresh-baked bread, the beet salad comes with roasted pecans and local blue cheese. Even the macaroni and cheese—freshly made—is noteworthy. For breakfast there are granola and pastries, made in-house. ⑤ *Average main: $10* ⊠ *14077A Hwy. 128, Boonville* ☎ *707/895–9477* ⊗ *No dinner.*

$$$$
AMERICAN
✕ **Table 128.** The restaurant at the Boonville Hotel takes small-town dining into the 21st century. Proprietor Johnny Schmitt and his kitchen prepare one prix fixe meal per night ($40 for three courses, $50 for four) and serve it up family-style, with platters of food brought to the table to be shared. Expect an expertly grilled or roasted meat (such as pork chops or flank steak), a sophisticated side (raddichio with polenta; heirloom bean ragout with salsa verde), and a soulful dessert (rhubarb galette; panna cotta with fresh berries). The lack of choices may feel limiting (menus are posted on the Web a few days in advance), but

this is essentially home cooking done at a high level with the freshest ingredients, and it's likely to satisfy most diners. $ *Average main: $40* ✉ *14050 Hwy. 128, Boonville* ☎ *707/895–2210* ⊕ *www.boonvillehotel. com* ⊘ *Closed Mon.–Thurs. Nov.–Apr; closed Tues. and Wed. May–mid-June; closed Tues. mid-June–mid-Oct. No lunch.*

$$$

HOTEL

▦ **Boonville Hotel.** From the street this looks like a fairly standard small-town hotel, but once you cross the threshold you start picking up on the laid-back sophistication that captures a lot of what's most appealing about Anderson Valley. **Pros:** stylish but homey; building is the town's main hub. **Cons:** service is friendly but not overly attentive—don't expect to be pampered; two-night stay required most weekends. **TripAdvisor:** "aesthetically pleasing slow down," "country charm," "warm and welcoming." $ *Rooms from: $185* ✉ *14050 Hwy. 128, Boonville* ☎ *707/895–2210* ⊕ *www.boonvillehotel.com* ⇋ *8 rooms, 7 suites* ❚❑❚ *Breakfast.*

$$$

HOTEL

▦ **The Philo Apple Farm.** Set in an orchard of organic, heirloom apples, the three cottages and one guest room here are tasteful, spare, and inspired by the surrounding landscape. **Pros:** pretty; quiet; country feel. **Cons:** occasionally hot in summer. **TripAdvisor:** "it does not get any nicer," "pure paradise," "best apple juice and jams anywhere." $ *Rooms from: $200* ✉ *18501 Greenwood Rd., Philo* ☎ *707/895–2333* ⊕ *www. philoapplefarm.com* ⇋ *1 room, 3 cottages* ❚❑❚ *Breakfast.*

LITTLE RIVER

14 miles north of Elk on Hwy. 1.

The town of Little River is not much more than a post office and a convenience store; Albion, its neighbor to the south, is even smaller. Along the winding road, though, you'll find numerous inns and restaurants, all of them quiet and situated to take advantage of the breathtaking ocean.

GETTING HERE AND AROUND

To reach Little River from San Francisco, exit Highway 101 at Cloverdale and follow Highway 128 northwest about 56 miles until it merges with Highway 1, then head north 7 miles. From the north, exit Highway 101 in Ukiah at Highway 253 West and follow it 17 miles to Boonville/Highway 128. Then travel along Highway 128 northwest 29 miles and Highway 1 north 7 miles to town. South Mendocino Coast Bus Route 75 (⊕ *www.4mta.org*) provides public transit.

EXPLORING

Van Damme State Park. Best known for its beach, this park is a prime abalone diving spot. Upland trails lead through lush riparian habitat and the bizarre **Pygmy Forest,** where acidic soil and poor drainage have produced mature cypress and pine trees that are no taller than a person. The visitor center has displays on ocean life and the historical significance of the redwood lumber industry along the coast. ✉ *Hwy. 1, 3 miles south of Mendocino* ☎ *707/937–5804* ⊕ *www.parks.ca.gov.*

WHERE TO EAT AND STAY

For expanded reviews, facilities, and current deals, visit Fodors.com.

$$$
FRENCH
★ **✕ Ledford House.** The only thing separating this bluff-top wood-and-glass restaurant from the Pacific Ocean is a great view. Entrées evoke the flavors of southern France and include hearty bistro dishes—stews, cassoulets, and pastas—and large portions of grilled meats and freshly caught fish (though it also is vegetarian friendly). The long bar, with its unobstructed water view, is a scenic spot for a sunset aperitif. ⑤ *Average main: $24 ✉ 3000 N. Hwy. 1, Albion ☎ 707/937–0282 ⊕ www. ledfordhouse.com ⊘ Closed Mon. and Tues. No lunch.*

$$$
B&B/INN **⌂ Albion River Inn.** Contemporary New England–style cottages at this inn overlook the dramatic bridge and seascape where the Albion River empties into the Pacific. **Pros:** great views; great bathtubs. **Cons:** newer buildings aren't as quaint as they could be. **TripAdvisor:** "absolutely perfect setting and views," "great dining," "beautiful welcoming to California."⑤ *Rooms from: $195 ✉ 3790 N. Hwy. 1, Albion ☎ 707/937–1919, 800/479–7944 ⊕ www.albionriverinn.com ⇗ 18 rooms, 4 cottages ❖❙ Breakfast.*

$$$
B&B/INN
★ **⌂ Glendeven Inn.** If Mendocino is the New England village of the West Coast, then Glendeven is the local country manor. **Pros:** picture-book pretty; elegant; romantic. **Cons:** not within walking distance of town; on the main drag. **TripAdvisor:** "better than you can imagine," "beautiful place," "a magical experience."⑤ *Rooms from: $165 ✉ 8205 N. Hwy. 1 707/937–0083, 800/822–4536 ⊕ www.glendeven.com ⇗ 6 rooms, 4 suites ❖❙ Breakfast.*

MENDOCINO

3 miles north of Little River on Hwy. 1; 153 miles from San Francisco, north on U.S. 101, west on Hwy. 128, and north on Hwy. 1.

Many of Mendocino's original settlers came from the Northeast and built houses in the New England style. Thanks to the logging boom, the town flourished for most of the second half of the 19th century. As the timber industry declined, many residents left, but the town's setting was too beautiful to be ignored. Artists and craftspeople began flocking here in the 1950s, and Elia Kazan chose Mendocino as the backdrop for his 1955 film adaptation of John Steinbeck's *East of Eden,* starring James Dean. As the arts community thrived, restaurants, cafés, and inns sprung up. Today, the small downtown area consists almost entirely of places to eat and shop.

GETTING HERE AND AROUND
From San Francisco, exit Highway 101 at Cloverdale and follow Highway 128 northwest about 56 miles and Highway 1 north 10 miles. You can also exit at Willits and head west on Highway 20 about 33 miles to Highway 1, then head south 8 miles to Mendocino. From Ukiah, use Highway 253 West 17 miles to Boonville, Highway 128 northwest 29 miles and Highway 1 north 7 miles. South Mendocino Coast Bus Route 75 (⊕ *www.4mta.org*) provides public transit.

EXPLORING
Ford House. The restored Ford House, built in 1854, serves as the visitor center for Mendocino Headlands State Park and the town. The house has a scale model of Mendocino as it looked in 1890, when it had 34

water towers and a 12-seat public outhouse. From the museum, you can head out on a 3-mile trail across the spectacular seaside cliffs that border the town. ⊠ *735 Main St., West of Lansing St.* ☎ *707/937–5397* ⊕ *www.mendoparks.org* ✉ *$2 suggested donation* ⊙ *Daily 11–4.*

Kelley House Museum. An 1861 structure holds this museum, whose artifacts include Victorian-era furniture and historical photographs of Mendocino coast's logging days. ⊠ *45007 Albion St.* ☎ *707/937–5791* ⊕ *www.kelleyhousemuseum.org* ✉ *$2* ⊙ *June–Sept., Thurs.–Tues. 11–3; Oct.–May, Fri.–Mon. 11–3.*

Mendocino Art Center. This art center has an extensive program of workshops, mounts rotating exhibits in its galleries, and is the home of the Mendocino Theatre Company. ⊠ *45200 Little Lake St.* ☎ *707/937–5818, 800/653–3328* ⊕ *www.mendocinoartcenter.org.*

WHERE TO EAT AND STAY

For expanded reviews, facilities, and current deals, visit Fodors.com.

$$$
AMERICAN

✕ **Cafe Beaujolais.** The yellow Victorian cottage that houses this popular restaurant is surrounded by a garden of heirloom and exotic plantings. A commitment to the freshest possible organic and local ingredients guides the chef here. The menu is eclectic and ever-evolving, but often includes free-range fowl, line-caught fish, and Niman Ranch beef. The bakery turns out several delicious varieties of bread from a wood-fired oven. ⑤ *Average main: $30* ⊠ *961 Ukiah St.* ☎ *707/937–5614* ⊕ *www. cafebeaujolais.com* ⊙ *No lunch Mon. and Tues.*

$$$$
B&B/INN
★

🛏 **Brewery Gulch Inn.** This tasteful inn gives a modern twist to the elegance of Mendocino. **Pros:** stylish; peaceful; intimate. **Cons:** must drive to town. **TripAdvisor:** "beautiful ocean views with a romantic feel," "the very best," "great service."⑤ *Rooms from: $330* ⊠ *9401 N. Hwy. 1, 1 mile south of Mendocino* ☎ *707/937–4752, 800/578–4454* ⊕ *www. brewerygulchinn.com* ⇌ *10 rooms, 1 suite* ⑩ *Breakfast.*

$$$
B&B/INN
Fodor's Choice
★

🛏 **MacCallum House.** Set on 2 flower-filled acres in the middle of town, this inn is a perfect mix of Victorian charm and modern luxury. **Pros:** best B&B around; excellent breakfast; great in-town location. **Cons:** new luxury suites on a separate property are less charming. **TripAdvisor:** "great restaurant," "perfect getaway," "lovely and romantic."⑤ *Rooms from: $179* ⊠ *45020 Albion St.* ☎ *707/937–0289, 800/609–0492* ⊕ *www.maccallumhouse.com* ⇌ *11 rooms, 13 suites, 7 cottages* ⑩ *Breakfast.*

NIGHTLIFE AND THE ARTS

Mendocino Theatre Company. The repertoire of this well-established company ranges all over the contemporary map, including works by David Mamet, Arthur Miller, Neil Simon, and local playwrights. Performances take place Thursday through Saturday evenings, with some weekend matinees. ⊠ *Mendocino Art Center, 45200 Little Lake St.* ☎ *707/937–4477* ⊕ *www.mendocinotheatre.org.*

The North Coast is famous for its locally caught Dungeness crab; be sure to try some during your visit.

SPORTS AND THE OUTDOORS

Catch-A-Canoe and Bicycles Too. Rent kayaks and regular and outrigger canoes here, as well as mountain and suspension bicycles. ⊠ *Stanford Inn by the Sea, Comptche-Ukiah Rd., off Hwy. 1* ☎ *707/937–0273* ⊕ *www.catchacanoe.com.*

FORT BRAGG

10 miles north of Mendocino on Hwy. 1.

The commercial center of Mendocino County, Fort Bragg is a working-class town that many feel is the most authentic place around; it's certainly less expensive than its neighbors to the south. The declining timber industry has been steadily replaced by booming tourism, but the city maintains a local feel since most people who work at the area hotels and restaurants also live here, as do many local artists. A stroll down Franklin Street (one block east of Highway 1) takes you past numerous bookstores, antiques shops, and boutiques.

GETTING HERE AND AROUND

From Highway 101 at Willits follow Highway 20 west about 33 miles to Highway 1 and go north 2 miles. South Mendocino Coast Bus Route 75 (⊕ *www.4mta.org*) buses service the town and region.

EXPLORING

★ **Mendocino Coast Botanical Gardens.** The gardens have something for nature lovers in every season. Even in winter, heather and camellias bloom. Along 3½ miles of trails, including pathways with ocean views and observation points for whale-watching, is a splendid profusion of flowers. The rhododendrons are at their peak from April through June; the dahlias begin their spectacular show in August and last until October. ⊠ *18220 N. Hwy. 1, 2 miles south of Fort Bragg* ☎ *707/964–4352* ⊕ *www.gardenbythesea.org* ✉ *$14* ⊙ *Mar.–Oct., daily 9–5; Nov.–Feb., daily 9–4.*

Museum in the Triangle Tattoo Parlor. At the top of a steep staircase, this museum is an unexpected nod to Fort Bragg's rough-and-tumble past. The two-room display shows a wonderful collection of tattoo memorabilia, including pictures of astonishing tattoos from around the world, early 20th-century Burmese tattooing instruments, and a small shrine to sword-swallowing sideshow king Captain Don Leslie. ⊠ *356-B N. Main St.* ☎ *707/964–8814* ✉ *Free* ⊙ *Daily noon–6.*

☾ **The Skunk Train.** Back in the 1920s, a fume-spewing gas-powered train car shuttled passengers along a rail line dating from the logging days of the 1880s. Nicknamed the Skunk Train, it traversed redwood forests inaccessible to automobiles. The reproduction that you can ride today travels the same route, making a 3½- to 4-hour round-trip between Fort Bragg and the town of Northspur, 21 miles inland. The schedule varies depending on the season and in summer includes evening barbecue excursions and wine parties. ⊠ *Foot of Laurel St., west of Main St.* ☎ *707/964–6371, 866/457–5865* ⊕ *www.skunktrain.com* ✉ *$49–$70.*

BEACHES

Glass Beach. The ocean is not visible from most of Fort Bragg, but go three blocks west of Main Street on Elm Street, and a gravel path leads to wild coastline where you can walk for miles along the bluffs. The sandy coves in the area you first reach from the road are called Glass Beach because this used to be the dumping ground for the city. That history is still apparent, although the pounding surf has pulverized the trash into a sparkling treasure. Look closely at the sand and you'll find the top layer is comprised almost entirely of sea glass, likely more than you've ever seen in one place before. You can gaze at the dazzling colors, but don't take any glass with you; it's now against the law. No swimming at this beach either, for safety's sake. **Amenities:** parking; toilets. **Best For:** sunset; walking. ⊠ *Elm St. and Old Haul Rd.*

MacKerricher State Park. This park begins at Glass Beach and stretches north for 9 miles, beginning with rocky headlands that taper into dunes and sandy beaches. The headland is a good place for whale-watching from December to mid-April. Fishing at Lake Cleone (a freshwater lake stocked with trout), canoeing, hiking, tide-pooling, jogging, bicycling, beachcombing, camping, and harbor seal watching at Laguna Point are among the popular activities, many of which are accessible to the mobility-impaired. Rangers, who lead nature hikes in summer, discourage swimming in the treacherous surf and remind those on shore to be vigilant for rogue waves and to never turn their backs on the sea. Dogs must be leashed. **Amenities:** parking; toilets. **Best For:** solitude; sunset; walking. ⊠ *Hwy. 1, 3 miles north of Fort Bragg* ☎ *707/937–5804* ✉ *$8 per vehicle.*

WHERE TO EAT AND STAY

For expanded reviews, facilities, and current deals, visit Fodors.com.

$ ✕ **Piaci.** The seats are stools and your elbows might bang a neighbor's,
ITALIAN but nobody seems to mind at this cozy little spot—this is hands down
the most popular casual restaurant around. The food is simple, mostly
pizza and calzones, but everything is given careful attention and comes
out tasty. Alongside the selective list of wines is a distinctive beer list
that has been given equal respect; noted are the origin, brewmaster,
and alcohol content for each brew. Dogs and their owners are welcome
at the tables outside. ⑤ *Average main: $13* ✉ *120 W. Redwood Ave.*
☎ *707/961–1133* ⊕ *www.piacipizza.com* ☉ *No lunch Sun.*

$$$ ⊡ **Weller House Inn.** It's hard to believe that this house was abandoned
B&B/INN and slated for demolition when it was purchased in 1994 and then
carefully restored into the loveliest Victorian in Fort Bragg. **Pros:** hand-
crafted details; radiant heat in the wood floors; friendly innkeepers.
Cons: some may find it too old-fashioned. **TripAdvisor:** "great room,"
"quiet and accommodating," "charming." ⑤ *Rooms from: $180* ✉ *524
Stewart St.* ☎ *707/964–4415, 877/893–5537* ⊕ *www.wellerhouse.com*
➥ *9 rooms* ❙❉❙ *Breakfast.*

SPORTS AND THE OUTDOORS

All Aboard Adventures. From late December through April All Aboard
Adventures operates whale-watching trips; they also offer fishing excur-
sions all year out of Noyo Harbor. ✉ *32410 N. Harbor Dr.* ☎ *707/964–
1881* ⊕ *www.allaboardadventures.com.*

Ricochet Ridge Ranch. Come here for private and group trail rides through
redwood forest and on the beach. ✉ *24201 N. Hwy. 1* ☎ *707/964–
7669, 888/873–5777* ⊕ *www.horse-vacation.com.*

REDWOOD COUNTRY

HUMBOLDT REDWOODS STATE PARK

20 miles north of Garberville on U.S. 101.

GETTING HERE AND AROUND

Access the park right off U.S. 101, about 43 miles south of Eureka and
20 miles north of Garberville. Contact Humboldt Transit Authority
(⊕ *www.hta.org*) for public transportation details.

EXPLORING

◐ **Avenue of the Giants.** Also known as State Highway 254, this route tra-
verses Humbolt Redwoods State Park south–north, branching off U.S.
101 about 7 miles north of Garberville and more or less paralleling
that road for 32 miles north to Pepperwood. Some of the tallest trees
on the planet tower over the stretch of two-lane blacktop that follows
the south fork of the Eel River.

Humboldt Redwoods State Park Visitor Center. At the visitor center
you can pick up information about the redwoods, waterways, and recre-
ational activities in the 53,000-acre park. One brochure describes a self-
guided auto tour of the park, with short and long hikes into redwood
groves. ✉ *Ave. of the Giants, 2 miles south of Weott* ☎ *707/946–2263
visitor center* ⊕ *www.humboldtredwoods.org* ✉ *Free; $8 day-use fee*

for parking and facilities in Williams Grove ⊙ Park daily; visitor center Apr.–Sept., daily 9–5; Oct.–Mar., daily 10–4

Founders Grove. One of the most impressive trees here—the 362-foot-long Dyerville Giant—fell to the ground in 1991; its root base points skyward 35 feet. You reach the grove via a ½-mile trail off Avenue of the Giants. ⊠ *Hwy. 254, 4 miles north of Humboldt Redwoods State Park Visitor Center*

Rockefeller Forest. The largest remaining old-growth coast redwood forest contains 40 of the 100 tallest trees in the world. ⊠ *Mattole Rd., 6 miles north of Humboldt Redwoods State Park Visitor Center*

FERNDALE

35 miles northwest of Weott; 57 miles northwest of Garberville via U.S. 101 north to Hwy. 211 west.

Though gift shops and ice-cream stores comprise a fair share of the businesses here, Ferndale remains a fully functioning small town. There's a butcher, a small grocery, and a local saloon (the westernmost in the contiguous United States), and descendants of the Portuguese and Scandinavian dairy farmers who settled this town continue to raise dairy cows in the surrounding pastures. Ferndale is best known for its colorful Victorian architecture; many shops carry a self-guided tour map that highlights the town's most interesting historical buildings.

GETTING HERE AND AROUND
Ferndale is about 15 miles south of Eureka and 35 miles northwest of Weott. Exit U.S. 101 at Highway 211 and follow it southwest 5 miles.

EXPLORING
Eel River Delta Tours. Two-hour boat trips examine the wildlife and history of the Eel River's estuary and salt marsh. (Don't be surprised if you get an informal answering machine when you inquire—this is laid-back Humboldt, and you will get a call back.) ⊠ *285 Morgan Slough Rd.* ☎ 707/786–4902.

Ferndale Historic Cemetery. A walk through the cemetery on the east side of town gives interesting insight into the hard, often short lives of the European immigrants who cultivated this area of California in the mid-18th century. The gravestones are worn, lovely, and sometimes imaginative (one is in the shape of a nubbly redwood log). The cemetery is lined by forest, and from the top of the hill there's a nice view of town, the surrounding farms, and the ocean. ⊠ *Bluff St. and Craig St.*

Ferndale Museum. The main building of this museum exhibits Victoriana and historical photographs and has a display of an old-style barbershop and another of Wiyot Indian baskets. In the annex are a horse-drawn buggy, a re-created blacksmith's shop, and antique farming, fishing, and dairy equipment. Don't miss the historic Bosch-Omori seismograph, installed in 1933 in Ferndale; it's still checked daily for recordings of earthquake activity. ⊠ *515 Shaw Ave.* ☎ 707/786–4466 ⊕ *www. ferndale-museum.org* ✑ *$1* ⊙ *June–Sept., Tues.–Sat. 11–4, Sun. 1–4; Oct.–Dec. and Feb.–May, Wed.–Sat. 11–4, Sun. 1–4.*

The Kinetic Sculpture Race. Memorial Day weekend's annual Kinetic Sculpture Race has artists and engineers (and plenty of hacks) building moving sculptures from used bicycle parts and other scraps, which they race from Arcata to the finish line in Ferndale. Contestants are judged as much on their creativity as on their ability to cross the finish line, and as a result sculptures have included the Albino Rhino and a 93-foot-long fish. ⊕ *www.kineticgrandchampionship.com.*

Ferndale Kinetic Museum. Stop by here to see a display of "vehicles, costumes, awards, and bribes" from past races. ⊠ *580 Main St.* ☎ *No phone* ✉ *Free, donation encouraged* ⊙ *Daily 10–5*

EUREKA

18 miles north of Ferndale; 66 miles north of Garberville on U.S. 101.

With a population of 28,606, Eureka is the North Coast's largest city. Over the past century, it has cycled through several periods of boom and bust—first with mining and later with timber and fishing—but these days, tourism is developing into a healthy sustaining industry. The town's nearly 100 Victorian buildings have inspired some to dub it "the Williamsburg of the West." Shops draw people to the renovated downtown, and a walking pier extends into the harbor.

GETTING HERE AND AROUND

U.S. 101 travels through Eureka. From Redding and U.S. 5, travel west along Highway 299 about 138 miles to U.S. 101; Eureka is 9 miles south. Eureka Transit buses (⊕ *www.eurekatransit.org*) travel on regular routes throughout town and connect with regional transit.

EXPLORING

Blue Ox Millworks. Blue Ox is one of only a handful of wood shops in the country that specialize in Victorian-era architecture, but what makes it truly unique is that it uses antique tools to do the work. The most modern tool here is a 1948 band saw. Lucky for curious craftspeople and history buffs, the shop doubles as a dusty historical park. Visitors can watch craftsmen use printing presses, lathes, and even a mill that pares down whole redwood logs into the ornate fixtures for Victorians like those around town. The museum is less interesting on Saturday, when the craftspeople mostly take the day off. ⊠ *1 X St.* ☎ *707/444–3437, 800/248–4259* ⊕ *www.blueoxmill.com* ✉ *$7.50* ⊙ *Weekdays 9–5, Sat. 9–4.*

Clarke Historical Museum. The Native American Wing of the Clarke Historical Museum contains a beautiful collection of northwestern California basketry. Artifacts from Eureka's Victorian, logging, and maritime eras fill the rest of the museum. ⊠ *240 E St.* ☎ *707/443–1947* ⊕ *www.clarkemuseum.org* ✉ *Donations accepted* ⊙ *Wed.–Sat. 11–4.*

Eureka Chamber of Commerce. You can pick up maps here with self-guided driving tours of Eureka's Victorian architecture, and also learn about organized tours. ⊠ *2112 Broadway* ☎ *707/442–3738, 800/356–6381* ⊕ *www.eurekachamber.com* ⊙ *June–Aug., Mon.–Thurs. 8:30–5, Fri. 8:30–4, Sat. 10–3; Sept.–May, Mon.–Thurs. 8:30–5, Fri. 8:30–4.*

◷ **Fort Humboldt State Historic Park.** The structure that gives this park its name was built in response to conflicts between white settlers and Native Americans. It no longer stands, but on its grounds are some reconstructed buildings, fort and logging museums, and old logging locomotives. At this writing the museums are closed due to earthquake damage, but the park, which is a good place for a picnic, remains open. ✉ *3431 Fort Ave.* ☎ *707/445–6547* ⊕ *www.parks.ca.gov* ▤ *Free* ◷ *Daily 8–5.*

QUICK BITES

Lost Coast Brewery & Cafe. This bustling microbrewery is the best place in town to relax with a pint of ale or porter. Soups, salads, and light meals are served for lunch and dinner. ✉ *617 4th St.* ☎ *707/445–4480* ⊕ *www. lostcoast.com.*

WHERE TO EAT AND STAY
For expanded reviews, facilities, and current deals, visit Fodors.com.

$$$
AMERICAN
Fodor'sChoice
★

✕ **Restaurant 301.** Eureka's most elegant restaurant, housed in the lovely Carter House, uses ingredients selected from the farmers' market, local cheese makers and ranchers, and the on-site gardens. Dishes are prepared with a delicate hand and a sensuous imagination—the ever-changing menu features a fresh fish offering daily, plus a fixed-price Discovery Menu with optional wine pairing from the restaurant's award-winning wine cellar (which has more than 3,500 bottles). ⑤ *Average main: $28* ✉ *301 L St.* ☎ *707/444–8062, 800/404–1390* ⊕ *www.carterhouse.com* ◷ *No lunch.*

$
AMERICAN
◷

✕ **Samoa Cookhouse.** Originally a cafeteria that fed 500 local mill workers, the cookhouse became a public restaurant in the 1950s—though not much but the clientele has changed. Take a seat at one of the long, communal tables, and waiters will bring bottomless, family-style bowls of whatever is being served at that meal. For breakfast that means eggs, sausage, biscuits and gravy, and the like. Lunch and dinner usually feature soup, potatoes, salad, and pie, plus daily changing entrées such as pot roast and pork loin. A back room contains a museum of logging culture, but really the whole place is a tribute to the rough-and-tumble life and hard work that tamed this wild land. Dieters and vegetarians should look elsewhere for sustenance. ⑤ *Average main: $16* ✉ *908 Vance Ave., near Cookhouse Rd., Samoa* ☎ *707/442–1659* ⊕ *www. samoacookhouse.net.*

$$
HOTEL

▦ **Abigail's Elegant Victorian Mansion.** Innkeepers Doug and Lily Vieyra have devoted themselves to honoring this National Historic Landmark (once home to the town's millionaire real-estate sultan) by decorating it with authentic, Victorian-era opulence. **Pros:** unique; lots of character; fun innkeepers. **Cons:** downtown is not within walking distance; bedrooms are a bit worn. **TripAdvisor:** "very nice visit," "a trip back in time," "a genuinely memorable experience." ⑤ *Rooms from: $105* ✉ *1406 C St.* ☎ *707/444–3144* ⊕ *www.eureka-california.com* ⇆ *4 rooms, 2 with shared bath* ⑪ *No meals.*

$$$
HOTEL
Fodor'sChoice
★

▦ **Carter House.** According to owner Mark Carter, his staff has been trained always to say yes; whether it's breakfast in bed or an in-room massage, someone here will make sure you get what you want. **Pros:** elegant; every detail in place; excellent dining at Restaurant 301, bar off the lobby. **Cons:** while kids are allowed, it's better suited for grown-ups. **TripAdvisor:** "beautiful cottage," "a historic property," "helpful staff." ⑤ *Rooms from: $159* ✉ *301 L St.* ☎ *707/444–8062, 800/404–1390* ⊕ *www.carterhouse.com* ↪ *22 rooms, 8 suites, 2 cottages* ○| *Breakfast.*

SHOPPING

Eureka has several art galleries and numerous antiques stores in the district running from C to I streets between 2nd and 3rd streets.

Eureka Books. Along with classics and bestsellers, this bibliophile's haven has an exceptional collection of used books on all topics. ✉ *426 2nd St.* ☎ *707/444–9593* ⊕ *www.eurekabooksellers.com.*

First Street Gallery. Run by Humboldt State University, this is the best spot for contemporary art by local and regional artists, with some national and international representation. ✉ *422 1st St.* ☎ *707/443–6363* ⊕ *www.humboldt.edu/first.*

SPORTS AND THE OUTDOORS

Hum-Boats. Kayak rental and lessons are available here, along with a variety of group kayak tours, including popular whale-watching trips ($75, December–June) that get you close enough to get good photos of migrating gray whales and resident humpback whales. ✉ *Dock A, Woodley Island Marina* ☎ *707/443–5157* ⊕ *www.humboats.com.*

TRINIDAD

21 miles north of Eureka on U.S. 101.

Trinidad got its name from the Spanish mariners who entered the bay on Trinity Sunday, June 9, 1775. The town became a principal trading post for the mining camps along the Klamath and Trinity rivers. Mining and whaling have faded from the scene, and now Trinidad is a quiet and genuinely charming community with ample sights and activities to entertain low-key visitors.

GETTING HERE AND AROUND

Access Trinidad via U.S. 101. If you're driving on Highway 5 south from Oregon, exit at Grants Pass and take U.S. 199 southwest to Crescent City (about 78 miles), then U.S. 101 south to Trinidad (another 66 miles). Redwood Transit System (⊕ *www.redwoodtransit.org*) provides bus service to Trinidad, Eureka, and nearby towns.

EXPLORING

Patrick's Point State Park. On a forested plateau almost 200 feet above the surf, Patrick's Point State Park has stunning views of the Pacific, great whale- and sea lion–watching in season, picnic areas, bike paths, and hiking trails through old-growth spruce forest. There are also tidal pools at Agate Beach, a re-created Yurok Indian village, and a small museum with natural-history exhibits. Because the park is far from major tourist hubs, there are few visitors (most are local surfers), which leaves the land sublimely quiet. In spruce and alder forest above the ocean, the park's three campgrounds have all amenities except RV hookups. In summer it's best to reserve in advance. Dogs are not allowed on trails or the beach. ✉ *U.S. 101, 5 miles north of Trinidad* ☎ *707/677–3570* ⊕ *www.parks.ca.gov* 🖃 *$8 per vehicle.*

BEACHES

☺ **Clam Beach County Park and Little River State Beach.** Together these make a park that stretches from Trinidad to as far south as one can see. The sandy beach here is exceptionally wide, perfect for kids who need to get out of the car and burn off some energy. Beachcombing and clamming are favored activities, as well as savoring fabulous sunsets. The two parks share day use facilities. **Amenities:** parking; toilets. **Best for:** solitude; sunset; walking. ✉ *Hwy. 1, 6½ miles south of Trinidad* ☎ *707/445–7651* ⊙ *Daily 5 am–midnight.*

WHERE TO EAT AND STAY

For expanded reviews, facilities, and current deals, visit Fodors.com.

$ ✕ **Katy's Smokehouse.** Purchase delectable picnic fixings at this tiny deli
SEAFOOD that has been doing things the same way since the 1940s, curing day-boat, line-caught fish with its original smokers. Salmon cured with brown sugar, albacore jerky, and smoked scallops are popular. Buy bread and drinks in town and walk to the waterside for alfresco snacking. Katy's closes at 6 pm. ⑤ *Average main: $10* ✉ *740 Edwards St.* ☎ *707/677–0151* ⊕ *www.katyssmokehouse.com.*

$$$ ✕ **Larrupin' Cafe.** Locals consider this restaurant one of the best places to
AMERICAN eat on the North Coast. Set in a two-story house on a quiet country road north of town, it's often thronged with people enjoying fresh seafood, Cornish game hen, or mesquite-grilled ribs. While the garden setting and candlelight stir thoughts of romance, service is sometimes rather rushed. ⑤ *Average main: $30* ✉ *1658 Patrick's Point Dr.* ☎ *707/677–0230* ⊕ *www.larrupin.com* 🍴 *Reservations essential* ⊙ *Closed Thurs. in winter. No lunch.*

$$$ 🏠 **Trinidad Bay Bed and Breakfast Inn.** Staying at this small Cape Cod–style
B&B/INN inn perched above Trinidad Bay is like spending the weekend at a friend's vacation house. **Pros:** great location above bay; lots of light. **Cons:** if all rooms are full, the main house can feel a bit crowded. **TripAdvisor:** "beautiful rooms," "amazing views," "a special place." ⑤ *Rooms from: $200* ✉ *560 Edwards St., Box 849* ☎ *707/677–0840* ⊕ *www.trinidadbaybnb.com* 🛏 *4 rooms* ⦿️ *Breakfast.*

$$$$ 🏠 **Turtle Rocks Oceanfront Inn.** This comfortable inn has the best view in
B&B/INN Trinidad, and the builders have made the most of it. **Pros:** great ocean views; comfy king beds. **Cons:** no businesses within walking distance; not as deluxe as you might expect for the price. **TripAdvisor:** "service was awesome," "breathtaking view," "great breakfast." ⑤ *Rooms from: $275* ✉ *3392 Patrick's Point Dr., 4½ miles north of town* ☎ *707/677–3707* ⊕ *www.turtlerocksinn.com* 🛏 *5 rooms, 1 suite* ⦿️ *Breakfast.*

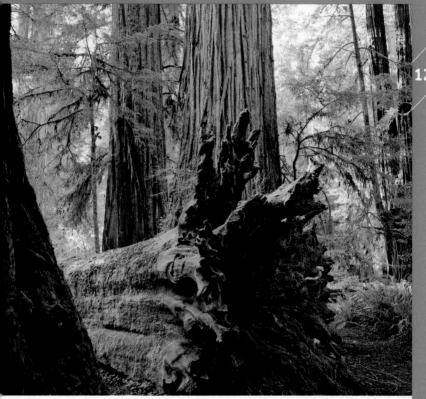

Redwood
National Park

WORD OF MOUTH

"Roosevelt elk were easy to find. Whenever we saw an odd collection of cars by the side of the road (or sometimes in the middle of the road!) and a lot of people with cameras, we knew we would see elk."

—Elnap29

WELCOME TO REDWOOD NATIONAL PARK

TOP REASONS TO GO

★ **Giant trees:** These mature coastal redwoods are the tallest trees in the world.

★ **Hiking to the sea:** The park's trails wind through majestic redwood groves, and many connect to the Coastal Trail running along the western edge of the park.

★ **Rare wildlife:** Mighty Roosevelt elk favor the park's flat prairie and open lands; seldom-seen black bears roam the backcountry; trout and salmon leap through streams, and Pacific gray whales swim along the coast during their biannual migrations.

★ **Stepping back in time:** Hike Fern Canyon Trail and explore a prehistoric scene of lush vegetation and giant ferns.

★ **Cheeps, not beeps:** Amid the majestic redwoods you're out of range for cell-phone service—and in range for the soothing sounds of warblers and burbling creeks.

1 Del Norte Coast Redwoods State Park. The rugged terrain of this far northwest corner of California combines stretches of treacherous surf, steep cliffs, and forested ridges. On a clear day it's postcard-perfect; with fog, it's mysteriously mesmerizing.

2 Jedediah Smith Redwoods State Park. Gargantuan old-growth redwoods dominate the scenery here. The Smith River cuts through canyons and splits across boulders, carrying salmon to the inland creeks where they spawn.

3 Prairie Creek Redwoods State Park. The forests here give way to spacious, grassy plains where abundant wildlife thrives. Roosevelt elk are a common sight in the meadows and down to Gold Bluffs Beach.

4 Orick Area. The highlight of the southern portion of Redwood National Park is the Tall Trees Grove. It's difficult to reach and requires a special pass, but it's worth the hassle—this section has the tallest coast redwood trees, with a new record holder discovered in 2006.

CALIFORNIA

12

GETTING ORIENTED

U.S. 101 weaves through the southern portion of the park, skirts around the center, and then slips back through redwoods in the north and on to Crescent City. Kuchel Visitor Center, Prairie Creek Redwoods State Park and Visitor Center, Tall Trees Grove, Fern Canyon, and Lady Bird Johnson Grove are all in the park's southern section. The graveled Coastal Drive curves along ocean vistas and dips down to the Klamath River in the park's central section. To the north you'll find Mill Creek Trail, Enderts Beach, and Crescent Beach Overlook in Del Norte Coast Redwoods State Park as well as Jedediah Smith Redwoods State Park, Stout Grove, Little Bald Hills, and Simpson-Reed Grove.

Updated
by Christine
Vovakes

Soaring to more than 300 feet, the coastal redwoods that give this park its name are miracles of efficiency—some have survived hundreds of years (a few live for more than 2,000 years). These massive trees glean nutrients from the rich alluvial flats at their feet and from the moisture and nitrogen trapped in their uneven canopy. Their huge, thick-barked trunks can hold thousands of gallons of water, reservoirs that have helped them withstand centuries of firestorms.

REDWOOD PLANNER

WHEN TO GO

Campers and hikers flock to the park from mid-June to early September. Crowds disappear in winter, but you'll have to contend with frequent rains and nasty potholes on side roads. Temperatures fluctuate widely throughout the park: the foggy coastal lowland is much cooler than the higher-altitude interior.

The average annual rainfall here is 90 to 100 inches, and during dry summer months thick fog rolling in from the Pacific veils the forests, giving redwoods a large portion of their moisture intake.

GETTING HERE AND AROUND

CAR TRAVEL

U.S. 101 runs north–south along the park, and Highway 199 cuts east–west through its northern portion. Access routes off 101 include Bald Hills Road, Davison Road, Newton B. Drury Scenic Parkway, Coastal Drive, Requa Road, and Enderts Beach Road. From 199 take South Fork Road to Howland Hill Road. Many of the park's roads aren't paved, and winter rains can turn them into obstacle courses; sometimes they're closed completely. RVs and trailers aren't permitted on some routes.

PARK ESSENTIALS

PARK FEES AND PERMITS

Admission to Redwood National Park is free. There's an $8 day-use fee to enter one or all of Redwood's state parks; for camping at these state parks it's an additional $35. To visit Tall Trees Grove, you must get a free permit at the Kuchel Information Center in Orick. Permits also are needed to camp in Redwood Creek backcountry.

12

PARK HOURS

The park is open year-round, 24 hours a day.

VISITOR INFORMATION

PARK CONTACT INFORMATION

Redwood National Park ⊠ *1111 2nd St., Crescent City* ☎ *707/465–7335* ⊕ *www.nps.gov/redw.*

VISITOR CENTERS

Crescent City Information Center. As the park's headquarters, this center is the main information stop if you're approaching the redwoods from the north. A gift shop and picnic area are here. ⊠ *Off U.S. 101 at 2nd and K Sts., 1111 2nd St, Crescent City* ☎ *707/465–7335* ⊕ *www.nps.gov/redw* ☉ *Mid-May–mid-Oct., daily 9–6; mid-Oct.–mid-May, daily 9–4.*

Hiouchi Information Center. Located in Jedediah Smith Redwoods State Park, 2 miles west of Hiouchi and 9 miles east of Crescent City off U.S. 199, this center has a bookstore, film, and exhibits about the flora and fauna in the park. It's also a starting point for seasonal ranger programs. ⊠ *Hiouchi Information Center, Hwy. 199* ☎ *707/458–3294* ⊕ *www.nps.gov/redw* ☉ *Late May–mid-Sept., daily 9–6.*

Jedediah Smith Visitor Center. Located off U.S. 199, this center has information about ranger-led walks and evening campfire programs in the summer in Jedediah Smith Redwoods State Park. Also here are nature and history exhibits, a gift shop, a pay phone, and a picnic area. ⊠ *Off U.S. 199* ☎ *707/458–3496* ⊕ *www.parks.ca.gov* ☉ *Late May–mid-Sept., daily 9–6; closed late Sept.–mid-May.*

★ **Prairie Creek Visitor Center.** This center, housed in a redwood lodge, has wildlife displays and a massive stone fireplace that was built in 1933. Several trailheads begin here. Stretch your legs with an easy stroll along Revelation Trail, a short loop behind the lodge. Pick up information about summer programs in Prairie Creek Redwoods State Park. There's a pay phone, nature museum, gift shop, picnic area, and exhibits on flora and fauna. ⊠ *Off southern end of Newton B. Drury Scenic Pkwy., Orick* ☎ *707/488–2039* ⊕ *www.parks.ca.gov* ☉ *Daily 9–5.*

★ **Thomas H. Kuchel Visitor Center.** Here you can get brochures, advice, and a free permit to drive up the access road to Tall Trees Grove. Whale-watchers will find the deck of the visitor center an excellent observation point, and bird-watchers will enjoy the nearby Freshwater Lagoon, a popular layover for migrating waterfowl. ⊠ *Off U.S. 101, Orick* ☎ *707/465–7765* ⊕ *www.nps.gov/redw* ☉ *Daily 9–5.*

Plants and Wildlife in Redwood

Coast redwoods, the world's tallest trees (a new record holder, topping out at 379 feet, was found within the park in 2006) grow in the moist, temperate climate of California's North Coast. These ancient giants thrive in an environment that exists in only a few hundred coastal miles along the Pacific Ocean. They commonly live 600 years—though some have been around for 2,000 years.

A healthy redwood forest is diverse and includes Douglas firs, western hemlocks, tan oaks, and madrone trees. The complex soils of the forest floor support a verdant profusion of ferns, mosses, and fungi, along with numerous shrubs and berry bushes. In spring, California rhododendron bloom throughout the forest, providing a daz-

zling purple and pink contrast to the dense greenery.

Redwood National Park holds 45% of all California's old-growth redwood forests. Of the original 3,125 square miles (2 million acres) in the Redwoods Historic Range, only 4% remain following the logging that began in 1850; 1% is privately owned and managed, and 3% is on public land.

In the park's backcountry, you might spot mountain lions, black bears, black-tailed deer, river otters, beavers, and minks. Roosevelt elk roam the flatlands, and the rivers and streams teem with salmon and trout. Gray whales, seals, and sea lions cavort near the coastline. And thanks to the area's location along the Pacific Flyway, an amazing 402 species of birds have been sighted here.

EXPLORING

SCENIC DRIVES

★ **Coastal Drive.** This 8-mile, partially paved road is closed to trailers and RVs and takes about one hour to drive one way. The slow pace alongside stands of redwoods offers close-up views of the Klamath River and expansive panoramas of the Pacific. From here you'll find access to the Flint Ridge section of the Coastal Trail.

SCENIC STOPS

Crescent Beach Overlook. The scenery here includes ocean views and, in the distance, Crescent City and its working harbor; in balmy weather this is a great place for a picnic. From the overlook you can spot migrating gray whales November through December and March through April. ⊠ *2 miles south of Crescent City off Enderts Beach Rd.*

★ **Fern Canyon.** Enter another world and be surrounded by 30-foot canyon walls covered with sword, maidenhair, and five-finger ferns. Allow an hour to explore the 0.25-mile-long vertical garden along a 0.7-mile loop. From the north end of Gold Bluffs Beach it's an easy walk, although you'll have to wade across a small stream several times (in addition to driving across streams on the way to the parking area). But the lush surroundings are otherworldly, and worth a visit when creeks aren't running too high. Be aware that RVs longer than 24 feet and all trailers are not allowed here. ⊠ *10 miles northwest of Prairie Creek Visitor Center, via Davison Rd. off U.S. 101.*

Lady Bird Johnson Grove. This section of the park was dedicated by, and named for, the former first lady. A 1-mile, wheelchair-accessible nature loop follows an old logging road through a mature redwood forest. Allow 45 minutes to complete the trail. ⊠ *5 miles east of Kuchel Visitor Center, along U.S. 101 and Bald Hills Rd.*

★ **Tall Trees Grove.** From the Kuchel Visitor Center, you can get a free permit to make the drive up the steep 14-mile Tall Trees Access Road (the last 6 miles are gravel) to the grove's trailhead (trailers and RVs not allowed). Access to the popular grove is first-come, first-served, and a maximum of 50 permits are handed out each day. ⊠ *Access road is 10-mile drive east of Kuchel Visitor Center, via U.S. 101; turn right at Bald Hills Rd. and follow it to access road.*

SPORTS AND THE OUTDOORS

HIKING

MODERATE

★ **Coastal Trail.** Although this easy-to-difficult trail runs along most of the park's length, smaller sections—of varying degrees of difficulty—are accessible via frequent, well-marked trailheads. The moderate to difficult DeMartin section leads past 5 miles of old-growth redwoods and through prairie. If you're up for a real workout, you'll be well rewarded with the brutally difficult but stunning Flint Ridge section, a 4.5-mile stretch of steep grades and numerous switchbacks that leads past redwoods and Marshall Pond. The moderate 4-mile-long Hidden Beach section connects the Lagoon Creek picnic area with Klamath Overlook and provides coastal views and whale-watching opportunities. *Moderate.* ⊠ *Flint Ridge trailhead: Douglas Bridge parking area, north end of Coastal Dr.*

KAYAKING

With many miles of often-shallow rivers and streams in the area, kayaking is a popular pastime in the park.

OUTFITTERS

Adventure's Edge. You can rent hard-shell kayaks here for $40 a day. In business since 1970, this Arcata outfitter also rents camping equipment and tents. ⊠ *650 10th St., Arcata* ☎ *707/822–4673* ⊗ *Mon.–Sat. 9–6, Sun. 10–5.*

CLOSE UP

Best Campgrounds in Redwood

Within a 30-minute drive of Redwood National and State parks there are nearly 60 public and private camping facilities. None of the four primitive areas in Redwood—DeMartin, Flint Ridge, Little Bald Hills, and Nickel Creek—is a drive-in site. Although you don't need a permit at these four hike-in sites, stop at a ranger station to inquire about availability. You will need to get a permit from a ranger station for camping along Redwood Creek in the backcountry. Bring your own water, since drinking water isn't available in any of these sites.

If you'd rather drive than hike in, Redwood has four developed campgrounds—Elk Prairie, Gold Bluffs Beach, Jedediah Smith, and Mill Creek—that are within the state-park boundaries. None has RV hookups, and some length restrictions apply. Fees are $35 in state park campgrounds. For details and reservations, call ☏ 800/444–7275 or check ⊕ www.reserveamerica.com.

Elk Prairie Campground. Adjacent to a prairie and old-growth redwoods, this campground is popular with Roosevelt elk. ⊠ 6 miles north of Orick on Newton B. Drury Scenic Pkwy. in Prairie Creek Redwoods State Park ☏ 800/444–7275.

Gold Bluffs Beach Campground. You can camp in tents or RVs right on the beach at this Prairie Creek Redwoods State Park campground near Fern Canyon. ⊠ At end of Davison Rd., which is 5 miles south of Redwood Information Center off U.S. 101 ☏ 707/488–2039.

Jedediah Smith Campground. This is one of the few places to camp—in tents or RVs—within groves of old-growth redwood forest. ⊠ 8 miles east of Crescent City on U.S. 199 ☏ 800/444–7275.

Mill Creek Campground. Mill Creek is the largest of the state-park campgrounds. ⊠ East of U.S. 101, 7 miles southeast of Crescent City ☏ 800/444–7275.

Nickel Creek Campground. An easy hike gets you to this primitive site, which is near tide pools and has great ocean views. ⊠ On Coastal Trail ½ mile from end of Enderts Beach Rd. ☏ 707/465–7335.

WHALE-WATCHING

Good vantage points for whale-watching include Crescent Beach Overlook, the Kuchel Visitor Center in Orick, points along the Coastal Drive, and the Klamath River Overlook. Late November through January are the best months to see their southward migrations; February through April they return and generally pass closer to shore.

The Inland Empire

EAST OF LOS ANGELES TO THE
SAN JACINTO MOUNTAINS

WORD OF MOUTH

"Callaway [and] Hart are some of my favorite wineries in Temecula, for the grounds, the restaurants, the special events and the wines. If you like sweet bubbles, Wilson Creek's Almond Champagne is lovely."

—fairygemgirl

WELCOME TO THE INLAND EMPIRE

TOP REASONS TO GO

★ **Wine Country:** The Temecula Valley is a mélange of rolling hills, faint ocean breezes, beautiful and funky wineries, lovely lodging options, and gourmet restaurants.

★ **The Mission Inn:** One of the most unique hotels in America, Riverside's rambling, eclectic Mission Inn feels like an urban Hearst Castle.

★ **Apple country:** Oak Glen is one of Southern California's largest apple-growing regions. Attend an old-fashioned hoedown, take a wagon ride, and sample Mile High apple pies and homemade ciders.

★ **Soothing spas:** The lushly landscaped grounds, bubbling hot springs, and playful mud baths of Glen Ivy are ideal spots to unwind, while Kelly's Spa at the historic Mission Inn provides a Tuscan-style retreat.

★ **Alpine escapes:** Breathe in the clean mountain air or cozy up in a rustic cabin at one of the Inland Empire's great mountain hideaways: Lake Arrowhead, Big Bear, and Idyllwild.

1 **The Western Inland Empire.** At the foot of 10,000-foot-high Mt. Baldy in the San Gabriel Mountains, the tree-lined communities of Pomona and Claremont are known for their prestigious colleges: California State Polytechnic University–Pomona and the seven-school Claremont college complex. Pomona is urban and industrial, but Claremont is a classic tree-shaded, lively, sophisticated college town that more resembles trendy sections of Los Angeles than the laid back Inland Empire.

2 **Riverside Area.** In the late 1700s, Mexican settlers called this now-suburban region Valle de Paraiso. Citrus-growing here began in 1873, when homesteader Eliza Tibbets planted two navel-orange trees in her yard. The area's biggest draws are the majestic Mission Inn, with its fine restaurants and unique history and architecture, and Glen Ivy Hot Springs in nearby Corona.

GETTING ORIENTED

Several freeways provide access to the Inland Empire from Los Angeles and San Diego. Ontario, Corona, and Temecula line up along Interstates 10 and 215; and Corona, Riverside, and San Bernardino lie along Highway 91. As a Los Angeles bedroom community, the area sees nasty freeway congestion on Highway 60 and Interstates 10 and 15, so try to avoid driving during rush hour, usually from 6 to 8 am and 4 to 7 pm.

3 San Bernardino Mountains. Lake Arrowhead and always-sunny Big Bear are the recreational centers of this area. Though the two are geographically close, they're distinct in appeal. Lake Arrowhead, with its cool mountain air, trail-threaded woods, and brilliant lake, draws a summertime crowd—a well-heeled one, if the prices in its shops and restaurants are any indication. Big Bear's ski and snowboarding slopes, cross-country trails, and cheerful lodges come alive in winter. Even if you're not interested in visiting the resorts themselves, the Rim of the World Scenic Byway (Highway 18), which connects Big Bear Lake and Lake Arrowhead at an elevation up to 8,000 feet, is a magnificent drive. On a clear day, you'll feel like you can see forever.

4 The Southern Inland Empire. Life is quieter in the southern portion of the Inland Empire than it is to the north. In this corner of Riverside County, towns such as Idyllwild and Temecula are oases of the good life for locals and visitors alike.

Updated by
Bobbi Zane

The Inland Empire, an area often overlooked by visitors because of its tangled freeways and suburban sprawl, has its charms. No more than a couple of hours' drive from metropolitan Los Angeles, you can ski a 7,000-foot mountain overlooking a crystal blue lake or go wine tasting at a vineyard cooled by ocean breezes.

At the heart of this desert and mountain region is Riverside, the birthplace of California's multimillion-dollar navel-orange industry—established in 1875—and home of the University of California at Riverside. The tree that started it all still flourishes on Magnolia Avenue. Today the streets of downtown buzz with people on their way to shop for antiques, eat in exciting restaurants, and listen to live jazz.

The scene is completely different northeast of Riverside, in the San Bernardino Mountains. There Big Bear Lake and Lake Arrowhead are set like bowls surrounded by wooded mountain peaks. To the south, in the San Jacinto Mountains just west of Palm Springs, Idyllwild is a popular year-round getaway with romantic cottages, an impressive collection of art galleries, and cozy restaurants. In the southernmost reaches of the Inland Empire, on the way from Riverside to San Diego, is what is known as the Southern California Wine Country around Temecula, a hip and trendy destination for oenophiles. This is also prime territory for hot-air ballooning, golfing, fine dining, and—of course—vineyard tours and wine tasting.

INLAND EMPIRE PLANNER

WHEN TO GO

The climate varies greatly depending on what part of the Inland Empire you're visiting. Summer temperatures in the mountains and in Temecula, 20 miles from the coast, usually hover around 80°F, though it's not uncommon for Riverside to reach temperatures over 100°F. From September to March this area is subject to increasingly high Santa Ana winds, sometimes strong enough to overturn trucks on the freeway. In winter, temperatures in the mountains and in Temecula usually range from 30°F to 55°F, and in the Riverside area 40°F to 60°F. Most of the ski areas open when the first natural snow falls (usually in November) and close in mid-March.

GETTING HERE AND AROUND

AIR TRAVEL

LA/Ontario International Airport (ONT) is the local airport. Aeromexico, Alaska, American, Delta, Southwest, United, and US Airways fly here.

Airport Contacts LA/Ontario International Airport ⊠ *Airport Dr., Archibald Ave. exit off I-10, Ontario* ☎ *909/937-2700* ⊕ *www.lawa.org.*

BUS TRAVEL

Greyhound serves Riverside, San Bernardino, and Temecula. The Foothill Transit Bus Line serves Pomona, Claremont, and Montclair, with stops at Cal Poly and the Fairplex. Riverside Transit Authority (RTA) serves Riverside and some outlying communities, as does OmniTrans.

Bus Contacts Foothill Transit ☎ *800/743-3463, 909/621-2126* ⊕ *www. foothilltransit.org.* **Omnitrans** ☎ *800/966-6428* ⊕ *www.omnitrans.org.* **Riverside Transit Authority** ⊠ *1825 3rd St.* ☎ *800/800-7821* ⊕ *www.riversidetransit. com.*

CAR TRAVEL

Avoid Highway 91 if possible; it's almost always backed up from Corona through Orange County.

Car Contact Caltrans Current Highway Conditions ☎ *800/427-7623* ⊕ *www. dot.ca.gov.*

TRAIN TRAVEL

■TIP→ Many locals use the Metrolink to get around, which is clean and quick, and generally a much nicer way to travel than by bus.

Metrolink has several Inland Empire stations on its Inter-County, San Bernardino, and Riverside rail lines. You can buy tickets and passes at the ticket vending machine at each station, or by telephone. 511 Travel Information Service is a phone- and Web-based service where you can get real-time traffic information and trip planning help. A recorded message announces Metrolink schedules 24 hours a day.

Train Contact Metrolink ☎ *800/371-5465* ⊕ *www.metrolinktrains.com.*

HEALTH AND SAFETY

In an emergency dial 911.

Emergency Services Big Bear Lake Sheriff ⊠ *477 Summit Blvd., Big Bear Lake* ☎ *909/866-0100.* **Parkview Community Hospital** ⊠ *3865 Jackson St., Riverside* ☎ *951/688-2211* ⊕ *www.pchmc.org.* **Rancho Springs Medical Center** ⊠ *25500 Medical Center Dr., Murietta* ☎ *951/696-6000* ⊕ *www. swhealthcaresystem.com.* **Riverside Community Hospital** ⊠ *4445 Magnolia Ave., Riverside* ☎ *951/788-3000* ⊕ *riversidecommunityhospital.com.* **St. Bernardine Medical Center** ⊠ *2101 N. Waterman Ave., San Bernardino* ☎ *909/883-8711* ⊕ *www.stbernardinemedicalcenter.org.*

RESTAURANTS

Downtown Riverside is home to a few ambitious restaurants, along with the chains you can find in most areas. The college towns of Claremont and Redlands focus on creative contemporary, ethnic, and traditional selections. Excellent innovative cuisine has become an art in Temecula, especially at the wineries, many of which showcase their products alongside fine dining. Your options are limited in the smaller mountain communities; typically each town supports a single upscale restaurant, along with fast-food outlets, steak-and-potatoes family spots, and perhaps an Italian or Mexican eatery. Universally, dining out is casual. *Prices in the reviews are the average cost of a main course at dinner or, if dinner is not served, at lunch.*

HOTELS

In the San Bernardino mountains, many accommodations are bed-and-breakfasts or rustic cabins, though Lake Arrowhead and Big Bear offer more luxurious resort lodging. Rates for Big Bear lodgings fluctuate widely, depending on the season. When winter snow brings droves of Angelenos to the mountains for skiing, expect to pay sky-high prices for any kind of room. Most establishments require a two-night stay on weekends. In Riverside, you might enjoy a stay at the landmark Mission Inn, a rambling Spanish-style hotel with elaborate courtyards, fountains, and a mixture of ornate Mission revival, Spanish baroque, Renaissance revival, and Asian architecture styles. In the Wine Country, lodgings can be found at wineries, golf resorts, and chain hotels. *Prices in the reviews are the lowest cost of a standard double room in high season. For expanded reviews, facilities, and current deals, visit Fodors.com.*

THE WESTERN INLAND EMPIRE

Straddling the line between Los Angeles and San Bernardino counties, the western section of the Inland Empire is home to some of California's oldest vineyards and original citrus orchards. Now a busy suburban community, it holds the closest ski slopes to metro L.A., Fairplex, where the L.A. County Fair is held each year, and Claremont, home to a collection of high ranking colleges.

POMONA

23 miles north of Anaheim on Hwy. 57; 27 miles east of Pasadena on I–210.

The green hills of Pomona, dotted with horses and houses, are perhaps best known as the site of the Los Angeles County Fair and of California State Polytechnic University–Pomona. Named for the Roman goddess of fruit, the city has a rich citrus-growing heritage.

GETTING HERE AND AROUND

Interstate 10 bisects the Western Inland Empire west to east. Points of interest lie at the base of the San Gabriel Mountains, north of the freeway. You can reach this area by public transportation, but you'll need a car to get around unless you plan to spend all your time in the

Claremont Village. Shuttle service is available to the L.A. metro area. Some areas are quite walkable, especially the Claremont colleges where you can stroll through parks from one school building to another.

ESSENTIALS

Visitor Information Pomona Chamber of Commerce ⊠ *101 W. Mission Blvd., #223* ☎ *909/622–8484* ⊕ *www.pomonachamber.org.*

EXPLORING

California Polytechnic University at Pomona. The university occupies 1,438 acres of the Kellogg Ranch, originally the winter home of cereal magnate W.K. Kellogg. Cal Poly specializes in teaching agriculture, and you can find rose gardens, avocado groves, many farm animals, and a working Arabian horse ranch. The Farm Store (⊠ *4102 University Dr. S.* ☎ *909/869–4906,* ☉ *Daily 10–6*) sells locally grown seasonal fruit and vegetables, campus-grown pork and beef, cheeses and other deli items, gift baskets, and plants grown in the university nursery. ⊠ *3801 W. Temple Ave.* ☎ *909/869–7659* ⊕ *www.csupomona.edu.*

Fairplex. The site of the Los Angeles County Fair (North America's largest county fair), the Fairplex exposition center has a 10,000-seat grandstand and numerous exhibit halls and outdoor spaces. The venue hosts open-air markets, antiques shows, swap meets, roadster shows, historical train and model train exhibits, horse shows and racing, dog shows, and the annual International Wine and Spirits competition. Fairplex also houses the **Wally Parks NHRA Motorsports Museum,** which pays tribute to the rich history of American motor sports with exhibits of vintage racing vehicles and has an amusing collection of tricked-out drag-racing cars. ⊠ *1101 W. McKinley Ave.* ☎ *909/623–3111, 909/622–2133 museum* ⊕ *www.fairplex.com* 🎟 *Museum $8* ☉ *Museum Wed.–Sun. 10–5.*

Wally Parks NHRA Motorsports Museum. Fairplex houses the Wally Parks NHRA Motorsports Museum, dedicated to the history of American motor sports with exhibits of vintage racing vehicles. The museum holds a collection of tricked-out drag racing cars. ⊠ *1101 W. McKinley Ave.* ☎ *909/622–2133* 🎟 *$8* ☉ *Wed.–Sun. 10–5*

W.K. Kellogg Arabian Horse Shows. The classic shows, started by Kellogg in 1926, are still a tradition on the CSU–Pomona campus. More than 85 of the purebreds live at the ranch, and the university presents exhibitions of the equines in English and Western tack the first Sunday of the month at 2 pm from October through May. Stable tours and pony rides take place after the show. ⊠ *3801 W. Temple Ave.* ☎ *909/869–2224* ⊕ *www.csupomona.edu/~equine* 🎟 *$4.*

WHERE TO EAT AND STAY

For expanded reviews, facilities, and current deals, visit Fodors.com.

$$$
AMERICAN
✕ **Pomona Valley Mining Company.** Perched on a hilltop near an old mining site, this rustic steak-and-seafood restaurant provides a great city views at night. Though somewhat dated, the decor reflects the local mining heritage. Authentic gold-rush pieces and 1800s memorabilia hang on the walls, and old lanterns adorn the tables. The food—heavy on steak and prime rib—is well prepared; consider trying the Pickin's Combo

appetizer, an extravaganza that includes coconut-beer shrimp, calamari, chicken fingers, and Buffalo wings. $ *Average main: $29* ✉ *1777 Gillette Rd.* 🕿 *909/623–3515* ⊕ *www.pomonavalleyminingco. com* ⊙ *Closed Mon. No lunch Tues.–Sat.*

$ 🛏 **Sheraton Suites Fairplex.** County-
HOTEL fair murals and whimsical carousel animals welcome you to this all-suites hotel at the entrance to Pomona's Fairplex. **Pros:** adjacent to convention center; clean rooms; comfortable beds; signature dog beds. **Cons:** parts of the hotel feel dated; not close to many restaurants. **TripAdvisor:** "great staff," "an oasis of comfort," "nice rooms and property." $ *Rooms from: $119* ✉ *601 W. McKinley Ave.* 🕿 *888/627–8074, 909/622–2220* ⊕ *www.sheraton.com* ↩ *247 suites* ⦿ *No meals.*

CLAREMONT

4 miles north of Pomona along Garey Ave., then 2 miles east on Foothill Blvd.

The seven Claremont colleges are among the most prestigious in the nation. The campuses are all laid out cheek-by-jowl; as you wander from one leafy street to the next, you won't be able to tell where one college ends and the next begins.

Claremont was originally the home of the Sunkist citrus growers cooperative movement. Today, Claremont Village, home to descendants of those early farmers, is bright and lively. The business district village, with streets named for prestigious eastern colleges, is walkable and appealing with a collection of boutiques, fancy food emporiums, cafés, and lounges. The downtown district is a beautiful place to visit, with Victorian, Craftsman, and Spanish-colonial buildings.

GETTING HERE AND AROUND

If you're driving, exit Interstate 10 at Indian Hill Boulevard, and drive north to Claremont. Parking can be difficult, although there are metered spots. Overnight parking is prohibited within the village; however there is a parking structure adjacent to the College Heights Packing House Fairplex that is also north of the freeway; exit Garey and drive toward the mountains.

ESSENTIALS

Visitor Information Claremont Chamber of Commerce ✉ *205 Yale Ave.* 🕿 *909/624–1681* ⊕ *www.claremontchamber.org.*

EXPLORING

Pomona College Museum of Art. This small museum on the campus of Pomona College exhibits significant contemporary art, works by old masters, and examples of Native American arts and artifacts. Highlights include the first mural painted by Mexican artist Jose Clemente Orozco in North America, first-edition etchings by Goya, and the Kress collection of 15th- and 16th-century Italian panel paintings. The Art

After Hours events on Thursday nights are lively and fun and often include local bands and music. ⊠ *333 N. College Ave.* ☎ *909/621–8283* ⊕ *www.pomona.edu/museum* ⊠ *Free* ☉ *Tues.–Sun. 12–5, Thurs. until 11.*

QUICK BITES

Bert & Rocky's Cream Company. This ice cream store is known for its innovative and simply sinful concoctions. Popular items include vanilla ice cream, the Elvis special with bananas and peanut butter, Tuscany marble, chocolate raspberry swirl ice cream, and cheesecake ice cream. ⊠ *242 Yale Ave.* ☎ *909/625-1852.*

13

★ **Rancho Santa Ana Botanic Garden.** Founded in 1927 by Susanna Bixby Bryant, a wealthy landowner and conservationist, the garden is a living museum and research center dedicated to the conservation of native-California plant species. You can meander here for hours enjoying the shade of an oak tree canopy or take a guided tour of the grounds, whose 86 acres of ponds and greenery shelter such specimens as California wild lilacs (ceanothus), big berry manzanita, and four-needled piñon. Countless birds also make their homes here. ⊠ *1500 N. College Ave.* ☎ *909/625–8767* ⊕ *www.rsabg.org* ⊠ *$8* ☉ *Daily 8–5.*

WHERE TO EAT

$$
ITALIAN

✕ **La Parolaccia.** This busy lunch or dinner spot has locals lining up on the weekends to get a table. Bustling waiters zip through a series of small rooms serving up fresh and beautifully seasoned items from an extensive Italian menu. Popular items include spaghetti with fresh salmon and eggplant, rigatoni with Italian sausage and sherry cream sauce, and risotto with seafood, white wine, and tomato sauce. Topping the desert list is bread pudding made with ciabatta bread and crème anglaise. ⑤ *Average main: $19* ⊠ *201 N. Indian Hill Blvd.* ☎ *909/624–1516* ⊕ *www.LaParolacciaUSA.com.*

$$$$
ITALIAN

✕ **Tutti Mangia Italian Grill.** College students have their parents take them to this corner storefront when they're in town visiting. The dining room, with tables well spaced, feels warm and cozy. Top choices include herb-crusted Atlantic salmon, grilled thick-cut pork chops, and veal shank. The lineup of small plates always entices. ⑤ *Average main: $32* ⊠ *102 Harvard Ave.* ☎ *909/625–4669* ⊕ *www.tuttimangia.com* ⚐ *Reservations essential* ☉ *No lunch weekends.*

$$
ECLECTIC

✕ **Walter's Restaurant.** With a menu that roams the globe from France to Italy to Afghanistan, Walter's is where locals gather to dine, sip wine, and chat. You can eat outside on the sidewalk, on the lively patio, or in a cozy setting inside. Wherever you sit, the owner, Nangy, will stroll by to make sure you're happy with your meal. He'll urge you to try the puffy Afghan fries with hot sauce, tabouleh salad, or lamb stew. Breakfast possibilities include omelets, sausage and eggs, and burritos; for lunch are salads, soups, pastas, kebabs, and vegetarian items. ⑤ *Average main: $21* ⊠ *310 N. Yale Ave.* ☎ *909/624–4914* ⊕ *waltersrestaurant.biz* ⚐ *Reservations essential.*

WHERE TO STAY

For expanded reviews, facilities, and current deals, visit Fodors.com.

$$$ ⚏ **Casa 425.** This boutique inn, perched on a corner opposite the Col-
B&B/INN lege Heights Lemon Packing House entertainment/shopping complex, is
Fodor's Choice the most attractive lodging choice in Claremont Village. **Pros:** bicycles
★ available; walking distance to attractions and restaurants; consider-
ate service; small plates served in evening. **Cons:** no on-street parking
overnight (free across street); occasional noise. **TripAdvisor:** "awesome
locale," "very lovely place," "relaxing and charming."⑤ *Rooms from:
$175* ✉ *425 W. 1st St.* ☎ *866/450–0425* ⊕ *www.foursisters.com* ⇝ *28
rooms* ⦿ *Some meals.*

$$ ⚏ **DoubleTree Hotel Claremont.** This is the hotel of choice in Claremont
HOTEL for parents visiting children attending the local colleges. **Pros:** conve-
nient to colleges; family friendly. **Cons:** small bathrooms. **TripAdvisor:**
"very nice property," "convenient and quiet," "nice oasis."⑤ *Rooms
from: $125* ✉ *555 W. Foothill Blvd.* ☎ *909/626–2411* ⊕ *www.
doubletreeclaremont.com* ⇝ *190 rooms.*

NIGHTLIFE

Being a college town, Claremont has lots of bars and cafés, some of
which showcase bands.

Flappers Comedy Club. A typical stand-up club, Flappers is a branch of a
Burbank club. Headliners such as Hal Sparks and Titus perform, as do
up-and-coming comedians. ✉ *532 W. 1st St.* ☎ *818/845–9721* ⊕ *www.
flapperscomedy.com* ⦿ *Closed Mon.–Wed.*

SPORTS AND THE OUTDOORS

SKIING **Mt. Baldy Ski Resort.** The 10,064-foot mountain's real name is Mt. San
Antonio, but Mt. Baldy Ski Resort—the oldest ski area in Southern
California—takes its name from the treeless slopes. It's known for its
steep triple-diamond runs. ■**TIP→ You can rent snow tubes and boards
here.** The Mt. Baldy base lies at 6,500 feet, and four chairlifts ascend to
8,600 feet. There are 26 runs; the longest is 2,100 vertical feet. Whenever abundant fresh snow falls, there's a danger of avalanche in out-of-
bounds areas. Backcountry skiing is available via shuttle in the spring,
and there's a school on weekends for kids ages 5 to 12. Winter or summer, you can take a scenic chairlift ride ($20) to the Top of the Notch
restaurant and hiking and mountain-biking trails. ✉ *8401 Mt. Baldy
Rd., Mt. Baldy* ☎ *909/982–0800* ⊕ *www.mtbaldyskilifts.com* ▱ *Full
day $69, half day $49* ⦿ *Snow season Nov.–Apr., weekdays 8–4:30,
weekends 7:30–4:30; summer season May–Oct., weekends 7–sunset.*

ONTARIO

Junction of I–10 and I–15, 6 miles east of Pomona.

Ontario has a rich agricultural and industrial heritage. The valley's
warm climate once supported vineyards that produced grape varietals
such as Grenache, Mourvèdre, and Zinfandel. Today, housing tracts and
shopping malls have replaced most of the vineyards. But the airport is
here, so you may well find yourself passing through.

GETTING HERE AND AROUND

Ontario lies between Interstate 10 to the north and Highway 60 (Pomona Freeway) to the south. Metrolink connects the L.A. area to the airport and other destinations, but driving is the best way to get around the area.

ESSENTIALS

Visitor Information Ontario Convention & Visitors Bureau ⊠ *2000 E. Convention Center Way* ☎ *909/937–3000* ⊕ *www.ontariocc.com.*

13

EXPLORING

Graber Olive House. Ontario's oldest existing business, Graber Olive House, opened in 1894 when, at the urging of family and friends, C.C. Graber bottled his meaty, tree-ripened olives and started selling them; they are still sold throughout the United States. Stop by the gourmet shop for a jar, then have a picnic on the shaded grounds. Tours are conducted year-round; in fall you can watch workers grade, cure, and can the olives. ⊠ *315 E. 4th St.* ☎ *800/996–5483* ⊕ *www.graberolives. com* ⊠ *Free* ☉ *Daily 9–5:30.*

WHERE TO STAY

For expanded reviews, facilities, and current deals, visit Fodors.com.

$$ 🏨 **DoubleTree by Hilton Ontario Airport.** A beautifully landscaped court-
HOTEL yard greets you at Ontario's only full-service hotel. **Pros:** clean;
☺ large rooms; free shuttle to airport and Ontario Mills Mall; choco-
★ late chip cookies. **Cons:** airport and freeway noise; Internet charge;
dated rooms. **TripAdvisor:** "staff was incredibly helpful," "comfort-
able," "good location." ⑤ *Rooms from: $126* ⊠ *222 N. Vineyard Ave.*
☎ *909/937–0900, 800/222–8733* ⊕ *www.doubletree.com* ⇱ *482 rooms*
🍽 *Breakfast.*

SHOPPING

☺ **Ontario Mills Mall.** The gargantuan Ontario Mills Mall is California's largest, packing in more than 200 outlet stores including Nordstrom Rack and Sax Fifth Avenue Off 5th. Also here are Carleton Day Spa, a 30-screen movie theater, the Improv Comedy Club and Dinner Theater, and two entertainment complexes: Dave & Buster's pool hall–restaurant–arcade, and GameWorks video-game center. Dining options include the kid-friendly Rainforest Cafe, Chipotle Mexican Grill, and a 1,000-seat food court. ⊠ *1 Mills Circle, 4th St. and I–15* ☎ *909/484–8301* ⊕ *www.ontariomills.com* ☉ *Mon.–Sat. 10–9, Sun. 11–8.*

RANCHO CUCAMONGA

5 miles north of Ontario on I–15.

Once a thriving wine-making area with more than 50,000 acres of wine grapes, Rancho Cucamonga—the oldest wine district in California—lost most of its pastoral charm after real-estate developers bought up the land for a megamall and affordable housing. Most of it is now a squeaky-clean planned community, but the wine-making tradition still thrives at the Joseph Filippi Winery.

GETTING HERE AND AROUND

Historic Route 66 (Foothill Boulevard) cuts east–west across Rancho Cucamonga. The community is best reached via Interstate 10.

EXPLORING

Joseph Filippi Winery. J.P. and Jared Filippi continue the family tradition that was started in 1922 at the Joseph Filippi Winery, crafting wines from Cabernet, Sangiovese, and Zinfandel grapes, among other varieties. You can taste up to five wines for $5. Daily tours take place at 1 pm, and a small museum chronicles the history of Rancho Cucamonga's wine making. ⊠ *12467 Base Line Rd.* ☎ *909/899–5755* ⊕ *www. josephfilippiwinery.com* ⊠ *Free* ☉ *Mon. noon–5, Tues.–Thurs. noon–6, Fri. and Sat. 11–7, Sun. noon–6.*

☾ **Victoria Gardens.** Classy Victoria Gardens feels a lot like Disneyland
★ with its vintage signs, antique lampposts, and colorful California-theme murals along 12 city blocks. At this family-oriented shopping, dining, and entertainment complex, stores such as Banana Republic, Abercrombie & Fitch, and Williams-Sonoma are flanked by a Macy's and a 12-screen AMC movie theater. After you're finished shopping, grab an ice cream at the Ben & Jerry's shop and linger in the 1920s-style Town Square, a relaxing little park with fountains, grass, and an old-fashioned trolley ($2 per ride). The busy restaurants here include the Cheesecake Factory, Lucille's Smokehouse Bar-B-Que, and the Yard House. The Victoria Gardens Cultural Center houses a 540-seat performing-arts center. ⊠ *12505 N. Mainstreet* ☎ *909/463–2830 info, 909/477–2775 Cultural Center* ⊕ *www.victoriagardensie.com* ⊠ *Free* ☉ *Daily 10–9; hrs vary for some establishments.*

WHERE TO EAT

$$$$ ✕ **The Sycamore Inn.** Flickering gas lamps and a glowing fireplace greet
STEAKHOUSE you at this rustic restaurant. Built in 1921, the Sycamore Inn occupies
★ the site of a stagecoach stop on Historic Route 66. The specialty here is USDA prime steak—portion sizes range from 8 to 22 ounces—but also on the menu are ahi tuna, Australian lobster tail, and Colorado rack of lamb. The impressive wine list includes selections from the best Napa and Sonoma wineries; France, New Zealand, Australia, and South America are also well represented. ⑤ *Average main: $32* ⊠ *8318 Foothill Blvd.* ☎ *909/982–1104* ⊕ *www.thesycamoreinn.com* ⚵ *Reservations essential* ☉ *No lunch.*

RIVERSIDE AREA

Historic Riverside lies at the heart of the Inland Empire. Major highways linking it to other regional destinations spoke out from this city to the north, south, and east.

CORONA

13 miles south of Ontario on I–15.

Corona's Temescal Canyon is named for the dome-shaped mud saunas that the Luiseño Indians built around the artesian hot springs in the

It's OK to get a little dirty at Glen Ivy Hot Springs, which offers a wide variety of treatments at its famous spa—including the red clay pool at Club Mud.

early 19th century. Starting in 1860, weary Overland Stage Company passengers stopped to relax in the soothing mineral springs. In 1890 Mr. and Mrs. W.G. Steers turned the springs into Glen Ivy Hot Springs, whose popularity has yet to fade.

GETTING HERE AND AROUND
Primarily a bedroom community, Corona lies at the intersection of Interstate 15 and Highway 91. The many roadside malls make it a convenient stop for food or gas.

EXPLORING

Fodor's Choice **Glen Ivy Hot Springs Spa.** Presidents Herbert Hoover and Ronald Reagan ★ are among the thousands of guests who have soaked their toes at the very relaxing and beautiful Glen Ivy Hot Springs. Colorful bougainvillea and birds-of-paradise surround the secluded canyon day spa, which offers a full range of facials, manicures, pedicures, body wraps, and massages; some treatments are performed in underground granite spa chambers known collectively as the Grotto, highly recommended by readers. The Under the Oaks treatment center holds a cluster of eight open-air massage rooms surrounded by waterfalls and ancient oak trees. Don't bring your best bikini if you plan to dive into the red clay (brought in daily from a local mine) of Club Mud. Admission gives you use of the property all day. Reserve in advance for treatments that run from $99 to $183 for 50 to 80 minutes. ⊠ *25000 Glen Ivy Rd.* ☎ *888/453–6489* ⊕ *www.glenivy.com* ✉ *Mon.–Thurs. $46, Fri.–Sun. $59* ⊙ *Apr.–Oct., daily 9–6; Nov.–Mar., daily 9–5.*

☺ **Tom's Farms.** Opened as a produce stand along Interstate 15 in 1974, Tom's Farms has grown to include a popular hamburger stand, furniture

Navel Oranges in California: Good as Gold

In 1873 a woman named Eliza Tibbets changed the course of California history when she planted two Brazilian navel-orange trees in her Riverside garden.

The trees (which were called Washington Navels in honor of America's first president) flourished in the area's warm climate and rich soil—and before long, Tibbett's garden was producing the sweetest seedless oranges anyone had ever tasted. After winning awards at several major exhibitions, Tibbets realized she could make a profit from her trees. She sold buds to the increasing droves of citrus farmers flocking to the Inland Empire, and by 1882, almost 250,000 citrus trees had been planted in Riverside alone. California's citrus industry had been born.

Today, Riverside still celebrates its citrus-growing heritage. The downtown Marketplace district contains several restored packing houses, and the Riverside Metropolitan Museum is home to a permanent exhibit of historic tools and machinery once used in the industry. The University of California at Riverside still remains at the forefront of citrus research; its Citrus Variety Collection includes specimens of 1,000 different fruit trees from around the world.

showroom, and sweet shop. You can still buy produce here, but the big draw is various attractions (most $) for the kiddies on weekends: tractor driving, Tom's mining company, a petting zoo, a children's train, a pony ride, free magic shows, face painting, and an old-style carousel. Of interest for adults is the wine-and-cheese shop, which has more than 600 varieties of wine, including many from nearby Temecula Valley; wine tasting ($5 for three samples) takes place daily 11 to 6. ⊠ 23900 Temescal Canyon Rd. ☎ 951/277–4422 ⊕ www.tomsfarms.com ☜ Free ☉ Daily 8–8.

RIVERSIDE

14 miles north of Corona on Rte. 91; 34 miles northeast from Anaheim on Rte. 91.

By 1882 Riverside was home to more than half of California's citrus groves, making it the state's wealthiest city per capita in 1895. The prosperity produced a downtown area of opulent architecture, which is well preserved today. Main Street's pedestrian strip is lined with antiques and gift stores, art galleries, salons, and the UCR/California Museum of Photography.

GETTING HERE AND AROUND
Downtown Riverside lies north of Highway 91 at the University Avenue exit. The hub holding the Mission Inn, museums, shops and restaurants is at the corner of Orange and Mission Inn Avenue. Park here and walk.

EXPLORING

Fodor's Choice ★ **Mission Inn Museum.** The crown jewel of Riverside is the Mission Inn, a Spanish-revival hotel whose elaborate turrets, clock tower, mission bells, and flying buttresses rise above downtown. Docent-led tours of the hotel are offered by the Mission Inn Foundation, which also operates an expansive museum with displays depicting the building's illustrious history. The inn was designed in 1902 by Arthur B. Benton and Myron Hunt; the team took its cues from the Spanish missions in San Gabriel and Carmel. You can climb to the top of the Rotunda Wing's five-story spiral stairway, or linger a while in the Courtyard of the Birds, where a tinkling fountain and shady trees invite meditation. You can also peek inside the St. Francis Chapel, where celebrities such as Bette Davis, Humphrey Bogart, and Richard and Pat Nixon tied the knot before the Mexican cedar altar. The Presidential Lounge, a dark, wood-panel bar, has been patronized by eight U.S. presidents. ⊠ *3696 Main St.* ☎ *951/788–9556,* ⊕ *www.missioninnmuseum.com* ⊠ *$2 inn; docent tours $12* ⊗ *Daily 9:30–4:30.*

Riverside Art Museum. Hearst Castle architect Julia Morgan designed this museum that houses a fine collection of paintings by Southern California landscape artists, including William Keith, Robert Wood, and Ralph Love. Major temporary exhibitions are mounted year-round. Docents conduct tours of the museum at 3 pm on Wednesday. ⊠ *3425 Mission Inn Ave.* ☎ *951/684–7111* ⊕ *www.riversideartmuseum.org* ⊠ *$8, free 1st Thurs. of month 6–9* ⊗ *Tues., Wed., Fri., and Sat. 10–4; Thurs. 2–4 and 6–9; Sun. noon–4.*

★ **UCR/California Museum of Photography.** With an impressive collection that includes thousands of Kodak Brownie and Zeiss Ikon cameras, this museum surveys the history of photography *and* the devices that produced it. Exhibitions—some of contemporary images, others historically oriented—are always top-notch and often incorporate photographs from the permanent collection. When not on display, works by Ansel Adams, Olindo Ceccarini, and other greats can be viewed by appointment. ⊠ *3824 Main St.* ☎ *951/827–4787* ⊕ *www.cmp.ucr.edu* ⊠ *$3* ⊗ *Tues.–Sat. noon–5.*

WHERE TO EAT AND STAY

For expanded reviews, facilities, and current deals, visit Fodors.com.

$$$
ITALIAN
Fodor's Choice
★
✕ Mario's Place. The clientele is as beautiful as the food at this intimate jazz and supper club across the street from the Mission Inn. The northern Italian cuisine is first-rate, as are the jazz bands that perform Friday and Saturday at 10 pm. Try the pear-and-Gorgonzola wood-fired pizza, followed by the star anise panna cotta for dessert. Jazz groups play weekend nights in the Lounge. ⑤ *Average main: $30* ⊠ *3646 Mission Inn Ave.* ☎ *951/684–7755* ⊕ *www.mariosplace.com* ⌖ *Reservations essential* ⊗ *Closed Sun.*

$
AMERICAN
✕ Simple Simon's. Expect to wait in line at this little sandwich shop on the pedestrians-only shopping strip outside the Mission Inn. Traditional salads, soups, and sandwiches on house-baked breads are served; standout specialties include the chicken-apple sausage sandwich and the roast lamb sandwich topped with grilled eggplant, red peppers,

and tomato-fennel-olive sauce. ⑤ *Average main: $10* ⊠ *3636 Main St.* ☎ *951/369–6030* ⚬ *Reservations not accepted* ⊘ *Closed Sun. No dinner.*

$$$
HOTEL
☺
Fodor's Choice
★

⚏ **Mission Inn and Spa.** One of California's most historic hotels, the inn grew from a modest adobe lodge in 1876 to the grand Spanish-revival hotel it is today. **Pros:** fascinating historical site; luxurious rooms; great restaurants; family friendly. **Cons:** train noise can be deafening at night. **TripAdvisor:** "romance," "beautiful historic hotel," "comfortable experience." ⑤ *Rooms from: $190* ⊠ *3649 Mission Inn Ave.* ☎ *951/784–0300, 800/843–7755* ⊕ *www.missioninn.com* ⚑ *239 rooms, 28 suites.*

NIGHTLIFE

Cafe Sevilla. A combination restaurant and nightclub, Cafe Sevilla has a huge tapas menu that includes the traditional small plates and entrée-size portions as well. The selection includes wild mushroom empanadas and paella Valenciana. There's live music for dancing nearly every night; on weekends the restaurant plays host to a Latin-Euro Top 40 dance club. ⊠ *3252 Mission Inn Ave.* ☎ *951/778–0611* ⊕ *www.cafesevilla. com* ⚏ *$10 cover charge most nights.*

REDLANDS

15 miles northeast of Riverside via I–215 north and I–10 east.

Redlands lies at the center of what once was the largest navel-orange-producing region in the world. Orange groves are still plentiful throughout the area. Populated in the late 1800s by wealthy citrus farmers, the town holds a colorful collection of Victorian homes.

GETTING HERE AND AROUND

Redlands straddles Interstate 10 north and south of the freeway at its intersection with Highway 30 (one of the main roads into the San Bernardino Mountains). You can check out the exhibits at the county museum and the Lincoln Memorial Shrine, just off the freeway before you reach the town, which is known for its elegant Victorian houses.

ESSENTIALS

Visitor Information Redlands Chamber of Commerce ⊠ *1 E. Redlands Blvd.* ☎ *909/793–2546* ⊕ *www.redlandschamber.org.*

EXPLORING

Asistencia Mission de San Gabriel. Franciscan Fathers built the Asistencia Mission de San Gabriel in 1819, but it functioned as a mission only for a few years. In 1834 it became part of a rancho and later served as a school and a factory. The county purchased the mission in 1925 and constructed the replica that stands today. The landscaped courtyard contains an old Spanish mission bell, and one building holds a small museum. ⊠ *26930 Barton Rd.* ☎ *909/793–5402* ⊕ *www.sbcounty.gov/ museum/branches/asist.htm* ⚏ *$2* ⊘ *Tues.–Sat. 10–3.*

Kimberly Crest House and Gardens. In 1897 Cornelia A. Hill built Kimberly Crest House and Gardens to mimic the châteaus of France's Loire Valley. Surrounded by orange groves, lily ponds, and terraced Italian gardens, the mansion has a French-revival parlor, a mahogany stair-case, a glass-mosaic fireplace, and a bubbling fountain in the form of Venus rising from the sea. Alfred and Helen Kimberly, founders of the Kimberly-Clark Paper Company, purchased the home in 1905, and their daughter, Mary, lived here until 1979. Most of the 22 rooms are in original condition. ⊠ *1325 Prospect Dr.* ☎ *909/792–2111* ⊕ *www.kimberlycrest.org* ⊠ *$10* ⊙ *Sept.–July, Thurs.–Sun. 1–4.*

Lincoln Memorial Shrine. The shrine houses the largest collection of Abraham Lincoln artifacts on the West Coast. You can view a marble bust of Lincoln by sculptor George Grey Barnard, along with more than a dozen letters and rare pamphlets. The gift shop sells many books, toys, and reproductions pertaining to the Civil War. ⊠ *125 W. Vine St.* ☎ *909/798–7636, 909/798–7632* ⊕ *www.lincolnshrine.org* ⊠ *Free* ⊙ *Tues.–Sun. 1–5.*

☺ **San Bernardino County Museum.** To learn more about Southern California's shaky history, head to this museum where you can watch a working seismometer or check out a display about the San Andreas Fault. Specializing in the natural and regional history of Southern California, the museum is big on birds, eggs, dinosaurs, and mammals. Afterward, have a light lunch at the Garden Café, open from 11 to 2. ⊠ *2024 Orange Tree La.* ☎ *909/307–2669* ⊕ *www.sbcounty.gov/museum* ⊠ *$8* ⊙ *Tues.–Sun., holiday Mon. 9–5.*

WHERE TO EAT

$$$$
ITALIAN
✕ **Joe Greensleeves.** Housed in the 19th-century brick Board of Trade building, this restaurant is homey and inviting. Wood-grilled steaks, chicken, duck, and fish make up most of the Italian-leaning menu. The long list of pastas and risottos includes lobster ravioli, chocolate fettuccini with chopped zucchini in Parmesan cheese sauce, and risotto with asparagus and saffron. Cell phones are not permitted in the dining room. ⑤ *Average main: $32* ⊠ *220 N. Orange St.* ☎ *909/792–6969* ⊕ *www.joegreensleevesrestaurant.com* ⌸ *Reservations essential* ⊙ *No lunch weekends.*

OAK GLEN

★ *17 miles east of Redlands via I–10 and Live Oak Canyon Rd.*

More than 60 varieties of apples are grown in Oak Glen. This rustic village, tucked in the foothills above Yucaipa, is home to acres of farms, produce stands, country shops, and homey cafés. The town really comes alive during the fall harvest (from September through December), which is celebrated with piglet races, live entertainment, and other events. Most farms also grow berries and stone fruit, which are available in summer. Most of the apple farms lie along Oak Glen Road.

GETTING HERE AND AROUND
Oak Glen is tucked into a mountainside about halfway up the San Berndardinos. Exit Interstate 10 at Yucaipa Boulevard, heading east to the intersection with Oak Glen Road, a 5-mile loop along which you'll find most of the shops, cafés, and apple orchards.

ESSENTIALS

Visitor Information Oak Glen Apple Growers Association ✉ *39600 Oak Glen Rd., Yucaipa* 🕾 *909/797–6833* ⊕ *www.oakglen.net.*

EXPLORING

Mom's Country Orchards. Oak Glen's informal information center is at Mom's Country Orchards, where you can belly up to the bar and learn about the nuances of apple tasting, or warm up with a hot cider heated on an antique stove. Organic produce, local honey, apple butter, and salsa are also specialties here. ✉ *38695 Oak Glen Rd.* 🕾 *909/797–4249* ⊕ *www.momscountryorchards.com* ☉ *Daily 10–6.*

> ### BEFORE YOU GO PICKING
>
> Be sure to call before visiting the farms, most of which are family run. Unpasteurized cider—sold at some farms—should not be consumed by children, the elderly, or those with weakened immune systems.

🕓 **Oak Tree Village.** This 14-acre children's park has miniature train rides, trout fishing, gold panning, exotic animal exhibits, a petting zoo, and several eateries. ✉ *38480 Oak Glen Rd.* 🕾 *909/797–4020* ⊕ *www. oaktreevillageoakglen.com* ☜ *$5* ☉ *Daily 10–5.*

🕓 **Riley's Farm.** Employees dress in period costumes at Riley's Farm, one of the most interactive and kid-friendly ranches in apple country. The farm hosts school groups from September to June. Individuals can join the groups by reservation. You can hop on a hayride, take part in a barn dance, pick your own apples, press some cider, or throw a tomahawk while enjoying living-history performances throughout the orchard. The farm is also home to Colonial Chesterfield, a replica New England–style estate where costumed 18th-century reenactors offer lessons in cider pressing, candle dipping, colonial games, and etiquette. The four-hour Revolutionary War Adventures are especially popular. Afterward, head to the Public House for a bite of colonial specialties. The warm apple pies are unforgettable. ✉ *12261 S. Oak Glen Rd.* 🕾 *909/797–7534* ⊕ *www.rileysfarm.com* ☜ *Free to visit ranch, $14 for school tour, fees vary for activities* ☉ *Mon.–Sat. 9–4.*

Rileys at Los Rios Rancho. This farm, with 50 acres of apple trees, has a fantastic country store where you can stock up on jams, cookbooks, syrups, and candied apples. Head into the bakery for a hot tri-tip sandwich before going outside to the picnic grounds for lunch. During the fall, you can pick your own apples and pumpkins, take a hayride, or enjoy live bluegrass music. On the rancho grounds, the **Wildlands Conservancy** preserves 400 acres of nature trails, open weekends from 8:30 to 4:30. From April through December, guided night walks take place on the third Saturday of the month. ✉ *39611 S. Oak Glen Rd.* 🕾 *909/797–1005* ⊕ *www.losriosrancho.com* ☉ *Oct. and Nov., daily 9–5; Dec.–Sept., Wed.–Sun. 10–5.*

WHERE TO EAT

$ ✕ **Apple Annie's Restaurant and Bakery.** You won't leave hungry from this
BAKERY country-western diner, known for its 5-pound apple pies and family-style seven-course dinners. The decor is comfortable and rustic; old guns and handcuffs hang on the walls alongside pictures of cowboys,

trail wagons, and outlaws. Standout dishes include the tuna melt and the Annie deluxe burger. $ *Average main: $12* ✉ *38480 Oak Glen Rd.* ☎ *909/797–7371* ◷ *Daily 8–7.*

$ ✕ **Law's Oak Glen Coffee Shop.** Since 1953, this old-fashioned coffee shop

AMERICAN has been serving up hot coffee, hearty breakfasts, and famous apple pies to hungry and grateful customers. The menu lists meat loaf, country-fried steak, and Reuben sandwiches. Service has been known to be slow, so if you're in a hurry, look elsewhere. $ *Average main: $8* ✉ *38392 Oak Glen Rd.* ☎ *909/797–1642.*

13

SAN BERNARDINO MOUNTAINS

One of three transverse mountain ranges that lie in the Inland Empire, the San Bernardino range holds the tallest peak in Southern California, San Gorgonio Mountain at 11,503 feet. It's frequently snowcapped in winter, providing the region's only challenging ski slopes. In summer the forested hillsides and lakes provide a cool retreat from the city for many locals.

LAKE ARROWHEAD

37 miles northeast of Riverside via I–215 north, to I–10 east, to Hwy. 30 and then Hwy. 330 north, to Running Springs, turn left on Hwy. 18 west.

Lake Arrowhead Village is an alpine community with lodgings, shops, outlet stores, and eateries that descend the hill to the lake. Outside the village, access to the lake and its beaches is limited to area residents and their guests.

GETTING HERE AND AROUND

The drive to Lake Arrowhead can be one of the most beautiful in Southern California as Highway 18, called the Rim of the World, travels a mountainside ledge at 5,000-foot elevation revealing a fabulous city view. At the Lake Arrowhead turnoff, you descend into a wooded bowl surrounding the lake. The village is walkable, but hilly. Scenic Highway 173 winding along the east side of the lake offers scenic blue water views through the forest. (In winter, check for chain control on this route.)

ESSENTIALS

Visitor Information Lake Arrowhead Chamber ✉ *28200 Hwy. 189* ☎ *909/337–3715* ⊕ *lakearrowhead.net.*

EXPLORING

Lake Arrowhead Queen. One of the few ways visitors can access Lake Arrowhead is on a 50-minute *Lake Arrowhead Queen* cruise, operated daily from the Lake Arrowhead Village marina. *909/336–6992* ⊕ *lake-arrowheadqueen.com* ✉ *$16.*

WHERE TO EAT AND STAY

For expanded reviews, facilities, and current deals, visit Fodors.com.

$ ✕ **Belgian Waffle Works.** This dockside eatery, just steps from the *Lake*
BELGIAN   *Arrowhead Queen*, is quaint and homey, with country decor and beau-
🕒   tiful lake views. The namesake waffles are crisp on the outside and
moist on the inside, topped with fresh berries and cream. Lunch is
also delicious—burgers, tuna melts, chili, meat loaf, chicken, and salads. Weekends at lunchtime can get crowded, so arrive early to snag a
table with a view. ⑤ *Average main: $9* ✉ *28200 Hwy. 189, Suite #150*
☎ *909/337–5222* ⊕ *belgianwaffle.com* ⌲ *Reservations not accepted*
⊗ *No dinner.*

$$$$ ✕ **Casual Elegance.** Owner-chef Kathleen Kirk charms locals and visitors
AMERICAN   with her inventive cuisine. The specialties include rack of lamb prepared
with an herb crust, crusted filet mignon with Stilton, and steak au
poivre. Dine by the fireplace for a particularly cozy experience. ⑤ *Aver-*
age main: $38 ✉ *26848 Hwy. 189, Blue Jay* ☎ *909/337–8932* ⊕ *www.*
casualelegancerestaurant.com ⌲ *Reservations essential* ⊗ *Closed Mon.*
and Tues. No lunch.

$$$$ ⛅ **Lake Arrowhead Resort and Spa.** This lakeside lodge is warm and comfy
RESORT   with fireplaces everywhere. **Pros:** beautiful lake views; delicious on-site
★   dining. **Cons:** some rooms have thin walls; resort amenity fee. **TripAdvi-**
sor: "nice place to relax," "great location," "beautiful."⑤ *Rooms from:*
$259 ✉ *27984 Hwy. 189* ☎ *909/336–1511, 800/800–6792* ⊕ *www.*
lakearrowheadresort.com ↩ *162 rooms, 11 suites.*

SPORTS AND THE OUTDOORS

McKenzie Waterski School. Summer ski-boat rides and waterskiing and
wakeboarding lessons are available through this school in summer.
✉ *28200 Hwy. 189* ☎ *909/337–3814* ⊕ *www.mckenziewaterskischool.*
com.

BIG BEAR LAKE

24 miles east of Lake Arrowhead on Hwy. 18.

When Angelenos say they're going to the mountains, they usually mean
Big Bear, where a collection of Alpine-style villages surrounds a 7-mile-
long lake. The south shore of the lake is busy with ski slopes, animal
parks, a gorgeous B&B, water sports, lodging, and restaurants. You'll
find quiet country walks, biking trails, and splendid alpine scenery
along the north shore.

GETTING HERE AND AROUND

Driving is the best way to get to and explore the Big Bear area. But
there are alternatives. The Mountain Area Regional Transit Authority
provides bus service to and in San Bernardino Mountain communities
and connects with public transit in San Bernardino.

ESSENTIALS

Visitor Information Big Bear Lake Resort Association ✉ *630 Bartlett Rd.*
☎ *909/866–7000, 800/424–4232* ⊕ *www.bigbearinfo.com.*

EXPLORING

🕒 **Alpine Slide at Magic Mountain.** Take a ride down a twisting bobsled
course in winter, or beat the summer heat on a dual waterslide at Alpine
Slide at Magic Mountain. The facility also has an 18-hole miniature golf

course, and go-carts. ⊠ *800 Wildrose La.* ☎ *909/866–4626* ⊕ *www. alpineslidebigbear.com* 🖀 *$5 single rides, $20 5-ride pass, $25 all-day snow play pass* ⊙ *Daily 10–4.*

Ⓒ **Big Bear Discovery Center.** Operated by the forest service, this nature

Fodor'sChoice center is the place to sign up for a canoe ride through Grout Bay. Natu-

★ ralist-led Discovery Tours include visits to the Baldwin Lake Ecological Reserve or Holcomb Valley, where a small gold rush took place more than a century ago. The center also has flora and fauna exhibits and a large gift shop. Center staffers provide maps and camping and hiking information. ⊠ *North Shore Dr., Hwy. 38, between Fawnskin and Stanfield Cutoff, 40971 North Shore Dr., Fawnskin* ☎ *909/382–2790* ⊕ *www.bigbeardiscoverycenter.com* 🖀 *Free* ⊙ *Thurs.–Mon. 8:30–4:30.*

Big Bear Marina. The paddle wheeler *Big Bear Queen* departs from the marina for 90-minute lake tours. The marina also rents fishing boats, Jet Skis, kayaks, and canoes. ⊠ *500 Paine Ct.* ☎ *909/866–3218* ⊕ *www. bigbearmarina.com* 🖀 *$18* ⊙ *Tours May–early Sept., daily at noon, 2, and 4; call to confirm.*

Ⓒ **Big Bear Rescue Zoo.** This rescue and rehabilitation center specializes in animals native to the San Bernardino Mountains. Among its residents are black and (nonnative) grizzly bears, bald eagles, coyote, beavers, mountain lions, gray wolves, and bobcats. An animal presentation takes place daily at noon and a feeding tour Thursday through Tuesday at 3. The facility was planning to move in 2013, so check before visiting. ⊠ *43285 Goldmine Dr.* ☎ *909/878–4200* ⊕ *www.moonridgezoo.org* 🖀 *$9* ⊙ *June–Sept., daily 10–5; Sept.–May, weekdays 10–4, weekends 10–5.*

Ⓒ **Time Bandit Pirate Ship.** Featured in the 1981 move *Time Bandits,* this small-scale replica of a 17th-century English galleon cruises Big Bear Lake daily from roughly April through October. The shop travels along the southern lakeshore to 6,743-foot high Big Bear Dam; along the way you'll pass big bay-front mansions, some owned by celebrities. A sightseeing excursion with the crew dressed up like pirates, the cruise is popular with kids and adults. There's a bar, but no dining onboard. ⊠ *Holloway's Marina and RV Park, 398 Edgemoor Rd.* ☎ *909/878–4040* ⊕ *www.bigbearboating.com/pirateship* 🖀 *$19* ⊙ *Confirmed tours daily at 2 in warm weather; call for additional times.*

WHERE TO EAT

$ ✕ **Himalayan Restaurant.** It's best to order family style at this no-frills

NEPALESE storefront restaurant so that everyone gets a taste of the many Nep-

Ⓒ alese and Indian delicacies. Standouts include the spicy mo-mo (pot stickers), daal (green lentils), lamb and shrimp-curry vindaloo, fish and chicken masala, and clay-oven-roasted tandoori meats and seafood, all supplemented by tangy garlic naan. Wash it all down with the perky teas and lemonades. Ⓢ *Average main: $12* ⊠ *672 Pine Knot Ave.* ☎ *909/866–2907* ⊕ *www.himalayanbigbear.com* ⌕ *Reservations essential* ⊙ *Closed Wed.*

$$$$ ✕ **Madlon's.** The menu at this cozy gingerbread-style cottage includes

FRENCH sophisticated dishes such as rack of lamb with port wine reduction, cream of jalapeño soup, and dry aged filet mignon with Drambuie sauce. All menu items have wine-pairing suggestions. Midweek prix-fixe three-course specials include wine. $ *Average main: $39* ✉ *829 W. Big Bear Blvd., Big Bear City* ☎ *909/585–3762* ⊕ *www.madlonsrestaurant. com* ⌂ *Reservations essential* ☉ *Closed Tues.*

WHERE TO STAY

For expanded reviews, facilities, and current deals, visit Fodors.com.

$$$
B&B/INN

⌖ **Apples Bed & Breakfast Inn.** Despite its location on a busy road to the ski lifts, the inn feels remote and peaceful, thanks to the surrounding pines. **Pros:** large rooms; clean; free snacks and movies; delicious big breakfast. **Cons:** some traffic noise; fussy decor; sometimes feels busy. **TripAdvisor:** "very frilly," "home away from home," "it is the complete package." $ *Rooms from: $196* ✉ *42430 Moonridge Rd.* ☎ *909/866–0903* ⊕ *www.applesbigbear.com* ↩ *19 rooms* ⏏ *Some meals.*

$$
B&B/INN
★

⌖ **Gold Mountain Manor.** This restored 1928 log mansion has a wide veranda under wooden eaves and Adirondack-style furnishings. **Pros:** gracious hosts; snow shoes and kayaks available; original art on walls. **Cons:** somewhat thin walls; 10-minute drive to the village; lots of stairs and narrow corridors. **TripAdvisor:** "excellent owner," "a luxurious respite of relaxation and charm," "oh so cozy." $ *Rooms from: $149* ✉ *1117 Anita Ave., Big Bear City 909/585–6997, 800/509–2604* ⊕ *www.goldmountainmanor.com* ↩ *4 rooms, 3 suites* ⏏ *Multiple meal plans.*

$$
HOTEL

⌖ **Northwoods Resort.** A giant log cabin with the amenities of a resort, Northwoods has a lobby that resembles a 1930s hunting lodge: canoes, antlers, fishing poles, and a grand stone fireplace all decorate the walls. **Pros:** pool heated in winter; ski packages available; beautiful grounds. **Cons:** parts of the hotel are showing their age; rooms can be noisy at night; rates fluctuate depending on whether there is snow. **TripAdvisor:** "great customer service," "friendly atmosphere," "good place to rest." $ *Rooms from: $139* ✉ *40650 Village Dr.* ☎ *909/866–3121, 800/866–3121* ⊕ *www.northwoodsresort.com* ↩ *140 rooms, 7 suites* ⏏ *No meals.*

$$
B&B/INN

⌖ **Windy Point Inn.** Perched on a point surrounded on three sides by water, Windy Point offers the best view and the most luxurious accommodations in the Big Bear area. **Pros:** secure parking; gracious hosts; privacy; views. **Cons:** remote from lake activities; windy at times. **TripAdvisor:** "idyllic lake getaway," "quiet and peaceful," "a breathtaking place to enjoy romance." $ *Rooms from: $145* ✉ *31094 North Shore Dr., Fawnskin* ☎ *909/866–2746* ⊕ *windypointinn.com* ↩ *5 rooms* ⏏ *Breakfast.*

SPORTS AND THE OUTDOORS

**BOATS AND
CHARTERS**

Pine Knot Landing Marina. This full-service marina rents fishing boats, pontoon boats, and kayaks and sells bait, ice, and snacks. The tour boat *Miss Liberty* leaves from the landing for a 90-minute tour ($20) of Big Bear Lake from late April through September. ✉ *439 Pine Knot Blvd.* ☎ *909/866–8129* ⊕ *pineknotmarina.com.*

**HORSEBACK
RIDING**

Baldwin Lake Stables. Explore the forested mountain on horseback on a group or private guided trail ride (one hour to a half day) arranged by this outfit. Reservations are required for private rides and suggested for all. ✉ *46475 Pioneertown Rd., Fawnskin* ☎ *909/585–6482* ⊕ *www. baldwinlakestables.com* 🖾 *$40 and up per person per hr.*

SKIING **Big Bear Mountain Resorts.** Two distinct resorts, Bear Mountain and Snow Summit, comprise Southern California's largest winter playground, one of the few that challenge skilled skiers. The complex offers 438 skiable acres, 55 runs, and 26 chairlifts, including four high-speed quads. The vibe is youthful at Bear, which has beginner slopes (training available) and the after-ski hangout The Scene. Snow Summit holds challenging runs and is open for night skiing. On weekends and holidays it's best to reserve tickets for either mountain. Bear rents skis and boards.

The resorts are open in summer for mountain biking, hiking, golfing, and some special events. The Snow Summit Scenic Sky Chair zips to the mountain's 8,200-foot peak, where View Haus ($), a casual outdoor restaurant, has breathtaking views of the lake and San Gorgonio Mountain. ✉ *Big Bear, 43101 Goldmine Dr., off Moonridge Rd.* ☎ *909/866–5766* ⊕ *www.bigbearmountainresorts.com* 🖾 *$56–$69.*

THE SOUTHERN INLAND EMPIRE

The southern end of the Inland Empire is devoted to the good life. Mile-high Idyllwild atop Mt. San Jacinto holds a renowned arts academy, charming restaurants, and galleries. It's also a good place to hike, mountain climb, and test high-altitude biking skills. Temecula, lying at the base of the mountain, is a popular wine region where you'll find vineyards, tasting rooms, fine dining, and cozy lodgings.

IDYLLWILD

44 miles east of Riverside via State Hwy. 60 and I–10 to State Hwy. 243.

Set in a valley halfway up Mt. San Jacinto, Idyllwild has been a serene forested getaway for San Diegans and Angelenos for nearly a century. The town's simple, quiet lifestyle attracts artists and performers as well as outdoor types who enjoy hiking, biking, and rock climbing.

GETTING HERE AND AROUND

There are two routes to Idyllwild from interstates; both are slow and winding, but they reward you with some great mountain views. From Interstate 15 south of Lake Elsinore, you can take Highway 74 to the top of the mountain. Scenic Highway 243 takes off from Banning on Interstate 10. Once you get to Idyllwild, you'll discover that you can walk nearly everywhere in the village. You'll need to drive to trailheads, fishing holes, and rock-climbing locations.

ESSENTIALS

Visitor Information Idyllwild Chamber of Commerce ✉ *54325 N. Circle Dr., Box 304* ☎ *951/659–3259, 888/659–3259* ⊕ *www.idyllwildchamber.com.*

EXPLORING

☾ **Idyllwild Nature Center.** At the center, you can learn about the area's Native American history, try your hand at astronomy, and listen to traditional storytellers. Outside are 3 miles of hiking trails, plus biking and equestrian trails and picnic areas. The park is pet friendly. ✉ *25225 Hwy. 243* ☎ *951/659–3850* ⊕ *www.rivcoparks.org/parks* 🅿 *$3* ⊙ *Tues.–Sun. 9–4:30.*

WHERE TO EAT

$$$$

FRENCH

✕ **Restaurant Gastrognome.** Elegant and dimly lighted, with wood paneling, lace curtains, and an oft-glowing fireplace, "The Gnome" is where locals go for a romantic dinner. The overall feel is French, but the menu goes beyond the Gallic, with entrées such as calamari almandine, sausage pasta, and lobster tacos. The French onion soup is a standout appetizer, and the roast duck with orange sauce and the Southwest-style grilled pork are excellent entrées. The crème brûlée makes for a sweet finale. For lighter dinner fare, check out the bar menu. 💲 *Average main: $32* ✉ *54381 Ridgeview Dr.* ☎ *951/659–5055* ⊕ *www.gastrognome. com* 🍽 *Reservations essential.*

THE ARTS

Idyllwild Arts Academy. The Idyllwild Arts Academy is a summer camp offering more than 60 workshops in dance, music, Native American arts, theater, visual arts, and writing. There are free summer concerts and theater productions featuring students and professional performers. ✉ *52500 Temecula Rd.* ☎ *951/659–2171* ⊕ *www.idyllwildarts.org.*

SPORTS AND THE OUTDOORS

FISHING

Lake Fulmor. The lake is stocked with rainbow trout, largemouth bass, catfish, and bluegill. To fish, you'll need a California fishing license and a National Forest Adventure Pass ($5 per vehicle per day). ✉ *Hwy. 243, 10 miles north of Idyllwild* ☎ *951/659–2117* ⊕ *www.fs.usda.gov/sbnf.*

HIKING

Humber Park Trailhead. Two great hikes begin at this site, the 2.5-mile Devils Slide Trail and the 2.6-mile Ernie Maxwell Scenic Trail. Permits ($5) are needed for both. ✉ *At top of Fern Valley Rd.* ☎ *951/659–2117* ⊕ *www.fs.usda.gov/recarea/sbnf/recarea/?recid=26483.*

Pacific Crest Trail. Access the trail at Highway 74, 1 mile east of Highway 371; or via the Fuller Ridge Trail at Black Mountain Road, 15 miles north of Idyllwild. Permits ($5 per day), required for camping and day hikes in the San Jacinto Wilderness, are available online or at the Idyllwild Ranger Station (✉ *Pine Crest Ave., off Hwy. 243* ☎ *951/659–2117*). ⊕ *www.fs.usda.gov/sbnf.*

EN
ROUTE

Winchester Cheese Company. If you're headed for Temecula via Route 74 east from Idyllwild, make a detour to Winchester Cheese Company for a taste of Jules Wesselink's famous Goudas, made from the raw milk of his Holstein cows. Take a tour, or sample one of six varieties, including a spicy jalapeño, in the tasting room. If you want to see the cheese-making process, call first. ✉ *32605 Holland Rd., Winchester* ☎ *951/926–4239* ⊕ *www.winchestercheese.com* 🎟 *Free* ⊙ *Weekdays 10–5, weekends 10–4.*

TEMECULA

Fodor's Choice ★ *43 miles south of Riverside on I–15; 60 miles north of San Diego on I–15; 90 miles southeast of Los Angeles via I–10 and I–15.*

Temecula, with its rolling green vineyards, comfy country inns, and first-rate restaurants, bills itself as the "Southern California Wine Country." The region is home to more than three dozen wineries, several of which offer fine dining, luxury lodging, and spas in addition to appealing boutiques, charming picnic areas, and, of course, award-winning vintages.

The name Temecula comes from a Luiseño Indian word meaning "where the sun shines through the mist"—ideal conditions for growing wine grapes. Intense afternoon sun and cool nighttime temperatures, complemented by ocean breezes that flow through the Rainbow and Santa Margarita gaps in the coastal range, help grapevines flourish in the area's granite soil. Best known for Chardonnay, Temecula Valley winemakers are moving in new directions, producing Viognier, Syrah, old-vine Zinfandel, and Pinot Gris varietals. Most wineries charge a small fee ($5 to $15) for a tasting that includes several wines. Most wineries are strung out along Rancho California Road, east of Interstate 15; a few newer ones lie along the eastern portion of De Portola Road. For a winery map, visit ⊕ *www.temeculawines.org.*

GETTING HERE AND AROUND

Interstate 15 cuts right through Temecula. The wineries lie on the east side of the freeway along Rancho California Road. Old West Temecula lies along the west side of the freeway along Front Street.

WINERY TOURS

Destination Temecula runs daily tours of wine country, with pickups at San Diego hotels and Old Town Temecula. Plan on a full day for these tours as they include stops at three wineries, a chance to explore Old Town, and picnic lunch. Rates run from $89 starting in Temecula and $97 round-trip from San Diego. If you plan to visit several wineries (and taste a lot of wine), catch the Grapeline Wine Country Shuttle, which operates daily with pickup at Temecula and San Diego hotels. The Vineyard Picnic Tour at $98 ($118 on Saturday) includes transportation, a wine-making demonstration, free tastings at four wineries, and a gourmet picnic lunch catered by Creekside Grill at Wilson Creek Winery.

ESSENTIALS

Tour Contacts Destination Temecula ⊠ *28475 Old Town Front St.* ☎ *951/695–1232* ⊕ *www.destem.com.* **Grapeline Wine Country Shuttle** ⊠ *43500 Ridge Park Dr., #204* ☎ *951/693–5755, 888/894–6379* ⊕ *www. gogrape.com* ▱ *$52 transportation only, $72 Sat.*

Visitor Information Temecula Valley Convention and Visitors Bureau ⊠ *28690 Mercedes St.* ☎ *951/491–6085, 888/363–2852* ⊕ *www.temeculacvb. com.*

EXPLORING

TOP ATTRACTIONS

Fodor'sChoice ★ **Hart Family Winery.** With Mediterranean varietals grown on 11 acres of vineyards in Temecula, Hart Family Winery is known for producing some of the best red wines in Temecula Valley. Joe Hart, one of the area's pioneer winemakers, creates small lots of big-flavored Zinfandel, Cabernet Sauvignon, and Sangiovese wines. The winery's purple tasting room is decked out with ribbons, medals, and awards. ✉ *41300 Avenida Biona* ☎ *951/676–6300* ⊕ *www.hartfamilywinery.com* ✉ *Winery free, tastings $10* ☉ *Daily 9–4:30.*

Old Town Temecula. Temecula is more than just vineyards and tasting rooms. For a bit of old-fashioned fun, head to Old Town Temecula, a turn-of-the-20th-century-style cluster of storefronts and boardwalks that holds more than 640 antiques stores, boutiques, and art galleries. ✉ *Front St., between Rancho California Rd. and Hwy. 79* ☎ *888/363–2852.*

☾ **Pennypickle's Workshop—Temecula Children's Museum.** If you have the kids along, check out the fictional 7,500-square-foot workshop of Professor Phineas T. Pennypickle, PhD. This elaborately decorated children's museum is filled with secret passageways, machines, wacky contraptions, and time-travel inventions. ✉ *42081 Main St.* ☎ *951/308–6370* ⊕ *www.pennypickles.org* ✉ *$4.50* ☉ *Tues.–Sat. 10–5, Sun. 12:30–5.*

★ **Ponte Family Estates.** Lush gardens and 350 acres of vineyards provide the welcome at this rustic winery inside a beautiful new barn. In the open-beam tasting room, you can sample six different varietals, including Cabernet Sauvignon, Syrah, Pinot Grigio, and Chardonnay. One area is devoted to an eye-popping marketplace selling ceramics, specialty foods, and gift baskets. The outdoor Restaurant at Ponte serves wood-fired pizza, salads, beef, and seafood daily for lunch and on Friday and weekends for dinner. ✉ *35053 Rancho California Rd.* ☎ *951/694–8855* ⊕ *www.pontewinery.com* ✉ *Winery free; tastings $12 weekdays, $20 weekends* ☉ *Daily 10–5.*

Fodor'sChoice ★ **Thornton Winery.** A rambling French Mediterranean–style stone building houses Thornton Winery, a producer best known for its sparkling wine. You can taste winemaker David Vergari's Brut Reserve and Cuvée Rouge at a table in the lounge, or along with some food at Café Champagne. Readers rave about the Syrah. On the weekend, take a free tour of the grounds and the wine cave. Summer Champagne jazz concerts ($55–$95) featuring performers such as George Benson, Herb Alpert, and David Benoit, and elaborate winemaker dinners ($120–$170) make this a fun place to spend an afternoon or evening. ✉ *32575 Rancho California Rd.* ☎ *951/699–0099* ⊕ *www.thorntonwine.com* ✉ *Winery free, tastings $12–$17* ☉ *Daily 10–5, winery tours weekends at 11, 12:30, 2, and 4.*

WORTH NOTING

Baily Vineyard & Winery. Winemaker Phil Baily is recognized for growing grapes that produce hearty red wines—Cabernet Sauvignon, Merlot, Cabernet Franc, Sangiovese, and a French-style Meritage. There's a gourmet gift shop and a restaurant, Carol's, that is locally popular for

13

lunch and dinner. ⊠ *33440 La Serena Way* ☎ *951/676–9463* ⊕ *www. bailywinery.com* ✉ *Winery free; tastings $5 weekdays, $10 weekends and holidays* ⊙ *Sun.–Fri. 11–5, Sat. 10–5.*

Callaway Coastal Vineyards. Established in 1969, Callaway is known for winemaker Craig Larson's reserve Chardonnays, red blends, and Merlots. Perched on a hill overlooking the vineyards, the Meritage Restaurant, open for lunch daily and dinner on weekends, serves tapas, salads, and sandwiches. ⊠ *32720 Rancho California Rd.* ☎ *951/676– 4001* ⊕ *www.callawaywinery.com* ✉ *Winery free, tastings $10, tours free with tasting or $5* ⊙ *Daily 10–5; tours weekdays at 11, 1, and 3, weekends 10–2 on the hr.*

Falkner Winery. With its wraparound deck overlooking the vineyards, this winery's Western-style barn is a great spot to enjoy Temecula's cool breezes. Falkner's Super Tuscan–style Amante, a blend of Sangiovese, Merlot, Cabernet Sauvignon, and Cabernet Franc grapes, has garnered great praise; the winery is also known for its Viognier, Chardonnay, and Syrah wines. The award-winning Pinnacle Restaurant, open for lunch daily, has a fabulous view. Winery tours are conducted at 11 and 2 on weekends. ⊠ *40620 Calle Contento Rd.* ☎ *951/676–8231* ⊕ *www.falknerwinery.com* ✉ *Winery free, tours $10, tastings $10–$15* ⊙ *Daily 10–5.*

Leoness Cellars. This is a casual farmhouse-style winery with a stone turret overlooking 20 acres of Cabernet Sauvignon grapes. The winery hosts private tours (reservations required) that include rides and walks through the vineyards, tastings, wine and cheese pairings, and a bit of chocolate with dessert wines. The popular restaurant here is open on Friday and weekends. ⊠ *38311 DePortola Rd.* ☎ *951/302–7601* ⊕ *www.leonesscellars.com* ✉ *Winery free, tastings $14, tours $14–$75* ⊙ *Daily 11–5.*

Miramonte Winery. Perched on a hilltop, Miramonte may be Temecula's hippest winery, thanks to the vision of owner Cane Vanderhoof, whose wines have earned dozens of awards. Listen to Spanish-guitar recordings while sampling the Opulente Meritage, a supple Sauvignon Blanc, or the sultry Syrah. On Friday and Saturday nights from 7 to 10, the winery turns into a hot spot with tastings of signature wines ($6 to $10) and beer, live music, and dancing that spills out into the vineyards. ⊠ *33410 Rancho California Rd.* ☎ *951/506–5500* ⊕ *www. miramontewinery.com* ✉ *Winery free, tastings $10, tours $20–$25* ⊙ *Tastings Sun.–Thurs. 11–6, Fri. and Sat. 11–10.*

Mount Palomar Winery. Opened in 1969, Mount Palomar was one of the original Temecula Valley wineries and the first to introduce Sangiovese grapes, a varietal that has proven perfectly suited to the region's soil and climate. The tasting room occupies a Spanish colonial–style building, an excellent setting for sampling a red Meritage blend, a white Cortese, and a cream sherry that is to die for. Shorty's Bistro, open for lunch daily and for dinner on Friday and weekends, presents live entertainment on Friday nights. ⊠ *33820 Rancho California Rd.* ☎ *951/676–5047* ⊕ *www.mountpalomar.com* ✉ *Winery free, tastings $10 Mon.–Thurs., $12 Fri.– Sun.* ⊙ *Mon.–Thurs. 10:30–6, Fri.–Sun. 10:30–7.*

13

WHERE TO EAT AND STAY

For expanded reviews, facilities, and current deals, visit Fodors.com.

$$$
AMERICAN

✕ **Baily's Fine Dining and Front Street Bar & Grill.** The family that owns Baily Winery also runs these two restaurants. Locals swoon over chef Neftali Torres's well-executed cuisine upstairs (dinner only) at Baily's Fine Dining. The menu varies according to his creative whims and might include chicken schnitzel drizzled in lemon-caper-wine sauce or salmon Wellington. Temecula Valley wines are well represented on the extensive list here. The fare is more casual—burgers, barbecue, soups, and salads—downstairs at Front Street, which often has live entertainment. $ *Average main: $25* ⊠ *28699 Front St.* ☎ *951/676–9567* ⊕ *www.oldtowndining.com* ◔ *No lunch at Baily's Fine Dining.*

$$$
ECLECTIC
Fodor's Choice
★

✕ **Café Champagne.** The spacious patio, with its bubbling fountain, flowering trellises, and views of Thornton Winery's vineyards, is the perfect place to lunch on a sunny day. Inside, the dining room is decked out in French country style, and the open kitchen turns out such dishes as braised boneless beef short ribs and cioppino. The reasonably priced wines served here include the signature Thornton sparklers. $ *Average main: $28* ⊠ *32575 Rancho California Rd.* ☎ *951/699–0088* ⊕ *www. thorntonwine.com/cafe.html* ⌔ *Reservations essential.*

$$
RESORT

▦ **Temecula Creek Inn.** If you want the relaxation of the wine country and the challenge of playing a championship golf course, this is the place for you. **Pros:** beautiful grounds; top golf course; clean, comfortable rooms. **Cons:** location away from Old Town and wineries. **TripAdvisor:** "romantic getaway," "upscale and relaxing," "so serene." $ *Rooms from: $169* ⊠ *44501 Rainbow Canyon Rd.* ☎ *951/694–1000, 877/517–1823* ⊕ *www.temeculacreekinn.com* ⇌ *130 rooms, 1 guesthouse* ⏻ *No meals.*

NIGHTLIFE

Pechanga Resort and Casino. Risk-takers can do a bit of gambling at this casino that also has several entertainment venues. The Showroom Theater presents stars such as Paul Anka, Wanda Sykes, and the Steve Martin Band. The intimate Comedy Club draws headliners and up-and-coming talent. ESPN and Showtime championship boxing matches draw thousands of fans. ⊠ *45000 Pechanga Pkwy.* ☎ *877/711–2946, 951/770–1819.*

SHOPPING

Rancho Fruit Market. You'll find lots of locally sourced produce such as Valencia oranges, avocadoes, and grapefruit at this little shop. Much is organic, and the prices are low. It's a cheerful spot. ⊠ *28670 Old Town Front St.* ☎ *951/676–5519* ◔ *Daily 9–6.*

Temecula Lavender Co. Owner Jan Schneider offers an inspiring collection of the herb that fosters peace, purification, sleep, and longevity. Bath salts, hand soaps, essential oil—she's got it all, even dryer bags to freshen up the laundry. ⊠ *28561 Old Town Front St.* ☎ *951/676–1931* ⊕ *www.temeculalavenderco.com* ◔ *Weekdays 11–5, weekends 10–6.*

Temecula Olive Oil Company. While you're shopping in Old Town, stop by the cool tasting room here for a sample of extra-virgin olive oils, bath products, and Mission, Ascalano, and Italian olives. ⊠ *28653 Old*

There's no more relaxing way to enjoy Temecula's wine country than by taking a peaceful hot-air balloon ride over the vineyards.

Town Front St., Suite H ☎ *951/693–0607* ⊕ *www.temeculaoliveoil.com* ⊘ *Daily 9:30–6.*

SPORTS AND THE OUTDOORS

GOLF
Temecula has several championship golf courses cooled by the valley's ocean breezes.

Redhawk Golf Club. Ron Fream designed the club's championship golf course. ⊠ *45100 Redhawk Pkwy.* ☎ *951/302–3850* ⊕ *www.redhawkgolfcourse.com* ⛳ *18 holes. 7,110 yds. Par 72. Green fee: $44/$55.*

Temeku Golf Club. The public is welcome on the Robinson-designed championship course at Temeku Golf Club. It's a challenging course with tiered greens and many blind spots. ⊠ *41687 Temeku Dr.* ☎ *951/694–9998* ⊕ *www.temekuhillsgolfcourse.com* ⛳ *18 holes. 6,636 yds. Par 72. Green fee: $45/$55.*

HOT-AIR
BALLOONING
California Dreamin'. Float serenely above Temecula's vineyards and country estates on an early-morning balloon adventure. The ride includes champagne, coffee, a pastry breakfast, and a souvenir photo. ☎ *800/373–3359* ⊕ *www.californiadreamin.com* ✉ *$138–$158.*

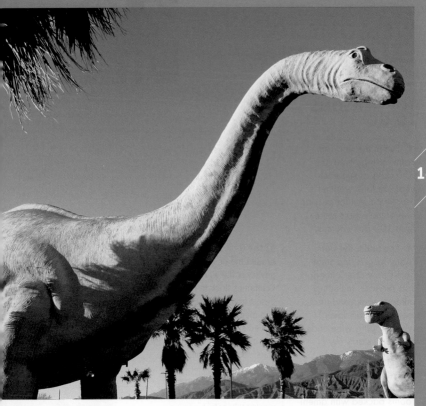

Palm Springs

AND THE DESERT RESORTS

WORD OF MOUTH

"I wasn't sure that there was going to be enough [in Palm Springs] to fill up a week. Boy was I wrong! Between swimming, hiking, poolside lounging, shopping, and a couple day trips to Joshua Tree National Park and the top of Mt. San Jacinto via the aerial tramway, we could have filled up two weeks."

—Sam_A

WELCOME TO PALM SPRINGS

TOP REASONS TO GO

★ **Fun in the sun:** The Palm Springs area has 350 days of sun each year, and the weather's usually perfect for playing one of the area's more than 100 golf courses.

★ **Spa under the stars:** Many resorts and small hotels now offer after-dark spa services, including outdoor soaks and treatments you can savor while sipping wine under the clear, starry sky.

★ **Personal pampering:** The resorts here have it all: beautifully appointed rooms packed with amenities, professional staffs, sublime spas, and delicious dining options.

★ **Divine desert scenery:** You'll probably spend a lot of your time here taking in the gorgeous 360-degree natural panorama, a flat desert floor surrounded by 10,000-foot mountains rising into a brilliant blue sky.

★ **The Hollywood connection:** The Palm Springs area has more celebrity ties than any other resort community. So keep your eyes open for your favorite star.

1 The Desert Resorts. Around the desert resorts, privacy is the watchword. Celebrities flock to the desert from Los Angeles, and many communities are walled and guarded. Still, you might spot Hollywood stars, sports personalities, politicians, and other high-profile types in restaurants, out on the town, at the weekly Villagefest, or on a golf course. For the most part, the desert's social, sports, shopping, and entertainment scenes center on Palm Springs, Palm Desert, and (increasingly) La Quinta.

2 Along Twentynine Palms Highway. The towns of Yucca Valley, Joshua Tree, and Twentynine Palms punctuate Twentynine Palms Highway (Highway 62)—the northern highway from the desert resorts to Joshua Tree National Park (⇨ see Chapter 15)—and provide visitor information, lodging, and other services to park visitors.

3 Anza-Borrego Desert. If you're looking for a break from the action, you'll find sublime solitude in this 600,000-acre desert landscape.

4 Joshua Tree National Park. This is desert scenery at its best and most abundant. Tiptoe through fields of wildflowers in spring, scramble on and around giant boulders, and check out the park's bizarre namesake trees (⇨ see Chapter 15).

GETTING ORIENTED

The Palm Springs resort area lies within the Colorado Desert, on the western edge of the Coachella Valley. The area holds seven cities that are strung out along Highway 111, with Palm Springs at the northwestern end of this strip and Indio at the southeastern end. North of Palm Springs, between Interstate 10 and Highway 62, is Desert Hot Springs. Northeast of Palm Springs, the towns of the Morongo Valley lie along Twentynine Palms Highway (Highway 62), which leads to Joshua Tree National Park (⇨ see Chapter 15). Head south on Highway 86 from Indio to reach Anza-Borrego State Park and the Salton Sea. All of the area's attractions are easy day trips from Palm Springs.

14

Updated by
Bobbi Zane

MANY MILLIONS OF YEARS AGO, the Southern Desert was the bottom of a vast sea. By 10 million years ago, the waters had receded and the climate was hospitable to prehistoric mastodons, zebras, and camels. The first human inhabitants of record were the Agua Caliente, part of the Cahuilla people, who settled in and around the Coachella Valley about 1,000 years ago.

Lake Cahuilla dried up about 300 years ago, but by then the Agua Caliente had discovered the area's hot springs and were making use of their healing properties during winter visits to the desert. The springs became a tourist attraction in 1871, when the tribe built a bathhouse (on a site near the current Spa Resort Casino in Palm Springs) to serve passengers on a pioneer stage highway. The Agua Caliente still own about 32,000 acres of desert, 6,700 of which lie within the city limits of Palm Springs.

In the last half of the 19th century, farmers established a date-growing industry at the southern end of the Coachella Valley. By 1900 word had spread about the health benefits of the area's dry climate, inspiring the gentry of the northern United States to winter under the warm desert sun. Growth hit the Coachella Valley in the 1970s, when developers began to construct the fabulous golf courses, country clubs, and residential communities that would draw celebrities, tycoons, and politicians. Communities sprang up south and east of what is now Palm Springs, creating a sprawl of tract houses and strip malls and forcing nature lovers to push farther south into the sparsely settled Anza-Borrego Desert.

PLANNING

WHEN TO GO

Desert weather is best between January and April, the height of the visitor season. The fall months are nearly as lovely, but less crowded and less expensive (although autumn draws a lot of conventions and business travelers). In summer, an increasingly popular time for European visitors, daytime temperatures may rise above 110°F (though evenings cool to the mid-70s); some attractions and restaurants close or reduce their hours during this time.

GETTING HERE AND AROUND
AIR TRAVEL
Palm Springs International Airport serves California's desert communities. Alaska, Allegiant, American, Delta, Frontier, Sun Country, United, US Airways, Virgin America, and WestJet all fly to Palm Springs, some only seasonally. Yellow Cab of the Desert serves the airport, which is about 3 miles from downtown. The fare is $3.25 to enter the cab and about $3 per mile.

Airport Information Palm Springs International Airport ⊠ *Kirk Douglas Way, off E. Tahquitz Canyon Way* ☎ *760/323-8299* ⊕ *www.palmspringsairport. com.*

Airport Transfers Yellow Cab of the Desert ☎ *760/340-5845* ⊕ *www. yellowcabofthedesert.com.*

BUS TRAVEL
Greyhound provides service to Palm Springs from many cities. SunBus, operated by the SunLine Transit Agency, serves the entire Coachella Valley, from Desert Hot Springs to Mecca.

Bus Contacts Greyhound ☎ *800/231-2222* ⊕ *www.greyhound.com.***SunLine Transit** ☎ *800/347-8628* ⊕ *www.sunline.org.*

CAR TRAVEL
The desert resort communities occupy a 20-mile stretch between Interstate 10, to the east, and Palm Canyon Drive (Highway 111), to the west. The region is about a two-hour drive east of the Los Angeles area and a three-hour drive northeast of San Diego. It can take twice as long to make the trip from Los Angeles to the desert on winter and spring weekends because of heavy traffic. From Los Angeles take the San Bernardino Freeway (Interstate 10) east to Highway 111. From San Diego, Interstate 15 heading north connects with the Pomona Freeway (Highway 60), leading to the San Bernardino Freeway east.

To reach Borrego Springs from Los Angeles, take Interstate 10 east past the desert resorts area to Highway 86 south to the Borrego Salton Seaway (Highway S22) west. You can reach the Borrego area from San Diego via Interstate 8 to Highway 79 through Cuyamaca State Park. This will take you to Highway 78 in Julian, which you follow east to Yaqui Pass Road (S3) into Borrego Springs.

TAXI TRAVEL
Yellow Cab of the Desert serves the entire Coachella Valley. The fare is $3.25 to enter a cab and about $3 per mile.

Taxi Contacts Yellow Cab of the Desert ☎ *760/340-5845* ⊕ *www. yellowcabofthedesert.com.*

TRAIN TRAVEL
The Amtrak Sunset Limited, which runs between Florida and Los Angeles, stops in Palm Springs.

Train Contact Amtrak ☎ *800/872-7245* ⊕ *www.amtrakcalifornia.com.*

14

HEALTH AND SAFETY

Never travel alone in the desert. Let someone know your trip route, destination, and estimated time and date of return. Before setting out, make sure your vehicle is in good condition. Carry a jack, tools, and towrope or chain. Fill up your tank whenever you see a gas pump. Stay on main roads, and watch out for horses and range cattle.

Drink at least a gallon of water a day (three gallons if you're hiking or otherwise exerting yourself). Dress in layered clothing and wear comfortable, sturdy shoes and a hat. Keep snacks, sunscreen, and a first-aid kit on hand. If you suddenly have a headache or feel dizzy or nauseous, you could be suffering from dehydration. Get out of the sun immediately and drink plenty of water. Dampen your clothing to lower your body temperature.

Do not enter mine tunnels or shafts. Avoid canyons during rainstorms. Never place your hands or feet where you can't see them: Rattlesnakes, scorpions, and black widow spiders may be hiding there.

Emergency Services Borrego Medical Center ⊠ 4343 Yaqui Pass Rd., Borrego Springs ☎ 760/767–5051 ⊕ www.borregomedical.org.**Desert Regional Medical Center** ⊠ 1150 N. Indian Canyon Dr., Palm Springs ☎ 760/323–6511 ⊕ www.desertmedctr.com.

TOUR OPTIONS

Desert Adventures conducts two- to four-hour red jeep tours ($100 to $200) on private land along the canyons and palm oases above the San Andreas earthquake fault. Other public tours include Painted Canyon/Mecca Hills and Joshua Tree National Park (⇨ see Chapter 15). Groups are small and guides are knowledgeable. Departures are from Palm Springs and La Quinta; hotel pickups are available.

Elite Land Tours offers two- to five-hour luxurious treks via Hummer and helicopter led by knowledgeable guides who take you to the San Andreas Fault, Joshua Tree, the Salton Sea, and other locations. Tours include hotel pickup, lunch, snacks, and beverages.

The city of Palm Desert offers four self-guided tours of its 150-piece Art in Public Places collection. Each tour is walkable or drivable. Maps are available at the Palm Desert Visitor Center and online (⊕ www.palm-desert.org/arts-culture/public-art). You can also take guided tours on the second Saturday of the month or by appointment for groups of four or more.

Tour Contacts Desert Adventures ⊠ 74-794 Lennon Pl., Suite B, Palm Desert ☎ 760/324-5337 ⊕ www.red-jeep.com.**Desert Safari Guides** ⊠ 2343 Bisnaga Ave. ☎ 760/861–6292 ⊕ www.palmspringshiking.com.**Elite Land Tours** ⊠ 540 S. Vella Rd. ☎ 760/318–1200 ⊕ www.elitelandtours.com.**Palm Desert Visitor Center** ⊠ 73-470 El Paseo, Suite 7-F, Palm Desert ☎ 760/568–1441 ⊕ www.palm-desert.org.

RESTAURANTS

During the season, restaurants can be busy, as many locals and visitors dine out every night, and some for every meal. An influx of talented young chefs has expanded the dining possibilities of a formerly staid scene. The meat-and-potatoes crowd still has plenty of options, but

The green revolution is proudly on display in many parts of the Palm Springs area.

you'll also find fresh seafood superbly prepared and contemporary Californian, Asian, Indian, and vegetarian cuisine; Mexican food abounds. Many restaurants have early-evening happy hours, with discounted drinks and small-plate menus. Restaurants that remain open in July and August frequently discount deeply; others close in July and August or offer limited service.

HOTELS

In general you can find the widest choice of lodgings in Palm Springs, ranging from tiny B&Bs and chain motels to business and resort hotels. All-inclusive resorts dominate in down-valley communities, such as Palm Desert. You can stay in the desert for as little as $80 or spend more than $1,000 a night. Rates vary widely by season and expected occupancy; a $200 room midweek can jump in price to $450 by Saturday.

Hotel/resort prices are frequently 50% less in summer and fall than in winter and early spring. From January through May prices soar, and lodgings book up far in advance. You should book well ahead for stays during events such as Modernism Week or the Coachella and Stagecoach music festivals.

Most resort hotels charge a resort fee (charged daily) that is not included in the room rate; be sure to ask about extra fees when you book. Many hotels are pet friendly and offer special services. Small boutique hotels and bed-and-breakfasts have historic character and offer good value; discounts are sometimes given for extended stays. Casino hotels can also offer good deals on lodging; check their ads before you book. Take care when considering budget lodgings; other than reliable chains, they may not be up to par.

The Desert Resorts

HOTEL AND RESTAURANT COSTS

Prices in the restaurant reviews are the average cost of a main course at dinner or, if dinner is not served, at lunch (excluding sales tax). Prices in the hotel reviews are the lowest cost of a standard double room in high season. Prices do not include taxes (as high as 14%, depending on the region).

NIGHTLIFE

Desert nightlife is concentrated and abundant in Palm Springs, where there are many straight and gay bars and clubs. The Fabulous Palm Springs Follies—a vaudeville-style revue starring retired professional performers—is a must-see. Arts festivals occur on a regular basis, especially in winter and spring. *Palm Springs Life* magazine (⊕ *www. palmspringslife.com*), available at hotels and visitor centers, has nightlife listings, as does the *Desert Sun* newspaper (⊕ *www.mydesert.com*). *Bottom Line Magazine* (⊕ *psbottomline.com*) and the *Gay Guide to Palm Springs* (⊕ *palmspringsgayinfo.com*) cover the lesbian and gay scenes.

THE DESERT RESORTS

The term "desert" resorts refers to the communities along or just off Highway 111—Palm Springs, Cathedral City, Rancho Mirage, Palm Desert, Indian Wells, Indio, and La Quinta—along with Desert Hot

Springs, which is north of Palm Springs off Highway 62 and Interstate 10.

PALM SPRINGS

90 miles southeast of Los Angeles on I–10.

A tourist destination since the late 19th century, Palm Springs evolved into an ideal hideaway for early Hollywood celebrities. They could slip into town, play some tennis, lounge around the pool, attend a party or two, and, unless things got out of hand, remain beyond the reach of gossip columnists. But the place really blossomed in the 1930s after actors Charlie Farrell and Ralph Bellamy bought 200 acres of land for $30 an acre and opened the Palm Springs Racquet Club, which soon listed Ginger Rogers, Humphrey Bogart, and Clark Gable among its members.

14

During its slow, steady growth period from the 1930s to 1970s, the Palm Springs area drew some of the world's most famous architects to design homes for the rich and famous. The collected works, inspired by the mountains and desert sands and notable for the use of glass and indoor–outdoor space, became known as Palm Springs Modernism. The city lost some of its luster in the 1970s as the wealthy moved to newer down-valley, golf-oriented communities. But Palm Springs reinvented itself starting in the 1990s, restoring the bright and airy old mid-century modern houses and hotels, and cultivating a welcoming atmosphere for gay visitors.

You'll find reminders of the city's glamorous past in its unique architecture and renovated hotels—for an overview, pick up a copy of *Palm Springs: Brief History and Architectural Guide* at the Palm Springs Visitor Center—and you'll see change and progress in the trendy restaurants and upscale shops. Formerly exclusive Palm Canyon Drive is now a lively avenue filled with coffeehouses, outdoor cafés, and bars.

GETTING HERE AND AROUND

Most visitors arrive in the Palm Springs area by car from the Los Angeles or San Diego areas via Interstate 10, which intersects with Highway 111 just north of Palm Springs. ■**TIP→** Tahquitz Canyon Way marks the division between north and south on major streets (e.g., North and South Palm Canyon Drive).

ESSENTIALS

Visitor Information Greater Palm Springs Convention and Visitors Bureau ⊠ *Visitor Center, 70-100 Hwy. 111, at Via Florencia, Rancho Mirage* ☎ *760/770– 9000, 800/967–3767* ⊕ *www.palmspringsusa.com* ☉ *Weekdays 8:30–5.***Palm Springs Visitor Information Center** ⊠ *2901 N. Palm Canyon Dr.* ☎ *760/778– 8418, 800/347–7746* ⊕ *www.palm-springs.org* ☉ *Daily 9–5.*

EXPLORING

☾ **Indian Canyons.** The Indian Canyons are the ancestral home of the Agua Caliente, part of the Cahuilla people. You can see remnants of their ancient life, including rock art, house pits and foundations, irrigation ditches, bedrock mortars, pictographs, and stone houses and shelters atop cliff walls. Short, easy walks through the canyons reveal palm oases, waterfalls, and spring wildflowers. Tree-shaded picnic areas

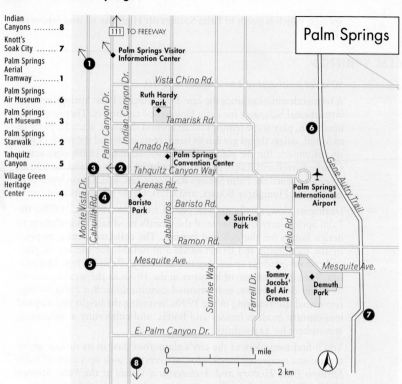

are abundant. The attraction includes three canyons open for touring:
Palm Canyon, noted for its stand of Washingtonia palms; Murray Canyon, home of Peninsula bighorn sheep and a herd of wild ponies; and
Andreas Canyon, where a stand of fan palms contrasts with sharp rock
formations. Ranger-led hikes to Palm and Andreas canyons are offered
daily for an additional charge. The trading post at the entrance to Palm
Canyon has hiking maps and refreshments, as well as Native American art, jewelry, and weavings. ⊠ *38520 S. Palm Canyon Dr., south of
Acanto Dr.* ☎ *760/323–6018* ⊕ *www.indian-canyons.com* ☞ *$9, ranger
hikes $3* ⊗ *Oct.–June, daily 8–5; July–Sept., Fri.–Sun. 8–5.*

ⓒ **Knott's Soak City.** For a break from the desert heat, head to Knott's. You'll
find 1950s-theme ambience complete with Woody station wagons, 13
waterslides, a huge wave pool, an arcade, and other family attractions.
The park also contains the full-service Fitness Point Health Club, where
you can take exercise classes—including water aerobics and yoga—use
the weight room, or swim. ⊠ *1500 S. Gene Autry Trail, south of Dinah
Shore Dr.* ☎ *760/327–0499, 760/325–8155 Fitness Point Health Club*
⊕ *www.knotts.com* ☞ *Park $33 ($22 after 3 pm); health club, $12 day
pass* ⊗ *Mid-Mar.–early Sept., daily; early Sept.–Oct., weekends. Opens
at 10 am, closing times vary.*

ELVIS IN PALM SPRINGS

Elvis's Honeymoon Hideaway—where the King and Priscilla lived during the first year of their marriage—is perched on a hilltop right up against the mountains in Palm Springs. The house, which is opened for tours, is a stunning example of Palm Springs Mid-Century Modern; it's rich in Elvis lore, photos, and furnishings. Docents describe the fabulous parties, celebrities, and some local legends. You can see some home movies of the loving couple, sit on the King's sofa, and strum one of his guitars. The house, built in 1962 by one of Palm Spring's largest developers, Robert Alexander, consists of four perfect circles, each set on a different level. At the time, *Look* magazine described it as the "house of tomorrow." (And indeed many features, like the huge kitchen with circular island, are standard in today's homes.) Tours are offered daily by appointment only; they're $25. Call ☎ 760/322–1192 or visit ⊕ *www.elvishoneymoon.com* for reservations.

14

☾ ★ **Palm Springs Aerial Tramway.** A trip on the Palm Springs Aerial Tramway provides a 360-degree view of the desert through the picture windows of rotating tramcars. The 2½-mile ascent through Chino Canyon, the steepest vertical cable ride in the United States, brings you to an elevation of 8,516 feet in less than 20 minutes. On clear days, which are common, the view stretches 75 miles—from the peak of Mt. San Gorgonio in the north, to the Salton Sea in the southeast. Stepping out into the snow at the summit is a winter treat. At the top, a bit below the summit of Mt. San Jacinto, are several diversions. Mountain Station has an observation deck, two restaurants, a cocktail lounge, apparel and gift shops, picnic facilities, a small wildlife exhibit, and a theater that screens a worthwhile 22-minute film on the history of the tramway. Take advantage of free guided and self-guided nature walks through the adjacent Mount San Jacinto State Park and Wilderness, or if there's snow on the ground, rent skis, snowshoes, or snow tubes (inner tubes or similar contraptions for sliding down hills). The tramway generally closes for maintenance in mid-September. ■TIP→ Ride-and-dine packages are available in late afternoon. The tram is a popular attraction; to avoid a two-hour or longer wait, arrive before the first car leaves in the morning. ⊠ *1 Tramway Rd., off N. Palm Canyon Dr. (Hwy. 111)* ☎ *760/325–1391, 888/515–8726* ⊕ *www.pstramway.com* ☜ *$23.95, ride-and-dine package $36* ☉ *Tramcars depart at least every 30 mins from 10 am weekdays and 8 am weekends; last car up leaves at 8 pm, last car down leaves Mountain Station at 9:45 pm.*

☾ Fodor's Choice ★ **Palm Springs Air Museum.** The museum's impressive collection of World War II aircraft includes a B-17 Flying Fortress bomber, a P-51 Mustang, a Lockheed P-38, and a Grumman TBF Avenger. Among the cool exhibits are model warships, a Pearl Harbor diorama, and a Grumman Goose into which kids can crawl. Photos, artifacts, memorabilia, and uniforms are also on display, and educational programs take place on Saturdays. Flight demonstrations are scheduled regularly. ⊠ *745 N.*

Gene Autry Trail, Hwy. 111 ☎ *760/778–6262* ⊕ *www.air-museum.org* 🎟 *$15* ⊙ *Daily 10–5.*

★ **Palm Springs Art Museum.** The museum displays contemporary and traditional art in bright, open galleries. The permanent collection includes a shimmering exhibition of contemporary studio glass, highlighted by works by Dale Chihuly, Ginny Ruffner, and William Morris. You'll also find handcrafted furniture by the late actor George Montgomery, an array of enormous Native American baskets, and works by artists like Allen Houser, Arlo Namingha, and Fritz Scholder; the museum also displays significant works of 20th-century sculpture by Henry Moore, Marino Marina, Deborah Butterfield, and Mark Di Suvero. The Annenberg Theater presents plays, concerts, lectures, operas, and other cultural events. ⊠ *101 Museum Dr., off W. Tahquitz Canyon Dr.* ☎ *760/322–4800* ⊕ *www.psmuseum.org* 🎟 *$12.50, free Thurs. 4–8 during Villagefest* ⊙ *Tues.–Sun. 10–5.*

Palm Springs Walk of Stars. Along the walk, more than 300 bronze stars are embedded in the sidewalk (à la Hollywood Walk of Fame) to honor celebrities with a Palm Springs connection. Frank, Elvis, Marilyn, Dinah, Lucy, Ginger, Liz, and Liberace have all received their due. Those still around to walk the Walk and see their stars include Nancy Sinatra, Kathy Griffin, and Adam West. ⊠ *Palm Canyon Dr., around Tahquitz Canyon Way, and Tahquitz Canyon Way, between Palm Canyon and Indian Canyon Drs.* ⊕ *www.palmsprings.com/stars.*

Tahquitz Canyon. On ranger-led tours of this secluded canyon on the Agua Caliente Reservation, you can view a spectacular 60-foot waterfall, rock art, ancient irrigation systems, and native wildlife and plants. Tours are conducted several times daily; participants must be able to navigate 100 steep steps. (You can also take a self-guided tour of the 1.8-mile trail.) A visitor center at the canyon entrance screens a video, displays artifacts, and sells maps. ⊠ *500 W. Mesquite Ave., west of S. Palm Canyon Dr.* ☎ *760/416–7044* ⊕ *www.tahquitzcanyon.com* 🎟 *$12.50* ⊙ *Oct.–June, daily 7:30–5; July–Sept., Fri.–Sun. 7:30–5.*

Village Green Heritage Center. Three small museums at the Village Green Heritage Center illustrate early life in Palm Springs. The **Agua Caliente Cultural Museum,** the centerpiece, traces the culture and history of the Cahuilla tribe with several exhibits. The **McCallum Adobe** holds the collection of the Palm Springs Historical Society. **Rudy's General Store Museum** is a re-creation of a 1930s general store. ⊠ *219–221 S. Palm Canyon Dr.* ☎ *760/778–1079* 🎟 *Agua Caliente free, McCallum $2, Rudy's $1* ⊙ *Agua Caliente weekdays 8–5; call for others.*

WHERE TO EAT

$$$$ ✕ **Copley's on Palm Canyon.** Chef Manion Copley prepares innovative
MODERN   cuisine in a setting that's straight out of Hollywood—a hacienda once
AMERICAN   owned by Cary Grant. Dine in the clubby house or under the stars in the garden. Start with appetizers such as roasted beet and warm goat cheese salad or one of the Hawaiian ahi tacos. Oh My Lobster Pot Pie is the biggest hit on an entrée menu that also includes an elegant rack of lamb crusted with parsley and lavender. Save room for Copley's sweet and savory herb ice creams. ⑤ *Average main: $33* ⊠ *621 N. Palm*

Canyon Dr., at E. Granvia Valmonte ☎ 760/327–9555 ⊕ www. copleyspalmsprings.com ⌂ Reservations essential ⊘ No lunch.

$$ ✕ **El Mirasol.** Chef Filipe Castaneda
MODERN opened his second Mexican res-
MEXICAN taurant at the north end of Palm
Springs in 2011—he's been serv-
ing overflow crowds for years at
a simple café at the other end of
town. His latest venture, within the
Los Arboles Hotel, which he owns,
is outside on a charming patio set
amid flower gardens and shaded by
red umbrellas. Castaneda prepares
classic combinations of tacos, tama-
les, and enchiladas, along with spe-
cialties such as double-cooked pork
and chicharrones (fried pork rinds)
with tomatillo salsa. Vegetarian
offerings include delightfully deli-
cate spinach enchiladas. $ Average
main: $18 ⊠ 140 E. Palm Canyon
Dr., at E. Avenida Olancha ☎ 760/459–3605.

> ### SINATRA AND THE DESERT
>
> Old Blue Eyes probably had more haunts in these parts than any other celebrity. He owned two homes, one of them a mid-century modern jewel (Twin Palms Estate, at 1148 East Alejo Road), and called this area home for more than five decades. He frequented Melvyn's Restaurant and Lounge at the Ingleside Hotel (200 West Ramon Road)—ask Melvyn to tell you about Sinatra's pre-wedding dinner with Barbara Marx in 1976—as well as Riccio's (then on East Palm Canyon Drive, but now at 495 North Palm Canyon Drive) and Lord Fletcher's (70–385 Highway 111, Rancho Mirage).

$$$$ ✕ **The Falls.** A mile-long martini menu lures a chic, moneyed crowd to
STEAKHOUSE this hot spot overlooking Palm Canyon Drive. Reserve well in advance
for one of the outdoor balcony tables to get the best view. The restau-
rant specializes in dry aged beef, but you can also get seafood and chops,
and there are vegetarian choices. Steaks and chops are prepared your
way with a selection of sides that includes mac and cheese, roasted pota-
toes, and steamed asparagus with hollandaise sauce. Go early for the
nightly happy hour (between 4 and 6:30), when items on the bar menu
are half price—or hang around late to catch the action at the Martini
Dome bar. $ Average main: $36 ⊠ 155 S. Palm Canyon Dr., near W.
Arenas Rd. ☎ 760/416–8664 ⊕ thefallsrestaurants.com ⌂ Reservations
essential ⊘ No lunch.

$$$$ ✕ **Le Vallauris.** A longtime favorite that occupies the historic Roberson
FRENCH House, Le Vallauris is popular with ladies who lunch, all of whom get a
★ hug from the maître d'. The menu changes daily, and each day it's hand-
written on a white board. Lunch entrées might include perfectly rare
tuna niçoise salad, or grilled whitefish with Dijon mustard sauce. Din-
ner might bring a sublime smoked salmon, sautéed calves' liver, roasted
quail with orange sauce, or rack of lamb. There are also weekly prix-fixe
menus, with and without wine, for lunch and dinner. The restaurant
has a lovely tree-shaded garden. On cool winter evenings, request a
table by the fireplace. $ Average main: $40 ⊠ 385 W. Tahquitz Canyon
Way, west of Palm Canyon Dr. ☎ 760/325–5059 ⊕ www.levallauris.
com ⌂ Reservations essential ⊘ Closed July and Aug.

$$$ ✕ **Matchbox Vintage Pizza Bistro.** The name says pizza, but this bistro
ITALIAN also serves interesting salads topped with grilled tuna, and a selection

of sandwiches with fillings like chicken with portobello mushrooms or Angus beef with Gorgonzola. Main courses include bone-in cowboy-cut pork chop, adult macaroni and cheese, and fish-and-chips. The pizzas are made just about any way you'd like, including vegetarian. On the second-floor overlooking the action on Palm Canyon Drive, this is a great place to go for cocktails and small plates. ⑤ *Average main: $24* ⊠ *155 S. Palm Canyon Dr., near W. Arenas Rd.* ☎ *760/778–6000* ⊕ *www.matchboxpalmsprings.com* ⊗ *No lunch Sun.–Wed.*

$$$
MODERN
AMERICAN
★

✕ **Purple Palm.** The hottest tables in Palm Springs are those that surround the pool at the Colony Palms Hotel, where the hip and elite pay homage to Purple Gang mobster Al Wertheimer, who reportedly built the hotel in the mid-1930s. Now it's a casual, convivial place where you can dine alfresco surrounded by a tropical garden. The dinner menu is about evenly divided between large plates—among them roasted Jidori chicken, bouillabaisse, or Angus rib-eye steak—and small plates like fried avocado, mussels and clams, and black truffle mac and cheese. The impressive wine list roams the globe. The restaurant is also open for breakfast and lunch. ■ **TIP→ A visit to the ladies room is a must for Paul Newman fans. The loo holds a fabulous black-and-white image of a very young Newman.** ⑤ *Average main: $31* ⊠ *572 N. Indian Canyon Dr., at E. Granvia Valmonte* ☎ *800/557–2187* ⊕ *www.colonypalmshotel.com* ⚐ *Reservations essential.*

$$$$
BASQUE
Fodor's Choice
★

✕ **Tinto.** The talented Jose Garces, a Food Channel Iron Chefs winner and the recipient of a James Beard Award, takes small plates to a new level at Tinto, his Spanish Basque wine bar in the Saguaro Hotel. Garces concocts such delightfully exotic items as bleu de Basque cheese, marinated white anchovies with pine nuts, succulent pork belly, and a mini short-rib sandwich with celery aioli. Order two or three plates per person and share, or select the chef's tasting menu, available with wine pairing. This is a fun place where tables are closely spaced, so dinner becomes a party. The extensive wine list showcases Spanish vintages. Weekday breakfast and weekend brunch are served. ⑤ *Average main: $55* ⊠ *1800 E. Palm Canyon Dr., at S. Sunshine Way* ☎ *760/323-1711* ⊕ *www.jdvhotels.com/dining/riverside/tinto* ⚐ *Reservations essential.*

$$$
INTERNATIONAL

✕ **The Tropicale.** Tucked onto a side-street corner, the Tropicale is a mid-century–style watering hole with a contemporary vibe. The bar and main dining room hold cozy leather booths while flowers and water features brighten the outdoor area. The menu roams the world with small and large plates, from the miso-glazed salmon rice bowl, to the Kahlua barbecue pork porterhouse with mashed plantains, to the carne asada pizza. ⑤ *Average main: $28* ⊠ *330 E. Amado Rd., at N. Calle Encilia* ☎ *760/866–1952* ⊕ *www.thetropicale.com* ⚐ *Reservations essential* ⊗ *No lunch.*

$$
MEDITERRANEAN

✕ **Zini Café Med.** One of the best people-watching spots in Palm Springs, this sidewalk café is a fine choice before or after seeing the Follies. The lunch and dinner menus feature a wide selection of small plates in addition to hearty items such as pasta, pizza, *pollo alla diavolo* (macadamia-crusted chicken breast), and veal scaloppini. On a separate tapas menu you can find some surprises: spicy chickpeas with Mediterranean chicken sausage, layered grilled artichoke, asparagus topped with a fried egg, or spicy lime drizzled shrimp. $ *Average main: $20* ✉ *140 S. Palm Canyon Dr., at La Plaza* ☎ *760/325–9464* ⊕ *www. zinicafe.com.*

WHERE TO STAY

For expanded reviews, facilities, and current deals, visit Fodors.com.

$$$
RESORT

▦ **Ace Hotel and Swim Club.** Take a trip back to the 1960s at the Ace: With the hotel's vintage feel and hippie-chic decor, it would be no surprise to find the Grateful Dead playing in the bar. **Pros:** Amigo Room has late-night dining; poolside stargazing deck; scooter rentals available on-site. **Cons:** party atmosphere not for everyone; limited amenities; casual staff and service. **TripAdvisor:** "hipster paradise," "vintage feel," "super relaxing." $ *Rooms from: $179* ✉ *701 E. Palm Canyon Dr.* ☎ *760/325–9900* ⊕ *www.acehotel.com/palmsprings* ⤴ *180 rooms, 8 suites* ▯ *No meals.*

> ### TRIBAL WEALTH
>
> The Agua Caliente band of Cahuilla Indians owns nearly half the land in the Palm Springs area. Wanting to encourage the railroad to bring their trains through the desert, Congress granted half the land to the railroad and the other half to the Native Americans. The Cahuilla were granted all the even-numbered one-square-mile sections—but they were unable to develop the land for years due to litigation. The resulting patchwork of developed and vacant land can still be seen today (though the Cahuilla are making up for lost time by opening new hotels and casinos).

$
HOTEL

▦ **Alcazar Palm Springs.** Amid an area known as the Movie Colony, Alcazar embodies the desert's popular mid-century-modern design style; the ample, blazing-white guest rooms here wrap around a sparkling pool. **Pros:** walking distance of downtown; parking on-site; bikes available. **Cons:** limited service; wall air-conditioners. **TripAdvisor:** "gorgeous setting," "beautiful boutique hotel," "charm and tranquility." $ *Rooms from: $79* ✉ *622 N. Indian Canyon Dr.* ☎ *760/318–9850* ⊕ *www. alcazarpalmsprings.com* ⤴ *34* ▯ *Breakfast.*

$
B&B/INN

▦ **Casa Cody.** The service is personal and gracious at this large B&B near the Palm Springs Art Museum; spacious studios and one- and two-bedroom suites hold Santa Fe–style rustic furnishings. **Pros:** family-size digs; friendly ambience; good value. **Cons:** old buildings; limited amenities. **TripAdvisor:** "perfect for a lazy weekend," "still holds its charm," "perfect setting for relaxation." $ *Rooms from: $99* ✉ *175 S. Cahuilla Rd.* ☎ *760/320–9346, 800/231–2639* ⊕ *www.casacody.com* ⤴ *16 rooms, 7 suites, 2 cottages* ▯ *Breakfast.*

$$$
HOTEL

▦ **Colony Palms Hotel.** This hotel has been a hip place to stay since the 1930s, when gangster Al Wertheimer built it to front his casino, bar, and brothel. **Pros:** glam with a swagger; attentive staff; all that history. **Cons:** high noise level outside; not for families with young children. **TripAdvisor:** "a piece of heaven," "great ambience," "wonderful retreat." $ *Rooms from: $179* ✉ *572 N. Indian Canyon Dr.* ☎ *760/969–1800, 800/577–2187* ⊕ *www.colonypalmshotel.com* ⤴ *43 rooms, 3 suites, 8 casitas* ▯ *No meals.*

$$
B&B/INN

▦ **East Canyon Hotel & Spa.** Serving a primarily gay clientele, this classy resort is the only one in the desert with an in-house, full-service spa exclusively for men. **Pros:** elegant laid-back feel; attentive service; complimentary poolside cocktails. **Cons:** spa is for men only. **TripAdvisor:** "an oasis in an oasis," "great vibe," "clean and relaxing."⑤ *Rooms from: $134* ⊠ *288 E. Camino Monte Vista* ☎ *760/320–1928, 877/324–6835* ⊕ *www.eastcanyonps.com* ⮌ *15 rooms, 1 suite* ⑩ *Breakfast.*

$$$　🔆 **Hyatt Regency Suites Palm Springs.** The best-situated downtown hotel
HOTEL　in Palm Springs, the Hyatt has rooms where you can watch the sun rise over the city or set behind the mountains from your bedroom's balcony. **Pros:** underground parking; the fireplace in the bar; baby services. **Cons:** lots of business travelers; some street noise. **TripAdvisor:** "nice hotel," "great location," "relaxing stay."⑤ *Rooms from: $174* ⊠ *285 N. Palm Canyon Dr.* ☎ *760/322–9000, 800/633–7313* ⊕ *www. hyattpalmsprings.com* ⮌ *197 suites* ⑩ *No meals.*

$$　🔆 **Movie Colony Hotel.** Designed in 1935 by Albert Frey, this intimate
B&B/INN　hotel evokes mid-century minimalist ambience. **Pros:** architectural icon; happy hour; cruiser bikes. **Cons:** close quarters; off the beaten path; staff not available 24 hours. **TripAdvisor:** "cute and convenient," "wonderful hidden gem," "stylish and low key."⑤ *Rooms from: $135* ⊠ *726 N. Indian Canyon Dr.* ☎ *760/320–6340, 888/953–5700* ⊕ *www. moviecolonyhotel.com* ⮌ *13 rooms, 3 suites* ⑩ *Breakfast.*

$$　🔆 **Orbit In Hotel.** Step back to 1957 at this hip inn, located on a quiet
B&B/INN　backstreet downtown. **Pros:** saltwater pool; in-room spa services; Orbitini cocktail hour. **Cons:** best for couples; style not to everyone's taste; staff not available 24 hours. **TripAdvisor:** "exceptional stay," "good old-fashioned service," "splendid oasis."⑤ *Rooms from: $149* ⊠ *562 W. Arenas Rd.* ☎ *760/323–3585, 877/996–7248* ⊕ *www.orbitin.com* ⮌ *9 rooms* ⑩ *Breakfast.*

$$$$　🔆 **The Parker Palm Springs.** A cacophony of color and over-the-top con-
RESORT　temporary art assembled by New York designer Jonathan Adler, this
★　hip hotel appeals to a stylish, L.A.-based clientele. **Pros:** fun in the sun; celebrity clientele; high jinks at the Palm Springs Yacht Club Spa. **Cons:** pricey drinks and wine; long walks in the hot sun to get anywhere. **TripAdvisor:** "beautiful setting," "pure escapism," "exceeded my expectations."⑤ *Rooms from: $285* ⊠ *4200 E. Palm Canyon Dr.* ☎ *760/770–5000, 800/543–4300* ⊕ *www.theparkerpalmsprings.com* ⮌ *131 rooms, 13 suites* ⑩ *Breakfast.*

$$$$　🔆 **Riviera Resort & Spa.** A party place built in 1958 and renovated in
RESORT　2008, the Riviera attracts young, well-heeled, bikini-clad guests who hang out around the pool by day and the Bikini Bar by night. **Pros:** personal beachy fire pits throughout the property; hip vibe; sublime spa. **Cons:** high noise level outdoors; party atmosphere; location at north end of Palm Springs. **TripAdvisor:** "love the lobby," "winded splendor," "it's Vegas in Palm Springs."⑤ *Rooms from: $259* ⊠ *1600 N. Indian Canyon Dr.* ☎ *760/327–8311* ⊕ *www.psriviera.com* ⮌ *406 rooms, 43 suites* ⑩ *No meals.*

$$$$　🔆 **Smoke Tree Ranch.** A world apart from Palm Springs' pulsating urban
ALL-INCLUSIVE　village, the area's most exclusive resort occupies 400 pristine desert
☾　acres, surrounded by mountains and unspoiled vistas. **Pros:** priceless
★　privacy; simple luxury; many recreation choices include horseback riding, lawn bowling, hiking, and jogging. **Cons:** no glitz or glamour;

limited entertainment options; family atmosphere not for everyone. **TripAdvisor:** "lovely property," "the real deal," "we are going back." [$] *Rooms from: $315* ⊠ *1850 Smoke Tree La.* ☎ *760/327–1221, 800/787–3922* ⊕ *www.smoketreeranch.com* ⤳ *49 cottages, includes 18 suites* ⊘ *Closed Apr.–late Oct.* ⦿ *Multiple meal plans.*

$

HOTEL

▦ **Vagabond Inn.** Rooms are smallish at this centrally located motel, but they're clean, comfortable, and a good value. **Pros:** quiet; kids stay free. **Cons:** limited amenities, facilities, and service. **TripAdvisor:** "great location," "no frills," "quiet." [$] *Rooms from: $62* ⊠ *1699 S. Palm Canyon Dr.* ☎ *760/325–7211, 800/522–1555* ⊕ *www.vagabondinn.com* ⤳ *117 rooms* ⦿ *Breakfast.*

$$$$

RESORT

★

▦ **The Viceroy Palm Springs.** Stepping into the Viceroy you're greeted with a bright, sunny white-and-yellow ambience, reminiscent of a sun-filled desert day. **Pros:** poolside cabanas; celebrity clientele. **Cons:** uneven service; popular wedding site. **TripAdvisor:** "drop-dead gorgeous," "excellent service," "friendly people everywhere." [$] *Rooms from: $330* ⊠ *415 S. Belardo Rd.* ☎ *760/320–4117, 800/327–3687* ⊕ *www. viceroypalmsprings.com* ⤳ *67 rooms, 12 villas.*

$$$$

B&B/INN

★

▦ **Willows Historic Palm Springs Inn.** Within walking distance of most village attractions, this luxurious hillside B&B is next door to the Palm Springs Art Museum and near dining and shopping options. **Pros:** ultra luxurious; sublime service. **Cons:** closed June–Sept.; pricey. **TripAdvisor:** "desert paradise," "mostly perfect," "beautiful." [$] *Rooms from: $325* ⊠ *412 W. Tahquitz Canyon Way* ☎ *760/320–0771, 800/966–9597* ⊕ *www.thewillowspalmsprings.com* ⤳ *8 rooms* ⦿ *Breakfast.*

NIGHTLIFE AND THE ARTS

NIGHTLIFE

Ace Hotel and Swim Club. Events are held here nearly every night, including film screenings, live concerts, DJs with dancing, parties, and seasonal entertainment. Many are free, and quite a few are family friendly. ⊠ *701 E. Palm Canyon Dr., at Calle Palo Fierro* ☎ *760/325–9900* ⊕ *www.acehotel.com.*

Casino Morongo. A 20-minute drive west of Palm Springs, this casino has 2,000 slot machines, video games, the Vibe nightclub, plus Vegas-style shows. ⊠ *49500 Seminole Dr., off I–10, Cabazon* ☎ *800/252–4499, 951/849–3080.*

Hair of the Dog English Pub. Drawing a young crowd that likes to tip back English ales and ciders, this bar is lively and popular. ⊠ *238 N. Palm Canyon Dr., near E. Amado Rd.* ☎ *760/323–9890.*

Spa Resort Casino. This resort holds 1,000 slot machines, blackjack tables, a high-limit room, four restaurants, two bars, and the Cascade Lounge for entertainment. ⊠ *401 E. Amado Rd., at N. Calle Encilia* ☎ *888/999–1995.*

Village Pub. With live entertainment, DJs, and friendly service, this popular bar caters to a young crowd. ⊠ *266 S. Palm Canyon Dr., at Baristo Rd.* ☎ *760/323–3265.*

Zelda's Nightclub. A Palm Springs institution, Zelda's moved south in 2010, but the high-energy DJs, dancing, and drinking are still going strong and the dance floor is still thumping with Latin, hip hop, and

CLOSE UP

Palm Springs Modernism

Some of the world's most forward-looking architects designed and constructed buildings around Palm Springs between 1940 and 1970, and modernism, also popular elsewhere in California in the years after World War II, became an ideal fit for desert living, because it minimizes the separation between indoors and outdoors. See-through houses with glass exterior walls are common. Oversize flat roofs provide shade from the sun, and many buildings' sculptural forms reflect nearby landforms. The style is notable for elegant informality, clean lines, and simple landscaping. Emblematic structures in Palm Springs include public buildings, hotels, stores, banks, and private residences.

Most obvious to visitors are three buildings that are part of the Palm Springs Aerial Tramway complex, built in the 1960s. Albert Frey, a Swiss-born architect, designed the soaring A-frame Tramway Gas Station, visually echoing the pointed peaks behind it. Frey also created the glass-walled Valley Station, from which you get your initial view of the Coachella Valley before you board the tram to the Mountain Station, designed by E. Stewart Williams.

Frey, a Palm Springs resident for more than 60 years, also designed the indoor–outdoor City Hall, Fire Station #1, and numerous houses. You

can see his second home, perched atop stilts on the hillside above the Palm Springs Art Museum; it affords a sweeping view of the Coachella Valley through glass walls. The classy Movie Colony Hotel, one of the first buildings Frey designed in the desert, may seem like a typical 1950s motel with rooms surrounding a swimming pool now, but when it was built in 1935, it was years ahead of its time.

Donald Wexler, who honed his vision with Los Angeles architect Richard Neutra, brought new ideas about the use of materials to the desert, where he teamed up with William Cody on a number of projects, including the terminal at the Palm Springs airport. Many of Wexler's buildings have soaring overhanging roofs, designed to provide shade from the blazing desert sun. Wexler also experimented with steel framing back in 1961, but the metal proved too expensive. Seven of his steel-frame houses can be seen in a neighborhood off Indian Canyon and Frances drives.

The Palm Springs Modern Committee sponsors Modernism Week in mid-February, when you can visit some of the most remarkable buildings in the area. The committee also publishes a map and driving guide to 52 historic buildings, which is available for $5 at the Palm Springs Visitor Information Center or at ⊕ *psmodcom.org*.

---

sounds from the 60s, 70s, and 80s. The club offers bottle service in the VIP Sky Box. ⊠ *611 S. Palm Canyon Dr., at E. Camino Parocela* ☎ *760/325–2375* ⊕ *www.zeldasnightclub.com* ⊗ *Closed Sun.*

GAY AND LESBIAN

The Dinah. In late March, when the world's finest female golfers hit the links for the Annual LPGA Kraft Nabisco Championship in Rancho Mirage, thousands of lesbians converge on Palm Springs for a four-day

Palm Springs is a golfer's paradise: the area is home to more than 125 courses.

party popularly known as The Dinah. ⇨ *Kraft Nabisco Championship in Rancho Mirage.* ☎ *888/923–4624* ⊕ *www.clubskirts.com.*

Hunter's Video Bar. Drawing a young gay and straight crowd, Hunter's is a clubbing-scene mainstay. ⊠ *302 E. Arenas Rd., at Calle Encilia* ☎ *760/323–0700* ⊕ *http://huntersnightclubs.com.*

Toucans Tiki Lounge. A friendly place with a tropical jungle in a rainforest setting, Toucans serves festive drinks and has live entertainment and theme nights. ⊠ *2100 N. Palm Canyon Dr., at W. Via Escuela* ☎ *760/416–7584.*

White Party Palm Springs. Held during spring break, the White Party draws tens of thousands of gay men from around the country to the Palm Springs area for four days of parties and events. ⊕ *jeffreysanker. com.*

THE ARTS
Annenberg Theater. Broadway shows, opera, lectures, Sunday-afternoon chamber concerts, and other events take place here. ⊠ *Palm Springs Art Museum, 101 N. Museum Dr., at W. Tahquitz Canyon Way* ☎ *760/325–4490* ⊕ *www.psmuseum.org.*

Fabulous Palm Springs Follies. For years the hottest ticket in the desert, the Follies sells out 10 weekly performances from November through May. The vaudeville-style revue, about half of which focuses on mid-century nostalgia, stars extravagantly costumed, retired (but very fit) showgirls, comedians, singers, and dancers. ⊠ *Plaza Theatre, 128 S. Palm Canyon Dr., at La Plaza* ☎ *760/327–0225* ⊕ *www.palmspringsfollies. com* ⊠ *$50–$93*

Modernism Week. Each February, the desert communities celebrate the work of the architects and designers who created the Palm Springs "look" in the 1940s, 1950s, and 1960s. Described these days as mid-century modern (you'll also see the term "desert modernism" used), these structures were created by Albert Frey, Richard Neutra, William F. Cody, John Lautner, and other notables. The 11-day event features lectures, a modernism show, films, vintage car and trailer shows, galas, and home and garden tours. ☎ 760/322–2502 ⊕ www.modernismweek. com.

Palm Springs International Film Festival. In mid-January this festival brings stars and more than 150 feature films from 25 countries, plus panel discussions, short films, and documentaries, to the Annenberg Theater and other venues. ☎ 760/322–2930, 800/898–7256 ⊕ www.psfilmfest.org.

Plaza Theatre. The Spanish-style Plaza Theatre opened in 1936 with a glittering premiere of the MGM film *Camille*. In the 1940s and 50s, it presented some of Hollywood's biggest stars, including Bob Hope and Bing Crosby. Home of the Fabulous Palm Springs Follies, it is favored by fans of old-time radio even in the off-season. ⊠ 128 S. Palm Canyon Dr., at La Plaza ☎ 760/327–0225 ⊕ www.psfollies.com.

SPORTS AND THE OUTDOORS
BICYCLING
Many hotels and resorts have bicycles available for guest use.

Big Wheel Tours. Rent cruisers, performance road bikes, and mountain bikes from this agency that also offers road tours to La Quinta Loop, Joshua Tree National Park, and the San Andreas fault. Off-road tours are available, too. The company have no retail outlet but will pick up and deliver bikes to your hotel and supply you with area maps. ☎ 760/779–1837 ⊕ www.bwbtours.com.

Palm Springs Recreation Division. This organization can provide you with maps of city bike trails. Printable versions of several routes are available on the website. ⊠ 401 S. Pavilion Way ☎ 760/323–8272 ⊕ www. palmspringsca.gov/index.aspx?page=752 ⊙ Weekdays 7:30–6.

GOLF
Palm Springs Desert Resorts Convention and Visitors Bureau. Palm Springs hosts more than 100 golf tournaments annually; the bureau's website posts listings. ⊕ www.palmspringsusa.com.

Affordable Palm Springs TeeTimes. This service matches golfers with courses and arranges tee times. If you know which course you want to play, you can book online up to 60 days in advance. ☎ 760/324–5012 ⊕ www.palmspringsteetimes.com.

Indian Canyons Golf Resort. Two 18-hole courses designed by Casey O'Callaghan, Amy Alcott, and William P. Bell, this spot, at the base of the mountains, is operated by the Aqua Caliente tribe. ⊠ 1097 E. Murray Canyon Dr., at Kings Rd. E ☎ 760/833–8700 ⊕ www. indiancanyonsgolf.com.

Tahquitz Creek Golf Resort. The resort has two 18-hole, par-72 courses and a 50-space driving range. Greens fees, including cart and refreshments, run $59 to $79. ⊠ *1885 Golf Club Dr., at 34th Ave.* ☎ *760/328–1005* ⊕ *www.tahquitzcreek.com.*

Tommy Jacobs' Bel Air Greens Country Club. This is a 9-hole executive course. The greens fee is $15 to $30 for walking; carts are $12. ⊠ *1001 S. El Cielo Rd., at E. Mesquite Ave.* ☎ *760/322–6062.*

SPAS

Spa Resort Casino. Taking the waters at this resort is an indulgent pleasure. You can spend a full day enjoying a five-step, wet-and-dry treatment that includes a mineral bath, steam, sauna, and eucalyptus inhalation. The program allows you to take fitness classes and use the gym and, for an extra charge, add massage or body treatments. During the week, the spa admission rate is $40 for a full day, less for hotel guests or if you combine it with a treatment; on weekends you cannot purchase a day pass without booking a treatment. ⊠ *100 N. Indian Canyon Dr., at E. Tahquitz Canyon Way* ☎ *760/778–1772* ⊕ *www. sparesortcasino.com.*

SHOPPING

Desert Hills Premium Outlets. About 20 miles west of Palm Springs in Cabazon lies this outlet center with more than 130 brand-name discount fashion shops, including J. Crew, Giorgio Armani, Gucci, and Prada. ⊠ *48400 Seminole Rd., off I–10, Cabazon* ☎ *951/849–6641* ⊕ *www.premiumoutlets.com.*

Uptown Heritage Galleries & Antiques District. A loose-knit collection of consignment and secondhand shops, galleries, and lively restaurants extends north of Palm Springs' main shopping area. The theme here is decidedly retro. Many businesses sell mid-century modern furniture and decorator items, and others carry clothing and estate jewelry. ⊠ *N. Palm Canyon Dr., between Amado Rd. and Vista Chino* ☎ ⊕ *www. palmcanyondrive.org.*

CATHEDRAL CITY

2 miles southeast of Palm Springs on Hwy. 111.

One of the fastest-growing communities in the desert, Cathedral City is more residential than tourist-oriented. However, the city has a number of good restaurants and entertainment venues with moderate prices.

GETTING HERE AND AROUND

Cathedral City lies due east of the Palm Springs International Airport. Much of the city is suburban/residential community with large and small malls everywhere. Main streets north and south are Landau and Date Palm; west to east are Ramon Road, Dinah Shore, and Highway 111.

EXPLORING

Boomers Palm Springs. At this theme park you can play miniature golf, drive bumper boats, climb a rock wall, drive a go-kart, swing in the batting cages, test your skill in an arcade, and play video games. ⊠ *67-700 E. Palm Canyon Dr., at Cree Rd.* ☎ *760/770–7522* ⊕ *www. boomerspark.com* ⊠ *$6–$8 per activity, $25 day passes* ☉ *Mon.–Thurs. 11–9, Fri. 11–10, Sat. 10–10, Sun. 10–11.*

Pickford Salon. This small museum inside a multiplex celebrates silent film star Mary Pickford. Items on display include her 1976 Oscar for contributions to the film industry, a gown she wore in the 1927 film *Dorothy Vernon of Haddon Hall,* and dinnerware from Pickfair, the Beverly Hills mansion she shared with actor Douglas Fairbanks. Pickford herself produced one of the film bios the Salon screens. ⊠ *Mary Pickford Theatre, 36-850 Pickfair St., at Buddy Rogers Ave.* ☎ *760/328-7100* ☎ *Free* ☉ *Daily 10:30 am–midnight.*

WHERE TO EAT

$$$

BISTRO

✕ **Cello's.** A favorite of locals and critics, this art-laden café in a strip mall serves modern twists on classics such as the crab Napoleon and smoked-trout appetizers, potato risotto, chicken caprese, and eggplant Parmesan. The voluptuous cioppino in a thick marinara sauce teems with shellfish. There's a community table with about eight chairs; sit here if you're dining alone or want to meet some locals. The owner, Bonnie Barley, is as friendly as they come. ⑤ *Average main: $23* ⊠ *35-943 Date Palm Dr., at Gerald Ford Dr.* ☎ *760/328–5353* ⚱ *Reservations essential* ☉ *No lunch.*

$$$

ITALIAN

✕ **Trilussa.** Locals gather at this San Francisco–style storefront restaurant for delicious food, big drinks, and a friendly welcome. The congenial bar is busy during happy hour, after which diners drift to their nicely spaced tables indoors and out. The long menu changes daily, but staples include antipasti, homemade pasta, pizza, risotto, veal, and fish. All come with an Italian accent. ⑤ *Average main: $27* ⊠ *68718 E. Palm Canyon Dr., at Monty Hall Dr.* ☎ *760/328–2300* ⚱ *Reservations essential.*

DESERT HOT SPRINGS

9 miles north of Palm Springs on Gene Autry Trail.

Desert Hot Springs' famous hot mineral waters, thought by some to have curative powers, bubble up at temperatures of 90°F to 148°F and flow into the wells of more than 40 hotel spas.

GETTING HERE AND AROUND

Desert Hot Springs lies due north of Palm Springs. Take Gene Autry Trail north to Interstate 10, where the street name changes to Palm. Continue north to Pierson Blvd., the town's center.

EXPLORING

Cabot's Pueblo Museum. Cabot Yerxa, the man who found the spring that made Desert Hot Springs famous, built a quirky four-story, 35-room pueblo between 1939 and his death in 1965. Now a museum run by the city of Desert Hot Springs—Yerxa was the town's first mayor—the Hopi-inspired adobe structure is filled with memorabilia of his time as a homesteader; his encounters with Hollywood celebrities at the nearby Bar-H Ranch; his expedition to the Alaskan gold rush; and many other events. The home, much of it crafted out of materials Yerxa recycled from the desert, can only be seen on hour-long tours. Outside, you can walk the beautiful grounds to a lookout with amazing desert views. ⊠ *67-616 Desert View Ave., at Eliseo Rd.* ☎ *760/329–7610* ⊕ *www.cabotsmuseum.org* ☎ *$11* ☉ *Tues.–Sun. 9–4.*

WHERE TO STAY

For expanded reviews, facilities, and current deals, visit Fodors.com.

$$$ 🏨 **The Spring.** Designed for those who want to detox, lose weight, or
HOTEL take special spa treatments, the Spring caters to guests seeking quiet
and personal service. **Pros:** Exquisite quiet; personal pampering; multi-
national clientele. **Cons:** far from everything; dinner not available;
adults only. **TripAdvisor:** "impeccable service," "private oasis," "very
relaxing." ⑤ *Rooms from: $209* ✉ *12699 Reposo Way* ☎ *760/251–
6700, 877/200–2110* ⊕ *www.the-spring.com* 🛏 *12 rooms* ⦿ *Breakfast.*

RANCHO MIRAGE

4 miles southeast of Cathedral City on Hwy. 111.

14

The rich and famous of Rancho Mirage live in beautiful estates and
patronize elegant resorts and expensive restaurants. Although many
mansions here are concealed behind the walls of gated communities
and country clubs, the grandest of them all, Sunnylands, the Annenberg
residence, is now open to the public as a museum.

The city's golf courses host many high-profile tournaments. You'll find
some of the swankiest resorts in the desert in Rancho Mirage—plus
great golf, and plenty of peace and quiet. For those truly needing to
take things down a notch further, the Betty Ford Center, the famous
drug-and-alcohol rehab center, is also here.

GETTING HERE AND AROUND

Due east of Cathedral City, Rancho Mirage stretches from Ramon Road
on the north to the hills south of Highway 111. The western border is
Da Vall Drive, the eastern one Monterey Avenue. Major cross east–west
streets are Frank Sinatra Drive and Country Club Drive. Most shopping
and dining spots are on Highway 111.

EXPLORING

The Annenberg Retreat at Sunnylands. The stunning 25,000-square-foot
winter home and retreat of the late Ambassador Walter H. and Leonore
Annenberg opened to the public in 2012. You can spend a whole day
enjoying the 9 glorious acres of gardens, or take a guided 90-minute
tour of the residence (reservations essential), a striking mid-century
modern edifice designed by A. Quincy Jones. Floor-to-ceiling windows
frame views of the gardens and Mount San Jacinto, and the expansive
rooms hold furnishings from the 1960s and later, along with impres-
sionist art (some original, some replicas). The history made here is as
captivating as the surroundings. Seven U.S. presidents—from Dwight
Eisenhower to Bill Clinton—and their First Ladies visited Sunnylands;
Ronald and Nancy Reagan were frequent guests. Britain's Queen Eliz-
abeth and Prince Philip also relaxed here, as did Princess Grace of
Monaco and Japanese Prime Minister Toshiki Kaifu. Photos, art, let-
ters, journals, and mementos provide insight into some of the history
that unfolded here. ✉ *37-977 Bob Hope Dr., south of Gerald Ford Dr.*
☎ *760/202–2260* ⊕ *www.sunnylands.org* 🎟 *Tours $35, tickets avail-
able online 2 wks in advance; visitor center and gardens free* ☙ *Sept.–*

May, Thurs.–Sun. 9–4; June and July, Thurs.–Sun. 7–2; free garden tours Fri. 10:30 ☉ *Closed Aug. and during retreats.*

Children's Discovery Museum of the Desert. With instructive hands-on exhibits, this museum contains a miniature rock-climbing area, a magnetic sculpture wall, make-it-and-take-it-apart projects, a rope maze, and an area for toddlers. Kids can paint a VW Bug, work as chefs in the museum's pizza parlor, and build pies out of arts and crafts supplies. Newer exhibits include a racetrack for which kids can assemble their own cars. ✉ *71-701 Gerald Ford Dr., at Bob Hope Dr.* ☎ *760/321-0602* ⊕ *www.cdmod.org* ✉ *$8* ☉ *Jan.–Apr., daily 10–5; May–Dec., Tues.–Sun. 10–5.*

WHERE TO EAT AND STAY

For expanded hotel reviews, facilities, and current deals, visit Fodors.com.

$$
MEXICAN
✕ **Las Casuelas Nuevas.** Hundreds of artifacts from Guadalajara, Mexico, lend festive charm to this casual restaurant, which has an expansive garden patio. Tamales and shellfish dishes are among the specialties. The tequila menu lists dozens of aged and reserve selections, served by the shot or folded into a margarita. There's live entertainment weekends. ⑤ *Average main: $20* ✉ *70-050 Hwy. 111* ☎ *760/328-8844* ⊕ *www.lascasuelasnuevas.com.*

$
RESORT
▦ **Agua Caliente Casino, Resort & Spa.** As in Las Vegas, the Agua Caliente casino is in the lobby, but once you get into the spacious, beautifully appointed rooms of the resort, all of the cacophony at the entrance is forgotten. **Pros:** gorgeous; access to high rollers room offered for $25; value priced. **Cons:** casino ambience; not appropriate for kids. **TripAdvisor:** "can't wait to return," "great rooms," "did not disappoint." ⑤ *Rooms from: $109* ✉ *32-250 Bob Hope Dr.* ☎ *888/999-1995* ⊕ *www.hotwatercasino.com* ⊅ *340 rooms, 26 suites* ▯❮◯ *No meals.*

$$$
RESORT
▦ **Rancho Las Palmas Resort & Spa.** The most family-friendly resort in the desert, this large venue holds Splashtopia, a huge water play-zone. **Pros:** family friendly; trails for hiking and jogging; nightly entertainment. **Cons:** second-floor rooms accessed by very steep stairs; golf course surrounds rooms; resort hosts conventions. **TripAdvisor:** "great relaxing stay," "awesome family time," "fun pool." ⑤ *Rooms from: $190* ✉ *41-000 Bob Hope Dr.* ☎ *760/568-2727, 866/423-1195* ⊕ *www.rancholaspalmas.com* ⊅ *422 rooms, 22 suites.*

$$$
RESORT
▦ **Westin Mission Hills Resort and Spa.** A sprawling resort on 360 acres, the Westin is surrounded by fairways, putting greens, and time-share accommodations. **Pros:** gorgeous grounds; first-class golf facilities; daily activity program for kids. **Cons:** rooms are spread out. **TripAdvisor:** "beautiful," "very nice," "rest and relaxation." ⑤ *Rooms from: $229* ✉ *71333 Dinah Shore Dr.* ☎ *760/328-5955, 800/937-8461* ⊕ *www.westinmissionhills.com* ⊅ *512 rooms, 40 suites* ▯❮◯ *No meals.*

NIGHTLIFE

Agua Caliente Casino. This elegant and surprisingly quiet casino contains 1,400 slot machines, 39 table games, an 18-table poker room, a high-limit room, a no-smoking area, and six restaurants. The Show, the resort's concert theater, presents acts such as Joel McHale, Music of ABBA, and Crosby, Stills and Nash, as well as live sporting events. ✉ *32-250 Bob Hope Dr., at E. Ramon Rd.* ☎ *760/321–2000* ⊕ *www. hotwatercasino.com.*

SPORTS AND THE OUTDOORS

Kraft Nabisco Championship. The best female golfers in the world compete in this championship held in late March. ✉ *Mission Hills Country Club* ☎ *760/324–4546* ⊕ *www.kncgolf.com.*

★ **Westin Mission Hills Resort Golf Club.** Of the two golf courses located here, the 18-hole, par-70 Pete Dye course is especially noteworthy. The club is a member of the Troon Golf Institute, and has several teaching facilities, including the Westin Mission Hills Resort Golf Academy and the *Golf Digest* Golf School. Greens fees are $165 during peak season, including a cart; off-season they are $85. ✉ *71-501 Dinah Shore Dr.* ☎ *760/328–3198* ⊕ *www.westinmissionhillsgolf.com.*

SHOPPING

River at Rancho Mirage. This shopping-dining-entertainment complex holds 20 high-end shops, including Hats Unlimited, Robann's Fine Jewelers, Cohiba Cigar Lounge, and Tulip Hill Winery tasting room, all fronting a faux river with cascading waterfalls. Also here are a 12-screen cinema, an outdoor amphitheater, and eight restaurants, among them Flemings Prime Steakhouse, Babe's Bar-B-Que and Brewery, and P.F. Chang's. ✉ *71-800 Hwy. 111, at Bob Hope Dr.* ☎ *760/341–2711* ⊕ *www.theriveratranchomirage.com.*

PALM DESERT

2 miles southeast of Rancho Mirage on Hwy. 111.

Palm Desert is a thriving retail and business community with popular restaurants, private and public golf courses, and premium shopping. Its stellar sight to see is the Living Desert complex.

GETTING HERE AND AROUND

Palm Desert stretches from north of Interstate 10 to the hills south of Highway 111. West–east cross streets north to south are Frank Sinatra Drive, Country Club Drive (lined on both sides with gated golfing communities), and Fred Waring Drive. Monterey Avenue marks the western boundary, and Washington Street forms the eastern edge.

EXPLORING

★ **El Paseo.** West of and parallel to Highway 111, this mile-long Mediterranean-style avenue is lined with fountains and courtyards, French and Italian fashion boutiques, plus Tommy Bahama's Emporium, Sax's Fifth Avenue, and Gucci. You'll find shoe salons, jewelry stores, children's shops, 23 restaurants, and nearly 20 art galleries. The strip is a pleasant place to stroll, window-shop, people-watch, and exercise your credit cards. During the season a free city-operated bright-yellow shuttle can take you from shop to shop or to your car in the parking lot. ⊠ *Between Monterey and Portola Aves.* ☎ *877/735–7273* ⊕ *www.elpaseo. com.*

☾ ★ **Living Desert.** Come eyeball-to-eyeball with wolves, coyotes, mountain lions, cheetahs, bighorn sheep, golden eagles, warthogs, and owls at the 1,800-acre Living Desert. Easy to challenging scenic trails traverse desert terrain populated with plants of the Mojave, Colo-

rado, and Sonoran deserts in numerous habitats. In recent years, the park has expanded its vision to include Africa. At the 3-acre African WaTuTu village, you'll find a traditional marketplace as well as camels, leopards, hyenas, and other African animals. Children can pet African domesticated animals, including goats and guinea fowl, in a "petting kraal." Gecko Gulch is a children's playground with crawl-through underground tunnels, climb-on snake sculptures, a carousel, and a Discovery Center that holds ancient Pleistocene animal bones. Elsewhere, a small enclosure contains butterflies and hummingbirds, and a cool model train travels through miniatures of historic California towns. ■TIP→ A garden center sells native desert flora, much of which is unavailable elsewhere. ⊠ *47-900 Portola Ave., south from Hwy. 111* ☎ *760/346–5694* ⊕ *www.livingdesert.org* ⊠ *$14.25* ☉ *June–Sept., daily 8–1:30; Oct.–May, daily 9–5.*

Palm Desert Golf Cart Parade. Each October, this parade launches the "season" with a procession of 80 golf carts decked out as floats buzzing up and down El Paseo. ☎ *760/346–6111* ⊕ *www.golfcartparade.com*

Santa Rosa and San Jacinto Mountains National Monument. Administered by the U. S. Bureau of Land Management, this monument protects Peninsula bighorn sheep and other wildlife on 280,000 acres of desert habitat. Stop by the visitor center for an introduction to the site and information about the natural history of the desert. A landscaped garden displays native plants and frames a sweeping view. The well-informed staffers can recommend hiking trails that show off the beauties of the desert. Free guided hikes are offered on Thursday and Saturday. ⊠ *51-500 Hwy. 74* ☎ *760/862–9984* ⊕ *www.ca.blm.gov/palmsprings* ⊠ *Free* ☉ *Thurs–Tues. 9–4.*

WHERE TO EAT AND STAY

For expanded hotel reviews, facilities, and current deals, visit Fodors. com.

$$$$
SEAFOOD
✕ **Pacifica Seafood.** Sublime seafood, rooftop dining, and reduced prices at sunset draw locals to this busy restaurant on the second floor of the Gardens of El Paseo. Seafood that shines in dishes such as butter-poached Maine lobster tail, grilled Pacific swordfish, and barbecued sugar-spiced salmon arrives daily from San Diego; the menu also includes chicken, steaks, and meal-size salads. Preparations feature

sauces such as orange-cumin glaze, Szechuan peppercorn butter, and green curry-coconut. The restaurant bar boasts a 130-bottle collection of vodka. ■ TIP→ **Arrive between 3 and 5:30 to select from the lower-price sunset menu.** ⑤ *Average main: $34* ⊠ *73505 El Paseo* ☎ *760/674–8666* ⊕ *www.pacificaseafoodrestaurant.com* ⌖ *Reservations essential* ⊘ *No lunch June–Aug.*

$$$$
RESORT
☾

⊞ **Desert Springs J. W. Marriott Resort and Spa.** With a dramatic U-shape design, this sprawling convention-oriented hotel is set on 450 landscaped acres. **Pros:** gondola rides to restaurants; Kids Club daily activities; lobby bar is a popular watering hole. **Cons:** crowded in season; extra charges; business-traveler vibe. **TripAdvisor:** "outstanding in every way," "family fun and friendly," "incredible customer service." ⑤ *Rooms from: $269* ⊠ *74-855 Country Club Dr.* ☎ *760/341–2211, 888/538–9459* ⊕ *www.desertspringsresort.com* ⇥ *833 rooms, 51 suites* ⏃ *No meals.*

THE ARTS

McCallum Theatre. The principal cultural venue in the desert, this theater stages productions from fall through spring. *Fiddler on the Roof* has played here; Lily Tomlin and Michael Feinstein have performed, and Joffrey Ballet dancers have pirouetted across the stage. ⊠ *73-000 Fred Waring Dr.* ☎ *760/340–2787* ⊕ *www.mccallumtheatre.com.*

SPORTS AND THE OUTDOORS

BALLOONING

Fantasy Balloon Flights. Operating sunrise excursions over the southern end of the Coachella Valley, Fantasy offers flights ($185 per person) that run from an hour to an hour and a half, followed by a traditional Champagne toast. ⊠ *74-181 Parosella St.* ☎ *760/568–0997* ⊕ *www. fantasyballoonflight.com.*

BICYCLING

Big Wheel Bike Tours. Palm Desert-based Big Wheel delivers rental mountain, three-speed, and tandem bikes to area hotels. The company also conducts full- and half-day escorted on- and off-road bike tours throughout the area, starting at about $95 per person. ☎ *760/779–1837* ⊕ *www.bwbtours.com.*

GOLF

Desert Willow Golf Resort. Praised for its environmentally smart design, this golf resort features pesticide-free and water-thrifty turf grasses. A public course, managed by the City of Palm Desert, has two challenging 18-hole links plus a golf academy. The greens fee is $150–185, including cart. ⊠ *38-995 Desert Willow Dr.* ☎ *760/346–7060* ⊕ *www. desertwillow.com.*

INDIAN WELLS

5 miles east of Palm Desert on Hwy. 111.

For the most part a quiet residential community, Indian Wells is the site of golf and tennis tournaments throughout the year, including the BNP Paribus Open tennis tournament. The city has three hotels that share access to city-owned championship golf and tennis facilities.

GETTING HERE AND AROUND

Indian Wells lies between Palm Desert and La Quinta with most of its hotels, restaurants, and shopping set back from Highway 111. Private country clubs and gated residential communities are tucked along back roads.

WHERE TO STAY

For expanded reviews, facilities, and current deals, visit Fodors.com.

> ### FROM DATES TO DOLLARS
>
> Originally several communities of humble date farmers, 15-square-mile Indian Wells has evolved into one of the country's wealthiest cities. The average family here has a six-figure annual income.

$$$
RESORT
☷ **Hyatt Grand Champions Resort.** This stark-white resort, set adjacent to the Golf Resort at Indian Wells, is one of the grandest in the desert. **Pros:** spacious rooms; excellent business services; butler service in some rooms. **Cons:** big and impersonal; spread out over 45 acres; noisy public areas. **TripAdvisor:** "really nice property and rooms," "very comfortable," "spectacular vistas."⑤ *Rooms from: $209* ⊠ *44-600 Indian Wells La.* ☏ *760/341–1000, 800/552–4386* ⊕ *www.grandchampions. hyatt.com* ⤳ *454 rooms, 26 suites, 40 villas* ⦿ *No meals.*

$$
RESORT
★
☷ **Miramonte Resort & Spa.** A warm bit of Tuscany against a backdrop of the Santa Rosa Mountains characterizes the smallest, most intimate, and most opulent of the Indian Wells hotels. **Pros:** romantic intimacy; gorgeous gardens; discreet service. **Cons:** adult-oriented; limited resort facilities on-site. **TripAdvisor:** "paradise in the middle of the desert," "so relaxing," "beautiful and charming."⑤ *Rooms from: $219* ⊠ *45-000 Indian Wells La.* ☏ *760/341–2200* ⊕ *www.miramonteresort.com* ⤳ *215 rooms* ⦿ *Some meals.*

$$$
RESORT
☺
★
☷ **Renaissance Esmeralda Resort and Spa.** The centerpiece of this luxurious resort, adjacent to the Golf Resort at Indian Wells, is an eight-story atrium lobby, which most rooms open onto. **Pros:** balcony views; adjacent to golf-tennis complex; kids club; bicycles available. **Cons:** higher noise level in rooms surrounding pool; somewhat impersonal ambience. **TripAdvisor:** "great pool," "very central," "perfect desert retreat."⑤ *Rooms from: $209* ⊠ *44-400 Indian Wells La.* ☏ *760/773–4444* ⊕ *www.renaissanceesmeralda.com* ⤳ *538 rooms, 22 suites* ⦿ *No meals.*

SPORTS AND THE OUTDOORS

GOLF

Golf Resort at Indian Wells. Adjacent to the Hyatt Grand Champions Resort, this complex includes the 7,050-yard Celebrity Course, designed by Clive Clark, and the 7,376-yard Players Course, designed by John Fought. Both courses consistently rank among the best public courses in California according to golfing magazines and websites. Off the courses, you can visit the Callaway Performance Center to have your swing evaluated or get fitted with quality golf clubs; you can seek out lessons at the golf school. Greens fees range from $75 to $180 depending upon the season. This being a public facility, it pays to reserve well in advance, up to 60 days. The resort's IW Club has a restaurant and a jazz café. ⊠ *44-500 Indian Wells La.* ☎ *760/346–4653* ⊕ *www. indianwellsgolfresort.com.*

TENNIS

BNP Paribas Open. Drawing 200 of the world's top players, this tournament takes place at Indian Wells Tennis Garden for two weeks in March. Various ticket plans are available, with some packages including stays at the adjoining Hyatt Grand Champions or Renaissance Esmeralda resorts. ☎ *800/999–1585* ⊕ *www.bnpparibasopen.com* ⊠ *$40 per day.*

LA QUINTA

14

4 miles south of Indian Wells, Washington St. off Hwy 111.

The desert became a Hollywood hideout in the 1920s, when La Quinta Hotel (now La Quinta Resort and Club) opened, introducing the Coachella Valley's first golf course. Old Town La Quinta is a popular attraction, the area holds dining spots, shops, and galleries.

GETTING HERE AND AROUND

Most of La Quinta lies south of Highway 111. The main drag through town is Washington Street.

WHERE TO EAT AND STAY

$$$$ × **Arnold Palmer's.** From the photos on the walls to the trophy-filled
MODERN display cases to the putting green for diners awaiting a table, Arnie's
AMERICAN essence infuses this restaurant—it's a big, clubby place where families gather for birthdays and Sunday dinners, and the service is always attentive. Among the well-crafted main courses are barbecued pork ribs, filet mignon with béarnaise sauce, and pan-seared sea scallops; desserts include the splendid Coachella date-bread pudding. The wine list is top-notch, and there's entertainment most nights. At Arnie's Pub, the more limited menu focuses on comfort food. ⑤ *Average main: $35* ⊠ *78-164 Ave. 52* ☎ *760/771–4653* ⊕ *www.arnoldpalmersrestaurant. com* ⚘ *Reservations essential.*

$$$ × **Hog's Breath Inn La Quinta.** Clint Eastwood watches over this replica of
AMERICAN his Hog's Breath restaurant in Carmel; his presence is felt in the larger-than-life photos that fill the walls of its bright dining room. The large selection of American comfort food ranges from barbecued baby back ribs to sole stuffed with crab and white Peking duck. The signature dish is the Dirty Harry dinner: chopped sirloin with capers, garlic mashed potatoes, and red cabbage, served with horseradish mushroom sauce. ⑤ *Average main: $25* ⊠ *78-065 Main St.* ☎ *760/564–5556, 866/464–7888* ⚘ *Reservations essential.*

$$$$ ⚏ **La Quinta Resort and Club.** Opened in 1926 and now a member of the
RESORT Waldorf-Astoria Collection, the desert's oldest resort is a lush green oasis set on 45 acres. **Pros:** individual swimming pools; gorgeous gardens; best golf courses in the desert. **Cons:** a party atmosphere sometimes prevails; spotty housekeeping/maintenance. **TripAdvisor:** "beauty in the high desert," "a quiet weekend," "relaxing."⑤ *Rooms from: $259* ⊠ *49-499 Eisenhower Dr.* ☎ *760/564–4111, 800/598–3828* ⊕ *www.laquintaresort.com* ⚓ *562 rooms, 24 suites, 210 villas.*

THE ARTS

La Quinta Arts Festival. More than 200 artists participate each March in a four-day juried show that's considered one of the best in the West. The event, held at La Quinta Civic Center, includes sculptures, paintings, watercolors, fiber art, and ceramics. Proceeds benefit arts programs in area schools. ⊠ *78495 Calle Tampico* ☎ *760/564–1244* ⊕ *www.lqaf.com* ✍ *$12, multi-day passes $15.*

SPORTS AND THE OUTDOORS

★ **PGA West.** A world-class golf destination where Phil Mickelson and Jack Nicklaus play, this venue includes three 18-hole, par-72 championship courses and provides instruction and golf clinics. Greens fees (which include a mandatory cart) range from $50 on weekdays in summer to $235 on weekends in February and March. Bookings are accepted 30 days in advance, but prices are lower when you book close to the date you need. ⊠ *49-499 Eisenhower Dr.* ☎ *760/564–5729 for tee times* ⊕ *www.pgawest.com.*

> ### THE FIRST CELEBRITY HOTEL
>
> Frank Capra probably started the trend when he booked a casita at the then new, very remote La Quinta Hotel (now Resort) to write the script for the movie *It Happened One Night*. The movie went on to earn an Academy Award, and Capra continued to book that room whenever he had some writing to do. A long line of Hollywood stars followed Capra's example over the years; the current list includes Oprah Winfrey, Adam Sandler, and Christina Aguilera.

INDIO

5 miles east of Indian Wells on Hwy. 111.

Indio is the home of the date shake, which is exactly what it sounds like: an extremely thick milk shake made with dates. The city and surrounding countryside generate 95% of the dates grown and harvested in the United States. If you take a hot-air balloon ride, you will likely drift over the tops of date palm trees.

GETTING HERE AND AROUND

Indio is east of Indian Wells and north of La Quinta. Highway 111 runs right through Indio, and Interstate 10 skirts it to the north.

EXPLORING

☾ **Coachella Valley History Museum.** Make a date to learn about dates at this museum inside a former farmhouse. The exhibits here provide an intriguing glimpse into irrigation, harvesting, and other farming practices; a time line and other displays chronicle how the industry emerged in the desert a century ago. ⊠ *82-616 Miles Ave.* ☎ *760/342–6651* ⊕ *www.coachellavalleymuseum.org* ✍ *$5* ☾ *Oct.–May, Thurs.–Sat. 10–4, Sun. 1–4.*

☾ **National Date Festival and Riverside County Fair.** Indio celebrates its raison d'être each February at this festival and county fair. The midmonth festivities include an Arabian Nights pageant, camel and ostrich races, and exhibits of local dates, plus monster truck shows, a demolition derby, a nightly musical pageant, and a nightly musical pageant, and a rodeo. Admission includes camel rides. ⊠ *Riverside County Fairgrounds, 82-503 Hwy. 111* ☎ *800/811–3247* ⊕ *www.datefest. org* ⊠ *$8.*

Shields Date Garden and Café. You can sample, select, and take home some of Shields's locally grown dates. Ten varieties are available, including the giant super-sweet royal medjools, along with specialty date products such as date crystals, stuffed dates, and confections. At the Shields Date Garden Café, you can try an iconic date shake, dig into date pancakes, or go exotic with a date tamale. Breakfast and lunch are served daily. ⊠ *80-225 Hwy. 111* ☎ *760/347–0996* ⊕ *www.shieldsdategarden.com* ⊙ *Store 9–5, café 6:30–2:30* ⊙ *No dinner.*

> **ROCKIN' AT COACHELLA**

The Coachella Valley Music and Arts Festival, one of the biggest parties in SoCal, draws hundreds of thousands of rock music fans to Indio for two weekends of live concerts and dancing each April. Hundreds of bands show up, including headliners such as Jack Johnson, the Raconteurs, Portishead, Roger Waters, and My Morning Jacket. Everybody camps at the polo grounds. Visit ⊕ *www. coachella.com* for details and tickets, which sell out months in advance.

14

WHERE TO EAT AND STAY

For expanded hotel reviews, facilities, and current deals, visit Fodors. com.

$$
SICILIAN
✕ **Ciro's Ristorante and Pizzeria.** Serving pizza and pasta since the 1960s, this popular casual restaurant has a few unusual pies on the menu, including cashew with three cheeses. The decor is classic pizza joint, with checkered tablecloths and bentwood chairs. Daily pasta specials vary but might include red- or white-clam sauce or scallops with parsley and red wine. $ *Average main: $2025* ⊠ *81-963 Hwy. 111* ☎ *760/347–6503* ⊕ *www.cirospasta.com* ⊙ *No lunch Sun.*

$$$
SOUTHWESTERN
✕ **Jackalope Ranch.** It's worth the drive to Indio to sample flavors of the Old West here, 21st-century style. Inside a rambling 21,000 foot building, holding a clutch of indoor/outdoor dining spaces, you may be seated near an open kitchen, a bar, fountains, fireplaces, or waterworks (both inside and out). Jackalope can be a busy, noisy place; ask for a quiet corner if that's your pleasure. The large menu roams the west, featuring grilled and barbecued items of all sorts, spicy and savory sauces, flavorful vegetables, and sumptuous desserts. Locals like the place, especially the bar; but some reviews complain that the quality of the food doesn't match the setting. $ *Average main: $26* ⊠ *80-400 Hwy. 111* ☎ *760/342–1999* ⊕ *www.thejackaloperanch.com* ⌲ *Reservations essential.*

$$$
HOTEL
☺
▥ **Fantasy Springs Resort Casino.** Operated by the Cabazon Band of Mission Indians, this family-oriented resort casino stands out in the Coachella Valley, affording mountain views from most rooms and the rooftop wine bar. **Pros:** headliner entertainment; great views from the rooftop bar; bowling alley; golf course. **Cons:** in the middle of nowhere; average staff service. **TripAdvisor:** "great desert casino," "valley ambience," "my favorite getaway." $ *Rooms from: $179*

✉ *84-245 Indio Springs Pkwy.* ☎ *760/342–5000, 800/827–2946* ⊕ *www.fantasyspringsresort.com* ⮞ *240 rooms, 11 suites.*

EN
ROUTE

Coachella Valley Preserve. For a glimpse of how the desert appeared before development, head northeast from Palm Springs to this preserve. It has a system of sand dunes and several palm oases that were formed because the San Andreas Fault lines here allow water flowing underground to rise to the surface. A mile-long walk along Thousand Palms Oasis reveals pools supporting the tiny endangered desert pupfish and more than 183 bird species. The preserve has a visitor center, nature and equestrian trails, restrooms, and picnic facilities. Guided hikes are offered. Note that it is exceptionally hot in summer here. ✉ *29200 Thousand Palms Canyon Rd.* ☎ *760/343–2733* ⊕ *www. coachellapreserve.org* ⊡ *Free* ⊙ *Visitor center daily 8–4.*

ALONG TWENTYNINE PALMS HIGHWAY

Designated a California Scenic Highway, the Twentynine Palms Highway not only connects two of the three entrances to Joshua Tree National Park (⇨ *see Chapter 15*), it also offers a gorgeous view of the high desert, especially in winter and spring when you may be driving beneath snowcapped peaks or through a field of wildflowers. Park entrances are located at Joshua Tree and Twentynine Palms. Yucca Valley and Twentynine Palms have lodging, dining options, and other services. If you see any strange artworks along the way, they might be created by artists associated with the avant-garde High Desert Test Sites (⊕ *www.highdeserttestsites.com*).

YUCCA VALLEY

30 miles northeast of Palm Springs on Hwy. 62/Twentynine Palms Hwy.

One of the high desert's fastest-growing cities, Yucca Valley is emerging as a bedroom community for people who work as far away as Ontario, 85 miles to the west. In this sprawling suburb you can shop for necessities, get your car serviced, and chow down at the fast-food outlets.

GETTING HERE AND AROUND

The drive to Yucca Valley on Highway 62/Twentynine Palms Highway passes through the Painted Hills and drops down into a valley. Yucca Valley is the first town you come to. Take Pioneertown Road north to the Old West outpost.

EXPLORING

☾ **Hi-Desert Nature Museum.** Creatures that make their homes in Joshua Tree National Park are the focus here. A small live-animal display includes scorpions, snakes, ground squirrels, and chuckwallas (a type of lizard). You'll also find rocks, minerals, and fossils from the Paleozoic era and Native American artifacts, and there's a children's room. ✉ *Yucca Valley Community Center, 57116 Twentynine Palms Hwy.* ☎ *760/369–7212* ⊕ *hidesertnaturemuseum.org* ⊡ *Free* ⊙ *Tues.–Sat. 10–5.*

Pioneertown. In 1946 Roy Rogers, Gene Autry, the Sons of the Pioneers (the music group for whom the town is named), and Russ Hayden built Pioneertown, an 1880s-style Wild West movie set complete with hitching posts, saloon, and an OK Corral. You can stroll past wooden and adobe storefronts and feel like you're back in the Old West. Or not: Pappy and Harriet's Pioneertown Palace, now the town's top draw, has evolved into a hip venue for indie and other bands. ⊠ *Pioneertown Rd., 4 miles north of Yucca Valley.*

WHERE TO EAT AND STAY

For expanded hotel reviews, facilities, and current deals, visit Fodors. com.

$$ ✕ **Pappy & Harriet's Pioneertown Palace.** Smack in the middle of a West-
MEXICAN ern-movie-set town is this Western-movie-set saloon where you can have dinner, relax over a drink at the bar, or check out some great indie and other bands—Leon Russell, Sonic Youth, the Get Up Kids, and Robert Plant have all played here, as have many Cali groups. The food ranges from Tex-Mex to Santa Maria–style barbecue to steak and burgers. No surprises but plenty of fun. ■TIP→ Pappy & Harriet's may be in the middle of nowhere, but you'll need reservations for dinner on weekends. ⑤ *Average main: $21* ⊠ *53688 Pioneertown Rd., Pioneertown* ☎ *760/365–5956* ⊕ *www.pappyandharriets.com* ⚱ *Reservations essential* ⊘ *Closed Tues. and Wed.*

$ ⊡ **Best Western Yucca Valley Hotel & Suites.** Opened in 2008, this hotel
HOTEL is a welcome addition to the slim pickings near Joshua Tree National Park; rooms are spacious, nicely appointed, and decorated in soft desert colors. **Pros:** convenient to Joshua Tree NP; pleasant lounge. **Cons:** location on busy highway; limited service. **TripAdvisor:** "convenient to Joshua Tree," "the basics are good," "clean and new." ⑤ *Rooms from: $100* ⊠ *56525 Twentynine Palms Hwy.* ☎ *760/365–3555* ⊕ *www. bestwestern.com* ⇨ *95 rooms* ⧄ *Multiple meal plans.*

TWENTYNINE PALMS

24 miles east of Yucca Valley on Hwy. 62, Twentynine Palms Hwy.

The main gateway town to Joshua Tree National Park (⇨ *see Chapter 15*), Twentynine Palms is also the location of the U.S. Marine Air Ground Task Force Training Center. You can find services, supplies, and limited lodgings in town.

GETTING HERE AND AROUND

Highway 62 is the main route to and through Twentynine Palms. Most businesses here center around Highway 62 and Utah Trail, 3 miles north of Joshua Tree's entrance.

ESSENTIALS

Visitor Information Twentynine Palms Chamber of Commerce and Visitor Center ⊠ *73484 Twentynine Palms Hwy.* ☎ *760/367–3445* ⊕ *www.visit29.org.*

14

EXPLORING

Oasis of Murals. The history and current life of Twentynine Palms is depicted in this collection of 20 murals painted on the sides of buildings. If you drive around town, you can't miss the murals, but you can also pick up a free map from the Twentynine Palms Chamber of Commerce.

29 Palms Art Gallery. This gallery features work by local painters, sculptors, and jewelry makers who find inspiration in the desert landscape. ⊠ 74055 Cottonwood Dr. ☎ 760/367–7819 ⊕ www.29palmsartgallery. com ۞ Wed.–Sun. noon–3.

WHERE TO STAY

For expanded reviews, facilities, and current deals, visit Fodors.com.

$
B&B/INN

29 Palms Inn. The funky 29 Palms is the closest lodging to the entrance to Joshua Tree National Park. **Pros:** gracious hospitality; exceptional bird-watching; popular with artists. **Cons:** rustic accommodations; limited amenities. **TripAdvisor:** "relaxing stop," "unique place," "cool spot in the desert." ⑤ Rooms from: $95 ⊠ 73-950 Inn Ave. ☎ 760/367–3505 ⊕ www.29palmsinn.com ⟳ 18 rooms, 5 suites ΙΟΙ Multiple meal plans.

$$
B&B/INN
★

Roughley Manor. To the wealthy pioneer who erected the stone mansion now occupied by this B&B, expense was no object, which is evident in the 50-foot-long planked maple floor in the great room, the intricate carpentry on the walls, and the huge stone fireplaces that warm the house on the rare cold night. **Pros:** elegant rooms and public spaces; good stargazing in the gazebo; great horned owls on property. **Cons:** somewhat isolated location; three-story main building doesn't have an elevator. **TripAdvisor:** "perfection in the desert," "a charmer," "best experience ever." ⑤ Rooms from: $135 ⊠ 74744 Joe Davis Rd. ☎ 760/367–3238 ⊕ www.roughleymanor.com ⟳ 2 suites, 7 cottages ΙΟΙ Multiple meal plans.

ANZA-BORREGO DESERT

Largely uninhabited, the Anza-Borrego Desert is popular with those who love solitude, silence, space, starry nights, light, and sweeping mountain vistas. This desert lies south of the Palm Springs area, stretching along the western shore of the Salton Sea down toward Interstate 8 along the Mexican border. Isolated from the rest of California by mile-high mountains to the north and west, most of this desert falls within the borders of Anza-Borrego Desert State Park, which at more than 600,000 acres is the largest state park in the contiguous United States. This is a place where you can escape the cares of the human world.

For thousands of years Native Americans of the Cahuilla and Kumeyaay people inhabited this area, spending their winters on the warm desert floor and their summers in the mountains. The first Europeans—a party led by the Spanish explorer Juan Baptiste de Anza—crossed this desert in 1776. Anza, for whom the desert is named, made the trip through here twice. Roadside signs along Highways 86, 78, and S2 mark the route of the Anza expedition, which spent Christmas Eve 1776 in what is now Anza-Borrego Desert State Park. Seventy-five years later thousands of immigrants on their way to the goldfields up north crossed the desert on the Southern Immigrant Trail, remnants of which remain along Highway S2. Permanent settlers arrived early in the 20th century, and by the 1930s the first adobe resort cottage had been built.

BORREGO SPRINGS

59 miles south of Indio via Hwys. 86 and S22.

The permanent population of Borrego Springs, set squarely in the middle of Anza-Borrego Desert State Park, hovers around 2,500. Long a quiet town, it's emerging as a laid-back destination for desert lovers. From September through June, when temperatures stay in the 80s and 90s, you can engage in outdoor activities such as hiking, nature study, golf, tennis, horseback riding, and mountain biking. If winter rains cooperate, Borrego Springs puts on some of the best wildflower displays in the low desert. In some years the desert floor is carpeted with color: yellow dandelions and sunflowers, pink primrose, purple sand verbena, and blue wild heliotrope. The bloom generally runs from late February through April. For current information on wildflowers around Borrego Springs, call Anza-Borrego Desert State Park's wildflower hotline (☎ 760/767–4684).

GETTING HERE AND AROUND

You can reach the Anza Borrego Desert from the Palm Springs area by taking the Highway 86 exit from Interstate 10, south of Indio. Highway 86, mostly not freeway, passes through Coachella and along the western shore of the Salton Sea. Turn west on Highway S22 at Salton City and follow it to Peg Leg Road, where you turn south until you reach Palm Canyon Drive. Turn west and the road leads to the center of Borrego Springs, Christmas Circle, where most major roads come together. Well-marked roads radiating from the circle will take you to the most popular sites in the park. If you are coming from the San Diego area, you'll need to drive east on Interstate 8 to the Cuyamaca Mountains, exit at Highway 79 and enjoy a lovely 23-mile drive through the mountains until you reach Julian; head east on Highway 78 and follow well-marked signs to Borrego Springs.

ESSENTIALS

Visitor Information Borrego Springs Chamber of Commerce ✉ *786 Palm Canyon Dr.* ☎ *760/767–5555, 800/559–5524* ⊕ *www.borregospringschamber. com.*

EXPLORING

★ **Anza-Borrego Desert State Park.** One of the richest living natural-history museums in the nation, this state park is a vast, nearly uninhabited wilderness where you can step through a field of wildflowers, cool off in a palm-shaded oasis, count zillions of stars in the black night sky, and listen to coyotes howl at dusk. The landscape, largely undisturbed by humans, reveals a rich natural history. There's evidence of a vast inland sea in the piles of oyster beds near Split Mountain and of the power of natural forces such as earthquakes and flash floods. In addition,

14

If you think the desert is just a sandy wasteland, the colorful beauty of the Anza-Borrego Desert will shock you.

recent scientific work has confirmed that the Borrego Badlands, with more than 6,000 meters of exposed fossil-bearing sediments, is likely the richest such deposit in North America, telling the story of 7 million years of climate change, upheaval, and prehistoric animals. They've found evidence of saber-tooth cats, flamingos, zebras, and the largest flying bird in the northern hemisphere beneath the now-parched sand. Today the desert's most treasured inhabitants are the herds of elusive and endangered native bighorn sheep, or borrego, for which the park is named. Among the strange desert plants you may observe are the gnarly elephant trees. As these are endangered, rangers don't encourage visitors to seek out the secluded grove at Fish Creek, but there are a few examples at the visitor center garden. After a wet winter you can see a short-lived but stunning display of cacti, succulents, and desert wildflowers in bloom.

The park is unusually accessible to visitors. Admission to the park is free, and few areas are off-limits. There are two developed campgrounds, but you can camp anywhere; just follow the trails and pitch a tent wherever you like. There are more than 500 miles of dirt roads, two huge wilderness areas, and 110 miles of riding and hiking trails. Many sites can be seen from paved roads, but some require driving on dirt roads, for which rangers recommend you use a four-wheel-drive vehicle. When you do leave the pavement, carry the appropriate supplies: a cell phone (which may be unreliable in some areas), a shovel and other tools, flares, blankets, and plenty of water. The canyons are susceptible to flash flooding, so inquire about weather conditions (even on sunny days) before entering. ■TIP→ Borrego resorts, restaurants, and the state park have Wi-Fi, but the service is spotty at best. If you need to talk to someone in the area, it's best to find a phone with a landline.

The sites and hikes listed below are arranged by region of the park and distance from the visitor center: in the valley and hills surrounding Borrego Springs, near Tamarisk Campground, along Highway S2, south of Scissors Crossing, and south of Ocotillo Wells.

Stop by the **visitor center** to get oriented, to pick up a park map, and to learn about weather, road, and wildlife conditions. Designed to keep cool during the desert's blazing hot summers, the center is built underground, beneath a demonstration desert garden containing examples of most of the native flora and a little pupfish pond. Displays inside the center illustrate the natural history of the area. Picnic tables are scattered throughout, making this a good place to linger and enjoy the view.

A 1½-mile trail through **Borrego Palm Canyon** leads to one of the few native palm groves in North America. The canyon, about 1 mile west of the visitor center, holds a grove of more than 1,000 native fan palms, a stream, and a waterfall. Wildlife is abundant along this route. This moderate hike is the most popular in the park.

Just a few steps off the paved road, the **Carrizo Badlands Overlook** offers a view of eroded and twisted sedimentary rock that obscures the fossils of the mastodons, saber-tooths, zebras, and camels that roamed this region a million years ago. The route to the overlook through Earthquake Valley and Blair Valley parallels the Southern Emigrant Trail. It's off Highway S2, 40 miles south of Scissors Crossing.

With a year-round stream and lush plant life, **Coyote Canyon,** approximately 4½ miles north of Borrego Springs, is one of the best places to see and photograph spring wildflowers. Portions of the canyon road follow a section of the old Anza Trail. This area is closed between June 15 and September 15 to allow native bighorn sheep undisturbed use of the water. The dirt road that gives access to the canyon may be sandy enough to require a four-wheel-drive vehicle.

The late-afternoon vista of the Borrego badlands from **Font's Point,** 13 miles east of Borrego Springs, is one of the most breathtaking views in the desert, especially when the setting sun casts a golden glow in high relief on the eroded mountain slopes. The road from the Font's Point turnoff can be rough enough to make using a four-wheel-drive vehicle advisable; inquire about road conditions at the visitor center before starting out. Even if you can't make it out on the paved road, you can see some of the view from the highway.

East of Tamarisk Grove campground (13 miles south of Borrego Springs), the **Narrows Earth Trail** is a short walk off the road. Along the way you can see evidence of the many geologic processes involved in forming the canyons of the desert, such as a contact zone between two earthquake faults, and sedimentary layers of metamorphic and igneous rock.

14

The 1.6-mile round trip **Yaqui Well Nature Trail** takes you along a path to a desert water hole where birds and wildlife are abundant. It's also a good place to look for wildflowers in spring. Pick up a self-guided brochure at the trailhead across from Tamarisk Campground.

Traversing a boulder-strewn trail is the easy, mostly flat **Pictograph/ Smuggler's Canyon Trail.** At the end is a collection of rocks covered with muted red and yellow pictographs painted within the last hundred years or so by Native Americans. Walk about ½ mile beyond the pictures to reach Smuggler's Canyon, where an overlook provides views of the Vallecito Valley. The hike is 2 to 3 miles round-trip and begins in Blair Valley, 6 miles southeast of Highway 78, off Highway S2, at the Scissors Crossing intersection.

Geology students from all over the world visit the Fish Creek area of Anza-Borrego to explore the canyon through **Split Mountain.** The narrow gorge with 600-foot walls was formed by an ancient stream. Fossils in this area indicate that a sea once covered the desert floor. From Highway 78 at Ocotillo Wells, take Split Mountain Road south 9 miles. ⊠ *Visitor center, 200 Palm Canyon Dr., Hwy. S22* ☏ *760/767-5311, 800/444-7275 campground reservations only, 760/767-4684 wildflower hotline* ⊕ *www.parks.ca.gov* ☑ *Free* ⊙ *Park daily, visitor center Thurs.–Mon. 9–5.*

Galleta Meadows. Flowers aren't the only things popping up from the earth in Borrego Springs. At Galleta Meadows camels, llamas, saber-toothed tigers, tortoises, and monumental gomphotherium (a sort of ancient elephant) appear to roam the earth again. These life-size bronze figures are of prehistoric animals whose fossils can be found in the Borrego Badlands. The collection, more than 50 sets of animals, is the project of a wealthy resident who has installed the works of art on property he owns for the entertainment of locals and visitors. Maps are available from Borrego Springs Chamber of Commerce. ⊠ *Borrego Springs Rd. from Christmas Circle to Henderson Canyon* ☏ *760/767-5555* ⊕ *www. galletameadows.com* ☑ *Free.*

WHERE TO EAT

$$
MODERN
AMERICAN
✕ **The Arches.** On the edge of the Borrego Springs Resort Golf Course, set beneath a canopy of grapefruit trees, the Arches is a pleasant place to eat. For breakfast you'll find burritos alongside standard fare such as pancakes and biscuits and gravy. At lunch, best enjoyed on the patio, sandwiches and salads are the main options. Dinner selections include seafood, steak, and pasta. ⑤ *Average main: $19* ⊠ *1112 Tilting T Dr.* ☏ *760/767-5700* ⊙ *Summer hrs vary; call ahead.*

$
MEXICAN
✕ **Carmelita's Mexican Grill and Cantina.** A friendly, family-run eatery tucked into a back corner of what is called "The Mall," Carmelita's draws locals and visitors all day, whether it's for a hearty breakfast, a cooked-to-order enchilada or burrito, or to tip back a brew at the bar. The menu lists typical combination plates (enchiladas, burritos, tamales, and tacos). Salsas have a bit of zing, and the *masas* (corn dough used to make tortillas and tamales) are tasty and tender. ⑤ *Average main: $12* ⊠ *575 Palm Canyon Dr.* ☏ *760/767-5666.*

$$$
MODERN
AMERICAN

✕**Krazy Coyote/Red Ocotillo.** The owners of the Palms at Indian Head operate these two restaurants together. Red Ocotillo serves breakfast (all the usual suspects) and lunch—burgers, Caesar salads, fish-and-chips, and the like. The more fancy Krazy Coyote serves rack of lamb, filet mignon, and other hearty standbys for dinner. What you eat is less important than the lovely 1950s-modern setting and the casual atmosphere. Dog-lovers will appreciate the canine menu, whose treats include peanut-butter dog cookies. ⑤ *Average main: $23* ✉ *2220 Hoberg Rd.* ☎ *760/767–7400* ♿ *Reservations essential* ⊘ *Closed Jul. and Aug.; Krazy Coyote no breakfast or lunch.*

WHERE TO STAY

For expanded reviews, facilities, and current deals, visit Fodors.com.

$$
RESORT

🏨 **Borrego Springs Resort and Spa.** Renovated in 2010, this quiet resort has spruced up its large rooms with luxury linens and amenities, flat-screen TVs, and some new furnishings. **Pros:** golf and tennis on-site; most rooms have good desert views. **Cons:** limited amenities; average service. **TripAdvisor:** "clean and quiet," "beautiful rooms," "escape to comfort and starry nights." ⑤ *Rooms from: $149* ✉ *1112 Tilting T Dr.* ☎ *760/767–5700, 888/826–7734* ⊕ *www.borregospringsresort.com* 🛏 *66 rooms, 34 suites.*

$$$
B&B/INN
★

🏨 **Borrego Valley Inn.** Desert gardens of mesquite, ocotillo, and creosote surround the adobe Southwestern-style buildings here. **Pros:** swim under the stars in the clothing-optional pool; exquisite desert gardens. **Cons:** potential street noise in season; not a good choice for families with young children. **TripAdvisor:** "something different and unique," "rustic charm," "a relaxing and tranquil getaway." ⑤ *Rooms from: $200* ✉ *405 Palm Canyon Dr.* ☎ *760/767–0311, 800/333–5810* ⊕ *www.borregovalleyinn.com* 🛏 *15 rooms, 1 suite* ⑩ *Multiple meal plans.*

SPORTS AND THE OUTDOORS

GOLF

Borrego Springs Resort and Country Club. The 27 holes of golf at this resort and country club are open to the public. Three 9-hole courses, with natural desert landscaping and mature date palms, can be played individually or in any combination. Greens fees are $40 to $65, depending on the course and the day of the week, and include a cart and range balls. ✉ *1112 Tilting T Dr.* ☎ *760/767–5700* ⊕ *www.borregospringsresort. com.*

Roadrunner Club. This club has an 18-hole par-3 golf course. The greens fee is $35, including cart. ✉ *1010 Palm Canyon Dr.* ☎ *760/767–5373* ⊕ *www.roadrunnerclub.com.*

Springs at Borrego. Part of an RV park complex, the Springs at Borrego has one 18-hole course; greens fees are $25 to $50, not including cart fees. ✉ *2255 DiGiorgio Rd.* ☎ *760/767–2004* ⊕ *www.springsatborrego. com.*

14

TENNIS

Anza Borrego Tennis Center. A tennis club that's also open for public play, this center holds four hard surface courts, a swimming pool, and clubhouse with snack bar. Daily rates are $10. ⊠ *286 Palm Canyon Dr.* ☎ *760/767–0577* ⊕ *www.springsatborrego.com* ☉ *Closed in summer.*

SHOPPING

Anza-Borrego State Park Store. You can find guidebooks and maps, clothing, desert art, and gifts for kids here, and the staff organizes hikes, naturalist talks, classes, research programs, and nature walks. Or they can help you organize your own visit. Proceeds from sales benefit preservation of the park and its resources. ⊠ *587 Palm Canyon Dr., #110* ☎ *760/767–4063* ⊕ *www.theabf.org* ☉ *Oct.–May 14, daily 10–4; May 15–Sept., weekdays 11–3.*

Borrego Outfitters. This contemporary general store stocks high-end outdoor gear from Kelty and Columbia, personal care items from Burt's Bees, footwear from Teva and Acorn, Speedo and Fresh Produce swimsuits, and tabletop and home-decor items. You can browse through racks of clothing and piles of hats, all suited to the desert climate. The off-season brings some great bargains. ⊠ *579 Palm Canyon Dr.* ☎ *760/767–3502, 760 /767–3502* ⊕ *www.borregooutfitters.com.*

SALTON SEA

★ *30 miles southeast of Indio via Hwy. 86S on western shore and via Hwy. 111 on eastern shore; 29 miles east of Borrego Springs via Hwy. S22.*

The Salton Sea, one of the largest inland seas on Earth, is the product of both natural and artificial forces. The sea occupies the Salton Basin, a remnant of prehistoric Lake Cahuilla. Over the centuries the Colorado River flooded the basin and the water drained into the Gulf of California. In 1905 a flood once again filled the Salton Basin, but the exit to the gulf was blocked by sediment. The floodwaters remained in the basin, creating a saline lake 228 feet below sea level, about 35 miles long and 15 miles wide, with a surface area of nearly 380 square miles. The sea, which lies along the Pacific Flyway, supports 400 species of birds. Fishing for tilapia, boating, camping, and bird-watching are popular activities year-round.

GETTING HERE AND AROUND

Salton Sea State Recreation Area includes about 14 miles of coastline on the northeastern shore of the sea, about 30 miles south of Indio via Highway 111. The Sonny Bono Salton Sea National Wildlife Refuge fills the southernmost tip of the sea's shore. To reach it from the recreation area, continue south about 60 miles to Niland; continue south to Sinclair Road, and turn west following the road to the Refuge Headquarters.

EXPLORING

☉ **Salton Sea State Recreation Area.** This huge recreation area on the sea's north shore draws thousands each year to its playgrounds, hiking trails, fishing spots, and boat launches. Ranger-guided bird walks take place on Saturday; you'll see migrating and native birds including Canada

Spa Life, Desert-Style

These days, taking the waters at a spa in Palm Springs is massively different from the experience imagined by the Cahuilla Indians when they first discovered the healing powers of their hot springs more than a century ago.

While you can still savor that tradition at the Spa Hotel, most desert spas including the Spa Hotel offer more, including signature treatments employing local materials such as clay, desert-dwelling plants, salts, or sugars. And some are considered world-class within their industry.

Here are some of the best spa options in the area.

The Viceroy Hotel Estrella Spa earns top honors each year for the indoor/outdoor spa experience it offers with a touch of Old Hollywood ambience. You can enjoy your massage in one of four outdoor treatment rooms in a garden, experience a Vichy shower massage, have a facial or pedicure fireside, or enjoy a couple's full-body treatment with lemon crystals in the spa's Ice Haus. Whatever the treatment, you can use the spa's private pool, dine on a spa lunch, even order a drink from the hotel's bar.

It's all about fun at the **Palm Springs Yacht Club in the Parker Hotel,** according to Commodore Stephanie Neely, who invites guests to play video games, use iPod Touches, select a book from the spa's library, or watch the game on TV poolside indoors. You can get a complementary shot of whiskey, vodka, or the Commodore Special while lounging in a poolside tent reminiscent of Somerset Maugham's colonial India. Get massages, body treatments, or a Daily Excursion (three treatments). Personal trainers can help you with your

workout in the gym; go get heated in the sauna or practice a little yoga poolside. When you're ready to crash, wander out to the outdoor café, the Deck, and order a burger and Pimm's. The salon at the PSYC, Jose Neira, caters to quite a few marquee names.

The Spring offers a laid-back alternative to other "more is more" resort spas. It also heads many national lists as a great place to get away from the urban world, and "focus on cleansing, detoxification, and rejuvenation," according to spa director Maria Lease. The setting is simple, as are the rooms. With day-spa services and multi-day packages, you can immerse yourself for four to five hours of personal pampering, plus spend time in the Finnish sauna and the mineral pools for which Desert Hot Springs is famous. You can get the most out of a signature treatment such as the European Power Polish that will send you home cleaned, exfoliated, stimulated, and ready for a deep massage. The Spring Day offers three hours of bliss.

Despite its funkiness, the **Feel Good Spa at the Ace Hotel** takes its services very seriously. Spa Director Lisa Ross spins a lot of magic to help "bring your bod back to the good ol' days of health and balance." Lotions, essential oils, rubs, and scrubs are organic botanicals here; you can even blend your own. The estheticians use a lot of local clay, mud, and sea algae in this 21st-century hippy hangout. The Ace offers a variety of choices of where to have your rubdown, but the coolest is inside one of the two yurts set up poolside. Ross says the yurts are popular in summer when groups of clients order up clay bakes, followed by outdoor showers and salt scrubs.

14

geese, pelicans, and shorebirds. On Sunday there are free kayak tours. ⚠ State budget cuts may result in the closure of some or all of this area; check before coming here. ✉ *100–225 State Park Rd., North Shore* ☎ *760/393–3052* ⊕ *www.parks.ca.gov* 💲 *$5* ⊙ *Park daily 8–sunset.*

Sonny Bono Salton Sea National Wildlife Refuge. The 2,200-acre wildlife refuge here, on the Pacific Flyway, is a wonderful spot for viewing migratory birds. There's an observation deck where you can watch migrating Canada geese. Along the trails you might view eared grebes, burrowing owls, great blue herons, ospreys, or yellow-footed gulls. ✉ *906 W. Sinclair Rd., Calipatria* ☎ *760/348–5278* ⊕ *www.fws.gov/saltonsea* 💲 *Free* ⊙ *Park Oct.–Feb., daily sunrise–sunset. Visitor center Oct.–Feb., weekdays 7–3, weekends 8–4:15; Mar.–Sept., closed weekends.*

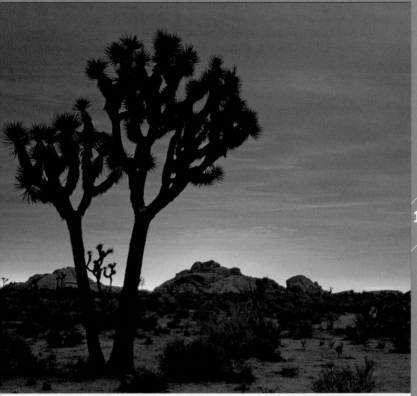

Joshua Tree National Park

WORD OF MOUTH

"The other place we really liked was Joshua Tree National Park. Its unique landscape and climbing opportunities made it one of our favorite places in California. Also, photography in the afternoon light in this park makes for phenomenal results."

—Elyse_Dorm

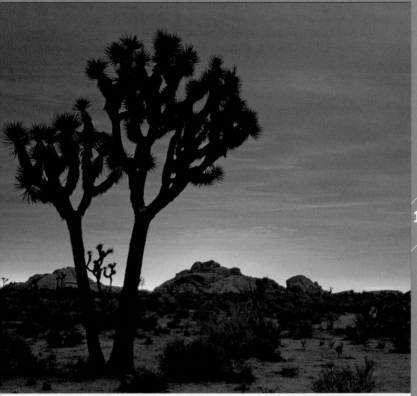

Joshua Tree National Park

WORD OF MOUTH

"The other place we really liked was Joshua Tree National Park. Its unique landscape and climbing opportunities made it one of our favorite places in California. Also, photography in the afternoon light in this park makes for phenomenal results."

—Elyse_Dorm

WELCOME TO JOSHUA TREE NATIONAL PARK

TOP REASONS TO GO

★ **Rock climbing:** Joshua Tree is a world-class site with challenges for climbers of just about every skill level.

★ **Peace and quiet:** Savor the solitude of one of the last great wildernesses in America.

★ **Stargazing:** You'll be mesmerized by the Milky Way flowing across the summer sky. For spectacular natural fireworks, visit in mid-August during the Perseid meteor shower and watch shooting stars streak overhead.

★ **Wildflowers:** In spring, the hillsides explode in a patchwork of yellow, blue, pink, and white.

★ **Sunsets:** Twilight is a magical time here, especially during the winter, when the setting sun casts a golden glow on the mountains.

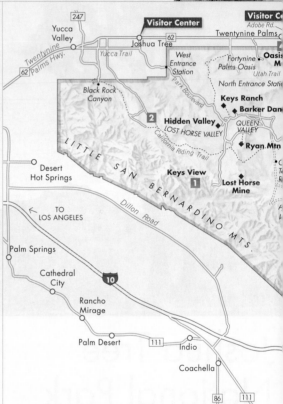

1 Keys View. This is the most dramatic overlook in the park—on clear days you can see Signal Mountain in Mexico.

2 Hidden Valley. Crawl between the big rocks and you'll understand why this boulder-strewn area was once a cattle rustlers' hideout.

3 Cholla Cactus Garden. Come here in the late afternoon, when the spiky stalks of the bigelow (jumping) cholla cactus are backlit against an intense blue sky.

4 Oasis of Mara. Walk the nature trail around this desert oasis, which the first settlers, the Serrano, dubbed "the place of little springs and much grass."

CALIFORNIA

Utah Trail Rd.

62

62

```
0          5 mi
0          5 km
```

15

PINTO   MOUNTAINS

3

PINTO   BASIN

◆ **Cholla
Cactus Garden**

HEXIE
MOUNTAINS

Pinto Basin Rd.

COXCOMB MOUNTAINS

Kaiser Road

EAGLE   MOUNTAINS

177

Visitor Center
◆ **Cottonwood Spring**
Bajada Nature Trail

COTTONWOOD MTS.   **Lost Palms Oasis**

Desert Center

10

Chiriaco
Summit

↙ TO
MECCA

GETTING
ORIENTED

Daggerlike tufts grace the branches of the namesake of Joshua Tree National Park in southeastern California, where the arid Mojave Desert meets the sparsely vegetated Colorado Desert (part of the Sonoran Desert, which lies within California, Arizona, and Northern Mexico). Passenger cars are fine for paved areas, but you'll need four-wheel drive for many of the rugged backcountry roadways. At the park's most popular sites, parking is limited. Joshua Tree does not have public transportation.

Updated by
Bobbi Zane

Ruggedly beautiful desert scenery attracts nearly 2 million visitors each year to Joshua Tree National Park, one of the last great wildernesses in the continental United States. Its mountains support mounds of enormous boulders and jagged rock; natural cactus gardens and lush oases shaded by tall fan palms mark the meeting place of the Mojave (high) and Sonora (low) deserts. Extensive stands of Joshua trees gave the park its name; the plants (members of the yucca family of shrubs) reminded Mormon pioneers of the biblical Joshua, with their thick, stubby branches representing the prophet raising his arms toward heaven.

JOSHUA TREE PLANNER

WHEN TO GO

October through May, when the desert is cooler, is when most visitors arrive. Daytime temperatures range from the mid-70s in December and January to mid-90s in October and May. Lows can dip to near freezing in midwinter, and you may even encounter snow at the higher elevations. Summers can be torrid, with daytime temperatures reaching 110°F.

GETTING HERE AND AROUND

CAR TRAVEL

An isolated island of pristine wilderness—a rarity these days—Joshua Tree National Park is within a short drive of 11 million Southern California residents. Most visitors, in fact, make the two-hour drive from the Los Angeles area to enjoy a weekend of solitude in 792,726 acres of untouched desert. The urban sprawl of Palm Springs (home to the nearest airport) is 45 miles away, but gateway towns Joshua Tree, Yucca

Valley, and Twentynine Palms are just north of the park. If you're staying in the Palm Springs area, you can enjoy the highlights of the park in one day, including a stop for a picnic at a scenic spot.

■TIP→ If you'd prefer not to drive, most Palm Springs area hotels can arrange a half- or full-day tour that hits the highlights of Joshua Tree National Park. But you'll need to spend two or three days camping here to truly experience the quiet beauty of the desert.

PARK ESSENTIALS
PARK FEES AND PERMITS

> **EXPLORING TIPS**
>
> The park is mostly roadless wilderness. Elevation in some areas of the park approaches 6,000 feet, and light snowfalls and cold, strong north winds are common in winter. There are no services within the park and little water, so you should carry at least a gallon of water per person per day. Apply sunscreen liberally at any time of the year. ■TIP→ Carry a cell phone for emergencies, but know that service is not very reliable.

Park admission is $15 per car, $5 per person on foot, bicycle, motorcycle, or horse. The Joshua Tree Pass, good for one year, is $30. Free permits—available at all visitor centers—are required for rock climbing.

PARK HOURS

The park is open every day, around the clock. The park is in the Pacific time zone.

VISITOR INFORMATION
PARK CONTACT INFORMATION

Joshua Tree National Park. ⊠ 74485 National Park Dr., Twentynine Palms ☎ 760/367-5500 ⊕ www.nps.gov/jotr.

VISITOR CENTERS

Cottonwood Visitor Center. Exhibits in this small center, staffed by rangers and volunteers, illustrate the region's natural history. The center also has restrooms. ⊠ Cottonwood Spring, Pinto Basin Rd. ⊕ www.nps.gov/jotr ☉ Daily 9–3.

Joshua Tree Visitor Center. This visitor center has interesting exhibits illustrating park geology, cultural and historic sites, and hiking and rock-climbing activities. There's also a small bookstore. Restrooms with flush toilets are on the premises, and showers are nearby. ⊠ 6554 Park Blvd., Joshua Tree ☎ 760/366-1855 ⊕ www.nps.gov/jotr ☉ Daily 8–5.

Oasis Visitor Center. Exhibits here illustrate how Joshua Tree was formed, reveal the differences between the park's two types of desert, and demonstrate how plants and animals eke out an existence in this arid climate. Take the 0.5-mile nature walk through the nearby Oasis of Mara, which is alive with cottonwood trees, palm trees, and mesquite shrubs. Facilities include picnic tables, restrooms, and a bookstore. ⊠ 74485 National Park Dr., Twentynine Palms ☎ 760/367-5500 ⊕ www.nps.gov/jotr ☉ Daily 8–5.

15

EXPLORING

SCENIC DRIVES

★ **Park Boulevard.** Traversing the most scenic portions of Joshua Tree, this well-paved road connects the north and west entrances in the park's high desert section. Along with some sweeping desert views, you'll see jumbles of splendid boulder formations, stands of Joshua trees, and Hidden Valley and Barker Dam, remnants of the area's wild and woolly past. From the Oasis Visitor Center, drive south. After about 5 miles, the road forks; turn right and head west toward Jumbo Rocks (clearly marked with a road sign).

> ### PLANTS AND WILDLIFE IN JOSHUA TREE
>
> Joshua Tree will shatter your notions of the desert as a wasteland. Life flourishes here, as flora and fauna have adapted to heat and drought. In most areas you'll be walking among native Joshua trees, ocotillos, and yuccas. One of the best spring desert wildflower displays in Southern California blooms here. You'll see plenty of animals—reptiles such as nocturnal sidewinders, birds like golden eagles or burrowing owls, and occasionally mammals like coyotes and bobcats.

HISTORIC SITES

☺ **Hidden Valley.** This legendary cattle-rustlers hideout is set among big boulders, which kids love to scramble over and around. There are shaded picnic tables here. ⊠ *Park Blvd., 14 miles south of West Entrance.*

Fodor's Choice
★ **Keys Ranch.** This 150-acre ranch, which once belonged to William and Frances Keys and is now on the National Historic Register, illustrates one of the area's most successful attempts at homesteading. The couple raised five children under extreme desert conditions. Most of the original buildings, including the house, school, store, and workshop, have been restored to the way they were when William died in 1969. The only way to see the ranch is on one of the 90-minute walking tours offered daily October to May. ⊠ *2 miles north of Barker Dam Rd.* ☎ *760/367–5555* ☞ *$5* ☺ *Oct.–May, daily at 10 and 1; Tues., Thurs., Sat. also at 7 pm.*

SCENIC STOPS

★ **Barker Dam.** Built around 1900 by ranchers and miners to hold water for cattle and mining operations, the dam now collects rainwater and is a good place to spot wildlife such as the elusive bighorn sheep. ⊠ *Barker Dam Rd., off Park Blvd., 14 miles south of West Entrance.*

Cholla Cactus Garden. This stand of bigelow cholla (sometimes called jumping cholla, since its hooked spines seem to jump at you) is best seen and photographed in late afternoon, when the backlit spiky stalks stand out against a colorful sky. ⊠ *Pinto Basin Rd., 20 miles north of Cottonwood Visitor Center.*

Cottonwood Spring. Home to the native Cahuilla people for centuries, this spring provided water for travelers and early prospectors. The area, which supports a large stand of fan palms, is a stop for migrating birds and a winter water source for bighorn sheep. A number of gold mills were located here, and the area still has some remains, including an *arrastra* (gold-mining tool)

> **LOOK, DON'T TOUCH—REALLY**
>
> Some cactus needles, like those on the cholla, can become embedded in your skin with just the slightest touch. If you do get zapped, use tweezers to gently pull it out.

and concrete pillars. You can access the site via a 1-mile paved trail that begins at sites 13A and 13B of the Cottonwood Campground. ⊠ *Cottonwood Visitor Center.*

Fortynine Palms Oasis. A short drive off Highway 62, this site is a bit if a preview of what the park's interior has to offer: stands of fan palms, interesting petroglyphs, and evidence of fires built by early American Indians. Since animals frequent this area, you may spot a coyote, bobcat, or roadrunner. ⊠ *End of Canyon Rd., 4 miles west of Twentynine Palms.*

★ **Keys View.** At 5,185 feet, this point affords a sweeping view of the Santa Rosa Mountains and Coachella Valley, the San Andreas Fault, the peak of 11,500-foot Mount San Gorgonio, the shimmering surface of Salton Sea, and—on a rare clear day—Signal Mountain in Mexico. Sunrise and sunset are magical times, when the light throws rocks and trees into high relief before bathing the hills in brilliant shades of red, orange, and gold. ⊠ *Keys View Rd., 21 miles south of west entrance.*

Lost Palms Oasis. More than 100 fan palms comprise the largest group of the exotic plants in the park. A spring bubbles from between the rocks, but disappears into the sandy, boulder-strewn canyon. As you hike along the 4-mile trail, you might spot bighorn sheep. ⊠ *Cottonwood Visitor Center.*

SPORTS AND THE OUTDOORS

HIKING

There are more than 191 miles of hiking trails in Joshua Tree, ranging from quarter-of-a-mile nature trails to 35-mile treks. Some connect with each other, so you can design your own desert maze. Remember that drinking water is hard to come by—you won't find water in the park except at the entrances. Bring along at least a gallon per person for all but the shortest hikes, more if the weather is hot. Before striking out on a hike or apparent nature trail, check out the signage. Roadside signage identifies hiking- and rock-climbing routes.

EASY

Cap Rock. This ½-mile wheelchair-accessible loop—named after a boulder that sits atop a huge rock formation like a cap—winds through fascinating rock formations and has signs that explain the geology of the

Mojave Desert. *Easy.* ✉ *Trailhead at junction of Park Blvd. and Keys View Rd.*

MODERATE

Fodor's Choice
★ **Ryan Mountain Trail.** The payoff for hiking to the top of 5,461-foot Ryan Mountain is one of the best panoramic views of Joshua Tree. From here you can see Mt. San Jacinto, Mt. San Gorgonio, Lost Horse Valley, and the Pinto Basin. You'll need two to three hours to complete the 3-mile round-trip. *Moderate.* ✉ *Trailhead at Ryan Mountain parking area, 16 miles southeast of park's west entrance or Sheep Pass, 16 miles southwest of Oasis Visitor Center.*

DIFFICULT

★ **Mastodon Peak Trail.** Some boulder scrambling is required on this 3-mile hike up 3,371-foot Mastodon Peak, but the journey rewards you with stunning views of the Salton Sea. The trail passes through a region where gold was mined from 1919 to 1932, so be on the lookout for open mines. The peak draws its name from a large rock formation that early miners believed looked like the head of a prehistoric behemoth. *Difficult.* ✉ *Trailhead at Cottonwood Spring Oasis.*

> **BEST CAMPGROUNDS IN JOSHUA TREE**
>
> Camping is the best way to experience the stark, exquisite beauty of Joshua Tree. You'll also have a rare opportunity to sleep outside in a semi-wilderness setting. The campgrounds, set at elevations from 3,000 to 4,500 feet, have only primitive facilities; few have drinking water. Black Rock and Indian Cove campgrounds, on the northern edge of the park, accept reservations up to six months in advance. Campsites elsewhere are on a first-come, first-served basis.

ROCK CLIMBING

Fodor's Choice
★ With an abundance of weathered igneous boulder outcroppings, Joshua Tree is one of the nation's top winter-climbing destinations. There are more than 4,500 established routes offering a full menu of climbing experiences—from bouldering for beginners in the Wonderland of Rocks to multiple-pitch climbs at Echo Rock and Saddle Rock. The best-known climb in the park is Hidden Valley's Sports Challenge Rock. A map inside the *Joshua Tree Guide* shows locations of selected wilderness and nonwilderness climbs.

The Mojave Desert

WITH OWENS VALLEY

WORD OF MOUTH

"There is plenty to see in the Mojave National Preserve—including lots of Joshua trees, sand dunes, volcanic rock, and flowers if you are there at the right time."

—tomfuller

WELCOME TO THE MOJAVE DESERT

TOP REASONS TO GO

★ **Nostalgia:** Old neon signs, historic motels, and restored (or neglected but still striking) Harvey House rail stations abound across this desert landscape. Don't miss the classic eateries along the way, including Bagdad Cafe in Newberry Springs, Emma Jean's Holland Burger Cafe in Victorville, and Summit Inn on the Cajon Pass.

★ **Death Valley wonders:** Visit this distinctive landscape to tour some of the most varied desert terrain in the world (⇨ Chapter 17, Death Valley National Park).

★ **Great ghost towns:** California's gold rush brought miners to the Mojave, and the towns they left behind have their own unique charms.

★ **Cool down in Sierra country:** Head up gorgeous U.S. 395 toward Bishop to visit the High Sierra, home to majestic Mt. Whitney.

★ **Explore ancient history:** The Mojave Desert is replete with rare petroglyphs, some dating back almost 16,000 years.

1 The Western Mojave. Stretching from the town of Ridgecrest to the base of the San Gabriel Mountains, the western Mojave is a varied landscape of ancient Native American petroglyphs, tufa towers, and hillsides covered in bright orange poppies.

2 The Eastern Mojave. Joshua trees and cacti dot a predominantly flat landscape that is interrupted by dramatic, rock-strewn mountains. The area is largely uninhabited, so be cautious when driving the back roads, where towns and services are scarce.

3 Owens Valley. Lying in the shadow of the Eastern Sierra Nevada, the Owens Valley stretches along U.S. 395 from the Mono–Inyo county line, in the north, to the town of Olancha, in the south. Tiny towns punctuate the highway, and the scenery is quietly powerful. If you're traveling between Yosemite National Park and Death Valley National Park or are headed from Lake Tahoe or Mammoth to the desert, U.S. 395 is your north–south corridor.

4 Death Valley National Park. This arid desert landscape is one of the hottest, lowest, and driest places in North America. From the surrounding mountains, you look down on its vast beauty. Down among the beautiful canyons and wide-open spaces, you'll find quirky bits of Americana, including the elaborate Scotty's Castle and eclectic Amargosa Opera House (⇨ *Chapter 17, Death Valley National Park.*).

GETTING ORIENTED

The Mojave Desert, once part of an ancient inland sea, is one of the largest swaths of open land in Southern California. Its boundaries include the San Gabriel and San Bernardino mountain ranges to the south; the areas of Palmdale and Ridgecrest to the west; Death Valley to the north; and Needles and Lake Havasu in Arizona and Primm, Nevada, to the east. The area is distinguishable by its wide-open sandy spaces, peppered with creosote bushes, Joshua trees, cacti, and abandoned homesteads. You can access the Mojave via Interstates 40 and 15, Highways 14 and 95, and U.S. 395.

16

Updated by
Reed Parsell

Dust and desolation, tumbleweeds and rattlesnakes, barren landscapes—these are the bleak images that come to mind when most people hear the word *desert*. But east of the Sierra Nevada, where the land quickly flattens and the rain seldom falls, the desert is anything but a wasteland.

The topography here is extreme; while Death Valley drops to almost 300 feet below sea level and contains the lowest (and hottest) spot in the Western Hemisphere, the Mojave Desert, which lies to the south, has elevations ranging from 3,000 to 5,000 feet. These remote regions (which are known, respectively, as low desert and high desert) possess a singular beauty, the vast open spaces populated with spiky Joshua trees, undulating sand dunes, faulted mountains, and dramatic rock formations. Owens Valley is where the desert meets the mountains; its 80-mile width separates the depths of Death Valley from Mt. Whitney, the highest mountain in the contiguous United States. Note: You may spot fossils at archaeological sites in the desert. If you do, leave them where they are; it's against the law to remove them.

MOJAVE DESERT PLANNER

WHEN TO GO
Spring and fall are the best seasons to tour the desert and Owens Valley. Winters are generally mild, but summers can be cruel. If you're on a budget, keep in mind that room rates drop as the temperatures rise.

GETTING HERE AND AROUND
AIR TRAVEL
Inyokern Airport, near Ridgecrest, is served by United Express from Los Angeles. Needles Airport serves small, private planes.

Contacts Inyokern Airport ⊠ *1669 Airport Rd., off Hwy. 178, 9 miles west of Ridgecrest, Inyokern* ☎ *760/377–5844* ⊕ *www.inyokernairport.com.***McCarran International Airport** ⊠ *5757 Wayne Newton Blvd., Las Vegas, Nevada* ☎ *702/261–5211* ⊕ *www.mccarran.com.***Needles Airport** ⊠ *711 Airport Rd., Needles* ☎ *760/326–5263.*

BUS TRAVEL

Greyhound provides bus service to Barstow, Victorville, Palmdale, and Needles; check with the chambers of commerce about local bus service, which is generally more useful to residents than to tourists.

Contact **Greyhound** ☎ *800/231–2222* ⊕ *www.greyhound.com.*

CAR TRAVEL

Much of the desert can be seen from the comfort of an air-conditioned car. Most visitors approach Death Valley (⇨ *Chapter 17)* from the west or the southeast. Whether you've come south from Bishop or north from Ridgecrest, head east from U.S. 395 on Highway 190 or 178. To enter Death Valley from the southeast, take Highway 127 north from Interstate 15 in Baker and link up with Highway 178, which travels west into the valley and then cuts north toward Highway 190 at Furnace Creek.

The major north–south route through the western Mojave is U.S. 395, which intersects with Interstate 15 between Cajon Pass and Victorville. U.S. 395 travels north into the Owens Valley, passing such relatively remote outposts as Lone Pine, Independence, Big Pine, and Bishop. Farther west, Highway 14 runs north–south between Inyokern (near Ridgecrest) and Palmdale. Two major east–west routes travel through the Mojave: to the north, Interstate 15 to Las Vegas, Nevada; to the south, Interstate 40 to Needles. At the intersection of the two interstates, in Barstow, Interstate 15 veers south toward Victorville and Los Angeles, and Interstate 40 gives way to Highway 58 west toward Bakersfield.

■TIP➔ For the latest Mojave traffic and weather, tune in to the Highway Stations (98.1 FM near Barstow, 98.9 FM near Essex, and 99.7 FM near Baker). Traffic can be especially troublesome Friday through Sunday, when thousands of Angelenos head to Las Vegas for a bit of R&R.

Contacts **Caltrans Current Highway Conditions** ☎ *800/427–7623* ⊕ *www. dot.ca.gov.*

TRAIN TRAVEL

Amtrak trains traveling east and west stop in Victorville, Barstow, and Needles, but the stations aren't staffed, so you'll have to purchase tickets in advance and handle your own baggage. The Barstow station is served daily by Amtrak California motor coaches that travel among Los Angeles, Bakersfield, and Las Vegas.

Contact **Amtrak** ☎ *800/872–7245* ⊕ *www.amtrakcalifornia.com.*

HEALTH AND SAFETY

In an emergency dial 911.

Let someone know your trip route, destination, and estimated time of return. Before setting out, make sure your vehicle is in good condition. Carry water, a jack, tools, and towrope or chain. Keep an eye on your gas gauge and try to keep the needle above half. Stay on main roads, and watch out for wildlife, horses, and cattle.

Drink at least a gallon of water a day (three gallons if you're hiking or otherwise exerting yourself). Dress in layered clothing and wear

HIKING IN THE MOJAVE DESERT

Hiking trails are abundant throughout the desert and along the eastern base of the Sierra, meandering toward sights that you can't see from the road. Some of the best trails are unmarked; ask locals for directions. Among the prime hiking spots is the John Muir Trail, which starts near Mt. Whitney. Whether you're exploring the high or low desert, wear sunblock, protective clothing, and a hat. Watch for tarantulas, black widows, scorpions, snakes, and other creatures.

comfortable, sturdy shoes and a hat. Keep snacks, sunscreen, and a first-aid kit on hand. If you have a headache or feel dizzy or nauseous, you could be suffering from dehydration. Get out of the sun immediately and drink plenty of water. Dampen your clothing to lower your body temperature. Do not enter abandoned mine tunnels or shafts, of which there are hundreds in the Mojave Desert. The structures may be unstable, and there may be hidden dangers such as pockets of bad air. Avoid canyons during rainstorms. Floodwaters can quickly fill up dry riverbeds and cover or wash away roads. Never place your hands or feet where you can't see them: rattlesnakes, scorpions, and black widow spiders may be hiding there.

Contacts BLM Rangers ☎ 760/326-7000 ⊕ www.blm.gov/ca.**Community Hospital** ✉ 555 S. 7th St., Barstow ☎ 760/256-1761 ⊕ www.barstowhospital. com.**Northern Inyo Hospital** ✉ 150 Pioneer La., Bishop ☎ 760/873-5811 ⊕ www.nih.org.**San Bernardino County Sheriff** ☎ 760/256-1796 in Barstow, 760/733-4448 in Baker.

HOURS OF OPERATION

Early morning is the best time to visit sights and avoid crowds, but some museums and visitor centers don't open until 10. If you schedule your town arrivals for late afternoon, you can drop by the visitor centers just before closing hours to line up an itinerary for the next day.

RESTAURANTS

Throughout the desert and the Eastern Sierra, dining is a fairly simple affair. Owens Valley is home to many mom-and-pop eateries, as well as a few fast-food chains. There are chain establishments in Ridgecrest, Victorville, and Barstow, as well as some ethnic eateries. *Prices in the reviews are the average cost of a main course at dinner or, if dinner is not served, at lunch.*

HOTELS

Hotel chains and roadside motels are the desert's primary lodging options. The tourist season runs from late May through September. Reservations are rarely a problem, but it's still wise to make them. *Prices in the reviews are the lowest cost of a standard double room in high season. For expanded reviews, facilities, and current deals, visit Fodors.com.*

TOUR OPTIONS

The Mojave Group of the Sierra Club regularly organizes field trips to interesting spots, and the San Gorgonio Sierra Club chapter also conducts desert excursions.

Contact Sierra Club ☎ *213/387–4287, 951/684–6203 for San Gorgonio chapter* ⊕ *www.sierraclub.com.*

VISITOR INFORMATION

Contacts Bureau of Land Management ⊠ *California Desert District Office, 22835 Calle San Juan De Los Lagos, Moreno Valley* ☎ *909/697–5200* ⊕ *www. blm.gov/ca.***California Welcome Center** ⊠ *2796 Tanger Way, Barstow* ☎ *760/253–4782* ⊕ *www.visitcwc.com/Barstow.***Death Valley Chamber of Commerce** ⊠ *860 Tecopa Hot Springs Rd., Tecopa* ☎ *760/852–4420* ⊕ *www. deathvalleychamber.com.***San Bernardino County Regional Parks Department** ⊠ *777 E. Rialto Ave., San Bernardino* ☎ *909/387–2757* ⊕ *cms.sbcounty. gov/parks.*

THE WESTERN MOJAVE

16

This vast area is especially beautiful along U.S. 395. From January through March, wildflowers are in bloom and temperatures are manageable. Year-round, snowcapped mountain peaks are irresistible sights.

PALMDALE

60 miles north of Los Angeles on Hwy. 14.

Before proclaiming itself the aerospace capital of the world, the town of Palmdale was an agricultural community. Settlers of Swiss and German descent, moving west from Illinois and Nebraska, populated the area in 1886, and most residents made their living as farmers, growing alfalfa, pears, and apples. After World War II, with the creation of Edwards Air Force Base and U.S. Air Force Plant 42, the region evolved into a center for aerospace and defense activities, with contractors such as McDonnell Douglas, Rockwell, Northrop, and Lockheed establishing factories here. Until the housing crisis and recent recession struck, Palmdale was one of Southern California's fastest-growing cities.

GETTING HERE AND AROUND

From the Los Angeles basin take Highway 14 to get to Palmdale. From the east, arrive via the Pearblossom Highway (Highway 18/138). Regional Metrolink trains serve the area from Los Angeles. Palmdale attractions are most easily seen by car, but you can see some of the town via local transit.

ESSENTIALS

Bus and Train Information Antelope Valley Transit Authority ☎ *661/945–9445* ⊕ *www.avta.com.*

Visitor InformationPalmdale Chamber of Commerce ⊠ *817 East Ave., Suite Q-9, Palmdale* ☎ *661/273–3232* ⊕ *www.palmdalechamber.org.*

EXPLORING

Antelope Valley Indian Museum. Notable for its one-of-a-kind artifacts from California, Southwest, and Great Basin native tribes, the museum occupies an unusual Swiss chalet–style building that clings to the rocky hillside of Piute Butte. To get here, exit north off Highway 138 at 165th Street East and follow the signs. ✉ *15701 E. Ave. M, Lancaster* ☎ *661/946–3045* ⊕ *www.avim.parks.ca.gov* ✆ *$3* ⊙ *Mid-Sept.–mid-June, weekends 11–4.*

Devil's Punchbowl Natural Area. A mile from the San Andreas Fault, the namesake of this attraction is a natural bowl-shaped depression in the earth, framed by 300-foot rock walls. At the bottom is a stream, which you can reach via a moderately strenuous 1-mile hike. You also can veer off on a short nature trail; at the top an interpretive center has displays of native flora and fauna, including live animals such as snakes, lizards, and birds of prey. ✉ *28000 Devil's Punchbowl Rd., south of Hwy. 138, Pearblossom* ☎ *661/944–2743* ✆ *Free* ⊙ *Park daily sunrise–sunset; center daily 8–4.*

St. Andrew's Abbey. This Benedictine monastery occupies 760 acres made lush by natural springs. The Abbey Ceramics studio, established here in 1969, sells handmade tile saints, angels, and plaques designed by Father Maur van Doorslaer, a Belgian monk whose work U.S. and Canadian collectors favor. The entertainment at the abbey's fall festival includes singing nuns and dancing monks. ✉ *31101 N. Valyermo Rd., south of Hwy. 138, Valyermo* ☎ *888/454–5411, 661/944–1047 ceramics studio* ⊕ *www.saintsandangels.org* ✆ *Free* ⊙ *Weekdays 9–12:30 and 1:30–4:30, weekends 9–11:45 and 12:30–4:30.*

Shambala Preserve. An 80-acre wildlife operation run by Hitchcock actress Tippi Hedren (*The Birds*), the sanctuary conducts safaris one weekend a month that bring participants as close as a foot away from the dozens of rescued exotic felines sheltered here. ✉ *6867 Soledad Canyon Rd., off Hwy. 14, Acton* ☎ *661/268–0380* ⊕ *www.shambala. org* ✆ *$50 minimum donation* ⊙ *Noon–3 once a month.*

WHERE TO STAY

For expanded reviews, facilities, and current deals, visit Fodors.com.

$
HOTEL
🏨 Best Western John Jay Inn & Suites. All rooms at this modern hotel have large desks and ergonomic chairs; suites have balconies, fireplaces, wet bars, and Jacuzzis. **Pros:** clean; good rates; spacious rooms. **Cons:** no on-site restaurant; ambulance noise from the hospital next door. **TripAdvisor:** "great staff," "nice place," "comfortable and convenient." ⑤ *Rooms from: $90* ✉ *600 W. Palmdale Blvd.* ☎ *661/575–9322* ⊕ *www.bestwestern.com* ⊳ *54 rooms, 13 suites* ⊗ *Breakfast.*

$$
HOTEL
🏨 Residence Inn Palmdale. Accommodations here range from studios to one-bedroom suites, all with full kitchens, sitting areas, and sleeper sofas. **Pros:** spacious rooms; close to town. **Cons:** no room service. **TripAdvisor:** "really nice room," "extremely friendly customer service," "great stay." ⑤ *Rooms from: $149* ✉ *514 W. Ave. P* ☎ *661/947–4204, 800/331–3131* ⊕ *www.marriott.com* ⊳ *90 suites* ⊗ *Breakfast.*

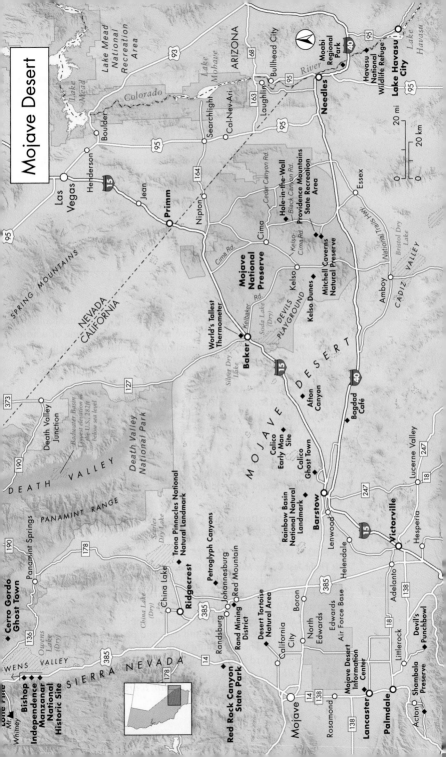

Mojave Desert

SPORTS AND THE OUTDOORS

ARIAL TOURS　**Brian Ranch Airport.** The school here offers introductory flights that allow you to pilot (with an instructor) two-seater ultralight aircraft across the Mojave. The airport's annual World's Smallest Air Show, held on Memorial Day weekend, draws aviation enthusiasts from around the country. ⊠ *34180 Largo Vista Rd., off Hwy. 138, Llano* ☎ *661/261–3216* ⊕ *www.brianranch.com* ⊇ *$40, 15-min flight; $75, 30 mins; $125, 1 hr.*

SKYDIVING　**Southern California Soaring Academy.** The academy operates sailplane rides (no engines!) over the scenic San Gabriel mountain pines, across the jagged San Andreas Fault, and over the sandy soil of El Mirage Dry Lake. Accompanied by a certified instructor, you'll learn the basics before handling the craft on your own. Reservations are required. ⊠ *32810 165th St. E, off Hwy 138, Llano* ☎ *661/944–1090* ⊕ *www. soaringacademy.org* ⊇ *$109–$250* ⊙ *Fri.–Mon. 9–sunset; Tues.–Thurs. by appointment.*

LANCASTER

8 miles north of Palmdale via Hwy. 14.

Lancaster was founded in 1876, when the Southern Pacific Railroad arrived. Before that, several Native American tribes, some of whose descendants still live in the surrounding mountains, inhabited it. Points of interest around Lancaster are far from the downtown area, and some are in neighboring communities.

GETTING HERE AND AROUND

From the Los Angeles basin take Highway 14, which proceeds north to Mojave and Highway 58, a link between Bakersfield and Barstow. Regional Metrolink trains serve Lancaster from the Los Angeles area. Local transit exists, but a car is the best way to experience this area.

ESSENTIALS

Transportation Contacts Antelope Valley Transit Authority ☎ *661/945–9445* ⊕ *www.avta.com.* **Metrolink** ☎ *800/371–5465* ⊕ *www.metrolinktrains. com.*

Visitor Information Destination Lancaster ⊠ *44933 Fern Ave., at W. Lancaster Blvd.* ☎ *661/723–6145* ⊕ *www.destinationlancasterca.org.*

EXPLORING

Air Flight Test Center Museum at Edwards Air Force Base. The museum at what many consider to be the birthplace of supersonic flight chronicles the rich history of flight testing. A dozen airplanes are on exhibit, from the first F-16B to the giant B-52D bomber. To visit, you must pass a security screening by providing your full name, Social Security number or driver's license number, and date and place of birth at least one week in advance. The 90-minute walking tours are open to the public on the first and third Friday of each month. ⊠ *405 S. Rosamond Blvd., off Yeager Blvd., Edwards* ☎ *661/277–3517* ⊕ *www.afftcmuseum.org* ⊇ *Free* ⊙ *1st and 3rd Fri. of each month, tours every 90 mins 9:30–3.*

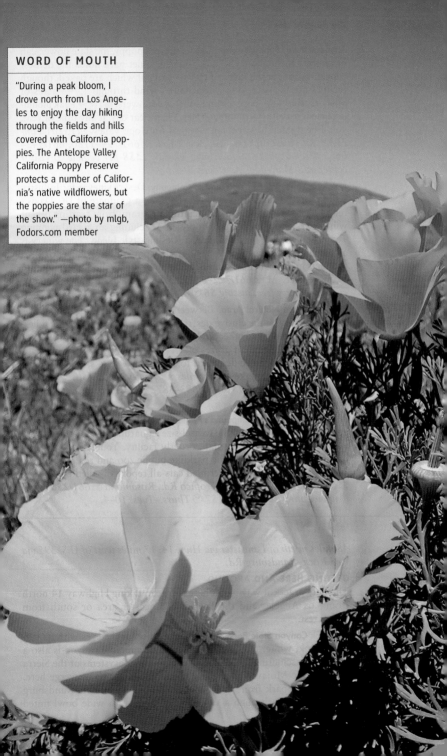

★ **Antelope Valley Poppy Reserve.** The California poppy, the state flower, can be spotted throughout the state, but this quiet park holds the densest concentration. Seven miles of trails—parts of which are paved, though inclines are too steep for wheelchairs—wind through 1,745 acres of hills carpeted with poppies and other wildflowers. ■TIP→ Peak blooming time is usually March through May. On a clear day at any time of year, you'll be treated to sweeping views of Antelope Valley. ⊠ *15101 Lancaster Rd., west off Hwy. 14, Ave. I Exit* ☎ *661/724–1180, 661/942–0662* ⊕ *www.parks.ca.gov/?page_id=627* ⊠ *$8 per vehicle* ⊙ *Visitor center mid-Mar.–mid-May, daily 9–5.*

Antelope Valley Winery and Buffalo Company. Desert vineyards? Industry scoffing hasn't deterred Cecil W. McLester, a graduate of UC Davis's renowned wine-making and viticulture program, from crafting decent wines—yes, from grapes grown on-site—including an award-winning Tempranillo and Paloma Blanca, a Riesling-style blend. The winery is also home to the Antelope Valley Buffalo Company, a producer of meat products made from its roaming herd in the Leona Valley. ⊠ *42041 20th St. W, at Ave. M* ☎ *661/722–0145, 888/282–8332* ⊕ *www.avwinery. com* ⊠ *Winery free, tasting $6* ⊙ *Wed.–Sun. 11–6.*

OFF THE BEATEN PATH

Desert Tortoise Natural Area. Between mid-March and mid-June, this natural habitat of the elusive desert tortoise blazes with desert candles, primroses, lupine, and other wildflowers. Arrive bright and early to spot the state reptile, while it grazes on fresh flowers and grass shoots. It's also a great spot to see desert kit fox, red-tailed hawks, cactus wrens, and Mojave rattlesnakes. ⊠ *8 miles northeast of California City via Randsburg Mojave Rd.* ☎ *951/683–3872* ⊕ *www.tortoise-tracks.org* ⊠ *Free* ⊙ *Daily.*

☾ **Exotic Feline Breeding Compound's Feline Conservation Center.** About a dozen species of wild cats, from the weasel-size jaguarundi to leopards, tigers, and jaguars, inhabit this small, orderly facility. You can see the cats (behind barrier fences) in the parklike public zoo and research center. The on-site museum's taxidermied cats all reportedly died of old age. ⊠ *Rhyolite Ave. off Mojave-Tropico Rd., Rosamond* ☎ *661/256–3793* ⊕ *www.cathouse-fcc.org* ⊠ *$7* ⊙ *Thurs.–Tues. 10–4.*

RED ROCK CANYON STATE PARK

48 miles north of Lancaster via Hwy. 14; 17 miles west of U.S. 395 via Red Rock–Randsburg Rd.

GETTING HERE AND AROUND

The only practical way to get here is by car, taking Highway 14 north from Los Angeles and the Palmdale/Lancaster area or south from Ridgecrest.

Red Rock Canyon State Park. A geological feast for the eyes with its layers of pink, white, red, and brown rock, this remote canyon is also a region of fascinating biological diversity—the ecosystems of the Sierra Nevada, the Mojave Desert, and the Basin Range all converge here. Entering the park from the south just beyond Red Rock–Randsburg Road, you pass through a steep-walled gorge to a wide bowl tinted pink by volcanic ash. Native Americans known as the Old People lived here some 20,000 years ago; later, Mojave Indians roamed the land for centuries. Gold-rush fever hit the region in the mid-1800s, and you can still see remains of mining operations in the park. In the 20th century, Hollywood invaded the canyon, shooting westerns, TV shows, commercials, music videos, and movies such as *Jurassic Park* here. Be sure to check out the Red Cliffs Preserve on Highway 14, across from the entrance to the Red Rock campground. ✉ *Ranger station, Abbott Dr., off Hwy. 14* ☎ *661/946–6092* ⊕ *www.parks.ca.gov* 🖃 *$6 per vehicle* ☉ *Daily sunrise–sunset; visitor center mid-Mar.–early June and early Sept.–Nov., Fri.–Sun. Call for hrs.*

RIDGECREST

28 miles northeast of Red Rock Canyon State Park via Hwy. 14; 77 miles south of Lone Pine via U.S. 395.

A military town that serves the U.S. Naval Weapons Center to its north, Ridgecrest has scores of stores, restaurants, and hotels. With about 25,000 residents, it's the last city of any significant size you'll encounter as you head northeast toward Death Valley National Park.

16

GETTING HERE AND AROUND

Come here by car so you can see regional attractions such as the Trona Pinnacles. Arrive via U.S. 395 or, from the Los Angeles area, Highway 14. The local bus service is of limited use to tourists.

ESSENTIALS

Transportation Contacts City Transit ☎ *760/499–5040* ⊕ *ci.ridgecrest.ca.us/transit.*

Visitor Information Ridgecrest Area Convention and Visitors Bureau ✉ *139 Balsam St., at Panamint Ave.* ☎ *760/375–8202, 800/847–4830* ⊕ *www.visitdeserts.com.*

EXPLORING

Fodor's Choice ★ **Petroglyph Canyons.** The two canyons, commonly called Big Petroglyph and Little Petroglyph, are in the Coso Mountain range on the million-acre U.S. Naval Weapons Center at China Lake. Each of the canyons holds a superlative concentration of ancient rock art, the largest of its kind in the Northern Hemisphere. Thousands of well-preserved images of animals and humans are scratched or pecked into dark basaltic rocks. The military requires everyone to produce a valid driver's license, Social Security number, passport, and vehicle registration before the trip (nondrivers must provide a birth certificate). ⊕ *www.maturango.org* 🖃 *$40; tours booked through Maturango Museum.*

Maturango Museum. The only way to see the amazing Petroglyph Canyons is on a guided tour conducted by the Maturango Museum. Tours ($40) depart from the museum February through June, and September or October through early December; call for tour times. Children under 10 are not allowed on the tour. The museum's interesting exhibits survey the area's art, history, and geology. ✉ *100 E. Las Flores Ave., at Hwy. 178* ☎ *760/375–6900* ⊕ *www.maturango.*

org ☎ *$5* ◷ *Daily 10–5. Tours Feb.–June and Sept. or Oct.–early Dec.; call for tour times*

Rand Mining District. The towns of Randsburg, Red Mountain, and Johannesburg make up the Rand Mining District, which first boomed with the discovery of gold in the Rand Mountains in 1895. Rich tungsten ore, used in World War I to make steel alloy, was discovered in 1907, and silver was found in 1919. The boom has gone bust, but the area still has some residents, a few antiques shops, and plenty of character. An archetypal Old West cemetery perched on a hillside looms over Johannesburg. ✉ *U.S. 395, 20 miles south of Ridgecrest, Randsburg.*

★ **Trona Pinnacles National Natural Landmark.** Fantastic-looking formations of calcium carbonate, known as tufa, were formed underwater along fault lines in the bed of what is now Searles Dry Lake. Some of the more than 500 spires stand as tall as 140 feet, creating a landscape so surreal that it doubled for outer-space terrain in the film *Star Trek V.*

An easy-to-walk ½-mile trail allows you to see the tufa up close, but wear sturdy shoes—tufa cuts like coral. The best road to the area can be impassable after a rainstorm. ✉ *Pinnacle Rd., 5 miles south of Hwy. 178, 18 miles east of Ridgecrest* ☎ *760/384–5400 Ridgecrest BLM office* ⊕ *www.blm.gov/ca/st/en/fo/ridgecrest/trona.3.html.*

OFF THE BEATEN PATH

Indian Wells Brewing Company. After driving through the hot desert, you'll surely appreciate a cold one at Indian Wells Brewing Company, where master brewer Rick Lovett lovingly crafts his Desert Pale Ale, Eastern Sierra Lager, Mojave Gold, and Sidewinder Missile Ales. If you have the kids along, grab a six-pack of his specialty root beer, black cherry, orange, or cream sodas. ✉ *2565 N. Hwy. 14, 2 miles west of U.S. 395, Inyokern* ☎ *760/377–5989* ☎ *$5 beer tasting* ◷ *Daily 9:30–5.*

WHERE TO STAY

For expanded reviews, facilities, and current deals, visit Fodors.com.

$
B&B/INN

🏠 **BevLen Haus Bed & Breakfast.** A central location, country-cute rooms, and sociable hosts make this mustard-color chalet-style B&B an appealing stop. **Pros:** low rates; good for solo travelers. **Cons:** only one of the three rooms is large enough for two people. **TripAdvisor:** "very special," "wonderful visit," "an oasis of cool." $ *Rooms from: $65* ✉ *809 N. Sanders St.* ☎ *760/375–1988, 800/375–1989* ⊕ *www.bevlen.com* ⬦ *3 rooms* ⦿ *Breakfast.*

THE EASTERN MOJAVE

Majestic, wide-open spaces define this region, with the Mojave National Preserve being one of the state's most remote but rewarding destinations.

VICTORVILLE

87 miles south of Ridgecrest on U.S. 395 off Bear Valley Rd.

At the southwest corner of the Mojave is the sprawling town of Victorville, a town rich in Route 66 heritage. Victorville was named for Santa Fe Railroad pioneer Jacob Nash Victor, who drove the first locomotive through the Cajon Pass here in 1885. Once home to Native Americans, the town later became a rest stop for Mormons and missionaries. In 1941, George Air Force Base (now an airport and storage area) brought scores of military families to the area, many of which have stayed on to raise families of their own. February, when the city holds its annual Roy Rogers and Dale Evans Western Film Festival and Adelanto Grand Prix, the largest motorcycle and quad off-road event in the country, is a great time to visit.

GETTING HERE AND AROUND

Drive here on Interstate 15 from Los Angeles or Las Vegas, or from the north via U.S. 395. Amtrak and Greyhound also serve the town. There are local buses, but touring by car is more practical.

ESSENTIALS

Transportation Information The Victor Valley Transit Authority ☎ 760/948–3030 ⊕ www.vvta.org.

Visitor Information Victorville Chamber of Commerce ✉ 14174 Green Tree Blvd., at St. Andrews Dr. ☎ 760/245–6506 ⊕ www.vvchamber.com.

EXPLORING

California Route 66 Museum. Fans of the Mother Road (as Steinbeck dubbed Route 66) will love this museum whose exhibits chronicle the famous highway's history. A book sold here contains a self-guided tour of 11 miles of the old Sagebrush Route from just north of Victorville in Oro Grande to Helendale. The tour passes by icons such as Potapov's Gas and Service Station and the once-rowdy Sagebrush Inn, now a private residence. ✉ 16825 D St., between 5th and 6th Sts. ☎ 760/951–0436 ⊕ www.califrt66museum.org ⌑ Free ☉ Mon. and Thurs.–Sat. 10–4, Sun. 11–3.

☾ **Mojave Narrows Regional Park.** In one of the few spots where the Mojave River flows aboveground, this park has two lakes surrounded by cottonwoods and cattails. You'll find fishing, rowboat rentals, a bait shop, equestrian paths, and a wheelchair-accessible trail. ✉ 18000 Yates Rd., north on Ridgecrest Rd. off Bear Valley Rd., Victorville ☎ 760/245–2226 ⊕ cms.sbcounty.gov/parks ⌑ $7 weekdays, $10 weekends and holidays.

Silverwood Lake State Recreation Area. One of the desert's most popular boating and fishing areas, 1,000-acre Silverwood Lake also has campgrounds and a beach with a lifeguard. You can rent boats; fish for trout, largemouth bass, crappie, and catfish; and hike and bike the trails. In winter, bald eagles nest in the tall Jeffrey pines by the shore. ✉ 14651 Cedar Cir., at Cleghorn Rd., off Hwy. 138, Hesperia ☎ 760/389–2303 ⊕ www.parks.ca.gov/?page_id=650 ⌑ $10 per car, $8 per boat ☉ May–Sept. daily 7–9, Oct.–Apr. daily 7–5.

WHERE TO EAT AND STAY

For expanded reviews, facilities, and current deals, visit Fodors.com.

$ ✕ **Emma Jean's Holland Burger Cafe.** This circa-1940s diner sits right on
AMERICAN U.S. Historic Route 66 and is favored by locals for its generous por-
★ tions and old-fashioned home cooking. Try the biscuits and gravy,

chicken-fried steak, or the famous Trucker's Sandwich, stuffed with roast beef, bacon, chilies, and cheese. The Brian Burger also elicits consistent praise. $ *Average main: $12* ⌧ *17143 N. D St., at Water Power Housing Dr.* ☎ *760/243–9938* ⊘ *Closed Sun. No dinner.*

$ ✕ **Summit Inn.** Elvis Presley is one of many famous customers who passed
AMERICAN through this kitschy diner perched atop the Cajon Pass. Open since 1952, the restaurant is filled with Route 66 novelty items, a gift shop, and vintage jukebox, which plays oldies from the 1960s. The food tends to generates positive reviews, and the funky decor and historic significance make it worth a stop. $ *Average main: $12* ⌧ *5970 Mariposa Rd., exit I–15 at Oak Hills, Oak Hills* ☎ *760/949–8688.*

$ ⌷ **La Quinta Inn and Suites Victorville.** If you're looking for a clean and com-
HOTEL fortable hotel with reasonable prices, this is a good choice. **Pros:** near shopping mall; clean rooms. **Cons:** near a busy freeway. **TripAdvisor:** "convenient and well appointed," "desert comfort," "quiet." $ *Rooms from: $94* ⌧ *12000 Mariposa Rd., Hesperia* ☎ *760/949–9900* ⊕ *www. lq.com* ⇆ *53 rooms, 22 suites* ⦿ *Breakfast.*

BARSTOW

32 miles northeast of Victorville on I–15.

Barstow was born in 1886, when a subsidiary of the Atchison, Topeka, and Santa Fe Railway began construction of a depot and hotel here. Outlet stores, chain restaurants, and motels define today's landscape, though old-time neon signs light up the town's main street.

GETTING HERE AND AROUND

Driving here on Interstate 15 from Los Angeles or Las Vegas is the best option, although you can reach Barstow via Amtrak or Greyhound. The local bus service is helpful for sights downtown.

ESSENTIALS

Transportation Information Barstow Area Transit ☎ *760/256–0311* ⊕ *www. barstow.org.*

Visitor Information Barstow Area Chamber of Commerce and Visitors Bureau ⌧ *681 N. 1st Ave., near Riverside Dr.* ☎ *760/256–8617* ⊕ *www. barstowchamber.com.* **California Welcome Center** ⌧ *2796 Tanger Way, off Lenwood Rd.* ☎ *760/253–4782* ⊕ *www.visitcwc.com* ⊘ *Daily 9–6.*

EXPLORING

TOP ATTRACTIONS

★ **Calico Early Man Site.** The earliest-known Americans fashioned the artifacts buried in the walls and floors of the pits here. Nearly 12,000 stone tools—used for scraping, cutting, and gouging—have been excavated here. The apparent age of some of these items (said to be as much as 200,000 years old) contradicts the dominant archaeological theory that humans populated North America only 13,000 years ago. Noted archaeologist Louis Leakey was so impressed with the Calico site that he became its director in 1963 and served in that capacity until his death in 1972. His old camp is now a visitor center and museum. The only way into the site is by guided tour (call ahead, as scheduled tours sometimes

Many of the buildings in the popular Calico Ghost Town are authentic.

don't take place). ⊠ *Off I–15, Minneola Rd. exit, 15 miles northeast of Barstow* ☎ *760/254–2248* ⊕ *www.blm.gov/ca/st/en/fo/barstow/calico. html* ☞ *$5* ⊙ *Visitor center Wed. 12:30–4:30, Thurs.–Sun. 9–4:30; tours Wed. 1:30 and 3:30, Thurs.–Sun. 9:30, 11:30, 1:30, and 3:30.*

Calico Ghost Town. Once a wild and wealthy mining town, Calico took off in 1881 when prospectors found a rich deposit of silver in the area, and by 1886 more than $85 million worth of silver, gold, and other precious metals had been harvested from the surrounding hills. Many buildings here are authentic, but the restoration has created a sanitized version of the 1880s. You can stroll the wooden sidewalks of Main Street, browse shops filled with Western goods, roam the tunnels of Maggie's Mine ($1), and take an enjoyable ride on the Calico-Odessa Railroad ($3). Calico is a fun and mildly educational place for families to stretch their legs on the drive between Los Angeles and Las Vegas. Festivals in March, May, October, and November celebrate Calico's Wild West theme. ⊠ *Ghost Town Rd., 3 miles north of I–15, 5 miles east of Barstow* ☎ *760/254–2122* ⊕ *www.calicotown.com* ☞ *$6* ⊙ *Daily 9–5.*

Casa Del Desierto Harvey House. This distinctive two-story structure—its Spanish name means "house of the desert"—was one of many hotel and restaurant depots opened by Santa Fe Railroad guru Fred Harvey in the early 20th century. In its heyday the building starred in Judy Garland's film *The Harvey Girls;* now it houses the Route 66 Mother Road Museum and the Western Railroad Museum. ⊠ *681 N. 1st Ave., near Riverside Dr.* ☎ *760/255–1890* ⊕ *www.route66museum.org* ☞ *Free* ⊙ *Fri.–Sun. 10–4. Guided tours by appointment.*

↻ **Goldstone Deep Space Communications Complex.** Friendly and enthusi-
Fodor's Choice astic staffers conduct guided tours of this 53-square-mile complex.
★ Tours start at the Goldstone Museum, where exhibits detail past and
present space missions and Deep Space Network history. From there,
you'll drive out to see the massive concave antennas, starting with
those used for early manned space flights and culminating with the
11-story-tall "listening" device and its always-staffed mission control room used to track spacecraft that have drifted beyond our solar
system. Appointments are required; contact the complex to reserve a
slot. ⊠ *Ft. Irwin Military Base, Ft. Irwin Rd. off I–15, 35 miles north
of Barstow* ☎ *760/255–8688* ⊕ *deepspace.jpl.nasa.gov/dsn/features/
goldstonetours.html* ⊡ *Free* ⊘ *Guided tours by appointment only.*

★ **Rainbow Basin National Natural Landmark.** Many science-fiction movies set
on Mars have been filmed at this landmark 8 miles north of Barstow.
Huge slabs of red, orange, white, and green stone tilt at crazy angles like
ships about to capsize; hike the washes, and you might see the fossilized
remains of mastodons and bear-dogs, which roamed the basin up to 16
million years ago. At times, only 4-wheel-drive vehicles are permitted.
If you have the time, park and hike. ⊠ *Fossil Bed Rd., 3 miles west of
Fort Irwin Rd. (head north from (I-15)* ☎ *760/252–6000* ⊕ *www.blm.
gov/ca/barstow/basin.html.*

WORTH NOTING

Afton Canyon. Because of its colorful, steep walls, Afton Canyon is often
called the Grand Canyon of the Mojave. It was carved over thousands
of years by the rushing waters of the Mojave River, which makes one of
its few aboveground appearances here. The dirt road that leads to the
canyon is ungraded in spots, so it is best to explore it in an all-terrain
vehicle. ⊠ *Off Afton Canyon Rd., 36 miles northeast of Barstow via
I-15* ⊕ *www.blm.gov/ca/st/en/fo/barstow/afton.html.*

↻ **Desert Discovery Center.** The center's main attraction is Old Woman Mete-
orite, the second-largest such celestial object ever found in the United
States. It was discovered in 1976 about 50 miles from Barstow. The center also has exhibits of fossils, plants, and local animals. ⊠ *831 Barstow
Rd., at E. Virginia Way* ☎ *760/252–6060* ⊕ *www.desertdiscoverycenter.
com* ⊡ *Free* ⊘ *Tues.–Sat. 11–4.*

Mojave River Valley Museum. Two blocks from the Desert Discovery Center, this complementary museum is crowded with exhibits that include
American Indian pottery, mammoth bones, and elephant tracks. Worth
a look outside are the iron-strap jail and rare Santa Fe Railroad drover's
car. ⊠ *270 E. Virginia Way, at Belinda St.* ☎ *760/256–5452* ⊕ *www.
mojaverivervalleymuseum.org* ⊡ *Free* ⊘ *Daily 11–4.*

Skyline Drive-In Theatre. When the sun sets in the Mojave, check out a
bit of surviving Americana at this dusty drive-in, where you can watch
the latest Hollywood flicks among the Joshua trees and starry night
sky in good old-fashioned stereo FM sound. ⊠ *31175 Old Hwy. 58*
☎ *760/256–3333* ⊡ *$6* ⊘ *Shows Wed.–Sun. at 7:30; closed Mon. and
Tues.*

↻ **Western American Rail Museum.** For a truly nostalgic experience, check
out the old locomotives and cabooses at this museum that houses

memorabilia from Barstow's early railroad days, as well as interactive and historic displays on railroad history. ⊠ *Casa Del Desierto, 685 N. 1st St., near Riverside Dr.* ☎ *760/256–9276* ⊕ *www.barstowrailmuseum. org* ⊠ *Free* ⊙ *Fri.–Sun. 11–4.*

WHERE TO EAT AND STAY

For expanded reviews, facilities, and current deals, visit Fodors.com.

$ ✕ **Bagdad Café.** Tourists from all over the world flock to the Route 66
AMERICAN eatery where the 1988 film of the same name was shot. Built in the
★ 1940s, the Bagdad serves burgers, chicken-fried steak, and seafood. The walls are crammed with memorabilia donated by visitors famous and otherwise. ⑤ *Average main: $12* ⊠ *46548 National Trails Hwy., at Nopal La., Newberry Springs* ☎ *760/257–3101.*

$$$ ✕ **Idle Spurs Steakhouse.** Since the 1950s this roadside ranch has been a
AMERICAN Barstow dining staple, and it's still beloved by locals. Covered in cacti
★ outside and Christmas lights inside, it's a colorful, cheerful place with a big wooden bar. The menu features prime cuts of meat, ribs, and lobster, and there's a great microbrew list. ⑤ *Average main: $23* ⊠ *690 Hwy. 58, at Camarillo Ave.* ☎ *760/256–8888* ⊕ *www.idlespurssteakhouse. com* ⊙ *No lunch weekends.*

$ ✕ **Slash X Ranch Cafe.** Burgers, cold beer, and chili-cheese fries in hearty
SOUTHERN portions lure visitors and locals to this rowdy Wild West-esque water-ing hole named for the cattle ranch that preceded it. Shuffleboard tables and horseshoe pits add to the fun, provided it's not too sizzling hot outside. ⑤ *Average main: $13* ⊠ *28040 Barstow Rd., at Powerline Rd.* ☎ *760/252–1197* ⊙ *Closed weekdays.*

$ 🏨 **Country Inn & Suites By Carlson.** A friendly and attentive staff make
HOTEL this chain hotel stand out in a town that has a sea of them. **Pros:** very clean rooms, engaged management. **Cons:** pricey for Barstow; nearest nightlife is two hours away. **TripAdvisor:** "quiet and friendly," "great service," "first class management." ⑤ *Rooms from: $119* ⊠ *2812 Len-wood Rd.* ☎ *760/307–3121* ⊕ *www.countryinns.com* ⤳ *121 rooms.*

BAKER

63 miles northeast of Barstow on I–15; 84 miles south of Death Valley Junction via Hwy. 127.

Death Valley's gateway to the central and western Mojave, the pit-stop town of Baker has several gas stations, some fast-food outlets, a few motels, and a general store that claims to sell the most winning Lotto tickets in California.

GETTING HERE AND AROUND

Baker sits at the intersection of I–15 and Highway 127. The only practi-cal way to get here is by car.

EXPLORING

thermometer. Baker's 134-foot-tall thermometer, the world's tallest such instrument, pays homage to the record U.S. temperature, 134°F, recorded in Death Valley on July 10, 1913. ⊠ *72157 Baker Blvd., near Death Valley Rd.*

PRIMM, NV

52 miles northeast of Baker, via I–15; 118 miles east of Death Valley, via Hwy. 160 and I–15; 114 miles north of Barstow, via I–15.

Amid the rugged beauty of the Mojave's landscapes, three casinos clustered on the Nevada side of Interstate 15 attract low rollers and travelers unable to hold off gambling until they arrive in Las Vegas.

GETTING HERE AND AROUND

Shuttles from the Las Vegas airport serve Primm; driving is another option. The three casinos are within walking distance of each other.

EXPLORING

Shopping the outlets and hitting the waterslide at Whiskey Pete's, the amusement park at Buffalo Bill's, or the casinos' video arcades are among the non-gambling diversions Primm offers.

WHERE TO STAY

For expanded reviews, facilities, and current deals, visit Fodors.com.

$

RESORT

Buffalo Bill's Resort and Casino. Decorated in the style of a Western frontier town, this hotel is the biggest and most popular in Primm. **Pros:** swimming pool and large amusement park; on-site restaurants and shops; comparatively exciting atmosphere. **Cons:** roller coaster noise at night; basic rooms seem a little worn. **TripAdvisor:** "fun place," "ok for the price," "great stay." $ *Rooms from: $90* ⊠ *31700 Las Vegas Blvd. S* ☎ *702/386–7867, 800/386–7867* ⊕ *www.primmvalleyresorts. com* 1,193 rooms, 49 suites.

SPORTS AND THE OUTDOORS

Primm Valley Golf Club. Hotel guests have privileges at the Primm Valley Golf Club, which has two 18-hole courses (Lakes and Desert) designed by Tom Fazio that rank among the top 100 in the nation. Expect to pay more than $100 a round in high season (spring and fall). ⊠ *1 Yates Well Rd., 4 miles south of Primm Valley Resort, Nipton, California* ☎ *702/679–5509* ⊕ *www.primmvalleygolf.com.*

MOJAVE NATIONAL PRESERVE

Between I–15 and I–40, roughly east of Baker and Ludlow to the California/Nevada border.

The 1.4 million acres of the Mojave National Preserve hold a surprising abundance of plant and animal life—especially considering their elevation (nearly 8,000 feet in some areas). There are traces of human history here as well, including abandoned army posts and vestiges of mining and ranching towns. The town of Cima still has a small functioning store.

GETTING HERE AND AROUND

The best way to see the preserve is by car. The fully paved Kelbaker Road bisects the park north–south; Essex Road gets you to Hole-in-the-Wall on pavement but is graveled beyond there.

EXPLORING

★ **Hole-in-the-Wall.** Created millions of years ago by volcanic activity, Hole-in-the-Wall formed when gases were trapped between layers of deposited ash, rock, and lava; the gas bubbles left holes in the solidified material. A member of the Butch Cassidy gang gave the area its name because it reminded him of his former hideout in Wyoming. You will encounter one of California's most distinctive hiking experiences here. Proceeding clockwise from a small visitor center, you walk gently down and around a craggy hill, past cacti and fading petroglyphs to Banshee Canyon, whose pockmarked walls resemble Swiss cheese. From there you head back out of the canyon, supporting yourself with widely spaced iron rings (some of which wiggle precariously from their rock moorings) as you ascend a 200-foot incline that deposits you back near the visitor center. The 90-minute adventure is mildly dangerous but wholly entertaining. ⊠ *From I–40, take Essex Rd. exit, drive north 10 miles to Black Canyon Rd., and continue north another 10 miles* ☎ *760/928–2572* ⊕ *www.nps.gov/moja* ☉ *Fri.–Sun. 9–4.*

★ **Kelso Dunes.** As you enter the preserve from the south, you'll pass miles of open scrub brush, Joshua trees, and beautiful red-black cinder cones before encountering the Kelso Dunes. These golden, fine-sand slopes cover 70 square miles, reaching heights of 600 feet. You can reach them via a ½-mile walk from the main parking area, but be prepared for a serious workout. When you reach the top of a dune, kick a little bit of sand down the lee side and listen to the sand "sing." North of the dunes, in the town of Kelso, is the Mission revival–style **Kelso Depot Visitor Center.** The striking building, which dates to 1923, was extensively renovated last decade and contains several rooms of desert- and train-themed exhibits. The Depot's restaurant, The Beanery, has an early- to mid-20th-century diner look that will have you reaching for your camera. ⊠ *For Kelso Depot Visitor Center, take Kelbaker Rd. exit from I–15 (head south 34 miles) or I–40 (head north 22 miles)* ☎ *760/928–2572, 760/252–6100* ⊕ *www.nps.gov/moja.*

Providence Mountains State Recreation Area. Budget cuts have resulted in the closure of this distinctive state park "until further notice," but you can still drive around the area and marvel at the desert vistas. The visitor center was also closed as of this writing, as was nearby **Mitchell Caverns.** ⊠ *Essex Rd., 16 miles north of I–40* ☎ *760/928–2586* ⊕ *www. parks.ca.gov/?page_id=26732.*

NEEDLES

I–40, 150 miles east of Barstow.

Along Route 66 and the Colorado River, Needles is a decent base for exploring Mojave National Preserve and other desert attractions. Founded in 1883, the town, named for the jagged mountain peaks that overlook the city, served as a stop along the Santa Fe railroad line.

GETTING HERE AND AROUND

Greyhound and Amtrak both pass through town daily, though most travelers arrive by car, either via Interstate 40 (east–west) or Highway 95 (north–south). Needles Area Transit is the local bus service.

ESSENTIALS

Bus Information Needles Area Transit ☎ 760/326-2113 ⊕ www. cityofneedles.com/transportation.asp.

Visitor Information Needles Chamber of Commerce ✉ 100 G St., at Front St. ☎ 760/326-2050 ⊕ www.needleschamber.com.

EXPLORING

El Garces Harvey House Train Depot. Stop and gawk at the crumbling 1908 train depot, one of the many restaurant–boardinghouses built by the Fred Harvey company, and imagine how magnificent this skeletal structure would look in the unlikely event it were restored. The shady city park out front has inviting benches. ✉ 900 Front St., at F. St. ☎ 760/326-5678.

Ⓒ   **Havasu National Wildlife Refuge.** In 1941, after the construction of Parker
Fodor'sChoice   Dam, President Franklin D. Roosevelt set aside Havasu National Wild-
★   life Refuge, a 24-mile stretch of land along the Colorado River between Needles and Lake Havasu City. Best seen by boat, this beautiful waterway is punctuated with isolated coves, sandy beaches, and Topock Marsh, a favorite nesting site of herons, egrets, and other waterbirds. You can see wonderful petroglyphs on the rocky red canyon cliffs of Topock Gorge. The park has 11 boat-access points; there's camping below Castle Rock. ■TIP→ Springtime is by far the best time to visit, as the river is more likely to be robust and wildflowers aflame. ✉ Off I–40, 13 miles southeast of Needles ☎ 760/326-3853 ⊕ www.fws.gov/ southwest/refuges/arizona/havasu.

Moabi Regional Park. This park on the banks of the Colorado River is a good place for swimming, boating, picnicking, horseback riding, and fishing. Bass, bluegill, and trout are plentiful in the river. The 600 campsites have full amenities. ✉ Park Moabi Rd., off I–40, 11 miles southeast of Needles ☎ 760/326-3831 ⊕ cms.sbcounty.gov/parks 🎫 Day use $10, camping $15–$40.

WHERE TO EAT AND STAY

For expanded reviews, facilities, and current deals, visit Fodors.com.

$ ✕ **River City Pizza.** Good grub is hard to find in Needles, but this inex-
PIZZA   pensive pizza place off Interstate 40 is a local favorite. Try the Vegetarian Deluxe pizza with a mug of cold lager or a glass of wine out on the small patio. 🟤 Average main: $14 ✉ 1901 Needles Hwy., at P St. ☎ 760/326-9191 ⊕ www.rivercitypizzaco.com.

$ ▦ **Best Western Colorado River Inn.** The spartan country western–style
HOTEL   rooms here are decorated in rich colors; expect the standard Best Western amenities. **Pros:** good rates; clean rooms; free calls; complimentary coffee. **Cons:** town's dead at night (and not much livelier during the day!); occasional train noise. **TripAdvisor:** "an oasis in the middle of nowhere," "clean and quiet," "great customer service." 🟤 Rooms from:

$77 ⊠2371 Needles Hwy. ☎760/326–4552, 800/780–7234 ⊕ www. bestwestern.com ⟳63 rooms |◎| Breakfast.

$ **RESORT** ⟳ ⊡ **Fender's River Road Resort.** On a calm section of the Colorado River, this funky little 1960s-era motel-resort—one of the best-kept secrets in Needles—caters to families with shade trees and an area with grills and picnic tables. **Pros:** on the river; clean rooms; peaceful; camping is $28–$40 a night. **Cons:** several minutes from the freeway; bare-bones amenities. **TripAdvisor:** "simply comfortable and relaxing," "friendly," "too much fun."[⑤] *Rooms from: $69 ⊠3396 Needles Hwy. ☎760/326– 3423 ⟳10 rooms, 27 campsites with full hookups.*

LAKE HAVASU CITY, AZ

Arizona Hwy. 95, 43 miles southeast of Needles in Arizona.

This wide spot in the Colorado River, created in the 1930s by Parker Dam, is accessed from its eastern shore in Arizona. Here you can swim; zip around on a Jet Ski; paddle a kayak; fish for trout, bass, or bluegill; or boat beneath the London Bridge, one of the desert's oddest sights. During sunset the views are breathtaking. Just be wary of coming here during March, when spring-breaking students definitely change the vibe.

16

GETTING HERE AND AROUND

Shuttles operate between here and Las Vegas, but as with other desert sites, traveling by car is the only practical way to go. Havasu Area Transit is the local bus service.

ESSENTIALS

Transportation Contacts Havasu Area Transit ☎ *928/453–7600.*

EXPLORING

London Bridge. What really put Lake Havasu City on the map was the piece-by-piece reconstruction in 1971 of London Bridge by town founder Robert P. McCulloch. Today the circa-1831 bridge, designed by John Rennie, connects the city to a small island. Riverbanks on both sides have numerous restaurants, hotels, RV parks, There's also a reconstructed English village whose quiet streets suggest that it has lost some of its luster. ☎ *928/855–4115 ⊕ www.havasuchamber.com* ⊡ *Free ⊙ Daily 24 hrs.*

WHERE TO EAT

$$$ **AMERICAN** ★ ✕ **Shugrue's.** This lakefront restaurant serves up beautiful views of London Bridge and the English Village, along with fresh seafood, steak, and specials such as Bombay chicken and shrimp, served with spicy yogurt sauce and mango chutney. [⑤] *Average main: $25 ⊠1425 N. McCulloch Blvd. ☎928/453–1400 ⊕ www.shugrues.com/lhc.*

SPORTS AND THE OUTDOORS

⟳ *Lake Havasu Dixie Bell.* The two-story, old-fashioned paddle-wheel boat, with air-conditioning and a cocktail lounge, takes its passengers on a one-hour narrated tour around the island. ☎ *928/453–6776 ⊕www. londonbridgeresort.com ⊡$20 ⊙ Tours daily at noon and 1:30.*

London Bridge Watercraft Tours & Rentals. Right on the beach, this outfitter rents personal watercraft such as Jet Skis and Sea-Doos. ⊠ *Crazy Horse Campground, 1534 Beachcomber Blvd.* ☎ *928/453–8883* ⊕ *www. londonbridgewatercraft.com.*

OWENS VALLEY

Along U.S. 395 east of the Sierra Nevada.

In this undervisited region, the snowcapped Sierra Nevada range abruptly and majestically rises to the west and the high desert whistles to the east.

LONE PINE

30 miles west of Panamint Valley via Hwy. 190.

Mt. Whitney towers majestically over this tiny community, which supplied nearby gold- and silver-mining outposts in the 1860s, and for the past century—especially from the 1920s through the 50s—the town has been touched by Hollywood glamour: several hundred movies, TV episodes, and commercials have been filmed here.

GETTING HERE AND AROUND

Arrive by car via U.S. 395 from the north or south, or Highway 190 from Death Valley National Park. No train or regularly scheduled bus service is available.

ESSENTIALS

Visitor Information Lone Pine Chamber of Commerce ⊠ *126 S. Main St., at Whitney Portal Rd.* ☎ *760/876–4444, 877/253–8981* ⊕ *www.lonepinechamber. org.*

EXPLORING

Alabama Hills. Drop by the Lone Pine Visitor Center for a map of the Alabama Hills and take a drive up Whitney Portal Road (turn west at the light) to this wonderland of granite boulders. Erosion has worn the rocks smooth; some have been chiseled to leave arches and other formations. The hills have become a popular location for rock climbing. There are three campgrounds among the rocks, each with a stream for fishing. ⊠ *Whitney Portal Rd., 4½ miles west of Lone Pine.*

Beverly and Jim Rogers Museum of Lone Pine Film History. Hopalong Cassidy, Barbara Stanwyck, Roy Rogers, John Wayne—even Robert Downey Jr.—are among the stars who have starred in westerns and other films shot in the Alabama Hills and surrounding dusty terrain. The marquee-embellished museum relates this Hollywood-in-the-desert tale via exhibits and a rollicking 20-minute documentary. ⊠ *701 S. Main St., U.S. 395* ☎ *760/876–9909* ⊕ *www.lonepinefilmhistorymuseum.org* ⌑ *$5* ⊙ *Mon.–Wed. 10–6, Thurs.–Sat. 10–7, Sun. 10–4.*

★ **Mt. Whitney.** Straddling the border of Sequoia National Park and Inyo National Forest–John Muir Wilderness, Mt. Whitney (14,496 feet) is the highest mountain in the contiguous United States. A favorite game for travelers passing through Lone Pine is trying to guess which peak is Mt. Whitney. Almost no one gets it right because Mt. Whitney is hidden behind other mountains. There is no road that ascends the peak, but you can catch a glimpse of the mountain by driving curvy Whitney Portal Road west from Lone Pine into the mountains. The pavement ends at the trailhead to the top of the mountain, which is also the start of the 211-mile John Muir Trail from Mt. Whitney to Yosemite National Park. At the portal, a restaurant (known for its pancakes) and a small store mostly cater to hikers and campers staying at Whitney Portal Campground. You can see a waterfall from the parking lot and go fishing in a small trout pond. The portal area is closed from mid-October to early May; the road closes when snow conditions require. ⊠ *Whitney Portal Rd., west of Lone Pine* ⊕ *www.fs.usda.gov/attmain/inyo.*

WHERE TO EAT AND STAY

For expanded reviews, facilities, and current deals, visit Fodors.com.

$ **✕ Alabama Hills Café & Bakery.** The extensive breakfast and lunch menus
AMERICAN at this eatery just off the main drag include many vegetarian items. Portions are huge. ⑤ *Average main: $10* ⊠ *111 W. Post St., at S. Main St.* ☎ *760/876–4675.*

$ **⊡ Dow Villa Motel and Hotel.** Built in 1923 to cater to the film indus-
HOTEL try (John Wayne slept here), Dow Villa is in the center of Lone Pine. **Pros:** clean rooms; great mountain views; in-room whirlpool tubs. **Cons:** somewhat dated decor; some rooms share bathrooms. **Trip-Advisor:** "very comfortable," "made us feel welcome," "beautiful view."⑤ *Rooms from: $105* ⊠ *310 S. Main St.* ☎ *760/876–5521, 800/824–9317* ⊕ *www.dowvillamotel.com* ⇆ *91 rooms* ⦿*No meals.*

16

MANZANAR NATIONAL HISTORIC SITE

U.S. 395, 11 miles north of Lone Pine.

GETTING HERE AND AROUND

There's no public transportation here; virtually everyone arrives by car.

EXPLORING

Manzanar National Historic Site. A reminder of an ugly episode in U.S. history, the former Manzanar War Relocation Center is where some 10,000 Japanese-Americans were confined behind barbed-wire fences between 1942 and 1945. Today not much remains of Manzanar but a guard post, the auditorium, and some concrete foundations. But you can drive the one-way dirt road past the ruins to a small cemetery, where a monument stands. Signs mark where the barracks, a hospital, a school, and the fire station once stood. An outstanding 8,000-square-foot interpretive center has exhibits and screens a short film. ■ TIP➔ This place has great bathrooms. ⊠ *U.S. 395, 11 miles north of Lone Pine* ☎ *760/878–2932* ⊕ *www.nps.gov/manz* ✉ *Free* ⊗ *Park daily dawn–dusk. Center Apr.–Oct., daily 9–5:30; Nov.–Mar., daily 9–4:30.*

CERRO GORDO GHOST TOWN

20 miles east of Lone Pine.

GETTING HERE AND AROUND

You can't visit Cerro Gordo without a car, and due to the rocky, steep roads you can't expect to make it here safely with a low-clearance undercarriage.

EXPLORING

Cerro Gordo Ghost Town. Discovered by Mexican miner Pablo Flores in 1865, Cerro Gordo was California's biggest producer of silver and lead, raking in almost $13 million before it shut down in 1959. Today, the privately owned ghost town offers overnight accommodations in the **Belshaw House** and the **Bunkhouse** for $150 per night (up to five people), billing itself the only bed-and-cook-your-own-breakfast ghost town in the world. Visit during the summer, as the 8,300-foot elevation proves impassable during the winter. Four-wheel-drive is recommended for the steep road into the ghost town. Admission includes a tour if arranged in advance. ⊠ *From U.S. 395 at Lone Pine, take Hwy. 136 for 13 miles to Keeler, then follow Cerro Gordo Rd. for 7½ miles. From Panamint Springs, drive 31 miles west on Hwy. 190 until it merges with Hwy. 136; drive 5 more miles to Cerro Gordo Rd.* ☎ *760/876–5030* ⊕ *www.cerrogordo.us.*

INDEPENDENCE

U.S. 395, 5 miles north of Manzanar National Historic Site.

Named for a military outpost that was established near here in 1862, Independence is small and sleepy. But the town has some wonderful historic buildings and is certainly worth a stop on your way from the Sierra Nevada to Death Valley (⇨ *Chapter 17*).

GETTING HERE AND AROUND

Greyhound passes through town, but most travelers arrive by car on U.S. 395.

ESSENTIALS

Visitor Information Independence Chamber of Commerce ⊠ *139 N. Edwards. St., U.S. 395* ☎ *760/878–0084* ⊕ *www.independence-ca.com.*

EXPLORING

Eastern California Museum. The highlights at this glimpse into Inyo County's history include the Paiute and Shoshone Indian basketry, the exhibit about the Manzanar internment camp, and the yard full of implements used by early area miners and farmers. ⊠ *155 N. Grant St., at W. Center St.* ☎ *760/878–0364* ⊕ *www.inyocounty.us/ecmuseum* 🖭 *Donations accepted* ☉ *Daily 10–5.*

Mt. Whitney Fish Hatchery. Here's a delightful place for a family picnic. Bring some change for the fish-food machines; the lakes are full of hefty, always-hungry breeder trout. Built in 1915, the hatchery was one of the first trout farms in California, and today it produces fish that stock lakes throughout the state. ⊠ *Fish Hatchery Rd., 2 miles north of town* 🖭 ⊕ *mtwhitneyfishhatchery.org* 🖭 *Free* ☉ *Thurs.–Mon. 9–4.*

A memorial honors the 10,000 Japanese-Americans who were held at the Manzanar War Relocation Center during World War II.

EN ROUTE

WHERE TO STAY

Ancient Bristlecone Pine Forest. About an hour's drive from Bishop you can view some of the oldest living trees on Earth, some of which date back more than 40 centuries. The world's largest bristlecone pine can be found in Patriarch Grove. ⊠ *Schulman Grove Visitor Center, White Mountain Rd. (from U.S. 395, turn east onto Hwy. 168 and follow signs for 23 miles)* 🖅 *$3* ☉ *Mid-May–Nov., shorter or longer as weather permits.*

BISHOP

U.S. 395, 43 miles north of Independence.

One of the biggest towns along U.S. 395, Bishop has views of the Sierra Nevada and the White and Inyo mountains. First settled by the Northern Paiute Indians, the area was named in 1861 for cattle rancher Samuel Bishop, who established a camp here. Paiute and Shoshone people reside on four reservations in the area.

GETTING HERE AND AROUND

To fully enjoy the many surrounding attractions, you must get here by car. Arrive and depart via U.S. 395 or, from Nevada, U.S. 6. Local transit provides limited service to nearby tourist sites.

ESSENTIALS

Bus Information Eastern Sierra Transit Authority 🕾 *800/922–1930* ⊕ *estransit.com.*

Visitor Information Bishop Chamber of Commerce ⊠ *690 N. Main St., at Park St.* 🕾 *760/873–8405* ⊕ *www.bishopvisitor.com.*

EXPLORING

☾ **Laws Railroad Museum.** The laid-back and wholly nostalgic Laws Railroad Museum celebrates the Carson and Colorado Railroad Company, which set up a narrow-gauge railroad yard here in 1883. Among the exhibits are a self-propelled car from the Death Valley Railroad and a full village of rescued buildings, including a post office, the original 1883 train depot, and a restored 1900 ranch house. Many of the buildings are chock-full of "modern amenities" of days gone by. ⊠ *200 Silver Canyon Rd., off U.S. 6, 4.5 miles north of town* ☎ *760/873–5950* ⊕ *www.lawsmuseum.org* ⊠ *$5 suggested donation* ⊙ *Daily 10–4.*

WHERE TO EAT AND STAY

For expanded reviews, facilities, and current deals, visit Fodors.com.

$ ✕ **Erick Schat's Bakkerÿ.** A bustling stop for motorists traveling to and
BAKERY from Mammoth Lakes, this shop is crammed with delicious pastries,
★ cookies, rolls, and other baked goods. The biggest draw, though, is the sheepherder bread, a hand-shaped and stone hearth–baked sourdough that was introduced during the gold rush by immigrant Basque sheepherders in 1907. That bread and others baked here are sliced to make the mammoth sandwiches the shop is also famous for. ⑤ *Average main: $8* ⊠ *763 N. Main St., near Park St.* ☎ *760/873–7156* ⊕ *www. erickschatsbakery.com.*

$$ ✕ **Whiskey Creek.** Since 1924, this Wild West–style saloon, restaurant,
AMERICAN and gift shop has been serving salads, warm soups, and barbecued steaks to locals and tourists. Sit on the shaded deck and enjoy one of the many available microbrews. ⑤ *Average main: $20* ⊠ *524 N. Main St., at Grove St.* ☎ *760/873–7174* ⊕ *www.whiskeycreekbishop.com.*

$$ ⌂ **Bishop Creekside Inn.** The nicest spot to stay in Bishop, this clean and
B&B/INN comfortable mountain-style hotel is a good base from which to explore the town or go skiing and trout fishing nearby. **Pros:** nice pool; spacious and modern rooms. **Cons:** pets not allowed. **TripAdvisor:** "very relaxing place to stay," "welcoming spot," "nice rooms." ⑤ *Rooms from: $150* ⊠ *725 N. Main St.* ☎ *760/872–3044, 800/273–3550* ⊕ *www. bishopcreeksideinn.com* ⇄ *89 rooms* ⍾ *Breakfast.*

Death Valley National Park

WORD OF MOUTH

"Death Valley early in the morning in the summer (or anytime) is spectacular. If you just drive through, and never hike Mosaic Canyon, or the myriad other wonderful walks into the rocks, you'll never really know what it holds."

—sylvia3

WELCOME TO DEATH VALLEY NATIONAL PARK

TOP REASONS TO GO

★ **Roving rocks:** Death Valley's Racetrack is home to moving boulders, an unexplained phenomenon that has scientists baffled.

★ **Lowest spot on the continent:** Stand on the lowest spot on the continent at Badwater, 282 feet below sea level.

★ **Wildflower explosion:** During the spring, this desert landscape is ablaze with greenery and colorful flowers, especially between Badwater and Ashford Mill.

★ **Ghost towns:** Death Valley is renowned for its Wild West heritage and is home to dozens of crumbling settlements including Ballarat, Cerro Gordo, Chloride City, Greenwater, Harrisburg, Keeler, Leadfield, Panamint City, Rhyolite, and Skidoo.

★ **Naturally amazing:** From canyons to sand dunes to salt flats and dry lake beds, Death Valley serves up plenty of geological treasures.

1 Central Death Valley. Furnace Creek sits in the heart of Death Valley—if you have only a short time in the park, head here. You can visit gorgeous Golden Canyon, Zabriskie Point, the Salt Creek Interpretive Trail, and Artist's Drive, among other popular points of interest.

2 Northern Death Valley. This region is uphill from Furnace Creek, which means marginally cooler temperatures. Be sure to stop by Rhyolite Ghost Town on Highway 374 before entering the park and exploring Moorish Scotty's Castle, colorful Titus Canyon, and jaw-dropping Ubehebe Crater.

3 Southern Death Valley. This is a desolate area, but there are plenty of sights that help convey Death Valley's rich history. Don't miss the Dublin Gulch Caves, or the famous Amargosa Opera House, where octogenarian ballerina Marta Becket still wows the crowds.

4 Western Death Valley.

Panamint Springs Resort is a nice place to grab a meal and get your bearings before moving on to quaint Darwin Falls, smooth rolling sand dunes, beehive-shaped Wildrose Charcoal Kilns, and historic Stovepipe Wells Village. On the way in, stop at Cerro Gordo Ghost Town, where you can view restored buildings dating back to 1867.

CALIFORNIA

GETTING ORIENTED

Death Valley National Park covers 5,310 square miles, ranges from 6 to 60 miles wide, and measures 140 miles north to south. Within the park, the Panamint Range parallels Death Valley to the west, the Amargosa Range to the east. Nearly all of the park lies in southeastern California, with a small eastern portion crossing over into Nevada.

17

Rhyolite (ghost town)
Beatty
374
95
TO LAS VEGAS

AMARGOSA RANGE

DEATH

Historic Stovepipe Well
Stovepipe Wells Village
Keane Wonder Mine
Salt Creek Interpretive Trail
190
Devils Cornfield
Harmony Borax Works Interpretive Trail
Visitor Center
Furnace Creek
1
Emigrant Canyon Rd.
Golden Canyon Interpretive Trail
Zabriskie Point
Twenty Mule Team Canyon
Artist's Palette
190
Devils Golf Course
Charcoal Kilns
Mahogany Flat
Natural Bridge
Natural Bridge Canyon
Badwater
Dante's View
Amargosa Valley
373
Death Valley Junction
TO PAHRUMP
127

VALLEY

Panamint City (ghost town)

Badwater Basin Lowest elevation in the U.S., 282 ft. below sea level

Tint indicates area below sea level
3
178
Shoshone

Ashford Mill (ruins)
127

Saratoga Spring
TO BAKER & I-15

Updated by
Reed Parsell

The desert is no Disneyland. With its scorching summer heat and vast, sparsely populated tracts of land, it's not often at the top of the list when most people plan their California vacations. But the natural riches of Death Valley—the largest national park outside Alaska—are overwhelming: rolling waves of sand dunes, black cinder cones thrusting up hundreds of feet from a blistered desert floor, riotous sheets of wildflowers, bizarrely shaped Joshua trees basking in the orange glow of a sunset, tiny pupfish that enthrall youngsters, and a silence that is both dramatic and startling.

DEATH VALLEY PLANNER

WHEN TO GO

Most of the park's 1 million annual visitors still come between late fall and early spring, taking advantage of moderate temperatures and the lack of rainfall. During these cooler months you will need to book a room in advance, but don't worry: the park never feels crowded. If you visit during summer, believe everything you've ever heard about desert heat—it can be brutal, with temperatures often topping 120°F. The dry air wicks moisture from the body without causing a sweat, so drink plenty of water. Bring sunglasses, a hat, and sufficient clothing to block the sun's rays and the wind. Flash floods are fairly common; sections of roadway can be flooded or washed away. The wettest month is February, when the park receives an average of 0.3 inch of rain.

GETTING HERE AND AROUND
CAR TRAVEL

It can take more than three hours to cross from one side of the park to another, so it's important to choose an entrance point that makes sense for what you want to see. If you're driving from Los Angeles, enter through the western portion along Highway 395; enter from the north at Beatty, Nevada, or via the central entrance at Death Valley Junction if you're coming from Las Vegas. Travelers from Orange County, San Diego, and the Inland Empire should access the park via Interstate15 North at Baker.

Distances can be deceiving within the park: what seems close can be very far away. Much of the park can be viewed on regularly scheduled bus tours, but these often don't allow time for hikes to sites not seen from the road, such as Salt Creek, Golden Canyon, and Natural Bridge. The best option is to drive to a number of the sites, get out of the car, and walk.

When driving in Death Valley, reliable maps are important, as signage is often limited or, in a few places, nonexistent. Other important accessories include a compass, a mobile phone (though these don't always work in remote areas), and extra food and water (3 gallons per person per day is recommended, plus additional radiator water). If you're able to take a four-wheel-drive vehicle, bring it: many of Death Valley's most spectacular canyons are otherwise inaccessible. Be aware of possible winter closures or driving restrictions due to snow.

Driving Information California State Department of Transportation Hotline. Call this hotline for updates on Death Valley road conditions. ☎ *916/445–7623, 800/427–7623* ⊕ *www.dot.ca.gov.* **California Highway Patrol.** The California Highway Patrol offers the latest traffic incident information. ☎ *800/427–7623 recorded info, 760/872–5900 live dispatcher* ⊕ *cad.chp.ca.gov.*

17

PARK ESSENTIALS

PARK FEES AND PERMITS

The entrance fee is $20 per vehicle and $10 for those entering on foot, bus, bike, or motorcycle. The payment, valid for seven consecutive days, is collected at the park's entrance stations and at the visitor center at Furnace Creek. (If you enter the park on Highway 190, you won't find an entrance station; remember to stop by the visitor center to pay the fee.) Annual park passes, valid only at Death Valley, are $40.

A permit is not required for groups of 14 or fewer, but if you're planning an overnight visit to the backcountry, complete a registration form at the Furnace Creek Visitor Center. Backcountry camping is allowed in areas that are at least 2 miles from maintained campgrounds and the main paved or unpaved roads and ¼ mile from water sources. Most abandoned mining areas are restricted to day use.

PARK HOURS

Most facilities within the park remain open year-round, daily 8–6.

TOURS

Death Valley & Scotty's Castle Adventure Tour. These 11-hour luxury motorcoach tours of the park pass through its most famous landmarks. Tours include lunch and hotel pickup from designated Las Vegas–area hotels. Tours depart Tuesday and Thursday at 7 am and cost $199 per person. ☎ *800/719–3768 Death Valley Tours, 800/566–5868, 702/233–1627 Look Tours.*

Furnace Creek Visitor Center tours. This center has the most tour options, including a weekly 2-mile Harmony Borax Walk and guided hikes to Mosaic Canyon and Golden Canyon. Less strenuous options include wildflower, birding, and geology walks, and a Furnace Creek Inn historical tour. The visitor center also offers orientation programs every half hour daily from 8 to 5. ⊠ *Furnace Creek Visitor Center, Rte. 190, 30 miles northwest of Death Valley Junction* ☎ 760/786–2331.

Pink Jeep Tours Las Vegas. Hop aboard a distinctive, pink four-wheel-drive vehicle with Pink Jeep Tours Las Vegas to visit places—the Charcola Kilns, the Racetrack, and Titus Canyon among them—that your own vehicle might not be able to handle. Pink Jeep tours last 9 to 10 hours from Las Vegas (you also can board at Furnace Creek) and cost up to $239. ☎ *888/900–4480* ⊕ *www.pinkjeep.com*

VISITOR INFORMATION

PARK CONTACT INFORMATION
Death Valley National Park *760/786–3200* ⊕ *www.nps.gov/deva.*

VISITOR CENTERS
Furnace Creek Visitor Center and Museum. The exhibits and artifacts here provide a broad overview of how Death Valley formed; you can pick up maps at the bookstore run by the Death Valley Natural History Association. This is also the place to sign up for ranger-led walks (available November through April) or check out a live presentation about the valley's cultural and natural history. The recently renovated center offers 12-minute slide shows about the park every 30 minutes. Your children are likely to receive plenty of individual attention from the enthusiastic rangers. Ongoing renovations to the center and museum are improving the displays and level of hands-on interactivity. ⊠ *Hwy. 190, 30 miles northwest of Death Valley Junction* ☎ *760/786–3200* ⊕ *www.nps.gov/deva* ☼ *Daily 8–5.*

Scotty's Castle Visitor Center and Museum. If you visit Death Valley, make sure you make the hour's drive north from Furnace Creek to Scotty's Castle. In addition to living-history tours, you'll find a nice display of exhibits, books, self-guided tour pamphlets, and displays about the castle's creators, Death Valley Scotty and Albert M. Johnson. Fuel up with sandwiches or souvenirs (there's no gasoline sold here anymore) before heading back out to the park. ⊠ *Rte. 267, 53 miles northwest of Furnace Creek and 45 miles northwest of Stovepipe Wells Village* ☎ *760/786–2392* ⊕ *www.nps.gov/deva* ☼ *Daily 8:30–5:30 (hrs vary seasonally).*

EXPLORING

SCENIC DRIVE

Artist's Drive. This 9-mile, one-way route skirts the foothills of the Black Mountains and provides intimate views of the changing landscape. Once inside the palette, the huge expanses of the valley are replaced by the small-scale natural beauty of pigments created by volcanic deposits.

It's a quiet, lonely drive, and shouldn't be rushed. Reach Artist's Palette by heading north off Badwater Road.

HISTORIC SITES

🕲 **Scotty's Castle.** This Moorish-style mansion, begun in 1924 and never completed, takes its name from Walter Scott, better known as Death Valley Scotty. An ex-cowboy, prospector, and performer in Buffalo Bill's Wild West Show, Scotty always told people the castle was his, financed by gold from a secret mine. In reality, there was no mine, and the house belonged to a Chicago millionaire named Albert Johnson, whom Scott had finagled into investing in the fictitious mine. Despite the con, Johnson and Scott became great friends. The house functioned for a while as a hotel and still contains works of art, imported carpets, handmade European furniture, and a tremendous pipe organ. Costumed rangers, with varying degrees of enthusiasm, re-create life at the castle circa 1939. Check out the Underground Tour, which takes you through a ¼-mile tunnel in the castle basement. ⊠ *Scotty's Castle Rd. (Hwy. 267), 53 miles north of Salt Creek Interpretive Trail* ☎ *760/786–2392* ⊕ *www.nps.gov/deva* ☒ *$15* ☾ *Daily 8:30–5, tours daily 9–5 (hrs vary seasonally).*

SCENIC STOPS

17

Artist's Palette. So called for the contrasting colors of its volcanic deposits, this is one of signature sights of Death Valley. Artist's Drive, the approach to the area, is one way heading north off Badwater Road, so if you're visiting Badwater from Furnace Creek, come here on the way back. The drive winds through foothills of sedimentary and volcanic rocks. About 4 miles into the drive, a short side road veers right to a parking lot that's a few hundred feet before the "palette," whose natural colors include shades of green, gold, and pink. ⊠ *off Badwater Rd., 11 miles south of Furnace Creek.*

Badwater. At 282 feet below sea level, Badwater is the lowest spot on land in the Western Hemisphere—and also one of the hottest. Stairs and wheelchair ramps descend from the parking lot to a wooden platform that overlooks a sodium chloride pool, a small but remarkably persistent reminder that the valley floor used to contain a lake. You can continue past the platform on a broad, white path that peters out after a half mile or so. Badwater is one of the most popular and easily accessible sites within the park. From this lowest point, be sure to look across to Telescope Peak, which towers more than 2 miles above the valley floor. ⊠ *Badwater Rd., 19 miles south of Furnace Creek.*

Fodor'sChoice ★ **Dante's View.** This lookout is more than 5,000 feet up in the Black Mountains. In the dry desert air you can see across most of 110-mile-long Death Valley. The view is astounding. Take a 10-minute, mildly strenuous walk from the parking lot toward a series of rocky overlooks, where with binoculars you can spot some of Death Valley's signature sites. A few interpretive signs point out the highlights below in the valley and across, in the Sierra. Getting here from Furnace Creek takes an hour—time well invested. ⊠ *Dante's View Rd., off Hwy. 190, 35 miles from Badwater, 20 miles south of Twenty Mule Team Canyon.*

Devil's Golf Course. Thousands of miniature salt pinnacles carved into surreal shapes by the desert wind dot this wildly varied landscape. The salt was pushed up to the earth's surface by pressure created as underground salt- and water-bearing gravel crystallized. Get out of your vehicle and take a closer look; you'll see perfectly round holes descending into the ground. ⊠ *Badwater Rd., 13 miles south of Furnace Creek. Turn right onto dirt road and drive 1 mile.*

Racetrack. Getting here involves a 27-mile journey over a rough dirt road, but the reward is well worth the trip. Where else in the world do rocks move on their own? This phenomenon has baffled scientists for years and is perhaps one of the last great natural mysteries. No one has actually seen the rocks in motion, but theory has it that when it rains, the hard-packed lake bed becomes slippery enough that gusty winds push the rocks along—sometimes for several hundred yards. When the mud dries, a telltale trail remains. The trek to the Racetrack can be made in a sedan, but sharp rocks can slash tires; a truck or SUV with thick tires, high clearance, and a spare tire are suggested. ⊠ *27 miles west of Ubehebe Crater via dirt road.*

Sand Dunes at Mesquite Flat. These dunes, made up of minute pieces of quartz and other rock, are ever-changing products of the wind-rippled hills, with curving crests and a sun-bleached hue. The dunes are the most photographed destination in the park, and you can see them at their best at sunrise and sunset. Keep your eyes open for animal tracks— you may even spot a coyote or fox. Bring plenty of water, and note where you parked your car: it's easy to become disoriented in this ocean of sand. If you lose your bearings, climb to the top of a dune and scan the horizon for the parking lot. ⊠ *19 miles north of Hwy. 190, northeast of Stovepipe Wells Village.*

Titus Canyon. This is a popular 28-mile drive from Beatty south along Scotty's Castle Road. Along the way you'll pass Leadville Ghost Town, petroglyphs at Klare Spring, and spectacular limestone and dolomite narrows at the end of the canyon. Toward the end, a gravel road will lead you into the mouth of the canyon. ⊠ *Access road off Scotty's Castle Rd., 33 miles northwest of Furnace Creek.*

Zabriskie Point. Although only about 710 feet in elevation, this is one of Death Valley National Park's most scenic spots, overlooking a striking panorama of wrinkled, multicolor hills. It's a great place to watch the sunrise, but it can be bustling any time of day. Pair it with a drive out to magnificent Dante's View. ⊠ *Hwy. 190, 5 miles south of Furnace Creek.*

SPORTS AND THE OUTDOORS

BIRD-WATCHING

Approximately 350 bird species have been identified in Death Valley. The best place to see the park's birds is along the Salt Creek Interpretive Trail, where you can spot ravens, common snipes, killdeer, spotted sandpipers, and great blue herons. Along the fairways at Furnace Creek Golf Club, you can see kingfishers, peregrine falcons, hawks, Canada geese, yellow warblers, and the occasional golden eagle—just remember to stay off the greens. Scotty's Castle attracts wintering birds from around the globe that are attracted to its running water, shady trees, and shrubs. Other good spots to find birds are at Saratoga Springs, Mesquite Springs, Travertine Springs, and Grimshaw Lake near Tecopa. You can download a complete park bird checklist, divided by season, at ⊕ *www. nps.gov/deva/naturescience/birds.htm*. Rangers at Furnace Creek Visitor Center often lead birding walks through Salt Creek between November and March.

FOUR-WHEELING

Maps and SUV guidebooks for four-wheel-drive and other backcountry roads (including the popular Cottonwood/Marble canyons, Racetrack, Eureka Dunes, Saratoga Springs, Warm Springs Canyon) are offered at the Furnace Creek Visitor Center. Remember: never travel alone and be sure to pack plenty of water and snacks. Driving off established roads is strictly prohibited in the park.

17

HIKING

Plan to hike before or after midday in the spring, summer, or fall, unless you're in the mood for a masochistic baking. Carry plenty of water, wear protective clothing, and keep an eye out for tarantulas, black widows, scorpions, snakes, and other potentially dangerous creatures. Some of the best trails are unmarked; if the opportunity arises, ask for directions.

EASY

Fodor's Choice
★

Darwin Falls. This lovely 2-mile round-trip hike rewards you with a refreshing waterfall surrounded by thick vegetation and a rocky gorge. No swimming or bathing is allowed, but it's a beautiful place for a picnic. Adventurous hikers can scramble higher toward more rewarding views of the falls. *Easy. ⊠ Access the 2-mile graded dirt road and parking area off Hwy. 190, 1 mile west of Panamint Springs Resort.*

Salt Creek Interpretive Trail. This trail, a ½-mile boardwalk circuit, loops through a spring-fed wash. The nearby hills are brown and gray, but the floor of the wash is alive with aquatic plants such as pickerelweed and salt grass. The stream and ponds here are among the few places in the park to see the rare pupfish, the only native fish species in Death Valley. Animals such as bobcats, fox, coyotes, and snakes visit the spring,

DID YOU KNOW?

One of the best ways to experience Artist's Palate—a beautiful landscape of colorful deposits—is by following Artist's Drive, a 9-mile one-way road through the area.

and you may also see ravens, common snipes, killdeer, and great blue herons. *Easy.* ⊠ *Off Hwy. 190, 14 miles north of Furnace Creek.*

MODERATE

Fall Canyon. This is a 3½-mile one-way hike from the Titus canyon parking area. First, walk ½ mile north along the base of the mountains to a large wash, then go 2½ miles up the canyon to a 35-foot dry fall. You can continue by climbing around to the falls on the south side. *Moderate.* ⊠ *Access road off Scotty's Castle Rd., 33 miles northwest of Furnace Creek.*

☺ **Mosaic Canyon.** A gradual uphill trail (4 miles round-trip) winds through the smoothly polished walls of this narrow canyon. There are dry falls to climb at the upper end. *Moderate.* ⊠ *Access road off Hwy. 190, ½ mile west of Stovepipe Wells Village.*

DIFFICULT

Fodor's Choice
★
Telescope Peak Trail. The 14-mile round-trip begins at Mahogany Flat Campground, which is accessible by a very rough dirt road. The steep and at some points treacherous trail winds through pinyon, juniper, and bristlecone pines, with excellent views of Death Valley and Panamint Valley. Ice axes and crampons may be necessary in winter—check at the Furnace Creek Visitor Center. It takes a minimum of six grueling hours to hike to the top of the 11,049-foot peak and then return. Getting to the peak is a strenuous endeavor; take plenty of water and only attempt it in fall if you're an experienced hiker. *Difficult.* ⊠ *Off Wildrose Rd., south of Charcoal Kilns.*

HORSEBACK AND CARRIAGE RIDES

TOURS AND OUTFITTERS

Furnace Creek Stables. Set off on a one- or two-hour guided horseback or carriage ride ($30–$65) from Furnace Creek Stables. The rides traverse trails with views of the surrounding mountains, where multicolor volcanic rock and alluvial fans form a background for date palms and other vegetation. Evening carriage rides take passengers around the golf course and Furnace Creek Ranch. Cocktail rides, with champagne, margaritas, and hot spiced wine, are available. The stables are open October through May only. ⊠ *Hwy. 190, Furnace Creek* ☎ *760/614–1018* ⊕ *www.furnacecreekstables.net.*

WHERE TO EAT

Prices in the reviews are the average cost of a main course at dinner or, if dinner is not served, at lunch.

$
CAFÉ
☺
✕ **Forty-Niner Cafe.** This casual coffee shop serves typical American fare for breakfast (except in the summer), lunch, and dinner. It's done up in a rustic mining style with whitewashed pine walls, vintage map-covered tables, and prospector-branded chairs. Past menus and old photographs decorate the walls. ⑤ *Average main: $15* ⊠ *Furnace Creek Ranch, Hwy. 190, Furnace Creek* ☎ *760/786–2345* ⊕ *www.furnacecreekresort.com.*

"I'd always wanted to photograph this remote location, and on my drive into Death Valley I was rewarded at Zabriskie Point with this amazing view." —photo by Rodney Ee, Fodors.com member

$$$
AMERICAN
Fodor's Choice
★

✕**Furnace Creek Inn Dining Room.** Fireplaces, beamed ceilings, and spectacular views provide a visual feast to match the inn's ambitious menu. Dishes may include such desert-theme items as crispy cactus fritters, and simpler fare such as salmon and free-range chicken and filet mignon all pair well with the signature prickly-pear margarita. There's a seasonal menu of vegetarian dishes, too. There's a minimal evening dress code (no T-shirts or shorts). Lunch is served, too, and you can always have afternoon tea in the lobby, an inn tradition since 1927. Breakfast and Sunday brunch are also served. Reservations are essential for dinner only. $ *Average main: $28* ✉ *Furnace Creek Inn Resort, Hwy. 190, Furnace Creek* ☎ *760/786–2345* ⊕ *www.furnacecreekresort.com* ⏶ *Reservations essential* ⊙ *Restaurant closed June–Sept.*

WHERE TO STAY

During the busy season (November through March) you should make reservations for lodgings within the park several months in advance. *Prices in the reviews are the lowest cost of a standard double room in high season. For expanded hotel reviews, visit Fodors.com.*

$$$$
HOTEL
Fodor's Choice
★

▦ **Furnace Creek Inn.** This is Death Valley's most luxurious accommodations, going so far as to have valet parking. **Pros:** refined; comfortable; great views. **Cons:** a far cry from roughing it; expensive. **TripAdvisor:** "clean and rustic," "great accommodations," "welcome oasis." $ *Rooms from: $375* ✉ *Furnace Creek Village, near intersection of Hwy. 190 and Badwater Rd.* ☎ *760/786–2345* ⊕ *www.furnacecreekresort. com* ⇆ *66 rooms* ⊙ *Closed mid-May–mid-Oct.* ⦿│*Breakfast.*

Plants and Wildlife in Death Valley

There's a general misconception that Death Valley National Park consists of mile upon endless mile of flat desert sands, scattered cacti, and an occasional cow skull. Many people don't realize that across the valley floor from Badwater—the lowest point in the Western Hemisphere—Telescope Peak towers at 11,049 feet above sea level. The extreme topography of Death Valley is a lesson in geology. Two hundred million years ago seas covered the area, depositing layers of sediment and fossils. Between 3.5 million and 5 million years ago faults in the Earth's crust and volcanic activity pushed and folded the ground, causing mountain ranges to rise and the valley floor to drop. The valley was then filled periodically by lakes, which eroded the surrounding rocks into fantastic formations and deposited the salts that now cover the floor of the basin.

Most animal life in Death Valley (51 mammal, 36 reptile, 307 bird, and three amphibian species) is found near the limited sources of water. The bighorn sheep spend most of their time in the secluded upper reaches of the park's rugged canyons and ridges. Coyotes often can be seen lazing in the shade next to the golf course and have been known to run onto the fairways to steal a golf ball. The only native fish in the park is the pupfish, which grows to slightly longer than 1 inch. In winter, when the water is cold, the fish lie dormant in the bottom mud, becoming active again in spring. Because they are wary of large moving shapes, you must stand quietly over a pool at Salt Creek to see them.

Botanists say there are more than 1,000 species of plants here (21 exist nowhere else in the world), though many annual plants lie dormant as seeds for all but a few months in spring, when rains trigger a bloom. The rest congregate around the few water sources. Most of the low-elevation vegetation grows around the oases at Furnace Creek and Scotty's Castle, where oleanders, palms, and salt cedar grow. At higher elevations you will find pinyon, juniper, and bristlecone pine.

$
B&B/INN
🏨 **Panamint Springs Resort.** Ten miles inside the west entrance of the park, this low-key resort overlooks the sand dunes and peculiar geological formations of the Panamint Valley. **Pros:** slow-paced; friendly; there's a glorious amount of peace and quiet after sundown. **Cons:** far from the park's main attractions. **TripAdvisor:** "quaint," "restful nights," "breathtaking vista." $ *Rooms from: $95* ⊠ *Hwy. 190, 28 miles west of Stovepipe Wells* 🕾 *775/482–7680* ⊕ *www.deathvalley.com/psr* 🛏 *14 rooms, 1 cabin* ⦿ *No meals.*

$$
HOTEL
🏨 **Stovepipe Wells Village.** If you prefer quiet nights and an unfettered view of the night sky and nearby sand dunes, this property is for you. **Pros:** intimate, relaxed; no big-time partying; authentic desert-community ambience. **Cons:** isolated; a bit dated. **TripAdvisor:** "stunning landscape," "good experience," "sweet oasis in the desert." $ *Rooms from: $140* ⊠ *Hwy. 190, Stovepipe Wells* 🕾 *760/786–2387* ⊕ *www. escapetodeathvalley.com* 🛏 *83 rooms* ⦿ *No meals.*

The Central Valley

HIGHWAY 99 FROM BAKERSFIELD TO LODI

WORD OF MOUTH

"We have many rivers that can be rafted. The closest river to Southern California and one of the best is the Upper Kern near Bakersfield. This was a fun day in June!"

— photo by Kim Brogan, Fodors.com member

WELCOME TO THE CENTRAL VALLEY

TOP REASONS TO GO

★ **Down under:** Forestiere Underground Gardens is not the flashiest tourist attraction in California, but it is one of the strangest—and oddly inspirational.

★ **Grape escape:** In the past two decades, Lodi's wineries have grown sufficiently in stature for the charming little town to become a must-sip destination.

★ **Port with authority:** Stockton has long been a hub for merchandise that is being transferred from roadway to waterway—or vice versa. Watch some of that commotion in commerce from the river-front downtown area.

★ **Go with the flow:** White-water rafting will get your blood pumping, and maybe your clothes wet, on the Stanislaus River near Oakdale.

★ **Hee haw!:** Kick up your heels and break out your drawl at Buck Owens' Crystal Palace in Bakersfield, a city some believe is the heart of country music.

1 Southern Central Valley. When gold was discovered in Kern County in the 1860s, settlers flocked to the southern end of the Central Valley. Black gold—oil—is now the area's most valuable commodity; the county provides two-thirds of California's oil production. Kern is also among the country's five most productive agricultural counties. From the flat plains around Bakersfield, the landscape grows gently hilly and then graduates to mountains as it nears Kernville, which lies in the Kern River valley.

2 Mid-Central Valley. The Mid-Central Valley extends over three counties—Tulare, Kings, and Fresno. Historic Hanford and bustling Visalia are off the tourist-traffic radar but have their charms. From Visalia, Highway 198 winds east 35 miles to Generals Highway, which passes through Sequoia and Kings Canyon national parks (⇨ *see Chapter 21*). Highway 180 snakes east 55 miles to Sequoia and Kings Canyon. From Fresno, Highway 41 leads north 95 miles to Yosemite National Park (⇨ *see Chapter 20*).

3 North Central Valley. The northern section of the valley cuts through Merced, Madera, Stanislaus, and San Joaquin counties, from the flat, abundantly fertile terrain between Merced and Modesto north to the edges of the Sacramento River delta and the fringes of the Gold Country. If you're heading to Yosemite National Park (⇨ *see Chapter 20*) from northern California, chances are you'll travel through (or near) one or more small gateway communities such as Oakdale.

GETTING ORIENTED

California has a diversity of delicious vacation possibilities. Among its many outstanding regions, however, the Central Valley is arguably the least inviting. This flat landscape, sometimes blistery hot and smelly, contains no famous attractions beyond its bountiful farmland, which few would regard as scenic except perhaps just before harvest. For many vacationers, it is a region to drive through as quickly as possible on the way to fabulous Sequoia, Kings Canyon, and Yosemite national parks (⇨ *see Chapters 20 and 21*). For those who have an extra day or two, whose tourism tastes don't demand Disneyland-level excitement, it can represent a pleasant diversion and provide insights into an enormous agricultural region. The valley is the vast geographical center of California, and from a breadbasket perspective, its proverbial heart.

18

Updated by
Reed Parsell

Among the world's most fertile working lands, the 225-mile Central Valley is important due to the scale of its food production but, to be honest, it lacks substantial appeal for visitors. For most people, the Central Valley is simply a place to pass through on the way to greater attractions in the north, south, east, or west. For those willing to invest some effort, however, California's heartland can be rewarding.

The Central Valley cuts through Kern, Tulare, Kings, Fresno, Madera, Merced, Stanislaus, and San Joaquin counties. It's bounded on the east by the mighty Sierra Nevada and on the west by the smaller coastal ranges. The agriculturally rich area is home to a diversity of birds; many telephone posts are crowned by a hawk or kestrel hunting the land below. Vineyards, especially in the northern valley around Lodi, and almond orchards, whose white blossoms make February a brighter month, are pleasant sights out motorists' windows. In the towns, historical societies display artifacts of the valley's eccentric past, concert halls and restored theaters showcase samplings of contemporary culture, and museums provide a blend of both. Restaurants can be very good, whether they be fancy or mom-and-pop. For fruit lovers, roadside stands can be treasure troves. Country-music enthusiasts will find a lot to appreciate on the radio and on stages, especially in the Bakersfield area. Summer nights spent at one of the valley's minor-league baseball parks—Bakersfield, Fresno, Modesto, Stockton, and Visalia have teams—can be a relaxing experience. Whether on back roads or main streets, people tend to be proud to help outsiders explore the Central Valley.

CENTRAL VALLEY PLANNER

WHEN TO GO
Spring, when wildflowers are in bloom and the scent of fruit blossoms is in the air, and fall, when the air is brisk and leaves turn red and gold, are the best times to visit. Many of the valley's biggest festivals take

place during these seasons. (If you suffer from allergies, though, beware of spring, when stone-fruit trees blossom.) Summer, when temperatures often top 100°F, can be oppressive. June through August, though, are the months to visit area water parks and lakes or to take in the air-conditioned museums. Many attractions close in winter, which can get dreary. Thick, ground-hugging tule fog is a common driving hazard from November through February.

GETTING HERE AND AROUND

AIR TRAVEL

The area's main airport is Fresno Yosemite International Airport (FYI), served by AeroMexico, Alaska, Allegiant, American, Delta, United, US Airways, and Volaris. Bakersfield's Kern County Airport at Meadows Field (BFL), served by United Express and US Airways, is the southern air gateway to the Central Valley. Regional airlines serve airports in Modesto and Visalia.

Airport Contacts Fresno Yosemite International Airport ✉ *5175 E. Clinton Way, Fresno* ☎ *559/621–4500, 800/244–2359 automated information* ⊕ *www.fresno.gov/discoverfresno/airports.***Kern County Airport at Meadows Field** ✉ *1401 Skyway Dr., Bakersfield* ☎ *661/391–1800* ⊕ *www.meadowsfield.com.*

BUS TRAVEL

Greyhound provides bus service to several major cities, and Orange Belt Stages provides coach service (and some Amtrak connections) to Bakersfield, Visalia, Hanford, and other large towns. KART buses serve Hanford, Visalia, and neighboring towns, with connections to Fresno on some weekdays.

Bus Contact Greyhound ☎ *800/231–2222* ⊕ *www.greyhound.com.***KART** ☎ *559/584–0101* ⊕ *www.mykartbus.com.* **Orange Belt Stages** ☎ *800/266–7433* ⊕ *www.orangebelt.com.*

CAR TRAVEL

Highway 99 is the main route between the valley's major cities and towns. Interstate 5 runs roughly parallel to it to the west but misses the major population centers; its main use is for quick access from San Francisco or Los Angeles. Major roads that connect the interstate with Highway 99 are Highways 58 (to Bakersfield), 198 (to Hanford and Visalia), 152 (to Chowchilla, via Los Banos), 140 (to Merced), 132 (to Modesto), and 120 (to Manteca).

Road Conditions California Department of Transportation ☎ *800/427–7623* ⊕ *www.dot.ca.gov.*

TRAIN TRAVEL

Amtrak's daily *San Joaquin* travels to Bakersfield, Hanford, Fresno, Merced, Modesto, and Stockton.

Train Contact Amtrak ☎ *800/872–7245* ⊕ *www.amtrakcalifornia.com.*

RESTAURANTS

Fast-food places and chain restaurants dominate valley highways, but away from the main drag, home-grown bistros and fine restaurants take advantage of the local produce and locally raised meats that are the cornerstone of California cuisine. Superb Mexican restaurants can

18

be found here, and Chinese, Italian, Armenian, and Basque cuisines are amply represented. *Prices in the reviews are the average cost of a main course at dinner or, if dinner is not served, at lunch.*

HOTELS

The Central Valley has many chain motels and hotels—utilitarian but clean and comfortable—but also a fair selection of upscale lodgings, small inns, and Victorian-style B&Bs. *Prices in the reviews are the lowest cost of a standard double room in high season. For expanded reviews, facilities, and current deals, visit Fodors.com.*

SOUTH CENTRAL VALLEY

BAKERSFIELD

110 miles north of Los Angeles via I–5 and Hwy. 99; 110 miles west of Ridgecrest via Hwy. 14 south and Hwy. 58 west.

Bakersfield's founder, Colonel Thomas Baker, arrived with the discovery of gold in the nearby Kern River valley in 1851. Now Kern County's biggest city—its 347,000 residents include the largest Basque community in the United States—Bakersfield probably is best known as Nashville West, a country-music haven closely affiliated with performers Buck Owens (who died here in 2006) and Merle Haggard (who was born here in 1937). It also has two very fine museums.

GETTING HERE AND AROUND

Arrive here by car via Highway 99 from the north or south, and via Highway 58 from the east or west. Amtrak and Greyhound provide train and bus service. GETbus operates local buses.

ESSENTIALS

Bus Contact GETbus ☎ *661/869–2438* ⊕ *www.getbus.org.*

Visitor Information Greater Bakersfield Convention & Visitors Bureau ⊠ *515 Truxton Ave.* ☎ *661/852–7282, 866/425–7353* ⊕ *www.visitbakersfield. com.* **Kern County Board of Trade** ⊠ *2101 Oak St.* ☎ *661/500–5376, 800/500–5376* ⊕ *www.visitkern.com.*

EXPLORING

Ⓒ ★ **California Living Museum.** A combination zoo, botanical garden, and natural-history museum, the emphasis here is on the zoo. All animal and plant species displayed are native to the state. Within the reptile house lives every species of rattlesnake found in California. The landscaped grounds—in the hills about a 20-minute drive northeast of Bakersfield—also shelter captive bald eagles, tortoises, coyotes, black bears, and foxes. ⊠ *10500 Alfred Harrell Hwy., Hwy. 178 east to Harrell Hwy. north* ☎ *661/872–2256* ⊕ *www.calmzoo.org* ⤳ *$9* ⊙ *Mar.–Oct., daily 9–5; Nov.–Feb., daily 9–4.*

Ⓒ ★ **Kern County Museum and Lori Brock Children's Discovery Center.** The 16-acre site is one of the Central Valley's top museum complexes. The indoor-outdoor Kern County Museum is an open-air, walk-through historic

The Central Valley

village with more than 55 restored or re-created buildings dating from the 1860s to the 1940s. "Black Gold: The Oil Experience," a permanent exhibit, shows how oil is created, discovered, extracted, and transformed for various uses. The Lori Brock Children's Discovery Center, for ages eight and younger, has hands-on displays and an indoor playground. ⊠ *3801 Chester Ave., at 38th St.* ☎ *661/852–5000* ⊕ *www.kcmuseum.org* 🎟 *$10* ☉ *Wed.–Sun. 10–5.*

> ### LOCAL LITERARY LEGENDS
>
> The Central Valley's cultural diversity and agricultural roots have woven a textured social fabric that has been chronicled by some of the country's finest writers, including Fresno native William Saroyan, Stockton native Maxine Hong Kingston, and *The Grapes of Wrath* author John Steinbeck.

WHERE TO EAT

$　✕ **Jake's Original Tex Mex Cafe.** Don't let the cafeteria-style service fool
MEXICAN　you; this is probably the best lunch place in Bakersfield. The chicken burritos and the chili fries (with meaty chili ladled on top) are superb; the coleslaw is a favorite, too. Locals rave about the chocolate cake—with good reason. Jake's is open for dinner, too. ⑤ *Average main: $9* ⊠ *1710 Oak St., near Truxton Ave.* ☎ *661/322–6380* ⊕ *www. jakestexmex.com* ⚐ *Reservations not accepted* ☉ *Closed Sun.*

$$　✕ **Uricchio's Trattoria.** This downtown restaurant draws everyone from
ITALIAN　office workers to oil barons—all attracted by the tasty food and casual atmosphere. *Panini* (Italian pressed sandwiches, served at lunch only), pasta, and Italian-style chicken dishes dominate the menu; the chicken piccata outsells all other offerings. ⑤ *Average main: $16* ⊠ *1400 17th St.* ☎ *661/326–8870* ⊕ *www.uricchios-trattoria.com* ☉ *Closed Sun. No lunch Sat.*

NIGHTLIFE AND THE ARTS

★　**Buck Owens' Crystal Palace.** Buck Owens is Bakersfield's local boy made good, and this venue is a combination nightclub, restaurant, souvenir store, and showcase of country-music memorabilia. Country-and-western singers perform here, as Owens did countless times before his death in 2006. A dance floor beckons customers who can still twirl after sampling the menu of steaks, burgers, nachos, and gooey desserts. Expect a cover charge some weeknights and most weekends. ⊠ *2800 Buck Owens Blvd., off Hwy. 178* ☎ *661/328–7500* ⊕ *www.buckowens.com* ☉ *Closed Mon.*

KERNVILLE

50 miles northeast of Bakersfield, via Hwys. 178 and 155.

The wild Kern River, which flows through Kernville en route from Mt. Whitney to Bakersfield, delivers some of the most exciting whitewater rafting in the state. Kernville (population 1,700) rests in a mountain valley on both banks of the river and also at the northern tip of Lake Isabella (a dammed portion of the river used as a reservoir and for recreation). By far the most scenic town in this region, Kernville has lodgings, restaurants, and antiques shops. The main streets are lined with Old West–style buildings, reflecting Kernville's heritage as a rough-and-tumble gold-mining town once known as Whiskey Flat. Present-day Kernville dates from the 1950s, when it was moved upriver to make room for Lake Isabella. The road from Bakersfield includes stretches where the rushing river is on one side and granite cliffs are on the other.

GETTING HERE AND AROUND

You get here from Bakersfield via Highway 178, and Highway 155 connects the town to Delano. There's no train line or regularly scheduled bus service.

ESSENTIALS

Visitor Information VisitKern.com ☎ *661/500–5376, 800/500–5376* ⊕ *www.visitkern.com.*

WHERE TO EAT AND STAY

For expanded reviews, facilities, and current deals, visit Fodors.com.

$
ITALIAN
✕ **That's Italian.** For northern Italian cuisine in a typical trattoria, this is the spot. Try the braised lamb shanks in a Chianti wine sauce or the linguine with clams, mussels, calamari, and shrimp in a white-wine clam sauce. ⑤ *Average main: $14* ⊠ *9 Big Blue Rd., at Kernville Rd.* ☎ *760/376–6020.*

$$$
B&B/INN
⌂ **Whispering Pines Lodge Bed & Breakfast.** Perched on the banks of the Kern River, this 8-acre property has units that are motel-style or in duplex bungalows; all have fireplaces, coffeemakers, and king-size beds. **Pros:** rustic setting; big breakfasts; great views; very clean. **Cons:** bungalows are quite pricey; town is remote. **TripAdvisor:** "nice place to relax," "amazing breakfast," "comfortable room with natural setting." ⑤ *Rooms from: $189* ⊠ *13745 Sierra Way* ☎ *760/376–3733, 877/241–4100* ⊕ *www.kernvalley.com/whisperingpines* ⇆ *17 rooms* ⍟ *Breakfast.*

SPORTS AND THE OUTDOORS

BOATING AND WINDSURFING
The Lower Kern River, which extends from Lake Isabella to Bakersfield and beyond, is open for fishing year-round. Catches include rainbow trout, catfish, smallmouth bass, crappie, and bluegill. Lake Isabella is popular with anglers, water-skiers, sailors, and windsurfers. Its shoreline marinas have boats for rent, bait and tackle, and moorings.

French Gulch Marina. This marina is near the dam on Lake Isabella's west shore. ☎ *760/379–8774* ⊕ *www.frenchgulchmarina.com.*

North Fork Marina. North Fork is in Wofford Heights, on the lake's north shore. ☎ *760/376–1812* ⊕ *www.northforkmarina.com.*

WHITE-WATER RAFTING
The three sections of the Kern River—known as the Lower Kern, Upper Kern, and the Forks—add up to nearly 50 miles of white water, ranging from Class I (easy) to Class V (expert). The Lower and Upper Kern are the most popular and accessible sections. Organized trips can last from one hour (for as little as $35) to more than two days. Rafting season usually runs from late spring until the end of summer.

Kern River Tours. This outfit leads several rafting tours, from half-day (from $105) to three-day ($868) trips navigating Class V rapids, and also arranges for mountain-bike trips. ☎ *800/844–7238* ⊕ *www.kernrivertours.com.*

18

Mountain & River Adventures. This outfit conducts calm-water kayaking tours as well as white-water rafting trips, leads mountain-bike excursions, and has a campground. In the wintertime, M&R rents snowshoes, cross-country skis, and other snow gear. ☎ 760/376–6553, 800/861–6553 ⊕ www.mtnriver.com.

Sierra South. Half-day Class II and III white-water rafting trips (starting at $70) are emphasized at Sierra South, which also offers kayaking classes and calm-water excursions. ☎ 760/376–3745, 800/457–2082 ⊕ www.sierrasouth.com.

MID-CENTRAL VALLEY

Flat and odor-challenged (there are countless cow operations here), this region's small towns offer oases of low-key urban pleasures, with decent restaurants and pleasant parks. Colonel Allensworth State Historic Park is its quietest but most worthy attraction.

COLONEL ALLENSWORTH STATE HISTORIC PARK

45 miles north of Bakersfield on Hwy. 43.

GETTING HERE AND AROUND

The easiest way to get here is by car. The park is off Highway 43, a 15-minute drive west of Highway 99.

★ **Colonel Allensworth State Historic Park.** It's worth the slight detour off Highway 99 to learn about and pay homage to the dream of Allen Allensworth and other black pioneers who in 1908 founded Allensworth, the only California town settled, governed, and financed by African-Americans. At its height, the town prospered as a key railroad transfer point, but after cars and trucks reduced railroad traffic and water was diverted for Central Valley agriculture, the town declined and was eventually deserted. Today, the restored and rebuilt schoolhouse, library, and other structures commemorate Allensworth's heyday, as do festivities that take place each October. The parking lot is open only on Fridays and weekends, but daily you can park nearby, walk over to the buildings, and peek in. ✉ 4129 Palmer Ave., off Hwy. 43; from Hwy. 99 at Delano, take Garces Hwy. west to Hwy. 43 north; from Earlimart, take County Rd. J22 west to Hwy. 43 south ☎ 661/849–3433 ⊕ www. cal-parks.ca.gov 🖼 $6 per car ☉ Daily sunrise–sunset; visitor center Fri.–Sun. 10–4; buildings open by appointment.

VISALIA

75 miles north of Bakersfield via Hwy. 99 north and Hwy. 198 east.

Visalia's combination of a reliable agricultural economy and civic pride has yielded the Central Valley's most vibrant downtown. If you're into Victorian and other old houses, drop by the city's visitor center and pick up a free map of them. A clear day's view of the Sierra from Main Street is spectacular, if sadly rare due to smog and dust, and even Sunday night can find the streets bustling with pedestrians.

Each spring the fruit orchards along the Blossom Trail, near Fresno, burst into bloom.

GETTING HERE AND AROUND

Highway 198, just east of its exit from Highway 99, cuts through town (and proceeds up the hill to Sequoia National Park). Greyhound and Orange Belt stop here, but not Amtrak. KART buses serve the locals.

ESSENTIALS

Visitor Information Visalia Visitor Center ⊠ *303 E. Acequia Ave., at S. Bridge St.* ☎ *559/334–0141* ⊕ *www.visitvisalia.org* ⊙ *Mon. 10–5, Tues.–Fri. 8:30–5.*

EXPLORING

Chinese Cultural Center. Housed in a pagoda-style building, the center mounts exhibits about Asian art and culture and documents the influx of Chinese workers to central California during the gold rush. Today, people of Chinese descent make up less than one half of 1% of the city's population. ⊠ *500 S. Akers Rd., at Hwy. 198* ☎ *559/625–4545* ☑ *Free* ⊙ *By appointment only.*

Kaweah Oaks Preserve. Trails at this 322-acre wildlife sanctuary off the main road to Sequoia National Park (⇨ *see Chapter 21*) lead past majestic valley oak, sycamore, cottonwood, and willow trees. Among the 134 bird species you might spot are hawks, hummingbirds, and great blue herons. Lizards, coyotes, and cottontails also live here. ⊠ *Follow Hwy. 198 for 7 miles east of Visalia, turn north on Rd. 182, and proceed ½ mile to gate on left side* ☎ *559/738–0211* ⊕ *www.sequoiariverlands.org* ☑ *Free* ⊙ *Daily sunrise–sunset.*

Mooney Grove Park. Amid shady oaks you can picnic alongside duck ponds, rent a boat for a ride around the lagoon, and view a replica of the famous *End of the Trail* statue. The original, designed by James Earl

Fraser for the 1915 Panama-Pacific International Exposition, is now in the Cowboy Hall of Fame in Oklahoma. ⊠ *27000 S. Mooney Blvd., Hwy. 63, 5 miles south of downtown* ⊠ *$7 per car, free in winter (dates vary)* ⊙ *Daily 8–sunset; sometimes closed Tues. and Wed.*

Tulare County Museum. This indoor-outdoor museum contains several re-created environments from the pioneer era. Also on display are Yokuts tribal artifacts (basketry, arrowheads, clamshell-necklace currency) as well as saddles, guns, dolls, quilts, and gowns. A new wing chronicles farm history and farm labor. ⊠ *Mooney Grove Park, 27000 S. Mooney Blvd., Hwy. 63, 5 miles south of downtown* ☎ *559/733–6616* ⊕ *www.co.tulare.ca.us/government/parks/museum.asp* ⊠ *Free with park entrance fee of $7* ⊙ *Weekdays 10–4, weekends 1–4.*

WHERE TO EAT

$ ✕ **Henry Salazar's Fresh Mex Grill.** Traditional Mexican food with a con-
MEXICAN   temporary twist is served at this restaurant that uses fresh ingredients from local farms. Bring your appetite if you expect to finish the Burrito Fantastico, a large flour tortilla stuffed with your choice of meat, beans, and chili sauce, and smothered with melted Monterey Jack cheese. Another signature dish is grilled salmon with lemon-butter sauce. Colorfully painted walls, soft reflections from candles in wall niches, and color-coordinated tablecloths and napkins make the atmosphere cozy and restful. $ *Average main: $12* ⊠ *123 W. Main St.* ☎ *559/741–7060* ⊕ *www.henrysalazars.com.*

$$$ ✕ **The Vintage Press.** Built in 1966, this is the best restaurant in the
EUROPEAN   Central Valley. Cut-glass doors and bar fixtures decorate the artfully
Fodor's Choice   designed rooms. The California–Continental cuisine includes dishes
★   such as crispy veal sweetbreads with a port-wine sauce, and a bacon-wrapped filet mignon stuffed with mushrooms. The chocolate Grand Marnier cake is a standout among the homemade desserts and ice creams. The wine list has more than 900 selections. $ *Average main: $30* ⊠ *216 N. Willis St.* ☎ *559/733–3033* ⊕ *www.thevintagepress.com.*

HANFORD

20 miles west of Visalia on Hwy. 198; 43 miles north of Colonel Allensworth State Historic Park on Hwy. 43.

Founded in 1877 as a Southern Pacific Railroad stop, Hanford had one of California's largest Chinatowns—the Chinese came to help build the railroads and stayed on to farm. If you arrive on a typically laid-back Hanford day, it might be hard to imagine the fatal skirmish that took place in 1880 between local settlers and railroad law agents over land titles. Known as the Mussel Slough Tragedy, the incident inspired Frank Norris's best seller *The Octopus.*

You can take a self-guided walking tour of Hanford with the help of a free brochure from its visitor agency, which also books driving tours ($85 per hour) in a restored 1930 Studebaker fire truck. One tour explores the restored buildings of Courthouse Square, whose art-deco Hanford Auditorium is a visual standout; another heads to narrow China Alley.

GETTING HERE AND AROUND

Highway 198 serves Hanford east to west, Highway 41 north to south. Amtrak trains serve Hanford, as do KART buses.

ESSENTIALS

Visitor Information Hanford Visitor Agency ✉ *113 Court St.* ☎ *559/582–5024* ⊕ *www.visithanford.com.*

EXPLORING

China Alley. Worth a brief look if you're in town—for the photo op, if nothing else—is this frozen-in-time street, the last remains of Hanford's once-bustling Chinatown. The centerpiece is the 1893 **Taoist Temple.** The alley's other buildings of note include the decaying L.T. Sue Herb building. ✉ *12 China Alley, off N. Green St.* ☎ *559/582–4508* ⊕ *www.chinaalley.com* ⊗ *Alley always accessible; temple tours 1st Sat. of month at noon.*

Hanford Carnegie Museum. Fashions, furnishings, toys, and military artifacts at this living-history museum tell the region's story. The facility is inside the former Carnegie Library, a Romanesque building dating from 1905. ✉ *108 E. 8th St., at N. Douty St.* ☎ *559/584–1367* ⊕ *www.hanfordcarnegiemuseum.org* 🎟 *$3* ⊗ *Tues.–Sat. 11–4.*

WHERE TO EAT AND STAY

For expanded reviews, facilities, and current deals, visit Fodors.com.

$ ✕ **La Fiesta.** Mexican-American families, farmworkers, and farmers all MEXICAN eat here, polishing off traditional Mexican dishes such as enchiladas and tacos. The Fiesta Special—for two or more—includes nachos, garlic shrimp, shrimp in a spicy red sauce, clams, and two pieces of top sirloin. $ *Average main: $10* ✉ *106 N. Green St.* ☎ *559/583–8775.*

$ ✕ **Niklana's.** Truck company bookkeepers Nichole Weed and Dalana BAKERY Church took the leap from passion to entrepreneurism when they opened this bustling breakfast and lunch spot in 2011. The duo's already deeply devoted patrons hail the crepes, cinnamon buns, soups, and sandwiches. $ *Average main: $9* ✉ *2459 N. 10th Ave., at E. Fargo Ave.* ☎ *559/410–8826* ⊗ *Closed Sun. No lunch Sat. No dinner.*

$ ⊞ **Comfort Inn Hanford.** Attentive service and generous breakfasts are HOTEL touted at this clean chain hotel, situated on the fringes of historic downtown. *Rooms from: $76* ✉ *10 N. Irwin St.* ☎ *559/584–9300* ⊕ *www.comfortinn.com* ⇋ *65.*

$ ⊞ **Irwin Street Inn.** Four tree-shaded, restored Victorian homes have been B&B/INN converted into spacious accommodations with comfortable rooms and suites. **Pros:** big rooms and bathrooms; funky decor; very unlike chain hotels. **Cons:** musty; mattresses can be uncomfortable; not much to do in town. **TripAdvisor:** "great place to stay and relax," "wonderful ambience," "nice rustic place." $ *Rooms from: $85* ✉ *522 N. Irwin St.* ☎ *559/583–8000* ⇋ *24 rooms, 3 suites* ⍟ *Breakfast.*

FRESNO

35 miles north of Hanford via Hwys. 43 and 99.

Sprawling Fresno, with nearly half a million people, is the center of the richest agricultural county in the United States. Cotton, grapes, and tomatoes are among the major crops; poultry and milk are also important. About 75 ethnic groups, including Armenians, Laotians, and Indians, live here. The city has a relatively vibrant arts scene, several public parks, and many low-price restaurants. The Tower District—with its chic restaurants, coffeehouses, and boutiques—is the trendy spot, though like the rest of Fresno it can look drab on a cloudy day. The Pulitzer Prize–winning playwright and novelist William Saroyan (*The Time of Your Life, The Human Comedy*) was born here in 1908.

GETTING HERE AND AROUND

Highway 99 is the biggest road through Fresno. Highways 41 and 180 also bisect the city. Amtrak trains stop here daily (and often). Fresno Area Express (FAX) provides comprehensive local bus service.

ESSENTIALS

Transportation Contacts FAX ☎ *559/621–7433* ⊕ *www.fresno.gov/discoverfresno.*

Visitor Information Fresno City & County Convention and Visitors Bureau ✉ *1550 E. Shaw Ave.* ☎ *559/981–5500, 800/788–0836* ⊕ *www.fresnocvb.org.*

EXPLORING

TOP ATTRACTIONS

☺ ★ **Forestiere Underground Gardens.** Sicilian immigrant Baldasare Forestiere spent four decades (1906–46) carving out an odd, subterranean realm of rooms, tunnels, grottoes, alcoves, and arched passageways that once extended for more than 10 acres between Highway 99 and busy, mall-pocked Shaw Avenue. Though not an engineer, Forestiere called on his memories of the ancient Roman structures he saw as a youth and on techniques he learned digging subways in New York and Boston. Only a fraction of his prodigious output is on view, but you can tour his underground living quarters, including bedrooms (one with a fireplace), the kitchen, living room, and bath, as well as a fishpond and auto tunnel. Skylights allow exotic full-grown fruit trees to flourish more than 20 feet belowground. ✉ *5021 W. Shaw Ave., 2 blocks east of Hwy. 99* ☎ *559/271–0734* ⊕ *www.undergroundgardens.com* ☺ *$14* ⊙ *Tours June–Aug., Wed.–Sun. 10–4; call or check website for other tour times* ⊙ *Closed Dec.–Feb.*

Fresno Art Museum. The museum's key permanent collections include pre-Columbian Mesoamerican art, Andean pre-Columbian textiles and artifacts, Japanese prints, Berkeley School abstract expressionist paintings, and contemporary sculpture. Temporary exhibits include important traveling shows. ✉ *Radio Park, 2233 N. 1st St., at E. Yale Ave.* ☎ *559/441–4221* ⊕ *www.fresnoartmuseum.org* ☺ *$5; free Sun.* ⊙ *Thur.–Sun. 11–5.*

Meux Home Museum. A restored 1889 Victorian, "the Meux" contains furnishings typical of an upper-class household in early Fresno. The house's namesake, Thomas Richard Meux, was a Confederate army doctor during the Civil War who became a family practitioner after moving to Fresno. The Meux can be viewed on guided tours only. ✉ *1007 R St., at Tulare St.* ☎ *559/233–8007* ⊕ *www.meux.mus.ca.us* ☺ *$5* ⊙ *Fri.–Sun. noon–3:30.*

Fresno Area

KEY

🛈 Tourist information

0   4 miles

0   6 km

WORTH NOTING

Blossom Trail. The 62-mile self-guided Blossom Trail driving tour takes in Fresno-area orchards, citrus groves, and vineyards during spring blossom season. The trail passes through small towns and past rivers, lakes, and canals. The most colorful and aromatic time to go is from late February to mid-March, when almond, plum, apple, apricot, and peach blossoms shower the landscape with shades of white, pink, and red. ✉ *Fresno* 🕾 *559/233–0836* ⊕ *www.goblossomtrail.com.*

Kearney Mansion Museum. The drive along palm-lined Kearney Boulevard is one of the best reasons to visit the museum, which stands in shaded 225-acre **Kearney Park.** The century-old home of M. Theo Kearney, Fresno's onetime "raisin king," is accessible only on guided 45-minute tours. ✉ *7160 W. Kearney Blvd., 6 miles west of Fresno off Hwy. 180* 🕾 *559/441–0862* ⊕ *www.valleyhistory.org* 💲 *Museum $5; park entry $5 (waived for museum visitors)* ⊘ *Park 7 am–10 pm; museum tours Fri.–Sun. at 1, 2, and 3.*

Legion of Valor Museum. Military-history buffs will enjoy this museum. It has German bayonets and daggers, a Japanese Namby pistol, a Gatling gun, and an extensive collection of Japanese, German, and American uniforms. The staff is extremely enthusiastic. ✉ *2425 Fresno*

St., between N and O Sts. ☎ *559/498–0510* ⊕ *www.legionofvalor.com* ✉ *Free* ☉ *Mon.–Sat. 10–3.*

☺ **Roeding Park.** Tree-shaded Roeding Park is a place of respite on hot summer days; it has picnic areas, playgrounds, tennis courts, horseshoe pits, and a zoo. A train, little race cars, paddleboats, a carousel, and other rides for kids are among the amusements at **Playland.** Children can explore attractions with fairy-tale themes at **Rotary Storyland.** ✉ *890 W Belmont Ave., at Olive Ave.* ☎ *559/498–1551* ⊕ *storylandplayland. com* ✉ *Roeding Park $5 per vehicle; Playland free (rides $1.50–$3); Storyland $5 ($3.50 kids 2–12 yrs)* ☉ *Park daily; Feb.–Nov., Playland weekends 10–6 and Storyland Fri.–Sun. 9–4, plus some holidays.*

Fresno Chaffee Zoo. The most striking exhibit at Fresno Chaffee Zoo is the tropical rain forest, where you'll encounter exotic birds along the paths and bridges. Elsewhere at the zoo live tigers, grizzly bears, sea lions, tule elk, camels, elephants, and hooting siamangs. Also here are a high-tech reptile house and a petting zoo. ✉ *894 W. Belmont Ave., east of Hwy. 99* ☎ *559/498–2671* ⊕ *www.fresnochaffeezoo.org* ✉ *$7* ☉ *Apr.–Sept., daily 9–6; Oct.–Mar., daily 9–4*

★ **Woodward Park.** The Central Valley's largest urban park, with 300 acres of jogging trails, picnic areas, and playgrounds in the city's northern reaches, is especially pretty in spring, when plum and cherry trees, magnolias, and camellias bloom. Outdoor concerts take place in summer. The **Shinzen Friendship Garden** has a teahouse, a koi pond, arched bridges, a waterfall, and Japanese art. ✉ *Audubon Dr. and Friant Rd.* ☎ *559/621–2900* ✉ *$5 per car Feb.–Oct.; additional $3 for Shinzen Garden* ☉ *Apr.–Oct., daily 6 am–10 pm; Nov.–Mar., daily 6–7.*

OFF THE BEATEN PATH

Old Town Clovis. The restored brick buildings of a former lumber-industry district now hold antiques shops, art galleries, restaurants, and saloons. At the visitor center (or online) you can access a walking-tour map. To get here from Fresno, head east on Herndon Avenue for about 10 miles to Clovis Avenue and drive south. Be warned that not much is open on Sunday. ✉ *Visitor center, 399 Clovis Ave., at 4th St., Clovis* ⊕ *www.visitclovis.com.*

WHERE TO EAT AND STAY

For expanded reviews, facilities, and current deals, visit Fodors.com.

$$
STEAKHOUSE

✗ **Tahoe Joe's.** This restaurant is known for its steaks—rib eye, strip, or filet mignon. Other selections include the slow-roasted prime rib, center-cut pork chops, and chicken breast served with a whiskey-peppercorn sauce. The baked potato that accompanies almost every dish is loaded tableside with your choice of butter, sour cream, chives, and bacon bits. Tahoe Joe's has two Fresno locations. ⑤ *Average main: $18* ✉ *7006 N. Cedar Ave., at E. Herndon Ave.* ☎ *559/299–9740* ⊕ *www.tahoejoes. com* ⚠ *Reservations not accepted* ☉ *No lunch* ⑤ *Average main: $18* ✉ *2700 W. Shaw Ave., at N. Marks Ave.* ☎ *559/277–8028* ⊕ *www. tahoejoes.com.*

$
HOTEL

▦ **Piccadilly Inn Shaw.** This two-story property has 7½ attractively landscaped acres and a big swimming pool. **Pros:** big rooms; nice pool; town's best lodging option. **Cons:** some rooms show mild wear; neighborhood is somewhat sketchy. **TripAdvisor:** "spacious rooms," "refreshing change from chain hotels," "elevated by good service." ⑤ *Rooms from: $89* ✉ *2305 W. Shaw Ave.* ☎ *559/348–5520, 888/286–2645* ⊕ *www. piccadillyinn.com/shaw* ⤶ *194 rooms, 5 suites.*

NIGHTLIFE AND THE ARTS

Fresno Philharmonic Orchestra. The orchestra performs classical concerts from September through June. ✉ *Saroyan Theatre, 730 M St., near Inyo St.* ☎ *559/261–0600* ⊕ *fresnophil.org.*

Roger Rocka's Dinner Theater. This Tower District venue stages Broadway-style musicals. ✉ *1226 N. Wishon Ave., at E. Olive Ave.* ☎ *559/266–9494, 800/371–4747* ⊕ *www.rogerrockas.com.*

Tower Theatre for the Performing Arts. The restored 1930s art-deco movie house, the anchor and namesake of the trendy Tower District of theaters, clubs, restaurants, and cafés, presents theater, ballet, concerts, and other cultural events. ✉ *815 E. Olive Ave., at N. Wishon Ave.* ☎ *559/485–9050* ⊕ *www.towertheatrefresno.com.*

SPORTS AND THE OUTDOORS

Kings River Expeditions. This outfit arranges one- and two-day whitewater rafting trips on the Kings River. ✉ *1840 W. Shaw Ave., Clovis* ☎ *559/233–4881, 800/846–3674* ⊕ *www.kingsriver.com.*

Wild Water Adventures. This 52-acre water park about 10 miles east of Fresno is open from late May to early September. ✉ *11413 E. Shaw Ave., off Hwy. 168, Clovis* ☎ *559/299–9453, 800/564–9453* ⊕ *www. wildwater.net* ⤶ *$28, $17 after 3 pm.*

18

NORTH CENTRAL VALLEY

Agriculture on a massive scale is what this flat region is all about. The vineyards around Lodi provide a more sophisticated vibe.

MERCED

50 miles north of Fresno on Hwy. 99.

Thanks to a branch of the University of California opening in 2005 and an aggressive community redevelopment plan, the downtown of county seat Merced is coming back to life. The transformation is not yet complete, but there are promising signs: a brewpub, several boutiques, a multiplex, the restoration of numerous historic buildings, and foot traffic won back from outlying strip malls.

GETTING HERE AND AROUND

The most scenic approach to Yosemite National Park, at least from the west, is via Highway 140 as it rambles through and past Merced. Most people arrive by car via Highway 99, but Amtrak also stops several times daily. The Bus provides transit service weekly except Sunday.

ESSENTIALS

Bus Contact The Bus ☎ *800/345–3111* ⊕ *www.mercedthebus.com.*

Visitor Information Visit Merced ✉ *710 W. 16th St.* ☎ *209/724–8104, 800/446–5353* ⊕ *www.yosemite-gateway.org.*

EXPLORING

Merced County Courthouse Museum. Even if you don't go inside, be sure to swing by this three-story former courthouse. Built in 1875, it's a striking example of Victorian Italianate style. The upper two floors are a museum of early Merced history. Highlights include ornate restored courtrooms and an 1870 Chinese temple with carved redwood altars. ✉ *621 W. 21st St., at N St.* ☎ *209/723–2401* ⊕ *www.mercedmuseum. org* 🖾 *Free* �8 *Wed.–Sun. 1–4.*

Merced Multicultural Arts Center. The center displays paintings, sculpture, and photography. The Big Valley Arts & Culture Festival, which celebrates the area's ethnic diversity and children's creativity, is held here in late September or early October. ✉ *645 W. Main St., at N St.* ☎ *209/388–1090* ⊕ *www.artsmerced.org* 🖾 *Free* �8 *Wed. and Thurs. 11–7, Fri. and Sat. 10–5.*

WHERE TO EAT AND STAY

For expanded reviews, facilities, and current deals, visit Fodors.com.

$$ ✕ **The Branding Iron.** Beef is what this restaurant is all about. It's the
STEAKHOUSE place where farmers and ranchers come to refuel as they travel through cattle country. Try the juicy cut of prime rib paired with potato and Parmesan-cheese bread. California cattle brands decorate the walls, and when the weather is nice, cooling breezes refresh diners on the outdoor patio. ⑤ *Average main: $20* ✉ *640 W. 16th St., between M and N Sts.* ☎ *209/722–1822* ⊕ *www.thebrandingiron-merced.com* �8 *No lunch weekends.*

$$ ✕ **DeAngelo's.** This restaurant, about 2 miles from downtown, is one
ITALIAN of the Central Valley's best. Chef Vincent DeAngelo, a graduate of the Culinary Institute of America, brings his considerable skill to everything from basic ravioli to calamari steak. Half the restaurant is occupied by Bellini's, a bar-bistro with its own menu, which includes brick-oven pizza. ⑤ *Average main: $20* ✉ *2000 E. Childs Ave., at Parsons Ave.* ☎ *209/383–3020* ⊕ *www.deangelosrestaurant.com* �8 *No lunch weekends.*

$$ ⛉ **Hooper House Bear Creek Inn.** This 1931 neocolonial home stands
B&B/INN regally at the corner of M Street; rooms are appointed with well-chosen antiques and big, soft beds. **Pros:** historic charm; friendly staff; good breakfast. **Cons:** front rooms can be noisy. **TripAdvisor:** "excellent service," "very friendly people," "historic charm." ⑤ *Rooms from: $139* ✉ *575 W. N. Bear Creek Dr., at M St.* ☎ *209/723–3991* ⊕ *www. hooperhouse.com* ⚮ *3 rooms, 2 cottages* ⋈ *Breakfast.*

SPORTS AND THE OUTDOORS

Lake Yosemite Regional Park. At this park surrounding a 387-acre irrigation reservoir, you can boat, swim, windsurf, water-ski, and fish. Paddleboat rentals and picnic areas are available. ✉ *N. Lake Rd. off Yosemite Ave., 5 miles northeast of Merced* ☎ *209/385–7426* 🖾 *$6 per car late May–early Sept.*

EN ROUTE

Castle Air Museum. You can stroll among dozens of restored military aircraft at this outdoor facility. The vintage war birds include the B-25 Mitchell medium-range bomber—best known for the Jimmy Doolittle raid on Tokyo after the attack on Pearl Harbor—and the speedy SR-71 Blackbird, used for reconnaissance over Vietnam and Libya. ⊠ *Castle Airport, 5050 Santa Fe Dr., 6 miles north of Merced, Buhach Rd. exit off Hwy. 99, Atwater* ☎ *209/723–2178* ⊕ *www.castleairmuseum.org* ✉ *$10* ☉ *Apr.–Sept., daily 9–5; Oct.–Mar., daily 10–4.*

MODESTO

38 miles north of Merced on Hwy. 99.

Modesto, a gateway to Yosemite *(⇨ see Chapter 20)* and the southern reaches of the Gold Country, was founded in 1870 to serve the Central Pacific Railroad. The frontier town was originally to be named Ralston, after a railroad baron, but as the story goes, he modestly declined—thus the name Modesto. The Stanislaus County seat, a tree-lined city of 201,000, is perhaps best known as the site of the annual Modesto Invitational Track Meet and Relays and the birthplace of producer-director George Lucas, creator of the *Star Wars* film series.

GETTING HERE AND AROUND

Highway 99 is the major traffic artery; Highway 132 heads east from here toward Yosemite National Park. United serves the airport here, and several Amtrak trains arrive daily. Modesto Area Express (MAX) is the local bus service.

ESSENTIALS

Airport Contacts Modesto City-County Airport ⊠ *617 Airport Way, off Mitchell Rd., south from Yosemite Blvd./Hwy 132* ☎ *209/577–5200* ⊕ *www.modairport. com.*

Bus Contacts MAX ☎ *209/521–1274* ⊕ *www.modestoareaexpress.com.*

Visitor Information Modesto Convention and Visitors Bureau ⊠ *1150 9th St., Suite C* ☎ *209/526–5588, 888/640–8467* ⊕ *www.visitmodesto.com.*

EXPLORING

Blue Diamond Growers Store. You can witness the everyday abundance of the Modesto area with a visit here; on offer are tasty samples, a film about almond growing, and many roasts and flavors of almonds, as well as other nuts. ⊠ *4800 Sisk Rd., at Kiernan Ave., off Hwy. 99* ☎ *209/545–6230.*

International Heritage Festival. The prosperity that water brought to Modesto has attracted people from all over the world. The city holds a well-attended International Heritage Festival in early October that celebrates the cultures, crafts, and cuisines of many nationalities. ☎ *209/521–3852* ⊕ *www.internationalfestivalmodesto.org.*

★ **McHenry Mansion.** A rancher and banker built the 1883 McHenry Mansion, the city's sole surviving original Victorian home. The Italianate mansion has been decorated to reflect Modesto life in the late 19th century. Its period-appropriate wallpaper is especially impressive.

18

The Central Valley is California's agricultural powerhouse.

⚠ A relatively minor fire damaged the mansion in December 2011; plans were afoot to reopen it for tours, possibly before repairs were completed, but check before heading here. ✉ *15th and I Sts.* ☎ *209/577–5341* ⊕ *www.mchenrymuseum.org* 🎟 *Free* ◷ *Tours Sun.–Thurs. 12:30–4.*

McHenry Museum. A repository of early Modesto and Stanislaus County memorabilia, the museum's displays include re-creations of an old-time dentist's office, a blacksmith's shop, a one-room schoolhouse, an extensive doll collection, and a general store stocked with period goods such as hair crimpers and corsets. ✉ *1402 I St., at 14th St.* ☎ *209/577–5366* ⊕ *www.mchenrymuseum.org* 🎟 *Free* ◷ *Tues.–Sun. noon–4.*

Modesto Arch. One of the broadest and most striking "welcome to downtown" signs you'll see, the Modesto Arch bears the city's motto: "Water, Wealth, Contentment, Health." ✉ *9th and I Sts.*

WHERE TO EAT AND STAY

For expanded reviews, facilities, and current deals, visit Fodors.com.

$
AMERICAN

✕ **Hero's Sports Lounge & Pizza Co.** Modesto's renowned microbrewery makes Hero's (formerly St. Stan's) beers. The 14 on tap include the delicious Whistle Stop pale ale and Red Sky ale. The casual restaurant serves a tasty beer-sausage nibbler and corned-beef sandwiches loaded with sauerkraut. $ *Average main: $12* ✉ *821 L St., at 9th St.* ☎ *209/524–2337* ◷ *Closed Sun.*

$$$
AMERICAN

✕ **Tresetti's World Caffe.** An intimate setting with white tablecloths and contemporary art draws diners to this eatery—part wineshop (with 500-plus selections), part restaurant—with a seasonally changing menu. The

Cajun-style crab cakes, served for lunch year-round, are outstanding. For a small fee, your waiter will uncork any wine you select from the shop. $ *Average main: $26* ✉ *927 11th St., at I St.* ☎ *209/572–2990* ⊕ *www.tresetti.com* ⊘ *Closed Sun.*

$
HOTEL 🔲 **Best Western Town House Lodge.** The downtown location is the primary draw for this hotel. **Pros:** perfect location; updated. **Cons:** staff's limited knowledge of town. **TripAdvisor:** "a pleasant surprise," "really nice employees," "very comfortable." $ *Rooms from: $63* ✉ *909 16th St.* ☎ *209/524–7261, 800/772–7261* ⊕ *www.bestwesterncalifornia.com* ⤳ *59 rooms* ⏺ *Breakfast.*

OAKDALE

15 miles northeast of Modesto on Hwy. 108.

Oakdale was founded as an orchard community and, in a real stretch, calls itself the Cowboy Capital of the World. Formerly the home of a Hershey's chocolate factory, the city continues to hold the Oakdale Chocolate Festival, on the third weekend in May. The main attraction of this sweet event, which attracts more than 50,000 people each year, is Chocolate Avenue, where vendors proffer cakes, cookies, ice cream, fudge, and cheesecake. The Oakland Chamber of Commerce can provide more details.

GETTING HERE AND AROUND
Reach Oakdale via Highway 108 from Modesto. Local transit is of little use to tourists.

ESSENTIALS
Visitor Information Oakdale Chamber of Commerce ✉ *590 N. Yosemite Ave., at E. A St.* ☎ *209/847–2244* ⊕ *www.oakdalechamber.com.*

EXPLORING

⟳ **Knights Ferry Recreation Area.** The featured attraction is the 355-foot-long
★ Knights Ferry covered bridge. The beautiful and haunting structure, built in 1863, crosses the Stanislaus River near the ruins of an old gristmill. The park has camping, picnic, and barbecue areas along the riverbanks, as well as three campgrounds accessible only by boat. You can hike, fish, canoe, and raft on 4 miles of rapids. ✉ *Corps of Engineers Park, 17968 Covered Bridge Rd., Knights Ferry, 12 miles east of Oakdale via Hwy. 108* ☎ *209/881–3517* ✑ *Free* ⊘ *Daily dawn–dusk.*

⟳ **Oakdale Cheese & Specialties.** You can sample the wares at this homey factory complex, which has tastings (try the aged Gouda) and cheese-making tours, a store, and a bakery. Outside are a picnic area and a petting zoo. ✉ *10040 Valley Home Rd., at River Rd.* ☎ *209/848–3139* ⊕ *www.oakdalecheese.com.*

SPORTS AND THE OUTDOORS
River Journey. Rafting on the Stanislaus River is a popular activity near Oakdale. River Journey will take you out for a few hours of fun. ✉ *14842 Orange Blossom Rd., off Hwy. 120/108* ☎ *209/847–4671, 800/292–2938* ⊕ *www.riverjourney.com.*

18

Sunshine River Adventures. To satisfy your white-water or flat-water cravings, contact Sunshine. ☎ *209/848–4800, 800/829–7238* ⊕ *www. raftadventure.com.*

STOCKTON

29 miles north of Modesto on Hwy. 99.

California's first inland port—connected since 1933 to San Francisco via a 60-mile-long deepwater channel—is wedged between Interstate 5 and Highway 99, on the eastern end of the Sacramento River delta. Stockton, founded during the gold rush as a way station for miners traveling from San Francisco to the Mother Lode and now a city of 292,000, is where many of the valley's agricultural products begin their journey to other parts of the world. The city has attempted to spruce up its riverfront area downtown, including building a spiffy minor-league baseball park for the Stockton Ports, but there remains much room for improvement.

GETTING HERE AND AROUND

Highway 99 (on the city's eastern side) and Interstate 5 (on the western side) are connected through downtown by Highway 4, so you can zip from place to place efficiently via freeways. Amtrak stops here, as does Greyhound. San Joaquin RTD (⊕ *www.sanjoaquinrtd.com*) provides local bus service.

ESSENTIALS

Visitor Information Stockton Visitors Bureau ⊠ *525 N. Center St.* ☎ *209/938–1555, 888/778–6258* ⊕ *www.visitstockton.org.*

EXPLORING

★ **Haggin Museum.** In pretty Victory Park, the Haggin has one of the Central Valley's finest art collections. Highlights include landscapes by Albert Bierstadt and Thomas Moran, a still life by Paul Gauguin, a Native American gallery, and an Egyptian mummy. ⊠ *1201 N. Pershing Ave., at Rose St.* ☎ *209/940–6300* ⊕ *www.hagginmuseum.org* ⌚ *$5* ⊗ *Wed.–Fri. 1:30–5, weekends noon–5; open until 9 on 1st and 3rd Thurs.*

Stockton Asparagus Festival. If you're here in late April, don't miss the asparagus festival. The food booths are the highlight of this waterfront event, as the more than 500 vendors collectively try to prove that almost any dish can be made (and made better) with asparagus. ☎ *209/644–3740* ⊕ *asparagusfest.com.*

WHERE TO EAT

$$$
EUROPEAN

✕ **Le Bistro.** This upscale restaurant serves modern interpretations of classic French cuisine—steak tartare, Grand Marnier soufflé—and warms hearts with a romantic atmosphere. ⑤ *Average main: $24* ⊠ *Marina Center Mall, 3121 W. Benjamin Holt Dr., off I–5, behind Lyon's* ☎ *209/951–0885* ⊕ *www.lebistrostockton.com* ⊗ *No lunch.*

$
CHINESE

✕ **On Lock Sam.** This Stockton landmark (it's been operating since 1898) is in a modern pagoda-style building with framed Chinese prints on the walls, a garden outside one window, and a sparkling bar area. One touch of old-time Chinatown remains: a few booths have curtains that can be drawn for complete privacy. The decor often gets trashed online, but the food's usually praised. $ *Average main: $11* ✉ *333 S. Sutter St., at E. Sonora St.* ☎ *209/466–4561.*

SPORTS AND THE OUTDOORS

Paradise Point Marina. The marina rents houseboats for cruising the California Delta waterways. The watercraft include highly relaxing patio boats. Off-season rates start at $750 for three days/two nights. ✉ *8095 Rio Blanco Rd.* ☎ *209/952–1000* ⊕ *www.sevencrown.com/lakes/.*

LODI

13 miles north of Stockton and 34 miles south of Sacramento on Hwy. 99.

Founded on agriculture, Lodi was once the watermelon capital of the country. Today it's surrounded by fields of asparagus, pumpkins, beans, safflowers, sunflowers, kiwis, melons, squashes, peaches, and cherries. It's also emerged as a wine-grape capital of sorts, producing Zinfandel, Merlot, Cabernet Sauvignon, Chardonnay, and Sauvignon Blanc grapes. For years California wineries have built their reputations on the juice of grapes grown around Lodi. Now the area that includes Lodi, Lockeford, and Woodbridge is a wine destination in itself, boasting about 40 wineries, many offering tours and tastings. Lodi still retains an old rural charm, despite its population of 62,000. You can stroll downtown or visit a wildlife refuge, all the while benefiting from a Sacramento River delta breeze that keeps this microclimate cooler in summer than anyplace else in the area.

GETTING HERE AND AROUND

Most of Lodi lies to the west of Highway 99, several miles east of Interstate 5. Buses and Amtrak trains stop here frequently. Although the Grape Line (☎ 209/333–6806) can get you around town and to many of the wineries, you are better off with your own vehicle.

ESSENTIALS

Visitor Information Lodi Conference and Visitors Bureau ✉ 115 S. School St. ☎ 209/365–1195, 800/798–1810 ⊕ www.visitlodi.com.

EXPLORING

★ **Jessie's Grove.** One of the standout wineries in the area is Jessie's Grove, a wooded horse ranch and vineyard that has been in the same family since 1863. In addition to producing outstanding old-vine Zinfandels, it presents blues concerts on various Saturdays from June through October. ✉ *1973 W. Turner Rd., west of Davis Rd.* ☎ *209/368–0880* ⊕ *www.jessiesgrovewinery.com* ☽ *Daily noon–5.*

Lodi Wine & Visitor Center. A fine place to sample Lodi wines (there's a tasting bar), the center has exhibits that chronicle Lodi's viticultural history. You can also buy wine here and pick up a map of area wineries to explore. ✉ *2545 W. Turner Rd., at Woodhaven La.* ☎ *209/365–0621* ⊕ *www.lodiwine.com.*

☺ **Micke Grove Regional Park.** This 258-acre, oak-shaded park, about 5 miles south of downtown, has a Japanese tea garden, picnic areas, children's play areas, softball fields, an agricultural museum, a golf course, and a water-play feature. Most rides and attractions at **Fun Town at Micke Grove,** a family-oriented amusement park, are geared toward children. Geckos and frogs, black-and-white ruffed lemurs, and hissing cockroaches found only on Madagascar inhabit "An Island Lost in Time," an exhibit at the **Micke Grove Zoo.** California sea lions, Chinese alligators, and a walk-through Mediterranean aviary are among the other highlights. (Micke Grove Golf Links, an 18-hole course, is next to the park.) ⊠ *11793 N. Micke Grove Rd., off Hwy. 99 Armstrong Rd. exit* ☏ *209/953–8800* ⛱ *Parking $5, Fun Town ride prices vary, zoo $4* ⊙ *Park daily 8–sunset; Fun Town daily 11–5, weekends and holidays Apr.–Sept., 11–6; zoo May–Sept., 10–6, Oct.–Apr., 10–5.*

Phillips Farms Fruit Stand/Michael David Winery. At this homey, kid-friendly complex, you can not only sample the affordable, robust Michael David wines but also cut flowers from the garden, eat breakfast or lunch at the café, and buy Phillips Farms and other local produce. ⊠ *4580 W. Hwy. 12, at N. Ray Rd.* ☏ *209/368–7384* ⊕ *www.lodivineyards.com* ⊙ *Daily 10–5.*

Woodbridge Winery. At huge Woodbridge, you can take a free 30-minute tour of the vineyard and barrel room and learn about the label's legendary founder, the late Robert Mondavi. ⊠ *5950 E. Woodbridge Rd., east of N. Hildebrand Rd., Acampo* ☏ *209/365–8139* ⊕ *www. robertmondavi.com/woodbridge/visit* ⊙ *Daily 10:30–4:30.*

WHERE TO EAT

$ ✕ **Habañero Hots.** If your mouth can handle the heat promised by the
MEXICAN   restaurant's name, try the tamales. If you want to take it easy on your taste buds, stick with the rest of the menu. ⑤ *Average main: $10* ⊠ *1024 E. Victor Rd., at N. Cluff Ave.* ☏ *209/369–3791* ⊕ *www.habanerohots. com.*

$$$ ✕ **Rosewood Bar & Grill.** Operated by the folks at Wine & Roses Hotel
AMERICAN   and Restaurant, this low-key downtown spot serves American fare with a twist, such as meat loaf wrapped in bacon, and daily seafood specials. The bar has a full-service menu, and live music on Friday and Saturday. ⑤ *Average main: $27* ⊠ *28 S. School St., at W. Oak St.* ☏ *209/369–0470* ⊕ *www.rosewoodbarandgrill.com* ⊙ *No lunch.*

WHERE TO STAY

For expanded reviews, facilities, and current deals, visit Fodors.com.

$$ ⌖ **The Inn at Locke House.** Built in 1865, this B&B was a pioneer doctor's
B&B/INN   family home and is on the National Register of Historic Places. **Pros:**
★   friendly; quiet; lovely. **Cons:** remote; can be hard to find. **TripAdvisor:** "charming B&B," "a delightful respite," "very nice and wonderful proprietors."⑤ *Rooms from: $145* ⊠ *19960 Elliott Rd.,Lockeford* ☏ *209/727–5715* ⊕ *www.theinnatlockehouse.com* ⇆ *4 rooms, 1 suite* ⦿⦿ *Breakfast.*

$$$ ⌖ **Wine & Roses Hotel and Restaurant.** Set on 7 acres amid a tapestry of
HOTEL   informal gardens, this hotel has cultivated a sense of refinement typically associated with Napa or Carmel. **Pros:** luxurious; relaxing; quiet.
★   **Cons:** expensive; isolated; some guests have said the walls are thin. **TripAdvisor:** "beautiful," "lovely stay," "dream vacation."⑤ *Rooms*

Lodi Lake Park is a great place to escape the Central Valley heat in summer.

from: $180 ✉ *2505 W. Turner Rd.* ☎ *209/334–6988* ⊕ *www.winerose. com* ⇌ *47 rooms, 4 suites* ⏐◎⏐ *Breakfast.*

SPORTS AND THE OUTDOORS

Lodi Lake Park. Even locals need respite from the heat of Central Valley summers, and Lodi Lake Park is where they find it. The banks, shaded by grand old elms and oaks, are much cooler than other spots in town. Swimming, bird-watching, and picnicking are possibilities, as is renting a kayak, canoe, or pedal boat. ✉ *1101 W. Turner Rd., at Mills Ave.* ☎ *209/333–6742* ⌫ *$5.*

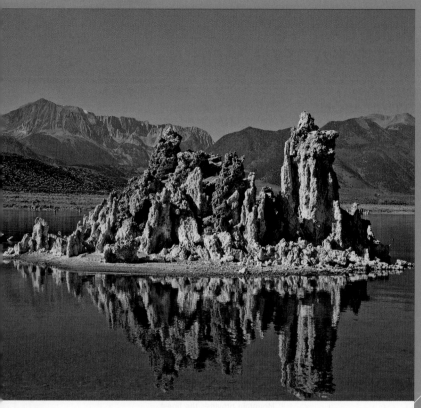

The Southern Sierra

AROUND SEQUOIA, KINGS CANYON, AND YOSEMITE NATIONAL PARKS

WORD OF MOUTH

"Mono Lake is an ancient saline lake. It is home to trillions of brine shrimp and alkali flies. You can see many limestone formations known as Tufa Towers, such as this, rising from the water's surface. Mono Lake is visited by millions of migratory birds each year."
— photo by Randall Pugh, Fodors.com member

WELCOME TO THE SOUTHERN SIERRA

TOP REASONS TO GO

★ **Strap 'em on:** Whether you walk the paved loops in the national parks (⇨ Chapter 20, Yosemite National Park, and Chapter 21, Sequoia and Kings Canyon National Parks) or head off the beaten path into the backcountry, a hike through groves and meadows or alongside streams and waterfalls will allow you to see, smell, and feel nature up close.

★ **Down you go:** Famous for its incredible snow-pack—some of the deepest in the North American continent—the Sierra Nevada has something for every winter-sports fan.

★ **Live it up:** Mammoth Lakes is eastern California's most exciting resort area.

★ **Pamper yourself:** Tucked in the hills south of Oakhurst, the elegant Château du Sureau will make you feel as if you've stepped into a fairy tale.

★ **Go with the flow:** Three Rivers, the gateway to Sequoia National Park, is the launching pad for white-water trips down the Kaweah River.

1 South of Yosemite National Park. Several gateway towns to the south and west of Yosemite National Park (⇨ Chapter 20), most within an hour's drive of Yosemite Valley, have food, lodging, and other services.

2 Mammoth Lakes. A jewel in the vast Eastern Sierra Nevada, the Mammoth Lakes area lies just east of the Sierra crest, on the backside of Yosemite and the Ansel Adams Wilderness. It's a place of rugged beauty, where giant sawtooth mountains drop into the vast deserts of the Great Basin. In winter, 11,053-foot-high Mammoth Mountain provides the finest skiing and snowboarding in California—sometimes as late as June or even July. Once the snows melt, Mammoth transforms itself into a warm-weather playground, with fishing, mountain biking, golfing, hiking, and horseback riding. Nine deep-blue lakes are spread through the Mammoth Lakes Basin, and another 100 lakes dot the surrounding countryside.

3 East of Yosemite National Park. The area to the east of Yosemite National Park (⇨ Chapter 20) includes some ruggedly handsome, albeit desolate, terrain, most notably around Mono Lake. The area is best visited by car, as distances are great and public transportation is negligible. U.S. 395 is the main north–south road on the eastern side of the Sierra Nevada, at the western edge of the Great Basin. It's one of California's most beautiful highways; plan to snap pictures at roadside pullouts.

GETTING ORIENTED

The transition between the Central Valley and the rugged Southern Sierra may be the most dramatic in California sightseeing; as you head into the mountains, your temptation to stop the car and gawk will increase with every foot gained in elevation. Although you should spend most of your time here in the national parks (⇨ Chapter 20, Yosemite National Park, and Chapter 21, Sequoia and Kings Canyon National Parks), be sure to check out some of the mountain towns on the parks' fringes—in addition to being great places to stock up on supplies, they have worthy attractions, restaurants, and lodging options.

19

4 **South of Sequoia and Kings Canyon: Three Rivers.** Scenic Three Rivers is the main gateway for Sequoia and Kings Canyon National Parks (⇨ Chapter 21).

Updated by
Reed Parsell

Vast granite peaks and giant sequoias are among the Southern Sierra's mind-boggling natural wonders, many of which are protected in three national parks. Mother Nature goes so far over the top in this region that it might wow you even more than California's more famous urban attractions.

Outside the national parks (⇨ *Chapter 20, Yosemite National Park, and Chapter 21, Sequoia and Kings Canyon National Parks*), pristine lakes, superb skiing, rolling hills, and small towns complete the picture of the Southern Sierra. Heading up U.S. 395 on the Sierra's eastern side, you'll be rewarded with outstanding vistas of dramatic mountain peaks, including Mt. Whitney, the highest point in the contiguous United States, and Mono Lake, a vast expanse of deep blue—one of the most-photographed natural attractions in California—that is struggling to survive.

PLANNING

GETTING HERE AND AROUND

AIR TRAVEL

Fresno Yosemite International Airport (FYI) is the nearest airport to the national parks; Reno–Tahoe is the closest major airport to Mammoth Lakes.

Airports Fresno Yosemite International Airport ⊠ *5175 E. Clinton Ave., Fresno* ☎ *559/621–4500, 559/498–4095* ⊕ *www.flyfresno.org.* **Reno–Tahoe International Airport** ⊠ *U.S. 395, Exit 65B, Reno, Nevada* ☎ *775/328–6400* ⊕ *www.renoairport.com.*

CAR TRAVEL

From San Francisco, heading east on Interstate 80 to 580 to 205E is the most efficient connecting route to Interstate 5 and Highway 99, which straddle the western side of the Sierra Nevada. To best reach the eastern side from the Bay Area, take Interstate 80 to U.S. 395, then head south.

To get to Mammoth Lakes in summer and early fall (or whenever snows aren't blocking Tioga Road), you can travel via Highway 120 (to U.S.

395 south) through the Yosemite high country; the quickest route in winter is Interstate 80 to U.S. 50 to Highway 207 (Kingsbury Grade) to U.S. 395 south; either route takes about seven hours.

■TIP→ Watch your gas gauge. Gas stations are few and far between in the Sierra, so fill your tank when you can. If you're traveling between October and May, heavy snow may cover mountain roads. Carry tire chains, know how to put them on (on Interstate 80 and U.S. 50 you can pay a chain installer $35 to do it for you, but on other routes you'll have to do it yourself), and always check road conditions before you leave.

Travel Reports Caltrans Current Highway Conditions ☎ 800/427–7623 ⊕ www.dot.ca.gov.

BUS TRAVEL
Greyhound serves Fresno, Madera, and other Central Valley towns west of the Sierra. Madera County Connection buses travel between Madera and Oakhurst (and Bass Lake). Eastern Sierra Transit Authority buses serve Mammoth Lakes, Bishop (⇨ Chapter 16), and other eastern Sierra towns.

Bus Contacts Eastern Sierra Transit Authority ☎ 800/922–1930 ⊕ www. easternsierratransitauthority.com. **Greyhound** ✉ Fresno ☎ 800/231–2222 ⊕ www.greyhound.com.**Madera County Connection** ✉ Madera ☎ 559/661–3040 ⊕ www.maderactc.com/pubtrans.html.

RESTAURANTS
Most small towns in the Sierra Nevada have at least one restaurant; with few exceptions, dress is casual. You'll most likely be spending a lot of time in the car while you're exploring the area, so pick up snacks and drinks to keep with you. With picnic supplies on hand, you'll be able to enjoy an impromptu meal under giant trees or in one of the eastern Sierra towns' municipal parks. *Prices in the reviews are the average cost of a main course at dinner or, if dinner is not served, at lunch.*

HOTELS
For visits to the Sierra Nevada's western side, book your hotel in advance—especially in summer—or you may wind up far from the action in the Central Valley. Booking in advance is less crucial for travel to the Eastern Sierra. In either area, keep in mind that rural and rustic does not always mean inexpensive. *Prices in the reviews are the lowest cost of a standard double room in high season. For expanded reviews, facilities, and current deals, visit Fodors.com.*

Hotel Contacts Mammoth Lakes Visitors Bureau Lodging Referral ☎ 760/934–2712, 888/466–2666 ⊕ www.visitmammoth.com.**Mammoth Reservations** ☎ 800/223–3032 ⊕ www.mammothreservations.com.

SOUTH OF YOSEMITE NATIONAL PARK

People heading to Yosemite National Park, especially those interested in seeing the giant redwoods on the park's south side, pass through Oakhurst and Fish Camp on Highway 41.

19

OAKHURST

40 miles north of Fresno on Hwy. 41.

Motels, restaurants, gas stations, and small businesses line Highway 41 in Oakhurst, the last sizeable community before Yosemite (⇨ *Chapter 20*)—the south entrance is 23 miles north of town—and a good spot to find provisions. Continue north on Highway 41 to get to Yosemite. Three miles north of town on Highway 41, then 6 miles east, lies honky-tonk Bass Lake, a popular spot in summer with motorboaters, Jet Skiers, and families looking to cool off in the reservoir.

GETTING HERE AND AROUND

At the junction of Highways 41 and 49, Oakhurst is a solid hour's drive north of Fresno. It's the southern gateway to Yosemite, so many people fly to Fresno and rent a car to get here and beyond. In town, there's no public transportation system of any consequence.

ESSENTIALS

Visitor Information Yosemite Sierra Visitors Bureau ☎ *559/683–4636* ⊕ *www.yosemitethisyear.com.*

WHERE TO EAT

$$$$
EUROPEAN
Fodor's Choice
★

✕ **Erna's Elderberry House.** Erna Kubin-Clanin, the grande dame of Château du Sureau, created this culinary oasis, stunning for its understated elegance, gorgeous setting, and impeccable service. Red walls and wood beams accent the dining room's high ceilings, and arched windows reflect the glow of candles. The seasonal six-course prix-fixe dinner can be paired with superb wines, with every course delivered in perfect synchronicity by the elite waitstaff. A short bistro menu is served in the former wine cellar. ⑤ *Average main: $95* ⊠ *Château du Sureau, 48688 Victoria La., off Hwy. 41* ☎ *559/683–6800* ⊕ *www.elderberryhouse. com* ⚱ *Reservations essential* ⊗ *No lunch Mon.–Sat.*

WHERE TO STAY

For expanded reviews, facilities, and current deals, visit Fodors.com.

$
HOTEL
☺

⊡ **Best Western Yosemite Gateway Inn.** Oakhurst's best motel has carefully tended landscaping and rooms with attractive colonial–style furniture and slightly kitschy hand-painted wall murals of Yosemite. **Pros:** reasonably close to Yosemite; clean; two pools, one heated; comfortable. **Cons:** chain property; some walls seem thin. **TripAdvisor:** "beautiful grounds," "great location," "nice clean room." ⑤ *Rooms from: $115* ⊠ *40530 Hwy. 41* ☎ *800/545–5462, 559/683–2378* ⊕ *www. yosemitegatewayinn.com* ⟿ *121 rooms, 16 suites.*

$$$$
RESORT
Fodor's Choice
★

⊡ **Château du Sureau.** You'll feel pampered from the moment you drive through the wrought-iron gates of this fairy-tale castle. **Pros:** luxurious; you'll feel pampered; great views. **Cons:** expensive; if you're not really into spas, it might not be worth your while. **TripAdvisor:** "a wonderful world away," "elegant," "beyond 5-star accommodations." ⑤ *Rooms from: $365* ⊠ *48688 Victoria La.* ☎ *559/683–6860* ⊕ *www.chateausureau.com* ⟿ *10 rooms, 1 villa* ⦿ *Breakfast.*

$$
B&B/INN
★

⊡ **Homestead Cottages.** Set on 160 acres of rolling hills that once held a Miwok village, these cottages (the largest sleeps six) have gas fireplaces, fully equipped kitchens, and queen-size beds. **Pros:** remote location;

quiet setting; friendly owners. **Cons:** might be a little *too* quiet for some. **TripAdvisor:** "awesome lodging," "lovely accommodations," "comfortable stay and kind hosts." $ *Rooms from: $155* ⊠ *41110 Rd. 600, 2½ miles off Hwy. 49, Ahwahnee* ☎ *559/683–0495, 800/483–0495* ⊕ *www.homesteadcottages.com* ⇨ *5 cottages, 1 loft.*

FISH CAMP

57 miles north of Fresno and 4 miles south of Yosemite National Park's south entrance.

As you climb in elevation along Highway 41 northbound, you see nothing but trees until you get to the small settlement of Fish Camp, where there's a post office and general store, but no gasoline (for gas, head 10 miles north to Wawona, in the park, or 17 miles south to Oakhurst).

GETTING HERE AND AROUND

Arrive here by car via Highway 41, from Yosemite National Park a few miles to the north, or from Oakhurst (and, farther down the road, Fresno) to the south. Unless you're on foot or a bicycle, a car is your only option.

EXPLORING

☺ **Yosemite Mountain Sugar Pine Railroad.** Travel back to a time when powerful steam locomotives hauled massive log trains through the Sierra. This 4-mile, narrow-gauge railroad excursion takes you near Yosemite's south gate; there's also a moonlight special, with dinner and entertainment ($48). Take Highway 41 south from Yosemite about 8 miles to the departure point. ⊠ *56001 Hwy. 41* ☎ *559/683–7273* ⊕ *www.ymsprr. com* ⊠ *$19* ☉ *Mar.–Oct., daily.*

WHERE TO STAY

$$ 🛏 **Narrow Gauge Inn.** The well-tended rooms at this family-owned property have balconies with great views of the surrounding woods and mountains. **Pros:** close to Yosemite's south entrance; nicely appointed rooms; wonderful balconies. **Cons:** rooms can be a bit dark; dining options are limited, especially for vegetarians. **TripAdvisor:** "quaint little find," "charming," "excellent restaurant." $ *Rooms from: $145* ⊠ *48571 Hwy. 41* ☎ *559/683–7720, 888/644–9050* ⊕ *www. narrowgaugeinn.com* ⇨ *26 rooms, 1 suite* ⍟ *Breakfast.*

B&B/INN

★

$$$$ 🛏 **Tenaya Lodge.** One of the region's largest hotels, Tenaya Lodge is ideal for people who enjoy wilderness treks by day but prefer creature comforts at night. **Pros:** rustic setting with modern comforts; good off-season deals; very close to Yosemite National Park. **Cons:** so big it can seem impersonal; pricey during summer; few dining options. **TripAdvisor:** "I want to go back," "Yosemite luxury," "well maintained." $ *Rooms from: $325* ⊠ *1122 Hwy. 41* ☎ *559/683–6555, 888/514–2167* ⊕ *www. tenayalodge.com* ⇨ *244 rooms, 6 suites.*

HOTEL

19

EL PORTAL

14 miles west of Yosemite Valley on Hwy. 140.

The market in town is a good place to pick up provisions before you get to Yosemite (⇨ *Chapter 20*). You'll find a post office and a gas station, but not much else.

GETTING HERE AND AROUND

The drive here on Highway 140 from Mariposa and, farther west, Merced, is the prettiest and gentlest (in terms of steep uphill and downhill portions) route to Yosemite National Park. Much of the road follows the Merced River in a rugged canyon. The Yosemite Area Regional Transportation System (YARTS; ⊕ *www.yarts.com*) is a cheap and dependable way to go between Merced and Yosemite Valley; all buses stop in El Portal, where many park employees reside.

WHERE TO STAY

For expanded reviews, facilities, and current deals, visit Fodors.com.

$$ **Evergreen Lodge at Yosemite.** Near Hetch Hetchy on Yosemite National
RESORT   Park's northwest side, this sprawling property set in the woods is perfect
☙   for families: The 90-cabin complex includes a playground, an amphitheater, a movie room, a restaurant, a gift shop, and an activities desk. **Pros:** near the underrated Hetch Hetchy; family atmosphere; clean cabins. **Cons:** about an hour's drive from Yosemite Valley. **TripAdvisor:** "unexpected delight," "restaurant is the best," "the great outdoors in style." ⑤ *Rooms from: $170 ⊠ 33160 Evergreen Rd.* ☎ *209/379–2606, 888/935–6343* ⊕ *www.evergreenlodge.com* ⇆ *90 cabins.*

$$$ **Yosemite View Lodge.** Just 2 miles outside the park's Arch Rock
B&B/INN   entrance, this modern property is the most convenient place to spend the night if you are unable to secure lodgings in the Valley. **Pros:** great location; good views; lots of on-site amenities. **Cons:** somewhat pricey for what you get. **TripAdvisor:** "lovely spot," "great location," "gorgeous view." ⑤ *Rooms from: $229 ⊠ 11136 Hwy. 140* ☎ *209/379–2681, 888/742–4371* ⊕ *www.yosemite-motels.com* ⇆ *279 rooms.*

MAMMOTH LAKES

30 miles south of eastern edge of Yosemite National Park on U.S. 395.

International real-estate developers joined forces with Mammoth Mountain Ski Area to transform the once sleepy town of Mammoth Lakes (elevation 7,800 feet) into an upscale ski destination. The Village at Mammoth is the epicenter of the recent development. Much of the architecture here is of the faux-alpine variety, but you'll find relatively sophisticated dining and lodging options. Winter is high season; in summer, room rates plummet.

GETTING HERE AND AROUND

The best way to get to Mammoth Lakes is by car. The town is a couple of miles west of U.S. 395. The Yosemite Area Regional Transportation System (YARTS; ⊕ *www.yarts.com*) provides once-a-day service between here and Yosemite Valley. The shuttle buses of Eastern Sierra Transit Authority (☎ 800/922–1930 ⊕ *www.estransit.com*) serve Mammoth Lakes, Bishop, and nearby tourist sites.

Highway 203 heads west from U.S. 395, becoming Main Street as it passes through the town of Mammoth Lakes, and later Minaret Road (which makes a right turn) as it continues west to the Mammoth Mountain ski area and Devils Postpile National Monument.

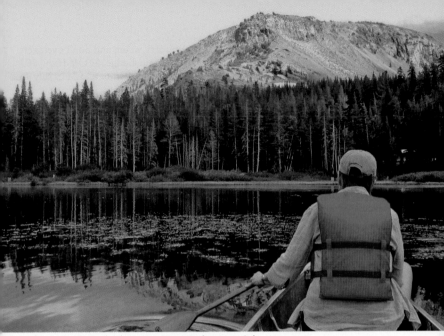
Twin Lakes, in the Mammoth Lakes region, is a great place to unwind.

ESSENTIALS

Visitor Information Mammoth Lakes Visitors Bureau ✉ *Welcome Center, 2510 Main St., near Sawmill Cutoff Rd.* ☎ *760/934–2712* ⊕ *www.visitmammoth. com.*

EXPLORING

Mammoth Lakes Basin. The lakes, reached by Lake Mary Road off Highway 203 southwest of town, are popular for fishing and boating in summer. First comes Twin Lakes, at the far end of which is Twin Falls, where water cascades 300 feet over a shelf of volcanic rock. Also popular are Lake Mary, the largest lake in the basin; Lake Mamie; and Lake George. Horseshoe Lake is the only lake in which you can swim.

Minaret Vista. The glacier-carved sawtooth spires of the Minarets, the remains of an ancient lava flow, are best viewed from the Minaret Vista, off Highway 203 west of Mammoth Lakes.

☾
Fodor's Choice
★

Panorama Gondola. Even if you don't ski, ride the gondola to see Mammoth Mountain, the aptly named dormant volcano that gives Mammoth Lakes its name. Gondolas serve skiers in winter and mountain bikers and sightseers in summer. The high-speed, eight-passenger gondolas whisk you from the chalet to the summit, where you can read about the area's volcanic history and take in top-of-the-world views. Standing high above the tree line, you can look west 150 miles across the state to the Coastal Range; to the east are the highest peaks of Nevada and the Great Basin beyond. You won't find a better view of the Sierra High Country without climbing. Remember, though, that the air is thin at the 11,053-foot summit; carry water, and don't overexert yourself. The boarding area is at the Main Lodge. ⊠ *Off Hwy. 203* ☎ *760/934–2571 information, 3850 gondola station* 💲 *$24* ☉ *July 4– Oct., daily 9–4:30; Nov.–July 3, daily 8:30–4.*

Village at Mammoth. This huge complex of shops, restaurants, and luxury accommodations is the town's tourist center. Parking can be tricky, even seemingly impossible. There's a parking lot across the street on Minaret Road; cross your fingers and pay attention to time limits.

WHERE TO EAT

$$$
STEAKHOUSE

✕ **The Mogul.** This longtime favorite the place to go when you want a straightforward steak and salad bar. The only catch is that the waiters cook your steak—and the result depends on the waiter's experience. But generally you can't go wrong. And kids love it. The knotty-pine walls lend a woodsy touch and suggest Mammoth Mountain before all the development. 💲 *Average main: $24* ⊠ *1528 Mammoth Tavern Rd., off Old Mammoth Rd.* ☎ *760/934–3039* ⊕ *www.themogul.com* ☉ *No lunch*.

$$$
AMERICAN

✕ **Petra's Bistro & Wine Bar.** The ambience at Petra's—quiet, dark, and warm—complements the carefully prepared meat main dishes and seasonal sides, and the more than two dozen California wines from behind the bar. The service is top-notch. Downstairs, the Clocktower Cellar bar provides a late-night, rowdy alternative—or chaser. 💲 *Average main: $28* ⊠ *6080 Minaret Rd.* ☎ *760/934–3500* ⊕ *www.petrasbistro.com* ⚑ *Reservations essential* ☉ *Closed Mon. No lunch.*

$$$
AMERICAN

✕ **Restaurant at Convict Lake.** Tucked in a tiny valley ringed by mile-high peaks, Convict Lake is one of the most spectacular spots in the eastern Sierra. Thank heaven the food lives up to the view. The chef's specialties include beef Wellington, rack of lamb, and pan-seared local trout, all beautifully prepared. The woodsy room has a vaulted knotty-pine ceiling and a copper-chimney fireplace that roars on cold nights. Natural light abounds in the daytime, but if it's summer, opt for a table outdoors under the white-barked aspens. Service is exceptional, as is the wine list, with reasonably priced European and California varietals. 💲 *Average main: $32* ⊠ *Convict Lake Rd. off U.S. 395, 4 miles south of Mammoth Lakes* ☎ *760/934–3803* ⊕ *www.convictlake.com* ⚑ *Reservations essential* ☉ *No lunch early Sept.–July 4.*

$$
WINE BAR

✕ **Side Door Café.** Half wine bar, half café, this is a laid-back spot for an easy lunch or a long, lingering afternoon. The café serves grilled panini sandwiches, sweet and savory crepes, and espresso. At the wine bar, order cheese plates and charcuterie platters, designed to pair with the 25 wines (fewer in summertime) available by the glass. If you're lucky, a winemaker will show up and hold court at the bar. 💲 *Average main: $18* ⊠ *Village at Mammoth, 1111 Forest Trail, Unit 229* ☎ *760/934–5200* ⊕ *www.sidedoormammoth.com.*

$$
AMERICAN

✕ **The Stove.** A longtime family favorite for down-to-earth, folksy cooking, this is the kind of place you take the family to fill up before a long car ride. The omelets, pancakes, huevos rancheros, and meat loaf won't win any awards, but they're tasty. The room is cozy, with gingham curtains and dark-wood booths, and service is friendly. Breakfast and lunch are the best bets here. ⑤ *Average main: $16* ✉ *644 Old Mammoth Rd.* ☎ *760/934–2821* ⚐ *Reservations not accepted* ☉ *No dinner Mon. and Tues.*

WHERE TO STAY

$
B&B/INN
🏨 **Alpenhof Lodge.** The owners of Alpenhof lucked out when developers built the fancy-schmancy Village at Mammoth across the street from their mom-and-pop motel, which remains a simple lodging offering basic comforts and a few niceties like attractive pine furniture. **Pros:** convenient for skiers; good price. **Cons:** could use an update; rooms above the pub can be noisy. **TripAdvisor:** "cozy hotel in stunning location," "nice 'Austrian' hotel," "a delightful retreat."⑤ *Rooms from: $119* ✉ *6080 Minaret Rd., Box 1157* ☎ *760/934–6330, 800/828–0371* ⊕ *www.alpenhof-lodge.com* ⬐ *54 rooms, 3 cabins.*

$$
B&B/INN
🏨 **Cinnamon Bear Inn Bed and Breakfast.** In a business district off Main Street, this bed-and-breakfast feels more like a small motel, with nicely decorated rooms, many with four-poster beds. **Pros:** comparatively quiet; affordable; friendly. **Cons:** a bit tricky to find; limited parking. **TripAdvisor:** "delicious breakfast," "a lovely friendly place," "quirky."⑤ *Rooms from: $149* ✉ *113 Center St.* ☎ *760/934–2873, 800/845–2873* ⊕ *www.cinnamonbearinn.com* ⬐ *22 rooms* ⚐ *Breakfast.*

$$$
RESORT
🏨 **Double Eagle Resort and Spa.** You won't find a better spa retreat in the eastern Sierra than the Double Eagle, which is in a spectacularly beautiful spot under towering peaks and along a creek, near June Lake, 20 minutes north of Mammoth Lakes. **Pros:** pretty setting; generous breakfast; good for families. **Cons:** expensive, remote. **TripAdvisor:** "beautiful spot," "great mountain getaway," "great location."⑤ *Rooms from: $229* ✉ *5587 Hwy. 158, Box 736, June Lake* ☎ *760/648–7004, 877/648–7004* ⊕ *www.doubleeagleresort.com* ⬐ *16 2-bedroom cabins, 16 cabin suites, 1 3-bedroom cabin.*

19

$$
RESORT
🏨 **Juniper Springs Lodge.** Tops for slope-side comfort, these condominium-style units have full kitchens and ski-in ski-out access to the mountain. **Pros:** bargain during summer; direct access to the slopes; good views. **Cons:** no nightlife within walking distance; no air-conditioning. ⑤ *Rooms from: $159* ✉ *4000 Meridian Blvd.* ☎ *760/924–1102, 800/626–6684* ⊕ *www.mammothmountain.com* ⬐ *10 studios, 99 1-bedrooms, 92 2-bedrooms, 3 3-bedrooms.*

$$
RESORT
🏨 **Mammoth Mountain Inn.** If you want to be within walking distance of the Mammoth Mountain Main Lodge, this is the place. **Pros:** great location; big rooms; a traditional place to stay. **Cons:** can be crowded in ski season; won't be around for many more years. **TripAdvisor:** "service at its best," "ski-in ski-out," "very conveniently located."⑤ *Rooms from: $129* ✉ *Minaret Rd., 4 miles west of Mammoth Lakes* ☎ *760/934–2581, 800/626–6684* ⊕ *www.mammothmountain.com* ⬐ *124 rooms, 91 condos.*

$$
RESORT
Fodor's Choice
★
🏨 **Tamarack Lodge Resort & Lakefront Restaurant.** Tucked away on the edge of the John Muir Wilderness Area, where cross-country ski trails loop through the woods, this original 1924 lodge looks like something out of a snow globe, and the lake it borders is serenely beautiful. **Pros:** rustic

but not run-down; plenty of eco-sensitivity; tons of nearby outdoor activities. **Cons:** thin walls; some main lodge rooms have shared bathrooms. **TripAdvisor:** "rustic hotel in beautiful spot," "lots of character," "wonderful helpful staff."⑤ *Rooms from: $169* ✉ *Lake Mary Rd., off Hwy. 203* ☎ *760/934–2442, 800/626–6684* ⊕ *www.tamaracklodge. com* ⟳ *11 rooms, 35 cabins.*

$$$ ⭒ **The Village Lodge.** At the epicenter of Mammoth's dining and nightlife
RESORT scene, this cluster of four-story timber-and-stone condo buildings nods to Alpine style, with exposed timbers and peaked roofs. **Pros:** central location; clean; big rooms; lots of good restaurants nearby. **Cons:** pricey; can be noisy outside. **TripAdvisor:** "beautiful room," "great condos in a great location," "city living in the mountains."⑤ *Rooms from: $189* ✉ *100 Canyon Blvd.* ☎ *760/934–1982, 800/626–6684* ⊕ *www.mammothmountain.com* ⟳ *277 units.*

SPORTS AND THE OUTDOORS

BICYCLING

Mammoth Mountain Bike Park. The park opens when the snow melts, usually by July, and has 70-plus miles of single-track trails—from mellow to super-challenging. Chairlifts and shuttles provide trail access, and rentals are available. Various shops around town also rent bikes and provide trail maps, if you don't want to ascend the mountain. ✉ *Mammoth Mountain Ski Area* ☎ *760/934–0706* ⊕ *www.mammothmountain.com.*

FISHING

The fishing season runs from the last Saturday in April until the end of October. Crowley Lake is the top trout-fishing spot in the area; Convict Lake, June Lake, and the lakes of the Mammoth Basin are other prime spots. One of the best trout rivers is the San Joaquin, near Devils Postpile. Hot Creek, a designated Wild Trout Stream, is renowned for fly-fishing (catch-and-release only).

Kittredge Sports. This outfit rents rods and reels and also conducts guided trips. ✉ *3218 Main St., at Forest Trail* ☎ *760/934–7566* ⊕ *www. kittredgesports.com.*

Sierra Drifters Guide Service. To maximize your time on the water, get tips from local anglers, or better yet, book a guided fishing trip with this service. ☎ *760/935–4250* ⊕ *www.sierradrifters.com.*

HIKING

Hiking in Mammoth is stellar, especially along the trails that wind through the pristine alpine scenery around the Lakes Basin. Carry lots of water; and remember, you're above 8,000-foot elevation, and the air is thin.

U.S. Forest Service Ranger Station and Welcome Center. Stop at the ranger station, just east of the town of Mammoth Lakes, for an area trail map and permits for backpacking in wilderness areas. ✉ *2510 Main St., Hwy. 203* ☎ *760/924–5500* ⊕ *www.fs.usda.gov/main/inyo.*

HORSEBACK RIDING

Stables around Mammoth are typically open from June through September.

Mammoth Lakes Pack Outfit. This company runs day and overnight horseback trips, or will shuttle you to the high country. ✉ *Lake Mary Rd., between Twin Lakes and Lake Mary* ☎ *888/475–8747* ⊕ *www. mammothpack.com.*

McGee Creek Pack Station. These folks customize pack trips or will shuttle you to camp alone. ☎ *760/935–4324, 760/878–2207, 800/854–7407* ⊕ *www.mcgeecreekpackstation.com.*

SKIING

In winter, check the On the Snow website or call the Snow Report for information about Mammoth weather conditions.

June Mountain Ski Area. In their rush to Mammoth Mountain, most people overlook June Mountain, a compact, low-key resort 20 miles north of Mammoth. Snowboarders especially dig it. Two freestyle terrain areas are for both skiers and boarders, including a huge 16-foot-wall super pipe. Best of all, there's rarely a line for the lifts—if you want to avoid the crowds but must ski on a weekend, this is the place. And in a storm, June is better protected from wind and blowing snow than Mammoth Mountain. (If it starts to storm, you can use your Mammoth ticket at June.) Expect all the usual services, including a rental-and-repair shop, ski school, and sports shop, but the food quality is better at Mammoth. Lift tickets cost $72, with discounts for multiple days. ✉ *3819 Hwy. 158, off June Lake Loop, June Lake* ☎ *760/648–7733, 888/586–3686* ⊕ *www.junemountain.com* ⌖ *35 trails on 500 acres, rated 35% beginner, 45% intermediate, 20% advanced. Longest run 2½ miles, base 7,510 feet, summit 10,174 feet. Lifts: 7.*

Fodor's Choice ★ **Mammoth Mountain Ski Area.** One of the West's largest and best ski areas, Mammoth has more than 3,500 acres of skiable terrain and a 3,100-foot vertical drop. The views from the 11,053-foot summit are some of the most stunning in the Sierra. Below, you'll find a 6½-mile-wide swath of groomed boulevards and canyons, as well as pockets of tree-skiing and a dozen vast bowls. Snowboarders are everywhere on the slopes; there are three outstanding freestyle terrain parks of varying technical difficulty, with jumps, rails, tabletops, and giant super pipes (this is the location of several international snowboarding and, in summer months, mountain-bike competitions). Mammoth's season begins in November and often lingers into May. Lift tickets cost $89. Lessons and equipment are available, and there's a children's ski and snowboard school. Mammoth runs free shuttle-bus routes around town and to the ski area, and the Village Gondola runs from the Village complex to Canyon Lodge. However, only overnight guests are allowed to park at the Village for more than a few hours. Warning: The main lodge is dark and dated, unsuited in most every way for the crush of ski season. Within a decade, it's likely to be replaced. ✉ *Minaret Rd., west of Mammoth Lakes* ☎ *760/934–2571, 800/626–6684, 760/934–0687 shuttle* ⌖ *150 trails on 3,500 acres, rated 30% beginner, 40% intermediate, 30% advanced. Longest run 3 miles, base 7,953 feet, summit 11,053 feet. Lifts: 27, including 9 high-speed and 2 gondolas.*

Tamarack Cross Country Ski Center. Trails at the center, adjacent to Tamarack Lodge, meander around several lakes. Rentals are available.

19

The all-day inclusive rate is $55. ✉ *Lake Mary Rd., off Hwy. 203* ☎ *760/934–5293, 760/934–2442* ⊕ *www.tamaracklodge.com.*

SKI RENTALS AND RESOURCES

★ **Footloose.** When the U.S. Ski Team visits Mammoth and needs boot adjustments, everyone heads to Footloose, the best place in town—and possibly all California—for ski-boot rentals and sales, as well as custom insoles (ask for Kevin or Corty). ✉ *3043 Main St., at Mammoth Rd.* ☎ *760/934–2400* ⊕ *www.footloosesports.com.*

Kittredge Sports. Advanced skiers should consider this outfit, which has been around since the 1960s. ✉ *3218 Main St.* ☎ *760/934–7566* ⊕ *www.kittredgesports.com.*

Mammoth Sporting Goods. This company rents good skis for intermediates and sells equipment, clothing, and accessories. ✉ *1 Sierra Center Mall, Old Mammoth Rd.* ☎ *760/934–3239.*

OntheSnow.com ⊕ *www.onthesnow.com/california/mammoth-mountain-ski-area/skireport.html.*

Snow Report. For information on winter conditions around Mammoth, call the Snow Report. ☎ *760/934–7669, 888/766–9778.*

EAST OF YOSEMITE NATIONAL PARK

Most people enter Yosemite National Park from the west, having driven out from the Bay Area or Los Angeles. The eastern entrance on Tioga Pass Road (Highway 120), however, provides stunning, sweeping views of the High Sierra. Gray rocks shine in the bright sun, with scattered, small vegetation sprinkled about the mountainside. To drive from Lee Vining to Tuolumne Meadows is an unforgettable experience, but keep in mind the road tends to be closed for at least seven months of the year.

LEE VINING

20 miles east of Tuolumne Meadows via Hwy. 120 to U.S. 395; 30 miles north of Mammoth Lakes on U.S. 395.

Tiny Lee Vining is known primarily as the eastern gateway to Yosemite National Park (summer only; ⇨ *Chapter 20*) and the location of vast and desolate Mono Lake. Pick up supplies at the general store year-round, or stop here for lunch or dinner before or after a drive through the high country. In winter the town is all but deserted, except for the ice climbers who come to scale frozen waterfalls. You can meet these hearty souls at Nicely's restaurant, where climbers congregate for breakfast around 8 on winter mornings. To try your hand at ice climbing, contact Doug Nidever (☎ *760/937–6922* ⊕ *www.themountainguide.com*), aka the Mountain Guide.

GETTING HERE AND AROUND

Lee Vining is on U.S. 395, just north of the road's intersection with Highway 120 and on the south side of Mono Lake. Yosemite Area Regional Transportation System (YARTS; ⊕ *www.yarts.com*) can get you here from Yosemite Valley, but you'll need a car to explore the area.

ESSENTIALS

Visitor Information Lee Vining Chamber of Commerce *760/647–6629*
⊕ *www.leevining.com.* **Mono Lake** ☎ *760/647–6595* ⊕ *www.monolake.org.*

EXPLORING

★ **Mono Lake.** Since the 1940s Los Angeles has diverted water from this lake, exposing striking towers of tufa, or calcium carbonate. Court victories by environmentalists have meant fewer diversions, and the lake is rising again. Although to see the lake from U.S. 395 is stunning, make time to walk about South Tufa, whose parking lot is 5 miles east of U.S. 395 off Highway 120. There during the summer you can join the naturalist-guided **South Tufa Walk,** which lasts about 1½ hours. The sensational **Scenic Area Visitor Center,** on U.S. 395, is open daily from June through September (Sunday–Thursday 8–5, Friday and Saturday 8–7), it's closed December through March and open weekends the rest of the year. The center's hilltop and sweeping views of Mono Lake, along with its interactive exhibits inside, make this one of California's best visitor centers. Rangers and naturalists lead walking tours of the tufa daily in summer and on weekends (sometimes on cross-country skis) in winter. In town at U.S. 395 and 3rd Street, the **Mono Lake Committee Information Center & Bookstore** has more information about this beautiful area. ⊠ *Hwy. 120, east of Lee Vining* ☎ *760/647–3044.*

**EN
ROUTE** **June Lake Loop.** Heading south from Lee Vining, U.S. 395 intersects the June Lake Loop. This gorgeous 17-mile drive follows an old glacial canyon past Grant, June, Gull, and other lakes before reconnecting with U.S. 395 on its way to Mammoth Lakes. The loop is especially colorful in fall. ⊠ *Hwy. 158 W.*

WHERE TO EAT AND STAY

For expanded reviews, facilities, and current deals, visit Fodors.com.

$ ✕ **Nicely's.** Artworks for sale decorate the walls of this vintage diner. The
AMERICAN country cooking isn't fancy—think blueberry pancakes for breakfast and chicken-fried steak for dinner—but this is a good spot for families with kids and unfussy eaters looking for a square meal. It's the kind of place where the waitress walks up with a pot of coffee and asks, "Ya want a warm-up, hon?" ⑤ *Average main: $15* ⊠ *U.S. 395 and 4th St.* ☎ *760/647–6477* ☉ *Closed Tues. and Wed. in winter.*

$ ✕ **Tioga Gas Mart & Whoa Nelli Deli.** This might be the only gas station in
AMERICAN the United States that serves cocktails, but its appeal goes way beyond
★ novelty. The mahimahi tacos are succulent, the gourmet pizzas tasty, and the herb-crusted pork loin with berry glaze elegant. Order at the counter and grab a seat inside or out. ⑤ *Average main: $14* ⊠ *Hwy. 120 and U.S. 395* ☎ *760/647–1088* ⊕ *www.whoanelliedeli.com* ☉ *Closed mid-Nov.–mid-Apr.*

$ ▦ **Lake View Lodge.** Enormous rooms and lovely landscaping, which
B&B/INN includes several shaded sitting areas, set this motel apart from its competitors in town. **Pros:** attractive; clean; friendly staff. **Cons:** could use updating. **TripAdvisor:** "convenient to Tioga pass," "no frills no fuss," "clean and comfortable." ⑤ *Rooms from: $89* ⊠ *51285 U.S. 395* ☎ *760/647–6543, 800/990–6614* ⊕ *www.lakeviewlodgeyosemite.com* ⬐ *76 rooms, 12 cottages.*

19

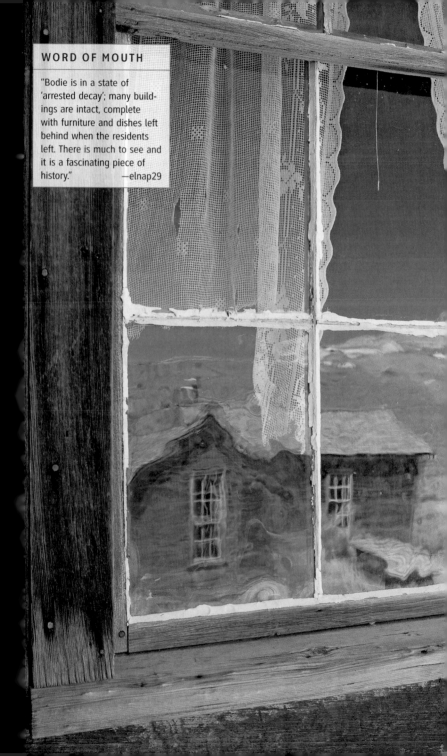

BODIE STATE HISTORIC PARK

23 miles northeast of Lee Vining via U.S. 395 to Hwy. 270.

The historic town of Bridgeport is the gateway to Bodie State Historic Park, and the only supply center for miles around. The scenery is spectacular, with craggy, snowcapped peaks looming over vast prairies. Tiny and for tourist purposes worth nothing more than a place to sleep and eat, Bridgeport's claim to fame is that most of the 1947 film-noir classic *Out of the Past* was filmed here. In winter, much of Bridgeport shuts down.

GETTING HERE AND AROUND

You need to get here by private car. About 15 miles north of Lee Vining (7 miles south of Bridgeport), look for signs pointing you east toward the ghost town, another 13 miles via Highway 270. The last 3 miles are unpaved, and possibly treacherous depending on erosion and the weather. You might need a snowmobile to get here in the winter.

EXPLORING

★ **Bodie Ghost Town.** The mining village of Rattlesnake Gulch, abandoned mine shafts, and the remains of a small Chinatown are among the sights at this fascinating ghost town. The town boomed from about 1878 to 1881, but by the late 1940s all its residents had departed. A state park was established here in 1962, with a mandate to preserve everything in a state of "arrested decay." Evidence of Bodie's wild past survives at an excellent museum, and you can tour an old stamp mill where ore was crushed into fine powder to extract gold and silver. The town is 23 miles from Lee Vining, north on U.S. 395, then east on Highway 270; the last 3 miles are unpaved. Snow may close Highway 270 from late fall through early spring. No food, drink, or lodging is available in Bodie. ⊠ *Main and Green Sts., Bodie* 🕾 *760/647–6445* ⊕ *www.bodie. com* 🖾 *Park $5, museum free* ⊘ *Park: late May–early Sept., daily 8–7; early Sept.–late May, daily 8–4. Museum: late May–early Sept., daily 9–6; early Sept.–late May, hrs vary.*

19

SOUTH OF SEQUOIA AND KINGS CANYON: THREE RIVERS

200 miles north of Los Angeles via I-5 to Hwy. 99 to Hwy. 198; 8 miles south of Ash Mountain/Foothills entrance to Sequoia National Park on Hwy. 198.

In the foothills of the Sierra along the Kaweah River, the serpentine hamlet of Three Rivers serves as the main gateway town to Sequoia and Kings Canyon national parks *(⇨ Chapter 21, Sequoia and Kings Canyon National Parks)*. Its livelihood depends largely on tourism from the parks, courtesy of two markets, a few service stations, banks, a post office, and several lodgings, which are good spots to find a room when park accommodations are full (or if you dislike camping and would like to save money).

GETTING HERE AND AROUND

From Memorial Day through Labor Day, you can ride the city of Visalia's Sequoia Shuttle (☎ 877/404–6473 ⊕ *www.ci.visalia.ca.us*) to and from Three Rivers, up to and down from Sequoia National Park. You probably should count on driving here yourself, however, via Highway 198. The town is slender and long, and to walk from your hotel to a restaurant might wear you out before you set foot in the national park.

WHERE TO EAT AND STAY

For expanded reviews, facilities, and current deals, visit Fodors.com.

$ ╳ **We Three Bakery.** This friendly, popular-with-the-locals spot packs
ECLECTIC lunches for trips into the nearby national parks; it's also open for breakfast. Baked goods for the windy road ahead, anyone? $ *Average main: $10* ⊠ *43688 Sierra Dr.* ☎ *559/561–4761.*

$$ ⊞ **Buckeye Tree Lodge.** Every room at this two-story motel has a patio
B&B/INN facing a sun-dappled grassy lawn, right on the banks of the Kaweah River. **Pros:** near the park entrance; fantastic river views; friendly staff. **Cons:** can fill up quickly in the summer; could use a little updating. **TripAdvisor:** "gorgeous location," "friendly people," "comfortable accommodations." $ *Rooms from: $123* ⊠ *46000 Sierra Dr., Hwy. 198* ☎ *559/561–5900* ⊕ *www.buckeyetree.com* ⇄ *11 rooms, 1 cottage* ❘○❘ *Breakfast.*

SPORTS AND THE OUTDOORS

RAFTING

Kaweah White Water Adventures. From April through July, this outfit conducts two-hour and full-day rafting trips, with some Class III rapids. Longer trips may include some Class IV. ☎ *559/561–1000, 800/229–8658* ⊕ *www.kaweah-whitewater.com* ◻ *$50 to $140 per person.*

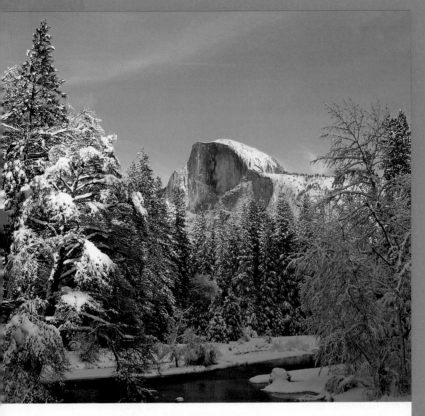

Yosemite National Park

WORD OF MOUTH

"I tried cross-country skiing for the first time in Yosemite. An avid downhill skier, I quickly learned that cross-country is more physically demanding, slower going, but scenically spectacular. I chose to use the time to find the perfect shot of Half Dome."

—photo by Sarah Corley, Fodors.com member

WELCOME TO YOSEMITE

TOP REASONS TO GO

★ **Wet and wild:** An easy stroll brings you to the base of Lower Yosemite Falls, where roaring springtime waters make for misty lens caps and lasting memories.

★ **Tunnel vision:** Approaching Yosemite Valley, Wawona Road passes through a mountainside and emerges before one of the park's most heart-stopping vistas.

★ **Inhale the beauty:** Pause to smell the light, pristine air as you travel about the High Sierra's Tiago Pass and Tuolumne Meadows, where 10,000-foot granite peaks just might take your breath away.

★ **Walk away:** Leave the crowds behind—but do bring along a buddy—and take a hike somewhere along Yosemite's 800 miles of trails.

★ **Powder your nose:** Winter's hush floats into Yosemite on snowflakes. Lift your face to the sky and listen to the trees.

1 **Yosemite Valley.** At an elevation of 4,000 feet, in roughly the center of the park, beats Yosemite's heart. This is where you'll find the park's most famous sights and biggest crowds.

2 **Wawona and Mariposa Grove.** The park's southern tip holds Wawona, with its grand old hotel and pioneer history center, and the Mariposa Grove of Big Trees, filled with giant sequoias. These are closest to the South Entrance, 35 miles (a one-hour drive) south of Yosemite Village.

3 **Tuolumne Meadows.** The highlight of east-central Yosemite is this wildflower-strewn valley with hiking trails, nestled among sharp, rocky peaks. It's a two-hour drive northeast of Yosemite Valley along Tioga Road (closed mid-October–late May).

4 **Hetch Hetchy.** The most remote, least visited part of Yosemite accessible by automobile, this glacial valley is dominated by a reservoir and veined with wilderness trails. It's near the park's western boundary, about a half-hour drive north of the Big Oak Flat Entrance.

CALIFORNIA

GETTING ORIENTED

Yosemite is so large that you can think of it as five parks. Yosemite Valley, famous for waterfalls and cliffs, and Wawona, where the giant sequoias stand, are open all year. Hetch Hetchy, home of less-used backcountry trails, is most accessible from late spring through early fall. The subalpine high country, Tuolumne Meadows, is open for summer hiking and camping; in winter it's accessible via cross-country skis or snowshoes. Badger Pass Ski Area is open in winter only. Most visitors spend their time along the park's southwestern border, between Wawona and Big Oak Flat Entrance; a bit farther east in Yosemite Valley and Badger Pass Ski Area; and along the east–west corridor of Tioga Road, which spans the park north of Yosemite Valley and bisects Tuolumne Meadows.

20

Updated by
Reed Parsell

By merely standing in Yosemite Valley and turning in a circle, you can see more natural wonders in a minute than you could in a full day pretty much anywhere else. Half Dome, Yosemite Falls, El Capitan, Bridalveil Fall, Sentinel Dome, the Merced River, white-flowering dogwood trees, maybe even bears ripping into the bark of fallen trees or sticking their snouts into beehives—it's all in Yosemite Valley.

In the mid-1800s, when tourists were arriving to the area, the valley's special geologic qualities, and the giant sequoias of Mariposa Grove 30 miles to the south, so impressed a group of influential Californians that they persuaded President Abraham Lincoln to grant those two areas to the state for protection. On Oct. 1, 1890—thanks largely to lobbying efforts by naturalist John Muir and Robert Underwood Johnson, the editor of *Century Magazine*—Congress set aside 1,500 square miles for Yosemite National Park.

YOSEMITE PLANNER

WHEN TO GO

During extremely busy periods—such as the 4th of July—you will experience delays at the entrance gates. ■ **TIP➜ For smaller crowds, visit midweek.** Or come mid-April through Memorial Day or mid-September through October, when the park is only a bit busy and the days usually are sunny and clear.

Summer rainfall is rare. In winter, heavy snows occasionally cause road closures, and tire chains or four-wheel drive may be required on the roads that remain open. The road to Glacier Point beyond the turnoff for Badger Pass is closed after the first major snowfall; Tioga Road is closed from late October through May or mid-June. Mariposa Grove Road is typically closed for a shorter period in winter.

GETTING HERE AND AROUND
BUS TRAVEL
Once you're in Yosemite you can take advantage of the free shuttle buses, which operate on low emissions, have 21 stops, and run every 10 minutes or so from 9 am to 6 pm year-round; a separate (but also free) summer-only shuttle runs out to El Capitan. Also during the summer, you can pay to take the morning "hikers' bus" from Yosemite Valley to Tuolumne or the bus up to Glacier Point. Bus service from Wawona is geared for people who are staying there and want to spend the day in Yosemite Valley. Free and frequent shuttles transport people between the Wawona Hotel and Mariposa Grove. During the snow season, buses run regularly between Yosemite Valley and Badger Pass Ski Area.

CAR TRAVEL
Roughly 200 miles from San Francisco, 300 miles from Los Angeles, and 500 miles from Las Vegas, Yosemite takes a while to reach—and its many sites and attractions merit much more time than what rangers say is the average visit: four hours. Most people arrive via automobile or tour bus, but public transportation (courtesy of Amtrak and the regional YARTS bus system) also can get you to the valley efficiently.

Of the park's four entrances, Arch Rock is the closest to Yosemite Valley. The road that goes through it, Route 140 from Merced and Mariposa, is a scenic western approach that snakes alongside the boulder-packed Merced River. Route 41, through Wawona, is the way to come from Los Angeles (or Fresno, if you've flown in and rented a car). Route 120, through Crane Flat, is the most direct route from San Francisco. The only way in from the east is Tioga Road, which may be the best route in terms of scenery—though due to snow accumulation it's open for a frustratingly short amount of time each year (typically early June through mid-October).

There are few gas stations within Yosemite (Crane Flat, Tuolumne Meadows, and Wawona; none in the valley), so fuel up before you reach the park. From late fall until early spring, the weather is especially unpredictable, and driving can be treacherous. You should carry chains.

PARK ESSENTIALS
PARK FEES AND PERMITS
The admission fee, valid for seven days, is $20 per vehicle or $10 per individual.

If you plan to camp in the backcountry or climb Half Dome, you must have a wilderness permit. Availability of permits, which are free, depends upon trailhead quotas. It's best to make a reservation, especially if you will be visiting May through September. You can reserve two days to 24 weeks in advance by phone (☎ *209/372–0740 or 209/372–0739*); a $5-per-person processing fee is charged if and when your reservations are confirmed. Requests must include your name, address, daytime phone, the number of people in your party, trip date, alternative dates, starting and ending trailheads, and a brief itinerary. Without a reservation, you may still get a free permit on a first-come, first-served basis at wilderness permit offices at Big Oak Flat, Hetch Hetchy, Tuolumne,

20

CLOSE UP

Plants and Wildlife in Yosemite

Dense stands of incense cedar and Douglas fir—as well as ponderosa, Jeffrey, lodgepole, and sugar pines—cover much of the park, but the stellar standout, quite literally, is the *Sequoia sempervirens*, the giant sequoia. Sequoias grow only along the west slope of the Sierra Nevada between 4,500 and 7,000 feet in elevation. Starting from a seed the size of a rolled-oat flake, each of these ancient monuments assumes remarkable proportions in adulthood; you can see them in the Mariposa Grove of Big Trees. In late May the valley's dogwood trees bloom with white, starlike flowers. Wildflowers, such as black-eyed Susan, bull thistle, cow parsnip, lupine, and meadow goldenrod, peak in June in the valley and in July at higher elevations.

The most visible animals in the park—aside from the omnipresent western gray squirrel—are the mule deer. Though sightings of bighorn sheep are infrequent in the park itself, you can sometimes see them on the eastern side of the Sierra Crest, just off Route 120 in Lee Vining Canyon. You may also see the American black bear, which often has a brown, cinnamon, or blond coat. The Sierra Nevada is home to thousands of bears, and you should take all necessary precautions to keep yourself—and the bears—safe. For one, do not feed the bears. Bears that acquire a taste for human food can become very aggressive and destructive and often must be destroyed by rangers.

Watch for the blue Steller's jay along trails, near public buildings, and in campgrounds, and look for golden eagles soaring over Tioga Road.

Wawona, the Wilderness Center in Yosemite Village, and Yosemite Valley in summer. From fall to spring, visit the Valley Visitor Center.

PARK HOURS

The park is open 24/7 year-round. All entrances are open at all hours, except for Hetch Hetchy Entrance, which is open roughly dawn to dusk. Yosemite is in the Pacific time zone.

TOURS

★ **Ansel Adams Photo Walks.** Photography enthusiasts shouldn't miss these 90-minute guided camera walks offered a few mornings each week by professional photographers. All are free, but participation is limited to 15 people. Meeting points vary. and advance reservations are essential. ☎ *209/372–4413, 800/568–7398* ⊕ *www.anseladams.com* ✉ *Free.*

🄲 **Wee Wild Ones.** Designed for kids under seven, this 45-minute program includes animal-theme games, songs, stories, and crafts. The event is held outdoors before the regular Yosemite Lodge or Curry Village evening programs in summer and fall; it moves to the Ahwahnee's big fireplace in winter and spring. All children must be accompanied by an adult. ☎ *209/372–1240* ✉ *Free.*

VISITOR INFORMATION

PARK CONTACT INFORMATION

Yosemite National Park ☎ *209/372–0200* ⊕ *www.nps.gov/yose.*

VISITOR CENTERS

Le Conte Memorial Lodge. This small but striking National Historic Landmark, with its granite walls and steeply pitched shingle roof, is Yosemite's first permanent public information center. Step inside to see the cathedral-like interior, which contains a library and environmental exhibits. To find out about evening programs, check the kiosk out front. ⊠ *Southside Dr., about ½ mile west of Curry Village* ⊗ *Memorial Day–Labor Day, Wed.–Sun. 10–4.*

Valley Visitor Center. Learn how Yosemite Valley's geology, vegetation, and human inhabitants at this visitor center. Don't leave without watching *Spirit of Yosemite*, a 23-minute introductory film that runs every half hour in the theater behind the visitor center. Strangely, the film shows no animals other than one deer. ⊠ *Yosemite Village* ☎ *209/372–0299* ⊗ *Late May–early Sept., daily 9–7:30; early Sept.–late May, daily 9–5.*

EXPLORING

HISTORIC SITES

Ahwahneechee Village. This solemn smattering of structures, accessed by a short loop trail behind the Yosemite Valley Visitor Center, is a look at what Native American life might have been like in the 1870s. One interpretive sign points out that the Miwok people referred to the 19th-century newcomers as "Yohemite" or "Yohometuk," which have been translated as meaning "some of them are killers." ⊠ *Northside Dr., Yosemite Village* ☞ *Free* ⊗ *Daily sunrise–sunset.*

Pioneer Yosemite History Center. Some of Yosemite's first structures—those not occupied by Native Americans, that is—were relocated here in the 1950s and 1960s. You can spend a pleasurable and informative half-hour walking about them and reading the signs, perhaps springing for a self-guided-tour pamphlet (50¢) to further enhance the history lesson. Weekends and some weekdays in summer, costumed docents conduct free blacksmithing and "wet-plate" photography demonstrations, and for a small fee you can take a stagecoach ride. ⊠ *Rte. 41, Wawona* ☎ *209/375–9531, 209/379–2646* ☞ *Free* ⊗ *Building interiors are open mid-June–Labor Day, Wed. 2–5, Thurs.–Sun. 10–1 and 2–5.*

20

SCENIC STOPS

★ **El Capitan.** Rising 3,593 feet—more than 350 stories—above the valley, El Capitan is the largest exposed-granite monolith in the world. Since 1958, people have been climbing its entire face, including the famous "nose." You can spot adventurers with your binoculars by scanning the smooth and nearly vertical cliff for specks of color. ⊠ *Off Northside Dr., about 4 miles west of the Valley Visitor Center.*

Fodor's Choice **Glacier Point.** If you lack the time, desire, or stamina to hike more than ★ 3,200 feet up to Glacier Point from the Yosemite Valley floor, you can drive here—or take a bus from the valley—for a bird's-eye view. You are likely to encounter a lot of day-trippers on the short, paved trail

Yosemite's Valley Floor

KEY

- ☖ Ranger Station
- ▲ Campground
- ⊼ Picnic Area
- ⊩ Restaurant
- ⌂ Lodge
- ☖ Trailhead
- ⚋ Restrooms
- ⁂ Scenic Viewpoint
- Walking/Hiking Trails
- Muir Trail
- Bicycle Path
- Valley Floor

Half Dome
8,836 ft.

Liberty Cap

Mist Trail

Nevada Fall

Emerald Pools

Vernal Fall

Footbridge

John Muir Trail

Clark Point

Mist Trail

Panorama Cliff

Sierra Point

Illilouette Gorge

Grizzly Peak

John Muir Trail

Mirror Lake

Washington Column

Road open only to bicycles and Shuttlebuses

bicycle path

Happy Isles Bridge

Upper Pines

Clarks Bridge

North Pines

Nature Center at Happy Isles

Royal Arch Cascade

Royal Arches

Lower Pines

CURRY VILLAGE

Road open only to bicycles and Shuttlebuses

Glacier Point
7,214 ft.

Panorama Trail

Curry Village Store

bicycle path

The Ahwahnee Hotel

Staircase Falls

Glacier Point Road

1/2 mi

Village Store

Auto Repair

Le Conte Memorial Lodge

Four Mile Trail

Pohono Trail

1/2 km

Medical Clinic

P.O.

Road open only to bicycles and Shuttlebuses

Moran Point

0

0

YOSEMITE VILLAGE

Yosemite Museum

Ahwahnechee Village

Ansel Adams Gallery

Valley Visitor Center

Chapel

Union Point

Sentinel Rock

Lower Yosemite Fall

bicycle path

Merced River

Yosemite Lodge

Four Mile Trail

Sentinel Fall

"This is us taking a break before conquering the top of Lembert Dome, while enjoying the beautiful view over Yosemite's high country." —photo by Rebalyn, Fodors.com member

that leads from the parking lot to the main overlook. Take a moment to veer off a few yards to the Geology Hut, which succinctly explains and illustrates how the valley looked like 10 million, 3 million, and 20,000 years ago. ⊠ *Glacier Point Rd., 16 miles northeast of Rte. 41* ☎ *209/372–1240.*

★ **Half Dome.** Visitors' eyes are continually drawn to this remarkable granite formation that tops out at more than 4,700 feet above the valley floor. Despite its name, the dome is actually about three-quarters intact. You can hike to the top of Half Dome on an 8.5-mile (one-way) trail whose last 400 feet must be ascended while holding onto a steel cable. For the past few years wilderness permits have been required (and checked on the trail). Back down in the valley, see Half Dome reflected in the Merced River by heading to Sentinel Bridge just before sundown. The brilliant orange light on Half Dome is a stunning sight.

Hetch Hetchy Reservoir. When Congress approved the O'Shaughnessy Dam in 1913, pragmatism triumphed over aestheticism. Some 2.4 million residents of the San Francisco Bay Area continue to get their water from this 117-billion-gallon reservoir, and spirited efforts are being made to restore the Hetch Hetchy Valley to its former, pristine glory. Eight miles long, the reservoir is Yosemite's largest body of water, and one that can be seen up close from several trails. ⊠ *Hetch Hetchy Rd., about 15 miles north of the Big Oak Flat entrance station.*

★ **Mariposa Grove of Big Trees.** Of Yosemite's three sequoia groves—the others being Merced and Tuolumne, both near Crane Flat well to the north—Mariposa is by far the largest and easiest to walk around.

GOOD READS

■ *The Photographer's Guide to Yosemite*, by Michael Frye, is an insider's guide to the park, with maps for shutterbugs looking to capture perfect images.

■ John Muir penned his observations of the park he long advocated for in *The Yosemite*.

■ *Yosemite and the High Sierra*, edited by Andrea G. Stillman and John Szarkowski, features beautiful reproductions of landmark photographs by Ansel Adams,

accompanied by excerpts from the photographer's journals written when Adams traveled in Yosemite National Park in the early 20th century.

■ An insightful collection of essays accompanies the museum-quality artworks in *Yosemite: Art of an American Icon*, by Amy Scott.

■ Perfect for beginning wildlife watchers, *Sierra Nevada Wildflowers*, by Karen Wiese, identifies more than 230 kinds of flora growing in the Sierra Nevada region.

Grizzly Giant, whose base measures 96 feet around, has been estimated to be one of the largest in the world. Perhaps more astoundingly, it's about 2,700 years old. On up the hill, you'll find many more sequoias, a small museum, and fewer people. Summer weekends are especially crowded here. Consider taking the free shuttle from Wawona. ⊠ *Rte. 41, 2 miles north of the South Entrance station.*

★ **Tuolumne Meadows.** The largest subalpine meadow in the Sierra (at 8,600 feet) is a popular way station for backpack trips along the Pacific Crest and John Muir trails. The setting is not as dramatic as Yosemite Valley, 56 miles away, but the almost perfectly flat basin, about 2½ miles long, is intriguing, and in July it's resplendent with wildflowers. The most popular day hike is up Lembert Dome, atop which you'll have breathtaking views of the basin below. Keep in mind that Tioga Road rarely opens before June and usually closes by mid-October. ⊠ *Tioga Rd. (Rte. 120), about 8 miles west of the Tioga Pass entrance station.*

WATERFALLS

Yosemite's waterfalls are at their most spectacular in May and June. When the snow starts to melt (usually peaking in May), streaming snowmelt spills down to meet the Merced River. By summer's end, some falls, including the mighty Yosemite Falls, trickle or dry up. Their flow increases in late fall, and in winter they may be hung dramatically with ice. Even in drier months, the waterfalls can be breathtaking. If you choose to hike any of the trails to or up the falls, be sure to wear shoes with no-slip soles; the rocks can be extremely slick. Stay on trails at all times.

■TIP→ Visit the park during a full moon and you can stroll without a flashlight and still make out the ribbons of falling water, as well as silhouettes of the giant granite monoliths.

Bridalveil Fall. This 620-foot waterfall is often diverted dozens of feet one way or the other by the breeze. It is the first marvelous site in Yosemite

Valley you will see if you enter via Route 41. ⊠ *Yosemite Valley, access from parking area off Wawona Rd.*

Nevada Fall. Climb Mist Trail from Happy Isles for an up-close view of this 594-foot cascading beauty. If you don't want to hike (the trail's final approach is quite taxing), you can see it—albeit distantly—from Glacier Point. Stay safely on the trail, as three people died in 2011 when they climbed over the railing and onto the slippery rocks. ⊠ *Yosemite Valley, access via Mist Trail from Nature Center at Happy Isles.*

Ribbon Fall. At 1,612 feet, this is the highest single fall in North America. It's also the first waterfall to dry up in summer; the rainwater and melted snow that create the slender fall evaporate quickly at this height. Look just west of El Capitan for the best view of the fall from the base of Bridalveil Fall. ⊠ *Yosemite Valley, west of El Capitan Meadow.*

Vernal Fall. Fern-covered black rocks frame this 317-foot fall, and rainbows play in the spray at its base. You can get a distance view from Glacier Point, or hike to see it close up. You'll get wet, but the view is worth it. ⊠ *Yosemite Valley, access via Mist Trail from Nature Center at Happy Isles.*

Fodor's Choice ★   **Yosemite Falls.** Actually three falls, they together constitute the highest waterfall in North America and the fifth-highest in the world. The water from the top descends a total of 2,425 feet, and when the falls run hard, you can hear them thunder across the valley. If they dry up—that sometimes happens in late summer—the valley seems naked without the wavering tower of spray. ∎TIP➔ If you hike the mile-long loop trail (partially paved) to the base of the Lower Falls in May, prepare to get wet. You can get a view of the falls from the lawn of Yosemite Chapel, off Southside Drive. ⊠ *Yosemite Valley, access from Yosemite Lodge or trail parking area.*

EDUCATIONAL OFFERINGS

CLASSES AND SEMINARS

Art Classes. Professional artists conduct workshops in watercolor, etching, drawing, and other mediums. Bring your own materials or purchase the basics at the Art Activity Center, next to the Village Store. Children under 13 must be accompanied by an adult. ⊠ *Art Activity Center, Yosemite Village* ☎ *209/372–1442* ⊕ *www.yosemitepark.com* 🖼 *Free* ⊙ *Early Apr.–early Oct., Mon.–Sat., 10 am–2 pm.*

Yosemite Outdoor Adventures. Naturalists, scientists, and park rangers lead multi-hour to multiday educational outings on topics from woodpeckers to fire management to pastel painting. Most sessions take place spring through fall, but a few focus on winter phenomena. ⊠ *Various locations* ☎ *209/379–2321* ⊕ *www.yosemite.org* 🖼 *$82–$465.*

RANGER PROGRAMS

Junior Ranger Program. Children ages 3 to 13 can participate in the informal, self-guided Little Cub and Junior Ranger programs. A park activity handbook ($4) is available at the Valley Visitor Center or the Nature Center at Happy Isles. Once kids complete the book, rangers present them with a certificate and a badge. ⊠ *Valley Visitor Center or the Nature Center at Happy Isles* ☎ *209/372–0299.*

Ranger-Led Programs. Rangers lead entertaining walks and give informative talks several times a day from spring to fall. The schedule is more limited in winter, but most days you can find a program somewhere in the park. In the evenings at Yosemite Lodge and Curry Village, lectures, slide shows, and documentary films present unique perspectives on Yosemite. On summer weekends, Camp Curry and Tuolumne Meadows Campground host sing-along campfire programs. Schedules and locations are posted on bulletin boards throughout the park.

SPORTS AND THE OUTDOORS

BICYCLING

One enjoyable way to see Yosemite Valley is to ride a bike beneath its lofty granite monoliths. The eastern valley has 12 miles of paved, flat bicycle paths across meadows and through woods, with bike racks at convenient stopping points. For a greater challenge but at no small risk, you can ride on 196 miles of paved park roads—but bicycles are not allowed on hiking trails or in the backcountry. Kids under 18 must wear a helmet.

TOURS AND OUTFITTERS

Yosemite bike rentals. You can arrange for rentals from Yosemite Lodge and Curry Village bike stands. Bikes with child trailers, baby-jogger strollers, and wheelchairs are also available. The cost is about $10 per hour. ⊠ *Yosemite Lodge or Curry Village* ☎ *209/372–1208* ⊕ *www.yosemitepark.com* ⊘ *Apr.–Oct.*

BIRD-WATCHING

Nearly 250 bird species have been spotted in the park, including the sage sparrow, pygmy owl, blue grouse, and mountain bluebird. Park rangers lead free bird-watching walks in Yosemite Valley one day each week in summer; check at a visitor center or information station for times and locations. Binoculars sometimes are available for loan.

20

HIKING

TOURS AND OUTFITTERS

Wilderness Center. This facility provides free wilderness permits, which are required for overnight camping (advance reservations are available for $5 and are highly recommended for popular trailheads in summer and on weekends). The staff here also provides maps and advice to hikers heading into the backcountry. ☎ *209/372–0308.*

Yosemite Mountaineering School and Guide Service. From April to November, Yosemite Mountaineering School and Guide Service leads two-hour to full-day treks, as well as backpacking and overnight excursions. Reservations are recommended. ⊠ *Yosemite Mountain Shop, Curry*

Village ☎ *209/372–8344* ⊕ *www.yosemitepark.com/Activities_Rock-Climbing.aspx.*

EASY

★ **Yosemite Falls Trail.** This is the highest waterfall in North America. The upper fall (1,430 feet), the middle cascades (675 feet), and the lower fall (320 feet) combine for a total of 2,425 feet and, when viewed from the valley, appear as a single waterfall. The ¼-mile trail leads from the parking lot to the base of the falls. Upper Yosemite Fall Trail, a strenuous 3½-mile climb rising 2,700 feet, takes you above the top of the falls. *Easy.* ⊠ *Trailhead off Camp 4, north of Northside Dr.*

MODERATE

★ **Mist Trail.** Except for Lower Yosemite Falls, more visitors take this trail (or portions of it) than any other in the park. The trek up to and back from Vernal Fall is 3 miles. Add another 4 miles total by continuing up to 594-foot Nevada Fall; the trail becomes quite steep and slippery in its final stages. The elevation gain to Vernal Fall is 1,000 feet, and to Nevada Fall an additional 1,000 feet. Merced River tumbles down both falls on its way to a tranquil flow through the valley. *Moderate.* ⊠ *Trailhead at Happy Isles.*

★ **Panorama Trail.** Few hikes come with the visual punch that this 8½-mile trail provides. The star attraction is Half Dome, visible from many intriguing angles, but you also see three waterfalls up close and walk through a manzanita grove. Before you begin, look down on Yosemite Valley from Glacier Point, a special experience in itself. *Moderate.* ⊠ *Trailhead at Glacier Point.*

DIFFICULT

Fodor's Choice
★ **John Muir Trail to Half Dome.** Ardent and courageous trekkers continue on from Nevada Fall to the top of Half Dome. Some hikers attempt this entire 10- to 12-hour, 16¾-mile round-trip trek in one day; if you're planning to do this, remember that the 4,800-foot elevation gain and the 8,842-foot altitude will cause shortness of breath. Another option is to hike to a campground in Little Yosemite Valley near the top of Nevada Fall the first day, then climb to the top of Half Dome and hike out the next day. Get your wilderness permit (required for a one-day hike to Half Dome, too) at least a month in advance. Be sure to wear hiking boots and bring gloves. The last pitch up the back of Half Dome is very steep—the only way to climb this sheer rock face is to pull yourself up using the steel cable handrails, which are in place only from late spring to early fall. Those who brave the ascent will be rewarded with an unbeatable view of Yosemite Valley below and the high country beyond. *Difficult.* ⊠ *Trailhead at Happy Isles.*

HORSEBACK RIDING

Reservations for guided trail rides must be made in advance at the hotel tour desks or by phone. For overnight saddle trips, which use mules, call ☎ 559/253–5673 on or after September 15 to request a lottery application for the following year. Scenic trail rides range from two hours to a full day; six-day High Sierra saddle trips are also available.

TOURS AND OUTFITTERS
Tuolumne Meadows Stables. Tuolumne Meadows Stables runs two-, four-, and eight-hour trips that start at $64, as well as four- to six-day camping treks on mules that begin at $625. Reservations are essential. ⊠ *Off Tioga Rd., 2 miles east of Tuolumne Meadows Visitor Center* ☎ *209/372–8427* ⊕ *www.yosemitepark.com.*

Wawona Stables. Wawona Stables has two- and five-hour rides starting at $64. Reservations are recommended. ⊠ *Rte. 41, Wawona* ☎ *209/375–6502.*

Yosemite Valley Stables. You can tour the valley and the start of the high country on two-hour, four-hour, and daylong rides at Yosemite Valley Stables. Reservations are strongly recommended for the trips, which start at $64. ⊠ *At entrance to North Pines Campground, 100 yards northeast of Curry Village* ☎ *209/372–8348* ⊕ *www.yosemitepark.com.*

RAFTING

Rafting is permitted only on designated areas of the Middle and South forks of the Merced River. Check with the Valley Visitor Center for closures and other restrictions.

OUTFITTERS
Curry Village raft stand. The per-person rental fee at Curry Village raft stand covers the four- to six-person raft, two paddles, and life jackets, plus a shuttle to the launch point on Sentinel Beach. ⊠ *South side of Southside Dr., Curry Village* ☎ *209/372–8319* ⊕ *www.yosemitepark. com* 🎫 *$20.50* ☉ *Late May–July.*

ROCK CLIMBING

Fodor's Choice ★ The granite canyon walls of Yosemite Valley are world renowned for rock climbing. El Capitan, with its 3,593-foot vertical face, is the most famous, but there are many other options here for all skill levels.

TOURS AND OUTFITTERS
Yosemite Mountaineering School and Guide Service. The one-day basic lesson at Yosemite Mountaineering School and Guide Service includes some bouldering and rappelling, and three or four 60-foot climbs. Climbers must be at least 10 and in reasonably good physical condition. Intermediate and advanced classes include instruction in first aid, anchor building, multi-pitch climbing, summer snow climbing, and big-wall climbing. There's a nordic program in the winter. ⊠ *Yosemite Mountain Shop, Curry Village* ☎ *209/372–8344* ⊕ *www.yosemitepark. com* 🎫 *$80–$190* ☉ *Apr.–Nov.*

20

WINTER SPORTS

ICE-SKATING
Curry Village Ice Rink. Winter visitors have skated at this outdoor rink for decades, and there's no mystery why: it's a kick to glide across the ice while soaking up views of Half Dome and Glacier Point. ⊠ *South*

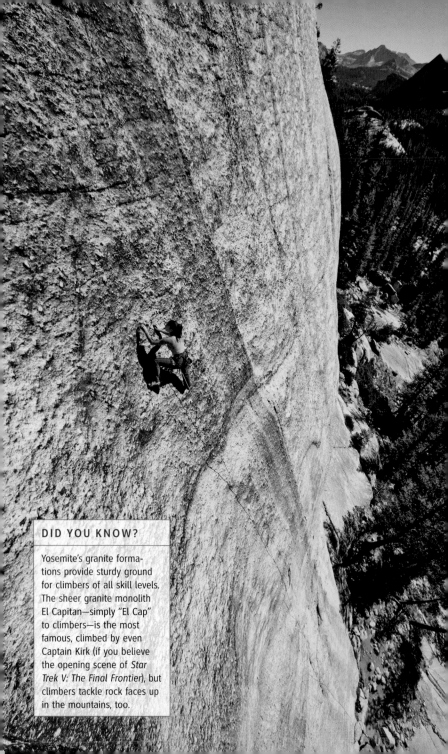

side of Southside Dr., Curry Village ☎ *209/372–8319* ☎ *$9 per session, $3 skate rental* ☺ *Mid-Nov.–mid-Mar. afternoons and evenings daily, morning sessions weekends (hrs vary).*

SKIING AND SNOWSHOEING

Badger Pass Ski Area. California's first ski resort has five lifts and 10 downhill runs, as well as 90 miles of groomed cross-country trails. Free shuttle buses from Yosemite Valley operate between December and early April, weather permitting. Lift tickets are $42, downhill equipment rents for $31, and snowboard rental with boots is $35. ⊠ *Badger Pass Rd., off Glacier Point Rd., 18 miles from Yosemite Valley* ☎ *209/372–8430.*

Yosemite Ski School. The gentle slopes of Badger Pass make Yosemite Ski School an ideal spot for children and beginners to learn downhill skiing or snowboarding for as little as $28 for a group lesson. ☎ *209/372–8430* ⊕ *www.yosemitepark.com*

Yosemite Mountaineering School. Yosemite Mountaineering School conducts snowshoeing, cross-country skiing, telemarking, and skate-skiing classes starting at $35. ⊠ *Badger Pass Ski Area* ☎ *209/372–8344* ⊕ *www.yosemitepark.com*

Yosemite Cross-Country Ski School. The highlight of Yosemite's cross-country skiing center is a 21-mile loop from Badger Pass to Glacier Point. You can rent cross-country skis for $23 per day at the Cross-Country Ski School, which also rents snowshoes ($22.50 per day), telemarking equipment ($29.50), and skate-skis ($27). ☎ *209/372–8444* ⊕ *www.yosemitepark.com*

WHERE TO EAT

In addition to the dining options listed here, you'll find fast-food grills and cafeterias, plus temporary snack bars, hamburger stands, and pizza joints lining park roads in summer. Many dining facilities in the park are open summer only. *Prices in the reviews are the average cost of a main course at dinner or, if dinner is not served, at lunch.*

20

$$$$ ✕**Ahwahnee Hotel Dining Room.** Rave reviews about the dining room's
EUROPEAN appearance are fully justified—it features towering windows, a 34-foot-
Fodor's Choice high ceiling with interlaced sugar-pine beams, and massive chandeliers.
★ Although many continue to applaud the food, others have reported that they sense a dip in the quality both in the service and in what is being served. Diners must spend a lot of money here, so perhaps that inflates the expectations and amplifies the disappointments. In any event, the $40 Sunday brunch is consistently praised. Reservations are always advised, and the attire is "resort casual." ⑤ *Average main: $38* ⊠ *Ahwahnee Hotel, Ahwahnee Rd., about ¾ mile east of Yosemite Valley Visitor Center, Yosemite Village* ☎ *209/372–1489* ⚑ *Reservations essential.*

$$$ ✕**Mountain Room.** Though good, the food becomes secondary when
AMERICAN you see Yosemite Falls through this dining room's wall of windows—
★ almost every table has a view. The chef makes a point of using locally

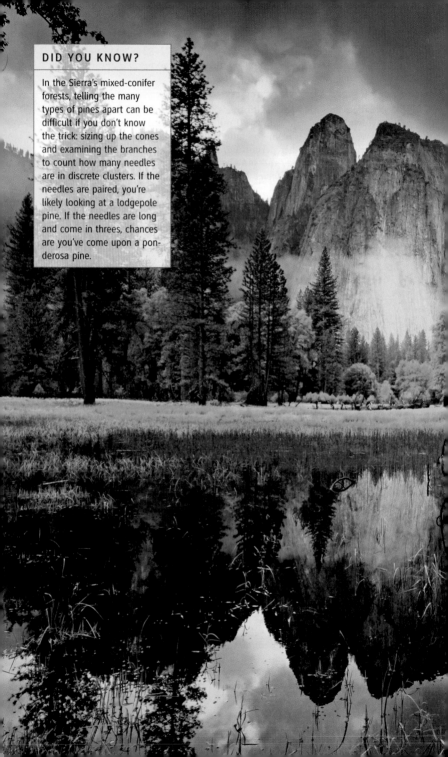

DID YOU KNOW?

In the Sierra's mixed-conifer forests, telling the many types of pines apart can be difficult if you don't know the trick: sizing up the cones and examining the branches to count how many needles are in discrete clusters. If the needles are paired, you're likely looking at a lodgepole pine. If the needles are long and come in threes, chances are you've come upon a ponderosa pine.

sourced, organic ingredients, so you can be assured of fresh vegetables. The Mountain Room Lounge, a few steps away in the Yosemite Lodge complex, has a broad bar with about 10 beers on tap. ⑤ *Average main: $23* ✉ *Yosemite Lodge, Northside Dr. about ¾ mile west of the visitor center, Yosemite Village* ☎ *209/372–1281* ⊙ *No lunch.*

$ ✕ **Tuolumne Meadows Grill.** Serving continuously throughout the day until
FAST FOOD   5 or 6 pm, this fast-food eatery cooks up breakfast, lunch, and snacks. Stop in for a quick meal before exploring the Meadows. ⑤ *Average main: $8* ✉ *Tioga Rd. (Rte. 120), 1½ miles east of Tuolumne Meadows Visitor Center* ☎ *209/372–8426* ⊙ *Closed Oct.–Memorial Day.*

$$ ✕ **Tuolumne Meadows Lodge.** At the back of a small building that contains
AMERICAN   the lodge's front desk and small gift shop, this restaurant serves hearty American fare at breakfast and dinner. The decor is ultra-woodsy, with dark-wood walls and red-and-white-checkered tablecloths. Meals are mostly of the meat-and-potato variety, but vegetarians' requests are honored. If you have any dietary restrictions, let the front desk know in advance and the cooks will not let you down. ⑤ *Average main: $18* ✉ *Tioga Rd. (Rte. 120)* ☎ *209/372–8413* ⚭ *Reservations essential* ⊙ *Closed late Sept.–Memorial Day. No lunch.*

$$$ ✕ **Wawona Hotel Dining Room.** Watch deer graze on the meadow while
AMERICAN   you dine in the romantic, candlelit dining room of the whitewashed
★   Wawona Hotel, which dates from the late 1800s. The American-style cuisine favors fresh ingredients and flavors; trout is a menu staple. There's also a Sunday brunch Easter through Thanksgiving, and a barbecue on the lawn Saturday evenings in summer. A jacket is required at dinner. ⑤ *Average main: $25* ✉ *Wawona Hotel, Rte. 41, Wawona* ☎ *209/375–1425* ⚭ *Reservations essential* ⊙ *Closed Jan. and Feb.*

PICNIC AREAS

Considering how large the park is and how many visitors come here— some 4 million people every year, most of them just for the day—it is somewhat surprising that Yosemite has so few formal picnic areas, though in many places you can find a smooth rock to sit on and enjoy breathtaking views along with your lunch. The convenience stores all sell picnic supplies, and prepackaged sandwiches and salads are widely available. Those options can come in especially handy during the middle of the day, when you might not want to spend precious daylight hours in such a spectacular setting sitting in a restaurant for a formal meal.

WHERE TO STAY

Prices in the reviews are the lowest cost of a standard double room in high season. For expanded hotel reviews, visit Fodors.com.

$$$$ ⌂ **Ahwahnee Hotel.** A National Historic Landmark, the hotel is con-
HOTEL   structed of sugar-pine logs and features Native American design motifs.
Fodor'sChoice   **Pros:** best lodge in Yosemite; helpful concierge. **Cons:** expensive rates;
★   some reports that service has slipped in recent years. **TripAdvisor:**

"splendid views," "rustic luxury in an incomparable location," "bucket list contender."⑤ *Rooms from: $485 ⊠ Ahwahnee Rd., about ¾ mile east of Yosemite Valley Visitor Center, Yosemite Village* ☎ *559/252–4848* ⊕ *www.yosemitepark.com* ↩ *99 lodge rooms, 4 suites, 24 cottage rooms.*

$ **Curry Village.** Opened in 1899 as
HOTEL a place for budget-conscious travelers, Curry Village has plain accommodations: standard motel rooms, simple cabins, and tent cabins with rough wood frames and canvas

walls. **Pros:** comparatively economical; family-friendly atmosphere. **Cons:** can be crowded; sometimes a bit noisy. **TripAdvisor:** "very comfortable," "amazing experience," "absolutely stunning."⑤ *Rooms from: $91 ⊠ South side of Southside Dr.* ☎ *559/252–4848* ⊕ *www.yosemitepark.com* ↩ *18 rooms, 390 cabins* ⊙ *No meals.*

$$ **Wawona Hotel.** This 1879 National Historic Landmark sits at Yosem-
HOTEL ite's southern end, a 15-minute drive from the Mariposa Grove of Big Trees. **Pros:** lovely building; peaceful atmosphere. **Cons:** few modern amenities; an hour's drive from Yosemite Valley. **TripAdvisor:** "old-world charm," "a can't miss experience," "beautiful."⑤ *Rooms from: $135 ⊠ Hwy. 41, Wawona* ☎ *559/252–4848* ⊕ *www.yosemitepark.com* ↩ *104 rooms, 50 with bath* ⊙ *Closed Jan. and Feb.*

$ **White Wolf Lodge.** Set in a subalpine meadow, the rustic accommoda-
HOTEL tions at White Wolf Lodge make it an excellent base camp for hiking the backcountry. **Pros:** quiet location; convenient for hikers; good restaurant. **Cons:** far from the valley; not much to do here. **TripAdvisor:** "rustic charm," "great high country lodging," "absolute heaven."⑤ *Rooms from: $100 ⊠ Off Tioga Rd. (Rte. 120), 25 miles west of Tuolumne Meadows and 15 miles east of Crane Flat* ☎ *559/252–4848* ↩ *24 tent cabins, 4 cabins* ⊙ *Closed mid-Sept.–early June.*

$$ **Yosemite Lodge at the Falls.** This 1915 lodge near Yosemite Falls more
HOTEL closely resembles a 1960s resort with its numerous two-story structures tucked beneath the trees. **Pros:** centrally located; dependably clean rooms; lots of tours leave from out front. **Cons:** can feel impersonal; appearance is little dated. **TripAdvisor:** "love the renovated rooms," "best location in the park," "old school Yosemite."⑤ *Rooms from: $124 ⊠ Northside Dr. about ¾ mile west of the visitor center, Yosemite Village* ☎ *559/252–4848* ⊕ *www.yosemitepark.com* ↩ *245 rooms.*

20

CLOSE UP

Best Campgrounds in Yosemite

If you are going to concentrate solely on valley sites and activities, you should endeavor to stay in one of the "Pines" campgrounds, which are clustered near Curry Village and within an easy stroll from that busy complex's many facilities. For a more primitive and quiet experience, and to be near many backcountry hikes, try one of the Tioga Road campgrounds.

National Park Service Reservations Office. Reservations are required at most of Yosemite's campgrounds, especially in summer. ☎ *800/ 436–7275* ⊕ *www.recreation.gov* ☉ *Daily 7–7.*

Bridalveil Creek. This campground sits among lodgepole pines at 7,200 feet, above the valley on Glacier Point Road. From here, you can easily drive to Glacier Point's magnificent valley views. ⊠ *From Hwy. 41 in Wawona, go north to Glacier Point Rd. and turn right; entrance to campground is 25 miles ahead on right side.*

Camp 4. Formerly known as Sunnyside Walk-In, this is the only valley campground available on a first-come, first-served basis. ⊠ *Base of Yosemite Falls Trail, just west of Yosemite Lodge on Northside Dr., Yosemite Village.*

Crane Flat. This camp on Yosemite's western boundary, south of Hodgdon Meadow, is just 17 miles from the valley but far from its bustle. ⊠ *From Big Oak Flat entrance on Hwy. 120, drive 10 miles east to campground entrance on right.*

Housekeeping Camp. Composed of three walls (usually concrete) and covered with two layers of canvas, each unit has an open-ended fourth side that can be closed off with a heavy white canvas curtain. You rent

"bedpacks," consisting of blankets, sheets, and other comforts. ⊠ *Southside Dr., ½ mile west of Curry Village.*

Lower Pines. This moderate-size campground sits directly along the Merced River; it's a short walk to the trailheads for the Mirror Lake and Mist trails. ⊠ *At east end of valley.*

Porcupine Flat. Sixteen miles west of Tuolumne Meadows, this campground sits at 8,100 feet. If you want to be in the high country, this is a good bet. ⊠ *16 miles west of Tuolumne Meadows on Hwy. 120.*

Tuolumne Meadow. In a wooded area at 8,600 feet, just south of its namesake meadow, this is one of the most spectacular and sought-after campgrounds in Yosemite. ⊠ *Hwy. 120, 46 miles east of Big Oak Flat entrance station.*

Upper Pines. This is the valley's largest campground and the closest one to the trailheads. Expect large crowds in the summer—and little privacy. ⊠ *At east end of valley, near Curry Village.*

Wawona. Near the Mariposa Grove, just downstream from a popular fishing spot, this year-round campground has larger, less densely packed sites than campgrounds in the valley. ⊠ *Hwy. 41, 1 mile north of Wawona.*

White Wolf. Set in the beautiful high country at 8,000 feet, this is a prime spot for hikers. ⊠ *From Big Oak Flat entrance, go 15 miles east on Tioga Rd.*

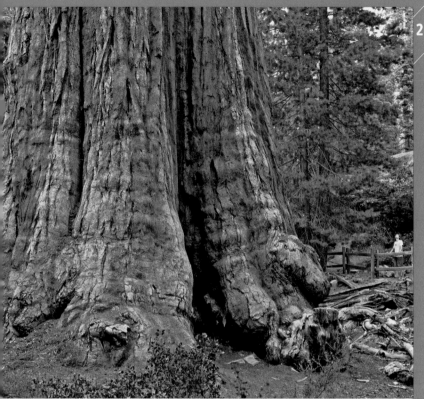

Sequoia and Kings Canyon National Parks

WORD OF MOUTH

"On arrival, I oriented myself at the Visitor's Center in Grant Grove Village, and then took a short hike in Grant's Grove, taking in the General Grant tree, among the other giant sequoias. Their size is mind boggling. . . . Next up was a drive along the Kings Canyon Scenic Byway. I highly recommend this beautiful drive."

—Iregeo

WELCOME TO SEQUOIA AND KINGS CANYON NATIONAL PARKS

TOP REASONS TO GO

★ **Gentle giants:** You'll feel small—in a good way—walking among some of the world's largest living things in Sequoia's Giant Forest and Kings Canyon's Grant Grove.

★ **Because it's there:** You can't even glimpse it from the main part of Sequoia, but the sight of majestic Mt. Whitney is worth the trek to the eastern face of the High Sierra.

★ **Underground explora-tion:** Far older even than the giant sequoias, the gleaming limestone for-mations in Crystal Cave will draw you along dark, marble passages.

★ **A grander-than-Grand Canyon:** Drive the twist-ing Kings Canyon Scenic Byway down into the jag-ged, granite Kings River Canyon, deeper in parts than the Grand Canyon.

★ **Regal solitude:** To spend a day or two hiking in a subalpine world of your own, pick one of the 11 trailheads at Mineral King.

1 **Giant Forest–Lodge-pole Village.** The most heavily visited area of Sequoia lies at the base of the "thumb" portion of Kings Canyon National Park and contains major sights such as Giant Forest, Gen-eral Sherman Tree, Crystal Cave, and Moro Rock.

2 **Grant Grove Village–Redwood Canyon.** The "thumb" of Kings Canyon National Park is its busiest section, where Grant Grove, General Grant Tree, Pan-oramic Point, and Big Stump are the main attractions.

3 **Cedar Grove.** Most visitors to the huge, high-country portion of Kings Canyon National Park don't go farther than Roads End, a few miles east of Cedar Grove on the canyon floor. Here, the river runs through Zumwalt Meadow, surrounded by magnificent granite formations.

4 **Mineral King.** In the southeast section of Sequoia, the highest road-accessible part of the park is a good place to hike, camp, and soak up the unspoiled grandeur of the Sierra Nevada.

5 **Mount Whitney.** The highest peak in the Lower 48 stands on the eastern edge of Sequoia; to get there from Giant Forest you must either backpack eight days through the mountains or drive nearly 400 miles around the park to its other side.

CALIFORNIA

GETTING ORIENTED

The two parks comprise 865,952 acres, mostly on the western flank of the Sierra. A map of the adjacent parks looks vaguely like a mitten, with the palm of Sequoia National Park south of the north-pointing, skinny thumb and long fingers of Kings Canyon National Park. Between the western thumb and eastern fingers, north of Sequoia, lies part of Sequoia National Forest, which includes Giant Sequoia National Monument.

McClure Meadow

Le Conte Divide

Le Conte Canyon

John Muir Trail

Bench Lake

MONARCH DIVIDE

Woods Creek Trail

Kings Canyon Scenic Byway

3 KINGS CANYON

Rae Lakes

Roads End Permit Station

Charlotte Lake

Visitor Center

Roaring River

KINGS-KERN DIVIDE

Table Mountain 13,630 ft.

Tyndall Creek

Whitney Portal

Stony Creek Village

Wuksachi Village

Visitor Center

5

Mount Whitney 14,491 ft.

Crystal Cave

1

Giant Forest Museum

General Sherman Tree

Bearpaw Meadow

John Muir Trail

Crabtree

Moro Rock

Buckeye Flat

Potwisha

Mount Kaweah 13,802 ft.

Mount Guyot 12,300 ft.

Rock Creek

Visitor Center

Little Five Lakes

Ash Mountain Entrance

KERN CANYON

Mineral King

4

Lookout Point Entrance

Cold Springs

Hockett Meadows

South Fork

Sheep Mountain 10,050 ft.

Kern Canyon

Updated by
Reed Parsell

Although *Sequoiadendron giganteum* is the formal name for the redwoods that grow here, everyone outside the classroom calls them sequoias, big trees, or Sierra redwoods. Their monstrously thick trunks and branches, remarkably shallow root systems, and neck-craning heights are almost impossible to believe, as is the fact they can live for more than 2,500 years. Many of these towering marvels are in the Giant Forest stretch of Generals Highway, which connects Sequoia and Kings Canyon national parks.

Next to or a few miles off the 43-mile road Generals Highway are most of Sequoia National Park's main attractions and Grant Grove Village, the orientation hub for Kings Canyon National Park. The two parks share a boundary that runs west–east, from the foothills of the Central Valley to the Sierra Nevada's dramatic eastern ridges. Kings Canyon has two portions: the smaller is shaped like a bent finger and encompasses Grant Grove Village and Redwood Mountain Grove (the two parks' largest concentration of sequoias), and the larger is home to stunning Kings River Canyon, whose vast, unspoiled peaks and valleys are a backpacker's dream. Sequoia is in one piece and includes Mt. Whitney, the highest point in the Lower 48 states (although it is impossible to see from the western part of the park and is a chore to ascend from either side).

SEQUOIA AND KINGS CANYON PLANNER

WHEN TO GO

The best times to visit are late spring and early fall, when temperatures are moderate and crowds thin. Summertime can draw hoards of tourists to see the giant sequoias, and the few, narrow roads mean congestion at peak holiday times. If you must visit in summer, go during the week. By contrast, in wintertime you may feel as though you have the parks all to yourself. But because of heavy snows, sections of the main park roads can be closed without warning, and low-hanging clouds can move in and obscure mountains and valleys for days. Check road and weather conditions before venturing out mid-November to late April.

GETTING HERE AND AROUND

CAR TRAVEL

Sequoia is 36 miles east of Visalia on Route 198; Kings Canyon is 53 miles east of Fresno on Route 180. There is no automobile entrance on the eastern side of the Sierra. Routes 180 and 198 are connected by Generals Highway, a paved two-lane road that sometimes sees delays at peak times due to ongoing improvements. The road is extremely narrow and steep from Route 198 to Giant Forest, so keep an eye on your engine temperature gauge, as the incline and congestion can cause vehicles to overheat; to avoid overheated brakes, use low gears on downgrades.

If you are traveling in an RV or with a trailer, study the restrictions on these vehicles. Do not travel beyond Potwisha Campground with an RV longer than 22 feet on Route 198; take straighter, easier Route 180 instead. Maximum vehicle length on Generals Highway is 40 feet, or 50 feet combined length for vehicles with trailers.

Generals Highway between Lodgepole and Grant Grove is sometimes closed by snow. The Mineral King Road from Route 198 into southern Sequoia National Park is closed 2 miles below Atwell Mill either on November 1 or after the first heavy snow. The Buckeye Flat–Middle Fork Trailhead Road is closed mid-October–mid-April when the Buckeye Flat Campground closes. The lower Crystal Cave Road is closed when the cave closes in November. Its upper 2 miles, as well as the Panoramic Point and Moro Rock–Crescent Meadow roads, are closed with the first heavy snow. Because of the danger of rockfall, the portion of Kings Canyon Scenic Byway east of Grant Grove closes in winter. For current conditions, call ☎ 559/565–3341 Ext. 4.

■ TIP➜ Snowstorms are common late October through April. Unless you have four-wheel drive with snow tires, you should carry chains and know how to apply them to the tires on the drive axle.

PARK ESSENTIALS

PARK FEES AND PERMITS

The admission fee is $20 per vehicle and $10 for those who enter by bus, on foot, bicycle, motorcycle, or horse; it is valid for seven days in both parks. U.S. residents over the age of 62 pay $10 for a lifetime pass, and permanently disabled U.S. residents are admitted free.

If you plan to camp in the backcountry, you need a permit, which costs $15 for hikers or $30 for stock users (e.g., horseback riders). One permit covers the group. Availability of permits depends upon trailhead quotas. Reservations are accepted by mail or fax for a $15 processing fee, beginning March 1, and must be made at least 14 days in advance (☎ 559/565–3766). Without a reservation, you may still get a permit on a first-come, first-served basis starting at 1 pm the day before you plan to hike. For more information on backcountry camping or travel with pack animals (horses, mules, burros, or llamas), contact the Wilderness Permit Office (☎ 530/565–3761).

PARK HOURS

The parks are open 24/7 year-round. They are in the Pacific time zone.

VISITOR INFORMATION

PARK CONTACT INFORMATION

Sequoia and Kings Canyon National Parks ⊠ 47050 Generals Hwy.(Rte. 198), Three Rivers ☎ 559/565–3341, 559/565–3134 ⊕ www.nps.gov/seki.

SEQUOIA VISITOR CENTERS

Foothills Visitor Center. Exhibits focusing on the foothills and resource issues facing the parks are on display here. You can also pick up books, maps, and a list of ranger-led walks, and get wilderness permits. ⊠ Generals Hwy. (Rte. 198), 1 mile north of the Ash Mountain entrance ☎ 559/565–3135 ☉ Oct.–mid-May, daily 8–4:30; mid-May–Sept., daily 8–5.

Lodgepole Visitor Center. Along with exhibits on the area's geologic history, wildlife, and longtime American Indian inhabitants, the center screens an outstanding 22-minute film about bears. You can also buy books and maps here. ⊠ Generals Hwy. (Rte. 198), 21 miles north of Ash Mountain entrance ☎ 559/565–4436 ☉ June–Oct., daily 7–6; Nov.–May, weekends 7–6.

KINGS CANYON VISITOR CENTERS

Cedar Grove Visitor Center. Off the main road and behind the Sentinel Campground, this small ranger station has books and maps, plus information about hikes and other things to do in the area. ⊠ Kings Canyon Scenic Byway, 30 miles east of park entrance ☎ 559/565–3793 ☉ Mid-May–late Sept., daily 9–5.

Grant Grove Visitor Center. Acquaint yourself with the varied charms of this two-section national park by watching a 15-minute film and perusing the center's exhibits on the canyon, sequoias, and human history. Books, maps, and free wilderness permits are available, as are updates on the parks' weather and air-quality conditions. ⊠ Generals Hwy. (Rte. 198), 3 miles northeast of Rte. 180, Big Stump entrance ☎ 559/565–4307 ☉ Summer, daily 8–6; mid-May–late Sept., daily 9–4:30; winter, daily 9:30–4:30.

SEQUOIA NATIONAL PARK

EXPLORING

SCENIC DRIVES

★ **Generals Highway.** One of the most scenic drives in a state replete with them is this 43-mile road, the main asphalt artery between Sequoia and Kings Canyon national parks. Named after the landmark Grant and Sherman trees that leave so many visitors awestruck, it runs from the Foothills Visitor Center north to Grant Grove Village. Along the way, it passes the turnoff to Crystal Cave, the Giant Forest Museum, Lodgepole Village, and Sequoia National Park's other most popular attractions.

Western Sequoia and Kings Canyon National Park

180 Kings Canyon Scenic Byway

South Fork Kings River

Lewis Creek Trail

Boyden Cave

Sheep Creek

Cedar Grove Visitor Center

Hume Lake

KINGS CANYON NATIONAL PARK

General Grant Tree

Crystal Springs

Sunset

Grant Grove Visitor Center

180

Big Stump Entrance

Redwood Mountain Overlook

Generals Highway

Stony Creek

SILLIMAN CREST

Eshom

Montecito Sequoia Lodge

REDWOOD CANYON

Stony Creek Village

Twin Lakes Trail

Dorst Creek

Wuksachi Village

Lodgepole Visitor Center and Village

Wolverton

Crystal Cave

General Sherman Tree

Kaweah River

Yucca Creek

Giant Forest Museum

Tharps Log

High Sierra Trail

CRESCENT MEADOW

Colony Mill Trail

Tunnel Log

Moro Rock

North Fork

ASH PEAKS

Potwisha

Buckeye Flat

Giant Forest Museum

SEQUOIA NATIONAL PARK

Foothills Visitor Center

Generals Highway

Ash Mountain Entrance

Atwell Mill

0   3 mi
0   3 km

198

River

○ **Three Rivers**

Kaweah River

Lookout Point Entrance

The lower portion, from Hospital Rock to the Giant Forest, is especially steep and windy. If your vehicle is 22 feet or longer, avoid that stretch by entering the parks via Route 180 (from Fresno) rather than Route 198 (from Visalia). And take your time on this road—there's a lot to see, and wildlife can scamper across at any time. △ Major roadwork will be ongoing for a few years between Foothills Visitor Center and Giant Forest Museum, which could delay your drive up to an hour each way.

SCENIC STOPS

Sequoia National Park is all about the trees, and to understand the scale of these giants you must walk among them. If you do nothing else, get out of the car for a short stroll through one of the groves. But there is much more to the park than the trees. Try to get up to one of the vista points that give you a panoramic view over the forested mountains. Whether you're driving south to north or north to south, Generals Highway (Route 198) will be your route to most of the park's sights. A few short spur roads lead off the highway to some sights, and Mineral King Road branches off Route 198 to enter the park at Lookout Point, winding east from there into the southernmost part of the park.

Crescent Meadow. John Muir called this the "gem of the Sierra." Walk around for an hour or two and you might decide that the Scotland-born naturalist was exaggerating a wee bit. Wildflowers bloom here throughout the summer. ⊠ *End of Moro Rock–Crescent Meadow Rd., 2.6 miles east off Generals Hwy.*

★ **Crystal Cave.** One of more than 200 caves in Sequoia and Kings Canyon national parks, Crystal Cave is unusual in that it's composed largely of marble, the result of limestone being hardened under heat and pressure. It contains several impressive formations that today are much easier to make out, thanks to an environmentally sensitive relighting project. Unfortunately, some of the cave's formations have been damaged or destroyed by early 20th-century dynamite blasting. The standard tour will give you 45 minutes inside the cave. ⊠ *Crystal Cave Rd., 6 miles west off Generals Hwy.* ☎ *559/565–3759* ⊕ *www.sequoiahistory.org* ☜ *$13* ⊙ *Mid-May–mid-Oct., daily 10–4.*

★ **General Sherman Tree.** Neither the world's tallest nor oldest sequoia, General Sherman is nevertheless tops in volume—and it is still putting on weight, adding the equivalent of a 60-foot-tall tree every year to its 2.7 million-pound mass. ⊠ *Generals Hwy. (Rte. 198), 2 miles south of Lodgepole Visitor Center.*

Mineral King. This subalpine valley sits at 7,800 feet at the end of a steep, winding road. The trip from the park's entrance can take up to two hours. This is the highest point to which you can drive in the park. ⊠ *End of Mineral King Rd., 25 miles east of Generals Hwy. (Rte. 198), east of Three Rivers.*

★ **Moro Rock.** Sequoia National Park's best non-tree attraction offers panoramic views to those fit and determined enough to mount its 350-ish steps. In a case where the journey rivals the destination, Moro's stone stairway is so impressive in its twisty inventiveness that it's on the National Register of Historic Places. The rock's 6,725-foot summit overlooks the Middle Fork Canyon, sculpted by the Kaweah River and approaching the depth of Arizona's Grand Canyon, although hazy air often compromises the view. ⊠ *Moro Rock–Crescent Meadow Rd., 2 miles east off Generals Hwy. (Rte. 198) to parking area.*

Tunnel Log. It's been almost 45 years since you could drive through a standing sequoia—and that was in Yosemite National Park's Mariposa Grove, not here. This 275-foot tree fell in 1937, and soon a 17-foot-wide, 8-foot-high hole was cut through it for vehicular passage that continues today. Large vehicles take the nearby bypass. ⊠ *Moro Rock–Crescent Meadow Rd., 2 miles east of Generals Hwy. (Rte. 198).*

EDUCATIONAL OFFERINGS

CLASSES AND SEMINARS

Evening Programs. In summer, the park shows documentary films and slide shows, and has evening lectures. Locations and times vary; pick up a schedule at any visitor center or check bulletin boards near ranger stations. ☎ *559/565–3341.*

★ **Seminars.** Expert naturalists lead seminars on a range of topics, including birds, wildflowers, geology, botany, photography, park history, backpacking, and pathfinding. Some courses offer transferable credits. Reserve in advance.

Sequoia Natural History Association. For information and prices, pick up a course catalogue at any visitor center or contact the Sequoia Natural History Association. ☎ *559/565–3759* ⊕ *www.sequoiahistory.org*

Sequoia Sightseeing Tours. The only licensed tour operator in either park offers daily interpretive sightseeing tours in a 10-passenger van with a friendly, knowledgeable guide. Reservations are essential. The company also offers private tours of Kings Canyon. ☎ *559/561–4489* ⊕ *www.sequoiatours.com* ✉ *$65 half-day tour, $88 full-day tour.*

RANGER PROGRAMS

Free Nature Programs. Almost any summer day, half-hour to 1½-hour ranger talks and walks explore subjects such as the life of the sequoia, the geology of the park, and the habits of bears. Giant Forest, Lodgepole Visitor Center, Wuksachi Village, and Dorst Creek Campground are frequent starting points. Check bulletin boards throughout the park for the week's offerings.

SPORTS AND THE OUTDOORS

The best way to see Sequoia is to take a hike. Unless you do so, you'll miss out on the up-close grandeur of mist wafting between deeply scored, red-orange tree trunks bigger than you've ever seen. If it's winter, put on some snowshoes or cross-country skis and plunge into the snow-swaddled woodland. There are not too many other outdoor options: no off-road driving is allowed in the parks, and no special provisions have been made for bicycles. Boating, rafting, and snowmobiling are also prohibited.

BIRD-WATCHING

More than 200 species of birds inhabit Sequoia and Kings Canyon national parks. Not seen in most parts of the United States, the white-headed woodpecker and the pileated woodpecker are common in most mid-elevation areas here. There are also many hawks and owls, including the renowned spotted owl. Species are diverse in both parks due to the changes in elevation, and range from warblers, kingbirds, thrushes, and sparrows in the foothills to goshawk, blue grouse, red-breasted nuthatch, and brown creeper at the highest elevations. Ranger-led bird-watching tours are held on a sporadic basis. Call the park's main information number to find out more about these tours.

Sequoia Natural History Association. The association's highly regarded Sequoia Field Institute conducts single-day and mulitiday "EdVenture" tours that include backpacking hikes, natural-history walks, and kayaking excursions. ☎ *559/565–3759* ⊕ *www.sequoiahistory.org.*

CROSS-COUNTRY SKIING
Wuksachi Lodge. Rent skis here. Depending on snowfall amounts, instruction may also be available. Reservations are recommended. Marked trails cut through Giant Forest, just 5 miles south of the lodge. ⊠ *Off Generals Hwy. (Rte. 198), 2 miles north of Lodgepole* ☎ *559/565–4070* 🕮 *$18–$25 ski rental* ☉ *Nov.–May (unless no snow), daily 9–4.*

HIKING
The best way to see the park is to hike it. The grandeur and majesty of the Sierra is best seen up close. Carry a hiking map—available at any visitor center—and plenty of water. Check with rangers for current trail conditions, and be aware of rapidly changing weather. As a rule of thumb, plan on trekking about a mile per hour.

EASY
★ **Congress Trail.** This easy 2-mile trail, arguably the best hike in the parks in terms of natural beauty, is a paved loop that begins near General Sherman Tree and winds through the heart of the sequoia forest. You'll get close-up views of more big trees here than on any other Sequoia hike. Watch for the clusters known as the House and Senate. An easy offshoot leads to Crescent Meadow, where in summer you can catch free shuttles back to the Sherman parking lot. *Easy.* ⊠ *Trail begins off Generals Hwy. (Rte. 198), 2 miles north of Giant Forest.*

★ **Crescent Meadow Trails.** John Muir reportedly called Crescent Meadow the "gem of the Sierra." Brilliant wildflowers bloom here by midsummer, and a 1.8-mile trail loops around the meadow. A 1.6-mile trail begins at Crescent Meadow and leads to Tharp's Log, a cabin built from a fire-hollowed sequoia. *Easy.* ⊠ *Trail begins end of Moro Rock–Crescent Meadow Rd., 2.6 miles east off Generals Hwy. (Rte. 198).*

MODERATE
Tokopah Falls Trail. This moderate trail follows the Marble Fork of the Kaweah River for 1.75 miles one way and dead-ends below the impressive granite cliffs and cascading waterfall of Tokopah Canyon. It takes 2½ to 4 hours to make the 3.5-mile round-trip journey. The trail passes through a mixed-conifer forest. *Moderate.* ⊠ *Trail begins off Generals Hwy. (Rte. 198), ¼ mile north of Lodgepole Campground.*

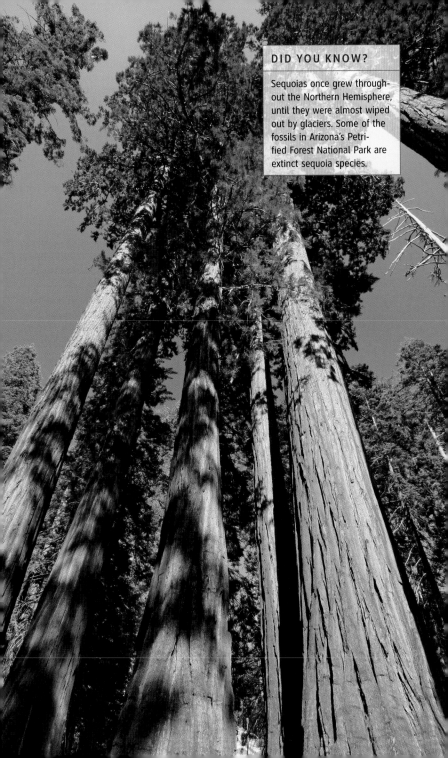

DIFFICULT

Mineral King Trails. Many trails to the high country begin at Mineral King. The two most popular day hikes are Eagle Lake and Timber Gap, both of which are somewhat strenuous. At 7,800 feet, this is the highest point to which one can drive in either of the parks. Get a map and provisions, and check with rangers about conditions. *Difficult.* ⊠ *Trailhead at end of Mineral King Rd., 25 miles east of Generals Hwy. (Rte. 198).*

HORSEBACK RIDING

Trips take you through redwood forests, flowering meadows, across the Sierra, or even up to Mt. Whitney. Costs per person range from $35 for a one-hour guided ride to around $250 per day for fully guided trips for which the packers do all the cooking and camp chores.

TOURS AND OUTFITTERS

Horse Corral Pack Station. Hourly, half-day, full-day, or overnight trips through Sequoia are available for beginning and advanced riders. ⊠ *Off Big Meadows Rd., 12 miles east of Generals Hwy. (Rte. 198) between Sequoia and Kings Canyon national parks* ☎ *559/565–3404 in summer, 559/564–6429 in winter* ☎ *$35–$145 day trips* ⊙ *May–Sept.*

Mineral King Pack Station. Day and overnight tours in the high-mountain area around Mineral King are available here. ⊠ *End of Mineral King Rd., 25 miles east of East Fork entrance* ☎ *559/561–3039 in summer, 928/855–5885 in winter* ⊕ *mineralking.tripod.com* ☎ *$30–$85 day trips* ⊙ *July–late Sept. or –early Oct.*

SLEDDING AND SNOWSHOEING

The Wolverton area, on Route 198 near Giant Forest, is a popular sledding spot, where sleds, inner tubes, and platters are allowed. You can buy sleds and saucers, starting at $8, at the Wuksachi Lodge (☎ *559/565–4070*), 2 miles north of Lodgepole.

You can rent snowshoes for $18–$25 at the Wuksachi Lodge (☎ *559/565–4070*), 2 miles north of Lodgepole. Naturalists lead snowshoe walks around Giant Forest and Wuksachi Lodge, conditions permitting, on Saturdays and holidays. Snowshoes are provided for a $1 donation. Make reservations and check schedules at Giant Forest Museum (☎ *559/565–4480*) or Wuksachi Lodge.

KINGS CANYON NATIONAL PARK

EXPLORING

SCENIC DRIVES

★ **Kings Canyon Scenic Byway.** About 10 miles east of Grant Grove Village is Jackson View, where you'll first see Kings River Canyon. Near Yucca Point, it's thousands of feet deeper than the much more famous Grand Canyon. Continuing through Sequoia National Forest past Boyden Cavern, you'll enter the larger portion of Kings Canyon National Park and, eventually, Cedar Grove Village. Past there, the U-shape canyon becomes broader. Be sure to allow an hour to walk through Zumwalt Meadow. Also, be sure to park and take the less-than-five-minute walks

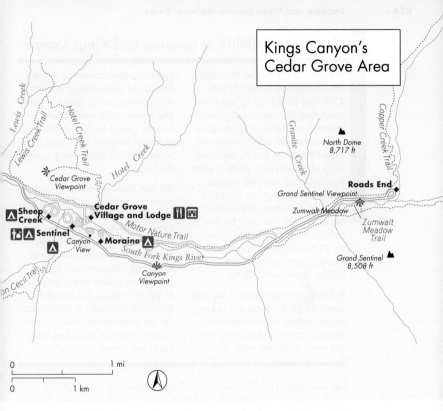

Kings Canyon's Cedar Grove Area

Lewis Creek — Lewis Creek Trail — Hotel Creek Trail — Hotel Creek — Granite Creek — Copper Creek Trail

North Dome 8,717 ft

Roads End
Grand Sentinel Viewpoint
Zumwalt Meadow

Cedar Grove Viewpoint

Sheep Creek

Cedar Grove Village and Lodge

Sentinel

Canyon View

Moraine

Motor Nature Trail

Zumwalt Meadow Trail

Grand Sentinel 8,508 ft

South Fork Kings River

Canyon Viewpoint

Don Cecil Trail

0 ——— 1 mi
0 ——— 1 km

to the base of Grizzly Falls and Roaring River Falls. The drive dead-ends at a big parking lot, the launch point for many backpackers. Driving the byway takes about one hour each way (without stops).

HISTORIC SITES

★ **Fallen Monarch.** This Sequoia's hollow base was used in the second half of the 19th century as a home for settlers, a saloon, and even to stable U.S. Cavalry horses. As you walk through it (assuming entry is permitted, which has not always been the case in recent years), check out how little the wood has decayed, and imagine yourself tucked safely inside, sheltered from a storm or protected from the searing heat. ⊠ *Trailhead 1 mile north of Grant Grove Visitor Center.*

SCENIC STOPS

Canyon View. There are many places along the scenic byway to pull over for sightseeing, but this special spot showcases evidence of the canyon's glacial history. Here, maybe more than anywhere else, you'll understand why John Muir compared Kings Canyon vistas with those in Yosemite. ⊠ *Kings Canyon Scenic Byway (Rte. 180), 1 mile east of the Cedar Grove turnoff.*

★ **Redwood Mountain Grove.** If you are serious about sequoias, you should consider visiting this, the world's largest big-tree grove. Within its 2,078 acres are 2,172 sequoias whose diameters exceed 10 feet. Your

CLOSE UP

Plants and Wildlife in Sequoia and Kings Canyon

The parks can be divided into three distinct zones. In the west (1,500–4,500 feet) are the rolling, lower elevation foothills, covered with shrubby chaparral vegetation or golden grasslands dotted with oaks. Chamise, red-barked manzanita, and the occasional yucca plant grow here. Fields of white popcorn flower cover the hillsides in spring, and the yellow fiddleneck flourishes. In summer, intense heat and absence of rain cause the hills to turn golden brown. Wildlife includes the California ground squirrel, noisy blue-and-gray scrub jay, black bears, coyotes, skunks, and gray fox.

At middle elevation (5,000–9,000 feet), where the giant sequoia belt resides, rock formations mix with meadows and huge stands of evergreens—red and white fir, incense cedar, and

ponderosa pines, to name a few. Wildflowers like yellow blazing star and red Indian paintbrush, bloom in spring and summer. Mule deer, golden-mantled ground squirrels, Steller's jays, mule deer, and black bears (most active in fall) inhabit the area, as does the chickaree.

The high alpine section of the parks is extremely rugged, with a string of rocky peaks reaching above 13,000 feet to Mt. Whitney's 14,494 feet. Fierce weather and scarcity of soil make vegetation and wildlife sparse. Foxtail and whitebark pines have gnarled and twisted trunks, the result of high wind, heavy snowfall, and freezing temperatures. In summer you can see yellow-bellied marmots, pikas, weasels, mountain chickadees, and Clark's nutcrackers.

options range from the distant (pulling off the Generals Highway onto an overlook) to the intimate (taking a 6- to 10-mile hike down into its richest regions, which include two of the world's 25 heaviest trees). ⊠ *Drive 5 miles south of Grant Grove on Generals Hwy. (Rte. 198), then turn right at Quail Flat; follow it 1½ miles to the Redwood Canyon trailhead.*

SPORTS AND THE OUTDOORS

CROSS-COUNTRY SKIING

Roads to Grant Grove are easily accessible during heavy snowfall, making the trails here a good choice over Sequoia's Giant Forest when harsh weather hits.

HIKING

You can enjoy many of Kings Canyon's sights from your car, but the giant gorge of the Kings River Canyon and the sweeping vistas of some of the highest mountains in the United States are best seen on foot. Carry a hiking map—available at any visitor center—and plenty of water. Check with rangers for current trail conditions, and be aware of rapidly changing weather.

Road's End Permit Station. If you're planning to hike the backcountry, you can pick up a permit and information on the backcountry at Road's End Permit Station. You can also rent or buy bear canisters, a must for campers. When the station is closed, you can still complete a self-service

Hiking in the Sierra Mountains is a thrilling experience, putting you amid some of the world's highest trees.

permit form. ⊠ *5 miles east of Cedar Grove Visitor Center, at the end of Kings Canyon Scenic Byway* ⊘ *Late May–late Sept., daily 7–3:30.*

EASY

Fodor'sChoice ★ **Zumwalt Meadow Trail.** Rangers say this is the best (and most popular) day hike in the Cedar Grove area. Just 1.5 miles long, it offers three visual treats: the South Fork of the Kings River, the lush meadow, and the high granite walls above, including those of Grand Sentinel and North Dome. *Easy.* ⊠ *Trailhead 4½ miles east of Cedar Grove Village turnoff from Kings Canyon Scenic Byway.*

MODERATE

★ **Big Baldy.** This hike climbs 600 feet and 2 miles up to the 8,209-feet summit of Big Baldy. Your reward is the view of Redwood Canyon. The round-trip hike is 4 miles. *Moderate.* ⊠ *Trailhead 8 miles south of Grant Grove on Generals Hwy. (Rte. 198).*

★ **Redwood Canyon Trail.** Avoid the hubbub of Giant Forest and its General Sherman Tree by hiking down to Redwood Canyon, the world's largest grove of sequoias. Opt for the trail toward Hart Tree, and you'll soon lose track of how many humongous trees you pass along the 6-mile loop. Count on spending four to six peaceful hours here—although some backpackers linger overnight (wilderness permit required). *Moderate.* ⊠ *Trail begins off Quail Flat. Drive 5 miles south of Grant Grove on Generals Hwy. (Rte. 198), then turn right at Quail Flat; follow it 1½ miles to the Redwood Canyon trailhead.*

DIFFICULT

★ **Hotel Creek Trail.** For gorgeous canyon views, take this trail from the canyon floor at Cedar Grove up a series of switchbacks until it splits. Follow the route left through chaparral to the forested ridge and rocky outcrop known as Cedar Grove Overlook, where you can see the Kings River Canyon stretching below. This strenuous 5-mile round-trip hike gains 1,200 feet and takes three to four hours to complete. For a longer hike, return via Lewis Creek Trail for an 8-mile loop. *Difficult.* ⊠ *Trailhead at Cedar Grove pack station, 1 mile east of Cedar Grove Village.*

HORSEBACK RIDING

One-day destinations by horseback out of Cedar Grove include Mist Falls and Upper Bubb's Creek. In the backcountry, many equestrians head for Volcanic Lakes or Granite Basin, ascending trails that reach elevations of 10,000 feet. Costs per person range from $35 for a one-hour guided ride to around $250 per day for fully guided trips for which the packers do all the cooking and camp chores.

TOURS AND OUTFITTERS **Cedar Grove Pack Station.** Take a day or overnight trip along the Kings River Canyon with Cedar Grove Pack Station. Popular routes include the Rae Lakes Loop and Monarch Divide. ⊠ *Kings Canyon Scenic Byway, 1 mile east of Cedar Grove Village* ☎ *559/565–3464 in summer, 559/337–2314 off-season* ⊠ *Call for prices* ☉ *May–Oct.*

Grant Grove Stables. A one- or two-hour trip through Grant Grove leaving from Grant Grove Stables is a good way to get a taste of horseback riding in Kings Canyon. ⊠ *Rte. 180, ½ mile north of Grant Grove Visitor Center* ☎ *559/335–9292 mid-June–Sept., 559/594–9307 Oct.–mid-June* ⊠ *$40–$60* ☉ *June–Labor Day, daily 8–6.*

SLEDDING AND SNOWSHOEING

In winter, Kings Canyon has a few great places to play in the snow. Sleds, inner tubes, and platters are allowed at both the Azalea Campground area on Grant Tree Road, ¼ mile north of Grant Grove Visitor Center, and at the Big Stump picnic area, 2 miles north of the lower Route 180 entrance to the park.

Snowshoeing is good around Grant Grove, where you can take naturalist-guided snowshoe walks on Saturdays and holidays mid-December through mid-March as conditions permit.

WHERE TO EAT

Prices in the reviews are the average cost of a main course at dinner or, if dinner is not served, at lunch.

SEQUOIA

$ ✕ **Lodgepole Market and Snack Bar.** The choices here run the gamut from CAFÉ simple to very simple, with the three counters only a few strides apart in a central eating complex. For hot food, venture into the snack bar. The deli sells prepackaged sandwiches along with ice cream scooped from tubs. You'll find other prepackaged foods and souvenirs in the market. $ *Average main: $5* ⊠ *Next to Lodgepole Visitor Center* ☎ *559/565–3301* ☉ *Closed late Sept.–mid-Apr.*

$$$ ✕ **Wolverton Barbecue.** Weather permitting, diners congregate on a
BARBECUE wooden porch that looks directly out onto a small but strikingly verdant meadow. In addition to the predictable meats such as ribs and chicken, the all-you-can-eat buffet has sides that include baked beans, corn on the cob, and potato salad. Following the meal, listen to a ranger talk and clear your throat for a campfire sing-along. Purchase tickets at Lodgepole Market, Wuksachi Lodge, or Wolverton Recreation Area's office. $ *Average main: $22* ⊠ *Wolverton Rd., 1½ miles northeast off Generals Hwy. (Rte. 198)* ☎ *559/565–4070, 559/565–3301* ☉ *Closed Mon.–Thurs. and early Sept.–mid-June. No lunch.*

$$ ✕ **Wuksachi Village Dining Room.** Huge windows run the length of the
AMERICAN high-ceilinged dining room, and a large fireplace on the far wall warms
★ both the body and the soul. The diverse dinner menu—by far the best in the two parks—includes filet mignon, rainbow trout, and vegetarian pasta dishes, in addition to the ever-present burgers. The children's menu is economically priced. Breakfast and lunch also are served. $ *Average main: $20* ⊠ *Wuksachi Village* ☎ *559/565–4070* ⌲ *Reservations essential.*

KINGS CANYON

$ ✕ **Cedar Grove Restaurant.** For a small operation, the menu here is sur-
AMERICAN prisingly extensive, with dinner entrées such as pasta, pork chops, and steak. For breakfast, try the biscuits and gravy, French toast, pancakes, or cold cereal. Burgers (including vegetarian patties) and hot dogs dominate the lunch choices. Outside, a patio dining area overlooks the Kings River. $ *Average main: $13* ⊠ *Cedar Grove Village* ☎ *559/565–0100* ☉ *Closed Oct.–May.*

$$ ✕ **Grant Grove Restaurant.** In a no-frills, open room, order basic Ameri-
AMERICAN can fare such as pancakes for breakfast or hot sandwiches and chicken for later meals. Vegetarians and vegans will have to content themselves with a simple salad. Take-out service is available. $ *Average main: $21* ⊠ *Grant Grove Village* ☎ *559/335–5500.*

WHERE TO STAY

Prices in the reviews are the lowest cost of a standard double room in high season. For expanded reviews, facilities, and current deals, visit Fodors.com.

SEQUOIA

$$$ ⌂ **Wuksachi Lodge.** The striking cedar-and-stone main building here is
HOTEL a fine example of how a structure can blend effectively with lovely
Fodor's Choice mountain scenery. **Pros:** best place to stay in the parks, lots of wildlife.
★ **Cons:** rooms can be small, main lodge is a few minutes' walk from guest rooms. **TripAdvisor:** "comfortable rooms," "great location," "beautiful setting." $ *Rooms from: $185* ⊠ *Wuksachi Village* ☎ *559/565–4070, 888/252–5757 reservations* ⊕ *www.visitsequoia.com* ⤴ *102 rooms.*

Mt. Whitney

CLOSE UP

At 14,494 feet, Mt. Whitney is the highest point in the contiguous United States and the crown jewel of Sequoia National Park's wild eastern side. The peak looms high above the tiny, high-mountain desert community of Lone Pine, where numerous Hollywood Westerns have been filmed. The high mountain ranges, arid landscape, and scrubby brush of the Eastern Sierra are beautiful in their vastness and austerity.

Despite the mountain's scale, you can't see it from the more traveled west side of the park because it is hidden behind the Great Western Divide. The only way to access Mt. Whitney from the main part of the park is to circumnavigate the Sierra Nevada via a 10-hour, nearly 400-mile drive outside the park. No road ascends the peak; the best vantage point from which to catch a glimpse of the mountain is at the end of Whitney Portal Road. The 13 miles of winding road leads from U.S. 395 at Lone Pine to the trailhead for the hiking route to the top of the mountain. Whitney Portal Road is closed in winter.

KINGS CANYON

$$$
HOTEL
🖼 **John Muir Lodge.** This modern, timber-sided lodge is nestled in a wooded area in the hills above Grant Grove Village and offers year-round accommodations. **Pros:** common room stays warm; it's far enough from the main road to be quiet. **Cons:** check-in is down in the village. **TripAdvisor:** "surprisingly comfortable," "peace and quiet in the forest," "terrific location and service." $ *Rooms from: $195* ✉ *Kings Canyon Scenic Byway, ¼ mile north of Grant Grove Village* ☎ *559/335–5500, 866/522–6966* ⊕ *www.sequoia-kingscanyon.com* ⤴ *24 rooms, 6 suites.*

Sacramento and the Gold Country

WORD OF MOUTH

"The twin mining towns of Nevada City and Grass Valley are two of my favorite towns in California. They both have many well preserved historical buildings, B&Bs, restaurants, and interesting shops."

—Otis_B_Driftwood

WELCOME TO SACRAMENTO AND THE GOLD COUNTRY

TOP REASONS TO GO

★ **Rush to the past:** Marshall Gold Discovery State Park and Hangtown's Gold Bug & Mine conjure up California's mid-19th century boom.

★ **Capital connections:** Sedate Sacramento offers enough attractions to engage out-of-towners for a day or two, especially its Capitol, historic Old Sacramento, and dining scene.

★ **Bon appetit:** Sacramento is home to the California state fair in July and many ethnic food festivals. Nevada City and environs are known for summer mountain music festivals and Victorian and Cornish winter holiday celebrations.

★ **Vintage calm:** With bucolic scenery and friendly tasting rooms, the Shenandoah Valley is the Gold Country's laid-back answer to Napa.

★ **Ups and downs:** Calaveras Big Trees State Park is filled with giant sequoias, and Moaning Cavern's main chamber is big enough to hold the Statue of Liberty.

1 Sacramento and Vicinity. The gateway to the Gold Country, the seat of state government, and an agricultural hub, Sacramento plays many important contemporary roles. About 2.5 million people live in the metropolitan area, which offers up more sunshine and lower housing costs than coastal California.

2 The Gold Country—South. South of its junction with U.S. 50, Highway 49 traces in asphalt the famed Mother Lode. The peppy former gold-rush towns strung along the road have for the most part been restored and made presentable to visitors with an interest in one of the most frenzied episodes of American history.

3 The Gold Country—North. Highway 49 north of Placerville links the towns of Coloma, Auburn, Grass Valley, and Nevada City. Most are gentrified versions of once-rowdy mining camps, vestiges of which remain in roadside museums, old mining structures, and restored homes now serving as inns.

22

GETTING ORIENTED

The Gold Country is a largely laid-back and lower-tech destination for those seeking to escape Southern California and the Bay Area. Sacramento, Davis, and Woodland are in an enormous valley bordered to the east by the Sierra Nevada mountain range. Foothill communities Nevada City, Placerville, and Sutter Creek were products of the gold rush.

Updated by
Reed Parsell

A new era dawned for California when James Marshall turned up a gold nugget in the tailrace of a sawmill he was constructing along the American River. Before January 24, 1848, Mexico and the United States were still wrestling for ownership of what would become the Golden State. With Marshall's discovery, the United States tightened its grip on the region, and prospectors from all over the world came to seek their fortunes in the Mother Lode.

As gold fever seized the nation, California's population of 15,000 swelled to 265,000 within three years. The mostly young, mostly male adventurers who arrived in search of gold—the 49ers—became part of a culture that discarded many of the conventions of the eastern states. It was also a violent time. Yankee prospectors chased Mexican miners off their claims, and California's leaders initiated a plan to exterminate the local Native American population. Bounties were paid and private militias were hired to wipe out the Native Americans or sell them into slavery. California was now to be dominated by the Anglo.

The gold rush boom lasted scarcely 20 years, but it changed California forever. It produced 546 mining towns, of which fewer than 250 remain. The hills of the Gold Country were alive, not only with prospecting and mining but also with business, the arts, gambling, and a fair share of crime. Opera houses went up alongside brothels, and the California State Capitol, in Sacramento, was built with the gold dug out of the hills.

Today the Gold Country is one of California's less expensive destinations, a region of the Sierra Nevada foothills that is filled with natural and cultural pleasures. Visitors come to Nevada City, Auburn, Coloma, Sutter Creek, and Columbia not only to relive the past but also to explore art galleries, shop for antiques, and stay at inns full of character. Spring brings wildflowers, and in fall the hills are colored by bright red berries and changing leaves. Because it offers many outdoor activities, the Gold Country is a great place to take the kids.

Visiting Old Sacramento's museums is a good way to immerse yourself in history, but the Gold Country's heart lies along Highway 49, which winds the 325-mile north–south length of the historic mining area. The highway, often a twisting, hilly, two-lane road, begs for a convertible with the top down.

22

PLANNING

WHEN TO GO

The Gold Country is most pleasant in spring, when the wildflowers are in bloom, and in fall. Summers can be hot: temperatures of 100°F are fairly common. Sacramento winters tend to be cool with occasionally foggy and/or rainy days; many Sacramentans drive to the foothills (or to the coast) to get some winter sunshine. Throughout the year Gold Country towns stage community and ethnic celebrations. In December many towns are decked out for Christmas.

GETTING HERE AND AROUND

AIR TRAVEL

Sacramento International Airport (SMF), which unveiled a new terminal in late 2011, is served by Aeromexico, Alaska, American, Delta, Frontier, Hawaiian, JetBlue, Southwest, United, and US Airways. A private taxi from the airport to downtown Sacramento costs about $40; the Super Shuttle fare is $25. Public buses *(see Bus and Light-Rail Travel)* are also an option.

Contacts Sacramento International Airport ⊠ *6900 Airport Blvd., 12 miles northwest of downtown off I-5, Sacramento* ☎ *916/929–5411* ⊕ *www.sacramento.aero/smf.* **Super Shuttle** ☎ *800/258–3826* ⊕ *www.supershuttle.com.*

BUS AND LIGHT-RAIL TRAVEL

Yolobus public buses No. 42A and 42B connect SMF airport and downtown Sacramento, West Sacramento, Davis, and Woodland. Greyhound serves Sacramento, Davis, Auburn, and Placerville. It's a two-hour trip from San Francisco's Temporary Transbay Terminal, at Folsom and Beale streets, to the Sacramento Greyhound Station, at Richards and Sequoia Pacific boulevards. Sacramento Regional Transit serves the capital area with buses and light-rail vehicles.

Contacts Greyhound ☎ *800/231–2222* ⊕ *www.greyhound.com.* **Sacramento Regional Transit** ☎ *916/321–2877* ⊕ *www.sacrt.com.* **Yolobus** ☎ *530/666–2837, 916/371–2877* ⊕ *www.yolobus.com.*

CAR TRAVEL

Interstate 5 (north–south) and Interstate 80 (east–west) are the two main routes into and out of Sacramento. From Sacramento, three highways fan out toward the east, all intersecting with historic Highway 49: Interstate 80 heads northeast 34 miles to Auburn; U.S. 50 goes east 40 miles to Placerville; and Highway 16 angles southeast 45 miles to Plymouth. Highway 49 is an excellent two-lane road that winds and climbs through the foothills and valleys, linking the principal Gold Country towns. Traveling by car is the only practical way to explore the Gold Country.

The Gold Country

Oroville
70
Lake Oroville
New Bullards Bar Reservoir
Downieville
TO RENO, NV →
89
NEVADA
CALIFORNIA
80
Truckee
49
20
Yuba City
99
Grass Valley · Nevada City
80
20
Empire Mine State Historic Park
28
Tahoe City
Lake Tahoe
Olivehurst
Colfax
49
South Lake Tahoe
Wheatland
70
65
89
Meyers
Lincoln
Auburn
Marshall Gold Discovery State Historic Park
50
Kirkwood
45
Sacramento see detail map
Rocklin
Roseville
Coloma
Woodland
5
Citrus Heights
Folsom Lake
Placerville
Hangtown's Gold Bug Park & Mine
80
Davis
50
Folsom
Summerset
49
88
Dixon
Rosemont
Shenandoah Valley
Cosumnes
16
Fiddletown
Plymouth
Elk Grove
Amador City · Sutter Creek
Tamarack
104
Ione
Jackson
99
88
Galt
Camanche Reservoir
Pardee Res.
Calaveras Big Tree State Park
108
Arnold
Isleton
Lockeford
12
San Andreas
Cold Spring
Lodi
New Hogan Reservoir
49
California Caverns
Murphys
Oakley
Lincoln Village
99
26
Calaveras
Angels Camp
Columbia
Moaning Cavern
Soulsbyville
Stockton
Linden
Sonora
Yosemite National Park
4
Jamestown
4
4
Manteca
108 120
Moccasin
Groveland
120
Lathrop
Stanislaus
Don Pedro Reservoir
49
205
Tracy
Ripon
120
Oakdale
108
132
580
Salida
Modesto
Waterford
132
Lake McClure
Livermore
580
99
Tuolumne
140
DIABLO RANGE
SAN JOAQUIN VALLEY
132
Mariposa
Turlock
Merced River
49
140
Livingston
140
Merced
99
Planada
0 20 mi
0 20 km

TRAIN TRAVEL

Amtrak trains serve Sacramento and Davis from San Jose, Oakland, and Emeryville (Amtrak buses transport passengers from San Francisco's Ferry Building to Emeryville). The trip takes 2½ hours. Amtrak also runs trains and connecting motor coaches from the Central Valley.

Contacts **Amtrak** ☎ *800/872-7245* ⊕ *www.amtrakcalifornia.com.*

HEALTH AND SAFETY

In an emergency, dial 911. Each of the following medical facilities has an emergency room open 24 hours a day.

Hospitals **Mercy Hospital of Sacramento** ✉ *4001 J St., Sacramento* ☎ *916/453-4545* ⊕ *www.mercygeneral.org.* **Sutter General Hospital** ✉ *2801 L St., Sacramento* ☎ *916/733-8900* ⊕ *www.suttermedicalcenter.org.* **Sutter Memorial Hospital** ✉ *52nd and F Sts., Sacramento* ☎ *916/733-1000* ⊕ *www. suttermedicalcenter.org.*

VISITOR INFORMATION

Contacts **Amador County Chamber of Commerce & Visitors Bureau** ✉ *115 Main St., Jackson* ☎ *209/223-0350* ⊕ *www.amadorcountychamber.com.* **El Dorado County Visitors Authority** ✉ *542 Main St., Placerville* ☎ *530/621–5885, 800/457-6279* ⊕ *visit-eldorado.com.* **Grass Valley/Nevada County Chamber of Commerce** ✉ *422 Henderson St., Grass Valley* ☎ *530/273-4667, 800/655-4667* ⊕ *www.grassvalleychamber.com.* **Mariposa County Visitors Bureau** ✉ *5158 Hwy. 140, Mariposa* ☎ *209/966-7081, 866/425-3366* ⊕ *www. yosemiteexperience.com.* **Tuolumne County Visitors Bureau** ✉ *542 W. Stockton Rd., Sonora* ☎ *209/533-4420, 800/446-1333* ⊕ *www.tcvb.com.*

RESTAURANTS

American, Italian, and Mexican are common Gold Country fare, but chefs also prepare ambitious European, French, and California cuisine. Grass Valley's meat- and vegetable-stuffed *pasties,* introduced by 19th-century gold miners from Cornwall, are one of the region's more unusual treats.

HOTELS

Full-service hotels, budget motels, and small inns can be found in Sacramento. Larger towns along Highway 49—among them Jackson, Placerville, Auburn, and Nevada City—have chain motels and inns. Many Gold Country bed-and-breakfasts occupy former mansions, miners' cabins, and other historic buildings.

HOTEL AND RESTAURANT COSTS

Prices in the restaurant reviews are the average cost of a main course at dinner or, if dinner is not served, at lunch (excluding sales tax). Prices in the hotel reviews are the lowest cost of a standard double room in high season. Prices do not include taxes (as high as 14%, depending on the region).

Contacts **Gold Country Inns of Tuolumne County** ⊕ *www.goldbnbs.com.* **Historic Inns of Grass Valley and Nevada City** ☎ *530/477-6634* ⊕ *goldcountryinns.net.* **Tour Amador County** ☎ *209/267-9249, 877/868-7262* ⊕ *www. touramador.com/accommodations.*

22

SACRAMENTO AND VICINITY

California's capital is one of the country's most ethnically diverse cities, with sizable Hmong and Ukrainian populations, among many others.

SACRAMENTO

87 miles northeast of San Francisco on I–80; 384 miles north of Los Angeles on I–5.

All around the Golden State's seat of government you'll experience echoes of the gold-rush days, most notably in Old Sacramento, whose wooden sidewalks and horse-drawn carriages on cobblestone streets lend the waterfront district a 19th-century feel. The California State Railroad Museums and other venues hold artifacts of state and national significance, and historic buildings house shops and restaurants. River cruises and train rides are fun family diversions for an hour or two.

Due east of Old Sacramento is downtown, whose noteworthy landmarks are the Capitol building and the surrounding Capitol Park. The convention center is also here. A persistent homeless problem and a scattering of boarded-up storefronts diminish the area's appeal somewhat.

Farther east, starting at about 15th Street, lies the city's most interesting neighborhood, midtown, a vibrant mix of genteel Victorian edifices, ultramodern lofts, and innovative restaurants and cozy wine bars. The neighborhood, which is so cool it's got its own magazine (⊕ *www.midtownmonthly.net*), springs to life on the second Saturday evening of the month, when art galleries hold open houses and the sidewalks are packed. A few intersections are jumping most evenings when the weather's good; they include the corner of 20th and L streets in what's known as Lavender Heights, the center of the city's gay and lesbian community.

GETTING HERE AND AROUND

Most people drive to Sacramento and get around by car. Taxis are a minor presence. Bike lanes abound, but often they come to sudden ends and leave riders in dicey circumstances.

Bus Travel Sacramento Regional Transit (⊕ *www.sacrt.com*) buses and light-rail vehicles serve the Sacramento area. The No. 30 DASH (Downtown Area Shuttle) bus links Old Sacramento, midtown, and Sutter's Fort.

Car Travel Assuming that traffic is not a factor, though it can be, Sacramento is a 90-minute drive from San Francisco (and a seven-hour drive from Los Angeles). Parking garages serve Old Sacramento and other tourist spots, but except on weekends street parking downtown can be difficult to find.

ESSENTIALS

Visitor Information Old Sacramento Visitor Information Center ⊠ *1002 2nd St., at K St.* ☎ *916/442-7644* ⊕ *www.oldsacramento.com* ☉ *Daily 10–5.* **Old Sacramento Events Hotline** ☎ *916/558-3912.* **Sacramento Convention and Visitors Bureau** ⊠ *1608 I St., Suite 600* ☎ *916/808-7777, 800/292-2334* ⊕ *www.discovergold.org.*

22

EXPLORING

California Automobile Museum. More than 150 vintage automobiles—including Model Ts, Hudsons, Studebakers, Pontiacs, and other bygone makes and models—are on display at this diverting museum that pays tribute to automotive history and car culture. A 1920s roadside café and garage exhibit re-creates the early days of motoring, and the friendly docents are ready to explain everything you see. The museum is near downtown and Old Sacramento, with ample free parking. ✉ *2200 Front St., 1 block off Broadway, Downtown* ☎ *916/442–6802* ⊕ *www. calautomuseum.org* 🎟 *$8* ☉ *Daily 10–6, 3rd Thurs. of the month, 10–9.*

☺ **California Museum.** Some of the exhibits at this celebration of all things California are high-tech and interactive, but there are also scores of archival drawers that you can pull out to see the real artifacts of history and culture—from the California State Constitution to surfing magazines. Board a 1949 cross-country bus to view a video on immigration, visit a Chinese herb shop maintained by a holographic proprietor, or find familiar names inducted into the annually expanded California Hall of Fame. There's also a café that's open weekdays until 2:30 pm. ✉ *1020 O St., at 11th St., Downtown* ☎ *916/653–7524* ⊕ *www. californiamuseum.org* 🎟 *$9* ☉ *Mon.–Sat. 10–5, Sun. noon–5.*

The California State Railroad Museum is North America's most popular railroad museum.

☺ **California State Railroad Museum.** Near what was once the terminus of the
Fodor's Choice   transcontinental and Sacramento Valley railroads, this 100,000-square-
★   foot museum—the best of its kind in the region, if not the country—
has 21 locomotives and railroad cars on display along with dozens of
other exhibits. You can walk through a post-office car and peer into
cubbyholes and canvas mailbags, enter a sleeping car that simulates
the swaying on the roadbed and the flashing lights of a passing town
at night, or glimpse the inside of the first-class dining car. One thousand vintage toy trains constitute a much-heralded permanent exhibit,
and the "Last Spike" room is compelling. Kids have lots of fun here,
especially in the big play area upstairs. ⊠ *125 I St., at 2nd St., Old
Sacramento* ☎ *916/445–6645* ⊕ *www.csrmf.org* 🖻 *$9* ☉ *Daily 10–5.*

★ **Capitol.** The lacy plasterwork of the Capitol's 120-foot-high rotunda has
the complexity and colors of a Fabergé egg. Underneath the gilded dome
are marble floors, glittering chandeliers, monumental staircases, reproductions of century-old state offices, and legislative chambers decorated
in the style of the 1890s (the Capitol was built in 1869). Guides conduct tours of the building and the 40-acre Capitol Park, which contains
a rose garden, an impressive display of camellias (Sacramento's city
flower), and the California Vietnam Veterans Memorial. ■TIP→ The
photogenic front of the building is best captured in late-afternoon light.
⊠ *Capitol Mall and 10th St., Downtown* ☎ *916/324–0333* ⊕ *www.
statecapitolmuseum.com* 🖻 *Free* ☉ *Daily 9–5; tours hourly 10–4.*

☺ **Central Pacific Railroad Passenger Station.** At this reconstructed 1876 depot
there's rolling stock to admire, a typical waiting room, and a small
restaurant. On weekends April through September, and for special

occasions October through December, a train ($10) departs hourly from the freight depot, south of the passenger station, making a 40-minute out-and-back trip between the Sacramento River and, less interestingly, Interstate 5. ✉ *930 Front St., at J St., Old Sacramento* ☎ *916/445–6645* 🖥 *$4, free with same-day ticket from California State Railroad Museum* 🕐 *Daily 10–4.*

★ **Crocker Art Museum.** The oldest art museum in the American West has a collection of art from Europe, Asia, and California, including *Sunday Morning in the Mines* (1872), a large canvas by Charles Christian Nahl depicting aspects of the original mining industry, and the magnificent *Great Canyon of the Sierra, Yosemite* (1871), by Thomas Hill. An expansion completed in 2010 tripled the Crocker's size; it now rivals San Francisco's best art museums in scope if not quite in permanent collections. ✉ *216 O St., at 3rd St., Downtown* ☎ *916/808–7000* 🌐 *www.crockerartmuseum.org* 🖥 *$10* 🕐 *Tues., Wed. 10–5, and Fri.–Sun.; Thurs. 10–9.*

★ **Governor's Mansion.** This 15-room house was built in 1877 and used by the state's chief executives from the early 1900s until 1967, when Ronald Reagan vacated it in favor of an upscale private residence. Many of the Italianate mansion's interior decorations were ordered from the Huntington, Hopkins & Co. hardware store, one of whose partners, Albert Gallatin, was the original occupant. Each of the seven marble fireplaces has a petticoat mirror that ladies strolled past to see if their slips were showing. State funding difficulties could lead to this site's closure or to diminished hours, so check before you visit. ✉ *1526 H St., at 16th St., Midtown* ☎ *916/323–3047* 🖥 *$5* 🕐 *Daily 10–5; tours hourly, last tour at 4.*

QUICK BITES

Tapa the World. As the name implies, this cozy bar and restaurant serves tapa—small plates of meats, seafood, chicken, and veggies shared at the table—daily from 11:30 am until midnight in the heart of midtown. Ⓢ *Average main: $12* ✉ *2115 J St., near 21st St., Midtown* ☎ *916/442–4353* 🌐 *www.tapatheworld.com.*

Old Sacramento Schoolhouse Museum. Sacramento's first school welcomed students in August 1849 and closed permanently four months later. Five years passed before another public school opened. Today it's a kid-friendly attraction that shows what one-room schoolhouses were like in the California Central Valley and foothills in the late 1800s.

☺ **State Indian Museum.** Among the interesting displays at this well-organized museum a few strides from Sutter's Fort is one devoted to Ishi, the last Yahi Indian to emerge from the mountains, in 1911. Ishi provided scientists with insight into the traditions and culture of this group of Native Americans. Arts-and-crafts exhibits, a demonstration village, and an evocative 10-minute video bring to life the multifaceted past and present of California's native peoples. ✉ *2618 K St., at 27th St.* ☎ *916/324–0971* 🌐 *www.parks.ca.gov* 🖥 *$3* 🕐 *Daily 10–5.*

☺ **Sutter's Fort.** German-born Swiss immigrant John Augustus Sutter ★ founded Sacramento's earliest Euro-American settlement in 1839. Audio speakers give information at each stop along a self-guided tour that includes a blacksmith's shop, bakery, prison, living quarters, and livestock areas. Costumed docents sometimes reenact fort life, demonstrating crafts, food preparation, and firearms maintenance. ⊠ *2701 L St., at 27th St., Midtown* ☎ *916/445–4422* ⊕ *www.parks.ca.gov* ⊒ *$5 most days, $7 on interpretive program days* ⊙ *Tues.–Sun. 10–5.*

WHERE TO EAT

$$$
ITALIAN
Fodor'sChoice
★

✕ **Biba.** Owner Biba Caggiano is a nationally recognized authority on Italian cuisine. The Capitol crowd flocks here for homemade ravioli, osso buco, grilled pork loin, and veal and rabbit specials. A pianist adds to the upscale ambience nightly. ⑤ *Average main: $28* ⊠ *2801 Capitol Ave., at 28th St., Midtown* ☎ *916/455–2422* ⊕ *www.biba-restaurant. com* ⌂ *Reservations essential* ⊙ *Closed Sun. No lunch Mon. or Sat.*

$
MEXICAN

✕ **Ernesto's Mexican Food.** Customers wait up to an hour for a table on Friday and Saturday evenings at this popular restaurant. Fresh ingredients are stressed in the wide selection of entrées, and the margaritas are especially refreshing. Sister restaurant **Zocalo** (⊠ *1801 Capitol Ave.,* ☎ *916/441–0303*) has a striking indoor-outdoor atmosphere and is a popular launching spot for nights out on the town. ⑤ *Average main: $14* ⊠ *1901 16th St., at S St., Midtown* ☎ *916/441–5850* ⊕ *www. ernestosmexicanfood.com.*

$$$$
AMERICAN
Fodor'sChoice
★

✕ **The Firehouse.** Consistently ranked by local publications as one of the city's top restaurants, this formal and historic restaurant has a full bar, courtyard seating (its signature attraction), and creative American cooking, such as char-grilled spring rack of lamb served with roasted French fingerling potatoes and baby artichoke and fava bean succotash. Visitors who can afford to treat themselves to a fine and leisurely meal can do no better in Old Sacramento—although they might also opt for the less-pricey **Ten 22.** Located a block away and under the same ownership as the Firehouse, it serves pizza and other fancified comfort food. ⑤ *Average main: $36* ⊠ *1112 2nd St., at L St., Old Sacramento* ☎ *916/442–4772* ⊕ *www.firehouseoldsac.com* ⊙ *No lunch Sat.*

$
ECLECTIC

✕ **The Park Downtown.** Atmosphere is what it's all about at this complex of sophisticated eateries across from Capitol Park. Ma Jong's Asian Diner has inexpensive fare, some suitable for vegetarians; the indoor-outdoor Park Lounge is a supermodern bar and dance club; and the Park To Go puts a classy spin on breakfasts and lunches for people to take away. ⑤ *Average main: $12* ⊠ *1116 15th St., at L St., Downtown* ☎ *916/492–1960* ⊕ *www.theparkdowntown.com.*

WHERE TO STAY

For expanded reviews, facilities, and current deals, visit Fodors.com.

$$
B&B/INN
★

▧ **Amber House Bed & Breakfast Inn.** This B&B about a mile from the Capitol encompasses two homes: the original house is a Craftsman-style home with five bedrooms, and the second is an 1897 Dutch colonial–revival home. **Pros:** midtown location; attentive service. **Cons:** a few blocks' walk from midtown's main drags. **TripAdvisor:** "bliss," "wonderful getaway," "amazing anniversary trip." ⑤ *Rooms from: $169* ⊠ *1315 22nd St., Midtown* ☎ *916/444–8085, 800/755–6526* ⊕ *www. amberhouse.com* ⇥ *10 rooms* ⓘⓄⓘ *Breakfast.*

$$$ ☷ **Citizen Hotel.** Billed as Sacramento's first luxury boutique hotel, the
HOTEL Citizen makes its home in the 1926 Cal Western Life building. **Pros:**
all the modern amenities with older-world charms; within easy walk-
ing distance of the Capitol and other downtown attractions. **Cons:**
pricey; smallish bathrooms. **TripAdvisor:** "lovely older hotel," "lots of
character and service," "charming."⑤ *Rooms from: $189* ✉ *926 J St.,
Downtown* ☎ *916/447–4460* ⊕ *www.jdvhotels.com* ⇆ *175 rooms, 23
suites* ❍❙*Breakfast.*

$$ ☷ **Delta King.** The best staterooms of this grand old riverboat, now per-
HOTEL manently moored on Old Sacramento's waterfront, are on the river side
toward the back. **Pros:** intimate; many historic sights nearby; creaky
floors add to ambience. **Cons:** area can be dull at night; amenities aren't
very modern; creaky floors. **TripAdvisor:** "quirky," "cute room," "an
enjoyable stay."⑤*Rooms from: $172* ✉ *1000 Front St., Old Sacra-
mento* ☎ *916/444–5464, 800/825–5464* ⊕ *www.deltaking.com* ⇆ *44
rooms* ❍❙ *Breakfast.*

$$$ ☷ **Hyatt Regency Sacramento.** With a marble-and-glass lobby and luxu-
HOTEL rious rooms, this hotel across from the Capitol and adjacent to the
★ convention center is arguably Sacramento's finest. **Pros:** beautiful Capi-
tol Park is across the street; some rooms have small balconies. **Cons:**
nearby streets can be dodgy at night; somewhat impersonal. **TripAdvi-
sor:** "business or pleasure," "beautiful view," "great staff."⑤ *Rooms
from: $195* ✉ *1209 L St., Downtown* ☎ *916/443–1234, 800/633–7313*
⊕ *www.hyatt.com* ⇆ *500 rooms, 24 suites.*

NIGHTLIFE AND THE ARTS
NIGHTLIFE
Blue Cue. A billiard lounge known for its large selection of single-malt
scotches, the Blue Cue is upstairs from the popular Mexican restaurant
Centro. ✉ *1004 28th St., at J St., Midtown* ☎ *916/441–6810* ⊕ *www.
bluecue.com.*

Fox and Goose. This casual pub with live music is a big draw for week-
end breakfasts. Traditional pub food (fish-and-chips, Cornish pasties)
is served on weekday evenings until 9:30. ✉ *1001 R St., at 10th St.,
Downtown* ☎ *916/443–8825* ⊕ *www.foxandgoose.com.*

Harlow's. Harlow's draws a young crowd to its art-deco bar-night-
club for live music after 9 pm. ✉ *2708 J St., at 27th St., Midtown*
☎ *916/441–4693* ⊕ *www.harlows.com.*

Streets of London Pub. A favorite among Anglophiles, Streets is open after
midnight every night. ✉ *1804 J St., at 18th St., Midtown* ☎ *916/498–
1388* ⊕ *streetsoflondon.net.*

THE ARTS
California Musical Theatre. The California Musical Theatre presents
Broadway shows at the Sacramento Community Center Theater. The
group presents its summer Music Circus offerings (think *Fiddler*,
Grease) at the spacious Wells Fargo Pavilion. ✉ *1419 H St., at 14th
St., Downtown* ☎ *916/557–1999* ⊕ *www.calmt.com.*

Crest Theatre. The art-deco Crest is a beloved venue for classic and art-
house films, along with concerts and other cultural events. ✉ *1013
K St., at 10th St., Downtown* ☎ *916/442–7378* ⊕ *www.thecrest.com.*

Sacramento Box Office. Tickets to major comedy, music, theater, and other cultural and sports events are sold through this online vendor. ⊠ *Downtown, Sacramento* ☎ *888/546–8561* ⊕ *sacramentoboxoffice.com.*

SHOPPING

Greater Sacramento is filled with shops you've heard of. To try something new, wander through Midtown, especially J, K, and L streets between 16th and 26th streets.

The Galleria at Roseville. The Sacramento region's largest shopping complex is a sprawling, heavily trafficked collection of chain stores and restaurants. It's always jumping. ⊠ *1151 Galleria Blvd., north of Sacramento off I–80 Exit 105A, Roseville* ⊕ *www.westfield.com/galleriaatroseville.*

Scout Living. The members of this collective are specialists in home accessories and antique, vintage, and modern furniture. Even if you're not looking to redecorate, the shop's a wonder to walk through. ⊠ *1215 18th St., at L St. Capitol Mall Alley, Sacramento* ☎ *916/594–7971,* ⊕ *www.scoutliving.com.*

WOODLAND

20 miles northwest of Sacramento on I–5.

In its heyday, Woodland was among California's wealthiest cities. Established by gold seekers and entrepreneurs, it later became an agricultural gold mine. The legacy of the old land barons can be seen in the restored Victorian and Craftsman architecture downtown; the best examples can be found south of Main Street on College, Elm, 1st, and 2nd streets. Budget cuts have led to extremely reduced hours for the Yolo Historical Museum (⊕ *www.gibsonhouse.org*) and the 1896 Woodland Opera House (⊕ *www.woodlandoperahouse.org*), so the town's undisputed top attraction is the delightful Heidrick Ag History Center.

GETTING HERE AND AROUND

Yolobus (⊕ *www.yolobus.com*) serves downtown Woodland from Sacramento, though most visitors arrive by car.

ESSENTIALS

Visitor Information Woodland Chamber of Commerce ⊠ *307 1st St., at Dead Cat Alley* ☎ *530/662–7327* ⊕ *www.woodlandchamber.org.*

EXPLORING

☺ ★ **Heidrick Ag History Center Tractor & Truck Museum.** This gigantic space provides a marvelous overview of the entire history of motorized agricultural vehicles. Souped-up and shiny, the antique threshers, harvesters, combines, tractors, and proto-tractors on display here look ready to service the farms of their eras all over again. And there's more. A separate wing surveys the evolution of the truck, with an emphasis on ones used for farm work. ⊠ *1962 Hays La., off County Rd. 102* ☎ *530/666–9700* ⊕ *www.aghistory.org* ⊠ *$8* ☾ *Mid-Mar.–early Nov., Wed.–Sun. 10–5; early Nov.–mid-Mar., 10–4 daily.*

DAVIS

10 miles west of Sacramento on I–80.

Davis began as a rich agricultural area and remains one, but it doesn't feel like a cow town. It's home to the University of California at Davis, whose students hang at downtown cafés, galleries, and bookstores (most of the action takes place between 1st and 4th and C and G streets), lending the city a vaguely cosmopolitan feel.

GETTING HERE AND AROUND

Most people arrive here and tour by car. Yolobus (⊕ *www.yolobus.com*) serves Davis from Sacramento. Downtown is compact and walkable. Touring by bicycle is also an option—Davis is mostly flat.

ESSENTIALS

Visitor Information Davis Chamber of Commerce ⊠ *640 3rd St., at E St.* ☎ *530/756–5160* ⊕ *www.davischamber.com.*

EXPLORING

University of California Davis. A top research university, UC Davis educates many of Wine Country's vintners and grape growers. Campus tours depart from Buehler Alumni and Visitors Center. On a tour or not, worthy stops include the well-tended **Arboretum** (⊕ *arboretum. ucdavis.edu*)—this is a major agricultural school, and it shows—and the **Mondavi Center for the Performing Arts** (⊕ *www.mondaviarts.org*), a striking modern glass structure that books top-tier artists. ⊠ *Visitor Center, Alumni La.* ☎ *530/752–8111* ⊕ *visit.ucdavis.edu* ☯ *Visitor-center weekdays 8–5, Sat. 10–2; campus tours Sat. at 11:30.*

THE GOLD COUNTRY—SOUTH

This hilly region has an old-timey vibe. It's rich with antiques shops, quaint coffee shops, and delightfully appointed Victorian B&Bs.

PLACERVILLE

10 miles south of Coloma on Hwy. 49; 44 miles east of Sacramento on U.S. 50.

It's hard to imagine now, but in 1849 about 4,000 miners staked out every gully and hillside in Placerville, turning the town into a rip-roaring camp of log cabins, tents, and clapboard houses. The area was then known as Hangtown, a graphic allusion to the nature of frontier justice. It took on the name Placerville in 1854 and became an important supply center for the miners. ("Placer" is defined roughly as valuable minerals found in riverbeds or lakes.) Mark Hopkins, Philip Armour, and John Studebaker were among the industrialists who got their starts here.

GETTING HERE AND AROUND

Placerville is a 45-minute drive east of downtown Sacramento via U.S. 50. There is no public bus link worth mentioning. You'll need a car to get here and around.

EXPLORING

Apple Hill. During the fall harvest season (from September through December), the members of the Apple Hill Growers Association open their orchards and vineyards for apple and berry picking, picnicking, and wine and cider tasting. Many sell baked items and picnic food. At other times of the year, various roadside stands sell produce and other items. The association's website has a map you can download. ⚠ Traffic on October weekends is often backed up. ⊠ *About 5 miles east of Hwy. 49; take Camino exit from U.S. 50* ☎ *530/644–7692* ⊕ *www. applehill.com.*

☾ **Hangtown's Gold Bug Park & Mine.** Hangtown's Gold Bug Park & Mine, ★ owned by the City of Placerville, centers on a fully lighted mine shaft open for self-guided touring. ■ TIP➔ An audio tour is included with admission and greatly enriches the experience. A shaded stream runs through the park, and there are picnic facilities. ⊠ *2635 Goldbug La., off Bedford Ave., 1 mile off U.S. 50* ☎ *530/642–5207* ⊕ *www.goldbugpark. org* 🖾 *$5* ☾ *Apr.–Oct., daily 10–4; Nov.–Mar., weekends noon–4. Gift shop Apr.–Oct., daily 10–4.*

WHERE TO EAT AND STAY

$ ✕ **The Cozmic Cafe.** Crowds convene here at any time of day for health-
VEGETARIAN ful wraps, burritos, sandwiches, salads, and the like, plus breakfasts (served anytime), smoothies, and coffee drinks. The portions are big, prices are low, and the ambience is distinctive. The eatery is in the 1859 Pearson's Soda Works Building and extends back into the side of a mountain, into what used to be a mineshaft. The live music here is among the best in the foothills, and an upstairs pub beckons with local wines and microbrews; unwind with yoga classes in the ballroom there before the evening's libations. ⑤ *Average main: $9* ⊠ *594 Main St., at Bedford Ave.* ☎ *530/642–8481* ⊕ *www.ourcoz.com.*

$$ 🛏 **Seasons Bed & Breakfast.** A 10-minute walk from downtown, one of
B&B/INN Placerville's oldest homes has been transformed into a lovely and relaxing oasis. **Pros:** quiet setting; attentive hosts; great breakfasts. **Cons:** B&B environment not for everyone. **TripAdvisor:** "beautiful escape," "top-notch service," "pampered beyond our wildest dreams."⑤ *Rooms from: $135* ⊠ *2934 Bedford Ave.* ☎ *530/626–4420* ⊕ *www.theseasons. net* ⊃ *1 room, 2 suites* ⧣⊙ *Breakfast.*

SHENANDOAH VALLEY

20 miles south of Placerville on Shenandoah Rd., east of Hwy. 49.

The most concentrated Gold Country wine-touring area lies in the hills of the Shenandoah Valley, east of Plymouth. Robust Zinfandel is the primary grape grown here, but vineyards also produce other varietals. Most wineries are open on weekend afternoons; several have shaded picnic areas, gift shops, and galleries or museums; all have tasting rooms. ■ TIP➔ This region is gaining steam as a less-congested alternative to the Napa Valley.

Continued on page 854

EUREKA! CALIFORNIA'S GOLD RUSH

When James W. Marshall burst into John Sutter's Mill on January 24, 1848, carrying flecks of gold in his hat, the millwright unleashed the glittering California gold rush with these immortal words:

"Boys, I believe I've found a gold mine!"

Before it was over, drowsy San Francisco had become the boomtown of the Golden West, Columbia's mines alone yielded $87,000,000, and California's Mother Lode—a vein of gold-bearing quartz that stretched 150 miles across the Sierra Nevada foothills—had been nearly tapped dry. Even though the gold rush soon became the gold bust, today you can still strike it rich by visiting the historic sites where it all happened.

Journey down the Gold Country Highway—a serpentine, nearly 300-mi-long two-lane route appropriately numbered 49—to find pure vacation treasure: fascinating mother lode towns, rip-roaring mining camps, and historic strike sites. In fact, in Placerville—as the former Hangtown, this spot saw so much new money and crime that outlaws were hanged in pairs—you can still pan the streams. And after you've seen the sights, the prospects remain just as golden: the entire region is a trove of gorgeous wineries, fun eateries, and Victorian-era hotels.

by: Reed Parsell and Robert I.C. Fisher

ALL THAT GLITTERED: '49ER FEVER

From imagination springs adventure, and perhaps no event in the 19th century provoked more wild adventures than the California gold rush of 1848 to 1855.

James Marshall

1856 U.S. quarter

John Sutter

GOLD IN THEM THAR HILLS California's golden lava was discovered purely by accident. Upon finding his cattle ranch had gone to ruin while he was away fighting in the Mexican-American War, New Jersey native James W. Marshall decided to build a sawmill, with John Sutter, outside the town of Coloma, 40 miles upstream of Sutter's Fort on the American River. To better power the mill, he had a wider siphon created to divert the river water and, one morning, spotted golden flakes in the trench. Rich fur magnate Sutter tried to keep the mother strike quiet, but his own staff soon decamped to pan the streams and the secret was out. The gold rush's impact was so profound that, practically overnight, it catapulted San Francisco into one of the nation's—and the world's—wealthiest cities.

BROTHER, CAN YOU SPARE AN INGOT? After Marshall, 37 at the time, saw his fledgling mill abandoned by workers who went to pan the streams, he left Coloma for almost a decade. During the 1860s he made some money as a vintner there—a dicey profession for a reported alcoholic. Eventually Marshall's wine business dried up, and he returned to prospecting in the 1870s. But without success. For six years starting in 1872, the state Legislature gave him a small pension as an acknowledgment of his gold rush importance, but for the last years of his life he was practically penniless. He died on Aug. 10, 1885, at age 74.w

THE GOLD CRUSH Before the gold rush ended, in 1855, it is estimated that it drew 300,000 people—Americans, Europeans, and Chinese—to the Sierra Nevada foothills to seek their fortune. Sadly, accidents, disease, and skirmishes with Native Americans took their toll on both the prospectors and the environment. In addition, the gold lust of '49er fever left more than a thousand murders in its wake (not counting the infamous "suspended" sentences meted out at Hangtown).

BOOM TO BUST

Jan. 24, 1848: James W. Marshall spies specks of bright rock in the streambed at his sawmill's site; Sutter certifies they are gold.
May, 1848: California's coastal communities empty out as prospectors flock to the hills to join the "forty-eighters."
Aug. 19, 1848: The *New York Herald* is the first East Coast newspaper to report a gold rush in California.
Oct. 13, 1849: California's state constitution is approved in Monterey. The state's new motto becomes "Eureka!"
1855: The California gold rush effectively ends, as digging for the precious mineral becomes increasingly difficult, and large corporations monopolize mining operations.

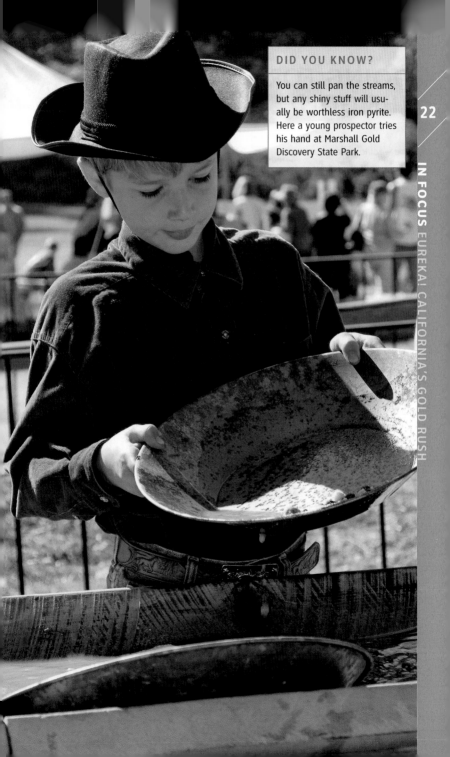

DID YOU KNOW?

You can still pan the streams, but any shiny stuff will usually be worthless iron pyrite. Here a young prospector tries his hand at Marshall Gold Discovery State Park.

GOING FOR THE GOLD

Marshall Gold Discovery State Park

If you want to go prospecting for the best sightseeing treasures in Gold Country, just follow this map.

Coloma

Empire Mine State Historic Park, Grass Valley: During the century that it was operating, Empire Mine produced some 5.6 million ounces of gold. More than 350 miles of tunnels were dug, most under water. Operations ceased in 1956, but today visitors to the 800-acre park can go on 50-minute guided tours of the mines and enjoy great hiking trails and picnic spots.

Marshall Gold Discovery State Historic Park, Coloma: Here's where it all began—a can't-miss gold rush site. See the stone cairn that marks the spot of James Marshall's discovery, the huge statue of him that rests on his grave site, and visit—together with crowds of schoolchildren—the updated museum, and more.

Hangtown's Gold Bug Park & Mine, Placerville: Put on a hardhat and step into the 19th century at Gold Bug, located a few miles south of Marshall's jackpot site. Take a self-guided audio tour of a mine that opened in 1888, or a special tour of a mine opened in the 1850s, and do some "placering" (panning for gold) yourself, outside the gift shop. "Fool's gold" (used for billiard tables and chalkboards) was mostly found here before digging stopped in 1942.

Man pans for gold during gold rush.

| Empire Mine State Historic Park | Gold sifting pan | Columbia State Historic Park |

Sutter Gold Mine: Between Amador City and Sutter Creek off Highway 49, this is the place to see how the so-called "Forty-Niner" individual prospectors were succeeded by large, deep-pocket mining companies. One-hour tours, offered daily April through most of October, take visitors deep into a hard-rock mine, where they can see ore veins that contain gold and learn the basics of hydraulic extraction.

Kennedy Gold Mine, Jackson: At 5,912 feet below ground, this is one of the world's deepest mines. Its head frame is one of the most dominant man-made sights along Highway 49's 295 miles. In operation from 1880 until World War II, the mine produced tens of millions of dollars of gold. One-hour tours, offered weekends and holidays from March through October, include a look inside the stately Mine Office.

Columbia State Historic Park

Columbia State Historic Park. Just north of Sonora, this is the best extant example of a gold rush-era town as it appeared in the mid-19th century. During its "golden" years, Columbia yielded more than $85 million in gold. Since World War II, the town has been restored. Fandango halls, Wells Fargo stage coaches, and a costumed staff bring a working 1850's mining town to life again.

Gold dollars

Mariposa Museum and History Center, Mariposa: Find all sorts of mining equipment, including a five-stamp ore mill, at this modest museum in the gold rush region's southernmost area. Also here is the fascinating California State Mining and Mineral Museum, home to a famous 13-pound golden nugget.

A PROSPECTING PRIMER

Grab any non-Teflon-coated pan with sloping sides and head up to "them thar hills." Find a stream—preferably one containing black sand—you can stoop beside, and then:

■ Scoop out sediment to fill your pan.

■ Add water, then gently shake the pan sideways, back and forth. This allows any gold to settle at the bottom.

■ Pick out and toss away any larger rocks.

■ Keep adding water, keep shaking the pan, and slowly pour the loosened waste gravel over the rim of the pan, making sure not to upend the pan while doing so.

■ If you're left with gold, yell "Eureka!" then put it in a glass container. Your findings may not make you rich, but will entitle you to bragging rights for as long as you keep the gold handy to show friends.

■ TIP➔ If you'd rather not pan on your own, plenty of attractions and museums in the Gold Country will let you try your hand at prospecting. See listings in this chapter for more details on these historic sites.

GETTING HERE AND AROUND

Reach the Shenandoah Valley by turning east on Fiddletown Road in Plymouth, between Placerville and Sutter Creek. You will need a car to explore the valley and its vineyards.

EXPLORING

Charles Spinetta Winery. Here, you can see a wildlife art gallery in addition to tasting the wine. The Zinfandel and Syrah are popular. ✉ *12557 Steiner Rd., off Shenandoah Rd.* ☎ *209/245–3384* ⊕ *www. charlesspinettawinery.com* ⊗ *Mon., Thurs., and Fri. 8–4; weekends 9–5.*

Shenandoah Vineyards. The gallery at this Sobon-affiliated winery (one of the valley's original four) displays contemporary art, and sells pottery, framed photographs, and souvenirs. ✉ *12300 Steiner Rd.* ☎ *209/245– 4455* ⊕ *www.sobonwine.com* ⊗ *Daily 10–5.*

Sobon Estate. Exhibits in the winery's Shenandoah Valley Museum illustrate pioneer life and wine making in the valley. The family-owned business is listed as a California State Historic Landmark. ✉ *14430 Shenandoah Rd., east of Ostrom Rd.* ☎ *209/245–4455* ⊕ *www. sobonwine.com* ⊗ *Daily 9:30–5.*

AMADOR CITY

6 miles south of Plymouth on Hwy. 49.

The history of tiny Amador City mirrors the boom-bust-boom cycle of many Gold Country towns. With an output of $42 million in gold, its Keystone Mine was one of the most productive in the Mother Lode. After all the gold was extracted, the miners cleared out, and the area suffered. Amador City now derives its wealth from tourists, who come to browse through its antiques and specialty shops, most of them on or just off Highway 49.

GETTING HERE AND AROUND

Park where you can along Old Highway 49 (a bypass diverts Highway 49 traffic around Sutter Creek and Amador City), and walk around this blink-and-you'll-miss-it town.

WHERE TO STAY

For expanded reviews, facilities, and current deals, visit Fodors.com.

$
B&B/INN
★

⊡ **Imperial Hotel.** The whimsically decorated mock-Victorian rooms at this 1879 hotel give a modern twist to the excesses of the era; the antique furnishings include iron-and-brass beds, gingerbread flourishes, and, in one room, art-deco appointments. **Pros:** comfortable; good restaurant and bar; tiny-town charm. **Cons:** the town's got no nightlife. **TripAdvisor:** "dinner is first class," "take a step back in time," "charming." ⑤ *Rooms from: $120* ✉ *14202 Old Hwy. 49* ☎ *209/267– 9172* ⊕ *www.imperialamador.com* ⇗ *6 rooms, 3 suites* � *Breakfast.*

SUTTER CREEK

★ *2 miles south of Amador City on Hwy. 49.*

Sutter Creek is a charming conglomeration of balconied buildings, Victorian homes, and neo–New England structures. The stores on Main Street (formerly part of busy Highway 49, which was rerouted around town) are worth visiting for works by the many local artists and craftspeople.

22

GETTING HERE AND AROUND

There are no public transportation options here, but Sutter Creek is very walkable once you've found a parking spot.

EXPLORING

Monteverde Store Museum. This store, opened 1896, is a relic from the past. Forty years ago, its final owner walked out without telling a soul and never returned, but you can still visit everything he left behind on the shelves including typical wares from the turn of the 20th century, an elaborate antique scale, and a chair-encircled potbellied stove in the corner. The store is open Thursday through Monday provided there are volunteers available. ⊠ *3 Randolph St.* ☎ *209/267–0493.*

Sutter Creek Visitor Center. The visitor center organizes walking tours and has a helpful website. ⊠ *71A Main St.* ☎ *209/267–1344, 800/400–0305* ⊕ *www.suttercreek.org.*

WHERE TO EAT AND STAY

$$
AMERICAN
✕ **Susan's Place.** Fresh produce, prompt and attentive service, and a lovely patio (especially so on warm summer evenings) distinguish this local favorite a half block off the main drag. The serving of wine is a big deal here; there's even a "mystery wine" option that leaves the bottle (or glass) choice up to the owner. Try the eggplant and Portobello mushrooms on grilled panini bread. $ *Average main: $16* ⊠ *15 Eureka St.* ☎ *209/267–0945* ☉ *Closed Mon.–Wed.*

$$
B&B/INN
★
🛏 **Eureka Street Inn.** The lead- and stained-glass windows and the original redwood paneling, wainscoting, and beams—and, oh yes, those gas-log fireplaces in most rooms—lend the Eureka Street Inn a cozy feel. **Pros:** quiet location; lovely porch; engaging owners; WiFi; large private bathrooms. **Cons:** only four rooms. **TripAdvisor:** "friendly and relaxing," "pleasant experience," "incredibly fantastic." $ *Rooms from: $125* ⊠ *55 Eureka St.* ☎ *209/267–5500, 800/399–2389* ⊕ *www. eurekastreetinn.com* ⟿ *4 rooms* ⦿ *Breakfast.*

$$
B&B/INN
★
🛏 **The Foxes Inn of Sutter Creek.** The rooms in this 1857 white-clapboard house are handsome, with high ceilings, antique beds, and armoires; five have gas fireplaces. **Pros:** lovely inside and out; friendly owners. **Cons:** pricey. **TripAdvisor:** "best bed and breakfast," "so close and so good," "absolutely fabulous." $ *Rooms from: $160* ⊠ *77 Main St.* ☎ *209/267–5882, 800/987–3344* ⊕ *www.foxesinn.com* ⟿ *5 rooms, 2 suites* ⦿ *Breakfast.*

$
HOTEL
🛏 **Sutter Creek Days Inn.** If you're on a budget, this hotel is a good choice; the rooms have coffeemakers, and most have queen-size beds. **Pros:** affordable; convenient; clean. **Cons:** can feel a bit impersonal. **TripAdvisor:** "simple but friendly," "clean and presentable," "well situated."

$ *Rooms from: $89* ⊠ *271 Hanford St.* ☎ *209/267–9177* ⊕ *www. daysinn.com/suttercreek* ⥲ *52 rooms* ⊙ *Breakfast.*

JACKSON

8 miles south of Sutter Creek on Hwy. 49.

Jackson wasn't the Gold Country's rowdiest town, but the party lasted longer here than most anywhere else: "girls' dormitories" (aka brothels) and nickel slot machines flourished until the mid-1950s. Jackson also had the world's deepest and richest gold mines, the Kennedy and the Argonaut, which together produced $70 million in gold. These were deep-rock mines with tunnels extending as much as a mile underground. Most of the miners who worked the lode were of Serbian or Italian origin, and they gave the town a European character that persists to this day. Jackson has pioneer cemeteries whose headstones tell the stories of local Serbian and Italian families.

GETTING HERE AND AROUND

Arrive here via automobile on Highway 49. You'll need a car to see Jackson and the nearby sites.

EXPLORING

St. Sava Serbian Orthodox Church. The terraced cemetery on the grounds of the handsome church is the town's most impressive burial grounds. ⊠ *724 N. Main St.*

WHERE TO EAT

$ ✕ **Mel and Faye's Diner.** For more than a half-century this roadside (loom-
AMERICAN ing over Highway 49 on a small hill) diner has been a local hangout, with its signature "Moo Burger" (so big it still makes cow sounds, presumably). Mel and Faye's son now runs the business and has supplemented the menu with slightly more sophisticated fare for breakfast, lunch, and dinner. $ *Average main: $10* ⊠ *31 Main St.* ☎ *209/223–0853* ⊕ *melandfayesdiner.com* ⊙ *Closed Tues. No dinner.*

ANGELS CAMP

20 miles south of Jackson on Hwy. 49.

Angels Camp is famous chiefly for its May jumping-frog contest, based on Mark Twain's short story "The Celebrated Jumping Frog of Calaveras County." The writer reputedly heard the story of the jumping frog from Ross Coon, proprietor of Angels Hotel, which has been in operation since 1856.

GETTING HERE AND AROUND

Angels Camp is at the intersection of Highway 49 and Highway 4, which from here heads northeast past Murphys up into the Sierra Nevada. You'll need a car to get here and around.

EXPLORING

Angels Camp Museum. Here you'll find gold-rush relics, including photos, rocks, petrified wood, old blacksmith and mining equipment, and a horse-drawn hearse. The carriage house out back holds 31 carriages and an impressive display of mineral specimens. ⊠ *753 S. Main St.*

☎ *209/736–2963* ⊕ *www.angelscampmuseumfoundation.org* ✉ *$5* ⊗ *Jan. and Feb., weekends 10–4; Mar.–Dec., daily 10–4.*

☾ **California Cavern.** A ½-mile subterranean trail winds through large chambers and past underground streams and lakes. There aren't many steps to climb, but it's a strenuous walk with some narrow passageways and steep spots. The caverns, at a constant 55°F, contain crystalline formations not found elsewhere, and the 80-minute guided tour explains local history and geology. Call ahead to check on hours of operation, which are subject to change. ⊠ *9 miles east of San Andreas on Mountain Ranch Rd., then about 3 miles on Cave City Rd.* ☎ *209/736–2708* ⊕ *www.caverntours.com* ✉ *$14.75* ⊗ *Mar. and Apr., daily 10–4; May–Oct., daily 10–5; Nov.–Feb. weekends 10–4.*

☾ **Moaning Cavern.** A 235-step spiral staircase leads into this vast cavern. More adventurous sorts can rappel into the chamber—ropes and instruction are provided. Otherwise, the only way inside is via the 45-minute tour, during which you'll see giant (and still growing) stalactites and stalagmites and an archaeological site that holds some of the oldest human remains yet found in America (an unlucky person has fallen into the cavern about once every 130 years for the last 13,000 years). ■TIP→ Caves are a great place to visit on rainy or especially hot days. Outside there are three zip lines, starting at $39 per person. ⊠ *5350 Moaning Cave Rd., off Parrots Ferry Rd., about 2 miles south of Vallecito* ☎ *209/736–2708* ⊕ *www.caverntours.com* ✉ *$14.75* ⊗ *May–Oct., daily 9–6; Nov.–Apr., weekdays 10–5, weekends 9–5.*

Fodor's Choice
★

MURPHYS

10 miles northeast of Angels Camp on Hwy. 4.

Murphys is a well-preserved town of white-picket fences, Victorian houses, and interesting shops that exhibits an upscale vibe, with its nearby wineries and free-spending Bay Area visitors. Horatio Alger and Ulysses S. Grant came through here, staying at Murphys Historic Hotel & Lodge when they, along with many other 19th-century tourists, came to see the giant sequoia groves in nearby Calaveras Big Trees State Park.

GETTING HERE AND AROUND
Although Murphys is 10 miles off Highway 49, the diversion on Highway 4 is worth it, as Murphys presents the Gold Country's most compact, orderly town, with enough shops and restaurants to keep most families busy for at least a half-day. You'll need to drive here, and parking can be a challenge on busy summer weekends.

EXPLORING
Calaveras Big Tree State Park. The Calaveras Big Tree State Park protects hundreds of the largest and rarest living things on the planet—magnificent giant sequoia redwood trees. Some are 3,000 years old, 90 feet around at the base, and 250 feet tall. There are campgrounds and picnic areas; swimming, wading, fishing, and sunbathing on the Stanislaus River are popular in summer. ⊠ *Off Hwy. 4, 15 miles northeast of Murphys, 4 miles northeast of Arnold, Angels Camp* ☎ *209/795–2334* ⊕ *www.parks.ca.gov/?page_id=551* ✉ *$6 per vehicle day use; campsites*

$20 ☉ Park daily sunrise–sunset day use. Visitor center May–Oct., daily 11–3; Nov.–Apr., weekends 11–3.

Ironstone Vineyards. Tours take you through the spectacular gardens and into underground tunnels cooled by a waterfall from a natural spring, and include a performance on a massive automated pipe organ. ■ **TIP→** It's worth a visit even if you don't drink wine. The winery schedules concerts during summer in its huge outdoor amphitheater, plus art shows and other events on weekends. On display is a 44-pound specimen of crystalline gold. Visit the deli for lunch. ⊠ *From Jones St. in town, head south on Scott St., 1894 6 Mile Rd.* ☎ *209/728–1251* ⊕ *www.ironstonevineyards.com ☉ Daily 10–5; open until 6 in summer.*

WHERE TO EAT AND STAY

$$
AMERICAN

✕ **Grounds.** Light entrées, grilled vegetables, chicken, seafood, and steak are the specialties at this bustling bistro and coffee shop. Sandwiches, salads, and homemade soups are served for lunch. The crowd is friendly and the service attentive. ⑤ *Average main: $18* ⊠ *402 Main St.* ☎ *209/728–8663* ⊕ *www.groundsrestaurant.com ☉ No dinner Mon.–Tues.*

$
HOTEL

🏨 **Murphys Historic Hotel & Lodge.** This 1855 stone hotel, whose register has seen the signatures of Mark Twain and the bandit Black Bart, figured in Bret Harte's short story "A Night at Wingdam." **Pros:** historical ambience; great bar; in the middle of downtown. **Cons:** dated; creaky. **TripAdvisor:** "historic and fun," "quaint and convenient," "homey." ⑤ *Rooms from: $109* ⊠ *457 Main St.* ☎ *209/728–3444, 800/532–7684* ⊕ *www.murphyshotel.com* ⤴ *29 rooms, 20 with bath.*

COLUMBIA

14 miles south of Angels Camp via Hwy. 49 to Parrots Ferry Rd.

Columbia is the gateway for Columbia State Historic Park, which is one of the Gold Country's most visited sites.

GETTING HERE AND AROUND

The only way to get here is by private automobile. Consider bringing picnic supplies, as there are several inviting spots within and around the town.

EXPLORING

ⓒ
Fodor's Choice
★

Columbia State Historic Park. Though definitely showing wear from state budget cuts, Columbia comes as close to a gold-rush town in its heyday as any site in the Gold Country. Usually, you can ride a stagecoach, pan for gold, and watch a blacksmith working at an anvil. Street musicians perform in summer. Restored or reconstructed buildings include a Wells Fargo Express office, a Masonic temple, stores, saloons, two hotels, a firehouse, churches, a school, and a newspaper office. At times, all are staffed to simulate a working 1850s town. The park also includes the **Historic Fallon House Theater,** where entertainment is presented much of the year. The town's two 19th-century historic lodgings, the Fallon Hotel ($) and City Hotel ($–$$) recently reopened; find out more at ⊕ *www.cityhotel.com.* ⊠ *11175 Washington St.* ☎ *209/532–0150* ⊕ *www.parks.ca.gov/?page_id=552* 🎟 *Free ☉ Daily 9–5.*

SONORA

4 miles south of Columbia via Parrots Ferry Rd. to Hwy. 49.

Miners from Mexico founded Sonora and made it the biggest town in the Mother Lode. Following a period of racial and ethnic strife, the Mexican settlers moved on, and Yankees built the commercial city that is visible today. Sonora's historic downtown section sits atop the Big Bonanza Mine, one of the richest in the state. Another mine, on the site of nearby Sonora High School, yielded 990 pounds of gold in a single week in 1879. Reminders of the gold rush are everywhere in Sonora, in prim Victorian houses, typical Sierra-stone storefronts, and awning-shaded sidewalks. Reality intrudes beyond the town's historic heart, with strip malls, shopping centers, and modern motels.

GETTING HERE AND AROUND

Sonora represents a bit of a parking challenge, what with its busy main drag (Washington Street, which is Highway 49) and its narrow, often very steep side roads.

EXPLORING

Tuolumne County Museum and History Center. The small museum occupies a historic gold rush–era building that served as a jail until 1960. Vintage firearms and paraphernalia, gold specimens, and MiWuk baskets are among the many artifacts on display. ⊠ *158 W. Bradford St., at Lower Sunset Dr.* ☎ *209/532–1317* ⊕ *www.tchistory.org* ✉ *Free* ⊙ *Weekdays 10–4, Sat. 10–3:30.*

WHERE TO EAT AND STAY

$
AMERICAN
✕ **Diamondback Grill and Wine Bar.** The bright decor and refined atmosphere suggest more ambitious fare, but burgers are what this place is about. Locals crowd the tables, especially after 6 pm, for the ground-meat patties, beer-battered onion rings, veggie burger, and fine wines. ⑤ *Average main: $11* ⊠ *93 S. Washington St., at Lineberg St.* ☎ *209/532–6661* ⊕ *www.thediamondbackgrill.com* ⊙ *Closed Sun.*

$$
B&B/INN
☷ **Barretta Gardens Bed and Breakfast Inn.** This inn is perfect for a romantic getaway, with elegant Victorian rooms varying in size, all furnished with period pieces. **Pros:** lovely grounds; yummy breakfasts; romantic. **Cons:** only seven rooms. **TripAdvisor:** "ultimate B&B," "cozy and charming," "great ambience." ⑤ *Rooms from: $155* ⊠ *700 S. Barretta St.* ☎ *209/532–6039, 800/206–3333* ⊕ *www.barrettagardens.com* ⇆ *7 rooms* ⑩ *Breakfast.*

JAMESTOWN

4 miles south of Sonora on Hwy. 49.

Compact Jamestown supplies a touristy view of gold rush–era life. Shops in brightly colored buildings along Main Street sell antiques and gift items. You can try your hand at panning for gold here or, if state budget cuts haven't forced its complete closure, visit Railtown 1897 (⊕ *www.railtown1897.org*), the local (mostly) outdoor railroad museum.

GETTING HERE AND AROUND

Jamestown is a car town. Highway 108 bisects the town east–west.

EXPLORING

☼ **Gold Prospecting Adventures.** You'll get a real feel (sort of) for the life of a prospector on the three-hour gold-panning excursions led by this outfit's congenial, steeped-in-history tour guides. You might even strike gold (people do) at the Jimtown Mine, and though it probably won't even cover your costs, you're likely to enjoy the experience, especially if traveling with kids. ⊠ *18170 Main St.* ☎ *209/984–4653, 800/596–0009* ⊕ *www.goldprospecting.com.*

WHERE TO STAY

For expanded reviews, facilities, and current deals, visit Fodors.com.

$$
HOTEL
🏨 **National Hotel.** The National has been in business since 1859, and the furnishings—brass beds, regal comforters, and lace curtains—are authentic but not overly embellished. **Pros:** wonderful historic feel; great brunches—especially the crepes. **Cons:** only nine rooms. **TripAdvisor:** "beautiful stay," "food is fantastic," "this place is a gem." ⑤ *Rooms from: $140* ⊠ *18183 Main St.* ☎ *209/984–3446, 800/894–3446 in CA* ⊕ *www.national-hotel.com* ⬐ *9 rooms* ❍ *Breakfast.*

MARIPOSA

50 miles south of Jamestown on Hwy. 49.

Mariposa marks the southern end of the Mother Lode. Much of the land in this area was part of a 44,000-acre land grant Colonel John C. Fremont acquired from Mexico before gold was discovered and California became a state.

GETTING HERE AND AROUND

Many people stop here on the way to Yosemite National Park, about an hour's drive east on Highway 140. YARTS (⊕ *www.yarts.com*), the regional transit system, is a cheap and dependable way to travel among Merced (off the Central Valley's busy Highway 99), Mariposa, and Yosemite Valley. YARTS partners with Amtrak so that riders on the Central Valley's San Joaquin line can detrain in Merced and catch a bus right at the train station. Otherwise, you'll need a car to get here.

WHERE TO EAT AND STAY

$$$
AMERICAN
✕ **Charles Street Dinner House.** Ever since Ed Uebner moved here from Chicago to become the owner-chef in 1980, Charles Street has been firmly established as the classiest dinner joint in town—plus, it's centrally located. The extensive menu includes beef, chicken, pork, lamb, duck, and lobster; recently a few vegetarian options were added. ⑤ *Average main: $25* ⊠ *Hwy. 140 and 7th St.* ☎ *209/966–2366* ⊕ *www.charlesstreetdinnerhouse.com* ☾ *No lunch.*

$
B&B/INN
🏨 **Little Valley Inn.** Historical photos and old mining tools add a little charm to this modern lodging, located about 7 miles south of Mariposa. **Pros:** quiet; comfortable; small. **Cons:** about an hour from Yosemite National Park. **TripAdvisor:** "nice comfortable stay," "charming rooms," "a mountain of hospitality." ⑤ *Rooms from: $115* ⊠ *3483*

Brooks Rd., off Hwy. 49 ☎ *209/742–6204, 800/889–5444* ⊕ *www. littlevalley.com* ⇀ *6 cabins, 1 suite* ⎮⊙⎮ *Breakfast.*

THE GOLD COUNTRY—NORTH

Gold has had a significant presence along this northern stretch of Highway 49, whose highlights include the bucolic Empire State Historic Park and Coloma, where the discovery of a few nuggets triggered the gold rush.

COLOMA

8 miles northwest of Placerville on Hwy. 49.

The California gold rush started in Coloma. "My eye was caught with the glimpse of something shining in the bottom of the ditch," James Marshall recalled. Marshall himself never found any more "color," as gold came to be called.

GETTING HERE AND AROUND

The only practical way to get here is by car. Once you've parked, it's easy enough to walk about town and see all the worthwhile sites.

EXPLORING

Ⓒ ★ **Marshall Gold Discovery State Historic Park.** Most of Coloma lies within the historic park. Though crowded with tourists in summer, Coloma hardly resembles the mob scene it was in 1849, when 2,000 prospectors staked out claims along the streambed. The town's population grew to 4,000, supporting seven hotels, three banks, and many stores and businesses. But when reserves of the precious metal dwindled, prospectors left as quickly as they had come. A working reproduction of an 1840s mill lies near the spot where James Marshall first saw gold. A trail leads to a sign marking his discovery. ■TIP→ **The museum is not as interesting as the outdoor exhibits.** ✉ *310 Back St., off Hwy. 49* ☎ *530/622–3470* ⊕ *www.parks.ca.gov/?page_id=484* ⊡ *$5 per vehicle, day use* ⊙ *Park daily 8–sunset. Museum daily 10–3.*

WHERE TO STAY

For expanded reviews, facilities, and current deals, visit Fodors.com.

$$
B&B/INN
Coloma Country Inn. Four of the rooms at this B&B on 2½ acres in the state historic park are inside an 1850s farmhouse, and two suites with kitchenettes occupy the carriage house. **Pros:** convenient to the park; quiet; leisurely ambience. **Cons:** no nightlife. **TripAdvisor:** "charming accommodations," "beautiful grounds," "pleasant and relaxing getaway." ⑤ *Rooms from: $125* ✉ *345 High St.* ☎ *530/622–6919* ⊕ *www.colomacountryinn.com* ⇀ *4 rooms, 2 suites* ⎮⊙⎮ *Breakfast.*

AUBURN

18 miles northwest of Coloma on Hwy. 49; 34 miles northeast of Sacramento on I-80.

Auburn is the Gold Country town most accessible to travelers on Interstate 80. An important transportation center during the gold rush,

Auburn has a small Old Town district with narrow climbing streets, cobblestone lanes, wooden sidewalks, and many original buildings. ■TIP→ Fresh produce, flowers, baked goods, and gifts are for sale at the farmers' market, held Saturday morning year-round.

GETTING HERE AND AROUND
You can get here via Amtrak or Greyhound. Otherwise, count on driving and needing a car to see all other Gold Country attractions.

EXPLORING
Bernhard Museum Complex. Party like it's 1889 at this diverting complex, whose main structure opened in 1851 as the Traveler's Rest Hotel and for 100 years was the residence of the Bernhard family. The congenial docents, dressed in Victorian garb, describe the family's history and 19th-century life in Auburn. ⊠ *291 Auburn–Folsom Rd., at Fairgate Rd.* ☎ *530/889–6500* ☏ *Free* ⊙ *Tues.–Sun. 11–4.*

🄫 **Gold Country Museum.** You'll get a feel for life in the mines at this museum whose highlights include a re-created mine tunnel, a gold-panning stream, and a reproduction saloon. ⊠ *1273 High St., off Auburn–Folsom Rd.* ☎ *530/889–6500* ☏ *Free to museum, $3 to pan for gold* ⊙ *Tues.–Sun. 11–4.*

Placer County Courthouse. Auburn's standout structure is the Placer County Courthouse. The classic gold-dome building houses the Placer County Museum, which documents the area's history—Native American, railroad, agricultural, and mining—from the early 1700s to 1900. ⊠ *101 Maple St., at Lincoln Way* ☎ *530/889–6500* ☏ *Free* ⊙ *Daily 10–4.*

WHERE TO EAT AND STAY
$
AMERICAN
✕ **Awful Annie's.** Big patio umbrellas (and outdoor heaters when necessary) allow patrons to take in the Old Town view from this popular spot for lunch or breakfast—one specialty is a chili omelet. Find an Awful Annie's outlet in nearby Lincoln. ⑤ *Average main: $10* ⊠ *160 Sacramento St., at Washington St.* ☎ *530/888–9857* ⊕ *www.awfulannies.com* ⊙ *No dinner.*

$$
ECLECTIC
✕ **Latitudes.** Delicious multicultural cuisine is served in an 1870 Victorian. The menu (with monthly specials from diverse geographical regions) includes meat entrées prepared with the appropriate Mexican spices, curries, cheeses, or teriyaki sauce. Vegetarians and vegans have several inventive choices, including tofu and tempeh dishes. Sunday brunch is deservedly popular. ⑤ *Average main: $16* ⊠ *130 Maple St., at Auburn-Folsom Rd.* ☎ *530/885–9535* ⊕ *www.latitudesrestaurant.com* ⊙ *Closed Mon. and Tues.*

$$
HOTEL
🛏 **Holiday Inn.** On a hill above the freeway across from Old Town, this hotel has a welcoming lobby and chain-standard but attractively furnished rooms. **Pros:** convenient; clean; large rooms. **Cons:** rooms near parking lot can be noisy. **TripAdvisor:** "on the way to Tahoe," "met expectations," "a nice friendly place." ⑤ *Rooms from: $124* ⊠ *120 Grass Valley Hwy.* ☎ *530/887–8787, 800/814–8787* ⊕ *www.auburnhi.com* ⇆ *96 rooms, 6 suites.*

Almost 6 million ounces of gold were extracted from the Empire Mine.

GRASS VALLEY

24 miles north of Auburn on Hwy. 49.

More than half of California's total gold production was extracted from mines around Grass Valley, including the Empire Mine, which, along with the North Star Mining Museum, is among the Gold Country's most fascinating attractions.

GETTING HERE AND AROUND

Highway 20 arrives here from Interstate 5 to the west and Interstate 80 to the east; otherwise, you'll likely get here via Highway 49 from Placerville. Gold Country Stage vehicles (☎ *530/447–0103* ◷ *Weekdays 7–6*) serve some attractions here. Expect to wait, though.

EXPLORING

Empire Mine State Historic Park. The hard-rock gold mine at Empire Mine State Historic Park was one of California's richest. An estimated 5.8 million ounces were extracted from its 367 miles of underground passages between 1850 and 1956. On the 50-minute tours you can walk into a mine shaft, peer into the mine's deeper recesses, and view the owner's "cottage," which has exquisite woodwork. With its shaded picnic areas and gentle hiking trails, this is a pleasant place for families. ⊠ *10791 E. Empire St., south of Empire St. exit of Hwy. 49* ☎ *530/273–8522* ⊕ *www.parks.ca.gov/?page_id=875* ⬛ *$5* ◷ *May–Aug., daily 9–6; Sept.–Apr., daily 10–5. Tours May–Aug., daily on hr 11–4; Sept.–Apr., weekends at 1 (cottage only) and 2 (mine yard only), weather permitting.*

Holbrooke Hotel. The landmark hotel, built in 1851, hosted entertainer Lola Montez and writer Mark Twain as well as a stream of U.S. presidents including Ulysses S. Grant. Its restaurant-saloon is one of the oldest operating west of the Mississippi. ✉ *212 W. Main St., at N. Church St.* ☎ *530/273–1353, 800/933–7077* ⊕ *www.holbrooke.com.*

Lola Montez House. In the center of town, on the site of the original, stands a reproduction of the home of Lola Montez, the notorious dancer, singer, and courtesan whose popularity with gold-rush-era miners derived from her suggestive "spider dance." Lola repaired to Grass Valley after wearing out her welcome in Europe, where her lovers included the composer Franz Liszt and the ill-fated King Ludwig of Bavaria. (Her calls for democracy contributed to Ludwig's overthrow and her banishment as a witch—or so the story goes.) Religion has recently found Lola: A local church bought her repro house in late 2011. ✉ *248 Mill St., at Walsh St.*

☺ **North Star Mining Museum.** Housed in the former North Star powerhouse, the museum displays the 32-foot-high enclosed Pelton Water Wheel, said to be the largest ever built. It was used to power mining operations and was a forerunner of the modern turbines that generate hydroelectricity. Hands-on displays are geared to children. There's a picnic area nearby. ✉ *10933 Allison Ranch Rd., north of Empire St. exit of Hwy. 49* ☎ *530/273–4255* ⊕ *nevadacountyhistory.org* ✐ *Donation requested* ⊙ *May–mid-Oct., daily 10–5.*

WHERE TO EAT AND STAY

$ ✕ **Cousin Jack Pasties.** Meat- and vegetable-stuffed pasties are a taste of
BRITISH   the region's history, having come across the Atlantic with Cornish miners and their families in the mid-19th century. The flaky crusts practically melt in your mouth. A simple food stand, Jack's is nonetheless a local landmark. ⑤ *Average main: $8* ✉ *100 S. Auburn St., at Main St.* ☎ *530/272–9230* ▬ *No credit cards.*

$$ ✕ **Villa Venezia Restaurant.** Pasta and seafood are the specialties served up
ITALIAN   in a cozy, warm Victorian building with an intimate patio area. Seafood stew is one of the most-ordered entrées. ⑤ *Average main: $21* ✉ *124 Bank St., at Stewart St.* ☎ *530/273–3555* ⊕ *www.villavenezia.info* ⊙ *No lunch Sat.–Thurs.*

$ ⌂ **Holiday Lodge.** This modest hotel is close to many of the town's main
HOTEL   attractions, and its staff can help arrange historical tours of Nevada City, Grass Valley, and the small town of Washington. **Pros:** good price; friendly staff. **Cons:** feels a bit dated. **TripAdvisor:** "great family environment," "good value," "comfortable and very clean." ⑤ *Rooms from: $77* ✉ *1221 E. Main St.* ☎ *530/273–4406, 800/742–7125* ⊕ *www. holidaylodge.biz* ⟿ *35 rooms* ✵ *Breakfast.*

NEVADA CITY

4 miles north of Grass Valley on Hwy. 49.

Nevada City, once known as the Queen City of the Northern Mines, is the most appealing of the northern Mother Lode towns. The iron-shutter brick buildings that line the narrow downtown streets contain antiques shops, galleries, boutiques, B&Bs, restaurants, and a winery. Horse-drawn carriage tours add to the romance, as do gas street lamps. At one point in the 1850s, Nevada City had a population of nearly 10,000—enough to support much cultural activity. Today, about 3,000 people live here.

GETTING HERE AND AROUND

Highway 20 arrives here from Interstate 5 to the west and Interstate 80 to the east; otherwise, you'll likely get here via Highway 49. Gold Country Stage vehicles (☎ 530/447–0103 ☉ Weekdays 7–6) serve some attractions here.

ESSENTIALS

Visitor Information Nevada City Chamber of Commerce ⊠ 132 Main St. ☎ 530/265–2692 ⊕ www.nevadacitychamber.com.

EXPLORING

Firehouse No. 1. With its gingerbread-trim bell tower, Firehouse No. 1 is one of the Gold Country's most distinctive buildings. A museum, it houses gold-rush artifacts and the altar from a Chinese joss house (temple). ⊠ 214 Main St., at Coyote St. ☎ 530/265–5468 ⊠ Donation requested ☉ May–Nov., Tues.–Sun. 1–4.

Miners Foundry. The Miners Foundry, erected in 1856, produced machines for gold mining and logging. The Pelton Water Wheel, a power source for the mines (the wheel also jump-started the hydroelectric power industry), was invented here. The cavernous building hosts plays, concerts, receptions, and other events. ⊠ 325 Spring St., at Bridge St. ☎ 530/265–5040 ⊕ www.minersfoundry.org.

Nevada City Winery. You can watch wine being created while you sip at the Nevada City Winery, where the tasting room overlooks the production area. ⊠ Miners Foundry Garage, 321 Spring St., at Bridge St. ☎ 530/265–9463, 800/203–9463 ⊕ www.ncwinery.com ⊠ Free ☉ Tastings Sun.–Thurs. noon–5, Fri. and Sat. noon–6.

Nevada Theatre. This redbrick edifice, constructed in 1865, is California's oldest theater building. Mark Twain, Emma Nevada, and many other notable people appeared on its stage. These days, plays and old films are presented here. ⊠ 401 Broad St., at Commercial St. ☎ 530/265–6161, 530/274–3456 for film showtimes ⊕ www.nevadatheatre.com.

WHERE TO EAT AND STAY

$$$
ECLECTIC
✕ **Friar Tuck's.** Popular Friar T's specializes in aromatic, interactive fondues and has an extensive seafood menu. The sparkling interior has a late-19th century ambience—it's one of Nevada City's best indoor spaces. ⓢ Average main: $23 ⊠ 111 N. Pine St., at Broad St. ☎ 530/265–9093 ⊕ friartucks.com ☉ No lunch.

$$$
AMERICAN
✕ **New Moon Cafe.** An attractively lighted room gives diners a cozy feeling, though loyal patrons have been known to complain about the high noise level. Organic flours and free-range meats are used when available. ⓢ Average main: $25 ⊠ 203 York St., at Commercial St.

☎ *530/265–6399* ⊕ *www.thenewmooncafe.com* ⊘ *Closed Mon. No lunch weekends.*

$ ✕ **South Pine Cafe.** Locals flock here, especially for brunch. Although
AMERICAN lobster and beef are on the menu, the real attention-grabbers are vegetarian entrées and side dishes, such as breakfast potatoes and apple-ginger muffins. A regional hit, South Pine also has branches in Grass Valley and Auburn. ⑤ *Average main: $11* ⊠ *110 S. Pine St., at Spring St.* ☎ *530/265–0260* ⊕ *www.southpinecafe.com* ⊘ *Daily 8–3.*

$$ ⛱ **Red Castle Historic Lodgings.** Handsome antique furnishings and Oriental rugs decorate the rooms of this 1857 Gothic-revival mansion, a fine
B&B/INN option for those who appreciate the finer points of Victorian interior
Fodor's Choice design. **Pros:** friendly owners; spectacular food; fascinating architecture;
★ hillside setting overlooking town. **Cons:** you'll get a workout walking up the hill from downtown. **TripAdvisor:** "romantic," "authentic historical experience," "very accommodating." ⑤ *Rooms from: $155* ⊠ *109 Prospect St.* ☎ *530/265–5135, 800/761–4766* ⊕ *www.redcastleinn.com* ⛽ *4 rooms, 3 suites* ⦿ *Breakfast.*

22

Lake Tahoe

WITH RENO, NEVADA

WORD OF MOUTH

"Lake Tahoe is quiet after Labor Day. The weather is beautiful and all of the activities . . . the hiking, touring the lake by paddlewheel boat, dining, and shopping, are still open and running."

—artjoanne

WELCOME TO LAKE TAHOE

TOP REASONS TO GO

★ **The lake:** Blue, deep, and alpine pure, Lake Tahoe is far and away the main reason to visit this high Sierra paradise.

★ **Snow, snow, snow:** Daring black-diamond runs or baby-bunny bumps—whether you're an expert, a beginner, or somewhere in between, there are many slopes to suit your skills at the numerous Tahoe-area ski parks.

★ **The great outdoors:** A ring of national forests and recreation areas, linked by miles of trails make Tahoe a nature-lover's paradise.

★ **Dinner with a view:** You can picnic lakeside at state parks or dine in restaurants perched along the shore.

★ **A date with lady luck:** Whether you want to roll dice, play the slots, or hope the blackjack dealer goes bust before you do, you'll find round-the-clock gambling at the casinos in Reno and on the Nevada side of the lake.

1 California Side. With the exception of Stateline, Nevada—which, aside from its casino-hotel towers, seems almost indistinguishable from South Lake Tahoe, California—the California side is more developed than the Nevada side. Here you can find both commercial enterprises—restaurants, motels, lodges, resorts, residential subdivisions—and public-access facilities, such as historic sites, parks, campgrounds, marinas, and beaches.

2 Nevada Side. You don't need a highway sign to know when you've crossed from California into Nevada: the flashing lights and elaborate marquees of casinos announce legal gambling in garish hues. But you'll find more here than tables and slot machines. Reno, the Biggest Little City in the World, has a vibrant art scene and a serene downtown RiverWalk. And when you really need to get away from the chip-toting crowds, you can hike through pristine wilderness at Lake Tahoe–Nevada State Park, or hit the slopes near Incline Village.

GETTING ORIENTED

In the northern section of the Sierra Nevada mountain range, the Lake Tahoe area covers portions of five national forests, several state parks, and rugged wilderness areas with names like Desolation and Granite Chief. Lake Tahoe, the star attraction, straddles California and Nevada and is one of the world's largest, clearest, and deepest alpine lakes. The region's proximity to the Bay Area and Sacramento to the west and Reno to the east draws thrill-seekers during ski season and summer, when water sports, camping, and hiking are the dominant activities.

23

TO SACRAMENTO AND
SAN FRANCISCO

80

Sugar
Bowl

Donner
Lake

Donner
Memorial
State Park

Truckee

89

267

Northstar-
at-Tahoe

Olympic
Valley

Squaw
Peak

Camp

Village at
Squaw Valley

Tahoe
National Forest

TO
RENO

Mtn Rose
10,776 ft.

Humboldt–
Toiyabe
National Forest

TO
RENO

431

Rose
Knob

Kings Beach
State Recreation
Area

Tahoe Vista

Carnelian Bay

Cedar Flat

28

Carnelian
Bay

Incline Village

2

Crystal
Bay

Kings
Beach

Crystal Bay

Brockway

Sand Harbor
Beach

Thunderbird
Lodge

395

Washoe
Lake

Lake Tahoe
Nevada
State Park

River

Tahoe City

Twin
Peaks

89

1

Tahoe Pines

Homewood

Tahoma

Meeks Bay

Rubicon

Rubicon
River

Rubicon
Peak

89

Emerald Bay
State Park

El Dorado
National
Forest

Sugar Pine Point
State Park

Rubicon
Bay

D. L. Bliss
State Park

Emerald Bay

Lake
Tahoe
el 6,229 ft.

CALIFORNIA
NEVADA

Glenbrook

Cave Rock

Lakeridge

Skyland

Snow Valley
Peak
9,214 ft.

28

50

Genoa Peak
9,150 ft.

Humboldt–
Toiyabe
National
Forest

Zephyr
Cove

C A R S O N   R A N G E

50

206

Genoa

Kingsbury

207

Stateline

East Peak

207

206

Jacks Peak

Fallen Leaf
Lake

Pope-Baldwin
Recreation
Area

South Lake
Tahoe

50

89

Meyers

TO PLACERVILLE
AND SACRAMENTO

5 mi

5 km

California

Updated by Christine Vovakes

Stunning Lake Tahoe is the largest alpine lake in North America, famous for its clarity, cobalt-blue water, and surrounding snowcapped peaks. Straddling the state line between California and Nevada, it lies 6,225 feet above sea level in the Sierra Nevada.

The border gives this popular resort region a split personality. About half its visitors are intent on low-key sightseeing, hiking, fishing, camping, and boating. The rest head directly for the Nevada side, where bargain dining, big-name entertainment, and the lure of a jackpot draw them into the glittering casinos.

The typical way to explore the Lake Tahoe area is to drive the 72-mile road that follows the shore through wooded flatlands and past beaches, climbing to vistas on the rugged southwest side of the lake and passing through busy commercial developments and casinos on its northeastern and southeastern edges. Another option is to actually go out *on* the 22-mile-long, 12-mile-wide lake on a sightseeing cruise or kayaking trip.

The lake, the communities around it, the state parks, national forests, and protected tracts of wilderness are the region's main draws, but other nearby destinations are gaining in popularity. Truckee, with an Old West feel and hot new restaurants, entices visitors looking for a relaxed pace and easy access to Tahoe's north shore and Olympic Valley ski parks. And today Reno, once known only for its casinos, attracts tourists with its buzzing arts scene, revitalized downtown riverfront, and campus events at the University of Nevada.

PLANNING

WHEN TO GO

A sapphire-blue lake shimmering deep in the center of an ice-white wonderland—that's Tahoe in winter. But those blankets of snow mean lots of storms that often close roads and force chain requirements on the interstate. In summer the roads are open, but the lake and lodgings are clogged with visitors seeking respite from valley heat. If you don't ski, the best times to visit are early fall—September and October—and late spring. The crowds thin, prices dip, and you can count on Tahoe being beautiful.

Most Lake Tahoe accommodations, restaurants, and even a handful of parks are open year-round, but many visitor centers, mansions, state parks, and beaches are closed from October through May. During those months, winter-sports enthusiasts swamp Tahoe's downhill resorts and cross-country centers, North America's largest concentration of skiing facilities. In summer it's cooler here than in the scorched Sierra Nevada foothills, the clean mountain air is bracingly crisp, and the surface temperature of Lake Tahoe is an invigorating 65°F to 70°F (compared with 40°F to 50°F in winter). This is also the time, however, when it may seem as if every tourist at the lake—100,000 on peak weekends—is in a car on the main road circling the shoreline (especially on Highway 89, just south of Tahoe City; on Highway 28, east of Tahoe City; and on U.S. 50 in South Lake Tahoe). Christmas week and July 4th are the busiest times, and prices go through the roof; plan accordingly.

GETTING HERE AND AROUND

AIR TRAVEL

The nearest airport to Lake Tahoe is Reno–Tahoe International Airport (RNO), in Reno, 50 miles northeast of the closest point on the lake. Airlines serving RNO include Alaska, American, Delta, Southwest, United, and US Airways. These airlines plus Frontier, Hawaiian, and JetBlue serve Sacramento International Airport (SMF), 112 miles from South Lake Tahoe. North Lake Tahoe Express runs buses ($40 one way, $75 round-trip) between RNO and towns on the lake's western and northern shores, plus Incline Village, Truckee, and Squaw Valley. South Tahoe Express runs buses ($27.50 one-way, $49 round-trip) between Reno–Tahoe Airport and resort hotels in the South Lake Tahoe area.

Airports Reno–Tahoe International Airport ⊠ *2001 E. Plumb La., off U.S. 395, Exit 65B, Reno, Nevada* ☎ *775/328–6400* ⊕ *www.renoairport.com.* **Sacramento International Airport** ⊠ *6900 Airport Blvd., 12 miles northwest of downtown off I–5, Sacramento, California* ☎ *916/929–5411* ⊕ *www.sacramento.aero/smf.*

Transfers North Lake Tahoe Express ☎ *866/216–5222* ⊕ *www.northlaketahoeexpress.com.* **South Tahoe Express** ☎ *775/325–8944, 866/898–2463* ⊕ *www.southtahoeexpress.com.*

BUS TRAVEL

Greyhound stops in Sacramento, Truckee, and Reno. BlueGO ($2 per ride) provides year-round local service in South Lake Tahoe, Nifty 50 Trolley service to parks and other attractions during summer. On the north shore, Tahoe Area Regional Transit (TART; $1.75) operates buses between Tahoma and Incline Village and runs shuttles to Truckee. RTC RIDE buses ($2) serve the Reno area. All local rides require exact change.

In winter, BlueGO provides free ski shuttle service from South Lake Tahoe hotels and resorts to various Heavenly Mountain ski lodge locations. Most of the major ski resorts offer shuttle service to lodgings near them.

Bus Contacts Greyhound ☎ *800/231–2222* ⊕ *www.greyhound.com.* **BlueGO** ☎ *530/541–7149* ⊕ *www.bluego.org.* **RTC RIDE** ☎ *775/348–7433* ⊕ *www. rtcwashoe.com.* **Tahoe Area Regional Transit (TART)** ☎ *530/550–1212, 800/736–6365* ⊕ *www.laketahoetransit.com.*

CAR TRAVEL

Lake Tahoe is 198 miles northeast of San Francisco, a drive of less than four hours in good weather and light traffic—if possible avoid heavy weekend traffic, particularly leaving the San Francisco area for Tahoe on Friday afternoon and returning on Sunday afternoon. The major route is Interstate 80, which cuts through the Sierra Nevada about 14 miles north of the lake. From there Highway 89 and Highway 267 reach the west and north shores, respectively. U.S. 50 is the more direct route to the south shore, a two-hour drive from Sacramento. From Reno you can get to the north shore by heading south on U.S. 395 for 10 miles, then west on Highway 431 for 25 miles. For the south shore, head south on U.S. 395 through Carson City, and then turn west on U.S. 50 (50 miles total).

The scenic 72-mile highway around the lake is marked Highway 89 on the southwest and west shores, Highway 28 on the north and northeast shores, and U.S. 50 on the east and southeast. Sections of Highway 89 sometimes close during snowy periods, usually at Emerald Bay because of avalanche danger, which makes it impossible to complete the circular drive around the lake. Interstate 80, U.S. 50, and U.S. 395 are all-weather highways, but there may be delays while snow is cleared during major storms. Interstate 80 is a four-lane freeway; much of U.S. 50 is only two lanes with no center divider. Carry tire chains from October through May, or rent a four-wheel-drive vehicle. Most rental agencies do not allow tire chains to be used on their vehicles; ask when you book.

Contacts California Highway Patrol ☎ *530/577–1001 South Lake Tahoe* ⊕ *www.chp.ca.gov.* **Caltrans Current Highway Conditions** ☎ *800/427–7623* ⊕ *www.dot.ca.gov.* **Nevada Department of Transportation Road Information** ☎ *877/687–6237* ⊕ *www.safetravelusa.com/nv.* **Nevada Highway Patrol** ☎ *775/687–5300* ⊕ *www.nvdpspub.gov/nhp/roadhazard.aspx.*

TRAIN TRAVEL

Amtrak's cross-country rail service makes stops in Truckee and Reno. Amtrak also operates several buses daily between Reno and Sacramento to connect with coastal train routes.

Train Contact Amtrak ☎ *800/872–7245* ⊕ *www.amtrak.com.*

HEALTH AND SAFETY

In an emergency dial 911.

Hospital Contacts Barton Memorial Hospital ✉ *2170 South Ave., at 4th St., South Lake Tahoe* ☎ *530/541–3420* ⊕ *www.bartonhealth.org.* **St. Mary's Regional Medical Center** ✉ *235 W. 6th St., at N. Arlington Ave., Reno, Nevada* ☎ *775/770–3000 general information* ⊕ *www.saintmarysreno.org.* **Tahoe Forest Hospital** ✉ *10121 Pine Ave., at Levon Ave., off Donner Pass Rd., Truckee* ☎ *530/587–6011* ⊕ *www.tfhd.com.*

OUTDOORS AND BACKCOUNTRY TIPS

If you're planning to spend any time outdoors around Lake Tahoe, whether hiking, climbing, skiing, or camping, be aware that weather conditions can change quickly in the Sierra. To avoid a life-threatening case of hypothermia, always bring a pocket-size, fold-up rain poncho (available in all sporting-goods stores) to keep you dry. Wear long pants and a hat. Carry plenty of water. Because you'll likely be walking on granite, wear sturdy, closed-toe hiking boots, with soles that grip rock. If you're going into the backcountry, bring a signaling device (such as a mirror), emergency whistle, compass, map, energy bars, and water purifier. When heading out alone, tell someone where you're going and when you plan to return.

If you plan to ski, be aware of resort elevations. In the event of a winter storm, determine the snow level before you choose the resort you'll ski. Often the level can be as high as 7,000 feet, which means rain at some resorts' base areas but snow at others.

BackCountry, in Truckee, operates an excellent website with current information about how and where to (and where not to) ski, mountain bike, and hike in the backcountry around Tahoe. The store also stocks everything from crampons to transceivers. For storm information, check the National Weather Service's website; for ski conditions, visit ⊕ *ontheSnow.com.* For reservations at campgrounds in California state parks, contact Reserve America. If you plan to camp in the backcountry of the national forests, you'll need to purchase a wilderness permit, which you can pick up at the forest service office or at a ranger station at any forest entrance. If you plan to ski the backcountry, check the U.S. Forest Service's recorded information for conditions.

Contacts and Information BackCountry ✉ *11400 Donner Pass Rd., at Meadow Way, Truckee* ☎ *530/582–0909 Truckee* ⊕ *www.thebackcountry.net.* **National Weather Service** ⊕ *www.wrh.noaa.gov/rev.* **Reserve America** ☎ *800/444–7275* ⊕ *www.reserveamerica.com.* **U.S. Forest Service** ✉ *Office, 35 College Dr., South Lake Tahoe* ☎ *530/543–2600 general information, 530/587–3558 backcountry recording* ⊕ *www.fs.fed.us/r5/ltbmu.*

TOUR OPTIONS

The 312-passenger *Tahoe Queen,* a glass-bottom paddle wheeler, departs from South Lake Tahoe daily for 2½-hour sightseeing cruises year-round by reservation and 3-hour dinner-dance cruises daily from late spring to early fall (weekly the rest of the year). Fares range from $46 to $75. In winter the boat becomes a waterborne ski shuttle: $125 covers boat transportation from South Lake Tahoe to the Hyatt Regency dock at Incline Village and back again, a bus transfer to Northstar Ski Resort, a half-day lift ticket, and breakfast. From May through September, the *Sierra Cloud,* a 41-passenger catamaran, departs from the Hyatt Regency beach at Incline Village and cruises the north shore area. The fare is $60. The 520-passenger MS *Dixie II,* a stern-wheeler, sails year-round from Zephyr Cove to Emerald Bay on sightseeing, lunch, and dinner cruises. Fares range from $39 to $69.

Also in Zephyr Cove, Tahoe Boat Cruises operates the *Woodwind II,* a 50-passenger catamaran that sails on regular and champagne cruises from April through October. Fares range from $34 to $49. The company's *Safari Rose,* an 80-foot-long wooden motor yacht, departs from Tahoe Keys Marina for half-day cruises around the lake; $105, including lunch.

Lake Tahoe Balloons flies over the lake from May through October; the hour-long trips cost $250. The entire experience takes four hours total.

Tour Contacts Lake Tahoe Balloons ☎ *530/544–1221, 800/872–9294* ⊕ *www.laketahoeballoons.com.* **MS *Dixie II*** ✉ *Zephyr Cove Marina, 760 U.S. Hwy. 50, near Church St., Zephyr Cove, Nevada* ☎ *775/589–4906, 888/896–3830* ⊕ *www.zephyrcove.com/cruises.* **Sierra Cloud** ✉ *Hyatt Regency Lake Tahoe, 111 Country Club Dr., Incline Village* ☎ *775/831–4386* ⊕ *www.awsincline.com.* ***Tahoe Queen*** ✉ *Ski Run Marina, 900 Ski Run Blvd., off U.S. 50, South Lake Tahoe* ☎ *530/543–6191, 888/896–3830* ⊕ *www.zephyrcove.com/cruises.* **Tahoe Boat Cruises** ✉ *Zephyr Cove Resort, 760 U.S. Hwy. 50, near Church St., Zephyr Cove* ☎ *775/588–1881, 888/867–6394* ⊕ *www.tahoecruises.com.*

RESTAURANTS

On weekends and in high season, expect a long wait in the more popular restaurants. And expect to pay resort prices almost everywhere. Some restaurants are only open 6 out of 12 months a year; during the "shoulder seasons" (from April to May and September to November), some places may close temporarily or limit their hours, so call ahead. Also, check local papers for deals and discounts during this time, especially two-for-one coupons. Many casinos use their restaurants to attract gamblers. Marquees often tout "$8.99 prime rib dinners" or "$1.99 breakfast specials." Some of these meals are downright lousy and they are usually available only in the coffee shops and buffets, but at those prices, it's hard to complain. The finer restaurants in casinos deliver pricier food, as well as reasonable service and a bit of atmosphere. Unless otherwise noted, even the most expensive area restaurants welcome customers in casual clothes. *Prices in the reviews are the average cost of a main course at dinner or, if dinner is not served, at lunch.*

HOTELS

Quiet inns on the water, suburban-style strip motels, casino hotels, slope-side ski lodges, and house and condo rentals throughout the area constitute the lodging choices at Tahoe. The crowds come in summer and during ski season; reserve as far in advance as possible, especially for holiday periods when prices skyrocket. Spring and fall give you a little more leeway and lower—sometimes significantly lower—rates. Check hotel websites for the best deals.

Head to South Lake Tahoe for the most activities and the widest range of lodging options. Heavenly Village in the heart of town has an ice rink, cinema, shops, fine dining restaurants, and simple cafés, plus a gondola that will whisk you up to the ski park. Walk two blocks south from downtown, and you can hit the casinos.

Tahoe City, on the west shore, has a small-town atmosphere and is accessible to several nearby ski resorts. A few miles northwest of the lake, Squaw Valley USA has its own self-contained upscale village, a gondola to the slopes, and numerous outdoor activities once the snow melts.

Looking for a taste of old Tahoe? The north shore with its woodsy backdrop is your best bet, with Carnelian Bay and Tahoe Vista on the California side. And across the Nevada border are casino resorts where Hollywood's glamour-stars once romped. *Prices in the reviews are the lowest cost of a standard double room in high season. For expanded reviews, facilities, and current deals, visit Fodors.com.*

SKIING AND SNOWBOARDING

The mountains around Lake Tahoe are bombarded by blizzards throughout most winters and sometimes in fall and spring; 10- to 12-foot bases are common. Indeed, the Sierra often have the deepest snowpack on the continent, but because of the relatively mild temperatures over the Pacific, falling snow can be very heavy and wet—it's nicknamed Sierra Cement for a reason. The upside is that you can sometimes ski and board as late as July (snowboarding is permitted at all Tahoe ski areas). The major resorts get extremely crowded on weekends. If you're going to ski on a Saturday, arrive early and quit early. Avoid moving with the masses: eat at 11 am or 1:30 pm, not noon. Also consider visiting the ski areas with few high-speed lifts or limited lodging and real estate at their bases: Alpine Meadows, Sugar Bowl, Homewood, Mt. Rose, Sierra-at-Tahoe, Diamond Peak, and Kirkwood. And to find out the true ski conditions, talk to waiters and bartenders—most of whom are ski bums.

The Lake Tahoe area is also a great destination for Nordic skiers. "Skinny" (i.e., cross-country) skiing at the resorts can be costly, but you get the benefits of machine grooming and trail preparation. If it's bargain Nordic you're after, take advantage of thousands of acres of public forest and parkland trails.

VISITOR INFORMATION

Contacts Lake Tahoe Visitors Authority ✉ *169 U.S. Hwy. 50, Stateline* ☎ *775/588–5900, 800/288–2463* ⊕ *tahoesouth.com.* **OntheSnow.com** ⊕ *www.onthesnow.com/california/skireport.html.***U.S. Forest Service** ☎ *530/587–2158 backcountry recording* ⊕ *www.fs.usda.gov/tahoe.*

THE CALIFORNIA SIDE

The most hotels, restaurants, ski resorts, and state parks are on the California side of the lake, but you'll also encounter the most congestion and developed areas.

SOUTH LAKE TAHOE

50 miles south of Reno on U.S. 395 and U.S. 50; 198 miles northeast of San Francisco on I–80 and U.S. 50.

The city of South Lake Tahoe's raison d'être is tourism: the casinos of adjacent Stateline, Nevada; the ski slopes at Heavenly Mountain; the beaches, docks, bike trails, and campgrounds all around the south shore; and the backcountry of Eldorado National Forest and Desolation Wilderness. The main road into town, however, shows less attractive features: a mix of older motels, strip malls, and low-rise prefab-looking buildings that line both sides of U.S. 50. Though there are plenty of places to stay, we haven't recommended many because they're not top choices. The small city's saving grace is its convenient location and bevy of services, as well as its gorgeous lake views.

GETTING HERE AND AROUND

U.S. 50, the main route into South Lake Tahoe, changes its name to Lake Tahoe Boulevard and is the major road through the city. Arrive by car or, if coming from Reno Airport, take the South Tahoe Express bus. BlueGO operates daily bus service in the south shore area year-round, plus a ski shuttle from the large hotels to Heavenly Ski Resort in the winter.

ESSENTIALS

Visitor Information Lake Tahoe Visitors Authority ⊠ *Visitor Center, 169 U.S. Hwy. 50, at Kingsbury Grade, Stateline, Nevada* ☎ *775/588–5900, 800/288–2463* ⊕ *ltva.org* ⊠ *Visitor Center, 3066 Lake Tahoe Blvd., at San Francisco Ave.* ☎ *530/554–5050.*

EXPLORING

ⓒ
Fodor'sChoice
★
Heavenly Gondola. Whether you ski or not, you'll appreciate the impressive view of Lake Tahoe from the Heavenly Gondola. Its eight-passenger cars travel from the middle of town 2.4 miles up the mountain in 15 minutes. When the weather's fine, you can take one of three hikes around the mountaintop and then have lunch at Tamarack Lodge. Heavenly also offers day care for children. ⊠ *4080 Lake Tahoe Blvd.* ☎ *775/586–7000, 800/432–8365* ⊕ *www.skiheavenly.com* 🎫 *$32* ⊙ *Hrs vary; summer, daily 10–5; winter, daily 9–4.*

Heavenly Village. At the base of the gondola the Heavenly Village is the centerpiece of South Lake Tahoe's efforts to reinvent itself and provide a focal point for tourism. Essentially a pedestrian mall, it includes some good shopping, a cinema, an arcade for kids, and the Heavenly Village Outdoor Ice Rink. ⊠ *U.S. 50 and Heavenly Village Way.*

WHERE TO EAT

$
ECLECTIC
✕ **Blue Angel Café.** A favorite of locals, who fill the dozen or so wooden tables, this cozy spot serves basic sandwiches and salads along with internationally inspired dishes like chipotle shrimp tacos and Thai curry. The café has Wi-Fi. 🖫 *Average main: $12* ⊠ *1132 Ski Run Blvd., at Larch Ave.* ☎ *530/544–6544.*

$
MEXICAN
✕ **The Cantina.** A casual Tahoe favorite, the Cantina serves traditional Mexican dishes—huge burritos, enchiladas, and rellenos—as well as stylized Southwestern fare such as smoked-chicken polenta with grilled vegetables, and crab cakes in jalapeño cream sauce. The bartenders make great margaritas and serve 30 different kinds of beer. 🖫 *Average main: $13* ⊠ *765 Emerald Bay Rd., Hwy. 89, at 10th St.* ☎ *530/544–1233* ⊕ *www.cantinatahoe.com* ⚐ *Reservations not accepted.*

$$$
ECLECTIC
✕ **Evan's American Gourmet Cafe.** Its excellent service, world-class food, and superb wine list make this the top choice for high-end dining in South Lake. Inside a converted cabin, the restaurant serves creative American cuisine that includes catch-of-the-day seafood offerings and meat dishes such as roasted rack of lamb with citrus couscous. Some

Continued on page 886

TAHOE A LAKE FOR ALL SEASONS

by Christine Vovakes

Best known for its excellent skiing, Lake Tahoe is a year-round resort and outdoor sports destination. All kinds of activities are available, from snowboarding some of the best runs in North America and gliding silently along the lakeshore on cross-country skis in winter, to mountain biking through lush forests and puttering around the alpine lake in a classic yacht in summer. Whatever you do—and whenever you visit—the sapphire lake is at the center of it all, pulling you out of your posh resort or rustic cabin rental like a giant blue magnet. There are many ways to enjoy and experience Lake Tahoe, but here are some of our favorites.

(top) Heavenly Mountain Resort, (bottom) Sand Harbor Beach.

WINTER WONDERLAND

Home to a host of world-famous Sierra resorts, Tahoe is a premier ski destination. Add sledding, ice skating, cross-country skiing, and jingly sleigh rides under the stars to the mix, and you begin to get a glimpse of Tahoe's cold-weather potential.

DOWNHILL SKIING AND SNOWBOARDING

Even if you've never made it off the bunny hill before, you should definitely hit the slopes here at least once. The Lake Tahoe region has the deepest snowpack in North America, and you can ski from Thanksgiving until it melts—which is sometimes July.

One of the top-rated resorts in the country, Olympic Valley's **Squaw Valley USA** hosted the 1960 Winter Olympics that put Tahoe on the map. A great classic resort is **Sugar Bowl**, where you can revel in a bit of Disney nostalgia while you swoop down the slopes. Walt helped start the resort, which opened in 1939 and had Tahoe's first chair lift.

Even if you're not hitting the slopes at South Lake Tahoe's **Heavenly Mountain**, be sure to take a ride on their **Heavenly Gondola** so you can take in awe-inspiring views of the frozen circle of white ice that rings the brilliant lake.

(top) Skiing in Lake Tahoe,. (above left) Cross-country skiing, (above right) Snow boarding at Heavenly Mountain.

SKI RESORT	LOCATION	TRAILS	ACRES	BEGIN.	INTER.	ADV./EXP.
CALIFORNIA						
Alpine Meadows	Tahoe City	100	2,400	25%	40%	35%
Heavenly Mountain	South Lake Tahoe	94	4,800	20%	45%	35%
Homewood Mountain	Homewood	60	1,260	15%	50%	35%
Kirkwood	Kirkwood	72	2,300	15%	50%	35%
Northstar-at-Tahoe	Truckee	97	3,000	13%	60%	27%
Sierra-at-Tahoe	South Lake Tahoe	46	2,000	25%	50%	25%
Squaw Valley USA	Olympic Valley	170	4,000	25%	45%	30%
Sugar Bowl	Truckee	95	1,500	17%	45%	38%
NEVADA						
Diamond Peak	Incline Village	30	655	18%	46%	36%
Mt. Rose Ski Tahoe	Incline Village	61	1,200	20%	30%	50%

CROSS-COUNTRY SKIING

Downhill skiing may get all the glory here, but Lake Tahoe is also a premier cross-country (or Nordic) skiing destination. "Skinny" skiers basically have two options: pony up the cash to ski the groomed trails at a resort, or hit the more rugged (but cheaper—or free) public forest and parkland trails.

Beautiful **Royal Gorge** is the country's largest cross-country ski resort. Other resorts with good skinny skiing include **Kirkwood, Squaw Valley USA, Tahoe Donner,** and **Northstar-at-Tahoe.** Private operators **Spooner Lake Cross Country** and **Hope Valley Cross Country** will also have you shushing through pristine powder in no time.

For bargain Nordic on public trails, head to **Sugar Pine Point State Park.** Other good low-cost cross-country skiing locations include **Donner Memorial State Park, Lake Tahoe—Nevada State Park,** and **Tahoe Meadows** near Incline Village.

CAUTION⚠ Cross-country skiing is relaxing and provides a great cardiovascular workout—but it's also quite strenuous. If it's your first time out or you're not in great shape, start out slow.

SLEDDING AND TUBING

Kirkwood, Squaw Valley USA, Boreal, Soda Springs, and many other Tahoe resorts have areas where you can barrel down hills on inflatable tubes. Some good non-resort sledding spots are **Tahoe National Forest** and **Tahoe Meadows,** near Incline Village.

ICE SKATING

Want to work on your triple lutz? You can skate seasonally at **Heavenly Village Outdoor Ice Rink,** or year-round at the **South Tahoe Ice Arena.** Other great gliding spots include **Squaw Valley USA's Olympic Ice Pavilion.**

WARMING UP

To defrost your ski-stiff limbs, take a dip in a resort's heated pool, de-stress in a hotel spa…or enjoy a brandy by the fire at a cozy restaurant. Our favorite places to warm up and imbibe include Graham's of Squaw Valley and Soule Domain, near Crystal Bay.

Lake Tahoe
Outdoor Activities

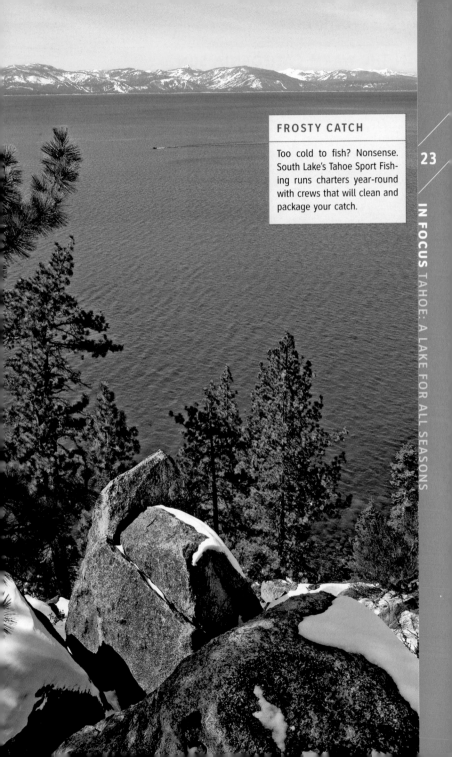

FROSTY CATCH

Too cold to fish? Nonsense. South Lake's Tahoe Sport Fishing runs charters year-round with crews that will clean and package your catch.

IN THE WARM CALIFORNIA SUN

Summer in Tahoe means diving into pure alpine waters, hiking a mountain trail with stunning lake views, or kayaking on glorious Emerald Bay. From tennis to golf to fishing, you can fill every waking moment with outdoor activity—or just stretch out on a sunny lakeside beach with a good book and a cool drink.

HIKING

The lake is surrounded by protected parkland, offering countless opportunities to take jaunts through the woods or rambles along lakeside trails.

One of the most unique hiking experiences in Tahoe is at Heavenly Mountain Resorts, where the **Heavenly Gondola** runs up to three nice trails. When you're done enjoying sky-high views of the lake, grab lunch at the nearby Tamarack Lodge.

Another out-of-the-ordinary option is a romantic moonlit trek. **Camp Richardson** has lots of trails and a long curve of lake to catch the moonlight.

In **Eldorado National Forest and Desolation Wilderness,** you can hike a small portion of the famous Pacific Crest Trail and branch off to discover beautiful back-country lakes. Nearby **Eagle Falls** has stunning views of Emerald Bay.

One of Tahoe's best hikes is a 4½-mi trail at **D.L. Bliss State Park;** it has lovely views of the lake and leads to bizarre **Vikingsholm** (*see box on next page*).

Other great places to hike in Lake Tahoe include **Sugar Pines Point State Park, Olympic Valley's Granite Chief Wilderness, Squaw Valley USA's High Camp, Donner Memorial State Park,** and **Lake Tahoe—Nevada State Park.**

You can pick up hiking maps at the **U.S. Forest Service** office at the **Lake Tahoe Visitor Center.**

HIT THE BEACH

Lake Tahoe has some gorgeous lakeside sunbathing terrain; get to perennial favorite **Kings Beach State Recreation Area** early to snag a choice spot. Or, if you never want to be far from the water, reserve one of the prime beachside spots at **D.L. Bliss State Park Campground.**

MOUNTAIN BIKING AND CYCLING

You don't need to be preparing for the Tour de France to join the biking fun. While there are myriad rugged mountain biking trails to choose from, the region is also blessed with many flat trails.

Truly intrepid cyclists take the lift up **Northstar-at-Tahoe** and hit the resort's 100 mi of trails. Another good option is **Sugar Pine Point State Park,** where you can hop on a 10-mi trail to Tahoe City.

Tahoe Sports in South Lake Tahoe is a good place for bike rentals and tips for planning your trip. **Cyclepath Mountain Bikes Adventures** in Truckee leads guided mountain biking tours, and **Flume Trail Bikes** on the Nevada side of the lake, near Glenbrook, rents bikes and operates a bike shuttle to popular trails.

LAKE TOURS AND KAYAKING

One of the best ways to experience the lake is by getting out on the water.

The *Tahoe Queen* is a huge glass-bottomed paddle-wheel boat that offers sightseeing cruises and dinner-dance cruises; in winter, it's the only water-borne ski shuttle in the world. The *Sierra Cloud, MS Dixie II,* and *Woodwind II* also ply the lake, offering a variety of enjoyable cruises. *(See Tour Options in the Planner section of this chapter for contact info.)*

Another enjoyable option is taking a throwback wooden cruiser from Tahoe Keys Marina in South Lake Tahoe to tour **Thunderbird Lodge,** the meticulously crafted stone mansion built in 1936 by socialite George Whittell.

For a more personal experience, rent a kayak and glide across **Emerald Bay. Kayak Tahoe** in South Lake Tahoe will have you paddling in no time.

VIKINGS?

As you kayak around Tahoe, you'll see many natural wonders…and a few manmade ones as well. One of the most impressive and strangest is **Vikingsholm**, a grand 1929 estate that looks like an ancient Viking castle. You can see it from **Emerald Bay** (which, appropriately, resembles a fjord), or hike to it via a steep one-mile trail.

(left top) Biking along the shore. (left bottom) Kayaking. (right) Steamboat cruise.

diners find the table spacing a tad close. Evan's is intimate, to be sure, but the food always pleases. $ *Average main: $30* ✉ *536 Emerald Bay Rd., Hwy. 89, at 15th St.* ☎ *530/542–1990* ⊕ *www.evanstahoe.com* ✪ *No lunch*.

$$$$
ASIAN
✕ **Kalani's.** Fresh-off-the-plane seafood gets flown directly from the Honolulu fish market to Heavenly Village's sexiest (and priciest) restaurant. The sleek, white-tablecloth dining room is decked out with carved bamboo, a burnt-orange color palette, and a modern-glass sculpture, all of which complement contemporary Pacific Rim specialties such as melt-from-the-bone baby back pork ribs with sesame-garlic soy sauce. Sushi selections with inventive rolls and sashimi combos, plus less expensive vegetarian dishes, add depth to the menu. $ *Average main: $33* ✉ *1001 Heavenly Village Way, at U.S. 50* ☎ *530/544–6100* ⊕ *www.kalanis.com* ✪ *No lunch weekdays in winter*.

$
AMERICAN
✕ **Red Hut Café.** A vintage-1959 Tahoe diner, all chrome and red plastic, the Red Hut is a tiny place with a wildly popular breakfast menu: huge omelets; banana, pecan, and coconut waffles; and other tasty vittles. A second branch, the only one that serves dinner (there's also a soda fountain), is also in South Lake, and there's a third location in Stateline. $ *Average main: $8* ✉ *2723 Lake Tahoe Blvd., near Blue Lake Ave.* ☎ *530/541–9024* ⊕ *www.redhutcafe.com* ⚏ *Reservations not accepted* ▭ *No credit cards* ✪ *No dinner at either location*.

$$
ITALIAN
✕ **Scusa! Italian Ristorante.** This longtime favorite moved recently, but the kitchen still turns out big plates of veal scallopine, chicken piccata, and linguine with clams—straightforward Italian-American food (and lots of it), served in an intimate dining room warmed by a crackling fire. The new location has an outdoor patio that's open in warm weather. $ *Average main: $18* ✉ *2543 Lake Tahoe Blvd., near Silver Dollar Ave.* ☎ *530/542–0100* ⊕ *www.scusalaketahoe.com* ✪ *No lunch*.

WHERE TO STAY

For expanded reviews, facilities, and current deals, visit Fodors.com.

$$$
B&B/INN
Fodor's Choice
★
🛏 **Black Bear Inn Bed and Breakfast.** South Lake Tahoe's most luxurious inn feels like one of the grand old lodges of the Adirondacks. **Pros:** intimate; serene, woodsy grounds; within walking distance of good restaurants. **Cons:** not appropriate for children under 16; pricey. **TripAdvisor:** "extremely accommodating," "amazing gardens," "great place to be pampered." $ *Rooms from: $225* ✉ *1202 Ski Run Blvd.* ☎ *530/544–4451, 877/232–7466* ⊕ *www.tahoeblackbear.com* ⇥ *5 rooms, 4 cabins* ⫶⊙⫶ *Breakfast*.

$$
HOTEL
☾
🛏 **Camp Richardson.** An old-fashioned family resort that is built around a 1920s lodge, this property features a few dozen cabins and a small inn, all tucked beneath giant pine trees on 80 acres fronting Lake Tahoe. **Pros:** lakeside location; wide choice of lodgings. **Cons:** dated style; no phones or TVs in some rooms. **TripAdvisor:** "retro stay right on the lake," "beautiful place to stay," "no wonder Lucky Baldwin lived here." $ *Rooms from: $105* ✉ *1900 Jameson Beach Rd.* ☎ *530/541–1801, 800/544–1801* ⊕ *www.camprichardson.com* ⇥ *27 lodge rooms, 40 cabins, 7 inn rooms, 212 campsites; 100 RV sites*.

$$
HOTEL
★
🛏 **Inn by the Lake.** Across the road from a beach, the "inn" is essentially a high-end motel, with spacious, spotless rooms and suites.

Pros: great value; stellar service; short drive from Heavenly Mountain. Cons: on busy Lake Tahoe Boulevard. **TripAdvisor:** "a heavenly holiday," "nice location," "very relaxing." $ *Rooms from:* $140 ✉ 3300 Lake Tahoe Blvd. ☎ 530/542–0330, 800/877–1466 ⊕ www.innbythelake.com ⟳ 90 rooms, 10 suites.

23

$$$
RESORT
★
Marriott's Grand Residence and Timber Lodge. You can't beat the location of these two gigantic, modern condominium complexes right at the base of Heavenly Gondola, smack in the center of town. **Pros:** central location; great for families; within walking distance of excellent restaurants. **Cons:** can be jam-packed on weekends. **TripAdvisor:** "great facilities," "great service," "perfect location and large rooms." $ *Rooms from:* $159 ✉ 1001 Heavenly Village Way ☎ 530/542–8400, 800/627–7468 ⊕ www.marriott.com ⟳ 431 condos.

$$
RESORT
Sorensen's Resort. Escape civilization by staying in a log cabin at this woodsy 165-acre resort within the Eldorado National Forest, 20 minutes south of town. **Pros:** gorgeous, rustic setting. **Cons:** nearest nightlife is 20 miles away in South Lake Tahoe. **TripAdvisor:** "cozy cabins," "amazing rustic hospitality," "gorgeous setting." $ *Rooms from:* $135 ✉ 14255 Hwy. 88, Hope Valley ☎ 530/694–2203, 800/423–9949 ⊕ www.sorensensresort.com ⟳ 2 rooms with shared bath, 35 cabins, 5 houses.

$$
HOTEL
Tahoe Seasons Resort. It's a 150-yard walk to California Lodge of Heavenly Mountain Resort from this all-suites time-share hotel, where every room has a two-person sunken hot tub. $ *Rooms from: $175* ✉ 3901 Saddle Rd. ☎ 530/541–6700 front desk, 800/540–4874 reservations ⊕ www.tahoeseasons.com ⟳ 160 suites.

NIGHTLIFE

Most of the area's nightlife is concentrated in the casinos over the border in Stateline. To avoid slot machines and blinking lights, try the California-side nightspots in and near Heavenly Village. The Marriott Timber Lodge bars are always dependable.

The Fresh Ketch. The lively bar at this popular seafood restaurant hosts bands on Tuesday, Thursday, and Friday year-round, Saturdays in summer. ✉ 2435 Venice Dr., off Tahoe Keys Blvd. ☎ 530/541–5683 ⊕ www.thefreshketch.com.

Mc P's Irish Pub & Grill. You can hear live bands—rock, jazz, blues, alternative—on most nights at Mc P's, across the street from the Heavenly Gondola. ✉ 4093 Lake Tahoe Blvd., near Friday Ave. ☎ 530/542–4435 ⊕ www.mcpspubtahoe.com.

SPORTS AND THE OUTDOORS

FISHING
Tahoe Sport Fishing. One of the area's largest and oldest fishing-charter services offers morning and afternoon trips. Outings include all necessary gear and bait, and the crew cleans and packages your catch. ✉ 900

Ski Run Blvd., off U.S. 50 ☎ *530/541–5448, 800/696–7797 in CA* ⊕ *www.tahoesportfishing.com.*

GOLF   **Lake Tahoe Golf Course.** The 18-hole, par-71 course also has a driving range. Greens fees cost from $64 to $84; a cart (mandatory Friday to Sunday) costs $25. Twilight rates drop as low as $39. ⊠ *2500 Emerald Bay Rd, Hwy. 89/U.S. 50* ☎ *530/577–0788* ⊕ *www.laketahoegc.com.*

HIKING   The south shore is a great jumping-off point for day treks into nearby Eldorado National Forest and Desolation Wilderness.

Desolation Wilderness. Trails at the 100-square-mile wilderness lead to gorgeous backcountry lakes and mountain peaks. It's called Desolation Wilderness for a reason, so bring a topographic map and compass, and carry water and food. In summer, you can access this area by boarding a boat taxi ($10 one way) at **Echo Chalet** (⊠ *9900 Echo Lakes Rd., off U.S. 50* ☎ *530/659–7207* ⊕ *www.echochalet.com*) and crossing Echo Lake. The Pacific Crest Trail also traverses Desolation Wilderness. ⊠ *El Dorado National Forest Information Center* ☎ *530/644–6048* ⊕ *www. fs.usda.gov/eldorado.*

Pacific Crest Trail. Hike a couple of miles on this famous mountain trail that stretches from Mexico to Canada. ⊠ *Echo Summit, about 12 miles southwest of South Lake Tahoe off U.S. 50* ☎ *916/285–1846, 888/728–7245* ⊕ *www.pcta.org.*

ICE-SKATING   **Heavenly Village Outdoor Ice Rink.** If you're here in winter, practice your
  ⓒ   jumps and turns at this rink between the gondola and the cinema. ⊠ *1001 Heavenly Village Way* ☎ *530/542–4230* ☑ *$20, includes skate rentals* ☉ *Nov.–Mar., daily 10–8, weather permitting.*

South Tahoe Ice Arena. For year-round fun, head to this city-operated NHL regulation size indoor rink where you can rent equipment and sign up for lessons. In the evening the lights are turned low and a disco ball lights up the ice. Call ahead to check on the irregular hours. ⊠ *1176 Rufus Allen Blvd.* ☎ *530/542–6262* ☑ *$9, plus $3 skate rental* ☉ *Daily.*

KAYAKING   **Kayak Tahoe.** Sign up for lessons and excursions (to the south shore, Emerald Bay, and Sand Harbor), offered from May through September. You can also rent a kayak and paddle solo on the lake. ⊠ *Timber Cove Marina, 3411 Lake Tahoe Blvd., at Balbijou Rd.* ☎ *530/544–2011* ⊕ *www.kayaktahoe.com.*

MOUNTAIN   **Tahoe Sports Ltd.** You can rent road and mountain bikes and get tips on
BIKING   where to ride from the friendly staff at this full-service sports store. ⊠ *Tahoe Crescent V Shopping Center, 4000 Lake Tahoe Blvd., near Heavenly Valley Way* ☎ *530/542–4000* ⊕ *www.tahoesportsltd.com.*

SKIING   If you don't want to pay the high cost of rental equipment at the resorts, you'll find reasonable prices and expert advice at Tahoe Sports *(see Mountain Biking, above).*

Fodor's Choice   **Heavenly Mountain Resort.** Straddling two states, vast Heavenly Moun-
  ★   tain Resort—composed of nine peaks, two valleys, and four base-lodge areas, along with the largest snowmaking system in the western United States—has terrain for every skier. Beginners can choose wide, well-groomed trails, accessed from the California Lodge or the gondola from

downtown South Lake Tahoe; kids have short and gentle runs in the Enchanted Forest area all to themselves. The Sky Express high-speed quad chair whisks intermediate and advanced skiers to the summit for wide cruisers or steep tree-skiing. Mott and Killebrew canyons draw experts to the Nevada side for steep chutes and thick-timber slopes. For snowboarders and tricksters, there are four different terrain parks.

The ski school is big and offers everything from learn-to-ski packages to canyon-adventure tours. Call about ski and boarding camps. Skiing lessons are available for children ages four and up; there's day care for infants older than six weeks. ⊠ *Ski Run Blvd., off U.S. 50* ☎ *775/586–7000, 800/432–8365* ⊕ *www.skiheavenly.com* ☞ *94 trails on 4,800 acres, rated 20% beginner, 45% intermediate, 35% expert. Longest run 5½ miles, base 6,540 feet, summit 10,067 feet. Lifts: 30, including 1 aerial tram, 1 gondola, 2 high-speed 6-passenger lifts, and 8 high-speed quads.*

Hope Valley Cross Country. Operating from a yurt at Pickett's Junction, Hope Valley provides lessons and equipment rentals to prepare you for cross-country skiing and snowshoeing. The outfit has 60 miles of trails through Humboldt–Toiyabe National Forest, 10 of which are groomed. ⊠ *Hwy. 88 at Hwy. 89, Hope Valley* ☎ *530/694–2266* ⊕ *www.hopevalleyoutdoors.com.*

★ **Kirkwood Ski Resort.** Thirty-six miles south of Lake Tahoe, Kirkwood Ski Resort is the hard-core skiers' and boarders' favorite south-shore mountain, known for its craggy gulp-and-go chutes, sweeping cornices, steep-aspect glade skiing, and high base elevation. But there's also fantastic terrain for newbies and intermediates down wide-open bowls, through wooded gullies, and along rolling tree-lined trails. Tricksters can show off in the Stomping Grounds terrain park on jumps, wall rides, rails, and a half-pipe, all visible from the base area. The mountain gets hammered with more than 500 inches of snow annually, and often has the most in all of North America. If you're into out-of-bounds skiing, check out Expedition Kirkwood, a backcountry-skills program that teaches basic safety awareness. Kirkwood is also the only Tahoe resort to offer Cat-skiing. If you're into cross-country, the resort has 80 km (50 miles) of superb groomed-track skiing, with skating lanes, instruction, and rentals. Nonskiers can snowshoe, snow-skate, and go dogsledding or snow-tubing. The children's ski school has programs for ages 4 to 12. ⊠ *1501 Kirkwood Meadows Dr., off Hwy. 88, 14 miles west of Hwy. 89, Kirkwood* ☎ *209/258–6000 downhill, 209/258–7248 cross-country, 209/258–7293 lodging information, 877/547–5966 snow phone* ⊕ *www.kirkwood.com* ☞ *65 trails on 2,300 acres, rated 15% beginner, 50% intermediate, 20% advanced, 15% expert. Longest run 2½ miles, base 7,800 feet, summit 9,800 feet. Lifts: 14, including 2 high-speed quads.*

Sierra-at-Tahoe. Often overlooked by skiers and boarders rushing to Heavenly or Kirkwood, Sierra-at-Tahoe has meticulously groomed intermediate slopes, some of the best tree-skiing in California, and gated backcountry access. Extremely popular with local snowboarders, Sierra also has six terrain parks, including a super-pipe with 17-foot walls. For nonskiers there's a snow-tubing hill. Sierra has a low-key atmosphere that's great for families. Kids and beginners take the slow routes in the Mellow Yellow Zone. ⊠ *1111 Sierra-at-Tahoe Rd., 12 miles from South Lake Tahoe off U.S. 50, near Echo Summit, Twin Bridges* ☎ *530/659–7453* ⊕ *www.sierraattahoe.com* ⌕ *46 trails on 2,000 acres, rated 25% beginner, 50% intermediate, 25% advanced. Longest run 2½ miles, base 6,640 feet, summit 8,852 feet. Lifts: 14, including 3 high-speed quads.*

POPE-BALDWIN RECREATION AREA

5 miles west of South Lake Tahoe on Hwy. 89.

To the west of downtown South Lake Tahoe, U.S. 50 and Highway 89 come together, forming an intersection nicknamed "the Y." If you head northwest on Highway 89, also called Emerald Bay Road, and follow the lakefront, commercial development gives way to national forests and state parks. One of these is Pope-Baldwin Recreation Area.

GETTING HERE AND AROUND

The entrance to the Pope-Baldwin Recreation Area is on the east side of Emerald Bay Road. In summer, BlueGO's Nifty 50 Trolley serves the area from South Lake Tahoe. From the northern and western communities, take a TART bus to Tahoma and transfer to the trolley. The area is closed to vehicles in winter, but you can cross-country ski here.

EXPLORING

Tallac Historic Site. Stroll or picnic lakeside, then explore **Pope House,** the magnificently restored 1894 mansion of George S. Pope, who made his money in shipping and lumber and played host to the business and cultural elite of 1920s America. There are two other estates here. One belonged to entrepreneur "Lucky" Baldwin; today it houses the **Baldwin Museum,** a collection of family memorabilia and Washoe Indian artifacts. The **Valhalla** (⊕ *www.valhallatahoe.com*), with a spectacular floor-to-ceiling stone fireplace, belonged to Walter Heller. Its Grand Hall and a lakeside boathouse, refurbished as a theater, host summertime concerts, plays, and cultural activities. Docents conduct tours of the Pope House in summer; call for tour times. In winter you can cross-country ski around the site. ⊠ *Hwy. 89* ☎ *530/541–5227* ⊕ *www. tahoeheritage.org* ☑ *Free; Pope House tour $5* ☉ *Grounds daily sunrise–sunset. Pope House and Baldwin Museum late May–mid-June, weekends 11–3; mid-June–early Sept., daily 11–4.*

🅒 **Taylor Creek Visitor Center.** At this center operated by the U.S. Forest Service you can visit the site of a Washoe Indian settlement; walk self-guided trails through meadow, marsh, and forest; and inspect the Stream Profile Chamber, an underground display with windows right into Taylor Creek (in fall you may see spawning kokanee salmon digging their nests). In summer U.S. Forest Service naturalists organize discovery walks and evening programs (call ahead). ⊠ *Hwy. 89, 3 miles north of junction with U.S. 50* ☎ *530/543–2674 June–Oct., 530/543–2600 year-round* ⊕ *www.fs.usda.gov/recmain/ltbmu/recreation* ☑ *Free* ☉ *Memorial Day–late Sept., daily 8–5; Oct., daily 8–4.*

Fjordlike Emerald Bay is quite possibly the prettiest part of Lake Tahoe.

EMERALD BAY STATE PARK

4 miles west of Pope-Baldwin Recreation Area on Hwy. 89.

GETTING HERE AND AROUND

The entrance to Emerald Bay State Park is on the east side of a narrow, twisty section of Highway 89. Caution is the keyword for both drivers and pedestrians. In summer, BlueGO's Nifty 50 Trolley serves the area from South Lake Tahoe. From the northern and western communities, take a TART bus to Tahoma and transfer to the trolley. The park is closed to vehicles in the winter.

EXPLORING

Fodor'sChoice ★
Emerald Bay. A massive glacier millions of years ago carved this 3-mile-long and 1-mile-wide fjordlike inlet. Famed for its jewel-like shape and colors, the bay surrounds Fannette, Tahoe's only island. Highway 89 curves high above the lake through Emerald Bay State Park; from the Emerald Bay lookout, the centerpiece of the park, you can survey the whole scene. This is one of the don't-miss views of Lake Tahoe. The light is best in mid- to late morning, when the bay's colors really pop. ⊠ *Hwy. 89* ☎ *530/525–7232* ⊕ *www.parks.ca.gov.*

Vikingsholm. A steep 1-mile-long trail from the Emerald Bay lookout leads down to Vikingsholm, a 38-room estate completed in 1929. The original owner, Lora Knight, had this precise copy of a 1,200-year-old Viking castle built out of materials native to the area. She furnished it with Scandinavian antiques and hired artisans to build period reproductions. The sod roof sprouts wildflowers each spring. There are picnic tables nearby and a gray-sand beach for strolling. The hike back up is hard (especially if you're not yet acclimated to the elevation), but there are benches and stone culverts to rest on. At the 150-foot peak of Fannette Island are the ruins of a stone structure known as the Tea House, built in 1928 so that Knight's guests could have a place to enjoy afternoon refreshments after a motorboat ride. The island is off-limits from February through June to protect nesting Canada geese. The rest of the year it's open for day use. ⊠ *Hwy. 89* ☎ *530/541–6498 summer, 530/525–3345 year-round* ⊕ *www.vikingsholm.com* ✉ *Day-use parking fee $8, mansion tour $8* ☉ *Late May–Sept., daily 10–4.*

SPORTS AND THE OUTDOORS

HIKING   **Eagle Falls.** Leave your car in the parking lot for Eagle Falls picnic area (near Vikingsholm; arrive early for a good spot), and head to these falls, a short but fairly steep walk-up canyon. You'll have a brilliant panorama of Emerald Bay from this spot, near the boundary of Desolation Wilderness. For a strenuous full-day hike, continue 5 miles, past Eagle Lake, to Upper and Middle Velma Lakes. Pick up trail maps at Taylor Creek Visitor Center in summer, or year-round at the main U.S. Forest Service Office in South Lake Tahoe, at 35 College Drive. ⊠ *Hwy. 89, South Lake Tahoe.*

D.L. BLISS STATE PARK

3 miles north of Emerald Bay State Park on Hwy. 89; 17 miles south of Tahoe City.

GETTING HERE AND AROUND

The entrance to D.L. Bliss State Park is on the east side of Highway 89 just north of Emerald Bay. In summer, BlueGO's Nifty 50 Trolley serves the area from South Lake Tahoe. From the northern and western communities, take a TART bus to Tahoma and transfer to the trolley.

EXPLORING

D.L. Bliss State Park. This park takes its name from Duane LeRoy Bliss, a 19th-century lumber magnate. At one time Bliss owned nearly 75% of Tahoe's lakefront, along with local steamboats, railroads, and banks. The park shares 6 miles of shoreline with Emerald Bay State Park; combined the two parks cover 1,830 acres, 744 of which the Bliss family donated to the state. At the north end of Bliss is Rubicon Point, which overlooks one of the lake's deepest spots. Short trails lead to an old lighthouse and Balancing Rock, which weighs 250,000 pounds and balances on a fist of granite. A 4.5-mile trail—one of Tahoe's premier hikes—leads to Vikingsholm and provides stunning lake views. Two white-sand beaches front some of Tahoe's warmest water. ⊠ *Hwy. 89* ☎ *530/525–3345, 800/777–0369* ⊕ *www.parks.ca.gov* ✉ *$8 per vehicle, day use* ☉ *Late May–Sept., daily sunrise–sunset.*

SUGAR PINE POINT STATE PARK

8 miles north of D.L. Bliss State Park on Hwy. 89; 10 miles south of Tahoe City.

GETTING HERE AND AROUND

The entrance to Sugar Pine Point is on the east side of Highway 89, about a mile south of Tahoma. In summer, BlueGO's Nifty 50 Trolley serves the area from South Lake Tahoe. From the northern and western communities, take a TART bus to Tahoma and transfer to the trolley for the short ride to the entrance. There's also a bike trail that links Tahoe City to the park.

EXPLORING

★ **Ehrman Mansion.** The main attraction at Sugar Pine Point State Park is Ehrman Mansion, a 1903 stone-and-shingle summer home furnished in period style. In its day it was the height of modernity, with a refrigerator, an elevator, and an electric stove. Also in the park are a trapper's log cabin from the mid-19th century, a nature preserve with wildlife exhibits, a lighthouse, the start of the 10-mile biking trail to Tahoe City, and an extensive system of hiking and cross-country skiing trails. If you're feeling less ambitious, you can relax on the sun-dappled lawn behind the mansion and gaze out at the lake. ✉ *Hwy. 89* ☎ *530/525–7982 mansion in season, 530/525–7232 year-round* ⊕ *www.parks.ca.gov* ✉ *$8 per vehicle, day use; mansion tour $8* ☉ *Mansion Memorial Day–Labor Day, daily 11–4.*

Sugar Pine Point State Park. Lake Tahoe's largest state park has 2,000 acres of dense forests and nearly 2 miles of shore frontage. A popular spot during snow season, Sugar Pine provides cross-country trails and winter camping on a first-come, first-served basis. Rangers lead three full-moon snowshoe tours from January to March. ✉ *Hwy. 89, 1 mile south of Tahoma* ⊕ *www.parks.ca.gov.*

TAHOMA

1 mile north of Sugar Pine Point State Park on Hwy. 89; 23 miles south of Truckee on Hwy. 89.

With its rustic waterfront vacation cottages, Tahoma exemplifies life on the lake in its quiet early days before bright-lights casinos and huge crowds proliferated. In 1960 Tahoma was host of the Olympic Nordic-skiing competitions. Today there's little to do here except stroll by the lake and listen to the wind in the trees, making it a favorite home base for mellow families and nature buffs.

GETTING HERE AND AROUND

Approach Tahoma by car on Highway 89, called West Lake Boulevard in this section. In summer, BlueGO's Nifty 50 Trolley serves the area from South Lake Tahoe. From the northern and western communities, take a TART bus to Tahoma. A bike trail links Tahoe City to Tahoma.

WHERE TO STAY

For expanded reviews, facilities, and current deals, visit Fodors.com.

$$
B&B/INN
★

⊞ **Tahoma Meadows B&B Cottages.** It's hard to beat this serene property for atmosphere and woodsy charm; it's a great retreat for families and couples. **Pros:** lovely setting; good choice for families; close to Homewood ski resort. **Cons:** far from the casinos. **TripAdvisor:** "exceptional service," "nice accommodations," "best breakfast ever." ⑤ *Rooms from: $149* ✉ *6821 W. Lake Blvd.* ☎ *530/525–1553, 866/525–1553* ⊕ *www.tahomameadows.com* ⇄ *16 cabins* ⑪ *Breakfast.*

SPORTS AND THE OUTDOORS

SKIING　**Homewood Mountain Resort.** Schuss down these slopes for fantastic views—the mountain rises across the road from the Tahoe shoreline. This smaller, usually uncrowded resort is the favorite area of locals on a fresh-snow day, because you can find lots of untracked powder. It's also the most protected and least windy Tahoe ski area during a storm; when every other resort's lifts are on wind hold, you can almost always count on Homewood's to be open. There's only one high-speed chairlift, but there are rarely any lines, and the ticket prices are some of the cheapest around—kids 5 to 12 ski for $10, and those 4 and under are free. The resort may look small as you drive by, but most of it isn't visible from the road. ✉ *5145 W. Lake Blvd., Hwy. 89, 6 miles south of Tahoe City, Homewood* ☎ *530/525–2992* ⊕ *www.skihomewood. com* ⇄ *60 trails on 1,260 acres, rated 15% beginner, 50% intermediate, and 35% advanced. Longest run 2 miles, base 6,230 feet, summit 7,880 feet. Lifts: 4 chairlifts, 4 surface lifts.*

TAHOE CITY

★　*10 miles north of Sugar Pine Point State Park on Hwy. 89; 14 miles south of Truckee on Hwy. 89.*

Tahoe City is the only lakeside town with a charming downtown area good for strolling and window-shopping. Stores and restaurants are all within walking distance of the Outlet Gates, where water is spilled into the Truckee River to control the surface level of the lake. You can spot giant trout in the river from Fanny Bridge, so-called for the views of the backsides of sightseers leaning over the railing.

GETTING HERE AND AROUND

Tahoe City is at the junction of Highway 28, also called North Lake Boulevard, and Highway 89 where it turns northwest toward Squaw Valley and Truckee. TART buses serve the communities along the north and west shores, and connects them to Truckee. Or you could arrive in Truckee via Greyhound bus or Amtrak, rent a car there, and drive to Tahoe City.

ESSENTIALS

Visitor Information North Lake Tahoe Resort Association ☎ *530/583–3494, 888/434–1262* ⊕ *www.gotahoenorth.com.*

EXPLORING

★　**Gatekeeper's Cabin Museum.** This museum preserves a little-known part of the region's history. Between 1910 and 1968 the gatekeeper who lived on this site was responsible for monitoring the level of the lake, using a hand-turned winch system (still used today) to keep the water at the correct level. Also on this site, the fantastic Marian Steinbach Indian Basket Museum displays 800 baskets from 85 tribes. ⊠ *130 W. Lake Blvd.* ☎ *530/583–1762* ⊕ *www.northtahoemuseums.org* ⊠ *$5* ⊙ *May–Sept., Wed.–Mon. 10–5; Oct.–Apr., Fri. and Sat. 11–5.*

Watson Cabin Living Museum. In the middle of town sits a 1909 log cabin built by Robert M. Watson and his son. Now a museum, it's filled with century-old furnishings and many reproductions. Docents are available to answer questions and will lead tours if you call ahead. ⊠ *560 N. Lake Blvd.* ☎ *530/583–8717, 530/583–1762* ⊕ *www.northtahoemuseums. org* ⊠ *$2 donation suggested* ⊙ *Late May–early Sept., Thurs.–Mon. 10–5.*

WHERE TO EAT

$$$ ✕ **Christy Hill.** Huge windows give diners here some of the best lake views
AMERICAN in Tahoe. The menu features solid Euro–Cal preparations of fresh seafood, filet mignon, or vegetarian selections. The extensive wine list and exceptionally good desserts earn accolades, as do the gracious service and casual vibe. If the weather is balmy, have dinner on the deck. In any season, this is the romantic choice for lake gazing and wine sipping. ⑤ *Average main: $24* ⊠ *Lakehouse Mall, 115 Grove St., at N. Lake Blvd.* ☎ *530/583–8551* ⊕ *www.christyhill.com* ⊙ *No lunch.*

$ ✕ **Fire Sign Café.** Watch the road carefully or you'll miss this great little
AMERICAN diner 2 miles south of Tahoe City on Highway 89. There's often a wait for breakfast and lunch, but it's worth it. The pastries are made from scratch, the salmon is smoked in-house, the salsa is hand cut, and there's real maple syrup for the many types of pancakes and waffles. Leave room for dessert; a fruit cobbler is almost always on the menu. ⑤ *Average main: $9* ⊠ *1785 W. Lake Blvd., at Fountain Ave.* ☎ *530/583–0871* ⌂ *Reservations not accepted* ⊙ *No dinner.*

$$$ ✕ **Wolfdale's.** Consistent, inspired cuisine makes Wolfdale's one of the
ECLECTIC top restaurants on the lake. Seafood is the specialty on the changing menu; the imaginative entrées merge Asian and European cooking (drawing on the chef-owner's training in Japan) and lean toward the light and healthful, rather than the heavy and overdone. Everything from teriyaki glaze to smoked fish is made in-house. Request a window table, and book early enough to see the lake view from the elegantly simple dining room. ⑤ *Average main: $27* ⊠ *640 N. Lake Blvd., near Grove St.* ☎ *530/583–5700* ⊕ *www.wolfdales.com* ⌂ *Reservations essential* ⊙ *Closed Tues. No lunch.*

WHERE TO STAY

For expanded reviews, facilities, and current deals, visit Fodors.com.

$$ ⊡ **Cottage Inn.** Avoid the crowds by staying in one of these charming
B&B/INN circa-1938 log cottages under the towering pines on the lake's west shore. **Pros:** romantic, woodsy setting; each room has a fireplace; full breakfast. **Cons:** no kids under 12. **TripAdvisor:** "lovely cottages," "nice location and facilities," "charming and comfortable." ⑤ *Rooms from: $145* ⊠ *1690 W. Lake Blvd., Box 66* ☎ *530/581–4073, 800/581–4073* ⊕ *www.thecottageinn.com* ⇆ *22 rooms.*

$$ ⊡ **River Ranch Lodge.** Tucked into a bend of the Truckee River, this inti-
HOTEL mate lodge is a short distance from major ski resorts and the town

center. **Pros:** beautiful river site; lounge with a gorgeous curved wall of windows. **Cons:** rooms fill quickly. **TripAdvisor:** "not bad at all," "retro charm," "cozy inn."⑤ *Rooms from: $120* ⊠ *Hwy. 89 at Alpine Meadows Rd.* ☎ *530/583–4264, 866/991–9912* ⊕ *www.riverranchlodge.com* ☞ *19 rooms* ⧇ *Breakfast.*

$$$ ⊞ **Sunnyside Steakhouse and Lodge.** The views are superb at this pretty
HOTEL little lodge right on the lake, 3 miles south of Tahoe City. **Pros:** com-
★ plimentary Continental breakfast and afternoon tea; most rooms have balconies overlooking the lake. **Cons:** can be pricey for families. **TripAdvisor:** "a great getaway spot," "friendly and lovely," "excellent in every way."⑤ *Rooms from: $200* ⊠ *1850 W. Lake Blvd., Box 5969* ☎ *530/583–7200, 800/822–2754* ⊕ *www.sunnysideresort.com* ☞ *18 rooms, 5 suites* ⧇ *Breakfast.*

SPORTS AND THE OUTDOORS

GOLF **Tahoe City Golf Course.** Golfers use pull carts or caddies at this 9-hole course, which opened in 1917. ■ **TIP➔** All greens break toward the lake. Though rates vary by season, the maximum greens fees are $40 for 9 holes, $75 for 18; a power cart costs $15 to $25. ⊠ *251 N. Lake Blvd.* ☎ *530/583–1516* ⊕ *www.tahoecitygolf.com.*

MOUNTAIN **Cyclepaths Mountain Bike Adventures.** This combination full-service bike
BIKING shop and bike-adventure outfitter offers instruction in mountain biking, guided tours, tips for self-guided bike touring, bike repairs, and books and maps on the area. ⊠ *10200 Donner Pass Rd., off I–80/Hwy. 89, Truckee* ☎ *530/582–1890* ⊕ *www.cyclepaths.com.*

RIVER **Truckee River Rafting.** In summer you can take a self-guided raft trip down
RAFTING a gentle 5-mile stretch of the Truckee River. The outfitters will shuttle
☺ you back to Tahoe City at the end of your two- to three-hour trip. On a warm day, this makes a great family outing. ⊠ *175 River Rd., near W. Lake Blvd.* ☎ *530/583–1111* ⊕ *www.truckeeriverrafting.com.*

SKIING **Alpine Meadows Ski Area.** The locals' favorite place to ski on the north
★ shore is also the unofficial telemarking hub of the Sierra. With 495 inches of snow annually, Alpine has some of Tahoe's most reliable conditions. It's usually one of the first areas to open in November and one of the last to close in May or June. Alpine isn't the place for arrogant show-offs; instead, you'll find down-to-earth alpine fetishists. The two peaks here are well suited to intermediate skiers, with a number of runs for experts only. Snowboarders and hot-dog skiers will find a terrain park with a super-pipe, rails, and tabletops, as well as a boarder-cross course. Alpine is a great place to learn to ski and has a ski school that teaches and coaches those with physical and mental disabilities. On Saturday, because of the limited parking, there's more acreage per person than at other resorts. ⊠ *2600 Alpine Meadows Rd., off Hwy. 89, 6 miles northwest of Tahoe City and 13 miles south of Truckee* ☎ *530/583–4232, 800/441–4423, 530/581–8374 snow phone* ⊕ *www. skialpine.com* ☞ *100 trails on 2,400 acres, rated 25% beginner, 40% intermediate, 35% advanced. Longest run 2½ miles, base 6,835 feet, summit 8,637 feet. Lifts: 14, including 1 high-speed 6-passenger lift and 2 high-speed quads.*

Squaw Valley USA has runs for skiers of all ability levels—from beginner trails to cliff drops for experts.

Tahoe Dave's Skis and Boards. You can rent skis, boards, and snowshoes at this shop, which touts the area's best selection of downhill rental equipment. ⊠ *590 N. Lake Blvd.* ☎ *530/583–0400.*

OLYMPIC VALLEY

7 miles north of Tahoe City via Hwy. 89 to Squaw Valley Rd.; 8½ miles south of Truckee via Hwy. 89 to Squaw Valley Rd.

Olympic Valley got its name in 1960, when Squaw Valley USA, the ski resort here, hosted the Winter Olympics. Snow sports remain the primary activity, but once summer comes, you can hike into the adjacent Granite Chief Wilderness, explore wildflower-studded alpine meadows, or lie by a swimming pool in one of the Sierra's prettiest valleys.

GETTING HERE AND AROUND

Squaw Valley Rd., the only way into Olympic Valley, branches west off Highway 89 about 8 miles south of Truckee. TART connects the Squaw Valley ski area with the communities along the north and west shores, and Truckee, with year-round public transportation. Squaw Valley Ski Resort provides a free shuttle to many stops in those same areas.

EXPLORING

High Camp. You can ride the Squaw Valley Aerial Tram to this activity hub, which at 8,200 feet commands superb views of Lake Tahoe and the surrounding mountains. In summer, go for a hike, sit by the pool, or have a cocktail and watch the sunset. In winter, you can ski, ice-skate, or snow-tube. There's also a restaurant, a lounge, and a small Olympic museum. ⊠ *Aerial Tram Bldg., Squaw Valley* ☎ *530/581–7278 High*

Camp ⊕ *www.squaw.com/the-village* ⧉ *Aerial Tram, $29* ⊙ *Daily; call for hrs.*

☺ **Village at Squaw Valley.** The centerpiece of Olympic Valley is a pedestrian mall at the base of several four-story ersatz Bavarian stone-and-timber buildings, where you'll find restaurants, high-end condo rentals, boutiques, and cafés. ⊠ *1750 Village East Rd.* ☎ *530/584–1000, 530/584–6205, 888/805–5022 condo reservations* ⊕ *www.squaw.com/the-village.*

WHERE TO EAT

$$$
ECLECTIC

✕ **Graham's of Squaw Valley.** Sit by a floor-to-ceiling river-rock hearth under a knotty-pine peaked ceiling in the intimate dining room in the Christy Inn Lodge. The southern European–inspired menu changes often, but expect hearty entrées such as fillet of beef with wild mushroom sauce, along with lighter-fare small plates like quail with red wine demi-glace. You can also stop in at the fireside bar for appetizers and wine from Graham's highly regarded wine list. ⑤ *Average main: $26* ⊠ *1650 Squaw Valley Rd.* ☎ *530/581–0454* ⊙ *Closed Mon. No lunch.*

$$
JAPANESE

✕ **Mamasake.** The hip and happening spot for sushi at Squaw serves stylized presentations. In the evening, sit at the bar and watch extreme ski movies, many of which were filmed right outside the window. Or drop in from 3 to 5 to enjoy the inexpensive afternoon special: a spicy-tuna or salmon hand roll and a can of Bud for five bucks. ⑤ *Average main: $16* ⊠ *1800 Village South Rd., off Squaw Valley Rd.* ☎ *530/584–0110* ⊕ *www.mamasake.com.*

$$$
AMERICAN
Fodor'sChoice
★

✕ **PlumpJack Café.** The best restaurant at Olympic Valley is also the finest in the entire Tahoe Basin, the epitome of discreet chic and a must-visit for all serious foodies. The menu changes seasonally, but look for roasted quail in an orange sauce, crispy sweetbreads, and butter poached lobster tail. Rather than complicated, heavy sauces, the chef uses simple reductions to complement a dish. The result: clean, dynamic, bright flavors. The wine list is exceptional for its variety and surprisingly low prices. A less expensive but equally adventurous menu, including lunch, is served at the bar. ⑤ *Average main: $28* ⊠ *1920 Squaw Valley Rd.* ☎ *530/583–1578, 800/323–7666* ⊕ *www. plumpjackcafe.com* ⧄ *Reservations essential.*

WHERE TO STAY

For expanded reviews, facilities, and current deals, visit Fodors.com.

$$$
HOTEL
Fodor'sChoice
★

🏨 **PlumpJack Squaw Valley Inn.** If style and luxury are a must, make PlumpJack your first choice. **Pros:** small; intimate; lots of attention to details. **Cons:** not the best choice for families with small children. **Trip-Advisor:** "perfect location," "best food and lodging in Tahoe," "great staff." ⑤ *Rooms from: $210* ⊠ *1920 Squaw Valley Rd.* ☎ *530/583–1576, 800/323–7666* ⊕ *www.plumpjacksquawvalleyinn.com* ⧖ *56 rooms, 8 suites* ⋈ *Breakfast.*

$$$
HOTEL

🏨 **The Village at Squaw Valley USA.** Right at the base of the slopes, at the center point of Olympic Valley, the Village's condominiums were built in 2000 and still look fresh. **Pros:** family-friendly; near Village restaurants and shops. **Cons:** claustrophobia-inducing crowds on weekends. **TripAdvisor:** "great location," "good service," "comfortable condo."

⑤ *Rooms from: $179* ✉ *1750 Village East Rd.* ☎ *530/584–1000, 866/818–6963* ⊕ *www.squaw.com/the-village/lodging* ⇆ *198 suites.*

SPORTS AND THE OUTDOORS

GOLF **Resort at Squaw Creek Golf Course.** This narrow, challenging 18-hole par-71 championship course was designed by Robert Trent Jones Jr. Greens fees range from $60 for afternoon play to $95 for prime time, and include the use of a cart. ✉ *400 Squaw Creek Rd.* ☎ *530/583–6300* ⊕ *www.squawcreek.com.*

HIKING **High Camp.** The Granite Chief Wilderness and the high peaks surrounding Olympic Valley are accessible by foot, but save yourself a 2,000-foot elevation gain by riding the Squaw Valley Aerial Tram to High Camp, the starting point for several hikes. Pick up trail maps at the tram building. High Camp offers sunset hikes in summer, and full moon hikes in winter. ☎ *530/583–6985* ⊕ *www.squaw.com.*

ICE-SKATING **Olympic Ice Pavilion.** Ice-skate here from late November to mid-March. A ride up the mountain in the Aerial Tram costs $29, plus $12 for skate rental and one hour of skate time. End your outing in the hot tub ($10). In summer, the pavilion converts into a roller-skating rink. Year-round, you get fabulous views of the lake and the Sierra Nevada. ✉ *1960 Squaw Valley Rd., High Camp, Squaw Valley* ☎ *800/403–0206, 530/581–7246* ⊕ *www.squaw.com.*

MINIATURE GOLF **Squaw Valley Adventure Center.** Next to the Olympic Village Lodge, on the far side of the creek, this activities center has an 18-hole miniature golf course, a ropes course, and sometimes a bungee trampoline, a ★ blast for kids. ✉ *1960 Squaw Valley Rd.* ☎ *530/583–7673* ⊕ *www. squawadventure.com.*

ROCK CLIMBING **Headwall Climbing Wall.** Before you rappel down a granite monolith, hone your skills at this challenging wall at the base of the Aerial Tram. ✉ *Squaw Valley Adventure Center, 1960 Squaw Valley Rd.* ☎ *530/583–7673* ⊕ *www.squawadventure.com.*

SKIING **Resort at Squaw Creek.** Cross-country skiers enjoy looping through the valley's giant alpine meadow. The resort rents equipment and provides trail maps. ✉ *400 Squaw Creek Rd.* ☎ *530/583–6300* ⊕ *www. squawcreek.com.*

Fodor's Choice ★ **Squaw Valley USA.** Known for some of the toughest skiing in the Tahoe area, this park was the centerpiece of the 1960 Winter Olympics. Today it's the definitive North Tahoe ski resort and among the top-three megaresorts in California (the other two are Heavenly and Mammoth). Although Squaw has changed significantly since the Olympics, the skiing is still world-class and extends across vast bowls stretched between six peaks. Experts often head directly to the untamed terrain of the infamous KT-22 face, which has bumps, cliffs, and gulp-and-go chutes, or to the nearly vertical Palisades, where many famous Warren Miller extreme-skiing films have been shot. Fret not, beginners and intermediates: you have plenty of wide-open, groomed trails at High Camp (which sits at the *top* of the mountain) and around the more challenging Snow King Peak. Snowboarders and show-off skiers can tear up

23

the three fantastic terrain parks, which include a giant super-pipe. Lift prices include night skiing until 8 pm. ⊠ *1960 Squaw Valley Rd., off Hwy. 89, 7 miles northwest of Tahoe City* ☎ *530/583–6985, 800/545–4350 lodging reservations, 530/583–6955 snow phone* ⊕ *www.squaw. com* ↝ *170 trails on 4,000 acres, rated 25% beginner, 45% intermediate, 30% advanced. Longest run 3.2 miles, base 6,200 feet, summit 9,050 feet. Lifts: 33, including a gondola-style funitel, a tram, 7 high-speed chairs, and 18 fixed-grip chairs.*

Tahoe Dave's Skis and Boards. If you don't want to pay resort prices, you can rent and tune downhill skis and snowboards at this shop. ⊠ *3039 Hwy. 89, at Squaw Valley Rd.* ☎ *530/583–5665* ⊕ *www.tahoedaves. com.*

TRUCKEE

13 miles northwest of Kings Beach on Hwy. 267; 14 miles north of Tahoe City on Hwy. 89.

Formerly a decrepit railroad town in the mountains, Truckee is now the trendy first stop for many Tahoe visitors. The town was officially established around 1863, and by 1868 it had gone from a stagecoach station to a major stopover for trains bound for the Pacific via the new transcontinental railroad. Freight trains and Amtrak's California Zephyr still stop every day at the depot right in the middle of town. Stop inside the depot for a walking-tour map of historic Truckee. Across from the station, where Old West facades line the main drag, you'll find galleries, gift shops, boutiques, old-fashioned diners, and several remarkably good restaurants. Look for outlet stores, strip malls, and discount skiwear shops along Donner Pass Road, north of the freeway. Because of its location on Interstate 80, Truckee is a favorite stopover for people traveling from the San Francisco Bay Area to the north shore of Lake Tahoe, Reno, and points east.

GETTING HERE AND AROUND

Truckee is just off Interstate 80 between Highways 89 and 267. Greyhound and Amtrak stop here, Enterprise and Hertz provide car rentals, and TART buses serve Truckee and north shore communities.

ESSENTIALS

Visitor Information Truckee Donner Chamber of Commerce and the California Welcome Center ⊠ *Amtrak depot, 10065 Donner Pass Rd., near Spring St.* ☎ *530/587–8808* ⊕ *www.truckee.com.*

EXPLORING

Donner Memorial State Park and Emigrant Trail Museum. The park and museum commemorate the Donner Party, westward-bound pioneers—about 90; historians debate the exact number—who became trapped in the Sierra in the winter of 1846–47 in snow 22 feet deep. Barely more than half the pioneers survived, some by resorting to cannibalism. The Emigrant Trail Museum details the Donner Party's plight, and other displays explain railroad development through the Sierra. In the park, you can picnic, hike, camp, and go boating, fishing, and water-skiing in summer; winter brings cross-country skiing and snowshoeing on groomed trails. Slated for a late-summer 2013 debut, a new High Sierra Crossing Museum will contain exhibits about the Donner Party, regional Native Americans, and railroad and transportation development through Donner Pass. ☒ *12593 Donner Pass Rd., off I–80, 2 miles west of Truckee* ☎ *530/582–7892 museum, 800/444–7275 camping reservations* ⊕ *www.parks.ca.gov* ☒ *$8 parking, day use* ☉ *Museum late May–early Sept., daily 9–4; closed Tues. and Wed. early Sept.–late May.*

OFF THE BEATEN PATH

23

Tahoe National Forest. Draped along the Sierra Nevada Crest above Lake Tahoe, the national forest offers abundant outdoor recreation: picnicking and camping in summer, and in winter, snowshoeing, skiing, and sledding over some of the deepest snowpack in the West. The **Big Bend Visitor Center** occupies a state historic landmark within the forest, 10 miles west of Donner Summit. This area has been on major cross-country routes for centuries, ever since Native Americans passed through trading acorns and salt for pelts, obsidian, and other materials. Between 1844 and 1860, more than 200,000 emigrants traveled to California along the Emigrant Trail, which passed nearby; you can see rut marks left by wagon wheels scraping the famously hard granite. Later the nation's first transcontinental railroad ran through here (and still does), as do U.S. 40 (the old National Road) and its successor, Interstate 80. Exhibits in the visitor center explore the area's transportation history. ☒ *49685 Hampshire Rocks Rd., Rainbow–Big Bend exit off I–80, Soda Springs* ☎ *530/426–3609, 530/265–4531* ⊕ *www.fs.usda. gov/tahoe* ☒ *Free* ☉ *Summer months only, hrs vary; call ahead.*

WHERE TO EAT

$$$
ECLECTIC

✕ **Cottonwood.** Perched above town on the site of North America's first chairlift, the Cottonwood restaurant is a veritable institution. The bar is decked out with old wooden skis, sleds, skates, and photos of Truckee's early days. The dining area serves an ambitious menu—everything from grilled New York strip steak to baby back short ribs with Cajun spices to butternut squash enchiladas, plus fresh-baked breads and desserts— but people come here mainly for the atmosphere and hilltop views. $ *Average main: $23* ☒ *10142 Rue Hilltop, off Brockway Rd., ¼ mile south of downtown* ☎ *530/587–5711* ⊕ *www.cottonwoodrestaurant. com* ☉ *No lunch.*

$$
ASIAN

✕ **Dragonfly.** Flavors are bold and zingy at this Cal-Asian spot, where every dish is well executed and stylishly presented. Southeast Asian cooking inspires most dishes, which you can savor in the bright, contemporary dining rooms—one for sushi—or an outdoor terrace overlooking Main Street and the train depot. Lunch is a bargain, and there are many choices for vegetarians. Look for the staircase: the restaurant is on the second floor, not at street level. $ *Average main: $22* ☒ *10118 Donner Pass Rd., at Spring St.* ☎ *530/587–0557* ⊕ *www. dragonflycuisine.com.*

$$
AMERICAN

✕ **FiftyFifty Brewing Company.** In this Truckee brewpub, warm red tones and comfy booths, plus a pint of the Donner Party Porter, will take the nip out of a cold day on the slopes. The lunch menu includes salads, burgers, and the house specialty, a pulled-pork sandwich. After 5 pm, you can tuck into barbecued ribs and pan-seared salmon. Order one of their inventive pizzas anytime. There's a full bar along with the brews, and lots of après-ski action. $ *Average main: $19* ✉ *11197 Brockway Rd.* ☎ *530/587–2337* ⊕ *www.fiftyfiftybrewing.com.*

$$$ ✕ **Moody's Bistro Bar & Beats.** Head here for contemporary-Cal cuisine
ECLECTIC in a sexy dining room with pumpkin-color walls, burgundy velvet banquettes, and art-deco fixtures. The earthy, sure-handed cooking features organically grown ingredients: look for ahi poke, snazzy pizzas bubbling-hot from a brick oven, pan-roasted wild game, fresh seafood, and organic grass-fed steak. Lunch fare is lighter. In summer dine alfresco surrounded by flowers. From Thursday through Saturday there's music in the borderline-raucous bar that gets packed with Truckee's bon vivants. $ *Average main: $23* ✉ *10007 Bridge St., at Church St.* ☎ *530/587–8688* ⊕ *www.moodysbistro.com.*

WHERE TO STAY

For expanded reviews, facilities, and current deals, visit Fodors.com.

$$$ 🏨 **Cedar House Sport Hotel.** Cedar House ups the ante for lodging at
HOTEL Tahoe: the clean, spare lines of the wooden exterior evoke a modern European feel, while energy-saving heating, cooling, and lighting systems, countertops made from recycled paper, and other green features emphasize the owners' commitment to sustainability. **Pros:** an environmentally friendly; comfortable; hip. **Cons:** some bathrooms on the small side. **TripAdvisor:** "excellent European feel," "ultra comfortable," "impeccable service." $ *Rooms from: $175* ✉ *10918 Brockway Rd.* ☎ *530/582–5655, 866/582–5655* ⊕ *www.cedarhousesporthotel. com* ⇥ *41 rooms* ❏*Breakfast.*

$$$$ 🏨 **Northstar-at-Tahoe Resort.** The area's most complete destination resort
RESORT is perfect for families, thanks to its many sports activities—from golf and tennis to skiing and snowshoeing—and its concentration of restaurants, shops, recreation facilities, and accommodations. **Pros:** array of lodging types; on-site shuttle, several dining options in Northstar Village. **Cons:** family accommodations are very pricey. **TripAdvisor:** "beautiful condos," "excellent skiing," "great location." $ *Rooms from: $229* ✉ *Hwy. 267, 6 miles southeast of Truckee, Box 129* ☎ *530/562–1010, 800/466–6784* ⊕ *www.northstarattahoe.com* ⇥ *250 units.*

$$$$ 🏨 **Ritz-Carlton Highlands Court, Lake Tahoe.** The first luxury hotel built in
RESORT the Tahoe area in decades, the Ritz-Carlton opened in December 2009. **Pros:** superb service; gorgeous setting. **Cons:** prices as breathtaking as the views; must go off-site for golf and tennis. **TripAdvisor:** "serene," "majestic beauty," "world class." $ *Rooms from: $819* ✉ *13031 Ritz-Carlton Highlands Court* ☎ *530/562–3000, 800/241–3333* ⊕ *www. ritzcarlton.com/laketahoe* ⇥ *153 rooms, 17 suites.*

$$ 🏨 **River Street Inn.** On the banks of the Truckee River, this 1885 wood-
B&B/INN and-stone inn was at times a boardinghouse and a brothel. **Pros:** nice rooms; good value. **Cons:** parking is a half block from inn. **TripAdvisor:** "thoughtful and supportive proprietors," "the ambience was exceptional," "great accommodations and service." $ *Rooms from: $130* ✉ *10009 E. River St.* ☎ *530/550–9290* ⊕ *www.riverstreetinntruckee. com* ⇥ *11 rooms* ❏*Breakfast.*

SPORTS AND THE OUTDOORS

GOLF **Coyote Moon Golf Course.** This course is challenging and beautiful, with no houses to spoil the view. Fees range from $95 to $149, including cart. ✉ *10685 Northwoods Blvd., off Donner Pass Rd.* ☎ *530/587–0886* ⊕ *www.coyotemoongolf.com.*

Northstar. The course here has open links–style play and tight, tree-lined fairways, including water hazards. Fees range from $45 to $80, including cart. ✉ *Hwy. 267, at Northstar Dr.* ☎ *530/562–3290* ⊕ *www. northstarattahoe.com.*

Old Greenwood. At north Lake Tahoe's only Jack Nicklaus signature course, the water hazards are trout streams where you can actually fish. The $100–$185 fee includes a cart. ✉ *12915 Fairway Dr., off Overland Trail Rd., off I–80, Exit 190* ☎ *530/550–7010* ⊕ *www.oldgreenwood. com.*

MOUNTAIN **Northstar-at-Tahoe.** In summer you can rent a bike and ride the lifts to
BIKING the mountain-biking park for 100 miles of challenging terrain. The lift ride is $42 for ages 13 and above; $27 for ages 9–12. The season extends from mid-June through September with varying hours. ✉ *Hwy. 267, at Northstar Dr.* ☎ *530/562–2268* ⊕ *www.northstarattahoe.com.*

SKIING Several smaller resorts around Truckee give you access to the Sierra's slopes for less than half the price of the big resorts. Though you'll sacrifice vertical rise, acreage, and high-speed lifts, you can ski or ride and still have money left over for room and board. These are great places for first-timers and families with kids learning to ski.

Boreal. These slopes have 480 skiable acres and 500 vertical feet of terrain visible from the freeway; lift-served snow-tubing and night skiing go until 9. ✉ *19749 Boreal Ridge Rd., at I–80, Boreal/Castle Peak exit, Soda Springs* ☎ *530/426–3666* ⊕ *www.rideboreal.com.*

Donner Ski Ranch. This ski park has 505 acres and 750 vertical feet and sits across from the more challenging Sugar Bowl (⇨ *below).* ✉ *19320 Donner Pass Rd., Norden* ☎ *530/426–3635* ⊕ *www.donnerskiranch. com.*

Northstar-at-Tahoe. With two tree-lined, northeast-facing, wind-protected bowls, this park is the ideal place in a storm, and just may be the best all-around family ski resort at Tahoe. Hotshot experts unfairly call the mountain "Flatstar," but the meticulous grooming and long cruisers make it an intermediate skier's paradise. Boarders are especially welcome, with awesome terrain parks, including a 420-foot-long superpipe, a half-pipe, rails and boxes, and lots of kickers. Experts can ski the steeps and bumps off Lookout Mountain, where there's rarely a line for the high-speed quad. Northstar-at-Tahoe's cross-country center has 25 miles of groomed trails, including double-set tracks and skating lanes. The school has programs for skiers ages four and up, and day care is available for tots two and older. The mountain gets packed on busy weekends but when there's room on the slopes, Northstar is loads of fun. ✉ *100 Northstar Dr., off Hwy. 267, 6 miles southeast of Truckee* ☎ *530/562–1010, 800/466–6784, 530/562–1330 snow phone* ⊕ *www.northstarattahoe.com* ⌐ *93 trails on 3,000 acres, rated 13% beginner, 60% intermediate, 27% advanced. Longest run 1.4 miles,* *base 6,330 feet, summit 8,610 feet. Lifts: 19, including a gondola and 6 high-speed quads.*

★ **Royal Gorge.** If you love to cross-country, don't miss Royal Gorge, which serves up 93 miles of 18-foot-wide track for all abilities, 65 trails on a whopping 9,172 acres, a ski school, and eight warming huts. Two trailside cafés and two lodges round out the facilities. Since it's right on the Sierra Crest, the views are drop-dead gorgeous, and the resort feels like it goes on forever. ⊠ *9411 Hillside Dr., off I–80, Soda Springs/ Norden exit, Soda Springs* ☎ *530/426–3871* ⊕ *www.royalgorge.com.*

Soda Springs. Along with 200 acres and 652 vertical feet, this ski park also has lift-served snow-tubing. ⊠ *10244 Soda Springs Rd., I–80 Soda Springs exit, Soda Springs* ☎ *530/426–3901* ⊕ *www.skisodasprings. com.*

Sugar Bowl. Opened in 1939 by Walt Disney, this is the oldest—and one of the best—resorts at Tahoe. Atop Donner Summit, it receives an incredible 500 inches of snowfall annually. Four peaks are connected by 1,500 acres of skiable terrain, with everything from gentle groomed corduroy to wide-open bowls to vertical rocky chutes and outstanding tree skiing. Snowboarders can hit two terrain parks with numerous boxes, rails, and jumps. Because it's more compact than some of the area's megaresorts, there's a certain gentility here that distinguishes Sugar Bowl from its competitors, making this a great place for families and a low-pressure, low-key place to learn to ski. It's not huge, but there's some very challenging terrain (experts: head to the Palisades). There's limited lodging at the base area. ⊠ *629 Sugar Bowl Rd., off Donner Pass Rd., 3 miles east of I–80 Soda Springs/Norden exit, 10 miles west of Truckee, Norden* ☎ *530/426–9000 information and lodging reservations, 530/426–1111 snow phone, 866/843–2695 lodging referral* ⊕ *www.sugarbowl.com* ⚲ *95 trails on 1,500 acres, rated 17% beginner, 45% intermediate, 38% advanced. Longest run 3 miles, base 6,883 feet, summit 8,383 feet. Lifts: 13, including 5 high-speed quads.*

Tahoe Dave's. You can save money by renting skis and boards at this shop, which has the area's best selection and also repairs and tunes equipment. ⊠ *10200 Donner Pass Rd., near Spring St.* ☎ *530/582–0900* ⊕ *www.tahoedaves.com.*

Tahoe Donner. Just north of Truckee, this park covers 120 acres and 560 vertical feet; the cross-country center includes 51 trails on 114 km (71 miles) of groomed tracks on 4,800 acres, with night skiing on Wednesday in January and February. ⊠ *11509 Northwoods Blvd., at Muhlebach Way* ☎ *530/587–9444* ⊕ *www.tahoedonner.com.*

CARNELIAN BAY TO KINGS BEACH

5–10 miles northeast of Tahoe City on Hwy. 28.

The small lakeside commercial districts of Carnelian Bay and Tahoe Vista service the thousand or so locals who live in the area year-round and the thousands more who have summer residences or launch their boats here. Kings Beach, the last town heading east on Highway 28 before the Nevada border, is to Crystal Bay what South Lake Tahoe is to Stateline: a bustling California town full of basic motels and rental condos, restaurants, and shops, used by the hordes of hopefuls who pass through on their way to the casinos.

GETTING HERE AND AROUND

To reach Kings Beach and Carnelian Bay from the California side, take Highway 89 north to Highway 28 north and then east. From the Nevada side, follow Highway 28 north and then west. TART provides public transportation in this area.

BEACHES

23

Kings Beach State Recreation Area. The 28-acre Kings Beach State Recreation Area, one of the largest such areas on the lake, is open year-round. The 700-foot-long sandy beach gets very crowded in summer with people swimming, sunbathing, jet-skiing, riding in paddleboats, spiking volleyballs, and tossing Frisbees. If you're going to spend the day, come early enough to snag a table in the picnic area; there's also a good playground. **Amenities:** food and drink; parking (fee); toilets; water sports. **Best For:** sunrise; swimming; windsurfing. ⊠ *8318 N. Lake Blvd., Hwy. 28, Kings Beach* ☎ *530/546–7248* ⌦ *$8 parking fee* ⊘ *Daily.*

WHERE TO EAT AND STAY

For expanded reviews, facilities, and current deals, visit Fodors.com.

$$$ ✕ **Gar Woods Grill and Pier.** The view's the thing at this lakeside stalwart,
ECLECTIC   where you can watch the sun shimmer on the water through the dining room's plate-glass windows or from the heated outdoor deck. Grilled steak and fish are menu mainstays, but be sure to try specialties like crab chiles rellenos and chipotle chicken salad. At all hours in season, the bar gets packed with boaters who pull up to the restaurant's private pier. ⑤ *Average main: $28* ⊠ *5000 N. Lake Blvd., Hwy. 28, Carnelian Bay* ☎ *530/546–3366* ⊕ *www.garwoods.com.*

$$ ✕ **Spindleshanks.** This handsome roadhouse, decorated with floor-to-ceil-
AMERICAN   ing knotty pine, serves mostly classic American cooking—ribs, steaks, and seafood updated with adventurous sauces—as well as house-made ravioli. On cold nights request seating near the crackling fireplace and enjoy a drink from the full bar or the extensive wine list. Reservations are recommended. ⑤ *Average main: $20* ⊠ *6873 N. Lake Blvd, Tahoe Vista* ☎ *530/546–2191* ⊕ *www.spindleshankstahoe.com* ⊘ *No lunch.*

$ ▦ **Ferrari's Crown Resort.** The family-owned and -operated Ferrari's
HOTEL   has straightforward motel rooms in a resort setting, great for families
   with kids. **Pros:** family-friendly; lakeside location. **Cons:** older facility. **TripAdvisor:** "everything we needed," "room was amazing," "beautiful view." ⑤ *Rooms from: $99* ⊠ *8200 N. Lake Blvd., Kings Beach* ☎ *530/546–3388, 800/645–2260* ⊕ *www.tahoecrown.com* ⇆ *71 rooms* ⏃*Breakfast.*

$$$$ ▦ **Shore House.** Every room has a gas fireplace, down comforter, and
B&B/INN   featherbed at this lakefront B&B in Tahoe Vista. **Pros:** waterfront hon-
★   eymoon cottage; massage appointments available. **Cons:** pricey (even off-season). **TripAdvisor:** "perfect for a romantic getaway," "relaxing," "Tahoe perfected." ⑤ *Rooms from: $265* ⊠ *7170 N. Lake Blvd., Tahoe*

Vista ☎ *530/546–7270, 800/207–5160* ⊕ *www.shorehouselaketahoe. com* �='' *8 rooms, 1 cottage* ⦿| *Breakfast.*

THE NEVADA SIDE

The difference on the Nevada side of the lake is, of course, gambling, with all its repercussions.

CRYSTAL BAY

1 mile east of Kings Beach on Hwy. 28; 30 miles north of South Lake Tahoe, U.S. 50 to Hwy. 28.

Right at the Nevada border, Crystal Bay has a cluster of casinos that look essentially the same, but have a few minor differences. These casinos tend toward the tacky, and most of the lodging is pretty lackluster.

GETTING HERE AND AROUND

From the California side, reach Crystal Bay via Highway 89 or 267 to Highway 28. TART serves the communities along the north and west shores.

EXPLORING

Cal-Neva Lodge. Bisected by the state line, the Cal-Neva Lodge opened in 1927 and has weathered many scandals. The largest involved former owner Frank Sinatra (he lost his gaming license in the 1960s for alleged mob connections). The secret tunnel that Frank built so that he could steal away unnoticed to Marilyn Monroe's cabin is definitely worth a look; call for tour times. ⊠ *2 Stateline Rd.* ☎ *800/225–6382* ⊕ *www. calnevaresort.com.*

Crystal Bay Club. Known for its classic steak and lobster dinner, the restaurant here has a distinctive open-truss ceiling. ⊠ *14 Hwy. 28, near Stateline Rd.* ☎ *775/833–6333* ⊕ *www.crystalbaycasino.com.*

Jim Kelley's Tahoe Nugget. Nearly 90 kinds of beer highlight the bar scene at Jim Kelley's Tahoe Nugget. In fact, they're the highlight of the entire casino, which has no table games, only slots and video poker. ⊠ *20 Hwy. 28, near Stateline Rd.* ☎ *775/831–0455.*

Tahoe Biltmore. A daily happy hour keeps this old favorite hopping. The circular Tahoe Biltmore sign is a 1962 "Googie-style" architectural riff off the Seattle Space Neeedle, which debuted the same year. ⊠ *5 Hwy. 28, at Stateline Rd.* ☎ *800/245–8667* ⊕ *www.tahoebiltmore.com.*

WHERE TO EAT

$$$ ✕ **Soule Domain.** Rough-hewn wood beams and a vaulted wood ceiling
ECLECTIC   lend high romance to this cozy 1927 pine-log cabin next to the Tahoe Biltmore. Chef-owner Charlie Soule's specialties include curried almond chicken, fresh sea scallops poached in champagne with kiwi and mango cream sauce, and a vegan sauté with ginger, jalapeños, and tofu, but you'll find the chef's current passion in the roster of nightly specials. Some find Soule Domain pricey, but if you're looking for a place with a sterling menu where you can hold hands by candlelight, this is it. Ⓢ *Average main: $26* ⊠ *9983 Cove Ave., ½ block up Stateline Rd.*

off Hwy. 28, Kings Beach ☎ *530/546–7529* ⊕ *www.souledomain.com*
⚐ *Reservations essential* ⊙ *No lunch.*

INCLINE VILLAGE

3 miles east of Crystal Bay on Hwy. 28.

Incline Village dates to the early 1960s when an Oklahoma developer bought 10,000 acres north of Lake Tahoe. His idea was to sketch out a plan for a town without a central commercial district, hoping to prevent congestion and to preserve the area's natural beauty. One-acre lakeshore lots originally fetched $12,000 to $15,000; today you couldn't buy the same land for less than several million.

23

GETTING HERE AND AROUND

From the California side, reach Incline Village via Highway 89 or 267 to Highway 28. From South Lake Tahoe, take U.S. 50 north to Highway 28 north. TART serves the communities along Lake Tahoe's north and west shores from Incline Village to Tahoma.

ESSENTIALS

Visitor Information Lake Tahoe Incline Village/Crystal Bay Visitors Bureau
✉ **969 Tahoe Blvd.** ☎ **775/832–1606, 800/468–2463** ⊕ **www.gotahoenorth.com.**

EXPLORING

Lakeshore Drive. Take this beautiful drive to see some of the most expensive real estate in Nevada. The route is discreetly marked: to find it, start at the Hyatt hotel and drive westward along the lake.

Fodor's Choice
★

Thunderbird Lodge. George Whittell, a San Francisco socialite who once owned 40,000 acres of property along the lake, built the lodge in 1936. You can tour the mansion and the grounds by reservation only, and though it's pricey to do so, you'll get a rare glimpse back to a time when only the very wealthy had homes at Tahoe. The lodge is accessible via a bus from the Incline Village Visitors Bureau, a catamaran from the Hyatt in Incline Village ($110), or a 1950 wooden cruiser from Tahoe Keys Marina in South Lake Tahoe, which includes Continental breakfast and lunch ($135). ☎ *775/832–8750 lodge info, 800/468–2463 reservations, 775/588–1881, 888/867–6394 Tahoe Keys boat, 775/831–4386 Hyatt Incline catamaran* ⊕ *www.thunderbirdlodge.org/tours* ⛁ *$39 bus tour, $110 & 135 for boat tours* ⊙ *May–Oct., Tues.–Sat., call for tour times.*

BEACHES

Lake Tahoe–Nevada State Park and Sand Harbor Beach. Protecting much of the lake's eastern shore from development, the park comprises several sections that stretch from Incline Village to Zephyr Cove. Beaches and trails provide access to a wilder side of the lake, whether you're into cross-country skiing, hiking, or just relaxing at a picnic. With a gently sloping beach for lounging, crystal clear water for swimming and snorkeling, and a picnic area shaded by cedars and pines, **Sand Harbor Beach** is so popular that it sometimes fills to capacity by 11 am on summer weekends. Boaters have two launch ramps. A handicap-accessible nature trail has interpretive signs and beautiful lake views. Pets are not allowed. **Amenities:** food and drink; parking ($12 mid-Apr.–mid-Oct.,

$7 rest of the year; toilets; water sports. **Best For:** snorkeling; sunset; swimming; walking. ✉ *Sand Harbor Beach, Hwy. 28, 3 miles south of Incline Village* 🕾 *775/831–0494* ⊕ *parks.nv.gov/parks/sand-harbor.*

WHERE TO EAT AND STAY

For expanded reviews, facilities, and current deals, visit Fodors.com.

$$$ ✕ **Frederick's.** Copper-top tables lend a chic look to the dining room
ECLECTIC at this intimate bistro. The menu consists of a mélange of European and Asian dishes, most of them prepared with organic produce and free-range meats. Try the braised short ribs, roasted duck with caramel-pecan glaze, or the deliciously fresh sushi rolls. Ask for a table by the fire. ⑤ *Average main: $28* ✉ *907 Tahoe Blvd., at Village Blvd.* 🕾 *775/832–3007* ⊕ *fredricksbistro.com* ⚐ *Reservations essential* ⊘ *Closed Sun. and Mon. No lunch.*

$$$ ✕ **Le Bistro.** Incline Village's hidden gem serves expertly prepared French-
FRENCH country cuisine in a relaxed, romantic dining room. The chef-owner makes everything himself, using organically grown ingredients. Expect such dishes as pâté de campagne, porcini mushroom bisque en croute, escargot, and herb-crusted roast lamb loin. Try the five-course prix-fixe menu ($50), which can be paired with award-winning wine selections. Service is gracious and attentive. Be sure to ask directions when you book, because the restaurant is hard to find. ⑤ *Average main: $30* ✉ *120 Country Club Dr., off Lakeshore Blvd.* 🕾 *775/831–0800* ⊕ *www.lebistrorestaurant.net* ⊘ *Closed Sun. and Mon. No lunch.*

$ ✕ **T's Rotisserie.** There's nothing fancy about T's (it looks like a small
SOUTHERN snack bar), but the mesquite-grilled chicken and tri-tip steaks are delicious and inexpensive—a rare combination in pricey Incline Village. It's mainly a take-out spot; seating is limited. ⑤ *Average main: $8* ✉ *901 Tahoe Blvd., at Village Blvd.* 🕾 *775/831–2832* ⊟ *No credit cards.*

$$$$ 🏨 **Hyatt Regency Lake Tahoe.** A full-service destination resort on 26
RESORT acres of prime lakefront property, the Hyatt has a range of luxurious accommodations, from tower-hotel rooms to lakeside cottages. **Pros:** incredible views; first-class spa. **Cons:** pricey (especially for families). **TripAdvisor:** "beautiful resort," "the best staff I have ever experienced," "nice room." ⑤ *Rooms from: $298* ✉ *111 Country Club Dr.* 🕾 *775/832–1234, 888/899–5019* ⊕ *www.laketahoe.hyatt.com* 🛏 *386 rooms, 36 suites.*

SPORTS AND THE OUTDOORS

GOLF **Incline Championship.** Robert Trent Jones Sr. designed this 18-hole, par-72 course with a driving range. The $179 greens fee includes an optional cart. ✉ *955 Fairway Blvd., at Northwood Blvd., north off Hwy. 28* 🕾 *866/925–4653* ⊕ *www.inclinegolf.com.*

Incline Mountain. This executive (shorter) 18-hole par 58 course has greens fees that start at $65, including optional cart. ✉ *690 Wilson Way, at Golfer's Pass, south off Hwy. 431* 🕾 *866/925–4653* ⊕ *www.inclinegolf.com.*

MOUNTAIN **Flume Trail Bikes.** You can rent bikes and get helpful tips from company,
BIKING which also operates a bike shuttle to popular trailheads. Ask about the secluded backcountry rental cabins for overnight rides. ✉ *Spooner*

Get to Sand Harbor Beach in Lake Tahoe–Nevada State Park early; the park sometimes fills to capacity before lunchtime in summer.

Summit, Hwy. 28, ¾ mile north of U.S. 50, Glenbrook ☎ *775/749–5349* ⊕ *www.theflumetrail.com.*

SKIING **Diamond Peak.** A fun family mood prevails at Diamond Peak, which has affordable rates and many special programs. Snowmaking covers 75% of the mountain, and runs are groomed nightly. The ride up the 1-mile Crystal Express rewards you with fantastic views. Diamond Peak is less crowded than the larger areas and provides free shuttles to nearby lodging. A great place for beginners and intermediates, it's appropriately priced for families. Though there are some steep-aspect black-diamond runs, advanced skiers may find the acreage too limited. For snowboarders there's a small terrain park. ⊠ *1210 Ski Way, off Country Club Dr.* ☎ *775/832–1177* ⊕ *www.diamondpeak.com* ☞ *30 trails on 655 acres, rated 18% beginner, 46% intermediate, 36% advanced. Longest run 2½ miles, base 6,700 feet, summit 8,540 feet. Lifts: 6, including 2 high-speed quads.*

Mt. Rose Ski Tahoe. At this park, ski some of Tahoe's highest slopes and take in bird's-eye views of Reno, the lake, and Carson Valley. Though more compact than the bigger Tahoe resorts, Mt. Rose has the area's highest base elevation and consequently the driest snow. The mountain has a wide variety of terrain. The most challenging is the Chutes, 200 acres of gulp-and-go advanced-to-expert vertical. Intermediates can choose steep groomers or mellow, wide-open boulevards. Beginners have their own corner of the mountain, with gentle, wide slopes. Boarders and tricksters have three terrain parks to choose from, on opposite sides of the mountain, allowing them to follow the sun as it tracks across the resort. The mountain gets hit hard in storms; check conditions before heading up during inclement weather or on a windy day. ⊠ *22222 Mt. Rose Hwy., Hwy. 431, 11 miles north of Incline Village, Reno* ☎ *775/849–0704, 800/754–7673* ⊕ *www.skirose.com* ⌖ *61 trails on 1,200 acres, rated 20% beginner, 30% intermediate, 40% advanced, 10% expert. Longest run 2½ miles, base 8,260 feet, summit 9,700 feet. Lifts: 8, including 2 high-speed 6-passenger lifts.*

> **TAHOE TESSIE**
>
> Local lore claims this huge sea monster slithers around Lake Tahoe. Skeptics laugh, but true believers keep their eyes peeled for surprise sightings.

Spooner Lake Cross-Country. You'll find superbly groomed tracks and fabulous views of Lake Tahoe while you skim along about 50 miles of trails on more than 9,000 acres. Two secluded cabins are available for rent for overnight treks. ⊠ *Spooner Summit, Hwy. 28, ½ mile north of U.S. 50, Glenbrook* ☎ *775/749–5349* ⊕ *www.spoonerlake.com.*

Tahoe Meadows Snowplay Area. This is the most popular area near the north shore for noncommercial cross-country skiing, sledding, tubing, snowshoeing, and snowmobiling. ⊠ *Hwy. 431, between Incline Village and Mt. Rose.*

ZEPHYR COVE

22 miles south of Incline Village via Hwy. 28 to U.S. 50.

The largest settlement between Incline Village and the Stateline area is Zephyr Cove, a tiny resort. It has a beach, marina, campground, picnic area, coffee shop in a log lodge, rustic cabins, and nearby riding stables.

GETTING HERE AND AROUND

From the north shore communities, reach Zephyr Cove by following Highway 28 along the eastern side of the lake. From South Lake Tahoe, take U.S. 50 north and then west. Public transportation isn't available in Zephyr Cove.

EXPLORING

★ **Cave Rock.** Near Zephyr Cove, this 75 feet of solid stone at the southern end of Lake Tahoe–Nevada State Park is the throat of an extinct volcano. Tahoe Tessie, the lake's version of the Loch Ness monster, is reputed to live in a cavern below the impressive outcropping. Cave Rock towers over a parking lot, a lakefront picnic ground, and a boat launch. The views are some of the best on the lake; this is a good spot to stop and take a picture. However, this area is a sacred burial site for the Washoe Indians, and climbing up to the cave, or through it, is prohibited. ⊠ *U.S. 50, 4 miles north of Zephyr Cove* ☎ *775/831–0494.*

WHERE TO STAY

For expanded reviews, facilities, and current deals, visit Fodors.com.

$$$
RENTAL
☺ **Zephyr Cove Resort.** Beneath towering pines at the lake's edge stand 29 cozy, modern vacation cabins with peaked knotty-pine ceilings. **Pros:** family-friendly. **Cons:** lodge rooms are very basic; can be noisy. **Trip-Advisor:** "a cabin with a beautiful view," "fresh peaceful scenery," "tranquility." $ *Rooms from: $199* ⊠ *760 U.S. 50, 4 miles north of*

Stateline ☎ *775/589–4907, 888/896–3830* ⊕ *www.zephyrcove.com* 🛏 *29 cabins.*

STATELINE

5 miles south of Zephyr Cove on U.S. 50.

Stateline is the archetypal Nevada border town. Its four high-rise casinos are as vertical and contained as the commercial district of South Lake Tahoe, on the California side, is horizontal and sprawling. And Stateline is as relentlessly indoors oriented as the rest of the lake is focused on the outdoors. This strip is where you'll find the most concentrated action at Lake Tahoe: restaurants (including typical casino buffets), showrooms with famous headliners and razzle-dazzle revues, tower-hotel rooms and suites, and 24-hour casinos.

GETTING HERE AND AROUND

From South Lake Tahoe take U.S. 50, also called Lake Tahoe Boulevard, north across the Nevada border to reach Stateline and its casinos. If coming from Reno's airport, take U.S. 395 south to Carson City, and then head west on U.S. 50 to the lake and head south. Or take the South Tahoe Express bus. BlueGO operates daily bus service in the south shore area year-round, plus a ski shuttle from the large hotels to Heavenly in the winter.

BEACHES

Nevada Beach. Although less than a mile long, this is the widest beach on the lake and especially good for swimming (many Tahoe beaches are rocky). You can boat and fish here, and there are picnic tables, barbecue grills, and a campground beneath the pines. This is the best place to watch the July 4th or Labor Day fireworks, but most of the summer the subdued atmosphere attracts families and those seeking a less-touristy spot. **Amenities:** parking ($7 fee); water sports; toilets. **Best For:** sunrise; swimming; walking. ⊠ *Elk Point Rd., off U.S. 50, 3 miles north of Stateline* ☎ *530/543–2600* ⊕ *www.fs.usda.gov/ltbmu* ⊗ *Daily late May–Oct.* ⌔ *No pets.*

WHERE TO EAT AND STAY

For expanded reviews, facilities, and current deals, visit Fodors.com.

$$$ FRENCH ✕ **Mirabelle.** Don't be put off by this restaurant's nondescript exterior. Inside there's an airy dining room with creamy yellow walls and white tablecloths. Enticing scents drift from the kitchen, where the Alsatian-born chef-owner, Camille Schwartz, prepares everything from puff pastry to meringues to homemade bread. Specialties include sautéed veal sweetbreads, garlicky escargot, and rack of lamb with fresh thyme. There's always a fresh fish entrée, plus a $29.50 prix-fixe "casual menu." ⑤ *Average main: $25* ⊠ *290 Kingsbury Grade, off U.S. 50* ☎ *775/586–1007* ⊕ *www.mirabelletahoe.com* ⊗ *Closed Mon. No lunch.*

$$ HOTEL 🏨 **Harrah's Tahoe Hotel/Casino.** The hotel's major selling point is that every room has two full bathrooms, each with a television and telephone, a boon if you're traveling with family. **Pros:** central location; great midweek values. **Cons:** can get noisy. **TripAdvisor:** "nice surprise,"

"amazing," "great location."[$] *Rooms from: $110* ⊠ *15 U.S. 50, at Stateline Ave.* ☎ *775/588–6611, 800/427–7247* ⊕ *www.harrahstahoe. com* ⤳ *470 rooms, 62 suites.*

$$ **▦ Harveys Resort Hotel/Casino.** The resort began as a cabin in 1944, and
HOTEL now it's Tahoe's largest casino-hotel. **Pros:** hip entertainment; just a few blocks south of the Heavenly Gondola. **Cons:** can get loud at night. **TripAdvisor:** "great rooms," "very nice," "not your typical casino hotel."[$] *Rooms from: $80* ⊠ *18 U.S. 50, at Stateline Ave.* ☎ *775/588–2411, 800/648–3361* ⊕ *www.harrahs.com* ⤳ *705 rooms, 38 suites.*

$ **▦ MontBleu.** The contemporary, slightly kitschy MontBleu has guest
HOTEL rooms with oversize tubs, king-size beds, and views of Lake Tahoe and the surrounding mountains. **Pros:** indoor pool; first-class spa; great specials online. **Cons:** looking careworn in places; can get noisy; some rooms overlook parking lot's glaring lights. **TripAdvisor:** "nice location," "many amenities," "great weekend stay."[$] *Rooms from: $99* ⊠ *55 U.S. 50* ☎ *775/588–3515, 800/648–3353* ⊕ *www.montbleuresort. com* ⤳ *328 rooms, 109 suites.*

NIGHTLIFE

Each of the major casinos has its own showroom, featuring everything from comedy to magic acts to sexy floor shows to Broadway musicals.

Harveys Outdoor Summer Concert Series. The casino presents outdoor concerts on weekends in summer with headliners such as Sugarland, Brad Paisley, the Rascal Flats, and Toby Keith. ☎ *800/427–7247* ⊕ *www. harveystahoe.com.*

South Shore Room. Old-school (Rick Springfield) and really old-school (Eric Burdon) rockers play Harrah's big showroom, along with relatively less nostalgia-oriented headliners such as Los Lobos and—combining most of the above attributes—Chickenfoot. ⊠ *Harrah's, 15 U.S. 50* ☎ *775/588–6611.*

Vex. You can dance the night away at this club with a semi-Vegas feel. ⊠ *Harrah's, 15 U.S. 50* ☎ *775/588–6611.*

SPORTS AND THE OUTDOORS

GOLF **Edgewood Tahoe.** This highly scenic lakeside course, 18 holes, par 72, has a driving range. The greens fee, $160–$240, includes an optional cart. ⊠ *100 Lake Pkwy., at U.S. 50* ☎ *775/588–3566, 888/881–8659* ⊕ *www.edgewood-tahoe.com.*

RENO

32 miles east of Truckee on I–80; 38 miles northeast of Incline Village via Hwy. 431 and U.S. 395.

Established in 1859 as a trading station at a bridge over the Truckee River, Reno grew along with the silver mines of nearby Virginia City and the transcontinental railroad that chugged through town. Train officials named it in 1868, but gambling—legalized in 1931—put Reno on the map.

Today a sign over the upper end of Virginia Street proclaims Reno "The Biggest Little City in the World." This is still a gambling town, with most of the casinos crowded into five square blocks downtown, but a thriving university scene and outdoor activities also bring tourists to the area.

Though parts of downtown are sketchy, things are changing. Several defunct casinos are being converted into condominiums, and downtown is undergoing an urban renewal, sparked by the development of the riverfront, with new shops, boutiques, and nongaming, family-friendly activities like kayaking on the Truckee River. Excellent restaurants have sprung up outside the hotels. Temperatures year-round in this high-mountain-desert climate are warmer than at Tahoe, though it rarely gets as hot here as in Sacramento and the Central Valley, making strolling around town a pleasure.

> ## RENO'S RIVERWALK
>
> Stroll along the Truckee River and check out the art galleries, cinema, specialty shops, theater, and restaurants that line this lively refurbished section of town near Reno's casino district.

23

GETTING HERE AND AROUND

Interstate 80 bisects Reno east–west, U.S. 395 north–south. Greyhound and Amtrak stop here, and several airlines fly into Reno-Tahoe International Airport. RTC Ride provides bus service in the greater Reno area.

ESSENTIALS

Bus Contact RTC Ride ⊠ *Transit Center, E. 4th and Lake Sts.* ☎ 775/348–0400 ⊕ *rtcwashoe.com.*

Visitor Information Reno-Sparks Convention and Visitors Authority ⊠ 4001 S. Virginia St. ☎ 775/827–7650, 800/367–7366 ⊕ www.visitrenotahoe. com.

EXPLORING

TOP ATTRACTIONS

Downtown RiverWalk. Once dilapidated, Reno's waterfront district got a gentrified makeover when the Downtown RiverWalk brought in street performers, art exhibits, shops, and a lovely park. The 2,600-foot-long Truckee River white-water kayaking course runs right through downtown and has become a major attraction for water-sports enthusiasts. On the third Saturday of each month, from 2 to 5, local merchants host a **Wine Walk.** The cost is $20; stop inside the RiverWalk's participating shops, galleries, and boutiques to refill your wine glass. In July look for stellar outdoor art, opera, dance, and kids' performances as part of the monthlong **Artown festival** (⊕ *www.renoisartown.com*), presented mostly in Wingfield Park, along the river. ⊠ *S. Virginia St. and the Truckee River* ⊕ *www.renoriver.org.*

Eldorado. Action packed, with lots of slots and popular bar-top video poker, this casino also has good coffee-shop and food-court fare. Don't miss the Fountain of Fortune with its massive Florentine-inspired sculptures. ⊠ *345 N. Virginia St., at W. 4th St.* ☎ 775/786–5700, 800/648–5966 ⊕ *www.eldoradoreno.com.*

☾ **Fleischmann Planetarium.** Digital star shows provide the glittering lights inside this facility that aims to make learning about astronomy entertaining for kids and adults. ⊠ *University of Nevada, 1650 N. Virginia*

St., near E. 15th St. ☎ *775/784–4811* ⊕ *www.planetarium.unr.nevada. edu* ✉ *Exhibits free, films and star shows $7* ⊙ *Mon.–Thurs. noon–5, Fri. noon–9, Sat. 10–9, Sun. 10–5.*

🐣 ★ **National Automobile Museum.** Antique and classic automobiles, including an Elvis Presley Cadillac, a Mercury coupe driven by James Dean in the movie *Rebel Without a Cause,* and the experimental and still futuristic-looking 1938 Phantom Corsair are all on display here. ✉ *10 S. Lake St., at Mill St.* ☎ *775/333–9300* ⊕ *www.automuseum.org* ✉ *$10* ⊙ *Mon.–Sat. 9:30–5:30, Sun. 10–4.*

★ **Nevada Museum of Art.** A dramatic structure designed by Will Bruder houses this splendid museum's collection, which focuses on themes such as the Sierra Nevada/Great Basin and altered-landscape photography. Important traveling exhibitions often come here. ✉ *160 W. Liberty St., and Hill St.* ☎ *775/329–3333* ⊕ *www.nevadaart.org* ✉ *$10* ⊙ *Wed. and Fri.–Sun. 10–5, Thurs. 10–8.*

★ **Peppermill.** A few miles from downtown, this casino is known for its excellent restaurants and neon-bright gambling areas. The Fireside cocktail lounge is a blast. ✉ *2707 S. Virginia St., at Peppermill La.* ☎ *775/826–2121, 800/648–6992* ⊕ *www.peppermillreno.com.*

WORTH NOTING

🐣 **Circus Circus.** Families with kids in tow head to this casino, where a midway above the floor has clowns, games, fun-house mirrors, and circus acts. ✉ *500 N. Sierra St., at W. 5th St.* ☎ *775/329–0711, 800/648–5010* ⊕ *www.circusreno.com.*

Harrah's. Occupying two city blocks, this landmark property has a sprawling casino and an outdoor promenade. ✉ *219 N. Center St., at E. 2nd St.* ☎ *775/786–3232, 800/648–3773* ⊕ *www.harrahsreno.com.*

Silver Legacy. A 120-foot-tall mining rig and video poker games draw gamblers to this razzle-dazzle casino. ✉ *407 N. Virginia St., at W. 4th St.* ☎ *775/329–4777, 800/687–8733* ⊕ *www.silverlegacy.com.*

WHERE TO EAT

$$$
AMERICAN
★
✕ **4th St. Bistro.** For deliciously simple, smart cooking, head to this charming little bistro on the edge of town. The chef-owner uses organic produce and meats in her soulful preparations of dishes like grilled Moroccan spiced chicken breast with garbanzo beans and couscous. Ocher-color sponge-painted walls and a roaring fireplace warm the white-tablecloth dining room. $ *Average main: $30* ✉ *3065 W. 4th St.* ☎ *775/323–3200* ⊕ *www.4thstbistro.com* ⊙ *Closed Sun. and Mon. No lunch.*

$
THAI
✕ **Bangkok Cuisine.** To eat well but not break the bank, come to this busy Thai restaurant and sample the delicious soups, salads, stir-fries, and curries. $ *Average main: $10* ✉ *55 Mt. Rose St., at S. Virginia St.* ☎ *775/322–0299* ⊕ *www.bangkokcuisinereno.com* ⊙ *No lunch Sun.*

$$$
FRENCH
✕ **Beaujolais Bistro.** Consistently spot-on, this restaurant serves earthy, country-style French food with zero pretension—classics like beef bourguignonne, roast duck, escargots, and steak frites béarnaise, all lovingly prepared and seasoned just right. Less expensive small plates are also on the menu, plus a nightly $39 prix-fixe offering. The airy dining

room has an inviting, casual vibe. $ *Average main: $28* ⊠ *130 West St.* ☎ *775/323–2227* ⊕ *www.beaujolaisbistro.com* ☾ *Closed Mon. No lunch weekends.*

$ ✕ **Chocolate Bar.** Part café, part cocktail bar, this hip little spot close to
CAFÉ the river makes killer truffles, chocolate fondue, fabulous fruity cocktails, gourmet appetizers, and stellar hot chocolate, served at a long curved bar or at several tables and leather banquettes. Chocolate Bar is open late each night for those craving dessert, a fabulous chocolate cocktail, or a simple, unadorned cognac. $ *Average main: $13* ⊠ *95 N. Sierra St., at W. 1st St.* ☎ *775/337–1122* ⊕ *www.thechocbar.com.*

WHERE TO STAY
For expanded reviews, facilities, and current deals, visit Fodors.com.

$ ⊞ **Eldorado.** In the middle of glittering downtown, the resort's huge
HOTEL tower has rooms overlooking either the mountains or the lights of the city. **Pros:** fun; good food; amusingly kitschy decor. **Cons:** noisy. $ *Rooms from: $65* ⊠ *345 N. Virginia St.* ☎ *775/786–5700, 800/648–5966* ⊕ *www.eldoradoreno.com* ↘ *679 rooms, 137 suites.*

$ ⊞ **Harrah's.** Of the big-name casino hotels in downtown Reno, double-
HOTEL towered Harrah's does a good job, with no surprises. **Pros:** sets the standard for downtown Reno; great midweek rates. **Cons:** huge property. **TripAdvisor:** "another wonderful stay," "it's almost all about the bed," "one of the few good ones downtown." $ *Rooms from: $67* ⊠ *219 N. Center St.* ☎ *775/786–3232, 800/648–3773* ⊕ *www.harrahs.com* ↘ *876 rooms, 52 suites.*

$ ⊞ **Peppermill.** A few miles removed from downtown Reno's flashy main
HOTEL drag, this property generates its own glitz with a dazzling neon-filled
★ casino. **Pros:** luxurious rooms; casino decor; good (and inexpensive) coffee shop. **Cons:** deluge of neon may be offputting to some. **TripAdvisor:** "the only place to stay," "always a great experience," "beautiful room." $ *Rooms from: $99* ⊠ *2707 S. Virginia St.* ☎ *775/826–2121, 800/648–6992* ⊕ *www.peppermillreno.com* ↘ *915 rooms, 720 suites.*

23

The Far North

WITH LAKE SHASTA, MT. SHASTA, AND LASSEN VOLCANIC NATIONAL PARK

WORD OF MOUTH

"Lassen is one of those best-kept-secret spots. It has a little bit of everything: peaks, waterfalls, snow, trees, awesome flowers, a mini Yellowstone, and not tons of folks everywhere."

—spirobulldog

WELCOME TO THE FAR NORTH

TOP REASONS TO GO

★ **Mother Nature's wonders:** California's Far North has more rivers, streams, lakes, forests, and mountains than you'll ever have time to explore.

★ **Rock and roll:** With two volcanoes to entice you—Lassen and Shasta—you can learn firsthand what happens when a mountain blows its top.

★ **Fantastic fishing:** Whether you like casting from a riverbank or letting your line bob beside a boat, you'll find fabulous fishing in all the northern counties.

★ **Cool hops:** On a hot day there's nothing quite as inviting as a visit to Chico's world-famous Sierra Nevada Brewery. Take the tour and then savor a chilled glass on tap at the adjacent brewpub.

★ **Shasta:** Wonderful in all its forms: lake, dam, river, mountain, forest, and town.

1 **From Chico to Mt. Shasta.** The Far North is bisected, south to north, by Interstate 5, which passes through several historic towns and state parks, as well as miles of mountainous terrain. Halfway to the Oregon border is Lake Shasta, a favorite recreation destination, and farther north stands the spectacular snowy peak of Mt. Shasta.

2 **The Backcountry.** East of Interstate 5, the Far North's main corridor, dozens of scenic two-lane roads crisscross the wilderness, leading to dramatic mountain peaks and fascinating natural wonders. Small towns settled in the second half of the 19th century seem frozen in time, except that they are well equipped with tourist amenities.

GETTING ORIENTED

The Far North is a vast area that stretches from the upper reaches of the Sacramento Valley north to the Oregon border and east to Nevada. The region includes all or part of eight counties with sparsely populated rural farming and mountain communities, as well as thriving small cities in the valley. Much of the landscape was shaped by two volcanoes—Mt. Shasta and Mt. Lassen—that draw amateur geologists, weekend hikers, and avid mountain climbers to their rugged terrain. An intricate network of high mountain watersheds feeds lakes large and small, plus streams and rivers that course through several forests.

24

Updated
by Christine
Vovakes

The wondrous landscape of California's northeastern corner, relatively unmarred by development, congestion, and traffic, is the product of volcanic activity. At the southern end of the Cascade Range, Lassen Volcanic National Park is the best place to witness the Far North's fascinating geology. Beyond the sulfur vents and bubbling mud pots, the park owes much of its beauty to 10,457-foot Mt. Lassen and 50 wilderness lakes.

The most enduring image of the region, though, is Mt. Shasta, whose 14,162-foot snowcapped peak beckons outdoor adventurers of all kinds. There are many versions of Shasta to enjoy—the mountain, the lake, the river, the town, the dam, and the forest—all named after the Native Americans known as the Shatasla, or Sastise, who once inhabited the region. The Far North's soaring mountain peaks, wild rivers teeming with trout, and almost unlimited recreational possibilities make it the perfect destination for sports lovers. You won't find many hot nightspots or cultural enclaves, but you will find superlative hiking and fishing.

FAR NORTH PLANNER

WHEN TO GO

Heat scorches the valley in summer. Temperatures above 110°F are common, but the mountains provide cool respite. Fall throughout the Far North is beautiful, rivaled only by spring, when wildflowers bloom and mountain creeks fed by the snowmelt splash through the forests. Winter is usually temperate in the valley, but cold and snowy in high country. A few favorite tourist attractions are closed in winter.

GETTING HERE AND AROUND
AIR TRAVEL

For the cheapest fares, fly into Sacramento ($\Rightarrow$ *Chapter 22, Sacramento and the Gold Country)* and then rent a car—you'll need one anyway—and drive north. Chico and Redding, both served by United Express, have small airports. Neither has shuttle service, but you can take a taxi for about $30 to downtown Redding and $21 to downtown Chico.

Air Contacts Chico Municipal Airport ⊠ *150 Airpark Blvd., off Cohasset Rd., Chico* ☎ *530/896–7200* ⊕ *www.chico.ca.us/airport/home_page.asp.* **Redding Municipal Airport** ⊠ *6751 Woodrum Circle, off Airport Rd., Redding* ☎ *530/224–4320* ⊕ *www.ci.redding.ca.us/transeng/airports/rma.htm.*

Ground Transportation Taxi Service, Chico ☎ *530/893–4444, 530/342–2929.* **Taxi Service, Redding** ☎ *530/246–0577, 530/222–1234.*

BUS TRAVEL

Greyhound buses stop in Burney, Chico, Red Bluff, Redding, Susanville, and Weed. Various transit authorities provide local bus transportation *(see individual town listings for details)*, though few tourists avail themselves of it.

Bus Contact Greyhound ☎ *800/231–2222* ⊕ *www.greyhound.com.*

CAR TRAVEL

Interstate 5 runs up the center of California through Red Bluff and Redding. Chico is east of Interstate 5 on Highway 32. Lassen Volcanic National Park can be reached by Highway 36 from Red Bluff or (except in winter) Highway 44 from Redding. Highway 299 connects Weaverville, Redding and Alturas. U.S. 395 leads from Susanville to Alturas. Highway 89 will take you from Mt. Shasta to Quincy. Highway 36 links Chester and Susanville. Check weather reports and carry detailed maps, warm clothing, and tire chains whenever you head into mountainous terrain in winter.

Road Conditions Caltrans Current Highway Conditions ☎ *800/427–7623* ⊕ *www.dot.ca.gov.*

TRAIN TRAVEL

Amtrak serves Chico, Redding, and Dunsmuir.

Train Contacts Amtrak ☎ *800/872–7245* ⊕ *www.amtrakcalifornia.com.*

RESTAURANTS

Redding, the urban center of the Far North, and college-town Chico have the greatest selection of restaurants. Cafés and simple eateries are the rule in the smaller towns, though trendy, innovative restaurants have been popping up. Dress is always informal. *Prices in the reviews are the average cost of a main course at dinner or, if dinner is not served, at lunch.*

HOTELS

Aside from the large chain hotels and motels in Redding and Chico, most accommodations in the Far North blend rusticity, simplicity, and coziness. Rooms in Redding, Chico, and Red Bluff usually are booked solid only during popular local events. Wilderness resorts close in fall and reopen after the snow season ends in May. For summer holiday weekends in towns such as Mt. Shasta, Dunsmuir, and Chester, and at camping sites within state or national parks, make lodging reservations well in advance. *Prices in the reviews are the lowest cost of a standard double room in high season. For expanded reviews, facilities, and current deals, visit Fodors.com.*

B&B Info California Association of Bed & Breakfast Inns ⊕ *www.cabbi.com/ region/Mount-Shasta.*

VISITOR INFORMATION

Contacts Lassen County Chamber of Commerce ⊠ *75 N. Weatherlow St., Susanville* ☎ *530/257–4323* ⊕ *www.lassencountychamber.com.* **Shasta Cascade Wonderland Association** ⊠ *1699 Hwy. 273, Anderson* ☎ *530/365–7500, 800/474–2782* ⊕ *www.shastacascade.com.* **Visit Siskiyou** ☎ *800/926–4865* ⊕ *www.visitsiskiyou.org.*

FROM CHICO TO MT. SHASTA

From the blooming almond orchards of the fertile Sacramento River valley, through the forested mountains and to the dominating peak of a dormant volcano, this section of the Far North entices tourists in all seasons.

CHICO

180 miles from San Francisco, east on I–80, north on I–505 to I–5, and east on Hwy. 32; 86 miles north of Sacramento on Hwy. 99.

Chico (which is Spanish for "small") lies in the Sacramento Valley and offers a welcome break from the monotony of Interstate 5. The Chico campus of California State University, the scores of local artisans, and the area's agriculture (primarily almond orchards) all influence the culture here. Chico's true claim to fame, however, is the popular Sierra Nevada Brewery, which keeps beer drinkers across the country happy with its distinctive microbrews.

GETTING HERE AND AROUND

Both Highway 99, coming north from Sacramento or south off Interstate 5 at Red Bluff, and Highway 32, going east off Interstate 5 at Orland, intersect Chico. Amtrak and Greyhound stop here, and United Express flies into the Chico airport. Butte Regional Transit's B-Line buses serve Chico and nearby towns. Anchored by a robust university scene, the downtown neighborhoods are great for walking.

ESSENTIALS

Bus Contact B-Line ☎ *530/342–0221, 800/822–8145* ⊕ *www.blinetransit.com.*

Visitor Information Chico Chamber of Commerce ⊠ *300 Salem St., at W. 3rd St.* ☎ *530/891–5556, 800/852–8570* ⊕ *www.chicochamber.com.*

EXPLORING

★ **Bidwell Mansion State Historic Park.** Built between 1865 and 1868 by General John Bidwell, the founder of Chico, this mansion was designed by Henry W. Cleaveland, a San Francisco architect. Bidwell and his wife welcomed many distinguished guests to their distinctive pink Italianate home, including President Rutherford B. Hayes, naturalist John Muir, suffragist Susan B. Anthony, and General William T. Sherman. A one-hour tour takes you through most of the mansion's 26 rooms. ⊠ *525 The Esplanade, at Memorial Way* ☎ *530/895–6144* 🖾 *$6* 🕙 *Mon. noon–5, weekends 11–5; last tour at 4* 🕙 *Closed Tues.–Thurs.*

★ **Bidwell Park.** The sprawling 3,670-acre Bidwell Park is a community green space straddling Big Chico Creek, where scenes from *Gone With the Wind* and the 1938 version of *Robin Hood* (starring Errol Flynn) were filmed. The region's recreational hub, it includes a golf course, swimming areas, and paved biking, hiking, and in-line skating trails. One of the largest city-run parks in the country, Bidwell starts as a slender strip downtown and expands eastward 11 miles toward the Sierra foothills. ⊠ *300 S. Park Dr., off Hwy. 99* ☎ *530/896–7800* ⊕ *www.bidwellpark.org.*

★ **Sierra Nevada Brewing Company.** This pioneer of the microbrewery movement still has a hands-on approach to beer making. Tour the brew house and see how the beer is produced—from the sorting of hops through fermentation and bottling. You can also visit the gift shop and enjoy a hearty lunch or dinner in the brewpub where tastings are available (for a fee). ⊠ *1075 E. 20th St., at Sierra Nevada St.* ☎ *530/345–2739* ⊕ *www.sierranevada.com* 🖾 *Free* 🕙 *Tours daily, call for times.*

WHERE TO EAT

$$$
STEAKHOUSE
✕ **5th Street Steakhouse.** Hand-cut steak is the star in this refurbished early 1900s building, the place to come when you're craving red meat and a huge baked potato. Exposed redbrick walls warm the small dining area. A long mahogany bar catches the overflow crowds that jam the place on weekends. Lunch is served on Friday only. No reservations are accepted on Friday and Saturday, but it's worth the wait. ⑤ *Average main: $27* ⊠ *345 W. 5th St., at Normal Ave.* ☎ *530/891–6328* ⊕ *www.5thstreetsteakhouse.com* 🕙 *No lunch Sat.–Thurs.*

$
AMERICAN
✕ **Madison Bear Garden.** This downtown favorite two blocks south of the Chico State campus is a great spot for checking out the vibrant college scene while enjoying a burger and a brew. ⑤ *Average main: $8* ⊠ *316 W. 2nd St., at Salem St.* ☎ *530/891–1639* ⊕ *www.madisonbeargarden.com.*

$$$
MEDITERRANEAN
✕ **Red Tavern.** With its burgundy carpet, white linen tablecloths, and mellow lighting, this is one of Chico's coziest restaurants. The Mediterranean-influenced menu, inspired by fresh local produce, changes seasonally. There's a great California wine list, and also a full bar. ⑤ *Average main: $24* ⊠ *1250 The Esplanade, at E. 3rd Ave.* ☎ *530/894–3463* ⊕ *www.redtavern.com* 🕙 *Closed Sun. No lunch.*

24

WHERE TO STAY

For expanded reviews, facilities, and current deals, visit Fodors.com.

$$$
HOTEL
★

Hotel Diamond. Crystal chandeliers and gleaming wood floors and banisters elegantly welcome guests into the foyer of this restored gem in downtown Chico near the university. **Pros:** refined; great location; excellent breakfast buffet included in room rate. **Cons:** pricey; not a good choice for families. **TripAdvisor:** "beautiful antique hotel," "quality service," "you will not be disappointed." $ *Rooms from: $175* ⊠ *220 W. 4th St.* ☎ *530/893-3100, 866/993-3100* ⊕ *www.hoteldiamondchico. com* ⇘ *39 rooms, 4 suites* ¶⊙¶ *Breakfast.*

$
B&B/INN

Johnson's Country Inn. Nestled in an almond orchard a five-minute drive from downtown, this Victorian-style farmhouse with a wraparound veranda is a welcome change from motel row. **Pros:** rural setting; antique furnishings; expected modern conveniences; beautifully maintained; serene walks. **Cons:** a car is essential. **TripAdvisor:** "quiet country setting," "beautiful home and grounds," "lovely people." $ *Rooms from: $95* ⊠ *3935 Morehead Ave.* ☎☎ *530/345-7829* ⊕ *www.chico. com/johnsonsinn* ⇘ *4 rooms* ¶⊙¶ *Breakfast.*

SHOPPING

Made in Chico. Made in Chico sells locally made goods, including pottery, olives, almonds, and Woof and Poof creations—whimsical home decor items, such as stuffed Santas, elves, animals, and pillows. ⊠ *127 W. 3rd St., between Main St. and Broadway* ☎ *530/894-7009.*

Needham Studios. Beautiful custom-made etched, stained, and beveled glass is created at Needham Studios. ⊠ *237 Broadway, at 3rd St.* ☎ *530/345-4718* ⊕ *www.needhamstudios.com.*

RED BLUFF

41 miles north of Chico on Hwy 99.

Historic Red Bluff is a gateway to Lassen Volcanic National Park. Established in the mid-19th century as a shipping center and named for the color of its soil, the town is filled with dozens of restored Victorians. It's a great home base for outdoor adventures in the area.

GETTING HERE AND AROUND

Access Red Bluff via exits off Interstate 5, or by driving north on Highway 99. Highway 36 is a long, twisting road that begins near the Pacific Coast and goes to Red Bluff, then east to the towns near Lassen Volcanic National Park. Greyhound buses stop here and also provide connecting service to Amtrak. TRAX (Tehama Rural Area Express) serves Red Bluff and neighboring towns.

ESSENTIALS

Bus Information TRAX ⊠ *Red Bluff* ☎ *530/385-2877* ⊕ *www.taketrax.com.*

Visitor Information Red Bluff–Tehama County Chamber of Commerce ⊠ *100 Main St., at Rio St.* ☎ *530/527-6220* ⊕ *www.redbluffchamber.com.*

EXPLORING

★ **William B. Ide Adobe State Historic Park.** Named for the first and only president of the short-lived California Republic of 1846, William B. Ide Adobe State Historic Park is on an oak-lined bank of the Sacramento River. The Bear Flag Party proclaimed California a sovereign nation, separate from Mexican rule, and the republic existed for 22 days before it was taken over by the United States. The republic's flag has survived, with minor refinements, as California's state flag. The park's main attraction is an adobe home built in the 1850s and outfitted with period furnishings. ⊠ *21659 Adobe Rd., at Park Pl.* ☎ *530/529–8599* ⊕ *www.parks.ca.gov/?page_id=458* ⊠ *$6 per vehicle* ☽ *Park and picnic facilities; adobe home and historic sites open Fri.–Sun., varying hrs.*

> **RED BLUFF ROUND-UP**
>
> Check out old-time rodeo at its best during the Red Bluff Round-Up. Held the third weekend of April, this annual event attracts some of the best cowboys in the country. For more information, visit ⊕ *www.redbluffroundup.com.*

WHERE TO EAT AND STAY

For expanded reviews, facilities, and current deals, visit Fodors.com.

$$ ✕ **Green Barn Steakhouse.** You're likely to find cowboys sporting Stetsons and spurs feasting on sizzling porterhouse, baby back ribs, and prime rib at Red Bluff's premier steak house. For lighter fare, there's rainbow trout or clam fettuccine. Don't miss the bread pudding with rum sauce. The lounge is usually hopping, especially when there's an event at the nearby rodeo grounds. Ⓢ *Average main: $19* ⊠ *5 Chestnut Ave., at Antelope Blvd.* ☎ *530/527–3161* ⚍ *Reservations not accepted* ☽ *Closed Sun.*

STEAKHOUSE

$ ⊞ **The Jeter Victorian Inn.** The four guest rooms of this 1881 Victorian home are elegantly decorated with antiques and period furnishings; two have private baths, and the Imperial Room has a Jacuzzi. **Pros:** quiet residential area; within walking distance of restaurants. **Cons:** no Internet access. Ⓢ *Rooms from: $85* ⊠ *1107 Jefferson St.* ☎ *530/527–7574* ⊕ *www.jetervictorianinn.com* ⇄ *4 rooms, 3 with bath; 1 cottage* ⵏⵔ *Breakfast.*

B&B/INN

REDDING

32 miles north of Red Bluff on I–5.

As the largest city in the Far North, Redding is an ideal headquarters for exploring the surrounding countryside.

GETTING HERE AND AROUND

Reach Redding from exits off Interstate 5 or via Highway 299, which originates near coastal Eureka and crosses Weaverville and Redding before heading northeast to Burney and Alturas. Highway 44 stretches from Susanville past Lassen Park's north entrance before ending in Redding. United Express serves the Redding airport. Amtrak and Greyhound make stops here.

24

Fisherman under Santiago Calatrava's striking Sundial Bridge next to Turtle Bay Exploration Park.

ESSENTIALS

Bus Information Redding Area Bus Authority ☏ 530/241-2877 ⊕ www.rabaride.com.

Visitor Information Redding Convention and Visitors Bureau ✉ 2334 Washington Ave., Suite B ☏ 530/225-4100, 800/874-7562 ⊕ www.visitredding.com.

EXPLORING

☺ Fodor's Choice ★ **Turtle Bay Exploration Park.** Here you find walking trails, an arboretum and botanical gardens, and lots of interactive exhibits for kids, including a gold-panning area and the seasonal butterfly exhibit. The main draw is the stunning **Sundial Bridge,** which links the Sacramento River Trail and the park's arboretum and gardens. Access to the bridge and arboretum is free, but there's a fee for the museum. ✉ 840 Sundial Bridge Dr., off Hwy. 44 ☏ 530/243-8850 ⊕ www.turtlebay.org ⤳ $14 for museum ☉ Apr.–mid-Sept., Mon.–Sat. 9–5, Sun. 10–5; mid-Sept.–Mar., Wed.–Sat. 9–4, Sun. 10–4.

WHERE TO EAT AND STAY

For expanded reviews, facilities, and current deals, visit Fodors.com.

$ SEAFOOD **✕ Buz's Crab.** This casual restaurant in central Redding shares space with a bustling seafood market where locals snap up fresh-from-the-ocean Dungeness crab in season. The fish-and-chips and seafood combos are popular, but crab is what keeps the customers coming back. ⑤ *Average main: $13* ✉ 2159 East St., at Pine St. ☏ 530/243-2120 ⊕ www.buzscrab.com.

$$$ STEAKHOUSE **✕ Jack's Grill.** Famous for its 16-ounce steaks, this popular bar and steak house also serves shrimp and chicken. A town favorite, the place is

usually jam-packed and noisy. $ *Average main: $23* ⊠ *1743 California St., at Sacramento St.* ☎ *530/241–9705* ⊕ *www.jacksgrillredding.com* ⊙ *Closed Sun. No lunch.*

$ ✗ **Klassique Kafe.** Two sisters run this small, bustling restaurant that
AMERICAN caters to locals looking for simple but hearty breakfast and lunch fare. The hot luncheon specials served daily might include butter beans and ham with corn bread, or chicken and dumplings. $ *Average main: $9* ⊠ *2427 Athens Ave., at Locust St.* ☎ *530/244–4939* ⊙ *Closed Sat. No dinner.*

$$ ☷ **The Red Lion.** Close to Redding's convention center and regional rec-
HOTEL reation sites, this hotel is a top choice for both business and vacation travelers. **Pros:** family-friendly; close to a major shopping area. **Cons:** busy area. **TripAdvisor:** "nice people," "awesome hospitality and comfortable beds," "convenient." $ *Rooms from: $119* ⊠ *1830 Hilltop Dr., Hwy. 44/299 exit off I–5* ☎ *530/221–8700, 800/733–5466* ⊕ *www. redlion.com* ⌕ *192 rooms, 2 suites.*

SPORTS AND THE OUTDOORS

Fly Shop. The Fly Shop sells fishing licenses and has information about guides, conditions, and fishing packages. ⊠ *4140 Churn Creek Rd., at Denton Way* ☎ *530/222–3555* ⊕ *www.flyshop.com.*

WEAVERVILLE

46 miles west of Redding on Hwy. 299.

A man known only as Weaver struck gold here in 1849, and the fledgling community that developed at the base of the Trinity Alps was named after him. With its impressive downtown historic district, today Weaverville is a popular headquarters for family vacations and biking, hiking, fishing, and gold-panning excursions.

GETTING HERE AND AROUND

Highway 299 becomes Main Street down the center of Weaverville. Take the highway either east from the Pacific Coast or west from Redding. Highway 36 from Red Bluff to Highway 3 heading north leads to Weaverville. Trinity Transit provides minimal local bus service plus a line that links Weaverville to Interstate 5 at Redding.

EXPLORING

Trinity County Courthouse. Trinity County Courthouse, built in 1856 as a store, office building, and hotel, was converted to county use in 1865. The Apollo Saloon, in the basement, became the county jail. It's the oldest courthouse still in use in California. ⊠ *Court and Main Sts.*

★ **Trinity County Historical Park.** For a vivid sense of Weaverville's past, visit the Trinity County Historical Park, especially its **Jake Jackson Memorial Museum,** which has a blacksmith shop and a stamp mill (where ore is crushed) from the 1890s that is still in use. Also here are the original jail cells of the Trinity County Courthouse. ⊠ *780 Main St., at Bartlett La.* ☎ *530/623–5211* ⊙ *Jan.–Mar., Wed. and Sat. noon–4; Apr., daily noon–4; May–Oct., daily 10–5; Nov. and Dec., Wed.–Sat. 11–4.*

Fodor'sChoice **Weaverville Joss House.** Weaverville's main attraction is the Joss House,
★ a Taoist temple built in 1874 and called Won Lim Miao ("the temple

of the forest beneath the clouds") by Chinese miners. The oldest continuously used Chinese temple in California, it attracts worshippers from around the world. With its golden altar, antique weaponry, and carved wooden canopies, the Joss House is a piece of California history that can best be appreciated on a guided 30-minute tour. The original temple building and many of its furnishings—some of which came from China—were lost to fire in 1873, but members of the local Chinese community soon rebuilt it. ⊠ *630 Main St., at Oregon St.* ☎ *530/623–5284* 🖾 *Museum free; guided tour $4* ☉ *Thurs. and Sun. 10–5; last tour at 4.*

WHERE TO EAT

$$
AMERICAN

✕ **La Grange Café.** In two brick buildings dating from the 1850s (they're among the oldest edifices in town), this eatery serves buffalo and other game meats, pasta, fresh fish, and farmers' market vegetables when they're available. There's a full premium bar, and the wine list is extensive. 💲 *Average main: $19* ⊠ *520 Main St.* ☎ *530/623–5325* ☉ *Hrs sometimes sporadic in winter.*

SPORTS AND THE OUTDOORS

Fly Stretch. Below the Lewiston Dam, east of Weaverville on Highway 299, is the Fly Stretch of the Trinity River, an excellent fly-fishing area.

Pine Cove Boat Ramp. This ramp on Lewiston Lake provides fishing access for those with disabilities—decks here are built over prime trout-fishing waters.

Weaverville Ranger Station. Check here for maps and information about hiking trails in the Trinity Alps Wilderness. ⊠ *360 Main St.* ☎ *530/623–2121.*

LAKE SHASTA AREA

★ *12 miles north of Redding on I–5.*

When you think of the Lake Shasta Area picture water, wilderness, dazzling stalagmites—and a fabulous man-made project in the midst of it all.

GETTING HERE AND AROUND

Interstate 5 north of Redding is the main link to the entire Lake Shasta area. Get to the dam by passing through tiny City of Shasta Lake. There is no local bus service.

ESSENTIALS

Shasta Cascade Wonderland Association ⊠ *1699 Hwy. 273, Anderson* ☎ *530/365–7500, 800/474–2782* ⊕ *www.shastacascade.com.*

EXPLORING

Lake Shasta. Twenty-one types of fish inhabit the lake, including rainbow trout and salmon. The lake region also has the largest nesting population of bald eagles in California. You can rent fishing boats, ski boats, sailboats, canoes, paddleboats, Jet Skis, and windsurfing boards at one of the many marinas and resorts along the 370-mile shoreline.

Fodor'sChoice
★

Lake Shasta Caverns. Stalagmites, stalactites, flowstone deposits, and crystals entice visitors to the Lake Shasta Caverns. To see this impressive spectacle, you must take the two-hour tour, which includes a catamaran ride across the McCloud arm of Lake Shasta and a bus ride up Grey Rock Mountain to the cavern entrance. The caverns are 58°F year-round, making them a cool retreat on a hot summer day. The most awe-inspiring of the limestone rock formations is the glistening Cathedral Room, which appears to be gilded. During peak summer months (June through August), tours depart every half hour; in April, May, and September it's every hour. A gift shop is open from 8 to 4:30. ⊠ *20359 Shasta Caverns Rd., off I–5, 17 miles north of Redding, Lakehead* ☎ *530/238–2341, 800/795–2283* ⊕ *www.lakeshastacaverns.com* ⊠ *$24* ☺ *June–Aug., tours on the ½ hr, daily 9–4; Apr., May, and Sept., tours on the hr, daily 9–3; Oct.–Mar., tours at 10, noon, and 2 daily.*

★ **Shasta Dam.** This is the second-largest concrete dam in the United States (only Grand Coulee in Washington is bigger). The visitor center has computerized photographic tours of the dam construction, video presentations, fact sheets, and historical displays. Hour-long guided tours inside the dam and its powerhouse leave from the center. ⊠ *16349 Shasta Dam Blvd., off Lake Blvd., Shasta Lake* ☎ *530/275–1554* ⊕ *www.usbr.gov/mp/ncao* ⊠ *Free* ☺ *Visitor center daily 8–5; call for tour times.*

SPORTS AND THE OUTDOORS

FISHING

The Fishen Hole. A couple of miles from the lake, this bait-and-tackle shop sells fishing licenses and provides information about conditions. ⊠ *3844 Shasta Dam Blvd., Shasta Lake City* ☎ *530/275–4123.*

HOUSEBOATING

Houseboats here come in all sizes except small. As a rule, rentals are outfitted with cooking utensils, dishes, and most of the equipment you'll need—you supply the food and the linens. When you rent a houseboat, you receive a short course in how to maneuver your launch before you set out. You can fish, swim, sunbathe on the flat roof, or sit on the deck and watch the world go by. The shoreline of Lake Shasta is beautifully ragged, with countless inlets; it's not hard to find privacy. Expect to spend a minimum of $350 a day for a craft that sleeps six. A three-day, two-night minimum is customary. Prices are often lower during the off-season (September through May). Bridge Bay Resort rents houseboats, fishing boats, ski boats, and patio boats. Shasta Cascade offers general information.

Bridge Bay Resort ⊠ *10300 Bridge Bay Rd., Redding* ☎ *800/752–9669.*

Shasta Cascade Wonderland Association ⊠ *Anderson* ☎ *530/365–7500, 800/474–2782* ⊕ *www.shastacascade.com.*

DUNSMUIR

10 miles south of Mt. Shasta on I–5.

Castle Crags State Park surrounds the tiny town of Dunsmuir, which was named for a 19th-century Scottish coal baron who offered to build a fountain if the town was renamed in his honor. The town's other major attraction is the Railroad Park Resort, where you can spend the night in restored railcars.

GETTING HERE AND AROUND

Reach Dunsmuir via exits off Interstate 5 at the north and south ends of town. When snow hasn't closed the route, you can take Highway 89 from the Lassen Park area toward Burney then northeast to Interstate 5 at Mt. Shasta. From there it's a 10-mile drive south to Dunsmuir. Amtrak stops here; Greyhound stops in Weed, 20 miles north. On weekdays, STAGE buses serve Dunsmuir.

> ### FINE FISHING
>
> The upper Sacramento River near Dunsmuir is consistently rated one of the best fishing spots in the country. Check with the chamber of commerce for local fishing guides.

ESSENTIALS

Bus Information STAGE ☎ *530/842–8295* ⊕ *www.co.siskiyou.ca.us.*

Visitor Information Dunsmuir Chamber of Commerce ✉ *5915 Dunsmuir Ave., Suite 100* ☎ *530/235–2177* ⊕ *dunsmuir.com.*

EXPLORING

★ **Castle Crags State Park.** Named for its 6,000-foot glacier-polished crags, which tower over the Sacramento River, this park offers fishing in Castle Creek, hiking in the backcountry, and a view of Mt. Shasta. The crags draw climbers and hikers from around the world. The 4,350-acre park has 28 miles of hiking trails, including a 2.75-mile access trail to **Castle Crags Wilderness,** part of the **Shasta-Trinity National Forest.** There are excellent trails at lower altitudes. Because of budget cuts, the state parks department proposed closing Castle Crags, but nonprofit groups hope to keep this stunning space open. Call ahead to check status. ✉ *6 miles south of Dunsmuir, Castella/Castle Crags exit off I–5* ☎ *530/235–2684* 🚗 *$8 per vehicle, day use.*

WHERE TO EAT AND STAY

For expanded reviews, facilities, and current deals, visit Fodors.com.

$$
MEDITERRANEAN
✕ **Café Maddalena.** The chef here gained experience working in top San Francisco restaurants before moving up north to prepare adventurous Mediterranean fare with a French influence. Selections change seasonally but always feature a vegetarian dish, along with entrées such as Pacific salmon with Meyer lemon sauce, and lamb shoulder with cassoulet. Wines from Spain, Italy, and France complement the meals. $ *Average main: $18* ✉ *5801 Sacramento Ave.* ☎ *530/235–2725* ⊕ *www.cafemaddalena.com* ☉ *Closed Mon.–Wed. and Jan.–mid-Feb. No lunch.*

$
HOTEL
☁
🚂 **Railroad Park Resort.** The antique cabooses here were collected over more than three decades and have been converted into cozy motel rooms in honor of Dunsmuir's railroad legacy. **Pros:** gorgeous setting; kitschy fun. **Cons:** cabooses can feel cramped; restaurant open mid-May through September. **TripAdvisor:** "what a fun place," "railroad buff's delight," "quite different." $ *Rooms from: $115* ✉ *100 Railroad Park Rd.* ☎ *530/235–4440* ⊕ *www.rrpark.com* 🛏 *23 cabooses, 4 cabins.*

MT. SHASTA

34 miles north of Lake Shasta on I–5.

GETTING HERE AND AROUND

Three exits off Interstate 5 lead to the town of Mt. Shasta. When snow hasn't closed the route, you can take Highway 89 from the Lassen Park area toward Burney then northeast to Mt. Shasta. The ski park is off Highway 89. Greyhound stops at Weed, 10 miles north; Amtrak stops at Dunsmuir, 10 miles south. There's no local bus system.

ESSENTIALS

Visitor Information Mt. Shasta Chamber of Commerce and Visitors Bureau
✉ *300 Pine St., at W. Lake St.* ☎ *530/926–3696, 800/926–4865* ⊕ *www.visitsiskiyou.org.*

EXPLORING

Mt. Shasta. The crown jewel of the 2.5-million-acre Shasta-Trinity National Forest, Mt. Shasta, a 14,162-foot-high dormant volcano, is a mecca for day hikers. It's especially enticing in spring, when fragrant Shasta lilies and other flowers adorn the rocky slopes. The paved road reaches only as far as the timberline; the final 6,000 feet are a tough climb of rubble, ice, and snow (the summit is perpetually ice packed). Only a hardy few are qualified to make the trek to the top.

The town of Mt. Shasta has real character and some fine restaurants. Lovers of the outdoors and backcountry skiers abound, and they are more than willing to offer advice on the most beautiful spots in the region, which include out-of-the-way swimming holes, dozens of high mountain lakes, and a challenging 18-hole golf course with 360 degrees of spectacular views.

WHERE TO EAT AND STAY

For expanded reviews, facilities, and current deals, visit Fodors.com.

$$
ECLECTIC
✕ **Lilys.** This restaurant in a white-clapboard home, framed by a picket fence and arched trellis, serves everything from steaks and pastas to Mexican and vegetarian dishes. Daily specials include prime rib and a fresh fish entrée. For innovative vegetarian fare try a *dal* burger, which is made with walnuts, fresh veggies, garbanzo beans, and rice. ⑤ *Average main: $19* ✉ *1013 S. Mt. Shasta Blvd., at Holly St.* ☎ *530/926–3372* ⊕ *www.lilysrestaurant.com.*

$
CAFÉ
✕ **Seven Suns Coffee and Cafe.** A favorite gathering spot for locals, this small coffee shop serves specialty wraps for breakfast and lunch, plus soup and salad selections. Pastries, made daily, include muffins and scones, and blackberry fruit bars in season. If the weather's nice, grab a seat on the patio. ⑤ *Average main: $8* ✉ *1011 S. Mt. Shasta Blvd., at Holly St.* ☎ *530/926–9701* ⊕ *www.mtshastacoffee.com.*

$$$
RENTAL
★
🏠 **Mount Shasta Resort.** Private chalets are nestled among tall pine trees along the shore of Lake Siskiyou, all with gas-log fireplaces and full kitchens. **Pros:** incredible views; romantic woodsy setting. **Cons:** kids may get bored. **TripAdvisor:** "fabulous views and surroundings," "it's all service and ambience," "beautiful." ⑤ *Rooms from: $169* ✉ *1000 Siskiyou Lake Blvd.* ☎ *530/926–3030, 800/958–3363* ⊕ *www.mountshastaresort.com* ⇥ *65 units.*

SPORTS AND THE OUTDOORS

HIKING   **Mt. Shasta Forest Service Ranger Station.** Check in here for current trail conditions and avalanche reports. ⊠ *204 W. Alma St., at Pine St.* ☎ *530/926–4511, 530/926–9613.*

MOUNTAIN   **Fifth Season Mountaineering Shop.** The shop rents skiing and climbing
CLIMBING   equipment and operates a recorded 24-hour climber-skier report. ⊠ *300 N. Mt. Shasta Blvd.* ☎ *530/926–3606, 530/926–5555* ⊕ *www. thefifthseason.com.*

Shasta Mountain Guides. These guides lead hiking, climbing, and ski-touring groups to the summit of Mt. Shasta. ☎ *530/926–3117* ⊕ *www. shastaguides.com.*

SKIING   **Mt. Shasta Board & Ski Park.** On the southeast flank of Mt. Shasta, this ski park has three triple-chair lifts and one surface lift on 425 skiable acres. Three-quarters of the trails are for beginning or intermediate skiers. The area's vertical drop is 1,435 feet, with a top elevation of 6,600 feet. The longest of the 32 trails is 1.75 miles. A package for beginners, available through the ski school, includes a lift ticket, ski rental, and a lesson. The school also runs ski and snowboard programs for children. There's night skiing for those who want to see the moon rise as they schuss. The base lodge has a simple café, a ski shop, and a ski-snowboard rental shop. ⊠ *Hwy. 89 exit east from I–5, south of Mt. Shasta* ☎ *530/926–8610, 800/754–7427* ⊕ *www.skipark.com* ☉ *Winter ski season schedule: Sun.–Wed. 9–4, Thurs.–Sat. 9–9.*

Mt. Shasta Nordic Center. The center, run by a nonprofit, maintains 15 miles of groomed cross-country ski trails. ⊠ *Ski Park Hwy., off Hwy. 89 (take I–5's McCloud exit)* ☎ *530/926–2142* ⊕ *www.mtshastanordic. org.*

THE BACKCOUNTRY

The Far North's primitive, rugged backcountry is arguably full of more natural wonders than any other region in California.

MCARTHUR–BURNEY FALLS MEMORIAL STATE PARK

Hwy. 89, 52 miles southeast of Mt. Shasta and 41 miles north of Lassen Volcanic National Park.

GETTING HERE AND AROUND

To see some stunning falls, head east off Interstate 5 on Highway 89 at Mt. Shasta. The drive is 52 miles. From Interstate 5 in Redding, head east 55 miles on Highway 299 to connect with Highway 89; follow signs 6 miles to the park. From Alturas, head west on Highway 299 for about 86 miles hook up with Highway 89.

EXPLORING

Fodor's Choice   **McArthur–Burney Falls Memorial State Park.** Just inside the park's southern
★   boundary, Burney Creek wells up from the ground and divides into two falls that cascade over a 129-foot cliff into a pool below. Count-less ribbonlike streams pour from hidden moss-covered crevices; resi-dent bald eagles are frequently seen soaring overhead. You can walk

a self-guided nature trail that descends to the foot of the falls, which Theodore Roosevelt—according to legend—called "the eighth wonder of the world." On warm days, swim at Lake Britton; lounge on the beach; rent motorboats, paddleboats, and canoes; or relax at one of the campsites or picnic areas. The camp store is open from early May to the end of October. ⊠ *24898 Hwy. 89, Burney* 🕾 *530/335–2777* 🖅 *$8 per vehicle, day use.*

ALTURAS

86 miles northeast of McArthur–Burney Falls Memorial State Park on Hwy. 299.

Alturas is the county seat and largest town in Modoc County. The Dorris family arrived in the area in 1874, built Dorris Bridge over the Pit River, and later opened a small wayside stop for travelers. As in the past, travelers today come to see eagles and other wildlife, the Modoc National Forest, and active geothermal areas.

GETTING HERE AND AROUND
To get to Alturas from Susanville take Main Street/Highway 36 south for about 4 miles; turn left at U.S. 395 and stay on that highway for 99 miles. From Redding, take the Lake Blvd./299E exit off Interstate 5, head east and stay on Highway 299 for 140 miles. Sage Stage buses serve Alturas from Redding and Susanville.

ESSENTIALS
Bus Information Modoc County Sage Stage 🕾 *530/233–3883, 530/233–6410* ⊕ *www.sagestage.com.*

Visitor Information Alturas Chamber of Commerce ⊠ *600 S. Main St.* 🕾 *530/233–4434* ⊕ *www.alturaschamber.org.*

EXPLORING
Modoc National Forest. Encompassing 1.6 million acres, Modoc National Forest protects 300 species of wildlife, including Rocky Mountain elk, wild horses, mule deer, and pronghorn antelope. In spring and fall, watch for migratory waterfowl as they make their way along the Pacific Flyway above the forest. Hiking trails lead to Petroglyph Point, one of the largest panels of rock art in the United States. ⊠ *Park Headquarters, 800 W. 12th St.* 🕾 *530/233–5811* ⊕ *www.fs.usda.gov/modoc.*

Modoc National Wildlife Refuge. The 7,021-acre Modoc National Wildlife Refuge was established in 1961 to protect migratory waterfowl. You might see Canada geese, sandhill cranes, mallards, teal, wigeon, pintail, white pelicans, cormorants, and snowy egrets. The refuge is open for hiking, bird-watching, and photography, but one area is set aside for hunters. Regulations vary according to season. ⊠ *U.S. 395, 1½ miles south of Alturas* 🕾 *530/233–3572* ⊕ *www.fws.gov/modoc/* 🖅 *Free* ⊙ *Daily dawn–dusk.*

WHERE TO EAT
$$ ✕ **Brass Rail.** Prix-fixe dinners at this authentic Basque restaurant include
SPANISH wine, homemade bread, soup, salad, side dishes, coffee, and ice cream. Steak, lamb chops, fried chicken, shrimp, and scallops are among the

24

best entrée selections. A lounge with a full bar adjoins the dining area. ⑤ *Average main: $20* ⊠ *395 Lake View Dr., at Lake Rd.* ☎ *530/233–2906* ☉ *Closed Mon.*

SUSANVILLE

104 miles south of Alturas via U.S. 395; 65 miles east of Lassen Volcanic National Park via Highway 36.

Susanville, established as a trading post in 1854, tells the tale of its rich history through murals painted on buildings in the historic uptown area. You can take a self-guided tour around the original buildings and stop for a bite at one of the restaurants now housed within them. If you'd rather work up a sweat, you can hit the Bizz Johnson Trail and Eagle Lake recreation areas just outside of town.

GETTING HERE AND AROUND

U.S. 395 connects Susanville and Alturas, about a 100-mile trip. From Red Bluff, take Interstate 5's Highway 36E/Fairgrounds exit and drive east for about 3 miles; turn left at Highway 36E and continue through the mountains for 103 miles. Lassen Rural Bus serves Susanville and surrounding areas on weekdays only.

ESSENTIALS

Bus Information Lassen Rural Bus ☎ *530/252–7433* ⊕ *www. lassentransportation.org.*

Visitor Information Lassen County Chamber of Commerce ⊠ *75 N. Weatherlow St., off Main St.* ☎ *530/257–4323* ⊕ *www.lassencountychamber.com.*

EXPLORING

Bizz Johnson Trail. Bizz Johnson Trail follows a defunct line of the Southern Pacific Railroad for 25 miles. Known to locals as the Bizz, the trail is open for hikers, walkers, mountain bikers, horseback riders, and cross-country skiers. It skirts the Susan River through a scenic landscape of canyons, bridges, and forests abundant with wildlife. ⊠ *Trailhead, 601 Richmond Rd., near N. Railroad Ave.* ☎ *530/257–0456* ⊕ *www.blm. gov/ca/eaglelake/bizztrail.html* ☒ *Free.*

Eagle Lake. Anglers travel great distances to fish the waters of large Eagle Lake, whose rainbow trout is prized for its size and fighting ability. Surrounded by high desert to the north and alpine forests to the south, the lake is also popular for picnicking, hiking, boating, waterskiing and windsurfing, and bird-watching—ospreys, pelicans, and many other waterfowl visit the lake. On land you might see mule deer, small mammals, and even pronghorn antelope—and be sure to watch for bald-eagle nesting sites. ⊠ *16 miles north of Susanville, Eagle Lake Rd. off Hwy. 139* ☎ *530/257–0456 for Eagle Lake Recreation Area, 530/825–3454 for Eagle Lake Marina* ⊕ *www.blm.gov/ca/eaglelake.*

WHERE TO EAT AND STAY

$ ✕ **Mazatlan Grill.** The sauces and tortillas are prepared on-site in this
MEXICAN friendly, family-run restaurant and lounge, which serves lunch and dinner daily. The dining room is simple and tidy, with comfortable upholstered booths. The extensive menu offers authentic, inexpensive

Lassen Volcanic National Park

TO BURNEY

89

44

TO REDDING

Entrance Station

Ranger Station

Manzanita Lake

89

CHAOS CRAGS

DEVASTATED AREA

Lassen Peak 10,457 ft.

BLUE LAKE CANYON

Sulfur Works

89

Bumpass Hell

Kings Creek

Koham Yah-mah-nee Visitor Center

Entrance Station

TO RED BLUFF AND CHICO

TWIN MEADOWS

Devil's Kitchen

READING PEAK

CORRAL MEADOW

Hat Mt.

DERSCH MEADOWS

Summit Lake North
Summit Lake South

GRASSY SWALE

Crater Butte

Fairfield Peak

FANTASTIC LAVA BEDS

PAINTED DUNES

Snag Lake

Cinder Cone

Ash Butte

Butte Lake

44

Prospect Peak 8,338 ft.

Pacific Crest Trail

Horseshoe Lake

Juniper Lake

Warner Valley

TO CHESTER AND SUSANVILLE

0   1/2 mi
0   1/2 km

Mexican fare ranging from fajitas and enchiladas to a vegetarian burrito. $ *Average main: $10* ✉ *1535 Main St., at Park St.* ☎ *530/257–1800.*

$ ⊞ **High Country Inn.** Rooms are spacious in this colonial-style motel on
HOTEL the eastern edge of town. **Pros:** great mountain views; heated pool. **Cons:** lots of traffic in the area. **TripAdvisor:** "everything was great," "quiet," "a very nice property." $ *Rooms from: $84* ✉ *3015 Riverside Dr.* ☎ *530/257–3450, 866/454–4566* ⊕ *www.high-country-inn.com* ⥰ *66 rooms* ○ *Breakfast.*

LASSEN VOLCANIC NATIONAL PARK

45 miles east of Redding on Hwy. 44; 48 miles east of Red Bluff on Hwy. 36.

24

GETTING HERE AND AROUND

Whether coming from the west or the east, reach the park's southern entrance via Highway 36E, and turn onto Highway 89 for a short drive to the park. The northwest entrance is reached via Highway 44 from Redding and Susanville. No buses serve the area.

EXPLORING

Chaos Jumbles. More than 350 years ago, an avalanche from the Chaos Crags lava domes scattered hundreds of thousands of rocks—many of them 2–3 feet in diameter—over a couple of square miles. ✉ *Lassen Park Rd., 2 miles northeast of the northwest entrance ranger station.*

Fodor'sChoice **Lassen Scenic Byway.** This 185-mile scenic drive begins in Chester and
★ loops through the forests, volcanic peaks, geothermal springs, and lava fields of Lassen National Forest and Lassen National Park, providing for an all-day excursion into dramatic wilderness. Parts of the road are inaccessible in winter. From Chester, take Route 36 west to Route 89 north through the park, then Route 44 east to Route 36 west. ☎ *800/427–7623.*

Fodor'sChoice **Lassen Volcanic National Park.** A dormant plug dome, Lassen Peak is the
★ focus of Lassen Volcanic National Park's 165.6 square miles of distinctive landscape. The peak began erupting in May 1914, sending pumice, rock, and snow thundering down the mountain and gas and hot ash billowing into the atmosphere. Lassen's most spectacular outburst occurred in 1915 when it blew a cloud of ash some 7 miles into the stratosphere. The resulting mudflow destroyed vegetation for miles in some directions; the evidence is still visible today, especially in Devastated Area. The volcano finally came to rest in 1921. Now fumaroles, mud pots, lakes, and bubbling hot springs create a fascinating but dangerous landscape that can be viewed throughout the park, especially via a hiked descent into Bumpass Hell. Because of its significance as a volcanic landscape, Lassen became a national park in 1916. Several volcanoes—the largest of which is now Lassen Peak—have been active in the area for roughly 600,000 years. The four types of volcanoes found in the world are represented in the park, including shield (Prospect Peak), plug dome (Lassen Peak), cinder cone (Cinder Cone), and composite (Brokeoff Volcano). Lassen Park Road (the continuation of Highway 89 within the park) and 150 miles of hiking trails provide access to many of these volcanic wonders. Caution is key here: signs warn visitors to

stay on the trails and railed boardwalks to avoid falling into boiling water or through dangerous thin-crusted areas of the park. Although the park is closed to cars in winter, it's usually open to intrepid cross-country skiers and snowshoers. The Kohm Yah-mah-nee Visitor Center, at the southwest entrance to the park, is open year-round. ⊕ *www.nps. gov/lavo* ⌦ *$10 per car, $5 per person if not in a car.*

Ⓒ **Sulphur Works Thermal Area.** Proof of Lassen Peak's volatility becomes evident shortly after you enter the park at the southwest entrance. Sidewalks skirt boiling springs and sulphur-emitting steam vents. This area is usually the last site to close because of snow. ⊠ *Lassen Park Rd., 1 mile from the southwest entrance ranger station.*

SPORTS AND THE OUTDOORS

HIKING   **Bumpass Hell Trail.** Boiling springs, steam vents, and mudpots highlight
Fodor's Choice this 3.2-mile round-trip hike. Expect the loop to take about three hours.
★ During the first mile of the hike there's a gradual climb of 500 feet before a steep 250-foot descent to the basin. You'll encounter rocky patches, so wear hiking boots. Stay on trails and boardwalks near the thermal areas, as what appears to be firm ground may be only a thin crust over scalding mud. *Moderate.* ⊠ *Trailhead at end of paved parking area off Lassen Park Rd., 6 miles from the southwest entrance ranger station.*

Fodor's Choice **Lassen Peak Hike.** This trail winds 2½ miles to the mountaintop. It's a
★ tough climb—2,000 feet uphill on a steady, steep grade—but the reward is a spectacular view. At the peak you can see into the rim and view the entire park (and much of California's far north). Bring sunscreen, water, and a jacket since it's often windy and much cooler at the summit. ■TIP➔ A multiyear restoration project means all or part of the trail will be closed at certain times, so call ahead. At this writing trail work was expected to be complete in 2014. *Difficult.* ⊠ *Trailhead past a paved parking area off Lassen Park Rd., 7 miles north of the southwest entrance ranger station* ☎ *530/595–4480.*

CHESTER

36 miles west of Susanville on Hwy 36.

The population of this small town on Lake Almanor swells from 2,500 to nearly 5,000 in summer as tourists come to visit. Chester serves as a gateway to Lassen Volcanic National Park.

GETTING HERE AND AROUND

Chester is on Highway 36E. When snow doesn't close Highway 89, the main road through Lassen Park, visitors can take Highway 44 from Redding to Highway 89 through the park and to Highway 36E and onto Chester and Lake Almanor. Plumas County Transit connects Chester to the Quincy area.

ESSENTIALS

Bus Information Plumas County Transit ⊠ *Chester* ☎ *530/283–2538* ⊕ *www. plumastransit.com.*

Lassen Volcanic National Park's King Creek Falls Hike, which takes you through forests and meadows dotted with wildflowers, is a good hike for nature photographers.

Visitor Information Chester–Lake Almanor Chamber of Commerce ✉ *529 Main St., at Farrar Dr.* ☎ *530/258–2426, 800/350–4838* ⊕ *www.lakealmanorarea. com.*

EXPLORING

Lake Almanor. Lake Almanor's 52 miles of shoreline lie in the shadow of Mt. Lassen, and are popular with campers, swimmers, water-skiers, and anglers. At an elevation of 4,500 feet, the lake warms to above 70°F for about eight weeks in summer. ✉ *Off Hwys. 89 and 36* ☎ *530/258–2426.*

WHERE TO EAT AND STAY

For expanded reviews, facilities, and current deals, visit Fodors.com.

$ ✕ **Kopper Kettle Cafe.** Locals return again and again to this tidy res-
AMERICAN taurant that serves home-cooked lunches and dinners. Head here for breakfast whenever you've got a hankering for scrambled eggs or biscuits and gravy. ⑤ *Average main: $13* ✉ *243 Main St., at Myrtle St.* ☎ *530/258–2698.*

$ ✕ **Maria's Mexican Restaurant.** A festive atmosphere prevails in this
MEXICAN family-friendly restaurant and lounge, where traditional south-of-the-border fare is served. It's one of the few restaurants in the area with a full bar, a great place to enjoy a margarita at the end of a long day spent hiking. ⑤ *Average main: $10* ✉ *159 Main St., at Willow Way* ☎ *530/258–2262* ⊙ *Closed Sun.*

$$ ⊡ **Best Western Rose Quartz Inn.** Down the road from Lake Almanor
HOTEL and close to Lassen Volcanic National Park, this small-town inn balances traditional decor and up-to-the-minute amenities like Wi-Fi. **Pros:** near national park; modern conveniences. **Cons:** standard rooms on the

pricey side. **TripAdvisor:** "comfortable," "great night's sleep," "friendly place to stay."⑤ *Rooms from: $120* ⊠ *306 Main St.* ☎ *530/258–2002, 888/571–4885* ⊕ *www.bestwesterncalifornia.com/chester-hotels* ⇥ *50 rooms* ❙○❙ *Breakfast.*

$ 🖼 **Bidwell House.** Some guest rooms at this 1901 ranch house have wood-
B&B/INN   burning stoves, claw-foot tubs, and antique furnishings; a separate
Fodor's Choice cottage with a kitchen sleeps six. **Pros:** unique decor in each room; beau-
★   tiful wooded setting; near Lake Almanor. **Cons:** not ideal for kids. **Trip-
Advisor:** "these folks know how to do hospitality," "peaceful place," "great breakfasts."⑤ *Rooms from: $115* ⊠ *1 Main St.* ☎ *530/258–3338* ⊕ *www.bidwellhouse.com* ⇥ *14 rooms, 12 with bath* ❙○❙ *Breakfast.*

QUINCY

67 miles southwest of Susanville via Hwys. 36 and 89.

A center for mining and logging in the 1850s, Quincy is nestled against the western slope of the Sierra Nevada. The county seat and largest community in Plumas County, the town is rich in historic buildings that have been the focus of preservation and restoration efforts. The four-story courthouse on Main Street, one of several stops on a self-guided tour, was built in 1921 with marble posts and staircases. The arts are thriving in Quincy, too: catch a play or a bluegrass performance at the Town Hall Theatre.

GETTING HERE AND AROUND

Quincy is on Highway 70 and is accessible from all directions via mountain roads. Highway 70 goes through the Feather River Canyon to Highway 149, then Highway 99 to Chico and Red Bluff, a 198-mile trip. From Quincy, Highway 70 connects to Highway 89 and then to Highway 36E toward Susanville in the east, or westward toward Chester and Lassen Park. Plumas County Transit serves Chester and Quincy. Lassen Rural Bus connects Quincy and Susanville.

ESSENTIALS

Bus Information Lassen Rural Bus ☎ *530/252–7433* ⊕ *www. lassentransportation.org.***Plumas County Transit** ☎ *530/283–2538* ⊕ *www. plumastransit.com.*

Visitor Information Quincy Chamber of Commerce ⊠ *464 Main St., at Bradley St.* ☎ *530/283–0188* ⊕ *www.quincychamber.com.*

EXPLORING

Plumas County Museum. The cultural, home arts, and industrial history displays at the Plumas County Museum contain artifacts dating to the 1850s. Highlights include collections of Maidu Indian basketry, pioneer weapons, and rooms depicting life in the early logging and mining days of Plumas County. Out in the Exhibit Yard are a working blacksmith shop, a restored goldminer's cabin, and a railroad exhibit. ⊠ *500 Jackson St., at Coburn St.* ☎ *530/283–6320* ⊕ *www.plumasmuseum.org* 🖾 *$2* ⊙ *Tues.–Sat. 10–4.*

Plumas National Forest. Plumas County is known for its wide-open spaces, and the 1.2-million-acre Plumas National Forest, with its high alpine lakes and crystal-clear woodland streams, is a beautiful example.

Hundreds of campsites are maintained in the forest, and picnic areas and hiking trails abound. You can enter the forest along Highways 70 and 89. ⊠ *U.S. Forest Service, 159 Lawrence St., near W. Main St.* ☎ *530/283–2050* ☯ *Office weekdays 8–4:30.*

WHERE TO EAT AND STAY
For expanded reviews, facilities, and current deals, visit Fodors.com.

$ ✕ **Sweet Lorraine's.** Hearty fare served in this casual, bustling restau-
AMERICAN rant in Quincy's historic downtown area includes meaty dishes like St. Louis ribs as well as vegetarian selections and lighter items; there's also a good selection of wines. If the weather is mild, dine alfresco on the patio. Ⓢ *Average main: $15* ⊠ *384 Main St., at Harbison Ave.* ☎ *530/283–5300* ☯ *Closed Sun. and Mon.*

$ 🏠 **Ada's Place.** This place is actually four uniquely beautiful cottages,
RENTAL secluded on a quiet street one block from the county courthouse and
Fodor's Choice downtown Quincy. **Pros:** on-site owners' meticulous upkeep. **Cons:** not
★ a good choice for children. **TripAdvisor:** "fabulous tranquil retreat," "a most wonderful oasis," "absolutely wonderful." Ⓢ *Rooms from: $100* ⊠ *562 Jackson St., near Court St.* ☎ *530/283–1954, 877/234–2327* ⊕ *www.adasplace.com* ⇆ *4 cottages.*

$ 🏠 **Feather Bed.** The quaint romanticism of an 1893 Queen Anne Victo-
B&B/INN rian plus proximity to Quincy's town center are the draws here. **Pros:** great location for exploring the town on foot. **Cons:** some rooms are small. **TripAdvisor:** "caring and nurturing place to stay," "friendly owners," "nice location." Ⓢ *Rooms from: $120* ⊠ *542 Jackson St.* ☎ *530/283–0102, 800/696–8624* ⊕ *www.featherbed-inn.com* ⇆ *5 rooms, 2 cottages* ⦿ *Breakfast.*

24

Travel Smart
California

GETTING HERE AND AROUND

Wherever you plan to go in California, getting there will likely involve driving, even if you fly. With the exception of San Diego, major airports are usually far from main attractions. For example, four airports serve the Los Angeles area—but three of them are outside the city limits. You'll find a similar situation in San Francisco, where it's a 30-minute-plus trip between any Bay Area airport and downtown. California's major airport hubs are LAX in Los Angeles and SFO in San Francisco, but satellite airports can be found around most major cities. When booking flights, it pays to check these locations, as you may find more convenient times and a better location in relation to your hotel. Most small cities have their own commercial airports, with connecting flights to larger cities—but service may be extremely limited, and it may be cheaper to rent a car and drive from L.A. or San Francisco.

FROM LOS ANGELES TO:	BY AIR	BY CAR
San Diego	55 minutes	2 hours
Death Valley		6 hours
San Francisco	1 hour 25 minutes	6 hours 30 minutes
Monterey	1 hour 10 minutes	5 hours 45 minutes
Santa Barbara	45 minutes	1 hour 45 minutes
Big Sur		5 hours 30 minutes
Sacramento	1 hour 25 minutes	6 hours 30 minutes

FROM SAN FRANCISCO TO:	BY AIR	BY CAR
San Jose		1 hour 10 minutes
Monterey	50 minutes	2 hours 10 minutes
Los Angeles	1 hour 25 minutes	6 hours 30 minutes
Portland, OR	1 hour 50 minutes	10 hours 30 minutes
Mendocino		3 hours
Yosemite NP/ Fresno	65 minutes	4 hours
Lake Tahoe/ Reno	65 minutes	4 hours

▌ AIR TRAVEL

Flying time to California is about 6 hours from New York and 4½ hours from Chicago. Travel from London to either Los Angeles or San Francisco is 11 hours and from Sydney approximately 14. Flying between San Francisco and Los Angeles takes about 90 minutes.

AIRPORTS

California's gateways are Los Angeles International Airport (LAX), San Francisco International Airport (SFO), San Diego International Airport (SAN), Sacramento International Airport (SMF), and San Jose International Airport (SJC). Oakland International Airport (OAK) is another option in the Bay Area, and other Los Angeles airports include Long Beach (LGB), Bob Hope Airport (BUR), LA/Ontario (ONT), and John Wayne Airport (SNA).

Airport Information Bob Hope Airport ☎ 818/840–8840 ⊕ www.burbankairport. com.**John Wayne Airport** ☎ 949/252–5200 ⊕ www.ocair.com.**LA/Ontario International Airport** ☎ 909/937–2700 ⊕ www.flyontario. com.**Long Beach Airport** ☎ 562/570–2600

⊕ www.lgb.org.**Los Angeles International Airport** ☎ 310/646–5252 ⊕ www.lawa.org/lax. **Oakland International Airport** ☎ 510/563–3300 ⊕ www.flyoakland.com.**Sacramento International Airport** ☎ 916/929–5411 ⊕ www.sacramento.aero/smf.**San Diego International Airport** ☎ 619/400–2404 ⊕ www.san.org.**San Francisco International Airport** ☎ 650/821–8211, 800/435–9736 ⊕ www.flysfo.com.**San Jose International Airport** ☎ 408/392–3600 ⊕ www.flysanjose.com.

FLIGHTS

United, with hubs in San Francisco and Los Angeles, has the greatest number of flights into and within California. But most national and many international airlines fly to the state. Southwest Airlines connects smaller cities within California, often from satellite airports near major cities.

Airline Contacts Air Canada ☎ 888/247–2262 ⊕ www.aircanada.com.**Alaska Airlines/Horizon Air** ☎ 800/252–7522 ⊕ www.alaskaair.com.**American Airlines** ☎ 800/433–7300 ⊕ www.aa.com.<**British Airways** ☎ 800/247–9297 ⊕ www.britishairways.com. **Cathay Pacific** ☎ 800/233–2742 ⊕ www.cathaypacific.com.**Delta Airlines** ☎ 800/221–1212 for U.S. reservations, 800/241–4141 for international reservations ⊕ www.delta.com.**Frontier Airlines** ☎ 800/432–1359 ⊕ www.frontierairlines.com. **Japan Air Lines** ☎ 800/525–3663 ⊕ www.jal.com. **JetBlue** ☎ 800/538–2583 ⊕ www.jetblue.com.**Qantas** ☎ 800/227–4500 ⊕ www.qantas.com.au.**Southwest Airlines** ☎ 800/435–9792 ⊕ www.southwest.com.**Spirit Airlines** ☎ 800/772–7117 ⊕ www.spirit.com. **United Airlines** ☎ 800/864–8331 for U.S. reservations, 800/538–2929 for international reservations ⊕ www.united.com.**US Airways** ☎ 800/428–4322 for U.S. and Canada reservations, 800/622–1015 for international reservations ⊕ www.usairways.com.

▌ BOAT TRAVEL

CRUISES

A number of major cruise lines offer trips that begin or end in California. Most voyages sail north along the Pacific Coast to Alaska or south to Mexico. California cruise ports include Los Angeles, San Diego, and San Francisco.

Cruise Lines Carnival Cruise Line ☎ 305/599–2600, 800/227–6482 ⊕ www.carnival.com. **Celebrity Cruises** ☎ 800/647–2251, 800/437–3111 ⊕ www.celebritycruises.com. **Crystal Cruises** ☎ 310/785–9300, 800/446–6620 ⊕ www.crystalcruises.com. **Holland America Line** ☎ 206/281–3535, 877/932–4259 ⊕ www.hollandamerica.com. **Norwegian Cruise Line** ☎ 305/436–4000, 800/327–7030 ⊕ www.ncl.com. **Princess Cruises** ☎ 661/753–0000, 800/774–6237 ⊕ www.princess.com. **Regent Seven Seas Cruises** ☎ 954/776–6123, 800/477–7500 ⊕ www.rssc.com. **Royal Caribbean International** ☎ 305/539–6000, 800/327–6700 ⊕ www.royalcaribbean.com. **Silversea Cruises** ☎ 954/522–4477, 800/722–9955 ⊕ www.silversea.com.

▌ BUS TRAVEL

Greyhound is the major bus carrier in California. Regional bus service is available in metropolitan areas.

Bus Information Greyhound ☎ 800/231–2222 ⊕ www.greyhound.com.

▌ CAR TRAVEL

There are two basic north–south routes in California: Interstate 5 runs inland most of the way from the Oregon border to the Mexican border; and U.S. 101 hugs the coast for part of the route from Oregon to Mexico. A slower but much more scenic option is to take California State Route 1, also referred to as Highway 1 and the Pacific Coast Highway, which winds along much of the California coast and provides an occasionally hair-raising, but breathtaking, ride.

From north to south, the state's east–west interstates are Interstate 80, Interstate 15, Interstate 10, and Interstate 8. Much of California is mountainous, and you may encounter winding roads, frequently cliffside, and steep mountain grades. In winter, roads crossing the Sierra from east to west may close at any time due to weather. Also in winter, Interstate 5 north of Los Angeles closes during snowstorms.

The flying and driving times in the accompanying charts represent best-case scenario estimates, but know that the infamous California traffic jam can occur at any time.

FROM LOS ANGELES TO	ROUTE	DISTANCE
San Diego	I–5 or I–15	127 miles
Las Vegas	I–10 to I–15	265 miles
Death Valley	I–10 to I–15 to Hwy. 127 to Hwy. 190	290 miles
San Francisco	I–5 to Hwy. 156 to U.S. 101	403 miles
Monterey	U.S. 101 to Salinas, Hwy. 68 to Hwy. 1	334 miles
Santa Barbara	U.S. 101	95 miles
Big Sur	U.S. 101 to Hwy. 1	297 miles
Sacramento	I–5	386 miles

GASOLINE

Gasoline prices in California vary widely, depending on location, oil company, and whether you buy it at a full-service or self-serve pump. It's less expensive to buy fuel in the southern part of the state than in the north. If you're planning to travel near Nevada, you can save a bit by purchasing gas over the border. Gas stations are plentiful throughout the state. Most stay open late (24 hours along major highways and in big cities), except in rural areas, where Sunday hours are limited and where you may drive long stretches without a chance to refuel.

ROAD CONDITIONS

Rainy weather can make driving along the coast or in the mountains treacherous. Some of the smaller routes over mountain ranges and in the deserts are prone to flash flooding. When the rains are severe, coastal Highway 1 can quickly become a slippery nightmare, buffeted by strong winds and obstructed by falling debris from the cliffs above. When the weather is particularly bad, Highway 1 may be closed due to mud and rock slides.

FROM SAN FRANCISCO TO	ROUTE	DISTANCE
San Jose	U.S. 101	50 miles
Monterey	U.S. 101 to Hwy. 156 to Hwy. 1	120 miles
Los Angeles	U.S. 101 to Hwy. 156 to I–5	403 miles
Portland, OR	I–80 to I–505 to I–5	635 miles
Mendocino	Hwy. 1	174 miles
Yosemite NP	I–80 to I–580 to I–205 to Hwy. 120 east	184 miles
Lake Tahoe/ Reno	I–80	220 miles

Many smaller roads over the Sierra Nevada are closed in winter, and if it's snowing, tire chains may be required on routes that are open, most notably those to Yosemite and Lake Tahoe. From October through April, if it's raining along the coast, it's usually snowing at higher elevations. Consider renting a four-wheel-drive vehicle, or purchase chains before you get to the mountains. (Chains or cables generally cost $30 to $70, depending on tire size; cables are easier to attach than chains, but chains are more durable.) If you delay and purchase them in the vicinity of the chain-control area, the cost may double. Be aware that most rental-car companies prohibit chain installation on their vehicles. If you choose to risk it and do not tighten them properly, they may snap—your insurance likely will not cover any resulting damage. Uniformed chain installers on Interstate 80 and U.S. 50 will apply them at the checkpoint for $35 or take them off for less than that. Chain installers are independent business people, not highway employees, and set their own fees. They are not allowed to sell or rent chains. On smaller roads, you're on your own. Always carry extra clothing, blankets, water, and food when driving to the mountains in the winter, and keep your gas tank full to prevent the fuel line from freezing.

Road Conditions Caltrans Current Highway Conditions ☎ 800/427–7623 ⊕ www.dot.ca.gov.

Weather Conditions National Weather Service ☎ 707/443–6484 northernmost California, 831/656–1725 San Francisco Bay area and central California, 775/673–8100 Reno, Lake Tahoe, and northern Sierra, 805/988–6610 Los Angeles area, 858/675–8700 San Diego area ⊕ www.weather.gov.

ROADSIDE EMERGENCIES

Dial 911 to report accidents on the road and to reach the police, the California Highway Patrol (CHP), or the fire department. On some rural highways and on most interstates, look for emergency phones on the side of the road. In Los Angeles, the Metro Freeway Service Patrol provides assistance to stranded motorists under nonemergency conditions. Call #399 on your cell phone to reach them 24 hours a day.

RULES OF THE ROAD

All passengers must wear seat belts at all times. A child must be secured in a federally approved child passenger restraint system and ride in the back seat until at least eight years of age or until the child is at least 4 feet 9 inches tall. Children who are eight but don't meet the height requirement must ride in a booster seat or a car seat. Unless otherwise indicated, right turns are allowed at red lights after

you've come to a full stop. Left turns between two one-way streets are allowed at red lights after you've come to a full stop.

Drivers with a blood-alcohol level higher than 0.08 who are stopped by police are subject to arrest, and police officers can detain those under 21 with a level of 0.05 if they appear impaired. California's drunk-driving laws are extremely tough—violators may have their licenses immediately suspended, pay hefty fines, and spend the night in jail.

The speed limit on many interstate highways is 70 mph; unlimited-access roads are usually 55 mph. In cities, freeway speed limits are between 55 mph and 65 mph. Many city routes have commuter lanes during rush hour.

Those 18 and older must use a hands-free device for their mobile phones while driving; those under 18 may not use mobile phones or wireless devices while driving. Texting on a wireless device is illegal for all drivers. Smoking in a vehicle where a minor is present is an infraction. For more information refer to the Department of Motor Vehicles driver's handbook at ⊕ *www.dmv.ca.gov.*

CAR RENTAL

When you reserve a car, ask about cancellation penalties, taxes, drop-off charges (if you're planning to pick up the car in one city and leave it in another), and surcharges (for being under or over a certain age, for additional drivers, or for driving across state or country borders or beyond a specific distance from your point of rental). All of these things can add substantially to your costs. Request car seats and extras such as GPS when you book.

Rates are sometimes—but not always—better if you book in advance or reserve through a rental agency's website. There are other reasons to book ahead, though: for popular destinations, during busy times of the year, or to ensure that you get certain types of cars (vans, SUVs, exotic sports cars).

■TIP→ Make sure that a confirmed reservation guarantees you a car. Agencies sometimes overbook, particularly for busy weekends and holiday periods.

A car is essential in most parts of California, though in compact San Francisco it's better to use public transportation to avoid parking headaches. In sprawling cities such as Los Angeles and San Diego, however, you'll have to take the freeways to get just about anywhere.

Rates statewide for the least expensive vehicle begin as low as $30 a day, usually on weekends, and less than $200 a week (though they increase rapidly from here). This does not include additional fees or the tax on car rentals, which is 8.75% in Los Angeles, 8.5% in San Francisco, and 7.75% in San Diego. Be sure to shop around—you can get a decent deal by carefully shopping the major car rental companies' websites. Also, rates are sometimes lower in San Diego; compare prices by city before you book, and ask about "drop charges" if you plan to return the car in a city other than the one where you rented the vehicle. If you pick up at an airport, there may also be a facility charge of as much as $12 per rental; ask when you book.

In California, you must have a valid driver's license and be 21 to rent a car; rates may be higher if you're under 25. Some agencies will not rent to those under 25; check when you book. Non-U.S. residents must have a license with text that is in the Roman alphabet that is valid for the entire rental period. Though it need not be entirely written in English, it must have English letters that clearly identify it as a driver's license. In addition, most companies also require an international license; check in advance.

If you dream of driving down the coast with the top down, or you want to explore the desert landscape not visible from the road, consider renting a specialty vehicle. Agencies that specialize in convertibles and sport-utility vehicles will

often arrange airport delivery in larger cities. Unlike most of the major agencies, the following companies guarantee the car class that you book.

Specialty Car Agencies Specialty Rentals ☎ 800/400–8412 *locations in San Francisco and Los Angeles* ⊕ *www.specialtyrentals.com*. **Beverly Hills Rent a Car** ☎ 800/479–5996 *several locations in Los Angeles* ⊕ *www. bhrentacar.com.* **Midway Car Rental** ☎ 800/824–5260 *several locations in Los Angeles* ⊕ *www.midwaycarrental.com.*

Major Rental Agencies Alamo ☎ 800/462–5266 ⊕ *www.alamo.com.* **Avis** ☎ 800/331–1212 ⊕ *www.avis.com.* **Budget** ☎ 800/527–0700 ⊕ *www.budget.com.* **Hertz** ☎ 800/654–3131 ⊕ *www.hertz.com.* **National Car Rental** ☎ 877/222–9058 ⊕ *www. nationalcar.com.*

▌ TRAIN TRAVEL

One of the most beautiful train trips in the country, Amtrak's *Coast Starlight*, begins in Los Angeles and hugs the Pacific Coast to San Luis Obispo before it turns inland for the rest of its journey to Seattle. The *California Zephyr* travels from Chicago to Oakland via Denver; the *Pacific Surfliner* connects San Diego and San Luis Obispo via Los Angeles and Santa Barbara with multiple departures daily; and the *Sunset Limited* runs from Los Angeles to New Orleans via Arizona, New Mexico, and Texas.

Information Amtrak ☎ 800/872–7245 ⊕ *www.amtrakcalifornia.com.*

ESSENTIALS

■ ACCOMMODATIONS

The lodgings we review are the cream of the crop in each price category. For a full list of the facilities that are available at each property, please see the expanded review on ⊕ *www.fodors.com*. We don't specify whether the facilities cost extra; when pricing accommodations, ask what's included and what costs extra. ⇨ *For price information, see the planner in each chapter.*

Most hotels require you to give your credit-card details before they will confirm your reservation. If you don't feel comfortable emailing this information, ask if you can fax it (some places even prefer faxes). However you book, get confirmation in writing and have a copy of it handy when you check in.

Be sure you understand the hotel's cancellation policy. Some places allow you to cancel without any kind of penalty—even if you prepaid to secure a discounted rate—if you cancel at least 24 hours in advance. Others require you to cancel a week in advance or penalize you the cost of one night. Small inns and B&Bs are most likely to require you to cancel far in advance. Most hotels allow children under a certain age to stay in their parents' room at no extra charge, but others charge for them as extra adults; find out the cutoff age for discounts.

Many B&Bs are entirely nonsmoking, and hotels and motels are decreasing their inventory of smoking rooms; if you require one, ask when you book if any are available.

BED-AND-BREAKFASTS

California has more than 1,000 bed-and-breakfasts. You'll find everything from simple homestays to lavish luxury lodgings, many in historic hotels and homes. The California Association of Bed and Breakfast Inns has about 300 member

properties that you can locate and book through its website.

Reservation Services Bed & Breakfast.com ☎ *512/322-2710, 800/462-2632* ⊕ *www. bedandbreakfast.com.* **Bed & Breakfast Inns Online** ☎ *310/280-4363, 800/215-7365* ⊕ *www.bbonline.com.* **BnB Finder.com** ☎ *212/480-0414, 888/547-8226* ⊕ *www. bnbfinder.com.* **California Association of Bed and Breakfast Inns** ☎ *800/373-9251* ⊕ *www.cabbi.com.*

■ COMMUNICATIONS

INTERNET

Internet access is widely available in urban areas, but it's usually more difficult to get online in the state's rural areas. Most hotels offer some kind of connection—usually broadband or Wi-Fi. Many hotels charge a daily fee (about $10) for Internet access. Cybercafés are located throughout California.

Contacts Cybercafés ⊕ *www.cybercafes. com.*

■ EATING OUT

California has led the pack in bringing natural and organic foods to the forefront of American cooking. Though rooted in European cuisine, California cooking sometimes has strong Asian and Latin influences. Wherever you go, you're likely to find that dishes are made with fresh produce and other local ingredients.

The restaurants we list are the cream of the crop in each price category. ⇨ *For price information, see the planner in each chapter.*

CUTTING COSTS

■ TIP➜ If you're on a budget, take advantage of the "small plates" craze sweeping California by ordering several appetizer-size portions and having a glass of wine at the bar, rather than having a full meal. Also, the better grocery and specialty-food stores have grab-and-go sections, with prepared foods on par with restaurant cooking, perfect for picnicking (remember, it rarely rains between May and October). At resort areas in the off-season (such as Lake Tahoe in October and May, or San Diego in January), you can often find two-for-one dinner specials at upper-end restaurants; check coupon apps or local papers or with visitor bureaus.

RESERVATIONS AND DRESS

Regardless of where you are, it's a good idea to make a reservation if you can. We only mention reservations specifically when they are essential (there's no other way you'll ever get a table) or when they are not accepted. For popular restaurants, book as far ahead as you can (often 30 days), and reconfirm as soon as you arrive. (Large parties should always call ahead to check the reservations policy.) We mention dress only when men are required to wear a jacket or a jacket and tie.

Online reservation services make it easy to book a table before you even leave home. OpenTable covers many California cities.

Contacts OpenTable ⊕ *www.opentable.com.*

WINES, BEER, AND SPIRITS

Throughout the state, most famously in the Napa and Sonoma valleys, you can visit wineries, many of which have tasting rooms and offer tours. Microbreweries are an emerging trend in the state's cities and in some rural areas in northern California. The legal drinking age is 21.

▌HEALTH

Do not fly within 24 hours of scuba diving. Smoking is illegal in all California bars and restaurants, including on outdoor dining patios in some cities.

▌HOURS OF OPERATION

Banks in California are typically open weekdays from 9 to 6 and Saturday morning; most are closed on Sunday and most

holidays. Smaller shops usually operate from 10 to 6, with larger stores remaining open until 8 or later. Hours vary for museums and historical sites, and many are closed one or more days a week, or for extended periods during off-season months. It's a good idea to check before you visit a tourist site.

▌MONEY

Los Angeles, San Diego, and San Francisco tend to be expensive cities to visit, and rates at coastal and desert resorts are almost as high. A day's admission to a major theme park can run as much as $80 per person, though you may be able to get discounts by purchasing tickets in advance online. Hotel rates average $150 to $250 a night (though you can find cheaper places), and dinners at even moderately priced restaurants often cost $20 to $40 per person. Costs in the Gold Country, the Far North, and the Death Valley/Mojave Desert region are considerably less—many fine Gold Country bed-and-breakfasts charge around $100 a night, and some motels in the Far North and the Mojave charge $70 to $90.

CREDIT CARDS

It's a good idea to inform your credit-card company before you travel. Otherwise, the credit-card company might put a hold on your card owing to unusual activity—not a good thing halfway through your trip. Record all your credit-card numbers—as well as the phone numbers to call if your cards are lost or stolen—in a safe place, so you're prepared should something go wrong. Both MasterCard and Visa have general numbers you can call (collect if you're abroad) if your card is lost, but you're better off calling the number of your issuing bank, since MasterCard and Visa normally just transfer you to your bank; your bank's number is usually printed on your card.

Reporting Lost Cards American Express ☎ 800/992-3404 in U.S., 336/393-1111 collect from abroad ⊕ www.americanexpress.com. **Discover** ☎ 800/347-2683 in U.S., 801/902-3100 collect from abroad ⊕ www.discovercard. com.**Diners Club** ☎ 800/234-6377 in U.S., 514/877-1577 collect from abroad ⊕ www. dinersclub.com. **MasterCard** ☎ 800/622-7747 in U.S., 636/722-7111 collect from abroad ⊕ www.mastercard.com. **Visa** ☎ 800/847-2911 in U.S., 303/967-1096 collect from abroad ⊕ www.visa.com.

▌ SAFETY

California is a safe place to visit, as long as you take the usual precautions. In large cities ask the concierge or desk clerk to point out areas on your map that you should avoid. Lock valuables in a hotel safe when you're not using them. (Some hotels have in-room safes large enough to hold a laptop computer.) Keep an eye on your handbag when you're out in public. Security is high (but mostly invisible) at theme parks and resorts.

▌ TAXES

Sales tax in California varies from about 7.25% to 9.75% and applies to all purchases except for food purchased in a grocery store; food consumed in a restaurant is taxed but take-out food purchases are not. Hotel taxes vary widely by region, from about 8% to 15%.

▌ TIME

California is in the Pacific time zone. Pacific daylight time (PDT) is in effect from mid-March through early November; the rest of the year the clock is set to Pacific standard time (PST).

▌ TIPPING

Most service workers in California are fairly well paid compared to those in the rest of the country, and extravagant tipping is not the rule here. Exceptions include wealthy enclaves such as Beverly Hills, La Jolla, and San Francisco as well as the most expensive resort areas.

TIPPING GUIDELINES FOR CALIFORNIA	
Bartender	$1 per drink, or 10%–15% of tab per round of drinks
Bellhop	$1–$5 per bag, depending on the level of the hotel
Hotel Concierge	$5 or more, if he/she performs a service for you
Hotel Doorman	$1–$2 if he/she helps you get a cab
Valet Parking Attendant	$2 when you get your car
Hotel Maid	$2–$3 per person, per day; more in high-end hotels
Waiter	15%–20% (20% is standard in upscale restaurants); nothing additional if a service charge is added to the bill
Skycap at Airport	$1–$3 per bag
Hotel Room-Service Waiter	15%–20% per delivery, even if a service charge was added since that fee goes to the hotel, not the waiter
Taxi Driver	15%–20%, but round up the fare to the next dollar amount
Tour Guide	10% of the cost of the tour, more depending on quality

▌ TOURS

Guided tours are a good option when you don't want to do it all yourself. You travel along with a group (sometimes large, sometimes small), stay in prebooked hotels, eat with your fellow travelers (the cost of meals is sometimes included in the price of your tour, sometimes not), and follow a schedule.

But not all guided tours are an if-it's-Tuesday-this-must-be-Yosemite experience. A knowledgeable guide can take you places that you might never discover on your own, and you may be pushed to see more than you would have otherwise. Tours aren't for everyone, but they can be just the thing for trips to places where making travel arrangements is difficult or time-consuming.

Whenever you book a guided tour, find out what's included and what isn't. A "land-only" tour includes all your travel (by bus, in most cases) in the destination, but not necessarily your flights to and from or even within it. Also, in most cases prices in tour brochures don't include fees and taxes. And remember that you'll be expected to tip your guide (in cash) at the end of the tour.

SPECIAL-INTEREST TOURS

BIKING

Bicycling is a popular way to see the California countryside, and commercial tours are available throughout the state. Most three- to five-day trips are all-inclusive—you'll stay in delightful country inns, dine at good regional restaurants, and follow experienced guides. The Northern California wine country, with its flat valley roads, is one of the most popular destinations. When booking, ask about level of difficulty, as nearly every trip will involve some hill work. Tours fill up early, so book well in advance.

■TIP→ Most airlines accommodate bikes as luggage, provided they're dismantled and boxed.

Contacts Napa and Sonoma Valley Bike Tours ⊠ 6795 Washington St., Bldg. B, Yountville ☎ 800/707–2453 ⊕ www. napavalleybiketours.com. **Bicycle Adventures** ⊠ 29700 S.E. High Point Way, Issaquah, Washington ☎ 800/443–6060 ⊕ www. bicycleadventures.com.

▌ VISITOR INFORMATION

The California Travel and Tourism Commission's website takes you to each region of California, with digital visitor guides in multiple languages, driving tours, maps, welcome center locations, information on local tours, links to bed-and-breakfasts, and a complete booking center. It also links you—via the Explore California menu—to the websites of city and regional tourism offices and attractions. *For the numbers and websites of regional and city visitor bureaus and chambers of commerce see the "Planning" sections in each chapter.*

Contacts California Travel and Tourism Commission ⊠ Box 1499, Sacramento ☎ 916/444–4429 information, 800/862–2543 brochures ⊕ www.visitcalifornia.com.

INDEX

PHOTO CREDITS

fotostock. 318, Brent Reeves/Shutterstock. 325, Robert Holmes. 332, Holger Mette/iStockphoto. 339, laurel stewart/iStockphoto. Chapter 8: San Francisco: 359-62, Brett Shoaf/Artistic Visuals Photography. 371, Brett Shoaf/Artistic Visuals Photography. 372 (top), Arnold Genthe. 372 (bottom), Library of Congress Prints and Photographs Division. 373 (left), Sandor Balatoni/SFCVB. 373 (right), Detroit Publishing Company Collection, Photography Collection, Miriam and Ira D. Wallach Division of Art, Prints and Photographs, The New York Public Library, Astor, Lenox and Tilden Foundation. 374, Brett Shoaf/Artistic Visuals Photography. 375 (top), Gary Soup/Flickr. 375 (bottom), Albert Cheng/Shutterstock. 376 (top), Sheryl Schindler/SFCVB. 376 (center), Ronen/Shutterstock. 376 (bottom), Robert Holmes. 381, Walter Bibikow/age fotostock. 387, travelstock44/Alamy. 389, Brett Shoaf/Artistic Visuals Photography. 390, San Francisco Municipal Railway Historical Archives. 397, Lewis Sommer/SFCVB. 406, Robert Holmes. 415, aprillilacs, Fodors.com member. 419, Rafael Ramirez Lee/iStockphoto. 426, yummyporky/Flickr. 427 (top), Lisa M. Hamilton. 427 (bottom), Lisa M. Hamilton. 444 (top), Fairmont Hotels & Resorts. 444 (center left), The Huntington Hotel. 444 (center right), David Phelps/Argonaut Hotel. 444 (bottom), Cesar Rubio/Joie De Vivre Hospitality. 445 (top), The Ritz-Carlton, San Francisco. 445 (center left and right), Joie de Vivre Hospitality. 445 (bottom), Cris Ford/Union Street Inn. 454, Rough Guides/Alamy. 457, Robert Holmes. Chapter 9: The Bay Area: 461 and 462, Robert Holmes. 463, Jyeshern Cheng/iStockphoto. 464, Brett Shoaf/Artistic Visuals Photography. 469, Robert Holmes. 483, Mark Rasmussen/iStockphoto. 485, Robert Holmes. 492, S. Greg Panosian/iStockphoto. 496 and 508, Robert Holmes. Chapter 10: The Wine Country: 515, Robert Holmes. 516, iStockphoto. 517, Robert Holmes. 518, Warren H. White. 524, Robert Holmes. 525 (top), kevin miller/iStockphoto. 525 (bottom), Far Niente+Dolce+Nickel & Nickel. 526 (top and bottom) and 527 (top), Robert Holmes. 527 (bottom), star5112/Flickr. 528 (top left), Rubicon Estate. 528 (top right and bottom right) and 529 (top and bottom), Robert Holmes. 530 (top), Philippe Roy/Alamy. 530 (center), Agence Images/Alamy. 530 (bottom), Cephas Picture Library/Alamy. 531 (top), Napa Valley Conference Bureau. 531 (second and third from top), Wild Horse Winery (Forrest L. Doud). 531 (fourth from top), Napa Valley Conference Bureau. 531 (fifth from top), Panther Creek Cellars (Ron Kaplan). 531 (sixth from top), Clos du Val (Marvin Collins). 531 (seventh from top), Panther Creek Cellars (Ron Kaplan). 531 (bottom), Warren H. White. 532 and 535, Robert Holmes. 545, Far Niente+Dolce+Nickel & Nickel. 548, Terry Joanis/Frog's Leap. 556, Chuck Honek/Schramsberg Vineyard. 558, Castello di Amorosa. 571, Robert Holmes. 572, Robert Holmes. 578-79, Robert Holmes. 580, Robert Holmes. Chapter 11: The North Coast: 589, Thomas Barrat/Shutterstock. 590 (all), Robert Holmes. 591 (top), Russ Bishop/age fotostock. 591 (bottom), Robert Holmes. 592, Janet Fullwood. 599, 605, and 609, Robert Holmes. Chapter 12: Redwood National Park: 619, iStockphoto. 620 (top), Michael Schweppe/wikipedia.org. 620 (center), Agnieszka Szymczak/iStockphoto. 620 (bottom), Natalia Bratslavsky/Shutterstock. 622, WellyWelly/Shutterstock. Chapter 13: The Inland Empire: 627, Mission Inn Hotel & Spa. 628, Hartford Family Wines. 629 (top), Robert Holmes. 629 (bottom), stevekc/Flickr. 630 , Edward Lin/iStockphoto. 639, Glen Ivy Hot Springs. 651, Robert Holmes. 656, Brett Shoaf/Artistic Visuals Photography. Chapter 14: Palm Springs: 657, toby fraley/iStockphoto. 658, JustASC/Shutterstock. 659 (top and bottom), Robert Holmes. 660, iStockphoto. 663, William Royer/iStockphoto. 675, David Falk/iStockphoto. 692, Brett Shoaf/Artistic Visuals Photography. Chapter 15: Joshua Tree National Park: 699, Eric Foltz/iStockphoto. 700 (top), Loic Bernard/iStockphoto. 700 (bottom), Eric Foltz/iStockphoto. 701 (top), Justin Mair/Shutterstock. 701 (bottom), Mariusz S. Jurgielewicz/Shutterstock. 702, Eric Foltz/iStockphoto. Chapter 16: The Mojave Desert: 707, Robert Holmes. 708, amygdala imagery/Shutterstock. 709, Robert Holmes. 710, San Bernardino County Regional Parks. 717, Merryl Edelstein, Fodors.com member. 723, Robert Holmes. 733, Paul Erickson/iStockphoto. Chapter 17: Death Valley National Park: 735, Bryan Brazil/Shutterstock. 737 (top), Igor Karon/Shutterstock. 737 (bottom), iofoto/Shutterstock. 738, Paul D. Lemke/iStockphoto. 744-45, James Feliciano/iStockphoto. 747, Rodney Ee, Fodors.com member. Chapter 18: The Central Valley: 749, Kim Brogan, Fodors.com member. 750, Gary Allard/iStockphoto. 751-72, Robert Holmes. 759-773, Robert Holmes. Chapter 19: The Southern Sierra: 775, Randall Pugh, Fodors.com member. 776, Craig Cozart/iStockphoto. 777 (top), David T Gomez/iStockphoto. 777 (bottom left and bottom right), Robert Holmes. 778, christinea78, Fodors.com member. 783, moonjazz/Flickr. 790, Douglas Atmore/iStockphoto. Chapter 20: Yosemite National Park: 793, Sarah P. Corley, Fodors.com member. 794, Yosemite Concession Services. 795 (top), Andy Z./Shutterstock. 795 (bottom), Greg Epperson/age fotostock. 796, Doug Lemke/Shutterstock. 801, Rebalyn, Fodors.com member. 803, Nathan Jaskowiak/Shutterstock. 808, Greg Epperson/age fotostock. 810-11, Katrina Leigh/Shutterstock. Chapter 21: Sequoia and Kings Canyon National Parks: 815 and 816, Robert Holmes. 817 (top), Greg Epperson/age fotostock. 817 (bottom) and 818, Robert Holmes. 825, urosr/Shutterstock. 829, Robert Holmes. Chapter 22: Sacramento and the Gold Country: 833 and 835 (top and bottom), Robert Holmes. 836, Andy Z./Shutterstock. 842, Marcin Wichary/Flickr. 849, Image Asset Management/age fotostock. 850 (left) and 850 (right), wikipe-

ABOUT OUR WRITERS

Native Californian **Cheryl Crabtree**—who updated the Central Coast and Monterey Bay Area chapters—has worked as a freelance writer since 1987. She has contributed to *Fodor's California* since 2003 and has also written for *Fodor's Complete Guide to the National Parks of the West*. Cheryl is editor of *Montecito Magazine*. Her articles have appeared in many regional and national publications, including *US Airways* in-flight magazine and *Santa Barbara Seasons*. She also authors regional travel apps for mobile devices, and has co-authored several travel books on Santa Barbara and the Central Coast. She currently lives in Santa Barbara with her husband, two sons, and Jack Russell terrier.

Finding the unexpected is Los Angeles freelance writer and frequent traveler **Kathy A. McDonald's** favorite assignment. A writer with peripatetic beats, she covers the film business, design, and destinations and is a frequent contributor to the entertainment trade paper *Variety* and other publications. Art galleries, modern architecture and thrift stores entice her; she rarely passes by a realtor open house or yard sale without stopping. For this edition she updated our Los Angeles and Orange County and Catalina Island chapters.

For more than 20 years **Reed Parsell** has written travel stories, for newspapers and magazines, about destinations throughout the world. In recent years he has written mostly about California attractions, and has updated the Mojave, Southern Sierra and Sacramento/Gold Country chapters for several years. He is the principal author of *Fodor's In Focus: Yosemite, Sequoia and Kings Canyon National Parks*. Reed, who lives in Sacramento with his wife and daughter, would like to point out that college buddy David S. Williams has been an invaluable companion on Fodor's research trips through the Mojave Desert and up and down the Eastern Sierra.

Freelance writer **Christine Vovakes**—who updated the North Coast, Lake Tahoe, Far North, and Travel Smart California chapters—has also contributed to *Fodor's National Parks of the West* and *Essential USA*. Her articles have appeared in many regional and national publications, including US Airways in-flight magazine, *Santa Barbara Seasons*, and annual visitor magazines in Ventura and Santa Barbara. She also authors regional travel apps for mobile devices, including *Big Sur & Monterey Bay and Santa Barbara—Ocean to Oaks,* and co-author *The California Directory of Fine Wineries, Central Coast and Napa/Sonoma Mendocino* books. She also co-authored the first edition of *The Insider's Guide to Santa Barbara* and *Hometown Santa Barbara.*

Bobbi Zane—who updated the Experience California, San Diego, Inland Empire, and Palm Springs chapters for this edition—grew up in Southern California, watching the region grow from its mostly rural roots into one of the most exciting places in the world. She now lives in historic Julian in San Diego County. Her articles on Palm Springs have appeared in the *Orange County Register* and *Westways* magazine. She has contributed to *Fodor's Complete Guide to the National Parks of the West, Fodor's San Diego,* and *Escape to Nature Without Roughing It*. A lifelong Californian, Bobbi has visited every corner of the state on behalf of Fodor's.